ACCESS 97
EXPERT SOLUTIONS

ACCESS 97
EXPERT SOLUTIONS

Stan Leszynski

Access 97 Expert Solutions

Copyright© 1997 by Que® Corporation.

Library of Congress Catalog No.: 95-72581

ISBN: 0-7897-0367-x

99 98 97   6 5 4 3 2 1

Interpretation of the printing code: The rightmost double-digit number is the year of the book's printing; the rightmost single-digit number, the number of the book's printing. For example, a printing code of 97-1 shows that the first printing of the book occurred in 1997.

Screen reproductions in this book were created using Collage Plus from Inner Media, Inc., Hollis, NH.

Information on the Office Developer Edition is based on beta software. Up-to-date information is available at **http://www.com/officedev**.

Credits

President
Roland Elgey

Publisher
Joseph B. Wikert

Publishing Manager
Fred Slone

Senior Title Manager
Bryan Gambrel

Editorial Services Director
Elizabeth Keaffaber

Managing Editor
Sandy Doell

Director of Marketing
Lynn E. Zingraf

Product Director
Kelly Marshall

Production Editor
Sherri Fugit

Editors
Sean Dixon
Cynthia Felando
Kate Givens
Kristin Ivanetich
Sydney Jones
Patrick Kanouse
Pat Kinyon
Bonnie Lawler
Maureen McDaniel

Product Marketing Manager
Kristine Ankney

Strategic Marketing Manager
Barry Pruett

Assistant Product Marketing Managers
Karen Hagen
Christy M. Miller

Technical Editors
Joe Risse
Mark Robinson
Bob Tackett

Technical Support Specialist
Nadeem Muhammed

Acquisitions Coordinator
Carmen Krikorian

Editorial Assistant
Andrea Duvall

Book Designer
Ruth Harvey

Cover Designer
Barb Kordesh

Production Team
Marcia Brizendine
Jessica Ford
Trey Frank
Brian Grossman
Julie Geeting
Dan Harris
Christy Hendershot
Daryl Kessler
Anjy Perry
Casey Price
Lisa Stumph
Marvin Van Tiem

Indexer
Chris Wilcox

Composed in *Helvetica Condensed* and *Stone Serif* by Que Corporation.

For Mom and Dad, who taught me the importance of God, love, family, friends, patience, hard work, and honesty in the only way that really matters—by example.

Prolog

Nine Months From Conception to Birth

A funny thing happened on the way to writing this book. A few weeks after I signed the contract, my wife Joan discovered she was expecting. This meant that the development of our first child and our first book would happen in parallel, and the timing couldn't have been worse.

For the first few months, Joan was not well. Morning sickness gave way to afternoon sickness, which would turn to evening sickness promptly at 6:00 p.m., and she couldn't work, eat, or sleep. Thus, many of her home responsibilities fell on me, and I couldn't write as often as I had hoped.

Likewise, as I started taking time away from my companies to write, they got sick too. I never realized that every decision, every problem, every idea, and every activity in my companies seems to be funneled through me. When I stopped going to work, the funnel blocked up, and the backup began. As the months went on, Joan got sicker, and my ventures got sicker too. I tried to remain oblivious to it all and just focus on writing, but for a time my life was as challenging as it's ever been.

At Month Five, things suddenly began to look brighter. Joan's illness broke and she was back on her feet. My evenings were free for writing instead of nursing and cleaning, allowing me to go in to my office by day. The redirection of effort pulled my business ventures out of chaos and got all cylinders firing again.

The fifth month, the baby and the book both began to really take shape. Now at the halfway point of both projects, each was showing real signs of life. The baby's arms and legs were strong, kicking and rolling around inside Joan—truly a marvel to behold. Likewise, this book was fully outlined, chapter edits from Que were stacking up, my staff was helping me hack out code routines, and Fred, the Publishing Manager, was kicking and rolling around too, trying to get me to work faster. Life was fairly good.

By Month Eight of both projects, there were clouds over our heads again. For her part, Joan had never realized how hard the final stage of pregnancy was. She was getting tired easily and having trouble sleeping. The baby had gone from a bump to a bowling ball and now was quite a load to carry.

And so it was with this book. What I thought would take five months was taking twice as long. I was constantly adding new topics, revising the outline, hitting technical roadblocks, and getting lost in style debates with my employees and peers. Like Joan, I was losing sleep too, laying awake at night composing sentences.

Time, however, marched on and swept us to the finish line. The baby grew very quickly the last month, as did my page count. The closer Joan got to delivery, the more desperate I was to finish writing—I was writing in bed, on airplanes, in restaurants, and everywhere else (sitting in the doctor's reception area together waiting for her checkup, I was writing chapter outlines on the back of a magazine while Joan quietly cheered, "Go! Go! Go!")

I finished writing almost the same instant the baby was born, and Joan and I both breathed loud sighs of relief. We each were free of our chosen burdens, and could begin to share the joys of post-delivery.

In retrospect, writing a book alone was much harder than I had envisioned. Most books are collaborative efforts of multiple authors or ghost writers, and now I know why. My book would have been easier to write with a co-author, just as Joan's pregnancy would have been easier if I had been around more often to help out. The life lesson expressed to us through these parallel experiences was the importance of teamwork and patience.

As you read these words, picture me in a rocking chair, reading Chapter 1, "Access As a Development Tool," aloud to my infant son.

Acknowledgments

The following people proved staunchly supportive of this venture and eagerly provided assistance when asked:

Tod Nielsen, chief of the Access tribe at Microsoft, cheerfully contributed many great stories and insights about the development and use of Access.

F. Scott Barker, a friend of the highest quality and a valued business associate, provided the late-night motivation calls that jolted me awake as I dozed off at the keyboard.

Fred Slone, my Publishing Manager at Que, deftly juggled my missed deadlines and resisted the overwhelming temptation to shackle me to my computer.

Don Roche at Que patiently chased me year after year before I let myself be tackled, and once I did he bravely gave me the freedom to write exactly the book I wanted, not the book that Que wanted.

Sid Stusinski, my second-in-command at Leszynski Company Inc., shouldered my weighty management burdens day after day so that I could write or research. Sid forfeited sleep, income, and family time in order to help me get this book done.

Roger Jennings, fellow Que author, razzed me for three years that I wouldn't really be *Somebody* until I wrote this book.

In addition to my primary support team, the following people contributed their time reviewing chapters, submitting sidebar ideas, and otherwise improving the content of this book:

Several of the developers on my staff—**Wade Webster**, **Sid Stusinski**, **Curt Whitaker**, and **Michael Beaton**—read and re-read my chapters, helping to improve their content and usability.

David Crosby, Development Manager at Washington Mutual Bank and the model of a great client, provided useful real-world perspectives and feedback.

Patti Leszynski, my sister and company Office Manager, huddled over CorelDRAW! and Visio creating many of the figures herein, and deftly juggled rushing chapters to FedEx as an additional duty on her already long list.

David Risher, of the Access group at Microsoft, contributed story ideas and moral support.

Michael Metzger, of MTX Inc., shared with me his company's war stories about application and database conversion.

Neil Black, of the Microsoft Jet group, eagerly checked every word of my SQL Server chapter.

Gregory Lucas, my attorney, who dotted the *i's*, crossed the *t's*, and made sure I was neither the abuser nor the abused in my business dealings with Que.

Of course, my greatest debt is to my wife, **Joan**, who spent two hundred evenings alone so that I could climb this mountain. She never complained or threatened, even when days passed where she had seen me for only a few minutes. Over the years, Joan has been consistently supportive of my business risks and responsibilities, and without her support I would be one tenth of what I am today. I could fill a book several times the size of this one with a list of her wonderful qualities, but suffice it to say that she's the best wife anywhere.

Both my parents and Joan's also deserve thanks. While I wrote, Joan's mother **Winnie** and father **Bob** fed and amused her. When we needed help around the house while I tickled the keyboard, my mother **Lois** went shopping for us and my father, **Stan Sr.**, mowed our lawn and fixed our cars.

Finally, there are scores of client companies and hundreds of their employees—far too many to mention here—who provided me and my staff with the fifteen years of development challenges that make *Access 97 Expert Solutions* a practical book based on real-life experiences. To all of them I say, "Thank you for choosing Leszynski Company Inc. as your development partner."

About the Author

Stan Leszynski is the original Access "Insider"—the first person outside of Microsoft to create an Access end-user solution with the Access 1.0 alpha release. Before Access had ever shipped to the public, Stan had created a complex Access application with a dozen users and half a million records for Bill Gates' second company, Corbis Corporation. Since those days, Stan and his staff have helped design and test every release of Access.

Leszynski Company, Inc., was started in 1982 to provide software design consulting and contract application development. They have worked with hundreds of clients and produced software products and solutions that sit on millions of desktops around the world. Some of the retail products Stan and his company have designed and developed are the 386MAX 6.0 and ASQ, two products for Qualitas, Inc. that together reached 1.5 million computers; the ActiveX Calendar Control shipped by Microsoft with Access versions 2, 95, and 97, which reached over ten million users; Microsoft's Internet Explorer Starter Kit, with more than twelve million copies distributed.

Leszynski Company, Inc. is a Microsoft Solution Provider specializing in Access, Visual Basic, SQL Server, and Visual C++ applications. Stan and his company have created over 100 custom Access applications for clients large and small, including Microsoft and AT&T.

Stan's second venture, Kwery Corporation, creates developer tools and ActiveX controls for the retail marketplace and distributes products built around the Leszynski Naming Conventions and Leszynski Development Framework. Kwery was the first company anywhere to ship an Access add-on product (called Access To Word).

Stan writes the Developer's View column for *Access/Visual Basic Advisor* magazine. He has also contributed to *PC Magazine*, *Microsoft Systems Journal*, and over a dozen Access and Visual Basic books, including Que's bestselling "Using Access" titles. Stan can also be regularly found speaking at TechEd, VBITS, and other Microsoft Office developer conferences around the world. In 1995 Stan and Access guru, F. Scott Barker, produced Microsoft Office developer conferences around the world. Their company, LBI, produces several conferences each year Europe and Asia.

Stan lives in Bellevue, Washington with his wife Joan. They have a new son, also named Stan in keeping with a family tradition going back three hundred years.

Leszynski Company, Inc.	**www.lciinfo.com**
Kwery Corporation	**www.kwery.com**
Leszynski Barker International	**www.lbiinfo.com**
Leszynski Development Framework	**www.ldfinfo.com**

We'd Like to Hear from You!

As part of our continuing effort to produce books of the highest possible quality, Que would like to hear your comments. To stay competitive, we *really* want you, as a computer book reader and user, to let us know what you like or dislike most about this book or other Que products.

You can mail comments, ideas, or suggestions for improving future editions to the address below, or send us a fax at (317) 581-4663. For the online inclined, Macmillan Computer Publishing has a forum on CompuServe (type **GO QUEBOOKS** at any prompt) through which our staff and authors are available for questions and comments. The address of our Internet site, the Macmillan Information SuperLibrary is **http://www.mcp.com** (World Wide Web).

In addition to exploring our forums, please feel free to contact me personally to discuss your opinions of this book: I'm **104470,324** on CompuServe, and I'm **klmarshall@que.mcp.com** on the Internet.

Thanks in advance—your comments will help us to continue publishing the best books available on computer topics in today's market.

Kelly Marshall
Product Director
Que Corporation
201 W. 103rd Street
Indianapolis, Indiana 46290
USA

 Note

Although we cannot provide general technical support, we're happy to help you resolve problems you encounter related to our books, disks, or other products. If you need such assistance, please contact our Tech Support department at 800-545-5914 ext. 3833.

To order other Que or Macmillan Computer Publishing books or products, please call our Customer Service department at 800-835-3202 ext. 666.

Contents at a Glance

Contents

5 Creating Naming Conventions 177

7   Understanding Application Architecture   267

8   Designing Effective Interfaces   325

Foreword

Access Expert Solutions—
My Perspective

By Tod Neilsen, General Manager of the Access Business Unit at Microsoft

---

Number Seven—

In 1994, I was doing the keynote address at an Access conference where Stan was also a featured speaker. I started my keynote with a slide called "The Top Ten Reasons I Came to This Conference." I thought I'd have a little fun at Stan's expense, so as Number Seven on my slide I put, "To learn how to properly spell Leszynski."

I didn't know at the time how Stan would respond, but I *did* know that he wouldn't sit back and just enjoy the notoriety. True to form, at Stan's first speech the next day he gave a presentation called "How to spell Leszynski using Microsoft Access objects," in which he ribbed not only our product but me personally. It turns out he had stayed up most of the night putting together these slides just to get even with me.

Stan is very competitive!

At the top of the pyramid of Access solution developers sit only a few people, and one of them is Stan Leszynski. Since the alpha release of Access 1.0, he has tirelessly stretched our product with applications for his clients, and bent our ears with his feedback.

When Stan told me his objectives for *Access 97 Expert Solutions*, I was elated. Within the Access group, we realize that we can never have enough resources to fully enlighten people on how to use our product. Thus, we rely heavily on the third-party marketplace to further explain and educate people on the depth of Microsoft Access.

One such information shortfall is the creation and articulation of standard practices for users of Access. I imagine that, if everyone were taught to drive with different rules of the road, the chaos on our streets would be unimaginable. Yet at Microsoft, we do not have the resources to train millions of people to "drive" our product, so each user drives

Access a little differently. Stan's passion is helping to create the "rules of the road" so that Access developers have fewer collisions, especially when developing applications for beginning to intermediate users. This book is his attempt to give people who are serious about Access a framework for approaching the application development process methodically.

While my position at Microsoft does not allow me to endorse the specific styles and approaches in this book, I *do* strongly endorse the discussions the book creates. Historically, debates about product features and benefits really heat up when someone puts an idea in motion (in print or in practice), where others can see it, try it, and critique it. For that, we at Microsoft have come to depend on Stan. His writing and speaking often seeds discussions that directly or indirectly influence our product.

For example, his publication of the original Access naming conventions sparked a broad debate on the subject, and three things happened:

1. Developers told Stan what they liked and didn't like about his style, and he improved it based upon their feedback. The style became so refined and well-regarded that we in the Access group even use it.

2. Developers who never realized the need for naming conventions entered the debate, and were enlightened to new development techniques as a result.

3. Users who read about naming conventions got a better understanding of the objects in Access and their roles in an application, and thus they came to better appreciate the richness of our product.

No doubt the same benefits will accrue to the marketplace from this book. The ideas that Stan sets forth—research and specification guidelines, application interface approaches, "Bulletproofing" techniques, and the like—will cause thousands of developers to review and discuss their own development style and tools as contrasted with Stan's ideas.

Stan is the first to admit that he doesn't care so much that people use the guidelines he writes down, but rather he cares deeply that people discuss his ideas enough to decide if they are right or wrong for them. In the end, the big winners of such debates are the users of Access applications, who will inherit more friendly and powerful "expert solutions" at the end of the process.

Preface

Why Expert Solutions?

So Much Wisdom in So Few Words

I was having a problem last year getting the design team together on a client's database project. A design team member at the client company summed up the reason that nobody would come to the meetings we had scheduled with them: "I don't trust any computer that I can pick up and carry."

This says a lot. First, it indicates the shock and disbelief that users encounter when they learn just how much work can really be done with a single Pentium machine running a good Access application. At that moment of discovery, an individual fears that his or her job will be lost to automation.

Secondly, his comment bears testimony to the inability of users and managers to properly budget for software development. If bigger is better, as our client implied, then buying a drive array for a minicomputer (which may cost as much as several thousand hours of our consulting time) is easier to justify than a custom programming effort.

Solution providers like my company, and in-house corporate developers as well, face a significant public relations challenge: to sway and correct the mistaken opinions like the one expressed here by our client. We can only do so by example—by creating custom applications that deliver high power at a low cost. Access helps us do this.

Fortunately, each day brings thousands more PC users into the fold of people who rave about the desktop computer revolution, and who are willing to trust Access and its champions with their critical data.

Let Me Be Your Coach

I believe that application developers are the intellectual athletes of the Cyber age. They improve their skills through dogged determination, constantly set new challenges for themselves, and develop their own disciplines and styles the same way as a tennis champion, golf pro, or Major League pitcher.

If you are such a developer, or want to be one, this book is my effort to volunteer as your coach. I believe that Access developers now have enough *raw information* available to them through books, magazines, and conferences. What is lacking is a proper *context* for the information. By this I mean that the features of Access and the techniques of its developers are the puzzle pieces. Even when you have all the pieces laid out in front of you, you still can't combine them into a solution without the wisdom to visualize the desired result. Thus, Access Expert Solutions is as much a *why* book as a *how-to* book, as I attempt to help you understand the value of skills in addition to the skills themselves, and help you mix the skills together to satisfy the needs of the solution.

The word "Expert" in the title is not meant to imply that the book is *for* experts, or even designed to make *you* into an expert. Instead, the word implies that I (your personal expert) am providing examples of how my team creates applications. The end result of what we do is an "expert solution," which is an application that does the following:

▶ satisfies the users' needs

▶ meets the budget

▶ is easy to use

▶ protects the data

When you have finished this book, your measure of success will be your ability to *create* an expert solution as opposed to your ability to engage in intellectual combat with other "experts."

A Dose of Reality

I sat down and tried to determine what differentiated successful application development projects from unsuccessful ones. I came up with what I felt were important points to cover here. What was not so easy, however, was to decide *how* to cover these points. I decided upon a style that hopefully entertains and stimulates.

I include real-world examples and stories in this book, in order to provide my opinions and techniques with some context. I also use fewer screen shots and more words than similarly-sized books. In many sections here, I'm more concerned with helping you create a *mental picture* of what I'm saying than I am with showing you a visual representation of the subject at hand. The reason is that my own personal style of teaching is influenced by the opportunity I've had to observe Microsoft at close proximity.

In Bill Gate's company, and in mine, we attempt to present our people with responsibilities and challenges that are just slightly beyond their current abilities, and trust that two things will happen:

1. *The job will get done*, because a bright and conscientious person will not rest until a challenge is surmounted and a solution is found.

2. *The person will learn something along the way.* The world is now too complex to rest long on a given skill set; workers must be adaptive to new challenges and technologies. "Give a person a code snippet, and they'll use it for a day; *teach* a person to code, and they'll code for a lifetime."

Thus, I don't want you to simply read what I am saying and paste my code samples into your applications. Instead, I want you to be slightly intrigued or intimidated by my words and ideas, so that you'll go forth to your keyboard or white board and either improve upon my suggested solution, or extrapolate what I've taught you into you own personal approach.

Regardless of your level of experience or skills, I cover some ground in this book that you probably have not yet trodden. Many good developers are not good planners, and many good planners want to learn to be developers. Thus, I try here to give each of these people new ideas and techniques that will *broaden* their skill base in addition to *deepening* it.

What I don't cover in this book are skills that I think you should have *before* you read a book of this kind, or skills that you can get from the Access documentation. For example, you will not find a chapter about macros here. I'm not ignoring the fact that you may be using macros in your applications—I simply believe that everything that can be said about macros is already in print somewhere else.

So Many Ideas, So Little Time

I tried to educate but not pontificate. Nevertheless, I can't discuss the unique discipline we bring to developing applications without feeling and conveying some pride in our methodology. Thus, I have leant my name to—and gambled my reputation on—ideas in this book such as the Leszynski Development Framework and the Leszynski Naming Conventions. Giving my ideas a name is not an ego play; rather, I expect that the marketplace will have better success in debating my ideas if it can describe them by name and point to their location in print.

It turns out that the experiences I want to share with readers fill more than one book, so along the way some concepts were scrapped. As one example, I had to trade out either the SQL Server chapter or the replication chapter. Because we've been doing client server applications with several versions of Access, but replication is rather new, I opted to write about the topic where I could add the most value by basing it on the largest number of hands-on experiences.

Where Do You Want Your Applications To Go Today?

In talking with the Access group, I found that Microsoft has identified the three major trends in the PC database marketplace:

1. *More people buy software suites than stand-alone products.* The fact that more people acquire Access through Office than singly means that Microsoft if forced to pay more attention each year to the interoperability between their products, and so must you and I. This means that we are no longer Access developers, we are Office developers.

   There aren't enough pages to talk about using Access in conjunction with all of the Office suite. However, I *do* help you understand how to approach development, how to design applications, how to work with users, and how to deliver solutions. Once you understand these issues in the context of Access, you can easily extrapolate each of these skills to use the other Office components or Visual Basic on your own.

2. *Access led the merger of programmable and user-oriented databases.* Until Access, there were database products for programmers and other database products for users. Access redefined the category by creating a product for *all* types of buyers. What this means to you is that you must work harder to protect users from becoming developers before their time. In other words, your Access application objects and data are sometimes exposed and not secure—you don't want users browsing through your objects and potentially changing them.

   In this book, I've tried to give you the techniques to create powerful applications with a product that many Information Technology departments still view as a simple end-user query tool. I believe that an expert solution restricts the *user* features of Access while utilizing its *development* features to the fullest potential.

3. *Users are getting more sophisticated.* The mysterious shroud around the programming hive in many companies has been lifted. Instead, your users know a little about Basic and question your coding decisions; they ask why your run-time application does not allow them to create ad hoc queries; and they want to add their own reports to your application after it's complete.

   Yet, I've tried here to provide tricks and techniques that allow you to create flexible applications while still protecting the underlying data, so that you can at least attempt to address *any* user request or challenge. Occasionally, I anticipate that you will thump on this book when asked to justify your approach to a problem, and say, "If you want to know why I did it this way, read this."

I put more time into this book than I actually had available to give. But once I started, there was no turning back—I was obsessed with creating a quality product that you would find valuable. Please let me know if I succeeded.

Introduction

In order to get the most value from your computer technology, and to prevent its misuse, you should create reusable systems and published standards. Everyone knows this fact, but few apply it. In the Access environment, some developers think a systematic approach to development is to use the form wizards so all their forms look similar. They neglect to take the next step, however, to ensure that their forms include help or status bar text for users, validation rules to protect the data, and event procedures to trap errors and changes in status. The difference between the two steps is the difference between using Access *well* and using Access *wisely*. I wrote this book to help you use Access wisely.

Why Doesn't My Computer Understand Me?

Computers and software get faster and more powerful with each passing release. But are these tools really getting *smarter?* My father has watched me upgrade my personal computers each year for the past 14 years and notes with each revision that he will buy a computer as soon as computers can understand his speech.

I think many of us dream—even expect—that computers will be able to converse with us in the not-too-distant future. But even at that point, will they really be any smarter? Will they understand only what Dad *says,* or what he actually *means?* The difference is important, especially with respect to data stored in a database. Imagine the difference between these requests:
"Hal, add a record to the contact table noting that I saw *fourteen* people today" and "Hal, add a record to the contact table noting that I saw *four teen* people today."

Ultimately, it is up to us as users to continue to adhere to the maxim that has pervaded the computer world since its beginning: garbage in, garbage out. If you ask a flawed question of the computer, you can expect a flawed answer. If you enter bad data into a database, you will make a bad decision based on the inaccurate report that comes out. This probably will be true in the future, when you are speaking to your machine, as it is today. Consequently, users and application developers—and not the computers themselves—are responsible for the quality of information that is stored in databases.

Deciding Whether This Book Is for You

What standardized approaches do you use to develop Access applications? If you are like most Access users and developers, you've not had the time or energy to even consider creating standard approaches, development tools, or reusable objects to make your time in Access more productive—simply learning to use Access well keeps you plenty busy. This book was written with your situation in mind.

Access is a product with multiple personalities. On the surface, a quick tour of Access leads you to believe that it was created primarily for database neophytes. Like a friendly personal assistant, Access helps you organize and store your information by using such features as the following:

- A well-organized Database window
- Wizards for constructing database objects
- A variety of built-in properties to define each object
- A simplified macro scripting language

However, below the surface lies a completely different persona—that of a workhorse just waiting to pull your heavy load with the following features:

▶ Automation waits to serve you when you need to program Access to print reports from within Visual Basic or to edit Access 97 table data while inside an Excel worksheet.

▶ The Visual Basic for Applications programming language gives you the building blocks for creating robust applications in Access 97 and for automating complex business processes.

▶ The Access relational data model and Structured Query Language (SQL) foundation allow you to make uncomplicated representations of complex data.

▶ The Jet Database Engine exposes programmable Data Access Objects that allow your program code direct access to database data and structures.

In Part I, "The Leszynski Development Framework," this book assumes you are comfortable working with the personal assistant side of Access. You should know your way around the Database window and understand the various Access objects. In Part II, "Expert Solutions Techniques," a slightly higher skill level is expected. You should be able to create basic tables, queries, forms and reports, and to apply the fundamentals of writing a VBA function or event procedure. With such a foundation in place, you are now ready to use this book to tame the workhorse persona of Access, or if you're using it already, to make it work even harder for you.

You will find this book valuable if you fit any of the following Access user profiles:

▶ *Beginning User Ready To Grow.* You are comfortable with the basics of Access and want a structured approach for moving to the next skill level.

▶ *Student.* You want to understand how applications are constructed and how to create and apply systematic approaches to their development.

▶ *Small Business Owner.* You need a real-world approach to collecting and managing data using Access so you can make better business decisions from the data, or you need to be able to speak conversantly with development staff or contractors who write your applications for you.

▶ *Business Application User.* You are on the receiving end of Access development, using custom applications to perform much of your work. You want to be able to understand the processes used by those who develop applications for you, so you can work with them closely to improve the quality of the products they give you.

▶ *Power User.* You desire to know more about Access and want to be challenged with new tips, techniques, and concepts.

▶ *Information Systems Developer.* You work in a development environment where reusable systems and standards have proven to be beneficial, and you want to learn the systems and standards for Access development.

▶ *Information Systems Manager.* You manage application developers and want methodologies for making them more successful and cost-effective, or you want to understand the effort required to create applications.

▶ *Solution Provider.* You need to deliver solutions to clients or coworkers quickly, and need techniques to ensure that you meet their expectations and budgets in the process.

▶ *Contract Programmer.* You create applications and write code for a living, and can increase the demand for your services by following techniques employed by other successful programmers.

These profiles match the majority of user types that are serious about Access as a productivity tool, or would like to be. You'll note that the list above does not include the casual home user or the user trying to create their first Access table or form. If you are trying to figure out how to create your first table, macro, or form, this book is less useful to you than step-by-step feature books like Que's *Using Access 97* by F. Scott Barker or *Using Access 97* by Jennings.

What Is an Expert Solution?

The term *expert solutions* in this book's title does not mean *solutions created by experts.* This book does not assume you are an expert nor that you want to be. Instead, the title is meant to imply that you'll learn about *solutions created using the processes employed by experts.* This book helps you learn how Access application experts work—their standards, philosophies, tools, and techniques—and how to apply such knowledge to your development.

What You Will Learn

Most software books are *feature-focused.* They walk you through the features of a tool with each chapter devoted to a specific technique or technology. They demonstrate features using a sample application that may or may not be relevant to your needs in an attempt to cover most of a product's features along the way.

This book takes a different approach. *Access 97 Expert Solutions* is *process-focused* instead of *feature-focused.* It recognizes that application development is a process with the following attributes:

▶ *It is alive.* Development has a beginning, a middle, and an end. It involves people, thus it is a living process that changes but can be controlled.

▶ *It is quantifiable.* The development process has opportunities, milestones, and pitfalls to be aware of along the way. Developers can be taught to recognize each of these.

▶ *It can be mastered.* If it can be standardized, written down, taught, and applied consistently, it can be mastered. The *process* of development is easier to master than the development techniques themselves.

▶ *It pays dividends.* If you master the development process, you achieve very important objectives. Because Access applications are virtually always built to save somebody time, money, or both, a successful development process will pay dividends in these areas. (And conversely, an unsuccessful one may cost more than it returns!)

In this book, you will spend time with both facets of the Access application development process: *theory* and *technique*. I personally don't believe that you can be successful unless you apply and understand both equally well. If you understand the theory of application development (the attributes listed previously), and do not apply them to your forms, reports, Visual Basic coding, and so on, you will still not create solid applications. On the other hand, if you have outstanding programming skills but do not understand how an application is constructed or how the development process flows, you will deliver incomplete or flawed solutions.

Consider a real-life analogy. First, picture an accountant named Mike. He has been to eight years of college and reads accounting books voraciously. He can spout tax law in a heartbeat, always knows the prime interest rate and the Dow Jones average, and teaches evening accounting classes at the local university. Mike is really good with theory.

However, the work he actually produces tells a different story. When you put him in charge of your taxes, he takes all your receipts and staples them together alphabetically instead of by category. He totals them in his head and regularly adds the numbers wrong. When filling out your tax forms he scratches out mistakes instead of erasing them. And he leaves his filing cabinet and office containing your personal financial records unlocked, even when he goes home. While competent in the theory of accounting, Mike is *not* good with technique.

Now, picture a second accountant, Mary. You send her your financial information and she produces a balance sheet for you in only two days. The report has been entered into a computer and has headers, footers, and perfect math. She makes several copies—for you, your spouse, and your banker—and sends them to you by registered mail. Mary is obviously a whiz at technique.

However, on reading your balance sheet, you notice that she hasn't adjusted your real estate asset holdings by subtracting the mortgage balances. She also placed liabilities before assets, in violation of published Generally Accepted Accounting Principles, and forgot to project your impending tax liability. While Mary is great at implementation, she is not good at theory. She understands how to produce results, but not *usable, accurate results.*

Access 97 Expert Solutions recognizes that there are many Access users, developers, and project managers that are like Mike or Mary, but not as many that have the best attributes of both. The following are the three primary reasons why few developers have mastered both the theory and technique domains within Access development:

▸ *Access is a young product.* It takes quite a lot of time and experimentation to understand how to apply this complex product to your specific needs or environment. Access has been available for about four years.

▸ *People are too busy.* Your company is probably either downsizing or right-sizing, and you are most likely past due on many of your personal and business obligations as well. So who has time in the 90s to truly master a business skill or hobby on their own?

▸ *Lack of leadership.* Many companies, small and large, use Access aggressively. Yet few have published stories about their successful approach to development or placed their applications in the public domain as learning tools. And many Access training materials are based upon a restatement of the Access manuals and not actual experience with the product in a business environment.

This book is the first ever to comprehensively document the theoretical side of Access development. It has two main parts (Part I and Part II), the first of which is primarily devoted to application development theory. In Part I, "The Leszynski Development Framework," you learn how to do the following:

▸ Plan your application.

▸ Research your users' needs and document them in a specification.

▸ Design your application with a logical layout.

▸ Consistently name and reference application objects.

▸ Design friendly and familiar user interfaces.

▸ Organize and reuse objects you've invested time in.

▸ Deliver your application to users, and support and upgrade it.

Part I pulls these application elements together into the *Leszynski Development Framework* (LDF), which reflects the belief stated in the first list in this topic: If it can be standardized, written down, taught, and applied consistently, it can be mastered. You can use the LDF blueprint over and over to guide your development process. Whether the application is large or small, LDF provides the rules to minimize your design time, management effort, and development problems on the project.

Part II, "Expert Solutions Techniques," concentrates on the technical side of development. Everyone loves tips and tricks, and you will find plenty there. But this book goes beyond the norm and shows how its tips and tricks map back to the theoretical half of the book. Thus, the tips and tricks provide practical examples of how to *implement* one or more of the theoretical points detailed in Part I. Taken together, the parts of this book combine to present the blending of theory and technique required to produce truly expert solutions.

Foundations for Expert Solutions

The information in this book is based on actual events and the lessons learned from them. I have collected real-life experiences from my work and from that of my development staff in shaping the content. Among us, we have created hundreds of PC applications in the last dozen years, about 100 of them in Access. I wanted the examples in this book—even in the theoretical chapters—to reflect real things that happen to real users and developers. I hope you find some small touchstone in each example that feels familiar and helps you see its applicability to your own situation or experiences.

Collecting Stories

Some of the more interesting examples and short stories collected for this book are used in the chapter sidebars where they are most relevant. Many of these stories were submitted by people in the Access development and marketing groups at Microsoft, and others solicited from prominent developers in the Access community. Where a credit is not noted, the example is mine or is by one of my employees.

Most of the Access applications developed by my company have development time budgets of between 200 and 500 hours, which means that they are user interface intensive, to the following extent that:

▶ Users of our applications are rarely allowed to work from the Database window.

▶ Menus and navigation routines are provided to guide users.

▶ All data entered into the system is validated.

▶ Most query capabilities and reporting needs are met by the application; users are not expected to skirt the application and use Access ad hoc.

▶ Every VBA procedure has error trapping.

▶ User and system documentation are created for each application.

These listed attributes are part of what I consider to be the minimum requirements for delivering a quality Access application to users. This book is intended to show you why each of these areas is important, and how to implement each in your development work.

I also applied a lot of personal experiences to the writing of this book. As the owner of a consulting firm, I have a payroll to meet and clients to satisfy. Without repeatable techniques, documented conventions, reusable objects, coding standards, and similar methodologies, I could not be organized, successful, and profitable while meeting all these objectives. I believe earnestly in the necessity of the information in this book, not from some abstract viewpoint but rather because my company uses every technique detailed in it.

Applying This Book to Access 2 and Access 95

If you've not migrated to Access 97 from Access 2, about 75 percent of this book is still useful to you. Almost all of the theoretical discussions in Part I, "The Leszynski Development Framework," apply to Access 2 development exactly as they are worded or with very minor modifications. Roughly half of the technique topics in Part II, "Expert Solutions Techniques," will still apply to Access 2 with the remainder specific to Access 97's enhancements.

Access 95 users will find that many features were left unchanged between the 95 and 97 versions, and thus the majority of topics in this book are applicable with no modification.

If you'd like to upgrade from Access 2 or Access 95 before using this book, use the guidelines provided in Appendix D, "Converting Existing Access Applications," on the CD-ROM.

Applying This Book to Other Microsoft Products

Because this book strikes a balance between the theory of development and the technique, much of its content can be extrapolated from Access into other environments. Indeed, I know very few Access developers that are not Office users, Visual Basic users, or FoxPro users—sometimes using all of these platforms together. Once you read and understand the methodologies in Part I of the book, you will be able to apply them from Access to your other development tools with little to no modification. For example, the discussion of application testing in Chapter 9, "Completing and Deploying a Solution," is relevant to any applications that use forms to collect information. Whether you are deploying your solution in Access, Excel, Visual Basic, or FoxPro, the approach detailed in that chapter will provide you with value.

If you use or mix both Access and Visual Basic, you will find this book especially useful because both of its major segments are appropriate to both tools. Because these two products have so many features in common (the use of forms, the Jet Database Engine, the Basic language, and so on), the development theory elements that Part I describes apply to your Visual Basic projects in an almost word-for-word fashion.

However, the real bonus comes in Part II. The tips and techniques for creating Jet databases, for coding conventions, for form data validation, for multiuser applications, and for code libraries can be applied to Visual Basic verbatim or with very few syntax or structure changes. Other topics in Part II, such as working with forms and client/server data, are implemented differently in Visual Basic than in Access. Nevertheless, with some modifications, the techniques in those topics can also be made applicable to Visual Basic.

Defining the Terms Used in This Book

Perhaps you purchased this book mostly for the LDF material, or you bought it to help you plan the transition from Access 2 or Access 95 to Access 97. Because many portions of this book are as equally appropriate to Access 2 and Access 95 as to Access 97, the terminology used in the book is intended to help you distinguish whether only one of these products, as opposed to all Access versions, is being discussed in a specific context:

Access. When this term is used with no clarification, the point being discussed applies to all versions of Access from Access 2 forward.

Access 2. Shorthand for the final 16-bit version of Access, formally Microsoft Access 2.0.

Access 95. Shorthand for the full product name of Access for Windows 95, which is technically also Microsoft Access 7.0.

Access 97. Shorthand for the full product name of Access for Windows 97, which is technically also Microsoft Access 8.x. In general, statements I make and development examples shown for Access 97 are appropriate to Access 95.

In addition, I also use the following terms and abbreviations throughout the book:

Access Basic, Basic, VBA, and *Visual Basic for Applications*. These terms are used interchangeably to represent the programming engine in Access 95 and 97. When

Access 2 is being discussed specifically, only the terms Access Basic and Basic will be used.

ActiveX, Automation. In 1996, Microsoft created an umbrella marketing brand called "ActiveX™" to describe component technologies. Thus, OLE controls became ActiveX controls, document objects became ActiveX documents, and so on. OLE Automation, however, became simply Automation as opposed to ActiveX Automation.

Application. An Access *database* is a collection of objects in a single file, but an Access *application* is a collection of objects in one or more files that are organized for the benefit of users and presented to them via an interface. An application usually includes forms, reports, menus, and VBA code.

Back-end/Front-end. Most Access solutions are constructed in two pieces. The term *front-end* denotes the portion of the application that resides on the user's workstation, usually a single database with forms, reports, queries, and application code. The term *back-end* describes the location of the data tables, commonly stored apart from the front-end in a Jet database on a file server or an ODBC data source on a database server machine.

Client. My perspective as a developer has always been as a consultant serving a client, so I frequently use this term to describe the users of an application. Whether the users of your applications are paying customers, coworkers within your firm, or your wife and children, this term is still applicable to the relationship between you and your users as you strive to service their needs.

 Note

When I use the term "client" in my speaking engagements, listeners often come up to me afterward and say, "I work in Information Technology, so my users are technically not my clients. Your terminology made me feel like the speech was oriented toward outside consultants rather than in-house developers."

In fact, many Information Technology groups that we work with have standardized the term "client" to describe the application users within their company that they develop for. Describing users with this term adds a tone of seriousness and professionalism to the relationship between developers and users, even within the same firm.

Full Access. This term denotes the retail version of Access—sold as a stand-alone product or with Office Professional—as contrasted with the "runtime" version provided by the Office Developer Edition (ODE).

IT. This abbreviation for Information Technology refers to the department within a company that is responsible for computer software development and management. In the past, the term Information Systems (IS) was used for such a department, and may also appear in the text of this book.

Jet. Shorthand for the Jet Database Engine, which provides all database services to Access. Jet can also be called by other clients like Visual Basic and Visual C++ without invoking Access.

LDF. Shorthand for the Leszynski Development Framework, a term used to describe the development philosophy detailed in Part I, entitled "The Leszynski Development Framework," and used to guide the development techniques described throughout the book. LDF is a formalized set of objectives, principles, and guidelines for application development.

LNC. Shorthand for the Leszynski Naming Conventions, a standardized approach to object names used throughout the book. LNC is described in detail in Chapter 6, "Leszynski Naming Conventions for Access."

Normalize/De-normalize. Normalization is a term related to the construction of relational databases that implies taking tabular data and creating from it one or more tables that convey the data relationships with the least amount of repeated data elements. Normalized tables are often described as having a parent/child/grandchild structure. To de-normalize (also called *flattening*) data tables means to combine data in related, normalized tables into a single, simplified table with repeated values. Normalization is described in more detail in Chapter 10, "Creating Expert Tables and Queries."

Office. Shorthand for Microsoft Office for Windows 97. Microsoft Office versions 4.x, which include Access 2, are not discussed in this book.

ODE. An abbreviation for the Office 97 Developer Edition, which has replaced the Access Developer's Toolkit as the distribution medium for the Access runtime and other tools.

Pseudocode. This term refers to a structural outline of Basic code logic using non-technical and non-executable language.

Schema. The data-oriented structure of a database—tables, queries, fields, relationships, indexes, and related properties—is usually described as an application's schema.

Screen. I use the terms *form* and *screen* interchangeably in this book to represent displayed form objects.

Solution. Within this book, this term is interchangeable with *application*. An Access-based solution consists of one or more files containing objects and a user interface. This term is important because the existence of a solution necessitates the existence of a related problem, and most Access applications are designed to solve a business problem or achieve a business objective.

Spec. This term is common shorthand for design specification, a document that details a development project as described in Chapter 4, "Creating Design Specifications."

VB, Visual Basic, VB 5, and *Visual Basic 5.* To avoid confusion, these four terms are used to describe the product Microsoft Visual Basic and are never used as a short-hand for Visual Basic for Applications (which is represented by the shorthand VBA). When the sentence is specific to 32-bit Visual Basic (4.x and 5.x) and does not apply to 16-bit version 3.x, the terms VB 5 or Visual Basic 5 will be used.

Understanding Other Conventions Used in This Book

This book uses standardized conventions in the following areas:

Typographic Conventions. All VBA code appears in `monospace font`, as do the names of Access objects, properties, methods, events, and other reserved words.

Object Names. Sample code and screen figures contain naming convention type tags (three or four standardized leading characters), such as "int" in the following:

```
Dim intWork As Integer
```

The tags are designed to help you understand the use and context of application and code objects when reading the examples, and are documented in Chapter 6, "Leszynski Naming Conventions for Access."

`Call` *Keyword.* The `Call` keyword in Access VBA is an optional syntax for running a `Sub` procedure, as in:

```
Call subname (argument1, argument2, ...)
```

Throughout the code examples in this book, I use this syntax with `Sub` procedures for two reasons: (a) It is easier when reading the example to determine what the code is doing, because "Call" is used in only this one context, and (b) the use of "Call" requires you to place the procedure's arguments in parentheses, again improving readability. (You can use `Call` with `Function` procedures also, but this is generally not done.)

Error Trapping. To minimize the clutter of code examples in the book, error trapping syntax is not shown in code listings unless relevant to the specific example. However, in practice, all your code should employ `On Error` statements, and the majority of the code on the CD-ROM reflects this belief. See Chapter 11, "Expert Approaches to VBA," for a complete discussion of error trapping.

Library Routines. Library code routines used in the code listings and sample databases in the book and on the CD-ROM are often derived from the Leszynski Company Inc. code library. Such routines begin with the "lci_" prefix characters. The databases shipped on the CD-ROM are self-contained, meaning that each holds all the code and library routines required to run the examples in it. Thus, more than one database contains the same library code routines. In actual practice, the common library routines would usually be located in a central library database or all in the application front-end database to avoid such duplication.

Break on All Errors Setting. Code in the sample databases on the CD-ROM may make use of a standard error-trapping methodology that allows errors to occur and then traps and manages such errors. Consequently, if your Access environment settings includes a Break on All Errors option setting of `True`, some routines on the CD-ROM drop into code when they are run. Make sure this option setting is cleared when running code included with this book.

From Here...

This introduction describes the organization of *Access 97 Expert Solutions*, the value you receive from it, and how to apply it beyond only Access 97. Because the flow from theory to technique as described here is much akin to crawling before walking, you should read Part I of this book, "The Leszynski Development Framework," if you can, before reading Part II, "Expert Solutions Techniques."

▶ To begin your study of application development theory, read Chapter 2, "Introducing the Leszynski Development Framework."

▶ For specific development techniques that you can apply to your application, start reading Chapter 10, "Creating Expert Tables and Queries."

The Leszynski Development Framework

Access as a Development Tool

1

C an every data manipulation problem be solved with Access? Are there any data-centric solutions where Access simply does not fit?

Of course, Microsoft's marketing mavens would have you believe that the answers to these two questions are an unquali-fied yes and no. My own answers to the questions are similar to Microsoft's, but slightly more qualified:

▶ Yes, Access can play a role in almost every PC data management scenario.

▶ Yes, there are a few data-centric solutions where Access or Jet cannot play a role.

To expand on these questions and their answers, I think it is beneficial to clarify how Access can best be used in a variety of circumstances. User and developer satisfaction with Access is not enhanced when Access is misused or applied when it's not appropriate.

Table Wizardry

About 30 percent of my company's Access development projects begin when a client hands us a large Excel worksheet filled with data and says, "This is out of control; move it to Access." Without a relational data model where one record can point to many other records, expressing information in a worksheet format quickly hits its limit.

The Access group at Microsoft heard about this data migration from our clients and other users and devised an elegant solution. Beginning with the 95 version, Access ships with the Table Analyzer Wizard that breaks Excel worksheets and other tabular data down into component Access tables, complete with relationships. Unfortunately for me, the wizard is so good that now some of our clients can migrate their data without our help!

 ### Tip

Access works your machine very hard, and can seem slow at times when running applications that rely heavily on forms and VBA code. I don't find that our clients are satisfied running our Access applications in 8 megabytes of RAM. Access is much more efficient in 12, 16, or ideally 32 megabytes. If you are committed to Access, consider whether or not your hardware is up to the challenge.

A test suite we ran to load Access included opening a complex application, checking user permissions, linking tables, and loading the main menu. The following list shows the length of time the test took on different hardware configurations:

486/50 with 8M RAM	78 seconds
486/50 with 16M RAM	28 seconds
586/90 with 32M RAM	7 seconds

Notice the substantial performance increases gained by spending a few hundred dollars on RAM or around $1,500 more on the higher-powered machine. When considering such extra hardware expenditures, evaluate the cost of time people spend waiting for their computers against the cost of the upgrade.

Access User Statistics

The registration card completed by purchasers of Access contains a short survey about the environment Access will be used in. Although Microsoft qualifies the validity of any information gleaned from registration cards by saying that experienced users return the cards more frequently than new users and thus skew the results, a summary of the survey information is still enlightening for our purposes in this chapter. (Note that the most recent statistics available from Microsoft were for Access 2.)

Sixty-two percent of the Access 2 survey respondents develop applications for use by others. Of these, 43 percent work in an IS/IT group in systems analysis, or doing PC support in their corporation. (The other 57 percent presumably create applications in an unofficial capacity.) Of the users that registered Access 2, 16 percent are also registered for Visual Basic or Visual Basic Professional (although there may be some overlap in these numbers).

Six percent of Access users responding are self-employed, 33 percent work for a company with fewer than 100 employees, and 41 percent work for a company with 1,000 employees or more. Perhaps the most interesting statistic is that 43 percent of registered buyers use Access at work only; 22 percent use Access at home only; and an impressive 35 percent use Access at both work and home.

While such information is not statistically significant, it does indicate a measurable diversity among Access users and their installations.

Access at Home

Four years ago, if you thought using Access 1.x at home was like using a sledgehammer to swat a fly, you were correct. At that time, home PC users lacked sophistication and most could not grasp the relational data model. Access had only a few wizards and thus a long learning curve. Few home PCs had the 16 megabytes of memory and 486 or 586 processors that Access demands.

Now the home marketplace is quite different. The explosion of *multimedia PCs*—machines with enough random access memory and processor horsepower to deal with complex sound and graphics—has brought suitable equipment for use with Access into many homes. Also, surveys show that one quarter of all home PC owners regularly take some of their work home to do on their computers; so the sophistication of home computer users has climbed steadily as a result. Finally, Microsoft Office Professional, of which Access is a part, is convenient for home users who want to use the same software at home that they have already learned to use at work.

If you use or intend to use Access at home, and you are reading this book, you most likely fit into one of the previous two categories: Either you are a business user bringing Access work home, or you are a home user, who knows Access through your job, and want your home machine to resemble your work machine. It is natural for you to reason that if Access can manage your business data, it can certainly handle your home data.

Just because personal computers at home are getting more powerful and their owners more adept, is Access necessarily the right tool for non-business projects? Microsoft thinks so. In Access 97, when you create a new database, you can select a template for the Database Wizard to use to meet your specific purpose. Some of these database templates are quite obviously designed for home PC users: Book Collection, Donations, and Household Inventory, to name a few (see Figure 1.1).

Fig. 1.1
Several database templates are included with the Access 97 Database Wizard.

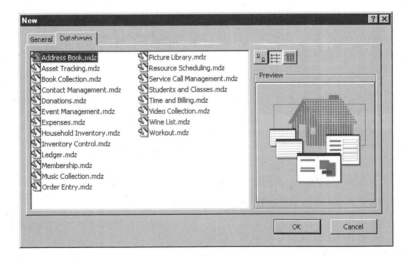

It is true that Access has the computational power to solve any challenge that a home computer user can throw at it. The real question is not whether Access can handle your needs, but rather whether you can handle Access. Because Access is powerful, it requires a greater expenditure of time to learn and money to provide it with adequate hardware than some simpler data-management products, such as Microsoft Works, for example.

Access *can* work for you as a personal database management system at home, but only if you commit to the following items:

▶ *Feed it hardware.* If your home computer does not have 16 megabytes of memory and a 486 or 586 processor running at 50 megahertz or higher, expect to spend a lot of time waiting for Access to complete form and reporting tasks.

▶ *Take the time to learn it well.* Like the proverbial hammer, you can pound a nail with Access or smash your thumb with it. Using complex Access applications at work is still easier than creating simple ones at home. Understand the processes of designing tables, of creating forms and reports, and of integrating them into applications before you commence your home database projects.

▶ *Conserve your time.* A home database project, like one for business, often starts small and then quickly gets more complex. Set simple objectives for yourself and try to avoid *feature creep,* or your family may start to wonder whether you'll ever leave the den!

▶ *Leverage the time of others.* If your home database project is similar to one of the templates that ships with Access, use the template as a starting point and modify the result rather than start from scratch. If you are a member of CompuServe, the Microsoft Network, or a similar forum, or participate in a local computer users' group, look for databases and applications created by others and released into the public domain. Somewhere, I imagine that someone has written a pretty good Access application for managing your Little League team, for example. If you can find out where it is and by whom it is offered, you can grab it, save yourself 50 hours of Access development, and devote that time to training your next star pitcher.

▶ *Share with your family.* As you learn new techniques, share them with members of your household. Even if you're not intimidated by Access, they won't use your application if they are intimidated by it. But remember that the Access training you received at work may not be appropriate for your spouse and children. Use simple, relevant examples and work slowly to keep others in your household interested in learning a product as complex as Access.

The following list details the features of Access 97 that are most appealing to home users. Use this to help you explore features with that you might not yet be familiar, such as:

▶ *Database Wizard.* It can help you create a database to manage home data by using a standard template; the resulting application can be modified.

▶ *Table Wizard.* This steps you through the process of creating commonly used tables and their relationships.

▶ *Form Wizard.* This tool saves hours of time by removing most of the tedious form layout work.

▶ *Assistant.* The Assistant character answers simple help requests and is designed to help new users feel less intimidated by the product.

▶ *Import Wizards.* Many home users keep their records in products that produce spreadsheet or text format files. The Import Wizards help you load such data into Access.

▶ *Easy queries.* Access 97 has a powerful SQL-based query engine, but provides home users with layers of usability features (query wizards, sortable datasheets, query filters, and the like) on top of that engine. This enables you to easily ask everyday personal questions, like "What is the oldest bottle of wine in my collection?"

▶ *Macros.* Even home users who can program in Basic often prefer the simple expediency of macro scripts.

▶ *Add-ins.* As more copies of Access enter the home market, third parties will produce additional tools and wizards appropriate for home users.

▶ *Export to Word.* Historically, home PC users spend more time in their word processing software than their database software. Access makes copying and merging data to Word easy.

▶ *Publish to the Web.* If you maintain a home page on the Internet for your Little League team, for example, Access' new Internet data publishing features help you keep the batting statistics online and up-to-date.

Many of the concepts in this book are more appropriate for complex business applications and are overkill for a home application. Other concepts still provide value to the creation of personal applications. For example, trapping and handling usage and application errors easily is as important for your children's telephone list solutions as for your boss's contact management database.

Access in Small Businesses

Access is best suited for small businesses. Microsoft had this market in mind when they started creating wizards in the Office product line. Because this market is comprised of people short on both time and money, they won't use Access if it can't solve their problems quickly and cost-effectively.

Many small business owners and managers use Access themselves as a productivity and decision-support tool. Often small businesses have only a few computer-literate employees on staff; the ability of Access to manage a few dozen simultaneous users is quite adequate. Business owners on a tight budget find that they, or a staff member, can learn enough about Access to produce a simple but effective custom application with a few weeks of training and a few more weeks of development time.

Of course, a very small business with one or two decision makers may not even need Access for the application development power it provides. Using Access interactively may be satisfactory for your needs in such a case. Even without an application and its forms, you can be productive with Access by entering data into table datasheets, running summary queries, exporting data to Excel for analysis, and printing reports. (The reasons for going beyond this direct interaction as your company grows and placing an application layer over the data becomes clear in Part I, "The Leszynski Development Framework.")

If you are automating data collection in your small business, you can have good results by using Access as your database platform, if you adhere to the following guidelines:

▶ *Don't scrimp on hardware.* Access works your machines very hard; you need to provide it with the highest performance computers you can afford. Because time is money in the business environment, especially in small businesses where both are in short supply, you want data entry, data management, and reporting operations to produce a minimum of *wait state* time. A wait state is when your hourly employees, and possibly customers on the phone with them, are sitting idly while the hourglass cursor or Access speedometer is displayed on the terminal and a process runs. We tell clients that there is no such thing as a computer *too* powerful for Access.

▶ *Keep the application running.* Your small business was built around its expertise in landscaping, home building, or accounting, and so on; not for its network management expertise. So leave the hardware stuff to hardware jockeys; hire good vendors to install, test, and support quality computers and networking for you. Buy a service contract from the vendor that guarantees a replacement server if yours fails. No matter how good your Access data and applications are, you're not making any money on them if your users can't get to them.

Tip

One of the best investments you can make in your business hardware is an *uninterruptible power supply* (UPS) for each machine, especially the server. These items protect your sensitive devices as well as your database records from the damage and information loss caused by storms and power outages. More importantly, many smaller office buildings and home offices are subject to minor power fluctuations, which are not detected by humans but lead to the premature demise of computer parts. A good UPS traps and smoothes these variances.

▶ *Designate an in-house expert.* Select someone on your staff with the skills, or at least the aptitude to learn, to maintain the datasets and applications you have in place. It is often more cost- and time-effective to contract out your application development work than to do it yourself, but once an application is in place, you will profit by having someone on staff and immediately available who understands the day-to-day maintenance, training, and support issues that arise.

▶ *Safeguard your data.* Creating daily backups of production databases, and keeping regular off-site backups as well, seem like obvious suggestions for business users of Access. Yet a majority of Access users, including many of our own clients, refuse to adhere to this wisdom. In no place is a data disaster more costly (as a percentage of revenue) than in a small business.

▶ *Train users well.* Because databases in small businesses traditionally have thinner security and application layers than those in larger companies, the probability that the garbage in, garbage out syndrome will afflict your data is much higher. To minimize affliction, inoculate your users with training. However, commercial software training classes are expensive, so investigate the various cost-cutting measures you can employ—books, video-based training, community college and user group classes, and having one student attend training to train the rest of the staff.

 Tip

Tie salary increases or one-time bonuses to employee training milestones. Many employees perceive computer classes as dull or even intimidating and need extra motivation to go to their first one. From an economic standpoint, it is cheaper for your business to give someone a $200 training bonus to attend a $700 course than to have that $20/hour worker spend 100 hours self-teaching Access, right?

▶ *Teach users to be interactive*. Your application development requirements are reduced if your users know how to use Access interactively to answer their questions without adding more queries and reporting to the application layer. While much of this book is devoted to strategies to protect the data from its users, the protection layer (application) is often thinnest in small businesses for economic reasons.

An application used in a large corporation may have scores of users; enabling so many users to get directly to the data creates a high probability that one of them will introduce erroneous records. In a small business, however, if only a handful of users work with your Access data, it may be cheaper to teach them how to do their own queries than to have your development contractor program a new query into the application each time your needs change. Because some validation may be bypassed with direct data access, enabling users to interact with critical company data is only successful if you also provide the appropriate training.

The most important features when using Access 97 in a small business are as follows:

▶ *Queries*. Access queries let you ask almost any question imaginable. In a small business, many strategic decisions are made by ad hoc querying and filtering of customer, competitor, market, and sales data.

▶ *Form Wizard*. Many business users prefer to create their Access tables manually, without the Table Wizard, in order to accommodate their company's specific needs, but few like to create form layouts manually.

▶ *Import Wizards*. Before adopting Access, many small businesses accumulate data in spreadsheets or in products that produce standard text format or DBF (dBASE) files. The Import Wizards help you convert such files into Access table data.

▶ *Startup properties*. Access 97 simplifies the process of controlling what happens when a user opens an application database. An *interactive database* becomes an *application database* when you add a switchboard form and some Startup options to control the flow.

▶ *Interoperability*. To make effective and rapid business decisions, small business workers often rely on, and become proficient with, the entire Office application suite. Access integrates its data well with both Excel and Word.

▶ *Macros*. Repetitive tasks can be automated easily without contract developers or expensive VBA training.

▶ *Multi-user*. Access makes data available to workgroups of multiple users by providing built-in record locking and contention management. Both are available in forms and table datasheets without any programming.

Access in Corporate Businesses

Many midsize and large companies rely heavily on Access, but none rely exclusively on Access. Companies of any significant size usually have complex data needs, multiple database platforms, competitive dynamics, and dozens to thousands of application users. In such an environment, no single product is sufficient to satisfy all needs. Access becomes one piece of an often complex puzzle of application development tools.

Virtually all automated companies with more than 100 employees have some in-house development staff. These departments are usually called *Information Systems* (IS) or *Information Technology* (IT). Often an "IT group" is composed of programmers becoming redundant by changing technology, as mainframe databases are brought to the desktop or to PC servers. Corporations with changing technology have the challenge of efficiently retraining their application development staff to use that technology. Access wins big in such a circumstance for two main reasons.

First, Access has a reasonable learning and implementation cycle. It is neither the easiest nor the hardest development tool to learn. There are enough books, videos, courses, and conferences built around Access that companies can shop competitively and select the best staff retraining option they can find. There are also thousands of consultants and contractors that can help the IT staff make the transition to Access without wandering in the dark.

Secondly, Access is extensible. Access fits well into corporate development models because it can be extended in the following ways:

▶ *Access interoperates with other applications.* Companies using Excel, Word, or both find Access easy to add to existing desktops. Users are comfortable with the Office-style user interface, appreciate the built-in data links between each of the products, and they enjoy features like drag-and-drop. The IT staff can use Automation to add extra capabilities to the exchange of information between these products.

▶ *Access supports add-ins and ActiveX controls.* Access now has robust support for add-in applications and ActiveX controls. IT developers can search the world for third-party extensions to address a specific feature deficit in Access. If no adequate product is found, IT can then create its own wizard, builder, add-in, or ActiveX control to help Access meet the defined need.

▶ *Access connects to existing data.* Using ODBC technology and ISAM drivers, Access can import or link to text file data, spreadsheet data, Xbase data, Paradox data, Web pages, and SQL-based data residing on platforms ranging from PC servers to mainframes. Companies can continue to use data stored in non-Access formats and easily can convert such data to native Access data when required.

1

▶ *Access uses Basic.* While Visual Basic for Applications is not the same as VAX Basic or Pick Basic or older MS Basic, many IT programmers have been writing in some dialect of Basic for years and find the transition to programming in Access only modestly challenging. Also, where Visual Basic is already part of an IT department's tool set, Access fits in well due to its many similarities to and compatibility with VB.

Corporations that are adding Access to their tools suite or replacing some of that suite with Access should adhere to the first five guidelines for small business implementation of Access. Don't scrimp on hardware; keep the application running; designate an in-house expert; safeguard your data; and train users well.

However, the sixth guideline given for small companies, teaching users to be interactive, is a debatable objective for users of corporate data. A production database in a corporate environment has scores or hundreds of users. If these users can add, edit, and delete data directly (and perhaps freely roam the Database window), the introduction of erroneous records may be significant. There is a better sixth guideline for corporate use of Access—*create solid applications.* The company must take its data very seriously and use IT or outside resources to create application layers over the data. An application layer protects data from accidents and misuse, and makes it usable by a broad user base.

 Tip

Much of this book is devoted to strategies that protect Access data from its users. Imagine back to your school days when you were learning about defensive driving. If you apply that mind-set—always be alert to potential problems—to your applications, you come up with a philosophy of *defensive development*, which is one of the pervasive themes in this book.

When using Access 97 in business, the features that are most appealing to corporate IT groups and other development staff are as follows:

▶ *Visual Basic for Applications.* Access is highly programmable because its VBA language provides the ability to write custom procedures and because it provides event notifications that can be detected from code. Also, existing code from Visual Basic or Excel VBA libraries can be easily ported to Access VBA code libraries.

▶ *Forms.* IT groups can create complex entry/edit forms to provide selective access to records, data validation, query-by-form capabilities, and spell checking of entered data.

> *Reports.* Corporate managers make many of their daily decisions from reports. Access lets them use graphical reports to filter the reports using queries and parameters and to connect the reports to linked external data.

> *SQL.* Most IT programmers have been exposed to SQL while working on minicomputer or mainframe databases and can quickly grasp the query capabilities of Access.

> *Interoperability.* Features like Automation from Access to Excel and Word or the new Publish to the Web Wizard give users flexibility when they publish and report company data. IT groups also appreciate the ability to drive Access via Automation from other Office applications or from Visual Basic in order to use Access as an external querying/reporting tool from non-Access applications.

> *Replication.* Access helps synchronize data sets for users on the go or in a distributed environment. This feature is extremely useful to companies with departmental databases, roving salespeople, and mobile executives.

> *Intranet capabilities.* Access applications can provide users with links to Web pages on a corporate intranet through hyperlinks on form controls and in table fields.

Although a powerful product, there are places in a corporate environment where Jet, the data back end of Access, hits the wall, runs out of performance horsepower, and must yield to more serious data management products. A common rule of thumb is that Access as a front end, with Jet as its back end, is limited to around 50 simultaneous users on one database. The key word here is *simultaneous*; Access can support many more casual users. Fortunately, in such a case, a well-designed database can be *upsized*, moving the data from Jet to SQL Server while continuing to use the Access application as the interface component. (See the Que book *Access 95 Client/Server Development* by Michelle A. Poolet and Michael D. Reilly for more information on upsizing.)

Access and Independent Software Vendors

Access 97 application files can now be locked (as MDE files) to prevent user modifications to code and objects. Additionally, the Office Developer Edition (ODE) product provides a runtime version of Access for distributing applications broadly and a setup wizard to create a setup program to aid such distribution. But even with these tools, can you create retail products built around Access? There are actually two distinct opportunities provided by Access to an *independent software vendor* (ISV).

ISVs and Retail Applications

The first business opportunity is to create retail applications using Access as the programming environment. Such products are usually distributed using the ODE. The advantages
of using Access over Visual Basic, Visual C++, and similar truly-compiled languages are as
follows:

▶ *Rapid development.* With all its built-in capabilities, Access is the fastest tool for
creating database structures, queries, forms, and other application elements.

▶ *Reporting.* The reporting capability of Access is flexible and cost-effective when
contrasted with the third-party extensions used for reporting in Visual Basic and
other tools.

▶ *Less expensive result.* Because Access can produce applications more quickly and
cheaply than the alternative tools, the price charged to consumers may be lower as
a reflection of the reduced investment. In a price-sensitive marketplace, this factor
can be important.

▶ *Source code.* Access applications, when distributed without a security layer, provide
the consumer the ability to modify the application objects and code to create a
customized product for themselves.

The following are some disadvantages when using Access to create a retail product:

▶ *Performance.* Access forms, reports, and code are not truly *compiled* into an executable file; thus, an Access application runs at a noticeably reduced speed than a
counterpart in executable format.

▶ *Disk space.* The runtime engine, the user interface and Jet database component
drivers, and the application database all consume disk space on the consumer's
computer.

▶ *Resources.* Access requires more system resources from the host machine than some
other development languages. Also, Access does not let you control and allocate
the resources it uses in order to tune the end product for different system configurations. An Access application running in 8M of RAM leaves few resources available
to other applications running at the same time.

Clearly, any decision to use Access as the basis of a retail product must involve weighing
the previously mentioned factors and any others you feel are relevant. In general, poor
performance of Access retail applications on some user machines is the most common
complaint voiced by ISVs and their customers. The availability of an Access application's
source code for customization and the accessibility of the Jet database structure and data
generate the most frequent praise.

A Retail Product Vendor's Story

"As a provider of electronic accounting products, MTX International, Inc. annually surveys its customers, and we found consistently over a 10-year period that our customers want more and better access to their accounting data. They also want cost-effective customization of their accounting solution as their business changes. We decided to develop a solution that meets both needs and decided that Access would be the database engine and user interface tool.

"We found that Access met the challenge of developing a serious accounting application because it offers these features: referential integrity, transaction processing, and integrated security. Another major element in our decision-making process was the speed at (*sic*) that they could get the product to market and start recovering the substantial development investment. The rapid nature of Access development met these criteria as well.

"Basing MTX Accounting on Access lets our customers extend their accounting system by modifying its Basic source code, so the customer never feels trapped in a limited solution. Finally, integration with the other Microsoft Office applications fulfilled a common user request to enable custom reporting capabilities in Word, Excel, and PowerPoint. We are pleased with Access as a development platform."

Michael Mullin, MTX, Inc.

ISVs and Add-in Applications

The second opportunity for ISVs is to produce add-in products for Access users. The most common add-ins are development tools linked to the Access environment (called *menu add-ins*), wizards (providing step-by-step assistance for creating objects), and builders (a dialog that helps create a property setting or otherwise simplifies a task).

User expectations for add-in products are different than those for a retail application product. Because the add-ins shipped with Access are built *using* Access, these provide the comparative benchmarks for both performance and usability. Users of add-ins don't necessarily expect the performance of a compiled executable application.

Add-ins are usually written in Access VBA and added to a user's Access environment via a setup mechanism that establishes a *reference*, in the case of a code library, or creates Windows registry entries, in the case of add-ins.

The market for Access add-ins has grown as users have become more sophisticated and are able to explore new ways to increase their productivity in Access. However, ISVs that create add-ins warn prospective entrants into this field that Microsoft has a history of taking functionality found in successful third-party products and adding it to their retail products, thus removing the demand for some ISVs' products after only a short time on the market. For example, my first retail Access add-in product was called Access To Word, a mail-merge wizard that let users perform powerful data merges into Word documents from Access 1.x. Most of the capabilities provided by my product were added to the subsequent releases of both Access and Word, rendering the add-in obsolete after only 18 months on the market.

An Add-In Vendor's Story

"FMS is the leading Microsoft Access add-in vendor with several popular products: Total Access Analyzer (a documentation program), Total Access Detective (an object comparison Wizard), Total Access Speller (a spell checker), and Total Access Statistics (a statistical analysis program). Overall, we are very pleased with the success of our product line. Obviously, our growth is directly tied to the success of Access in the marketplace, and we're fortunate to have invested in a product that became the Windows database standard. However, the success of Access was not quite so obvious when we began supporting it in early 1993.

"Our first product, Total Access Analyzer, shipped for Access 1.1 in July 1993. It was an immediate success and led to the development of additional products for Access 2.0. In the shrink-wrap software business, including retail products and add-ins, a huge investment is required up front before the first copy is sold, so the risk is substantial. The success of our first products enabled us to continue developing more and upgrading existing products.

"One of the most difficult tasks we face is creating products quickly for each new version of Access. With new versions of Access appearing every 12 to 18 months, our products need to be quickly developed and marketed before the next version eliminates the previous version's add-ins. Realistically, our products have life cycles of under 12 months. Such an aggressive schedule requires intense efforts to understand each new Access version and create products that take best advantage of the new features.

"The other risk we face is the potential that a competitor may create a product similar to ours (or better) before we can get to market. If this happens, a considerable investment can be lost. A final risk is that Microsoft will include the features from our add-in in a release of Access, making our product unnecessary in the marketplace.

> "Nonetheless, we are happy to be in the Access add-in business. It is a profitable business for us, and has the added benefit of giving us instant credibility in our consulting engagements (the other half of our business). Add-ins remain an important part of FMS's strategic plan and we anticipate launching several add-ins for Access 97."
>
> Luke Chung, FMS, Inc.

Access as Part of an Integrated Solution

Access is an excellent tool for multifaceted solutions that involve integration with other Microsoft applications. Access 97 communicates better than ever before with its siblings in Microsoft Office, because of the following features:

▶ *Drag-and-drop.* You can drag-and-drop form data, cells from a table datasheet, and entire table and query objects into Excel worksheets and Word documents. Conversely, you can drag-and-drop Excel cells into Access to create a new table. You can also drop Access objects onto the Windows desktop to create shortcuts to databases.

▶ *Save as Rich Text Format.* You can save the output of a table datasheet, a form, or a report as a Rich Text Format (RTF) file that can be loaded into Word with the formatting preserved.

▶ *Mail Merge Wizard.* Using this wizard, you can link a Word mail merge document to data in Access and retrieve the latest data from Access whenever you print your Word merge document.

▶ *Save as an Excel worksheet.* You can save the output of a table datasheet, a form, or a report as an Excel file with the formatting preserved—everything from fonts to report group levels.

▶ *Excel AccessLinks.* The AccessLinks add-in program in Excel lets you create Access forms and reports using data in Excel and to easily export data from Excel into Access tables.

▶ *E-mail attachments.* Using the SendObject macro action or File Send... menu selection, you can attach an Access datasheet, form, report, or module to an e-mail message as a Rich Text Format file, an Excel worksheet, or a text file.

▶ *Common interface elements.* The new Office 97 Assistant and Command Bar features provide a common set of user interface construction tools that let users interact with the different office applications through consistent metaphors.

Here is an example of integrating Access with Excel, e-mail, and Word to provide a complete solution. The Pencil Pushers Office Supply company has four employees. Dave, the salesperson, uses Access to log prospect records as he contacts new businesses or receives a referral from an existing customer. When Dave qualifies a prospect and converts the prospect to a customer by assigning a customer number, the Access application detects this and sends an e-mail to Kathy, the store manager, with the information about the new customer account.

Once a month, Dave's assistant, Sarah, creates a flyer in a Word document by exporting Access product information from the inventory database. Then, using Word's mail merge features, she produces letters and envelopes based on the Access customer data, and sends a mailing to all existing customers. When customers call in to place orders, Shannon, the order clerk, keys the orders into Access and uses the data to manage inventory stocking levels and shipping schedules for the orders.

Once monthly, Kathy prints various sales reports from Access for the company meeting and reviews the company's performance with Dave, Sarah, and Shannon. She also exports the same reports to Excel where she reviews the data by customer, region, and product, and makes month-to-month comparisons against similar worksheets she saved from previous months.

Figure 1.2 shows the main application switchboard for the hypothetical application used to manage the Pencil Pushers company data. The switchboard layout is similar to Access 97's default switchboard style applied by the Database Wizard.

Fig. 1.2

The main switchboard for this Pencil Pushers Office Supply solution includes data export options linking to other Microsoft Office applications.

Of course, significantly more complex examples can be constructed showing how Access data can flow into other applications and integrate with other environments. Writing Automation code in Access VBA against the object models exposed by various other Microsoft products lets your applications insert schedule items into Schedule+ to create PowerPoint slides displaying Access data, to pull project schedules from Microsoft Project into Access tables, and to drive Microsoft Graph to present Access data visually.

Access and Visual Basic Together

During Access 2's reign, a significant two-way migration of developers occurred. Many Access developers realized that the investment they had made in learning Access Basic enabled them to learn Visual Basic more easily and added another powerful product to their skill set. From the other direction, most Visual Basic programmers adopted the Jet Database Engine as their preferred file-server database technology and fell into using Access to create the database structures and saved queries, and to provide users with ad hoc reporting.

Thus, many Access developers became Visual Basic developers, and the reverse. This trend will not be reversed with the 97 versions of both of these products; it will only accelerate. The following are three key areas to be aware of whether both products are to be used by you or your team of developers:

Visual Basic for Applications. Both Visual Basic 5 and Access 97 utilize the same programming language engine. Program code developed in either environment can be easily ported to the other. The benefits are legion, and they include the following:

▶ You can create one common code library with procedures that work in both environments.

▶ Developers can be trained in one language and can use it in multiple products, including Access 97, Excel 97, Project 97, PowerPoint 97, Visual Basic 5, and Word 97.

▶ You can quickly prototype applications destined for Visual Basic 5 in Access 97 using the Table and Form Wizards and some simple navigation code, then preserve any VBA code in a demo when moving it over to VB 5.

Jet Database Engine. Visual Basic 5 makes even broader use of Jet through the same Data Access Objects coding language as Access 97 uses. VB 5 also includes many databound controls, so more and more developers will create multifaceted solutions that use both Access 97 and VB 5 against the same back-end database in Jet.

> **α Note**
> The Jet developers at Microsoft are separate from the Access developers there and consider serving the needs of Visual Basic users as important as serving the needs of Access users.

Automation. The OLE communication wire between Access 97 and Visual Basic 5 runs in both directions:

▶ You can use Visual Basic 5 to drive Access 97 as an Automation server for editing table data or printing database reports from within a VB 5 application.

▶ You can create applications in VB 5 that are specifically designed to be OLE servers to Access 97, enhancing the capabilities of Access 97 while providing the faster performance of a compiled application.

▶ You can build ActiveX controls in Visual Basic or Visual C++, or buy them and use the same control and code to extend both Access 97 and VB 5. Both products are *host containers* for ActiveX controls (OCX files).

One of the biggest challenges for developers using both of these Microsoft tools—deciding whether to use Access or Visual Basic as the primary language for a project—has not gotten any easier with their 32-bit releases. See the "Selecting the Tools" section of Chapter 3, "Preparing for Development," for a discussion of this dilemma.

From Here...

This chapter gives you a feeling of how Access fits into your workday or personal projects. You should better understand now what the capabilities of Access are and what your obligations are to be successful when using Access to meet your specific needs, some of which may be the following:

▶ For an understanding of how to plan, research, and stage your Access development cycle, refer to Chapter 3, "Preparing for Development."

▶ To begin learning the actual techniques of application development, read Chapter 10, "Creating Expert Tables and Queries."

▶ For more information on the use of the Automation capabilities of Access, see Chapter 11, "Expert Approaches to VBA."

▸ The application layer that often distinguishes a small business application from a corporate-grade application is better defined in Chapter 17, "Bulletproofing Your Application Interface."

▸ For additional tips on using the development environment in Access, plus information on building add-ins, read Chapter 20, "Applying Development Shortcuts."

chapter 2

Introducing the Leszynski Development Framework

In this chapter

◆ **The basic foundations of the application development process**

◆ **The Leszynski Development Framework (LDF), a simple set of application development process guidelines**

◆ **Forty-five common-sense principles to apply as you design and develop applications**

E ach year, the application development process becomes more complex as Office and related technologies become more powerful. Additionally, development timelines keep getting shorter and development staffs smaller as a decade of corporate downsizing takes its toll. Mastering the application development role in such a challenging environment requires a formalized, proven, repeatable approach to development. In this chapter, I itemize the formalized approach my company has devised.

A Company with a *VIEW*

I started my first company when I was 23, mostly because I didn't travel in a circle of friends brave enough to tell me what a silly idea it was to go into business fresh out of college with no business experience. In order to stay afloat, I had to get very organized very quickly.

During times when database development work was slow in coming, I spent time organizing my company and planning its future. After a while, friends were asking me to help them get their small firms organized as well. Eventually, we formalized the process of helping each other get businesses started and organized by founding a nonprofit group to help startup companies do business planning. Our group provided free seminars and training for small businesses.

For the training events, I developed a curriculum I called "*VIEWing Your Company's Future.*" I used the acronym *VIEW* to stand for a four-step planning process I designed:

1. *Visualize.* The first step is to "brainstorm"—to visualize all of the possible options for a project or enterprise.

2. *Investigate.* The second step is to explore each of the brainstormed ideas for feasibility—to "flesh out" the details.

3. *Eliminate.* The third step is to remove from consideration or defer those ideas that are not the most practical or profitable.

4. *Write.* The final step is to formalize the project plan in writing.

When I would speak on this methodology to business people, I was surprised by how well-received the concept was. To me, it was simply common sense.

From this experience, I learned an important lesson about how people approach complex endeavors—they use outlines and checklists. Business people, programmers, even your children all feel less intimidated by a task when given a simple list of common-sense bullet points to work from.

I survived the early days of PC software development by devising simple methodologies to keep my projects organized. However, as my company moved into the 90s, software tools and development projects were becoming so complex that simple common-sense approaches didn't provide enough structure.

The Evolution of Access

Before Access, my company built most of our applications with only one tool—we chose either R:BASE, dBASE, Clipper, or Visual Basic as the platform for any single project. But when Access came along, we discovered that having *both* Access and Visual Basic in our toolkit let us create applications more powerful and complex than we ever had with a single product.

Not long after the first release of Access, Excel got the Basic language and became its own robust application development tool, and SQL Server became available on Windows NT. It seemed that, suddenly, every few months we were adding another tool to our development environment.

At some point in this evolution, it became apparent to our clients that Microsoft's application-building tools had reached the level where we could create with them complete solutions at the departmental or even enterprise level, and that these solutions would replace the previous applications written with C or Cobol code. Suddenly, we weren't writing simple budgeting databases or spreadsheets—we were creating budgeting *environments* that included multiple accounting modules, mail merge letters, spreadsheet exports, and links to historical corporate budget data (in short, we were writing "mission-critical" applications with Office).

With these newly complex development tools and projects came the need for a better overall vision of how to develop effective applications, and the Leszynski Development Framework (LDF) was born. LDF is simply a formalized set of objectives, principles, and guidelines that I built to help my staff create quality software solutions.

This chapter introduces the core objectives, principles, and guidelines of LDF. The *implementation* of the framework (examples of turning the guidelines into methodologies) is explored and documented throughout this book.

 Note

In common usage, the term *framework* refers to an abstraction—a unified set of related concepts. In contrast, a methodology is a set of policies, procedures, processes, techniques, and tools that fit within the framework.

One or more methodologies can be derived from or influenced by a single framework. A management team creates a framework and a development team works from a methodology that fits that framework.

For example, the framework for financial accounting in American business is clearly defined. The notion of a chart of accounts, the system of debits and credits, and the reporting concepts of profit/loss and balance sheets are widely stated and understood. However, there is no single methodology used to implement this framework;

> different accounting departments, CPA firms, and software packages define and use different techniques for applying the concepts found in the framework.
>
> In this book, I define the conceptual *framework* of LDF in this chapter. In the remainder of the book, I include techniques, tools, and templates that fit within the framework, forming the *methodology* that I use for application development within my own company.

My hope, in sharing LDF with you, is that you use it as a set of base guidelines and expand upon it to create your own team development framework. I also expect you to use the practical methodologies included in this book as examples that you can apply or extend toward your project development efforts.

 Note

I sometimes use the terms *developer* and *programmer* interchangeably in this chapter and elsewhere in this book to describe someone who creates solutions. In practical terms, however, the term developer actually implies a higher skill set than does programmer. Programmers often work within a very narrow range of tasks and tools (writing Cobol reports for months on end, for example), while a solution developer (in the LDF sense) must possess the skills to design and deploy solutions in addition to coding them.

Foundation Elements for Access Development

LDF or any development philosophy cannot exist in a vacuum. There are certain givens that are central to all application development endeavors and that dictate the environment for any methodological approach to working with software tools like Access.

Before describing LDF, let's explore the external factors that affect it. The following list highlights some of the fundamental attributes of the development process. A development style like LDF should attempt to address these aspects of development that are common to all projects:

> *The needs of the users.* Users provide the sparks that ignite each development effort. The needs of the users must be addressed by the solution, or the solution will fail. Thus, accurately capturing and describing users' needs should be addressed by a good development framework.

The use of multiple tools and platforms. You cannot give the users what they need if your tools do not provide the necessary capabilities. A development framework should not prescribe a specific set of tools, otherwise the maxim "When all you have is a hammer, everything looks like a nail" becomes true and you might try to make one tool do everything.

Instead, a framework must support working with multiple tools. Thus, a development style for Access should be part of, or leveraged from, a larger set of style guidelines that apply to related databases (like SQL Server) and related languages (like Visual Basic and Excel VBA).

Current trends in the marketplace. If everyone is writing code a certain way, and you are not, or if you still build a single application database when all other developers are creating a front-end/back-end mix, your framework is clearly out of step. A development style must recognize trends in the marketplace and be adaptive to them.

One example of this adage is provided by the interface standards established by Microsoft Office applications. The Office interface standard seems to change with each Office release; a framework and its methodologies must be reviewed and modified accordingly at such times.

Other Defined Frameworks. There are good, published techniques for researching users' needs, managing development, and delivering applications. Any framework you adopt or create will have some contrasts and some similarities with these other approaches.

Within one organization, there may actually be many defined frameworks with multiple methodologies under them. For example, the PC database development style and the mainframe development style may each be a subset or derivation of a grander, corporate framework for database development.

The next few topics define more clearly these foundation elements within the context of Access application development. Before you can understand the principles of LDF, you must understand the environment that we will apply it.

Understanding the Users' Predicament

The users' needs are the top priority. On the surface, this statement sounds like an obvious introduction to any development framework. However, many pressures can cause development projects to stray away from this precept, including the following:

Lack of institutional support. Developers are always charged with satisfying the users' needs as a top priority. However, the same developers are not always given the proper facilities, policies, training, staff, and tools to execute this task successfully.

User Confusion. Many corporate computer users are simply overwhelmed by the current state of technology and technical change. They aren't able to communicate their needs well to developers, or they're simply afraid to try.

Budget Realities. When a project starts hitting the budget wall, features start to get cut or abbreviated. Sometimes, the users do not secure enough capital for the developers at the outset to fund their desired solution.

At other times, development projects or development staffs are mismanaged and the money runs out too soon through no fault of the users. In this scenario, the users end up having to trade away features in order to minimize a budget disaster that they didn't create.

LDF places the users first by recognizing the severity of these pitfalls and by emphasizing developer training and tools to address and correct them. LDF also believes that users must invest their own time and effort in the development process in order to be protected from these pitfalls. See the section "Element 1—User and Business Requirements" later in this chapter for LDF's approach to these issues.

Generally Accepted Development Conventions

Lost in the rush to produce new solutions and keep the existing ones running, many developers and Information Technology *(IT)* groups dream about standardizing their development policies, techniques, and tools but never have the time to bring the dream to reality. For them, the next best thing is to cobble together a compendium from guidelines that are publicly available and most closely match their needs.

There is plenty of material available for such an effort. The free exchange of ideas in the Access community gains more and more momentum daily, as the ubiquity of CompuServe as an information focal point is displaced by the Internet, magazines, conferences, user groups, and so on.

Sometimes, as more ideas are exchanged, more consensus develops and developers in aggregate begin to evolve toward the same style. For example, even the simplest Access application these days has separate data (back-end) and interface (front-end) database files. This style was not universally accepted among Access developers in the days of Access 1.0, but it is now.

More often than not, the free exchange of ideas produces more than one good idea on the same topic, and developers divide into camps around the best of these ideas. No clear standard emerges; instead, the market provides a list of good ideas to choose from, without any clear strategy for piecing these ideas together.

Once, accountants suffered from a similar discord and found that they could reduce the confusion in their industry by adopting and applying written guidelines (called *Generally Accepted Accounting Principles*). *GAAP* has given accountants a methodology for solving many of their style disputes and a common framework for the presentation of information.

Ideally, a good software development style should do no less. It should synthesize the best of what the market does and pull these ideas together into written guidelines. More importantly, however, it must make the ideas *fit* together to achieve a common objective or vision. A development standard should also add ideas that take the high road—principles that most developers know they should observe but don't always make the time for. For example, LDF takes this high road by saying, "Place a comment block at the top of each procedure," and "Every project should have a written specification."

The first step toward a GAAP-like standard for Access developers is for someone to provide ideas that synthesize the generally accepted development conventions. LDF does this and creates a list that can be used as a focal point for debate among developers. Active discussion of the ideas here will help this framework evolve into a document consensus of application development precepts.

Understanding Access' Role in Your Projects

Access is almost always at a pivotal location in applications where it's a component. However, this pivotal role can become either larger or smaller over time. Thus, any understanding of how Access fits into a project must be tempered by an understanding of the entire life cycle of the project and Access' changing role throughout that life cycle.

At one end of the spectrum, consider a departmental application for tracking information about shippers and shipping rates. The application has a central database and five users. Users enter information into shipper and pricing tables and run queries to determine the best shipper to use for a specific shipment, based on a combination of cost and locale. Access is very good at solutions like this, and if the department does not grow rapidly, the needs don't change dramatically; this stand-alone application can go through its five-year life span virtually unchanged.

An example like this provides fodder for developers who ask, "Why do I need a development methodology? I can hack out a quick solution to this shipping data problem by using any development style or none at all. Besides, I'll be around for the next five years to debug it if something goes wrong." It is quite hard to argue with such a utilitarian attitude given these facts, so I'll capitulate and admit that this developer's attitude serves him well *in this scenario*. However, very few applications live in such a vacuum where the users can guarantee that their needs won't change, and the developer can guarantee that he won't leave.

Exploring the other end of the continuum, imagine a departmental budgeting application that is distributed to all five departments in a company. These departments share a single database but will each have a slightly different interface to match their unique budgeting requirements. This application has complex needs such as data validation and auditing, segmentation of features and data ownership by department—reporting that produces detailed budget spreadsheets, and links to corporate accounting data.

Clearly, this type of application cannot simply be slapped together as in the previous example. Access' role in this project is not as the only component but rather as a facilitator, bringing together information from, or serving data to, several external components. Developers working on an application in this capacity must understand how to augment Access with other tools and how to have Access provide the best interaction with these other tools.

Consequently, understanding the role of Access in a project like this one involves:

▸ Understanding the users' needs in exacting detail.

▸ Accurately identifying which needs can be met by Access and which features must be provided by other tools.

▸ Defining the hardware and other enterprise infrastructures that will host the Access application.

▸ Mapping the data items in the entire system and determining their attributes and usage.

▸ Understanding the life cycle of the project and how Access fits in at the end of the cycle as compared to the beginning.

Viewed at a conceptual level, development of this complex project would be more successful if guided by a framework that takes into account the many facets of Access-centric database solutions. A good development framework can help you create large solutions by providing a direction for each of the critical tasks in creating the solution: research, design, management, coding, deployment, and enhancement.

Microsoft Office Compatible

In 1993, Microsoft created a definition of Office compatibility and a set of criteria for software that is qualified to wear this mantle. Access applications can be sent to a testing lab and receive certification as Office Compatible (*OC*). This certification enables the application to display the OC logo, an advantageous marketing attribute for a retail application.

> **Note**
>
> To find out about the requirements for certifying your applications as Office Compatible, send an e-mail with your information request to **offcomp@microsoft.com**. If you are creating an add-in, tool, or industry-specific application that will be sold in the retail marketplace, membership in this program can provide substantial marketing benefits.

2

Should developers that aren't doing retail applications care about being Office Compatible? In terms of the actual certification process, no. However, the OC specification provides some guidelines for building Windows-style interfaces; these guidelines can be used as a framework for designing Access application interfaces.

Unfortunately, OC doesn't outline database-specific application interfaces and provides no guidelines for interface issues involved in creating, editing, saving, and searching for records. Thus, developers must extend OC by creating their own guidelines for situations that OC doesn't discuss.

Chapter 8, "Designing Effective Interfaces," discusses the Office Compatible guidelines in more detail and discusses how to supplement them with interface guidelines for your database-centric applications. The general tenet of OC, that Access application interfaces should look and feel like other Windows applications, has been incorporated into LDF and should be incorporated into your solutions.

Microsoft Solutions Framework

The Microsoft Solutions Framework (MSF) is the mindset employed and taught by Microsoft Consulting Services. Microsoft defines MSF as "the reference guide for building and deploying distributed enterprise systems based on Microsoft tools and technologies."

MSF provides a well-defined framework that describes development *as a process*, meaning that MSF enumerates high-level guidelines that provide structure to the development of your own internal methodology. MSF is not a methodology itself, because it does not include policy documents, tools, reusable objects, templates, or similar components.

MSF is based on several core concepts, including

> ▶ An *application model* that views an application as a compilation of reusable objects and services, structured in three layers:
>
> **1.** User Services
>
> **2.** Business Services
>
> **3.** Data Services

Note

If you are not familiar with this three-tiered layering model, see Chapter 7, "Understanding Application Architecture," for a description.

▶ A *process model* that is focused primarily on the management of milestones, with the following as the four primary ones:

1. Vision and Scope Document Complete
2. Functional Specification Complete
3. Code Complete
4. Release

The MSF model encourages multiple, iterative releases of each of these listed deliverables, with short time spans between each release.

▶ A defined *development team* composition with six clearly delineated roles:

1. *Product Management*. Team members performing this role define the solution and act as the user advocate throughout the process.
2. *Program Management*. Team members performing this role write the functional specifications and oversee the development effort to achieve successful implementation of that specification.
3. *Development*. Team members performing this role provide the actual development resources to code the solution.
4. *Test and Quality Assurance*. Team members performing this role review the application to ensure that it is fit for deployment.
5. *User Education*. Team members performing this role create the user documentation and provide hands-on instruction, if necessary.
6. *Logistics*. Team members performing this role validate the infrastructure, deploy the application, and provide ongoing support.

MSF does not conflict with LDF. In fact, the two frameworks coexist just fine, because MSF is at a higher level than LDF. MSF can work for smaller projects and development teams but is not tuned for them. It was derived from experiences on very large projects inside Microsoft and their largest customer companies.

LDF, by contrast, is structured for development teams of one to ten people, working on projects taking hundreds of hours instead of thousands. Over the long term, as MSF and LDF both expand to include wider audiences and a broader range of projects, they will overlap or possibly even collide, but Access developers should still be able to benefit from elements of both.

Introducing LDF

So far in this chapter, I've laid some of the groundwork for the Leszynski Development Framework by clarifying the unique environmental factors that provide its foundation. To summarize, these are the pervasive factors in Access application development that LDF deems important:

> *Know the users' requirements.* All projects start with the users' statement of their needs. LDF places the needs of the users above development considerations and does not let process mechanics distract developers from the users' objectives.

> *Utilize generally accepted development conventions.* LDF does not try to swim against the tide with respect to generally accepted development trends, such as three-tiered architecture and Hungarian-style object-naming rules.

> *Understand Access.* LDF assumes that Access cannot be used properly in an application until its role in both the short-term and long-term versions of the solution is defined. LDF encourages a focus on where Access' strong and weak points lie with respect to the needs of each unique solution.

> *Mimic Microsoft Office.* LDF encourages an interface standard that matches accepted Office interface conventions wherever practical.

> *Dovetail with Microsoft Solutions Framework.* LDF provides a migration path to MSF by bringing the same discipline to smaller, Access-centric projects that MSF brings to large client/server projects.

LDF takes these base assumptions and builds upon and around them, applying these two attitudes to each: common sense and consistency.

Defining a Common-sense Approach to Development

If you are a sophisticated developer, to hear me say that every project should have a design document, and that every design process should include a representative sample of actual users seems like I'm stating the obvious. It should be obvious to you if you've been developing for a while, but remember, pearls of wisdom like this are not obvious until you have tried the alternate approaches and failed with them. New developers that have not yet been through the trial-and-error process can be saved some distress by applying a framework that bypasses it.

LDF attempts to distill the sometimes-complex development process into a set of simple guidelines and techniques that read much like everyday common sense. In this respect, LDF provides a middle ground between the extremes that frameworks often drift toward:

▶ Some frameworks get bogged down in their own seriousness, and never leave the drawing board. The endless discussions of infinite levels of philosophy and detail eventually wear down the designers until they give up the project.

▶ Other frameworks are based on wonderfully interesting but vague ideas that are untested in the real world. You'll find these in magazine articles and posted in the public domain. Their hallmark features are that they sound quite interesting in theory and include attractive diagrams, but they have no guidelines for practical implementation and no basis in business reality.

LDF adheres to the middle ground and common-sense kernel by passing all of its concepts through the following filter:

Will it work for most developers most of the time? Any framework element that does not apply to 80 percent of all developers and 80 percent of their applications is suspect as to its value. It is not possible to please all of the people all of the time with any framework, but LDF attempts to appeal to the practical majority rather than the philosophical minority.

Is it easy to understand and apply? The development team of the '90s should include application users at both ends of the construction process; users help define the requirements, and the same users help test the solution. The best framework is one that not only appeals to the sentiments of developers, but one that can be grasped by sophisticated users as well. LDF strives to build an environment where users understand *how* a solution is built; only then are they able to map their needs into the available processes and technologies.

Does it have an economic benefit? In the final analysis, all business solutions are about money—spending money on development to save money in the workflow. Any element of a framework that does not tie-in easily to a measurable economic benefit becomes problematic. LDF attempts to stay focused on the long-term cost savings gained by standardization, communication, planning, and competence in the development process.

It would be easy for me to reduce LDF to a ten-point bulleted list of common-sense approaches to Access development. However, at this level you would have only a teaser, rather than a complete fabric of information that you could actually use. Ultimately, all developers want more than just a sneak peek.

At the other end of the spectrum, I could summarize every one of the individual ideas and tips in this book into a bulleted LDF outline that would span dozens of pages. This approach would be counterproductive to the nature of the framework by providing excessive detail and leaving no discretion to developers in the use of its principles.

I've struck a middle ground instead of either of these options. My framework provides statements and objectives, and this book provides examples of implementations of the principles. Taken as a whole, you can use my ideas to guide much of your development process, or you can simply use them as seeds for the creation of your own guidelines.

Defining a Consistent Development Style

The purpose of any framework is to pull together related concepts and to make them work harmoniously. The roots of LDF are in our actual application development experiences. The pieces fit together not because they've been forced, but because they reflect the actual development environment that my staff and I have created around us. Thus, the laboratory for my concepts is my consulting company, and none of our ideas escape from the lab until they have been through the "clinical trials" of hands-on use.

This brings to LDF a healthy consistency and a lack of gaps or inherent contradictions. It also enables LDF to move beyond the theoretical to the practical.

For example, many development styles include these two maxims:

1. Create reusable code where possible.
2. Create reusable tools to make development easier.

   Both of these common guidelines are noble and useful, and each is a part of LDF. However, when you apply these concepts in the *real world*, an evolution occurs that creates a third point:

3. Create reusable tools to write reusable code.

The third point is a consistent and logical outflow of the first two. Further, this book attempts to be consistent in its efforts to demonstrate LDF to you with practical examples. Thus, Chapter 20, "Applying Development Shortcuts," gives you specific techniques that you can use to apply the three LDF principles listed above to your own work, by describing how to do these three things.

1. Create code libraries.
2. Create builders.
3. Create builders to write code for code libraries.

Professionals in any field will tell you that the path to success is to find a system that works and to continually refine it toward a state of perfection. As you sit reading this, my staff is continuing to use and refine LDF toward that lofty state.

Defining the Elements of LDF

The fact that this entire book is a living example of LDF makes it hard for me to distill the framework into one single section. My staff learns LDF not simply by reading bulleted lists and policy documents, but through team meetings, client interaction, training sessions, and hands-on implementation. Nevertheless, you do not have the luxury of dropping by my office, so I must enumerate the *essence* of LDF in the remainder of this chapter. LDF is best expressed by the model shown in Figure 2.1.

Fig. 2.1

This diagram graphically reflects the composition of the Leszynski Development Framework.

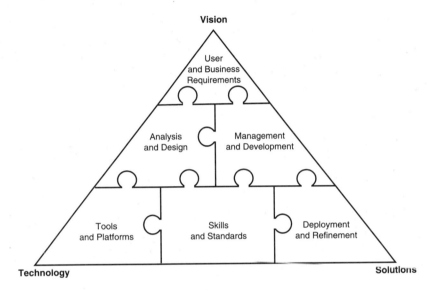

I call each of the segments of the diagram in Figure 2.1 an *element*. One element does not equate to one group of people or one block of processes. Instead, one element is a collection of *concepts* that are related to each other. Taken together, these six elements include all of the primary notions that I believe are critical to application development:

User and Business Requirements. Automated solutions are not built to provide developers with job security; they are created to solve a business problem identified by one or more users (the user requirements) or identified in the company's strategic vision (the business requirements).

Analysis and Design. If you define the problem incorrectly you will build the wrong solution. The processes of analysis and design are an art form that differentiates the developer as coder from the developer as business counselor.

Management and Development. I link these concepts inexorably because each is wholly dependent on the other. A good manager with a bad development team will never deliver a quality product, and a good development team that is mismanaged will never ship a solution on time.

Tools and Platforms. I've placed much emphasis thus far in the book on the importance of using Access for what it does best, and providing it with appropriate hardware to run on. Access and its developers are captive to the overall architecture of the enterprise and the workstations of its users.

Skills and Standards. If a project's needs do not match well with the skills of its developers, calamity is the likely result. In a similar vein, development team interaction often drifts toward anarchy unless the team is provided with a clear set of policies and standards to apply to their work.

Deployment and Refinement. Shipping a solution is only half of the battle. Most applications have a multi-year life span and go through several major version releases. Developers must build into today's solution an easy migration path to tomorrow's solution.

Each of these elements is described in much greater detail in the pages that follow. A document that summarizes LDF that can be used as a starting point for evolving LDF to fit your development environment is found on the CD-ROM as LDF-SUMM.DOC.

I've chosen the triangular layout of the LDF diagram to emphasize two points:

1. *There is interdependence between the framework's elements.* Each of the six elements in the diagram is related to the other five by their common membership in the framework and their role in the application development process. Yet, some elements are more strongly related than others. The layout of the diagram and the connection points emphasize these relationships.

   For example, note the position of the *Analysis and Design* element. This element connects to the other four elements that are critical players on its stage: The analysis process quantifies the user's requirements, and the design process balances these requirements against the available tools, the skills of the developers, and the composition of the development team and its managers.

2. *There are three primary factors that wrap around the framework.* Outside of the framework elements are three super elements that I call *factors*. These factors are the highest-level conceptual elements that surround the solution development process:

   ▶ *Vision.* At the pinnacle of the solution diagram is the *Vision* factor, which no business can operate without. Vision rises above the users' conception of a specific solution to encompass the strategic objectives of the entire enterprise.

   This pervasive vision of where a company is going is often distilled into a *Mission Statement*, which is a written corporate statement of purpose. Any automated solution, large or small, should in some way feed this stated corporate direction. Thus, any prospective development task that cannot be justified as a legitimate brick in a company's wall of mission and vision must be questioned as to its reason for consideration.

▶ *Technology*. At the second apex point in the diagram is the *Technology* factor. While the element Tools and Platforms relates directly to technology at a solution implementation level, technology as a factor in the diagram refers to technology as a *force* within the enterprise.

The *Technology element* (Tools and Platforms) of Access solutions is embodied in software tools, servers, networked workstations, and database records, but the *Technology factor* of the enterprise includes *all* of its machines (from fork-lifts to jet airplanes) and *all* of its tools (such as the Internet and satellites).

Put another way, a database-centric solution is not merely a collection of records, but rather a collection of records *about* things that are important to the company, such as products, people, or places. In some way or another, the information items stored by the Access technology are always related in a larger fashion to the company's other technologies. (In the current example, *products* are manufactured by the company's machines, *people* call in on its telephone system, and *places* are connected to the company location by trucks and trains.)

▶ *Solutions*. At the third convergence point in the diagram lies the *Solutions* factor. As with its sibling factors Vision and Technology, this is a high-level item. It embodies not simply the current solution, but the mix of solutions in the enterprise.

Just as your proposed software solution must dovetail with the business vision and technology components of the enterprise, so must it mesh with the pool of existing solutions spread throughout the entire organization. This isn't to say that each individual solution must communicate data with all others; such a goal would be both pointless and impossible. Instead, each solution is a building block, and you should be able to define and detail its relationship to the other building blocks in the enterprise.

The remainder of this chapter details the six elements of the Leszynski Development Framework diagram. Each element in LDF is exemplified by *precepts*, or statements that convey an objective, fact, or guideline. Not all precepts apply to every project, and you do not need to agree with all precepts in order to derive value from its parent element or from the framework.

LDF attempts to keep precepts at a broad level because they provide guidelines for behavior without necessarily specifying the actual behavior itself. For example, Element 2, Design Precept 3 states, "Every project should have a written plan." This precept provides a rule without specifying an implementation strategy to fulfill it, so you need to create your own execution blueprint for this guideline or use the examples I provide in Chapter

4, "Creating Design Specifications," and Appendix B, "Design Specifications," which is on the CD-ROM.

Element 1—User and Business Requirements

This element of LDF is placed at the top of the diagram for a reason. LDF adheres strongly to the belief that all automated solutions should be driven by a clearly defined set of user requirements, and that these should dovetail into the larger needs of the business (see Figure 2.2).

Fig. 2.2
User and business requirements drive solutions.

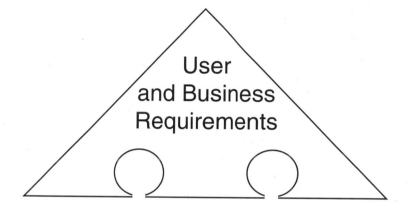

User Requirement Precepts

Some development projects start with a user or users stating a set of needs to the development team. Other development efforts are the brainchild of Information Technology staffers who see a shortcoming in a current business system. Still other solutions are (wrongly) implemented because someone got excited about applying an interesting new technology to a workgroup. It doesn't matter who *conceives* the need, but it does matter who *defines* the need. Users must be actively involved in the design and review process of an automated solution, from conception through deployment, and the business management layer that pays for the solution must require that the project be cost-justified before it begins.

User Precept 1—All Solutions Must Start with a Defined Need

Step One for a new development project is when someone says one of the following:

"This is what we are missing..."

"This is what we have that doesn't work well for us..."

"There is this great new technology that may benefit us..."

The core of any automated solution must be a human or business need (or both). The success of the automation project depends on the degree that the needs are properly defined before starting and how well they are satisfied after completion.

LDF requires that developers stay focused on the users' needs and the needs of their company during design and development. This focus helps to keep coders from taking technology tangents, introducing ad hoc feature redesigns, and other common distractions. A solution process that begins with the third phrase in the previous list is likely to fail, because a fascination with technology, as opposed to a defined user or business need, is driving the solution design process. Thus, this precept really is saying: All solutions must start with a defined need rather than a fascination with technology or a sales call from a vendor.

User Precept 2—Prioritize All Needs Before Beginning

When users have defined their needs as a new project concept, the users' manager and the development manager must prioritize the concept against other pending projects in the same budgetary unit (workgroup, department, or similar segment). No company can afford to implement all good ideas; trade-offs must always be made to allocate finite budgets and manpower to the most pressing needs.

In addition to weighing the proposed project against other proposed development efforts, managers should try to weigh each need *within* the project against the other needs. As the user requirements are defined, the weighting must be maintained so that it is easier to decide which features will be kept and which deferred if inadequate funds are available to satisfy all listed needs. Many projects die of bloat by trying to do too much with too little time and money.

User Precept 3—Define the Problem Before Defining the Solution

Users must commit an up-front effort to define their problems, needs, hopes, and objectives in detail at the beginning of the research phase. Developers can lead users astray with technology tangents that cause a project to stray from the original vision. This situation is less likely if the vision is clearly specified early on.

When defining the project objectives, try to withhold discussion of tools, technologies, budgets, and other constricting facts. Design an ideal system first, unencumbered by constraining factors, then fit the solution to budget realities later.

Several problem-definition steps occur early in project planning:

1. Describe the concept
2. Determine the scope
3. Select the players
4. Answer the key questions

These and other steps in the design process are detailed in Chapter 3, "Preparing for Development."

User Precept 4—The Solution Will Not Be Used if It Does Not Fit the Need

The user is unlikely to use a solution that does not solve the defined business problem no matter how powerful, easy to use, or well-designed it is. A system that "misses the mark," even slightly, with respect to the users' defined needs falls into disuse almost immediately.

Consider how often you, as a developer, purchase tools and utilities to assist you with your work, only to find them missing a feature you deem critical. You quickly reduce or remove your dependence on the tool once you have found its fatal flaw. Remember that users respond to your application with very similar behavior.

Business Requirement Precepts

A development project must feed one of the company's strategic objectives, such as "Reduce head count" or "Improve customer satisfaction," in addition to a defined set of user needs. Otherwise, the application will be branded rogue and its users selfish due to the lack of tie-in with larger objectives.

Business Precept 1—All Solutions Must Tie to the Corporate Vision

After defining the users' needs for a new project, test the defined needs against the department's or company's overall needs. A project can be successful in the short term if it fits the needs of a workgroup, but it cannot be successful in the long run unless it fits a broader need or objective.

Users must help developers understand how their proposed solution fits into the big picture and must be able to justify the project to those up the corporate hierarchy at higher levels.

Business Precept 2—Secure Support from the Highest Possible Level

In the current climate of rapid and regular business reorganizations, a project in process can quickly be swept away into oblivion by the tide of restructuring. This point reinforces the precept that a project that feeds the corporate vision has greater longevity and support in high places than one that serves a compartmentalized need.

Determine who the highest-level beneficiary of a project in the company is, then involve that person in the project. If the solution project hits a political or financial roadblock later, the blockage will often be cleared quickly by the highly placed champion.

Note

I call the highest-level beneficiary of an application the *ultimate user*, as defined further in Chapter 3, "Preparing for Development." An example of the highest-level beneficiary is the manager of the department that initiates the project, or perhaps an executive that will use reports produced by the proposed system.

Element 2—Analysis and Design

A thorough analysis and design effort is a critical factor in the success of most projects (see Figure 2.3). When done well, it launches the project ship riding high in the water; when done poorly or skipped, the project begins sinking before it even leaves port.

Fig. 2.3

A thorough analysis and design is critical.

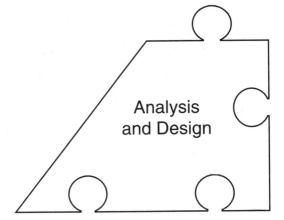

Analysis Process Precepts

The analysis of existing processes and research into users' needs is often maligned. Developers and users both find it tedious. Executives don't understand why it takes so long to define the solution to an obvious problem, so the definition phase is often underfunded. Yet, the solution surgeons may operate on the wrong problem if they don't perform the proper diagnostic procedures.

Analysis Precept 1—Understand the Players in the Game

A design effort must be done by a *design team*. Such a team usually includes core members (developers and user representatives) and peripheral members (user and management reviewers).

Much of the success of a project relates directly to the quality of its design team. Here are five keys to composing a successful design team:

1. Make sure the users are properly represented.

2. Make sure important factions outside of the work group (upper management and Information Technology) are properly represented.

3. Do not include either too many users or too many managers, or the process slows to a crawl.

4. Keep the pace brisk or attention wanes.

5. Assign homework to team members to spread the load and limit time spent in meetings.

In LDF, the design process includes participation by and input from each of these parties:

Program Manager

Project Manager

Development Manager

Developers

Ultimate Users

User Representatives

Users

Information Technology Liaison

Support Personnel

These roles and their responsibilities are described in detail in the "Selecting the Players" section in Chapter 3, "Preparing for Development."

Analysis Precept 2—Formalize the Research Process

There is a correct way and a wrong way to do research. The success of a research effort depends on the level of organization of the researchers, their ability to meticulously dissect processes, and their political skills when interviewing affected parties.

The key pitfalls to avoid in a research and design effort are:

Inadequate Information. The researcher does not probe past the surface and find all the facts needed to support a good solution design.

Misleading Information. The researcher does not get a balance of opinions, or lets one user's input sway the design too strongly, or makes an erroneous inference from information provided.

LDF provides three models for performing automated solution research:

1. The Workflow Analysis
2. The Data Chase
3. The Reports Analysis

See "Researching Automated Solutions" in Chapter 3, "Preparing for Development," for clarification of these research models.

Analysis Precept 3—Beware of Tool Biases

Whenever possible, the discussion of development tools should come late in the design process. Early in the design process, focus on the problem being solved, not on the technology that will be used to solve it.

In smaller organizations, Access may be the tool of choice and your project design will be constrained by its selection from the outset. Larger organizations, however, will have several layers of standards:

▶ A desktop database standard (such as Access).

▶ A PC database engine standard (such as Jet used with Visual Basic or C++).

▶ A client/server standard, such as SQL Server.

▶ A legacy data storage standard, such as mainframe DB2 databases.

Developers may have an inkling of the appropriate tool or tool mix for a particular project early in the design phase but should not express this bias to the users or let the bias affect the research and design process. See "Selecting the Tools" in Chapter 3, "Preparing for Development," for more information on determining the development platform.

System Design Precepts

Developers without a plan are wanderers in the solution development desert, looking for a direction. A strong, written design specification document is one of the core elements of LDF. The document must be comprehensive and clear.

Design Precept 1—A Bad Design Always Yields an Inadequate Solution

A project that begins by pointing in the wrong direction ends up in the wrong location. To create a quality solution, the users' needs must be accurately defined and the system design must describe an application that fills these needs.

Users must be encouraged to vocalize all of their thoughts and perceptions related to a proposed solution, without fear of ridicule by the development team, fellow workers, or management. Developers, on the other hand, must remain attentive during the processes of brainstorming, research, and specification writing—the tasks that historically bore many programmers.

In addition, the developers writing the project plan must have the skill set necessary to produce an accurate, technically feasible plan that solves the business problem as defined by the users.

Design Precept 2—Always Get the Data Structure Right

The backbone of a database project is a set of data records. If the data records are flawed, the entire database may be worthless. Imagine an order database with a field for credit card numbers that's missing an expiration date field. Or picture how databases that use two-digit years in their records will not be able to adapt to the turn of the century coming just around the corner.

Forms are easier to change than data and reports easier than forms. Data structures are the hardest component to change in a deployed system, so make certain that the table structures are accurate the first time around.

Design Precept 3—Every Project Should Have a Written Plan

Developers and users bring distinctly different skills and perceptions to the design table. To presume that each group understands what the other is saying is as dangerous as assuming that parents and their teenagers communicate from the same mindset.

A common rapid application development scenario involves users giving a developer a spreadsheet of data and some hand-drawn reports, and saying, "Move the spreadsheet data to a database, create an entry form, and add a report that looks like this spreadsheet." To some developers, this qualifies as a written plan, but LDF is more demanding than such developers.

Developers and users have a better chance of minimizing misunderstanding and disagreement when they all work from the same written plan. Every development project has a minimum set of information that should be either researched in detail, or discussed and dismissed. See Chapter 4, "Creating Design Specifications," and on the CD-ROM, Appendix B, "Design Specifications," for a complete discourse on these elements and the layout of a good written design specification.

Design Precept 4—Plan for Growth

Most applications follow a somewhat generic evolutionary path as their life span progresses. Good applications are built to support an easy migration to each new level of that evolution, and every application should have a long term (multi-year) growth or maintenance plan.

An application that is built with a short time window in mind often suffers from a nearsighted design process and is antiquated when the time window expires. With an architecture that is not extensible, such an application may cost more to revise than to simply replace (rewrite).

In contrast, if an application is engineered to grow, moving it from one stage in its life cycle to the next stage requires a process of extension, but not renovation.

Here are the ten LDF stages in the average life cycle of a database-centric application, as described fully in Chapter 3, "Preparing for Development":

1. Design
2. Prototyping
3. Application Development
4. Testing
5. Initial Deployment
6. Product Refinement
7. Expanded Deployment
8. Upsizing
9. Product Maturity
10. Obsolescence and Death

Many developers think that a project is completed when it gets into the hands of the users (stage 5 on this list). However, you'll note from the list that the fifth stage is only halfway through a good application's life cycle. The more of these stages that are defined in the original project plan, the more likely the application will be well-constructed and evolve smoothly into each new stage.

Design Precept 5—Keep the Users in Tow

LDF places high value on user involvement in most facets of the design, development, testing, and deployment process. Users can be an extension of the development team, as well as its masters.

In the course of system design, developers are often inclined to take seeds (ideas, problems, or process descriptions) from the users to define the solution from these seeds, deserting the users when issues arise that present complex decision points. LDF states that it is better to stop and educate the users on issues that are important to them, and involve them in the decision process, than to act as their proxy.

If the users' sense of ownership and participation in the design process begins to lessen, so does their commitment to the overall success of the project. Also, their ability to successfully blame the developers for every problem throughout the project is enhanced when developers shoo them away and create the application autonomously.

Design Precept 6—Communicate Important Concepts Visually

One good diagram is worth a thousand words, or more. Throughout the design process and in the written plan, use drawings and diagrams to clarify key concepts. Visual aids are proven to stimulate the creative process, communicate difficult concepts, and guide discussions in group meetings.

Consider these points:

▶ The most important visual aid for developers is a database diagram. The database structure is the foundation of the application and guides much of the design and development of the system.

▶ The most important visual aids for users are the form mockups. Users interact with the application primarily through its forms.

▶ The most important visual aids for development managers are project plans. A commonly used visual representation of a project plan is a Gantt chart, which is a diagram that displays project tasks, their timing, and their dependencies. (Gantt charts can be produced with Microsoft Project.)

▶ The most important visual aid for project managers is a process flow diagram. Properly understanding the improved work flow and its benefits is critical when defining and funding a solution.

▶ The most important visual aids for management and the ultimate users are report mockups. The final value of most systems is reflected in the quality of information coming out of its printer.

Each of these diagrams should be prominently included in the specification document.

Design Precept 7—Application Design Is Its Own Project

A design effort must be budgeted separately from a development effort. This ensures that researching and writing a plan is itself a *project*, complete with its own team, management, milestones, and deliverable (a specification document). This also ensures that the research effort explores multiple options for resolving the stated problem or need, because the planners' judgment is not clouded with the foreknowledge of the target development budget or timeline.

When following the LDF research and design model, the design budget for a project is usually at least ten percent of the overall project cost. See Chapter 4, "Creating Design Specifications," for information on how to cost-justify the design effort.

Design Precept 8—Create the Budget Last

Establishing the development budget before the research begins automatically limits the scope of the design team's vision and places blinders on the research process. Instead, the research effort should proceed as if development money were unlimited (or at least ample), with an eye toward designing the best possible solution to the problem. Then, at the end of the design process, the budgetary realities are introduced, and three determinations are made in order to fit the design and the budget together:

1. Which features are critical but can be deferred to future releases?

2. Which features are not critical and can be deferred indefinitely?

 Note

Witness my careful choice of words in the second point. No feature that is dear to the users should ever be *canceled*, which removes it from consideration and the design plan. Instead, features that are not affordable now are "deferred indefinitely," which keeps them in the plan for future review and resuscitation if economics change later.

3. What alternatives exist to costly features that provide a legitimate benefit?

It's important to understand the ramifications of the third point. Some developers scoff when I state that design discussions should downplay budget realities. They feel that it is wasteful of effort to discuss a feature that the users obviously cannot afford.

I see the situation differently. The purpose of a design phase is to define a problem and its possible solutions. Stifling discussion during design meetings is a bad idea. Many times I have seen users describe some grandiose feature that they clearly cannot afford, only to hear another member of the design team redefine the need or the application's approach to it and concoct an affordable alternative. Without an environment that encourages free and open debate, the design phase will not be comprehensive.

Chapter 4, "Creating Design Specifications," provides a thorough discussion of budgeting in the section "Budgeting from a Specification."

Design Precept 9—Plan for Data Mobility

Do not presume that the data you key into a Jet database will always reside only in that Jet database. Data that has value often migrates into other database platforms, analytical tools, and storage structures. Thus, you must carefully weigh any aspects of a database layout that decrease its portability.

Here are two examples of data structures that are limiting to migration:

Platform-dependent object names. Placing spaces or special characters in table or field names in an Access database can make it difficult to copy or move the data into another platform that does not support one or both of these conventions.

Note

As part of Chapter 6, "Leszynski Naming Conventions for Access," I discuss how to keep object names portable between Access/Jet and SQL Server.

2

Application-dependent data structures. Specific applications may benefit from a customized data structure, but when the data is exported to another environment, the data structure becomes problematic. For example, a data table that must store dates, but serves an application that concerns itself mostly with the month portion of the date, may use three fields for storage of the value (month, day, and year). Copying this data to a mainframe for use by the corporate ad hoc query tool may require special export or query logic to recombine the date information so that users can view and test it as a complete date when querying.

Design Precept 10—Never Throw Any Data Away

Today's critical information may be tomorrow's minutiae, and data taken for granted when collected may provide a wealth of information at some point in the future. It is not always possible to accurately predict the future value of today's collected data.

As a consequence, LDF maintains that no valid data should ever be discarded. Records are not deleted; they are *archived*. See my discussions of archive tables and data warehouses in Chapter 7, "Understanding Application Architecture," for more information on LDF's obsession with saving copies of every data item.

Also, as critical information is modified, consider making backup copies of the affected records before the changes are made. Chapter 15, "Protecting and Validating Data," exemplifies this with an illustration of archiving deleted records.

Design Precept 11—Focus on Usability

Most applications are used by people with diverse computer skills. Developers must be aware of the spectrum of users' skills and abilities when designing a system's interface. An application's design must focus on creating a tool that can be mastered by anyone in the user community, not a tool that is comprehensive only to developers and power users.

Forms are the primary user interface element in an application; thus, techniques for maximizing usability under this precept will usually apply to forms. Chapters 13, "Mastering Combo and List Boxes," through 17, "Bulletproofing Your Application Interface," expand this precept into hands-on techniques for building forms that are powerful yet highly usable.

Element 3—Management and Development

The application rubber meets the road here. After days or months of planning, debate, and definition, the development effort begins. LDF views management personnel and development personnel as two legs of the project's structure; if both legs are not present and solid, the project cannot stand up (see Figure 2.4).

Fig. 2.4
Management and development support a project's structure.

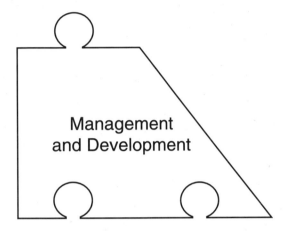

Project Management Precepts

PC database projects often have no hands-on management personnel. Instead, one or a handful of developers are beholden directly to the users for their input, motivation, and feedback. LDF maintains that full-time developers should not manage the workflow like this, nor directly control the budgeting, milestones, and delivery of an application.

The following points refer specifically to the management of the development process and its team.

Management Precept 1—No Development Team Should Be Smaller than Three People

Small applications can be created by a single person. In many corporate departments, one PC support person provides both hardware and software support, and his or her job definition may include creating database applications. But however tempting it is to enable a person like this to solo on a project, LDF maintains that the smallest logical team for a development effort has these three roles:

A Development Manager. Developers need two kinds of help once development begins:

▶ First, they need someone to buffer them from the users. Questions and issues crop up during development on both the technical side and in the users' camp. These issues require time to research and manage, and the most efficient model for this is to use the management side of the development team rather than distracting an actual coder.

▶ Second, programmers need to be prodded to stay on schedule. Coders can get lost in both the wizardry and the pitfalls of their technology and need to be managed and motivated toward deadlines in order to stay focused.

A development manager fills both of these roles and, in doing so, creates a much higher probability of a timely delivery of the solution.

 Note

In some cases, the role of project manager and development manager fall on the same person, which can work fine if the project manager is technically sophisticated (see the following precept).

A Developer/Programmer. All development requires at least one, undistracted, dedicated coder. (If the roles of manager and coder absolutely *must* fall to the same person in a small department or company, that person must be very talented in order to determine when to wear the programmer hat and when to wear the manager hat.)

A Tester. Developers should not do the final testing on their own work. Ever. Period. (See the related precept under the Deployment element.)

Management Precept 2—The Development Manager Must Be a Technologist

If the opinions of the readers of this book reflect the composition of developers in the real world, they are evenly divided between the beliefs that the leader of a development team should be an outstanding business manager or a brilliant technologist.

Of course, someone with *both* talents is automatically qualified for the position, and such a combination is preferred in a development manager. Assuming, however, that such a joint skill set is rare, LDF chooses to weight the technology bent as a higher factor than the management skills.

Why? Consider the example of the military. Never are civilians brought in and made into generals. Working your way through the ranks is the only valid course of advancement that earns you the respect of your peers and crew, and provides you with an understanding of the processes and people you must control.

So it is with development teams. There is little regard in programming circles for management personnel at all and even less for development managers who have not themselves been developers. Thus, the natural job path for a development manager is up through the ranks of development. Having reached the management role, the manager should not forswear all coding, at the risk of getting out of touch with the needs of the development staff and the options for the users.

Management Precept 3—The Development Manager Must Not Be a Full-Time Developer

A quick reading of the prior precept might lead you to believe that the development manager should also be a developer, but LDF maintains the such a position is best filled by an *ex-developer*. The development manager should have a development background and should still dabble with technology, in order to properly understand the processes used to create solutions.

However, a development manager should be involved in only a small amount of actual *current* development. Fulfilling development responsibilities in addition to business responsibilities tends to give a manager two conflicting job roles. Of the two roles, management is the more important one.

While they may not participate in the actual development of mission-critical code, managers should be part of the review process for code and architecture, as detailed in Chapter 9, "Completing and Deploying a Solution."

Development Precepts

Most developers define or innately follow a fairly consistent development style. The style will have "repeatable" techniques and guidelines; some of them will probably be quite detailed. For example, Chapter 20, "Applying Development Shortcuts," describes several methodologies for controlling application object versions in a multi-developer environment. Most development teams will follow one of the methodologies described in that chapter and will employ a detailed team development policy.

However, it would not be appropriate for LDF to prescribe one version control methodology over another. In keeping with the synopsis nature of LDF precepts, the development principles reflected in this element are at a high level and do not concern themselves with implementation details.

Development Precept 1—Develop in Rings Around the Processes

The core application processes (data management routines such as end-of-month postings) are the hardest elements of a system to design, write, and test. Because these processes can evolve as they are developed, you should not finalize an interface before creating the processes it surrounds.

LDF encourages an early focus on the interface in order to facilitate user reviews and feedback (see the "Prototyping" section of Chapter 3, "Preparing for Development").

However, this is only to solidify the interface *from a layout standpoint*; it is difficult for users to finalize an interface until its processes are completed.

If significant development resources are available, it is possible to code interfaces and processes in parallel, with the developers sharing information closely. If not, the team must code interfaces in *rings* around the processes, bringing each process to a state of solidity first, then developing its related interfaces.

 Note

This precept is akin to eating the dessert *after* the meal (saving the best for last). Many developers find form and report development faster and more rewarding (the dessert) than slogging through core processes (the meal) and do this fun work first. This precept ensures that developers finish all of their broccoli before starting on the ice cream.

Development Precept 2—Coordinate Team Efforts

Consistency of development style, as touted by the focus on standards in the *Skills and Standards* element of LDF, is only half of the development equation. An equally important area of focus is consistent management of the development process and the players in it.

Coding assignments must be delegated in a way that balances the skills currently held by each of the development team members against the skills that they may want or need to acquire during the current project. A development manager must deftly juggle the skills and schedules of the team members and also the project's deliverables and milestones. Creating a reliable model for delegation and coordination of all these tasks can improve the harmonious functioning of the team. These intricacies of project management are detailed further in Chapter 9, "Completing and Deploying a Solution."

Development Precept 3—Develop Toward Functional Milestones

Creating code and application objects can be a joyous creative effort one day and a tedious debugging morass the next. Developers are more successful in surmounting the tangents, distractions, and pitfalls of coding if they stay focused on specific objectives.

Project tasks should be doled out in bite-size chunks, with reasonable and regular milestones attached. Milestones for team members should mesh so that at various intervals, team members can meet to review progress and note specific components that have been completed. Identifying component completion as it occurs allows the unit testing process to occur parallel with the development effort, which very favorably impacts development timelines.

The management of milestones is discussed in Chapter 9, "Completing and Deploying a Solution."

Element 4—Tools and Platforms

Solutions that look great on paper must, when implemented, conform to the reality of the infrastructure on which they depend. The capabilities of the tools, languages, operating systems, and other environmental elements have a significant impact on the actual implemented solution (see Figure 2.5).

Fig. 2.5
Tools and platforms.

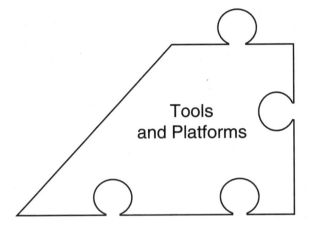

Tools Precepts

LDF can apply in many different development environments, but it is obviously a database-focused framework. Presuming that you use Jet and Access for data and interface services, you may or may not require any additional tools to complete the solution.

Tools Precept 1—Minimize the Use of Tools that Slow Execution

Too many programmers love to burden applications with gadgets, widgets, and good-looking extensions that ultimately slow the solution down more than they increase productivity. Developers must resist both their urges, and those of the users, to employ application devices that have a negative performance impact such as voice, video, large or complex graphics, and some types of ActiveX controls. This is especially true where reasonable alternatives exist.

 Note

A good example of the scenario mentioned in the preceding paragraph was found in tabbed forms. While alternatives to a tabbed layout (toggling control visibility or using multiple pages) have always existed in Access, many developers insisted on trying to emulate tabs with graphics or ActiveX controls because it made forms more attractive. Such efforts usually were quirky or slow.

Fortunately, this struggle was not lost on Microsoft, and we inherited an intrinsic tab control with Access 97.

Developers must make conscious performance tradeoffs when enabling user features. For example, on slower machines, the negative performance impact of operations like sending e-mail messages in the background from a database application may require a creative but equally functional alternative approach, such as writing messages to a table and sending all queued messages late at night.

Tools Precept 2—Grow Your Own Tools When You Are Able

As a tool builder by nature (read Chapter 20, "Applying Development Shortcuts"), LDF reflects my inherent bias with respect to automating the development process. It is absolutely true that homemade tools are more expensive than retail tools, *in the first use*. However, the real cost is measured over the long-term, not up front.

Consider why custom solutions are developed:

▶ A suitable retail solution could not be found.

▶ The users insisted on self-reliance (ownership of the code and processes).

If you are the developer of such a custom solution, why would you choose to suffer the ills that you protect your users from (compromising on features and not having ownership of code) by purchasing and using retail tools that don't work precisely as your needs dictate?

Note

There are, of course, plenty of good tools on the market that may match your needs precisely. LDF doesn't argue against purchasing a tool that does exactly what you need, only against compromising with a less-than-perfect match if you are capable of writing your own tool in-house.

Platform Precepts

Because Access is not a cross-platform solution, the developer knows much about the environment that an application will be deployed in without ever asking the users.

Windows, Office, MAPI, and other environmental factors can usually be assumed as a given. Nevertheless, developers must still consider the various configurations of machinery and connectivity when creating the solution.

Platform Precept 1—Hardware Is Cheaper than Idle Time

We frequently see companies spend 30 to 50 thousand dollars on a custom solution, only to load it onto 486 computers with 8M of memory. In this scenario, users are waiting (and waiting, and waiting...) for each application process to complete. A company that budgets hundreds of thousands of dollars for mainframe memory and does not spend a few thousand dollars on PC RAM is wasting valuable human capital by forcing people to wait for their machines.

Assume that an average worker costs a company $40,000 each year in wages and benefits and spends all day working on the computer. Suppose also that purchasing a new computer for this worker costs $5,000. The worker would need to produce 12.5 percent more work each year (40,000 divided by 5,000) to recoup the cost of the machine in one year. In an environment where each PC upgrade nets the buyer an average computing speed increase of 100 percent, it does not seem hard to justify the purchase of new equipment based on this math.

Platform Precept 2—Empower and Protect the Data

The platform and infrastructure that the application rides must treat the data with the seriousness that it deserves. Database records are often mission-critical, and the databases that contain them must be adequately supported by the users' hardware.

LDF maintains that the network infrastructure for a database application must provide these features:

Reliability. Low-quality network hardware can drop packets of data, poor servers may crash disks often or suffer power surges, and applications run on a serverless workgroup are only as solid as the workstation with the database. Each of these situations may result in database corruption. A database application demands a stable and reliable platform.

Security. In addition to the security layer in Access, the network and workstation infrastructure should restrict the ability of unauthorized users to get near the database and application files. As a simple example, users should log off of their workstations when they go home.

Performance. A development team's reputation suffers when their good application is placed on a bad (slow) network, server, or workstation.

Redundancy. In a perfect world, all servers are mirrored and perfectly redundant. If this is not possible, regular backups are the minimum level of network-level redundancy mandated by any database application.

Element 5—Skills and Standards

As with any other team of people working together, a development team needs a clear set of policies and standards to apply to their work (see Figure 2.6). Only minor variances of coding and architectural styles, and sometimes development skills, can be tolerated if the team is to succeed collectively.

Fig. 2.6

A development team needs clear policies and standards.

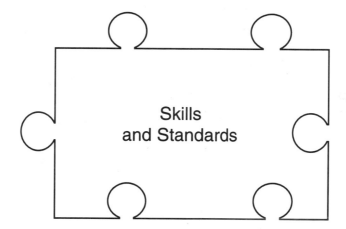

The goal of this standardization effort can be exemplified as follows: Four developers, using the published style for their development team, could each work on a quarter of an application. When their components are combined, the application would have a single, consistent appearance to all of the objects and code.

Developer Skills Precepts

No framework can legitimately mandate that only expert coders work on a project; we all have to start at the bottom of the skills ladder and work up. However, LDF *does* expect that policies will be created to help elevate the skill levels of all developers on a team, with an eye toward building a balanced staff of experts.

Skills Precept 1—Every Developer Is a Business Doctor

Fundamental to LDF is the belief that solution developers must have a broader knowledge base than simply writing code. Just as a doctor must learn anatomy, someone who solves business problems for a living should understand how business processes work.

LDF's leaning in this respect can be summarized this way:

> *Every programmer should be an analyst.* Developers are most successful at satisfying users' needs if they can dissect the environment where the users work, understand the fundamental processes, and grasp the full impact and nuances of the designed solution.

Every analyst should be a consultant. I tend to think of an *analyst* as someone who can understand a problem, and a *consultant* as someone who can suggest multiple plausible solutions to the problem.

Every consultant should be a psychologist. An application consultant must, by definition, be able to work with a team of users to define their needs, arbitrate their discussions, and build team camaraderie. In complex environments, developers that interact deeply with users must be as adept at understanding and managing disparate personalities as a corporate psychologist.

As team members move from programmers to analysts to consultants to psychologists, they evolve from the ability to code what is in a specification to the ability to truly understand how people work and how to automate it. They become able to envision the problems an application will solve and to suggest enhancements to processes and application designs, and can then offer alternative solutions in the course of development. A careful reading of Part I of this book, "The Leszynski Development Framework," can help you to move up the skills ladder this way.

Skills Precept 2—Establish Skills Metrics

How do you maintain a high-quality and balanced development team? By setting and testing against skill level hurdles. Ideally, both new hires and existing team members can be challenged with creative examinations or tasks that demonstrate the areas that are ripe for improvement.

Aptitude tests for programmers are a bit awkward to create and apply. The most successful means for measuring aptitude and charting areas for improvement that I've found are these:

Code Reviews. A senior developer or development manager should regularly analyze code produced by each developer and provide constructive feedback on areas for improvement and methodology.

 Note

This review process is not solely relevant to skills enhancement; code reviews should be a regular part of the quality assurance process when building applications.

Peer reviews. Development teams often share code, ideas, and objects among themselves. In this scenario, each developer learns the strong and weak points of the other developers with respect to their skills and their ability to contribute to the team. If the team climate supports it without political fallout, having developers review one another in an open or closed forum gives each developer the benefit of a skill review by other developers.

Chapter 9, "Completing and Deploying a Solution," discusses these types of reviews in more detail.

Of course, another type of skill review comes from the users of the application, who find its feature deficiencies and application bugs. The nature of these deficiencies and defects speaks volumes about the skills and motivation of the programmers that created them.

Skills Precept 3—Invest Wisely in Skill Enhancement

Developers usually learn on the job. All too often, developers are thrust into a project in progress on their first day of work and given immediate milestones to achieve. The pressure of such a situation is not conducive to a quality learning experience.

As an alternative, companies can send new (and existing) team members to expensive classes and conferences for training. If the quality of information provided by such an event is marginal, as many are, the company loses twice: The developer is dispirited, and the team has lost productive time.

In between these extremes, teams must place a high priority on contriving a training model that is cost- and time-efficient and make sure that developers who are eager to move themselves up the skills ladder are given the effective tools and reviews to do so.

 Tip

In my company, we've found that developers receive enormous value from teaching each other new skills that are appropriate to our specific projects and tool mix. We hold a "teach-in" each Friday, where one developer trains the rest of the team on a specific skill targeted in advance as an area of current need.

Development Standards Precepts

LDF maintains that development teams should apply rigorous discipline to the creation and implementation of a uniform development style throughout the team, and if possible, throughout the organization.

Standards Precept 1—Create Intelligent Development Conventions

The LDF position on the value of a consistent object-naming strategy is made apparent in Chapter 5, "Creating Naming Conventions," Chapter 6, "Leszynski Naming Conventions for Access," and in Appendix C, "Leszynski Naming Conventions for Microsoft

Solution Developers" on the CD-ROM. One of the core principles of LDF is that any developer should be able to understand code and objects created by any other developer on the same team.

In addition to object names, development conventions can specify common standards for code layout (see Chapter 11, "Expert Approaches to VBA") and for coding techniques (see Chapter 20, "Applying Development Shortcuts").

Standards Precept 2—Use a Consistent Application Architecture Model

Development team members must implement the architecture of a solution based on a commonly accepted model for the team. How objects are built, where they are located, and how they communicate with each other must not be determined on a per-object, per-project basis.

Here are simple examples of important architectural considerations:

▶ How and when is denormalization allowed for performance reasons?

▶ Are indexes optimized for entry/edit operations or for analysis and reporting?

▶ What are the location, security, and maintenance models for different types of data tables?

▶ How are data tables separated from the interface database?

These and other application architecture concepts are detailed in Chapter 7, "Understanding Application Architecture."

Standards Precept 3—Apply a Consistent Interface Standard

Companies should create a *style guide* that determines the standards for the look and feel of forms, reports, alerts, and other user interface elements. The guide should include specifications for the visual presentation of application elements. Here is an example of some areas that should be included:

▶ Standards for colors and other visual properties.

▶ How form and report labels and controls align.

▶ Standards for button text and bitmaps, and button size, location, and accelerators.

▶ Standardized form and report headers and footers.

▶ Standards for wording of dialog boxes, alerts, and messages.

Chapter 8, "Designing Effective Interfaces," and Chapter 16, "Presenting Data to Users," each contain detailed discussions of application interface element standardization.

Standards Precept 4—Apply a Consistent Navigation Model

Very few companies run on a single application or a single developer. Instead, multiple solutions are created by multiple coders. The challenge in this environment is for each application to work like one another (as much as is practical). Companies and their users are both affected negatively if each application requires a significant retraining of users to understand the construction, navigation model, and usage.

LDF suggests that development teams create standards for how users interact with application objects and base these standards on generally accepted interface standards where applicable. See Chapter 14, "Navigating in Forms and Applications," for examples of this precept in action.

Standards Precept 5—Apply a Consistent Development Model

Many coding projects are executed in a state of chaos. Developers (and sadly, even development managers) are often so focused on their technology, the project timelines, or the budding solution that they forget to apply appropriate controls and techniques for smoothing development and deployment.

LDF suggests that development teams pay attention to defining organizational techniques that can prevent emergencies and distractions. A consistent operational model for the development environment that prescribes how to back up source code, manage ownership of objects, configure a development workstation, and organize a code repository can provide a critical layer of organization for the entire team.

Standards Precept 6—All Standards Should Be Written Down or Online

Development standards must be written down or available in online resources like help files or Web pages. Create a standards document, index it, publish it, distribute it, and subject it to regular review and feedback. Treat is as your *Developer's Handbook*.

Your document should explain not only the *What* of the style, but also the *Why*—for each element of the style, note why that element is logical and necessary.

 Tip

With the availability of inexpensive tools to create online documentation (viewers, readers, help compilers, multimedia authoring systems, and Office's new Web publishing features), development teams have few excuses left for not having their development policies and examples available interactively for the benefit of the entire team.

Standards Precept 7—Enforce Consistent Usage of Standards

Team leaders and development managers must be charged not only with creating a compendium of policies and procedures for all developers, but with enforcing the policies.

Each team must determine which development conventions are important to enforce. Here are examples of standards that foster the objective of consistency across a team:

▶ Standards for the rules and tools used to design database structures.

▶ Strategies for naming application objects.

▶ A set of common terms and abbreviations.

▶ Policies for object descriptions, code comments, code structure, and team communication.

Other examples of development styles and standards are found scattered throughout this book.

Standards Precept 8—Creating Standards Is a Team Project

Debates on standardization can go on almost forever; thus, creating standards as a team is not always practical. Nevertheless, a written draft of any proposed standards should be reviewed by all developers or a carefully selected representative sample. Software developers are among the most apolitical of all creatures and many bristle when standards created higher up are forced upon them.

Element 6—Deployment and Refinement

As defined in Chapter 3, "Preparing for Development," an application's useful life is usually measured in years, with multiple revisions occurring along the way. LDF maintains that half or even less of a total project's time and monetary outlay is applied to the first release. As a result, developers must stay committed to the success of a project long after the last line of code for version 1.0 is completed. The development team must shepherd or participate in the deployment and installation of the solution, and in its ongoing maintenance (see Figure 2.7).

Fig. 2.7
Deployment and refinement.

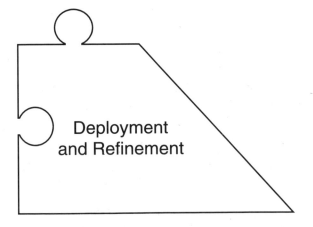

Deployment Precepts

Preparing to ship an application to users brings with it the elation of a milestone (code complete) achieved, but also the burdens of testing, documentation, setup, and training. Depending on the size of the development team, coders may not be involved in these efforts. In smaller firms, however, it is likely that the development and deployment teams include the same people.

Deployment Precept 1—Developers Make Inadequate Testers

Never, ever, let the person who coded a routine act as the only tester for that process. Developers in general are not very good testers, and a developer testing his or her own code should be the first line of defense only, never the last one.

Some people are simply born to test. They try the oddest combinations of interaction with the application; they seem to be able to sniff out bugs with their eyes closed, and they have a critical eye for consistency. People like this should be sought out, cultivated, and revered by development teams, because having a knack for testing is truly a rare gift.

Chapter 9, "Completing and Deploying a Solution," discusses this testing personality and the testing process in significant detail.

Deployment Precept 2—Involve the Users in Deployment

For any size project, involve some of the users in the testing process for the application. Many developers dismiss users as too unsophisticated to be good testers, or too difficult to manage as a test team. However, such developers overlook the many benefits provided by the participation of users.

Similarly, users can sometimes effectively assist each other with application setup and training, offloading some of these responsibilities from the development team.

Chapter 9, "Completing and Deploying a Solution," details the value of user participation in deployment, and how to manage the process.

Deployment Precept 3—Strive to Make Users Self-Supporting

Ten years ago, many Information Technology department workers tied their sense of worth and job satisfaction to the degree of dependence between the users and them. A phone constantly ringing with bug reports, training requests, and change orders was seen as a status symbol.

Today, most developers would rather focus on building new solutions and learning new technologies than maintaining old ones, and thus are motivated to minimize the distractions they get from users. A combination of good training, solid applications, a high-quality design team, wise testing processes, and smart development policies and tools can make this happen.

See Chapter 8, "Designing Effective Interfaces," and Chapter 17, "Bulletproofing Your Application Interface," for more details on creating applications that educate and assist the user toward self-sufficiency. Chapter 9, "Completing and Deploying a Solution," provides general insights into useful testing and training approaches.

Refinement Precepts

What we and many other developers used to call *maintenance mode* (a state where the application feature set does not grow, only bugs are fixed) is no longer an inevitable state for an application. With new releases of tools coming on an annual basis, and hardware upgrades following at an equally frantic pace, merely maintaining an application is not logical. Instead, significant periodic upgrades of major applications is an instituted policy in many companies.

Refinement Precept 1—Cycle Your Updates

Unless an application is so broken that users cannot derive any value from it, do not fix problems or add features each time a user request is generated. Software builds should be released at reasonable intervals, in response to a body of work rather than a single change.

For applications that are widely deployed, the internal cost of distributing and retraining a new release is high. This cost must be weighed against the benefit of a release in order to gauge whether the timing is right.

See Chapter 9, "Completing and Deploying a Solution," for more information on staging the release of application updates.

Refinement Precept 2—Leverage Your Investment

Writing reusable code instead of static code and creating reusable objects instead of canned objects adds very little extra time to a development effort, yet provides significant financial benefits to a company. As any particular application grows and morphs into new releases, developers should be able to leverage off of existing components in the application when constructing the new releases or other applications.

LDF advocates creating reusable code and objects as part of the development team's library. Additionally, however, developers should understand the growth plan for each object *captive* to an application, and design the object to provide the simplest possible upgrade path in the future.

From Here...

This chapter provides the groundwork for every chapter that follows in the book, because the framework described here pervades the examples and practices in each chapter.

The chapters early in this book provide additional information derived from LDF on a conceptual level, including these:

▶ Chapter 3, "Preparing for Development," expands the analysis precepts in LDF into practical research techniques.

▶ Chapter 4, "Creating Design Specifications," describes how the LDF design precepts can be applied to the creation of a specification document.

▶ In Chapter 5, "Creating Naming Conventions," the LDF penchant for written standards is expanded into one specific area of development.

The chapters later in the book move from theory to practice by showing how LDF, taken to its logical conclusion, becomes actual coding and development techniques:

▶ Chapter 17, "Bulletproofing Your Application Interface," provides hands-on techniques for applying LDF guidelines to real-world development.

▶ The LDF tools precepts are embodied in the wizards and builders shown in Chapter 20, "Applying Development Shortcuts."

Preparing for Development

3

We've all heard that "Most people don't plan to fail, they fail to plan." As an Access developer or an advanced user, this quote is certainly pertinent to your work. It's likely that you learned to work with Access through trial and error, so you probably develop applications in much the same way. Most developers have not been trained in the value and process of planning, and many dislike it as a result. However, developers who do not plan regularly find themselves embroiled in development projects that never seem to end, as feature enhancement requests and problem reports continue to pour in.

Moving the Window

When contractors were building the current house that my wife Joan and I designed, we visited every day to see their progress and to check the work against the plans we had drawn. On one visit, we noted that the sun was setting right where we had located the fireplace, and Joan commented, "We should have put the window there instead." So, the next day, I met the framing contractor at the site and talked through our options for swapping the fireplace and the window next to it. Because the house was only roughly framed, the cost and time impact were minimal, so we made the change and ended up with a better design.

Sometimes when I'm sitting in my family room looking out the relocated window, I try to imagine living in the house the way we had first framed it, and then suddenly deciding to move the fireplace and the original window. Two complete walls would come down, wires and pipes would move, and the deck would be modified. The cost would be astronomical (at least 100 times as much as the original revamp), and the chaos would be exasperating.

There are many parallels between this tale and the software development process. First, our vigilance saved us money and disappointment—we would have certainly enjoyed our house less without the relocated window. Similarly, users of software applications that discover design shortfalls equally early in a process can initiate a change, but would never be able to afford that same change if they caught it later in the development phase.

Secondly, the cost differential of changing a feature of a house early versus after completion is about the same as that of changing a software program feature. It can cost as much as 100 times more to change a software feature at the end of development as in the design phase. So, the correct time to make sure you are delivering to your users what they want is in the framing stage of the application, not after they've moved in.

Given that your habit probably is to take a few report and form sketches produced by your users and begin coding, how can I convince you to create plans and designs for your database applications before you start coding? I'll employ three techniques in the next two chapters that will help make my argument more persuasive:

Keep it simple. Entire handbooks are written on software design, but I think the essence of the process can be distilled into a much smaller space. Ultimately, the way you approach project planning and the plan document itself are very tailored to your firm, your project, and your users; all you probably really want me to do is hit the high points. That's what I'll do.

Give you the tools. The information in these two planning-related chapters has been distilled into checklists, outlines, and document templates located on the CD-ROM. You can use them as tools to guide your planning process. This should jump start your planning efforts, and make it easier for you to adopt good habits.

Automate the process. Every developer likes to use tools, so I've provided you with an automated design tool that helps you lay out your schema in Excel, and then build the Access database automatically. The LCI Schema Builder tool is on the CD-ROM and is explained in Chapter 4, "Creating Design Specifications," and Chapter 10, "Creating Expert Tables and Queries." Once you understand it, you can modify and use it for your own projects.

Even if you already create detailed project plans, you should still find enough interesting tips, techniques, and tools in this chapter and the next one to help you rethink or refine your process.

The information in this chapter is relevant to all parties in a development process, from management and development to users. However, the chapter generally speaks from the perspective of the development manager or primary developer.

Planning Your Project

A database application project quickly takes on a life of its own and can grow in scope like a weed: quickly and in all directions. Careful planning can provide a control and budgeting mechanism for such growth.

Planning a business application is more like detective work than science. The design team begins with an incomplete set of facts about how a process works, how it could be improved, and then embarks on a discovery phase to fill in the missing information. As Figure 3.1 implies, the process is complicated by the fact that users don't always invest the time and mental energy necessary in application design to provide the following essential information:

▶ Accurate details about the workflow or process that will be automated

▶ Complete descriptions of the desired system features

▶ A long-range vision for the automated solution

Instead, users normally provide brief descriptions of their current workflow and a list of their objectives for an automated solution. The users' lack of technical skills often means that their descriptions are inaccurate or incomplete; thus, the design detectives must fill in the gaps between what users say and what they really mean. The design team then must propose extensions and alternatives to the users' wish lists, based upon its members' greater knowledge of business processes and technology.

Fig. 3.1

During the application design process, this information must be discovered and detailed.

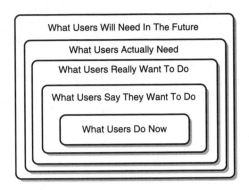

When projects are spearheaded by developers, as is often the case in flat organizations with few management layers, caution must be exercised that the users and managers do not get the impression that they need not be involved in the project beyond creating an initial wish list. In fact, the involvement of users and managers throughout the project is critical to its success. I try to get my clients to realize the following two points about Access projects before we get started:

▶ *There is no free lunch.* Try to imagine getting a custom-made suit or a custom-built house without being involved in the design process, inspecting the work, testing the fit, and so on. The odds are very high that the final product would not meet your needs and expectations, and you would not be satisfied with the result.

Custom software development is no different. Users and managers must invest time in the application's design, review, testing, and deployment in order to reap the highest benefits of the project. Users must also commit time to their training at the end of the deployment phase so that they do not misuse or under-utilize the application.

▶ *The enemy's name is Feature Creep.* Even good planning still seems to miss one or more important fields or features. Depending on where the project is in the development cycle when the shortfall is discovered and enhancement requests created, it may be unwise to implement them in the current release. Changes in features or scope (called *feature creep* in development circles) usually expand the original delivery timeline and budget, and if rushed can decrease the stability of the application; they are to be discouraged after development has begun.

Developers and project managers must work hard to discern critical feature requests from nice-to-have features, and must be able to say no convincingly to any non-critical features after development has started (see the sidebar). Designers of the application must take their responsibility seriously to create a comprehensive and final, design and project plan early in the process.

If you can communicate the preceding two points to those who benefit from the development project, you can start the design process off with the correct team mindset.

A "Pisa" the Puzzle

Try as we might to indoctrinate our clients with the mindset described in this section, they nevertheless regularly surprise us with significant enhancement requests late in a project development cycle. Sid, one of my staff members, tries to handle such change requests firmly with the following analogy:

"Assume that your software project is a ten-story building, and I'm your builder. At this point in the project, I've completed the majority of your building—frame, wiring, plumbing, windows, and walls. What you're asking me to do now is to stop and add five more stories to your building. That means you want me to rip out all of the wiring, plumbing, and framing on the tenth floor and connect the five new stories to it.

"Not only were the wiring, plumbing, and structure of the building designed for ten stories, not fifteen, making it very hard for me to safely add the additional footage, but the foundation of the building was poured with ten stories in mind. If I add five more stories without rebuilding the foundation, your building could begin to sink and tip. You don't really want me to build you another Leaning Tower of Pisa, do you?"

While slightly whimsical, Sid's analogy is appropriate and paints the correct picture—adding last-minute features to an application without backing up to the beginning and fitting the features in correctly may undermine the entire integrity of the solution. It is the responsibility of developers/designers to elicit from the users enough information to determine accurately what the feature set of the application should be, and it is incumbent on the users to be clear and comprehensive about their long-term needs early in a project's design process.

Some business processes cry out for automation and are easy to computerize. Others are not so linear and can challenge developers and their tools. Of course, the more complex the project, the more intensive the planning effort.

Describing the Concept

One of the three following circumstances usually initiates discussion of an application development project:

  ▶ *A business process is re-engineered.* Forces outside a particular workflow often influence the need to automate that workflow. When larger computers are replaced with desktop computers, manual operations are mechanized, and an organization grows rapidly. Or, downsizing and layoffs require increased productivity from fewer workers, and managers look to custom software applications to automate or improve business processes.

▶ *Competitive pressures increase.* If the competition is automated or is hot on your heels and chasing your customers, the pressure mounts to streamline specific processes. Most business people remember how two areas in their company were probably the first to automate: accounting and sales. The accounting department, under the competitive pressures of the prosperous 80s, needed personal computers to count its beans better and to get the company more nutrition from each bean. The sales department got prospect and customer management software before most other departments even got personal computers in order to improve the sales closing rate in the face of better-automated competitors.

▶ *Someone with a budget gets fed up.* If an influential worker or manager voices a complaint often enough, whether it is about the difficulties of finding specific information or trying to decipher an unintelligible report, someone with unencumbered money in a budget may eventually hear the cries for help.

Whether initiated by one of these forces or others, early discussions of an application usually involve workers and managers within a single department. A workflow issue becomes a frequent point of discussion at departmental meetings, or even the water cooler, until someone determines that the problem can be overcome with a customized software solution.

Next, the tone of the discussions usually shifts quickly from problem-oriented to solution-oriented, with users contributing ideas and feedback about improving the current situation or process. Often at this point, hard copy documentation of the problem or solution crops up, such as reports with manual notations showing additional desired data.

The original discovery phase should produce the following twofold result:

1. A detailed project wish list that captures all relevant user input
2. A simple project-proposal paragraph stating the problem and the contemplated solution

With the beginning of a project proposal at hand, discussions can begin in earnest about the feasibility of the project.

Determining the Scope

Before discussing a project's specifics, you should help its users and managers to understand the phases that an application goes through during its lifetime. People who have not been through the complete application life cycle may be surprised to learn how many total stages there are to an automated solution. Each of the phases is described in the section "Understanding an Application's Life Cycle" later in this chapter. Try to get all parties in the project to think past the first release and to consider the total life of the project when doing the design work.

 Tip

My company is still supporting two DOS-based database applications we wrote in 1986. Do not underestimate the useful life of a good application.

I like to ask my clients in the first design meeting what their five-year plan for the application is. The first reaction is normally something like this: "We have to upgrade Access every 18 months and our hardware at the same time, so we will rethink the application in 18 months as well. For now, let's just get something out there that works." Clearly, the amount of time and energy they expect to devote to the project is limited by their short expectations of its useful life.

After further prodding, however, I can usually get such clients to admit more about their long-term needs, often something like the following:

▶ "We would really like to share the data with the salespeople working from home in two years."

▶ "We'll be doubling the department next year and most of the new employees will use this system."

▶ "The marketing department needs its own system much like this one sometime in the future."

With information at hand about the users' long-range plans, the nature of the project often changes dramatically. In the example statements above, each one introduces a slightly different wrinkle into your approach to the project:

▶ *Replication and Security.* To share the data with the salespeople working remotely in the future causes you to think more now about replication, security, distribution, and concurrency issues.

▶ *User Load.* More attention must be paid to performance up front when the user load will be increasing rapidly—in this case, the application must handle doubling the department. Multiuser issues, database administration, and the timeliness of report data become more urgent as well.

▶ *Common Data Structure.* If we know that Marketing will have "its own system much like this one" in the near future, it is much cheaper in the long run to expand the data structure now to include support for the future marketing users, even if the front-end extensions to the application are not added for their benefit until later.

If your users can come to see the project as a five-year project instead of one with a shorter horizon, their interest and willingness to invest time in the project increases, and your chances for a successful long-term result improve. You can also effect long-term cost savings in a project by building it with room to grow from the start, making future modifications easier. See the section "Planning for Growth" later in this chapter for more information.

Selecting the Players

> **Career Moves**
> "When we visit with our customers, it always amazes me to hear about the background of the people developing applications with our product. For many companies, the first people that were able to requisition and purchase personal computers became the most computer-literate and eventually inherited enough software support or development responsibilities that they were edged out of their original job and into a de facto Information Technology role. Thus, if you dig into the background of many corporate Access gurus, you'll find that it wasn't long ago that they were the company travel agent, bookkeeper, or shipping clerk!"
>
> Tod Nielsen, General Manager, Microsoft Access Business Unit

People power is the fuel of application design and development. Depending on the scope of a project, there are many key players on the team. No project is solely dependent on the skills of the developer; the design effort is affected by the capabilities of each member of the team, and how well they interact. A solution project team may include a mixture of people with the following responsibilities:

Program Manager. This person is at the top of the pyramid and is the funnel through which the empowerment and money for the project flows. This person is usually accountable for the project's success to someone high in the organization; it is important to keep him or her happy and informed throughout the project. This individual
understands how the project fits into larger programs and plays an advisory, rather than a hands-on, role in the design.

Project Manager. This person is the drill sergeant for the project; the one who spearheads the design, selects the players, drives the team, solves mechanical issues, and sets the priorities and milestones. For smaller companies or smaller projects, the program manager and project manager may be the same person. Alternatively, the development manager can serve as project manager.

Development Manager. For projects with more than one developer, one person should be designated as the development manager. This person coordinates communication between the development team and the project manager. In a larger project, this role is not the same as that of the lead developer, who serves as primary technician or technical architect on a project. Instead, the development manager is at the balance point between business processes (meeting budgets and timelines, managing group dynamics, motivating people, and so on) and technical skills (measuring the program against the design, finding creative solutions, selecting tools, and so on).

Developers. These are the construction workers of application building, pulling the bricks and mortar of bits and bytes together into a cohesive product. Sometimes, developers latch on to specific projects or even go looking for them, which is the reverse direction from the ideal. The development team should be chosen after the project planning indicates what skill set is required by the project's coders.

Ultimate Users. This is the highest level in the organization where outputs from the application are utilized. In some cases, the program manager is the ultimate user, providing the reason for his or her interest in the project. Sometimes, the ultimate user or users are even higher in an organization. For example, many users may interact with an accounting application, but if the Chief Financial Officer makes strategic decisions based on reports produced by the application, he or she would be the ultimate user.

User Representatives. This group is the voice of the masses who will use the application every day. It represents the application users and must make decisions for, and communicate the wants of, the entire user base. Whether the user community is 20 people or 300, I try to keep this group to between five and ten people. Larger groups can become ineffective.

Users. This group comprises the data entry people, accounting clerks, personnel, or other users that will be interacting with the application on a daily basis. In the design phase, this group is represented by a few selected individuals, but often more members of the user group are involved in testing and all are involved in training and deployment.

Information Technology Liaison. Most Information Technology departments are overloaded. They were behind when vacuum-tube computers first shipped, and they're still behind. As a result, Access projects are often done outside the realm of IT on a departmental level, using contract resources, departmental support people, or programmers on loan from IT. Although IT has only a supporting role in such a project, they should provide someone to participate in project meetings at various key points to make sure IT is represented when discussions include areas within its domain, such as ongoing support, hardware resources, and integration with other corporate databases.

Support Personnel. Departmental projects may be deployed and supported by departmental, divisional, or corporate support personnel. Sometimes these personnel groups don't even know about a project's existence until the rollout ends up on their To Do list. A more effective strategy is to allow the support personnel to review the specification and application as they are constructed, making recommendations on how to minimize the maintenance and support burden that the application will create. Support personnel often have unique insights on how users think and work, as well as how applications fail.

Figure 3.2 shows the relationships of project team members to each other. Within the user pyramid, power flows from both ends to the middle; the user representatives are empowered by the ultimate users and the users to ensure that their needs are met by the application. In the development pyramid, power flows downward through the various management levels to development.

Fig. 3.2
The application development process involves many team players.

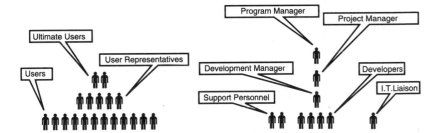

A large development project may have different people filling each role described here. In a smaller project, the team is usually smaller as well. The program manager and project manager positions often fall on the ultimate user who initiates the project. The development manager and the developers might be the same (one) person, and all the users may be part of the user representatives group. If no IT liaison is present and the developer provides support, the smallest reasonable project group consists of manager, developer, and users.

 Note

In the past, application development teams usually had a position called Systems Analyst, a person who was technically sophisticated but was also qualified to

> research and design new systems. I believe that every good PC application developer should strive to have the skills of a Systems Analyst.
>
> In the design team that I define here, the development manager performs the systems analysis role, or all of the developers share the role if they are qualified to do so.

3

When assembling a team of developers, bear in mind that there are dangers in using either too few or too many developers for an application. On the skinny side, one developer doing a 500- or 1,000-hour project is likely to become a little bored or overwhelmed toward the end. A project of this size may be complex enough to benefit from a mix of skills and experience rather than the talents of a single person.

At the opposite end of the spectrum, the coordination and communication layers that accrue when multiple developers write an application can slow down a small project. The addition of source code management in Access 97 provides more control in a multi-developer environment than was previously available, but smaller teams still tend to be more successful with Access development than larger ones. (I discuss multi-developer issues in Chapter 20, "Applying Development Shortcuts.")

 Tip

For my development projects, I try to target a ratio of no more than one developer for every 200 hours of project scope and one developer or more for every 500 hours.

Answering Key Questions

The project design process usually starts with a feasibility meeting where users and managers discuss the current process and how it can be improved. Developers can often add value to such a meeting, and you should try to attend them. The discussion at this point should be focused on the following five overview questions:

What needs to be done? From the treetops, what is the current problem? Who has the problem, and what is the proposed solution?

Why does it need to be done? What will the tangible benefits to the users and company be?

Who will do it? What planning, management, and development resources will be used?

Who will pay for it? What budget(s) will cover both the direct and indirect costs of development and implementation?

When does it need to be completed? Is there some major milestone date driving the project completion, or is as soon as possible the mandate?

If a project concept survives this feasibility meeting, a project manager is formally appointed by the program manager to coordinate users and developers and to see the application through development to its delivery. An initial design meeting is scheduled to bring user representatives together with the development manager and selected developers to discuss the application's features and usage. It is important in the initial meeting to establish the scope of the project and to build the good team chemistry necessary for an enjoyable project.

An Initial Meeting

One of my development leads, Sid, and I recently attended an initial design meeting with a project manager and user representatives to begin designing a complex client application. As development manager for the project, I was leading the meeting, so I asked Sid to record his observations about the flow of the meeting, hoping that it would provide a case study for this chapter. The following are his comments and my annotations:

▶ "Stan begins the meeting by getting people to introduce themselves and talk about their jobs."

I try to build team spirit in the design group from the start and get people comfortable with us and each other.

▶ "Stan explains his understanding of the purpose and goals for the project and allows people to rebut."

I establish the foundation for the project and make sure everyone is heading in the same direction.

▶ "Stan asks people to describe their current workflow."

It is important to get the users to detail the current workflow before they describe how they want to computerize it, so that developers understand the business process to be automated. At this point, users show current data items or reports, or are given a homework item to pull together documentation of the current workflow for the next meeting.

▶ "Stan draws several table grids on the white board and people discuss basic data structures."

Based on the description or documentation of the current workflow, I can determine the basic data structures that are needed. I never try to talk about database design theory, normalization, indexing, and other concepts until very late in the design cycle. In the beginning, I want to keep it simple and talk through the data as if it were to be contained in simple spreadsheets or presented in a simple tabular report, which are concepts most knowledgeable workers understand.

▶ "Stan walks through each data item and asks people to think of related items."

I try to move people past their original concept of the data structure, to get them thinking about information that is related to, or flows from, the information they expected to gather.

▶ "Stan draws a process flow diagram on the white board."

Toward the end of the initial meeting, I like to start people thinking about and discussing how users will interact with the new database application—the features and the sequence of using the features.

This initial project design meeting lasted about four hours. When the meeting began, we had a simple wish list for a new application. By the end, we had added some definition to the items on the wish list, designed a rough application flow and data structure, and given the user representatives a list of open issues and research assignments to complete before the next meeting.

Depending on the number of attendees and the project complexity, an average application development project can consume 20 to 100 or more hours of design meetings. I employ the following two techniques to try to limit the total time spent in meetings:

▶ *Disperse the meetings around logical milestones in the research effort.* I am leery to deploy any product that was designed solely in meetings. I believe that someone, usually one or more developers, should augment the user representatives' input by doing on-site research into the users' workflow and needs. This allows a technical person to observe actual processes that exist and understand the infrastructure that the application rides on. Techniques for on-site research are detailed in the "Researching Automated Solutions" section later in this chapter. For an average project, I've found that we usually have at least three design meetings with the user committee, with additional research and design work ongoing between each meeting.

▶ *Give people homework so they come to meetings prepared.* Like any other business meeting, if the leader has an agenda, users come prepared, and all parties leave with specific action items for the next meeting, then application design meetings are shortened significantly. I usually appoint a meeting scribe at each meeting and have that person zealously clackity-clacking on a laptop computer taking meeting notes throughout the discussions. As soon as possible after the meeting, we produce a summary document with action items and send it to the project team members. Action items that flow from a design meeting and are due at the next meeting usually involve: research by design team members into existing processes; gathering copies of existing reports as input to the new system; gathering user feedback on specific, suggested enhancements, and so on.

 Tip

Providing user committee members with homework assignments between meetings gives them a sense of involvement in the design and development process, which fosters team spirit and commitment to the project. It also reduces the probability of boredom with the process, which can lead to design errors or omissions.

Figure 3.3 shows the cycle of design meetings and how it is mixed with hands-on research into existing processes.

Fig. 3.3

Most application design processes follow a flow similar to this.

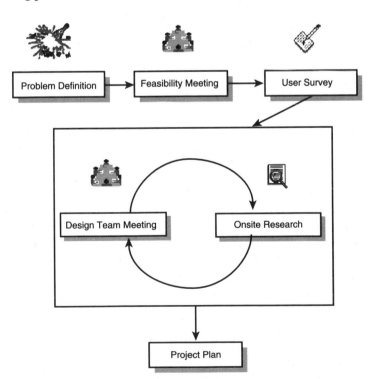

> α **Note**
> Diagrams are the lifeblood of application design meetings; thus a meeting room without a white board is mostly useless to a design team.

The first homework item for the project team comes between the feasibility meeting and the first design meeting. After the project is approved for a design phase, I send a survey document we have developed to all attendees expected at the first design meeting. The recipients are expected to complete the questions pertinent to them before the meeting.

The main sections on the survey are described as follows to help you understand project pre-planning. The complete survey document itself has more than 40 questions. It is on the CD-ROM as Appendix A, "Database Software Project Pre-planning."

Project Overview. Here, the planners detail their objectives for the automated solution, the condition of any current system and the reasons why it needs to be enhanced, and a project summary. This information provides the foundation for the new system and people's expectations of it.

Feasibility. The planners answer questions about the financing of the project, detail how the company and targeted individuals will benefit from the new application, and provide other cost-justification information. This section helps the team build an *executive summary,* which is used to sell and fund the project.

Milestones. The questions in this section establish the expected start and end points for a proposed project timeline and explain factors driving the milestone dates.

Hardware/Software. In this section, the planners detail the workstation, network, and server capabilities that may affect the project. Responses in this section help you establish whether the existing infrastructure will support the proposed application. The respondents also detail expected and future development tool guidelines.

Users. To understand what the load on the system will be, the survey asks about the number of total users, the number of concurrent users, the frequency of user activity in the system, and so on.

Points of Contact. Here, respondents list the parties that are responsible for various elements of the project, including design meetings, design approval, finance, testing, training, and deployment.

> ## Don't I Get to Vote?
>
> Over the years, I've noticed a trend regarding the delegation of computer responsibilities in midsize companies. When we do multiuser database projects in such firms, we often coordinate deployment issues with the person we call the *net admin* (network administrator). All too often, I ask the net admin how he or she inherited responsibility for the computer infrastructure only to hear this answer: "I wasn't here the day they voted on the position, so I guess everyone voted for me." In some firms, managing computer hardware or development vendors is not seen as an enviable position because neither has a reputation for reliability; so someone who does not want the job often gets stuck with it due to company politics.
>
> This statistic serves to emphasize the fact that, in the early phase of a development project, people by nature often try to shift responsibilities from themselves onto others. Thus, the moral is: Be alert and in attendance at company meetings, or you may find yourself elected in absentia to a position you don't want!

Application Features Summary. This survey section asks for an explanation of the primary features and functions expected from the system at various milestones over the next five years.

Application Tables. In responding to this section, people list the primary data tables and their expectations for the elements that will be stored, the size of the tables at various application life cycle milestones, and the source of data for the tables.

Application Screens. Respondents are asked here to describe or sketch the primary system screens, and to detail user interface guidelines or considerations affecting screen forms.

Application Reports. In this section, people are asked to describe the primary reports to be generated by the system, and the record selection criteria and sorting options.

Application Processes. Usually, the collection of data in a system is augmented by code routines that manipulate the data. In this section, people discuss conversion, posting, uploading, and similar critical processes expected in the application. Data validation and security needs are also sketched out here.

Training. Readers are asked to describe the level of training they would expect for this system, and that individuals will supervise, provide, and attend the training.

Support. Concerns related to supporting the users and keeping the system running smoothly are detailed here. Vendor obligations are listed, if the development is to be contracted outside the company, as are the responsibilities of the company's Information Technology group.

Some of these survey items provide the framework information that helps to shape the design process. For example, having a constrained delivery date at the outset often limits the final feature set. Other survey items map to items on the final specification and provide discussion points for the design meetings.

Understanding an Application's Life Cycle

Most database applications stay in use for several years, so initial design and development is only part of the total scope. Enhancements, a widening of the user base, performance tuning, archiving aged data, and other upkeep consume ongoing resources. In the early stages of a project, it is important to communicate these facts to the project team.

Caution

My experience with database projects indicates that up to two thirds of an application's total cost and labor still lie ahead after the initial version is delivered. Companies rarely budget time or money properly for these ongoing efforts.

You should also make sure the system's designers and users understand the complex dynamics involved in developing, deploying, and maintaining a database application. Figure 3.4 diagrams a system's life cycle.

Fig. 3.4

The life cycle of a non-trivial database application may be several years.

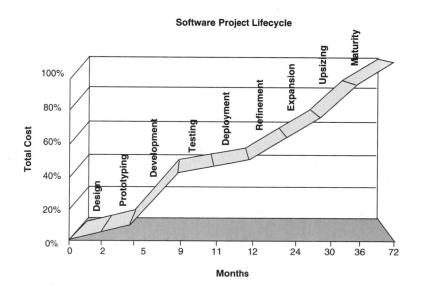

At each stage in an application's life cycle, there are different project characteristics and development requirements.

Design

The process of designing an application has two primary components, as indicated by the two chapters on the subject in this book (this chapter and Chapter 4, "Creating Design Specifications"). They are as follows:

▶ *Project scope and research.* This component involves meetings and investigations that take a project vision and fill in its details.

▶ *Application design documentation.* This effort involves the creation of a written design specification.

While all of the following phases of a project are important, I devote this entire chapter to the subject of design because it is the most critical to both the short term and long term success of the project.

The design phase rarely takes less than a month and can run into several months, even for a small project. The time frame is not always a reflection of the complexity of the project; often it is a reflection of the availability of the design team for meetings or the difficulty of the research effort.

Designing Slowly

While I noted previously that an application design process may take several months, my company actually has two client projects that have each been in the design phase for over a year. One of the projects is moving slowly due to the unavailability of design team members and the complex nature of the project (financial services). The other is in a state of constant redesign, as its industry (health care) is changing rapidly.

The most dangerous part of very long design phases is that project team members can get bored after several months, and the quality of the discussions and design effort may decline.

At the end of the design phase, a preliminary design document exists as described in Chapter 4. Costs are then applied to the development time estimates to arrive at a total project cost. This cost is measured against budgets to see whether features must be deferred or removed.

Prototyping

With a design in hand, too many developers begin immediately coding in earnest. In my life cycle model, however, the application development phase is a step removed from the design phase. I believe that, before you code, it is prudent to do a sanity check to determine if what the designers say they want is, in fact, what they need.

> **Tip**
>
> Software development studies I have read indicate, as does my own experience, that at least half of the problems and deficiencies in a software project are attributable to poor design as opposed to poor coding. A prototype can help you catch design deficiencies early.

One of the biggest mistakes a project team can make is to believe that, at the end of the design phase, their design is 100 percent accurate and coding can begin. In such an environment, a missing feature invariably comes to light well into the development cycle, with negative consequences. To steer clear of such adversity, I try to introduce two reviews at the beginning of the development phase, as shown in Figure 3.5.

Fig. 3.5

An application's design can be validated by having users review prototypes.

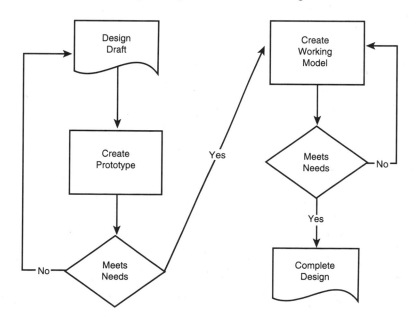

You'll notice in Figure 3.5 that the design is reviewed twice. The first review is the prototype phase, where designers review form mockups in an attempt to discover missing or erroneous tables and fields. The second review is what I call the *working model,* which I'll talk about in a moment and whose purpose is to verify the design of the forms.

Two forces are at play in the prototyping phase. First, giving designers additional reviews of the design increases the odds that it will be correct when development starts. Secondly, if designers are allowed to change their minds now, it's hard to stop them from doing so throughout the project. The dual reviews that we build into our projects are an attempt to balance these two polarized forces; designers get two extra trips to the wishing well, then they are cut off.

Because Access provides you with great leverage through its online assistants—its wizards—you can usually prototype even a complicated project fairly quickly. The two most important components in a prototype are the following:

▶ *Database Structure (schema).* The underpinnings of a database application are data tables, which you need to construct at this stage. The decision point for you is whether to build a comprehensive schema as per the design document (tables, properties, indexes, and queries), or to simply create tables and fields with minimal information in order to get the prototype out quickly. Both strategies are viable.

If you complete the schema to match the spec, your prototype takes longer to deliver, but you have one component of the project almost complete. On the other hand, if you produce a minimal schema and the users change their minds about the structure after reviewing the prototype, you have to discard or replace less of your work because you have completed less of it. Both strategies are viable, and you can use different ones for different projects.

▶ *Forms.* People on the project design team who are heavily *visual* as a personality trait give you better feedback when viewing screens than design documents. A visual person is the type that needs to see something in 3-D to truly comprehend it. (These types of people abound in marketing and sales departments, for example.) They browse specification listings or screen mockups in your design meetings and say that everything looks fine, but when the test build is delivered and their "visual" tendencies kick in, they tend to throw a lot more feedback into a project. Unfortunately, feedback so late in the cycle can rarely be accommodated. In contrast, the prototype phase enables the design team to visually see the application structure early enough in the project to have an impact without radically changing the timeline.

Prototypes do not need to have navigation, validation, or any other code components— usually just a copy of each data bound form. Your goal for each of the forms is to make it comprehensive, but stop short of completion. Comprehensive means that all the controls are included, the layout or location of the controls is accurate (though not necessarily precise), and all databound forms in the user interface are reflected. Interface design guidelines for the project should be reflected in the forms, but only enough for the purposes of the prototype. The forms have no code written for them yet.

You can give users a tour of the prototype in a design meeting, or they can be given a reviewer's guide that tells them how to open each form from the Database window, what to look for during their review, and what kind of feedback is expected. Reviewers need to be alert for missing features, but a few minor change requests made at this point in the project can usually also be accommodated with a minimal impact on the budget and timeline.

The real purpose of prototyping has nothing to do with forms, which are reviewed again later in a second review. The primary purpose at this point is to confirm the schema. You create form prototypes here to give the non-technical person windows to view the data structure through. In the prototype, the user is looking at the schema by reviewing the controls placed on the forms.

The entire design team should review the prototype. Although the team normally includes a representative sample of the users of the application, it is ideal to gather feedback on the prototype from as many users as possible, sometimes even beyond the design team.

After feedback from the prototype is collected, create a list showing all of the relevant input received. The design team should meet to debate what input from the list becomes part of the project plan and what is discarded or deferred. Any schema changes that are approved are trickled into the schema and the prototype forms.

It is important to stress to reviewers that this is their final opportunity for input with respect to objects missing from the core database structure. After reviewing your sample screens, they may not have another opportunity to change tables and fields until the next major release of the application, which may be a year or more in the future.

After the prototype review, take the prototype forms and add enough event code to allow users to navigate through the application. Your objective is to create a working model that is an expanded prototype for the purpose of reviewing the forms and the application flow they enforce. The following are the components that I include in a working model:

> *Switchboard Menus.* Draft the application's main and subsidiary switchboard menu forms to help organize the application flow from one form to the next. These forms don't need to be fancy or fully functional; simply use buttons that accurately get people to the correct forms in the correct workflow. The buttons can be replaced later with the actual list boxes, tabs, graphic buttons, and other controls that make up each final switchboard.

Data Forms. The forms you created for the prototype need basic navigation elements added to them and placeholders for any other form features. For example, a working model form should have all the buttons on it that are stipulated in the design. The buttons that navigate to other forms should be allowed to do so, but none of the buttons need graphics, tool tips, and other frills in order to permit the user to review the model. Buttons that initiate data processing events should be on the forms as placeholders but not yet enabled with event code.

Dialog Forms. Although the first prototype build had only databound forms so that users could review the schema with them, users need to see mockups of most forms in the working model. Forms that assist with navigation are required in order to properly review the application. However, these forms also do not need to be fully functional. For example, when the user chooses to create a new record, your application may show a dialog listing various available record types in a list box. Your model should display this form with the list box in the appropriate place and with OK and Cancel buttons, but the list box does not need to be loaded with items. Only the OK button needs to be enabled so that users can review the navigation and move on.

The working model build has none of the following features:

▶ *User Assistance Elements.* The forms in the model do not have toolbars, menu bars, shortcut menus, help, control tips, status bar text, or similar niceties. Buttons that may be graphical later are textual at this point. No control magic is in place, such as hiding or disabling controls in a particular context or changing combo box row sources on-the-fly.

▶ *Validation.* No validation is provided by the forms. If any entered data is validated at this point, the validation comes from table-level rules in the schema, not from form code.

▶ *Processing.* The model does not include import or export routines, automation such as mail merges, or any bulk posting or processing of records.

▶ *Reports.* There are two good reasons to leave reports out of the working model. The first is time; a complex application can have a hundred or more reports, and building review copies of each of these reports is tedious work and can slow the project at this critical point. If the specification is adequate, this step adds little value to the project because report designs can be changed later more cheaply than form designs; your time should be prioritized in favor of forms.

The second reason to skip reports is human nature. It seems that people can reach agreement on the layout of forms more easily than they can on reports. I theorize that this is because forms are transitory digital concepts, but reports are tangible, physical objects, and often are the objects against which the success of the project is measured. I've been in meetings where all eight people had different ideas about how a particular report should look, and each was happy to defend his or her position for the rest of the afternoon.

▶ Leaving reports out of the model prevents the introduction into the modeling process of this potentially time-consuming tangent. If you hold reports development until later in the project, there is less time available in the development cycle for people to endlessly iterate report layouts, and they are forced to come to a quick resolution on any remaining design issues. Of course, if time allows, there is nothing inherently wrong with adding draft versions of the more important reports to this model instead of skipping them.

▶ If report mockups are not included in the working model, the design team should at least review the report layouts in the final specification document during the critique of the working model. The purpose of this final report review is to ensure that: Fields reflected in the report designs are included in the table designs; and, report designs accurately reflect the needs of the users.

The need for the working model arises from the fact that at least 50 percent of an average application's development budget and time is spent on forms. Because forms are so expensive, the team is highly motivated to try to prevent building and coding each form or form feature more than once. The energy spent creating and reviewing the working model is almost always less than the energy consumed by skipping this step and getting your first user feedback regarding forms at the alpha release stage much later in the development cycle.

Users should be looking for the following items in their review of a working model:

Form Layouts. Do the forms reflect the desired layout of text, controls, subforms, and so on?

Form Navigation. Does the user move through the application in the appropriate order to match the workflow? Does the application provide a branch from each form to any related forms or processes and back?

Usability. A good database design may be hard to express at the user interface level, so users must confirm that the representation in the working model is a suitable way to work with their data.

Capturing User Feedback

When we distribute a working model to reviewers, we sometimes employ audio tape to capture their feedback. We have reviewers turn on a pocket (hand held) dictation machine and make verbal comments as they move through the model. This method is highly accurate when capturing user opinion, and also very time-efficient. The technique captures more information about the application than a reviewer commonly writes down or keys in when reviewing a form. Also, the reviewer can move freely though the application, unencumbered by pauses to manually note issues and questions, which speeds up the review process. The tapes are then reviewed by the development or design team.

Microsoft employs a similar technique as they design products. Early models of a product's interface are given to the corporate usability lab, which brings in users from the Seattle area and videotapes their attempts to use and navigate through the product model. These video tapes are later reviewed by product managers and developers, who can witness prospective users' attempts to comprehend the product's interface.

When the prototype and working model have been reviewed, the development team should have sufficient feedback to consider the design phase complete. Depending on the feedback received, application objects or processes may need to be redesigned, and the modified design may need to be reviewed again.

After incorporating the final feedback into the specification document, the design should be considered closed for purposes of the first release. The next chapter details what the design document itself should look like at this point. The project manager is responsible for minimizing user enhancement requests after this moment.

Based on the redefined feature set, the project manager and development manager revise and finalize the project timeline and budget, complete with development milestones and schedules for testing and deployment.

Application Development

The development phase of a project is totally dependent on the design phases that came before it. Without a comprehensive design spec, developers have to guess about how the designers intended a feature to work. Also, if the design is vague, the timelines established for development will be in error, and the developers may find themselves out of time and money before the work is done.

The primary challenges that arise during the development process are:

Selecting tools and styles. Development cannot begin until the developers agree on the set of development languages, equipment, tools, conventions, and styles that are to be utilized by the development team.

Division of Labor. Allocating work to multiple developers, developing different application components in parallel, and combining them into a cohesive application can provide interesting challenges for the development manager.

Managing against milestones. The development manager must provide direction and motivation to the development team to assure that project milestones for completion are met.

Managing user expectations. Once development has begun, users are excitedly awaiting their new toy and often require regular and detailed progress reports. Users also often use this time to plot feature enhancements and then attempt to dictate them to the design team.

Chapter 9, "Completing and Deploying a Solution," further describes how to execute and manage the development process, and Part II of this book, "Expert Solutions Techniques," includes detailed tips and techniques for use during the development stage.

Testing

At the completion of initial development, the testing cycle begins. The simplest testing process involves the following two stages:

▶ *Developer Testing.* Users should not be burdened with the testing process until the application is considered solid by the development team. Coders should test their work as they complete logical units or objects. At the end of development, the integrated application is tested by the development team and other available technical personnel.

▶ *User Testing.* The testing release to representative users has three primary objectives. The first is to verify that the feature set is complete and the users' needs are met by the application. If development has taken long enough that the process being automated has changed or if developers have implemented a feature poorly, this is the users' chance to catch it.

The second objective is to deploy the application on user machines for purposes of testing the application against the infrastructure. The application must be deployed to selected users to ensure that it is easy to configure and runs reliably on a variety of workstations. Users chosen for the testing process may represent only a fraction of the total user base for the application, and are usually chosen for their above-average technical abilities.

The third objective of user testing is to hunt down and kill bugs. Multiple users with different tasks to manage should be involved in the process, and the process should follow detailed testing guidelines to ensure that the application is given a complete workout.

The testing process, and the importance of user involvement in it, is discussed in greater detail in Chapter 9, "Completing and Deploying a Solution."

Initial Deployment

This phase of the project is the most exciting for both developers and users. After months of work by all parties, the application is launched. Whether it reaches orbit or crashes is determined by the following factors:

The suitability of the application to the needs of the users. If the design process was flawed, the developers' interpretation of the feature set in error, or the application unreliable or buggy, then its acceptance will be poor.

The commitment of the users to adopt the application. Even the best application can be unsuccessful if the user community fails to embrace it. Problems I sometimes see in this area include the following:

▶ Users are too busy to learn and adopt a new technology. Such users often need a management directive to undergo training and begin using the application.

▶ Users are slow to change and fall back into their old habits and methods after a few weeks of attempting to use the new application. Users sometimes behave this way when they are intimidated by an application. Such users commonly require extra training to become more comfortable with the new system before they will use it.

▶ Environments, priorities, or skills have changed since the project was conceived. An example is a budgeting application that was designed when users were unsophisticated with Excel, but have since become Excel whizzes and prefer to do budgeting interactively. They now find a budgeting application constraining.

The successful deployment of the application. If the initial deployment involves long waits for available deployment staff to set up each workstation or is fraught with technical glitches, users get a sour first taste of the application. In contrast, users who run a SETUP.EXE program from the company's application server, install the system on their machine without a hitch, and begin using it right away are much happier and more supportive of the project.

At the end of successful deployment of the application's first release, the project is usually considered complete with respect to the initial design, timeline, and budget. The project team may or may not be relieved of their responsibilities, and the ongoing support may shift from the developers to a support staff. However, this does not mean the application has matured, only that it has reached its first plateau. More growth and change lie ahead.

3

> α **Note**
>
> The life cycle phases I have detailed up to this point have been at a *microcosmic* (step-by-step) level. From here forward, the phases I list are *macrocosms*, which are meant to include by inference each of the preceding steps. In other words, the steps from design through deployment that I have just described were for release Version 1.0. For each future release version, as detailed in the following life cycle stages, each of the steps taken to create Version 1.0 may be repeated.

Product Refinement

The first year or so of life for an application usually is not quiet, but neither is it dramatic. As users become more productive with the application, they discover problems with the software or initiate ideas for enhancing it. Also, much can happen in a company in one year, often necessitating some changes in the application to keep it in step with business process changes.

At some point, the To Do list for the application becomes significant enough to warrant another release, usually Version 1.1. The process for creating this release varies depending on several factors, including the following:

The existence of a design document. In some cases, the specification for the original release described necessary Version 1.1 enhancements. Such features were either deferred from the original release to meet time or budget goals, or were not required until some point after the first deployed release but were documented anyway. In other cases, the features for Version 1.1 are derived from user requests generated as they use the first released version. These user requests that were not planned in the original spec document must each undergo feasibility analysis, research, design, and approval processes.

The availability of the original developers. If the original developers are available, fixes and enhancements can be coded more quickly and cheaply than if a development team unfamiliar with the application is used.

> **Caution**
>
> For a complicated application, it can easily take five or even ten times as long for a new developer to modify a feature as it would take the original developer. Use of standardized and documented development conventions can smooth the transition of a project from the original developers to maintenance developers. Good development standards are exemplified by the naming conventions described in Chapter 5, "Creating Naming Conventions," and Chapter 6, "Leszynski Naming Conventions for Access," and by the coding style defined in Chapter 11, "Expert Approaches to VBA."

The Scope of Work. Releases during the first year of life usually include both bug fixes and minor enhancements. If the release includes deferred features or significant enhancements, the scope of work can sometimes equal or surpass that of the original version. Usually, however, the refinement phase sees several smaller releases (1.1, 1.2, and so on) rather than one comprehensive makeover.

The Available Budget. New version refinements are often under-budgeted, with the scope of work constrained by cost factors.

Because the refinement phase is the time to work out the kinks, as well as to keep the application current with the users' needs, more than one application version may be released during this phase. This phase usually goes on for a year or more after initial deployment. Because each release version is a redeployment, it requires the same design effort, prototyping, testing, and other tasks as were required by the initial release; the only difference is one of scope. Each release also requires a project team, although it may include fewer people than the original release.

Expanded Deployment

A successful application often gains momentum as its feature set is improved and balanced to match the users' needs. As the users become more comfortable with it, they become reliant on it as well and the importance of the application within the workgroup increases. From this point, through the first or second year of life, it is not uncommon for one of the following three things to happen:

▶ Someone suggests that the application would be useful to other departments in the organization. For example, a prospect management system for sales may be applicable with minor changes to the supplier tracking functions in manufacturing. Thus, one application becomes two.

▶ The workgroup would like to allow the application to benefit a broader audience and requests additional features to support the new users. For example, managers often decide that they want to get online with the data rather than receive only hard copy reports of it; thus they request expanded querying, graphing, and reporting capabilities.

▶ Similar workgroups in other branches or locations of the company request a connection to the existing application. For example, people in the accounting group may want online access to data in an inventory receiving application located in the warehouse.

Whatever the reason, the application is suddenly facing a dramatic bump in the number of total users and possibly in concurrent users as well. If the original design team expected this, the project plan may include some plans for handling the growth. The data schema and application may even have been created with *hooks* to enable additional users and features to be added easily, or with extra fields required by the expanded user base.

In rare cases, a well-built application can be deployed to additional users with no coding changes. However, to accommodate growth, the application is usually modified in this phase. As with product refinement, a new release requires design, prototyping, development, and testing processes. However, this expanded deployment phase adds an increased burden on resources beyond that required during refinement.

The refinement builds of the product most likely implemented features requested by existing users, so a minimum additional training and support burden was generated. In this expansion phase however, a body of completely new users is added—users who require hand-holding during deployment to their machines and training on the application from scratch. Further, if the user base increases, any ongoing support costs and workloads suddenly increase as well.

Upsizing

With the application deployed to a greater number of users, it is likely that Access is now being taxed at or near the limits of its comfort zone. Any further expansion of the user base requires the discussion about moving the application from the Access shared MDB file metaphor to a client/server metaphor. If the initial deployment was quite wide, Access was strained from the start; this phase sometimes comes in place of the expanded deployment phase instead of after it.

The client/server model provides the application with the following two tangible improvements:

Performance. Users can expect faster performance from a file server database than a Jet database under a substantial concurrent user load. The growth curve here also becomes more flat than in the file server model because each additional user usually has a very nominal effect on performance on the server product.

Integrity. Access databases can become corrupted, whereas server databases are historically more stable. Also, server databases can integrate security from the workstations with the security of the database or share security layers across multiple databases. Finally, backups and transaction rollbacks are usually facilitated better by server products.

When the application goes to client/server, does this take Access out of the loop? The answer varies and is treated more fully in Chapter 19, "Exploring Client/Server Issues." Regardless, the phase always requires additional programming and the full gamut of release version steps from design through deployment, as seen in previous builds.

Many applications never achieve the user base to support this phase, and so their users continue to work quite contentedly in Access/Jet throughout the life cycle of the project.

Product Maturity

Somewhere during the second or third year of an application, the application is probably considered *mature.* Multiple minor revamps have been done and usually at least one major expansion, and the application has been useful enough to the company to have paid back its cost.

Throughout the maturity phase, the primary requirements of the application are as follows:

Upgrades. With each release of Access, the application and data must be converted and the feature set brought current. In some cases, processes are modified or re-coded to take advantage of new features, so each upgrade of an application can take as little as a week or as much as several hundred development hours.

Reconfiguration. As new workstations are added and network topologies changed over time, the application must be reinstalled and sometimes modified and retested.

Tuning. Even without the dramatic increases in the user base described above, most applications see a slow, steady increase of users logging in. At regular intervals, perhaps every six months, the application should be reviewed to see whether opportunities exist to retune it for the current workload and workflow.

Data Maintenance. At periodic intervals, usually once or twice a year, many applications require that the data be archived to a storage server or old transactions cleared from the tables. Additionally, at these intervals managers might want to get data summaries produced to aid in tasks such as budget analysis or audit preparation.

3

> **Caution**
>
> A dangerous trap lurks at this phase because the application has become stable, which to some users and developers can translate into antiquated. In other words, some people believe that when an application is no longer being changed, it is non-dynamic and outmoded. Such people look for ways to rework or replace the system, to keep life interesting or to provide themselves with make-work projects and job security. Often, reality is quite the opposite of their perception; an application that needs no major changes does its job perfectly, and thus is producing a superior return on investment for its company and a stable environment for its users.

How long can people use the same Access application? Nobody can be sure at this point because Access has been available for only three years. However, I am comfortable projecting that many applications we have created in the past three years will be in use five years from now.

Obsolescence and Death

I noted previously that application planners should work with at least a five-year horizon in mind. Nevertheless, most applications eventually reach a point where they should be scrapped.

The reason for scrapping an application is not usually that the application does not perform its function well, but rather that either the function has changed or new tools have come to light. The pace of business competition and technological change almost guarantees that one of these situations will occur.

For example, a sales prospecting package written in Access may provide several years of outstanding performance and value to the company. However, at some point in the future, one of the following three things will happen:

▶ *The company restructures and changes the way that sales information is managed.* The application can no longer accommodate the new workflow and requires a major rewrite. At the point where radical surgery is needed on an application, it is often better to scrap the old code and write a new application from scratch. For example, this scenario is common in industries with lots of mergers and acquisitions.

The company acquires a sales prospecting package. For all its strengths, Access cannot match the performance of vertical or retail programs written in Visual C++ or similar languages. At some point, the company may find that a commercially available application provides much of the functionality of the Access application and runs faster or has lower support costs.

A different toolset is selected. On the way to client/server (usually in the upsizing phase described earlier), Access sometimes loses out to Visual Basic or Visual C++ for the creation of the user interface, and the original application is replaced. Sometimes the creation of a similar project in a different language produces enough improved components that are useful in the application that it makes sense to move it to the other platform.

Regardless of the disposition of the application, data is virtually never thrown away. The Access data needs to be ported, at obsolescence, to a new platform or kept online for analysis because it has historical value. Chapter 7, "Understanding Application Architecture," discusses managing warehouses of such historical data.

Researching Automated Solutions

Having completed our detour through an application's life cycle, let's return to the design process. At this point, the design team has completed its survey and debated the results in one or more initial design meetings. At each meeting, issues are discussed that cannot be resolved without field research, making it prudent for developers to perform hands-on investigation between the meetings.

Doing on-site research involves meeting with the users, dissecting existing processes, and keeping good notes and audit trails that feed the design effort. Doing this research well involves a balance of the following skills:

Patience. Sometimes the process of observing an existing workflow or tracking down a data item can involve waiting for an event or individual or wading through many records or report pages. When doing research, you are captive to the search for information and the parties that control it, and you must wait until they can work with you or be able to watch them work through fairly lengthy processes.

Politics. Observing how people work and getting them to explain it to you takes good interpersonal skills. You are probing into each contact's business life as a psychiatrist would probe their personal life, and so they will tell you their true thoughts and feelings only if they trust you and they are comfortable with your presence.

Diligence. Tracking data items throughout a company can be detailed work as data splits, merges, and changes usage. You must be thorough and alert, or you will miss key facts.

In this section, I detail my three approaches for digging out the business facts necessary to create a solid application design. The approaches are not mutually exclusive; each is valid alone or in conjunction with the others. Figure 3.6 shows the relationship between the flow of information in an organization and the three research approaches I use.

Fig. 3.6

I use some combination of these three approaches when researching the database needs of an organization.

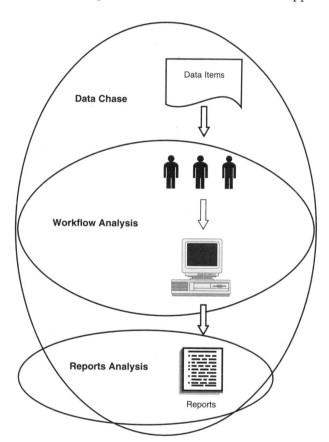

Workflow Analysis

Workflow analysis is the process of watching people do their jobs or even doing the work with them. This process is basically like walking a mile in someone's shoes in order to gain insight about how to improve their workday. You are looking to discover the human side of a business process.

To do workflow analysis, spend time with potential users of the new system and note the processes they use throughout the workday that are relevant to the proposed application. Observe the flow of information across each person's desk or workbench, paying close attention to the following areas:

> *How each worker interacts with other workers.* What information does each worker have that others do not? What information do they all have in common? How does information get from one worker to another? Whom do workers go to for answers to their questions?

> *How each worker interacts with existing technology.* What automated processes are used now? How will the application fit into or replace these processes? What do the workers like and dislike about each automation device or automated process?

> *How each worker interacts with company data.* Where does each worker get important data? How does the data change as it passes through people and processes? How do workers use data to make decisions?

In visiting with the potential users of the new system, make note of habits or repetitive behavior as they do their work. Many people who have mastered their jobs are not even aware of some of the things they actually do each day; some actions become *motor memory* and are done without thinking. You need to be observant to catch work habits as they are manifested, and ask enough questions to understand how the habit might become automated through software.

Ask workers what parts of their current workflow they think are the most efficient. If these processes are manual, try to discover how they might be computerized.

Delve into inefficiencies in existing systems as well. Ask people for their top gripes about their workflow and suggestions for improvement. If any processes are automated, review the existing applications and make notes about the good and bad points.

 Tip

When doing on-site research, I try to have lunch with the workers in their normal environment at least once. Meals and other work breaks provide a relaxed, social forum where people can be encouraged to talk about the work environment without distraction. Also, the interplay between multiple workers often produces better quality ideas.

The Data Chase

The essence of the *data chase* is to identify which data items are of primary importance in the new system and to follow those data items through their life cycle in the company. An individual data item (a *datum*) can take many paths through a company, change along the way, and be utilized by more than one process. Whereas a workflow analysis exposes you to only the processes that are to be automated, the data chase may involve following data items through workflows and processes outside the scope of the current application in order to understand the data better.

To start this procedure, identify which data items are important enough to warrant a data chase. The best way to make this identification is to ask the ultimate users of the new system to highlight items in the application's output that they will be using to guide their critical decision making. The accuracy of information that is used for management decisions should be a top priority of the new application. Performing a data chase on such items helps ensure that they are handled correctly as they travel through the organization.

After identifying critical data items, work backwards from the reports or other output of the current system that produces these outputs. Trace the data items through each process that uses them all the way back to their original source. After mapping how the data items flow within the organization, contrast how they will flow when the application you are designing is implemented. Also note which fail-safes are required to ensure their accuracy.

Tracing a Data Item

Here is an example of a data chase from my recent experience. The ultimate user of one of our newly designed systems—an accounting controller to be exact—required that the new application compute the average weighted cost per pound paid for goods entering the manufacturing process. The data chase on cost and weight information coming from the factory floor to accounting led me backwards through the following objects and locations:

▶ The current costing report contains computed cost per pound information and is used by the controller for vendor purchase decisions.

▶ The costing report is produced by an accounting clerk. She prints a receiving report from the minicomputer and enters the data into a costing worksheet where she calculates the pricing information. She rekeys the pricing information into a personal computer to print the costing report.

> ▶ A minicomputer database program captures the cost and weight of items as they are received into the factory. The minicomputer produces a receiving summary report that shows loads received.
>
> ▶ Information is keyed into the minicomputer from receiving tickets generated at the receiving dock. Receiving tickets are handwritten from the vendor's bill of lading provided by the truck driver.
>
> ▶ If the receipt comes in as a transfer from another warehouse for the company, the original receiving ticket is delivered with the load, or an adjusted one is provided in the case of a partial load.
>
> You can see that the data used by the accounting staff begins at the ground floor of the building five stories below and is handwritten from a vendor document (so it *actually* begins at the vendor site). In the case of an intercompany transfer of goods, the data items may actually begin in another state.
>
> You probably also noted that the process described had several inefficiencies (such as rekeying data into a PC from a minicomputer report) and suffered from lack of data validation (such as the lack of verification of vendor weights on receipts). The data chase we used in this case provided many useful insights into the origin, movement, and quality of this important data.

Several things can happen to a datum during its life in the company:

Absorption. A piece of information can enter the company, only to be absorbed into other information. The original detail is lost or archived. For example, assume that a company providing telephone connections to the Internet (called an Internet Service Provider) bills customers for connection time using a monthly rate. Data about each incoming call to a customer's account is accumulated by the telephone equipment into a file. At the end of the month, all connection records run through a process where the end time for each connection is subtracted from the start time, and the computed number of minutes for each connection (plus the date) is written to a billing record. The billing records are summed to a total number of minutes, which is shown as information on the customer invoice. The connection clock time information is then discarded, having been absorbed into the billing records.

Dormancy. Some data comes into a company and then into a computer system, and then is never used. Such data is usually accumulated for future growth or as protection in the case of an audit or lawsuit, but usually remains dormant for its entire life. For example, the receiving dock at a company logs packages into a software application as they are delivered. The license plate number of the truck making the delivery is recorded in the system. Under normal circumstances, this information is not reported or queried in any fashion; it is only kept as a contingency.

Transmutation. In some cases, data mutates while passing through an organization. The original data item may or may not be kept, but the transmuted value becomes the only one of importance. For example, a European company receives shipments from an American supplier whose shipping documents indicate each shipment's weight in pounds. When the shipping documents are entered into the receiving application, the application immediately converts the weight value from pounds to kilograms and stores only the latter value. Thus, the weight data item on the hard copy has been transmuted in the course of entry into a computer system.

Transmission. For many data items, the way they enter the organization is the way they end up on reports coming out of computer systems. No physical change takes place to the data itself; the data is simply transmitted intact through the company from start to finish.

As you run the data chase and observe data items going through one of these states listed, remember to ask the users whether what you observe is actually the desired result. This is especially true of transmuted data, which is sometimes transformed wrongly, but the error is not noticed until a data chase brings it to light.

Reports Analysis

The *reports analysis* provides a third research approach, and is often the only method many developers employ. Database projects are frequently initiated by managers who complain about existing reports or see room for improvement in them. These managers drive design meetings that are focused on improving the reports, and they keep the meetings oriented toward the outputs from the new system rather than other features.

Even in this supposedly paperless decade, most business decisions are still made from a hard copy, and one of the primary objectives of most database systems is still to produce reports. Thus, there is nothing inherently wrong with focusing on reports. Good report analysis work includes analyzing not only the current and desired reports, but also existing ledgers, spreadsheets, and other printed materials that might be relevant to the targeted reports from the new system.

Caution
Of the three types of research, reports analysis is the least comprehensive and usually should be done in conjunction with a workflow analysis, a data chase, or both.

As you perform reports analysis, keep the following items in mind:

Understand how people make decisions based on the reported information. How are the reports used? Who reviews them, and who ultimately uses them? At what point in a process flow are decisions actually made from the reports? What other reports contribute to those decisions?

Think beyond the stated request. Do the existing or requested reports present the data in its most accurate and useful fashion? Simply because your ultimate users tell you to produce a given set of reports, do not lose sight of the fact that the best solution may be different from what is being requested. Using your insight into technology and into the business processes that you have researched as part of the workflow analysis, be alert for improvements that can be made to the suggested result. For example, managers that request several specific reports may actually be more effective with a single report that rolls up requested data into summary data. Alternatively, hands-on managers may be more effective with the data if you export it to a spreadsheet for detailed analysis, instead of providing a hard copy report.

Understand where the data comes from. If you cannot perform a data chase on the contents of the requested reports, try to at least have someone explain to you how each reported item moves from its source to the report. If the new system you are creating does not have complete control of the accuracy of the reported data, try to determine or suggest how such accuracy can be assured.

At the conclusion of reports analysis, you should have a stack of existing reports that need to be re-automated, and every item on each report should be annotated with your findings about the item's source and flow within the company. You should also have produced report mockups of the new reports to come from the new application. These mockups should show the source and flow of any data items that are new and not reflected on the existing reports.

 Tip

I find that Excel is a very convenient tool for creating report mockups. Excel's grid layout makes creating columnar representations easy; you can create report mockups without building a data structure, enter sample data items, use formulas to show subtotals and sums, and make changes and reprint mockups quickly when creating printed review copies for meetings.

Sometimes, the reports coming from a system are its only reason for existence. In such an event, most of the design effort is invested in the reports, and the layout of screens and database structures is left to the developer. The reports become your primary design document in this case, so make sure you note on the report designs the standard schema information for each item: data type, maximum width, input mask, required validation, and so on. Also, make sure to have the design team discuss the sort order, selection criteria, subtotals, and totals required.

Planning for Growth

Your application may deploy smoothly and work as planned and yet find itself struggling in a year or so under a large data load or user volume. If the design team did not commit to long-range planning for the application or was simply wrong in its growth projections, your application may outlive its usefulness sooner than planned.

In one of the final group design meetings, make sure to cover the topic of the application's expected growth over time. In my experience, design teams usually underestimate the acceptance of an application and thus miscalculate the application's requirements for growth and flexibility. For example, assume that a prospect management system developed for marketing was projected to add 1,000 new prospects per month or around 24,000 records over the first two years. As the application becomes better known throughout the company, the expanded deployment phase that we discussed above kicks in. Suddenly salespeople begin using the system to track existing customers, and the Human Resources department jumps on board and tracks job candidates using the software. The difference between expected and actual load, both for data items and users, greatly exceeds expectations, as shown in Figure 3.7.

Fig. 3.7
An application's actual growth in record count and user count often exceeds the expected growth.

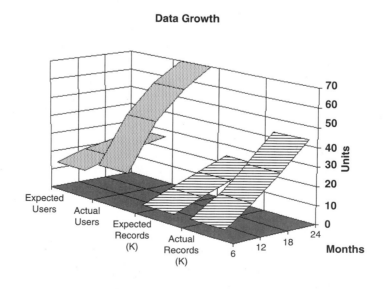

Data Growth

Without proper growth planning, the marketing application has three potential short-comings:

Managing additional records. The data volume in the application will be twice what was expected during the first two years; performance may suffer.

Managing additional users. The user load on the system will be three times what was expected; multiuser problems may accrue.

Managing disparate data. When the additional departments began using a system that was not precisely designed for their needs, they placed data items in the most appropriate fields they could find. However, some of the needed fields did not exist, and important data may be strewn in comment fields or left out.

It is very likely that the design team could have seen this situation coming and planned for it with better research. Discussions in design meetings about the hypothetical expansion of the system might have highlighted its potential for growth.

As you design an application, the following are some areas to include in your design discussions to allow the application to cope with growth:

Consider the upside potential. If the design team properly understands the application's life cycle, they more readily expend effort thinking about the load on the application two or three years out. The upside potential of an application is not limited to its total records and total users. Be sure to also consider a widening of scope that includes adoption by different groups with modestly different workflows or data needs (see the sidebar). Planning for more users usually involves careful consideration of issues, such as security, managing multiple logins, record locking strategies, table and index workloads, and so on.

Whose Project Is This, Anyway?

Twice in the past few months, I have been involved in design work for clients and found that the original project scope was really only the tip of the iceberg. By asking the right questions and doing on-site research, we were able to save the clients much extraneous effort.

Client A asked us to build a database to track people qualified as public relations contacts for their products. The original project team was created in one isolated product group, so we asked them if any other product groups in the company already had similar databases. The response was, "No, not to our knowledge." In doing the legwork of workflow analysis, however, we checked around the company

---

> and discovered several contact databases dispersed across other departments, and two more in the marketing department alone! What started as a small, isolated database became a company-wide project to coordinate the needs of many different groups of users, all wanting and trying to track PR contacts.
>
> At Client B, an initial design meeting was called for sales department personnel to discuss a proposed application for managing resellers. In the meeting, I asked whether they knew of any other departments in the company that would benefit from the database. One of the attendees spoke up: "I do some work in marketing, too, and they need a database just like this." All jaws dropped as it became apparent that nobody had talked to other departments in the company to see whether efforts, costs, and code could be shared.

3

Add future fields now. If you perform the proper growth planning, you will see areas in the application, especially the data structure, where changes will need to be made in the future to accommodate the growth. If possible, include any fields or field changes in the database structure up front so that those changes will not need to be made later. It is better to have dormant tables and fields in the schema from the first day than to try to retrofit new objects on the four-hundredth day. For example, we recently wrote a sales management application for a small company. Their salespeople were not on commission so they felt no need to track the identification of the salesperson with the sales order. We added fields to the database anyway for salesperson and commission rate. When the client changed their compensation model and asked for these additions to the system a year later, we did not have to change the table structure, because the required fields were already there. We only had to expose the dormant fields on the order entry form and sales report.

Make all data fields adaptable. The database, and the interface tied to it, should support virtually limitless flexibility in the configuration of data. Any values that are codified—for example, state abbreviations as placeholders for place names, should be driven off of lookup tables. The lookup tables feed combo boxes on the entry/edit forms, and new values can be easily added (as opposed to hard-coding multiple values in the RowSource property, which can't be changed without a developer). As another example, numeric fields that are set to the Integer data type in the beginning often need to be changed to enable Long Integer values later, as the amount of data or maximum values expand; so, consider using wider fields from the beginning if growth is expected.

Tip

We create most client databases as if they will hold international data at some point in the future, even if the client tells us that they don't think the feature is required. Only a few changes are needed, including a wider state field to hold province names, the addition of a country field, rules that enable both alphabetic and numeric characters in ZIP Code (postal code) fields, and wider telephone number fields. If the application eventually needs to hold information from Canada or Mexico or even farther away, such a database requires no expensive modifications, but instead only minor user interface changes.

Note that the concept of an English-based database containing international data in its tables is not the same as distributing an application internationally into a non-English user base.

Tune for performance. One of the final steps in the application development process is to review the application looking for performance bottlenecks, and to optimize the application. In the rush to ship, or on a tight budget, this step is sometimes overlooked or deferred. As the application database and its user base grow, the lack of solid indexing and other performance-related features will be sorely missed. Your application stands the test of time and growth better if you make the effort to optimize its performance in advance.

Keep only current data in the production tables. Data, like many other commodities, has a useful shelf life. At some point, the need to have a record easily accessible is dramatically diminished, and the record can be archived. Consider creating archive routines in your applications to move all old or closed records from a production table to an archive table (or even an archive database) at regular intervals. You can create union queries that join the archive and live tables together if the users still need to occasionally query across all historical records. Chapter 7, "Understanding Application Architecture," discusses storage of historical data.

Tip

If an application has data that has an identifiable expiration date, check for that date during each login and display a reminder to the user that it's time to archive the data. For example, much data is reported on an annual (calendar) basis, and at the end of the year, annual reports are run (in January). In such an application, a reminder set for February 1, telling the user to archive the previous year's data, is appreciated.

Document your work. I would guess that one year after an application has been deployed, its developers have forgotten half of everything they knew about the project. For them, or anyone else, to work on future versions of the application, good system documentation is important. System documentation should describe the structure of the database, the relationships between the data tables, and other nuances about the application's structure. Wherever possible, annotate a project's source code or project notes with comments as you work that explain non-standard approaches to problems and situations. These notes help clarify the system to yourself or others at a future point in the life cycle.

If the data will be upsized to SQL Server or another platform in the future, several additional considerations enter the mix. Record indexing strategies, record fetching and locking in forms, and other areas of the application are approached differently when the back end will change from Jet to an ODBC data source. See Chapter 19, "Exploring Client/Server Issues," for more information.

Selecting the Tools

It is said that a crafts person is only as good as his or her tools. Certainly, this adage holds true in the application development trade. Using tools that are unstable or difficult to work with can radically delay a project's timetable, and nothing is more frustrating for a developer than trying to get a product to do a task that it's not suited to do.

While Access is obviously a capable platform for data-centric applications, the following are two questions each design team must ask as it selects tools for a project:

▶ What tools could we use in place of Access?

▶ What tools could we use in addition to Access?

Concluding that Access should be a project's platform tool must not be a capricious decision. The project team should make the determination by considering both questions, as the following section explains.

Evaluating Access Against Other Tools

When asking if Access is the right tool for the job, the job must first be defined. In other words, too many project teams decide on Access at the feasibility meeting rather than completing the design and *then* talking about the toolset. While I'm a big fan of Access, neither it nor any other product is the perfect tool for every single job. Trying to make Access do a job it is not suited for ultimately produces negative sentiments among all parties: designers, developers, and users.

Comparing Access and Visual Basic

One of the most common questions asked about Access is, "How do I choose whether to use Access or Visual Basic for my project?" Because both products have powerful, and similar, capabilities, the answer is not easy to come by. When determining which of these tools is appropriate for your project, consider each of the similarities and differences between the products.

In the latest release of each of these products, there are more features in common than different features with respect to application development. Some of the most important similarities between Access and Visual Basic are the following:

Jet. The Jet Database Engine was loosely integrated with Visual Basic 3, but by VB 4, Jet was a key component in the product's strategy.

Visual Basic for Applications. The programming language in the two products for similar features is often identical; you use the same code and coding techniques in both.

Forms. Both VB and Access rely heavily on a similar forms-centric metaphor for creating applications. The visual structure of the forms, the nature and use of controls, and the event model and coding strategies for both products are nearly identical. Additionally, both products now enable the use of non-displayed forms as class definitions.

Data Binding. Both products provide the capability to seamlessly work with data in a database by managing the database connections and the record loading and saving tasks for the user. The implementation of these features, however, is different. Access binds the form to a data source and controls inherit the binding, while VB binds the controls themselves to another control that points to the data. The difference in metaphor makes programming databound and client/server solutions different in the two products.

Extensibility. In the past, VB was heavily reliant on third-party extensions (VBXs) to increase its interface capabilities, while Access forms were less extensible. Beginning with VB 4 and Access 95, both products began supporting ActiveX controls in a similar fashion (although VB supports complex control nesting while Access does not). In addition, both products can use wizards and other add-ins, although the implementation of this extensibility is different between the products, and a single add-in does not work in both environments without modification.

Source Code Control. Both VB 5 and Access 97 now can share a common installation of a Visual SourceSafe server for object version control.

Menus. The implementation of menus in VB has historically been a bit cleaner than in Access, with menus as programmable objects. Access 97's new command bars now bring menus more in sync with the VB model.

Remote Data Objects. Visual Basic provides direct connectivity to ODBC data sources through an ActiveX control. This enables very powerful query processing capabilities on remote data servers. Access 97 provides the same direct data access through its ODBCDirect feature.

③

While the two products have much in common, Visual Basic has several key features that differentiate it from Access:

Richer Event Model. Visual Basic forms and their controls have more events than in Access forms, and the management of the events is different (for example, Access forms save records automatically but VB requires the developer to programmatically control database events). In general, Visual Basic provides more control over the interface when responding to the user-generated and Windows events. VB also provides a more substantial implementation of the *Multiple Document Interface* (MDI) standard for forms.

Executable File Format. VB applications are compiled into an executable file, which provides better performance than the code storage model provided by Access. Compiled VB applications also run on machines with less RAM and slower processors than are required for Access. An additional benefit to VB compiled code—that it does not allow users to view the source—has been removed as a shortcoming of Access through the addition of the MDE file format in Access 97.

Remote Automation. VB 5 enables you to create reusable components based on Automation technology, and to install, manage, and share those components.

Access also has several unique features not found in Visual Basic:

Ad Hoc Capabilities. Visual Basic is a tool for creating a *sealed* (compiled) deliverable to users. The delivered application has only the user interfaces and features that were created by the developer, and no ad hoc capabilities. Access applications, on the other hand, can be delivered sealed, using the runtime, or can be used in full Access to let users exploit design, querying, and reporting features found on the menus and toolbars.

Queries. Visual Basic provides a Visual Data Manager add-in application that enables developers to create new databases, tables, and relationships, but Access provides a more robust, interactive schema design interface.

Reports. The Access reports designer is more tightly integrated with the product than the Crystal Reports component bundled with VB, and provides more powerful reporting options. For example, Access reports can be built with custom wizards, modified through code, or contain subreports, whereas such features are not found in VB.

Subobjects. Only Access provides the ability to create embedded subforms and subreport objects.

Data Binding. Access list box and combo box controls can be bound directly to data, while these objects must be loaded and refreshed via program code in VB.

Datasheets. Access provides a handy datasheet grid for viewing and sorting multiple records, while VB provides inferior grid capabilities via the DBGrid control.

Macros. Access still provides this entry-level programming feature to perform quick coding tasks and to automate repetitive operations.

Security. Database security is integrated into the Access interface. Designing database security in Visual Basic is programmatic only, and requires the use of Access for an interface.

Table 3.1 provides a decision table showing which product is stronger when you are considering specific application development benefits.

Table 3.1　Comparing Access and Visual Basic

Requirement	Access	Visual Basic
Fast execution	Very dependent on hardware for its performance	Compiled executable gives faster performance, especially on form loads
Rapid development	Wizards and powerful interface assist rapid development	Richer feature set and steeper learning curve add more development time
Application disk space	The smallest databound application, setup, and supporting files takes 18 megabytes	The smallest databound application, setup, and supporting files takes 4 megabytes
User interface	Centered around databound forms with Access-managed events	Complex, non-databound forms with compound ActiveX and subforms controls and control arrays

Requirement	Access	Visual Basic
Learning curve	Access has fewer total development features and is thus faster to learn	If you are new to object-centric development, VB can take longer to master than Access
Database orientation	Easy to build database objects and work with data	Slower for building database objects and viewing data
Development and maintenance costs	Access applications are cheaper to build and easier to change	A VB application costs more to build and must be recompiled after a change

3

⚛ Tip

In my experience, a Visual Basic application takes roughly twice as much money and time to produce as a similar Access application due to the factors shown in Table 3.1.

In reality, almost half of all our client projects involve both Access and Visual Basic together in some capacity, so the decision to use one or the other in a project is not mutually exclusive. Many projects that start with one of these tools end up using both within the first year after deployment. Figure 3.8 shows the relationship between these products in many of our installations.

Fig. 3.8

Access, Visual Basic, Jet, and SQL Server are frequently mixed together in an integrated application.

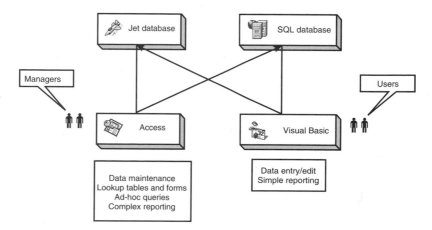

I can summarize our approach to the decision between these two products in the following sentences:

▶ If you need to deploy a fast-running application with a locked feature set to a wide audience using slower hardware and you have an appropriate budget, Visual Basic may be the best choice.

▶ If you need to deploy an application quickly and inexpensively or provide users with access to the source objects and ad hoc capabilities to create new objects or analyze data, Access is the best choice.

Comparing Access and Visual FoxPro

There are about five million people that use a variation of the Xbase language, a catchall term that includes dBASE, CA-Clipper, and FoxPro. Microsoft's acquisition of FoxPro was designed to provide access to that large base of developers as much as it was to obtain a tool that fit a particular product strategy. As such, Visual FoxPro (*VFP*), while an excellent product, does not integrate as smoothly with Office as Access does.

Despite their very different origins, VFP has evolved from humble DOS roots and has become a capable Windows development platform. Access and VFP now have several primary features in common:

Graphical Interface. Both products provide similar, but not identical, interfaces for creating tables and queries. Both also provide graphical tools for building forms and reports, but based on somewhat different paradigms.

SQL and Rushmore. Each product has borrowed from the other in these areas. Rushmore (a set of query optimization algorithms) was pioneered in FoxPro, but added to Access with version 2. Access had a stronger original implementation of SQL, but VFP now supports a rich SQL syntax.

Object-centric Metaphor. Both products build on the object model with objects as building blocks that contain properties, methods, and events. VFP actually provides a richer object model than Access at this time due to a stronger focus on user-definable classes.

Regardless of these similarities, at the core these products are worlds apart where developers spend much of their time—in code. The FoxPro code model is built on an Xbase design, now more than a decade old, while Access shares common VBA engines and syntax with the rest of Microsoft Office. I believe that Access remains a better choice for most new projects that do not rely heavily on meeting one of the following three criteria:

Cross-platform Support. Access does not, and may not ever, support non-Windows platforms such as the Macintosh. If an application must run on DOS, Macintosh, and UNIX machines in addition to Windows, FoxPro is the logical choice.

Utilize legacy code. Corporations that have a large investment in Xbase code can port that code into a VFP application much faster than creating a new Access application from scratch.

Create an executable. As with VB, a VFP project can be compiled into a single executable file that simplifies the delivery of an application to end users and provides speed improvements over Access.

VFP can share data in Access using ODBC, and Access can share data in VFP using installable ISAM technology, so it is possible for these two tools to coexist within a single project, as required.

Comparing Access and SQL Server

In Chapter 19, "Exploring Client/Server Issues," you will find detailed information about how Access and SQL Server can coexist within a project. SQL Server is only a back-end data storage and retrieval tool and does not provide a user interface for non-developers, so it cannot replace Access as a tool for building the user interfaces in an application. For our purposes here, I presume that you have already decided to use Access for forms, reports, and code and you're trying to decide whether to use Jet or SQL Server for your back-end data storage.

Both products provide you with the ability to create tables and queries (called *views* in SQL Server). Your application can use these objects in each platform in any of several fashions, but usually via table attachments or through Open Database Connectivity (ODBC) links. Because both products provide effective data repositories, the key difference lies in only one word: server.

When your application asks Jet (a non-server platform) to return records, the application interface makes the determination about how to find the records. As a result, the interface and the computer it resides on do the processing work to filter and sort the requested data. Conversely, when your application asks SQL Server for records, the server product makes the decisions involved in selecting and sorting records, then sends only the requested records back to your interface. The difference in these methods can be significant with the server returning results ten times faster or more depending on the question asked, the structure of the data, and the supporting hardware.

Here are a few areas where you might find that SQL Server makes a better back-end choice than Jet for your application:

High User Load. Jet handles 20 or 30 concurrent users quite well, but past that point the performance may suffer. If many concurrent users—as opposed to *total* users—are expected, a data server is a better choice.

Remote Connections. Because the server performs the hard work of selecting which records to return to the client (user interface), the load on the client application, and the amount of data traveling between the two components across a network or telephone line is less than with a central MDB data file. When users are accessing data over phone lines or wide area network connections, a server can provide much better performance than Jet.

Tightly Controlled Data. SQL Server provides richer models than Jet for security, transaction control, and backup/recovery; in applications where the data is massively mission critical, these features may weigh heavily in favor of SQL Server in the platform decision.

Some applications include a mix of both Jet databases and SQL Server databases for a variety of reasons. For example, sometimes we clone server data in a Jet database nightly to give managers a database to run ad hoc queries against without encumbering the busy server or exposing its raw data. In other cases, we use Jet databases as a hub for data that we don't want to put on the server, such as data that must be imported, exported, or reprocessed frequently or perhaps connected via ISAM drivers to other sources like FoxPro. Finally, in some installations, the server stores transaction data and provides transaction control, while lookup values and data extractions are stored locally in Jet for performance or convenience reasons.

Comparing Access and Excel

Many projects that end up in a database begin in a spreadsheet. Users find that logging data into Excel is quick and easy due to the tabular layout. Often, the spreadsheet grows out of control as more and more data is entered, and the type of data includes records that force duplication of entry. In this scenario, Excel becomes inadequate as a data storage receptacle for many reasons with the following four as the most critical:

1. *Tabular Layout.* Placing all available data in one worksheet is not the appropriate option when the data involves records that have a parent-child relationship. The user either places all the data in one worksheet, which causes duplication of the parent record data, or creates two data worksheets or ranges, which solves the data duplication but does not allow the user to enforce the relationship (cascading deletes are not available in Excel, for example).

2. *Queries.* Excel provides the ability to quickly sort the data on multiple columns and to search for specific data items, but does not approach the power of the Access

query engine. Also, sorting data in Excel physically reorders the data, which may be cumbersome for the user.

3. *Validation.* Excel provides the rudimentary forms technology, but cannot provide the rich event model, data binding, and form control properties necessary to aggressively validate items as they are keyed in.

4. *Reporting.* Excel can print tabular data with headers, footers, and other conveniences, but does not easily provide the grouping, sorting, and aggregate mathematics that make Access reporting so powerful.

When the data load exceeds Excel's capabilities, you can use the Access Table Analyzer Wizard to move the data from Excel into one or more Access tables, then build an application atop the data. As part of the Access solution, users or developers may choose to continue to use Excel, but as a reporting and analysis tool, rather than for data storage.

Extending the Reach of Access

After it is clear that Access is suited for the primary role in a project, the supporting parts must be cast. With Visual Basic for Applications residing in several Microsoft products, the acceptance of tools like Excel and Project as part of an application toolset has risen dramatically among developers. Also, the availability of more Automation server applications that can be invoked from Access, and the tools to build them, has increased the ways that a developer can extend Access, as has the continued expansion of the third-party add-in market.

The following three primary categories of tools effectively augment Access as a development platform:

Microsoft Office. With the advent of Office 4, my staff stopped thinking of themselves as Access developers and began to refer to themselves as Office developers. Very few of our Access-centric solutions involve *only* Access. If some of the output data from a system can be easily summarized, has a strong statistical bent to it, or is financial in nature, dumping virtual reports from Access into Excel has more appeal to some managers than a hard copy.

Conversely, some managers like to have us take textual or tabular information and create Word reports or data merges from Access using Automation. The messaging and scheduling capabilities of the new Outlook component in Office provide programmable engines that can be addressed from VBA code as well.

For development teams, the investment made in learning Access quickly reaps dividends when the same Basic skills can be translated for use with other products. Thus, the effort of creating an Excel VBA extension to an Access application is not significantly greater for an Access developer than doing the same amount of work in Access itself.

Automation Servers. The power of OLE extends outside the realm of Microsoft Office. Programs from other software companies, such as Shapeware's Visio, can be controlled from Access applications using Automation and provide powerful additional capabilities to meet specific development needs. If a suitable third-party product cannot be found, Visual Basic or Visual C++ can be used to create a custom Automation server for Access to call for solving a unique problem.

Access has a form and report container control specifically for working with ActiveX controls. The availability of these third-party extensions is growing at a brisk pace. As with external Automation servers, you can create ActiveX controls in Visual Basic or Visual C++ if your project's needs warrant a totally unique extension to Access.

Add-ins. Several vendors have been producing Access add-ins for a number of years, and each year more jump aboard. The primary add-ins to date have been wizards, which are oriented toward end users. Some wizards make for viable application extensions. As more wizards and other add-ins are created, some will invariably be designed as components that integrate well with a host application. Also, developers can create custom wizards and add-ins themselves using VBA code and Access forms.

Other types of add-ins will become more common as more vendors enter the Access marketplace. Code libraries, reusable objects, and development tools are some of the extensions that will make application development easier and less expensive.

With the variety of options for extending Access, few database applications you create will utilize Access alone, and even fewer will not use Access at all.

From Here...

In this chapter, we built a firm foundation for the application development process. Without solid research and planning, the design of your application may be inaccurate or incomplete, and the project consumes more time and money than should be required.

▶ To learn how to take the information gleaned in the research and planning phase and turn it into a design document and project plan, see Chapter 4, "Creating Design Specifications."

▶ For details on how to organize an application's features and components based on the results of the design phase and how to store archived information, read Chapter 7, "Understanding Application Architecture."

▶ To learn how to manage a project toward successful completion of the objectives created in the planning stage, read Chapter 9, "Completing and Deploying a Solution."

▶ For techniques to extend Access using Automation, see Chapter 11, "Expert Approaches to VBA."

▶ To review an example of a project pre-planning survey, see Appendix A, "Database Software Pre-planning," on the CD- ROM.

chapter 4

Creating Design Specifications

4

In this chapter

◆ **How to produce specifications quickly**

◆ **How to make them comprehensive**

◆ **Topics to consider for inclusion in the document**

◆ **What tools to use in the authoring process**

T he pace and economics of development projects today do not allow for the thick specification documents of days gone by. In this chapter, I'll describe how to survive the specification process and how to produce a useful control document for application development.

Staring at Blank Pages

"During the development of Access 1.0, we spent a lot of time defining the structure and format of all of our specifications and internal design documents. In fact, one could argue that we spent an inordinate amount of time. The very first printing of the Cirrus (Access 1.0) design document was over 200 pages long, with all the proper sections and headings, yet every page simply had the words 'Text to Come' on it."

Tod Nielsen, General Manager, Microsoft Access Business Unit

When I was in high school and life was simpler, my friend Dave and I would jump into my car each day after school and drive. It didn't matter where we went, we just liked to drive. While this is a nice way to pass an afternoon, I would not recommend it as a metaphor for application development. Some developers sit down at the computer without any greater sense of direction than Dave and I had. They don't know where they're going either; they just like to code.

To prevent unstructured wandering, whether on the road or the keyboard, you use maps. The map of an application (see Figure 4.1) is called a design specification (spec), and a well-written spec saves money and time for developers and their employers or clients.

Fig. 4.1

A specification is the map of an application, providing the boundaries and also the direction of travel.

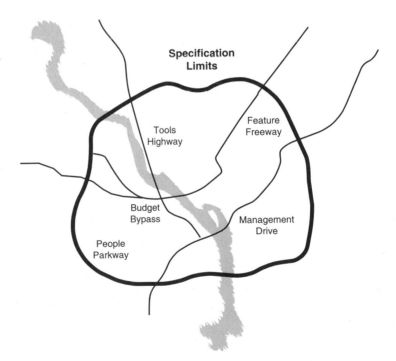

One common perception is that a spec provides the development boundaries for programmers who are apt to wander unless given a map denoting where to go, how to get there, and by when. This notion was true back when coders were salaried and could measure delivery times in years. In those days, a thick spec ensured the following:

▶ Users got back from their IT shop what they expected to get because IT was an independent department over which they could exercise little or no control.

▶ Coders had their job security spelled out for them by virtue of the endless pile of thick project specs on their desks.

The modern paradigm is different—we now work in a world where many coders are consultants, contractors, or staff developers who work for—or at least are accountable to—the users. And development times are now measured in person hours, not months or years. In the current scenario, the spec still protects the users and helps ensure that they get what they asked for. In addition, a spec also protects the developers, but no longer by providing job security. Instead, developers should now use specs to do the following:

▶ To review and test the feasibility of the proposed solution up front to avoid hitting technical walls later in the project.

▶ To rein in the development project from the common feature creep that users are wont to introduce, starting about midway through a project.

▶ To compute the cost of the feature set to see whether it can be delivered in the required budget. This is an important issue because budgets always seem to precede the spec these days, whereas the reverse was often true in the past.

On the highest plane, a spec is the bridge between the disparate worlds of user and developer and provides a common reference point and communication tool for both. In my company, we simply won't do a large development project without a defined spec. Any client who won't commit to a good design phase is dooming us to fail, so why start?

Each But Not Both

One common type of miscommunication in the solution design process arises when users speak in non-technical terms—developers hear in technical terms. For example, when users try to describe to developers the criteria requirements for a query operation driving a data sheet, data export, form, or report, the two sides don't always apply the same meaning to the terms "and" and "or."

Consider the following predicament (derived from one of our application development projects). The users need a contact management system with parent contact person records (with fields like `ContactID`, `ContactName`, and so on) pointing to multiple child records for contact events (`ContactID`, `EventDate`, `EventType`, and the like). Assume that Mr. Gill Bates is in the contact table and that there are two contact event child records for Gill: one with an `EventType` of "Letter" and one for "Call."

Next, assume the users tell you that they want their new contact management system to produce a report showing "any prospect that has received a letter or a call." As a developer, you will focus on the "or" in their request and mentally picture an `OR` operator in an SQL `WHERE` clause, with the SQL selecting the distinct `ContactID` values from the parent table where the child records match `EventType = 'Letter'` `OR EventType = 'Call'`. This query will return all parent records that have child records of type letter, call, or both.

What the users actually envisioned from their request was that the report would show all contact persons who received either a letter or a call, but not a letter in addition to a call (as is the case with Gill Bates). In their vocabulary, the term "or" means "one or the other but not both," because if they wanted both they would have asked for "a letter *and* a call." In contast, you and other developers thinking in terms of the SQL language will envision "one or the other or both" to solve their request when you hear them say "or."

The point here is that without a spec document, the developer creating the report is unlikely to clearly understand an issue like this. Equally important, though, is the fact that a written spec does not by itself solve this communication problem. Only a specification that is detailed enough to define the query behind the report and show sample data for the report will provide users with the opportunity to catch the developers' misinterpretation before coding begins.

With the days of largesse in software development efforts gone (if you've been around for awhile you may recall the era of million-dollar mainframe software projects), the tight budgets of the '90s often require a software project to be built like a cheap movie: shot in one take (see Figure 4.2). This leaves little margin for error in the development cycle and requires a good project specification "script" to work from to ensure success.

When I ask a new client or another solution developer why they don't do good specifications for their projects, the most common answer I get is a simple one, "We don't have a good formula for doing specs." They fear the 300-page document syndrome or some unreadable, complex technical tome and so they simply shelve the idea. My goal for this chapter is to provide that "good formula" that makes it easy for you to decide how you want to configure and write specifications.

Fig. 4.2
If an application was a feature film, the specification would be the script.

Preventing Development Problems with a Specification

There is basically no such thing as a specification that is too detailed—some of our larger clients have produced more than 300 page specs for us to work from. The majority of Access applications do not have the complexity or budget to warrant such monolithic documents, however. The key objective is to have the specification—and the research process that creates it—clarify users' goals to developers and describe the tools and techniques to achieve the goals. Quality, not quantity, is the objective, and the hallmarks of a quality design document are comprehension and clarity.

In an application development project, both the users and developers are at risk. The users stand to lose money, productivity, and perhaps even customers if the project is not successful. An in-house developer stands to lose his or her reputation or perhaps even their job, while contract developers may lose an important client, and often actual cash, when a project goes awry. All of these parties are better protected by a good design document.

The degree of protection the spec document provides lies in the balance struck between user interests and developer interests. As an example, our specifications have always included milestone dates related to various phases of the project (recall the application phases such as prototyping from Chapter 3, "Preparing for Development"). These dates were originally intended to protect our clients by providing them with a written obligation that we would deliver portions of the project on specified dates.

Over time, however, we expanded this model to include the subsidiary milestones within each phase that require client involvement, such as reviewing the prototype or providing testing effort. We added these dates to protect ourselves because documented milestones require clients to commit to delivering their portion of the project on specified dates. This enables us to schedule our time better and to hold them accountable if they negatively affect the project timeline.

Generally, the benefits derived from a good spec fall into the following three areas:

▶ Time benefits

▶ Cost benefits

▶ Communication benefits

Saving Time with Specifications

In the old frontier of the American West, gunmen were said to have "itchy trigger fingers" if they were too quick to draw their pistol. In the new frontier of technology, too many programmers have "itchy coding fingers" and are too quick to begin coding a project without defining it. Nothing is more frustrating to the itchy-fingered developer than to laboriously plod through spec development, because this takes time away from the joy of coding. However, the time spent on design work seems always to save an equal or greater amount of time on recoding and reworking features of a project, thus justifying the cost for the effort.

 Tip
Successful developers understand and support the spec process because it protects them from the least enjoyable type of development work: rework.

Project time savings accrue from a specification in the following areas:

Less time is spent managing the project. With a good specification, the program manager has a clearly defined set of expectations for the project manager, who has clearly defined expectations for the development manager, and so on down the chain. At each level of management, a minimum amount of time is spent discerning who is doing what and when it is due, and if a written spec is being used as the project plan.

Less time is spent on clarification. At each decision point in development where a developer feels that the specification is mute or unclear about a particular feature, the developer must contact one or more user groups or design team members for clarification. This process can be time-consuming and accumulate into a substantial time block over the life of a project. Clearly defined specification notations reduce or eliminate the need for these communication tangents.

Less time is spent on testing. A clear specification details not only what the application will do but what it enables with respect to user interaction. As the application is developed and the initial testing is done by the developers, the more clear the spec is on the subject of user interaction, the more accurately the testing process can emulate real-world usage. This way, developers can catch more coding and usability problems up front, before the slower and bulkier user testing process begins.

Less time is spent on training and documentation. To a minor degree, a well-written spec can serve as an outline for both the system (developer) documentation and the user documentation. The spec text used to describe features can sometimes be expanded into the documentation of those features. If a system is created for sophisticated users, in some cases the amount of training they require can be substantially reduced by simply having them read the specification to determine how the application works.

Less time is spent debating feature implementation. When developers work from handwritten design meeting notes or from their recollection of a user request, the features they deliver may not match user expectations. Even with a written specification, communication missteps can occur. In general, however, an application will be delivered to users for review and testing with less disparity between the expected features and the delivered features when a spec document is involved.

Less time is spent debating feature creep. We have a company strategy to reduce feature creep that essentially says: When you are painted into a corner by a new user request, thump on the spec and shout, "That feature is not in here!" It is easier to convince users and their managers to defer a feature addition when you can convey to them that they've already completed the application design and agreed to its feature set in total (in other words, they already had their chance).

 Tip

For added leverage, have the design team members sign or initial the final specification document. You have a much stronger position from which to resist enhancement requests when you can point to the signature of the requester and say, "But you agreed *in writing* that this was the final design."

> Remember that, even in spite of your best efforts to control feature expansion, you may lose the battle in an environment where "the customer is always right" is the prevailing maxim. Your only insurance policy when feature expansion occurs is a time and money allocation in the specification document for contingencies. See the section "Estimating Project Costs" later in this chapter for more information.

In a perfect world, each spec is comprehensive and limiting enough that it need not, and cannot, be changed once development begins. In the real world, change is inevitable, but having a spec at least helps to clearly identify the deviation from the original intent.

Saving Money with Specifications

It seems obvious to say that a good design specification will save money because the application can be built in one pass instead of multiple iterations. And yet, the importance of this point cannot be overstated. An equally important point lurks within it: A good specification helps determine whether the project should be done at all.

I've seen projects that survive the research phase, are written up into a brief specification, and then are developed. Further into the development process, issues that were not properly clarified in the specification crop up and begin to slide the time frame and cost of the project outward. In a project with a very tight budget, any such perturbation may be enough to "break the bank"—in other words, to make it apparent to management that the project cost is going to exceed its budget and trigger an immediate cancellation of the project. A substantial amount of capital and human energy is thrown out when this happens. All parties would have been better served by an accurate spec that showed the true effort, budget, and intent that the project should not be initiated with the presently available financial resources.

The cost of creating a spec is not always trivial. The litmus test for the success of the effort is whether management feels that the investment was recouped by cost savings elsewhere in the project. Such cost savings may accrue in several areas, such as in the following:

> *Prioritizing Features.* Often different users, or factions of the user community, have "pet" features that they are deeply committed to but that are not necessarily cost-efficient or provide a positive cost/benefit ratio for the company as a whole. Project managers trying to limit an application budget must often make difficult decisions about cutting some of these pet features while steering clear of the negative political ramifications that follow. With a spec at their disposal, managers can make

more informed decisions about the cost and worth of each feature when making such trade-offs.

Technology Sharing. One way to reduce the cost of a development project is to use components developed for other applications or to create components in the application that can be used elsewhere in the company. When communicating a project idea to others in the company, a written spec is much more effective than verbal descriptions for discovering what common objects and code routines might exist elsewhere in the organization that can be reused for the new project.

Precise Budgeting and Contracting. In general, a spec with feature and cost breakdowns provides a superb budgeting framework for the manager. Also, any coding that an outside vendor does is much easier to manage if the spec contains explicit detail about the timing and cost of each feature. Contract programmers can be assigned specific project areas as defined in the spec, provide a cost bid against those areas as detailed, and get paid based on the clearly described set of release dates and feature milestones.

Timely Delivery. If time is money within a business organization, then the timely delivery of a project is generally considered to be more cost-efficient than its late delivery. A project guided by a specification that defines time deadlines and milestones has a higher probability of being delivered on time than a project managed with no clear blueprint.

Empirically measuring the economic value of a spec is difficult because the cost of the problems it prevents cannot be calculated if the problems never occur. It takes foresight on the part of project management and the design team to commit to the process and believe in it, despite their inability to measure its worth precisely.

Enhancing Communication with Specifications

The process of researching, creating, and reviewing the specification forces the design team to discuss features and functionality at a very detailed level. Subtle features that may be taken for granted—for example, the location and wording of form command buttons—will end up on the agenda for discussion and definition.

When nothing is left to chance, the possibility for acrimony and contention between the developers and users is mostly removed. However, project timing and budgets rarely allow for the rich level of detail that can prevent all situations leading to communication gaps. Throughout the spec process, you will have to make decisions about the appropriate level of detail in each section and for each feature. In general, of course, more detailed specifications enhance communication among project team members.

Do You Speak My Language?

Simply having a specification is not always enough to aid your success. The specification must also be written in a manner that is not ambiguous and uses language that all parties can understand. Also, members of the design team who are aware of the communication challenges in application development must review the specification. The following example provides a good illustration.

On a recent client project, time pressures allowed us only a brief, but precise (or so we thought), specification. The application would track employee information, and each record included the following fields:

```
EmployeeName

SupervisorName

ManagerName
```

We were told that each employee had a supervisor, and each supervisor a manager. For convenience, the client wanted us to store the manager's name in the table even though it could have been joined in from a lookup on the supervisor name.

From this design, we inferred that the terms "supervisor" and "manager" when used by the client were literal references to the fields in the system of the same name. Thus, everywhere in the system where the client told us to display or report the employee's manager, we used the field called `ManagerName`. The client approved the screens during the prototype phase, but during testing, they complained that the manager information was not correct on reports.

It turned out that in their vocabulary, even though an employee record contained a manager's name, only supervisors truly had a manager. For employees, their supervisor served as their manager. Thus, every place in the system where we had displayed or printed `ManagerName` needed to be changed to show `SupervisorName` if the employee involved was not a supervisor. The extra time, confusion, expense, and ill will that this miscommunication generated was tremendous, and the project was delivered late as a result.

In reviewing the process to determine how we could have avoided the situation, it turned out that what we put in the specification would have had to be incredibly detailed to trap this problem because the client's misuse of his own terminology would have confused all but the most thorough review process. The solution in this case may have been to lay out the forms and reports on the specification, displaying actual employee data records for the company. Team members at that point possibly might have noted that we were putting the manager's name where they expected to see the supervisor's name in some cases.

As you prepare your specifications, be alert to such potential communication pitfalls.

Communication gaps occur most often when you work with forms and reports and less often in application structures and processes for several reasons:

▶ A strong design phase using the techniques described in Chapter 3, "Preparing for Development," usually yields a good, solid schema design. If you create table designs, review them with the team, and test sample data records against the structure—the odds are good that the data structure will be solid.

▶ Users are not adept at visualizing forms and reports; therefore, they historically provide the majority of their feedback on these objects at or after the prototype stage. If budgets do not allow for including form and report designs in the specification, as is frequently the case, the spec will include only functional descriptions of these objects. Later, when the users first see the prototypes, they will be apt to make changes, some of which deviate from the original design.

Peeling the Onion

"Too often, our users tell us what they want an application to do, but they are unable to put into words how they want the screen forms to match the workflow. If we attempt to document (in a spec) what we think the users want to help them review the spec from a usability standpoint, then additional requirements and clarifications often come to light. We call this process 'peeling off the next layer of the onion.'

"Poor screen navigation and awkward usability will cause an application to be unsuccessful faster than you can say, 'I should have done a spec.' I have seen applications with only a marginal data structure design become quite successful in spite of themselves, simply because they were easy to use. Placing menu and screen navigation designs in the project spec enables the users to compare the developers' interpretation of their needs with their actual business needs."

David M. Crosby, Senior Applications Consultant, Washington Mutual Bank

▶ Users depend on developers more and more these days for the layout of these objects. With smaller budgets in this era of downsizing and because the time burden on design teams to lay out these objects can be significant, many project teams rely on the expertise of the developer to design forms or reports. ("Just give it your best shot," we're often told.) Depending on how adept the developer is at second guessing the users, this may or may not lead to some reworking later based on the user feedback received from the prototypes.

▶ Users also depend on developers to be aware of the current standards or generally accepted metaphors for interface design, such as the Office Compatible standard discussed in Chapter 8, "Designing Effective Interfaces."

▶ High-level managers (the ultimate users referred to in the previous chapter), are famous for tuning reports over and over in an attempt to perfect the data presentation. If these users participate in the spec development and review process, they can usually get the reports they want at a lower price than if they iterate later.

 Tip

Some kind of layout for form and report objects—even hand-drawn—will improve the communication of features through the spec. This point is discussed further in the section "Using Tools in the Design Process" later in this chapter.

Specs also enhance communication between the management members of the design team. A spec that details project timelines and costs provides a powerful management tool for budgeting cash outflows, scheduling personnel resources for each project phase, estimating overall life cycle cost, and creating delivery schedules. The program manager for the project rarely keeps in touch with the day-to-day machinations of the application's development. Instead, he or she will often select milestones from the project spec and periodically review the development progress against those milestones with the project manager.

For the project manager, the spec provides the major benchmarks that define the success or failure of a project. With the spec as the ruler, the manager can quickly determine at deployment whether the feature set was delivered and whether the timing and cost targets were met.

Pulling the Research Together

A spec based on faulty or limited research is no better than a map made without walking its territory. Before you create the specification, you must complete your research using the guidelines described in Chapter 3, "Preparing for Development." The strategies presented in that chapter are intended to convince you to be thorough in your research practices. Remember that if you cut corners on the research, the spec will be less accurate as a result.

The outputs from the research phase of the project will be threefold, as follows:

An understanding of the existing process. When research is complete, the design team should have a detailed grasp of the current processes that will be enhanced or replaced by the new system.

An understanding of the existing infrastructure. During the research phase, an analysis is made of the technology that will host the new solution.

A detailed wish list from the users. The research phase will accumulate and will document user needs that the new system must meet.

The first step in creating a specification from the research data is to clarify and prioritize the requested feature set. While features may be cut later in the specification process as cost estimates are attached to them, some feature requests that are simply not worth even putting in the spec may stand out after the research effort. For example, a feature that obviously does not fit cleanly with the other features and creates a large coding and integration burden with respect to the expected benefit may be killed or deferred before it ever gets onto the spec. Try to determine at this stage which of the *requested* features are actually *required* features.

The second step is to mix the features into a cohesive model. Like puzzle pieces, all the user requirements must be laid out and fitted together into an application design that provides the needed benefits while employing the simplest possible interface at the lowest cost.

The third step is to define a plan for implementing the development (see Figure 4.3). Human resource requirements, computing infrastructure needs, timelines and milestones, tools and techniques to use, and responsible parties must all be determined.

The specification process can be lengthy for large projects, but for any project, the probability of the development effort's success is directly proportional to the amount of time spent creating a detailed specification for that effort. With job performance often tied to a mission-critical software application, both users and developers have much to lose from a sloppy specification process.

Fig. 4.3
Pulling the research data into a spec follows this flow.

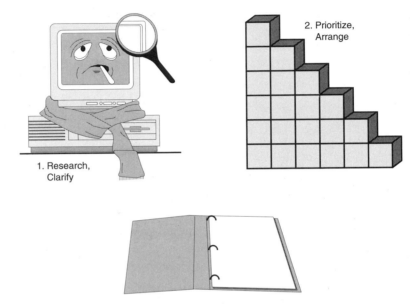

1. Research, Clarify

2. Prioritize, Arrange

3. Write the Spec

Elements of a Specification Document

The needs of the project, your development style, design team mechanics, and similar factors will affect the organization of information that you place in each design specification. There is no particular reason to be rigid in your formatting or to have each specification match the layout of a previous one.

I believe that there is a minimum set of information that each specification should include, or at least that the design team should consider for inclusion. This minimum set of specification sections includes:

1. Executive Summary
2. Application Processes
3. Project Mechanics and Management
4. Data Structures and Rules

5. Screen Forms

6. Reports

7. Appendixes

The flow of these document sections reflects our standard approach, which puts the three sections that managers and executives are most likely to read first and the technical information after them. In your specs, I recommend that the Executive Summary remains the first section, as is standard practice for business documents. The placement of the other sections is not fixed, however, and you can vary the order to suit a particular project.

The spec outline that follows provides a top-level view of the organization and content of my suggested specification layout. I provide more detailed descriptions of each topic in the spec document example in Appendix B on the CD-ROM, "Design Specifications." You should read that appendix—file SPECSHEL.DOC on the CD-ROM—before using the following outline for your own specifications.

Topics in the "Executive Summary" Section

An Executive Summary provides a clear, accurate, and concise synopsis of the project by highlighting the project's functionality, justification, and cost.

1A. Overview

Identified Problems

Proposed Solution

Project Scope

1B. Justification

Cost Justification

Return on Investment

1C. Resource Requirements

Human Resources

Physical Resources

Capital Resources

Topics in the "Application Processes" Section

This section describes the solution from a functional standpoint, including the software's primary tasks and the processing algorithms for the tasks.

2A. Solution Description

2B. Primary Processes

2C. Application Navigation

Launching the Application

Interface Philosophy

Navigation Map

2D. Initial Data Conversion

Source of Initial Data

Converting and Validating Initial Data

2E. Links to Other Systems

Downloads

Uploads

Merges and Links

2F. Security Requirements

Workgroup Security

Application Security

2G. Multiuser Issues

Topics in the "Project Mechanics and Management" Section

This section describes how the project will be managed and delivered.

3A. Project Management Overview

3B. Architecture and Tools

Platform

Development Tools

Reusable Components

3C. Equipment Requirements

Client Configuration

Server Requirements

Connectivity

Equipment Upgrades

3D. Application Deployment

User Definition

Review Builds

Testing

Unit Testing

System Testing

Test Plan

Preloading Data

Training

Installation

Online Documentation

User Documentation

System Documentation

Database Administration

Administrators

Backup Policies

Disaster Recovery

Adding Users

Localization

Ongoing Support

Supporting Users

Reporting Problems and Enhancement Requests

Problem/Enhancement Resolution Guidelines

Future Releases

3E. Project Management

Affected Users and Related Parties

Project Timelines

Responsible Parties

Project Administration

Issue Management

Risk Management

Coding and Documentation Standards

Spillover

Future Phases

3F. Financial Mechanics

Costing

Third Parties

Contractual Issues

Topics in the "Data Structures and Rules" Section

This section provides the blueprint for the database structure by describing the data tables and business rules.

4A. Data Models and Diagrams

4B. Schema Definition

Table Structures

Stored Views

Table Relationships

Business Rules

4C. Data Load

Initial Volumes

Future Volumes

Topics in the "Screen Forms" Section

This section provides the form designs and describes the standards and guidelines that affect form design.

5A. UI Guidelines

Form Layouts

System Messages

Fonts and Point Sizes

Colors

Buttons

Switchboard Menus

Bar Menus

Shortcut Menus

Toolbars

Keyboard and Mouse

Status

Terminology

5B. Structural Information

(name of the first form)

Purpose

Mockup

Data Source

Navigation

Controls

Events and Procedures

Properties

Validation

(name of the second form)

(repeat the topics above)

Topics in the "Reports" Section

This section provides the report designs and describes the standards and guidelines that affect report design.

6A. UI Guidelines

Report Layouts

Fonts and Point Sizes

Colors

Bar Menus

Shortcut Menus

Toolbars

Terminology

6B. Structural Information

(name of the first report)

Purpose

Mockup

Data Source

Navigation

Controls

Events and Procedures

Properties

(name of the second report)

(repeat the topics above)

Topics in the "Appendix"

Attach any supporting documents to the end of the specification that are too large or cumbersome to embed in the related section. Some examples follow:

Data Diagrams

Database Schema

Process Flow Diagrams

Form Mockups

Report Mockups

Project Timeline

Test Plan

Design Team Notes

History Application

History Data

Integration Information

Future Phases

Budgeting from a Specification

For prospective users, the design process's primary challenge is to define and clarify the short- and long-term feature sets for the application. Philosophically, the developer's primary design challenge is the same; but in practical terms, the developer's primary challenge is actually to properly estimate the time and cost budgets for the project—in other words, to tell the users whether they can afford what they have requested and when they will have it.

Notice that I mentioned time and cost budgets, as if they are equally important. In fact they are, but not to the same audience. At the completion of the design, users are now very excited about their new application and would like to have it completed as soon as possible. Thus, their main focus is on the time budget—the delivery milestones for the application.

Conversely, managers are primarily concerned with monetary budgets, and are usually content to delay the completion of the project if the cost can be reduced, either through using less-expensive development resources or using some existing company resources. Thus, for the developer, the budgeting process involves finding a balance between the speedy delivery of the application and the most cost-effective delivery methods.

4

Estimating Project Costs

The cost of a project is equal to the number of hours of work multiplied by the labor cost per hour. Right? True, yet with such a simple formula at its heart, the project costing process is frequently inaccurate and developers who do similar work day after day still seem unable to accurately cost their work. When a project is not completed on budget, the blame is placed on the developers for either working too slowly or poorly estimating the scope of work. Several other factors may actually be to blame, however, such as the following:

> *Lack of control.* If the users change the scope of work along the way, the developer has little hope of delivering within the original budget. Preventing such a situation is the goal of creating and enforcing an explicit specification.

> *Development difficulties.* Everyone who works with computer software understands the difficulties posed by software bugs, hardware problems, program incompatibilities, poor documentation, and busy technical support telephone lines. As the developer encounters such problems during development, he or she should immediately communicate them to the project manager so that he or she is aware of issues that may affect the budget or timeline but that are only partially within the control of the development team. Project budgets should always carry a contingency factor that allocates some money and time to cover a reasonable number of such obstacles.

Once these two factors are eliminated—the first by good design and the second by contingency budgeting—then the responsibility for meeting a project budget again lies with the development team, and accurately so. Therefore, when you apply development time estimates to a spec, your numbers had better be accurate, or you will paint yourself into a corner.

If you create Access applications on an ongoing basis, your ability to estimate project costs should be high. The knowledge you gain from developing each application should carry forward to the estimates for the next application. If your estimates of future project time requirements are to be based on historical development times, you must keep good project logs and records while you develop each application. The information in your records will eliminate any guesswork when you compute project times for new projects.

For example, you may find that with your combination of development style and tools, you can produce the average Access form for an application in two hours. As you budget a new project, you can list each form in the specification then apply the two hours per form to start the time budgeting process. You would then modify the budget based on the deviation of each specific form's complexity from that of the average two-hour form and account for any special needs of the application, such as enhanced validation or processing.

It is very simple to keep good project time information. In my company, we log time in an Access database against individual projects and their components (see Figure 4.4). At the end of each project, we can query the database and determine how time was spent by project, by developer, and by feature. This information helps us to determine where time was misspent on a particular project but also helps us to develop rules of thumb for budgeting projects in general. We apply these rules of thumb to application budgets as our starting point then adjust them based on the specific project requirements. (Project time analysis is also discussed in Chapter 9, "Completing and Deploying a Solution." That chapter also describes the SpecItem column shown in the figure.)

Table 4.1 shows the rules of thumb that we use to devise the time requirements for various deliverables in an Access application. These numbers represent our factors for the standard of an object in an average application; we use these factors as a starting point for budgeting in our specification documents. You may use them for informational purposes or perhaps for budgeting your first Access project, after which time you will develop your own benchmarks based on your own user base, techniques, and experiences.

Note that the table data is based on our approach to Access expert solutions development as reflected in this book and may not be indicative of your approach or that desired by your users. Also, some actual object development times will vary far from these averages due to their feature set in a specific project. For example, forms for lookup tables are usually very simple and take less time than the average shown in the table, while complex forms with background processes and user interface tricks may take several times the average hours. The table merely provides numbers to use when starting the budgeting process.

Fig. 4.4
Database records in Access can be used to log and analyze project time.

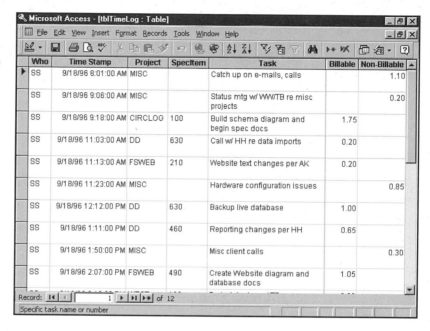

Table 4.1   Development Time Guidelines Used for Access Application Objects

Object Type	Budget Hours
One data table (1)	0.5
One form switchboard menu (2)	2.0
One record list form (3)	3.0
One data entry/edit form	3.0
One summary report	1.0
One detail report	1.5
One lookup table form	1.0

(1) A data table includes the overhead of schema items related to the table, such as properties, indexes, relationships, and standard (default) queries.
(2) Clients usually request that switchboard menus include an application- or company-specific graphic image that we create or clean up.
(3) The record list form is a Get form we commonly create so that users can list, sort, and find records. See Chapter 16, "Presenting Data to Users," for an example of this type of form.

How did I arrive at the numbers in Table 4.1? In our early days of Access development, we created a set of target times for object development. Over the years, in project post-mortem meetings, we have reviewed our time estimates and adjusted them to reflect our experiences up to and including that project.

To further legitimize the information in Table 4.1, I was curious to see if our own statistics would defend our rules of thumb, so for this chapter, I reviewed time log information for 11 of my company's recent Access projects. The results are summarized in Table 4.2, which shows the averages of the actual time expended per object when developers created the first release of the 11 selected projects (note that our time log data did not support statistics for every object type listed in Table 4.1). I selected average small projects that were not overly complex, so your actual development time for objects may vary wildly in either direction from these numbers.

Table 4.2   Average Development Time per Object for 11 Leszynski Company, Inc. Access Applications

Object Type	Average Hours
One data table (1)	0.2
One form switchboard menu (2)	3.0
One record list form (3)	3.5
One data entry/edit form	4.5
One report	1.5

1) A data table includes the overhead of schema items related to the table, such as properties, indexes, relationships, and standard (default) queries.

(2) Clients usually request that switchboard menus include an application- or company-specific graphic image that we create or clean up.

(3) The record list form is a Get form we commonly create so that users can list, sort, and find records. See Chapter 16, "Presenting Data to Users," for an example of this type of form.

What my calculations in Table 4.2 show is that for several object types, the actual time expended was greater than the average budgeted time we applied to our specs from Table 4.1. This is a tangible manifestation of feature creep—our estimates were less than the actual time requirements because users changed the design of the interface during development in almost every project reviewed. As developers, we budget a project based on the time it should take to do the work, but change requests or technical problems can cause the actual time to exceed our estimate.

If the budgeted time and actual time consumed by object development for our reviewed projects were not equivalent, you're probably wondering where the money came from to pay the difference. In the analyzed cases, and in most others in my company's experience, the money for a budget shortfall or change of scope comes from one of these sources:

▶ *Contingency.* If a specification includes a contingency amount to cover unforeseen circumstances, and there are few of these during the course of development, there will be a positive balance in the contingency budget at the end of the project. This amount often pays for minor enhancement requests or budget shortfall.

 Tip

When you create a project budget, add up all the time items and then apply a contingency factor to the total budget to allow some extra money for minimal design changes and unforeseen problems. Depending on the nature of the project, we typically include a Contingency line item on the budget that equals between five and 20 percent of the total project budget.

▶ *Other Budgets.* If developing certain objects in an application proceeds faster than expected, extra time and money will be left in the budget to cover the development of objects that take longer than anticipated.

▶ *Change of Budget.* If you have properly implemented a methodology for budgeting against a spec document within your organization, you should have a license to formally request an increase in the budget to cover change requests initiated by the design team.

▶ *Developer Contribution.* In a few cases, we have gifted time against our invoices to cover a change request that we felt had merit and could not be added to the client's budget. My developers, at their discretion, can give away a small percentage of the time on a large project for an established client if the free hours serve to maintain an amicable relationship or ensure the success of a project. This is an investment we make in the client/consultant partnership that we attempt to forge for each project.

Table 4.2 also provides an additional interesting statistic. Notice that the time it takes us to create tables and the database schema (0.2 hours) is dramatically less than the amount of time we budget (0.5 hours). This results from the fact that our budget times still reflect the assumption that tables and indexes are built manually, when in fact we generally use our LCI Schema Builder to complete the process much faster. This tool is described in

Chapter 10, "Creating Expert Tables and Queries," and provides a dramatic example of the economic benefit of development add-ins.

Table 4.3 gives statistical information for the time spent on each project component for the same 11 projects in Table 4.2. The second column in the table shows the overall average actual total time we expended on each project element. The third column shows the overall average percentage of a project's time that we spent on each element. You can use these percentages as guidelines to help you begin your own spec budgeting process.

For the data in Table 4.3, the average total project time was 203 hours for the 11 projects, the smallest project reviewed was 103 hours, and the largest project was 398 hours. (The totals in the second column add to 225 hours as opposed to the average project size of 203 due to statistical mechanics.)

Table 4.3   Average Development Time per Project for Elements of 11 Leszynski Company, Inc. Access Applications

Project Feature	Average Hours	Average Percent
Design, specification, management	56	28
Supporting UI code (1)	19	9
Schema development	6	3
Forms development	49	21
Reports development	19	9
Processing code (2)	35	12
Testing, deployment, training (3)	41	18

(1) Supporting UI code is the user interface and library code that is not related to a specific form, such as navigation, generic validation, error management, and login.
(2) Processing code includes routines that are specific to the application's purpose, such as accounting processes or upload/download routines.
(3) Integration/beta testing time is reflected in this item, but time for unit testing of each application object is buried in the object development times. Remember also that our business model offloads much of the testing to users; in environments without access to users as testing resources, the percentage of project resources spent on testing may be much larger.

Bear in mind that a single time record on our time logs may sometimes include work on several objects, so the numbers shown in the previous three tables may be mildly skewed due to members of my staff lumping several work items into one time log entry. Also note that the nature and complexity of projects that come to us as a firm may have no correlation to the type of projects that you do—some of the things we do with Access are rather complex. Despite the caveats, the information above should help you to understand the time burden of Access development.

Thanks to Microsoft's successful advertising about the ease of using Access, your clients and users will think that you can generate an Access application in a few dozen hours. While you may be able to create a simple application in 30 to 100 hours, creating an expert solution takes much more time. Our standard answer when a new client calls and asks, "How long does it take to create an Access application?" is "The average high-quality application takes 200 to 500 hours." We sometimes create, or see others create, Access applications that require more than 1,000 hours.

 Note

The previous tables provide you with insight into how time on a project is distributed. If you add up the overhead numbers in Table 4.3 (design, administration, deployment), you'll see that the average overhead per project for the selected 11 applications was 97 hours, or 46 percent of the total using the percentage column. Many developers do not take these overhead items into consideration when they create a project plan and consequently end up with inaccurate time budgets.

Because the analyzed projects were not large and could not benefit from economies of scale, the overhead as a percentage was quite large. The percent of total project time spent on overhead decreases somewhat as projects get larger than those summarized here.

Factors that Constrain Project Budgets

Ideally, the project cost budget is a factor solely of the scope of work. In a perfect world, you would simply take the final specification and apply costs to the features. The reality is different, however; a project's pricing is affected by numerous factors, such as the following:

Competing Estimates. In a competitive bidding situation, the users may have conducted the project research autonomously and could be asking multiple developers to bid on the project. Your understanding of the competition and bidding process will affect the budget you create for a project under such circumstances. I enjoy these situations the least of almost any element of my business and will not participate in a bidding war for a project.

Not only is it financially and politically dangerous for me to tailor my fees on a per-project basis, but I also have found that clients who manage development projects this way are often unsuccessful in their development efforts. An application is a different creature than the hardware that it runs—with too many variables and other dynamics as the process unfolds—and therefore cannot be bid as accurately or as tightly as a piece of hardware or a repair service.

Tip

If you must participate in competitive bidding for projects, don't bid on projects that have an incomplete or vague specification—you will lose money. If you see weaknesses in the spec that you are asked to bid, show these shortcomings to the client and try to have the spec reworked. Both you and your client are put in better positions as the accuracy of the spec improves.

Previous Projects. In organizations that rely heavily on custom software applications, users and managers develop a historical sense of the cost of various software features. At the end of a design phase, such sophisticated design teams will already have a targeted project cost in mind and will be pressuring the developer to deliver the project within that estimate.

Tip

If you can afford to do so, run away from projects where users and managers have established the budget without the help of developers.

Budget Allocation. Nothing is more frustrating for a developer than to have the budget fixed before the feature set is defined, but business processes unfortunately sometimes work this way. For us, the established budget for a project is mentioned in perhaps 40 percent of the initial meetings we have regarding a development project for a new client. This has the undesirable effect of setting user expectations before design has even begun, risking that the client probably won't get all the features they desire or require and reducing some of the design team's enthusiasm.

If the budget and the expected feature set do not match in the first meeting, we raise a red flag at that early stage. The users have two options in this scenario. First, they can continue to design as if budget is not an issue, which produces a better design spec, then select only the features they can afford from the spec. The unfunded remainder of the spec becomes the growth plan for future phases. Alternatively, the design team can remain prejudiced by available money and explore other options throughout the design process that will produce the solution that is affordable rather than ideal.

External Funding. In cases where the project is not financed directly by the users, the budget may be truly immutable. For example, projects that are funded by grants, charitable gifts, government contracts, and so on often have no budgetary flexibility. The users in such a case often feel as though the specification process is a waste of precious, limited capital, and the developer often limits the discussion of features to fit the budget, leaving the client with an application but no growth plan.

Regardless of early perceptions of the development budget, I feel strongly about research-ing and specifying a project as if the development budget were not an issue. In fact, I prefer to talk only about the budget for the design and specification phase until the spec document is done. This simply means that I try to convince clients to expend the time and money to first create a long-term project plan that meets the determined user and business needs, regardless of cost.

Only with this approach are users assured that all their needs will be considered, dis-cussed, and researched. In a cost-centric model, ideas are thrown out too early in the process strictly due to someone's determination that they are not economically feasible. If an idea is dismissed so capriciously, it does not even receive the benefit of the developer's wisdom in seeking alternative, less costly approaches to arrive at the same features, and the users lose out.

A Penny Saved Is Ten Cents Wasted

To illustrate my point about the dangers of undercutting the specification budget, I will describe a situation I have seen many times in my consulting career.

For our average medium-sized Access projects, the research and specification work is completed in around 100 hours. Assume that in this amount of time, we can design a system that matches the users' needs. If, instead, we are forced into a more economical 40-hour design phase and charged with designing a system that matches the users' budget, the quality of the specification and the final product will be dramatically reduced.

In the small picture, the client thinks they have saved a few thousand dollars as a result of the 60 hours of deleted specification work. In the big picture, however, the client has cut off the research and discussion of features prematurely. In a year or two, information that was not included in the original spec will come to light, and the application will be changed at a cost equal to ten times the few thousand dollars initially saved.

Adjusting Features to Match the Budget

In cases where a budget amount is predetermined and the budget and features do not match, the developer is placed in a tricky situation. Having painstakingly worked with the design team to craft a good application plan, the developer must now consider changing or removing features from the current version of the application to meet a budget target. The developer has several alternatives to choose from when trying to deliver the feature set within the prescribed budget, such as the following:

Defer or Stage Features. The design team can refine the specification to allow for a staged implementation—over several years, if necessary—rather than all at once. This approach leaves the users with a design document that includes a definition of not only the application they will get now but also a road map to guide them (eventually) to the application they wanted when they initiated the project.

Unfortunately, it is usually more costly to implement a feature after the application's initial delivery because the application will be in use (perhaps even mission-critical) and will contain data. Thus, the overall (long-term) budget impact of deferring features is greater than expanding the current budget to cover such features.

Three Months of Designing, Ten Years of Coding

One of my most satisfying development projects was a (DOS-based) circuit management application we did for a telecommunications company. When the project started in 1986, I was able to convince the company of the importance of a good design phase, so most of their staff was involved with my staff in a series of design meetings that went on for several months. The philosophy we adhered to in the meetings was the one I describe in this chapter, where we assumed that we had a data problem to solve and an open-ended budget for solving it.

At the end of the design phase, we had produced a comprehensive plan that incorporated not only their current needs but everyone's best guess regarding their future needs. A budget was created that enabled us to deliver a majority of the desired features within the first year and to structure the application so that the nonimplemented features could be inserted later.

After deployment, the client called periodically over the next several years, as money became available, and asked us to implement more of the features from the original design. In each case, when we went to add the features, we were able to "hook" them in to the existing application easily because we had created an available "slot" for each future feature to occupy. For example, we placed fields in the first version of the data structure that we knew we wouldn't use for several years. Creating them up-front was cheaper than adding them after the system was in production.

Our foresight, and the client's, paid off handily as the application grew because new features fit into the design quickly and cost-effectively in a fashion unlike the all-too-common "gut and rebuild" approach that must be used to expand software not written with a growth potential built-in.

As I write this in 1996, we are still supporting and expanding this application guided by the original project spec, and it is still serving the client well after ten years of use.

4

Wait for changes in tools. The cost of a feature is affected by the tools used to deliver it. As the tools become smarter, the cost of features that depend on those tools may go down. In such a case, it is cheaper on the overall budget to defer a feature and retrofit it into the application than to deliver it in the initial release. For example, we have a client who wanted us to add management features to their current Access application for compound documents developed with various Office applications. We persuaded them that it was cheaper to wait for the second version of the application, when we could use the document Binder capabilities of Office 95, than to have us program a document management system immediately using Access 2 and Automation code.

Use available components. If you can deliver a defined feature of an application with off-the-shelf software or by modifying a third-party application sold with source code, the project budget can be favorably affected and the users will still get their desired features. Another alternative is to modify portions of an existing application within the company or to raid other in-house applications or your personal code base for components already in use that can be reused in the new application.

Expand the user base. Sometimes an application design can be expanded to include more users with similar but distinct needs. As a result of expanding the user base, budgets belonging to those added users can be tapped for the extra money to complete the original project design, plus the additions. This approach is usually a desperate act on the part of the project manager, used to salvage a specification when the budget for it is cut back late in the design process and the project's viability is placed in jeopardy. It essentially amounts to getting your neighbors to help you buy a nicer car than you can afford by making them co-owners. In some circumstances, however, we have legitimately expanded the user base and budget in a way that favorably impacted an entire organization (for example, getting the Sales department to join in the design, funding, and usage of the Marketing department's contact management application).

Prioritize features. I like to have design teams consider the relative importance of each feature as they determine the application's feature set and document the rankings. Later, if the budget axe looms, it is a relatively easy process for the developer to identify and remove the features the users deem least necessary to meet a specific budget target.

 Tip

Where possible, create a project budget as an amalgamation of component budgets with costing applied to each major element. With this process, you can easily mix and match features to meet the allocated funding for the project and budget for the future addition of any deferred features.

You can even apply project time for overhead items like testing and contingency at the component level.

Of course, budget compromises are never pleasant for either developers or users, but they are a fact of life.

Using Tools in the Design Process

From a mechanical standpoint, creating a design spec can be as simple as typing large volumes of information into a Word document. A better approach is to select the appropriate tool for each component of a spec document, and to combine the outputs from the tools into the final spec. This way, you can leverage the best features of a variety of tools as you try to achieve the following objectives:

▶ Producing a quality, readable, and usable document that guides the development effort. An example of these objectives is the inclusion of report mockups in a specification.

▶ Creating data and methodologies that extend beyond the hard copy specification and can be used during development. For example, it would be good if the tool that produces the project tasks and timeline component of the spec document can be used as a task management tool throughout the project.

Spec development is a two-way communication process between users and developers—users request various features and developers tell them what's realistic and affordable. Because the communication *is* two-way, it helps to communicate in a language that all parties understand. We prefer to use a toolset for spec authorship that is familiar to our users and clients, so we use Office and other widespread Microsoft products as much as possible. Thus, our clients usually own the same tools we use to create spec documents. The following are two benefits:

> *We can work on site* at any client workstation during the design process if the client has the same tools we use in our office (Excel, for example).

> With good direction, *design team members can directly participate* in creating and editing the specification document and components, and spec files can be passed back and forth within the design team for revision.

This section lists several of the components of a spec and the suggested tools you can use to create the component. It is not meant to be a reviewer's guide to all available tools for each specific task. Instead, I describe the tools that work best for us after employing a broad variety of methodologies over the years. If you disagree with my choice of particular tools, the examples here of various processes should still be of value to you, regardless of the tool you employ in the process.

Creating Database Diagrams

In my opinion, the business diagramming war is over and Visio won. I really like the product and I find it easy to use for creating almost any kind of business diagram, including navigation maps, process flow charts, and database relationship diagrams for specifications. Figure 4.5 shows a sample database diagram created in Visio.

One of Visio's strengths is the ability to use Automation to create drawings via program code. As an example, you can create a database schema in Access, or definition in Excel, then build a drawing of the schema in Visio using VBA code. Your code would simply automate Visio to rough out a diagram by programmatically creating a drawing object for each named table.

In the specification outlined previously, the "Navigation Map" topic refers to a flow diagram of a user's interaction with the application interface through forms. Such a diagram shows each form in the application and a visual depiction of how the user moves between the forms. The map's purpose is to show how the application branches and flows based on button clicks and menu/toolbar selections. Navigation map diagrams are also easily created with Visio, as shown in Figure 4.6. (Refer to Appendix B, "Design Specifications," on the CD-ROM for more information on navigation maps.)

Fig. 4.5
Visio is an effective tool for creating database structure diagrams.

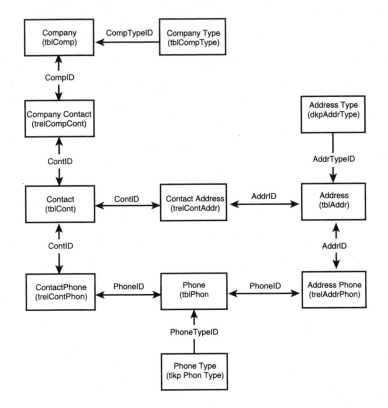

Fig. 4.6
You can use Visio or a similar drawing tool to create the navigation map diagram used in specifications.

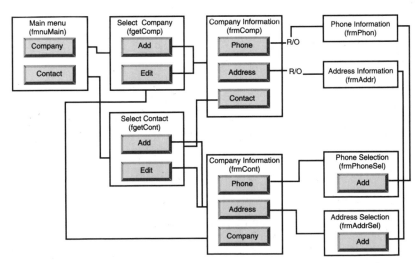

Other options for creating simple drawings in your spec include the following:

▶ Drawing Tools in Microsoft Office. Organization Chart, Paint, WordArt, Word's drawing tools, and so on

▶ Retail Drawing Tools. CorelDRAW!, PageMaker, and so on

In addition to using drawing programs, you can create database structure diagrams using database design tools, as described in the next section.

Creating Data Structure Documents

Your specification should include documentation for tables and fields. This information is best expressed in tabular format, so I standardized years ago on a system of building table definitions in Excel. The ease of printing, reordering, and outlining in Excel makes the process of schema design quick and simple, and we can e-mail Excel files to our clients for review with certitude that they own the program and know how to use it.

We begin by building a worksheet with columns for the most important Access data structure properties, such as Table Name, Field Order, Field Name, Data Type, and Description. Then, we or the design team populate the worksheet from the information gleaned in the research phase (see Figure 4.7).

Fig. 4.7

You can use Excel to create a database schema design worksheet.

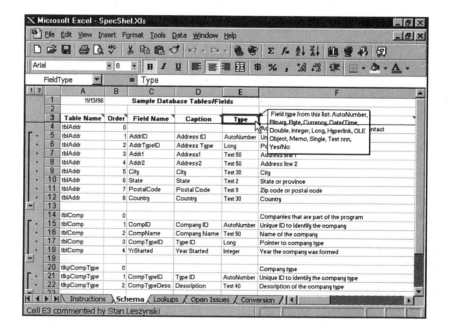

Depending on your style and needs, you can expand the worksheet shown to include more detail about the data structure, such as Format, Validation Rule, Default Value, and other field attributes.

 Tip

I prefer to order the tables and fields alphabetically by name when defining the schema but to place the primary key and foreign key field(s) at the top of each table listing. Reading through object names alphabetically is easier when reviewing the specification. I include a Field Order column in the worksheet so I can sort on this attribute just before the spec is finalized, to reflect the actual desired field order in the table.

Figure 4.7 also demonstrates the following benefits you inherit from using Excel for schema design worksheets according to our template:

Outlining. Using Excel's outline feature, you can expand and collapse each table definition, making it easier to navigate and use design worksheets for large databases.

Cell Notes. To assist any reader in understanding the content of the worksheet, you can include cell notes.

Properties. You can create a column in the worksheet for each field property available in Access or only those you deem important enough to put in the spec.

Lookups. We create a separate worksheet in the workbook for designing lookup tables to show the columns of each expected table. Design team members can enter the lookup table data directly into the worksheet quickly and easily. Later, we can then copy the table values from Excel into the new database before release.

Conversion Map. If an existing application is being upgraded into or replaced by the new application, it is convenient to use Excel to log the information required to convert existing data into the new schema. We place an additional worksheet in the spec workbook to record the table structure of the existing system and note the name of the new table and field that each data item will be moved to when it populates the new application.

Bulk Operations. Designing in Excel provides enormous flexibility when performing bulk operations, like a copy and paste of a block of fields repeated in multiple tables, or a global rename of a field. (Contrast the ease of renaming one field that appears in ten tables in the Excel template as opposed to renaming the same field in each table in an Access-based prototype of the new database.)

The file SPECSHEL.XLS on the CD-ROM provides you with a version of our Excel design spreadsheet that you can use as a template for your project designs.

Using the power of VBA and Automation, my company has created a tool that takes our database designs in Excel once a specification is frozen and automatically builds the Access database from it. This saves us dozens of hours of schema-creation work per project. The code that provides this feature is discussed in Chapter 10, "Creating Expert Tables and Queries," and is included on the CD-ROM.

Of course, you have options other than Excel for creating the table structure documents in your spec:

> *Word Tables.* You can mimic the Excel layout shown in Figure 4.7 in a Word document, creating one Word table per data table and showing the fields on the left and the properties across the top.

> *Word Outline.* You can bypass a tabular metaphor and simply list each table in the specification document with each field below it then each property listed (nested) within the field information, all using Word's outline view.

> *Database Design Tools.* Advanced database design tools, such as ERwin from Logic Works and InfoModeler from Asymetrix, assist you with table and field design and can provide both diagrammatic and tabular representations of database structures. Some of these tools (InfoModeler, for example) can create an Access database from the design document, much like our Excel tool described here.

> *Access Tables.* Many developers like to prototype a data structure directly in Access then print the structure using the built-in Documenter or similar tool. I personally find this approach difficult to implement, given the poor output of the Documenter and Access' limited ability to support the dynamics of the design process (for example, you can't easily search and replace table definitions to change a field name in an Access mockup, or quickly locate all occurrences of the Integer-type fields).

Creating Form Mockups

The Access Form Wizard provides a handy tool for creating form mockups during the design phase. Members of the design team can even participate directly in this process because it is quite simple. Once the database structure is shelled-out in Access, run the Form Wizard against the structure to create draft form mockups. Drag the controls to their desired locations to make the mockups match the users' requirements. Alternatively, you can create form mockups in Access before the tables are created by using unbound forms and controls.

On the form mockups, add controls to reflect the data source for the form. Add any additional text boxes, labels, command buttons, and other controls that make up the form, and then print the form mockup to include it in the specification. For mockups, you do not write any code nor set most form or control properties.

Of course, you can also do form mockups in drawing programs, such as Microsoft Paint. You can even do form mockups by hand, having members of the design team draw them on paper.

Designing Report Mockups

As with forms, report mockups are easily done using the wizards in Access. I find three liabilities in such a strategy:

1. *Time Expended.* Too often, when designers or developers try to mock up reports in Access, they tend to spend too much time beautifying the report and trying to get just the right look and layout. By the time the report mockup is completed, a significant portion of the development effort for the report has been expended, which pulls too much development time forward into the design phase.

2. *Communication.* Most potential users of the application are probably not Access literate and therefore only a limited subset of the design team, and even fewer management-level reviewers will be able to review and modify the designs online.

3. *Sample Data.* Report mockups are clearer for reviewers if they contain sample data. For mockups built in Access to display sample data, tables must be built and populated. Again, the time investment in this effort is imprudent.

To solve these problems, I gravitate to one of two other tools: Excel or Word. You can lay out simple columnar reports in Excel very quickly using the cells and grids, and sample data with totals or other calculations are easily expressed. We give Excel report mockups to members of the design team to review and revise online because Excel is widely distributed and well known among our clients.

You can also create complex report layouts in Word documents and populate them with sample records by typing or pasting data from an existing system. It is as easy to send Word mockups around for review as it is with Excel files, with the further benefit in Word that each reviewer can make use of the revision marks feature to show his or her contribution to the final design.

As with forms, you can also design report mockups using drawing programs such as Microsoft Paint, drawing them by hand on plain paper, or even sketching them out on cocktail napkins!

A Picture Is Worth a Thousand Words

One of my clients years ago was a flamboyant and energetic entrepreneur who owned several small companies. In most of the systems we developed for him, he would be classified as the ultimate user of the application because reports that were run at almost any level in the company trickled up through the management layers and were reviewed by him.

Because this client spent so much time reading reports, he took a keen interest in the layout and content of each report. Near the end of each application design process, we would ask him to lead the design meeting for defining report layouts. In the meeting, he would review the data structures then go to the white board and draw in a frenzy, erasing sections wildly and using different colored pens to add emphasis to his masterpiece.

At the end of this spectacle, he would have produced a drawing of exactly what he wanted to see on a particular report. His administrative assistant would then enter the room, shoot an instant picture of the white board, and leave, at which time the client erased the board and began drawing the next report.

The photos were included in the specifications as the final report mockups for us to use during development!

Describing Code Processes

Code processes are usually described using a technique called "pseudocode," which simply means to describe a coding need without using application-specific terms. Every developer has a different style for writing pseudocode, and there is no single correct way to do it. The objective when writing pseudocode is to describe a process using terms that will be clear to both the nontechnical readers of the spec document and to the developers.

As an example, the process for exporting invoice records to an external billing system could be pseudocoded as shown in Listing 4.1. Note that one line in the listing does not map directly to one line of program code—it is up to the developer to make the translation between the English-like pseudocode and the programming language used to implement it. It is also up to the developer to create object names, add code comments, and place error trapping in the final code.

Listing 4.1 Pseudocode for a Billing Export

```
Create an export file name
 Add "I" plus the current date as YYMMDD, plus a ".DAT" extension
Open the export file name for output
 If the filename exists, prompt the user to overwrite
  If No to overwrite, generate an alert and exit
Create a recordset with all non-exported invoice records,
   sort the recordset by invoice number
 If no records are returned, generate an alert and exit
Loop for each record in the recordset
 Print the following items to the export file, separated by commas
  Patient ID
  Invoice date, in quotes
  Invoice number
  Invoice amount, with two decimal places but no dollar sign
  Carriage return
 Get the next record in the recordset
End of loop
Close the recordset
Close the export file
Alert the user that the export was successfully created
End
```

I prefer to create the pseudocode directly in the specification document. Writing pseudocode in Word is easy, and using a fixed-width font like Courier makes the indentation of the processes visually evident.

 Tip

When the specification is approved, copy all the pseudocode routines to a new, empty Word document. Then, write a macro to go down line-by-line, adding an apostrophe to the beginning of each line. Now you can take the pseudocode and paste it into the Access module editor, using it as a guiding outline while you write your code. The leading apostrophes turn each pseudocode line into a code comment that is innocuous to the Access compiler. You can delete such comments at the end of the coding process when they have outlived their usefulness.

Preparing Project Timelines

Simple project timeline documents are often prepared in Excel worksheets. You can lay out milestone dates, expand and collapse outlines of related tasks, and print selectively with ease. Excel's weakness in the area of project planning lies in the difficulty of creating and maintaining dependencies on project dates.

If you are more adventurous, you can create your project plans in Microsoft Project or similar project management software. Project enables you to set up and maintain links between tasks, making it simple to slide an entire phase forward in time if one component of that phase is delivered late or postponed.

Project also makes it easy to assign times to each task and to sum the task times into time budgets by phase. See Figure 4.8 for a sample application development plan done with Project.

Fig. 4.8

Microsoft Project is useful for creating and maintaining application development timelines.

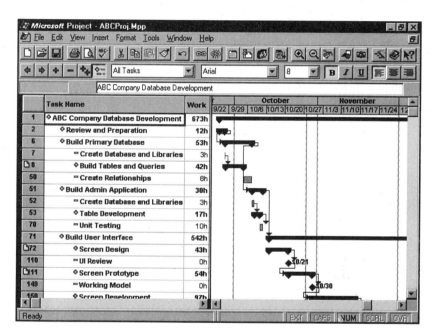

Using the Binder for Specifications

The Binder application in Office can be used to group some or all of the components of your specification documents. Because a specification can have many different components and the Binder works primarily with Excel and Word files, you may or may not be able to make use of this technology.

If you create spec components with software whose outputs can be embedded into Word documents as document objects (such as Visio drawings), you will be able to place Word files in your Binder whose purposes are to contain drawings or other outputs from other programs. With this technique, you can take advantage of the cross-file printing in the Binder.

From Here...

This chapter described in detail the process for turning design information into a written specification. Coupled with the spec template files SPECSHEL.DOC, SPECSHEL.XLS and Appendix B, "Design Specifications," included on the CD-ROM, you should now have the tools and techniques you need to create solid application specs.

▶ To refresh your knowledge of the research and design processes that come before specification writing, review Chapter 3, "Preparing for Development."

▶ For a complete discussion of user interface issues that you should consider and document in the specification, see Chapter 8, "Designing Effective Interfaces."

▶ To see how to build database tables automatically from the specification design worksheet described here, go to Chapter 10, "Creating Expert Tables and Queries."

▶ For a list of questions that you should answer before you begin to develop a project spec, see on the CD-ROM Appendix A, "Database Software Pre-planning."

chapter 5

Creating Naming Conventions

5

In this chapter

◆ Why are object naming conventions important?

◆ What are the guidelines for creating naming conventions?

◆ What are the components of a naming convention?

◆ How are naming convention components assembled and applied?

One Access application consists of many objects. While developing an application, you might see and use each object's name dozens or hundreds of times. To help you manage and reference so many different objects, consider developing standard rules for naming them. Any object name you see and use over and over should be both informative and familiar (as some say, "easy on the eyes").

Basic Organization

> ## Sorting Tables and Queries
>
> In the original release of Access 1.0, many lists displayed tables and columns sorted together; for example, the Add Table dialog box in query design view. In such lists, it was difficult or impossible to differentiate a table from a query and knowing the object type was an important part of creating accurate queries. This challenge led many people, including us, to look for a way to clarify the two object types.
>
> Some people would put a lowercase q at the beginning of query object names so they stood out from tables. Others would use the q convention and also put a lowercase t in front of table names. Because we were already using a three-letter control naming convention from our form design work in Access and Visual Basic, we decided to apply that convention to database object names as well, and we began using qry to prefix query names and tbl for tables. This solved the problem of identifying object types within a single mixed list.
>
> Starting with Access 2, many dialog boxes that list tables and queries together included option buttons at the bottom of the dialog box to filter the list to show only one of the object types at a time. Nevertheless, in Access versions 2 through 97 the queries and tables are still listed together in the object selection screen of the Form and Report Wizards and in other places, so the need for a naming convention for these objects has not diminished.

While most serious developers live and die by their programming conventions, some are casual about issues like consistent object naming. To find out if the issue of naming conventions is important to you, take the following test.

In the Database window in Figure 5.1, can you identify:

▸ The main switchboard menu?

▸ Which form is for customer entry and which is for customer editing?

▸ Which forms are used to maintain lookup tables?

▸ Which forms are subforms and shouldn't be opened from the Database window?

If you were frustrated that the object names in Figure 5.1 were not very descriptive, you will get valuable information from this chapter. For me, an application filled with names like those above is as difficult to navigate through as a messy garage!

Fig. 5.1

These form names do not provide adequate information.

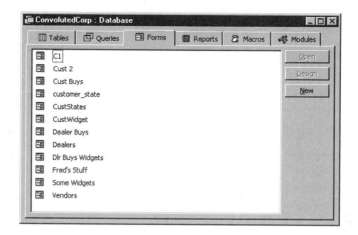

To continue illustrating the value of naming conventions, next consider the Database window in Figure 5.2. The objects are the same, but the names follow a standardized convention. Even if you don't know the specific naming conventions used, I'll bet you can infer a lot about each object's important properties from the object names and identify the items on the list above.

Fig. 5.2

These form's names specific naming conventions.

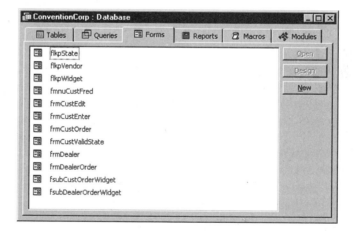

The specific conventions used in Figure 5.2 are described in the next chapter, but you probably determined quite easily which forms were standard forms, which menu was the switchboard menu, which conventions were for lookup tables, and which form was actually a subform.

Notice that two types of naming conventions were applied in the example. The first, and most obvious, convention is the standardization of the object base names. c, Cust, and Customer, all meaning the same thing, were standardized to Cust. The Cust portion of the names was moved to the beginning of each base name so the customer objects would each sort with their peers. Also, the random use of singular and plural was stopped, and the names were made more descriptive.

The second, and equally important convention is the addition of leading characters denoting the type of the forms. Many programming naming conventions have in common the standardization of the base object name and the addition of descriptive information on one or both ends of the base name.

The example provided by the contrasting form names previously is equally applicable to the other named elements of an Access application. Any object in your application that you view or refer to frequently—database objects, form and report controls, procedure names, and VBA variables—is a candidate for naming conventions.

I use the terms "naming conventions" and "style" interchangeably throughout this chapter. Naming conventions and other key development foundation items are each a part of your overall development style.

Why Use Naming Conventions?

The motivation for creating naming conventions to work with your development tools usually derives from specific problems or situations you encounter. The previous example from my experience with Access (differentiating table and query names) is probably familiar to you as well.

There are other and more compelling reasons for developing and using naming conventions in an application. A description of each of the most important reasons follows.

Reverse Engineering an Application

When you look at an application that someone else has written or revisit your own after some period of time, the overall structure should make sense to you almost immediately. If not, you will waste time researching and reviewing it or chasing down documentation—if it even exists. While good naming conventions cannot help you to immediately infer the complex workings of the SQL in a query or help you read an intricate code module if you don't speak Basic, they give you at least an immediate treetop view of an application's architecture.

Suppose I'm visiting a client and they need me to give them an opinion on the viability of an accounting application they've written. In a perfect world, they would sit the application's developer down with me and take me step-by-step through the facets of the solution. In the real world, however, they will place me alone in front of a computer and give me only a few hours to understand their situation and make a recommendation, because whatever objective they have was probably due yesterday.

Thanks to the enhanced Database window introduced in Access 97 that displays object descriptions entered by the developer, I am in a better position to understand the objects than I was with previous versions of Access. But screen real-estate is limited and descriptions are usually terse, so if this client has followed good naming conventions, I can also learn much about the application from its object names.

If the hypothetical client used my naming conventions, the Database window for tables might look something like the one in Figure 5.3 and from it I could divine the following:

▶ The application tracks customer and order information. (Okay, I didn't really need naming conventions to figure that out.)

▶ The master product list resides in a Microsoft SQL Server database (tsql).

▶ Order information is collected in a local table (tbl) and also summarized into a work table (tsum), perhaps for management reporting or batch checksums.

▶ There are several lookup tables (tlkp) to fill combo and list boxes during data entry.

▶ The user makes temporary backups of the order table (zttbl) on a daily basis.

▶ The customer table is currently under development (_tbl) and not in production.

Fig. 5.3

The table names in this Database window are self-documenting.

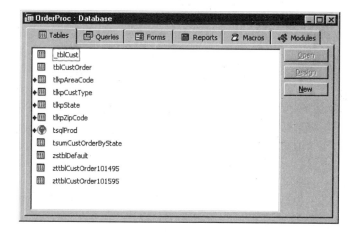

Team Development

When multiple developers are working on the same project, having a common methodology helps pull them together as a team. With a written set of standards and objectives, individuals can work together more effectively as in the following:

▶ Predefined standards remove the variability introduced by individual styles and prevent the "turf wars" that can occur when champions of conflicting styles get together.

▶ Predefined standards ensure that objects are interchangeable among team members. Developers can share objects created by each other and understand them more easily through their knowledge of the standards applied to the objects during development.

▶ New team members feel less intimidated when the expectations for them are clearly defined (as in, "Please code to this written standard"). Existing team members can be reassigned to new responsibilities with an equally clear sense of direction.

▶ Departing team members can be replaced with less expense because their replacements can quickly understand the inherited application's architecture and code.

When creating application development standards, including naming conventions, the expected benefit for team development can be summarized this way: Any member of the team should be able to quickly navigate and comprehend the application's object and program structure as if it were his or her own.

The code shown in Listing 5.1 provides an illustration of these points. Reading this code for the first time, you should easily see what the author intends for the code to do (to sum up data items from a transaction table). Not only are the base names descriptive, but the prefixes in front of the variable names also enable the reader to know the context of a variable when it's seen anywhere in the same code routine.

Listing 5.1   AES_NAMG.Mdb—Dim Statements Using Specific Conventions

```
Public Function CustOrdrSum(rlngCustID As Long) As Currency

    Dim curOrdrSum   As Currency
    Dim dbs          As Database
    Dim rstOrdrSum   As Recordset
    Dim varValidTest As Variant

    Set dbs = CurrentDb()
    Set rstOrdrSum = __
      dbs.OpenRecordset("SELECT * FROM tblCustOrdr WHERE CustID = " _
      & rlngCustID, dbOpenDynaset)
    rstOrdrSum.MoveFirst

    Do While Not rstOrdrSum.EOF
       curOrdrSum = curOrdrSum + rstOrdrSum!Amount
       rstOrdrSum.MoveNext
    Loop
    CustOrdrSum = curOrdrSum

End Function
```

Making Access Easier to Use

Users new to naming conventions and similar standards often complain that the conventions require extra time to implement and that they slow down the pace of development. While it is true that any new system involves an investment of time to learn, good standards will always save time, not cost time, in the long run. Also, applying consistent standards eventually becomes second-nature and requires minimal or no extra development effort.

Consider the Object Browser in Access 97. When you create a new form and view it in the Object Browser dialog box, you'll see exactly 154 built-in methods and properties listed for the form. The list is quite crowded before you've written one line of code. After you have written several code procedures in the form module, using the Object Browser to find those procedures among the several hundred total method and property items listed can be very time consuming. Figure 5.4 shows two code procedures (`Validate` and `WidgetCost`) aligned alphabetically with other items in the Object Browser.

Fig. 5.4

These two functions sort in the Object Browser by their names.

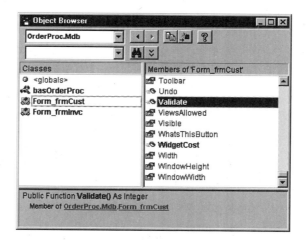

Now let's apply a simple naming convention to the two procedures in Figure 5.4. Because these are form module procedures (often called "code behind forms"), we will prefix all the form's functions (and subs) with `cbf`. Placing these characters before the name sorts all form procedures with this naming convention together in the Object Browser. Figure 5.5 shows how the new sort order makes it much easier to go quickly to a specific routine or to find a routine when you don't know its precise name because all the form's procedures sort together.

Fig. 5.5

These two functions sort in the Object Browser by their type.

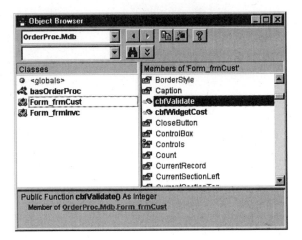

As a further example, consider what happens when you rename a table (or field, form, or any other object) in an application; for example, changing the table name CustOrdr to CustOrder. You will have to globally find and replace every reference to the original name CustOrdr in all of your code. When you do so, the name may occur in other contexts than as a table name, making for a slow replacement process as you read through each match and check the context. For example, in Listing 5.2, you may only want to change one of the four references to CustOrdr—the one that is a table reference—during your bulk replace operation.

Listing 5.2   AES_NAMG.Mdb—Basic Function with Multiple Occurrences of the String *CustOrdr*

```
Public Function CustOrdrArchive() As Integer

  Dim dbs     As Database
  Dim CustOrdr As Recordset

  Set CustOrdr = dbs.OpenRecordset("CustOrdr", dbOpenDynaset)
...
```

If, however, a unique naming convention was applied so that the table name was originally tblCustOrdr, the code in Listing 5.2 would have one reference to the target string (in the OpenRecordset method), not four. Your find and replace operation would be more precise and more rapid.

Leveraging Your Techniques

The final benefit in the list of naming convention justifications is the ability to extend your development environment and techniques by leveraging your naming conventions. Good object naming habits should enhance your ability to document an application, create tools and utilities, create reusable code libraries, and otherwise increase your productivity.

For example, with Access, you can create powerful add-ins and other tools using Visual Basic for Applications code. My company tapped into this power and developed our own set of documentation tools to analyze databases and create documentation files. The documentation routines take quite some time to run on large databases and produce large output files.

Because we use naming conventions, we can selectively disable documenting entire groups of objects by their type, thus saving time and disk space. Specifically, we might tell the documentation routines only to document entry/edit forms and their subforms (our objects with prefixes of `frm` and `fsub`), and to skip all switchboard menus (`fmnu`), dialog forms (`fdlg`), and all lookup table forms (`flkp`).

As another example, assume you use a common set of lookup tables and their forms in most of your applications, and you give these objects unique character prefixes. You could write a simple wizard to import specific objects from a master database. Your wizard could look to a template database and import all the lookup-type objects from there. If naming conventions are used, lookup objects are easily identified because all lookup forms in your template database might begin with `flkp` and all lookup tables with `tlkp`. It's not hard for your wizard to grab such lookup tables and forms on demand based on their unique prefix characters.

Even if you don't create your own tools, naming conventions facilitate better use of the tools in Access itself. For example, in the introductory section of this chapter, I demonstrated standardizing the abbreviation for `Customer` to `Cust` throughout a particular application. With this kind of standardization in place, all customer tables, queries, forms, reports, and macros in a system should have the string `Cust` in their base name somewhere. (In fact, in my world, even VBA variables that worked with the customer-related objects would have `Cust` somewhere in their name.)

Therefore, if you were looking for a particular set of program routines in your application, you could use the Access search engine to search all modules for the string `Cust`. You would quite successfully find all code routines for customer objects if you used such a convention consistently. Applying naming conventions to your daily work this way can be quite a time saver.

Naming Convention Considerations

I summarized the objectives I think of as most important when developing a naming convention. Before choosing or developing a style of your own, first list your own objectives if they are different from mine. Next, decide what considerations will affect the development of your conventions.

To create a style, keep the following four considerations in mind:

> ▶ *Be consistent.* If you take the trouble to create a naming style, apply it uniformly over a long period of time. Don't change elements of the style every time someone lobs a criticism or suggestion at it (see the sidebar). The reason you create a style is to guide your long-term development strategy and to provide a foundation of common elements across multiple projects and applications. Therefore, your naming conventions should be more like a rock foundation than sand.

For example, I've used Apvd as an abbreviation for Approved in database structures for at least ten years. In our dBASE and R:BASE days when names were very short, we needed the space. Now, Access lets us use longer names, but we still use Apvd. Why? Because consistency makes our lives easier.

When clients call and say, "We'd like to create a status report driven by approval date—where do we start?" I don't have to think hard or dig for their documentation or restore their application from a tape. Instead, I can tell them immediately to look in their structure for the field ApvdDate. Whether their application is one or ten years old, I know the answer without looking it up because we've always used that name and spelling, and we probably always will.

Of Hobgoblins and Small Minds

While my efforts over the last several years to help standardize VBA naming conventions have met with mostly favorable reception, there have been a few detractors as well. And, much to my amusement, a large portion of the people who tirade against naming conventions include some variation of this same quote in their messages to me, year after year: "Consistency is the hobgoblin of small minds."

I wonder if people who use this quote for their purposes truly believe what it says. Do they really conclude that all people who choose to drive consistently on the right side of the road and stop at red lights have small minds? Do they think that things like consistently on-time airline arrivals and departures are a sign of low intellect among airline pilots and FAA personnel?

I could go on, but obviously from my perspective, consistency is in no way an evil thing. Using naming conventions faithfully does not imply that you are small-minded and a shallow thinker. Quite the opposite is true—it shows that you are smart enough to create repeatable systems to automate your mundane tasks, free up your rather large mind, and float unhindered toward higher purposes!

As a footnote, I find it equally amusing that not one person who has used this quote against naming conventions has actually used the exact quote correctly. It reads, "A foolish consistency is the hobgoblin of little minds" (Ralph Waldo Emerson). Notice that Emerson wasn't actually against consistency, only the foolish use of it. But, of course, people who twist this quote for their own purposes can't be expected to quote him consistently, right?

5

▶ *Plan ahead.* If you know where the feature sets of your development products are going or have a long-term development strategy, let such information influence your naming conventions. Ideally, you never want to be forced to rename objects or rewrite code in a production application over its life span.

For example, we wrote our original naming conventions for Access years ago. With a limited set of object and variable types, we probably could have gotten by with one or two character naming prefixes as many developers do. We expected that someday other Microsoft Office applications would have much of the same capabilities as Access, so we used three characters in our object descriptors to give ourselves room to grow.

Now, several years later, our Access naming conventions are used in, or must coexist with, objects, procedures, and variables in Excel, Word, and so on (see Appendix C, "Leszynski Naming Conventions for Microsoft Solution Developers" on the CD-ROM). One- and two-character naming conventions would now be too limiting to develop a cross-application style for so many products, so we're glad we planned ahead.

▶ *There is no single correct answer.* Different developers have different goals. Different users have different needs. Consequently, there are many ways to approach development styles, and no specific naming convention is the correct one. What you are looking for is a tool that works for you now and later, not an answer to philosophical programming questions. As you will see in the following sections, naming conventions can be short or long, lead and follow object names, use many characters or few, and so on. No single approach works for everyone—there are as many approaches to naming conventions as there are creative thinkers.

> **An Abundance of Styles**
> In my dBASE and R:BASE days, there were few published styles and little debate on the subject, so we just used a style that worked best for us and kept it to ourselves. The Access and VBA worlds present a different situation. Since the publication of our original Access naming conventions in 1992, we have received hundreds of e-mail and telephone suggestions and have reviewed more than a dozen other Access naming conventions, some derived from ours and others completely different. Developers, and even casual users, seem very interested in the subject and have widely differing opinions.

> ▶ *Weigh the build versus borrow decision.* With many people interested in the subject, there are obviously several standards from which to choose. The one proposed in the next chapter has unique merits that will be described later, but it may not have value to you specifically. If not, you are left at a fork in the road facing the age-old build versus borrow decision.

Up one fork of the road (build) is the hard task of creating your own naming conventions. You can do this from scratch, using the objectives, considerations, and techniques learned in this chapter. Or you can review other published conventions and extract from them parts that meet your needs, filling in the gaps and creating a hybrid.

Up the other fork in the road is the decision to take an existing convention (borrow) and apply it as is. If you are new to Access development, this route may be the easiest. You can ask other developers for suggestions on what style they use. Also, you can check the Access forum on CompuServe (GO MSACCESS and search for the keyword naming), surf the Internet, browse other books by Access developers, and review the major Access and Visual Basic periodicals.

With a foundation of objectives and considerations, let's delve into the specific mechanics of naming conventions. You will want to consider each of the topics in the remainder of this chapter as you develop your style.

Creating Object Base Names

If you used no naming conventions at all, each object would still have a name of some sort. For tables, queries, and other database objects, these names are usually descriptive, such as Salespeople or FriendsOfMine. For program variables, programmers are usually more economical: The classic Dim I As Integer statement for loop variables comes to mind. You could call this starting point (Salespeople, FriendsOfMine, or I) the initial name, primary name, base name, or perhaps root name. For our purposes here, I use the term base name to describe the starting point when you name a particular object.

A strategy for selecting, abbreviating, capitalizing, and organizing object base names is, in and of itself, a naming convention. Therefore, if you do nothing more than create a consistent approach to base names, you have authored a development style for yourself. What topics would you include in a convention for base names? Let's examine the needs of specific Access objects.

 Note

Whether or not to use capitalization and punctuation schemes in your object names is discussed in the "Capitalizing and Punctuating" section that follows the discussions of individual object naming strategies. Normally, styles for capitalization and punctuation are applied uniformly within a convention rather than varying by object type.

Table Base Names

When naming tables, your standard should specify a desired target length for names. Some developers prefer things very terse and use the shortest name they can read. (Although that doesn't ensure that others can read it!) One Access naming convention I reviewed suggested limiting table names to eight characters to be compatible with dBASE and FoxPro formats! I find such short names to be totally non-intuitive to read and would not recommend such a restrictive approach unless you routinely move your Access data to a platform with shorter name restrictions.

I spent a decade working on products with eight-character names and I'm happy to be free of that bondage. While most users can infer that `CustInfo` is the customer information table, far fewer will recognize that `InStTxSl` is the table for "in-state taxable sales," because it could just as easily be the "installed steel in Texas's silos."

At the other end of the spectrum, some developers prefer longer names that are fully descriptive. Long names may even refer to the source or range of the data. Examples include `MainEuropeanCustomerData`, `north region sales summary from db2`, and `WidgetProductionStatisticsFirstQuarter1997`. While these names are valid in Access, they become rather unwieldy when you use them in your application—for example, in the query grid or in SQL statements and other strings in VBA code.

For table names, as with most things in life, moderation is probably the best approach. If you create a set of standard abbreviations for your development (see "Abbreviating

Object Names" later in this chapter) and remove extraneous words, you can create table names that are not overly long and yet are fully descriptive. I prefer to keep table names to 15 characters or fewer through the use of standard abbreviations. At most, I use a 30 character absolute limit for my table names, so they can upsize eventually to SQL Server without exceeding that product's length limitation.

Another justification for modest table name lengths is that table names often become part of the base name for other objects that depend on them, thus long table names breed even longer names for queries, forms, and reports. For example, a table `Customer` would probably have several queries based on it, like `CustomerSalesSummary`, `CustomerByRegion`, for instance. The longer the table name, the longer the names derived from it.

The final consideration affecting table name length is a very pragmatic one. The Access user interface provides limited real estate in property pages, combo boxes, and other objects that list table names. Table names wider than the display space that Access provides are difficult to view and work with in the user interface. Table 5.1 shows the default width in average characters displayed by the Access 97 user interface in various places. As you can see from the different widths listed, table names longer than 30 characters are routinely truncated, and even those longer than 15 characters will sometimes be trimmed when displayed.

Table 5.1   Default Average Display Width of Table Names

User Interface Item	Default Width (Characters)
Form Record Source Property	30
Form/Report Wizard Source Object	25
Query Design Grid Field List	15
Query Design Grid Table Combo	17
Macro Action Argument	32

In addition to the areas listed in Table 5.1, table names appear in your query SQL statements and in your VBA code as `Recordset` sources and SQL parameters. Table names are the most widespread object names in a typical application. Something that gets that much usage deserves a few moments of your quality thought when you give it a name.

Finally, I prefer to keep my table names singular (`Customer`) rather than plural (`Customers`). By implication, a table is always plural because it contains more than one record, so why waste one or more characters (to form a plural) everywhere you use its name? Whether you prefer singular or plural names, remember to pick one approach and apply it uniformly. I frequently see other developers mix and match singular and plural object names, and some confusion can arise when users try to decide whether they should enter more than one record in tables with singular names or only in tables with plural names.

In the discussion of table name length above, I noted three sample table names that were long enough to be problematic for us. I'll now restate those names, along with a suggestion of how I would rename them based on the factors we've just considered, as follows:

- `MainEuropeanCustomerData`. I find `CustEurope` equally effective. `Main` and `Data` seem redundant. (What else would be in a table but data?) Also, I can apply an abbreviation to `Customer`.

- `North region sales summary from db2`. I much prefer mixed case names without spaces, so I would use `tsumNRegionSaleDB2` instead. I can abbreviate `North`, use one of my standard tags (`tsum`) for summary tables to convey the fact that this is not raw data, and eliminate `From` to save keystrokes with no loss of meaning.

- `WidgetProductionStatisticsFirstQuarter1997`. I can use my standard abbreviation (see the following section) to shorten `Statistics`, assume that most users know it's a production-oriented database and drop `Production`, and shorten the year and period. That leaves me with the name `WidgetStats97Q1`. Why did I move the quarters after the year? See the section "Sorting Object Names" later in this chapter for an explanation.

An object naming convention rarely stops with base names, but if you have no need for more elaborate conventions, simply apply the forethought described in this section to table names to develop standards for good base names and make your application development and usage more pleasant.

Table Field Base Names

The considerations discussed in the preceding "Table Base Names" section apply to any discussion of field names as well, including the following:

- Keep the names short but readable.
- Use standardized abbreviations.
- Be consistent in applying singular versus plural.

Because a table holds many different types of information and a field holds only one, it is easier to shorten field names than table names. Whatever target you select for table name length, your field name standard length should be less than or equal to, but not longer than, the standard for table names. Like table names, field names appear in the user interface in property dialog boxes, the query grid, the macro action grid, and so on, and each of these areas has display-width limitations for object names. You will find that sticking with field names around 20 characters long removes most annoying truncations in the Access 97 user interface.

One common discussion that arises during the development of field naming conventions involves the order of compound elements in the name. Some compound name ordering questions are easily resolved—LastName is generally thought to be a more readable field name than NameLast. Other names are equally adequate in any order, such as date field names like ClosedDate versus DateClosed. And, because field names usually appear in the Access user interface in natural order rather than sorted, the sort order of field names does not have a large impact on your development.

If you opt for the style ApvdDate and ClosedDate, you are placing more weight on the content part of the base name rather than the data type. If you opt instead for DateApvd and DateClosed, you are placing more emphasis on the type of field. I view this latter style as the more dangerous of the two because when you carry it out to its logical conclusion, it may lead to confusing names. For example, CommentMgr is a name for the Manager Comment field that places emphasis on the type, and this name is less accurate than MgrComment. A type-based construction becomes essentially unworkable beyond date and time fields.

Query Base Names

As noted in the "Table Base Names" section earlier in this chapter, many query names are built around the primary table or tables in the query. Therefore, query names are longer on average than table names. One reason I had suggested 15 character table names is so that the length of query names built around short table names will also be reasonable.

Refer to Table 5.1 where I listed maximum display sizes for table names, and note that the Access 97 interface provides 30 characters or fewer of table name display space by default. In every case, the user interface areas in the table listing can also display query names, so to keep query names to 30 characters, building them around table base names of 10 to 15 characters is a good rule of thumb.

Having decided on a target length for query names, applying the standard can become a challenge. It is harder to be terse with query names than table names because queries perform actions on data or change the presentation of data. A good query name must express the actions it performs on the data. To solve this problem without being verbose, I prefer to use prefix and suffix characters placed around the query base name to express the query's actions succinctly, rather than including action information in the base name.

For example, a query to delete all dormant sales prospects could have a base name like Cold Prospects Delete or perhaps DeleteDormantSalesProspects. For my tastes, these are both too wordy, and they marry the action too closely to the base name. My preferred approach would be to keep the base name simple, SalesProsCold, and describe the action using a prefix or suffix. Using this approach, the base name describes a group of records independent of the action so it can be reused in various related objects. Adding an action prefix or suffix to this query would allow for multiple "flavors" of the same base name: qselSalesProsCold, qdelSalesProsCold, and qupdSalesProsCold.

Finally, I prefer to keep my query names singular (Customer) rather than plural (Customers) because a query is usually plural by its nature. Select a pluralization scheme for your queries and apply it uniformly.

Form and Report Base Names

Because form and report names are less widespread throughout both your application and the Access user interface (they appear mainly in OpenForm/OpenReport actions and in the Database window), you have more leeway on the length of their names than with other object names. Access allows object names up to 64 characters long, but few people find that such long names are usable in practice.

You may want to establish a name length standard for form and report names. Like queries, forms and reports are based most often on a source table or tables and the object name derived from the source table names. Therefore, I would suggest using the same name length guidelines you establish for query names as your form and report name guidelines. More important than discussing length is establishing rules for constructing the names of these objects.

There can be many different kinds of forms. Forms can be dialog boxes, switchboard menus, data entry screens, record edit screens, form/subform combinations, record selection lists, floating (pop-up) text or utilities, and more. Similarly, reports can provide detail, summaries, computations (totals, averages, and the like), access to legacy (mainframe) data, and so on. Therefore, how to convey a form's or report's purpose to users and developers without being wordy should be the primary focus of your conventions for these objects.

Consider a form to edit customer orders. It is possible to create an Access form with customers on the main form, orders in the subform, and order details in the subform's subform. The driving table for the main form is the customer table, but the primary purpose of the form is to get to the order details. So, is the form's base name Customer, CustomerEdit, CustomerOrder, Customer Order Detail Edit, or one of a dozen other possibilities? This is an example of the types of problems you should think through clearly as you create your naming conventions. Good conventions should help you and your co-developers approach such problems with ease.

How would I solve this specific dilemma? Our conventions require that the base name of the primary table be a part of the form or report name. It could be argued that the primary table here is the one that provides the most detail to the form (`CustOrdrDet` on the subform), not the one driving the main form (`Cust`). Therefore, I would name the form `frmCustOrdrDet`; if there were two varieties of the form, I'd use `frmCustOrdrDetAdd` and `frmCustOrdrDetEdit`.

Similar questions arise for reports and can be addressed with the same approach. The standards you create for form base names should be applied to reports in identical fashion. Report names tend to be even longer than query and form names because you will often have several types of a particular report: a detail version, a summary version, and versions that group, sort, and total differently to meet specific needs. Your standard should address how to differentiate these versions with a minimum number of characters; a good abbreviation system will be especially useful here.

Subform and subreport naming conventions sometimes specify that the base name of the parent form is reflected in the base name of the subform or subreport. This strategy becomes challenging, however, if you create subforms/subreports that reside in more than one form/report. Your naming convention for subforms and subreports should address how to handle this contingency, most commonly by giving the subform/ subreport a base name that describes the data that it's bound to, not the parent object(s).

Control Base Names

When you create a bound control on an Access form or report, the control automatically inherits the field name of the bound `ControlSource` as its name. This approach is adequate for most purposes and relieves any responsibility from you for assigning a base name that may be lacking in two areas.

The first concern is a practical one. You cannot evaluate some expressions on forms and reports when the name of the control is the same as the name of a table field in the object's `recordset`. For example, if the following expression is used as the `ControlSource` for a report control named `Qty` in a report whose `RecordSource` also contains a `Qty` field, the report displays `#Error` instead of the proper calculation:

```
=IIf([Qty]<100,"Low",[Qty])
```

The situation created here is called a circular reference, in that Access does not know whether to evaluate `[Qty]` in the expression as the table field with that name or the control with that name. Giving the report control a name that's different from the bound field name, such as `txtQty`, solves the problem.

The second concern is more esoteric, but in the same vein. Philosophically, should the name of a control, that is an object, be the same as that of a field, which is also an object but of a different class? I would argue no.

The objective of naming bound controls differently from their related fields is easily implemented simply by applying a naming convention to the control name. Thus, the control's base name can be exactly the same as the bound field's name with the addition of prefix characters to prevent circular references.

For unbound controls, determining the approach for base names is not quite so obvious. An unbound control may accept user inputs, display the result of an expression, or provide program code with a temporary workspace for values. Thus, my recommendation would be to apply the same logic stated previously for naming table fields. For example, if your naming convention would produce a field name of `LastName` rather than `NameLast`, you would use the same rules to produce an unbound control base name `FullName` as opposed to `NameFull`.

5

Macro Base Names

Macro names are even less widespread in your application than form and report names. They appear primarily in event properties for forms and reports where Access 97 by default displays about 30 characters of space. You may want to consider this character count as a reasonable limit for macro names.

As part of your development strategy, you may have already decided how related actions will be grouped into macros. One common approach is to place all the macros for a specific form or report into one macro group. If you follow this convention, the macro base name would include the base name of the associated form or report. If you create individual macros for each form or report event, consider showing the event name or an abbreviation in the macro name, for example `mfrmCustCurrent` and `mfrmCust_AftUpd`.

Because creating distinct macros for each form or report control event could lead to hundreds of macros, you will most likely group such macros together by control or even by form. If you are grouping by control, consider including both the form and control name in the macro name for clarity—`mfrmCustTxtCustName`, or perhaps `mfrmCust_txtCustName`.

Table 5.2 shows examples of abbreviated form and report event names that keep the macro names as short as possible.

Table 5.2 Examples of Abbreviations for Event Names

Form/Report/Control Event	Abbreviation
Activate	Actv
AfterDelConfirm	AftDC
AfterInsert	AftIns
AfterUpdate	AftUpd
ApplyFilter	AppFlt
BeforeDelConfirm	BefDC
BeforeInsert	BefIns
BeforeUpdate	BefUpd
Change	Change
Click	Click
Close	Close
Current	Currnt
DblClick	DClick
Deactivate	Deactv
Delete	Delete
Enter	Enter
Error	Error
Exit	Exit
Filter	Filter
Format	Format
GotFocus	GotFoc
KeyDown	KeyDn
KeyPress	KeyPr
KeyUp	KeyUp
Load	Load
LostFocus	LstFoc
MouseDown	MseDn
MouseMove	MseMv
MouseUp	MseUp
NoData	NoData

Form/Report/Control Event	Abbreviation
NotInList	NIList
Open	Open
Page	Page
Print	Print
Resize	Resiz
Retreat	Retrt
Timer	Timer
Unload	Unlod
Updated	Updat

5

Notice how the number of characters used in the abbreviations is not fixed. Rather, my goal in this example is to express the event name as clearly as possible in four to six characters, targeting the least number of characters to maintain readability. For an expanded discussion of abbreviations, see the section "Abbreviating Object Names" later in this chapter.

The names of generic macros (not attached to one object) are subject to much the same discussion as are modules, so refer to the discussion of module base names in the following section.

Module Base Names

Module names are usually meaningless to users (who never view your code), so they often follow the convention that is most convenient for the application developers. Your coding standards may already dictate how related procedures will be grouped into modules. In such a case, the module name will or should reflect the type of procedures it contains. You or fellow developers should be able to quickly determine the most logical module to look in to find a specific code routine. To accomplish this, your module names will generally be longer and more specific than names of other objects, for example, basAPIRoutines_FromMSDN or basAPIRoutines_Registry.

Unlike the organization of macros discussed above, you usually will not place procedures for one specific form or report into a module; such code would be stored instead with the form or report. If some need arose to group procedures for a specific object together, however, these guidelines for including the object's base name in the module name would apply.

Procedure Base Names

Naming code procedures (functions and subs) is often a very whimsical task. Some applications involve hundreds of procedures and thousands of lines of code, yet the average developer gives no more than a second of thought to naming a new procedure. Procedure names are often repeated (called) in many other procedures, so they become more unwieldy as they grow longer. On the flip side, procedure names usually cannot be descriptive in a mere 10 or 15 characters. Your naming convention should prescribe techniques to find a balance between names that are too long and too short. Using abbreviations can help keep your procedure names short.

Some developers create a naming convention of leading or trailing characters to delineate functions from subs. You should consider whether this technique is useful for you or not. In practical application, subs sometimes become functions later (see Chapter 11, "Expert Approaches to VBA"). Therefore, I don't identify the type of procedure in the name (such as subLogin), but it would be a perfectly legitimate thing to do if it suited your needs.

It may also be useful for you to formalize the construction of your procedure names. Consider these three function names, which all could describe the same function:

```
DatabaseName()
GetDatabaseName()
DbsNameGet()
```

There is nothing inherently wrong with any of these names. The function name DatabaseName() is too broad for my liking, however, because I can't tell by looking if it retrieves or sets a database name. The second option, GetDatabaseName(), is better because the leading action verb tells me more specifically what the function does.

If I consistently apply the philosophies in this chapter, however, I should arrive at a preference for the name DbsNameGet() for two reasons. First, the name begins by describing the object then the action. Because I prefer my object names to achieve some end result with respect to sorting, this convention causes similar routines to sort by object. DbsNameGet() and DbsNameSet() would sort together in procedure lists; the alternate construction GetDbsName() and SetDbsName() would cause them to sort farther apart by action. In general, I prefer first to place the object name then place the verb when naming procedures. You should decide for yourself whether you prefer this order or the reverse.

Second, the name includes a standard abbreviation to keep it short. In this case, the abbreviation used is the most readily available—our descriptor for database objects.

Capitalizing and Punctuating

On the surface, it would seem nonsensical to ask the question: "Who doesn't use upper- and lowercase mixtures in their object names?" The answer may surprise you.

As an example, before version 6.0, SQL Server's default installation mode made it case sensitive with respect to object names, including table and field names. This led Access developers who intended to migrate the database schema to SQL Server later to prefer lowercase names for tables and fields. Otherwise, when the application was upsized to the server, mixed-case object names had to be changed to lowercase and supporting objects and code had to be modified to reflect the rename. With SQL Server 6.x, however, the default (and preferred) installation mode is case insensitive, making it easier to upsize Access databases to the product without any name changes.

Also, I have met many developers who are religious about economizing keystrokes. Such people often work with lowercase object names to save their pinkie fingers thousands of visits to the Shift key on the keyboard each day. Conversely, developers who cut their teeth in the years before personal computers can remember terminals that had no lowercase letters. They may work mostly in uppercase out of habit.

Considering these points, it is true that the majority of developers work with mixed case when naming objects. Each independent part of an object's name is treated as a proper name, with the initial letter capitalized. Thus, a customer's personal information goes into a table named CustomerPersonalInformation or perhaps tblCustInfoPers.

The following are two caveats to consider with this simple capitalization rule:

▶ Other elements of your naming conventions do not automatically use mixed case simply because your base names do.

▶ Some people can't read object names clearly with only mixed case; they prefer punctuation.

Simply because your base names use upper- and lowercase does not automatically mean that your naming conventions should be mixed case. Some naming convention elements (leading items) are actually more effective in lowercase, as in the descriptor tbl in the previous paragraph. See the section "Applying Naming Conventions to Your Work," later in this chapter for a discussion on this point.

Also, mixing case may not automatically make object names readable. Some developers prefer to use additional punctuation to further improve readability. The first and most obvious option is to add spaces to names. Evaluate carefully whether or not this is a good option for your application and your overall style. Adding spaces to object names means that you will have to bracket the names (for example, [Customer Info]) when working with the objects in VBA code, macros, and expressions.

Spaces also remove the ability to easily upsize the application to a server platform, because virtually none of them support embedded spaces in object names. Finally, spaces in names make it more difficult for you to create tools or Data Access Object routines that involve any string parsing (separating component items), because you have to look for both brackets and multiple spaces in object names when grabbing them from inside a string or string variable.

In addition to spaces, I am basically sour on any kind of punctuation in object names except for underscores. This ensures that I can move data from the Access application to other platforms without a rename. For example, SQL Server allows only letters, digits, $, #, and underscores in names. Visual FoxPro is even more restrictive, allowing only letters, digits, and underscores.

I also frown on using characters in one context that have a different meaning in another context; I would rather be more consistent even if Access doesn't require me to be. For example, the apostrophe is a comment marker in VBA code but a valid character in Access object names. If I see apostrophes in object names, my brain thinks that the part of the name after the apostrophe is a comment! You will have to decide just how restrictive to make your naming conventions in this respect.

When punctuating names by using underscores, consider whether they should be allowed at all locations in a name or only in certain contexts. Although a table named `tbl_Customer_Info_Archive` is certainly readable, I don't want to spend my life adding that many underscores to all object names as I type. In the discussion of qualifiers and suffixes later in this chapter, you will see that underscores may be of great value in specific contexts.

Abbreviating Object Names

Earlier in the chapter you discovered that using standardized abbreviations can be useful in shortening object names without losing meaning. Typically, when the design phase of an application is completed and table and field names are being finalized, you should look for opportunities to apply your standard abbreviations or to create new abbreviations needed for the project. The tables in the "Standardized Terminology" section in Chapter 6, "Leszynski Naming Conventions for Access," show a list of some of the standardized abbreviations my company has created and used consistently over the years.

Abbreviations that we use tend to fall in the three- to five-character range, although some variances occur for clarity. Few words require more than five characters to convey the original word with no loss of readability or meaning. Also note how many characters you can eliminate in an object name when you use abbreviations—in the case of `admin` as a short form of `administration`, nine characters are saved.

When creating standard abbreviations, some developers establish restrictive rules for abbreviating. For example, I've seen conventions using a rule like this: Remove all vowels past the first character until five characters remain. If the abbreviation has fewer than five characters, add back vowels from left to right until a five-character length is achieved. Table 5.3 shows a few of our standard abbreviations and the revised abbreviation using the stated, stricter rule.

Table 5.3   Leszynski Company Abbreviations Contrasted with Strict, 5-character Consonant-centric Abbreviations

Term	Our Abbreviation	Revised Abbreviation
accounting	Actg	Accnt
administration	Admin	Admns
approved	Apvd	Apprv
authorized	Auth	Athrz
beginning	Beg	Bgnnn
building	Bldg	Bldng
record	Rec	Recrd

Witness the dramatic difference in abbreviations using the harsh rule. The revised abbreviations are, in my opinion, less obvious than our original versions in four of the six cases. Abbreviating `beginning` as `bgnnn` is particularly unusable. As opposed to a firm abbreviation rule, our approach to abbreviating is more pragmatic: Using as few characters as possible, convey the full term using characters from the term or an acceptable shorthand. (The "acceptable shorthand" clause lets us use commonly accepted contractions like `xsfr` for `transfer`.)

This example drives home an important point about abbreviations and, by inference, about naming conventions in general: Your rules for naming objects should be flexible enough to serve the ultimate objectives, not restrictive for their own sake.

Sorting Object Names

At this point in the chapter, you've wallowed through the philosophy of object base names, how to shorten them, and how to standardize abbreviations. With a strategy for shorter and meaningful base names in place, the remaining piece of the puzzle is a strategy for ordering the components of base names.

I showed the example of shortening the table name
`WidgetProductionStatisticsFirstQuarter1997` to `WidgetStats97Q1`. Why did I select this
particular order for segments of the name? I did it with sorting in mind.

By design, the Access Database window and various combo box lists in Access sort object
names alphabetically. When I name related objects (those with similarities in the base
name), I want them to sort close together so that they appear consecutively in ordered
lists. So, the first rule I apply is to start with the most important part of the name at the
left. If every object dealing with widgets begins with `Widget`, the objects will sort together.
Next would come the second most important part of the name, then the third, and so
forth.

Notice in the example at hand that I changed the trailing `FirstQuarter1997` portion of the
example table name to `97Q1`, a convention that ensures that similar object names will sort
by year, then quarter, producing a list like this:

`WidgetStats96Q3`

`WidgetStats96Q4`

`WidgetStats97Q1`

`WidgetStats97Q2`

 Tip
In the prior example, I abbreviated 1996 and 1997 in the object names as 96 and
97. For objects that have a short lifespan, such abbreviations are acceptable. However, if your objects or data will persist past the turn of the century, you should
begin using full year designations now, otherwise sort orders will be affected in
2000. For example, "99" items will sort *after* "00" items, but "1999" items will properly sort before "2000" items (all other things being equal).

Figure 5.6 shows a well-ordered Database window for which consideration has been
given to making the query names sort in a logical sequence.

Fig. 5.6

These query names sort in a logical sequence.

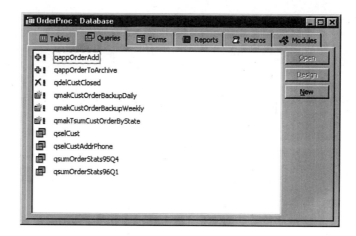

Developing Naming Convention Tags

With conventions firmly in hand for object base names, you can proceed to creating the wrappers around the base name that provide extra information and capabilities. The most important, in my view, are tags (see Figure 5.7).

Fig. 5.7

The form controls in this list are easily identified by their three-character tags.

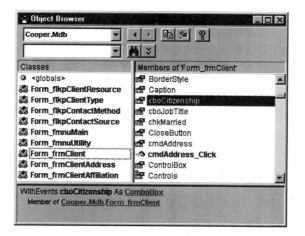

In the 80s, a Microsoft programmer named Charles Simonyi wrote a paper titled, "Program Identifier Naming Conventions," which some people point to as the beginning of formalized C language naming conventions. Actually, Simonyi's article was narrowly confined to (non-object-oriented) C programming and concentrated on philosophical as well as practical issues. Nevertheless, it was one of the first times in print that the issue of variable names was analyzed broadly. The paper also popularized the terms "tag" (a short prefix) and "qualifier" (a scope limiter placed after the tag), that are still in common use today. (Although before the terms existed, programmers were still using the concept. For example, we used one-character variable tags in our dBASE and R:BASE work starting in 1984.)

For our purposes here, I'll use tag to mean a set of characters placed against an object base name to characterize it. In object-oriented programming terms, the tag is somewhat analogous to an identifier for the "class" (a definition of a unique object type). The biggest challenges for you as you define your naming style are to define the following:

▶ Whether to use tags

▶ Where tags should be placed

▶ The size for the tags in number of characters

▶ The specific tags themselves (I discuss qualifiers in the "Using Qualifiers and Suffixes" section later in this chapter)

You can place tags before (as in `qselCust` or `qdelCustClosed`; see Figure 5.8) or after (as in `Cust_QSel` or `CustClosed_QDel`; see Figure 5.9) an object's base name. As examples throughout this chapter have shown, I have standardized tag placement to come before the object name for my style. To be fair, however, I will discuss both placements in the following section. Placing tags in front of object names is sometimes called "Hungarian Notation" in reference to Charles Simonyi's nationality.

Fig. 5.8

These query names have leading tags and sort by type.

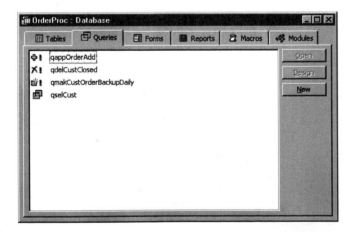

Fig. 5.9

*These query names
have trailing tags and
sort by base name.*

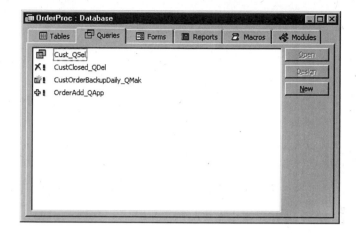

Fig. 5.9

*These query names
have trailing tags and
sort by base name.*

Why Use Tags on Names?

Why use tags at all? In an environment like Access, where terms such as object, class, and property are becoming more and more important, a base name by itself does not convey enough information for many developers. It can be very convenient to encapsulate within an object's name information about the type of the object (that is, its class and primary properties).

For example, reading through VBA code that executes a saved query whose name has no type information, you would have to look at the Database window to determine the type of query (indicated by its icon). A query name with a type tag on its base name, such as qdel for a delete query, is instantly recognizable in your code as to its type or class. This can provide programming benefits such as enhanced program readability and fewer coding errors.

In addition to these advantages for VBA programmers, the following are a few other benefits of tags:

▶ Leading tags on tables and queries cause them to sort by object type in lists where the objects are combined in the Access user interface (for example, all qry objects, then all tbl objects).

▶ Leading tags on database objects cause them to sort by the type (the tag) first and the name second, grouping items by their class and properties.

▶ Highly detailed leading tags on objects cause them to sort by subtype within their type group (for example, all qapp append queries, then all qdel delete queries, then all qmak make-table queries, and so forth).

▶ Highly detailed trailing tags on database objects provide object type information with a minimum of extra characters and no penalty on sort order.

▶ Tags on form and report controls remove ambiguity (they differentiate the control name from its bound field).

▶ Tags on program variables remove any need to review a variable's Dim statement to discern its type. They also remove the danger of assignment errors (where a variable's value is affected unintentionally through math with or assignment to a non-identical type).

As the examples above imply, you can have tags that are broad (qry for query) or detailed (qdel for delete query). You must weigh the advantage of the detailed versions—they are more informative—against the added cost of creating, learning, using, and maintaining a larger number of tags.

The placement of tags can become a hotly debated issue as you standardize: Are tags that precede a name better for us than those that follow the name? As the listings in the previous figures point out, tags placed on objects in sorted lists cause them to sort by type before name. But casual users are least interested in an object's type, so they will be the first to deride leading tags.

Some programmers also prefer to scan an object list and see the base name as the primary sort order. With such individuals around, you might opt for trailing tags.

 Note

To recap, programmers who are more interested in an object's properties than its name (as I am) will usually opt for the leading tag scheme, while coders who are focused on base names will place tags after that element.

If you have decided to use tags, next you need to determine which objects should be tagged. Consider each of the following Access objects as candidates for tags, and note the order of the list:

▶ Program variables and structures

▶ Queries

▶ Form controls

▶ Report controls

▶ Forms

▶ Reports

▶ Tables

▶ Macros

▶ Modules

▶ Procedures

▶ Fields

I have ordered this list based on my experience reviewing many different conventions and talking with other developers. The list sorts from the most frequently to the least frequently used object naming conventions. In other words, most developers who use tags use them in VBA program code (the first item in the list), while very few developers who use tags use them on table fields (the last item in the list). The following is a short summary of each item on the list.

> *Program variable and structure tags* are the most widely used tags. As I mentioned earlier, the Microsoft FoxPro documentation even suggests variable type tags for FoxPro users. Most C programmers have used type tags for many years (some influenced by the Charles Simonyi paper referred to earlier in this chapter). As they become, or work with, Access developers, they influence the acceptance of tags for VBA variables and structures (used here to mean arrays, constants, and type definitions). The overwhelming majority of programmers who use tags in Access Basic coding place them in front of the base name. See Figure 5.10 for an example of leading variable tags.

Fig. 5.10

This VBA code demonstrates variable declarations that use type tags.

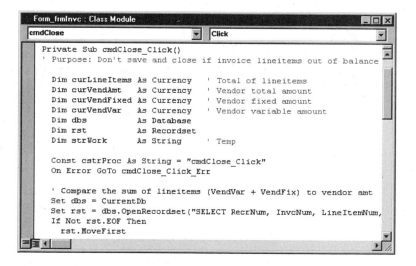

```
Form_frmInvc : Class Module                                    _ □ ×
cmdClose                          ▼   Click                          ▼
    Private Sub cmdClose_Click()
    ' Purpose: Don't save and close if invoice lineitems out of balance

        Dim curLineItems  As Currency    ' Total of lineitems
        Dim curVendAmt    As Currency    ' Vendor total amount
        Dim curVendFixed  As Currency    ' Vendor fixed amount
        Dim curVendVar    As Currency    ' Vendor variable amount
        Dim dbs           As Database
        Dim rst           As Recordset
        Dim strWork       As String      ' Temp

        Const cstrProc As String = "cmdClose_Click"
        On Error GoTo cmdClose_Click_Err

        ' Compare the sum of lineitems (VendVar + VendFix) to vendor amt
        Set dbs = CurrentDb
        Set rst = dbs.OpenRecordset("SELECT RecrNum, InvcNum, LineItemNum,
        If Not rst.EOF Then
            rst.MoveFirst
```

Query tags are also commonly used by advanced Access developers. Because queries perform actions (delete, update, and so on), their type is vitally important, so tags on query names usually convey the underlying action (see Figure 5.11). The other reason cited by most developers for query tags is to differentiate them from tables in certain lists and SQL statements (as noted in an early example in this chapter).

Fig. 5.11

Tags on query names cause them to sort separately from tables in wizard lists.

Form and report control tags help to distinguish the control's name from its ControlSource (if any), eliminating ambiguous references that can occur in code and in control expressions. As an added benefit, because leading control tags sort controls by their type in the Object Browser, control events sort similarly (see Figure 5.12).

Fig. 5.12

Tags on control names cause their events to sort by the tags first.

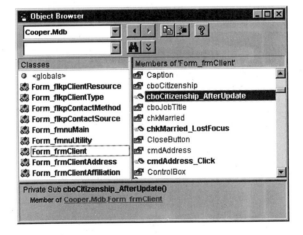

Form and report tags help to differentiate the various styles of forms and reports that can be created in Access. Different developers prefer different levels of detail in their form tags, but most who use tags distinguish databound forms (entry/edit) from subforms and from navigation forms (switchboard menus and dialog boxes), as shown in Figure 5.13. Less variety exists in report tags, which usually distinguish reports from subreports, and sometimes differentiate detail reports from summaries.

Fig. 5.13

These form tags provide a high degree of specific information about the type of form.

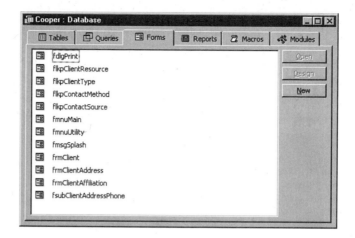

Table tags are lauded by developers who use them because different types of tables are often singled out for different treatments. For example, all summary tables (with a `tsum` tag) in an application might be deleted each night and rebuilt from mainframe data. Some developers prefer to keep their table names "pure," however, and use tags elsewhere in the application but not for tables. Figure 5.14 shows a database with table tags.

> **α Note**
>
> Refer to Appendix C, "Leszynski Naming Conventions for Microsoft Solution Developers," on the CD-ROM for insight into the difficulties provided when trying to standardize table tags in an application with multiple data platforms (Jet and SQL Server, in this case).

Fig. 5.14

Leading table tags group these tables by the type of data they contain or their role in the database.

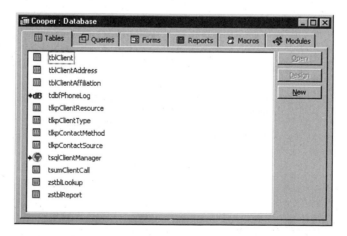

Macro tags are used by developers who rely heavily on macros and, to a lesser degree, by developers who write mostly VBA code. Before Access 97's command bars, the one constant about macros was that all developers used them to create menus. Therefore, many developers will identify menu macros by using tags (see Figure 5.15). Also, you can use an appropriate base name and tag combination scheme to specify macros for form and report events, as shown in the section "Macro Base Names" earlier in this chapter.

Fig. 5.15

These macro tags clearly identify form macros, general macros, menu macros, and report macros.

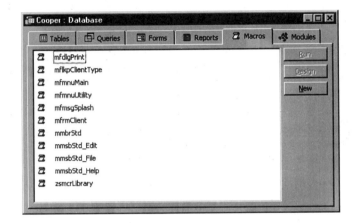

Module tags are one of the least necessary elements of an object naming strategy. Module names are not necessarily meaningful to users. Because module names usually do not appear in an application's user interface and application users are often excluded from the Database window, developers tend to give modules names that are descriptive only to coders as a matter of practice. Tags may not be necessary in such a scenario, however. If developers use tags to add additional detail, the tags tend to prescribe the type of procedures found in the module, as in the example in Figure 5.16.

Procedure tags are not frequently used. Descriptive function and subnames usually do not need clarification. One exception is my use of the tag cbf to group procedures in code behind forms and reports distinctly from event procedures. A few developers will prefix function names to designate a procedure's scope or return value (see Figure 5.17). Although this practice is not common, you should at least consider whether it has value in your situation.

Fig. 5.16
Module tags usually mean more to the developer than to the user.

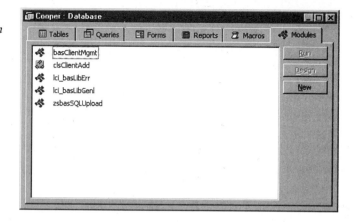

Fig. 5.17
Procedure tags can indicate a procedure's return value.

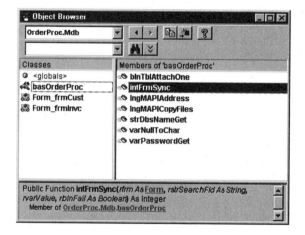

Field tags are also infrequently implemented. A few developers favor tagging a field name with the field's data type, but this strategy has a dangerous inherent risk and I dislike it. If the data type of a field changes, for example, from Integer to Long Integer as the user's needs expand, the field name must be changed throughout the application when the data type (and tag) changes. This includes changing all related queries, forms, reports, macros, and code—a very difficult process.

An alternative scheme to field data type tags that some developers use is to create a unique tag for each table in the database, for example cu_ for tblCustomer, and attach the tag to each field in that table. This strategy makes tables and their queries more self-documenting, and those who use it strongly believe in it.

I do not use the table name tag approach, however, unless requested by my client because I tend to design databases more around the concept of an integrated data dictionary. This concept states that a specific field name must represent the same data type and data content in all tables that contain it, thus counteracting the use of field tags that represent table names. In other words, the customer identifier field should be CustID in both the Cust and CustOrdr tables, rather than using a convention like cu_CustID and co_CustID for this primary key/foreign key pair. (While Jet does not strictly enforce a data dictionary in Access, you can apply the concept yourself through good schema design techniques. See Chapter 10, "Creating Expert Tables and Queries," for more information.)

Choosing Tag Length and Placement

Some developers use tags that are as short as a single character. While this certainly economizes on keystrokes, such tags are not very intuitive except in limited cases. For example, there are 11 intrinsic variable types in Access 97 VBA (not including the Data Access Objects, user-defined types, and specific object types), few enough that you could conceivably create a single-character tag for each.

Many developers like single-character tags because they use a minimum of keystrokes when added to an object's name. I feel that one-character tags are too obscure and limiting. (The limit is the 26 letters of the alphabet, which doesn't allow enough room for growth.) For an example of single character tags, see the Microsoft Visual FoxPro help file, which shows suggested single-character variable tags for FoxPro developers. In the FoxPro convention, the tag c is used for Character variables and the letter y denotes Currency types (see Table 5.4). An Access naming convention based on this model might use s for String variables and c for Currency. Most users would not find this notation intuitive at first glance, however.

Table 5.4 Single-Character Variable Tags Recommended by Microsoft in the Visual FoxPro Documentation

Variable Type	Tag
Array	a
Character	c
Currency	y
DateTime	t
Date	d
Double	b
Float	f

Variable Type	Tag
General	g
Logical	l
Numeric	n
Object	o
Unknown	u
Window	w

Like me, many developers find that single-character and even double-character prefixes are not intuitive enough to serve as tags and that three- and four-character tags are more useful. This tag length is the most prevalent across the majority of published Access styles, although those who use this style admit that it introduces quite a few extra keystrokes into development efforts. If you're not averse to even more keystrokes, your style could conceivably use more than four characters for tags.

Caution

Be aware that you cannot use reserved words as object names, so only the second syntax below is legal as a naming convention in Access:

```
Dim int As Integer
Dim intWork As Integer
```

Table 5.5 shows several different tags for selected Access objects, culled from various naming convention documents that Access developers have sent to me over the past two years. Note that none of the tags exceed five characters and that different developers often come up with very similar tags.

Table 5.5   Selected Tags from Various Access Naming Conventions

Object Type	Tag
QueryDef Variable	q
QueryDef Variable	q_
QueryDef Variable	qd
QueryDef Variable	qdf
QueryDef Variable	qdf_
QueryDef Variable	qry

continues

Table 5.5   Continued

Object Type	Tag
String Variable	s
String Variable	s_
String Variable	str
String Variable	str_
String Variable	sz
TextBox Control	otxt_
TextBox Control	t_
TextBox Control	tbx
TextBox Control	txt
TextBox Control	txt_

As I noted in the previous section, you can place tags before (as in qryStateCapitol) or after (as in StateCapitol_qry) the base name. Most developers place them at the front, but in some naming conventions, tags trail the name. Both the primary benefit and the primary liability of leading tags are the same: The sort order of objects is affected.

In my experience, the best approach to deciding on a placement strategy for yourself is to create two small, similar applications. Use the leading tag convention in one and the trailing tag convention in the other. Comparing the pluses and minuses of the two approaches after actually using them in a hands-on experiment is the best input for making your decision.

Creating Object Tags

At this point, you have decided on a tagging strategy that includes length and placement. With such guidelines in place, you must create the tags themselves. The following are four rules of thumb that I suggest you apply to the process:

▸ *Abbreviations must be intuitive.* In the section "Abbreviating Object Names" earlier in this chapter, I proposed guidelines for creating abbreviations. The discussion is appropriate to creating tags as well. The general rule propounded in that section is: Your rules for naming objects should be flexible enough to serve the ultimate objectives, not restrictive for their own sake.

I'll restate the rule here with tags in mind: To create tags, begin with the full word that the tag will abbreviate or a generally accepted shorthand of the word. Remove nonessential characters until you reach the target length and the remaining tag is the clearest representation of the original word.

For example, if you had targeted three characters as a tag length, removing the vowels from `table` to produce `tbl` is the obvious choice for creating a tag because `tbl` is probably more recognizable to a majority of users as `table` than `tab` or `tbe` or `tle` would be. The example gets more complex, however, with the word `checkbox`. Removing characters to produce a viable three character tag would produce both `chk` and `cbx` as logical and usable choices. Therefore, you need more rules to break the tie.

Follow the crowd when it suits you. Unless you have a legitimate need to be unique, your conventions should probably lean toward one or more of the existing popular conventions. That way, you can use the other convention(s) as your guide through the gray areas if you so desire. In the `checkbox` example from above, the tag `chk` would be a preferable choice over `cbx` if you remember that Microsoft has used `chk` as a sample tag in their Visual Basic manuals for several years.

Remember what problem you are solving. We have explored how naming conventions should always fit the objectives you designate for them. For example, if object sort order is a primary objective for your tags, you would favor tag characters that fed this objective over all others.

Assume you have created unique tags for each type of query (`qapp` for append, `qdel` for delete, and so forth). In this model, select queries using `qsel` or `qry` tags would sort below most other types of queries. If your stated objective for query tags is to have most primary (select) queries at the top of each query list, your tag for select queries would need to sort above `qapp`, which is alphabetically the first query tag. Therefore, you would need a select query tag of `q_ry` or `qaaa` or a similar device to suit this purpose.

As a second example, if your objective for database object tags was solely to differentiate tables from queries in merged lists and you used trailing tags, using `_t` after table names and `_q` after query names would achieve that stated objective. You would have no need for tags beyond the simple two character model, and typing `_tbl` or `_Table` after base names may be a wasted effort for you.

Define the big picture. Your naming convention may need to dovetail into other conventions in your organization. For example, if you are creating an Access naming convention in a company where a Visual Basic naming convention already exists, objects in Access that are common to both products (Check Box controls, for example) would inherit the existing Visual Basic tags. (I can think of nothing more chaotic in a development team than multiple conventions.) Also, your naming convention may need to allow for a growth path into conventions for other platforms. See the section "Considering Other Platforms" later in this chapter for a more detailed discussion of this objective.

5

If you've gotten the impression that there is no single simple rule for creating tags, you're right. The process is unique to your needs and experience as an individual developer or development team.

Using Prefixes to Clarify Tags

By definition, a tag describes the type of the object. Some objects can have attributes (essentially properties) other than their type that give them additional capabilities. For example, a VBA variable in Access 97 can have a scope, Public or Private, in addition to its data type. Further, it may be helpful to you to denote static variables with a prefix in front of the tag, such as the following:

```
Static sintSubtotal As Integer
```

In your naming convention, you should consider whether it is important to add such identifiers to your tags to describe scope and similar attributes. I call an identifier that precedes a tag a "prefix," which you could essentially define as a clarification string placed on an object tag.

How you use and define prefixes depends on your needs. There are several places in Access where extra qualification of a tag can be useful, and prefixes are obviously helpful in such cases. Table 5.6 lists examples. There may be other areas where your own needs and development style lead you to create specific prefixes for specific needs.

Table 5.6   Areas in Access Where Tag Prefixes Are Useful

Object Type	Prefix Use
Tables	To denote specific table characteristics, such as system tables, archive copies, work in progress, and so on.
Queries	Same as for tables.
Forms	Same as for tables. Also, you could debate whether a subform is a form object with a prefix in front of the form tag (for example, sfrm) or a unique object type that requires only a distinct tag (like fsub). I lean toward the latter.
Reports	Same as for forms.
Macros	Same as for tables.
Modules	To designate specific attributes of the module. For example, you could create specific prefixes to denote modules containing only API calls, constant declarations, company library routines, and so on.

Object Type	Prefix Use
Controls	To designate more specific information about generic controls. For example, an Unbound Object Frame in Access can contain various kinds of OLE objects. You could create prefixes to differentiate PaintBrush picture object frames (pfrb) from Excel worksheet object frames (xfrb).
Procedures	To designate procedure scope (Public versus Private versus Static). Also, when creating public library routines, some developers use a unique prefix (in our case, lci_ for Leszynski Company, Inc.) to clearly designate such routines.
Variables	To designate variable scope (Public versus Private versus Static) or the type of variable passed as a parameter (ByRef versus ByVal).

Because a prefix often equates to an object property, any object that can have multiple properties can legitimately have multiple prefixes. Thus your conventions will need to prescribe ordering rules for using multiple prefixes. For example, your program code requires a public (a p prefix) string array (an a prefix) of parts.

The two options for prefix order are pastrPart or apstrPart; you will have to select one of these orders. Creating an integer variable to index this array is a bit more problematic, however, because it would require three prefixes: p for public, a for array, and i for index. Thus, you could create six combinations of prefix orders from these prefixes, including paiintPart, piaintPart, and aipintPart. Your convention should detail how to decide which prefix order is appropriate when such compounding occurs.

Using Qualifiers and Suffixes

A "qualifier" is a naming extension that provides context to the specific use of an object. Unlike prefixes, which detail properties of the object (for example, that the variable has global scope), qualifiers describe how the object is being used in context. For example, assume you need three VBA variables to track movement through an array: the first item, the current item, and the last item. You could consider using the qualifiers First, Curr, and Last at the end of the object names to make the names unique and their purpose obvious while retaining the same base name:

```
iaintPartCurr

iaintPartFirst

iaintPartLast
```

Placing the qualifier after the base name like this allows the object base names (Part) to sort together. An alternate construction would place the qualifiers after the tags rather than the base name to drive the sort order differently:

```
iaintCurrPart

iaintFirstPart

iaintLastPart
```

If qualifiers in your style always came at the end of the object name, they would actually be a type of suffix. I find the term "qualifier" superior to suffix, however, because it is location-neutral—qualifiers may come before a base name, depending on your style. Further, you may want your naming convention to include both "qualifiers" and suffixes. This construction can get slightly complicated for its users, but the qualifier would still describe the use and the suffix would designate still other information about the object.

For example, your company creates separate queries on a per-state basis so that state sales managers can review their employees' performance daily. While this operation could be done with parameter queries, your company has specific reasons to make a different saved query for each state. Your naming convention could dictate that state abbreviations are legitimate suffixes so that your queries could look like the following list (note that the names in the list also include the qualifiers Best and Worst):

```
qsumSalesmanPerfBest_AK

qsumSalesmanPerfBest_AL

...

qsumSalesmanPerfBest_WY

qsumSalesmanPerfWorst_AK

qsumSalesmanPerfWorst_AL

...

qsumSalesmanPerfWorst_WY
```

In the example above, I use underscores to offset the suffix from the qualifier. The reason is that I want the qualifiers Best and Worst to be easily recognized when the names are read because the difference between the meaning of these two qualifiers is substantial. Some developers also prefer to use underscores before all qualifiers and all suffixes to pull them further from the base name. You should consider whether or not this is a good strategy for your style.

Considering Other Platforms

Your naming convention may legitimately be able to exist in a vacuum. If you are an independent developer and expect to be working only in Access for many years, you could create a development style that was Access-centric. Most developers use a variety of tools, however, which introduces both a problem and an opportunity.

The problem is that developing multiple styles can be time-consuming, learning the styles and keeping them separated at development time can be challenging, and styles with overlapping elements can breed confusion. For example, what if the same tags in two different platforms have two different meanings for a perfectly good reason?

The opportunity presented is for you to create a style that transcends products and dictates how you deal with common objects wherever they may reside. This task becomes easier with each release of Microsoft Office as the individual products in the suite begin to have more features and objects in common.

5

For example, in addition to Access, you can create Check Box controls in the other Office applications as well as Visual Basic and Visual FoxPro. As you create naming conventions for each of these tools, you will be best served by standardizing your tag for `CheckBox` across all these products. Your developers will only have to remember one `CheckBox` tag for all of the VBA host applications.

As a contrary example, prior to Office 97 there was a `Label` control type in Access, Excel, Visual Basic, and Visual FoxPro, while PowerPoint called the same control a `StaticText` control and Word called it a `Text` control. When you create a naming convention in an environment such as this and your convention must account for the disparate control names different products give to the same object, you have a significant problem to solve. Four solutions are available to you, as follows:

1. *The product majority rules.* You can decide to use one convention for all products you consider relevant, such as Microsoft Office, Microsoft Project, Visual Basic, and Visual FoxPro. The single convention will be the one that is most appropriate for the majority of the products.

2. *Your majority rules.* If you use only a subset of the tools listed in the item above, select a convention that is most appropriate for the majority of the products that you actually use.

3. *Different products, different standards.* You could also make a compelling case for using the exact terminology of each product in its conventions. Thus, different names across products for the same object would result in different tags.

4. *Predict the future.* If you can make an educated or informed guess regarding the direction of the majority of tools you must use, build the convention for the future, not the present. For example, if you had assumed that the Text control in Word would eventually become a Label similar to that used in Access, you would have let your Access conventions dictate the conventions used in Word over the previous few years.

The best argument in favor of cross-platform conventions is the ability to move your code from host to host and to create common code libraries. Because VBA is standardized across the Office suite, VBA code is now quite portable across the products.

If your company does work in both Visual FoxPro and Access 97, having a fairly common set of naming conventions across these platforms will make it easier to move data structures or application objects from one of these platforms to the other.

Applying Naming Conventions to Your Work

As defined in this chapter, five components are generally used in naming conventions:

Prefixes

Tags

Base names

Qualifiers

Suffixes

These components are usually arranged in some derivative of the following form:

[prefix(es)] tag [base name] [qualifier] [suffix]

The brackets indicate optional syntax elements. Notice in the syntax diagram that the tag is required even though the base name is not. Once you adopt a naming convention that uses tags, you cannot mix and match such usage. Either every object has a tag or none have any—you should not break this model. Therefore, the tag becomes more critical than the base name, and in a case where the tag is not ambivalent, it can be used by itself.

For example, in the code snippet below, there is only one Database object and one Recordset in the procedure. While a base name on each variable would make the code more clear, especially Cust on the Recordset variable, the tag is obviously even more useful:

```
Dim dbs As Database
Dim rst As Recordset
...
Set rst = dbs.OpenRecordset("tblCust", dbOpenDynaset)
rst.MoveFirst
```

Table 5.7 provides a syntax diagram of the various combinations of these components. The diagram will help you understand that some combinations of components can be nonsensical, like putting a puzzle piece in the wrong place. Of course, the terms used for these components and the component layout described in this chapter are suggestions only, derived from my experience. Your naming convention components may not resemble those in the table in every respect. The spaces between components are added for readability and are not part of the actual usage. The use of upper- and lowercase for the component placeholders is explained following the table.

Table 5.7   Logical Object-Name Component Combinations

Components	Description
BaseName	Without a naming convention, this is all you have.
tag BaseName	The simplest and most common construction.
BaseName Tag	An alternate approach, to sort by base name.
prefix BaseName	This construction would only be useful if you were never using tags.
prefix tag BaseName	Provides more detail on the object.
BaseName Prefix Tag	An alternate approach, to sort by base name.
prefix tag BaseName Qualifier	Provides the most detail on the object.
prefix tag qualifier BaseName	A variation on the qualifier location.
BaseName Prefix Tag Qualifier	An alternate approach, to sort by base name.

To each of the items in the table, a suffix could also be added, subject to the discussion in the previous "Using Qualifiers and Suffixes" section.

Notice also in the table the careful use of upper- and lowercase as applied to the component placeholders. I use lowercase tags, prefixes, and qualifiers when they begin the object name, but mix the case on them—as well as qualifiers and suffixes—when they trail the base name. You may choose to employ a different capitalization or punctuation strategy than this.

When prefixes and tags begin the object name, I want to read past them quickly to get to the first (uppercase) character of the base name. For example, I find the name zttblCust easier to read than either ztTblCust or ZTTBLCust. When any naming conventions, whether prefixes, tags, qualifiers, or suffixes, trail the base name, they may be more readable when mixed case is used. For example, I think that `intCustFirst` is a more friendly variable name than `intCustfirst`.

 Tip

After you define a naming convention, write it down for the benefit of all developers who will be asked to use it. A clearly documented convention (such as the one shown in the following chapter) should leave little room for variance of style between different developers working on the same team or project. Even if you work alone, having a written reference is better than trying to remember a complex set of conventions.

If you understand how to use the Windows help compiler included with the Office 97 Developer Edition, you can easily turn your naming convention documentation into a help file. See the file `LNC97DEV.HLP` on the CD-ROM for an example. Alternatively, you could publish your naming conventions on your corporate intranet using HTML documents.

If you adopt or create a set of naming conventions, should you apply it retroactively to any existing applications? The answer depends on the following two questions:

What is the longevity of the system? If an application has a potential life span of one or two years, retrofitting a naming convention into it is not very cost effective. Because naming conventions benefit developers more than users, a system that has already been deployed to users should not be modified retroactively to include developer features.

Can you afford it? A naming convention retrofit can take a hundred hours of work or more in a substantial application, so there must be development time and money available to cover the effort. If you decide to retrofit, the most cost-effective approach is to include the renaming of objects and rewriting of code as part of a major application upgrade because resources already will be budgeted into the upgrade cycle to retest the application. Because name changes are very pervasive in an application, strong testing after the process is crucial.

From Here...

This chapter includes many thought-provoking questions for you and your development team. If you intend to standardize naming conventions as a result of this discussion, you may want to answer the questions I posed and prototype a naming convention now before you proceed further into the development framework issues in subsequent chapters. Alternatively, reviewing the following areas of the book will also be helpful as you develop your naming conventions:

▶ Read Chapter 6, "Leszynski Naming Conventions for Access," which describes in detail the answers my company came up with to the questions in this chapter. That chapter is the current update of the most widely published Access naming convention style.

▶ For a practical application within Visual Basic for Applications of many of the naming convention techniques discussed in this chapter, see Chapter 11, "Expert Approaches to VBA."

▶ For a strategy you can use to develop tools (wizards and builders) to apply your naming conventions automatically during your development work, see Chapter 20, "Applying Development Shortcuts."

▶ To read a document that proposes cross-platform naming conventions for all of Microsoft Office and other Microsoft developer products, see Appendix C, "Leszynski Naming Conventions for Microsoft Solution Developers," on the CD-ROM.

chapter 6

Leszynski Naming Conventions for Access

6

In this chapter

◆ An overview of the Leszynski Naming Conventions, a standardized set of naming guidelines for Access application objects

◆ Naming convention elements for Access application objects such as tables, forms, reports, and so on

◆ Suggestions for standardizing the documentation in your VBA code procedures

◆ Techniques for creating your own naming convention elements for your special needs

◆ A methodology for consistently abbreviating key development terms and using standardized terminology in your object names

I t's amusing to look at applications you wrote a year or two ago. If you're constantly improving yourself and learning new techniques, the approaches demonstrated in your older applications can seem outdated now, almost embarrassing. However, even if your development style today is different from yesterday, it would be nice to still be able to understand the structure of applications you wrote in the past and to be able to debug or upgrade their code. These tasks are facilitated by the use of standardized naming conventions.

Cartoon Chaos

"I learned the value of naming conventions years ago. Before I was at Microsoft, I was working on an accounting application for a client and needed to hire a contractor to do some of the work on the project. At the time, I didn't have any formal naming conventions, or a specific structure or style that I wanted the code to look like—I just wanted the app to work. Well, the contract coder did his part of the application, and it seemed to work fine. Some time later, however, I had to modify the application, and I couldn't figure out what the code did. For example, his code looked like this:

```
Barney = 500
Do While Fred < Barney
...
Fred = Wilma + 1
...
Loop
```

"My confusion stemmed from the fact that he had named all of his objects and variables after cartoon characters, and they had no consistency or link to the application at all!"

Tod Nielsen, General Manager, Microsoft Access Business Unit

Developers by nature have a love/hate relationship with naming conventions. Such standards are often seen as slowing the development process, increasing the size of object names and files, and stifling true programming creativity. And yet, without order, the laws of entropy invariably draw every project toward incoherent *spaghetti code* (or perhaps *spaghetti objects*). Thus, few developers would argue against the need for an ordered approach to development, but they want the least intrusive system.

Sorry, but you can't have it both ways! A system that is comprehensive and applied consistently will also, by nature, be intrusive. If you want to apply a naming convention to your objects, you will incur a penalty of a few keystrokes every time you type an object name. For a detailed explanation of why the small pain of extra keystrokes produces a large gain, refer to "Why Use Naming Conventions?" in Chapter 5, "Creating Naming Conventions."

In Chapter 5, I describe the methods you might use when creating your own naming conventions; you may want to review that chapter before proceeding for two reasons:

▶ If you decide to create your own conventions, Chapter 5 suggests approaches and lays out rules of thumb that will increase your chances of success.

> ▶ Alternatively, if you decide to borrow my conventions (Leszynski Naming Conventions), you will better understand the thought processes that went into creating them.

In this chapter, I detail for you the *Leszynski Naming Conventions* (LNC), a set of standardized approaches to naming objects during Access development. These naming conventions were born of necessity because some members of my staff would spend all day in Access development, year after year. They were also born of a different need—a void that existed in the marketplace due to a lack of consensus about development styles among leading Access developers.

LNC began in the days of Access 1.0, when it was referred to as L/R (the Leszynski/ Reddick conventions). The L/R conventions were distributed broadly—with over 500,000 copies in print, and they have become the most widely used conventions in the Access community. Over the last few years, we have received feedback about L/R from hundreds of developers and companies, and we have tried to incorporate some of their input, as well as our ongoing experiences, into LNC.

6

LNC improves upon the previous Access style by considering developers who work with multiple Microsoft development tools. Access, Visual Basic, Office, SQL Server, and other Microsoft products have more in common in their 97 versions than in any previous iterations. Consequently, this Access style dovetails with the LNC development style for the Microsoft toolset, as detailed in Appendix C, "Leszynski Naming Conventions for Microsoft Solution Developers," which is on the CD-ROM.

I will use the terms *naming conventions*, *style*, and *LNC* interchangeably throughout this chapter.

Naming Conventions: A Primer

Naming conventions is one of the foundation elements of your overall development style. We developed our naming conventions primarily to achieve the following four objectives (as described in detail in Chapter 5, "Creating Naming Conventions"):

> ▶ To be able to quickly understand an application's structure and code by making object names more informative

> ▶ To simplify team development of applications by creating a standardized vocabulary for all team members

> ▶ To improve the ability to work with Access objects, including enforcing object name sort orders, creating self-documenting program code, and enhancing find-and-replace capabilities

> ▶ To increase the ability to create tools for Access development work and to create code libraries across various VBA platforms

To meet these objectives, we create and apply consistent naming conventions to the Access objects. The following are target objects for naming conventions:

Tables

Table fields

Queries

Forms

Form controls

Reports

Report controls

Macros

Modules

Classes

Procedures

Variables

Constants

User-defined types

Because object names are the foundation upon which you build your entire application, it is almost impossible to change them once you begin development. Therefore, you will not find it cost-effective or time-efficient to retrofit naming conventions into your existing applications. For new applications, however, you should apply these conventions consistently from the moment you create your first object in a new database application file.

Leading Tags

Our naming conventions rely primarily on leading tags, which are several characters placed before an object's name (for example, `qryOrderByMonth`). This approach, known as *Hungarian Notation,* is defined in Chapter 5, "Creating Naming Conventions." Leading tags provide the following benefits:

▶ The first thing you see about an object when you see its name is the leading type tag, which is often more important than the name itself.

▶ Leading tags drive the ordering of object names in Access lists, sorting first by type and then by base name.

▶ Leading tags are consistently located in the same place in an object's name, making them easier to find by parsers and other tools.

Trailing Tags

If you are averse to Hungarian Notation for some reason and prefer trailing tags, LNC will still work for you. However, LNC prescribes no standard for locating and punctuating trailing tags. You will have to decide to offset them with underscoring (`OrderByMonth_qry`), by capitalization (`OrderByMonthQry`), or by some other technique.

Using trailing tags on database objects is problematic when your application also contains VBA code. The primary justification given by developers who prefer trailing tags on database objects is that it allows the objects to sort by base names rather than tags in ordered lists. However, such developers often still use *leading* tags and prefixes in their VBA code because there is no compelling argument for trailing tags on VBA objects such as variables. If you mix your styles like this, be prepared to justify your lack of consistency.

Because some developers, especially newer ones, prefer to minimize the complexity of a naming convention, LNC provides two levels for Access users. Level One has the minimum realistic subset of tags but provides lesser detail about the application. It is intended for users whose work is centered around the Database window and who develop database objects rather than applications. Level Two provides greater detail and the flexibility to create extensions. It is intended for application developers building expert solutions.

Access Object Types

For purposes of this chapter, I have created the following standardized terminology for grouping objects. I will use these group names when discussing naming conventions:

Database Objects:

Database Window Objects:

Tables

Table fields

> Queries
>
> Forms
>
> Reports
>
> Macros
>
> Modules
>
> Classes

Database Control Objects:

> Form controls
>
> Report controls

VBA Objects:

Procedures

Variables

Constants

User-defined types

Structuring Object Names

In LNC, object names are constructed using the following syntax for Level One:

    [prefix(es)] [tag] BaseName [Qualifier] [Suffix]

For Level Two, the syntax varies slightly:

    [prefix(es)] tag [BaseName] [Qualifier] [Suffix]

The brackets indicate optional syntax elements. Notice that, for Level One, the *BaseName* element is required and the *tag* is optional in some cases. At Level Two, the *tag* element is required even though the *BaseName* is not in some cases. (This will be explained later in this chapter; see "Naming Conventions for VBA Objects.") Table 6.1 shows sample object names using these constructions.

Table 6.1　Object Names Constructed in LNC Format

Object Name	Prefixes	Tag	BaseName	Qualifier	Suffix
tblCust		tbl	Cust		
qsumSalesPerfBest_WA		qsum	SalesPerf	Best	_WA
plngRecNumMax	p	lng	RecNum	Max	
ialngPartNum	ia	lng	PartNum		

Note in the syntax diagrams that the case of each element reflects its case in actual use. The element *tag* is in lowercase because the tags themselves are always lowercase.

What Is a Prefix?

A *prefix* is an identifier that precedes a tag and clarifies it narrowly. Prefixes describe one or more important properties of an object. For example, a Long Integer variable that is public in scope (declared Public) has a prefix p, as in plngRecNumMax. Prefixes are one or two characters long and lowercase. Multiple prefixes can be used together on one object, as in ialngPartNum, where i and a are both prefixes.

What Is a Tag?

A *tag* is a character phrase placed against an object base name to characterize it. In object-oriented programming terms, the tag is basically an identifier for the class. At Level One, tags define an object's general class: for example, qry for a query of any type. At Level Two, tags define the specific subclass: for example, qdel for a delete query.

Note that the word *class* here refers to a naming convention construction, not an object model construction. For example, there is only one Query (or QueryDef) class object in Access, and the data action (delete, update, and so on.) is determined by its SQL statement rather than its class. LNC prescribes several tags for this one Access class.

Tags are three or four characters long for readability and to allow for the hundreds of combinations necessary as the Microsoft Office object model grows over time. They are always to the left of the base name and in lowercase, so that your eye reads past them to the beginning of the base name.

6

Tags are ideally created to mnemonically represent the word they abbreviate, such as "frm" for "form." However, some tags may not seem fully mnemonic for two reasons. First, the most appropriate, or obvious tag for a particular object may already be assigned to another object. Second, common objects (those with similar properties and usage) may exist in multiple Microsoft applications; therefore, the tag for one may be used to represent similar objects in other products, even if the names differ. For example, an Access Rectangle object is almost identical in structure and purpose to a Visual Basic Shape object. Because our Visual Basic conventions have existed longer than our Access conventions, I used the Visual Basic Shape object tag shp to also represent the Access Rectangle.

What Is a Base Name?

When you name a particular object, the *base name* is the starting point—it is a name you would use anyway if you had no naming conventions. For example, you might use Customer as the name for a table filled with customer records. The LNC guidelines for creating base names is driven by a set of guidelines discussed in the section, "Creating Database Object Base Names," later in this chapter.

What Is a Qualifier?

A *qualifier* is an extension following the base name that provides context to the specific use of an object. Unlike prefixes, which detail properties of the object (for example, that the variable has public scope), qualifiers describe how the object is being used in a context. For example, plngRecNumMax is obviously the maximum record number in an application that could also have variables for the minimum (plngRecNumMin) and current (plngRecNumCur) record numbers. Qualifiers are short and written in upper- and lowercase, using the list in Table 6.2.

Table 6.2   Suggested LNC Qualifiers

Qualifier	Usage
Curr	Current element of a set
Dest	Destination
First	First element of a set
Hold	Hold a value for later reuse
Last	Last element of a set
Max	Maximum item in a set

Qualifier	Usage
Min	Minimum item in a set
Next	Next element of a set
New	New instance or value
Old	Prior instance or value
Prev	Previous element of a set
Sub	Subform/subreport (Level One only)
Src	Source
Temp	Temporary value

What Is a Suffix?

Suffix elements provide specific information about the object and are only used as "tie breakers" when more detail is required to differentiate one object name from another. These are the only elements in the syntax for which our naming conventions do not specify standardized values. You will create suffix items as needed by your company, development team, or application. For example, a series of queries that summarized the best sales performance by state would need the state name in the object name to properly qualify it, as in qsumSalesPerfBest_AK. Placing the state name at the very end of the name as a *suffix* item allows the entire collection of related queries to sort together, like this:

```
qsumSalesmanPerfBest_AK
qsumSalesmanPerfBest_AL
...
qsumSalesmanPerfBest_WY
```

Because the suffix is the last piece of information in a name, it can be easier for the eye to find if delimited from the rest of the object name with an underscore, as shown. Use of the underscore is optional.

Creating Database Object Base Names

The building blocks of your Access application are its database objects. When you create a base name for an object, consider its purpose, the approaches used in naming associated objects, and the following rules of thumb.

Rules for Base Names

Observe the following rules when developing a base name for a new database object:

▸ Spaces are not allowed in any object name. Spaces create a multitude of problems with consistency, readability, and documentation. Where the readability of a space is required, use an underscore instead.

▸ Object names begin with a letter and should only include letters, digits, and underscores. The use of special characters in object names is disallowed in order to comply with the naming rules of both VBA and Microsoft SQL Server. This allows your Basic variable names to include database object base names, and your entire Access schema to be easily upsized to a more powerful SQL Server platform.

▸ Object names use mixed case to add readability to the name. (Previously, some developers used all lowercase names to allow for upsizing to Microsoft SQL Server. Starting with version 6.0, that product is now installed case-insensitive and will allow you to maintain upper- and lowercase in object names that are moved to the server from Access.)

▸ The only syntax element that can have multiple capital letters is the base name. A qualifier or suffix begins with a single capital letter unless it is an abbreviation: for example, `qsumSalesmanPerfBestUSA`. If you need to see the elements of a name clearly (prefixes, tag, base name, qualifier, and suffix), LNC allows the use of underscores as separators: `qsum_SalesmanPerf_Best_USA`.

▸ Object names are usually singular (`Widget`) rather than plural (`Widgets`). By implication, tables, queries, forms, and reports are plural because they usually work with more than one record. Why restate the obvious?

▸ An object's base name should include the base names of any associated table objects, if practical. This rule is explained next.

The first two rules also apply to the other naming convention elements: prefixes, tags, qualifiers, and suffixes. These elements should never include spaces or special characters.

You should abbreviate object base name elements wherever possible using a standardized abbreviation table such as Table 6.17 in the later section "Standardized Abbreviations." You can extend LNC with your own standard abbreviations as well. You should create and use standardized terminology in your applications wherever possible; for examples, see the later section "Standardized Terminology."

Base Name Length Limits

LNC includes some constraints and suggestions for object name lengths.

I *target* table name lengths at a 15-character maximum for the following two reasons:

▶ Short names (15 characters or less) will fully display within the default column width of the Access query design grid.

▶ Query, form, and report names usually include the base name(s) of the primary table object(s) they relate to and will be too long to use if the table base names are long.

Beyond the 15-character target, I *absolutely limit* table name lengths to 30 characters, which maintains compatibility with the table name length limit in SQL Server. For other objects, I *target* a 30-character limit as well because Access shows no more than the first 30 characters of object names in the default width of any of its lists or property grids.

Compound Base Names

An object name that is driven by a table must include the base name of that table. Thus, for the `tblCust` table, the primary query would be `qryCust`, the primary form `frmCust`, and so forth. Queries, forms, and reports that are sourced from multiple tables should reflect the base names of all the tables if it is practical. If not, you must decide which tables are the primary tables and list as many as possible in the name.

Generally, in a multi-table query, form, or report, the most "important" tables are not necessarily the first and second, but more often the first and last. So, a query joining `tblCust` to `tblAddr` to `tblPhone` to get the phone numbers for customers would be named `qryCustAddrPhone` if the address information is included in the query result. If the address information is used simply to join to the phone numbers and is not displayed, the query would be simply `qryCustPhone`.

Bound control base names on forms and reports are always equivalent to the base name of the bound field (the `ControlSource`). For example, a text box tied to the `LastName` field is named `txtLastName`.

Field Base Names

As a part of standardizing terminology, I adhere to the concept of a centralized data dictionary. This principle dictates that any fields in the data structure having the same name must have the same properties and data purpose. For example, if the `LastName` field in `tblCust` is of type `Text` 30 and holds the customer last name, then any other field

6

named `LastName` in the same application must have the same type, length, properties, and purpose. If your application needs last name fields for both customers and dealers, this rule dictates that you name them differently (such as `CustLastName` and `DlrLastName`).

Applying the centralized data dictionary principle also means that table fields do not get leading prefixes or tags because I prefer my data dictionaries to be platform-neutral. That way, a field does not have to be renamed if data is upsized or ported to a platform with different data types. A table is still called a table in SQL Server, so moving `tblCust` there from Access would not require renaming.

However, if `tblCust` had a field `lngCustID` defined as a Long Integer in Access, moving the database to SQL Server would require a field rename to `intCustID` because SQL Server uses the data type name `Integer` to mean the same as the Access Long Integer. Because renaming fields affects all dependent objects and code, avoid it at all costs. Therefore I would call the field simply `CustID`.

If field tags are part of your development style and you must use them, LNC provides the tags listed in Table 6.3.

Table 6.3 Database Field Object Tags

Data Type	Tag
AutoNumber (Random non-sequential)	idn
AutoNumber (Replication ID)	idr
AutoNumber (Sequential)	ids
Binary	bin
Byte	byt
Currency	cur
Date/Time	dtm
Double	dbl
Hyperlink	hlk
Integer	int
Long	lngz
Memo	mem
Ole	ole
Single	sng
Text (Character)	chr
Yes/No (Boolean)	bln

As much as is practical, LNC maps similar Jet and SQL Server data types to the same tag so that the data structure can be upsized with a minimum of object name changes. See Appendix C on the CD-ROM, "Leszynski Naming Conventions for Microsoft Solution Developers," for an expanded discussion of this subject.

Unlike tags, qualifiers and suffixes are acceptable in field names because they describe the object's data purpose and not its type.

Ordering Base Name Elements

Object base name elements should be ordered from left to right with respect to their importance, readability, and desired sort order. In the example from the previous paragraph, CustLastName is a better name than LastNameCust because the group name portion (Cust or Dlr) carries greater weight in an object's name than the specific item name (LastName or PhoneNum). Think of Cust as the name of a collection of customer-related items and this rule becomes clear—what you are really saying is that CustLastName is analogous to Cust(LastName) or Cust.LastName in *Collection.Object* terminology.

Some of you will naturally carry this example to its extreme and say that the Customers collection really has a Names collection with multiple elements, including Last, thus the representation of that idea as Cust.Name(Last) would lead to the field name CustNameLast instead. Such a construction model still fits within the rules of LNC, and I won't debate you against using it. In practice, however, such names often become fairly unreadable, even if they are accurate.

Naming Conventions for Database Objects

In Level Two of LNC, the following Access (and Jet) database objects require tags:

Tables

Queries

Forms

Form controls

Reports

Report controls

Macros

Modules

Classes

Level One also recommends that you place tags on every object name. However, Level One recognizes that nondevelopers may prefer to save time, effort, and complexity by leaving tags off objects where the context is obvious while viewing the Database window. Thus, Level One users are required only to place the qry tag on queries in order to differentiate them from tables in any combined lists, such as the Choose the Table or Query combo box on Form and Report Wizards. Placing tags on other objects in the preceding list is optional.

Caution

I described earlier how difficult it can be to propagate name changes throughout a database, so if you are a casual user now but expect to become a developer later—and thus migrate from Level One of LNC to Level Two—you would be unwise to leave tags off any object names. Use the Level Two tags now on all objects.

Tags for Database Window Objects

Table 6.4 lists the Level One tags for Database window objects. Note that only one tag exists for each object type.

Table 6.4   Level One Database Window Object Tags

Object	Tag
Class module	cls
Form	frm
Macro	mcr
Module	bas
Query	qry
Report	rpt
Subform	fsub
Subreport	rsub
Table	tbl

Though Level One is the simplified naming model, it is necessary to provide tags to identify subform and subreport objects specifically. The distinction between objects and subobjects is critical for nondevelopers who navigate using the Database window. Because it is not appropriate to open subforms and subreports directly from the Database window, they must be clearly identified and grouped using tags. Table 6.5 lists the Level Two tags for Database window objects.

Table 6.5   Level Two Database Window Object Tags

Object	Tag
Class module	cls
Form	frm
Form (class module)	fcls
Form (dialog box)	fdlg
Form (lookup table)	flkp
Form (menu/switchboard)	fmnu
Form (message/alert)	fmsg
Form (subform)	fsub
Form (wizard main)	fwzm
Form (wizard subform)	fwzs
Macro	mcr
Macro (for form/report)	m[*obj*]
Macro (bar menu)	mmbr
Macro (general menu)	mmnu
Macro (shortcut menu)	mmct
Macro (submenu/drop-down)	mmsb
Module	bas
Query	qry
Query (form/report source)	q[*obj*]
Query (append)	qapp
Query (crosstab)	qxtb
Query (data definition)	qddl
Query (delete)	qdel
Query (form filter)	qflt
Query (lookup)	qlkp
Query (make table)	qmak

continues

Table 6.5   Continued

Object	Tag
Query (select)	qsel
Query (SQL pass-through)	qspt
Query (union)	quni
Query (update)	qupd
Report	rpt
Report (detail)	rdet
Report (sub)	rsub
Report (summary)	rsum
Table	tbl
Table (attached Btrieve)	tbtv
Table (attached dBASE)	tdbf
Table (attached Excel)	txls
Table (attached Fox)	tfox
Table (attached Lotus 1-2-3)	twks
Table (attached ODBC)	todb
Table (attached Paradox)	tpdx
Table (attached SQL Server)	tsql
Table (attached text)	ttxt
Table (lookup)	tlkp
Table (many-to-many relation)	trel
Table (summary information)	tsum

The tags for Level Two provide rich detail about the objects and sort objects with similar attributes. For example, lookup tables and their maintenance forms are often used repeatedly in multiple applications. The tags tlkp and flkp clearly identify these objects, making it easy for you to perform tasks such as importing all lookup-related objects from an existing database into a new one when using the object list in the Access Import dialog box.

> **Tip**
>
> If you like the idea of using tags to sort objects but still need access to the base name of the object, place each object's unmodified base name in its `Description` property. When you need to view database objects sorted by their base name, sort the Database window using the Description column. To add a description to a database object, highlight the object in the Database window and select <u>V</u>iew <u>P</u>roperties.

In two special cases in Table 6.5, as indicated by the `[obj]` placeholder, the conventions prescribe a single character tag added to the front of the full object name (including the tag) of a related object. This situation occurs when

a macro is created solely for a particular form or report, as in `mfrmCust`

or

a query is created solely to serve as the `RecordSource` for one particular form or report, as in `qfrmCust`

6

Tags for Form and Report Control Objects

Table 6.6 lists the Level One tags for control objects on forms and reports.

Table 6.6   Level One Form and Report Control Object Tags

Control	Tag
Label	`lbl`
Other types	`ctl`

These Level One control tags provide no differentiation of control type other than to distinguish labels, which do not interact with the user, from controls that can display or modify data. This level of detail is inadequate for applications where VBA code will be written behind forms or reports.

Table 6.7 lists the Level Two tags for control objects on forms and reports. A different tag is provided for each built-in control type. VBA code written behind forms and reports using this convention will reflect a control's type in its event procedure names (for example, cboState_AfterUpdate). The automatic sorting provided by this notation in the Access form and module design windows can be very helpful during development. The table lists controls by their Access internal names rather than by more commonly used terms.

Table 6.7   Level Two Form and Report Control Object Tags

Control	Tag	TypeOf
Bound object frame	frb	BoundObjectFrame
Chart (graph)	cht	ObjectFrame
Check box	chk	CheckBox
Combo box	cbo	ComboBox
Command button	cmd	CommandButton
Custom control	ocx	CustomControl
Detail (section)	det	Section
Footer (group section)	gft[n]	Section
Form footer (section)	fft	Section
Form header (section)	fhd	Section
Header (group section)	ghd[n]	Section
Hyperlink	hlk	Hyperlink
Image	img	Image
Label	lbl	Label
Line	lin	Line
List box	lst	ListBox
Option button	opt	OptionButton
Option group	grp	OptionGroup
Page (tab)	pge	Page
Page break	brk	PageBreak
Page footer (section)	pft	Section
Page header (section)	phd	Section
Rectangle	shp	Rectangle
Report footer (section)	rft	Section
Report header (section)	rhd	Section
Section	sec	Section

Control	Tag	TypeOf
Subform/Subreport	sub	Subform
Tab	tab	TabControl
Text box	txt	TextBox
Toggle button	tgl	ToggleButton
Unbound object frame	fru	ObjectFrame

The placeholder [n] in the headers and footers for reports indicates the GroupLevel index, as in gft0 for the first group footer.

All control tags are three characters long.

Appendix C, "Leszynski Naming Conventions for Microsoft Solution Developers," on the CD-ROM includes a listing of tags for ActiveX controls that can be used in Access applications.

Prefixes for Database Objects

The following list describes the database object prefixes and their usage. With the exception of zz for backup copies of objects, these prefixes are Level Two (i.e. developer) elements only.

_(underscore)   Use this prefix for objects that are incomplete and under development. When the Database window is sorted by object name, this prefix sorts objects to the top where they are immediately recognized as unfinished and unusable. When the object is ready for testing or deployment, remove the underscore. This prefix is not used with form and report controls.

zh   Use this prefix to denote system objects, which are objects that should be hidden from the user by default. System objects provide the infrastructure for an application; they are used by application code or by other objects but are not meant for user interaction. For example, you would use this prefix on a form's hidden text box that is used to compute a value or on a hidden table that logs system errors from VBA code.

Note that Access has its own prefix with a similar meaning. Items prefixed with USys are not for user interaction and are not displayed in the Database window by default. In past versions of Access, it was necessary to use USys instead of zh to prevent the display of system objects in the Database window. With Access 97, you can use the zh prefix, combined with setting the object's Hidden property to True, to hide the system object. If the system object should not be hidden, use the zs prefix instead.

zs

Use this prefix to denote displayed system objects, which are for use by developers and application code only, but should be displayed in the Database window. If the system object should be hidden, use the zh prefix instead.

zt

Use this prefix for temporary objects that are created programmatically. For example, a query written out from VBA code, used in code, and then deleted by the code, would have a zt prefix. Any database object labeled with zt showing in the Database window should be deleted before each repair and compact of a database because, by definition, it is probably left over from an abnormally terminated process.

zz

This prefix denotes backup copies of objects that you keep in the Database window for reference or possible reuse. Items with this prefix should be reviewed periodically to determine their value and deleted if no longer necessary.

Note that most of these database object prefixes use z as the first character. Database objects with such prefixes sort to the bottom of the Database window, below the user- or developer-oriented objects that are accessed more frequently.

Using Menus and Toolbars

Menu macros behave differently than standard macros; thus, they fall under separate guidelines when you create their names. Menu macros are used either for bar menus or for shortcut menus.

When creating menu macros, bar menu macros should be prefixed with mmbr, submenus (drop-down) with mmsb, and shortcut menus with mmct. The tags for command bar menu objects are similar: mbr for a menu bar (which includes its submenus), mct for a shortcut menu (also now called a *pop-up*), and tbr for a toolbar object.

Detailed tags like these will help greatly when you are selecting from a list of menus to assign to the MenuBar or ShortcutMenuBar properties of a form or in the Startup properties dialog box. This convention also sorts menu macros by type in the Database window.

Because any saved submenu macro can be selected as the primary object in a shortcut menu, this convention gives you the flexibility to create *component* submenus, which can be called from both multiple bar menus and multiple shortcut menus and thus reused. The structure of command bar menus is different from that of menu macros; you cannot create a component submenu and use it by name in multiple bar menus. You can, however, make a copy of a submenu to another bar menu when customizing toolbars.

Database Object Name Examples

Table 6.8 shows examples of database objects, applying the various conventions in this section.

Table 6.8   Database Object Naming Convention Examples

Object	Description
zhtxtUser	Hidden system text box
mfrmCust	Macro for form
zttfoxCustHist	Temporary Fox attachment
qupdCustBal_Dlr	Update customers that are dealers
trelCustAddrPhone	Link many addresses to phones

Creating VBA Object Base Names

When creating VBA object base names, remember that the base name must be descriptive even in the absence of its tag. For many programmers, the syntax `Dim I As Integer` for a loop variable is quite acceptable. Within LNC, however, the variable named `I` would become `iintLoop`. Single character variable names, especially without tags, are not allowed. Instead, create a list of short and standardized work variables to handle common daily needs. Table 6.9 suggests the LNC approach to commonly used variables.

Table 6.9   Standardized LNC Work Variables

Variable	Description
blnRet	Captures a `True` or `False` return value from a function call
cccDebug	A conditional compilation constant for turning conditional debugging on and off
dbsCurr	Database object variable for the current Access database (`CurrentDB`)

continues

Table 6.9 Continued

Variable	Description
iintLoop	A counter for For...Next loops
intMsg	Captures a return value from a MsgBox() function call
intResult	Holds the result of math operations (also dblResult, lngResult, and so on)
intRet	Captures a numeric return value from a function call (also dblRet, lngRet, and so on)
intWork	Used for any temporary work (also dblWork, lngWork, and so on)
strMsg	Used to build long message box strings
strOrder	Used to build long SQL ORDER BY strings
strSQL	Used to build long SQL strings
strWhere	Used to build long SQL WHERE clauses

Rules for Base Names

Creating VBA object base names involves observing the same rules listed in the earlier section "Rules for Base Names" for creating database object base names, as follows:

▸ Spaces are not allowed in any object name.

▸ Object names begin with a letter and should only include letters, digits, and underscores.

▸ Object names use mixed case to add readability to the name.

▸ The only non-abbreviated syntax element that can have multiple capital letters is the base name.

▸ Object names are usually singular rather than plural.

▸ An object's base name should include the base names of any objects it is built on if practical.

Note that the last rule is an expanded version of the corresponding rule for database objects, which states that table base names should propagate into names of dependent objects. In VBA, that rule expands to require a reference in variable names to objects of any type that they relate to. For example, a RecordSet variable created on tblCust should be named rstCust. Also, if a string array variable of part numbers astrPartNum has an Integer index variable, its name should include the array's base name: iaintPartNum.

Base Name Lengths

There is no rule limiting variable name length, but common sense would dictate that variable names longer than 15 or 20 characters waste a lot of keystrokes. The VBA module editor shows roughly the first 30 characters of a procedure name by default, so 30 is suggested as the target maximum procedure name length.

Abbreviate VBA object base name elements wherever possible using a standardized abbreviation table, such as in Table 6.17 in the later section "Standard Abbreviations." You can extend LNC by creating your own standard abbreviations as well. You should create and use standardized terminology in your applications wherever possible; for examples see the later section "Standardized Terminology", later in this chapter.

Compound Base Names

Procedure base names follow the construction *ObjectVerb*, where the *Object* portion describes the primary object type affected (often the same as the primary argument), and *Verb* describes the action. This style sorts functions and subs by their target object when shown in ordered lists:

```
FormCtlAdd

FormCtlGet

FormCtlSet

FormPropAdd

FormPropGet

FormPropSet
```

Naming Conventions for VBA Objects

In Level Two of LNC, the following VBA objects require tags:

- ▶ Variables
- ▶ Type structures
- ▶ Constants

Optional tags also are available for some types of procedures. By definition, if you are a Level One user, LNC assumes that you are not writing VBA code. If you are creating procedures, you are a Level Two user and should always apply Level Two tags and prefixes throughout your application.

In the syntax diagram earlier, I noted that base names are optional in some Level Two constructions. When programming in VBA in Level Two, the *tag* element is always required, but the *base name* is optional for local variables only. For example, a procedure that declared only one form object variable could legitimately use the variable name `frm`, which is a tag without a base name. Type structures, constants, and variables that have module-level or public scope must have both a tag and base name.

Tags for Variables

Visual Basic for Applications variable tags are noted in Table 6.10, Table 6.11, and Table 6.12, grouped by type of variable.

Table 6.10   Tags for VBA Data Variables

Variable Type	Tag
Boolean	bln
Byte	byt
Conditional Compilation Constant	ccc
Currency	cur
Date	dtm
Double	dbl
Error	err
Integer	int
Long	lng
Object	obj
Single	sng
String	str
User-Defined Type	typ
Variant	var

In the previous table, note that Conditional Compilation Constant, Error, and User-Defined Type are not true data types (created with `Dim name As type`) but rather programming concepts. A Conditional Compilation Constant variable is a flag of type `Boolean`, an Error variable is a `Variant` created with the `CVErr()` function, and user-defined types are unique constructs.

Table 6.11   Tags for VBA Object Variables

Object	Tag
Application	app
Assistant	ast
Collection	col
CommandBar	cbr
CommandBars	cbrs
Control	ctl
Controls	ctls
CustomControl	ocx
CustomControlInReport	ocx
DoCmd	dcd
Form	frm
Forms	frms
GroupLevel	lvl
Module	bas
Modules	bass
Page	pge
Pages	pges
Reference	ref
References	refs
Report	rpt
Reports	rpts
Screen	scn
Section	sec

Table 6.12   Tags for Data Access Object Variables

Object	Tag
Connection	cnc
Connections	cncs
Container	con

continues

Table 6.12 Continued

Object	Tag
Containers	cons
DBEngine	dbe
Database (any type)	dbs
Database (Btrieve)	dbtv
Database (dBASE)	ddbf
Database (Excel)	dxls
Database (FoxPro)	dfox
Database (Jet)	djet
Database (Lotus 1-2-3)	dwks
Database (ODBC)	dodb
Database (Paradox)	dpdx
Database (SQL Server)	dsql
Database (Text)	dtxt
Databases	dbss
Document	doc
Documents	docs
Dynaset	dyn
Error	err
Errors	errs
Field	fld
Fields	flds
Group	gru
Groups	grus
Index	idx
Indexes	idxs
Parameter	prm
Parameters	prms
Property	prp
Properties	prps
QueryDef (any type)	qdf

Object	Tag
QueryDef (Btrieve)	qbtv
QueryDef (dBASE)	qdbf
QueryDef (Excel)	qxls
QueryDef (FoxPro)	qfox
QueryDef (Jet)	qjet
QueryDef (Lotus 1-2-3)	qwks
QueryDef (ODBC)	qodb
QueryDef (Paradox)	qpdx
QueryDef (SQL Server)	qsql
QueryDef (Text)	qtxt
QueryDefs	qdfs
Recordset (any type)	rst
RecordSet (Btrieve)	rbtv
RecordSet (dBASE)	rdbf
RecordSet (dynaset)	rdyn
RecordSet (Excel)	rxls
RecordSet (Fox)	rfox
RecordSet (Lotus 1-2-3)	rwks
RecordSet (ODBC)	rodb
RecordSet (Paradox)	rpdx
RecordSet (snapshot)	rsnp
RecordSet (SQL Server)	rsql
RecordSet (table)	rtbl
RecordSet (text)	rtxt
Recordsets	rsts
Relation	rel
Relations	rels
Snapshot	snp
Table	tbl
TableDef (any type)	tdf
TableDef (Btrieve)	tbtv

6

continues

Table 6.12   Continued

Object	Tag
TableDef (dBASE)	tdbf
TableDef (Excel)	txls
TableDef (FoxPro)	tfox
TableDef (Jet)	tjet
TableDef (Lotus 1-2-3)	twks
TableDef (ODBC)	todb
TableDef (Paradox)	tpdx
TableDef (SQL Server)	tsql
TableDef (Text)	ttxt
TableDefs	tdfs
User	usr
Users	usrs
Workspace	wsp
Workspaces	wsps

The tags dyn, snp, and tbl in Table 6.12, for dynaset, snapshot, and table objects are directly relevant to users of Access 1 and Access 2. Starting with Access 95, these object types are allowed only as a subtype of recordset variables, thus the recordset tags rdyn, rsnp, and rtbl.

In Tables 6.11 and 6.12, tags for collection variables are made by adding s after the tag for the object type stored in the collection.

Even though I noted previously that a tag by itself is a legitimate variable name, some variable tags shown (such as int) are reserved words and will not compile in VBA—such tags require a base name.

Creating Automation Variables

Table 6.13 lists the LNC tags for Automation server variables.

Table 6.13   Tags for Automation Server Variables

Object	Tag
Access.Application	accapp
DAO.DBEngine	daodbe
Excel.Application	xlsapp
Excel.Chart	xlscht
Excel.Sheet	xlssht
Graph.Application	gphapp
MAPI.Session	mpimps
MSForms.DataObject	fmsdoj
MSForms.UserForm	fmsufm
MSProject.Application	prjapp
MSProject.Project	prjprj
OfficeBinder.Binder	bndbnd
Outlook.Application	otlapp
PowerPoint.Application	pptapp
SchedulePlus.Application	scdapp
SQLOLE.SQLServer	sqlsvr
TeamManager.Application	mgrapp
Word.Application	wrdapp
Word.Basic	wrdbas

6

Note that variables for objects in the object hierarchy of a referenced type library can be dimensioned directly by class, as in this line:

```
Dim xlsapp As Excel.Application
```

Alternately, if the variable is created with *late binding* (i.e., as a generic object) rather than *early binding* (as an object class), the prefix o is added to denote an object variable:

```
Dim oxlsapp As Object
Set oxlsapp = CreateObject("Excel.Application")
```

Our naming convention for entry point variables into Automation server applications follows this syntax:

applicationtag [entrypointtag] primaryobjecttag BaseName

The item *applicationtag* is a three-character notation for the server application, and *entrypointtag* is three characters denoting the entry point used. The *entrypointtag* is optional and should be used when clarification is necessary (when variables for several entry points are declared in the same procedure), or when the entry point is not the standard Application object. The *primaryobjecttag* describes the ultimate class of the object (the one you intend to address with the variable). The *BaseName* is optional and clarifies the use of the variable, as with other VBA variables.

For example, the following code creates an Excel `Range` object and manipulates it.

```
Sub SalesCheck()
  Dim xlswksSales As Excel.Worksheet
  Dim xlsrngYTD As Excel.Range
  Set xlswksSales = GetObject("C:\Data\Sales.Xls", "Excel.Sheet")
  Set xlsrngYTD = xlswksSales.Range("YTDSales")
  If xlsrngYTD.Value < 100000 Then
    MsgBox "Sales are lame.", vbOKOnly, "Get to Work!"
  End If
  Set xlswksSales = Nothing
End Sub
```

In this example, the `Range` object is technically several layers deep in the application hierarchy, and a purely accurate combination of tags and code structure would yield this line of code, which actually runs:

```
Set xlsappwkbwksrngYTD = _
    xlsapp.ActiveWorkbook.Worksheets("Sales").Range("YTDSales")
```

In practice, of course, such nomenclature is unwieldy, and the shorter style is more friendly yet still accurate.

I prefer to show the server name in the variable declaration for clarity of code—while both lines below will run, the second is less ambiguous:

```
Dim xlsrng As Range
Dim xlsrng As Excel.Range
```

See the section "Creating Your Own Tags," later in this chapter, for more discussion of Automation syntax.

Prefixes for Variables

The prefixes for VBA variables can be categorized into two groups: prefixes for scope and all other prefixes. Because the model for variable scope changed somewhat between Access 2 and 95, I will discuss scope prefixes first. The following prefixes are ordered by increasing (broader) scope.

No prefix   Use no prefix for variables that are local to a procedure.

s   Place this prefix before variables that are declared locally to a procedure with a `Static` statement.

m   Use this prefix for module-level variables that are declared with `Dim` or `Private` statements in the Declarations section of a module.

p   Use this prefix to denote variables declared as `Public` in the `Declarations` section of a form or report module. Such variables are publicly available to other procedures in the same database only.

g   Use this prefix to denote variables declared as `Public` in the `Declarations` section of a standard module. Such variables are truly global and may be referenced from procedures in the current or other databases.

When used, scope prefixes always begin a variable name and precede any other prefixes.

In addition to scope, there are other characteristics of variables that can be identified by prefixes, as follows:

a   Use this prefix to denote a variable that is declared as an array, including a `ParamArray` argument to a function.

c   This prefix is placed before constants defined with the `Const` statement.

i   Use this prefix to denote a variable (usually of type `Integer`) that serves as an index to an array or an index counter for a `For...Next` loop.

o   This prefix is placed before object variables that reference Automation servers through *late binding* (and `Object` variable), where the tag denotes the type of server.

r   Use this prefix for variables that are arguments (parameters) passed to a procedure and declared as `ByRef`, or not declared as either `ByRef` or `ByVal` (including a `ParamArray`), which implies `ByRef`.

t   Use this prefix to describe a variable that is declared as a user-defined `Type` structure. The variable should inherit the base name from the original declaration for the type.

v   Use this prefix for variables that are arguments (parameters) passed to a procedure and declared as `ByVal`.

Because a prefix provides a very detailed description of a variable, the number of allowable prefix combinations is limited, as shown in Table 6.14.

Table 6.14   Allowable Prefix Combinations

Any One of These...	...Can Come Before This
s, m, p, g, r, v	a
m, p, g	c
s, m, p, g, r, v	e
s, m, p, g, r, v	i
s, m, p, g, r, v	ia
s, m, p, g, r, v	o
m, p, g	t

Variables require a unique prefix when declared Public in a widely distributed application. See the "Tags and Prefixes for Procedures" section that follows for more information.

Naming Constants

Access 95 introduced sweeping changes in the area of constants. The changes most relevant to naming conventions include the following:

- ▶ A constant can now be assigned a data type when it is defined.
- ▶ All constants have been renamed and carry a tag of ac, db, or vb to identify their primary functional area.
- ▶ Constants can now be created with the Variant data type.

When creating constants, use a scope prefix (if appropriate), the prefix c, and the suitable tag for the constant's data type. To properly synchronize the tag and the data type, do not let Access assign the type; always use the full Const *name* As *datatype* syntax.

Constants require a unique prefix when declared Public in a widely distributed application. See the following section for more information.

Tags and Prefixes for Procedures

Whether to prefix and tag procedure names and how to do so are debatable subjects. This style neither requires nor encourages placing characters before a procedure name except in the situations discussed next.

Prefixes for Procedures

Procedures can have scope similar to that of variables—s (Static), m (Private), p (Public), or g (global Public). LNC supports the use of these scope prefixes on function names if they solve a particular need and are used consistently throughout an application.

If you are creating software for retail, for inclusion in the public domain, or for some other form of broad distribution, LNC requires that you prefix Public variables, constants, and procedures with a unique author prefix identifying you or your company. The prefix consists of two or three unique characters and an underscore and prevents your object names from conflicting with others in databases on a user's machine.

To create an author prefix, use your personal or company initials. For example, author prefixes for my companies are lbi_ for Leszynski Barker Inc., lci_ for Leszynski Company Inc., and kwc_ for Kwery Corporation. Before using your selected prefix, make an effort to determine if the prefix is already widely in use.

Tags for Procedures

The LNC style prescribes the following naming convention tags for procedures:

cbf   Use this tag on procedure names for code behind a form or report that is Private to the object. This tag clearly differentiates such procedures from Property procedures and event procedures.

mtd   Use this tag to differentiate class method procedures, which are method procedures defined in a class module, and Public procedures in a form or report object (which are de-facto methods).

prp   Use this tag on Property procedure names defined with Property Get, Property Let, and Property Set statements. This tag clearly differentiates such procedures from functions, subs procedures, and event procedures.

LNC does not require or suggest assigning a data type tag to functions to reflect their return value. However, if you have a specific need to tag procedures to reflect their return value type, use the appropriate tags from the earlier section "Tags for Variables" in this chapter, and apply them consistently to all procedures in an application.

Using Macros Instead of VBA

Occasionally, you might have a good reason to use macros to create action scripts. If so, apply the rules described earlier for VBA procedure base names to your macro base names. Macro groups in the Database window should utilize the macro prefixes and tags previously noted. Individual macros within a macro group do not have prefixes or tags except for event macros.

All macros for a specific form or report should be placed into one macro group with the form or report name as the macro base name. Within the macro group, create standard macros and event macros for the form or report. If a macro is tied to a form or report event, show the event name or an abbreviation in the macro name. For example, you would store macros related to `frmCust` in macro group `mfrmCust`. Event macro names in the group might include `Form_Current` and `txtLastName_Change`.

Macros that are not specific to a form or report should hold actions that have some common functionality or purpose. Use the same grouping methodology (related items together) that you would apply to locate procedures in VBA modules.

Visual Basic for Applications Object Name Examples

Table 6.15 shows examples of VBA variables applying the various conventions in this section.

Table 6.15   VBA Variable Name Examples

Declaration	Description
`Dim oxlsaBudget As Object`	Excel.Application
`Function lci_ArraySum (ParamArray _` `ravarNum() As Variant) As Double`	Company identifier
`Public giaintPartNum As Integer`	Global index into array
`Const clngCustNumMax As Long = 10000`	`Const` for max `CustID`
`Function FileLock(ByVal vstrFile As _` `String) As Boolean`	`ByVal` argument

Creating Your Own Tags

What do you do when LNC doesn't address a particular object naming need? First, contact me at **stanl@kwery.com** and let me know why so that we can improve the style for the benefit of all users. Second, consider whether what you are trying to do is covered by the style in some other way. For example, in your development team you call tables that link two other tables in a many-to-many relationship *linking* tables, and you want to create a new table tag, `tlnk`, as a result.

On examination of all table tags, you will find `trel` already exists, defined as "Table (many-to-many relation)," which is the correct tag for what you need. Even though the nomenclature is not exactly what you use, it is better to use an existing tag than to create another one.

Finally, when other options are exhausted, you can create a custom tag to address your need. When creating a custom tag, use the following guidelines:

▶ Do not redefine an existing tag. No matter how badly you really want the three or four character combination for your own purpose, never reuse a defined tag.

▶ Do not change the rule for tags. Stay within the three to four character range followed by LNC.

▶ Use the conventions in existing tags as your guide for the new one. For example, all table tags start with `t`, all query tags with `q`, and so on. Any new tags you make for these objects should begin with the correct letter. See Table 6.16 for guidelines on standard tag components. Note that some of the examples are from the solution developer's version of LNC (see Appendix C, "Leszynski Naming Conventions for Microsoft Solution Developers," on the CD-ROM). Tag components that can be easily inferred from the tags in this chapter are not listed in the table (for example, the component `fox` for FoxPro can be inferred from the tags `tfox` and `dfox`).

When you create a new tag, use a character combination that is mnemonic enough to uniquely shorten the word the tag represents, and only use characters from the root word or a generally accepted shorthand.

Table 6.16   Some Standard Tag Components

Item	Segment	Example	Location
bar	br	pbr	anywhere
database/databound	d	dout	leading
definition	df	qdf/tdf	anywhere
footer	ft	fft	anywhere
form	f	fdlg	leading
header	hd	fhd	anywhere
macro	m	mmnu	leading
MAPI	mp	mpm	leading
module	b	bas	leading
query	q	qsel	leading

continues

Table 6.16   Continued

Item	Segment	Example	Location
report	r	rdet	leading
set	st	rst	anywhere
table	t	tdf	leading
view	vw	lvw	anywhere

To create tags for object variables pointing to Automation server applications, start with the three-character MS-DOS file extension for the files created by the server application if unique and applicable (for example, xls for Excel files). If not unique, create a meaningful abbreviation of the application name. Add to the three-character abbreviation a single character for the actual object that serves as the entry point for the application, such as sht for "sheet" in Dim xlssht As Excel.Sheet.

For example, to create a tag for Automation with Shapeware's Visio program, which is an OLE server, use either vsd (the data file extension) or vis (a good mnemonic for Visio) as the basis for the tag, then add app for Application because the entry point to Visio's automation engine is a call to Visio.Application. Thus the tag and its use in variable declarations would look like the following:

```
Dim ovisapp As Object
Dim ovisdocHouse As Object
Set ovisapp - CreatcObject("Visio.Application")
Set ovisdocHouse = ovisapp.Documents.Open("C:\VISIO\HOUSE.VSD")
```

VBA Coding Conventions

In addition to object-naming conventions, LNC proposes several standardized coding conventions for VBA procedures. The use of standardized coding conventions makes your code more readable when you are debugging, doing a code review for yourself or another developer, or documenting an application.

Coding conventions and style issues that are not specifically related to object names are detailed in Chapter 11, "Expert Approaches to VBA."

Code Comments

There are as many in-line VBA code commenting styles as there are Basic coders. Whatever convention you use, the keys are to be terse yet descriptive and be consistent.

LNC suggests placing the following minimum set of comments at the beginning of each procedure:

Purpose—Briefly describe the purpose of the procedure.

Arguments—List the arguments to a function and how they are to be used.

Return Value—Describe what the return value of a `Function` procedure signifies.

Authors—Name the creator, the date created, the last editor, and the date last edited.

Comments placed on the same line as code should be separated from the code by two spaces. Comments placed on their own line should be no longer than 60 characters so they are displayed fully in the Access default module design view size.

Trapping Errors

Every procedure that can fail, which is virtually every procedure with more than a few lines, should have an error trap. You can create an error trap by placing the following line at the beginning of the procedure, after the header comments and before any other statements:

```
On Error GoTo procname_Err
```

The marker `procname` should be replaced with the full procedure name. The error handler is placed at the bottom of the procedure, denoted with the label `procname_Err`. At the end of the error handler, control is returned somewhere in the procedure, usually to a line label name `procname_Exit`, that precedes a block of code immediately above the error handler.

To turn off error trapping during program debugging, LNC suggests that you place the `On Error` statement inside a conditional compilation directive such as the following:

```
#If pcccDebug Then
   On Error Goto 0
#Else
   On Error Goto procname_Err
#Endif
```

Before running an application, you can enable or disable error trapping by setting the value of `pcccDebug` to -1 (`True`) or 0 (`False`) in the Conditional Compilation Arguments text box on the Module tab of the Tools Options dialog box.

Standardized Abbreviations

Table 6.17 lists some of my standard abbreviations for use in building object names. This is not a comprehensive list and is meant only to give you a starting point for your own taxonomy.

Table 6.17   Standardized Object Name Abbreviations

Abbreviation	Description
Acct	account
Actg	accounting
Addr	address
Admin	administration
Agmt	agreement
Amt	amount
Anal	analysis
Apvd	approved
Arch	archive
Arvl	arrival
Asst	assist(ant)
Atty	attorney
Auth	authorized
Avg	average
Beg	beginning
Bilg	billing
Bldg	building
Busn	business
Char	character
Comm	comment
Cont	contact
Corp	corporate, corporation
Ctrl	control
Ctry	country
Cty	county

Abbreviation	Description
Cur	currency
Curr	current
Cust	customer
Dept	department
Desc	description
Det	detail, details
Devlpmt	development
Disc	discount
Dlr	dealer
Empe	employee
Engrg	engineering
Exec	executive
Extd	extend, extended
Extn	extension
Fin	finance, financial
Genl	general
Glbl	global
Int	interest
Intl	international
Inv	inventory
Invc	invoice
Loca	location
Mfg	manufacturing
Mgmt	management
Mgr	manager
Mkt	market
Mktg	marketing
Mon	month
Mtg	meeting
Mtl	material
Mtls	materials

continues

6

Table 6.17   Continued

Abbreviation	Description
Num	number
Ofc	office
Ofcr	officer
Op	operation
Ops	operations
Ordr	order
Othr	other
Perd	period
Pers	personal, personnel
Phon	phone
Phys	physical
Pmt	payment
Prim	primary
Prnt	print
Proj	project
Pros	prospect, prospective
Qty	quantity
Rec	record
Recd	received
Rem	remark
Schd	schedule, scheduled
Secy	secretary
Seq	sequence
Srce	source
Stat	status
Stats	statistics
Std	standard
Sum	summary, summaries, summation
Super	supervise, supervisor
Svc	service

Abbreviation	Description
Titl	title
Tran	transaction
Ttl	total
Var	variable
Ver	version
Whse	warehouse
Whsl	wholesale
Xsfr	transfer
Xsmn	transmission
Xsmt	transmit

Standardized Terminology

When creating code comments, object names, help files, and system documentation, it is important to use terms that have an accepted and nonambiguous meaning. Build a list of standardized terms for your specific industry or application to ensure consistency. Table 6.18 provides a short list of standardized terminology. These terms are not required by LNC; they are only examples.

Table 6.18   Examples of Standardized Terminology

Term	Description
Add	To create a new record. Select Add, Create, Enter, or New, and be consistent.
Beg	The start of a process.
Close	To close an open object.
Comment	A more familiar term for text originating with a human than Remark or Notes.
Desc	A description, often a long text string.
Edit	To change or modify.
Editor	The last person to change a record.
End	The end of a process.

continues

Table 6.18   Continued

Term	Description
Flag	A programming item with a fixed set of values, usually True/False (a Boolean).
Key	An index used to find a record.
Max	The maximum, better than Most.
Min	The minimum, better than Least.
Open	To open an object.
Owner	The creator of a record, process, or object.
Save	To commit a record.
User	The person currently running an application.

From Here...

This chapter details comprehensive standardized naming conventions for Access. Application development examples found throughout the book will use these naming conventions.

▶ For a detailed discussion of questions asked during the creation of these naming conventions, read Chapter 5, "Creating Naming Conventions."

▶ To see the practical application within VBA of many techniques discussed in this chapter, go to Chapter 11, "Expert Approaches to VBA."

▶ In-house development tools can apply naming conventions automatically. To learn how to build such tools, refer to Chapter 20, "Applying Development Shortcuts."

▶ To read an expanded document that proposes cross-platform naming conventions for all of Microsoft Office and other Microsoft developer products, see Appendix C, "Leszynski Naming Conventions for Microsoft Solution Developers," on the CD-ROM.

Understanding Application Architecture

7

You can't build a reliable application unless you use or create a good set of components and combine them appropriately. This chapter teaches you about application ingredients.

Solution Development

> ### Multiple Personalities
>
> "When we were designing the first release of Access, many people on the Access team didn't see the need for separate report objects in the product. As we had already decided that users would be able to print forms, all we really needed to do was to enable forms with sorting, grouping, and a few other report-specific features, and presto—forms would have both personalities.
>
> "Ultimately, we deserted the concept as too confusing for users, because it would give forms quite a few more features and properties to wade through. To this day, however, we're not convinced that it was a bad idea."
>
> Tod Nielsen, General Manager, Microsoft Access Business Unit

I used to enjoy rock and ice climbing in my youth. You can take two approaches to scaling a rock face:

Plan the route. With binoculars in hand, the climbing team stands back from the rock wall and carefully reviews the challenge, determining the most interesting and realistic route through the various obstacles. Part of the enjoyment of climbing this way involves successfully negotiating the selected route, thus validating the planning process.

Start climbing. By contrast, some climbers prefer to simply grab the first visible handhold, pull themselves up a few inches, then hang there and chart their path to the next handhold or ledge. The adrenaline rush of hanging in space with no clear sense of direction provides much of the satisfaction in this variation of the sport.

Many programmers employ the second approach when climbing their coding cliffs. With an objective in hand (solving a described business need), they begin building tables, and then layer application objects on top in whatever order suits them. For these developers, some of the satisfaction of building an application lies in surmounting the unforeseen hurdles that crop up when developing with no clear direction.

Unfortunately, in this ad hoc variation of both solution development and rock climbing, it is easy to navigate into obstacles that are not surmountable. Having reached an unplanned barrier, the climber or developer must then pull back and find another direction around the problem. On the rock face, this involves "down climbing," which is much more difficult and dangerous than "up climbing." In solution development, this involves reworking or replacing objects that have been partially developed, which is embarrassing and wasteful.

When I was teaching others to rock climb, I would try to stress to them that there is no shame in choosing the first approach (planning) over the second approach (ad hoc). Excluding the radically macho types, most people can be taught to derive as much raw enjoyment from the sport using a thoughtful approach as from a random one, and with less risk.

And so it is with developers. Programming a solution should not be like unstructured rock climbing or playing a video game—the thrill must not be linked to the resolution of short-term hurdles, but rather to conquering the overall business problem.

 Note

I believe that an important milestone in the maturation of an application developer is when he or she learns to derive satisfaction from the creation and execution of a solid development plan.

I discussed planning automated solutions to business problems in Chapters 3, "Preparing for Development," and 4, "Creating Design Specifications." You might recall that I focused on these main concepts in the two chapters:

▸ Discovering and documenting the needs of the users

▸ Understanding an application's life cycle and designing the application for growth

▸ Creating an effective team process for defining and deploying the application

With a grasp of these issues and a development plan in hand, you are ready to begin creating application objects, right? Not so fast. While successful design means creating a good plan, effective development does not mean blindly executing the plan. Rather, the planning process takes grains of sand (facts) and assembles them into a rock wall (the project); but there are multiple routes (project plans) that would get the team up and over the top to the completed solution. The developer's mission is to find the best route to the solution by mixing and matching these ingredients:

Access Application Objects. These are tables, queries, forms, command bars, code procedures, and so on.

External Components and Services. Some applications can benefit from external services like ActiveX Controls, Automation servers, e-mail messaging, and Windows API calls.

Methodologies. Development efforts and teams are more successful when employing consistent, stated methodologies for application organization, development techniques, and project management.

In this chapter, we will explore how to blend these ingredients successfully and define the conceptual issues that impact how you select a route up an application development cliff. Along the way, I will expose various elements of the Leszynski Development Framework (LDF) approach to application architecture. (Recall from Chapter 2, "Introducing the Leszynski Development Framework," that LDF Standards Precept 2 says, "Use a Consistent Application Architecture Model.")

Dissecting the Parts of an Application

An Access-centric application may have scores or even hundreds of objects. On the surface, the fundamental relationship between these objects is straightforward—queries build on tables, forms get data from queries, and so on.

Looking at application objects as if they were construction materials puts them in a different light, however. You can't build a house with only one shape of wood or a single type of nail. Neither can you build an application with one kind of table or form. It is important to understand the subtle and not-so-subtle "types," or "subclasses," of application objects available for constructing a solution.

Classifying Access Application Components

Much of the work of defining the attributes of application objects occurs at development time. A specification may call for a data-entry form and describe the layout of controls and list of events that will populate the form, yet the developer retains some discretion about exactly how to empower the form to achieve the stated objectives.

It is useful for developers to create standard definitions of different Access object types and their roles. These standard object types become the building blocks of applications. The definitions are not rigid and can be modified at development time to suit particular user needs. The definitions are clear and precise, however, to achieve these two results:

To provide planners and users with application building blocks. Users and design team members—especially the nontechnical members—greatly appreciate being given a list of application building blocks and their definitions and being told to request the appropriate object type for each need when writing a design specification. This process brings users and developers closer together in terms of a common language, and helps users to understand the tools in the developer's satchel.

To allow developers to create object templates and reusable object engines. Once common objects have been defined, developers can create standard library versions of the objects and use them as a starting point or template when building an application-specific version of the object type.

Let's consider a simple example. Historically, users of database-centric applications have been exposed to their data through forms that display a single record at a time. This was for technical reasons (limitations in mainframe terminal software), business reasons (the safety of exposing users to a limited set of data), and usability reasons (to minimize user confusion). If your users have this background, they may not be aware of the flexibility of Access forms to present data in various layouts unless so instructed. To allow such users to help design the correct application for their needs, they must be made to understand the difference in capabilities and relevance between single-record, continuous, form/subform, and datasheet form object types.

To create a set of application building blocks, enumerate and describe the standard object types that your development team will use. For example, LDF uses the following attributes to define application object types:

> *Name.* Each object type should have formal name and naming convention guidelines. For example, when you create an object definition to apply to all application main switchboards, you could designate that such objects always be called `fmnuMain`.

> *Formal Definition.* A short, formal definition quickly describes the object to potential users. For example: The main switchboard menu in each application will be provided by a modal form that contains an application graphic and two controls, a combo box control that lists option types, and a list box control that shows options within the selected type. The main switchboard won't have a bar menu or toolbar and will have OK and Quit buttons.

> *Primary Attributes.* Any traits of the object that are formalized should be recorded for the benefit of developers. Here is an example of a formalized attribute definition: Developers must enter a `Description` property value for each field in transaction tables, but system tables and temporary tables do not require field descriptions. Each transaction table will contain the fields `CreatedAt` and `CreatedBy`—logging the creation and creator of each record—and `ChangedAt` and `ChangedBy`—capturing the last edit date and initiating user.

> *Rules for Use.* Your guidelines may define how to mix each standard object type into an application in an appropriate manner. For example: Archive tables that store historical records must reside in a database on the server named Graveyard.

> *Standard Template.* If a template object is created for reuse (such as a standard form template used as a starting point for new switchboard menus), its location and usage should be documented for the benefit of the entire development team. For example: Standardized templates for form objects should be stored in a database of templates located with other development library objects.

Note

I'm using the term *template* here in a broader sense than Access does. A form or report template to Access is an object designated in the Options dialog as a Form Template or Report Template. In my parlance, a template object may be used in this fashion as well or may also be used by developers as a source object that is copied, renamed, and modified to create a new object.

Standard Bearer. Often a specific object type is assigned to a development team member who determines, disseminates, champions, and enhances the object's definition and templates. Such a person is sometimes called an Object Librarian or Code Librarian.

In the next six sections, I review the six primary Access objects and define the various LDF application object types for each object. The LDF object type designations are summarized in Tables 7.1 and 7.2.

Note

These designations are my own—no industry standard classifications have been defined for PC database application objects. You may use my designations as they are or use them only as seeds for your own definition discussions.

Table 7.1   LDF Application Object Types

Tables	Queries	Forms	Reports
Archive	Control Source	Alert	Detail
Log	Family View	Class Module	Export
Lookup	Filter	Dialog	Subreport
Relation	Form Source	Lookup	Summary
Summary	Grand Join	Query-By-Form	Template
Supporting	Lookup	Subform	
System	Report Source	Switchboard Menu	
Temporary	Summary	Template	
Transaction		Wizard/Builder	

Notice that the LDF object types named in Table 7.1 are often more concerned with user interaction and application requirements than the internal workings of Access. For example, a crosstab query is a legitimate query type in Access; but from an application construction standpoint, the purpose of the query is usually to provide records to a Detail Report or Summary Report. Thus, LDF places more importance on the fact that the query is a Report Source type rather than being constructed as a crosstab.

When you create your own standard object classifications, you may find that object types have subtypes, and that these subtypes deserve clarification in your architecture model. For example, Table 7.1 notes the LDF form type Query-By-Form, which actually has more than one subtype (such as the Get form I describe in Chapter 16, "Presenting Data to Users").

Table 7.2   LDF Programming Object Types

Macros	Modules
AutoExec	Application
AutoKeys	Class Module
Event	Declaration
Macro Group	Library
Menu	Process

Defining Table Types

The majority of Access tables hold raw data, as entered by users or application processes. I term these *transaction tables* because their records describe real-life events: buying, selling, consuming, moving, counting, meeting, inspecting, fixing, calling, and so on. (Some traditional relational database terminologies call these base tables.)

I group transaction tables into three categories (see Figure 7.1):

Native. Native tables reside in the user's interface database and serve one of two purposes:

▶ In a single-user, single-file application, native transaction tables log actual data entry. The front-end and back-end databases are combined to make the application transportable, to achieve a performance objective, or to simplify the application architecture.

▶ In any kind of application, native (local) transaction tables may store "system" transactions (generated by application code), temporary transactions, and so forth. For example, the user of an inventory application may regularly import warehouse receipt information from a portable bar-code reader into a local transaction table, and then audit and adjust the table data before posting it to the back-end database file or database server.

Linked. A linked transaction table resides in a back-end database—which may be located on the user's local drive—on a shared drive on another workstation, on a file server at the current location, or even on a server across the globe. Jet's ISAM driver layer allows linked tables to be maintained in Jet or non-Jet formats, thus allowing Access to use or share data in formats created by other database software packages. The user's interface (front-end application) database only contains a link to each remote table; thus, schema changes are not possible from the user session of the application.

Server. Transaction tables may also reside on a database server and provide data to forms via ODBC table links or program code. Developers can make use of a technology called "pass through" to send SQL commands directly through the ODBC layer to a variety of database server engines without using table links. When server data is presented on a form, it may be presented in a real-time, updatable fashion (through table links), or via transactions that "check out" and "check in" records from and to the server via program code. See Chapter 19, "Exploring Client/Server Issues," for an enhanced discussion of these techniques.

Fig. 7.1

I catalog transaction tables in an application into these three groups.

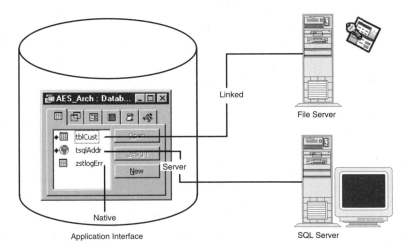

Sprinkled around transaction tables in the database schema are other table types that serve as supporting players. LDF groups nontransaction tables using the following terms and capabilities:

Archive Tables. Many database systems remove a record from an active table when the record has aged past a certain point, or when a transaction is "closed" (has reached the end of its usefulness). A common design methodology involves moving such records from a transaction table to an archive table (or history table), which serves as a repository for aged data.

 Tip

An additional use for archive tables is to store deleted records for later review or retrieval. Deleted data records are usually stored in separate tables from aged (archived) records. See Chapter 15, "Protecting and Validating Data," for an expanded discussion of saving deleted records.

Log Tables. Application events that repeat over and over and are of significance for auditing, accounting, or other user-monitoring are noted in log tables. These tables are reviewed periodically for the management or development information they can provide. An example of a log table is a table that is updated each time data is imported from a mainframe into the application database. At import time, a record is written to the table with the date, time, and statistics from the process. Such information may later prove useful to developers or managers.

Lookup Tables. Combo and list box values in data-entry forms are usually filled from tables that map short key values to longer display strings. These tables, called lookup tables, translate string information that is important to users into numbers or very short strings that are stored in the transaction tables. Storing numbers or short strings allows for quicker data access, localization or redefinition of supporting strings, a smaller data storage footprint, and similar benefits.

An example lookup table is a list of states that contains the Postal Service short code and the full state name, with the short code stored in the data tables and the long string values "looked up" for display and reporting.

Relation Tables. In a relational database like Access, a single record cannot have multiple parent records in another table by direct linkage. A relationship where such many-to-many connections exist must use a third table to list the identifying keys of the records that are joined. Such a table is most commonly called a relation table, junction table, intersect table, or linking table.

For example, assume an application with tables for companies and people. One company can be the parent of many people, but one person can work at multiple companies. Thus, the relationship between the tables is many-to-many and requires an intermediate relation table to enable query joins (see Figure 7.2). Chapter 10, "Creating Expert Tables and Queries," explores this type of table in detail.

Fig. 7.2

An example of a many-to-many table relationship with a relation table between the data tables.

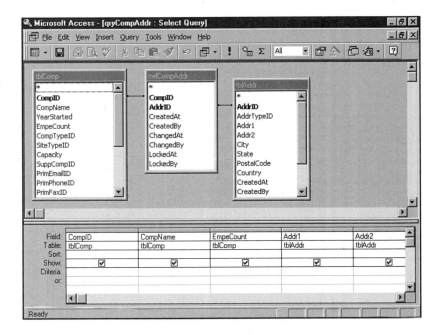

Summary Tables. Data that must be presented to users in summary form is often reorganized to make it more presentable or easier to use. Summary tables provide information pulled from one or more tables and then denormalized (a single record is created from multiple joined records) or summarized (aggregate queries are run to group data and only the summary results are stored). This type of data processing is often performed when creating executive reporting systems or data warehouses (as described in the section "Access and Data Warehousing" later in this chapter) or when creating interim results that are used in other application processes.

For example, each call to your Customer Service department is logged in a table containing the customer number as the link to the customer table. A summary query for this data joins the tblCall table with the tblCustomer table, groups and counts the calls by customer number, and creates a summary table containing one record per customer with these fields: CustomerNumber, CustomerName, and TotalCalls.

Supporting Tables. Some data tables are mostly static (nontransactional) yet contain more information than would be found in a standard lookup table. These tables usually provide ancillary support to one or more features in your application; I call them supporting tables.

For example, your application uses a table of employee names to validate logins and stamp records. Because the data entry processes do not use the table, I would not call it a transaction table. It is hidden from nonadministrative users, thus it is somewhat like a system table (defined following). The `EmployeeID` field values from this table are stored in transaction tables, however, which map back to this table for the full employee name, so the table is somewhat like a lookup table. Further, because each employee record in this table is stamped with the most recent login date and time for the employee, it has some characteristics of a log table. This table has many of the characteristics of table types that I have defined, but it also provides such a broad array of support to its application that the best term for it is supporting table.

System Tables. LDF uses the moniker "system tables" to describe tables that provide information to program routines only and not to users. An example is a table with standardized message strings that provides customized messages for alerts generated by program code. These message strings are created by the developer and are used only from code, thus there is no user interface or user interaction.

Temporary Tables. Some application processes require the creation of work tables that may be displayed to the user or accessed from program code then deleted at the completion of a process. We call these temporary, or temp, tables.

For example, your application contains a code routine to import records from an external Excel file each week. One approach your code could use is to call the `TransferSpreadsheet` method and import the spreadsheet as a new table, clean up the data in the import table, and then append the imported records to a transaction table. The imported (temporary) table would then be deleted. Figure 7.3 diagrams these various table types.

Depending on your tastes, you can define tables and their purposes more broadly than I have here (for example, transaction and supporting tables only) or devise terminology that is much more detailed than the LDF list. You may also find yourself adding new types of table definitions over time as your application needs dictate. Defining table types and their roles in an application provides a good foundation for developing policies and procedures, as well as a common syntax for developers and application designers.

Fig. 7.3
*The LDF table types
and the Access objects
that use them most
frequently.*

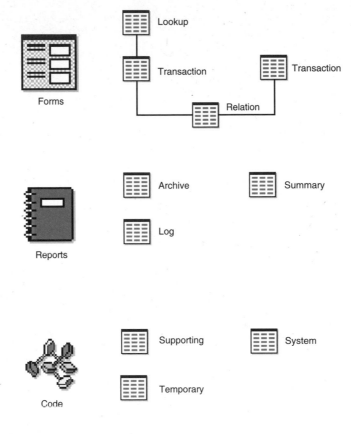

Defining Query Types

Access intrinsically defines nine types of queries:

▶ Append

▶ Crosstab

▶ Data Definition

▶ Delete

▶ Make Table

▶ Pass-Through

▶ Select

▶ Union

▶ Update

A query inherits its basic personality from its type, as listed here, and from its source tables. Access strictly defines the personality of each of the listed Access query types, requiring little additional characterization by the developer.

In addition to a query's Access type or action, however, there is a purpose for the object that is related to its role in its host application. The needs of your applications or development style may dictate specific query type definitions. The following list is the expanded type terminology that LDF uses for queries:

> *Control Source.* A query that supplies records to a combo box or list box control's list provides the minimum subset of rows and columns required to build the list, and usually sorts the data. Control source queries often use the Union operator to combine values from multiple tables or to add an "All" or "New" marker to the list (see examples of this in Chapter 13, "Mastering Combo and List Boxes").

> *Family View.* I use the term "family view query" to describe a join that brings together all related data elements, excluding their lookup table values (see also the definition of grand join later). In other words, a family view shows one or more parent records and every related (child) record from the parent downward to some logical point in the relationship tree (see Figure 7.4). A family view may include a record's children, grandchildren, and even deeper related records. Alternatively, a family view may join records from sibling tables, where one record in a table matches to one record in a second table.

Fig. 7.4

A family view query joins parents and children.

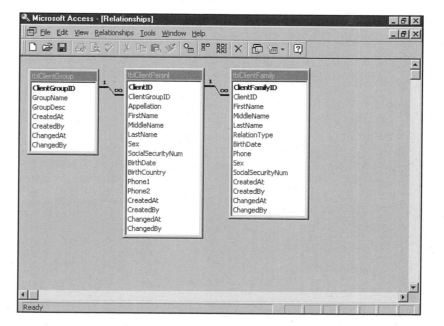

Filter. A filter query specifies a record restriction that is used as a form filter with the OpenForm method or Filter property.

Form Source. By my definition, a form source query is used to supply records to a form's RecordSource property and must meet certain criteria:

▶ It (usually) must be updatable.

▶ It must be optimized for performance.

▶ It must provide only the minimum number of fields and records valuable to the form.

Grand Join. I use the term "grand join" to describe a query that brings in related and supporting information from the top of a relationship downward or sideways. A grand join query usually includes a parent table, its child and grandchild tables, and all lookup tables required to translate ID values into user-viewable strings (see Figure 7.5). A grand join may also bring together data in a transaction table with its related logs and other supporting tables.

Fig. 7.5

A grand join query includes multiple generations plus related lookup values.

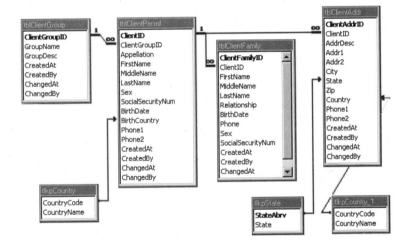

Report Source. A report source query provides data to a report. This kind of query usually combines several related tables with their lookup table values (making it a variation on a grand join query). Alternatively, this query is a type of summary query (defined following) that performs aggregation of data records.

Lookup Table. Datasheets and forms based on lookup tables are usually sourced from a query that sorts the lookup values for a cleaner presentation.

Summary. A summary query uses the Group By clause and one or more of the SQL aggregate functions like Average(), Count(), and Sum() to create a condensed view of transaction data.

While the query types listed here are most often constructed as select queries, a query of a specific LDF type can be defined using various action types (as an example, a family view query might be built as a select, append, or make table query).

Defining Form Types

If you have to choose to put effort into creating standardized object definitions for only one type of Access object, you should choose forms. These objects are the primary device for allowing user interaction with data and, as such, provide the most visible and heavily used application elements.

The most important forms in your application are data entry/edit transaction forms. Often, one transaction form provides both of these capabilities; in other cases, an application's needs dictate a separation of entry and edit tasks into form pairs. You will want to consider creating form templates for these two form varieties and standardizing button designations, navigation code, validation styles, and property definitions. You can use the form templates and their code as the basis for creating new objects. Alternatively, some developers create customized form wizards to build forms matching their company's standardized layouts.

Forms are extremely versatile and thus are used to create other types of application object subclasses. They add functionality to your application by providing a medium for collecting information (as data), displaying information (as messages), and enabling the flow (as switchboard menus). In addition to entry/edit transaction forms, LDF defines these other form types and creates standards for using each type:

Alert. An alert or message form performs services similar to the MsgBox() function by communicating a short informational or warning string to the user, but usually expands on the capabilities of the intrinsic function by providing additional data, graphics, text, or buttons. For example, Figure 7.6 shows a helpful alert that appears at the end of an import process.

7

Fig. 7.6

Custom alert forms
can provide more
information and
features than a simple
`MsgBox()` *dialog.*

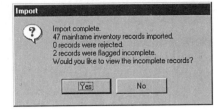

Class Module. Access uses the forms engine to create class modules—custom objects that provide extensions to your application via custom properties and methods. For example, a class module called `fclsNameFix` could be defined in your application with first, middle, and last names as custom properties and include a procedure to return a combined name string from these properties via a custom method that concatenates the component parts.

> **α Note**
>
> A class module that is displayed to the user can be created as a form class module, and technically any form or report that has code is loosely defined as a class module. However, Access 97 now provides class module objects that are a subtype of the module object. Use this type of class module when your object won't have a display view.

Dialog. A dialog form collects settings or other nontransactional information that can be gathered on a single, often unbound, pop-up form. Usually a dialog form asks a question or collects information that is critical to application flow or a programmatic process. Figure 7.7 shows a sample dialog form.

Fig. 7.7

A dialog form collects
information from the
user but does not save
the information to a
transaction record.

Lookup Table. LDF provides this separate designation for forms that allow entry and editing of lookup table values. Because of the special connection between lookup table keys and transaction data, these forms have a limited audience (usually database administrators only) and narrowly defined validation code (disallowing the deletion of values in use). For example, a form to edit values in a lookup table of inventory product types must contain a procedure that prevents the administrator from deleting a type used in any transaction records.

Query By Form. Most applications include a mechanism for presenting users with a simple format for selecting and operating on record subsets. My application model approaches this task using a standardized type of query-by-form object that we call a Get form. See Chapter 16, "Presenting Data to Users," for a complete description of this type of form.

 Note

Access's new Filter By Form and Filter By Selection capabilities remove some of the value of homemade query-by-form and other record selection forms.

Subform. A subform is a variation of the entry/edit form definition and inherits many of the attributes of its containing (parent) form.

Switchboard Menu. Forms used as button or list menus are easily defined, standardized, and made into template objects.

Template. Access uses a template form to prescribe the properties that a new form will inherit. The current template is defined using the Form Template option on the Options dialog. A template exists in an application solely to aid the developer; it has no interaction with users.

Wizard/Builder. Wizard forms follow specific formulae for construction and for look-and-feel and can be created to provide users with a development tool or to direct an application process. Wizard form definitions follow a question-and-answer metaphor and should mimic the layout and flow of Access' own wizards. A builder form is usually a single dialog that assists users in the creation of a property or application value.

It can be helpful to design teams to provide them with hardcopy examples of each form type defined for your organization. This allows the team to understand Access'—and the developers'—abilities with respect to forms, helping the team design more usable and capable applications overall.

Defining Report Types

When defining the capabilities and properties of your organization's standard report types, it will be tempting to gravitate to one of two extremes. At one end is the belief that reports have no attributes worth standardizing, because they are always defined by the users. At the other end of the spectrum is the temptation to define report subclasses for a wide variety of data sources, grouping and sorting algorithms, distribution methods, and user communities.

Because reporting is more heavily user-driven than form design, many developers evolve a hands-off attitude to reporting standards and let the design team create reporting object definitions on a per-application basis. LDF mostly leans this way, based on the belief that reports are the most widely visible and used component in most applications and thus should be custom tailored to the users' needs. Thus, LDF defines the following minimum set of standard report types simply to provide a standardized vocabulary to guide the design process:

Detail. Also termed a transaction report, this report type makes up the bulk of an application's reporting by dumping data elements in a tabular layout. For each user community, we create a general definition for this subclass that provides guidelines for layout, fonts, and other properties, events, and so on.

Export. Reports that are created specifically to provide data to the Office Links feature of Access (to be exported to either Excel or Word) should be defined with standardized attributes that provide the best possible look and layout in the receiving application. For example, a report designed for export has no need for fancy control border styles that are not carried to the Word document. (See Chapter 18, "Creating Expert Reports," for an example of an export report that is designed specifically to be published on the Web.)

Subreport. A subreport can be embedded in either a detail or summary report, and can be of either a detailed transaction or summary nature. It inherits many of the attributes of the containing (parent) report even if it groups the data differently.

Summary. A summary, or rollup, report is usually based on a summary query and groups and sorts data with totaling.

Template. Access uses a template report to prescribe the properties that a new report will inherit. The current template is defined using the Report Template option on the Options dialog. A template exists in an application solely to aid the developer; it has no interaction with users.

Chapter 18, "Creating Expert Reports," discusses additional reporting issues and techniques.

 Note
One reality of application development is that the report design process never ends. Whenever the ultimate users of a report (usually managers) have a slow day,

> an infusion of new management, or a corporate restructuring meeting, reports tend to get redesigned in the process.

Defining Macro Types

The distinct flavors of macros are readily discernible to any Access developer. They do not require a complex level of definition except for naming conventions and a strategy for enforcing and phrasing the Comment property strings. Access macro objects are grouped under LDF using these type designations:

AutoExec. Each application may have one of these macros, whose purpose is well defined. (The Startup property Display Form can now be used to replace the AutoExec macro.)

AutoKeys. This optional macro provides keyboard shortcuts defined for developers, users, or both.

Event. Although VBA has become the event handler of choice for most developers, macros can still be used to provide actions to form and report event properties.

Macro Group. A macro group includes one or more macros that provide shared routines to the application in the same manner as a standard module provides multiple shared VBA code procedures.

Menu. A menu macro can create a bar menu, a drop-down menu (also called a submenu), or a shortcut menu. These macros are still supported in Access 97, although the newer command bar technology has replaced them.

These macro definitions are primarily programming constructions and have no impact on users, thus they are not usually described to the application's design team. For example, the team can effectively define application menus even without understanding what technique is used to program them.

Defining Module Types

Modules are grouping objects whose use is completely arbitrary—in theory, all the code for one application could be placed in a single standard module. Developers are well served by using modules to create smaller subsets of grouped procedures, however. LDF defines procedure groups using modules with these personalities:

Application. I place all the code that is specifically tailored for an application into a single application module (or sometimes several modules) that clearly group the functions defined for application processes. For example, a simple phone list application may have a module `basPhoneList` containing all primary routines for the application.

Class Module. A class module is implemented in Access as an object whose procedures define custom properties or methods. Refer to Chapter 12, "Understanding Form Structures and Coding," which discusses both form-based and module-based class modules.

Library. For procedures that I reuse across multiple applications, I create small library modules that group several procedures related by attributes, such as a single type of target object (list box routines, for example) or related functionality (all data import routines). Consequently, I might create a separate library module `lci_basLibLst` for generic `ListBox` routines. See Chapter 20, "Applying Development Shortcuts," for more information on library procedures and modules.

Process. A process module contains all the procedures required for a specific application process, and is a subset of the application module type defined previously. For example, `basEndOfMonth` may contain all of the related routines that post accounting transactions monthly.

Because these groupings are arbitrary and the implementation is flexible, you will most likely group procedures slightly differently from one application to the next (with the exception of library procedures which, by definition, tend to remain static across applications).

Identifying Non-Access Application Components

Access applications do not exist in a vacuum; they inherit some of the characteristics of their operating environment, such as screen resolution from the workstation and window display attributes from the operating system. For more complex applications, Access can also be made to interact with a variety of external components to create a robust solution that taps into readily available feature providers.

Let's review the primary common components that Access can reach out and use to extend its abilities:

ActiveX Controls. Access forms and reports can serve as hosts for custom controls, which are simply embeddable OLE servers. Thus, you can buy or create very powerful task engines written as OCX files and coded with all the power of Visual Basic or Visual C++.

Automation Servers. Using Visual Basic or Visual C++, your organization can create Automation server programs that provide an unlimited range of extensions to Access applications and are driven by VBA code.

Business Objects. As I describe in the "Access and Three-Tiered Architecture" section later in this chapter, the current vogue in client/server application topology includes isolating certain program operations into a middle layer of data validation and processing. In an enterprise with these componentized business objects, Access can sometimes be made to take advantage of such process engines (for example, if they are coded as Automation servers or DLL files).

Code Libraries. The ability to reference an Access code library file from an application provides you the opportunity to extend each application with centralized code engines and shared wizards.

Data Services. Access can be made to use external (non-Jet) data services by directly calling either the ODBC API, the RDO API, or ODBCDirect from VBA code.

 Note
ODBCDirect is a new client/server connection technology added to Access 97 that allows for connections to ODBC data sources without using any resources of the Jet Database Engine. If you are a Visual Basic programmer, you will have first been exposed to the concept of going directly to ODBC for data services while working with the RDO (Remote Data Objects) technology introduced in VB4.

7

Executables. Your code can call the Shell() function in Access to start another executable application. This operation can be as simple as starting the Windows Calculator, or as complex as "chaining" from Access to an accounting module written in Visual Basic or Visual C++.

Office Applications. Using Automation, your Access application can take advantage of the capabilities of Excel, Graph, OLE Messaging, Outlook, Project, PowerPoint, Schedule+, Word, and other Microsoft applications.

Windows API. Within the Windows Application Program Interface are functions that return a host of workstation and operating system information tidbits and provide linkage to the screen, the Clipboard, the keyboard, and so forth.

Design and development teams must be made to understand this full gamut of extensions available to Access and not limit their design cosmos only to that provided by Access' feature list.

Exploring Application Architecture Arrangements

Once you have defined the functional requirements of an application, you must list the appropriate set of application building blocks and organize the selected blocks into an application architecture.

 Note

I'm using the term "application architecture" loosely in this chapter to describe the conceptual and physical arrangement of objects and processes that make up an Access solution. In this context, the term means how elements and processes in an application are organized. Within application architecture, LDF includes these object-related subsets: data architecture (as detailed in the section "Deciding Where the Data Will Reside," that follows), code architecture (described in the section "Fitting VBA Code into the Architecture" later in this chapter), and interface architecture (discussed in the section "Defining User Interface Elements" later in this chapter).

In contrast, some current client/server vocabularies define application architecture more narrowly than I do here and separate it from the related solution construction concepts of data architecture and business architecture.

Not every application contains every object type you have defined as part of your standards, although most of your sizable applications will contain a majority of your defined Access object types as well as one or more of the external components described in the previous section.

You can represent the mix of components in your application visually in an application architecture diagram, a simple example of which is shown in Figure 7.8. This diagram provides a view of the component mix in a robust Access-centric application. Application architecture diagrams can be drawn to be much more complex than this example, showing procedures within modules, modules within objects, indexes within tables, and so forth.

This type of architecture diagram provides a conceptual view of the application, as opposed to a logical view. At the conceptual level, components are shown based on their functionality or contributions. At the logical level, the actual physical location of objects is noted, including the machine, drive, and directory.

Fig. 7.8

This simplified Access application architecture diagram shows the various application components.

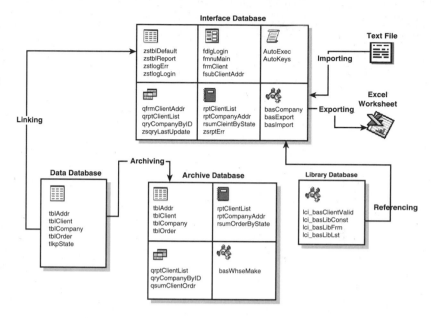

Certain logical (physical) considerations come into play when you design an Access solution, such as locating library routines and other shared objects. You can design an Access application using virtually any layout that your network infrastructure supports. Figure 7.9 shows the extreme layout options as contrasted with the most common (balanced) scenario for Access solutions.

Fig. 7.9

Several physical topologies may be used for combining Access components into an application.

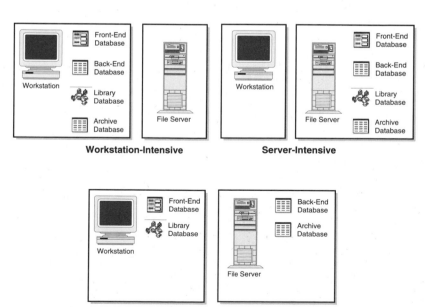

7

Note

Physical layout considerations are limited by Access's current inability to directly call class module interfaces located in a referenced database. Specifically, Access cannot call custom methods and properties of form or standard class modules in referenced database library files by referencing the class, as in this line:

```
AES_Lib.Form_fclsNameFix.prpNameFirst = "Bob"
```

This limitation prevents you from creating class modules as service objects that are referenced in the same fashion as library code and wizard forms. See the section "Segregating Solution Services" later in this chapter for more information.

Deciding Where the Data Will Reside

Most developers currently engineer their Access applications in two parts: the front-end application database file with form, report, and program objects, and the back-end data file with tables that are linked to the front-end (see the sidebar and Figure 7.9). This model creates a file server database application, detaching the shared data (located on a shared drive for multiuser support) from the application objects (placed on a local hard drive for better performance).

A Not-So-Fond Attachment

In the original version of Access (1.0), using table attachments to separate application objects from data storage was something of a challenge. For example, there was no add-in like the current Linked Table Manager to manage table attachments and Access' performance issues were not yet documented.

I remember the first Access 1 application we created during early alpha testing. It was a database to manage information about graphical images. We used dynasets (now called recordsets) in those early days to fetch table data programmatically from attached tables. This revealed a serious performance drawback because the FindFirst method did not use indexes.

Looking for a specific record in a large table with FindFirst took more than 40 seconds. We next changed all of our DAO coding to use Table objects (now table-type recordsets) against a database object pointing to a named back-end file to use the Seek method to find records. The same single-record search took only four seconds.

> Based upon what we learned from this experience, we redefined our application architecture model to include a reliance on specific DAO coding methods whenever recordset searches were involved. Many architectural decisions and standards derive from such real-world application needs and experiences.

While the separation of data from the interface allows for multiuser data access, some applications require deeper consideration of data architecture, which defines the types of data elements and their optimal locations. In addition, a discussion of the various roles that data can play in the application is often relevant when "architecting" an Access solution.

Mixing Tables, Links, and Direct Access

In the "Defining Table Types" section earlier in this chapter, I hinted at the variety of tables that you can construct in an application. While my list of definitions may not be comprehensive for your specific development needs, it nevertheless represents the majority of table types in common usage.

Not all table types are optimally located in the back-end database and linked to the front-end. Generally, certain tables obviously belong in the back-end and others in the front-end. In some applications, you may put some tables in their own distinct database.

When structuring an application with a variety of table types, you must consider several facets of the application's environment to determine the best architecture for locating the tables:

Performance. Dividing the transaction tables in an application into multiple database files spread across multiple different file servers may help to achieve load balancing. This may provide performance benefits in some cases, but also increases the complexity of the application architecture.

For example, a huge inventory table of products may be more efficient if allocated to its own drive or server, separated from the related customer and order information. This would allow the index pages for the table potentially to completely fit in the server's disk cache if it is not competing with the indexes of the other tables.

Security. In some data distribution schemes, it may be useful to place nonsecured data tables in a separate back-end file from secured data. This not only eases the database administration burden, it may also produce a minor performance gain.

For example, encrypting a database adds a five or ten percent performance penalty to the use of the database. If the company's lookup tables can be exposed unencrypted to all users, removing them from the encrypted back-end and placing them in their own unprotected database may improve their access time.

Enterprise Architecture. Tables are sometimes distributed in related sets that accomplish a specific enterprise objective. For example, an organization wanting to maintain only one copy of each of its lookup tables for states, sales regions, and district managers may want to place such lookup tables in a different database from production data. This strategy allows users from multiple applications to more easily link to a single shared "lookup database" and provides administrators the benefit of supporting only one version of each of the tables.

You can also locate archive and summary tables in a separate database file, especially if such tables comprise part of your company's data warehousing strategy.

Physical Topology. The performance differential between a file server database (like Access) and a database server (like SQL Server) sending the same data to a client application can be significant. One reason is architectural—a data request to a database server is processed with less network traffic than one to a file server because no index pages are sent to the client. The other reason is physical—a file server machine is often not assigned the same amount of RAM for caching or top-of-the-line disk access as is a database server. This second shortfall can be corrected to some extent by providing users with the fastest possible network connections and a file server with a fast CPU, plenty of RAM cache, and fast drives.

You may infer from reading the previous list that some application architectures favor more than one database back-end file. After you've grouped related tables into a database file, the database can then be easily classified by its type. The LNC designations for back-end files as defined by their primary content are listed here:

Archive. You can improve transaction database performance by regularly moving records into history tables in an archive database. For example, two specific types of archive databases—the data warehouse and the data mart—are described near the end of this chapter.

Lookup. In many applications, placing lookup tables into one or more separate back-end files provides for easier administration of the values, improved sharing of the tables across multiple distinct applications, and sometimes improved performance when accessing the records.

Transaction. This type of database file is the live data containing the primary transaction tables.

> ⚛ **Tip**
>
> When moving large numbers of records from a transaction database to the history tables in an archive database, it's good practice to compact the transaction database. Compacting the database will defragment the file and free up the space previously occupied by the deleted records.

Figure 7.10 shows three common table distribution architectures that may improve data access times. The multidisk model allocates a separate disk to the transaction database apart from the supporting databases. The multiserver model places the separate database disks on separate server machines. The multifile model simply copies the central lookup database to the user's workstation at regular intervals for improved performance.

Fig. 7.10

You can distribute data tables using three different physical layout models that each involve multiple back-end files.

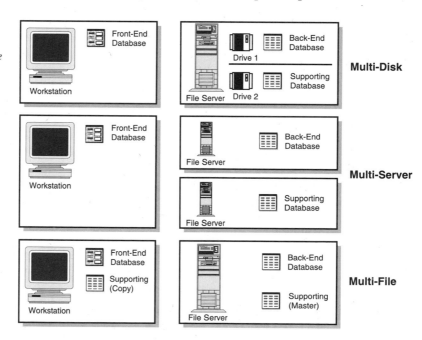

Table 7.3 reviews the list of LDF table types from earlier in this chapter and notes the logical locations for each type in your application's architecture. The table groups the archive and lookup database types under the heading "Supporting."

Table 7.3   Preferred Locations for Various Table Types

Table Type	Local UI File	Transaction Back-End	Supporting Back-End
Archive			X
Log	X	X	X
Lookup		X	X
Relation		X	X
Summary		X	X
Supporting		X	X
System	X	X	X
Temporary	X		
Transaction		X	

Once you have decided which tables in an application are to be native to the interface database and which are linked, the application architecture is complete with respect to table objects exposed to users. Nonexposed data tables (those accessed directly through code with the OpenDatabase method and not linked into the front-end database) may also deserve consideration with respect to application architecture.

For example, assume that login routines in your company's Access library provide a common login form object for use in each application. The company maintains a centralized database with a table holding login information: user names, rights, mailbox names, and so forth. The login process in each application checks the supplied password and assigns application variables (e-mail name, rights, and so on) based on information in the login table in the communal database. This database is part of the application architecture for referencing applications even though it is used only from code and not exposed to the users. (Chapter 17, "Bulletproofing Your Application Interface," includes a login form and code that demonstrates this exact scenario.)

Balancing Tables, Queries, and SQL

At the highest level, by considering application architecture, you can describe the location of objects and their relationships. At a more detailed level, your architectural analysis proceeds to forms, reports, controls, data access code, and so forth, because the architectural decisions made at the higher level trickle into the configuration of these application elements.

Providing Records to Forms and Reports

The manner in which you provide records to forms and reports will be directly affected by the table architecture you've mapped for the application. If the application's data layout includes a database server, for example, you are presented with far different options for supplying rows to forms than if its architecture is solely the Access/Jet file server model.

Forms and reports include a powerful variety of options for collecting their records. Data can be served to these objects via some combination of the following:

- ▶ Tables
- ▶ Queries
- ▶ SQL statements
- ▶ Filters
- ▶ Program code

The location and structure of each form or report's source data may impact how you balance these sources. In most cases, however, your decision regarding the appropriate record selection mechanism for a form or report will not be based on the location of the data but instead will weigh factors such as the following:

Performance. Improving form load performance has been, and will continue to be, a primary focus of any Access application developer's efforts.

When performance is an issue, using a saved query as a record source for any form or report that cannot be based directly on a table will usually provide better performance than an SQL statement saved with the object. This is true for tables located in either the front-end or any back-end data file because Jet's query storage model includes saving a query optimization plan with the query definition.

 Note

In previous versions of Access, the execution plan for the data source of a form or control was only saved in the database if a named query was used. In Access 97, the execution plan for a raw SQL statement used as a RecordSource or RowSource property is also saved with the form definition, reducing some of the necessity of using saved queries for these properties.

Documentation. From the perspective of developers' documentation, SQL statements provide more value than saved queries because they can be extracted along with other form or report properties during the documentation process. They can also quickly be viewed in the Properties dialog in form design by using the `Shift+F2` combination to zoom.

In light of the performance liability's removal of using SQL statements (see the previous Note), you can now choose to use an SQL statement over a saved query to make the documentation process easier and suffer no performance penalty.

Containment. SQL statements as record sources do provide extra value over queries when viewed from the perspective of object-centric development. An SQL record source for a form or report travels with its parent object when the object moves to another location, allowing forms and reports to be more self-contained. Database window clutter is also lessened when individual query objects are not created for each form and report in the application.

You can see that no single factor helps you make the decision about constructing `RecordSource` properties. Instead, your decision will be based on applying the listed considerations to the specific needs of each object, on an application-wide design model created to ensure a consistent approach across the development team, and on performance considerations defined after testing various architectures on your specific application.

For any given form, there is usually only one possible source of records. (In a replicated environment, this may not be true per se, but there will nevertheless be a best source.) For reports, an application with a repository (warehouse) of data provides you with a more complex decision process:

▶ A specific data item may exist in both the transaction database and the archive database.

▶ Historical records may exist only in the archive database.

▶ Today's records may exist only in the transaction database.

Figure 7.11 helps to diagram this predicament. It shows that some records in the archive table are no longer in the transaction table, and that the records added on 10/11/95 to the transaction table have not been copied to the archive table.

For each report in this architecture, you will need to compare the report's primary objective against the data architecture. The currency of data may be important enough to warrant reporting off of the live transaction tables even at the expense of slowing other users. Alternatively, if a specific report can be run off the nonlive data in a repository, it will have access to historical records much older than are found in the transaction database.

Fig. 7.11

Records in a non-replicated archive table will not exactly match those in its source transaction table.

Four common records —

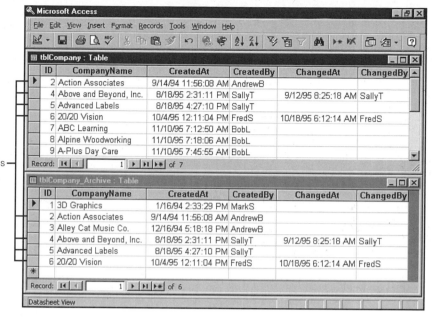

Providing Records to Controls

Drilling down from forms and reports into their dependent objects, consider next the example provided by combo box and list box controls. A number of different vehicles can provide the records for these controls:

Table or Query. A single table, a saved query, and an SQL statement are each legitimate RowSource property settings.

Value List. A delimited list of items can be supplied to combo and list boxes.

Function. You can create a callback function to supply values from a recordset. A callback is a specifically structured, user-defined function, as discussed in Chapter 13, "Mastering Combo and List Boxes."

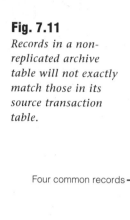 **Note**

It is also possible to load a combo box with the list of fields for a table, query, or SQL statement using the Field List value for the RowSourceType property, but this feature is not relevant to the discussion at hand.

For each combo or list box control, the decision on which of these data sources to use as a record source will be impacted by the larger architectural decisions. For example, a combo box based on a small, native table in the front-end file will load quickly from either a table or a query, thus confronting you with an architectural decision:

▶ You can base the combo box on the entire local table and simply not display the columns in the combo box that contain unneeded fields.

▶ Alternatively, you can build a query to restrict the number of columns actually fetched from the table.

In contrast, moving the same table to the back-end file and linking the front-end to the table will cause the combo box to load more slowly than when it is native due to the network traffic incurred when fetching the records. Your architectural decision here is simplified—layering a query on top of the table to restrict the number of columns and rows pulled down the network pipeline becomes an obvious architectural choice.

As a third scenario to this combo box example, imagine that the application architecture placed this same table of values as a text file on a shared server, rebuilt each day by some external process. Once again, your approach to loading the data into a combo box is affected by the application architecture. You now need to prototype and test several of the available options before you are able to make an informed architectural decision on the fastest and most logical approach. The options include:

▶ Creating a table link to the text file and pointing the combo box's RowSource to the link

▶ Importing the text file into a table each time the file changes

▶ Creating a callback function for the combo box to load the file from a table link

▶ Creating a callback function for the combo box to load the text file directly from disk using VBA's file input syntax

▶ Creating a form event procedure to build a value list from the text file on disk

 Note

A file that mimics a data table, like the mainframe-produced text file described here, is often called a flat file.

You can see that the architecture of the application impacts your decisions involving data access, from query construction to form RowSource properties to VBA coding against the DAO. At every point in the application where table rows are fetched, you must consider your alternatives for grabbing those rows in light of the application's data layout.

Confronting Complex Architectural Decisions

Spreading data tables across multiple database files, disk drives, and even file servers (refer to Figure 7.10) seems on the surface to be an appropriate direction considering the current industry penchant for componentization. Indeed, a data distribution strategy may provide performance and maintenance benefits to a widely used application. Then again, the trouble may not outweigh the benefits.

Consider the complex ramifications of separating lookup tables into a distinct file on a different server from the production tables. The performance of reads and writes to the tables may be positively affected by such a strategy in these ways:

- ▶ Because lookup tables are accessed frequently by every user, a large burden is shifted off of the server that manages the production (transaction) data. This may positively impact the performance of the production tables.

- ▶ Lookup tables are not large and thus may end up entirely in cache if their server machine has enough RAM, providing a performance boost to their users.

- ▶ The application front-end workstation is able to separate the data read operations going to each of the two servers using distinct Jet threads, which may improve performance.

- ▶ Because joins between data and lookup tables point to two different drives, the application is not "fighting against itself" for disk reads.

Negative performance factors are also built in to this strategy, including the following:

- ▶ Additional system resources are consumed on each application workstation by the maintenance of multiple database connections and Jet cache partitions.

- ▶ Access's security and record locking mechanisms must divide their efforts and attention across two different database files instead of a central one.

- ▶ The user's workstation must manage network connections and traffic going to two different server machines.

Taking these factors into account, the real performance increase or decrease of this scenario is virtually impossible to estimate. You would need to benchmark the problem with test cases before finalizing your architecture plan.

Of course, performance is only part of the equation in this example. Diffusing application tables across multiple databases and servers solves and creates a variety of non-performance problems as well, including extra security and maintenance burdens and opportunities. Building a well-tuned application involves exploring each of these issues and making decisions that best fit the combined personalities of the application, its users, and the infrastructure available to it.

Fitting VBA Code into the Architecture

The concept of application architecture trickles to even the lowest level of an application—program code. Code architecture can be considered as the "site plan" for the VBA elements of the application architecture.

Code architecture has three primary components:

Coding Style. Each developer or development team develops an approach to coding and a look and feel for their VBA routines.

Location of Code. A code component in an application can be placed in one of a few different cubbyholes.

Role of Code. A single code routine has a very quantifiable responsibility in an application.

Defining Your Coding Style

Your coding style for VBA development is defined by your techniques for authoring individual procedures. Your style is reflected in your consistent approaches to these code components:

Error Handling. The way you trap and manage error events has an impact on the structure of your code.

Code Comments. Comments can be lengthy or brief, at the top of the routine or the bottom, following a code line or before it, and so forth.

Indentation. Your preferences for indentation of code will impact its look and readability.

Naming Conventions. A naming style should provide each of your applications with a consistent dialect for identifying object attributes.

Libraries. Using the same shared code base in multiple projects may affect the structure of each project.

Data Access. Developers often create and reuse a standardized style or approach to fetching and working with data. As opposed to the other listed style elements, however, the way data is fetched and presented is often tailored by project.

Figure 7.12 shows examples of these coding style elements.

Fig.7.12

This diagram shows the various elements of a VBA code procedure.

Error Handling ——

Naming ——

Code Comments ——

Code Libraries ——

Data Access ——

```
Microsoft Access - [Form_fdlgLogin : Class Module]
File  Edit  View  Insert  Debug  Run  Tools  Window  Help

cmdOK                                         Click

Private Sub cmdOK_Click()
' Purpose: Validate the user name and password

On Error GoTo cmdOK_Click_Err
Const cstrProc As String = "cmdOK_Click"

Dim dbs        As Database
Dim rst        As Recordset
Dim intRet     As Integer
Dim varBackEnd As Variant

' The back-end path is a saved default
varBackEnd = DFirst("BackEndData", "zstblDefault")
intRet = lci_UserValidate(Me!txtUserName, Me!txtPW, varBackEnd)
Beep
Select Case intRet
  Case -1
    lci_gstrCurrentUser = Me!txtUserName  ' Set global user name
    Set dbs = CurrentDb
    Set rst = dbs.OpenRecordset("zstlogLogin", dbOpenDynaset)
    rst.AddNew

Ready
```

Coding style is one of the most consistent elements of application architecture, meaning that the coding model used by your development team should not change much between applications. As you design the architecture of an application, review your coding style elements from the previous list and determine whether each existing style item will fit the current project unmodified, with modifications, or not at all. Issues related to coding style are discussed further in Chapter 11, "Expert Approaches to VBA."

Locating Code Routines

In contrast to code style, the concept of code architecture has a broader impact on an application. Whereas style issues apply to the attributes of code lines within a procedure, the code architecture determines the organization of the procedures themselves within the application.

Access cares less about where its code lives than developers do, so as you craft an application, you will consider the location of code routines as related to these issues:

Performance. You can locate a specific piece of code in a form or report module, a class module, a standard module, or a library module. For a given application, one of these scenarios may produce a performance benefit over the others.

7

Maintenance. The common practice of grouping routines based on their shared purpose or attributes is a convenience rather than a necessity, designed primarily to aid with maintenance and documentation. Your application can group routines into modules using any model that proves effective.

Modularity. Stand-alone code routines can be moved between applications more easily when they are not attached to objects. Alternatively, code for objects is usually more effectively relocated when stored with its related object.

Most of your applications will follow a similar code architecture because the opportunities for locating code are limited. To establish the appropriate layout of code, you must first identify which of these criteria a routine fits best:

Object-Specific. Code written specifically for a form, report, or class definition is most often stored with the object.

Application-Specific. These code routines are tailored for an application and are not generally usable outside of the application.

Generic. You can use generic code routines in a variety of applications and under slightly differing circumstances, due to their use of arguments.

Figure 7.13 shows how these various types of code routines interweave.

After you discern the primary type of a routine, the decision where to locate it is mostly straightforward. See Chapter 11, "Expert Approaches to VBA," for an expanded discussion of the decision points for locating code.

Defining a Procedure's Role

In addition to the style and location of code, the purpose of each VBA object comes into play when defining code architecture. Unlike objects such as tables, which drive the architecture of the application, code routines derive their traits from the architecture of the application. Thus, the role of code in an application is clearly defined. Nevertheless, a varying degree of architectural decisions are always left to the developer.

For example, the data entry/edit needs of a table determine the needs of a specific form bound to it. That form's needs then dictate a list box control to manage the presentation of lookup data related to the table. This list box requires callback code (described in Chapter 13, "Mastering Combo and List Boxes") to provide its RowSource.

Fig. 7.13

An example of a code hierarchy that employs object-specific code (relevant to one object), application-specific code (relevant to the database), and generic code (the calling database is irrelevant).

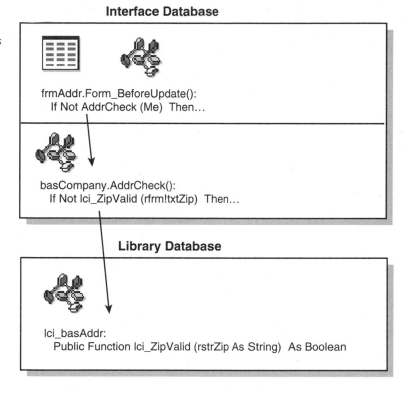

Interface Database

frmAddr.Form_BeforeUpdate():
   If Not AddrCheck (Me) Then…

basCompany.AddrCheck():
   If Not lci_ZipValid (rfrm!txtZip) Then…

Library Database

lci_basAddr:
   Public Function lci_ZipValid (rstrZip As String) As Boolean

The application has already made most of the code architecture decisions for this example procedure for you:

▸ It must be structured as a callback (callback functions have an Access-defined, fixed structure).

▸ It must provide specific records from a specific table, and in a specific order.

Thus, the only architectural decisions left to the developer are simple ones:

▸ Where to locate the procedure (in the form's module or in a standard module?)

▸ What to name the procedure

▸ Whether the procedure will be tied to the source table or generic

As a contrasting example, the code architecture of a data import routine is less tightly defined. Assume that your application requires the weekly import of a flat file (a simple ASCII text file) that is created from your company's mainframe. You must craft a procedure to open the file, grab each line, parse and validate the items, and post the items to an application table. As you design this routine, several different approaches will achieve the stated objective, leaving you to choose from a variety of layouts:

▶ You can create one large procedure or several smaller procedures that "chain" to each other.

▶ You can validate each field in the code as it is loaded or validate each record as it is committed.

▶ On validation failure, you can abort the load, present the record to the user for cleanup, post the record to a holding table, or post the record to the target table anyway but flagged as invalid.

▶ You can create one or more Jet transactions wrapped around the load process.

▶ Your procedure can display status to the user as records load or remain silent until completion.

▶ And so on...

The challenge of coding this single procedure exposes you to several decision points. You must consider the different alternative approaches to the stated problem and define an appropriate architecture for the VBA solution to it. The way you create this definition will be influenced by three factors:

▶ The availability of existing historical or library code to solve the problem

▶ Your, or your team's, development style and preferences

▶ Specific needs as dictated by the users or environment in which the application resides

Thus, the code architecture subset of application architecture presents you with the greatest number of decisions at the mechanical level (defining what each line of code does) and the least number of decisions at the structural level (where to locate code and how to relate it to other objects).

Defining the Role of External Data

Almost no application is an island with a fixed dataset. Instead, data enters an application from outside it via the following mechanisms:

Data Entry. The standard mechanism for entering records into tables is for users to key data into forms. Data can also be entered into tables directly from non-keyboard hardware, such as bar code readers, flatbed scanners, analog/digital monitoring cards, and so on.

External Posting. Data sometimes is posted to a back-end database without using the designated front-end application. In Access, this is accomplished when an affiliated application appends records to back-end tables via queries, table links, or code.

Data Sharing. Jet's ISAM drivers allow your application to link to FoxPro, Btrieve, and other types of data files. This way, your application can access data created with programs that use non-Jet file formats.

Imports. Data can be pulled into an application by code routines that fetch data from external files.

As you map the data layer in an application, you must confront each of these possible data sources and find the optimal mix for the specific application.

Posting Data from External Sources

Data sent from an external source to your application provides a specific set of challenges, the most urgent of which are these questions:

▶ What mechanism ensures that records coming from an external source are valid in your host database?

▶ How are record locking and data currency issues managed if new external data come into your system while users are online?

As an example, assume that your application manages inventory data but that a different application catalogs the orders that actually consume the inventory items. To reconcile a product's inventory records against the transactions that consume them, the order details must be sent from the order entry database to your application's database.

If the external database can submit records to your application while users are querying or reporting data, the information users see may not be current. Imagine the situation that arises when a user prints two reports consecutively that have a relationship to each other. If the external data is loaded into your application at the time lag between printing the first and second report, only the second report will contain the posted information and will not balance to the first report printed minutes before it.

This is one small example of the issues that arise when external data can "raid" your system in the background. As you build your system, you must be aware of such issues and resolve them to the benefit of both of the interacting applications.

 Tip

I'm strongly in favor of letting the host application control all of the data that comes into its tables. If possible, I build the implantation of remote data so it is driven from the destination database as an *import* rather than as an export from the external application.

Sharing Data with Other Programs

You can easily establish table links with other programs' databases in Access. This ease may fade quickly, however, if the purpose of the links is to edit data.

For example, several retail contact management and accounting products are created in FoxPro, whose database tables can be linked to your Access application. You have no knowledge of, or control over, the manner in which the retail application locks edited records, refreshes data in your linked recordset, or builds indexes, however. Thus, the potential for collision and confusion exists when multiple users of your Access application interact with data that is simultaneously managed by users of the separate retail application that owns the data.

 Tip

Pulling data from an external data source without fully understanding its layout and structure may lead to an improper or inaccurate representation of that data to your users.

In confronting these challenges, you must consider the architectural options available when you work with databases that are not "owned" by your application:

▶ Use table links to read data from external sources but not to write to them and require that all data entry be done through the appropriate (host) application.

▶ Write extra-robust concurrency control and error handling mechanisms to help detect and correct in a friendly fashion any lock contentions created by your users' interaction with the external data.

▶ Use the links only to import the required external data into your application at regular intervals and provide your users with access only to the imported copies of the data.

Architectural decisions like these require that you understand not only the needs of your application but also the workings and capabilities of the host system managing the external data. Creating the layout of an Access application with active links to external data requires a team effort between your development team and the team that maintains the external database.

 Tip

"Raiding" an external data store without a cooperative effort involving your development team and the owners of that data may create a negative political climate between the two teams.

Importing External Data

Data located in external data sources can be easily imported into your application if the data source is supported by a Jet ISAM driver. Jet's capabilities to link to data sources as diverse as Paradox tables and delimited text files greatly reduces the complexity of imports involving supported data formats.

 Note

Access 97 includes new ISAM drivers that link to HTML-based information and Microsoft Exchange data stores.

The prevailing architectural issue that derives from imports of external records is data integrity. Any data that is not keyed into your application's tables through one of the application's forms is suspect in its accuracy and should be checked on the way in.

 Tip

As external data is brought into your application's database, subject each record to the same stringent tests that are applied to records keyed-in by the application's users through forms. You can buffer external data's entry into your application by loading it to a temporary table and validating it there before posting it to transaction tables.

Consider the following scenario. Your company's mainframe exports a delimited file each week containing customer order information. Your application's users need to import the information and report it as part of their weekly account balancing process. The file is denormalized and contains the order header information merged with each order detail record.

The least costly approach to this task is to import the orders from the file into a table each week using the TransferText method in a piece of program code. The import's target table can then serve as the RecordSource for a related report, which groups and sorts the data to suppress display of the redundant fields. Importing the data into a table allows indexes to be created, which improves printing performance over simply linking to the external text file.

7

In this model, the impact on your application's architecture is the addition of four objects:

- ▶ An import procedure or macro
- ▶ A destination table
- ▶ An index or indexes
- ▶ A report

The downside of a simple import like this is that data in the file is not validated before being printed. On its own, Access makes its best effort to pull the text file data into table fields, but is not able to check the data for validity beyond simple data type testing (in other words, Access will not import a long integer value into an Integer type field).

A more solid approach would be to import the data via a code routine that validates each field as it is posted to the target tables. Notice the pluralization of table into tables in this model because you can also use the import routine to normalize the order data into parent and child records. In this model, your application architecture is impacted by the addition of the following objects:

- ▶ An import procedure
- ▶ A validation procedure that applies business rules to each data item
- ▶ A destination table for order headers
- ▶ A destination table for order details
- ▶ An error log table to hold messages describing all records that failed the import or validation process
- ▶ A report to dump the error log table information at the end of the import process
- ▶ An index or indexes
- ▶ A query to provide the joined parent and child records to the report's RecordSource
- ▶ A report

Notice that the numbers and types of objects required in the second scenario greatly exceed those produced by the first scenario. Taking the proper and most robust approach to the import problem adds complexity to your application's architectural layout, but is always worth the extra effort if data accuracy is improved.

Charting the Data's Destination

Where an application's data comes from is quite important to you as a developer. What is more important to the application's users, however, is where the data goes to. Possible "To" destinations for application data include the following:

Queries. Users may review data online in query datasheets or form datasheets bound to a query. A query result set usually is presented directly to users in these fashions when it needs to be edited but does not need to be printed. Some decision-support systems also allow users to query data directly from a query-by-form interface or Access' query grid.

Forms. Forms primarily service the "from" side of a data flow, used by data-maintenance personnel who enter or edit records. Forms can also serve the role of presenting data to decision makers in a summary format or as an ordered subset of records. In this model, the form is a data destination and may even serve as a report by virtue of its printable layout.

Datasets that are presented for review or analysis on forms are usually filtered based on criteria entered by the user. The filter mechanism may be query parameters, a query-by-form object, or Access' native form filtration features.

Reports. The majority of data presentation from an application is provided by reports. Hardcopy reports are the norm, but with the print preview capabilities of Access, you can lay out a report that is primarily viewed on-screen as well.

When defining an application's architecture, decisions are often made with the specific intent of enabling the reporting process. For example, complex data may be regularly summarized or flattened (denormalized) into additional table objects to facilitate a reporting objective.

Exports to External Applications. Exporting Access data to external databases may facilitate an objective of the system but will also require a thoughtful review of the impact on the architecture. Routines may be required to help the user select the export dataset, to group and order the data, to copy the data out of Access, and to provide the user with feedback on the success of the process.

In addition, exporting data may add additional table or query objects that support the process by formatting or grouping the records for export. As an example, a batch history table may log each export batch by date, time, and range of record keys that were exported.

Links from External Applications. Exposing Access data to other applications (usually Access applications) provides a method for sharing the valuable information in your application with personnel outside of its circle of active users.

Caution

Be aware that your architecture must provide a provision for restricting a linked user from making changes to your data. You must enable this blockade by providing remote users with read-only rights to the data, usually by applying an Access security layer.

Database Replication. Data created and stored in one database can be shared with additional databases though replication. Copying records from an application's database to a member of its replica set does not actually constitute a final destination for the data, but rather another repository from which the user can pull the data to its destination using any other techniques in this listing.

Note the architectural impact of charting these various data destinations—giving users the ability to extract, review, or print records in a database requires adding new objects. It also requires discussions of the attributes of those objects and of the relationship of the objects to the remainder of the application.

Deciding How Users Will Interact with a Solution

Defining the architecture of an application includes considering the data and code attributes discussed previously in this chapter. The effort also includes considering the roles of various interface elements in the solution:

▶ What are the application's interface objects?

▶ How will the user navigate through the interface?

▶ What data is exposed by the interface?

These questions are addressed in the sections that follow.

Defining User Interface Elements

Almost all of a user's interaction with an application is through forms. Forms are the gateway to data records, provide the mechanism for displaying switchboard menus and selection dialogs, and can now be used to provide programmable class objects. Nevertheless, contemplating an application's interface architecture is a broader effort than simply deciding on a list of forms. Access exposes other features to developers to use when defining an interface's structure:

Menus and Toolbars. Defining the balance between menu options, toolbar buttons, and command buttons is an interface architecture discussion.

Keyboard Shortcuts. It is a conceptual leap (albeit a small one) to consider remapping the keyboard as an architectural issue. Nevertheless, the task involves both program code objects and macro objects, which are indeed a part of the application's architecture.

Access Interface Elements. Access provides the ability to change the application window's title caption, to set the status bar text, and to display message boxes and the Office Assistant. These are distinct, programmable interface elements, but they play a very minor role in any discussion of architecture because they are present in Access whether or not they are used.

Controls. Defining the properties of the form controls that reside in a host object will have the biggest impact on any architectural discussion involving controls. Nevertheless, I noted earlier in the chapter that the definition of a control can affect architecture by requiring a source query object as well as related code objects.

Most application data elements have interface (presentation) prerequisites that require the designer to explore interface options. These options lead to decision points. Decision points produce object definitions that add more elements to the architecture. Thus, the interface subset of your application's architecture flows directly from the stated needs and wishes of the users and their data.

> **Note**
> The following chapter provides a thorough discussion of the user interface objects that make up an application's interface architecture. The chapter also discusses the properties and roles of interface objects within an application's blueprint. Thus, I limit the discussion of these objects in this section.

Considering Navigation Philosophies

A primary consideration in your application's interface architecture is: How will my users navigate between features? In fact, before you can define form objects for an application, you must first answer this question and produce a policy from the answer.

For example, an application for sophisticated users who regularly review and print data could contain only a list of queries displayed on a form's list box. Users could run one or more specific queries as required to audit or correct data records, tile or otherwise rearrange the datasheet windows, and even print the query datasheets. These objects have no navigation requirements except for allowing the user to open and close them.

In contrast, an entry/edit application for unskilled data entry personnel must use forms as the lenses to data. Each form has an enforced navigation plan and contains record validation code. Selecting forms, opening and closing forms, and moving between forms are all regulated by the application's structure.

The difference in numbers and types of objects in these two example applications is significant, as is the coding complexity. Thus, any decisions about the types of objects used to present data in an application—and the manner in which users move between these objects—will create the paradigm under which the objects and their roles are defined.

Delimiting the navigation and presentation elements of an interface involves debating and defining these attributes:

Navigation Elements. How do the application's users select a direction to travel? Do they use a switchboard or a bar menu, a toolbar button or a command button, or perhaps even a keyboard shortcut? Is the database window provided or hidden? Interface architecture must define such navigation parameters for an application.

Navigation Flow. How will users move from a record to its related data? How will they go back to where they came from? How does the navigation between objects match the physical workflow? The navigation paradigm in interface architecture must include a definition of the user's flow from task to task.

Navigation Objects. From the definition of navigation elements derives actual navigation objects (forms, buttons, menus, toolbars, and the like). These objects become part of the interface architecture.

Even though detailing the architecture of data tables, indexes, and queries has the largest overall impact on the structure of an application, the definition of interface objects, their roles, and their navigation has the most visible impact.

 Note

Because forms are the most visible, and arguably the most important, objects in an application, I devote considerable space to their design and usage in this book. The discussion of form navigation started in this section continues in the following chapter, carries on to Chapter 14, "Navigating in Forms and Applications," and is completed in Chapter 17, "Bulletproofing Your Application Interface."

Understanding How Users Work with Data

Closely related to the discussion of navigation methods and objects is a discussion of data entry and data editing objects. Forms and datasheets provide the primary tools for these tasks as well as the majority of interface objects in an application's structure.

For a specific application there are appropriate and inappropriate approaches to take when presenting data items to users. Selecting the most suitable approach is facilitated by an understanding of how users interact with data items. There are five primary means:

Batch Operations. Depending on an application's purpose and data, some users may spend all day simply keying data into one or more forms. The quantity and type of form objects called for in such an application will be determined by the needs and skills of these users.

For example, users keying order information into a system from hardcopy order sheets may find it efficient to enter an entire batch of order header records into a form, then open a different form and enter the related batch of order details. This model contrasts sharply with an equally relevant architecture where each order is entered in total into a single form/subform object before moving to the next order sheet. Determining which of these two models to follow involves investigating the workplace and the workflow of the users.

Bulk Operations. Users sometimes perform bulk manipulations of data items or records, including updates, deletions, imports, and similar aggregate processes. For such operations, users must have an interface they can use to select the appropriate dataset for processing, review and confirm the bulk operation before it is initiated, and review and confirm the result of the operation.

Direct Access. Users who are editing or reviewing existing records are primarily interested in going directly to a specific record. The manner in which users select a record and open a form or forms pointing to it can vary depending on the needs of the users and style of the developers, with repercussions at the architectural level. See Chapter 16, "Presenting Data to Users," for a comprehensive discussion of this subject.

Random Browsing. For users who simply want to review the records in a table, you must provide them with admittance to the records while minimizing their ability to negatively affect those records, especially in aggregate (bulk deletions should be restricted, for example). In other words, showing users multiple records in a table datasheet, query datasheet, form datasheet, or continuous form each has assets and liabilities from the standpoints of usability and data integrity.

7

Selective Browsing. Users often need to browse a defined subset of records. Defining the mechanism for enabling users to select a restricted dataset will have repercussions on the interface architecture.

In Access, there is usually more than one interface device available for addressing a defined need. For example you can provide selective browsing with a table datasheet with filtration options, a query, a form, and so forth. Your determination of which interface devices to use for each need impacts the structure of an application.

Fitting Access into New Paradigms

The database industry is replete with buzzwords describing the current technologies and paradigms. One hot concept is "replication," which was added to Access 95 and enhanced in Access 97.

Access can facilitate two other popular database concepts as well, but only to a limited extent. The following concepts are:

Three-Tier Architecture. This term describes the methodology of separating business rules (data validation) from both the application interface and its data, creating a third layer (tier) of solution services.

Data Warehousing. As the term implies, all of the historical data produced by one or more related systems can be merged and stored in a repository. This repository is used to house current and aged data together to enable retrieval and statistical analysis of all items gathered throughout the lifetime of a system.

Let's fit Access into these new models.

Access and Three-Tiered Architecture

Enabling the three-tier model in its pure form requires a client application and a database server. The client application provides "user services" and the database server provides "data services." Between these two engines lies a group of objects providing "business services" (see the sidebar), a collective term for processes that provide these capabilities to an application:

▶ Data selection

▶ Data validation

▶ Data protection

▶ Bulk and batch processing

Applying this new paradigm to Access is not possible in a purist sense because Access does not fully support the client/server data distribution model, but a discussion of it may nevertheless prove informative.

Tongue-Tying Three-Tiered Terminology

I've been struggling with how to present the three-tier model simply to our clients. Ideally, because they are accustomed to the terminology "front-end" and "back-end," I'd like to be able to refer to the new business services layer as the "middle-end." In practice, however, this phrase has not proven popular.

Alternatively, I merged the terms "business services" and "middle-end" and came up with "business-end." This phrase quite effectively enjoys a different meaning, however, and refers to the active terminus of a device (as in "He ended up on the business-end of his enemy's sword"). Once again, I produced confusion rather than clarification.

Amusingly enough, the phrase that has made the most sense to many of my clients is one with which they are already familiar. What does a business services engine do? It validates and manipulates records by itself—in other words, it autonomously "processes" data. A business services layer is simply a set of objects for "automatic data processing." Thus, the simplified three-tier model I show to clients looks like this:

User Interface→Automatic Data Processing→Data Storage

The term "automatic data processing" was in style twenty years ago when I was in college and originally referred to any work done by a computer. Now I use it to describe the magic processes in the middle-tier of a database structure. Life sometimes spins in circles.

7

Segregating Solution Services

To adhere to three-tier architecture, your Access application would need to locate all services for data validation, bulk processing, and security in a separate application, ideally on a separate server from the database (see Figure 7.14). Why the separate location? Because the object-centric development model dictates that you reuse code when possible in an organization. Some of the code that is embodied in a business services object (or, simply, business object) may have value to more than a single application and database.

Fig. 7.14

A business object for data validation acts as a gatekeeper between the client application and the data.

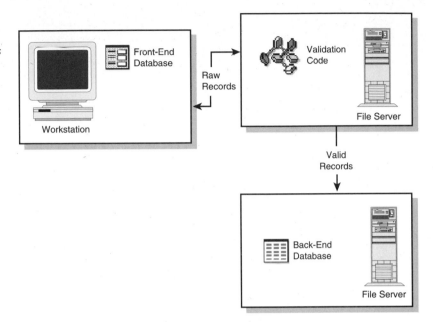

As an example, several applications in a single company may rely on one central database of customer information. A good role for a business object is to validate a customer number against the customer database and tell the user if the customer number is active, discontinued, or nonexistent. Many client applications within the company could call a single, central business service to perform this task.

In Automation, Microsoft has created an ideal model for enabling these business services. Using Visual C++ or Visual Basic, a developer can easily create an OLE-enabled business object. To use this object from Access, your user interface front-end application needs simply to reference the server application and to contain the appropriate code to control the Automation server. If you have written VBA code to propel Excel from Access, you will grasp that this is a straightforward process.

Thus, Access might refer to our imaginary business object for customer number inquiry in the current example simply as the following code:

```
Dim oappCustInq As Object   ' A business object
Dim oclsCustNum As Object   ' A class in the object
Set oappCustInq = CreateObject("CustInquiry.Application")
Set oclsCustNum = oappCustInq.clsCustNum
blnValid = oclsCustNum.mtdNumIsValid(lngCustNum)
```

Note

As with other Automation objects, the fictional CustInquiry server application in the code sample would contain properties and methods (referred to as interfaces or members) that you could view in Access's Object Browser dialog.

In this sample code, the server CustInquiry exposes a class object called clsCustNum with a method mtdNumIsValid. The server provides a validation routine that is tied to a database back-end but independent of any front-end applications that call it.

 Note

You can use Access itself as your business rules server because you can remotely automate it. Create a class module in a database separate from your application and drive the module via Automation code from the current session of Access to the remote session. The remote session provides the business services. However, you may find that Visual Basic or Visual C++ produce faster-executing business objects than Access.

7

Locating Access in a Three-Tiered Model

Because Access uses Jet for its data services, enabling the three-tier model precisely as defined is not possible. Jet is a file-server database engine that relegates the work of the data services tier to the user's workstation. In other words, the user's CPU provides both the user services and the data services, as shown in Figure 7.15.

Fig. 7.15

The client workstation does the majority of the data retrieval work in an Access/Jet application.

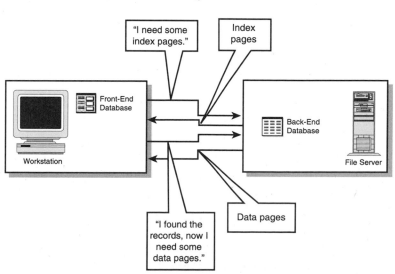

For practical purposes, the work of business services is also usually consigned to the user's workstation in an Access-centric model. While it is possible to create remote Automation objects that reside on a business server and to have these objects handle all data management tasks by virtue of their own connections to a Jet database, such an architecture may not provide tangible benefits when contrasted to the amount of work to create and maintain it and the horsepower requirements of the workstations that will use it. Because the user interface portion of an application would need connections to Jet tables (to fill combo boxes and so forth) and the business services objects would need their own connections to the same data, this paradigm would prove awkward and taxing for a file server database. Nevertheless, the possibilities are interesting and you can explore this opportunity to see if you like it.

By removing Jet from the picture and using Access as a front-end for SQL Server or another ODBC back-end database server, you can establish a structure that more closely resembles a true three-tier model. Moving data between the server and Access forms via the business service objects provides the appropriate middle layer of validation and data manipulation. (See Chapter 19, "Exploring Client/Server Issues," for more discussion on using Access with SQL Server.)

So, how do you make the most of this new paradigm today without creating an overly complex application architecture? The answer is in the objects. The primary features of a business object are that it is the following:

▶ Data-aware

▶ Automatic

▶ Self-contained

Thus, if you create stand-alone, smart, reusable objects in your Access applications to provide data-manipulation and data-protection services for your users, you are going down the right path. I'm not guaranteeing that if you create a class form or class module (as detailed in Chapter 12, "Understanding Form Structures and Coding") or library code (see Chapter 20, "Applying Development Shortcuts") to do validation work that your code will be 100 percent portable into a client/server business object in a year or two. But your code won't be far off, either.

Here are a few examples of how to apply the ideas of three-tier paradigm to Access today, within its limitations:

Create a standard login form. Users virtually always log in to a server database. Start users logging in to your applications now, using a standardized login form and user validation table shared by all your Access applications. Read Chapter 17, "Bulletproofing Your Application Interface," for further discussion of my views on standardized logins and their attributes and techniques.

Validate objects with code. I devote an entire chapter (Chapter 15, "Protecting and Validating Data") in this book to validation issues specifically because of the importance of writing good validation code in your applications, including applications that employ the three-tier model. The business services layer's primary job is to enforce business rules, and you can begin to apply this concept now by encapsulating reusable business rules for saving records in each form module's code or in centralized standard, class, or library modules.

Centralize your data access. Assume you have four forms that each contain a combo box with states. In Access, you can create an SQL string as the RowSource property of each combo box. The new paradigm dictates instead that you create a query to fetch and sort the state values, and have each of the forms call the same query. This centralizes the several independent calls to fetch data into a call to one object (the query). In the future (assuming features in Access change), the query could be replaced with a call to a single central business service or data service routine on a server that fetches the list of states for every application in the organization.

Centralize common code. Any routines that could someday better reside in a business services object should be currently centralized into a module within your application. For example, assume that several forms in your application contain customer order details and that as each of these forms save customer order data they recompute the order total and place it in a data field. Even if the logic to perform this task is very simple code (perhaps a DSum() function), consider centralizing the code into one public procedure and calling it from each of the four forms as needed. This model more closely matches the way your application would handle the transaction in a three-tier model, with your forms calling a business object to compute the order total as part of its record save processes. Implementing the procedure as a method on a class object approximates the three-tier model even more closely.

α **Note**

If you think that I've provided you with conflicting directives in this book regarding self-contained objects, you're correct. In one breath, I've suggested that you create objects that stand alone and can be used in other applications (such as an order entry form with all of its code in the form module). Yet in the next breath, I'm telling you to move routines out of the form and into public procedures where they can be shared by other forms. While there is certainly no single correct answer to this conundrum, in general I will sacrifice self-containment for the opportunity to reuse business services code.

Access and Data Warehousing

Where should old data live? The answer depends on who needs the data and how they need to see it. Earlier in this chapter, I noted that you should move aged records (and perhaps deleted records) to archive tables if the transaction tables they reside in suffer from reduced performance as a result of large record counts.

Whether or not you choose to move historical data out of active tables or keep it there, the important point here is never to throw any legitimate transaction records away (see the sidebar). Even data that may seem trivial may prove valuable in an audit, a merger, or for statistical analysis.

 Note

I use the concept of data warehousing here to primarily define a location for histori-cal information, mostly because of the nature of Access. In common usage, the term does not require that all data in a warehouse be aged. In its broadest sense, the concept of warehousing is really about accessibility—how to expose large amounts of data to users for ad-hoc research through Decision Support Systems and Executive Information Systems.

The concept of data warehousing simply means something like this: Keep all of your data stored together in a clean, dry place. Let's dissect this phrase:

All of your data. A data warehouse is a one-stop data shop, a database that collects all of the records entered into a specific system or group of related systems from the time of the system's inception to the present. (I'll define "present" a little further on.)

Together. Not only do you want to keep together all the data items from a specific system, but your warehouse may include mixing data from multiple systems that have a logical relationship. For example, although customers, their orders, and the company's inventory are managed by three different systems, it may still be benefi-cial to store all historical records from all three systems together, by virtue of their strong kinship.

A clean, dry place. Metaphorically, I'm hinting at the importance of providing a good, quality location for the data and making sure the data itself is of good qual-ity. This means that you should keep the data warehouse well organized in a cen-tral location available to all users on a machine responsive enough to provide adequate performance and should back it up regularly.

You must also ensure that users cannot edit, update, or delete records from the warehouse in a manner that would circumvent the original business rules. The data in the warehouse must be as accurate and trustworthy as it was in its original system.

Grandma's Warehouse

Have you ever been to a farm? Farmers never throw anything away. They're clever enough to know that an old piece of wire may fix the tractor, which in turn may save the year's crop. (They're also resourceful enough to actually fix the tractor with the wire, in the dark, in a hailstorm...)

One delight of my youth was exploring the attics and barns of my grandmother's farm. The dusty corners and creaky trunks held secrets and surprises from years long past. I believed that I might even find the Holy Grail somewhere in Grandma's warehouses of clutter, there was so much neat stuff there. Grandma saved everything.

Which is probably why, in my application development efforts, I save everything, too. We've not thrown any client's data records away in 14 years—instead, we build archive tables that eventually are moved to archive databases, that eventually are moved to archive tapes, but that never are moved to the dumpster. And often our clients don't even know we're doing this for them.

Thus, when a client's needs change and they tell me that they wish they'd saved more historical data because they now need to analyze some trend or research some problem, I take them to Stan's Data Attic and pull their archive tapes out of one of my creaky trunks. The client smiles, and somewhere in Heaven, Grandma smiles, too.

You can easily apply the concept of data warehousing to Access applications. At periodic intervals, your administrator can run a routine that copies records from the application database to the warehouse database. Tie this routine to a button on the administration menu or to a process that runs frequently, such as a daily posting or backup routine.

The most simplified model of a warehouse posting routine follows this flow:

1. For a table, create a recordset that contains records that have not been sent to the warehouse yet (their date archived field is `Null`).

2. Append each of the records in the recordset to the matching table in the warehouse. Flag each record's date archived field so that it is not sent to the warehouse again in the future.

3. Delete records from the table that exceed a specified threshold, such as records that have been warehoused, are more than a year old, and are not needed for any ongoing reporting tasks.

4. Repeat the three steps for each table in the database.

 Note

There are multiuser concerns during the warehousing operation. For example, if the process runs in the background and a user has saved edits to an order record but not yet saved the order details, the parent record could be copied to the warehouse but an unsaved child record may not be (the copy on disk, not in the form, would go to the warehouse). Information in the warehouse will be out of synchronicity. Thus, it is preferable for the administrator to run the warehousing routine only after securing an exclusive lock on the source database or at least on the records to be warehoused.

The simplified model I've provided for this illustration conveys the concept of warehousing, but is actually not robust enough for most real-world situations. Its shortfall is that it does not include a provision for records that are changed in the source database after they are warehoused. If this is an issue in your implementation, you will need to modify my logic steps to include updating a record in the warehouse if it has changed in the source database since it was last archived (warehoused). (One helpful technique to aid this is to time-stamp records as they change, as is described in Chapter 17, "Bullet-proofing Your Application Interface.")

If this seems a bit like writing your own custom replication, it is. Unfortunately, Access' current implementation of replication does not facilitate the warehousing paradigm. Two problems exist:

▶ Because a replica database must match the schema of its design master, you cannot replicate several different databases into one warehouse.

▶ Replication, by its nature, will mimic the deletion of records from the active database in the warehouse database, preventing you from ever deleting aged data after it is warehoused.

After you've built the structure and code to create a data warehouse, you need to provide users with access to it. Here are some simple rules to follow:

Provide a map. Users cannot use historical data for research or other purposes if they do not understand what it means. Because your applications normally shield users from the database schema, many of them will not be comfortable navigating in the maze of archive tables. To ease their burden, create data maps and other documentation describing the tables, fields, relationships, and perhaps examples of how to answer common questions.

Secure the data. The accuracy of history data must not be lessened by allowing users to edit or otherwise alter it. The entire warehouse should be secured for read-only access by all interactive users.

Restructure the data for easy ad-hoc querying. Warehouse data is often "flattened" for easier querying by nonsophisticated users, meaning that parent-child relationships are denormalized from multiple tables into a single table or single query (using the grand-join query object types described in the section "Defining Query Types" earlier in this chapter). Extra indexes are often added to the "flat" table to increase performance on the most commonly interrogated fields.

In some companies, subsets of cleaned-up warehouse data are moved to smaller, self-contained databases from which the users do their research. These subsidiary repositories of orderly, simplified history data for widespread consumption are called "data marts."

For example, a data warehouse contains all of a company's inventory information, including movement of items through inventory, related customer orders, and manufacturing data. The Quality Assurance department would like to analyze inventory shrinkage by researching trends in items lost, stolen, or broken. All information related to inventory reductions could be flattened and copied to a data mart database from which these users would do their research.

Note

Though I noted earlier that implementing replication for the creation of data warehouses is problematic, it would be possible to replicate information from the data warehouse into the shrinkage data mart described in this example. Using Access 97's new partial replication feature, you could synchronize selected shrinkage records from the data warehouse out to the data mart based on SQL criteria.

Create canned reports and queries. You should be able to identify the top ten or twenty questions that users most often ask of the historical data and create saved reports and/or queries to provide them with the ability to ask these questions repeatedly.

Tip

Query parameters are a handy device when you build saved queries for users to interrogate data marts and warehouses. Query parameters make it easy for users to enter a value or range of values to tailor the result set of a canned query or its report. For example, placing parameters like `[Enter From Date]` and `[Enter To Date]` on a date value in a warehouse query causes Access to produce dialogs that prompt users for these values.

Alert users to currency. Using an `AutoExec` macro or `Startup` property, or as part of the login process, you can alert users to the timeliness of the data when they enter a mart or warehouse. In an alert, tell users when the database or specific tables in it were last updated with records from the related production systems.

Of course, users making decisions based on historical data will not be well served if the data is not robust and current. When you build a data warehouse, you must make certain to update the warehouse frequently and to ensure that the data is accurate and comprehensive.

From Here...

In this chapter, we reviewed the techniques for selecting a route up the application development cliff. Your rope should now be stronger and you should slip and fall less given your new understanding of application architecture issues and the following:

▶ It is very difficult to create a good application architecture without first creating a solid application design, as detailed in Chapter 3, "Preparing for Development," and Chapter 4, "Creating Design Specifications."

▶ You can learn more about how tables interact and relate by reading Chapter 10, "Creating Expert Tables and Queries."

▶ Read Chapter 11, "Expert Approaches to VBA," to learn more about where to locate code in an application.

▶ Many of the form techniques described in Chapters 12 through 17 clarify the concepts of data validation, form structures and capabilities, navigation, and interface architecture described in this chapter.

▶ For more information on Access' role in a client/server application model, see Chapter 19, "Exploring Client/Server Issues."

▶ Chapter 20, "Applying Development Shortcuts," has more information on techniques for creating shared library procedures and modules.

chapter 8

Designing Effective Interfaces

8

In this chapter

◆ **How to simplify the display of complex database concepts to users**

◆ **How to adhere to commonly accepted Office interface guidelines**

◆ **How to provide friendly database interaction using the tools and features available in Access**

◆ **How to convey status and progress information to users**

I've struggled in vain over the years to find a good discussion of the issues involved in developing user interfaces for database applications, so I've written my own here. Sure, there are quite a few resources available from Microsoft and others that remind you that all Windows dialog boxes should have OK and Cancel buttons, or tell you to how to add a keyboard accelerator to a button. But nobody bothers to discuss the deeper philosophical issues specific to databases. Does Cancel undo the changes that are visible on screen, or the edits that have been most recently saved as well? Does OK save the current record and prepare for another one, or does it close the form?

I see users of custom Access solutions grapple with these kinds of usability issues day after day. Writing code is so consuming for most developers that they end up scrimping on the amount of attention given to the part of the application that the user actually sees. In this chapter, I'll lay the foundation for your interface design efforts and define the issues that are most important to creating a highly usable expert solutions.

> **Look and Feel**
>
> "In the Access group, we have two full-time graphic designers who are empowered to find ways to make the Access interface friendlier and easier to use. (They also come in real handy when we're creating Access T-shirts and other partyware!)"
>
> Tod Nielsen, General Manager, Microsoft Access Business Unit

No doubt you've seen what I call a "rainbow form?" Someone in your company or at an Access user group meeting comes up and proudly wants to show you their application. When you see it, you wonder if you've drifted into a Picasso exhibit: blue prompts, red messages, and yellow rectangles, all on a black background.

Designers of rainbow forms and similarly ineffectual interface elements demonstrate that they have lost track of one of the key tenets of application design: The success of any application will be determined by how well it solves a business problem, not by how it looks, what technology it employs, or how sophisticated the core code is. While visually enhancing an application is not a bad thing *per se*, the use of illustrative fonts and colors rates very low on my list of "Important Concepts In Business Process Reengineering."

Creating a friendly and usable Access application involves mixing together multiple components, such as:

A solid *design* that mirrors or improves workflow for the user.

A set of *tables and queries* that collect data and organize it for users.

Forms that organize related information items.

Controls that display individual data elements.

Code routines that manipulate or validate records and application objects.

Reports that reveal the data and its trends to decision-makers.

Not coincidentally, the flow of this list matches the outline of this book—creating expert solutions is about creating and mixing each of these elements well. However, of the elements on the list, forms have the most interaction with users and consume the majority of your development effort.

Thus, a big part of this book is devoted to forms. But before you can master creating powerful and complex forms, you should understand and inherit the body of interface design work that has already been done on behalf of your users. If they have ever seen Windows 95 or Office, they have already been exposed to paradigms originated from years of usability research at Microsoft. Rather than invent your own interface paradigm, why not simply borrow Microsoft's?

To some extent, you don't have a choice but to inherit it, because the toolset in Access defines the limits of your user interface, and the toolset dovetails into the Windows paradigm. (Just try building your own unique menu bar control in C++, getting it to nest and dock in Access and paint correctly, and making it communicate its events to VBA, and you'll quickly determine that the Access extensibility model does *not* include letting developers redefine the user interface paradigm.)

On the other hand, you are no longer stuck with only the interface elements that are built-in to Access. Anything you can code into an ActiveX control and teach to behave well on an Access form or report becomes a component of your own personal user interface construction kit. Thus, if your users really don't like the way a standard Windows List Box control works, you can make them a new one.

However, it is not economically prudent to build all of your own form classes and controls from scratch. Nor is it particularly exciting to experiment with font, color, and effect properties simply to spice up an application. Thus, the majority of your applications will make use of certain Access and Windows defaults. In this chapter, I clarify and classify those defaults for you, and help you determine how to mix and match them to achieve the highest degree of usability and user satisfaction.

Unfortunately, the Windows styles only take your application part of the way down the road. Conveying database-type concepts to users of an Access form is more complex than, for example, configuring a printer in a Windows dialog box. As a result, I'll also discuss in this chapter how to go beyond the Windows interface metaphor and establish your own enhanced interface metaphor for expert solutions.

8

Exploring Essential Interface Concepts

Because of the serious needs of database applications as detailed throughout this book (entering valid data, protecting data from erroneous interaction, displaying complex data simply, and so on), you should place quite a bit of emphasis on user interface elements during your design and development work. My own interaction with database application users tells me that perhaps 75 percent of all of their problems and frustrations stems from the following three things:

- ▶ The application *was not* able to do what the user expected or wanted.
- ▶ The application *was* able to do what the user expected or wanted, but he or she couldn't figure out how to initiate it.
- ▶ The application *failed* or *did not allow* a process to continue, and the user couldn't figure out what to do to correct the situation.

Note

You're probably wondering what comprises the remaining 25 percent of user frustration with database applications. Mostly these issues: application or Access bugs, setup/configuration issues, and inadequate performance.

The first item can't be corrected with good interface design; application enhancements are required when the application has feature limitations. When you design an application according to the LDF precepts in Chapters 2 through 4, you end up with a planned feature set that matches the users needs.

The second and third areas of frustration *can be* corrected by designing better interfaces. When you have properly defined the feature set for an application, the next step is to expose these features to users through a well-engineered interface. A good application interface (Access or otherwise) survives these tests:

It is easy to use. Users should be able to enter, edit, delete, and report information quickly, accurately, and efficiently—those are the primary functions of a database application. New users should be able to move smoothly through the feature set, and advanced users should have shortcuts and back doors that move them along even faster.

It is easy to learn. Training costs in corporate America are high and getting higher. Your application will be more self-explanatory if it matches the users' workflow already in place or a new workflow that the users helped to design.

It is easy to explore. The interface should enable users to wander through the features in a non-destructive fashion, and enable them to cancel out of an operation or undo a transaction where practical as they learn the system.

It follows established paradigms. Adhering to the Windows look and feel removes a significant percentage of the training burden. You should never again have to teach a user how to do File, Print within an application.

It is consistent. Where possible, the screens, commands, and terms used in the application should map to established standards already familiar to the users. Synchronize your application's interface elements with the rest of your development team and with other applications known to the users. While one benefit is consistency for the users across multiple applications, another is the ability to reuse interface objects across applications.

It is appealing. You don't need to use soft pinks and trendy mauves to make an application interface attractive. Usability studies show that users prefer spartan over complex and subtle over gaudy. Stick with the basics of Windows: subtle 3-D effects, two or three colors on a form, standardized menu metaphors, textual button captions, and so forth.

It is friendly. If your application uses jargon, it should be business terms familiar to the users. Don't use technical terms known only to those in the coding cave. Also, the interface's messages (status text, alerts, and dialogs) should guide and educate users, never discourage or punish them.

It is precise. Users need feedback from an application in order to know what it is doing and how much they can trust it. A good interface tells the user what is happening using factual metrics ("Now posting record 7 of 21"), tells them where to go next (by disabling irrelevant features or using a Wizard-type metaphor with Next and Back options), and keeps them in charge ("Are you sure you want to delete the record: Jones Company?").

It matches the real world. If you've defined the user requirements well, the interface should naturally map to the users needs. It should improve processes where possible, but only in ways that make sense to the users. For example, a process that takes six steps manually will probably take six steps on the computer; if you try to roll all six steps into a single one, your application may end up bypassing a critical part of the process flow entirely (such as the ability to cancel the process after the third step).

It takes extra effort to create forms that are uncluttered, functional, and consistent, but the effort is worthwhile if user satisfaction is higher as a result. Visit Chapters 13 though 17 for specific lessons on creating expert forms that meet the criteria listed here.

While part of creating good interfaces is adhering to feature sets that are realistically programmable and commonly recognizable, the other part of the job is to match the users' workflow. These two objectives don't always meet. I have yet to see an interface metaphor for managing contact information—for example, where the Windows interface style, the limitations of relational database structures, and the complexity desired by users didn't collide. It is very difficult to automate certain types of information in one or two Windows standard screens. Nevertheless, you are obligated to try.

As you mesh standard interface components with the needs of your users, first consider how the users work, and then ponder the interface requirements afterward. Discern from the users the following:

- ▶ What are their skills and habits?
- ▶ What applications do they use now?
- ▶ What do they like and dislike about their current software toolset?

▶ What job are they ultimately trying to do with your application?

▶ What shortcuts do they need when in a hurry?

▶ How do they locate information?

▶ How do they enter and edit information?

▶ How do they verify and audit information?

▶ Do they multitask or single-task?

▶ Do users job share? Equipment share?

▶ What are their abort patterns? When and why do they have to cancel or rollback processes?

▶ How do they deal with interruptions, keep their place when they go to lunch, and recover from disasters?

Each of these scenarios should be accommodated by your interface. And not every one of them can be accommodated from the Windows style guide. For example, assume that processing a batch of transactions in your new system will take two hours and must be supervised by a human. If the process starts at 4 P.M. and the user must leave at 5, does your application facilitate pausing the process in mid-stream and restarting where it left off? (Forget for a moment the repercussions for the data in this scenario; I'm asking an interface question.)

And if you are able to accommodate a pause in the process, how does the user restart it the next morning? The Windows/Office interface style has no standard menu option for Restart, no Resume Where I Left Off toolbar button, and no terminology for processes like these. You are on your own in areas like this, and such scenarios are common when you create database applications. That's why asking the right questions and planning an effective interface model is so important in Access solutions. You must create standard approaches to non-standard problems, and deploy them in your application or in all of the applications for a specific workgroup.

Here are some practical tips to keep handy as you sit in front on your blank paper preparing to lay out the forms for your next application:

Avoid visual overload. Use tabs, multipage forms, or pop-up forms to limit the amount of information placed on a single form. Users tend to think that even a functionally simple form is complicated if it looks crowded. If an application has many features, group them by workgroup, workflow, process, periodicity, or into whatever bins are logical, and present the options in these subsets to users.

Layout forms on a grid. Your forms will seem less crowded if the controls align in groups and along the same vertical plane. The Windows interface standard attempts to place labels left-aligned in a dialog box, and does the same with the text box and other controls that they attach to. The Access Options dialog provides a good example of screens that align cleanly and do not appear "scattered."

Compose message strings with the help of a user. Alerts are one of the most important components of your application, because they must convey bad news in the least intimidating and most information manner possible. Sit down with a user whose advice you trust and work together on the working of success, failure, and inquiry messages generated by the system. Your messages should be professional and informational, as discussed in Chapter 17, "Bulletproofing Your Application Interface."

Prototype the interface. Create a mockup of your interface model and sit through its review with several prospective users. See where they are confused or delighted. Note carefully the questions they ask, the actions they attempt, the habits they exhibit.

Use the right controls. For most information, there is a correct and incorrect way to present it to users. Learning the correct approach means first learning what works best for users, and next learning how to code it. For example, long lists of Check Box controls have generally been replaced in Windows interfaces with a *list constructor*—a list with available options next to a list box of selected options, with selection buttons in between. Many of your users have seen and used this metaphor in other applications and will expect it in yours (see Chapter 16, "Presenting Data to Users," for instructions on how to build one).

Avoid feature overkill. Avoid these temptations: to sneak neat new features into the application in order to "surprise" the users (they probably don't like surprises); to ship a feature before it really works correctly (take it out or delay the release); to waste time extending the interface with a feature that looks more appealing but doesn't save anybody any actual time or money; or to expect that the users will read the documentation before they use the system (it had better be self-explanatory).

Designing Friendly, "Office-like" Forms

For several years, Microsoft has had an initiative to convince authors of Windows-based software to follow the user interface metaphor defined in Office. The program is called Office Compatible, and is largely responsible for the fact that all of the Office applications have similar interface metaphors, as do many third-party Windows products. For example, why did <u>V</u>iew, <u>O</u>ptions in Access 2 become <u>T</u>ools, <u>O</u>ptions in Access 95? To become Office Compatible.

The Office Compatible specification defines several elements that make up a minimally standardized document-centric Windows application. Those that are relevant to your Access applications follow:

> *Main Menu Bar.* Office Compatible products should employ a main menu bar that is substantially similar to the one found in Office. The menu names, options, and access keys must not be redefined from their Office usage.

What this means to your Access solutions is that you should always attempt to solve a usability problem first with a built-in option on the menu bar. As a specific example, if users need to be able to create a new transaction on a specific form, consider adding the menu bar item <u>I</u>nsert to your custom menu because the term is familiar to users and part of the Office standard. Do not place on the menu the options that Access places there; instead, add a custom option <u>T</u>ransaction to the Insert drop-down. This is preferable to creating a totally new menu structure such as an <u>A</u>dd menu.

 Note

You have probably noticed that the menu terminology standard for Office-type menus employs a mix of nouns (<u>F</u>ile and <u>T</u>ools) and verbs (<u>E</u>dit and <u>V</u>iew) along the menu bar. This mixture provides you with no clear signal as to how your menus should be structured. In other words, should you have an <u>I</u>nsert menu bar option with <u>T</u>ransaction on the drop-down, or a <u>T</u>ransaction menu bar item with <u>I</u>nsert on the drop-down? The section "Conveying Database Issues to Users" later in this chapter addresses this issue in more detail.

According to the Office standard, application-specific bar menu options should always be located between <u>T</u>ools and <u>W</u>indow on the main menu bar. If the <u>W</u>indow option is not shown in your form or application, then your custom options go to the left of <u>H</u>elp. For example, if your application form will show the built-in <u>F</u>ile, <u>E</u>dit, <u>R</u>ecords, and <u>H</u>elp menu bar items, and your users also need a customized menu for transaction posting, the <u>P</u>ost menu option would go between <u>R</u>ecords and <u>H</u>elp.

Figure 8.1 shows the Office-standard menu options for working with Access forms. Wherever it is practical, you should find a home for your custom menu options under one of these menu bar items.

Fig. 8.1

Standard Access bar menu items for forms.

Drop-down Menus. As with menu bar items, you should only show the built-in drop-down menu items relevant to your application and workflow. Also, any built-in features that you do use should not be redefined.

For example, your application needs an option to save the current transaction batch. Under Office Compatible guidelines, you would not be allowed to move Save from the File menu to another menu, nor would you be able to change the shortcut key for it from Ctrl+S or redefine Ctrl+S to do something different in your application than File, Save. You would, however, be able to use File, Save unchanged (visually) to allow users to save their batch. You would also be able to change Save to Save Batch, which adds clarity without redefining the functionality. Figure 8.2 shows this amended option.

Fig. 8.2

Customizing a built-in menu option like File Save is acceptable if the meaning or intent of the action does not change substantially.

8

Shortcut Menus. Office Compatible doesn't tell you what to put on a shortcut menu, only that they are a useful interface concept and they must look and work like those in Office when employed. Because your shortcuts for Access applications will be built using the same command bar engine as is found in the rest of Office, the proper look and feel of shortcuts is guaranteed.

As for the commands on a shortcut menu, good Windows application design policy states that a shortcut menu should have the five to ten most commonly used options appropriate for the current context. In your Access application forms, these will usually be record-oriented navigation and disposition options like Next Record or Delete Record. See the shortcut menu discussion in Chapter 14, "Navigating in Forms and Applications."

Standard Dialog Boxes. Office Compatible mandates the use of the standard Windows dialog boxes for Open, Save, and Print. In earlier versions of Access, developers often coded their own versions of these dialog boxes around Windows API calls. Now, the Office Developer Edition tools include an ActiveX control that provides hooks into the Windows version of these dialog boxes without the need for

API code. See the section "Using Windows Common Dialog Boxes" later in this chapter for more information.

 Tip
You can read the entire Office Compatible specification online at **http://www.microsoft.com/office/compatible/prepare.htm.** At that location, you can also request a hard copy of the specification from Microsoft.

While Office Compatible provides a good framework for the basic elements of interface design, it is mute on database-specific problems and issues that are common to you and me. In areas where it is mute, you must still establish your own standards. See the discussion of database interface issues in "Conveying Database-specific Issues to Users" later in this chapter.

In addition to these interface elements discussed by the Office Compatible guidelines, there are several commonly-accepted Windows metaphors for designing interface elements. The next six sections provide more information on common Windows interface guidelines that will help shape the look of your application interfaces.

Employing Standard Windows Terminology

I can't begin a discussion of Windows interface issues without defining the basic terms that are relevant to such discussions and listing the commonly accepted interface practices you should use. There are quite a few terms and concepts that Microsoft has standardized over the years for use by Windows application developers. However, I'll only mention those that are important specifically to Access solution creators in an effort to keep things uncomplicated.

The following terms should be standardized in your application, both in the message that you show on the screen, in the training materials, in the Help file, and in the printed documentation. This glossary matches the terminology used in Microsoft's product documentation and includes usage examples:

Cancel. Your users should be able to terminate a process or abort a dialog box in several ways (not necessarily all in the same context): by pressing the Esc key, by clicking the Cancel button, by closing a dialog box with the Close button or Control Box, or by choosing Edit, Undo. Each of these is a *cancel* operation. Example: "Cancel the Post dialog box to abort the upload."

Check. To *check* is what users do to select the affirmative state on a Check Box, Option Button, or Toggle Button control, or on a drop-down menu option that supports on/off states. The opposite of this process is to *clear* (technically, to uncheck) the selection. Example: "Check the Dealer item to indicate that the contact is also one of our authorized dealers."

Choose. A user *chooses* a menu option, Command Button control, or hyperlink by clicking it (see also *click* and *select* following). Example: "Choose Tools Add-Ins to view the list of company wizards."

Clear. This is what a user does by removing all text from a control such as a text box or combo box (contrast this with *delete* following). Also use *clear* to indicate the removal of a check box selection (see also *check* previously). Example: "To survive validation, you must select a valid State value or clear the combo box."

Click. This is what happens when the user presses a mouse button over any control (including buttons, hyperlinks, list box items, and tabs) or menu/toolbar option. A click also occurs when a user presses a Command Button control with Enter or Spacebar on the keyboard. Example: "Click the Online Documentation hyperlink for more information."

Delete. To *delete* is to permanently remove an item that has been saved, such as a database record. *Delete* is an operation with larger scope than *clear*, defined previously. Example: "Do not delete a customer from the system without approval from your manager."

Dialog Box. Do not refer to a *dialog box* as simply a "dialog." A dialog box is a form that is modal and collects information that affects the configuration of the application environment or the user's flow through the application. In an Access context, a dialog box is usually less functional than a *form* and is rarely data bound. Example: "Click OK in the Post dialog box to continue with the upload."

8

Double-click. This is what happens when the user presses a mouse button twice in rapid succession over any control. Access provides both `Click` and `DblClick` event procedures for most form objects, so do not use a double-click to launch an event in your application when a single click will suffice (consider the example of hyperlinks, which require only one click). Example: "Double-click the company logo in the About dialog box to see the credits."

Open. This is what happens when a user *clicks* or *chooses* (both defined previously) a bar menu item that drops *open* to expose an attached drop-down menu. Example: "Open the Tools menu and review the options listed there."

Select. A user *selects* an option in a list box, check box, or combo box. This term is usually applied in the context of picking one data value over others, as contrasted with *choose*, which applies to navigation events. A user also *selects* text in a control by highlighting it with either the mouse or keyboard. Example: "Select the appropriate delivery option for the customer from the list."

Type. This is what the user does from the keyboard with the non-navigation keys. The term "enter" is often used in its place, but can confuse users who relate it to the Enter key on the keyboard. Example: "Type your name in User ID and Click OK to login."

If you use these terms as found in the Office product documentation, your application and its materials will already speak a language that users understand, and you will have no retraining or clarification expense when teaching them to use your solution.

Executing Actions from the Keyboard

As you design applications, do not presume that your users enjoy reaching for the mouse every few seconds. Take advantage of the built-in Access keyboard programming features and leverage them to make using your applications (via the keyboard) more friendly.

By default, all Windows application menu commands are accessible from the keyboard, often in more than one fashion. For example, in Access you can select File Close with the keystrokes Alt+F and C (called *access keys*), or with Ctrl+W (called a *keyboard shortcut*). If you use command bars to create your own custom application menus, you should provide access keys for any menu options you devise.

Access keys are for selecting menus by name, menu drop-down commands, dialog box options, and command buttons, and they utilize the Alt key plus a letter. As an example, assume that you are adding a custom Post menu bar option with a Batch option on its drop-down. Here are the general rules to follow when defining the access key combination for a menu bar item (Post):

1. Use the first letter if the keystroke will be unique. Because there is no Alt+P combination on the Access bar menu system, you could safely assign this access key to Post.

2. Use the most distinctive available consonant if the first letter is already in use. For example, if your custom bar menu option was Reconcile instead of Post, Alt+R would be unavailable because it belongs to the built-in Records menu bar item, so you would use the Alt+C as the access key instead.

3. Use the first available letter, if the first two options fail you.

When creating menu access keys for drop-down menu options, follow these rules:

1. Use the first letter of the most important word. In the case of Batch, the choice of B is obvious. If the menu item was Audited Invoices, I would opt for "I" instead of "A," delegating Invoices the more important term in the option.

2. If the access key from the most important word is taken, use the first letter of the first word.

3. If both of these options fail you, use the first available letter within the most important word.

Access keys used for command buttons, option buttons, and other form controls are also termed *accelerators*, such as Alt+N to click the New button in the Database window. The rules for assigning the hot key in an accelerator are the same as listed for access keys. Access keys and accelerators usually operate on visible options, while function keys can have broader scope. Thus, when creating a shortcut to jump directly to an application form, process, or dialog box (this is often called a "back door"), assign the task to a function key (or other "keyboard shortcut," described next) as opposed to an accelerator.

 Note

If an accelerator on a form control utilizes the same keystroke sequence assigned to a displayed bar menu item, the keystroke will go to the form and not the menu.

Keyboard shortcut keys, in contrast to accelerators, execute an option whether or not the menu or button for the action is displayed. Keyboard shortcuts involve the Ctrl key in conjunction with the Shift key, a function key, and/or another keyboard character. The section "Defining Keyboard Shortcuts" in Chapter 20, "Applying Development Shortcuts," details all of the keyboard shortcuts built in to Access and describes how to create your own with an AutoKeys macro.

So when do you utilize keyboard shortcuts and accelerators in an application? The answer is that you can create as many keyboard mappings as are valuable to your users. The two most common scenarios are:

▶ *To remap the keyboard for power users.* Custom keystrokes can be assigned to make work easier for users who are able to remember a custom key mapping, or who understand the accelerator designation shown on forms (the accelerator key is underlined).

▶ *To remap the keyboard to an existing standard.* If your users are coming from a previous keyboard-centric environment and have certain keystrokes ingrained in their work habits, you can teach Access to accommodate those habits. For example, if the mainframe terminal system used a Function key plus U to upload a batch of transactions, you can map the Upload button on the corresponding Access form to Alt+U to help users who have memorized the old keystroke sequence. (Typing keys automatically without having to think consciously about their meaning is called *motor memory*; it is important that you consider the collective motor memory of your user base when designing an application.)

 Tip

Users with keystrokes in their motor memory can be dangerous when learning your new system if some of your accelerators and shortcuts work differently than the keystrokes in the users' memories. During application planning, always query users to determine what keystrokes they use most often in the system you are replacing and in other systems that they will continue to use. If the keystrokes can be remapped in Access to perform the same function, users will be appreciative.

If, on the other hand, the keystrokes they used in a prior system perform a different action in Access, determine what the risk to the application is if users mistakenly press the old key sequence in the new application. You may need to remap certain keystroke sequences to be inert in Access to prevent accidents in the new system. Alternatively, you can place MsgBox function code in the keystroke sequence to ask the user if they want to proceed with the operation; this provides a layer of protection from the negative aspects of motor memory. The section "Trapping Dangerous Keystrokes" in Chapter 17, "Bulletproofing Your Application Interface," shows how to disable built-in keyboard shortcuts that may be dangerous to your specific users.

To create an accelerator key or access key, place the ampersand (&) character before the designated character in the caption of the menu item or control. For example, to use Alt+P for your custom Post menu bar option described earlier in this section, enter &Post as the menu item's name when you build the command bar. When you enter an accelerator in the Caption property of a Label control bound to another form control, pressing the accelerator jumps to that control. For example, an accelerator in the label of a text box will move focus to the text box.

 Caution

When the focus moves to a boolean-state control (check box, option button, or toggle button) via an accelerator, the control's value is automatically toggled (checked or cleared, whichever is the opposite of the current state). When focus moves to a Command Button control via an accelerator, the button is automatically clicked.

Figure 8.3 demonstrates the three user interaction scenarios described in this section as follows:

1. *Access Keys*. The menu bar attached to the form displays a custom <u>P</u>ost menu option. The keystroke sequence Alt+P is used to open the menu item and display its attached drop-down menu. The underlined access key designation is assigned via the & character in the menu item's name.

2. *Accelerator Keys*. Each editable control on the form shown has been given an accelerator key, as shown by the underline in the label caption. For example, when the user presses Alt+I, the focus on the form moves to Customer ID. When the user presses Alt+C, the focus moves to the Credit Approved check box *and* the check box is clicked (its selection state reverses).

   Additionally, the Next Record and Previous Record embedded toolbar buttons on the form have also been given accelerator keys, so that the user can simply press Alt+> and Alt+< to move between records. This is an example of a non-displayed accelerator, because the keystrokes are enabled via the `Caption` property of each button, but the bitmap on the button suppresses the display of (but not the functionality of) the caption.

> **Tip**
>
> To enable the use of the Alt+> and Alt+< navigation keystrokes for users, I actually used the captions &, and &. on the command buttons. Because the user would actually have to press the Shift key in order to get to the < and > symbols on the keyboard, I've used the unshifted versions of these keys as the actual accelerators to save the users wasted keystrokes.

3. *Keyboard Shortcuts*. Using the `AutoKeys` macro, the shortcut Ctrl+P has been designated as the "print" action keyboard shortcut for the application. In the macro group, the macro named `^P` contains the action `RunCode`, which executes a "helper function" called `PrintFromShortcut`. (A helper function is simply a `Public` function in a standard module whose purpose is to execute code in a form module.) In the present case, the task of the `PrintFromShortcut` helper is to execute the "print" action for the current form, as defined by the form itself. Thus, the model I'm using is to create a custom method procedure `mtdPrint` in each form in the application, and to have the helper function call that method when Ctrl+P is pressed:

```
Call Forms(Screen.ActiveForm.Name).mtdPrint
```

8

This technique allows each form to define its own version of "printing" and act accordingly and to have Ctrl+P initiate the action without any awareness of the current form's name or abilities.

 Note

Keyboard shortcuts that are applied uniformly across an application can be built in the AutoKeys macro group. To create a keyboard shortcut that is unique to a form, you can monitor the keyboard for the designated keystroke sequence using the form's KeyDown event. A procedure that monitor's the keyboard for specific key-strokes is called a "keyboard handler"; this type of procedure is described in Chapter 17, "Bulletproofing Your Application Interface."

Fig. 8.3

This form employs all three types of Windows-standard keyboard extensions: access keys, accelerators, and shortcut keys.

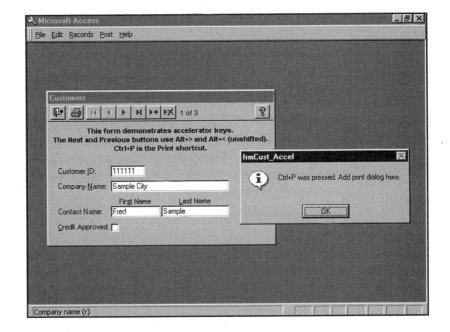

Note

This first release of Access 97 has some limitations with respect to keyboard short-cuts. The shortcomings are a reflection of the difficulty involved in bringing the Office command bar model into Access. I suspect that these deficiencies will be fixed in a future major or minor release of Access (perhaps even by the time you read this). Here are the problems:

▸ You cannot set the Shortcut Text property (create a keyboard shortcut) for a custom command bar item—the property is disabled. The workaround is to create an AutoKeys macro action for the keystroke.

▸ You can set the Shortcut Text property for a built in command bar item, but the property setting is ignored. The workaround is also to use AutoKeys.

▸ In order to be able to use menu access keys, the Control Box property on a form must be set to Yes. If the property is set to No, you can still execute menu options with the mouse but not from the keyboard. This limitation applies to both built-in and custom menus.

▸ An accelerator key on a toolbar button only executes if the text is shown on the button. If the display property for the control allows only the graphical view, the accelerator is inert. This limitation applies to both built-in and custom toolbars. Accelerators on command buttons embedded on forms do not have this limitation and will execute correctly even if only the bitmap is displayed.

8

Understanding the Windows Menu Metaphors

Menu systems in Windows applications employ the following components:

Bar Menu. Most applications always display one *menu bar*, usually at the top of the screen. When you create a custom bar menu option, it should be a single word and should be located just to the left of the <u>H</u>elp menu option on your menu (in other words, not to the left of any built-in Access standard bar menu options, except for <u>H</u>elp). See Figure 8.4.

 Tip

With Access 97, menu objects can now be "docked" at any of the four edges of the Access window. Figure 8.4 shows a menu bar and toolbar that have been located at the edges of the Access window. The menu also contains a custom <u>P</u>ost option in the proper location next to <u>H</u>elp.

Fig. 8.4

Access command bar objects can be docked at any edge of the Access window.

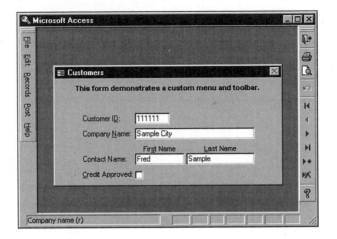

Drop-down. Also called a *pull-down*, this menu appears when you select a bar menu item. Items on a drop-down menu are usually no more than three words, and are spelled with initial capital letters. If your drop-down menu items have some logical relationship, keep related items within a group (denoted with a horizontal bar on the menu).

Cascading Menu. Also called a *tear-off* menu, this is a second level of drop-down that cascades from a parent drop-down. The presence of a cascading menu is indicated by the arrow character (▶) next to the parent menu option.

Shortcut Menu. Also called *pop-up* or *context* menus, these are the free-floating menus that appear with a right-click of the mouse. These are essentially a dismembered drop-down, with the same attributes and style.

Toolbar. As a general rule, a toolbar consists of a related set of command buttons grouped in a horizontal or vertical strip. Toolbar buttons are usually graphical, but there is no reason you cannot place textual buttons or even non-button controls on your toolbars.

You can create each of these types of menus using the new command bar technology in Access 97. While command bars come with some modest limitations and quirks, they are an effective tool for you to enhance your application interfaces. See Chapter 14, "Navigating in Forms and Applications," for examples of command bars at work and tutorials on how to create and program them.

Maximizing the usability of your application's menu system interface involves finding an appropriate balance between these different menu components. The balance point between menu options, toolbar buttons, and buttons on forms is a hard one to find. It is generally accepted as an application design goal for Windows applications that every option on a form button, toolbar button, and shortcut menu is available on the bar menu as well. This rule was designed to achieve two goals:

▶ Users who do not (or can not) use the mouse effectively can execute any application action from the bar menu by using keyboard access keys.

▶ Users can turn off the display of toolbars and not reduce the functionality of the application.

In your Access applications, providing a bar menu option for each button and shortcut menu item is not a goal you will pursue with the same vigor as developers of mass-appeal retail software applications, for three reasons:

1. *Some applications do not benefit from repeated functionality*, such as having a toolbar button and a menu option that do the same thing. In highly complex custom applications, duplicate execution methods actually produce "feature clutter," which proves more confusing than helpful for users.

2. *The rule of thumb that every form action has a menu option does not apply to modal forms.* If you prefer the one-form-at-a-time approach presented in this book, each form is a self-contained object that essentially behaves as a modal dialog box (it exclusively owns the entire interface). This enables you to choose whether a form will have a menu at all or not, because modal forms in Windows applications need not have a menu bar. You must, however, provide the user with important features via buttons on the form if you remove the menus via modality. (As an example, witness the fact that the form in Figure 8.3 in the previous section is mostly self-contained and, with a few more buttons, could be free of any dependence on the bar menu.)

3. *Creating custom menus on a per-form basis is time-consuming.* Most application development projects must look for ways to be cost-efficient, and sticking with generic menus, toolbars, and buttons is one common method employed. When you create a custom action that applies only to a single form, you may not have the time or money available to add a feature to the menu system for the benefit of one form.

Given this information, how do you decide where to locate application features within the menu system? Use these guidelines:

▶ *Follow the Navigation Paradigm.* The invocation method for many features will be determined by the navigation strategy for the application. The navigation strategy determines if users primarily use actions embedded on forms, toolbar buttons, or menu bar selections to execute processes and move within an application. See the section "Choosing a Navigation Paradigm" later in this chapter for a discussion of navigation issues.

8

▶ *Provide Textual Information.* In general, I've found that creating new toolbar button graphics in order to service application-specific features is self-defeating. Creating custom graphics is time-consuming, and users have a hard enough time remembering the meaning of all of the current button graphics in Office without having to learn new ones for each custom application. One solution is to add custom application features to the toolbar using buttons with text instead of graphics. For simple applications, this may work; however, toolbars quickly become crowded in this scenario.

The end result is that features unique to an application should generally be placed within the bar menu system. This gives you the space to use several words to describe the custom option, to allow some forms to be used without the display of toolbars, and to remove the requirement that coders also serve as graphic artists.

▶ Focus on Usability. For any given application feature, as you debate whether to initiate it from a form button, toolbar button, shortcut key, or menu option, consider which of these methods provides the highest usability. If users perform a certain task once a month, burying it on a cascading drop-down in the menu system does not negatively impact their workflow.

On the other hand, a feature that users activate every few minutes as they work with a form should be as close to the users' fingertips as possible. This usually means that you will employ a button embedded on a form and possibly an action tied to keystrokes as well.

Chapter 14, "Navigating in Forms and Applications," and Chapter 17, "Bulletproofing Your Application Interface," provide many screen figures that exemplify different menu, toolbar, and form button layouts.

Using Windows Common Dialog Boxes

Within Access, dialog boxes like Open, Save and Print are inherited by calling an external service—they are no longer built-in to the Access code. Thus, to perform a File Open menu action, Access asks Windows, "Please display your standard Open dialog box and send me back the user's selection." Your application can make use of these standard Windows interface elements as well.

If your application requires users to jump to an external document, locate the back-end database, or insert a document into an OLE Object table field, an expert solution should go beyond simply providing the user with a File Name text box. The standard metaphor to apply here is to create a Browse... button on the form and call the Windows Open dialog box. By passing the appropriate arguments to the dialog box, you can direct the user to a particular folder or filter the list of files shown.

With Access 97, using the standard Windows dialog boxes for Open, Save, Print, Font, and Color is enabled by placing the ActiveX control COMDLG32.OCX on the form and using VBA code to initiate the desired dialog box and to dispose of the result. The common dialog box control file is supplied with the Office Developer Edition. Once you have installed it on your system, you add it to a form by selecting Insert, ActiveX Control... and clicking the Microsoft Common Dialog Box Control.

When your application needs to provide any of the standard services in the control to users, there is no reason to write complex code or re-invent the existing Windows metaphor. The code in Listing 8.1 shows how easily the Open dialog box in the Common Dialog Box Control is displayed and the user's selection returned to the form.

Listing 8.1 AES_UI.Mdb—Calling the Common Open Dialog Box

```
With Me!cdlg
  .DialogTitle = "NorthWind Database"  ' Window caption
  .FileName = " NorthWind.Mdb"  ' Initial/returned filename
  .Filter = "Access Databases (*.mdb)|*.mdb"  ' Type filter combo
  .FilterIndex = 1  ' Seed for Type filter combo
  ' Set return value parameters
  .Flags = cdlOFNFileMustExist Or cdlOFNPathMustExist
  .InitDir = SysCmd(acSysCmdAccessDir) & "Samples"
  .ShowOpen
  If Len(.FileName) > 0 Then
    Me!txtFileName = .FileName
    Me!txtFileTitle = .FileTitle
  End If
End With
```

8

Figure 8.5 shows the dialog box produced by this code. Note how the initial values for the dialog box title, file name, and other options were passed from the code to the dialog box.

Fig. 8.5

This Windows common dialog box was displayed by form code.

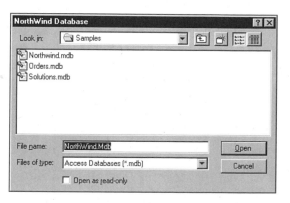

Note

An ActiveX control that is properly installed on your system and entered into the Windows Registry can be inserted into a form and referenced by code. However, to address the control's *type library* (object model definition) from program code, you may need to set a reference to the control file in the References dialog box. For example, the code in Listing 8.1 references constants declared in the control's type library such as `cdlOFNFileMustExist`. These constants are not available simply by adding the control to a form; you must also add a reference. See Chapter 11, "Expert Approaches to VBA," for further discussion of type libraries and references.

Whenever possible, use established interface metaphors like the Windows common dialog boxes in your applications. Reusing application components familiar to Office users provides a common interface for your users across all of their tasks.

Selecting Fonts and Colors to Use

Deciding how to use fonts and colors in Access is simple—you just accept the defaults. If you do that, you can create forms that are simple and match the Windows standard. The Access control defaults set most controls to black text on a white background, with the exception of Command Button controls and form sections that inherit their colors from the Windows desktop scheme (how they do it is described in the next section).

A Colorful Story

Remember how I introduced you to the concept of *rainbow forms* in the introduction to this chapter? In preparing for this section, I decided to unarchive one of the many client applications we've debugged or enhanced over the years that provided our office with a sense of artistic ambiance as a result of its forms.

As an example of what *not* to do in your applications, consider what I found in the relatively simple application written by a neophyte corporate developer and sent to us for rework. The `BackColor` property settings used on the forms included:

128	Dark Red
255	Red
32768	Dark Green
32896	Olive Green
65280	Light Green

65535	Light Yellow
8388608	Dark Blue
8388736	Dark Magenta
8421376	Dark Cyan
16711680	Light Blue
16711935	Light Magenta
16776960	Light Cyan
16777215	White

That's right, 13 different text box and section background colors were in use in the application, and ten of them appeared at one time *on a single form!* Sound dizzying? It was.

The `ForeColor` property settings in the application showed only a slightly less enthusiastic variety:

0	Black
128	Dark Red
255	Light Red
8388608	Dark Blue
16711680	Light Blue
16777215	Bright White

If you think that laptop users have a hard time seeing light blue text on a light cyan background in a sunny office, you're completely right.

Mercifully, the application made use of (only) five different fonts, less than many applications we've seen but still too many for my tastes (the use of Arial Rounded and System were unnecessary):

Arial

Arial Rounded

MS Sans Serif

System

Times New Roman

The lesson in this story is that the colors and fonts did nothing to add value to the application. They added value only to the job of the programmer, who spent an extra few days colorizing the application and got paid for his time. In fact, the excessive gaudiness of the application actually made it more difficult to use and highly distracting to walk past when on-screen.

8

For each new control you create, Access' default font setting is MS Sans Serif 8. Oddly, the default font of Windows is Arial 8, which Access correctly uses for report controls. So, if you want your forms to be more Windows-compliant (and to print better as well), change your control defaults for all form controls except for command buttons to Arial 8 (command button and title bar captions are the two places where Windows uses MS Sans Serif font).

In pre-95 versions of Windows and Access, bold font was used more readily for label captions and so on, but this emphasis has been removed. You will not want to use bold in your application interface unless you prescribe an application-specific use for the attribute and explain this need to your users.

 Note

The use of bold text on a phrase or setting words to all capital letters is referred to in user-interface parlance as *shouting*. Do not make your applications shout at users without a good reason.

Does this mean that any colors and fonts other than the Windows defaults are an anathema? Not necessarily. The key is to emphasize visual elements in moderation, and to apply valid logic when varying from the standards. For example, there may be group captions on your forms that are more usable when bold emphasis is applied to them, or a warning message displayed on a form may be more obvious in blue or red. But the properties you use for basic data entry/edit form control should not be changed from the Windows defaults.

 Note

In Chapter 18, "Creating Expert Reports," I note that it is acceptable to vary from the standard form background color of gray when forms are intended for printing as reports. In this scenario, using a white background facilitates printing.

Making Use of the System Color Scheme

You probably know that you can go into the Windows Control panel and change the coloration of your desktop, but you may not know that your Access application can be designed to inherit the color scheme you create there.

For example, open Access and create a new form. Leave the form open on the screen. Now open the Control Panel on the Start menu, open the Display Properties dialog box, change the Scheme setting on the Appearance tab, and apply the change. Does your Access form's background reflect the color change? Yes, it does.

When users modify the look of their desktop, they will expect all well-behaved applications to inherit the change. For your system to keep pace, you must assign the appropriate values to the color properties of Access form elements. Fortunately, Access does some of the work for you.

For Command Button controls, Access sets the ForeColor by default equal to the button text color setting for the current desktop (the property value is –2147483630). For form detail sections, Access sets the property to –2147483633, which tells it to inherit the 3-D Objects color from the desktop color scheme. For all other controls, Access hardwires the color property settings to Black (0) on Bright White (16777215).

To enable other form controls to change color dynamically to synchronize with the Windows desktop, you set the BackColor, BorderColor, and ForeColor properties equal to specific numeric values, as shown in Table 8.1.

Table 8.1   Color Property Settings that Prescribe System Defaults

Object	Property Value
3-D Dark Shadow	-2147483627
3-D Face	-2147483633
3-D Highlight	-2147483628
3-D Light	-2147483626
3-D Shadow	-2147483632
Active Window Border	-2147483638
Active Window Title Bar	-2147483646
Application Background	-2147483636
Button Text	-2147483630
Desktop	-2147483647
Dimmed (Disabled) Text	-2147483631
Highlight	-2147483635
Highlight Text	-2147483634
Inactive Window Border	-2147483637
Inactive Window Title Bar	-2147483645

8

continues

Table 8.1   Continued

Object	Property Value
Inactive Window Title Bar Text	-2147483629
Menu Bar	-2147483644
Menu Text	-2147483641
Scroll Bar	-2147483648
Title Bar Text	-2147483639
Tooltip Background	-2147483624
Tooltip Text	-2147483625
Window	-2147483643
Window Frame	-2147483642
Window Text	-2147483640

You can misuse these property values easily, because Access allows you to enter any setting listed in the table for any color property on any control. For example, you can assign the Highlight Text color value -2147483634 to the ForeColor property of a command button instead of the appropriate Button Text color value. You'll have to determine which combinations make sense for your application.

You will usually accept Access' suggestion that command buttons and form sections inherit their scheme from Windows. This allows your Access forms to follow suit when a display style change is made.

You may also want to teach other controls to inherit the Windows defaults. To do this, you override the Access default property settings for form controls and establish new defaults that mimic the Windows desktop. For example, assume that you do not want your Text Box controls to display black text in a white window regardless of the display environment; instead, you want the control's colors to change when the Windows desktop changes in the same manner that text boxes built-in to Access and Windows change. Follow these steps:

1. Create a new Text Box control on a form.

2. Set the Fore Color property value of the control to -2147483640, which tells Access to apply the desktop scheme color for Window Text to the control.

3. Set the Back Color property value of the control to -2147483643, which tells Access to apply the desktop scheme color for Window to the control.

4. Select F̲ormat, Set C̲ontrol Defaults from the menu. This teaches Access to apply these two property settings to all text boxes created from this time forward.

5. Follow this same strategy for any other form controls that you want to build custom default settings for.

Make sure that you consider the ramifications of any unique color settings that users may apply. For example, accepting Access' default text box setting of black text on a white background may be expedient in organizations where users are discouraged from changing their desktop display. In cases where a user can change the Windows color scheme for Window Text to white, your Access forms will display white text on a white background and become unusable. In this kind of environment, forcing the text box attributes to inherit the Windows attributes would prove more usable.

Guiding Users Through the Application

Forms are usually the most critically important objects in your application, for the reasons that follow:

▸ Forms are the most visible part of your application, seen by all users and leaving good or bad impressions depending on whether they serve or frustrate them.

▸ Forms are the only line of defense between users and data fields, providing data formatting and validation to keep information accurate as it is entered and edited.

▸ Forms consume a large percentage, usually more than half, of an application's development budget.

Because forms are so important, you must make them easy to use and easy to move within and between. After you sketch out an application's forms and their properties, ask these questions:

▸ How will users move forward from each form to the next one? What interface method will they employ, and what checks will the application do to make sure the move is allowed?

▸ How will users move backward through the application? Is it as easy as moving forward? Should there be shortcuts to move back to the "top" of the application in one jump?

▸ How does navigation enforce or assist the workflow? Can operations occur out of their required sequence?

As you create and enforce an application flow, you will combine various interface elements: buttons, menus, toolbars, shortcuts/accelerators, windows (forms), messages, and dialog boxes. Knowing which element is most appropriate for an application task is important to crafting an expert interface.

Choosing a Navigation Paradigm

My preferred user interface model directs users through forms, one by one, or at least limits them to some small, manageable group of related forms at the same time. This model is called *Single Document Interface* (SDI) in contrast to the *Multiple Document Interface* (MDI) model that Microsoft Office applications, including Access, employ by default. The MDI model is acceptable for slides and documents, but data-bound forms really cry out to be structured into a cohesive application.

In fact, one of the stated design goals for Windows 95 was to define more of an SDI model for users, based on feedback from Windows 3.x usability testing, which showed that users become overwhelmed when too many options are presented. Notice, for example, how the Windows Explorer doesn't let you tile multiple drive listings as File Manager did, or how linear the Start menu is when compared to Program Manager.

Consider the following problems that can arise when you allow your users to open multiple Access forms at random:

▶ Users can enter dependent data out of sequence. For example, they might try to enter child records before the parent.

▶ Users can open multiple forms that point to the same record, introducing possible record-locking challenges.

▶ Users can open too many forms at the same time, affecting application performance or losing track of their workflow.

▶ Users can keep multiple unsaved records open, usually by minimizing forms on the desktop without saving their edits. This situation prevents other users from seeing current data.

▶ Users can lock records, usually by minimizing forms that have edited records in an unsaved state (depending on the form's locking model). This potentially locks other users out of specific records for an unreasonable period of time.

Applying interface techniques that circumvent these and other situations is the responsibility of both the design and development teams. All of Chapter 14, "Navigating in Forms and Applications," is devoted to issues that arise as you create navigation methodologies for your application. Refer to that chapter for a complete exploration of navigation strategies. For our purposes here, I'll summarize the key points as follows:

▶ Your application should enable users to move in only directions that are safe in the current context.

▶ Your application should make it clear to users how to move one step forward or one step backwards.

▶ Your application should prevent users from overwhelming themselves with too many simultaneous objects or tasks.

You achieve these objectives by creating menu bar, toolbar, shortcut, or embedded navigation options for the user to click, and then teaching the application to provide the user with interaction within the specified set of objects valid for a given context, and nothing more.

The best approach is to create a standard navigation interface paradigm for your workgroup or enterprise, then create as many reusable objects as you can and employ them in multiple applications. The navigation library code and library toolbars shipped with many of the sample databases in this book is one example of this strategy.

If your navigation model is highly restrictive, you will end up building applications that utilize the runtime version of Access or at least adequately protect the data from misuse and the user from confusion. A restrictive interface usually removes the Database window and is modeled around one or more switchboard menu forms such as the one shown in Figure 8.6. Applications that provide a switchboard menu must provide users with a path to every important system feature via the menu system.

Fig. 8.6

A highly restrictive application provides users with a list of available features so they don't have to wander in the Database window.

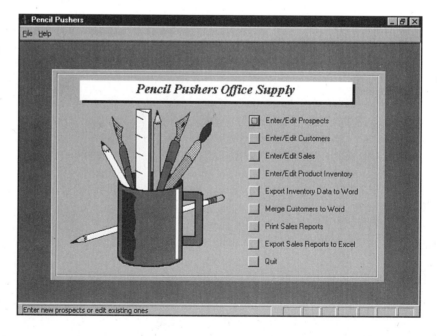

Users of an application that restricts and controls navigation will primarily be given a single task to perform at one time. This follows the SDI paradigm and reduces user confusion and application misuse. The application interface shown in Figure 8.7 provides an example of a restrictive environment oriented toward completing a single task before moving to another object. The user can only move to another process by completing the current process (closing the form, in this case).

Fig. 8.7

A Single Document Interface application model displays only one form at a time.

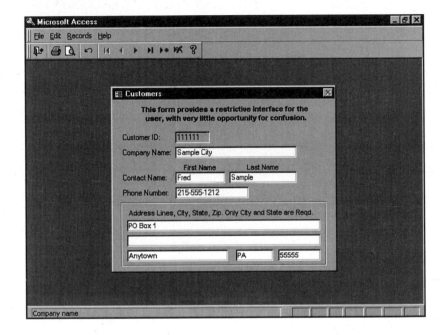

Of course, you can create hybrid navigation systems that deviate from the simple model in the following ways:

▶ *Allow users to open several related forms at one time but not all forms simultaneously.* Consider an order entry application where users only need to be able to move to a customers form, a customer contacts form, and a contact schedule form. You could create a toolbar with three buttons, one for each form, and devise an attractive graphical icon for each form. Place each icon and its related form name on a toolbar button and locate the toolbar at the bottom of the Access window, and you will have successfully created a user interface that visually matches the Windows 95 interface style based on a task bar. See the example in Figure 8.8.

▶ *Allow users to move only between related forms.* For example, you could build a navigation chain where users could go from the customer form to the order form to the product form, but in no other direction and only in a linear fashion.

Fig. 8.8
An Access toolbar that mimics the Windows 95 task bar interface style.

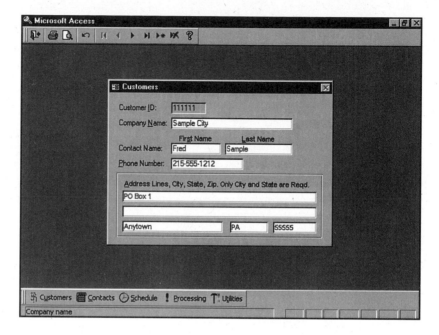

▶ *Allow users to work within a single form window.* Using subforms or a tab control, you could create a multi-page, multi-purpose form window that users move within to accomplish a task. Each screen would represent different but related sets of data. This metaphor resembles the Access wizards.

Other opportunities for creating a navigation model are limited only by your imagination, your skills, and the needs of your users and their data.

Accommodating Keyboard-centric Users

Accommodating keyboard-centric users should be of concern to you as you develop your applications. If you've been developing applications only in the Windows era, you may live with one hand glued to the mouse. However, not all of your users will mimic that style.

Before Windows, there was DOS. Before DOS, there were terminals (okay, I *am* simplifying a little bit). And what did people do with terminals all day? Enter and review database records. No word processing. No worksheets with graphics. No e-mail. Just databases.

So when these users try to use your application, they will try to figure out how the keyboard works with it; if the keyboard doesn't work well, you will have missed an important usability opportunity.

Accommodating keyboard users involves providing a minimum set of functionality that includes the following:

▶ *Utilize keyboard shortcuts.* Keyboard-centric users will expect your application to support certain standard Windows keyboard usability guidelines. Included in this list are keyboard shortcut keys (such as Ctrl+P to print), accelerator keys (such as Alt+N on your form's New Invoice button), and access keys for custom menu options (such as Alt+R to open your Records option on the menu bar). The section "Executing Actions from the Keyboard" earlier in this chapter describes these techniques in detail.

▶ *Create a flow that matches its task.* Users moving through an application using the keyboard will expect the Tab key to move focus to the next logical control. I say "next logical control" because many developers fail to consider how the tab order of their form controls can be an important usability issue.

Consider a form with Name, Address, City, State, ZIP, and Telephone Number Text Box controls. On average, a developer will display these controls in the order I just used, and users pressing the Tab key will expect to move through the controls in that order as well. However, this display-order flow may not be appropriate in an application where the users are telephone-bound and ask the customer for their telephone number as the first question on a new order call. Simply because there exists a good reason to display the telephone number halfway down the form does not mean that the user must grab the mouse to get there when the phone rings. It is quite simple to create a tab sequence for the form that begins in the Telephone Number control in the middle of the form and then jumps upwards to the Name field.

When you have completed the design of a form, always remember to establish a navigation sequence through the form that is reasonable for the task at hand and matches the users' workflow.

▶ *Provide intelligent navigation.* Keyboard centric users not only enjoy being able to press Tab to move between controls accurately, but they want to move between pages and forms as well. Access has some particularly bad habits with respect to tabbing inside multi-page forms and forms with subforms. Keyboard users can create anomalous pagination (displaying two partial pages instead of one complete page) or become "trapped" in a subform, unable to tab out. Both of these issues are frequent enough complaints of Access users that I address them in detail in Chapter 15, "Protecting and Validating Data."

▶ *Provide intelligent assistance.* You can also aid keyboard-centric users by providing a little clever code here and there to make their job more enjoyable. An example follows that documents this point.

Consider the form shown in Figure 8.9, which provides a prime example of a candidate for the status of "keyboard-optimizable." The form is a dialog box whose purpose is simply to help a user find a product when only a few characters are known.

Fig. 8.9

This form, properly coded, is very friendly to keyboard users.

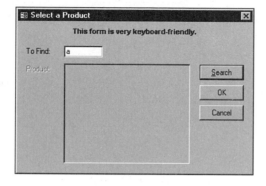

Here is how a user interacts with the form:

1. The form opens and focus is on the To Find text box. The Search button is the default button for the form (the button that is clicked when Enter is pressed).

2. The user types a string of characters to search for and presses Enter. The default button (Search) is clicked automatically and the code in Listing 8.2 runs. The code creates an SQL string that populates the list box with matching product names. If any matching products are found, the code does this: the list box is enabled; the focus is moved to the list; the first item in the list is selected; and the default button is changed from the Search button to the OK button, as shown in Figure 8.10.

Fig. 8.10

All products containing the letter "a" are listed in the list box simply by pressing Enter.

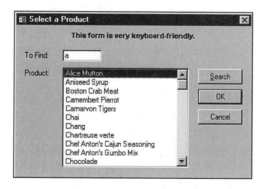

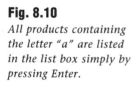

Listing 8.2   AES_UI.Mdb—Executing a Simple Search from a Search Button

```
Private Sub cmdSearch_Click()

  ' Create the search string
  Me!lstProduct.RowSource _
    = "SELECT ProdName, ProdID FROM tblProd" _
    & " WHERE ProdName Like '*" & Me!txtFind & "*'" _
    & " ORDER BY ProdName"
  Me!lstProduct.Requery  ' Run the search
  If Me!lstProduct.ListCount = 0 Then  ' No matches found
    Me!txtFind.SetFocus
  Else  ' Matches were found
    Me!lstProduct.Enabled = True
    Me!lstProduct.SetFocus
    Me!lstProduct.Selected(0) = True
    Me!cmdOK.Default = True
  End If

End Sub
```

3. The user scrolls through the list to the desired record and presses Enter. The default button (OK) is clicked automatically, the form closes, and the product value is passed to the calling routine.

Notice that the user has quickly located a product record without ever removing his or her fingers from the home position on the keyboard—no special shift keys (Alt, Ctrl, or Shift) or mouse usage was required. Because the code routine sets the focus to the list box and the first item in it, the user can navigate in the list using the first character of the list items—thus the cursor movement keys are not even required. To use this dialog box to select the product Aniseed Syrup, here are the keystrokes required once the dialog box has loaded: A Enter A Enter. That's all.

An application that is engineered correctly for the keyboard will allow a keyboard-centric user to perform a standard task faster than a mouse-centric user could perform the same task.

Using the Appropriate Window

By now you've determined that you will probably be creating applications that are very document-centric (to use the Office term), and thus concern themselves with a single document (database record or entry form) at a time. If you consider the parent record in relationship to the primary *document*, then child and grandchild records of that parent are essentially *subdocuments*. Within this model, you should strive to present a user with plenty of information about the document and its family, while isolating them from other non-related documents at the same time.

Note

Based on our discussions thus far about MDI versus SDI, it should not come as a surprise to you that the AppWizard in Visual C++, when creating a new database application, employs the Single Document Interface by default. Its developers recognized that even in retail-quality applications, if the document is data centric then it should be modal.

Access provides several different varieties of forms (windows) to use for the data collection tasks, as follows:

▶ *Single Forms.* A single form provides exactly one parent record, and may or may not have detail (child) records in a related pop-up or embedded subform. For data records of any complexity, this form is the only object that is appropriate.

▶ *Continuous Forms.* Forms that display multiple records really come in two varieties: continuous and datasheet. Each is appropriate for some tasks. For example, a continuous form can show unbound controls and can use non-linear control layouts, while a datasheet gives users more control over the display of columns and cells but is more difficult to add program code to.

As a general rule, I prefer to use continuous forms to view summary information or to browse records rather than as entry/edit devices. This is especially true when the continuous form will use multiple rows of controls for a single record, which often produces forms that are visually confusing for users. If a form has very few fields, it can be effectively displayed in a continuous mode, as shown by the subform in Figure 8.11.

Fig. 8.11
The subform on the tab is uncomplicated and makes a good candidate for using the continuous display mode.

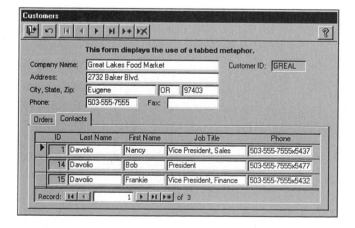

Chapter 16, "Presenting Data to Users," contains a lengthy discussion contrasting the continuous, the single record, and datasheet form layout models.

▶ *Modal Forms*. Any of the prior forms in this list can be displayed modally, either via form properties (Popup and Modal) or the acDialog argument on the OpenForm method. Modality is really not a form style; it is a display style. If you do not want users to do anything else besides work in the current document, its form should be displayed modally.

 Note

Modality is different from, but in some ways related to, border style. In Access, a form's border can be sizable or fixed. In general, you do not want to write the code to rearrange a form's layout when its border size changes, so you will not use the Sizable argument for Border Style unless the form is a datasheet.

Even if a form's border is not sizable, it does not automatically make the form modal. To enforce form modality, you set the PopUp and Modal properties to Yes.

▶ *Dialog Forms*. A dialog is a modal, fixed size, single-purpose form, usually designed to collect information at a branch point in the application flow. If your application is highly modal, every form is essentially a dialog box, but in the true sense a dialog box has less user interaction and capabilities that an entry/edit form. A dialog box usually has several selections or options, along with an OK/Cancel button pair or a Close button. Refer back to Figure 8.10 for an example of a dialog form that gathers information important to the application's flow but is not bound to a data table.

Tip

With the new tab control, you can create complex tabbed dialogs that resemble the Options dialog box in Access and other Property dialog boxes in Windows.

When you use dialog forms, there are two common interface elements that you may want to employ:

1. *Ellipses Points*.... Placing these marks at the end of a button or menu caption indicates that the selection will show a dialog box to collect information and then return to the current screen.

Ellipses points can also be used on a button within a dialog box to show that an additional dialog box (called a *Gosub dialog*) will be called. For an example of this see the Browse... button on the Hyperlinks/HTML tab in the Access Options dialog box.

   2. *Chevrons (>>).* These marks at the end of a button caption indicate that there are additional strings or controls that can be displayed in the dialog box. Clicking the button with chevrons expands the height of the dialog box to show the additional information. For an example, see the Advanced>> button in the Access Startup properties dialog box.

Providing Clues and Cues to Users

When first establishing our Access interface standards, we wanted to develop a technique for alerting users to the controls that must be filled in on a specific form in order to survive validation. We created forms demonstrating several different types of visual clues and surveyed a subset of our clients to gather their usability feedback on these forms.

Here is a quick summary of the interface devices we tested to denote required fields and the general response from us and our users:

   Changing the label font (using bold, italics, or color for instance), met with a very negative response because few combinations are as pleasant to read as the defaults of Arial and MS Sans Serif as plain text.

   Widening a control's border created a non-symmetrical look to the form, with some controls "leaping" off of the form.

   Noting in the status bar text that the value required was effective but too subtle—it was easily missed.

   Appending information to the caption, such as an asterisk or an "(r)" for "required" was effective but made the captions more difficult to read.

   Prefixing the caption of required fields with an asterisk, which is unobtrusive to the caption and the flow of the form, was the universal favorite and the technique we still employ today.

Figure 8.12 shows the various techniques we tested for denoting required elements on forms. See Chapter 15, "Protecting and Validating Data," for a discussion on implementing our chosen strategy for flagging required fields. That chapter also discusses other techniques to help users discern the minimum set of information required by an application process.

8

Fig. 8.12

Various approaches for helping users determine if an entry is required by a form control.

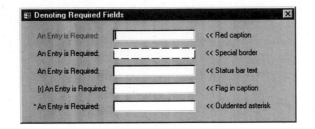

Enumerating our research process for you should help you see how pioneering interface decisions are made. When you create your design and development standards, and there are no existing metaphors to follow, you must create your own model. As you create any interface standard that is untried or uniquely different from accepted norms, you must prototype the standard on a body of users and weigh their feedback.

Beyond the problem of telling users what values are required, you have several similar usability challenges as you craft your interface. You must teach the users how the application works and also give them some clues regarding what the program expects of them.

You can place helpful information in your interface in a variety of locations. The assistance text can tell users what to do next, what kind of information to enter in a control, what happens when a button is clicked, what to expect during a process, or what the status is of the current process. Here are a few ways to convey such information to the user via the forms interface:

Status Bar Text. Each control on your form should have information in the `StatusBarText` property for the control. Most users are familiar with the purpose of the status area of the screen and will look there for advice.

Control Tip Text. You can add floating *tooltips* to almost any form control. The tip can provide information about the data entry requirements of the control or the process that clicking the control will initiate.

Control Groupings. In some cases, you can economize on form text or communicate a dependency by grouping several controls together with a Rectangle or Line control and creating one label to describe the data entry requirements for the entire control group.

Check Box, Option Group, Combo Box, and List Box controls. Of course, these control types limit the data entry options for the user and therefore prove very useful for conveying data entry requirements.

> **α Note**
>
> Control tips have, unfortunately, become less useful in Access 97 than they were in Access 95. While both versions accept 255 characters of text in the property setting, only Access 95 actually displays all of the text. In the 95 release, control tip text is wrapped within a rectangular box and the entire string is shown in an attractive manner. In Access 97, tip text does not wrap. It displays on a single line and truncates when it reaches the end of the screen. Thus the amount of text you can display is limited by screen resolution (slightly over 100 characters in 640×480 mode). This horizontal display is also not as visually attractive than in the previous boxed layout.
>
> These controls do not have a `ControlTipText` property: `Line`, `PageBreak`, `Rectangle`, `Subform`, and `Tab` (although tab pages do have the property).

Form Messages. Depending on the amount of empty space on your form, you can often provide detailed messages using labels on the form, or a single label with text that changes based on context, much like a status bar.

Figure 8.13 shows an example of several of these visual clues provided on a single form. Expanded examples of these and other communication techniques are detailed in Chapter 17, "Bulletproofing Your Application Interface."

You will also want to make use of custom help files when your application development process allows. Map the `HelpContextID` property of each form to a topic in the custom help file that explicitly describes the form's usage and requirements (see the sidebar).

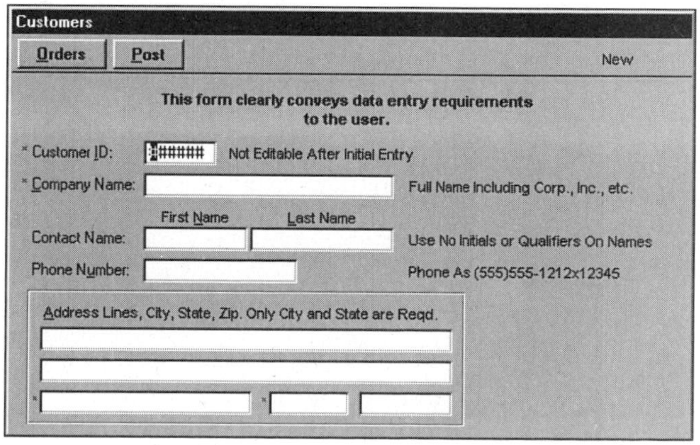

Fig. 8.13

This form explicitly indicates field formats, required fields, control groupings, and other data entry requirements.

A Hidden Smile

There is an actual Help topic in the Access 95 help file whose title is "Make my computer smile." To find the topic, search for "smile" on the Find tab in Help. Here is the text:

1. Type a colon, and then type a right parenthesis.

2. Repeat until the desired level of machine happiness is achieved.

Unfortunately, the topic is gone from Access 97's Help and I haven't found its replacement.

Conveying Database-specific Issues to Users

Database application forms often provide very interesting interface challenges. The reason is that it's sometimes very hard to explain to users how an action on a form translates into an action against the data. In this section, I'll provide a few examples of this challenge to get you thinking about the subject. However, each application, user group, and enterprise has unique attributes, so it's not possible for me to cover here even a fraction of the kinds of hurdles that will arise as you develop your applications. All I can do here is spark your interest in the subject of database-centric interfaces in the hope that you will budget the time and mental effort required to properly address these situations as they arise.

As our first example, consider this challenge: When your application's user is entering multiple records as a batch, is it possible for the user to cancel the entire batch? If so, how do you convey this to the user within the Windows interface metaphor? If you simply follow the model for dialog boxes and place OK and Cancel buttons on the form, how does the user know that Cancel will undo multiple records as opposed to only the current record? If you follow the Access model instead of the Windows model, your form will have a control box and close button, both of which save the batch as the form closes. The user will have no clear idea how to perform a "cancel" operation.

The problem arises because there is no distinction in the Windows model between a minor cancellation and a major cancellation—Windows thinks only in terms of OK and not OK, and Access inherits this model. In the current example, your application will need to go beyond the Windows standard and provide more information, perhaps through two buttons: Cancel Record and Cancel Batch.

Similarly, consider the problem of the way Access handles record saves. When the user moves from a parent record into its related child records on an embedded subform, the parent record is saved automatically (called an *autocommit*). From the user's perspective, the transaction is only half complete—the invoice header has been entered but not the detail records, for example. Yet from Access' perspective, many things have happened without any direct command from the user:

▸ The parent record was saved to a table.

▸ An ID number was generated for the parent record; this ID will trickle into all child records as the link to the parent.

▸ Validation routines ran as the parent was saved.

▸ Audit information may have been written to a log showing the creation of the record.

None of these actions are bad per se: the point here is simply that the user was not asking for these events to happen yet. From the perspective of the user's workflow, saving the parent seems most logical when the complete transaction (including the children) has been entered.

When the parent record is saved before the entire group of related records is entered, the concept of "undo" becomes very confusing for users. Assume that the user simply wants to cancel the invoice he or she is entering. Access and Windows provide no default metaphor for this, because neither facilitates batches of information or form-based transactions. In the current example, it would be nice if the user could simply tell Access to cancel the transaction. Unfortunately for both the user and the developer, when a record autocommits early in the workflow, the only way to undo the record later is to delete it. This means extra coding work for the developer and confusing alerts to wade through for the user.

It takes time and effort to craft an elegant expert solution that hides these issues from non-sophisticated users, but the effort is usually a prudent investment in the success of a project. Here are some common approaches you can take to the problems posed by form data entry transactions:

> *Make your forms think in terms of batches.* If the concept of batch entry, batch validation, and batch cancellation are useful to your application, you must code your forms with this metaphor in mind. It is possible to make empty copies of production tables and bind entry forms to the empty copies. This causes the user to perform data entry into "holding bins" as opposed to live tables. If the holding bins are in the local (user interface or *front-end*) database, the developer has an easy job when the user decides to cancel a transaction—simply clear the work tables.

Provide adequate information. OK and Cancel buttons are simply ineffectual in a database application. In the current example, the user will receive much more value from the form if its buttons say, "Save Entire Transaction" and "Cancel Entire Transaction."

Shield the user from what's really happening. The user doesn't care that canceling an invoice and its detail initiates one or more deletion events, so why display this information? When a record opened for editing is deleted, you obviously want to confirm that the user intends to proceed, and to echo back the deletion status. In contrast, deleting records as part of undoing an entry batch can be coded as a silent operation.

Consider another significant issue in database interfaces: bulk processing. Users in a manual system can perform an operation or two on a batch of data, then decide to revert back to a previous data set by simply throwing away some new paperwork and pulling the old papers back from file drawers. For all of its power, Access doesn't think in these terms unless you tell it to.

Assume the following scenario:

1. The user imports into the application a file of information dumped out of the mainframe.
2. After loading, the application code audits the imported records and produces a problem report.
3. The user edits the problem records using a form, and prints a hard copy report showing the imported information.
4. The user runs a routine to process existing records in the system by applying cost items to them from the imported data.
5. The application code produces summary records that recap the processing in the previous step and post the summary information to a transaction table.
6. The user runs a process to update master total records with the summary information placed in the transaction table.

Up through step 3, this process can be canceled quite easily and the application can purge itself of any trace of the interrupted process. What happens, however, if the user discovers serious problems after step 5 and wants to cancel? While you can wrap a specific code process in a transaction in your application, Access does not maintain a transaction log after your code has completed. Access has no knowledge of the relationship between the workflow steps in the list, and so it has no idea how to help the user cancel several, or even one, of the steps.

An expert approach to multi-step operations like this one requires that the developer creates the transaction log that allows the process to be undone and writes the code to support the change of heart. The entire process can be run on a copy of the affected records and the changes inserted into the live data after step 6 has run to completion. Alternatively, the code can secure an exclusive lock on the database, backup the key tables, and execute the steps.

In either case, the key point here is not so much the problem itself as the limitations in Access that it exposes. Access does very well when thinking in terms of *records*, but you have to teach it everything you want it to know about *processes*. Then, you have to expose the processes to users.

A final confusing database-specific issue to consider when creating your interface involves terminology. Should you have an Insert menu bar option with Transaction on the drop-down, or a Transaction menu bar item with Insert on the drop-down? Does the user understand what a "rollback" is or should you be using the terms "revert" or "undo?" Semantic questions arise constantly when creating database applications, and the majority of them have no established standard nor one single correct approach. The key to your success will be to work with the users of the application and developers of similar applications to make sure that the application fits the needs and semantics of the user's workflow as much as possible.

From Here...

There are many interesting challenges that arise in the course of developing user interface layers over data. One of my favorite aspects of custom application development is the constant variety of challenges presented by the need to automate a workflow we've never attacked before.

In this chapter, you've acquired important knowledge for designing complex application forms and other interface elements. Here are other tools this book provides for becoming a designer of expert interfaces:

- ▶ Chapter 3, "Preparing for Development," discusses how to effectively coordinate a design effort that includes both users and developers.
- ▶ Read Chapter 14, "Navigating in Forms and Applications," for an expanded discussion of the navigation issues introduced in this chapter.
- ▶ Chapter 15, "Protecting and Validating Data," describes user interface techniques that smooth out the entry, editing, and deletion of records.

▶ The text and figures in Chapter 16, "Presenting Data to Users," provides you with several options for the layout of your forms.

▶ Chapter 17, "Bulletproofing Your Application Interface," expands on the issues raised in this chapter related to controlling application flow, enforcing modalilty, improving keyboard interaction, and providing feedback to users.

chapter 9

Completing and Deploying a Solution

9

In this chapter

◆ Techniques for successful project management

◆ Testing a solution well to ensure a quality product

◆ Effectively educating application users

◆ Distributing the application to users smoothly

◆ Encouraging and collecting user feedback

F ew situations in life reward us for good planning alone; instead, the successful execution of the plan is the result that most endeavors are judged by. So too with application development. In spite of your good research, planning, and coding efforts, a project can fail or fall short of its mark. I'll focus on five key areas in this chapter to help you prevent such situations.

> ## Counting Critters
>
> "To keep life interesting, we established various milestones in the Access 95 development process, with prizes to members of the team that achieved each milestone. One such benchmark was a designated prize for reporting the ten thousandth bug.
>
> "One of the testers (I'll call him Bob to protect his dignity) decided he really wanted the prize for this bug count milestone, so he wrote a very clever program on his machine. Starting at bug 9,950, his program monitored bug reports as they were being submitted to the server, watching for that critical bug number 9,999. When his program saw the magic number, it immediately sent in a bug he had been holding back, in order to clinch him the coveted slot number 10,000.
>
> "Bob's program ran perfectly, and late one Saturday night, it saw number 9,999 go by, launched on cue, and submitted the winning bug report. However, before Bob came back in on Monday, some of his fellow testers noticed that he had submitted the prize-winning report on a night when he was not even in the building, and they suspected foul play. For fun, they moved Bob's bug from 10,000 to 10,001 and placed one of their own in the winning slot.
>
> "In the days that followed, people who were in on this nefarious plot would wander by Bob's office and peer in, chuckling to themselves as Bob groped through his code line by line to try to figure out what had gone wrong and how it could have fired one number too late!"
>
> Tod Nielsen, General Manager, Microsoft Access Business Unit

All too often, developers and users with the best of intentions miss the mark with respect to deploying a successful and useful application. While all parties apply the appropriate amount of good intentions and effort, they miss a few critical opportunities, and the development effort ends in diminished success or outright failure.

In my experience, development efforts that produce poor applications or user satisfaction do so as a result of some combination of the following factors:

Developers didn't listen to users. In design meetings, while users were carefully describing their needs, the technical members of the design team were thinking about the technology they would use for coding the solution or some new approach they could take to the problem or which existing objects they could re-use—in short, they were thinking ahead to the programming effort when they should have been participating in the design effort.

Developers listened to users but didn't apply what they heard. Possibly, the developers heard the users loud and clear during the design phase and then took the license during development to improve the solution by changing or adding features autonomously. If developers do this without proper user review and approval, there is a chance that they will move further away from solving the users' problems instead of creating an improved solution.

Users gave developers bad information. During the design meetings, users were simply unable to speak a common language with the developers, and what was said by the user representatives was received in a completely different form by the development representatives.

For example, users describing queries required in their system often state that they want to find all data matching Criterion A *and* Criterion B (in other words, they want information that matches the first criterion together with information that matches the second criterion). While the users said "and," from a developer's standpoint they really meant an OR operator at the code (SQL) level. Thus, these two groups are speaking different dialects, and the success of the queries will be tied to whether the developers knew that the users were speaking "Userese" and not "Developerese."

Poor management or a lack of management led the project astray. Sometimes, the boat wants to go a certain way and the wind wants it to go that way, but the captain, nevertheless, insists on steering a different course. Project managers have the ability and the right to overrule both the users and developers when charting the course. Sometimes they produce a better application as a result, and at other times, the quality suffers. Alternately, development teams run amuck without qualified management may produce solutions that display technical brilliance but do not accomplish their stated mission.

9

Nobody compared the outputs to the inputs. Sometimes, an application's unsuitability to its audience is not noticed until it is deployed. An inadequate solution should never end up in the hands of the users because it should be properly reviewed during the development and testing processes for compliance with the original project plan. Similarly, the project plan should have been reviewed for compliance with the user's actual needs before the development effort began.

The application was not properly tested. Because of time constraints, poor management, inexperienced developers, or a flawed deployment methodology, an application may be released without being properly tested. If so, many of those nasty critters called "bugs" may be roaming around in the application waiting to spring on unsuspecting users.

What can be done to dodge these bullets and produce the best possible solution? In Chapter 3, "Preparing for Development," I described methodologies that system designers can use to minimize the occurrence of flawed design processes and communication problems. In this chapter, I'll assume that the design plan is solid and show how to turn the plan into a shipped application.

Managing Application Development

> ## Sign of the Times
> I saw this sign at Microsoft: "All tasks that are due yesterday must be fully assigned by noon tomorrow."

As the sidebar alludes, there never seems to be enough time in an Access development project to do a perfect job. The low cost of Access and the machines that run it produces a mindset that Access development can be done quickly and inexpensively. With time and money constraints in place from the beginning of a project, the project has no chance of success unless it is directed by someone competent in budgeting, time management, motivation, problem solving, and team coordination.

Developers are an independent lot and are often creative and liberal types with disdain for traditional business hierarchies. Nevertheless, application development must be structured and respected like any other business process.

As I alluded in Chapter 3, even a development effort involving only one programmer will be more successful if that lone coder is managed by someone else. When programmers are freed from user interruptions and deployment planning, they can focus exclusively on the creation of the solution.

Creating a Time Budget from the Specification

In Chapter 4, "Creating Design Specifications," I describe in minute detail an approach for creating design specifications. One element of a high-quality specification is a detailed itemization of the component objects that comprise the solution, and the application's primary tasks.

Generally, the project time and monetary budgets are based upon the listings of objects and tasks in the design document. The manager's primary role at the beginning of the development process is to refine the time budget and object listings into a finite and detailed project work plan.

If the project tasks were assigned time estimates in the specification, the manager can extrapolate the maximum calendar time required for development. Adding all of the time elements and dividing by the average length of a workday would produce the number of person-days required in a one-person, linear development model.

Of course, most development projects involve more than a single developer. Consequently, the manager's initial mission is far more complex than simply defining a time budget in days. Rather, the manager must proceed according to the following plan:

1. Itemize objects and processes to the lowest reasonable level of detail.

2. Define the time budget for each itemized object and process.

3. Assign a developer to each object and process.

4. Define the order in which each developer will execute his or her defined tasks.

5. Balance the assignment of tasks and times to synchronize the completion of all tasks.

6. Revise the schedule to manage dependencies within developers and between developers. Establish interim and final milestones for the project (this process is described in the following section).

7. Launch the development process and manage the development effort against the plan. Revise the plan and reassign tasks as required.

In the "Preparing Project Timelines" section of Chapter 4, I introduced the concept of placing time estimates by task into a project plan. At the highest level, a sample project plan looks like the one shown in Figure 9.1.

When a detailed plan exists for a project, I use the plan as a time budget by breaking each task into what I call *SpecItems*, which are detailed tasks (objects or processes) on a specification. Each SpecItem on a project is a measurable unit of work with distinct attributes and a prescribed time budget. On projects that have a finite amount of hours (and/or dollars) associated with them, creating time budgets at this detailed subitem level greatly increases the ability to manage available resources against the budget.

9

α Note

The term "SpecItem" is my own. You can replace it with any term that provides the equivalent meaning to your development team, such as *task*, *item*, *subitem*, *workitem*, or *element*.

Figure 9.2 shows a portion of the project plan from Figure 9.1 that includes the SpecItem number and time budget for each task.

Fig. 9.1

You can create development project timelines using tools like Microsoft Project.

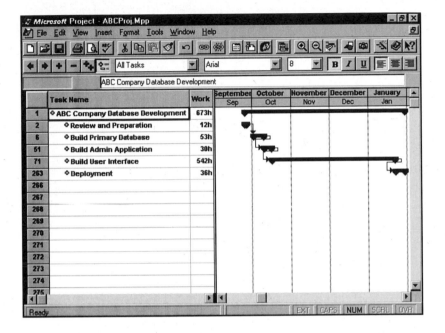

Fig. 9.2

A project plan that shows individual time budget items (SpecItems).

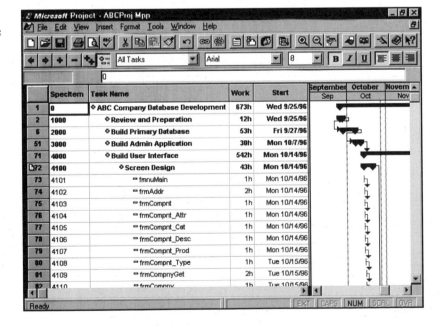

Note

If you want to create a time budget with SpecItems for your project and are not concerned with a visual or hardcopy timeline, you can use Excel instead of Project to create the grid portion of the information shown in the figure.

The SpecItem numbers can be used to track time against the project by requiring that each time-keeping entry made by a developer against the project includes the task (SpecItem) identifier. See the section "Performing Progress Reviews" later in this chapter.

Establishing Project Responsibilities and Milestones

The project manager's initial planning effort (as defined in the previous section) includes assigning tasks to developers and creating a plan for each developer to accomplish those tasks. A manager performing such a planning process must take many factors into account:

> *The nature of each task.* Before assigning tasks to developers, the manager must define the technical needs and complexities of the individual tasks. Development tasks, especially the creation of core processes, often require a unique level of experience or mix of skills during their creation. The completion of the development effort on-time and on-budget is often contingent on the ability of the manager to define the required skills for each task and to match coders to tasks.

 Tip

This process of matching skills to tasks may be more successful if the manager encourages the involvement of members of the development team.

Additionally, I mentioned in Chapter 3 the objective that development managers should also possess a high level of development skills themselves. Nowhere in the management process is the need for these skills more obvious than when the manager is estimating the time for each development task and matching the tasks to the skills of the programming team members. A manager who is only a "business" person and not familiar with the nuances and details of the development process will not be able to successfully create an accurate and detailed development plan.

The skills of each developer. In organizations with multiple developers, it can be difficult for the manager to assess the skill level of each developer with regular frequency. Nevertheless, in order to properly match skills with tasks, the manager must create and apply a review or measurement system that helps to monitor and record the aptitude and abilities of each team member.

The developers' schedules. Developers that work on more than one project simultaneously may quickly suffer from overload. Most developers I have known tend to prefer a structured, balanced workload that is narrowly focused around a small number of defined tasks and short-term milestones.

A manager must have access to up-to-date schedules and availability for each developer on the team in order to efficiently delegate tasks.

The relationship between tasks. There is no value in a development plan that assigns dependent tasks out of sequence or assigns them to many different developers. It is incumbent on the manager to define and map the dependencies between objects, code routines, and processes so that they are completed in the proper order.

The timing of related tasks. In order to successfully establish and achieve project milestones, managers must coordinate the completion of related tasks. The development plan must stage the availability of related objects to occur at the same milestone.

For example, in order to produce an interim build of the accounts receivable portion of an application for review by the users, a defined set of tables, queries, forms, and reports must be completed by the same time milestone.

 Note

When creating separate development efforts to run in parallel, I've found that the simplest organization is to have three development teams. First, all of the teams work together on the tables, code libraries, and application infrastructure. Then, one team works on forms, one on reports, and one on core processes.

Whichever team is done first with their list inherits the early testing work and the creation of user-education materials and deployment plans.

When creating a project development plan, interim milestones can be built around status points (a percentage complete, a specific number of objects created, or a subset of functionality demonstrable), or they can be built around the completion of named project components. When dependencies exist between objects or processes, it is useful to define functional subsets or components of an application, and to manage the completion of each component as its own miniature product.

Thus, the accounts receivable, accounts payable, and payroll components of an application may each be managed as if they were a full project. The development of these components can be run successively or can be staged consecutively if enough resources are available. The management of application components requires careful timing of interim deliveries and may also require component-level review, documentation, and testing efforts.

Whether interim milestones are based on measurable progress or the completion of identifiable components, they provide several types of value to the users and developers:

> *Interim reviews.* If milestones are coordinated in a way that allows developers to combine their work and create an interim *build* of the application that functions with reasonable stability, the build can be demonstrated to users. This allows users and managers to measure progress against the timeline and also to discern if the requested features are being implemented in the way that was intended.

> Interim reviews provide the opportunity to intercept mistakes in design and direction at regular stages in the development process.

> *Interim closure.* For developers, slogging through weeks of coding may not produce a sense of satisfaction or fulfillment if the results of the effort are not regularly made visible. Interim milestones allow developers to see the results of their work (individually and collectively) and to feel that they have actually checked some items off of their lists and made measurable progress.

 Tip

Interim milestones are a good place to locate team-building exercises like project review meetings, training and other skills enhancement, or rewards and social events.

> *Project pacing.* Left to their own devices, coders may fall into the same trap that other workers do and defer elements of their work to a future date closer to the final milestone. When enough work is deferred to the end of the project, there is no chance that the project will be completed on time.

> The presence of interim milestones prevents this situation. At any interim milestone, it is easy for the manager to determine which developers are not on schedule and to take immediate action to remedy the situation.

Note

Does the previous point mean that the timely delivery of a project is related to the number of milestones in the project? Not precisely. A project with an overload of milestones can become bogged down in preparing for milestones, creating interim builds, and coordinating user reviews, all of which may slow the progress of development rather than help it.

In the "Prototyping" section of Chapter 3, I noted that it can be useful to include at least two interim milestones in the development of every application:

User interface review. This build of the application provides the users with the opportunity to review the layout of screens before their code is created. For this milestone, screen forms are prototyped and their visual attributes are developed.

Working model. At this stage, the application forms and navigation elements have been built to a degree that allows users to interact with them. Users can test the flow of the application against the original navigation map and can determine if the forms contain the required attributes to solve their data entry and editing needs.

Complex applications may benefit from a few more milestones. For example, a review of report prototypes can often prove useful in applications with extensive reporting needs. Also, applications that have highly involved processes may benefit from a user review of the process logic when it is finalized.

 Tip

Users are not usually adept at reviewing the code or pseudocode for a process. Instead, the best way to enable a review of a process is to work with the users to dummy up a set of input data, run the process against the data, and then analyze the outputs from the process to determine if it is working as desired.

For example, an inventory control routine includes code to balance the running inventory balance to stock-on-hand (called physical count) information entered into the system. To assist users in reviewing this process, the developer would need to help the users enter sample records for initial product quantities, then create stocking-level adjustment records, and then run the inventory balancing process and review the output records.

When a project development plan has been created, it is important to share it not only with the developers but with the users as well. Users on the design team that are involved in the interim milestones must be made aware of the timing of their involvement and the amount of energy that will be required of them. When developers deliver the application to users for review at interim milestones, it is critical that the user feedback comes back on time, or the development timeline may be affected.

 Note

The only thing more frustrating to a development manager than coders that are behind on a deadline is users that are behind on a deadline. The development manager rarely has the authority to force the users to complete their obligations to a project.

Users involved in the testing process must also block out the testing phase on their calendars and check their availability early in the development process.

Identifying Pitfalls and Priorities

When creating a project timeline, the manager must attempt to foresee events that can derail that timeline. The ideal development model is one where all of the coders have all required skills and knowledge, sit down at their workstations, and proceed undistracted through the coding effort. However, this virtually never happens.

Some missed deadlines are a result of poor coding effort or a skills deficiency on the part of the development team. But there are other roadblocks that can crop up in the course of development:

> *A corporate directional change.* When corporate priorities change, the importance of specific projects may be re-evaluated, and the financial commitment to them may be reduced. When the wind shifts direction, a development manager may find himself or herself in a very difficult position. On the one hand, the corporate direction no longer supports rapid completion of the current project. On the other hand, users probably still want and need the solution, and discarding the work in process would be wasteful. Solving this dilemma requires solid political and budgeting skills on the part of the manager.

A change in personnel. When the composition of the development team changes suddenly, the harmonious flow of a project is disrupted. The loss of a single programmer may require alteration of the schedules of all other programmers on the team.

The loss of a staff member is only one of the personnel dangers confronting a project manager. Another is a change in the attitude of a programmer or the team. A reduction in corporate loyalty or team spirit can cause a coder to work at a slower pace than was budgeted, and a personal situation at home can reduce the workday or workweek.

α Note

The *addition* of a coder to the team can actually slow a project. Over the long term, an extra person usually increases the performance of the team, but in the short term, the new hire requires equipment, training, reviews, and motivation. Depending on the new person's skills, there may be a net drain on the project timeline rather than a net contribution. The best time to add a new person to a development team is in the short space between projects.

Alterations in the users' needs. In this fast-paced business environment, users and companies are constantly redefining themselves in order to stay competitive. When this redefinition occurs in the middle of a project, users often come to the project manager with change requests.

Depending on the scope of the user request, some or all of the work done to date may be invalidated. In this situation, managers must be careful to state and enforce the maxim that, when users change the project definition, "all bets are off" with respect to the original budget and timeline.

α Note

Never casually agree to finish a project redesigned during development on the same timeline and budget as the original project. *Stop all development*, go back to the drawing board, and recalculate all deadlines and costs. If possible, involve the members of the original design team in this process.

Changes in Technology. Few situations are more frustrating for managers and developers than to have a nearly completed project and to discover that an improvement in technology is available to apply to the project. When this happens, the manager must weigh the value of revamping the project to the new technology against the impact on the timeline.

Microsoft's release cycles are not closely guarded secrets, so managers should be able to reliably plan around new releases of Office and Windows and to budget for the impact of any mid-project upgrades.

A more frustrating situation is exemplified in the Visual Basic environment, where developers depend heavily on add-on products (VBX and OCX controls). Sometimes, we have been in the middle of coding our own VBX or OCX extension in C for a project, only to find that a third party has released a retail control that provides the same functionality we are coding. As Access becomes more reliant on ActiveX control extensions and other add-ins, this example will be more common in the Access environment as well.

Unreliable Technology. It seems that almost every project has its own "development hell"—a feature that cannot be made to work as designed or a major technical snafu. Because each Microsoft product has its own unique screen repainting peculiarities, event model, and built-in bugs, not every feature in the design plan can be coded to match the users' expectations; attempting to do so can introduce project delays.

Compounding this are the inevitable hardware issues that regularly plague development teams. One workstation seems to always be down or floundering (at least that's what happens in our office), so a project manager should not budget time as if all programmers can keep their hardware running all of the time. Even in very stable hardware scenarios, simply upgrading hardware components can cause a loss of productivity (for example, new drivers must often be located and installed or hardware settings must be tuned).

Time Conflicts. Creating an accurate time budget for a project requires knowing about the company's schedule and the work calendar of each developer. Managers often fail to plan for the standard time losses, like company meetings or social functions, training events, developers' vacation plans, holidays, and so forth that occur during a development phase.

Of course, to release a solution on time, the development manager must be able to expect or predict situations like the ones listed and to include in the project plan contingency tactics to apply when the situations occur.

In addition to contingency planning for situations that reduce productivity, managers should prioritize development efforts to ensure that the most important items are completed first, when possible. This situation ensures that a project that is late, runs out of money, or loses key staff is not abandoned because its most critical features are missing; instead, it can at least be delivered in a reduced form.

As you prioritize individual project elements, these three different attributes should cause an element's priority to be escalated:

Mission Critical. Any feature that is critical to the operation of other features, the core processes of the application, or the primary needs of the users should receive top priority.

Highly Complex. The features that are the most complex in a system should be delegated to the most proficient and reliable coders.

High Priority. The features that are most urgent for the users (their "top ten" wish list) should be given the heaviest weighting when creating project plans.

Tasks with one or more of these listed attributes should be slotted for completion earlier in the project rather than later. At the point where the most difficult and important issues are completed, much of the project stress for both users and developers goes away, so it is important to reach this milestone as early as possible in a project's lifecycle.

After reading this topic, it should now be apparent why I emphasize the need for a project manager to provide support to the coders. The complexities of project planning, project management, and problem resolution in even small applications often exceed the career interests or job descriptions of technical personnel.

Measuring Development Progress

Having had the privilege to work with many bright coders over the years, I've observed that each has his or her own artistic gifts. Some coders are brilliant at doing what they know but poor at solving new problems. Some programmers learn slowly but never forget, while others understand everything instantly but have no retention.

With so much variety, there is no single test you can give a programmer (or yourself) that measures development aptitude against a finite scale. The real proof of skills is in the quality and solidity of the solution components created.

If you must try to measure the abilities, and the growth in abilities, of programming team members, you must do it by analyzing the products they create. Evaluating skills based on criteria like the following can prove useful:

▶ Adherence to the specification

▶ User satisfaction

▶ Number of bugs

▶ Originality of contributions

▶ Coding style and throughput

Of course, benchmarks such as those listed can also be used to judge the quality and status of a development *project* in addition to that of developers (see the sidebar). In order to determine the percentage of a project that is completed, the development manager must periodically review the completion status of each project element and the quality of that element.

Is It Done Yet?

I heard a software company executive in the '80s once say something to this effect: the first 90 percent of software development is easy; it's the last 90 percent that kills you.

He was expressing his frustration with a process that has been the same as long as I have been in the business—when you *think* you're done coding, you're *really* only about halfway done. There always seems to be one more change or one more bug on the list, and as you cross items off the list other people are adding to it.

In the end, there is always a philosophical mind game where developers go through the product after they've decided to ship it and go down the open issues list reclassifying every open item. A quirk that never got corrected becomes a *feature*; a feature that got dropped at the last minute is hyped as a compelling reason to anticipate next year's upgrade, and the unfixed bugs are cataloged blandly as *known issues* near the bottom of the README file and blamed on the operating system.

Mostly as a result of time pressures, every software product ships with bugs, and the important question becomes not *"How many?"* but rather *"How severe?"*

α Note

The previous statement in no way means that developers should capitulate and stop striving for zero-defect applications. Because we have done it, I know that it is possible to write software that has no defects *known to users*. The bugs that were in the application were actually found by developers doing future upgrades but were never discovered by any users. This is as close to perfection as software ever gets.

Performing Progress Reviews

All projects should have either a time or cost budget, and most have both because time and money intertwine in business. As the manager performs interim progress reviews of a project, he or she must gauge progress by comparing the current status against the milestones and budgets established at the beginning of the development phase.

If a project plan is designed for what I call *progress budgeting*, it has a defined mixture of milestones and lists the expected status of each application process and object at each milestone. Determining the current state of a project relative to its completion is a matter of determining the current status of each object with respect to its nearest milestone.

For example, assume a project plan with progress budgeting defines the 40-percent-complete milestone for a project in terms of the completion of coding against a defined list of objects and processes. The status of the project with respect to the 40 percent mark is determined by the status of each object or process as compared to its expected status at the 40 percent milestone. Table 9.1 shows an example of such progress. For the project in the table, the application is assumed to be 40 percent complete when the three listed forms are completed.

Table 9.1   Status of a Project As Measured by Completion of Specified Objects

Object	Actual Percent Complete
frmCust	80%
frmAddr	100%
frmOrder	90%
Average	90%
Project	90% × 40% × 36% actual project completion

A second type of budgeting is what I call *time budgeting*, which measures all progress on a project in terms of hours (or dollars derived from the cost of the hours). Time budgeting assumes that each element of the project has an associated time projection. If the projections are good, it is safe to say that when the time budget for an item is consumed, the item is complete (because the allocated time or money available for it has been used up).

To measure project progress using SpecItems, developers must record their time at the SpecItem level. For example, Figure 9.3 shows how a developer might record his time against the SpecItems shown in Figure 9.2.

Fig. 9.3

An Access table for logging development time by project and SpecItem.

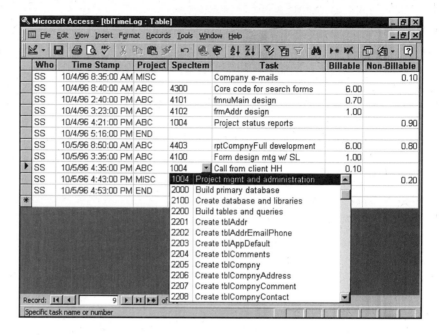

In this example, project status is measured by collecting time records in an Access table and then running a query with time grouped and summed by SpecItem in order to measure the hours accrued against each item. If the original time estimates were good, the number of hours expended against one SpecItem divided into the number of hours budgeted should indicate the percentage complete.

Performing Code Reviews

An Unfavorable Comment

The need for code reviews is indicated by the following quote, which we found in a code comment in an application inherited from a client:

```
' I'm writing this on my last night here.
' The code's not working and I'm sick and tired and giving up.
' This should have been thought out more clearly before I started.
```

Clearly, the person writing this code comment was disgruntled and was a lame duck. You cannot expect people in such a situation to do their best work. Discovering this comment during our code review indicated to us that we must carefully review the commented routine—and any other routines written by this same person—because the code quality may have been affected by the negative personal attitude.

As the sidebar indicates, if only one person writes a routine, reviews the routine, and tests the routine, the routine is completely a reflection of that person's skills and attitudes. If, however, someone else reviews the routine, the quality of the code can be brought up to a standard that better reflects the abilities of the entire team or the goals for the project.

A *code review* is simply the process of carefully reading code routines associated with a process or object, looking for areas that can be improved. Code procedures are often drafted, then coded to completion, and then optimized, and a code review can occur at any or all of these milestones.

 Tip

If a chunk of code can only be reviewed one time in a project, it should be reviewed when the coder thinks it's completely done and perfected. While an early code review (an architectural review given soon after a code routine is drafted) is very useful to see if the content is appropriate to the task at hand, too many code changes take place between this point and application completion for an early review to be useful as the only review.

It is often easiest to perform a code review at one of the project milestones, when an identifiable set of routines have been completed. (The strategy for defining project milestones and creating interim builds was discussed earlier in this chapter.) Any set of code delivered as part of an interim build is fair game for a review unless otherwise noted.

 Tip

All code reviews should occur before the testing cycle. When testing begins, the code should be complete from the perspective of both the programmer *and* the manager.

Properly commented code can be useful during a thorough code review. It can sometimes be very difficult to determine exactly what a piece of code is doing without appropriate comments.

Conversely, managers must not get in the habit of reviewing code by simply reading the comments. A comment is not a valid indicator of the quality of the code that follows it, nor are comments even guaranteed to be accurate because coders often forget to revise comments as they revise code.

In a perfect world, all code in a project would be reviewed before shipment to the users. However, there is rarely enough time or budget in a project to allow for this. Routines should be prioritized for review using the same criteria as was described previously in this chapter for ordering the flow of development. Thus, routines that are mission critical, highly complex, or a top priority for the users should be reviewed first.

What should the reviewer look for when scrutinizing code routines? A good coder can often spot bugs or logic flaws while reading another person's code. The reviewer should also note the following:

Poorly Structured Code. As detailed in Chapter 5, "Creating Naming Conventions" and Chapter 11, "Expert Approaches to VBA," development teams generally create and apply standards for commenting code, naming objects in code, locating and structuring code routines in relation to their parent objects, using common and library routines, and so on. Any code found during the review that does not match the standards established in these areas should be flagged for rework by the coder.

 Tip

You can imagine how difficult it would be for a manager to review the code of ten different developers who used ten different coding styles. Code reviews are made much more difficult when consistent coding styles are not enforced throughout the team.

Inefficient Code. There is often more than one way to programmatically address a specific task, and simply because the coder has used a different style than would have been employed by the reviewer does not mean that the routine is flawed.

However, a savvy reviewer should ideally know the most optimal way to achieve a specific result in code and should note any code found during the review that does not take this path.

Incomplete Code. Whereas a coder may be working on a specific engine routine or application process, the reviewer is usually a management person or senior coder more in tune with the big picture. Because reviewers are more aware than coders of the overall project scope and features, they must apply this knowledge to the review process and make certain that the reviewed code matches the features intended for it in the design document.

Thus, one focus of the review is to make certain that all of the users' needs are met by the code and that none have been overlooked.

Redundant Code. Coders are encouraged to reuse routines between them and to communicate with each other as new routines are placed in the central repository. Nevertheless, reviewers are generally in a better position to know what shared routines are available to a team than any single coder is.

A reviewer should be alert to the specific tasks performed by each code routine and should ask two questions while reading it:

▸ Does this routine perform a generic task? (If so, it should probably be moved to the library so it can be reused in the current and other applications.)

▸ Does this routine perform a task already available in the library? (If so, it should be replaced by the existing shared routine.)

Flawed Code. The reviewer should ideally be the first tester of the code, in the sense that the reviewer should be sophisticated enough to apply failure scenarios to code during a review and determine if the scenario is covered in the code. For example, a good reviewer reading a routine that creates a disk file should be sophisticated enough to instinctively check the code for proper handling of failure scenarios like an existing file of the same name, or a target drive that is read-only, and so on.

It is tempting to perform a code review from printed hardcopy code listings or in Word documents with revision marks enabled. Either of these options enables the reviewer to easily make notes and annotations. However, because reviewing code involves jumping to related routines and sometimes even running the code to follow a logic trail, most code reviews are actually performed online.

 Tip

When reviewing code online, you can use comment marks (an apostrophe) to make comments directly in the code. Create a standard notation that the original programmer can search for at the end of the review in order to read each review comment. For example, I place 'SL at the beginning of my code review comments inserted into code.

Performing Architecture Reviews

A review of an application's architecture is different than an audit of its code. An architectural review is concerned with the layout of objects, the dependencies between objects, and the flow from one object to the next.

This type of review is usually done at some interim milestone near the midpoint of the project. When the application is half completed, the table structures, form and report shells, and primary code routines should have been at least outlined and located within the solution. The reviewer should be able to divine if these objects are structured properly and match the intended and optimal design and usage.

> **Tip**
>
> In Chapter 4, "Creating Design Specifications," I describe how to create a *navigation map* for an application. The architectural review of a solution should include comparing the application against the navigation map from the design document. The reviewer should make sure that the application flow envisioned by the users was actually implemented in the solution.

Testing Access Applications

A Tester's Vocabulary

Various incarnations of this list of definitions have crossed my desk over the years. I've edited the lists and added a few items of my own:

Bug: A programmer's term for a feature that the user doesn't understand. Also, a user's term for a feature that can't be demonstrated when the programmer is watching.

Computer: A device designed to speed and automate the creation of errors in data.

Debugging: The process of fixing bugs that the programmer can easily remedy and then define the rest as features.

Hardware: The parts of a computer that can be kicked.

Keyboard: A device used for entering errors into an application's data.

Language: A system of organizing and defining error messages.

Programmer: Someone who exists to annoy users.

Quality Control: The process of ensuring that an application does not end up with an overabundance of quality.

Software: Thousands of tiny gremlins called bits running around inside a computer magically doing stuff.

User: Someone who exists to annoy programmers.

9

Some developers love to test applications, others do not. Some are better at it than others. Because there is no value in an untested routine, either to the rest of the development team or to the users, each developer must constantly strive to become a better tester of his or her own code.

Unfortunately, the testing process is often underbudgeted because a common perception is that a good coder or team should not be creating bugs in the first place. This is a misconception. First, all humans make mistakes, and thus all coders have bugs in their completed work. Secondly, a software application is a complex collection of code and objects interacting with users and data. There are many different combinations of such interactions to test and many different things that can go wrong in the interaction.

While random testing done by a good tester finds many of the problems in an application, it is wiser to proceed with testing according to a plan.

Creating a Test Plan

The quality of your product is directly affected by the quality of the testing performed on it. Notice that I said quality, not quantity. While a thousand robots or test scripts pounding on your application may eventually find every problem in it, one well-directed human generally finds as many issues and in less time.

Consequently, in the same fashion as a specification was created to provide the developers with a map to use during development, a test plan can be created to provide a map for use by the testers. The biggest danger in random testing is that a feature or feature set will be overlooked and untested. Testers working from a comprehensive plan are unlikely to generate this problem.

The most basic test plan is simply a list of the elements of an application: objects, features, and processes. A tester working from a comprehensive list of application elements verifies that each item on the list works as designed and is free from errors. A broader test plan includes suggestions for *how* to test each object, feature, and process.

 Note

If you prefer a formal definition for test plan, I offer this:

A list of every feature in the application, and every logical feature grouping, with a strategy for triggering each feature/group from every possible user-interface approach and internal circumstance. By following a test plan, a user unfamiliar with an application should be directed to use every feature in it in conjunction with every logical combination of data state (such as empty record, full record, valid record, invalid record) and initiation method (including keyboard, mouse, cascading code events, thresholds/triggers, and timers).

To determine if a feature works as designed, the tester must have a copy of the design document to test against. If the design document is not detailed and specific or one does not exist at all, the tester is forced to either guess as to the intended workings of a feature or ask a user or designer of the system for input on the intended behavior. Neither of these options is efficient or accurate. Consequently, we've just bumped into another benefit of a written specification: it provides the framework for a testing plan.

To write a basic test plan, make an outline list of the high level features in your application. For an Access application, the outline might be organized by bar or switchboard menu features. Next, fill in the outline with each feature that can be accessed in that area of the product. Remember to include features on menus, buttons, and those triggered by events. The outline might look something like this:

- Menu option or feature
  - Expected result
    - Activity
      - Expected result
    - Activity
      - Expected result
    - Activity...
- Menu option or feature...

Using the structure shown, here are some actual entries from a test plan:

- Select menu item: Enter Invoice
  - Result: Form loads on blank record
    - Select menu item/button: File New Invoice
      - Result: Save current record, goto new record
    - Select menu item/button: File Print
      - Result: Preview Invoice report for current record

You can see that even a simple feature list like this helps organize the testing process, provides the testers with a structure for recording issues discovered or objects certified, and enables managers to track testing progress.

With a basic test plan, we are relying on the abilities of the tester to try all possible variations of data and interaction with the system in order to properly test a feature. Skilled testers may function adequately in this scenario because they have seen many applications fail and know what to look for. Lesser-skilled testers, however, may not be able to properly anticipate all the different ways a user might interact with a feature and may not test well from a basic plan.

Writing a more comprehensive test plan than a simple outline takes additional time. Creating this test plan generally involves using the specification as an outline of features and objects, as well as adding details that are specific to the testing process. To create the details, browse the application and add to the plan the menu options, toolbar and form buttons, keystroke sequences, and events that could be triggered by a user at a given point. The objective is to come up with a document that lists each possible action that can be initiated by the user or via an event initiated by the user. In other words, this outline should list everything that can be accomplished using the application.

It is also helpful to review the code in an application with an eye toward branch points, subroutine calls, automated features (like timers), or feature combinations (such as dependent features), and then to add information to the test plan about how to test these internal code processes. What you are looking for here are areas in the application where events can either collide with each other, or be spawned by other events, or fail in an ungraceful manner.

Continuing on, add text to the plan, in appropriate places, that describes in detail how to properly evaluate whether or not each listed feature or function is working correctly. Note that the objective here is to convey to a tester, who may not be either a developer or user of the application, an understanding of the interaction of events amongst themselves or events between the users and the system. While it is assumed that testers of your applications are trained on the application's workings first, they still may not understand what a feature should *do*, only how to *use* it.

As a final step, read through your test plan and add notations about resource requirements for each individual test item. For example, if performance testing is an objective for the testing process, as it is in most database applications, someone needs to build a sample database (called a "test case") of sufficient size to allow the application to be tested under load. Someone also needs to configure the machines on which the performance tests will be run.

 Note

As a rule of thumb, you can assume that your users will upgrade their Access product, their client machine, or their database server machine, or all of the above, every 12 to 24 months. Thus, you would want to simulate in testing the data load that will be placed on your application 24 months from now in order to appropriately test under the future load that will be placed on your application using the user's current hardware configuration.

For example, in an invoicing system that will be logging 70 orders per day, you should add 33,600 records (70 × 20 working days × 24 months) to the system as dummy records so that performance can be tested for queries and reports using the full data load.

Another area involving additional resource requirements for your test plan might include calling APIs or other external programs from your application. For example, if the application is e-mail enabled, you need to test the mail functionality of the application in an environment that simulates that of the users. Thus, if your users include both Novell Netware and Windows NT users, you need to provide resources to your testers that include networks of both these varieties with e-mail services on which to test the application. You may also have to test more than one variety of mail services, such as Microsoft Mail and Exchange servers.

 Tip
Remember to include usage of notebook/laptop computers as an element of your testing. In an application that has local data, allows the replication of central data locally, or allows the users to make their own local copy of the data, a machine can be removed from the network and still use the application. In such a case, any dependencies your application has on the network (for example, the e-mail server or shared code libraries) must be tested in a non-network scenario.

As an example of a comprehensive test plan, presume that your application has a customer form. On the customer form is a combo box for the CustType field. The test plan for this single control would include the following suggestions:

1. Enter a value not on the list, you should receive an alert. Did you receive an alert? Was the alert accurate? Was the value disallowed?

2. Delete a value from the combo box, you should receive an alert. Did you receive an alert? Was the alert accurate? Was the delete disallowed?

3. When you enter a new record on the form, the CustType value should default to the customer type value for that CustID in the Customer table. Was the default entered? Can you select a value other than the default? Does the default reset on a new record?

4. When you change the CustID value on the form from one customer number to a different one, the value in the combo box should be replaced with the default value matching the new ID. Was the default entered? Can you select a value other than the default?

5. Does the control provide quality status bar text and a What's This help message? Is the control described in the application's help file? Can you easily find the topic?

6. Does the control behave the same whether entered and exited via a mouse click, Tab, or Shift+Tab?

You can see that the mere process of testing a single combo box control can have many steps. Compound this test action list by every control on every form, then add different data scenarios to the test, and also factor in the interaction *between* the various controls, and you will quickly understand why the testing process for a fairly standard Access application can take weeks.

Stalking the Wild Tester

If your team can afford dedicated testers, you have solved one of the biggest problems in software development: how to ensure that applications are properly and thoroughly tested. If, instead, your testers are also developers, then you face the significant burden of making the developers into *good* testers.

 Note
There is no correlation between a person's ability to write code and his or her ability to test. These skill sets are completely independent.

Historically, developers are not good testers for one single reason: they make too many assumptions. This is the reason why developers are very poor at testing their own code and only marginally better at testing code written by others. Here are some of the traditional (and flawed) assumptions that a developer makes when testing an application:

"No developer would write code like that." In some cases, a tester thinks that he or she should test for a specific situation, only to dismiss the situation as inconceivable by reasoning that no developer with any reasonable level of skill would knowingly code the stated situation. The flaw in this logic is twofold. First, all developers do not think alike; therefore, it *is* conceivable that someone else would write a block of code that you would not write. Secondly, people make mistakes, so the problem you do not expect to find may be there simply as the result of an accident.

"No user would do that." Another fatal miscalculation is to expect that users are rational creatures, when in actual fact they may not always be. Users might use the application tired, angry, distracted, rushed, drunk, untrained, or in any of a number of other mental states. As such, they interact with the application in ways that a tester must strain to visualize.

"Access takes care of that." By knowing the capabilities of Access, a developer often assumes that the application makes use of a specific Access trait and does not bother to test the affected application feature.

For example, a developer may take for granted that the deletion of a record deletes its child records (and thus not test this) because the referential integrity provided by Jet takes care of this under certain circumstances. However, a good tester never makes such an assumption and tests everything.

"That's not programmatically possible." A savvy developer often knows the various ways that a specific code routine can fail, and tests those areas. The developer then assumes that there are some ways that a routine cannot fail and skips testing those areas.

In fact, it is often surprising to developers that routines that cannot be made to fail in the test lab can be made to do so quite easily in the field. A simple example is provided by a routine that works on a recordset built from a lookup table. The author of the code wrote the routine with sample data in the table, and the tester tested the routine with the same sample records. When the table was emptied of sample data and the application shipped to users, the routine failed because the scenario of an empty recordset was not conceived during either development or testing.

You can do several things to learn how to be a better tester or to help your development team improve their testing skills:

Have a developer perform a technical support role. Making a developer the designated direct contact for users on an application he or she worked on provides a fantastic learning experience for that developer.

First, the developer becomes humbled by learning how many bugs were actually coded and shipped. This embarrassment can prod the coder on to improved diligence and self-monitoring in the future.

Secondly, the developer gets to learn how users think. The users call and describe how a bug or confusing situation is reproduced, and the developer is awed by the things that users do to the application that he or she never anticipated.

Finally, the support role is often so distracting and unpleasant for a developer that the manager can use the threat of it as a carrot in the future: the coder with the highest bug count for this application will be the designated technical support contact for the application.

Educate the developer on testing methodology. Have the best testers on the team constantly training the other members of the team in the hopes of making all developers into good testers.

Provide good test management. Creating good test plans, test assignments, deadlines, and management structures for each testing effort gives any developers involved in the testing a fighting chance of becoming better in the role.

Furnish adequate motivation. Telling developers that finding bugs makes the application better for users (which is a valid statement) should ideally provide sufficient incentive to motivate them to test aggressively. However, sometimes more inducement is required. The testing process can be managed as a competition, complete with target bug counts and a system of rewards for hitting the targets and fixing the bugs. Alternately, performance and salary reviews can take into consideration the quality of code written by a developer.

A great tester is able to meticulously, almost instinctively, examine each feature of an application and find its flaws. He or she can also contrive situations that are quirky but logical and reflect the strangest interaction a user can have with an application (see the sidebar).

 Note

The best tester is not simply a thorough tester but a crazed one. In my experience, great testers are slightly deviant when compared to normal people—they have a sadistic bent and enjoy breaking other people's code and confidence. With a different upbringing or personality, the best tester on your team would probably have turned out as one of those people who write software viruses or hack into secret military systems for fun!

Testing Time

One of my employees, Sid, fits the definition of a great (and slightly maniacal) tester. When he was helping test our retail ActiveX clock control product, I caught him placing 50 clocks on a single Access form, each set to a different time zone, size, or color combination.

> I disingenuously asked him, "Do you really think a user would ever do that?" His reply was the kind that separates great testers from good testers: "It doesn't matter if the users will ever do it, our product should be good enough to handle this situation anyway."

Setting Up a Test Machine

We've explored what qualifies a person to be a tester, but what qualifies a machine to be a test machine? I see three configuration-related mistakes commonly made when testing Access applications:

▶ *The test machines are much faster than the users' machines.* When this happens, issues related to reduced workstation performance are not discovered in testing.

▶ *The hardware configuration of the test machines does not match the average configuration of the users' machines.* In this scenario, the testing process does not accurately reflect the real world. One common example of this is where developers program and test on a Windows NT network or high-resolution monitors and then deploy to users in a Novell-based environment or a standard VGA workstation configuration.

◆ *The software configuration of the test machines does not match the average configuration of the users' machines.* A common example of this was seen after Microsoft released the Jet 2.5 upgrade in November 1994. After that time, most developers were working with this version of Jet on their machines but were often shipping applications to a user base still working with Jet 2.0, and compatibility problems arose.

The first maxim in configuring a test machine should be to reproduce the average user workstation as closely as possible.

After you've tested on the average user machine, test on machines that reproduce the most extreme user equipment scenarios. First, test on a machine that is very underpowered and boasts a simple configuration. A 486/33 with 8M of RAM, running in 16 colors with only default Windows fonts is a good candidate to test on.

Issues that can be discovered on a machine like this include:

▶ The use of non-standard fonts in the application that are not available on the test machine may cause some strings to display wrong or be sized poorly.

▶ Application graphics that make use of a high-resolution color palette may not display well on the minimum palette.

▶ Processes that run slowly on slow machines may require the addition of wait messages or status gauges to note progress.

▶ Some processes may run so slowly as to be unusable.

Next, test on a state-of-the-art machine, one that runs at blinding speed, has a variety of popular software products installed on it, has hardware options like a CD-ROM and sound, and runs in the highest available screen resolution. This test machine helps you discover the following:

▶ Forms created for 640×480 resolution may not display correctly at higher resolutions. (For example, the font display calculations that take place at higher resolutions cause some strings in label controls to be truncated on some video cards.)

▶ Processes that convey ongoing status to users may run so fast that no status message is displayed. For example, a data loading routine that shows its progress on the status bar may run so fast that the messages cannot be seen by the user. If this routine has no confirmation alert at the end of the process, the user may have no way of knowing that the process ran at all.

▶ Hardware conflicts can arise as systems get more complicated. For example, an Access application that uses the autodialer to dial the modem may have trouble finding a modem installed on a machine with two modems.

Finally, it is wise to always test an application on what I call a "clean machine." Such a computer reflects a new PC with a minimum of software on it. We create a clean machine by reformatting the disk drive and installing Windows 95 on the drive and nothing more.

Note that I don't install Office or Access on the clean machine. An Access application you ship with an ODE runtime setup should, in theory, be self-sufficient, and your users should be able to run the setup and the application on a machine containing nothing more than Windows. Of course, if your application is meant for users of the full Access product, you'll have to install Access (but not Office) on your clean machine in order to make it a valid test configuration.

 Tip

When you must develop applications on a machine that will also be subject to non-standard software, beta test copies of products, and so forth, it is wise to create two development environments on your machine. This is done by making the machine dual boot—run two copies of Windows. Keep one copy of Windows unpolluted, as

> close as possible to the configuration of a clean machine—and do your development and testing in this environment.
>
> It is also possible to create a dual boot machine that has both Windows NT and Windows 95 on it. You could use NT as your development environment and keep the Windows 95 environment unpolluted as a test environment.

Managing the Testing Process

Whether the testing process involves one tester or multiple testers, the objective is the same: do not allow any feature to be overlooked. Sometimes I see clients give an application to their staff and say something like this: "Genie, you test inventory; Mary, you test the general ledger; and Mike, you test accounts payable." In the end, we discover that the individual features were tested but not their interaction because that aspect of testing was overlooked by all parties. For example, an inventory receipt transaction generates a payable item; Genie thought that Mike would test this under payables testing, and Mike thought that Genie would test it via the inventory receipts.

 Note

The paradox of delegating the testing responsibility even afflicts Microsoft. When they were creating Windows NT version 4.0, I witnessed confusion there over whether the application groups should test their products on the new operating system, or whether the operating system group itself was responsible for compatibility testing.

9

From these examples, you can see that it is important to make sure every feature is included on the test plan and that every feature is delegated to at least one person for testing.

You may need to modularize the test process for the benefit of multiple testers so that two testers do not overlap on the same feature and miss another one altogether. Most applications should be tested both empty (as it will be delivered to users) and full (with 24 months worth of sample data loaded in). You can assign these tasks to two different people and have a parallel testing process.

As an alternate example, you might break your testing task delegation into modules based on the experience of the tester. For example, the old adage that developers make poor testers can be carried further to say that a tester that knows a lot about the feature may also make a poor tester. Thus, if your tester is highly literate in accounting, do not delegate that person to test the invoicing system. Use an accounting neophyte to do the testing of this element instead. This tester brings no preconceptions about how things should work and more closely recreates the scenario of the least-skilled user that may use the application.

 Note

I don't mean to infer in the previous paragraph that only persons ignorant in an application's purpose should be testing it. The point I'm making is that the people with the least number of preconceptions are often the best testers. Thus, an accounting neophyte will utilize the application in ways different from someone well versed in accounting and accounting software. The neophyte's testing efforts will often uncover usability, data protection, and process flow shortcomings that the accounting expert may breeze right past.

On the other hand, an accounting neophyte may not fully understand the workflow being automated by the system, and thus an accounting expert may provide better testing of the finer features of an application.

Ideally, the most favorable testing environment is one that solicits input from users at both of these ends of the skills spectrum.

Understanding the Types of Testing

Many developers and managers think that all testing happens at the end of application development. If the developers are also serving as testers, this model provides a good allocation of resources because coders are not distracted from the development effort while it is ongoing. They can shift gears mentally from coding to testing at the end of the project.

In a more optimal environment, where testers and developers are not the same people, it is better to have the testing process running parallel to the development process (to the extent that it can be).

There are several kinds of testing commonly defined in the software industry:

> *Unit testing.* Unit testing is done at the level of a unit of work—an object, a process, or a feature. The developer performs unit testing when he or she is *code complete* on the unit of work. In larger teams, it can be helpful to have a tester initiate unit testing immediately upon completion of a feature by the developer, while the developer moves on to the coding of another feature.

Unit testing is done to look for bugs and to verify that the feature or process matches the original design. It can be easier to correct problems discovered in the application if they are identified and corrected at the unit level instead of after the application components have been pulled together into a more complex mix.

Integration testing. This testing stage watches the progress of the application development cycle and jumps in whenever all of the units within a functional area are completed. The entire functional area is tested to make sure its units fit and work together.

The way that features are combined for this type of testing is at the discretion of the manager. For example, there are several discernible functional units within the accounts payable module of an accounting system. A functional unit, for testing purposes, could be defined as the processing of checks. Another option is that the manager could wait to begin integration testing until all payables processes are complete, or testing could even be held until the payables and general ledger modules are both complete because they interact.

 Tip

Because of the incomplete state of the application at the time of unit testing, it may be difficult to involve users in that process. However, by the time integration testing is in motion, parts of the application are stable enough that it may be possible to involve users in the testing process.

An added benefit of involving users at this stage is that they can compare the features to the specification (and to their expectations for the solution) well before the application components are combined for final testing.

System testing. System testing does not begin until every facet of the application is completed, often including supporting components like setup, online help, and documentation. In this phase, the application is tested as if actually in use. See the discussion in the section that follows, "Involving Users in the Testing," to see how closely this process can mimic actual use.

In system testing, all features of an application must be touched and tested. The two earlier testing stages should have validated that the features in the system match the users' expectations and work in conjunction with related features. At this stage, the testing process has other objectives:

▶ To determine if the performance of the application is adequate.

▶ To enter test data into the system and emulate real-world usage as much as possible.

▶ To test the application under heavy user, process, or data loads.

▶ To test application installation and deployment features.

▶ To determine if the usability of the application is acceptable.

▶ To discern if the application solves the business problem originally targeted when the design process began.

Obviously, in a smaller team, there may be few or no testers designated to help with these efforts. In such a case, developers provide the testing resources, and their success is directly correlated with their ability to function as qualified testers and with their understanding of the testing process as described here.

Involving Users in the Testing

The deployment mentality applied by developers in years past saw them saying to users: "You'll have the application when it's good and ready." Development teams feared they would lose their shroud of mystery if they exposed any elements of the development or testing processes (or an application's flaws) to the users.

The newer model I'm advocating says this to users instead: "Help us to make the application good and to determine when it's ready." Users that are realistic about the budgets and timelines they help to throw at developers must also be realistic in their approach to testing—they must not form a negative opinion of the development team simply because it asks for help with testing or because a few bugs are found in the process.

Thus, the trend I've already established in this book of involving users in design and ongoing reviews carries logically to testing as well.

The benefits of involving users in the testing process outweigh the frustrations, which arise mainly from the communication gaps that occur when developers/testers attempt to talk about technical issues with users (or when users attempt to do the same with developers/testers).

 Note

I've found that a user's "bug" is sometimes a developer's "by design" behavior. During testing, it can sometimes be difficult to determine what a serious flaw is and what is simply a shortcoming because different members of the project team may have different perceptions about an item's severity.

Before pulling users into a testing process, establish a mediation or management strategy that will help "triage" issues discovered and rate their priority, so as to minimize hostile debates between users and developers.

The primary benefits of user involvement in testing are:

▶ Additional manpower is added to the testing process but is not reflected on the budget as a development cost.

▶ Users are becoming trained on the application while they are testing it.

▶ The application is tested on a wider variety of hardware and software configurations than are available in the test lab.

▶ Users are better able to concoct "real world" scenarios to test under than are developers/testers.

Here are the primary pitfalls to avoid when adding users to the testing team:

▶ Involving users in the testing process too early can poison their attitude. For this reason, most testing processes tend to define two different milestones. The first is an *alpha testing* release, which occurs when all known features are complete and integrated into the application. There may be many bugs lurking in this release; thus, it should be reviewed by developers or qualified testers and not necessarily distributed to prospective users. When the deficiencies found in the alpha release are fixed and the application is more robust, the *beta testing* release cycle begins where one or more staged versions are released to users for testing.

▶ Users are apt to suggest minor improvements and enhancements in the course of their testing. The development manager must be careful to defer these requests to future phases and not let developers spend time allocated for debugging on adding new features.

▶ Users can quickly fatigue from a rigorous testing process or may be pulled from testing by the demands of their other daily duties and thus may only prove valuable for a limited amount of time.

▶ It takes time to coordinate the user testing effort. As a result, it may not make sense for one developer to manage the testing efforts of only a few users. One professional tester can sometimes provide the same quality of testing effort as several users. On the other hand, if one member of the development team can manage the involvement of 10 or 20 user-testers, the testing effort has gained significant momentum and the effort's return-on-investment is high.

 Tip
I've found that it can be helpful to create a reward process for users when you are motivating them to test out a new system because users are often too busy or intimidated to volunteer for such an effort.

For example, I might see if the client will include in the project budget money for printing a few T-shirts sporting a big roach and stating that "I killed Inventory System bugs." These shirts would be awarded to the users who provided the most usability or problem feedback during testing.

Bear in mind, however, that for some development teams the word "bug" is an abomination and is disallowed because it has negative connotations with respect to the development team's reputation. In such an environment, a more politically correct reward idea may be required. For example, instead of the roach shirt idea, consider a shirt with a cartoonish programmer-type figure on it and the words "Honorary Inventory System development team member."

Tracking Testing Discoveries

Once testing begins, the testers need a way to track problems discovered during the testing. Obviously, in a pinch, a Windows Notepad document is better than handwritten notes, and a spreadsheet or outlined Word document is better than a Notepad file. The best solution, however, is for testers to have access to an issues database into which they can log problems, suggestions, and shortcomings found during the testing.

Visual What?

With Microsoft's emphasis on the term "visual" (witness Visual Basic, Visual C++, and Visual Java), it was only a matter of time before the term became a running joke. With the advent of the Internet, so many people at Microsoft were using Notepad to edit their HTML Web pages that they recently began to jokingly refer to Notepad within the company as "Visual Notepad, the HTML Editor."

The power of a central issues database lies in the fact that it can be shared by testers and developers. Developers can query the database at any point to see the newly entered issue records, and testers can view previously entered issue records and determine the latest status information entered into them by the developers.

 Note

Notice my politically correct term for the tracking system—I prefer the term "issue" to "bug" for two reasons. First, there is a negative connotation (and subjective nature) to the classification "bug." Secondly, a good issue management system should not only be used at the end of development to track bugs. It can also be used throughout development to prioritize to-do items, record enhancement requests, and log technical discussions.

If you don't need to be politically correct within your team or your system actually is only used for bugs, you can use fun terms like "Bug Base" or "Ant Farm" to describe your tracking system.

Table 9.2 shows samples of the data fields that we use in our internal issue tracking system:

Table 9.2   Table Fields Useful for Managing Issues that Are Discovered During Development and Testing

Field	Description
IssueID	Unique record ID
IssueType	Type of issue (see Table 9.3)
Priority	Urgency, between 1–3
ProjectName	Name of the application
ProjectArea	Object, task, or process name
ProjectSubArea	Subsidiary object, task, or process name
ProjectVersion	Version or build number that the issue came up in
Platform	Hardware or software environment necessary to recreate the issue
ShortDescription	Description of the issue
LongDescription	Long description of the issue and steps to reproduce it
Status	Current status of the issue (see Table 9.5)
StatusSetBy	Person that set the current status
StatusSetAt	Date/time the current status was set
StatusVersion	Version number matching the current status
StatusDueAt	Target date/time for changing to the next status

continues

Table 9.2   Continued

Field	Description
IssueDueAt	Date/time the issue must be closed
WorkLog	Detailed history of how the issue evolved, was resolved, and/or was retested
SupportingInformation	Names of files or documents that provide more information
ReportedBy	Person who originally reported the issue
ReportedAt	Date/time the issue was originally reported
CreatedBy	Person that created the record
CreatedAt	Date and time the record was created
ChangedBy	Person that changed the record last
ChangedAt	Date and time the record was last changed

 Note

A database with the issue management system tables found in Tables 9.2, 9.3, and 9.4 is on the CD-ROM as file AESISSUE.MDB.

Table 9.3 suggests codes that can be used to designate a type categorization (IssueType) for each issue record.

Table 9.3   Lookup Values for Assigning *IssueType* Values to Issue Records

Code	Description
Application Bug—Fatal	Data is lost or the application or system crashes. The user cannot use the application.
Application Bug—Major	A specific object or process is unusable or unstable but the application does not crash.

Code	Description
Application Bug—Minor	There is a logic flaw in a process or an error alert is generated. The application is usable but requires fixing in the next release.
Assistance Request	The user requires information or training about a feature or is unsure about how to use portions of the application.
Cosmetic Problem	There is a display or printing problem related to colors, fonts, sizing, layout, or spelling.
Documentation/Help Problem	There is a flaw in the user education materials for the application.
Enhancement Order (Approved)	An enhancement request for the system that has already been discussed with management and approved for inclusion in the next release.
Enhancement Request (Wish)	A suggestion for improving the application that should be considered in the next design review.
Incomplete Feature	A feature in the application does not match the specification, documentation, or design documents.
Platform/Infrastructure Problem	The user's machine does not run the application well or behaves differently after installing the application.
Setup/Installation Problem	There were problems installing the application on a machine or a user could not set up the application at all.

Each issue can go through many designated status field values. Table 9.4 suggests status codes that you can use to track the current status of each issue record.

Table 9.4   Lookup Values for Assigning Issue Status

Status	Description
New	New issue, needs to have a status assigned
ToDo	Assigned to developer for action, management for review, or tester for more information
Test	Fixed or added, needs to be tested or retested
Failed	Failed test or retest, reassigned to developer for rework
Deferred	Deferred to another version
Denied	No action will ever be taken
Closed	Closed and deployed or awaiting deployment

All issues in this example begin life with a status of *New* and proceed through multiple interim rankings until they are closed; a closed issue has a status of either *Denied* or *Closed*.

 Note

The previous issue tracking table and the forms and reports that work with it can be expanded slightly to serve as an issue management system for the development process as well. To use this system for management of development, add information to the issue records to tie the issue to the specification (SpecItem), to budget time for the issue, to measure coding progress, and so on.

This issue tracking system serves multiple purposes:

▶ It serves as a repository for tracking legitimate bugs that must be fixed before the application ships.

▶ It serves as a single place to capture all information specific to an individual issue (for example, an issue record can store the file name of the sample file generated while reproducing a problem).

▶ It provides an area to store issues that are not critical to shipping the application immediately but should be considered for future revisions of the application.

Keeping issue information in a database offers the pluses of sorting, reporting, querying, and so on but requires that the testers load Access and a sometimes large issue management application on their system in addition to the application being tested.

> **Tip**
>
> In order to leave as many system resources available as possible for testing, we decided to invest in the development of our own Visual Basic/Jet issue tracking system. The compiled VB executable interface can be kept open on the testers' and developers' desktops at all times because it has a smaller memory footprint than an Access-based system.
>
> With Access 97's support for ASP files, you now can actually build an issue management system that doesn't even require a Visual Basic entry system. Instead, testers can submit issues using Internet Explorer and a Jet-literate Web page.

Logging issues into the tracking system is more of an art than a science. In some sense, a tester describing a bug to a developer is much like a sighted person describing an object to an unsighted person—the tester must describe in enough detail for the developer to re-create the exact incident that is being logged. In addition, the tester may be wise to include keystroke-by-keystroke reproductions of the issue, sample data used to generate to issue, sample files generated from the issue, or any other supporting materials that allow the developer to quickly re-create the situation being reported. There is basically no such thing as too much information coming from the tester to the developer in this respect.

Closing the Testing Phase

An application seems to never really be done. Users, testers, and developers are all quite adept at suggesting new features or defining modifications to existing processes.

The development manager has three significant challenges when trying to move the application from the testing stage to the deployment stage:

> *Controlling regression. Regression* is the situation where a change (usually a "fix") to a program feature affects another aspect of the program. The most common scenario is when a developer corrects a bug but creates another one in the process.
>
> Controlling regression requires that a developer or development manager properly determine the scope of a fix or addition and test to the limit of that scope. In other words, it is not sufficient to test the modified piece of code; all related features that could conceivably be affected by the change must be tested as well.

Minimizing feature creep. Users and developers involved in the testing or fixing process must be restrained from adding new features to the system or changing the functionality of existing features.

Developers and users must be made to understand that the repercussions of a last-minute feature change include possible changes to related features, retesting related features for regression, and changes to documentation and training materials.

Prioritizing open issues. When time and resources are running out, the development manager must be able to wisely triage issues as they are reported. Bugs should be given a severity rating and developers should always fix the most severe bugs first each day. The development manager must often assign a drastic cutoff point for shipping that states something like this: "When no bugs of severity 1 or 2 have been reported for two days, all open priority 3 bugs will be deferred to future releases and the application will be shipped."

Past some point in the testing phase, feature change requests must similarly be deferred to future releases.

Regardless of their status, many applications ship to users simply because the project deadline has been reached or the allotted resources for the project have been consumed. At some point, if an application is reasonably stable and the primary bugs have been fixed, it may need to be released to the users simply to allow the involved parties to move on to other projects. While this situation is not ideal, it certainly does provide the impetus for bringing a project to closure.

Avoiding Common Problems

Here are some concepts to apply to the testing process that can help you catch more problems:

Randomizing. A test plan provides direction to the testers in terms of listing the features to be tested. However, a tester must usually test the features multiple times using different approaches. Testers should randomize the testing of features to ensure that each feature is comprehensively tested from different access methods and feature combinations.

Volume Testing. The application must be tested under a significant load that re-creates the burden that the users will place on it. The important concept in volume testing is that the data not be homogenous. Simply creating a record in the data table and appending the table to itself several times in order to produce ten thousand identical test records is not sufficient for the purposes of your testing. As much as possible, the sample data should approximate what will be created by the users in reality, with a variety of record content such as all fields filled, some fields filled, only required fields filled, maximum values filled, minimum values filled, and so on.

Regression. One of the most important areas in testing is the retesting of issues once they are purportedly fixed. The scope of a particular issue may be broader than was thought by either the tester or the developer. Retesting a particular feature, once it has been addressed, may not satisfactorily note if other issues were generated by fixing the first issue. When retesting a fixed feature, work around the feature into related areas of the application, covering sufficient breadth to test all possible repercussions of the coding.

For example, an import routine that loads data into a database incorrectly, once fixed, must not only be retested on the offending import file to see if the data now imports correctly. It must also be retested on all files in the test suite in case fixing the application so that one file loads prevented other files from loading.

> **Note**
>
> It is hard to overstate the importance of this concept. At a recent conference, a Microsoft speaker stated that the majority of serious bugs in one of the Microsoft Office products were introduced late in the development cycle by fixing lesser bugs and improperly retesting the fix.

Configuration Testing. While your development environment may include only Pentiums, you must also test for the lowest common denominator machine in your user base. Therefore, if there is any possibility that users will be using your application on an 8M 486/33 machine, you have to find a test machine with this configuration to perform the test.

Automated Testing. In some cases, you may add value to your testing process by the use of macro recorders or keyboard automation programs such as Microsoft Test to automate some elements of the process. Mostly, however, I have found that testing database applications is different from testing retail applications because issues of usability and comprehension that are paramount to the applications cannot be addressed by an automated testing suite. (Automated programs are best when used to test for repetitive issues like memory leaks and fatal feature pairs.)

Having tested scores of Access applications, I asked my staff to help me make a list of the most common deficiencies we encounter when testing applications or when helping clients test theirs. The following list provides a "cheat sheet" (also reproduced on the

CD-ROM in the document PRE-SHIP.DOC) that you can add to your test plans to help you catch common problems (the order of the list items is inconsequential):

Lack of User Assistance Items. Developers often forget to add user niceties like status bar text, control tips, and What's This Help to their forms.

Missing Error Traps. Some developers use their own discretion when deciding whether or not to add error trapping to a specific routine. If they guess wrong and the routine fails, the application flow can be negatively affected. In general, every VBA routine should have an error handler.

Font Management Problems. Developers often have fonts installed on their systems that are not installed in user workstations. The use of non-standard fonts in an application causes strings to display oddly when deployed.

When sizing labels and other controls on forms, you should leave a little extra space in the control for potential font size differences introduced by different resolutions. The displayed width of a string of characters is slightly different at 1024×768 than at 640×480, and characters are sometimes truncated between the resolutions.

 Note

The default Font Size setting in the Windows Control Panel is Small Fonts. You may want to test your applications using the Large Fonts setting as well in order to determine if any display problems will accrue to your forms under such a setting.

Color Problems. The user's workstation color scheme must be correctly inherited by the application or the application will not match the look of other installed applications. If the application has hard-coded colors that override the desktop default colors, you must verify that they look adequate under each shipped Windows color scheme.

 Tip

Review the Access Help topic "Set color properties to Microsoft Windows system colors" for information on how to pull attributes of the current desktop color scheme into the `BackColor`, `BorderColor`, or `ForeColor` properties of objects. To find this topic, look under "colors" in the Help Index.

Object Sizing Problems. Developers that work in 800×600 resolution or higher often forget to check the size of their forms, reports, and datasheets in standard resolution before shipping. As a result, oversized forms sometimes "bleed" off of a user's screen.

Problems with Table Links. Some developers include the data tables in the application database during development and then use the Database Splitter add-in to create the back-end database just before shipping. While this technique is sound, it must be done before testing begins; otherwise, problems that result from separating the application into two databases (table-type recordsets no longer work, for example) will not be discovered prior to shipping.

Also, your application must provide for management of table links by the user when installing a new version or when remapping links to a data back-end that has moved.

Data Currency Problems. Make sure that any process that displays data retrieves the latest data. As a common example, if a list of records is shown on a form or control, when a new record is added through the application to the form or control's record source, the list must be requeried to immediately reflect the change.

Testing with Loaded Tables Only. Very frequently, developers build and test an application with sample data and then delete all the data before shipping to the users. If the application was never tested with empty tables, errors are often generated as soon as the users install and load the system.

Improper Propagation of Changes. When changes are made late in a development or testing cycle to object names, table field data types, or other application attributes, developers often forget to change all references in the application to the changed objects.

Hard-coded References. Routines that load disk files, open database objects against remote databases, or dynamically link tables often contain a hard-coded path or file name. If the users' workstation directories or network mappings are not exactly the same as the developers', such references can fail.

Keyboard Tab Orders. Many developers are mouse-centric in their work and forget that PC users that pre-date the mouse still rely heavily on the keyboard. Always check the tab order of controls on forms for proper flow and ensure that form buttons and common features are available with accelerator keys (Alt plus another key).

Data Type Mismatches. The dreaded "Type Mismatch" alert is all too common to users of Access and Visual Basic applications. Developers often assume that users would never enter a value into a field that was inappropriate for that field and fail to ensure that form and code processes react gracefully to type mismatches in entered data. Common scenarios to test include entering a string in a numeric field or a nonsensical date in a date/time field.

Event Management Issues. When newer developers are working with Access, they often do not fully understand the event model in it. Problems in an application sometimes result from using events or features related to events improperly.

For example, the `ValidationRule` properties exist at both the field and record level in a table and in a form as control properties. Jet also provides other engine-level validation features such as the `Required` property. The way that these different features interact with each other and with a form's `BeforeUpdate`, `AfterUpdate`, `Close`, and other events can provide both developers and testers with interesting challenges.

Compiling/Syntax Checking. Just prior to shipping an application, make sure it is properly compiled. Beginning with Access 95, this provides the dual benefit of checking the syntax of all code (even behind forms) and creating a compiled version of the VBA code that is run when the application is used.

Required Files Not in the Setup. Access applications frequently call functionality outside of Access itself, such as e-mail or scheduling routines. Never assume that your user has current copies of DLL, OCX, or other files required by your application. Always create a setup program for your application that copies all necessary files to the user's target machine or checks for their presence.

All too often, brilliant application designs go astray in the implementation for the simplest of reasons, and the reason is often that the developers failed to provide enough testing to ensure that users were provided with a solid, quality application. Don't detract from the reputation of your team or its application by scrimping in this area.

Educating Your Users

Prior to deploying a tested application, the users must be taught how to work with it. However, small development teams often cannot spare a person to provide several days of hands-on training.

Two points made in this book assist in solving this situation. First, according to the principles listed in Chapter 17, "Bulletproofing Your Application Interface," your objective for an application should be that it educates and guides the users as they use it. This approach, coupled with an online help file and printed documentation, often serves as a surrogate for formal user training. (Additionally, users that have participated in testing are often partially trained by the time the application ships. These users can train other users.)

The second point regarding education derives from the structure of the design team as described in Chapter 3, "Preparing for Development." User representatives on the design team are intimately involved in the project research and design; they have participated in the ongoing reviews during development, and they helped with the testing. Thus, by ship time, these "super users" may have a significantly detailed knowledge of the application and can provide the training in place of developers.

Few development project plans these days budget for the creation of a training manual. Thus, the user documentation must additionally serve as a training document. When you create your user documentation, bear in mind how it might be used and strive to make it comprehensive.

Also, applications are frequently tested using sample data from a real or fictional scenario (called a *test case*). Supplying this sample data to the users for group or self-education can serve to shorten their learning curve.

 Tip

If the application ships loaded with real data, the users should be trained on a copy of that data as the test case. This allows the training environment to closely mimic the actual work environment.

If the application is shipped without data, the test case does not provide a comprehensive educational example because it does not show users how to configure the system and seed it with initial values. Consider if the users will have any trouble migrating from the test case to an empty database, and include extra information in the training to help them through this situation.

Shipping a Completed Application

When the testing is completed and the users have been trained, it is time to create and test a setup to use to deploy the application. Many developers mistakenly assume that the Setup Wizard in the ODE provides the only option for creating an Access application setup. In this section, I'll describe your options for deploying a solution.

Here are the different techniques that you can use to deliver Access applications to your users:

Pull files from a server. Because some Access applications consist of nothing more than a single interface database file, users can be given instructions to copy the file from a central server onto their local drive. (Alternately, they can run a DOS batch file that was created for the purpose.)

Because this technique involves no setup script language, it is only useful when there are no ActiveX controls to copy or register and no special DLL files or Windows registry entries required by the application. Also, all tables in the interface database should be pre-linked to the back-end database.

Push files from a server. Using Microsoft Systems Management Server or another automated distribution system, it is possible to copy files from a server to each target workstation automatically. As with the previous option, this is only useful when the installation is uncomplicated.

The target workstations must be shared on the network (so that the application file can be pushed from a central location) or taught to run a setup script at login (so that the application file can be pulled from the central location).

Use the Acme setup engine. The Acme setup engine is at the heart of the ODE Setup Wizard. The Setup Wizard creates a setup table (STF) file that provides the instructions that drive the setup process. Acme setup uses a set of dialog boxes that are built in to the setup engine.

Acme provides you with some flexibility with respect to how files are copied and registered because you can modify the setup table file and the list of files to install in order to handle special setup needs. On the downside, there is no scripting language and the structure of the setup table file is not documented.

Use the Windows Setup Toolkit. We've used Microsoft's Setup Toolkit to create our setups for about six years, even prior to Access and even in place of the Setup Wizard. This setup utility is part of the Windows SDK and is built around a combination of C and Microsoft Test technology. It provides good flexibility in crafting custom setups because you can write setup scripts in a simple scripting language and create custom dialog boxes using the C Resource Editor.

Because the setup scripts are in ASCII files, they can be easily written and tested, as well as modified over the phone when performing technical support for the setup. As an additional bonus, the supporting files for this tool are very small and provide the smallest floppy disk footprint of any of the available setup engines.

On the minus side, this technology is now antiquated and unfriendly—the setup scripts and configuration files must all be built manually, the toolkit is poorly documented, and it is cryptic to debug.

Use the Visual Basic Setup Toolkit. Like the ODE, Visual Basic ships with a Setup Toolkit and a Setup Wizard. While the Setup Wizard is specific to VB projects and not useful for building an Access setup, the Toolkit can be used for any purpose including Access applications. It is simply a template with VB forms and code that you can modify and compile to create a custom setup executable.

The strength of this Toolkit is that it provides you with the flexibility to create forms and code to do virtually anything from the setup program. If you do not need this much power, however, your setup bears the burden of the large VB run-time DLL on the first setup disk, and you have to write program code to provide many of the capabilities built in to serious setup tools like InstallShield.

Use InstallShield. Now shipping with Microsoft's C++ product, the InstallShield SDK enables you to build powerful setup routines. If your application has special configuration needs, this tool is a good option to use.

InstallShield setups have a scripting language with scores of statements and functions and several built-in, configurable dialog boxes. The script is compiled before you ship for security and execution speed.

Use a third party setup tool. There are several other commercial setup utilities with much the same capabilities and mechanics as InstallShield. Each has strengths and shortcomings.

Why are there so many options for building setups? In my opinion, it is because no single tool has really found the correct balance of features yet. Each of the options I've listed has strong and weak points, but none provide *all* of the features that I want in a single setup engine:

- A very small floppy disk footprint for the setup files.
- Scripts that are simple to debug on the user's machine when setup fails.
- Built-in forms with large spaces for custom text and built-in hooks to a custom setup help file.
- A wizard that steps me through the creation of a setup and knows the different needs of VB, Access, and C applications.
- Help with the creation of registry entries for tools like ActiveX controls and custom builders.
- Assistance with the creation, management, and installation of customized application initialization (INI) files.

9

Table 9.5 provides a short summary of when you might choose to use each setup technique I've listed previously.

Table 9.5 Comparing the Different Setup Approaches

This Option...	Is Best for...
Pull files from the server	Instantly creating the simplest form of setup
Push files from the server	Providing central control of distribution/updates
Acme (ODE) setup	Building setups quickly with a wizard and doing minor customization
Windows Setup Toolkit	Building very small setups with modifiable scripts and file lists
Visual Basic Setup Toolkit	Creating custom forms and code for the setup
InstallShield	Using a robust setup language with built-in dialog boxes

Regardless of the tool you use, creating a quality setup for your application adds technical and visual value to the application and increases its reception by users. A professional setup program shows the users that you are serious about a quality distribution mechanism for the solution. Here are the important points to consider when deploying your application with a custom setup:

Explain what the application does. If your setup utility allows it, ensure that the user is installing the desired application by providing a brief description of the application in addition to its name on the setup welcome dialog box.

For example, showing an application title string "Homer" in the setup dialog boxes may be less useful than showing "Homer (Home Relocation Database)."

Check for disk space. Always make certain that the user's drive has room for the application. (Setups built with the ODE Acme engine provide automatic disk space checking.)

Assist the user with selecting a destination. You should always seed the setup program with a suggested target directory. In some installations it is desirable to have the setup force the application into a hard-coded destination so that all user workstations have the same configuration.

Tip

The Change Folder button is automatically added to the main setup dialog box in an Acme setup created by the ODE Setup Wizard. You can remove this button and hard-code the destination for your application by changing one flag in the setup table (SETUP.STF) file. Find the line in the setup table file with a Type value of AppSearch, and change the second boolean flag in this line from yes to no as shown in these before and after examples:

```
C:\Homer<C:\Program Files\Homer>,HOMER.MDB,,128,no,yes,
C:\Homer<C:\Program Files\Homer>,HOMER.MDB,,128,no,no,
```

Refer to Figure 9.7 for an example of the AppSearch value in a setup table file.

Show the user progress. When the setup engine is busy for more than a few seconds, show the user the progress of the setup or a wait message so that he or she knows that something is happening and the machine is not frozen.

Provide an uninstall. The ideal setup tool assists the user with removing an application from a workstation as well as installing it.

Don't cut corners when building a friendly, solid setup for your application. For users not involved in the design or testing processes, the first impression of your application is generated by the setup.

Customizing Acme Setups

When working with Acme-based setups created by the ODE Setup Wizard, you can modify the configuration settings that are stored in the setup table (STF) file built by the Setup Wizard. Open the file using Excel, tell the Text Import Wizard that the file is tab delimited, and click Finish. Once the file is open, change the required values and save the file over itself *in the original tab delimited format.*

The format of the STF file is complex and cryptic, and explaining it fully is beyond the scope of this chapter. Even worse is the fact that documentation for the Acme setup engine is not made publicly available by Microsoft. You have to experiment with the file format by changing values and observing the repercussions.

Caution

Each line in the STF file below the header section is indexed with a unique Object ID (labeled `ObjID` in the file). This identifier is used to reference a specific line in the file from other lines. Because of the intricate relationships utilizing these references, do not add or delete lines in the file until you fully understand how to find and modify any other lines that reference the affected `ObjID` values.

Figure 9.4 shows the heading section of a sample STF file created to install a single Access database file.

Fig. 9.4

The ODE Setup Wizard produces an STF setup control file with this structure in the top section.

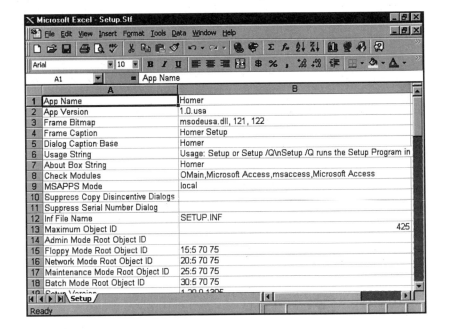

Note in the figure of the setup table file that the application name string you supply to the setup wizard ("Homer" in this example) is plugged into the file and used for dialog box captions and dialog box messages (as reflected by these values that were set to the string Homer: App Name, Frame Caption, Dialog Caption Base, and About Box String). These four values are examples of settings that you could change manually after running the wizard to further customize your setup.

For example, Figure 9.5 shows the welcome dialog box from an Acme setup sample. The Frame Caption string from SETUP.STF is displayed in the title bar of the setup parent window, and the Dialog Caption Base string is displayed in the dialog box message. The ODE

Setup Wizard sets these two options to the same string (the one you type in as the application name). As an example of customizing this setup, you could manually change the Dialog Caption Base value in the STF file, re-save the file, and cause the welcome dialog box to appear as shown in Figure 9.6 instead.

Fig. 9.5

A setup created by the Setup Wizard produces a default welcome dialog box.

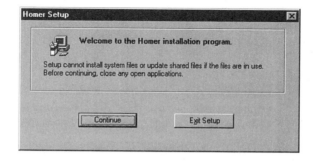

Fig. 9.6

Manual modifications to the setup table (STF) file can provide a customized welcome dialog instead of the default dialog box.

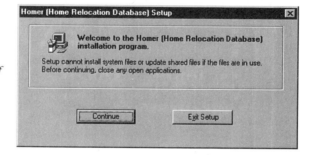

Figure 9.7 shows the detail section of a sample STF file created to install a single Access database file. Note that each element to be installed by the setup is described on a detail line in the STF file. You can reverse-engineer the structure of STF files and determine how to customize these detail lines.

Ensuring User Satisfaction

A user's satisfaction with your application is first affected by the smoothness of the setup process (or lack thereof). Here are some suggestions to make this process easier:

▶ Test the setup on several workstations before deploying it to the entire user base. A setup that works fine in testing may not work on the average user's configuration; testing the setup on several machines before shipping it out to all users helps minimize setup surprises.

▶ Organize the deployment process by building a target list naming all users that are expected to install the application. Manage installations against this list by notifying all users when the setup is ready, where it is located, and how to get help if they have trouble. Then, contact all users on the list at a later date to ensure that each was able to successfully install the application.

▸ Provide on-site support during the primary setup push. If possible, encourage all users to block out time on a particular day for running the setup, and have a developer available throughout that day to provide immediate support for installation or initial login problems.

Fig. 9.7

The ODE Setup Wizard produces an STF setup control file with this structure in the detail section.

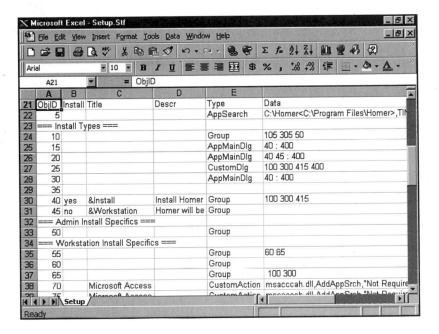

Unless they have been involved in design or testing, individual users are naive about the application during the first few weeks they are using it. It is important that the development manager provides resources to support users in this critical phase and not leave them abandoned.

During the development phase, the development manager can select a designated trainer or trainers for the application; these trainers should be recruited from the pool of "super users" from the design or testing teams. This approach provides good support for new users without encumbering developers. If there are no super users to provide peer-to-peer handholding and support, the development manager must provide one or more developers to fill this role.

Users may have comments during the installation of the application, as well as after they have installed the application and are using it. The deployment process or the application itself should provide a mechanism for users to submit feedback about the application, its installation, and its usage. See the following section for more information.

Reporting User Problems and Issues

For a developer, the job is only half done when the application ships. Ongoing maintenance and enhancement often consume more time and resources than creating the initial version of an application. The development manager is responsible for producing and implementing a plan to manage each successive release of the application. Information gathered from users of the application once in production is one of the most useful inputs to the creation of an upgrade plan.

All marketing hyperbole and developers' good intentions aside, one of the realities of software development is that every commercial product and custom application ships with at least one bug. Development tools are too powerful, development projects too complex, and development time frames too short to allow software developers the achievement of that Nirvana called *zero-defects*.

In Chapter 17, "Bulletproofing Your Application Interface," I stress that your applications should provide a device for collecting ongoing user feedback, both about bugs and about any other issue relating to the use of the application. Feedback mechanisms for users include:

▶ A table in the application database where users can log comments, for example a form available on the <u>H</u>elp menu.

▶ An e-mail account where users can send comment messages.

▶ A voice mailbox for recording user insights.

▶ User group meetings where users can interact and share insights about how they use an application.

9

 Tip

In Chapter 17, I note that some feedback devices are not exposed to users. For example, the automatic logging of system errors to a table can happen in the background.

Table 9.6 shows the structure of a sample table for logging user feedback directly into a database. You can provide a form where the user can create feedback records in the table and load the form from an option on the <u>H</u>elp menu, a custom toolbar button, or a keyboard shortcut.

Table 9.6 Table Fields Useful for Collecting User Feedback About an Application

Field	Description
FeedbackID	Unique record ID
IssueType	Type of issue (see Table 9.3)
ProjectName	Name of the application
ProjectArea	Object, task, or process name
ProjectSubArea	Subsidiary object, task, or process name
ProjectVersion	Version or build number that the issue was discovered in
Platform	Hardware or software environment necessary to re-create the issue
ShortDescription	Description of the issue
LongDescription	Long description of the issue and steps to reproduce it
ResolutionStatus	Resolution code, for example *Sent to Issues System*, *Solved*, *Discarded*
ResolutionStatusAt	Date/time of ResolutionStatus
CreatedBy	Person that created the record
CreatedAt	Date and time the record was created
ChangedBy	Person that changed the record last
ChangedAt	Date and time the record was last changed

 Note

The fields in the table mirror the fields in the issue tracking system designed in the earlier section "Tracking Testing Discoveries" in order to allow items from the feedback table to be copied into the issue system's table for development action. The IssueType field values in this table should be the same as those used in the larger issue management system; refer to Table 9.3 for codification examples.

A database with the feedback table shown in Table 9.6 is on the CD-ROM as file AESISSUE.MDB.

Users need to be able to provide their feedback, but they also should be made to feel that the feedback has been received and has value. If users provide a bug report or suggestion on a system, it can be valuable to send the user an e-mail notification that the input was received and thanking him or her for the feedback. (Replies to incoming e-mails or voice mails can often be generated automatically using modern technology, thus sparing a developer the burden of managing this process.)

Another key element in user satisfaction is to provide users that submit input with disposition information on the input. If a user submission is tracked through its life cycle, it is not difficult to notify users about the resolution of the issue that they generated. In the example provided earlier in this chapter, when an issue submitted by a user and stored in the issue tracking system receives a status code of Deferred, Denied, or Closed, the submitting user could be sent an automatic e-mail from the issue system describing the final status and the reason for it.

From Here...

In this chapter, we explored the techniques for solidifying an application before shipping through the use of rigorous testing. I also described issues relating to the management of project deadlines.

▶ For an understanding of where deployment issues fit into the overall framework of application development, see Chapter 2, "Introducing the Leszynski Development Framework (LDF)."

▶ Review Chapter 3, "Preparing for Development," for details on how to discern and document user needs before beginning development.

▶ Chapter 4, "Creating Design Specifications," provides a tutorial on the specification authoring process and the creation of project plans and budgets.

▶ Applications built according to the bulletproofing principles in Chapter 17, "Bulletproofing Your Application Interface," are generally easier to use and thus require less user training during deployment.

PART

II

Expert Solutions Techniques

chapter 10

Creating Expert Tables and Queries

In this chapter

◆ A review of Access 97's new database engine features

◆ A tutorial on database design using a real-world example

◆ Techniques for cataloging and finding data items with keywords

◆ Tips for optimizing your queries for faster performance

◆ An example of controlling the Data Access Objects to create database components programmatically

◆ An introduction to working with Web-based data tables

E ach important new fact that flows into an organization must find a place to live. Frequently, a database provides just such a residence. The tabular structure of a database allows facts to be collected (organized), protected (validated), and dissected (analyzed) in an orderly fashion.

With the Jet database engine, you can collect specific data and then develop an application layer over the data using the non-Jet components in Access. Before you build your forms, reports, and program code, however, you should always make sure you have created a solid data structure as their foundation. This chapter covers the key elements of providing a solid data structure.

He's Attached to His Data

"Many demos I gave of Access 1.0 to members of the press went something like my meeting with Stewart Alsop of InfoWorld. My goal was to show Stewart several of the exciting features in Access, but in order to do this, I wanted to show him the product using some of his existing data.

"He willingly pointed me to some of his data (stored in a non-Microsoft product's format), which I imported into Access and began to browse. While I was showing him how easy it was to make ad-hoc queries on the data, his eyes went "I never noticed that before, can we drill-down into this data?". For the next hour, we queried, sorted, filtered, and printed his records as he analyzed and trended his company information, not once noticing that we had spent the entire time focusing on his data and had barely even discussed any specific features in Access!"

Tod Nielsen, General Manager, Microsoft Access Business Unit

The Jet database engine, a standalone component that ships with Access, provides the advanced data management features that you would expect from a market-leading product like Access: "engine-level" rules (automatically enforced at the record and field-level), relationships between primary and foreign keys to maintain data integrity (called "referential integrity"), and cascading updates and deletes based on established relationships.

Of course, simply having these features in your applications does not make them into expert solutions. Creating an effective and optimized application involves properly applying the powerful features of Jet. You must know when and how to use the built-in features, as well as how to write code that goes beyond the limitations of the built-in features.

 Note

Lest you think that the Jet engine was built only for use with Access, Jet 3.5 actually ships with Access/Office, Merchant Server, Picture It, Publisher, Team Manager, Visual Basic, Visual C++, and Visual J++.

In fact, if you look in the files shipped with Microsoft's home management application, Bob, you'll find MSAJT110.DLL—yup, it's Jet!

In addition to knowing how best to use Jet, building an expert solution involves structuring the data to provide the optimal combination of usability and performance. There are some basic rules to use when creating relational database structures (brush up on the concept of "normalization" if you do not already know it or read "Design Step 1—Modeling the Data Structure" in this chapter). In addition to the basic rules, many data management scenarios are unique to a specific application and require the traditional brainstorming session at the whiteboard to discover the best approach.

In this chapter, I've tried to pull together examples relevant to the areas in Jet where I see developers struggling the most frequently. This chapter covers table and query concepts designed to help you resolve common database management and structure predicaments. The techniques here catapult you to a higher level of database productivity and your applications to a higher level of performance. Unfortunately, the art of good database design and structure cannot be covered in a single chapter, so I have used my discretion in selecting poignant examples of data management challenges.

 Note

In this chapter, I will often use the term "schema" to refer to the overall design of a database.

Reviewing the Best of the New Features

With the number of significant changes made to Access itself between versions 2 and 95 and 97, you would expect the list of recent feature additions in Jet to be quite lengthy. However, the biggest changes in Jet have taken place "under the hood" rather than to the features list or object model.

In the past, Access called the Jet database engine DLL directly, which made each version of Access "hard-wired" to a version of Jet and created the necessity to call the version of Jet directly from Access Basic. With the removal of Access Basic and its replacement with VBA came the opportunity to add proper support to Access for an object-centric model. Now, VBA communicates with the *type library* for the Data Access Objects in DAO350.DLL to determine what objects, properties, methods, and events are available for database work. It does so in the same fashion that VBA looks to any other referenced type library in your Access application (from Excel to ActiveX controls) to discern how to use them and to compile code against them. One of the services that DAO provides is access to the Jet engine.

10

 Note

A type library is a file that lists descriptions of the object model (objects, properties, and methods) of a program or service provider. Chapter 11, "Expert Approaches to VBA," provides an enhanced explanation of these files.

> For the purposes of this chapter, think of the DAO type library as the organizer of database services on Access's behalf. If Access needs to work with an MDB file, it asks DAO to work with Jet to link to the file and manipulate its data. On the other hand, if Access needs to work with an ODBC data source, it asks the DAO to initiate ODBCDirect functionality instead.

DAO has undergone a structural revamp to expose it as a 32-bit in-process Automation server. This server engine is implemented in the DAO350.DLL file, which provides data services to Access. DAO can provide services for Access to talk to ODBC data sources (such as SQL Server) and to the Jet engine routines stored in the primary Jet DLL MSJET35.DLL. Thus, Access's dependency on Jet has diminished in favor of a dependency on multiple data services provided by the Data Access Objects library.

Why should you care about this improvement? Because any product that fully utilizes VBA now can call the DAO; thus, any code and data structures you build or prototype in Access can be shared with or moved to other VBA-centric components of your applications. As an example, you can process data in Access and send it to Excel using tricky DDE or slow Automation, *or* you can now alternately create a database in Access, write and test your DAO code there, and then copy and paste it into Excel, running it directly from Excel VBA.

You should also care about the fact that DAO provides access to more than one type of back-end server through a common syntax. Thus, you can now create applications that create a recordset against Jet, move the data from Jet to another back end supported by the DAO, and do this without changing any of your code. This is a significant improvement in the way you can code.

There are several improvements in DAO/Jet that are noteworthy. Let's look first at the ones that you inherit in your applications but have no control over. Here are some of the internal changes that should make your data operations faster:

Larger Cache Size. Previous versions of Jet never grabbed more than 4M of RAM for cache. Jet now grabs half of all available memory for its cache when Access starts up, with no upper limit on the cache size, and dynamically sizes the cache as more memory becomes available. Jet also uses a new caching algorithm that keeps the most frequently used data in the cache longer.

Automatic Transactions. In the past, if you wanted to force Jet to cache a series of repetitive recordset operations, you had to create a transaction in your code. Now, Jet caches looping recordset operations automatically and only writes to the disk when the cache needs to be flushed.

Note

> This does *not* remove the need for transactions that provide the ability to undo an operation, but it does remove the need to add transactions whose only purpose is to provide speed.

Multiple Threads. Jet now uses three separate, parallel process threads: one for read-ahead operations, one for write-behind (buffered writes), and one for managing the record cache. This addition begins to truly capitalize on the newer 32-bit hardware platforms.

More FoxPro Logic. Access 2 saw the addition of FoxPro's Rushmore query processing logic to Jet. This process was completed with Jet 3.0 (Access 95) by the addition of FoxPro's best sorting algorithms.

Page Clustering. In previous versions of Jet, two contiguous pages often did not contain data from the same table. Jet now attempts to allocate table space in clusters of eight pages at one time, which places chunks of data from one table in close proximity. When Jet is doing a table-scan (forward read) to fetch data or pre-fill a cache, disk head movement is significantly reduced by this model.

Page Reallocation. Jet has optimized the algorithm that recycles pages when records are deleted. In a multi-user scenario with frequent deletions of data, a user other than the one performing the deletion usually suffers the performance penalty as the space freed by the deletion is recouped. This process is much faster now.

Faster retrieval of long values. Memo and OLE Object table data has always been stored in separate internal tables from the remainder of the parent record. Starting with Jet 3.0 (Access 95), this table structure was optimized and indexes are now better used to retrieve this additional data.

Index Improvements. Indexes now handle more concurrent users, reducing the frequency of index page locks. Indexes are also optimized during a compact operation, so you may want to compact your databases more frequently than in the past.

Transaction Management. Transactions may now partially commit in the background when they begin to consume too many file locks on a server.

Searching and Sorting. Query speed has been improved when using the <> operator. The sorting algorithm for ORDER BY statements has also been improved.

Table/Record Deletions. Deleting a table with DROP or removing some or all of the records in it with DELETE has been optimized.

10

Some of the enhancements in the prior list were introduced in Access 95 and enhanced in Access 97.

In addition to internal changes, Jet and DAO also include some improvements that are exposed to developers. Many of the exposed enhancements deal with ODBCDirect (as described in Chapter 19, "Exploring Client/Server Issues,") or with replication; this section will introduce the ones that don't.

Two new objects have been added to the DAO object model: the Connection object and the Errors collection. The Connection object is used to create a connection to an ODBC data source, bypassing Jet. This object facilitates ODBCDirect and is discussed in Chapter 19, "Exploring Client/Server Issues."

The Errors collection improves upon the single-dimension structure provided by the Err and Error$ functions by allowing for the accumulation of more than one data access error. The benefits of the collection structure become immediately apparent when performing operations against ODBC data sources, which can generate multiple error messages per error event. (See Chapter 19 for more information on the Errors collection.)

DAO 3.0 introduced a new EditMode property, which applies to RecordSet objects. This property shows the current status of the edit buffer of the recordset. The *edit buffer* holds either the current field values (after an Edit method has been invoked on the recordset) or the new field values being entered (after an AddNew method). Compare the value returned by this property to the following constants:

dbEditNone (0). There is no information in the edit buffer, and no add or edit is in progress.

dbEditInProgress (1). An Edit method has been issued, and unsaved edits to the current record are in the edit buffer.

dbEditAdd (2). An AddNew method has been issued, and unsaved entries to a new record are in the edit buffer.

The new CancelUpdate method works well in conjunction with EditMode. CancelUpdate discards the information in the edit buffer but does not move the record pointer. To cancel an edit in prior versions of Access, you had to move the record pointer off of the dirty record without issuing an Update method and then move back, which made for slightly sloppy code. Now you can cancel changes explicitly, as the example in Listing 10.1 shows.

Listing 10.1   AES_Tbl.Mdb—Using *CancelUpdate* to Discard an Edit

```
' Get a value from the user
varWork = InputBox("Enter new name or Esc to cancel:", "Edit", rst!CompName)
If Len(varWork) = 0 Then  ' User pressed Esc
  If rst.EditMode <> dbEditNone Then  ' Edit in progress
    rst.CancelUpdate
  End If
Else  ' Make the change
  ' Make certain the current record is being edited
  If rst.EditMode = dbEditNone Then  ' No edit in progress
    rst.Edit
  End If
  rst!CompName = varWork  ' Set the value
  rst.Update
End If
```

An additional new property for recordset objects is `AbsolutePosition`. This property provides the relative record number of the current record within the recordset. The setting is a zero-based long integer value that is read (to detect the current position) or written (to move the record pointer). The setting returns –1 to indicate that there is no current record (the recordset is empty).

 Note

The `AbsolutePosition` setting is analogous to the record number shown in the navigation buttons control on a form and should be taken just as lightly. In a relational database, a record's location in a recordset is informational only and should not be used to identify or refer to the record.

You should use the `Bookmark` property of a record if you need to store its location in the recordset and return to it later and use the primary key or other designated unique value of the record to identify it to users.

10

Another new property added to DAO 3.0 was the `RecordsAffected` attribute of a `QueryDef` or `Database` object. Immediately following an action query (delete, insert, or update), `RecordsAffected` describes the number of records that were impacted, as shown in Listing 10.2.

Listing 10.2   AES_Tbl.Mdb—Counting Records Affected by an Update

```
Set dbs = CurrentDb
strSQL = "UPDATE tblComp SET Employees = (Employees + 1)" _
  & " WHERE CompID BETWEEN 4 AND 6"
dbs.Execute strSQL
Debug.Print dbs.RecordsAffected
```

Tip

This property also works with data in ODBC data sources and can be extremely useful when used against server data. See Chapter 19, "Exploring Client/Server Issues," for examples.

DAO 3.0 also introduced the GetRows method of a RecordSet object, which creates a variant array from a selection of data. The only argument to the method is the number of records to fetch from the target object. The array is dynamically sized to two dimensions, with the first containing fields and the second containing rows. Here is a syntax example:

```
varComp = rst.GetRows(5)
```

GetRows starts fetching information at the current position of the recordset pointer and grabs as many records as are specified. After the fetch, the pointer is relocated to the record after the last one retrieved.

As with all array measurements, call the UBound function to determine the size of the array after a GetRows. Because GetRows rebuilds the array each time it is called, UBound will indicate how many records were actually fetched. See the example in Listing 10.3 for clarification.

Note

If you attempt to retrieve a record that cannot be fetched because it has been deleted from the recordset, GetRows does not generate an error. Instead, it retrieves records up to the problem record and stops there. Always compare the bounds of the target array with the number of records requested to make sure that they are the same. If they are not, there was a problem with a fetch or the end of the recordset was reached.

Because no error is generated when the expected number of rows is *not* fetched, you can request more records than are left in the recordset without generating an error. However, calling GetRows again once the recordset pointer is at EOF *will* generate an error.

Listing 10.3   AES_Tbl.Mdb—Using the *GetRows* Method to Fill an Array from Data

```
Sub GetRowsDemo()
' Purpose: Demonstrate the new GetRows method
```

```
Dim dbs     As Database
Dim iintCol As Integer
Dim iintRow As Integer
Dim rst     As Recordset
Dim varComp As Variant

Set dbs = CurrentDb
Set rst = dbs.OpenRecordset("tblComp", dbOpenDynaset)
rst.MoveLast    ' Pull the entire table into the buffer
rst.MoveFirst   ' Set the starting position

varComp = rst.GetRows(rst.RecordCount) ' Get all rows
' Increment the UBound by 1 to compensate for zero-based arrays
Debug.Print CStr(UBound(varComp, 1) + 1) & " fields returned"
Debug.Print CStr(UBound(varComp, 2) + 1) & " records returned"
' Dump the contents of the array
For iintRow = 0 To UBound(varComp, 2)
  For iintCol = 0 To UBound(varComp, 1)
    Debug.Print varComp(iintCol, iintRow);
  Next iintCol
  Debug.Print
Next iintRow

End Sub
```

Running the code in Listing 10.3 produces the output shown in Figure 10.1.

Fig. 10.1
This Debug window shows the results of dumping an array populated with the GetRows *method on a recordset.*

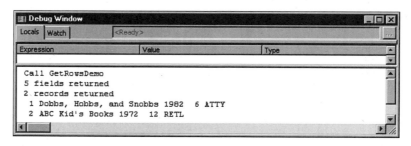

Caution

You can build very large arrays with this method, either by fetching many rows into the array or by including Memo or OLE Object fields in the source recordset. Be careful not to create arrays that use so much memory that they reduce the performance of your application.

Exploring Complicated Data Management Situations

While no two business problems are solved by exactly the same database structure, there are various *types* of data tables that are common to most databases. You will usually include tables with these purposes in each business application database:

Transaction (or base) Tables. These tables hold the raw data entered by users or generated by application processes.

Lookup Tables. Lookup tables provide the supporting values that validate data entry and allow short keys stored in transaction tables to represent longer display values.

Relation Tables. These tables provide the pointers that allow a relational data structure to support many-to-many links between records.

In addition to these designations, there are other types of tables that play supporting roles in an application. Some applications need tables to archive historical data or to log events, while other applications make use of various types of summary, temporary, or work tables. As you evolve standard approaches to designing and building databases, you will develop your own definitions and standards for the various application tables commonly used in your environment.

 Note

Review Chapter 7, "Understanding Application Architecture," for a detailed description of the various other categories I use to classify application tables.

One of the keys to creating a solid and effective database structure is to understand these various roles of tables (and queries) and how to optimize their use. There are many decision points when designing a database structure and usually more than one way to solve a specific problem.

I see several challenging situations arise frequently during database construction efforts. In the next few sections, I distill these common situations into examples that help you understand the structural challenges posed by data tables and prepare you to address similar challenges when they appear in your applications.

Designing a Database—An Example Using an Everyday Situation

The more database applications you create, the more likely you are to bump into one of the most common problems in database construction: the creation of a contact management system. Such a system provides us with several widespread real-world problems to address here, as exemplified when you try to classify the relationships between companies, people, and the extra information for both the companies and the people.

When I approach any database design project, I usually create several diagrams of the relationships between the data items. Database diagrams (often called "data models") help to convey data dependencies visually and provide an easy format for discussion and review.

Tip

When designing a database application, a whiteboard is the most important tool besides a computer. A complex database design session involves a team of designers doing a lot of drawing and erasing.

You cannot create database diagrams until you've determined the basic "entities" (real-world objects) and "attributes" (the properties of the entity objects) that will be stored in the database. For example, company information is one type of *entity* in a contact management system. This information has *attributes* that include name, number of employees, date established, and so on. (In Access terminology, you will distill entity information into one or more *tables* and the attributes into table *fields*.)

Design Step 1—Modeling the Data Structure

When modeling a new database, create a list of standard steps to follow that work best for your development team. You must explore the various structures for data items and their relationships and distill the structure that provides the best combination of practicality and performance.

Here is an example of simple steps that you might follow in a data modeling process:

1. *List the entities (groups of data) that must be accommodated by the application.* These groupings will become one or more tables in the final database, but at design time you should think only in terms of data items and the relationships between them.

   For our sample contact management system, Table 10.1 lists the primary entities.

Table 10.1   Primary Entities in a Contact Management System

Entity	Description
Companies	The top of the data pyramid in the system
Contacts	People, many of whom work at companies
Addresses	Both companies and people possess these
Telephones	Companies and people have phones

2. *Describe the relationships between the entities.* Often, there are mutual dependencies between data items, as in the case of companies that have multiple people (employees or related parties), and people that can work at multiple companies.

   One simple way to describe database relationships is to use the language of objects and their roles (a technique called "Object Role Modeling" has developed around this approach, as exemplified in products like Asymetrix's InfoModeler). Here is an example of sentences that describe objects (entities) and their roles:

▶ A company can have one or more addresses.

▶ An address can house one or more companies.

▶ A company can employ one or more people.

▶ A person can work at one or more companies.

▶ A person can have one or more work addresses.

▶ A work address houses one or more people.

▶ A person can have one or more home addresses.

▶ A home address houses one or more people.

▶ A work address has one or more phone numbers.

▶ A home address has one or more phone numbers.

▶ A person has one or more direct (non-address) phone numbers.

▶ A roving (cellular or car) telephone can be shared by more than one person.

Figure 10.2 displays a diagram that visually represents the described relationships (roles) between the entities. Notice that the diagram includes our modeling language.

Fig. 10.2

This diagram uses modeling language to convey the complex relationships between database entities.

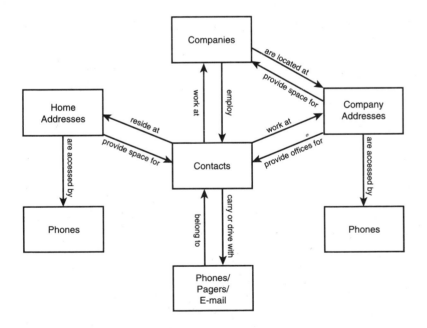

Tip

It is easier to involve users in the design process when you use database diagrams modeled with English-like syntax than with diagrams that are highly technical.

3. *Describe the attributes for the entities.* Once you have a rough idea of the data groupings and relationships, determine what details must be collected for each entity. For example, address information usually includes a location name, one or two address lines, and information about the city, state, and postal code.

During this process, note any areas where information will be duplicated or defines its own entity. As an example, here are some of the attributes you could track for people, as follows:

> First name
>
> Middle name
>
> Last name
>
> Date of birth
>
> Job title
>
> Telephone numbers

At this point in your modeling, you should begin to think in terms of tables and fields and begin to collect sample field values. Figure 10.3 shows the initial tabular layout that you might create using the information about people in the prior list. The table `tblCont` contains the contact information.

Closely analyzing the items that are known about each person yields a discovery that the telephone number actually repeats more than once for each person. The next step addresses this.

4. *Determine how entity information can be "normalized."* "Normalization" is a formal process applied to database structures that involves determining how to group and structure the data to best fit the relational model. (Jet is based on the relational database structure model and facilitates normalized tables.)

 Note

Because normalization is a formal process, much written material exists about it from both the philosophical and implementation standpoints. Thus, I chose to not turn this chapter into yet another full treatise on the rules of normalization.

Fig. 10.3

The known information about people has been turned into a tabular layout.

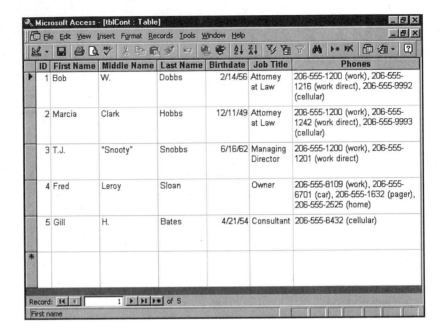

From a practical standpoint, the essence of the normalization process can be summed up in a few simple techniques—I'll summarize them here and note how they apply to the sample data at hand.

A. *Ensure that each attribute does not contain repeating data,* which makes data difficult to address using SQL statements.

In the case of information about people, recording multiple phone numbers in a single record for a person makes the data difficult to work with. A better approach would be to create several separate records for each person, with one phone number per record. Figure 10.4 shows the data from Figure 10.3 reworked according to this approach. The information about communication points (phones) for the contact people has been extracted to `tblCommPoint`.

B. *Ensure that each group of entity information is uniquely identifiable.* Access performs better, and your data is easier for users to work with if each piece of information can be located by addressing it with a unique identifier. (In Access terminology, the term "primary key" describes such an identifier.)

In the case of information about people, attributes like "Social Security Number" provide a unique identifier for each person, so such an attribute may make a good primary identifier if the data included no non-Americans. A unique identifier that may serve to locate one record in a table is called a *candidate key*. A table may have multiple candidate keys, and you will select one of them to serve as the primary key.

In our contact management database, we will not know a Social Security Number value for each person in the contact table, so we let Access assign unique, arbitrary `AutoNumber` identifiers instead. This identifier is also shown in Figure 10.4.

Fig. 10.4

Phone number information from the tabular layout in Figure 10.3 has been moved into a separate child table to allow for multiple values per person.

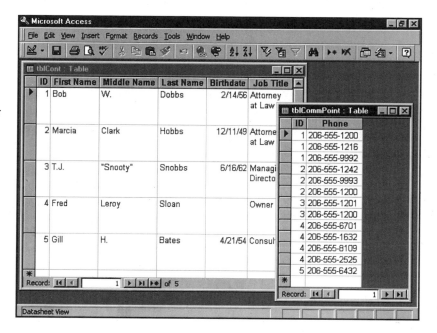

C. *Ensure that there is only one record for each unique identifier.* Simply giving each existing person a primary designator does not provide value if the unique identifier does not permanently identify one specific record in the table. The next step is to make sure that each unique identifier will always identify only a single record.

For example, we've let Access assign each person in Figure 10.4 an ID field value. The value currently uniquely identified one record in the table. But what would happen if a person in the contact table held two jobs? Two records would be required in the table for the person, with each attribute (field) identical in the two records except for the job title. This suddenly removes the ability to uniquely identify a single record with the primary identifier in the ID field. To prevent this situation, we must create a separate entity (job title record) for each title so that these attributes can be stored independently and then relate the titles back to people. This allows each person and ID number to appear only once in the person table.

10

D. *Ensure that all data in a record is related to the primary key.* Often, data "creeps" into a table that has relevance to the table record but is actually relevant by virtue of its association with a specific table field. Data of this sort is usually a candidate for a child table rather than inclusion in the data table.

For example, assume that you use a specified carrier to ship information to each of your contacts, and the carrier varies by state. Thus, for each contact address table record, it would be useful to track the carrier name in addition to the state value (for example, each address in Arizona would have "UPS" in the carrier field, while each address in Oregon would have "FedEx"). However, from a conceptual standpoint, the carrier attribute is a function of the state, *not* of the address record. Thus, the carrier value is not dependent on the primary key of the address record in the way that other elements of the address are. Consequently, it is appropriate to move the carrier information from the address table into a state/carrier table instead.

When each record is unique within a table, contains a unique identifier, and does not contain data that is unrelated to the unique identifier, your database structure is essentially "normalized."

α **Note**

The formal process of normalizing a database design includes several levels ("forms") of the state of normalization. The level attained in the previous discussion is called "third normal form," where unique keys identify records of non-repeating, non-compound, related data items.

Achievement of the third normal form is commonly used as the objective when designing a relational database system. There is a total of five levels of normalization that can be attained, but most database designers stop at third normal form for practical reasons. Consult a book on relational database theory if you are interested in learning about the fourth and fifth normal forms.

E. *Describe the structure of the attributes.* Once you have firmed-up the descriptions of entities and their attributes, define the characteristics of the attributes. In Access terms, this equates to determining the properties for each defined field.

As an example, names stored for people need to be given a data type (Text), a length in characters, rules for testing the data on entry and editing, and so on.

When defining a database structure, one of the most important attributes of a field is whether or not it participates in a relationship. Fields that constitute a unique record identifier (*primary key*) may need to link to similar fields in related tables (*foreign keys*). The fields that constitute primary key/foreign key pairs have common attributes, such as the same data type and, usually, the same name.

Tip

If you follow the commonly accepted database design wisdom that favors a centralized (also called "integrated") *data dictionary*, you use the same name for each field in a primary key/foreign key pair.

A data dictionary is simply the definition of a database's objects and their relationships, and an integrated data dictionary is one that treats fields that appear in different tables but have the same purpose as one field definition. The centralized definition of such a common field requires that the field's name and other properties are the same in each occurrence of the field.

When you apply the previous rules to the other entities in this data model, you discover that the final database structure closely resembles the role model you originally diagrammed in Figure 10.2. Figure 10.5 shows the base tables you end up with after normalizing the attributes for companies and people. (The base table names reflect the abbreviations "Comp" for *company*, "Cont" for *contact*, "Addr" for *address*, and "Phon" for *phone*.)

Fig. 10.5

This contact management system structure has been normalized to provide a relational data structure.

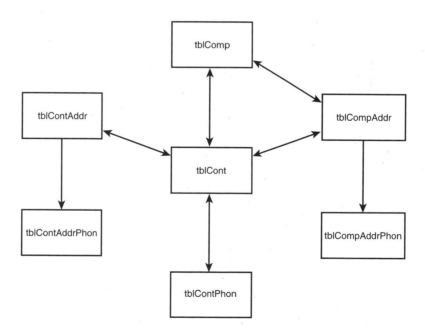

10

Notice in the figure that once you've normalized the structure, the database objects in the diagram are identified as tables rather than collections of attributes. When you have gotten to this point in the design process, it is wise to "concept test" the preliminary tables using sample records (this does not need to be done in Access, it can be done on paper or a whiteboard). Additionally, once a database design has been drafted at the table level, you can begin to consider the primary key identifiers for the records in each table, and the foreign key fields that will provide the links between the tables.

The example database design now includes the primary objects in the database. The next step is to identify and resolve the unique challenges presented by the finalized design.

Design Step 2—Answering the Tough Questions

When you have created a draft model of the database structure, you still don't have the answers to all of the database structure issues. You've survived the first round of the design battle, but the seeds have been sown for the more serious questions to be asked.

During your detailed application research efforts (as described in Chapter 3, "Preparing for Development"), you discovered the various types of data that must be stored by the contact management system. Now, further along in the design process, you must review the design notes and determine what non-standard data items and relationships were discussed during the research. You must make certain that the design facilitates these issues. As an example, during the design of this contact management system, a user stated that the system needed to store pager numbers in addition to other telephone numbers. You would review the design at this point to determine if the proposed database structure and table tblContPhon will accommodate this type of data or not. If not, you may need to revise the proposed structure.

The first question to ask yourself when reviewing a proposed data model is, "Does this model accommodate all relationships between entities?" Sometimes, an initial database design has an overabundance of join lines (relationships) between tables and can be simplified. At other times, data models get more complex as more "What if?" scenarios are run against it.

Take the example of the relationship between companies and people. Our current model assumes that people and companies are directly related. In this scenario, there is a direct relationship between one company and many people and also between one person and many companies (a person can hold two jobs, right?).

Inherent in this scenario, however, is this limitation: although a person works for a company, a person usually works at one primary company location each day. How does this model provide information about the relationship between people and specific company addresses? In other words, assume that Bob works at Jones Company, and Jones

Company has three locations. When you join Bob's contact record to Jones Company's record and then join Jones Company's record to its addresses, by inference, Bob works at all three addresses. A good data management model must be smarter than this and allow you to indicate which of the three addresses relates to Bob.

To confront this issue, you may have to alter the data structure, the relationships between entities, or both. In this specific case, you have these options for organizing the data:

▶ People can relate directly to companies and inherit all of the addresses of the companies.

▶ People can relate directly to company addresses only. By inference, a person works at the company that owns the address.

▶ You can maintain both relationships: Between the person and the company, and between the person and the work address, as designated in Figure 10.6.

Fig. 10.6

This diagram shows how records of people in the database have a relationship to companies and a relationship to one or more addresses for the company.

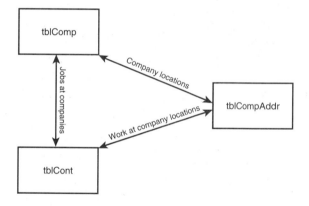

Notice that the third option creates a type of circularity in the data. While the relationships shown in Figure 10.6 *do* reflect the real world, they make querying the data and keeping entry and edits synchronized more of a challenge for the developer.

A second type of unaccommodated data relationship comes to light in further analysis. Thus far, we've provided for telephones that are attached to addresses, with the addresses attached to companies. In this layout, how does a user enter a toll-free or central switchboard number for a company, which are essentially address-independent telephones?

One approach is to provide direct numbers for companies in the same way that we've provided for direct numbers attached to people. This situation allows telephones to belong to companies without the need of an address relationship.

An alternate approach would be to restrict the data entry through a policy stating that all company telephone numbers entered into the system *must* be assigned to an address, even if this designation is somewhat arbitrary. Therefore, a toll-free phone number would be assigned to the corporate headquarters address, the marketing/sales office address, or another reasonable candidate.

A third question to ask at this point in the data model review is, "Does the data structure accommodate and allow orphaned records?" Certainly a telephone number or address record without a parent person or company is devoid of context, and thus these records should not be allowed to exist without a parent. People, however, present a different challenge: How do you track people in the database that do not have a relationship to a company (retired persons, homemakers, the self-employed, and so on)?

Answering this question means that one of two situations must be allowed, as follows:

1. People must be allowed into the database even if they have no matching company or company address entities. To enable this, there cannot be a referential integrity requirement in the database that insists each person belongs to at least one company.

2. People that have no parent company must relate to a phantom company record entered into the database simply to preserve the data integrity. To enable this scenario, one ("dummy") company record must be entered that provides the required parent record for all contact people that have no actual relationship to a company entity.

Either of these options is viable, and which one you choose is determined by personal preference or by the needs of the database platform and the application.

Going through this type of analysis provides new insight into the data structure and allows you to refine your model to match the world it must function in. Without this type of analysis, a database design that looks good often does not provide an adequate storehouse for its data. I often see database designs that seem adequate to the designers but are challenged by the users the very first day—"Hey, Mr. Developer, how do I enter *this* kind of information into the system?"

Design Step 3—Implementing Relation Tables

Our preliminary data design now provides for a variety of relationships between entities. Some of these relationships are two-way, called "many-to-many relationships," as in the case of companies and people. Expressing many-to-many relationships in a conceptual diagram can be done with table join lines that point in both directions, as in Figure 10.6 and others in this chapter.

However, when translating the conceptual diagram to an actual database structure, it becomes apparent that Access does not provide a way to store pointers between two tables in a many-to-many relationship in either one of the tables themselves. In other words, the relationships between the three tables in Figure 10.6 cannot be expressed in Access using only the three tables. Instead, a third table (commonly called a "relation table") must be located between two tables with a many-to-many relationship to provide the linkage.

Figure 10.7 shows how most of the table relationships in this current sample database structure require the presence of a relation table to maintain the many-to-many links.

Fig. 10.7

Many-to-many relationships in a database are facilitated by inserting relation tables between the base tables.

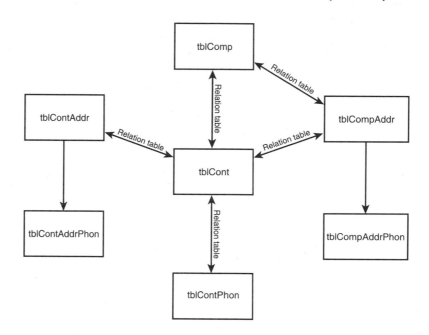

In general, an intermediary relation table consists of nothing more than records with foreign key values pointing back to the primary keys of the two tables it relates to. In other words, the relation table trelCompCont that you build to link tblComp to tblCont would contain a company ID and a contact ID in each record, as shown in Table 10.2. (The Comment item in the table is for explanatory purposes and is not in the data structure.)

Table 10.2   Entries in a Relation Table Allow for Many-to-Many Data Relationships

CompID	ContID	Comment
100	1	Bob (1) works at Jones Company (100)
100	2	Fred (2) also works at Jones Company (100)
101	1	Bob (1) also works at Smith Company (101)

10

Note

A relation table usually does not allow more than one instance of a defined relation-ship between two records; thus, the two foreign key values in the relation-table record can often constitute a primary key for the table.

Relation tables add a layer of complexity to a system, albeit a necessary one. At every point in your data diagram where a two-way arrow is used to indicate a many-to-many relationship, a relation table is required.

For a developer, the presence of relation tables introduces extra objects into table joins and thus provides additional performance challenges during development. For users, ad-hoc queries can be confusing due to the presence of the intermediary table and may add an additional training burden when deploying the system (see "Creating Complex Queries" later in this chapter).

Design Step 4—Expanding and Contracting the Roles of Tables

Hopefully, you're keeping up with me so far. We're three topics into the database design tutorial, with two topics to go. Now might be a good time to stretch and grab a hot drink to sip while you read further.

By definition, a relation table need not contain attributes other than the two keys of the linked records. However, once a relation table is in place, it can provide you with a handy storage device that solves certain data problems.

For example, in the discussion of the relationship between companies and their people, we have not defined how to store the job title for each person at each company. A rela-tion table between companies and people provides the natural home for such a data item because the job title is specifically a function of the intersection between a person and a company. Thus, you could expand the relation table trelCompCont shown in Table 10.2 in the previous section to include the job title, as shown in Table 10.3. (As before, the Com-ment column is for clarification and is not in the data table.)

Table 10.3   A Relation Table Can Also Store Attributes for a Specified Relationship

CompID	ContID	Title	Comment
100	1	Clerk	Bob's title at Jones Company
100	2	VP Finance	Fred's title at Jones Company
101	1	Bookkeeper	Bob's title at Smith Company

Carrying this example further, we find that people relate to company addresses in the same manner, in that they have a specific relationship to each address. (Physicians provide a good example of this situation because they often work at two or more clinics, with one being the primary location.) Thus, you locate an address type descriptor in each record of the relation table between people and addresses. Continuing the example of physicians, "Primary Office" and "Fridays Only" would be common address type descriptors found in the relation table.

Just as reviewing a database structure can lead to the addition of tables (such as relation tables), a complete analysis of a database design often finds opportunity for contraction as well. Sometimes, two tables that are similar in form and function can be combined into a single table.

For example, you've noticed by now that the use of separate address tables for people and companies introduces some redundancy into the database structure. The same is true of the three tables for telephone numbers. Each of these provides an opportunity to consolidate data items. However, before you blindly consolidate, consider the unique circumstances in each case.

For addresses, a given address is uniquely identified by a primary key, and its relationship to its parent is managed within a relation table. Thus, you could combine the addresses for people and companies into a single table, while keeping the two separate relation tables that identify the links between addresses and their owners. Because the address table does not store the foreign key of its owner, the table can serve multiple masters without compromising its data. In other words, the first record can be an address for Bob, while the second record can as easily be the address for Jones Company. Because the "parentage" of the address record is outside of it in a relation table, the address table itself doesn't care whose addresses it stores.

A more complicated example is provided by direct telephones. The data diagram for this information (refer to Figure 10.7) shows a many-to-many join between people and phones, as well as one-to-many joins between addresses and phones. (The relationship between addresses and phones is one-to-many rather than many-to-many because a telephone number cannot be related to more than one address record.) At first blush, you may be tempted to merge the three telephone structures into a single table. However, a single telephone number in the merged table would then belong to only one of the following types of parent record: company, contact, or address.

Figure 10.8 shows one option for restructuring the tables to support this kinship. In the diagram, a separate field is placed in the telephone table tblCommPoint for each type of parent. While this structure is effective, it is not easy to use (the table reflects only one kind of data, but it has a different foreign key field for each of its different parents).

10

Fig. 10.8

The second, third, and fourth fields in this table are each a foreign key and reflect the fact that each table record has one of three possible parents.

Comm. Point ID	Company Address ID	Contact Address ID	Contact ID	Phone/E-mail
1	1			206-555-1200
2			1	206-555-1216
3			2	206-555-1242
4			3	206-555-1201
5			1	206-555-9992
6			2	206-555-9993
7			4	206-555-6701
8	2			206-555-8109
9		3		206-555-2525
10			4	206-555-1632
11			5	206-555-6432

tblCommPoint : Table

Record: 1 of 11

A different approach to this problem involves creating an all-purpose foreign key field that serves as a pointer to any parent. Because this field can only have one data type, the primary key values of the three different parents must all be the same data type. For example, a telephone table with a single foreign key field might include two records, one which has the company address table as its parent and the other that is related to the contact address table. Table 10.4 shows these two records. (The Comment column is for clarification and is not in the data table.)

Table 10.4   The Structure of a Table that Has Two Parents

ParentID	PhoneID	Number	Comment
100	1251	555-1212	Number for a company. `ParentID` points to the company table.
768	1252	555-1313	Number for a contact person. `ParentID` points to contact table.

In both of these situations described for telephones, a condition called "multiple parentage" has been created because a specific record could be participating in any of several different relationships. While structures such as the two previously described are sometimes necessary and certainly provide economies of scale when storing and querying data, they are confusing to work with.

 Note

In this particular example, you solve the problem of multiple parentage by removing the foreign keys from the combined telephone table altogether and by using relation tables instead. Using a relation table helps to keep the actual data table "clean," without any fields to provide the "hack" that allows telephone records with different parents to exist in the same table. In the current example, this means that each telephone record has a unique ID only and no field that points to its parent. Instead, between the company address table and the telephone table there is a relation table. Also, between the contact address table and the telephone table lies a different relation table. Table 10.5 lists the required objects in this model.

Table 10.5   This Mix of Tables Supports Multiple Parentage for a Telephone Table

Table	Purpose
Company Address	Company addresses
Company Address Phone	Company addresses related to telephones
Telephone	Both company and contact telephones
Contact Address	Contact addresses
Contact Address Phone	Contact addresses related to telephones

 Note

A database structure built around relation tables allows you to change the model as the database grows without restructuring the actual base table. All future changes to the storage approach take place in the relation table instead. For example, adding warehouse address information to the structure listed in Table 10.5 would require the addition of a warehouse address table and a table to relate the addresses to telephones, but no change would be needed in the telephone table.

The previous discussion was necessary because of the existence of one-to-many linkages between addresses and telephones. If there is a many-to-many relationship between your data items, the use of a relation table is mandated automatically and determines the structure.

10

Further exploration of the database structure can often provide additional opportunities for improvement. Ideally, good database design teams should generally catch all data structure issues and opportunities early in the design process. Nevertheless, some people simply think better from a picture and will generate new ideas only once structure diagrams like those in the figures in this chapter are available.

In the case of our current example, as we review our drafted structure we note that no provision has been made for accommodating additional technology available for contacting people, specifically pagers and e-mail. The first temptation might be to create another table or tables to store the contact points. On closer examination, however, you find that the relationship between people or companies and direct phones is quite similar to that between people or companies and other communication points.

Only three changes must be made in order to accommodate additional communication (contact) points into the structure already designed for telephone numbers:

1. The table, field, and related relation table must be renamed to reflect the revised contents. Up to now, we've been describing a telephone table. In our sample database, we'll rename the fields and table for telephone information to reflect the concept "communication point" instead.

2. The field width of the telephone number field must be widened to allow e-mail addresses, which are longer. Table 10.6 shows the new mixture of sample communication point records. (The Comment column is for clarification and is not in the data table.)

Table 10.6   This Table Contains Different Varieties of Communication Points

CommPointID	CommPoint	Comment
7	206-555-1212x145	A telephone number
8	206-555-4666	A pager number
9	Bob@Jones.Com	An e-mail address

3. An additional field must be added to the relation table to allow for differentiation between phones, pagers, and e-mail addresses. Each relationship between a person and a communication point for that person should convey the type of contact information that it stores. Table 10.7 shows some relation table records that join contact people to communication point records.

Table 10.7   Sample Relation Table Records that Describe the Relationship Between Contacts and Their Direct Contact Points

ContID	CommPointID	CommPointType
456	7	Direct line
102	8	Pager

In the previous four sections, we've analyzed the nature of the contact management data and the data relationships in the proposed structure and found ways to get more data into less tables. We've done so partly by combining data tables and shifting organizational work to relation tables. A finalized data structure that solves the problems described in the four sections is shown in Figure 10.9.

Fig. 10.9

This data structure accommodates multiple parents for the tblAddr *and* tblCommPoint *tables and displays the many-to-many relationships.*

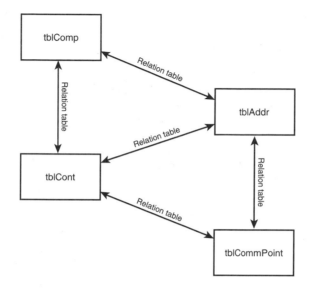

> ## α Note
>
> At this stage, you may want to launch Access and review the tables in the sample database for this chapter: AES_TBL.MDB. The tables in the database reflect the final schema design shown in Figure 10.9 and include sample records.

Design Step 5—Defining the Supporting Tables

Once the core data structure is defined, you must revisit each entity (table) in the database and extrapolate the supporting information required by its attributes (fields).

The most predominant types of supporting information in a database structure are lookup table values. Lookup tables provide several benefits to a database structure:

▶ They store the values that can be used for validation of entered data (such as through limit-to-list combo boxes on forms).

▶ They allow short codes to be saved in base tables and then translated into longer, more descriptive strings when displaying or reporting the data.

▶ They allow the descriptive strings to be revised without altering the base table data as the world changes or an application is deployed in different language bases.

10

▶ They provide a central mechanism for storing, securing, and maintaining departmental or company-wide value lists.

Database designers must walk a fine line when using lookup tables. The use of these tables provides a solid, centralized manner for enforcing data integrity in the database. Thus, it's tempting to use them for every field that has non-variable values.

The temptation to use lookup tables to validate and populate certain fields in a database can become extreme and can lead to an overabundance of such tables in the database. (As an example, I once saw a people table that had a Number of Children field fed by a lookup table. The lookup values were: "1," "2," "3," "4," "5," and "6 or more." Because this data was not fed into the computer based on a hard copy document with similar values, I saw no benefit in this structure over a validation rule in the table that simply enforced a non-negative number range instead.)

There is no art to creating lookup tables, as the majority of them have only one or two fields—a key value and a display string. (When the key value is self-explanatory, no additional display string is required.)

The example of the United States postal codes provides a common scenario. We now have short state abbreviation code values ("AK," "AZ," and so on) that are defined and maintained by the U.S. Postal Service, and these are used by the majority of database systems. However, even before the government's involvement, most computer system designers chose to define and store a shorter value for states ("Alas," "Ariz," and the like) in the base table data and then translate the short code to a full string via a lookup table as needed.

At the simplest level, some lookups have only one field. Lookup tables of this type are not intended to translate short codes into longer strings (as with the previous state example). Instead, single-field lookups provide only one purpose: data entry validation. Tables of this type are used to populate combo boxes on entry forms in order to limit the values placed in a field by users.

At a more complex level, lookup tables can present a slightly more intricate set of opportunities. Consider the decision whether to include multiple fields in a single lookup table in order to accommodate multiple uses or to create several lookup tables instead.

An example of this situation is presented by address records. We have defined previously in this chapter a structure where addresses that are attached to people can indicate personal addresses or company addresses. Thus, it is useful to catalog each relationship between address records and people by type (such as "home"). This type of code is stored in the relation table between people and addresses.

Consider that addresses are collected in the database for companies *and* individuals. In order to create a single lookup table that can be used for both types of addresses, a flag field must be placed in the lookup table to use when building filtered sublists from the table's records.

Figure 10.10 shows the lookup table for address types, with a flag field captioned Company/ Contact that allows for the creation of one value list for company addresses (where the field equals "C") and a different list for personal addresses (where the field equals "P").

Fig. 10.10

These lookup table values are flagged to allow them to populate more than one value list.

Address Type ID	Company/Contact	Address Type
BUSNWK	P	Business or Employer
CORPBR	C	Corporate - Branch
CORPHQ	C	Corporate - Headquarters
CORPSB	C	Subsidiary or Affiliate
CORPSL	C	Sales or Field Office
HOMEPR	P	Home - Primary
HOMESC	P	Home - Secondry
HOMEVC	P	Home - Vacation
RETAIL	C	Retail Shop

tlkpAddrType : Table

Record: 1 of 9

The benefit of the layout shown in the figure is that it allows you to build two combo or list sources from a single lookup table. By distinctly selecting the Address Type ID values based upon a Company/Contact flag value of "C" or "P," a list of address types for a specific purpose can be built.

Notice that the table in the figure includes Address Type ID values that could easily be grouped into two levels of detail (in other words, broken into two lookup fields). Addresses for companies are of the flavor *corporate* or *retail* (their Address Type ID begins with either "CORP" or "RETAIL"), and addresses for people are for *home* or *work* (their Address Type ID begins with either "BUSN" or "HOME"). Codifying these lookup values in one field provides the easiest maintenance, as well as ease of readability and querying of the base table data.

For example, consider the fact that you could find all business addresses for individuals by using a WHERE clause criteria of AddrTypeID LIKE "BUSN*" in the address table. You would not need to join the address table to the lookup table in this scenario to answer the question because the lookup value stored in the address table is descriptive. In contrast, if the lookup table ID values were numeric and that number was stored in the address table, the number itself would not have any descriptive value. Every query with criteria based on the lookup table information would require joining the lookup table to the addresses.

10

An additional opportunity provided by lookup tables is to redefine a single lookup table to include multiple disparate value types. This can be accomplished through the addition of a flag field to the table to provide the classification used for selecting only a subset of the lookup vales at any given time.

α Note

In the previous example, the flag field `Company/Contact` was used to select a subset of information from the lookup table in order to populate two different types of combo boxes from the same table. I have seen developers take this example to extremes by combining all of an application's lookup tables into a single table when performance-tuning a slow-running application. The table contains a short code and long code field, as well as a flag field for type in each record. All lists in the application query the master lookup table with a `WHERE` clause against the type value to grab the specific records they need.

The basis for this strategy is a performance theory stating that a single lookup table serving multiple needs performs better than multiple tables. A file server dedicated to an application keeps the most commonly used tables for that application (and their indexes) in cache memory at all times. The theory postulates that a combined lookup table would be used so frequently that it would always exist in the RAM cache, thus increasing form performance.

I am not advocating that you structure your databases in this manner and combine all of your lookups into a single table. However, I document the performance theory for you here so that you can explore it as an option when attempting to speed up your solutions.

Reviewing all of the fields in our sample database layout, we find the need for six lookup tables. Adding these lookup tables into the database structure, plus the field information and relation tables defined in the prior steps, helps us to arrive at a final database structure. The structure and its relationships, once built, appear as in Figure 10.11.

By using the example of a contact management system with several many-to-many relationships, I've provided a set of real-world database needs that illustrates some of the challenges you will face when defining a database layout. If you are new to Access application development, you may feel that the example provided is somewhat extreme, and the type of structure shown in the figure is rare. In actual fact, business data storage needs very frequently require the kind of analysis and approaches detailed in the previous five sections. With minor adjustments, you will find yourself using the techniques here in your applications over and over again.

Fig. 10.11
This Access Relationships window shows the final normalized and optimized data structure resulting from the discussions in this chapter.

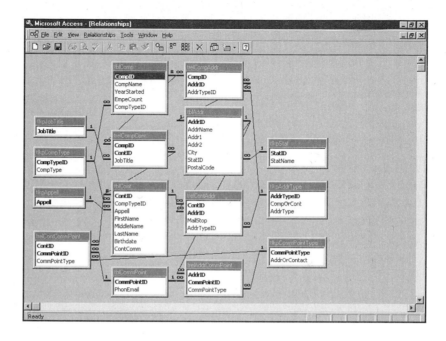

Under-normalizing a Database

Previously discussed in this chapter was the importance of a well-organized database structure, following the rules of "normalization." Most of the time, you will strive to create a database that adheres to the proper usage of parent, child, lookup, and relation tables. Sometimes, however, there are specific tables, or even specific databases, that you may choose not to split into the lowest possible level of component parts.

The consequence of not splitting tables is repeated data. If a table of data is not broken down into its smallest logical units, the same data items may occur more than once in the table. In Table 10.8, the names of contact persons have not been separated from their telephone information into an independent table, so the same person's name is duplicated in multiple telephone records.

Table 10.8   This Table is Under-normalized Because the Repeating Name Data Should Be in a Different Table

AddrID	FirstName	LastName	Telephone
142	Bob	Hopeful	206-555-1212x145
143	Bob	Hopeful	206-555-4466
144	Bing	Crawford	206-555-1896

10

Data that is not fully normalized is commonly referred to as "under-normalized," "de-normalized," or "flattened." Here are a few scenarios where an under-normalized database layout may prove valuable:

The data must be easy to query. If a database is built primarily to enable ad hoc inquiries into the data, users may find the process simpler when a small number of tables must be joined in order to answer any specific question. While a simplified data structure wastes disk space (by repeating information) and sometimes data entry effort, it enables users to browse data, export it, or build queries against it easily because they can quickly ascertain the data's layout.

Most important to this need is the removal of lookup tables from the schema, thus requiring the storage of complete strings in the actual data records. For example, the lookup table for company types in our sample contact management system causes the storage of a short code like "ATTY" for law firms in the base table record. Users performing ad-hoc queries against such data won't know to enter this value as a criteria for law firms because a code of "LAW" or "LEGL" might be equally appropriate depending on how lookup values are assigned. Doing away with the lookup table and its short codes requires the storage of the full description "Attorney/Legal" in the data record; this allows users to search for either of these common words and find matching companies.

Reporting performance is critical. In a system where reports are run with extreme frequency, and the reports include multiple levels of grouping and sorting, the reporting operations may run faster when based on simplified tables as opposed to queries that join multiple tables.

In this scenario, multiple parent, child, relation, and lookup tables may be combined to create one very large table for reporting. Because duplicate data fields are introduced by the combination, report group levels must be used against the table to hide the duplication.

The data must match that in another system. When an Access database or application provides an intermediate step between other data storage systems, the structure of the Access database may be simplified to match the input source or output destination.

For example, assume that an Access database is used to collect financial transactions that are exported to a complex Excel worksheet for analysis. Because the worksheet cannot provide the same normalized data model that Access provides, it will probably be structured as one large table of values. There may be no point in normalizing the Access entry database because then code would be required to de-normalize it immediately after entry so that it can be exported.

Under-normalizing a database structure often occurs as you design it. You determine at design time that the structure should be flat to serve the purposes in the previous list. Alternately, you can *de-normalize* an existing database by creating additional tables that store the flattened versions of the normalized data. The flattened tables may be stored in the back-end database, created in a separate database, or exported to another data storage system.

The most common use of flattened tables is in data warehousing, a concept described in Chapter 7, "Understanding Application Architecture." Data warehouses are created by making copies of production data on a regular basis and restructuring the copied data to provide the best possible ease-of-use for researchers. Oftentimes, the restructure involves flattening (combining) several related tables into one.

An alternative to flattening data by appending it into new table structures is to flatten the data with queries instead. Multiple tables can be added to a single query, which produces a datasheet of the combined data that can be used for statistical analysis or reporting.

The determination to use flattened tables versus flattening queries is made based on these factors:

Performance. Tables that are pre-built provide faster access to data and search results than queries that combine multiple tables to get the same result.

Timeliness of Data. Flattened tables are usually built at intervals, rather than as an ongoing application process because the aggregation of data can be time-consuming. Thus, queries run against production data provide current, real-time information, whereas flattened tables are only current up to the time they were created.

Editing Ability. Complex queries that flatten data usually generate a result set that is read-only. If the flattened data must be directly edited in the flattened view, a flattened table will provide this capability when a query cannot.

 Caution

Editing flattened data is a one-way street—changes to the flattened data are not reflected in the source tables from which it came. Worse still, the changes will be lost the next time the flattened data is rebuilt from the source data. It is rare that users would be allowed to edit copies of historical data.

It can be useful to create and save a set of queries that flatten the data in every database you build. This provides users or system administrators with a starting point for data research and analysis, rather than requiring them to create complex joins themselves every time multiple tables are required in the result set. You can document for your users how to do research into the data by using the saved queries.

Using saved queries for data analysis does have certain limitations. For example, in the sample database for this chapter, the creation of *family join* and *grand join* queries that flatten all the data into a single datasheet is problematic, because the complex data structure as expressed in Figure 10.11 does not allow you to see *all* information in the database with a single simple query. This problem is discussed further in "Creating Complex Queries" later in this chapter. (Refer to Chapter 7, "Understanding Application Architecture," for the join terminology such as the family join I use to describe queries.)

Nevertheless, saved queries that pull together commonly used views of data can be built and used as report sources or for ad-hoc queries. An example of such a query from the sample contact database is shown in Figure 10.12; the query combines company records with their addresses and the phone numbers for the addresses. This type of query would commonly be used to search for address or phone information or print phone list reports.

Fig. 10.12
This query "flattens" related table data into a single structure for easier analysis.

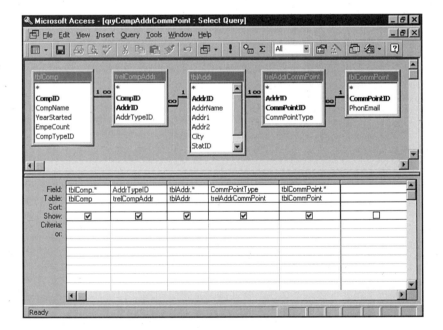

Cataloging and Finding Record Attributes

As you structure a database, you frequently find that a single data record needs to collect multiple attributes related to the record. This is usually referred to as "keywording" the data records. The challenge of keywording crops up regularly as you build expert solutions.

Keywording a data record involves attaching multiple attributes of the same type to a specific record. The simplest way to give a record multiple attributes is to place the attributes in a delimited string in a text field within the record. Using our contact information example, a field could be added to the people table to catalog each person's favorite foods, and the field could contain delimited values like those shown in Table 10.9.

Table 10.9   Assigning Multiple Keywords to a Single Record

ContID	FirstName	Favorites
1	Bob	Ham; Pizza

 Note

Access's new multi-select list box control is an excellent device for capturing this type of keyword information on forms. See the example in "Using Multi-select List Boxes" in Chapter 13, "Mastering Combo and List Boxes."

When multiple values are concatenated in a single field this way, the data structure is not normalized with respect to the rules provided in "Designing a Database" earlier in the chapter. Also, saving, extracting, and finding individual values within the delimited keyword list usually involves quite a bit of programmatic overhead in the application. Data structured this way provides several problems for the developer as well as the users. Some of these problems are:

Indexes cannot be used to find a value. Building an index on a concatenated field has no value because your searches on the field will always be looking for a subset of the field (one value), rather than the entire value (which matches the index).

Searching for values always involves a string search with LIKE. To find records with the keyword value "ham" a user must search the field using LIKE "*ham*", prompting an "in-string" search that must match individual characters within the field to the passed criteria. This type of search is the least efficient use of Jet.

Memo *fields are the slowest fields to retrieve.* If the delimited string values may exceed the 255-character length limit of an Access Text field, the Memo type must be used instead. Memo fields are not stored with the containing table but instead are placed by Jet in a separate table; hence, retrieving them is slower than retrieving other field types.

Users do not know what values are legitimate to search for. Without writing code, there is no way to give users a list of all keyword values that are logged in the field,

10

because using GROUP BY on concatenated values simply yields unique concatenated values and not unique individual values.

If the concatenated keyword data were instead stored with only one value per field, a GROUP BY SQL statement against the field would yield a unique list of all values in use.

The data must be queried in a precise fashion. Thoughtful validation must be applied to data entered into concatenated lists in order to ensure that it's stored in a way conducive to searching.

Imagine a user wanting to find all people that are fond of ham. To search using LIKE "*ham*" would not produce accurate results, because such a search would find "champagne" and "hamburgers" in the keyword strings in addition to "ham." Consequently, a user would need to know that the desired keyword value ended with a delimiter and would need to actually search for LIKE "*ham;*" instead. Users should not be expected to know such nuances in the data.

This type of search would also prove inaccurate unless the following validation was applied to the entered data:

1. Each value in the list must be followed by a delimiter but allow no spaces between the value and its delimiter ("ham;pizza" and "ham; pizza" are fine but "ham ; pizza" must not be allowed because a search for "ham;" would then fail).

2. The last value in a list must also be delimited so that a value appears the same anywhere in the field. Thus, if "ham" is the last value in a list of person's favorite foods, it must still be entered as "ham;" or it will not appear in the search results. In the case of Bob's data in Table 10.9, the delimiter would need to be added to the last value in the list—"pizza"—as shown in Table 10.10.

Table 10.10   Each Keyword in a Delimited List Must Be Delimited the Same Way

ContID	FirstName	Favorites
1	Bob	Ham; Pizza;

Despite their shortcomings, delimited lists can provide a simple way to store repeating values that are homogeneous. Data structured this way is also very easy to query using AND and OR logic—simply request all people records where the keyword values are LIKE "*ham;*" OR LIKE "*pizza;*".

When the number of records or keywords is large, the ability to search the attribute data using indexes can be valuable. Similarly, you may determine that you want the keyword values in a normalized structure, or you may determine that writing the code to deal with delimited keyword strings is too much work. In these instances, using a separate keyword table for the values may prove more effective.

At the simplest level, a keyword table is like any other child table in a parent-child relationship. Continuing with our example of people's favorite foods, a child table for food favorites would need only a foreign key field with the parent record's ID value and a keyword field. Unlike the single field with repeating values, a keyword field that stores a single value can be indexed for performance and can also be used in SELECT DISTINCT statements for creating lists of available values or for computing keyword statistics with functions like Count. Table 10.11 shows the information for Bob's favorite foods from Table 10.10 removed from his contact record and placed in a keyword table structure.

Table 10.11   Multiple Keywords Stored Using a Normalized Structure

ContID	Favorite
1	Ham
1	Pizza

At a more complex level, the use of keyword tables presents a dilemma for developers when there are a significant number of keyword types available in the data (for example, you want to track keywords for favorite films in addition to keywords for favorite foods). If a single record can have multiple different types of keyword values attached to it, the developer will be inclined to create one keyword table for each keyword type—one for foods, as shown in Table 10.11, and another one for films.

When the number of different keyword types is small and there is no need in the project plan to add future keyword types to the system, the most "pure" data structure is provided by using a separate table for each type of keyword. Thus, cataloging favorite foods and favorite films would involve two keyword tables. If, on the other hand, the data structure must provide growth and flexibility, combining keywords into a single table is worth exploring.

Let's use the example at hand to clarify the point. Assume that the design requires that a single person in our sample database can have many different types of favorites: favorite foods, favorite films, favorite colors, favorite leaders, and so on. If we create a keyword table for each of these favorites, we have an easy database to manage but also a cluttered structure—the database cannot be extended to handle another type of favorite without adding an additional keyword table.

10

If, on the other hand, we create a single favorites table, we will need to supply a field for the "type of favorite" in order to clarify the nature of each keyword. Figure 10.13 shows an example of such a table. Notice that the structure we defined in Table 10.11 has been expanded to include a favorite type code.

Fig. 10.13

This keyword table contains both a type field and a value field.

Contact ID	Favorite Type	Favorite Value
1	Color	Blue
1	Color	Red
1	Food	Ham
1	Food	Pizza
1	Movie	Blade Runner
1	Movie	Die Hard
2	Color	Blue
2	Food	Ham
2	Food	Lasagna
2	Food	Yams
2	Movie	Lost Horizon

Record: 1 of 11

I describe records following this metaphor as "tag/value pairs" (the type code for the keyword is the "tag"). Structuring records in this fashion allows for infinite flexibility in the actual data because additional tags can be created by the user during entry or by a system administrator as an addition to a lookup table. In either case, tags can come and go without any change to the schema.

The challenge in a tag/value pair layout comes from the need to query the data. Looking for any individual value in the keyword table presents no problem because the search criteria is not compound and thus only one record per parent is found. In other words, the following SQL statement would yield a list of parent ID records for people that like pizza:

```
SELECT ContID FROM tblFav
WHERE FavType = "Food" AND FavValue = "Pizza"
```

It is also not difficult to find people that like ham *or* pizza using tag/value pairs. Any of the queries in Listing 10.4 provides the desired result.

Listing 10.4   Three Approaches to Finding Tag/Value Pair Keyword Records Matching Ham or Pizza

```
SELECT DISTINCT ContID FROM tblFav
  WHERE FavType = "Food" AND FavValue IN ("Ham", "Pizza")

SELECT DISTINCT ContID FROM tblFav
WHERE (FavType = "Food" AND FavValue = "Ham")
   OR (FavType = "Food" AND FavValue = "Pizza")
```

```
SELECT DISTINCT ContID FROM tblFav
WHERE (FavType = "Food")
```

A more difficult situation arises when you want to find all people that enjoy ham *and* pizza. Of course, the following SQL string returns no records because it is nonsensical given the data structure:

```
SELECT DISTINCT ContID FROM tblFav
WHERE (FavType = "Food" AND FavValue = "Ham")
  AND (FavType = "Food" AND FavValue = "Pizza")
```

The problem here is that there's no way to use a single simple SELECT statement to answer the question because the target values are not in a single record; they are in more than one keyword record, but the AND operator applies the compound criteria to each single record. Thus, more sophisticated queries must be crafted to answer the compound question.

One option is to "flatten" the data so that it looks more like a single record and then use a standard compound WHERE clause against the virtual record. A SQL statement that accomplishes this is shown below, and the query in design view is in Figure 10.14.

```
SELECT DISTINCT tblFav.ContID
FROM tblFav
  INNER JOIN tblFav AS tblFav_1 ON tblFav.ContID = tblFav_1.ContID
WHERE tblFav.FavType="Food" AND tblFav.FavValue="Ham"
  AND tblFav_1.FavType="Food" AND tblFav_1.FavValue="Pizza"
```

Fig. 10.14

This query tricks Access into performing a multi-keyword search by joining multiple copies of the same base table.

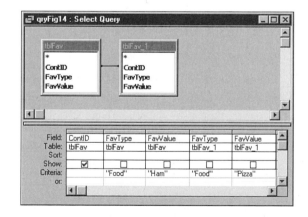

This method is limited because the SQL statement must include one copy of the base table for each major criterion, and must be rewritten for each request to reflect the number of FavType values that will be searched. In other words, expanding the previous query to include people whose favorite colors include *blue* would require an additional copy of tblFav in the join and the addition of the criterion: AND tblFav_2.FavType="Color" AND tblFav_2.FavValue="Blue".

If the number of criteria options you must present to users can be limited, you can actually create one parameterized version of this query for each unique number of criteria, and save and reuse these queries. This creates an ad-hoc search capability against saved queries that can be used by unsophisticated users. Thus, the query in Figure 10.14 previously could be redesigned, as shown in Figure 10.15, to use parameters and saved as qryFav_2Criteria. Additional canned queries qryFav_3Criteria, qryFav_4Criteria, and so on could also be created, each with an additional copy of tblFav to apply criteria against.

Fig. 10.15

This parameterized query follows the same search model as in Figure 10.14 but uses criteria arguments passed in by the user.

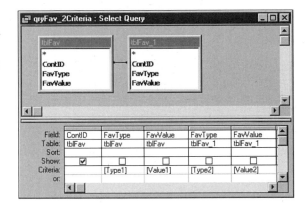

α Note

Depending on your system configuration, Jet should have no trouble joining several copies of a table to itself in this fashion. Access had no problem running a version of this query for me that contained ten copies of tblFav and thus accepted twenty parameters to test ten tag/value pair criteria.

A canned query like this can be run from code easily, because the code does not need to write any SQL statements but instead must simply set the query's parameters as shown in Listing 10.5.

Listing 10.5   Setting Query Parameters from Code

```
Set dbs = CurrentDb
Set qdf = dbs.QueryDefs("qryFav_2Criteria")
qdf!Type1 = "Food"
qdf!Value1 = "Ham"
qdf!Type2 = "Food"
qdf!Value2 = "Pizza"
Set rst = qdf.OpenRecordset()
```

Self-joining a table to copies of itself in this fashion does not always provide the best performance and is limited to the number of self-joins that the user's system resources can accommodate.

 Note

A self-join is inefficient because it creates a "cross-product" result set, meaning that each value in the table is joined to all other matching values. For example, if there are six values for the ID number 1, each of the records with this ID is joined to itself plus the other five. This produces a total of 36 (six multiplied by six) records in the join's result set. As you continue to add more copies of a table to the self-join, this growth continues geometrically.

There are two alternative approaches to this style, both of which involve dynamically creating SQL statements in code that test the desired criteria. The first SQL statement approach utilizes Jet's ability to perform a *sub-select* (a query within a query). In Jet, sub-selections are handled with the IN operator, as in the example in Listing 10.6.

Listing 10.6   A Sub-select Query Using an *IN* Clause

```
SELECT * FROM tblCont
WHERE tblCont.ContID IN
    (SELECT tblFav.ContID FROM tblFav
      WHERE tblFav.FavType = "Food"
        AND tblFav.FavValue = "Ham")
  AND tblCont.ContID IN
    (SELECT tblFav.ContID FROM tblFav
      WHERE tblFav.FavType = "Food"
        AND tblFav.FavValue = "Pizza")
```

In the syntax shown, the primary SELECT statement takes the result of two sub-select statements and joins them together to find only the records that match both criteria sets.

 Note

In my testing, Jet had no problem running a query of this style with ten IN clauses compounded together, but this type of query will eventually run out of resources at some finite number of criteria (and it's not very fast).

A better approach to tag/value queries that involve "and" comparisons involves the intriguing approach of using "or" comparisons and then counting the matches to find the correct target number. In other words, find all people who like ham or pizza and count the matches, and only select the people who matched to both criteria.

Figure 10.16 shows the query design to achieve this. The SQL statement for the query must be rewritten from code for each use in order to place the appropriate criteria into the WHERE clause and the appropriate number into the match for the Count, as shown in Listing 10.7.

Listing 10.7   AES_Tbl.Mdb—A Sub-select Query Using an *IN* Clause

```
SELECT ContID FROM tblFav
WHERE (FavType = "Food" AND FavValue = "Ham")
   OR (FavType = "Food" AND FavValue = "Pizza")
GROUP BY ContID
HAVING Count(ContID) = 2
```

Fig. 10.16

A GROUP BY query that counts record occurrences provides a handy device to find keyword values.

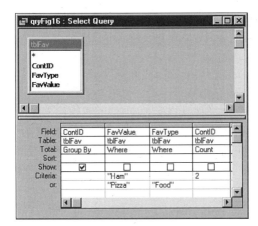

α **Note**

In the previous syntax, note the difference between the HAVING clause and the WHERE clause. WHERE is applied to the base records in the table, while HAVING is applied to the data *after* it has been restricted and grouped. HAVING is essentially a WHERE clause restriction against the aggregated result set.

While each of the techniques in this topic is viable and useful, none are simple to use for ad-hoc queries. Either the user must understand the type codes and values available in the data in order to ask the appropriate question, or Basic code must be run to write a SQL string into a query object that drives the search. In either case, querying keyword data is usually facilitated in an application by the use of a form that places a "wrapper" around the complex process of selecting and using multiple keywords.

Tip

Test each of these techniques against the actual data in your application before determining the one to use. Depending on the type of data, the number of records in the keyword table, the uniqueness of keyword table indexes, the average number of keywords used in a search, the average users' hardware, and other factors, one technique here may show a significant performance increase over the others. In general, the technique using HAVING will run the fastest.

Also, when repeated operations must be run against the results of the keywords search, use INSERT INTO or SELECT INTO in the SQL string to place the chosen ID values in a temporary table and then base forms or other processes on the temporary table to avoid running the keyword search more than once.

Building High-powered Queries

Once you've mastered the challenge of refining your database table layouts, your next hurdle becomes mastering the retrieval of information from the tables. Not all applications allow users to browse, sort, or filter table datasheets to scrutinize data attributes. Instead, filtered views of data are provided to users through forms and reports. The data retrieval engine for these forms and reports is Jet's query processor.

Understanding the optimal way to utilize this query processor, as well as the nature of queries themselves, will assist you in creating expert solutions.

Creating Faster Queries

Queries are the "big machines" that run the factory of your application. They provide the horsepower for record selection on forms and reports, along with data analysis, record exports, and bulk operations. Consequently, you should always spend some time at the end of your application development cycle "tuning" your queries to make them run as fast as possible.

Here a few guidelines for getting the best performance from queries:

> *Update Jet's statistics regularly.* Jet maintains a set of "statistics" (summary information) about the base tables involved in a query. This information is used when Jet is trying to determine the shortest execution path for a query.

> Over time, the statistics underlying a query may change. For example, in a join between two tables, one table may have more records than the other when the query is first created, but over time the situation can reverse and the second table

10

can become larger than the first. This disparity is not reflected in the query's saved execution plan and is not corrected until the statistics are updated.

Query statistics are updated when a query is saved and when the database is compacted. Thus, periodically compacting the back-end database in an application keeps query performance from degrading.

 Note

Data operations may slow down over time as the database file becomes "fragmented," with table records scattered over many different locations in the MDB file and perhaps many different locations on disk. In this scenario, compacting helps to speed up queries and other table data retrieval because it copies all records for each table into a contiguous area within the database file and copies all index entries into contiguous order by primary key (this is called "clustering").

Create plenty of indexes. Indexes add performance to query record selection operations, to record seeks in code, and to data sorting. You should create indexes on any field that will be used to locate data in SQL statements or recordset operations, including fields used in WHERE and ORDER BY clauses; however, there is one caveat.

The minor caveat is that index values must be written when a record is added or edited. Writing an index entry takes time; thus, the more indexes you have on a record, the more time it takes to save the record. If optimizing data entry operations is a primary consideration in your application, you may opt to err on the side of under-indexing a table in order to speed up record saves at the expense of record retrieval.

 Tip

Even though sorting in queries utilizes indexes where available, sorting is one of the greatest performance hits on a query. Use sorting only when required, and never use sorting in a query that will be subordinated inside another query—when nesting queries, apply sorting in the highest level query only.

Because the Jet group put some effort into improving sort performance in Jet 3.5, this tip is less urgent than in pre-97 releases of Access. You may no longer need to think of sorting as a serious performance negative, but you will still want to minimize where it occurs in your applications.

Utilize the best indexes. An index is highly "selective" when a single index value returns very few records. (Obviously, a primary key is the *most* selective type of index because it always returns a single record.) When creating queries, use the most selective index available; a field with a "No Duplicates" index provides faster access to data than a field with "Duplicates OK."

As another example, a query that selects records based on a criteria on the State field may return many records because such an index will not be highly selective. If practical, build the query around a more selective indexed field for better performance (City is more highly selective than State, and Postal Code more selective than City, and so on).

Also, when a field occurs in both sides of a join, placing a restriction on the field from the "one" table will generally provide better performance than placing the same criteria on the foreign key field in the "many" table. In our current sample data for this chapter, we would expect better performance restricting ContID in tblCont than if we restrict it in trelContAddr when these two tables are joined.

Utilize the best join strategy. Avoid joining on fields with Null values. Queries with Null values in an index may not qualify for certain highly-optimized index merge operations used by the Jet query optimizer.

Also, make certain that the linked fields on both sides of each join are indexed and are as selective as possible. Queries may also run faster when the two fields that are joined are of the exact same data type.

Use Rushmore optimization to its best advantage. Rushmore query optimization is applied when multiple indexed column comparisons are used in the selection criteria. Create indexes on columns that participate in these kinds of compound criteria in queries or SQL, as shown here:

```
column1 operator expression1 OR column2 operator expression2
column1 operator expression1 AND column2 operator expression2
```

The placeholder *operator* indicates a SQL comparison using <, >, =, <=, >=, <>, BETWEEN, IN, or LIKE.

Minimize the use of expressions in queries. Expressions in queries are evaluated for each record in the result set and can significantly slow down query execution. In some instances, adding an expression to a query is the only way to properly format or evaluate the underlying data. However, before adding an expression to a query, make certain that you have eliminated alternate, and perhaps speedier, approaches to the problem.

For example, consider the following SQL statement to select invoice records and display the month portion of the invoice date field:

10

```
SELECT
  InvcNum,
  InvcDate,
  Month([InvcDate]) As InvcMon
FROM tblInvc
```

This query must process the Month function for each record in the underlying table. Depending on the reason for the function, there may be alternative approaches that allow the function's removal from the query, as follows:

1. If the function is used to provide a value for a criteria against the query, consider passing different comparison values to the query that remove the need for the function. For example, assume that the Month function was chosen for use in the previous query so that the query can contain a WHERE clause like this:

   ```
   WHERE InvcMon BETWEEN 10 AND 12
   ```

   As it turns out, you discover that the application containing this query only contains a year's worth of invoices at one time in the invoice table. Thus, a more efficient query can be created (without the Month expression) by simply passing a range of dates within the current year to the query, rather than passing in month numbers:

   ```
   WHERE InvcDate BETWEEN 10/1/96 AND 12/31/96
   ```

 Note

I once saw timing tests for Access 2 that measured the difference between an expression in a comparison (such as our WHERE Month([InvcDate]) BETWEEN 10 AND 12) and a direct comparison (such as WHERE InvcDate BETWEEN 10/1/96 AND 12/31/96). The test showed the direct comparison variation as more than 100 times faster than the expression-based comparison!

I have not attempted to duplicate these timing tests in Access 97, but it is safe to say that the performance differential between the two techniques, if not quite as extreme, will still be measurably significant.

2. If the expression is provided to format the data for display, consider formatting the data in the target form or report instead. For example, the expression can be moved from the query to the ControlSource property of a report TextBox control, like this:

   ```
   =Month([InvcDate])
   ```

   You also want to optimize the use of expressions in nested queries. When one query is inside another (in other words, a "container" query holds a "contained" query), try not to use expressions in the contained query or to apply criteria at the container query level to the expression in the contained query. For example, you don't want to nest the query in the current example inside another query and use a criteria against the expression field, as in the following SQL statement where the contained query creates InvcMon and the container inspects it:

```
SELECT
  InvcNum,
  InvcMon
FROM (SELECT
        InvcNum,
        InvcDate,
        Month([InvcDate]) As InvcMon
      FROM tblInvc)
WHERE InvcMon BETWEEN 10 AND 12
```

Include only the needed fields in the query result. Using the SELECT * syntax on a large table in order to work with only two fields is wasteful of disk access, network traffic, and workstation resources. In general, it's best to only include in a query the fields that are actually required by the process using the result set.

OLE Object- and Memo-type fields are the slowest to retrieve from a table and should not be included in a query's result set unless specifically necessary.

Avoid open-ended restrictions. Query criteria that uses one of these operators—>, >=, <, and <=—may run faster if two operators are used instead. This allows for "bracketing" of index values instead of scanning indexes from a stated value to the end of the index tree. To choose a second value for bracketing, select a value that is the highest (or lowest, depending on the equality operator) known value in the index or a value beyond it. Thus, of the following restrictions, the first one will run the slowest:

```
WHERE InvcNum > 1000
WHERE InvcNum > 1000 AND < 1000000
WHERE InvcNum BETWEEN 1001 AND 1000000
```

10

Use aggregation wisely. GROUP BY queries are among the slowest performers in your applications. Always include the bare minimum number of fields in this type of query as are required for the task at hand.

When using GROUP BY on a query with joined tables, place the GROUP BY and SQL aggregate functions (SUM, AVG, and so on) on fields in the same table, if possible. For example, if you joined tlkpStat to tblAddr in order to count the number of address records for each state, the first query in Listing 10.8 would run faster than the second because the grouping and counting are both applied to the same table.

Listing 10.8   Two SQL Approaches to Grouping and Counting Addresses by State

```
' This query groups and counts on the StatID field in tlkpStat
SELECT
  tlkpStat.StatName,
  tlkpStat.StatID,
  Count(tlkpStat.StatID) AS CountOfStatID
FROM tlkpStat
  INNER JOIN tblAddr ON tlkpStat.StatID = tblAddr.StatID
GROUP BY
  tlkpStat.StatName,
  tlkpStat.StatID

' This query groups on the StatID field in tlkpStat and counts on tblAddr
SELECT
  tlkpStat.StatName,
  tblAddr.StatID,
  Count(tblAddr.StatID) AS CountOfStatID
FROM tlkpStat
  INNER JOIN tblAddr ON tlkpStat.StatID = tblAddr.StatID
GROUP BY
  tlkpStat.StatName,
  tblAddr.StatID;
```

It is also generally faster to use Count(*) rather than Count(*fieldname*) in an aggregate query expression; thus, the function Count(tlkpStat.StatID) in the previous example would be faster as Count(*).

Finally, if paired values are being grouped, try grouping only one half of the pair instead and using the First aggregate function on the second value. In our current example from Listing 10.8, StatID and StatName are both in the grouping so that the state name is displayed in the result. Changing the phrase SELECT tlkpStat.StatName to SELECT First(tlkpStat.StatName) as shown in Listing 10.9 allows tlkpStat.StatName to be removed from the grouping.

Listing 10.9   Using the *First* Function to Remove One Criterion from the *GROUPBY*

```
SELECT
  First(tlkpStat.StatName) As StatName,
  tlkpStat.StatID,
  Count(tlkpStat.StatID) AS CountOfStatID
FROM tlkpStat
  INNER JOIN tblAddr ON tlkpStat.StatID = tblAddr.StatID
GROUP BY
  tlkpStat.StatID
```

Understanding Join Types

Access provides effective capabilities for joining multiple data tables based on the SQL model. Understanding the various join options allows you to create more useful and powerful queries in your applications.

Essentially, you can join tables according to one of two models:

INNER JOIN. This type of join relates a field (or fields) in one table with a field (or fields) in a second table and returns joined records from both tables only where the field values match on both sides of the join.

OUTER JOIN. An outer join is not the opposite of an inner join, it is a superset of it. An outer join relates a field (or fields) in one table with a field (or fields) in a second table and returns joined records from both tables according to the following formula:

1. All of the records from one of the two tables (the designated "driving table") are returned into the result set, as determined by the direction of the join— see the following *outer join* type descriptions.

2. For each record in the result set, if matching join field values are found in the second table, data from the matching record in that table is appended to the record in the result set.

3. If no matching record is found in the joined table, Null values are added to the result set's record in the columns where values would have existed if a match was found.

Because an outer join has a *driving table*, it is described as driven from either the "right" or the "left," as defined by the direction of the *one* and *many* sides of the join line in the visual representation of the query layout (the Access query grid):

LEFT OUTER JOIN. Using the LEFT JOIN syntax designates the table on the left side of the join as the *driving table* (as represented by the SQL syntax or visual representation). All records in this table will appear in the result set along with data from the records in the right-side table in the join having ID values that match to the driving table.

RIGHT OUTER JOIN. Using the RIGHT JOIN syntax designates the table on the right side of the join as the *driving table* (as represented by the SQL syntax or visual representation). All records in this table will appear in the result set along with data from the records in the left-side table in the join having ID values that match to the driving table.

10

I'll quickly illustrate these join types. Assume that our sample data from the contact management system includes records for five contact people in `tblCont` (ID values 1 through 5), but only two of them have been assigned personal preferences in the table of favorites `tblFav` (ID values 1 and 2).

Figure 10.17 shows an example of a simple multi-table query that joins these two tables with an inner join. The datasheet returned shows only the records that have matching join field (ID) values in both tables.

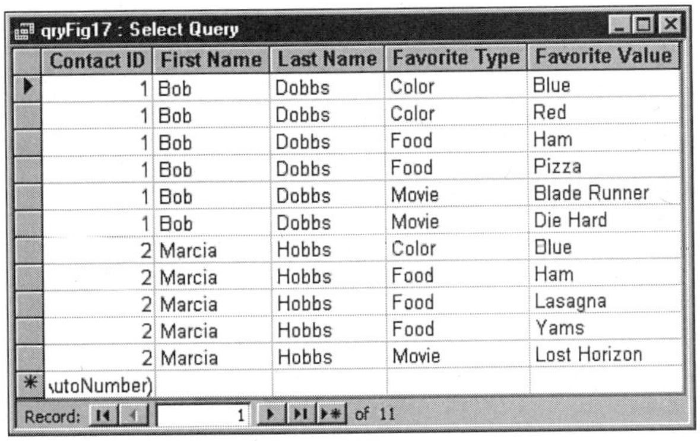

qryFig17 : Select Query

Contact ID	First Name	Last Name	Favorite Type	Favorite Value
1	Bob	Dobbs	Color	Blue
1	Bob	Dobbs	Color	Red
1	Bob	Dobbs	Food	Ham
1	Bob	Dobbs	Food	Pizza
1	Bob	Dobbs	Movie	Blade Runner
1	Bob	Dobbs	Movie	Die Hard
2	Marcia	Hobbs	Color	Blue
2	Marcia	Hobbs	Food	Ham
2	Marcia	Hobbs	Food	Lasagna
2	Marcia	Hobbs	Food	Yams
2	Marcia	Hobbs	Movie	Lost Horizon
utoNumber)				

Record: 1 of 11

Fig. 10.17
This datasheet results from an inner join on `tblCont` and `tblFav`, showing only the items that are common between them.

Listing 10.10 shows the join syntax behind the query shown in Figure 10.17.

Listing 10.10 AES_Tbl.Mdb—The Inner Join Query that Produces the Figure 10.17 Datasheet

```
SELECT
  tblCont.ContID,
  FirstName,
  LastName,
  FavType,
  FavValue
FROM tblCont
  INNER JOIN tblFav ON tblCont.ContID = tblFav.ContID
```

Figure 10.18 takes the same query and executes it using `LEFT JOIN` syntax, which returns all records from the driving table `tblCont` joined to any matching rows in `tblFav`.

Listing 10.11 shows the join syntax behind the query shown in Figure 10.18.

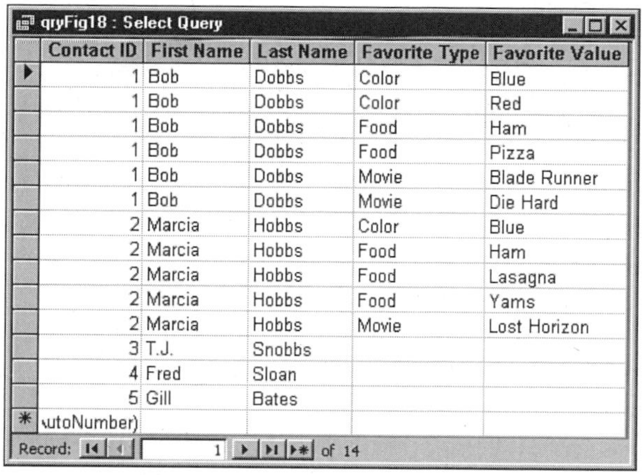

qryFig18 : Select Query

Contact ID	First Name	Last Name	Favorite Type	Favorite Value
1	Bob	Dobbs	Color	Blue
1	Bob	Dobbs	Color	Red
1	Bob	Dobbs	Food	Ham
1	Bob	Dobbs	Food	Pizza
1	Bob	Dobbs	Movie	Blade Runner
1	Bob	Dobbs	Movie	Die Hard
2	Marcia	Hobbs	Color	Blue
2	Marcia	Hobbs	Food	Ham
2	Marcia	Hobbs	Food	Lasagna
2	Marcia	Hobbs	Food	Yams
2	Marcia	Hobbs	Movie	Lost Horizon
3	T.J.	Snobbs		
4	Fred	Sloan		
5	Gill	Bates		
utoNumber)				

Record: 1 of 14

Fig. 10.18
This datasheet results from a left outer join on `tblCont` *and* `tblFav`*, which returns all the records for* `tblCont`.

Listing 10.11 AES_Tbl.Mdb—The Left Outer Join Query that Produces the Figure 10.18 Datasheet

```
SELECT
  tblCont.ContID,
  FirstName,
  LastName,
  FavType,
  FavValue
FROM tblCont
  LEFT OUTER JOIN tblFav ON tblCont.ContID = tblFav.ContID
```

Notice that the layout of the query remained the same—only one join type keyword ("`INNER`") changed (to "`LEFT OUTER`") to facilitate a completely different type of relationship between the tables.

Note

Applying the third join type ("`RIGHT OUTER`") to the two tables in this example would produce the same result as with the inner join, because when `tblFav` becomes the driving table there are no values in it that are *not* in `tblCont`; thus, only records with ID values 1 and 2 show up in the resulting set.

A child table in a database usually always contains values that are linked to its parent table. Thus, it is rare that a right outer join is used from a child to a parent because there is no benefit from including all child records in a join regardless of a matching parent. Because of this situation, the most common join type in a relational database is a left outer join from a parent table to its child, with the parent as the driving table.

When multiple tables are included in a join, the join statements become "nested." Nesting involves the use of parentheses to track the grouping of SELECT statements and JOIN statements when there are more than one of each in the SQL. Nested joins are simple to create in the query design grid by dragging multiple tables into the grid. When writing nested joins from code, however, you must pay attention to the compound nesting (parenthetical grouping) prescribed in the syntax, as in the example of a four-table join in Listing 10.12.

Listing 10.12   Use Parentheses to Group Join Statements Where More Than One Appear in the SQL

```
SELECT
  table1.field1,
  table2.field2,
  table3.field3,
  table4.field4
FROM table1 INNER JOIN
      ((table3 INNER JOIN table4 ON table3.field3 = table4.field3)
    INNER JOIN table2 ON table2.field2 = table3.field2)
  ON table1.field1 = table2.field1
```

This syntax flow reflects the nesting code generated by the query design grid. When creating nested joins from code, you may prefer to make your code more readable by using the syntax structure shown in Listing 10.13. The syntax in the listing is supported by Jet but is easier to read than the syntax generated by the query grid in Listing 10.12.

Listing 10.13   The Join Statement in Listing 10.12 Rewritten for Readability

```
SELECT
  table1.field1,
  table2.field2,
  table3.field3,
  table4.field4
FROM table1 INNER JOIN
  (table2 INNER JOIN
    (table3 INNER JOIN table4
      ON table3.field3 = table4.field3)
    ON table2.field2 = table3.field2)
  ON table1.field1 = table2.field1
```

You can create highly complex inner joins in Jet, using either code or the query design grid. However, outer joins are much more limited. For example, you cannot have multiple tables outer-joined to the same table. In other words, the query design in Figure 10.19 is not allowed in Jet SQL.

Fig. 10.19

This type of multiple outer join query is disallowed by Jet.

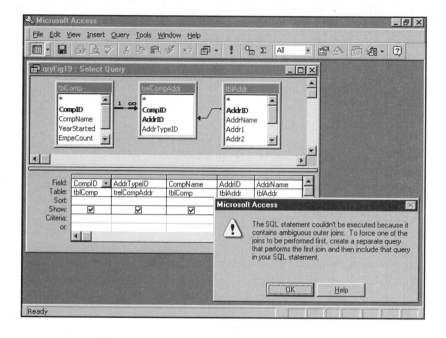

You can, however, have one table that is inner-joined to another table and whose result set is then outer-joined to still other tables. From a SQL perspective, this means that an INNER JOIN can create a virtual "driving table" for a LEFT JOIN or RIGHT JOIN but not the reverse. Thus, the relationship in Figure 10.21 is allowed, but not the relationship in Figure 10.20.

Fig. 10.20

A query like this that attempts an inner join nested in an outer join is disallowed by Jet.

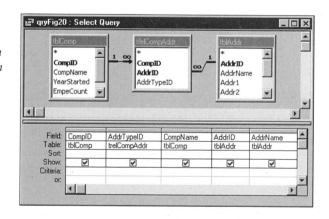

10

Fig. 10.21

Jet allows queries like this with an outer join driving an inner join.

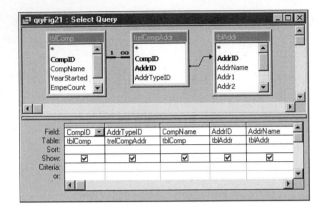

Notice that joining tables in any of the examples thus far involved an equivalence where a value in one table must exactly equal the matching value in another table (`table1.field1 = table2.field1`). Joins involving equal comparisons are termed "equi-joins." All table joins in the Access query design view are "equi-joins," meaning that the linked fields between two tables are compared for equality when the join is run.

In the SQL view of query design or in program code, you can create joins that aren't equi-joins, that cannot be expressed in the query design grid, and that do not use the = operator. Such queries join tables by using field comparisons with the non-equality join operators, such as >=.

To create advanced queries for compound comparisons, use this syntax:

```
SELECT
   field1,
   field2
FROM table1 INNER JOIN table2
   ON table1.field1 operator table2.field1
```

The designation *operator* indicates a relational comparison operator: >, >=, <, <=, and <>.

A join using an inequality operator on record key values has limited usefulness and may produce nonsensical results, but an inequality join on non-key values can be useful in statistical analysis of data. Using our contact database to build an example, the syntax in Listing 10.14 is a standard inner join that uses an equivalence and says, "Show me the state name for the state in address record 1."

Listing 10.14 A Standard Inner Join Using an Equi-join

```
SELECT
   tblAddr.AddrID,
   tblAddr.StatID,
   tlkpStat.StatName
```

```
FROM tlkpStat
  INNER JOIN tblAddr ON tlkpStat.StatID = tblAddr.StatID
WHERE tblAddr.AddrID=1;
```

The syntax in Listing 10.15 takes the join from Listing 10.14 and simply changes the equality operator = in the join to <>. The join now says, "Show me the state names that are *not* used by address record 1." The result set of the join contains a record for every state lookup value *except* the state in address record 1.

Listing 10.15   The Join in Listing 10.14 Expressed with an Inequality in the Join

```
SELECT
  tblAddr.AddrID,
  tblAddr.StatID,
  tlkpStat.StatName
FROM tlkpStat
  INNER JOIN tblAddr ON tlkpStat.StatID <> tblAddr.StatID
WHERE tblAddr.AddrID=1;
```

A final join strategy available in program code but not the query design grid allows you to join tables on multiple fields in a compound relationship that does not depend on the AND operator. Normal multi-field join operations use AND to link two compound field join statements, but the following example using OR to compound the links is also valid in Jet SQL:

```
SELECT
  table1.field1,
  table2.field3
FROM table1 INNER JOIN table2
  ON table1.field1 = table2.field1
  OR table1.field2 = table2.field2
```

Again, the utility of this type of statement is limited to somewhat obscure data analysis joins.

In the sample database for this chapter, some very common data management challenges with respect to joins are exhibited. First and foremost is how to express the relationships between the tables within SQL statements and the query design window. The driving queries that produce most of the figures in this chapter are included in the sample database.

Figure 10.22 shows the relationships built for the sample contact management database. Note that while building relationships between the tables, I also defined referential integrity information for the relationships. Referential integrity is the use of the database engine or code to maintain the linkage between parent and child data in two tables.

10

Referential integrity in Jet involves the establishment of cascading update and deletion rules, which are reflected by Access's display of the *one* and *many* symbols at the ends of the join lines in the Relationships window. I defined cascading updates for all one-to-many relationships in the sample database.

Fig. 10.22

This Access Relationships window shows a complete database structure with defined relationships and referential integrity.

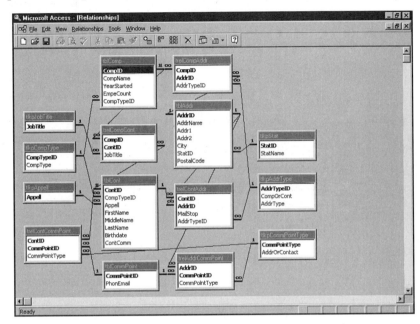

The database diagrams you create during the design phase express relationships *conceptually*, while the relationships you create in Access itself are specifically for data management and to aid in building queries. Here are two specific examples of the difference:

▶ The database diagrams built during a design phase often show that there must be one-to-many relationships between each lookup table and its related base table(s). Often, one-to-many relationships on a database diagram become left joins in the database structure. In the case of a lookup table, however, you do not want to define a left join relationship from it to its base table in Jet, because the presence of the left join from the lookup to the base table makes the use of any other left joins against the base table impossible. (Refer to Figure 10.20 and its related text for clarification of this point.)

Instead, define the relationship between a lookup and its base table(s) as an inner join of type one-to-many.

▶ When moving from database diagrams to Access relationships, a primary key–foreign key association between a base table and a relation table should not be established as a left outer join, even though this situation would conceivably produce the desired result in a query. Problems arise because a relation table consists of two foreign keys, one for each of the related tables. You will not be able to build a left join from each of the two parent (base) tables into the relation table without generating a `Query contains ambiguous outer joins` error message (refer to Figure 10.19).

Instead, define the relationship in Access between a base table and its relation table(s) as an inner join of type one-to-many.

As an additional preference item for lookup tables, I define cascading updates from a lookup table to its base table(s), but I do not define cascading deletes. When a system administrator changes a lookup table value, I want the new value to cascade into all related transaction table entries. On the other hand, a lookup table value that exists in transaction data should never be *deleted* because live data records would be left orphaned. Thus, I disallow cascading deletions from lookup tables into base table data because I assume that the deletion of a lookup table value is an error on the part of the database administrator, and I do not want this error to cascade into any base table records.

Creating Complex Queries

Relying heavily on relation tables and inner joins, as in our example database, causes significant data-retrieval challenges. With inner joins, records are retrieved based upon the presence of a common key in both joined tables. When one of the two tables does not possess a common key value, neither record is returned. When working with data structured like our contact information, this situation can produce undesirable results. For example, people with no addresses are not displayed in the results of a query inner-joining people and their addresses.

Union queries and sub-queries provide you with the tools you need to solve this problem. Consider the queries in Figures 10.23 and 10.24. The query in the first figure (Figure 10.23) returns a list of people and their addresses. This query is an inner join and thus will not list people that have no address records.

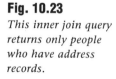

Fig. 10.23

This inner join query returns only people who have address records.

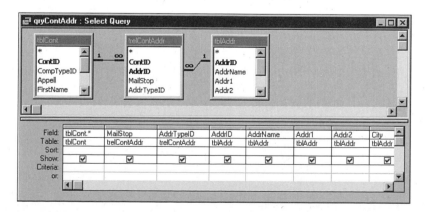

Fig. 10.24

This query uses a subquery only to return people with no address records.

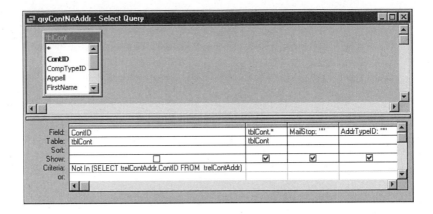

The second query (Figure 10.24) returns only people with *no* addresses, by virtue of this query criteria:

```
WHERE tblCont.ContID Not In
  (SELECT trelContAddr.ContID FROM trelContAddr)
```

This criteria returns records that are in the contact table but *not* in the relation table that links contacts to addresses, thus listing contacts without addresses. In order to display *all* contacts, whether or not they have addresses, the UNION keyword is applied to append the results of the two queries I've just shown, as in the statement in Listing 10.16.

Listing 10.16   AES_Tbl.Mdb—A Union Query that Appends People with No Addresses to People with Addresses

```
SELECT DISTINCTROW
  tblCont.*,
  trelContAddr.MailStop,
  trelContAddr.AddrTypeID,
  tblAddr.AddrID,
  tblAddr.AddrName,
  tblAddr.Addr1,
  tblAddr.Addr2,
  tblAddr.City,
  tblAddr.StatID,
  tblAddr.PostalCode
FROM tblCont
  INNER JOIN
    (tblAddr INNER JOIN trelContAddr
      ON tblAddr.AddrID = trelContAddr.AddrID)
  ON tblCont.ContID = trelContAddr.ContID
UNION
SELECT DISTINCTROW
  tblCont.*,
  "" AS MailStop,
  "" AS AddrTypeID,
  "" AS AddrID,
```

```
      "<none>" AS AddrName,
      "" AS Addr1,
      "" AS Addr2,
      "" AS City,
      "" AS StatID,
      "" AS PostalCode
FROM tblCont
WHERE tblCont.ContID Not In
   (SELECT trelContAddr.ContID FROM trelContAddr)
```

 Note

Notice that there are placeholder fields (as expressions) in the second SELECT statement in this query. When creating a union query, each participating SELECT statement must return the same number of fields as the first statement.

Consider, however, that there are *three tables* joined in the first SELECT string, but only a *single table* in the second SELECT string. Thus, there is a need for the number of fields in both result subsets to match, so the dummy expressions in the second SELECT string are added to facilitate this.

Figure 10.25 shows the result of the query in Listing 10.16. Note that the contact person Gill Bates, who has no address, *is* displayed in the result set.

 Note

In the figure, I've reordered the fields from the order shown in the prior SQL statement to show you how the address data is returned by the union.

Fig. 10.25

A union query between people that have addresses and people that don't displays all people records.

ContID	Appell	FirstName	LastName	AddrTypeID	AddrID	AddrName	Addr
1	Mr.	Bob	Dobbs	BUSNWK	1	Seattle Office	123 Anyst
2	Ms.	Marcia	Hobbs	BUSNWK	2	Redmond Office	456 S. 7th
3	Miss	T.J.	Snobbs	BUSNWK	1	Seattle Office	123 Anyst
4	Mr.	Fred	Sloan	BUSNWK	3	Supermall	3322 S. Ir
4	Mr.	Fred	Sloan	HOMEPR	4	Easy Sleep Cor	1400 S. E
5	Mr.	Gill	Bates			<none>	

Record: 6 of 6

10

Tip

You should establish a style that defines how much clutter you prefer in the Database window with respect to compound queries and their component parts. If you prefer a sparse style, you would create complex queries that perform all required operations in their SQL statement, as shown in my previous example.

If, on the other hand, you have no objection to littering the Database window with query components, you might create each of the two SELECT strings shown in Figures 10.23 and 10.24 and save them as two stored queries and then define your UNION query to simply join the results of the component queries, as in this example:

```
SELECT * FROM qryContAddr
UNION
SELECT * FROM qryContNoAddr
```

An additional structural challenge exemplified by the current sample contact database structure is that our design allows a given attribute table to service more than one parent table (this is called "multiple parentage"). For example, the contact point table tblCommPoint contains phone numbers for address records, as well as direct (non address-related) phone numbers for contact persons.

To properly utilize tables structured this way, you must be careful not to join each of the parent tables to the shared child table in query design. While multiple parentage is an acceptable database layout strategy, queries that utilize it improperly suffer from "circular references" and will not produce accurate results.

Consider the following scenario. Each person in our database can have phone numbers that are attached to the person's address and also phone numbers that are attached directly to the person (such as a cellular phone). You want to create a query that shows each person's address-related telephones alongside their direct phones.

Following the data structure, your first inclination would be to create the query shown in Figure 10.26. This query properly reflects the question you are attempting to answer but in doing so exhibits a circular reference from tblCommPoint to both the address and the contact tables. While this query does not generate an error, it also generates no matching records.

The more appropriate solution to the problem is to add a second copy of the telephone number table to the query so that each parent table can reference its own child table. This layout allows one parent to find its matches in tblCommPoint and the other parent to find its own matches in the aliased tblCommPoint_1, as shown in Figure 10.27. The results of the query are shown in Figure 10.28.

Fig. 10.26

This query contains a circular reference to tblCommPoint *and returns no records.*

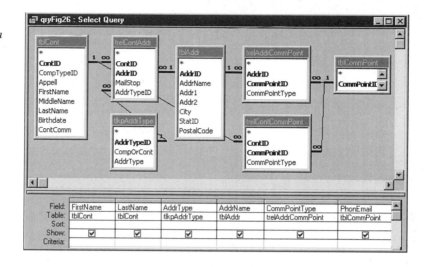

Fig. 10.27

Placing two copies of tblCommPoint *into the query from Figure 10.26 removes the circular reference.*

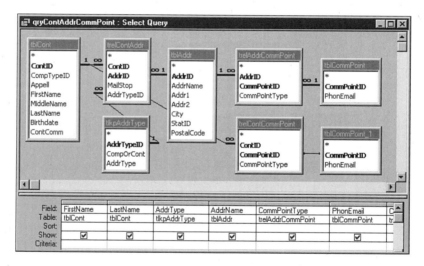

10

No discussion of high-powered query options would be complete without a mention of GROUP BY (aggregate) queries. Queries that "roll up" or summarize data are highly valuable when studying and manipulating data.

As you group records in a query, you can apply SQL aggregate functions to the data to affect the rollup and to provide additional information about the data in the query's result set. The SQL aggregate functions apply to a group of records called a *domain*.

When grouping data, one domain equates to the all of the records in the base table that constitute (roll-up to) a single record in the aggregate result set. In other words, assume that an address table has six records, three for Washington and three for Oregon. When a GROUP BY query is run against this data to group by the State field, the query's result set will have two records (one per unique state). However, each of the two records will be based on a different domain of three records each (the data records for that state). Thus, any domain aggregate function applied in the query will be first applied to the records in the Oregon domain and then to the Washington domain.

Fig. 10.28

The results of running the query in Figure 10.27 show address-related phone numbers and direct phone numbers for people.

First Name	Last Name	Address Type	Address Name	Comm. Point Type
Bob	Dobbs	Business or Employer	Seattle Office	Phone - Corporate
Bob	Dobbs	Business or Employer	Seattle Office	Phone - Corporate
Bob	Dobbs	Business or Employer	Seattle Office	Phone - Corporate
Marcia	Hobbs	Business or Employer	Redmond Office	Phone - Corporate
Marcia	Hobbs	Business or Employer	Redmond Office	Phone - Corporate
T.J.	Snobbs	Business or Employer	Seattle Office	Phone - Corporate
T.J.	Snobbs	Business or Employer	Seattle Office	Phone - Corporate
Fred	Sloan	Business or Employer	Supermall	Phone - Corporate
Fred	Sloan	Business or Employer	Supermall	Phone - Corporate
Fred	Sloan	Business or Employer	Supermall	Phone - Corporate
Fred	Sloan	Home - Primary	Easy Sleep Condominiums	Phone - Home
Fred	Sloan	Home - Primary	Easy Sleep Condominiums	Phone - Home
Fred	Sloan	Home - Primary	Easy Sleep Condominiums	Phone - Home

qryContAddrCommPoint : Select Query
Record: 1 of 13

Understanding this functionality is important because many Access users misconstrue how aggregate functions, especially First() and Last(), are applied to the underlying records. Essentially, the process is as follows:

1. Records are sorted according to the fields in the GROUP BY clause in the statement, sorting from left to right.

2. Each block of records that constitutes a domain is identified. These blocks are the groups of records identified by the lowest level of grouping.

3. Aggregate functions are applied to each domain, and the results are displayed as a record in the result set.

Here are the domain aggregate functions that can be used in queries:

Avg(). This function computes the average of a field in the records in the domain.

Count(). This function counts the number of records in the domain.

First(). This function returns a field in the first record in the domain. In a relational database, the concept of "first" is not specifically defined because table records are assumed to have no discernible order in their raw state. For practical purposes, however, Access usually uses the order in which records were created to select the first and last record in the domain.

Last(). This function returns a field in the last record in the domain, where "last" is defined based on the same criteria described for the First() function.

Max(). This function computes the largest value in a field in the domain.

Min(). This function computes the smallest value in a field in the domain.

StDev(). This function computes the standard deviation of a field in the records in the domain.

Sum(). This function computes the sum of a field in the domain's records.

Var(). This function computes the variance of a field in the records in the domain.

Using our sample contact database, assume that we want to find all people that have two or more direct phone numbers (cellular and car phones). Figure 10.29 shows a GROUP BY query that answers the question.

Fig. 10.29

This query uses a count to find people that have more than one direct phone number.

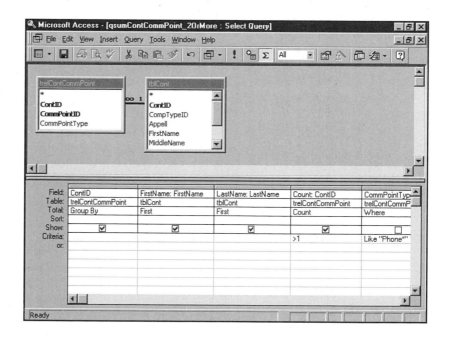

The SQL statement in Listing 10.17 drives the query shown in the figure.

Listing 10.17 AES_Tbl.Mdb—The SQL for the Query in Figure 10.29 Uses the SQL *Count* Function

```
SELECT
    trelContCommPoint.ContID,
    First(tblCont.FirstName) AS FirstName,
    First(tblCont.LastName) AS LastName,
    Count(trelContCommPoint.ContID) AS Count
```

```
FROM tblCont
   INNER JOIN trelContCommPoint ON tblCont.ContID = trelContCommPoint.ContID
WHERE trelContCommPoint.CommPointType Like "Phone*"
GROUP BY trelContCommPoint.ContID
HAVING Count(trelContCommPoint.ContID) > 1;
```

Driving the DAO from Program Code

As the name implies, the most important function of the Data Access Objects is to provide you with a way to manipulate data and the container objects that store it. For many developers, the DAO's ability to create a `Recordset` object attached to a `Database` object is the only part of this engine that they see.

Lurking within the DAO's object model, however, is the gateway to the actual structure of your Jet databases. The DAO can be made to perform these tasks in addition to manipulating recordsets:

> Explore the structural information about the Access forms, reports, macros, and modules in a database file

> Dissect the details of a data access error condition

> Create and update security profiles for a database file

> Create and modify tables, queries, relationships, indexes, and database properties

> Connect directly to ODBC data sources, bypassing Jet (see Chapter 19, "Exploring Client/Server Issues," for more on this)

Because many of the listed tasks can be performed from the Access user interface, their utility is marginal. For example, I rarely see developers creating and modifying security settings from program code written against the DAO. However, other features of the DAO can be downright exciting, especially the ability to create new tables and fields.

In the next two sections, I provide you with a practical example of writing DAO-based code. The example derives from the "Creating Data Structure Documents" section in Chapter 4, "Creating Design Specifications." In that chapter, I explained that I like to draft our database designs in Excel. Excel as a design tool provides easy sorting, grouping, dragging, copying, automating, printing, and similar tasks that are useful during the design process. At the end of the design process, I am left with a workbook filled with information and no database structure. I solve this problem with DAO code.

Structuring and Importing Schema Design Information

From Access, I've written code to extract the database design from Excel and build the tables listed there. The code for this is not complex, but the benefit is huge. My team members can spend several weeks at a customer site working with the users, designing the database structure in Excel and writing the specification document in Word. When the design is complete and approved by the users and by me, we simply run our Schema Builder tool against the workbook and produce a new database. For a large application, the tool can save several hours of typing table definitions from the specification document.

 Note

The Schema Builder tool is provided on the CD as SCHEMA.MDB, and the specification worksheet that drives it is there as well, in SPECSHEL.XLS.

Here is an outline of how the Schema Builder tool works:

1. *Populate a specification worksheet with a database definition.* During the design phase, we create an Excel worksheet that contains table and field attribute information. A worksheet is a handy tool because it can easily be modified on a laptop during design meetings, e-mailed to design team members for review, and quickly searched/audited in aggregate. Prototyping the database structure in Access during the design phase takes significantly more time than doing so in a worksheet.

2. *Populate a table in the Schema Builder with the design information.* We run a routine in the Schema Builder to import the specification information from the Excel worksheet into an Access definition table where it can drive the database-building process.

3. *Create tables and properties based on the database definition.* The main Schema Builder routines are run and use the information in the definition table to create tables, fields, properties, and indexes.

The starting point for the schema building process is an Excel worksheet created during the application design phase. The schema definition worksheet is shown in Figure 10.30.

The columns in the Excel worksheet match the items of information required by Jet to build a database structure, plus some informational items that are useful in the design and specification process. The columns we use in our design worksheet are listed in Table 10.12.

10

Fig. 10.30

The Excel schema design worksheet used by the Schema Builder tool.

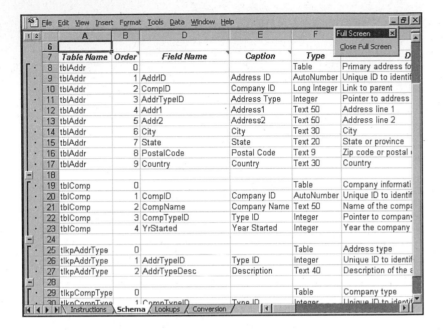

Table 10.12   The Columns in Our Excel Database Design Worksheet

Column	Contains
Table Name*	Table name
Order*	Field order within the table
Field Name*	Field name
Caption*	Field Caption property
Type*	Field data Type and Size properties
Description*	Field Description property
Ctl	Default control type to use for this field on forms
Index*	Type of index for this field
Reqd*	Field Required property
Linkage	Relationship of this field to a parent
Format*	Field Format property
Decimals*	Field DecimalPlaces property
Default*	Field DefaultValue property
Input Mask*	Field InputMask property
Value Source	Source of lookup values for field

Column	Contains
Validation*	Field `ValidationRule` property
Comments	Field comments

** These items are translated into Jet database property values by the Schema Builder and used during database creation. Worksheet columns in the table not noted with * are informational for developers but not used by the tool.*

Extracting the information from Excel is a simple matter of using Automation code. Each of the columns in the worksheet that will provide structure information to the Schema Builder is named as a range in Excel, so the tool can extract information from the worksheet based on range names and place the information into an Access work table.

The extraction process is table driven so that a developer can customize it for each operation. The process is as follows:

1. The developer determines the columns that he or she is interested in importing and flags the columns for import in a configuration table `lci_sb_tblXLSImportMap`. The table is shown in Figure 10.31. The table contains a record for each field in the database definition table that drives the Schema Builder. In turn, the fields in the database definition are mapped to Jet field properties (`AllowZeroLength`, `Attributes`, and so on). A field in the definition table holds information about one field's property in the database to be built.

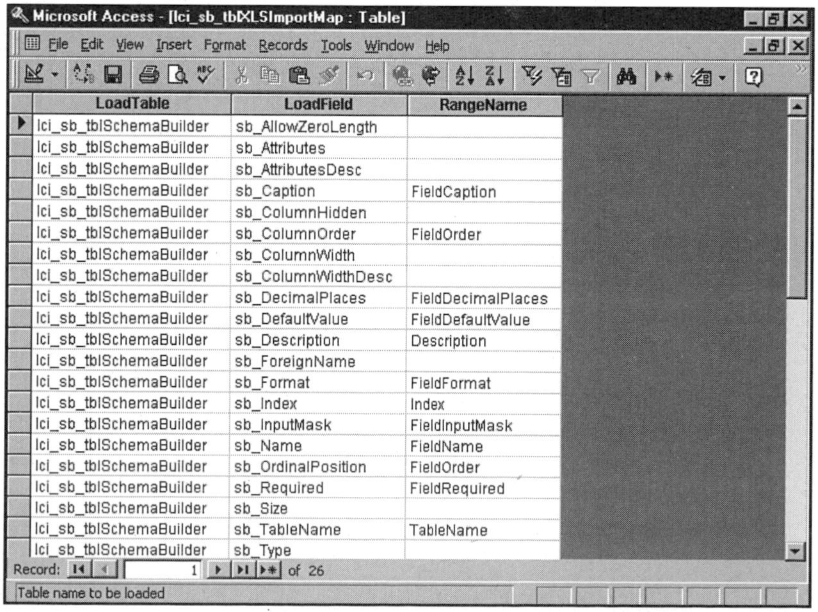

Microsoft Access - [lci_sb_tblXLSImportMap : Table]

LoadTable	LoadField	RangeName
lci_sb_tblSchemaBuilder	sb_AllowZeroLength	
lci_sb_tblSchemaBuilder	sb_Attributes	
lci_sb_tblSchemaBuilder	sb_AttributesDesc	
lci_sb_tblSchemaBuilder	sb_Caption	FieldCaption
lci_sb_tblSchemaBuilder	sb_ColumnHidden	
lci_sb_tblSchemaBuilder	sb_ColumnOrder	FieldOrder
lci_sb_tblSchemaBuilder	sb_ColumnWidth	
lci_sb_tblSchemaBuilder	sb_ColumnWidthDesc	
lci_sb_tblSchemaBuilder	sb_DecimalPlaces	FieldDecimalPlaces
lci_sb_tblSchemaBuilder	sb_DefaultValue	FieldDefaultValue
lci_sb_tblSchemaBuilder	sb_Description	Description
lci_sb_tblSchemaBuilder	sb_ForeignName	
lci_sb_tblSchemaBuilder	sb_Format	FieldFormat
lci_sb_tblSchemaBuilder	sb_Index	Index
lci_sb_tblSchemaBuilder	sb_InputMask	FieldInputMask
lci_sb_tblSchemaBuilder	sb_Name	FieldName
lci_sb_tblSchemaBuilder	sb_OrdinalPosition	FieldOrder
lci_sb_tblSchemaBuilder	sb_Required	FieldRequired
lci_sb_tblSchemaBuilder	sb_Size	
lci_sb_tblSchemaBuilder	sb_TableName	TableName
lci_sb_tblSchemaBuilder	sb_Type	

Record: 1 of 26

Table name to be loaded

Fig. 10.31

The Schema Builder imports values from the design worksheet that match the range names in the `RangeName` *column in this configuration table.*

2. The Schema Builder code looks at the configuration table to determine which fields to extract from the Excel worksheet. If the field is flagged in the configuration table by virtue of a value in the `RangeName` column, the tool looks for the matching range name in Excel and imports values from it.

3. The tool iterates through the worksheet and grabs the targeted information, placing each value in a destination table `lci_sb_tblSchemaBuilder` in the Access database. This is the definition table used by the Schema Builder. The name of the target definition table field for the information extracted from the worksheet is listed in the configuration table's `LoadField` column.

The process of importing from Excel is table-driven so that a developer can customize a worksheet for a particular project and still import the worksheet by changing values in the configuration table. For example, a client may be excited about using the worksheet to help us design their database but may want to simplify the worksheet by removing certain fields such as `Format` and `Validation`. Users often expect that we will create these properties during database development using our discretion. A reduced-scope worksheet can still be imported by the tool by removing the appropriate `RangeName` values from the configuration table.

Using a configuration table also allows the system to grow later. The table in the figure has field names in the schema definition table (in the `LoadField` column) that do not have a corresponding range (yet) in the design worksheet. Because our code is generic, however, and reads the configuration table, adding more columns to the worksheet to match fields in the definition table would require only the entry of the corresponding range name in the configuration table. No code would need to be changed.

 Tip

When you create tools or design application processes, try to make them easily reconfigurable like the example described here. Using values in a database table or enumerated constants in code are two ways to provide configuration information to a process that can easily be modified later without changing program logic.

The extraction code that is guided by the configuration table to pull information from the Excel worksheet is shown in the next three listings. All three listings combine to make the extraction routine `lci_sb_XLSDefnGet()`. I have removed variable declarations and simplified the listings to make them more readable, but you can infer the workings of a variable from its LNC tag and base name. For the complete code, see the example database on the CD-ROM.

Note

If you are interested in DAO coding but not concerned with learning the mechanics of Excel Automation, skip ahead to the section "Building a Database from Code."

Listing 10.18 shows the setup portion of the import routine. The code creates recordsets for the configuration table and for the definition table where the imported information will be placed. The code also opens an Automation instance of Excel and opens a schema worksheet.

Listing 10.18   Schema.Mdb—This Code Begins the Process of Importing Excel Data into an Access Table

```
Set dbs = CurrentDb

' Get list of ranges to import
' This recordset contains the records from the configuration table
'    that list a range name to import
Set rstXLSMap = dbs.OpenRecordset _
  ("SELECT * FROM lci_sb_tblXLSImportMap WHERE LoadTable = '" _
  & cstrSchemaTbl & "' AND RangeName IS NOT NULL", dbOpenSnapshot)
rstXLSMap.MoveLast

' The strCol array will hold the column number represented by each range
' The array is populated in Listing 10.18
ReDim strCol(rstXLSMap.RecordCount)  ' Array for ranges to import

' Get the target table
' This recordset will receive the new definition records created
'    with information from the worksheet
Set rstBuilder = dbs.OpenRecordset(cstrSchemaTbl, dbOpenDynaset)

' Open the schema worksheet
Set xlsapp = CreateObject("Excel.Application")
xlsapp.Workbooks.Open "C:\Data\Schema.Xls"
Set xlswkb = xlsapp.ActiveWorkbook
Set xlswks = xlswkb.Worksheets("Schema")
rstXLSMap.MoveFirst
```

10

The second block of Excel import code is shown in Listing 10.19. To facilitate the import, the worksheet row that holds the column headers (row 7 in Figure 10.30) has been given a range name of "Headers." The code in the listing identifies this row and places its number in a variable intHeadingRow. The variable is referenced by the import code to determine the starting row for the import process (in other words, the data to import starts on the row after the header row).

Next, the code populates an array with the column numbers that go with the range names to be imported. Each import range in the worksheet was originally defined as one column. The code pulls the column letter, such as "E," from the range and puts it into the array. This column letter is used later when walking down the rows in the worksheet, because the import code must read an entire row by cells in order to create one row for the Access table. To move across one worksheet row and only extract specific cells, the column letters in the array are used to create half of a target cell's address; the row number provides the other half of the address.

Listing 10.19   Schema.Mdb—This Code Establishes an Array and Other Variables that Map the Excel Data for Import

```
' Extract the dimensions of the Headers range
' Knowing where the header range is tells us where the data to import starts
' A range reference looks like this: =Schema!$7:$7
strWork = xlswkb.Names("Headers").RefersTo
intLoc = InStr(1, strWork, "!$")
intHeadingRow = Mid(strWork, intLoc + 2, 1)

iintLoop = 1

' Loop through the import range list and build an array with column
'    designations, one for each range to import
Do Until rstXLSMap.EOF
  intWorksheet = Len(xlswks.Name)   ' Length of worksheet name
  ' The RefersTo property returns the bounds of the range
  '    referred to by the range name, like =Schema!$7:$7
  strWork = xlswkb.Names(rstXLSMap!RangeName).RefersTo
  If Left(strWork, intWorksheet + 3) = "=" & xlswks.Name & "!$" Then
    ' Extract the letter of the range column, such as E
    strWork = Mid(strWork, intWorksheet + 4)
    intLoc = InStr(1, strWork & ":", ":")
    ' Add the column reference to the column array
    strCol(iintLoop) = Left(strWork, intLoc - 1)
  End If
  rstXLSMap.MoveNext
  iintLoop = iintLoop + 1
Loop

' Find last row in worksheet (as measured by column A data)
intRowMax = xlswks.Range("A1:A1").SpecialCells(xlLastCell).Row
```

The final portion of the import routine is shown in Listing 10.20. This code uses the values and objects established in the previous two listings to loop through the worksheet, extracting cell values and loading them into the database definition table in Access.

The code loops from the first data row (after the header row) to the end of the active area of the worksheet. As it loops, it creates a row/column cell address from the saved array values built in the previous listing and pulls a value from the identified cell. The cell's value is loaded into the Access database definition table.

Listing 10.20   Schema.Mdb—Desired Cells in the Worksheet Are Identified and Used to Populate the Access Table

```
' Loop through each row in the worksheet that has field definitions
For iintRow = intHeadingRow + 1 To intRowMax

   ' Only proceed if the first cell in the row has data
   If Not IsEmpty(xlswks.Range("A" & iintRow).Value) Then
      rstXLSMap.MoveFirst
      iintLoop = 1
      rstBuilder.AddNew   ' Create a definition table record
      ' Loop through the list of ranges to import
      Do Until rstXLSMap.EOF
         ' Load the destination table with the worksheet value
         ' A Boolean field like Required in the definition table must be
         '   translated from the text on the worksheet, all other values
         '   are stuffed into the table verbatim
         Select Case rstBuilder.Fields(rstXLSMap!LoadField).Type
            Case dbBoolean   ' Convert Yes/No on worksheet into Boolean
               rstBuilder(rstXLSMap!LoadField) = _
                  (xlswks.Range(strCol(iintLoop) & CStr(iintRow)).Value = "Yes")
            Case Else
               rstBuilder(rstXLSMap!LoadField) = _
                  xlswks.Range(strCol(iintLoop) & CStr(iintRow)).Value
         End Select
         rstXLSMap.MoveNext
         iintLoop = iintLoop + 1
      Loop
      rstBuilder.Update
   End If
Next iintRow

xlsapp.Application.[Quit]
Set xlsapp = Nothing
```

α Note

The Excel code in the previous listing is "legacy" code, something we wrote years ago and continue to milk. It has not been upgraded to newer versions of Excel over the years and may not reflect the best approach under Excel 97. Because this chapter is not an Excel tutorial, I did not spend time optimizing the extraction code; you should feel free to do so.

After running the code in the three listings in this section, the schema definition information has been pulled from Excel into an Access table. The populated table is shown in the section that follows.

Building a Database from Code

In the previous section, we explored Automation code to run an extraction process that pulled database definition information from an Excel worksheet. The Excel information was transferred to an Access definition table called `lci_sb_tblSchemaBuilder`, as shown in Figure 10.32.

Fig. 10.32

This database definition table contains enough information to allow the Schema Builder to build a complete database.

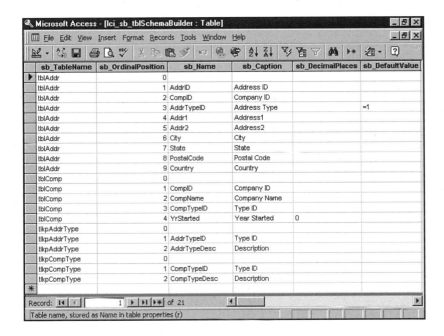

sb_TableName	sb_OrdinalPosition	sb_Name	sb_Caption	sb_DecimalPlaces	sb_DefaultValue
tblAddr	0				
tblAddr	1	AddrID	Address ID		
tblAddr	2	CompID	Company ID		
tblAddr	3	AddrTypeID	Address Type		=1
tblAddr	4	Addr1	Address1		
tblAddr	5	Addr2	Address2		
tblAddr	6	City	City		
tblAddr	7	State	State		
tblAddr	8	PostalCode	Postal Code		
tblAddr	9	Country	Country		
tblComp	0				
tblComp	1	CompID	Company ID		
tblComp	2	CompName	Company Name		
tblComp	3	CompTypeID	Type ID		
tblComp	4	YrStarted	Year Started	0	
tlkpAddrType	0				
tlkpAddrType	1	AddrTypeID	Type ID		
tlkpAddrType	2	AddrTypeDesc	Description		
tlkpCompType	0				
tlkpCompType	1	CompTypeID	Type ID		
tlkpCompType	2	CompTypeDesc	Description		

Record: 1 of 21

Table name, stored as Name in table properties (r)

 Note

The process described here depends on a database definition table, but the table need not be populated from Excel. The techniques here can still provide value to your development process even if you are not interested in designing databases in a worksheet.

As long as you can populate the database definition table with the required information, you can run the Schema Builder routines against it. To populate the table without Excel, you could import schema information from another modeling program such as InfoModeler, key the information in by hand, or create an Access form to help you define the table and field layouts that populate the table.

The database definition table shown in the figure provides the information for the schema creation process, a process that involves DAO code. The process simply iterates through the records in the schema definition table and builds a database structure from the information.

The following four listings divulge the majority of the core code in the Schema Builder. I have removed variable declarations, error trapping, and special scenario testing in order to simplify the listings to make them more readable. You can infer the type of a variable from its LNC tag and the purpose from the name or value assignment. For the complete code, see the example database on the CD-ROM.

The driving routine for the creation of tables and fields is in Listing 10.21.

Listing 10.21   Schema.Mdb—This Routine Takes Schema Definition Information from a Table and Creates New Tables and Fields

```
Public Function lci_sb_TblCreate() As Boolean
' Purpose:    Create new tables from field definitions in a table

   Const cstrSchemaTbl = "lci_sb_tblSchemaBuilder"

   Set dbs = CurrentDb
   ' Get table names
   Set rstTblDefn = dbs.OpenRecordset _
      ("SELECT sb_TableName, sb_Description FROM " & cstrSchemaTbl _
        & " WHERE sb_TableName IS NOT NULL AND sb_OrdinalPosition = 0" _
        & " ORDER BY sb_TableName", dbOpenSnapshot)

   ' Loop through definition table
   Do Until rstTblDefn.EOF

      ' Note: Jet requires that we create the table and fields first,
      '    then add the properties after the table is appended

      ' Create the new table
      varTbl = rstTblDefn!sb_TableName
      Set rstFldDefn = dbs.OpenRecordset _
        ("SELECT * FROM " & cstrSchemaTbl _
          & " WHERE sb_TableName = '" & varTbl & "' AND sb_OrdinalPosition > 0" _
          & " ORDER BY sb_OrdinalPosition", dbOpenSnapshot)
      Set tdf = dbs.CreateTableDef(varTbl)

      ' Loop through one table's fields and create them
      Do Until rstFldDefn.EOF
         ' Create fields
         blnRet = lci_sb_FldCreate(rstFldDefn, tdf)  ' Create one field
         rstFldDefn.MoveNext
      Loop

      dbs.TableDefs.Append tdf  ' Append table to database
      ' Cannot add custom property to table until after it's appended
      dbs.TableDefs.Refresh
      intRet = lci_sb_TblPrpCreate(tdf, "Description", dbText _
        , rstTblDefn!sb_Description)
```

10

continues

Listing 10.21   Continued

```
    ' Loop through one table's fields and create properties
    rstFldDefn.MoveFirst
    Do Until rstFldDefn.EOF
      ' Add field properties
      Set fld = tdf.Fields(rstFldDefn!sb_Name)
      blnRet = lci_sb_FldPrpCreate(rstFldDefn, fld)   ' Create properties
      If blnRet And Not IsNull(rstFldDefn!sb_Index) Then
        Call lci_sb_IdxCreate(rstFldDefn, tdf)   ' Create field index
      End If
      rstFldDefn.MoveNext
    Loop

    rstTblDefn.MoveNext
  Loop

End Function
```

The flow of the code in the listing is dissected as follows:

1. *Create the table list.* A recordset `rstTblDefn` is created that contains the table names to be built. The recordset grabs records from the definition table that are flagged as table definition records; my flagging strategy uses a value of 0 in the column order position to designate a table definition record. Records with a non-zero column order value are field definition records and follow after the table definition. Refer to Figure 10.32 for clarification.

2. *Create a table.* Each new table is defined by creating a `TableDef` object variable, using this line:

   ```
   Set tdf = dbs.CreateTableDef(varTbl)
   ```

   To build a table using DAO code, you must first create a `TableDef` object, as shown. Then you must add fields to the table object's `Fields` collection (see step 3 following). Finally, you must use the `TableDefs.Append` method to add the defined table to the database structure (see step 4).

3. *Create the fields.* After a table is created, its fields are added. The field information for one table is gathered from the definition table by creating a second recordset `rstFldDefn`. This recordset is looped and each new field for the table is created by the function `lci_sb_FldCreate()`, as described in Listing 10.22.

4. *Save the table.* Jet requires that a table and its fields be added to the database structure before properties such as the field caption can be added. Once the code has created and named a table, created and named the fields, and assigned field data types, it adds the table to the database like this:

   ```
   dbs.TableDefs.Append tdf   ' Append table to database
   ```

   The DAO does its best to keep information current for the benefit of your program code, but over the years I have seen instances where code can get ahead of the object structure it is creating in Jet. To prevent this, I habitually refresh DAO collections after populating them, as shown in this line from the listing:

```
dbs.TableDefs.Refresh
```

5. *Add the properties.* After a table and its basic field definitions are saved to the database structure, you can add property information to either. The code in the listing makes a second pass through the recordset of table fields in order to attach properties to each field. The work is done by a subordinate function, `lci_sb_FldPrpCreate()`, that is described in Listing 10.23:

```
Set fld = tdf.Fields(rstFldDefn!sb_Name)
blnRet = lci_sb_FldPrpCreate(rstFldDefn, fld)  ' Create properties
```

6. *Create the indexes.* After properties for a field are added, the field's definition information is inspected to see if the field will be indexed. If so, an `Indexes` collection object is created using the code for `lci_sb_IdxCreate()` in Listing 10.24:

```
Call lci_sb_IdxCreate(rstFldDefn, tdf)  ' Create field index
```

7. *Repeat.* Steps 2 through 5 are repeated for each table listed in the controlling recordset of table names (`rstTblDefn`).

The looping routine in the previous listing calls several subordinate functions that use DAO code to create database objects. The first function called creates fields in the target table, as shown in Listing 10.22.

Listing 10.22   Schema.Mdb—DAO Code to Create New Fields in a Table Definition

```
Public Function lci_sb_FldCreate(rrstDefn As Recordset _
  , rtdf As TableDef) As Boolean
' Purpose:   Create a new field based on definition table
' Arguments: rrstDefn:=Schema definition recordset
'            rtdf:=Tabledef to create field in

  Dim fld    As Field    ' New field
  Dim intRet As Integer  ' Returned by field type enum

  Set fld = rtdf.CreateField(rrstDefn!sb_Name)
  intRet = lci_sb_FldSizeGet(rrstDefn!sb_TypeDesc)  ' Get TEXT size or -1
  If intRet <> -1 Then  ' Only set Size if one was returned
    fld.Size = intRet
  End If
  intRet = lci_sb_FldTypeToEnum(rrstDefn!sb_TypeDesc)  ' Get field type
  fld.Type = intRet
  rtdf.Fields.Append fld  ' Append field to table

End Function
```

10

To create a new field, the code in the previous listing first creates a new field object and names it:

```
Set fld = rtdf.CreateField(rrstDefn!sb_Name)
```

Next, the code sets the size and data type of the field. Two functions are called to help with this process: `lci_sb_FldSizeGet()` and `lci_sb_FldSizeToEnum()`. The first function simply takes the field type description from the definition table, such as "TEXT 12," and extracts the field size ("12") for use by the Jet `Size` property. The second function uses this same field type string but translates the field type (such as "TEXT") into an integer value that specifies a valid Jet `Type` property (for example, a `Text` field is represented internally by the Jet field type value 10).

Finally, the code in the listing adds the new field to the table definition:

```
rtdf.Fields.Append fld   ' Append field to table
```

For each new field that is added to the table, several properties must be set to the values described in the definition table. The properties include `Caption`, `DefaultValue`, and `ValidationRule`. Each of these properties must be created and appended to the new field after the table is saved to the database structure.

The code in Listing 10.23 shows how to create new properties and their values or set the value of existing properties. Notice the differentiation I made in the previous sentence: between *new* and *existing* properties. When a new field is created, it comes with a base set of properties provided by Jet, plus you can add your own. The difference is not immediately obvious when exploring Access.

In a nutshell, Jet has a core set of properties that define a field. For example, the properties from the definition table described in this section that are native to Jet are:

```
AllowZeroLength

DefaultValue

Required

Size

Type

ValidationRule

ValidationText
```

These properties can be set directly during creation of a new field using the syntax:

```
fieldobject.property = value
```

In contrast, Jet is not aware by default of properties that Access creates to benefit the Access interface or application model. Jet allows Access to add *custom properties* to a `Field` object, and after they are added Jet treats them as its own. Here are the properties the Schema Builder adds via the database definition table that are actually custom Access properties and not native to Jet:

    Caption

    DecimalPlaces

    Description

    Format

    InputMask

 Tip

> To see all of the properties that are native to Jet, browse the `Field` object in the DAO library via the Object Browser.

Because several properties that are known to Jet are created via the Schema Builder, the routine `lci_sb_FldCreate()` in Listing 10.22 could continue defining Jet-specific properties before appending the field to the new table. Alternately, the Jet-specific and the Access custom properties can all be added at the same time. I have opted for the latter model but either is equally appropriate.

Listing 10.23 shows the routine that is called by the Schema Builder to add property values to a new field. The routine, `lci_sb_FldPrpCreate()`, accepts a pointer to the newly created field and adds the ten property values from the definition table recordset to the field. (The listing only shows one of the ten properties to save space; the syntax for each removed item is similar to the one shown.)

The second routine in the listing, `lci_sb_FldPrpCreateOne()`, is called by the first routine (`lci_sb_FldPrpCreate()`) to do the actual work of property creation. Notice how the routine can set both Jet (native) and Access (custom) properties. The dual personality is provided by the error trapping in the routine. The function first attempts to set the prescribed property value, assuming that the property exists:

```
rfld.Properties(rstrPrpName).Value = rvarPrpValue
```

If the property does exist, as in the case of `AllowZeroLength` and other native properties listed above, the property value is set by this line and no error is generated. On the other hand, if the property is a custom Access property, it will not exist for a new field until it is explicitly created. The code in Listing 10.23 handles this by creating and appending the new property to the field like this:

```
Set prp = rfld.CreateProperty(rstrPrpName, rintPrpType, rvarPrpValue)
rfld.Properties.Append prp
```

Listing 10.23   Schema.Mdb—DAO Code to Create New Properties in a Field Definition

```
Public Function lci_sb_FldPrpCreate(rrstDefn As Recordset _
  , rfld As Field) As Boolean
' Purpose:   Add field properties based on definition table
' Arguments: rrstDefn:=Schema definition recordset
'            rfld:=Field to add properties to

  Dim blnRet As Boolean  ' Property creator return value

  ' AllowZeroLength property
  If Not IsNull(rrstDefn!sb_AllowZeroLength) Then
    blnRet = lci_sb_FldPrpCreateOne(rfld, "AllowZeroLength" _
      , dbInteger, rrstDefn!sb_AllowZeroLength)
  End If
  ' …All other field properties are created here;
  '   the code has been removed…

End Function


Function lci_sb_FldPrpCreateOne(rfld As Field, rstrPrpName As String _
  , rintPrpType As Integer, rvarPrpValue As Variant) As Boolean
' Purpose:    Create one field property
' Arguments: rfld:=Field to create property on
'            rstrPrpName:=Property name
'            rintPrpType:=Property type
'            rvarPrpValue:=Property value

  Const cstrErrPrpNonExistent = 3270
  Dim prp As Property

  Err.Clear  ' Next line will generate an error if no property
  rfld.Properties(rstrPrpName).Value = rvarPrpValue
  If Err <> 0 Then  ' Property not found
    If Err <> cstrErrPrpNonExistent Then  ' Non-handleable error
      GoTo lci_sb_FldPrpCreateOne_Exit
    Else  ' Property not found
      Err.Clear  ' Next lines will generate an error if property info invalid
      Set prp = rfld.CreateProperty(rstrPrpName, rintPrpType, rvarPrpValue)
      rfld.Properties.Append prp
      If Err <> 0 Then  ' Abort
        GoTo lci_sb_FldPrpCreateOne_Exit
      End If
    End If
  End If

End Function
```

The final missing puzzle piece in the origination of a new database from DAO-centric code is the creation of indexes. The Schema Builder checks the controlling recordset to see if the index information for the table is not blank. If it is not, the routine in Listing 10.24 is called to create and append an index to the new table.

Listing 10.24   Schema.Mdb—This Routine Creates a New Index Programmatically

```
Public Sub lci_sb_IdxCreate(rrstDefn As Recordset, rtdf As TableDef)
' Purpose:    Create a new index based on definition table
' Arguments: rrstDefn:=Schema definition recordset
'                rtdf:=Tabledef to create index for

  Dim fld As Field
  Dim idx As Index

  Select Case rrstDefn!sb_Index
    Case "PK"
      Set idx = rtdf.CreateIndex("PrimaryKey")
      Set fld = idx.CreateField(rrstDefn!sb_Name)
      idx.Primary = True
      idx.Fields.Append fld
      rtdf.Indexes.Append idx
    Case "D"
      Set idx = rtdf.CreateIndex(rrstDefn!sb_Name)
      Set fld = idx.CreateField(rrstDefn!sb_Name)
      idx.Fields.Append fld
      rtdf.Indexes.Append idx
    Case "U"
      Set idx = rtdf.CreateIndex(rrstDefn!sb_Name)
      Set fld = idx.CreateField(rrstDefn!sb_Name)
      idx.Unique = True
      idx.Fields.Append fld
      rtdf.Indexes.Append idx
  End Select

End Sub
```

10

Notice in the listing the specific steps required to create an index. You must first create and name an Index-type object:

```
Set idx = rtdf.CreateIndex("PrimaryKey")
```

An Index object is actually a collection of the fields that make up the index. Thus, you must next create a field to place in the index, using the CreateField method:

```
Set fld = idx.CreateField(rrstDefn!sb_Name)
```

If an index field will serve as the primary key of the table, set the index's Primary property value accordingly:

```
idx.Primary = True
```

Otherwise, set this value to `False`, and use the `Unique` property to specify whether (`True`) or not (`False`) the index allows duplicate values:

```
idx.Unique = True
```

Finally, your code must add the field to the index and the index to the table:

```
idx.Fields.Append fld
rtdf.Indexes.Append idx
```

Figure 10.33 shows a table that was created directly from an Excel-based definition by the Schema Builder shown in this section.

Fig. 10.33

The Schema Builder created this table and its properties from information in Excel.

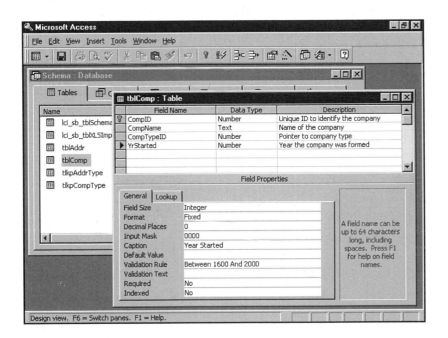

> **Tip**
>
> It took only one second of execution time for the Schema Builder to create the four tables shown in the definition table in Figure 10.32. We've used this tool to create a database with over a hundred tables in just a few minutes. Compare the few minutes to the manual entry time that would be required to build a hundred tables in the Access interface, and you'll quickly see why programming the DAO can be so rewarding.

Whether or not you choose to use the tool described in this section, the techniques that it demonstrates are exciting and powerful. Few database products provide you with as much control of the database objects and their properties as does Access coupled with the Data Access Objects engine. Not only does coding against the DAO object model allow you to create database objects as shown here, you can modify the properties of objects in bulk, write your own documentation routines, or export your database structure to another platform—all using VBA code.

From Here...

In this chapter, you've explored some of the issues that crop up regularly when designing and building tables and queries. A solid, intelligent database structure is one of the fundamental elements of an expert solution.

▶ Creating well-designed databases is almost impossible without a good research and design phase at the outset of a project, as detailed in Chapter 3, "Preparing for Development."

▶ Review Chapter 7, "Understanding Application Architecture," for the terminology used to describe tables and queries. This chapter also describes data warehousing and the need for special data structures to support the use of the warehouse.

▶ Chapter 13, "Mastering Combo and List Boxes," puts your optimized queries to good use in application forms.

▶ To explore issues involved in the use of tables and queries in a client/server environment, see Chapter 19, "Exploring Client/Server Issues."

10

chapter 11

Expert Approaches to VBA

In this chapter

◆ **A summary of the best new VBA features for coders**

◆ **A tour of the Access Application object model**

◆ **Examples of code that manipulate the Access object model through Automation**

◆ **Suggestions for creating well-structured code and for creating a consistent development style**

◆ **Tips for making your application code run as rapidly as possible**

I f you're still relying on macros in your application development, I suspect that Access 97 will cause you to change your style. The enhanced power, flexibility, and usability of the latest release of VBA are impossible to ignore, and a well-constructed expert solution is usually teeming with custom objects and procedures. This chapter shows you how to use VBA effectively.

Basic Priorities

"Removing Embedded Basic (the Access 2 code engine) from Access 95 and inserting Visual Basic for Applications in its place was akin to a heart, lung, and liver transplant on our product all at once. The effort was extraordinarily complex and required more than five person-years of development time.

"Yet, when most users look at the result, they get more excited about the color-coded syntax in the code editor than the more substantial—and more painful—enhancements that VBA brought to the product."

Tod Nielsen, General Manager, Microsoft Access Business Unit

As Tod's introductory sidebar implies, changing the coding engine in Access from Access Basic (also called *Embedded Basic* or *EB*) to Visual Basic for Applications (*VBA*) was no simple task. EB had much in common syntactically with its siblings Visual Basic 3 and the Visual Basic for Applications in Excel and Project, but was based on a different engine. EB was woven into Access at a very low level, and some of it was written in Assembler for the best performance. VBA, in contrast, is a service external to Access, much like the Jet Database Engine, and is written entirely in C.

Microsoft was highly motivated to move to one common Basic dialect and engine for all of its development applications. The benefits of this standardization to you as a developer are threefold:

Reduced learning curve. Microsoft is distributing Basic more widely each year, adding it to everything from the entire Office suite to its Internet browsers and servers. As a solution developer, you can now learn one rendition of the Basic language and one development interface, then carry your skills and experience with Access VBA into your work with other VBA host products.

Code Portability. One of the current developer buzzwords is *reusable objects,* a term that describes self-contained *servers* (or something that provides *services* to an application). In order for a code procedure to qualify as a reusable object, you must be able to carry code from one host application into another to use it unmodified. VBA provides this capability.

Shared Resources. By sharing a centralized coding and runtime environment, multiple tools and applications on your machine share the same dynamic link libraries and type libraries. The performance of your workstation improves when you have fewer resources loaded to memory, and this speeds up your development efforts. Disk space consumption, application deployment efforts, and version control issues are all favorably impacted as well when multiple applications on your machine share central services.

The Access team took a courageous leap by pulling VBA into Access. To understand the magnitude of the effort, you must first understand that VBA thinks in terms of *projects*, or integrated work sets of *classes* (code and objects). The project-centric metaphor integrates well with Visual Basic and other hosts, but in the case of Access proved particularly problematic. The Access environment provided an especially difficult environment for the following assumptions made by VBA:

▶ *VBA wants to treat all code in memory as one project.* Access does not provide an environment quite this simple, because your application can use wizard or library code external to the current project.

▶ *VBA wants a project to be used by a single user and saved in aggregate.* The Access environment is far from this metaphor, because database objects can be modified, saved, or deleted by multiple users simultaneously.

▶ *VBA wants only code, not objects, to be changed during application execution.* Access confuses VBA by allowing code in one object (an open form, for example) to be executing while a different object (new report, for example) is being created.

Pulling VBA into Access meant teaching the two components to get along despite these and other differences in approach and structure.

While the Basic language and its interface may now be mostly standardized, the way people write code certainly is not. Throughout this book, I use the term *style* to refer to *your* unique approach to application development. One of the aspects of your personal style is how you write code.

For example, there is more than one way to name objects, more than one way to compose code comments, and more than one way to perform file operations. The more time you spend writing application code, the more likely you are to develop standardized approaches to development of Basic code routines.

Standardizing your approach to VBA coding requires that you first understand the best way to apply its features. This chapter provides a discussion of the issues involved in creating consistent and reliable VBA code. Here, we explore the important aspects of VBA development and investigate techniques that make your development work more productive.

11

 Note

This chapter is *not* a VBA tutorial. It assumes that you have some familiarity with writing Basic code in Access and want to learn new features and approaches. You can prepare for this chapter by reading the VBA lessons in Que's *Access 97 Power Programming* by F. Scott Barker.

Implementing Major New VBA Features

There's a lot more to VBA in Access than just color-coded syntax. There were some very important changes and additions to Access' coding language between versions 2 and 95. I'll summarize them in case you missed them:

▶ The *improved code editor* allows you to view procedures in a module continuously and to set Watch expressions during program execution. It also provides automatic code indentation.

▶ A *line continuation character* (_) makes writing readable code much easier.

▶ You can create *references* to type libraries, other databases, and similar providers of external services. A reference from one Access database to another database or external service is a pointer that allows code in the current database to call objects and procedures in the referenced file.

 Note

A *type library* is a file that lists descriptions of the object model (objects, properties, and methods) of a program or service provider. A type library can be embedded within a dynamic link library (DLL) or ActiveX control (OCX) file, or can be stored in a stand-alone (TLB or OLB) file.

▶ *Automation* of Access from a controller application has been made possible by exposing the Application object.

▶ By creating Public variables and Property procedures in forms and reports, these objects can act as *class modules*, or templates that define the properties of object variables.

▶ The New *keyword* enables your code to create an instance of an object at the time of definition, and multiple instances of the same object class.

▶ The Optional *and* ParamArray *keywords* provide more flexibility in passing arguments to procedures. The Optional keyword is used in a procedure declaration to indicate that the procedure can be called without the argument. The ParamArray keyword is also used in procedure declarations and indicates that the argument to be passed in the specified position will be an array.

▶ *Conditional compilation* allows your program to react to global flags at compile time and only compile selective chunks of code.

▶ Several *new data types* expand the realm of coding possibilities: Boolean (representing True and False), Byte (representing 0 to 255), and Date (representing a date and time). These types come with corresponding conversion functions: CBool(), CByte(), and CDate().

▶ *User-defined data types* are now more flexible: you can nest one user-defined type within another, and you can ReDim arrays within user-defined types.

▶ The *With statement* reduces code clutter and enhances readability and performance. With establishes an instant object pointer (variable) and allows your code to reuse that pointer over and over.

▶ A *For Each statement* allows your code to loop through a collection or array and visit all members.

▶ The *KeyPreview property* of forms allows your code to detect keyboard events passed to the form before the keystroke is received by the target control.

▶ A *CancelEvent method* provides you with another mechanism to nullify an event procedure that is in process.

▶ The *Array() function* creates an instant Variant array from a list of values.

▶ Variant variables can now be *error variables* of type vbError, and you can create and detect these variables with the new CVErr() and IsError() functions.

▶ *File handling* improvements include the addition of the functions and statements FileCopy (copies a disk file), FileDateTime() (returns a file's date stamp), FileLen() (returns the length of a file in bytes), GetAttr() (returns a file's attributes), and SetAttr (sets a file's attributes).

▶ Detection of *object types and states* is easier with these new functions: IsArray() (tells whether a variable represents an array), IsError() (tells whether a variable is of type vbError), IsMissing() (tells whether an optional argument was passed to a procedure), and IsObject() (tells whether a variable is an object type).

▶ You can work with *Windows registry settings* from code by using the functions and statements DeleteSetting (deletes a registry section or key), GetAllSettings() (returns an array of registry key settings), GetSetting() (returns an individual registry key setting), and SaveSetting (saves or creates a registry key entry).

▶ The *Nz() function* enables you to easily convert a Null value to another value or string.

▶ The *TypeName() function* returns a string value that describes the type definition of a variable.

▶ *Startup and environmental options* can be set and retrieved from code. This allows your code to read and write property settings found in the Startup dialog and the Options dialog box.

The Access 97 release of VBA offers the following additional enhancements:

▶ Forms can now be stored without a code module or any binding to VBA (see the discussion of *lightweight forms* in Chapter 12, "Understanding Form Structures and Coding").

▶ VBA module *storage requirements* (for both disk and RAM) have been reduced from their bloated Access 95 footprint.

▶ The `Module` *object and* `Modules` *collection* provide you with programmatic access to VBA source code (see Chapter 20, "Applying Development Shortcuts," for more information).

▶ Your code can now add, remove, and inspect references via a `References` *collection*.

▶ The Debug window Locals tab now displays *local variables* and their values. Structured items like arrays, objects, and user-defined types are displayed in a hierarchical model.

▶ *Debugging commands have been moved* from the Run menu to a new Debug menu, and an option to Compile and Save All Modules has been added. A new Step Out command on this menu tells your code to execute the current procedure and all procedures it calls and then pause when this operation is done.

▶ When your code is paused during execution, you can hover the mouse over a variable or expression in the paused code and Access displays an *Auto Data Tip* (like a tool tip) containing the current value of the item.

▶ The new *Auto List Members* feature shows a list of members (objects, properties, methods, and constants) for an object name you have typed in the module editor.

▶ *Property procedures* now allow `Optional` arguments in their declaration. This gives your code more flexibility when calling custom class properties. In any type of procedure, `Optional` arguments can now be given a data type rather than being restricted to the `Variant` type.

▶ When you type a recognized command in the module editor followed by a space or an open parenthesis, Access now displays a small floating syntax diagram (called *Auto Quick Info*) that describes the syntax of the command.

▶ Pressing Shift+F2 on the name of a variable, procedure, or object in the module editor jumps to *the most appropriate definition* assistance for that item. For example, Shift+F2 on a variable name jumps to its declaration line and Shift+F2 on an object name loads the Object Browser and locates the object's definition.

▶ You can *press F5* in a `Sub` procedure to instantly begin executing the procedure or the form the procedure resides in, or press *F8* to begin single-stepping through the procedure from the beginning.

▶ You can set *bookmarks* in the module editor that place a marker at a code line, then you can cycle through the markers to return to marked locations. Code bookmarks are not saved when the database closes.

Learning about these new VBA features comes faster than actually *understanding* how to apply them. The new traits have broad applicability and can be mixed and matched in various ways when you are concocting creative code solutions. In the next few sections, I focus on the new features that are the most useful in application development.

Using the Application Object Model Enhancements

Access 95 introduced the Application object, which is a pointer to the current application (database file). The Application object allows Access to support the Automation object model and exposes more of Access to calling programs. As a result, you can now automate an Access application from any VBA code (Access or non-Access).

The Forms collection (pointers to each open form in an application) and the Reports collection are now contained within the new Application object, and the DoCmd and Screen objects have also been attached to it. These are all objects that you are familiar with from the days of Access 1, with these notable changes:

▶ References to the former DoCmd *actions* have been replaced by references to *methods* of the DoCmd object, as in this line:

```
Application.DoCmd.OpenForm "frmAutomation"
```

▶ DoCmd.DoMenuItem has been replaced by the RunCommand method, which translates menu options into unique integer values.

Refer to the DoCmd or Screen objects from code in a controlling application by directing your code toward their Application object parent. For example, you can use the following lines of code to work with these objects in an Access application serving as an Automation server whose instance is referenced by the Application object variable accappNwind:

```
accappNwind.DoCmd.SelectObject acForm, "Main Switchboard"
If accappNwind.Screen.ActiveForm.Name = " Main Switchboard" Then...
```

Putting Access to Work via Automation

You refer to the Application object or a variable built on it when you need to address the entire application, one of its settings, or one of its primary subordinate objects. Access exposes the Application object to code within the current database file so that you can affect the current database and also uses this object type as the primary interface to an "instance" of Access acting as an Automation server.

You can refer to an `Application` object from three different places:

> *From within the current Access application.* Use the `Application` object reference as a portal to its collections, methods, and properties in the current application. You can specify the keyword `Application` to improve code clarity, but within the current application a reference to the keyword is redundant and unnecessary. Thus, the three syntaxes in Listing 11.1 perform the same task on the current application, but the first one is the easiest to code; the second is the most readable; and the third is nonsensical in that it creates an object variable where one is not required.

Listing 11.1 Three Ways to Address a Member of the Application Object

```
Debug.Print CurrentObjectName

' The explicit variation
Debug.Print Application.CurrentObjectName

' Utilizing an object variable
Dim appCurr As Application
Set appCurr = Application   ' Points to the current Application object

Debug.Print appCurr.CurrentObjectName
```

> *From another VBA application.* A "controller" or "controlling" application is one that can refer to the Access object library (MSACC8.OLB) and act as an Automation controller driving Access as a server. For example, Excel, Project, and Visual Basic have this capability.

> *From another session of Access.* This feature enables you to modularize your applications and share objects between Access applications. For example, several different applications could use Automation code to launch a shared reporting application and print a customer report.

You drive Access as an Automation server by using the `Application` object as the entry point to *instantiate* (create an *instance*) of Access from VBA code. From within Access, Office, Project, or Visual Basic VBA code, create an object variable using the `Access.Application` object with `Dim`. Directly referencing an application's type in the `Dim` statement is called *early binding*, as contrasted to using an `Object` variable (*late binding*). Early binding produces the fastest-executing code:

```
Dim accappNwind As Access.Application
Set accappNwind = CreateObject("Access.Application.8")
```

Your VBA project must have a reference to the Access object library MSACC8.OLB in order to bind to the `Access.Application` object. The code shown previously is best in an environment where users could have more than one version of Access on their workstation. The explicit version number in the `CreateObject` call assures that the code instantiates the desired Access version.

If versioning is not a concern, your code can use the `New` keyword to launch an instance of whatever the Windows registry considers the default version of Access:

```
Dim accappNwind As New Access.Application
```

Caution

The `AutoExec` macro and startup form declared in the Startup properties execute in an Automation instance of Access as they would in a normal user instance. You generally will not want an application used as an Automation server to have either of these objects. (For example, for purposes of the sample code in this section, you need to disable the startup form in Northwind.)

Access is an *out-of-process* OLE server, defined as, "a stand-alone, executable program that runs in its own address space." Access meets this definition because it must serve the needs of controller applications as well as desktop users. (In contrast, an ActiveX control is an example of an *in-process* server, defined as a DLL, OCX, or other file that always requires a host or controlling application.)

Tip

An Automation session between a controller application and Access as a server requires a *connection* (a communication pipeline) between the two players. You can improve the performance of Automation operations by optimizing connection usage. See the section "Speeding Up Automation" later in this chapter for hints.

Once you've created an object variable that points to an Access `Application` object, Access is running as an Automation server and the properties and methods of the `Application` object can be referenced, as in this example:

```
' Open a database
accappNwind.OpenCurrentDatabase "C:\Office\Samples\Northwind.Mdb"
' Print a report by referring to its Application parent
accappNwind.DoCmd.OpenReport "Catalog"
```

When a new Automation instance of Access is created, the instance is by default *not visible*. (The Visible property of the application is False; in actual fact, the instance is minimized—not invisible.) If you need to display the instance to the user, you can set the Visible property to True. If not, the instance remains minimized until closed.

A programmatic instance of Access terminates when the procedure that created it goes out of scope, or when you set the object variable to Nothing:

```
Set accappNwind = Nothing
```

However, there are caveats to the previous paragraph. A server instance of Access may not close if there is a *process* pending. In this context, a process is anything that the server deems unfinished business. Also, if an instance of Access is opened invisible (minimized) and then set to Nothing, the instance closes correctly. However, if the user interacts with the instance (maximizes it and opens a form, for example) before it is set to Nothing, the instance does not close, because the user interaction has started an open process that must be completed before the server can close.

Both of these situations can be remedied by good coding. You can explicitly close a remote application instance from the calling code and force it to terminate with the Quit method. Alternately, closing the current database releases any pending processes and allow the instance to close on cue, as shown in Listing 11.2.

Listing 11.2   Two Ways to Close an Automation Instance of Access

```
' These two commands consistently close the server
accappNwind.CloseCurrentDatabase
Set accappNwind = Nothing

' As do these two
accappNwind.Quit
Set accappNwind = Nothing
```

 Tip

Of the two syntax options, Quit is the more reliable and consistent with the Automation model.

Listings 11.3 and 11.4 clarify the previous points by providing two Automation examples.

Listing 11.3   AES_VBA.Mdb—Creating an Access Server Instance with Automation

```
' This code block demonstrates how an open process will not terminate
Dim accappNwind As Access.Application
Set accappNwind = CreateObject("Access.Application.8")
accappNwind.OpenCurrentDatabase "C:\Office\Samples\Northwind.Mdb"
' At this point, Visible is False

' Display the server and a form in it
accappNwind.Visible = True
accappNwind.DoCmd.OpenForm "Main Switchboard"

' At this point, if the user clicks a button on the Northwind
'   switchboard, the server instance opens a pending process


' Closing the variable does NOT close the server because a process
'   is pending; you need to use CloseCurrentDatabase or Quit first
Set accappNwind = Nothing
```

Listing 11.4   AES_VBA.Mdb—Creating an Access Automation Server Instance to Print a Report

```
' This code block shows an example of Automation to print
Dim accappNwind As Access.Application
Set accappNwind = CreateObject("Access.Application.8")
accappNwind.OpenCurrentDatabase "C:\Office\Samples\Northwind.Mdb"

' At this point, Visible is False
' You do not need to display the server to run a process in it
accappNwind.DoCmd.OpenReport "Summary of Sales by Quarter"

' Close the instance
accappNwind.Quit
Set accappNwind = Nothing
```

Figure 11.1 shows a conceptual representation of the Application object and its members from the standpoint of behaving as an Automation server.

Fig. 11.1

Automation of Access is facilitated through the exposed Application *object.*

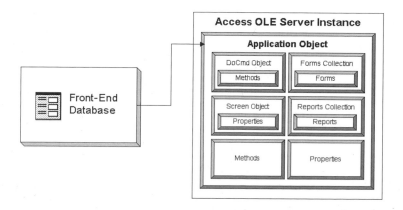

We've touched on several properties and methods of an `Application` object in this section. The next two sections provide a complete rundown of all of the new properties and methods available.

Setting an Application Object's Properties

Properties of the current database's `Application` object or of an object variable referring to an Access instance can be read (and sometimes set) from VBA code. When referring to properties in an Automation application instance, you must prefix the property name with the object variable name, as in:

```
If accappNwind.Visible = True Then
```

When referring to properties of the *current* application, the keyword `Application` is optional. Thus, the following two lines are equivalent:

```
MenuBar = "lci_mbrSimple"
Application.MenuBar = "lci_mbrSimple"
```

The following list describes the primary properties of the `Application` object that are of interest when doing VBA coding or Automation. Read-only properties are denoted with *RO* and read/write with *RW*:

> *CodeContextObject Property (RO)*. From a form module, you can use the `Me` property to refer to the object that contains the currently executing line of code. However, `Me` is not valuable from code that is executing *outside* of the form or report. Instead, the `CodeContextObject` property returns an object pointer to the object currently running the code (or macro). Listing 11.5 clarifies how this works when the code has a call tree.

Listing 11.5 *CodeContextObject* —Points to the Object at the Top of the Call Tree

```
' This code is in form frmOne
Private Sub cbfCustCheck()
  Call Form_frmTwo.cbfCustFlag
End Sub


' This code is in form frmTwo
Public Sub cbfCustFlag()
  Call ErrorMsg()
End Sub


' This code is in a standard module
Public Sub ErrorMsg()
  ' This statement displays "frmOne"
  Debug.Print CodeContextObject.Name
End Sub
```

CurrentObjectName Property (RO). Within an application, there is always one database object currently active. This property provides the name of that object, or the name of the object selected in the Database window, if it has focus.

CurrentObjectType Property (RO). This property describes the object type of the database object referred to by the `CurrentObjectName` property. The setting for this property will either be one of the object type intrinsic constants (`acForm`, `acMacro`, `acModule`, `acQuery`, `acReport`, and `acTable`) or −1 if no object is open or selected.

Note

If the current object is a child of one of the six database object types (for example, a property dialog of a form in Design view, or a menu for a form in Browse view), `CurrentObjectName` and `CurrentObjectType` refer to the parent object.

Caution

If the current object is the Database window, the `CurrentObjectName` and `CurrentObjectType` properties refer to the object currently selected in the window, *even if the object is not open*. You should be careful to detect the state of the object before trying to manipulate it. Use code like the following:

```
If SysCmd(acSysCmdGetObjectState, CurrentObjectType _
  , CurrentObjectName) = 0 Then
  '   Object is closed, do nothing
Else
  ' Do something here
End If
```

DBEngine Property (RO). This property provides a gateway to the Data Access Objects hierarchy within an application from a referencing application. Remotely automating the DAO enables you to create new databases or database objects from code.

Note

DAO code in a remote application runs much slower than in the current application, so you should generally only access the `DBEngine` property of the current database instead of a remotely automated database. Your code can use the `OpenDatabase` method of the current application to directly access an external database without relying on Automation.

Forms Collection (RO). The collection of open forms for an application can be accessed via its parent `Application` object.

IsCompiled Property (RO). This property is `True` when all of the modules in the project (database) are in a compiled state.

MenuBar Property (RW). This property names the command bar menu or menu macro that provides the current custom default menu bar. You can set the property to change the current menu bar from code, or assign an empty string ("") to the property to re-enable the application's default menu bar.

Modules Collection (RO). This collection contains all open standard and class modules in an application.

References Collection (RO). All established references for the current application are stored in this collection.

Reports Collection (RO). This collection hangs from the parent `Application` object and points to all open reports for an application.

ShortcutMenuBar Property (RW). The `ShortcutMenuBar` property names the command bar menu or menu macro that provides the current custom default shortcut menu for forms and form controls. You can set the property from code to change the current menu, or assign an empty string ("") to the property to re-enable the application's default shortcut menu.

 Note

The setting of the `MenuBar` and `ShortcutMenuBar` properties at the `Application` object level overrides the setting provided in the Startup options dialog box for the database.

Also, forms and reports have a `MenuBar` property and a `ShortcutMenuBar` property, which override the `Application` object's settings for these properties while the form or report is displayed.

UserControl Property (RW). The `UserControl` property of an application object is `True` if the current instance of Access was launched by a user and `False` if launched by an Automation controller. You can check this property from processes in an application to determine whether to perform specific actions or not.

For example, assume you've got a reporting application that contains a process to print a batch of month-end reports. When the user activates this process from within the reporting application, your code displays status information on the status bar as each report is printed. However, when you use Automation to launch the reporting application invisibly from another application, there is no need for the status bar code to run. The reporting application could contain code like the following to disable the status display when running as an Automation server:

```
If Application.UserControl = True Then
   ' Display the status messages here
End If
```

Visible property (RW). This property determines the visibility of an Automation instance of Access. When True, the Access application window is displayed. When set to False, the application instance is minimized, and objects opened in the application are not displayed to users.

Notice that functions and statements that you are probably already familiar with from prior versions of Access are now related to the Application object. For example, DBEngine is now a property of the Application object, even though you usually reference it directly instead of using Application.DBEngine. The value of this structure is that you can create an Application object variable for an Automation instance of Access and reference any application properties through that object variable.

 Tip

To explore the Application object in more detail, view it in the Object Browser dialog box by selecting it from the Classes list in the Access library.

Applying Methods to an Application Object

Just as property settings enable you to define or retrieve the *characteristics* of an Application object instance, *methods* enable you to run functions that make the object perform tasks. Some of the tasks are important when using Access as an Automation server, and others are more useful within the current application.

As with properties, the object prefix Application is not required when making a reference to a method in the database containing the code line. For databases opened through Automation, the calling code should reference these methods through the Application object variable that points to the instance:

```
Set accappNwind = CreateObject("Access.Application.8")
accappNwind.OpenCurrentDatabase "C:\Office\Samples\Northwind.Mdb"
```

Here are the `Application` object's methods:

AccessError Method. When you want to retrieve the string associated with an error number without actually invoking the error, you can use this method by passing it a valid error number:

```
' Returns "File not found"
Debug.Print AccessError(53)
```

After an error, these statements return the same error number:

```
Err.Description
AccessError(Err.Number)
Application.AccessError(Err.Number)
```

 Note

The `AccessError` method returns Access, Jet, and VBA error messages in Access 97, but does *not* return Jet error messages in Access 95.

AddToFavorites Method. This method adds a hyperlink for the current database to the Favorites folder on the current workstation.

BuildCriteria Method. This method takes three arguments and creates a properly delimited criteria string that can be used in SQL statements, `Find` methods, and form `Filter` property settings. The first argument is a field name from a table or query, and the second is an Access intrinsic constant describing the data type of the field. Use the data type constants for DAO fields (such as `dbBoolean`, `dbByte`, and `dbInteger`) as the second argument.

The third argument specifies a non-delimited comparison to apply to the field. The comparison can contain multiple criteria but they must all apply to the named field. Thus, the following examples are legitimate calls to `BuildCriteria`:

```
' The method returns "CategoryID=6 Or CategoryID=7 Or CategoryID=8"
Me.Filter = BuildCriteria("CategoryID", dbLong, "6 or 7 or 8")
```

```
' This variation demonstrates BuildCriteria against a recordset
rst.FindFirst BuildCriteria("CategoryID", dbLong, "Between 6 And 8")
```

CloseCurrentDatabase Method. This method is used primarily to perform a remote close of a database opened inside an Automation instance of Access. For example, you must close a database before repairing it, so these commands would prove useful:

```
accappNwind.CloseCurrentDatabase
accappNwind.DBEngine.RepairDatabase "C:\Office\Samples\Northwind.Mdb"
```

You also can use this method on the current local application to close the database and terminate the application without closing Access.

CodeDb, CurrentDb Methods. These methods are used in code to return a database object that refers to the database containing the currently executing code procedure, or the database that initiated the procedure. Use CodeDb to create a database object that refers to the library database when running library code. CurrentDb returns a pointer to the database containing the calling procedure that initiated the library code (the currently open database).

 Note

When Access is running as an Automation server application, you might expect CurrentDb to point to the controlling application. However, both CurrentDb and CodeDb in this context return the server database.

Create, Delete Methods. The functions for creating forms and reports from code and for adding or removing their controls are actually methods of the Application object. This structure enables you to use the methods to create new objects in server databases under Automation control. The actual Create and Delete methods are:

CreateControl. Create a new control on a form.

CreateForm. Create a new form.

CreateGroupLevel. Create a report grouping or sorting expression.

CreateReport. Create a new report.

CreateReportControl. Create a new control on a report.

DeleteControl. Delete a control from a form.

DeleteReportControl. Delete a control from a report.

CurrentUser Method. This function returns the name of the currently-logged user, or *Admin* if security is not enabled.

DDE Methods. These six DDE methods (formerly functions) are also attached to the Application object: DDEExecute, DDEInitiate, DDEPoke, DDERequest, DDETerminate, DDETerminateAll. DDE is a precursor to Automation, left over from previous versions of Access.

DefaultWorkspaceClone Method. A DAO Workspace object is created when an Access database is opened (either locally or remotely). This workspace is called the *default*

11

workspace; it is secured based on the currently logged user and his or her access rights (or lack thereof).

With the `DefaultWorkspaceClone` method, you can make a clone of the default workspace in a secured environment without initiating an additional login requiring a user name and password. Instead, the current user name and password for the default workspace are copied into its clone. This method is useful when you need to initiate parallel transactions by using multiple `Workspace` objects.

Domain Methods. You probably think of the domain methods as functions of the current database, because you are familiar with using them in expressions and SQL strings. Now, these can be applied to any `Application` object:

> `DAvg` *Method.* This method computes the average of a field or expression in a specified range of records.

> `DCount` *Method.* `DCount` counts the number of records in a specified domain (set of records).

> `DFirst, DLast` *Methods.* These methods return the first or last value from a range of fields or expressions in a specified set of records.

> `DLookup` *Method.* This method returns the value from a field or expression in a specified record.

> `DMax, DMin` *Methods.* These methods calculate the maximum or minimum value of a field or expression across a specified range of records.

> `DStDev, DStDevP` *Method.* These two methods compute a standard deviation for a field or expression across multiple records. `DStDevP` utilizes the entire population, while `DStDev` uses a representative sample.

> `DSum` *Method.* `DSum` computes the sum of a field or expression across a domain.

> `DVar, DVarP` *Method.* These two methods compute a variance for a field or expression across a record domain, with `DVarP` analyzing the entire population and `DVar` selecting a representative sample.

As methods of the `Application` object, these functions can be used from VBA against Automation server applications as well. In this example, values from the `Orders` table in the automated database (not the controller) are summed as follows:

```
varFreight = accappNwind.DSum("Freight", "Orders")
```

Echo Method. This method performs the task formerly achieved by the `DoCmd Echo` statement and enables or disables the automatic repainting of the Access application window after each change to the screen. For example, these lines turn off screen repaints (the first line targets the local application, and the second affects an Automation instance of Access):

```
Application.Echo False
accappNwind.Echo True
```

You can add an optional second argument after the `True` or `False` echo argument to write a string to the status bar, as in this example:

```
Application.Echo True, "Process complete."
```

Eval Method. This method acts as a function, evaluating the expression passed to it and returning a result as if the expression were run as a line of code. A common use of this method is to pass values from a form or table to the function that represent executable code expressions. For example, your code creates a variable `strEval` and places this string into it from code or a table field:

```
strEval = "DSum('Freight', 'Orders')"
```

The following `Eval` method call would return the correct result of the `DSum` method passed to it:

```
varFreight = Eval(strEval)
```

FollowHyperlink Method. As defined in Chapter 10, "Creating Expert Tables and Queries," Access 97 is aware of hyperlink addresses that point to disk files, information within a file, an object, or a Web page. This method jumps to a specified hyperlink address, as in the following Access-based example:

```
Application.FollowHyperlink "C:\Office\Samples\Northwind.Mdb" _
    , "Form Categories"
```

GetOption Method. You can retrieve the settings displayed in the Access Options dialog box with this method. `GetOption` returns a `Variant` value containing the named setting, as in this example:

```
varOpt = Application.GetOption("Arrow Key Behavior")
```

 11

 Note

The option values that can be retrieved with this method (or set with `SetOption`) are detailed in Access' online help system under the topic "Set Options from Visual Basic."

This method cannot read or set options displayed on the Modules tab of the Options dialog box.

GUIDFromString, StringFromGUID Methods. A Globally Unique Identifier (GUID) is a 16-character value that uniquely identifies a Windows object. In Access, GUIDs are used as `Replication ID` table field values, and are stored in a table as a `Byte` array. You can bind a form control in Access to an `AutoNumber` field of type `Replication ID`, but you cannot retrieve the value from that control into a variable without converting it to a string using the `StringFromGUID` function. Use the corollary `GUIDFromString` function if you need to convert a string value back into a `Byte` array.

hWndAccessApp Method. This method returns the unique *window handle* of an application instance, in the same way the `hWnd` property returns the window handle of an application's form and report child windows. A *window handle* is a pointer to a window that is used as an argument in calls to the Windows API.

HyperlinkPart Method. This method is new to Access 97 and returns the specified component part of a formatted `Hyperlink` field value. See Chapter 10, "Creating Expert Tables and Queries," for information on the structure of a hyperlink. This function returns a specified piece of the three-part link string, as in this example:

```
' The following call returns "LCI"
Application.HyperlinkPart ("LCI#www.lciinfo.com#Resume",acDisplayText)
```

LoadPicture Method. This method accepts a path and file name argument and converts the image in the file into a picture object. Picture objects are not supported directly by Access; this method is provided so that pictures can be submitted by Access to custom controls that support a `Picture` property.

NewCurrentDatabase Method. Apply this method to an `Application` object variable that references the non-current Access instance in order to create a new, empty database. This method is useful when creating databases programmatically and accepts the path and file name of the new database as its argument.

 Note

You can only use this method against an Automation instance of Access; you cannot create a new database through the current `Application` object. Close the currently open database in the server instance using the `CloseCurrentDatabase` method before issuing this command.

```
accappNwind.CloseCurrentDatabase
accappNwind.NewCurrentDatabase "C:\Data\Horses.Mdb"
```

Nz Method. This function allows your code to return a specific value or string when an evaluated `Variant` value is `Null`. For example, the following code returns a string when the tested variable is `Null`:

```
MsgBox Nz(varInput, "No value entered")
```

OpenCurrentDatabase Method. After you've created an Automation instance of Access through code, you apply this method to open a database within it. Supply a database path and name, and an optional argument of `True` or `False` to specify whether the database is opened exclusively (omitting the argument opens the database shared):

```
accappNwind.OpenCurrentDatabase "C:\Office\Samples\Northwind.Mdb" _
    , True
```

Note

Close the currently open database with the `CloseCurrentDatabase` method before issuing this command.

Quit Method. This method quits the current Access session completely, in the same manner as <u>F</u>ile, E<u>x</u>it from the menu system. This command is primarily used to create code attached to an application's Quit or Exit button, or to close an Automation instance of Access.

Following the `Quit` method, you can add an optional argument to indicate how to deal with any database objects that are open but not saved. The values are `acExit` to save nothing, `acPrompt` to display a save dialog box for each open (and dirty) object, or `acSaveYes` to save objects automatically. The default is `acSaveYes`.

RefreshDatabaseWindow Method. When an object is created, renamed, or deleted from program code, the change is not reflected in the visible database window until the user refreshes the window by moving off of the current tab and back. This method updates the Database window on demand.

RefreshTitleBar Method. After you make a programmatic change to an application's title bar, you must repaint the title bar with this method to display the change. The Access title bar now supports changes to the control box icon (using the `AppIcon` property) and title text (using the `AppTitle` property). See Chapter 17, "Bulletproofing Your Application Interface," for an example of these two database properties and this method.

11

Run Method. One of the most powerful methods of the `Application` object, `Run` enables you to execute a named procedure in the current or a remote database. In either case, the procedure must have been declared as `Public` and be located in a standard module. Because you cannot create a reference to an Access database from a non-Access controller application (to use Access as a library database), `Run` enables you to start an Access server instance from VB or another Office application and execute code in it.

Following the procedure name, specify any arguments required by the procedure, as in this example:

```
accappReports.Run "ReportToPrinter", "rptCustList"
```

If you have created a reference to another Access database, you can refer to a procedure in the database using the database's project name and the `Run` method, like this:

```
' The current database has a reference to StdRpts.Mdb, which has
'    a project name of StandardReports set via its Tools Options dialog
Application.Run "StandardReports.ReportToPrinter", "rptCustList"
```

There are good performance reasons for applying this method. See the section "Improving VBA Performance" later in this chapter.

> α **Note**
>
> Return values sent back by a function called with the `Run` method are discarded.
>
> Chapter 20, "Applying Development Shortcuts," discusses this method in greater detail.

RunCommand Method. This new function replaces the `DoCmd.DoMenuItem` syntax by providing a unique integer value to trigger each menu option. `RunCommand` also provides a useful shorthand for building command bar menus and buttons. The following example compares the old and new approaches to executing a menu selection:

```
' Size to Fit Form command, the old way
Application.DoCmd.DoMenuItem acFormBar, 7, 6, , acMenuVer70
' The new way
Application.DoCmd.RunCommand acCmdSizeToFit
```

SetOption Method. The opposite of `GetOption`, this method sets a value programmatically that is normally accessed via the Options dialog box. The following example sets the behavior of the arrow keys in datasheets and forms to Next Character (which can be reflected by the value 1 because of its location within the 0-based option group):

```
Application.SetOption "Arrow Key Behavior", 1
```

SysCmd method. This method performs a variety of tasks, including returning system information about the Access environment, manipulating text or the progress meter on the status bar, or detecting the state of an object. For example, you can determine whether a particular form is open in an Automation instance of Access by using this code from the controlling application:

```
If accappNwind.SysCmd(acSysCmdGetObjectState, acForm, _
  , "Main Switchboard") = acObjStateOpen Then
    ' Do something
End If
```

The powerful methods of the Application object enable you to manipulate Automation instances of Access to perform almost any task.

Using Non-Access Objects

You've seen, in the previous topics, how Access provides an exposed object structure that can be addressed from program code. The other Office applications also expose their internal structures in a similar fashion and allow program code to propel them remotely.

Applications usually expose their components to Automation through the use of a file that contains Automation-specific descriptions of their objects (classes), properties, and methods. Such files usually have one of these extensions:

DLL, for Dynamic Link Library

OLB, for Object Library

TLB, for Type Library

Table 11.1 lists the components of Office and Visual Basic that can be automated or shared and their Automation definition (type library) file names. Use the References option on the Tools menu in an Access module to create a reference to the type library for a component that you want to browse in the Object Browser or write Automation code against.

Table 11.1   Components of an Office-Centric Development Environment that Can Be Automated

Product	Type Library	Entry Point
Access 8	MSACC8.OLB	Access.Application.8
Binder 8	MSBDR8.OLB	OfficeBinder.Binder.8
DAO 3.5	DAO350.DLL	DAO.DBEngine.35

continues

Table 11.1   Continued

Product	Type Library	Entry Point
Excel 8	EXCEL8.OLB	Excel.Application.8 Excel.Chart.8 Excel.Sheet.8
Graph 8	GRAPH8.OLB	MSGraph.Application.8
MAPI—OLE Messaging 1	MDISP32.TLB	MAPI.Session.1
Outlook 8	MSOUTL8.OLB	Outlook.Application.8
PowerPoint 8	MSPPT8.OLB	PowerPoint.Application.8
Project 4	PJ4EN32.OLB	MSProject.Application.4 MSProject.Project.4
Schedule+ 7	SP7EN32.OLB	SchedulePlus.Application.7
SQL OLE 6.5	SQLOLE65.TLB	SQLOLE.SQLServer.6.5
Word 8	MSWORD8.OLB	Word.Application.8

See Chapter 10, "Creating Expert Tables and Queries," for an example of Automation code written against Excel's object model.

In addition to the listed Automation servers, there are several support files that provide extensions to Office applications by attaching themselves to the host application's object model and behaving like intrinsic features. Table 11.2 lists such files.

Table 11.2   Office Extensions that Are Hosted

Product	Type Library	Provides
Forms 2	FM20.DLL	Form controls, properties, and methods
Office 8	MSO97.DLL	Assistant, command bars
VBA	VBA332.DLL	Collections, errors
VBA Editor	VBEEXT1.OLB	Project editor, references

The hosted extensions listed in Table 11.2 do not require explicit Automation to use; they become part of the host's object model. Thus, if your Access application contains a reference to MSO97.DLL, the Office objects are directly available to your program code, as demonstrated by the Office FileSearch object in Listing 11.6.

Listing 11.6   AES_VBA.Mdb Using the New *FileSearch* Object Hosted Inside Access

```
Private Sub cmdSearch_Click()

  With FileSearch
    .NewSearch
    .FileName = "Northwind.Mdb"
    .FileType = msoFileTypeDatabases
    .LookIn = "C:\"
    .MatchTextExactly = True
    .SearchSubFolders = True
    If .Execute(SortBy:=msoSortByFileName _
      , SortOrder:=msoSortOrderAscending) > 0 Then
      Me!txtNWPath = .FoundFiles(1)
    Else
      Me!txtNWPath = Null
      Beep
, SortOrder:=msoSortOrderAscending)
      MsgBox "Could not find Northwind, enter the path yourself." _
        , , "Sorry"
    End If
  End With

End Sub
```

Similarly, VBA editing services are provided to Excel by VBEEXT1.OLB. If your Excel application references this file, it can issue commands like the following based on objects in the referenced object library:

```
strName = Application.VBE.ActiveVBProject.Name
```

 Note

Access has its own forms engine and does not rely on the MSForms objects in FM20.DLL, which create forms in Excel, Outlook, PowerPoint, and Word. You do not use this DLL from Access.

Access also provides its own VBA editor, thus you also do not need to reference VBEEXT1.OLB, which provides the VBA editing services for the rest of Office.

11

Applying Conditional Compilation

By default, when you compile Access VBA code, every line in all of the application's modules (when using <u>D</u>ebug, Compile All <u>M</u>odules or <u>D</u>ebug, Compile and Sa<u>v</u>e All

Modules) or all of the application's *open* modules (with <u>D</u>ebug, Compile Loa<u>d</u>ed Modules) is parsed and converted to pseudo code. If you have code that is relevant only in specific situations, you can tell Access to ignore compilation of that chunk of code in other situations. This default creates less compiled code (with an according performance increase) and also provides you with the capability to give your application multiple personalities with the flick of a switch.

The *switch* in this case is called a Conditional Compilation Constant (abbreviated as *CCC* here), which is the global flag (or flags) that you pass to your code to facilitate the branching required for conditional compilation. Branching is achieved by testing the conditional constant with a special conditional If statement.

VBA provides this syntax for use with conditional compilation.

```
#If...Then
#ElseIf...Then
#Else
#End If
```

When one of these #If statements detects the appropriate setting of the named CCC, it branches accordingly, as in Listing 11.7.

Listing 11.7   AES_VBA.Mdb—Code Can Be Conditionally Compiled Based upon the Setting of a Global Constant

```
#If lci_gcccDebug Then   ' Debug mode
   Application.SetOption "Break on All Errors", True
   MsgBox "Debugging is on."
#Else
   MsgBox "Debugging is off."
#End If
```

To create Conditional Compilation Constants, enter one or more of them in the Options dialog box on the Advanced tab, as shown in Figure 11.2. If you are declaring more than one CCC flag, separate the values with colons.

After you enter CCC flag values in the Options dialog box, compile all of the module code in the application. Some code may be excluded from the compiled code block based on the entered flags. The Options dialog box preserves the value of the flags between sessions of the current database, but not between different databases.

Fig. 11.2

Conditional Compila-
tion Constant values
are entered in the
Options dialog box.

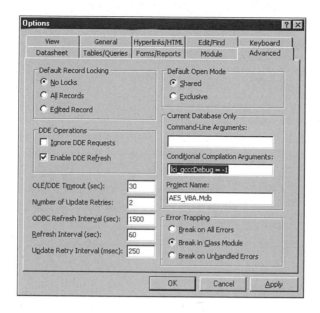

α Note

The CCC argument entered into the Options dialog box cannot make use of intrinsic constants or expressions; you can only set the CCC value to a positive or negative integer, like this:

```
lci_gcccDebug = 0   ' This is valid in the Options dialog
lci_gcccDebug = False ' This is not valid in the dialog
```

The #If statement treats a CCC variable value of 0 as False and any non-zero value as True.

Only the special #If statements listed previously can reference a declared CCC, you cannot reference a conditional flag from any other VBA statement (not even in the Debug window). The inverse is also true: A conditional #If statement can only reference conditional constants and literal values in its statements, as in the examples in Listing 11.8.

11

Listing 11.8   *Conditional Compilation Syntax Examples*

```
' These are valid in code
#If lci_gcccDebug = True Then...  ' Comparison to constant
#If lci_gcccDebug = "DebugOn" Then...  ' Comparison to literal
```

continues

Listing 11.8   Continued

```
' These are not valid
#If lci_gcccDebug = DebugGet() Then...  ' Calls user-defined function
MsgBox CStr(lci_gcccDebug)  ' CCC in non-conditional statement
```

Note in the previous code that a CCC value is being compared to a string value on one line. While CCC values cannot be non-numeric in the Options dialog box, they can be assigned non-numeric values when declared in module code. CCC flags are declared in program code with the #Const declaration. Such declarations should be declared at the module level and are private to the module. A conditional constant so defined has scope only within its module, so the following command is not allowed:

```
Public #Const lci_gcccDebug = False
```

Thus, you can only configure conditional statements at the *module level* from code—the only way to create *application-wide* CCC values is from the Options dialog box. This means that you must set application-wide conditional constants in the dialog box and then recompile the application manually.

 Note

Your application can haR multiple Conditional Compilation Constants in each module and can apply global CCC values from the Options dialog box in addition to the presence of CCC values in modules.

Beginning with Access 97, you can also change CCC values from code and recompile for them to take effect, as in this example:

```
Application.SetOption "Conditional Compilation Arguments" _
  , "lci_gcccDebug = 1"
RunCommand acCmdCompileAndSaveAllModules
```

Here are some suggestions on how to make use of this feature in your code:

Conditional Debugging. You can create code that includes and excludes specific statements related to debugging. See the section "Handling Runtime Errors" later in this chapter.

Conditional Code Blocks. There is no need to compile all of the code in an application into every release if some functionality goes unused by a subset of the user base. Instead, identify blocks of code that are not relevant to specific users; wrap that code in a conditional #If statement, and compile more than one version of the application based on different compilation constant settings.

As an example, assume that your application has two primary user types: data-entry and administrative. There are entire administrative procedures in the application that are not used by the data-entry people. You could place all of the code within the administration procedures inside a conditional statement that caused the procedures' code to be ignored when compiling, like this:

```
Sub EndOfMonth()
' When gcccAdmin is False, none of the following code is compiled

  #If gcccAdmin Then
    ' All administrative procedure code goes in here
  #End If

End Sub
```

Multiple-personality Objects. As you expand your use of component objects, you can create class modules (see Chapter 12, "Understanding Form Structures and Coding") or standard forms that serve more than one purpose. By placing blocks of code in a form's event or module procedures inside of conditional statements and adding the related conditional constant to the form's Declarations section, you effectively create a single form that behaves differently depending on how it is compiled.

There are still instances when you need more flexibility in handling conditional operations than is provided by conditional compilation. In situations where you need to set a conditional flag from a table, the Windows registry, an initialization file, or user interaction, global variables in standard If and Case statements provide flexibility still not available in the new conditional statements.

Exploring New Features Elsewhere in This Book

There are several powerful new VBA features that are described in detail elsewhere in this book as they are used in development techniques. They are:

- ▶ *Collections.* Access now enables you to build your own custom containers of object pointers called *collections*. This feature is described in detail in Chapter 12, "Understanding Form Structures and Coding."

- ▶ *Property Procedures.* Using the Property procedure syntax, you can create custom properties in forms. This allows forms and class modules to act as class definitions that can be reused for multiple purposes by changing their properties. This feature is described in detail in Chapter 12, "Understanding Form Structures and Coding."

- ▶ *The New Keyword.* New is an addition to the Dim statement that provides the capability to start a new, separate object instance of an object. This syntax is also demonstrated in Chapter 12, "Understanding Form Structures and Coding."

▶ *Keyboard Handlers.* The `KeyPreview` form property helps VBA routines to detect incoming keystrokes. See the discussion of this feature in Chapter 15, "Protecting and Validating Data."

▶ *Reading and Writing Options.* Application options and startup settings are exposed to your VBA code, as described in Chapter 17, "Bulletproofing Your Application Interface."

▶ *Programmatic Manipulation of Code.* Chapter 20, "Applying Development Shortcuts," describes how to use the new `Module` object to read and write VBA code from code that is executing.

Refer to the specific chapters noted for in-context demonstrations of these new features.

Developing with Visual Basic for Applications

If many of your days (and, as is very often the case, your *nights*) are spent writing VBA code, you may find that you've developed habits, "rules-of-thumb," shortcuts, conventions, and other style elements. Perhaps you've never formalized them, and even change them periodically for variety. Nevertheless, you've probably discovered that consistency can make your life easier.

For example, in both EB and VBA, you can use a variable in an assignment statement without ever declaring it with `Dim` (if the `Option Explicit` switch is not in the parent module). Access creates a `Variant` variable for you on-the-fly, using its best guess to select the data type, as in this example:

```
varWork = 10
MsgBox VarType(varWork)   ' Shows 2, which is an Integer
```

Such code is dangerous because Access is selecting the type for you. If you had really intended for this new variable to be a `Long Integer` and simply forgot to declare it, Access has possibly set your code up for failure (an overflow or type mismatch) later on by making it an `Integer`.

By contrast, in earlier and in the current versions of Access, placing an `Option Explicit` statement in each module forces the compiler to alert you to undefined variables. Many coders adopt the use of this statement as a standard policy after their first negative experience with a type mismatch between non-declared variables.

 Tip
You can now set the Require Variable Declaration option in the Options dialog box to force the automatic addition of an `Option Explicit` line to each new module.

Adopting a policy that says, "Do not use any undeclared variables," is an example of creating your personal coding style. The remainder of this chapter discusses issues that frequently arise in the course of VBA development. An understanding of the issues and techniques provides you with a solid foundation to define your coding style, by creating a set of standardized approaches to VBA.

Structuring Basic Code Procedures

dCOMMENTS

Years ago when we did dBASE development, one of our clients required us to aggressively comment our code. I've always been one to put a lot of code comments in a routine, but this client was extreme even by my standards—every code "block" (as they defined it, a group of related commands like an IF...ENDIF chunk) was preceded with a section comment, and each *line* of code required an in-line comment. This yielded programs like this:

```
* Check for the number 5
IF LEN(sInput) = 5  && Entered the number 5
   DO Fiver  && Run Fiver.Prg to handle the number 5
ELSE  && Didn't enter the number 5
   DO NoFiver  && Run NoFiver.Prg to handle other numbers
ENDIF  && End of block
```

Their intentions were actually good. dBASE was the kind of program where you could solve a particular problem a variety of ways, and different coders created radically different solutions to the same problem. For our client, maintaining code developed by outsiders was virtually impossible without good documentation and code comments. However, I think they went a little overboard.

By the time we stopped working with them, I'd been corrupted—I was adding parenthetical comments to my meeting notes, shopping lists, and letters to friends. Their commenting style had even trickled into my personal habits!

11

To me, the word *coding* is such an appropriate designation for what many developers do, because creating procedures involves uniquely mixing characters, numbers, and algorithms into a block of text that virtually nobody besides yourself can read. Reading another person's routines *can* be much like cracking a secret code.

There *is* a positive reason for this situation—the Basic language is flexible enough and Access is powerful enough to allow different developers with different styles to solve a stated problem in different ways. Flexibility yields diversity.

Chapter 5, "Creating Naming Conventions," provided you with some insights into the thought processes involved in designing a development style. Alternately, you might simply choose to use the style *du jour* in your code, expressing today's mood and not fitting some larger plan.

If you have any of the following three needs, however, I would suggest you consider creating a consistent VBA coding style:

> *Someone must maintain your code later.* If you mostly "fight fires" and crank out quick chunks of code to fill some short-term need, consistency and readability of code are not your biggest concerns. On the other hand, whether you or anyone else must debug, enhance, or convert any of your code in the future, readability and consistency of structure are big issues.

> *You work on a development team.* The only thing worse than going into code you wrote last year and having trouble figuring it out is going into code your team members wrote this morning and having the same trouble. Teams that must debug each others' code, support each others' code, and review each others' code should be highly motivated to approach development with consistent styles.

> *You need to train people.* I've met many developers who balk at coding styles that tend to "beautify" code, as if clean code is for neophytes. In fact, much of my code *is* for neophytes: It becomes the basis for magazine articles, book chapters, or speeches; it is reverse-engineered by our clients when they are teaching themselves to code; and, it is reviewed by new employees and contractors on my team to learn the company style. If any of these needs match yours, you should be more apt to favor a standardized coding style.

What are some of the elements of a VBA coding style? At the highest level, a primary style consideration is how to name procedures, variables, and the objects they work with, as exemplified by the conventions in Chapter 6, "Leszynski Naming Conventions for Access," and Appendix C, "Leszynski Naming Conventions for Microsoft Solution Developers, which is on the CD-ROM."

Another very high-level style decision is selecting how you structure and locate code routines within an application. See Chapter 7, "Understanding Application Architecture," for a discussion of this topic.

At a more detailed level, there are several style decisions that you must make for each procedure and line of code that you write, as detailed in the following section.

Indenting Code

Access' default indentation level is 4 characters. While this makes code look extremely clean and readable, I find that the text moves across the screen too quickly in complex applications. Consider this example:

```
Sub Demo()
    Dim varname...
        For Each...
            Select Case...
                With object...
                    .property =...
                    If...
                        Do...
```

You can see that editing a procedure like this in a module window that is not maximized to fill an SVGA screen quickly crowds critical code segments off the right edge of the screen.

At the other extreme, some developers code with no indentation. Let's take the same example and left-align it:

```
Sub Demo()
Dim varname...
For Each...
Select Case...
With object...
.property =...
If...
Do...
```

I've had to clean up both kinds of code, and I would much prefer to deal with too much indentation rather than none at all, which produces code that is nearly impossible to audit or debug. My personal style is a two-character indent, striking a compromise between both extremes shown here. Whether you adopt this indentation level for yourself or choose another, apply your choice consistently.

Indentation can also be used for alignment of information *within* code lines, and some coders do go slightly nuts when aligning code. For example, the comments in the following Case statement are all aligned:

```
Select Case Err.Number
  Case 52, 53, 64, 75, 76  ' Path/file error or not found
    lci_FileExists = cintErrNoFile
  Case 57, 68, 71          ' No device or disk
    lci_FileExists = cintErrNoDev
  Case 70                  ' No permission
    lci_FileExists = cintErrNoPerm
End Select
```

11

Most people don't find code like this much more readable, and some even find it annoying. I tend to use special alignment selectively, favoring it when it improves readability. For example, I don't generally align comments unless I'm writing code for printed publication, but I do like to arrange `Dim` statements for readability in all my code:

```
Const cstrProc As String = "lci_AppBoAECheck"
Dim blnBreak   As Boolean
Dim strMsg     As String
```

Wrapping Code Lines

Wrapping long lines of code is a whole new ball game with the introduction of a line continuation character into VBA. Long lines of code are now much easier to manage. Formerly, code lines would disappear off the right edge of the screen, a situation that could only be avoided if they were painstakingly concatenated, as in this example:

```
strMsg = "An error has occurred, please contact Technical Support."
strMsg = strMsg & " Send e-mail to TechSupp or call extension 12345"
strMsg = strMsg & " for immediate aid."
```

Life is much better now. Although concatenating strings still involves matching quote pairs before continuing to the next line, long lines of code are easier to build and read with a continuation mark:

```
strMsg = "An error has occurred, please contact Technical Support." _
    & " Send e-mail to TechSupp or call extension 12345" _
    & " for immediate aid."
```

Notice three conscious style decisions I made when wrapping the lines of code:

1. I indented the continued lines to provide a better visual clue of what is happening in the code.

2. The string concatenation operator (&) is placed at the beginning of the continued line rather than the end of the previous line. This is another very immediate visual clue when browsing code that the statement is part of a multiline command.

3. Developers often forget to include a space when they are continuing long strings, jamming words together when two lines are reassembled. We've standardized on placing the space at the beginning of the continuation string rather than the end of the previous line, where it may bleed off the screen and be harder to locate in a code review.

I made these style decisions after trying various strategies and deciding which one worked best for my team and my clients. You can employ the same methodology to create your own policy.

Tip

You should also consider how to locate commas in long delimited lists. You can choose to locate them at the end of the line or the beginning, as in these examples:

```
' The comma trails the first line
DoCmd.OpenForm "Customers", , , "CompanyName Like '*market*'", _
    acReadOnly, acDialog

' The comma wraps to the second line
DoCmd.OpenForm "Customers", , , "CompanyName Like '*market*'" _
    , acReadOnly, acDialog
```

As with the use of leading spaces in the prior example, my team prefers the second alternative shown. Placing the comma at the beginning of the continued line is an immediate visual clue that the line is a continuation, even in the absence of any indentation.

On the road that leads to a consistent style, SQL statements introduce another fork. Depending on how much SQL you create, you may decide to standardize your approach or to ignore the issue completely. Consider the statement shown in Listing 11.9.

Listing 11.9   A Long SQL Statement Syntax Line Without Indentation

```
strSQL = "SELECT zstlogErr.ErrWhen, zstlogErr.ErrProcName," _
& " zstlogErr.ErrUserName, zstlogErr.ErrNumber," _
& " zstlogErr.ErrDescription FROM zstlogErr WHERE" _
& "(zstlogErr.ErrWhen >= #1/1/96#) AND" _
& "(zstlogErr.ErrNumber = 3146) ORDER BY zstlogErr.ErrWhen;"
```

The previous statement is what your English teacher used to call a run-on sentence, one that never seems to end. Worse yet, the statement shown is a *very* short SQL string. SQL statements in complex applications can go for 50 or a 100 lines.

Contrast the previous example with the code in Listing 11.10, which is at the extreme opposite end of the spectrum with respect to indentation.

11

Listing 11.10   A Long SQL Statement Syntax Line with Indentation

```
strSQL = "SELECT   zstlogErr.ErrWhen," _
             & " zstlogErr.ErrProcName," _
             & " zstlogErr.ErrUserName," _
             & " zstlogErr.ErrNumber," _
             & " zstlogErr.ErrDescription" _
    & " FROM   zstlogErr" _
```

continues

Listing 11.10   Continued

```
       & " WHERE    (zstlogErr.ErrWhen >= #1/1/96#)" _
             & " AND" _
             & " (zstlogErr.ErrNumber = 3146)" _
       & " ORDER BY zstlogErr.ErrWhen;"
```

If I'm trying to find an error or insert a change in a long SQL statement, especially one that I didn't personally write, the second style of formatting can save several minutes of confusion.

 Note

Don't worry about a performance penalty for the indenting scheme shown—Jet optimizes the extra spaces out. Also, if you use code like this to create a new `QueryDef` object in a database, when you go to Design view in the query you'll find that Jet has removed your indentation and spaces in favor of its own wrapping model. Your painstakingly precise alignment is not saved in the `QueryDef`.

Using named procedure arguments provides a third option for standardizing the wrapping of code, because their use frequently produces multiline statements. Wrapping long commands with named arguments enables you to sort the arguments by name, which can improve readability and make reviewing or debugging a statement much easier. Consider the following statement that reorders the arguments to `OpenForm` alphabetically for readability and uses the indentation and line continuation styles described previously:

```
DoCmd.OpenForm "frmCust" _
  , DataMode:=acReadOnly _
  , WhereCondition:="CompanyName Like '*market*'" _
  , WindowMode:=acDialog
```

None of the style decisions involved in wrapping long code lines could be considered mission-critical or make your code run any faster or slower. Thus, standardizing an approach to this task is more important for team development than when coding in a solo environment.

Sprinkling Your Code with Comments

In the chapter on the Leszynski Naming Conventions (Chapter 6), I included suggestions for procedure-level code comments. Basically, you should consider standardizing the type of information you put at the top of each procedure and the information's layout. Consistent code comments are very useful when reading your own or another person's code.

> ### Audit Trail Ad-Nauseum
> One time at a client site, I noted that their IT group placed revision comments at the top of each of their code routines. The comments looked something like this:
>
> ```
> ' FSB 1/10/94 Created procedure
> ' FSB 1/14/94 Finished procedure
> ' ALC 4/12/94 Converted dynasets to snapshots for performance
> ' FSB 10/1/94 Added new error trapping model
> ```
>
> I didn't disagree with the idea in principle, but I did notice that some of the comment blocks got very long, which required you to press PgDn several times from the top of a procedure just to see the first line of code. As I was reviewing and debugging their code, I found that these comments got in the way and did not add value. Even worse, I found some procedures that were totally empty *except for* comments, with the last one reading something like this:
>
> ```
> ' ALC 2/14/96 Procedure abandoned, code removed
> ```
>
> This seemed to indicate that they placed a higher value on their comments than they did on their code!

Here are some examples of commonly used procedure heading comments:

Arguments. Describe the arguments passed to the procedure by type, restrictions, or disposition.

Authors. Name the original author and the creation date, and the last editor and edit date.

Called By. List other routines that rely on this routine.

Calls. List other routines that are called by this routine.

Example of Use. Show a sample line of code calling the procedure.

Open Issues. List incomplete items or areas targeted for improvement.

Owner. Name the owner of the procedure (*library* routines often have a designated owner who must approve all changes).

Purpose. Describe the purpose of the procedure.

Return Value. Describe the value returned by a Function to its calling routine.

Here is an example of a reasonable amount of comment information, taken from the top of one of our routines:

```
Public Sub lci_ErrLog(rlngErr As Long, rstrProc As String _
   , rstrDesc As String)
```

```
' Purpose:    Write an error log record to zstlogError
' Arguments:  rlngErr:=Error number
'             rstrProc:=Module and procedure name
'             rstrDesc:=Err.Description or similar string to log
' Authors:    Created 11/10/95 SWL  Edited 3/2/96 WOW
' Example:    lci_ErrLog(Err.Description, cstrProc, Err.Description)
' Called By:  lci_ErrMsgStd
' Calls:      lci_IsBlank
```

If you are inclined to keep a revision history in your procedures (see the previous sidebar), consider placing the comments at the bottom of procedures just before the End Sub or End Function statement, rather than at the top. The information is still available when needed but is less obtrusive.

For *in-line* code comments, your options are to create comments as independent lines or to add comments to the ends of code lines. Both are useful, and some developers prefer to mix and match them. Other teams use only full-line comments, in order to make reviewing code or stripping comments easier.

In either case, I generally find that the location of the comment is less important than what it says. There is a fine balance between too many comments and too few, and the judgment of what is *too much* or *too little* is in the eye of the individual reader of the code.

 Tip

When I'm reading others' code, I tend to expect a comment every five or ten lines as an average, depending on the complexity of the routine. If there are too few comments, I find it impossible to browse the code by simply reading the comments, which I will do when looking for a specific feature or simply trying to understand the general flow of the routine.

Listing 11.11 provides an example of in-line code comments that help to clarify the values in an If block for readers who are not the original coder. The If, ElseIf, and Else values are all explained:

Listing 11.11   Using Comments to Clarify Each *If*, *ElseIf*, and *Else* Statement

```
If olngHelpID = -1 Then  ' No Help button
  MsgBox strMsg, vbOKOnly + vbCritical, lci_gcstrAppTitle
ElseIf olngHelpID = 0 Then  ' Use the default ID
  MsgBox strMsg, vbOKOnly + vbCritical, lci_gcstrAppTitle _
    , lci_gcstrAppHelp, lci_gcintAppErrHelpID
ElseIf olngHelpID > 0 Then  ' Use the argument ID
  MsgBox strMsg, vbOKOnly + vbCritical, lci_gcstrAppTitle _
```

```
        , lci_gcstrAppHelp, olngHelpID
  Else   ' Error, bad ID
    MsgBox "Problem@Invalid value '" & CStr(olngHelpID) _
        & "' passed to error handler '" & mcstrMod & "." & cstrProc _
        & "'.", vbOKOnly + vbCritical, lci_gcstrAppTitle
  End If
```

One commenting technique that has helped us a lot is to standardize how our developers note open issues in code. When we stop coding at a certain point, "comment-out" an On Error statement for testing purposes, or want to record an open issue in the code, we use two exclamation marks, like this:

```
lci_ErrLog_Err:
   '!!TODO Add support for log to file if back-end not found
   Beep
   ...
```

Before we ship an application, we search all of its code for our custom '!! marker and review the attached comments to see whether any of them indicate work that must be finished before releasing the application.

 Note

> If you place comments in your code, they must be as accurate as the code itself, and they must be modified when the code changes in order to keep them accurate. Misleading comments are worse than none at all.

Another handy commenting technique is to place comment blocks at the top of the Declarations section of each module that describes the module, its purpose, and the procedures in the module. Such a record serves as a quick reference for the entire module, as shown in Listing 11.12.

Listing 11.12   AES_VBA.Mdb—Module Comments Serve as a Quick Reference for the Module

```
' lci_basLibErr, Version 1/31/96
' Standard error handling routines
' Copyright (c) 1995-96 Leszynski Company, Inc.
' May not be used without permission
' All routines here should start with 'lci_Err'
' Library dependencies:
'   lci_basLibGen1.lci_IsBlank()
'   lci_basLibInit.gstrCurrentUser
' Index:
'   lci_ErrLog      - Write error log record to zstlogError
'   lci_ErrMsgFixup - Remove @ signs from an Err.Description string
'   lci_ErrMsgStd   - Standard error message display
```

11

Handling Runtime Errors

One of the most intimidating facets of the development process is the way that no program ever seems able to be perfected. Some testing cycles seem to go on forever, as developers fix bugs and create bugs in the same keystrokes. There always seems to be one more thing keeping the software from being done.

When the solution finally does ship, it is presupposed that the users will find ways to make it misbehave. However, not all *problems* are *bugs*. There are several reasons why processes or code in an application can fail:

Unforeseen Circumstances. Events can occur that are beyond the scope of the design document or the coder's vision. For example, a programmatic routine to import data from a mainframe export file into Access tables will break if the mainframe programmer rearranges the data file's structure without notifying the Access programmer.

Infrastructure Problems. Network hiccups, a full disk drive, tight memory resources, and other mechanical problems with the user's operating environment can cause your application to fail or generate an error.

User Interaction. No matter how good a development team's testing abilities are, some user somewhere will find a combination of keystrokes, a sequence of events, or a set of data values that are not accommodated comfortably by the application.

Coding errors. I said earlier that not *all* problems are bugs, but certainly *some* of them are. In larger applications, it is just not possible to test every unique scenario or review every line of code, and this situation leaves small ticking time bombs scattered within the program.

When an application fails for one of the listed reasons, Access, Jet, or VBA generates an internal error event and expresses this occurrence to your code. If you have not designated a mechanism for handling these error notifications, Access stops and displays the offending line of code (or alternately displays its own error alert if no code is running).

You tell Access how to deal with error conditions by placing On Error statements in your code. There are several derivatives of the On Error statement:

```
On Error Goto 0

On Error Goto labelname

On Error Resume Next
```

In general, good development practice requires that you use the On Error Goto labelname variation in most code routines. It must name a line label as a jump destination when an error occurs. Below the line label, you place your error management code (called an *error handler*).

The standard flow of error handling in a procedure is shown in Listing 11.13.

Listing 11.13   The Commonly Used VBA Error-Handling Structure

```
proctype procname()
  On Error GoTo procname_Err
  ' The general code would be here

procname_Exit:
  ' The cleanup code would be here
  Exit proctype

procname_Err:
  ' The error handler code would be here
  Resume procname_Exit

End proctype
```

When an error occurs, control goes from the offending line (which does not complete execution) to the error handler (shown in the listing with the `procname_Err` label) and runs the statements there. To terminate your error-handler code block, you have three choices:

`Resume Next`. This statement causes code to resume execution at the line following the one that generated the error. Remember that the offending line *itself* never ran, so this statement enables your routine to skip a line of code that may be critical. Use it with care.

`Resume labelname`. This command branches out of the error handler and resumes execution at the named label. In the previous listing, it causes the routine to jump to the `procname_Exit` label and leave the routine. However, you could use this statement to create more complex handlers that jump to various locations within a procedure depending on specific error numbers, as shown in Listing 11.14.

11

Listing 11.14   Code Can Branch from an Error Handler to Various Locations in the Procedure

```
Select Case Err.Number
  Case 52, 53, 64, 75, 76   ' Path/file error or not found
    Resume ErrNoPath
  Case 57, 68, 71  ' No device or disk
    Resume ErrNoDisk
  Case Else  ' Unspecified error
    Resume ErrOther
End Select
```

Resume. This statement resumes execution where the original error occurred; in other words, it retries the offending line of code. You can use this when you've trapped a specific type of error in an error handler and rectified it. As an example, when you check for database properties in Jet that are created by Access, they may not yet exist when your code looks for them. You can create the missing property in the error handler and Resume, as in Listing 11.15:

Listing 11.15   AES_VBA.Mdb—A Customized Error Handler Can Check for a Specific Error by Number

```
Public Sub lci_AppIconCheck()
' Purpose: Try to locate and set the application icon

  On Error GoTo lci_AppIconCheck_Err
  Const cintErrPrpNotFound As Integer = 3270
  Dim dbsCurr As Database
  Dim prpIcon As Property    ' User-defined property
  Dim strIcon As String      ' Icon filename

  ' If the property does not exist, the next line jumps to _Err
  strIcon = dbsCurr.Properties("AppIcon")   ' Get the icon

  ' The rest of the code would be here

lci_AppIconCheck_Exit:
  Exit Sub

lci_AppIconCheck_Err:
  If Err.Number = cintErrPrpNotFound Then
    Set prpIcon = dbsCurr.CreateProperty("AppIcon", dbText _
      , "C:\Office\Access\Default.Ico")
    dbsCurr.Properties.Append prpIcon
    Resume   ' And retry the offending line
  Else
    ' The standard error handler would be here
  End If

End Sub
```

In addition to On Error Goto labelname, you can issue the On Error GoTo 0 statement to turn off error handling in the current procedure. When an error occurs while this command is in effect, VBA goes backwards through the call tree looking for a procedure with an error handler and executes the first one it finds. If it finds none, Access itself responds to the error by providing an alert.

For example, Listing 11.16 shows nested routines, with only the parent routine enabling an error handler. The child routine instead uses On Error Goto 0, which tells it to find an available handler or use Access' handler. When the child routine fails, the routine in the parent is triggered to supplant it.

Listing 11.16   AES_VBA.Mdb—A Demonstration of *On Error Goto 0* Passing Errors to the Next Available Handler

```
' The parent routine
Private Sub cmdGoto0_Click()
' Purpose: Demonstrate ramifications of On Error Goto 0
' Calls:   cbfGoto0

  ' This routine has an error trap
  On Error GoTo cmdGoto0_Click_Err
  Const cstrProc As String = "cmdGoto0_Click"

  Call cbfGoto0  ' Goto the subordinate routine

cmdGoto0_Click_Exit:
  Exit Sub

cmdGoto0_Click_Err:
  Call lci_ErrMsgStd(Me.Name & "." & cstrProc, Err.Number _
    , Err.Description, True)
  Resume cmdGoto0_Click_Exit

End Sub


' The child routine in the same form
Sub cbfGoto0()
' Purpose:   Shows how an error here is passed up the call tree
' Called By: cmdGoto0_Click

  On Error GoTo 0  ' Error goes to parent's handler or Access
  DoCmd.OpenForm "frmBogusName"  ' Not a real form, triggers an error

End Sub
```

Caution

The use of `On Error Goto 0` can be terribly dangerous. When a routine fails but passes its error to a higher-level handler, all context is lost and the higher error handler essentially inherits the blame for the code that failed. This makes debugging very difficult.

11

`On Error Goto 0` was formerly used to turn off error handling in order to enable debugging. The new Break on All Errors option setting provides a better mechanism for debugging, leaving `On Error Goto 0` with limited usefulness.

The third error-handling syntax is the `On Error Resume Next` statement, which enables you to momentarily discontinue error handling and simply ignore any resulting errors. The line that produced the error will not complete, but execution resumes at the line follow-ing the offender. This command is used when you consciously want to skip a statement or block of code and not be notified if it fails to run.

For example, it's a good coding policy to close open Jet objects (recordsets, databases, and so on) before leaving a procedure. However, if you are exiting a procedure due to an error, the objects you are trying to close may not ever have gotten created within the procedure; thus, you may generate *another* error while trying to bail out after an error. `On Error Resume Next` solves this situation by simply skipping statements that could cause such problems:

```
procname_Exit:
    On Error Resume Next
    rst.Close
    dbs.Close
    Exit Sub
```

Error-handling code can be as simple as giving the user a message and giving up, as in this example:

```
procname_Err:
    MsgBox "Error: "& cstr(Err.Number) & " " & Err.Description,,"Oops!"
    Resume procname_Exit  ' Abort the procedure
```

Alternatively, some routines need rather complex error handling. Here are three ex-amples of situations where you may want to provide advanced (smarter) error recovery than simply halting the procedure:

> *Working with files.* Disk file input/output routines can accrue a variety of problems, from the inability to open an output file on a read-only drive to attempting to locate a file that has been moved. Your code can trap for specific errors related to file operations and sometimes provide the user with a resolution path rather than giving up.
>
> For example, a routine that opens a disk file should not abort if the file is not found. Instead, your error handler can check for an `Err.Number` of 53 ("File not found") and display the common dialog for opening files, instructing the user to locate the missing file. If a valid filename is returned, the error handler can then `Resume` to the line that initially failed and continue onward.
>
> *Working with recordsets.* Recordset operations can generate unique and trappable errors, not all of which are fatal per se. Your error handler can contain various snares to capture specific errors and act accordingly.
>
> For example, an `Update` method applied to a recordset that bumps into a lock cre-ated by another user generates error number 3260 ("Couldn't update..."). When your error handler detects this error, it could ask the user whether she wants to

wait 10 seconds and try the update again, or move onward. If the user chooses to wait, each time the update is retried until the lock clears generates another error and its dialog, so the user can choose to wait indefinitely until the lock clears rather than simply aborting the routine.

 Tip

Some recordset operations legitimately should be discarded completely if one operation fails. However, others can be continued even in the presence of a partial failure. In such a case, your code should be smart enough to detect the error, determine that it is not fatal, and move past the problem record to the next record in the recordset and continue processing.

Client/server processes. Client/server routines may return multiple errors when ODBC is involved. They might also suffer from Automation errors, record lock contentions, connection timeouts, and various other aberrations. When working within this metaphor, your error-trapping code must rise to the occasion.

See Chapter 19, "Exploring Client/Server Issues," for an example that involves trapping multiple ODBC errors in Jet's Errors collection.

How your application displays error conditions to users is an area where your personal development style is reflected in your application. Your error messages may be as terse as simply displaying the Err.Description property of the Error object in a message box. Alternatively, error displays can be as elaborate as drawing a custom form that shows error context information, a suggested resolution, and a telephone extension or e-mail address to use for immediate support.

 Tip

If your users see several error messages more frequently than others, you can create strings of extra information to display for these specific errors to provide them with extra help. Keep the strings in a table with the error number as the key, then open an error alert form filtered to show only the specific message text for the error in process.

Alternatively, create help topics for the most frequent errors and call the help topics from your error handler.

You can discern which errors occur most frequently by logging all errors to a database table as they occur. See Chapter 17, "Bulletproofing Your Application Interface," for more information on this technique.

11

Here are the most common problems related to error handling that I see in applications:

Unhandled Errors. Errors that are not properly trapped are challenging for the user because they may be quite intimidated by some of Access' default messages. Such errors are also challenging for the coder because they don't contain enough context information to explain where the error is occurring and thus are difficult to debug (this is especially true in runtime applications). No matter how good of a developer or tester you are, you cannot predict, with certainty, all the different ways an application may fail.

 Note

In a professional-grade expert solution, even the smallest code routine has an error handler.

Recursion. It is possible to create code routines that have the proper error trapping yet can be made to loop back on themselves, sometimes infinitely. Consider the code in Listing 11.17, which looks innocuous but contains a hidden bomb.

Listing 11.17   Code that Runs in an Infinite Recursive Loop When It Fails

```
wsp.BeginTrans
' Recordset code would go here
wsp.CommitTrans

ErrSample_Exit:
  Exit Sub

ErrSample _Err:
  ' Code would display error message here
  wsp.Rollback  ' This line will fail if no open transaction
  Resume ErrSample_Exit
```

The code in the listing works fine as long as there is an open transaction to roll back. If, however, an error is generated *before* the BeginTrans statement has been issued, when the code drops to this error handler and tries to process the Rollback statement, a second error condition is generated before the first is resolved; this situation cannot be handled properly because the error handler is already in the middle of a process, so Access volunteers its own error alert, producing a circular situation, which is sloppy at best and dangerous at the worst.

> **Tip**
> The solution to the problem just demonstrated is to set a flag (for example,
> `blnInTrans = True`) whenever you open a transaction, and check the flag in the
> error handler before rolling back the transaction, as in this example:
>
> ```
> ' The following replaces the single line: wsp.Rollback
> If blnInTrans Then
>    wsp.Rollback
> End If
> ```

Break On All Errors. This setting is very useful, but is not the panacea for all testing ailments. The first problem is that there are times when you legitimately want your code to handle some errors cleanly and to break on others. However, this option setting assumes that every error is bad and cannot be configured at a level lower than global. Thus, your testing efforts drop to code lines that are not offensive or wrong simply because all error handling is turned off.

For example, imagine a line of code that looks for a database property, like this:

```
str = dbsCurr.Properties("AppTitle")  ' Get the title
```

This line generates an error if the property is not found by Jet, a situation that still reflects a valid state (no setting has been entered for the Application Title of the database). Your application may not consider this a problem, and choose to simply discard it in the error handler. With Break On All Errors enabled, however, this line generates an error every time it is run.

The second shortcoming in this option setting is that it is very black and white—you either drop to code or not. You cannot configure a rich testing environment with it.

The solution to these situations is to use conditional compilation instead of Break On All Errors when you need extra control. You can provide wrappers around your error handlers that emulate the work of Break On All Errors but provide more flexibility; in the following example, each routine enables or disables error handling based on a flag in its module:

```
#If mcccDebug = False Then  ' Module-level debug mode
   On Error GoTo procname_Err
#End If
```

To make error handling easier to code and more flexible in your application, you can create and reuse one or more standard error-handling routines. For example, you can create a routine to handle file I/O errors, and a different one for recordset errors. You can call these routines as library functions from your error handler or paste the code into the handlers as required.

11

You also can create a standard routine for error messages and logging. The code in Listing 11.18 shows our standard library routines for displaying error messages to the user and capturing the error condition in a table. Our standard routine is complex, but even if you choose not to use it, you benefit from understanding how our approach works.

Figure 11.3 shows an alert generated by the routine in the listing.

Fig. 11.3

This custom error alert is drawn by a library display routine.

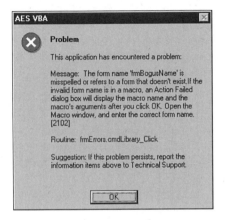

Listing 11.18   AES_VBA.Mdb—A Central Library Routine for Error Message Display

```
Public Sub lci_ErrMsgStd(rstrProc As String, rlngErr As Long _
  , rstrDesc As String, rblnLog As Boolean _
  , Optional ovarResol As Variant, Optional olngHelpID As Long = -1)
' Purpose:   Standard error message display
' Arguments: rstrProc   :=Module and procedure name
'            rlngErr    :=Err number
'            rstrDesc   :=Error description
'            rblnLog    :=True/False=add to error log table
'            ovarResol  :=Resolution string, if Missing uses global
'            olngHelpID :=Help context ID, -1=none (default)
'                       , 0=app default, >0=ID to call
' Example:   Call lci_ErrMsgStd(Me.Name & "." & cstrProc, Err.Number _
'                  , Err.Description , True, "Compact the database.", 128)
' Calls:     lci_ErrLog
' Pseudo Code:
'   1. Build the Problem message section from the argument values
'   2. Add Jet/ODBC information from the Errors collection
'   3. Add a standard resolution string and app title string
'   4. Show the message with the appropriate message box buttons
'   5. Log the error to a table if requested

  On Error GoTo lci_ErrorMsgStd_Err
  Const cstrProc As String = "lci_ErrMsgStd"
  Dim errJet    As Error
  Dim strDAOMsg As String
  Dim strMsg    As String
```

```
    strMsg = "Problem@" & lci_gcstrAppErrIntro & vbCrLf & vbCrLf
    strMsg = strMsg & "Message:   " & lci_ErrMsgFixup(rstrDesc) _
      & " [" & CStr(rlngErr) & "]" & vbCrLf & vbCrLf
    strMsg = strMsg & "Routine:   " & rstrProc

    ' If Jet errors were found, add them to the message
    If DBEngine.Errors.Count > 1 Then
      If DBEngine.Errors(DBEngine.Errors.Count-1).Number = rlngErr Then
        For Each errJet In DBEngine.Errors
          With errJet
            strDAOMsg = strDAOMsg & "  " _
              & lci_ErrMsgFixup(.Description) _
              & " [" & CStr(.Number) & " in " & .Source & "]"
          End With
        Next
        strMsg = strMsg & vbCrLf & vbCrLf & "Details:" & strDAOMsg
      End If
    End If

    If IsMissing(ovarResol) Then
      strMsg = strMsg & "@Suggestion: " & lci_gcstrAppErrResol
    Else
      strMsg = strMsg & "@Suggestion: " & ovarResol
    End If

    If olngHelpID > -1 Then  ' Will have Help button, add help text
      strMsg = strMsg & " " & lci_gcstrAppErrHelp
    End If
    Beep
    If olngHelpID = -1 Then  ' No Help button
      MsgBox strMsg, vbOKOnly + vbCritical, lci_gcstrAppTitle
    ElseIf olngHelpID = 0 Then  ' Use the default ID
      MsgBox strMsg, vbOKOnly + vbCritical, lci_gcstrAppTitle _
        , lci_gcstrAppHelp, lci_gcintAppErrHelpID
    ElseIf olngHelpID > 0 Then  ' Use the argument ID
      MsgBox strMsg, vbOKOnly + vbCritical, lci_gcstrAppTitle _
        , lci_gcstrAppHelp, olngHelpID
    Else  ' Error, bad ID
      MsgBox "Problem@Invalid value '" & CStr(olngHelpID) _
        & "' passed to error handler '" & mcstrMod & "." _
        & cstrProc & "'.", _
        vbOKOnly + vbCritical, lci_gcstrAppTitle
      GoTo lci_ErrorMsgStd_Exit
    End If

    If rblnLog Then
      Call lci_ErrLog(rlngErr, rstrProc, strMsg)
    End If

lci_ErrorMsgStd_Exit:
  On Error Resume Next
  Exit Sub

lci_ErrorMsgStd_Err:
  ' In a failure, this routine should not call itself
  Beep
```

continues

Listing 11.18   Continued

```
strMsg = "Problem@This application has encountered a problem '" _
    & Err.Description & " [" & CStr(Err.Number) _
    & "]' in the error display handler '" & mcstrMod _
    & "." & cstrProc & "'." & "@" & lci_gcstrAppErrResol
MsgBox strMsg, vbOKOnly + vbCritical, lci_gcstrAppTitle
Resume lci_ErrorMsgStd_Exit

End Sub
```

Here are the highlights of the routine in the listing:

> *Context.* The name of the procedure where the error occurred is supplied as an argument (`rstrProc`) so that appropriate context can be shown to the user in the custom message.

> `MsgBox()` *Formatting.* The code that builds the display string for the `MsgBox()` function adds two @ characters to the custom string. These are VBA formatting characters that divide a message box string into three parts.

> The part before the first @ is shown as a bold header. The part between the middle @ characters is shown as a non-bold string separated from the first string by a blank line. The final portion is displayed after another blank line. Figure 11.4 shows the result of issuing a `MsgBox` statement in the Debug window using this new feature.

Fig. 11.4

Using the formatting character (@) produces this customized `MsgBox()` *alert.*

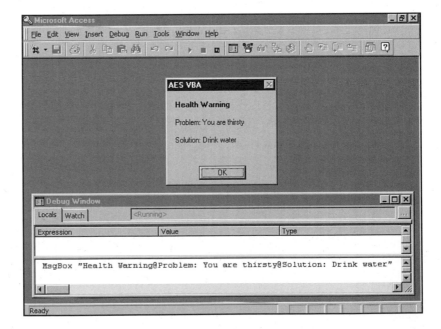

Note

In Access 95, the `MsgBox()` function inserted the word Solution in bold as a header line before the text in the third substring (after the second @). This feature has been removed from Access 97; you can no longer create a second bolded header in the message box.

Errors Collection. ODBC routines can generate multiple error strings, which Jet captures in its `Errors` collection. If multiple errors are in the collection, the routine adds the extra strings to the message body.

Global String Constants. To allow for configuration of the library routine on a per-application basis, the "suggested resolution" string displayed to the user is stored in a constant `lci_gcstrAppErrResol` that can be changed for each database, as is the standard string that tells the user how to get help: `lci_gcstrAppErrHelp`. The default (global) resolution suggestion string can be overridden by passing in an optional argument (`ovarResol`).

Help Contexts. The VBA `MsgBox()` function now accepts an optional help file name and context ID, enabling you to provide targeted help for specific situations by adding a Help button to the message box and jumping to a specific topic from it. The listed routine gets the application's help file name from an application constant `lci_gcstrAppHelp`, and the help context ID to call comes in via its argument list (as `olngHelpID`).

Error Logging. If the calling procedure requests to have the error logged (using `rblnLog`), the routine calls `lci_ErrLog`, another library routine whose job it is to append the user ID, error number, description, and offending procedure name to a log table `zstlogErr`. (This technique for error logging is also discussed in Chapter 17, "Bulletproofing Your Application Interface.")

Avoding Recursion. If the error message routine fails, it should not call itself again, leading to infinite recursion. Thus, any errors generated in the procedure itself must be managed directly in the error handler.

There are more subtleties to handling runtime errors than were listed in this topic, but they all involve variations on the ideas I've presented here. Handling errors properly is a development chore that must be taken seriously and a talent that is cultivated through hands-on experience.

11

Optimizing Your Basic Code Routines

I'll admit, quite candidly at this point, that some of the techniques for creating expert solutions create slower code, not faster code. For example, a Basic loop that calls out to a library function in each iteration of the loop runs more slowly than one that calls a chunk of code embedded directly inside the loop. Therefore, as you create modular code according to my model, you are possibly slowing your applications.

A counterbalance to this point is that, as your coding expertise increases, you can offset the speed losses in one area with speed gains in another by writing better code. Additionally, as the VBA compiler improves with age, the compilation process becomes more sophisticated at optimizing your code, and thus its architecture becomes less important. All things considered, the performance of your applications is more strongly affected by database operations than VBA code execution speed. Thus, the place to optimize your application first is in data access.

When you do get around to reviewing your code for VBA performance bottlenecks, keep in mind the primary VBA performance negative in Access 97 applications: uncompiled code. VBA decompiles the code in your application when any of these events occurs:

A code change in any module.

The addition or deletion of any form or report.

The addition or deletion of any form control or report control.

Renaming a form, report, or control.

Changing the name of the database file.

Renaming a procedure.

Code in an uncompiled state must be recompiled as it is run. An uncompiled application is a certain breeding ground for performance complaints.

Your code can check the compilation state of the application using the new IsCompiled property, as shown in Listing 11.19:

Listing 11.19   AES_VBA.Mdb—Handling an Uncompiled Application with *IsCompiled*

```
If Application.IsCompiled = False Then
  Beep
  If MsgBox("This application is decompiled and my run slowly." _
    & " Would you like to recompile the application now?" _
    , vbYesNo, lci_gcstrAppTitle) = vbYes Then
    ' Recompile the application. Note that this requires opening
    '   a module, which may be dangerous in a production application
    DoCmd.OpenModule "lci_basLibInit"
```

```
        Application.RunCommand acCmdCompileAndSaveAllModules
        DoCmd.Close acModule, "lci_basLibInit", acSaveNo
    End If
End If
```

Access 97 uses a new "compile on demand" model which tests a module's compilation state as it's loaded into memory (when a procedure that resides in it is first called). If the module is not compiled, Access compiles it first (but does not save the compiled state). This takes time. Before you ship, and whenever you make a change to an application already deployed, compile the *entire* application. Open any module (form or standard) and select Debug, Compile and Save All Modules.

 Note

Report and form code is now saved in a compiled state if you compile it before you save the object. Thus, form and report code either run *faster* than in Access 2 (if compiled), or *slower* (if not compiled), but rarely at the same speed as in the version of Access that most of us use for performance metrics.

The next two sections provide additional performance considerations.

Improving VBA Performance

In addition to the standard admonitions discussed elsewhere in this chapter (including remember to compile your code before shipping and use conditional compilation to selectively exclude code), there are several less potent techniques that can add incremental performance benefits to your applications. Applied together, they may provide a noticeable speed improvement:

Unscatter Procedures. When VBA runs a procedure, it loads all the code in the procedure's module into memory. You should group procedures with this in mind—the old approach of a single library module in an application may be a lesser performer than a score of much smaller library modules that each hold only a few, related routines.

Thus, if procedure SubOne calls procedure SubTwo, having SubTwo in the same module as SubOne will provide the fastest execution of both. It can be useful to map the dependencies in your code and organize procedures into modules that group the dependencies as much as is practical.

Reuse object variables and object references. If an object is referenced more than once within a procedure, create an object variable to designate the object, and use the variable in all references. For example, a form control reference

`Forms!frmCust!txtCustName` used repeatedly in the same procedure is much less efficient than assigning the reference to a `TextBox` variable `txt` and referring to the variable instead.

In the same vein, you can enhance the speed of references to objects through the use of the `With` statement. See the example in the following section "Speeding Up Automation."

Release object variables as soon as possible. In the "Speeding Up Automation" section that follows, I note the importance of releasing an Automation session's `Application` (or other entry point) variable as soon as it is unneeded. This same maxim applies to *any* variable of *any* object type, such as `Form`, `Control`, `Recordset`, and similar variables. You do not have to wait until the end of a procedure to release an object variable; instead, as soon as it is *unneeded*, set it to `Nothing`.

Use `Me` to refer to the current form. Any reference to the `Forms` collection (such as `Forms("frmCust")` or `Forms!frmCust`) must look outside of the current form to the `Application` object to resolve the reference, whereas the `Me` designator is resolved within the form's name space.

Use `Run` to call library routines. When your code calls a routine in a referenced library database, you can use the `Run` method described earlier in this chapter instead of calling the remote procedure directly. Doing so loads only the module from the library database that contains the called procedure. In contrast, calling a library procedure without `Run` loads from the referenced database all modules that have any procedures that are in the call tree of the called routine, even if they are not needed in the current context. This concept is explained further in Chapter 20, "Applying Development Shortcuts."

Restrict your use of the `Variant` data type in expressions or assignments. Access must do an internal type conversion from a `Variant` to its underlying type in order to use it in math or string operations. This analysis slows the processing of the expression when compared to using variables of the more specific type. For example, the `Mid()` function used on a `Variant` variable executes more slowly than the corresponding `Mid$()` function on a `String` variable.

Optimize array memory. Rather than creating arrays with fixed dimensions, start with empty arrays and `ReDim` the array larger on demand. When an upper-end array element is no longer needed, `ReDim` the array smaller with the `Preserve` keyword to recoup array memory. Clear an array completely with the `Erase` statement as soon as it is unneeded.

Compile On Demand. Make sure that the Compile On Demand option on the Module tab of the Options dialog box is selected. With this setting on, Access compiles an entire module only when it's actually called. With this setting off, Access compiles a module as part of its call tree processing, which means that if a module loads into memory to run, every module for every procedure that's called by any procedure in the loading module is compiled at that time. This can be a significant slowdown to an application, as you saw in Access 95 which used the call tree processing compilation model.

Create and reuse constants. A constant is tokenized during the compile and does not need to be analyzed again at runtime. If you use a static value more than once in a procedure or module, consider assigning it to a constant. Also, use the intrinsic Access constants where appropriate.

 Tip

There are quite a few new intrinsic constants that you can use in your code, such as days (vbWednesday, et. al.), keyboard characters (from vbKeyA to vbKeyZ), and the long-desired carriage-return/linefeed combination (vbCrLf). Browse the Access, DAO, and VBA libraries in the Object Browser to see the available constants.

Economize. Access stores the uncompiled version of your VBA code in the database file, which increases the file's size and consumes disk space. If the file size of your application is an issue of concern, you can create an MDE file (contains no source code) as described in Chapter 17, "Bulletproofing Your Application Interface." If you intend to preserve the source code in your application, you can strip the application of everything that could be considered excess baggage, as in the following:

▶ Remove all comments.

▶ Delete all blank lines and extra spaces.

▶ Combine multiple code lines using colons between the statements.

▶ Remove line continuations.

These techniques will reduce the overall size of the application file.

11

𝛼 **Note**

In the past, conventional wisdom said that economizing code with such techniques made the code run faster. With VBA's new compilation model, this is no longer true. There is no performance gain from making your (raw) source code more sparse.

Minimize repaints. While an iterative loop is running in code, it might be nice to display to the user a counter on the status bar or on a form showing the progress. However, each update of a visual object in Access causes a screen repaint on part or all of the screen, which slows the application significantly. Consider showing status increases at larger intervals (every 100 records instead of each one), or turning off application repaints altogether during processing, until the final results are displayed.

 Note

To disable screen repaints, set the `Painting` property of a form to `False`, or set the `Application` object's `Echo` property off.

There are literally dozens more small VBA optimization techniques, but the performance benefits of each is marginal when contrasted with the benefits from optimization of other elements of an application, such as form loading, Automation, and data access.

Speeding Up Automation

An Automation session sends information back and forth between the server and controller through *connections*. Connections are managed automatically (you cannot see them), but due to the way Automation works, they are re-created for each message sent back and forth.

However, you can trick Automation into keeping a connection open by using the new `With` statement, as in Listing 11.20.

Listing 11.20   AES_VBA.Mdb—Optimizing Automation Code Using *With*

```
Dim accappNwind As Access.Application
Set accappNwind = CreateObject("Access.Application.8")
accappNwind.OpenCurrentDatabase "C:\Office\Samples\Northwind.Mdb"

With accappNwind
  .Visible = False
  With .DoCmd
    .OpenReport "Summary of Sales by Quarter"
    .OpenReport "Summary of Sales by Year"
  End With
  .Quit
End With

Set accappNwind = Nothing
```

> **Note**
>
> Using `With` to keep a connection open increases the speed of your code only if *early binding* is used (the object variable is declared by type). In a *late-bound* variable (declared as `Object`), the `With` statement shows no performance benefit and may actually run slower. (See the section "Putting Access to Work via Automation" earlier in this chapter to review the definitions of these terms.)

Your Automation work also performs better if you apply these techniques:

Batch your requests. Opening and closing an Automation session is very resource- and time-intensive. Try to create an application flow that opens a remote Access (or other Automation server) session and performs all pending tasks within the single session, instead of opening and closing Automation sessions multiple times.

Run the session minimized. An Automation instance of Access can be run with its `Visible` property set to `False`, which keeps the application minimized on the desktop. Without the need to repaint the screen regularly, actions within the session may execute faster.

Obviously, you must also give your Automation-enabled application a fighting chance to perform by providing it with a machine with 16M of RAM or greater.

From Here...

In creating this chapter, I had to identify the concepts that would provide you with the *most* food for thought and overall benefit as you develop Access applications. The scope of VBA, however, is quite large and provides many more opportunities for exploration than were visited here. Many other chapters in this book demonstrate VBA's features while in the process of teaching their own solution:

Chapter 7, "Understanding Application Architecture," describes the role of VBA in applications from a theoretical perspective.

Chapters 12 through 16 make extensive use of VBA to enable the expert forms techniques described there.

Several VBA techniques that help make an application more usable and friendly are shown in Chapter 17, "Bulletproofing Your Application Interface."

Chapter 19, "Exploring Client/Server Issues," uses VBA code and the DAO's connectivity to demonstrate using Access as a database server front-end.

The wizards, builders, and code libraries described in Chapter 20, "Applying Development Shortcuts," make use of the coding techniques detailed in this chapter.

chapter 12

Understanding Form Structures and Coding

12

In this chapter

◆ Use proper syntax when referencing form and control objects

◆ Dissect and modify the structure of a form object

◆ Create and use custom form properties

◆ Implement forms as reusable class modules

◆ Use VBA collections to work with forms and controls

F orms are the gateway to your data, and they help determine the ongoing quality of the data. Good form design ranks with good database design as one of the two most important components of an expert solution. The four chapters following this one provide a wealth of techniques for creating expert forms for your applications. However, before you can apply the techniques in those chapters, you must first possess some basic form development skills.

Form Layouts at Your Fingertips

In the 1980s, R:BASE from Microrim was one of the leading database development products, and I was an R:BASE consultant in those pre-Access days. One thing I loved about R:BASE was that it stored definitions for forms and reports as text strings in a database table that was neither hidden nor locked. Once you figured out the data structures of these tables, you could do wondrous things to form and report designs manually.

For one thing, you could edit any form's definition directly. Because the form development interface was slow to load, it was actually faster to change a form definition directly by typing `EDIT * FROM SysForm WHERE SysFName = 'Product'` and manually editing the layout information. If you were really bold, you could update layout properties by running SQL `UPDATE` queries against these form and report layout tables, for example, to change the default `PageSize` property of all reports at once.

You could even use the definition tables to ask questions about your form and report data structures. For example, you could review the `PageSize` property for every report in the database by simply typing `SELECT * FROM SysRep WHERE SysRData LIKE 'PageSize%'`. Finally, you could easily write program code that walked through the form and report definition tables and produced documentation on all of those objects.

So, naturally, when I got my Access 1.0 alpha copy, I began looking for the form and report definition tables. Coming up empty handed, I asked the Access team how to locate them so that I could create a documentation add-in for Access. They thought I was nuts and explained to me that the concept of exposing form and report structures went against two key Microsoft philosophies: (a) do not expose more of the product innards than necessary to the users because that would also expose the information to the competition, and (b) minimize support calls by protecting users from product features that, when used wrongly, could make their applications unusable.

To this day, the storage format of form and report definitions is not documented for developers. Perhaps Access forms load faster and support call frequency is lower as a result, but I still miss direct access to the information!

Using the Form Wizards in Access, you can shell out a usable form in a few minutes. For some users, when the wizard is finished, the form development is finished. For developers of expert forms, however, the work has just begun.

I use the term *expert form* to describe a form that meets a set of strict criteria for usability and functionality. If your application meets any of the following tests, you should be creating expert forms for your users:

Multi-User Needs. Will the application be used by more than one person and could multiple users be working with data in the same table at the same time?

Validation Required. Does the application contain data that is important enough to require the prevention of data entry/edit errors or mistaken deletions?

Usability Concerns. Will any of the application's users be less skilled with Access than the developers who created it?

Must Be User-Friendly. Will your database be used only by developers and power users? If not, the forms must be easy to understand and self-explanatory.

If you answered *yes* to any of these questions, you should take your application's forms quite seriously. Forms are the primary user interaction component of your application and will play a key role in the success or failure—and consequently the acceptance—of the application.

The tangible tests for qualifying as an Access expert form using my ruler include the following:

▶ The form is easy to understand from the first time it is used. The layout of the form is logical and fits a familiar paradigm for the user.

▶ The user is never lost with respect to getting help and assistance or knowing what is happening when a process is running.

▶ The user cannot enter incomplete data into the system, especially if the data would result in erroneous reports or other negative consequences.

▶ The user receives accurate and constructive feedback when errors occur or problems arise.

▶ The form is optimized for the best possible performance.

The conceptual basis for expert forms, some of the simple techniques for creating good forms, and the importance of the items in the previous list are all discussed in various sections in Part I of this book, especially in Chapter 8, "Designing Effective Interfaces."

In this chapter and the next four, I will explore advanced, hands-on techniques for creating forms that meet the preceding tests and provide the highest level of usability possible, as follows:

12

▶ This chapter provides an overview of forms, including form development and coding tips, and a discussion of some new features, such as collections and form class modules.

▶ Chapter 13, "Mastering Combo and List Boxes," describes techniques for adding power and flexibility to forms through the advanced use of Combo and List Box controls.

▶ Chapter 14, " Navigating in Forms and Applications," shows how to build applications that control the user's navigation through forms and how to make effective use of menus and toolbars.

▶ Chapter 15, "Protecting and Validating Data," discusses techniques for ensuring that forms allow only valid user interaction with application data.

▶ Chapter 16, "Presenting Data to Users," details expert form strategies for displaying and working with multiple records and with filtered record sets.

How to Refer to Forms and Controls

Before delving into the advanced form techniques, I'll answer a common question: Why are there so many ways to refer to a form and its controls in Access? There are five different syntax variations for referencing a member of the Forms collection, as follows:

```
Forms!formname
Forms![formname]
Forms("formname")
Forms(expression)
Forms(indexnumber)
```

 Note

The Forms collection includes only open forms. See the section "Working with Form Design Information" later in this chapter to learn how to work with forms that are not open.

With this syntactic flexibility comes some confusion. In addition, the list of syntax options gets even longer when you consider the Me identifier, which is shorthand for "the form in which this piece of code is running." Let's sort through these options and make some sense of them.

Note

Starting with Access 95, another syntax variation was introduced for referring to forms. The syntax applies to forms that have been opened via program code as class objects and prefixes the form name with `Form_`, as described in the section "Using Forms as Class Modules" later in this chapter.

Object References with a Bang (!)

The exclamation point is also called the *bang,* as in the spoken phrase "`Forms` bang `frmCust`" to express `Forms!frmCust`. Throughout Access, the bang stands for, "look at a member of the object's default collection," even though its name is not necessarily specified. Put another way, think of the bang as a syntax to find an object or property that you have named (such as a form), and the dot as a reference to an object or property that Access has named (such as `BackColor`). So the default member of the `Forms` object is a collection of loaded forms, each of which you named; thus, the syntax `Forms!formname` is legitimate.

 Note

An interesting sidelight to this syntactic structure is that you can have an object name that is the same as a property name and use the appropriate syntax to refer to the desired item. Assume that you name a form control `Filter`, even though using reserved words as object names is not a good policy. The first syntax below refers to the `Filter` control, while the second refers to the form's `Filter` property:

```
Me!Filter   ' Looks in the default collection (Controls) for the named control
Me.Filter   ' Looks for a property with this name
```

Moving down one level, consider one specific form within the `Forms` object. The form has more than one collection—it has both `Properties` and `Controls`. In order for the bang to work, one collection must be designated as the default. In this case, the Access team at Microsoft coded the `Controls` collection as the built-in default, so the syntax pairs in Listing 12.1 are equivalent for a form assigned to the variable `frmCust`.

12

Listing 12.1   Form Syntax Pairs that Are Equivalent

```
' Create a form object variable
Dim frmCust As Form
Set frmCust = Forms!frmCust

' Now contrast equivalent syntaxes

frmCust.Controls!controlname    ' Use the Controls collection name
frmCust!controlname             ' Drop the default collection name

frmCust.Controls![controlname]  ' Brackets are optional...
frmCust![controlname]           ' ...and used when the name has spaces

frmCust.Controls("controlname") ' The controlname must be in quotes...
frmCust("controlname")
frmCust(expression)             ' ...or as a variable or expression

frmCust(indexnumber)            ' Used if you know the index number...
frmCust.Controls(indexnumber)   ' ...of the control in the collection
```

 Note

In the examples in Listing 12.1, I used the object variable `frmCust` created at the top of the routine to make the code faster and more readable but the use of fully qualified references to the parent form in each of the displayed syntaxes is equally valid, as in:

```
Forms!frmCust.Controls!controlname
```

In contrast, because the `Properties` collection is not the default collection for a `Form` object, you could not refer to it directly with a bang; thus, the following syntax is *not* valid:

```
frmCust!propertyname   ' Not valid
```

 Note

My example here is complicated by the fact that Access allows members of an item's `Properties` collection to be referred to directly with a *dot*, as in `frmCust.propertyname`. This is an anomaly/feature specific to properties; nevertheless, my example is still accurate and serves to illustrate the issue at hand.

With several options to choose from, the decision points used to determine how to specify collection members on forms and other objects are as follows:

▶ Use the bang when the object name (form name, control name, and so on.) is known in advance, as in `Forms!frmCust`, for two reasons: (a) it is the shortest structure, thus requiring the least keystrokes, and (b) Access VBA compiles the absolute relationship between the objects and executes the code faster than other syntax variations.

 Note

If you have written any code against the Data Access Objects, you have already noticed that Jet supports and derives a performance boost from the bang syntax shortcut as well. The default member of a `Recordset` object is its `Fields` collection; thus, the following syntaxes are legitimate for a `Recordset` object `rst`:

```
rstCust.Fields!fieldname    ' Use the Fields collection name
rstCust!fieldname           ' Drop the default collection name
```

▶ Use the `objectname.collectionname(membername)` syntax when the `membername` item will be replaced at runtime, usually with an object name stored in a variable or other expression that evaluates to an object name. However, this syntax produces slower code than using the bang. You can also use a quoted object name string as the `membername`, but if you know the name you should be using the bang.

▶ The syntax structure, `collectionname(indexnumber)`, is only useful when looping through all the members of a collection, such as controls on a form. When Access builds a collection, it assigns an `indexnumber` to represent an item's location in the collection at a *point in time*. Because this number is random and transitory, it should not be saved in your code or used as a future reference to an item.

 Note

Visual Basic developers will wonder why my syntax diagrams do not include the following two syntactic formulations familiar to them:

```
controlname
Me.controlname
```

With the addition of the VBA engine, Access now allows both of these types of references. However, they do not execute as fast as references with a bang. The Access group still prefers to use the bang for collection member references and the dot for property references, so I follow suit. The use of a non-qualified control name is also an ambiguous object reference, and I prefer my code more explicit. Consider this code:

```
Dim txtCompanyName As TextBox
Set txtCompanyName = Me!txtCompanyName
MsgBox txtCompanyName.BackColor
```

Does the `MsgBox` statement in the sample refer to the form control directly or to the object variable that represents it? Only Access knows, thus this coding model is imprecise and potentially dangerous.

 Tip

The discussion of form references in this section and those that follow is directly relevant to working with reports as well. Substitute the objects `Form` and `Forms` with `Report` and `Reports` in the section, and the information provided is equally accurate.

Using the *Me* Designator

Starting with Access 2, the reference `Me` became an acceptable surrogate for the reference `Form` in Basic code. Nevertheless, I come across many Access users who have not yet made the switch to `Me`.

`Me` refers to the object that is running the current code, while `Form` refers to the `Form` property (the self-awareness or "form-ness") of the current form. In many cases, they are the same thing and are treated the same by Access, as when the following lines of code are placed in a form module:

```
MsgBox Me.Name     ' Show the form name
MsgBox Form.Name   ' Show the form name
```

Both of these code lines get a pointer to the form that contains the code; then they look at the `Name` property of the referenced object, so both produce the same result (for example, the string `frmCust`). However, there are also situations in which the two identifiers behave differently. The difference stems primarily from the fact that `Me` is only available from Basic code, while `Form` is available elsewhere in the form.

Technically, `Me` can be thought of as a `Private` form module-level VBA variable of type `Form`, created when a specific instance of a form is opened. Like a `Private` variable, `Me` has limited scope and is only available in the code behind its own form. `Me` always points to the form that contains the code procedure in which it is referenced, regardless of whether that form is the active form.

Like `Me`, the designator `Form` is available in Basic code. Additionally, `Form` can also be used in other elements of a form, including properties (such as the `ControlSource` and event properties of controls), and when referring to a form from code in other forms, from code in standard modules, and from macro actions.

Use the following points to understand the conceptual difference between Me and Form:

Me is like an object variable; thus, it only has scope within a form's module.

Form is like a property; thus, it can be referenced in any place in Access where you can reference other form properties. Technically, the designator, Form, is shorthand for the following reference to the "form-ness" of a form:

```
Forms!formname.Form
```

The following are three examples of the different usage of the two designators:

In Basic code behind a form, both Me and Form produce the same result. These four code lines are interchangeable:

```
Me.Caption = "Customer"     ' Set the form caption
Form.Caption = "Customer"   ' Set the form caption

Call FrmCaptionSet(Me, "Customer")     ' Set the form caption
Call FrmCaptionSet(Form, "Customer")   ' Set the form caption
```

In form properties, including event properties, Me is not available because it acts like a variable, so Form is the only option. For example, in the ControlSource of a form's text box, only the following first syntax is legitimate:

```
=[Form].[Filter]   ' Retrieves the form's Filter property
=[Me].[Filter]     ' Generates a #Name? error
```

As an additional example, in the BeforeUpdate event property of a form, only the first syntax of the following two will work because Me is once again out-of-scope in the second one:

```
=FrmRecStamp([Form],Now())   ' Runs the function successfully
=FrmRecStamp([Me],Now())     ' Generates an error at runtime
```

When referring to form controls from outside the form, Me is also not usable, and Form must be appended to an explicit reference to an open form in order to access the Form property. Form is critically important—and most frequently used—when referring to controls on a subform because it points to the Form property of the form inside the Subform control, providing access to controls and properties in that subform like this:

```
strPhone = Forms!frmCust!subCustPhone.Form!txtPhone
```

Noting that Form is more widely useful than Me in forms, which has the more limited scope, you are inclined to ask: "Under which circumstances is Me recommended?" Because you could use Form in all instances where Me also works, why not use it all of the time and discard Me? I offer the following three reasons for using Me where it is allowed:

12

▶ It makes for standardized, generic code. Code using Me can be moved from a form module to a report module to a class module with no changes, whereas references to Form would have to be changed to Report or Me in such cases. Code with Me is also compatible with Visual Basic and other VBA hosts, which use the same syntax.

▶ It is more broadly appropriate. Form is an Access construct, and Me is a VBA syntax element.

▶ It is slightly shorter to type and easier to understand in context than Form.

The following are a few final hints for using Me in your form (and report and class) modules:

▶ Whenever you write code that could be ambiguous, see if you can use Me to clarify it and thereby reduce errors in your code. For example, the following two lines of code placed in a form module will perform identically on a form that has the focus. However, if the form running the code shown is not the active form (does *not* have the focus), the first line will close the active form, whatever it may be, while the second line will always close the form *that contains the code*, which is the desired result.

```
DoCmd.Close  ' Closes the form with the focus
DoCmd.Close acForm, Me.Name  ' Closes the form running this code line
```

▶ It is prudent to change any lingering references in form modules in your applications from Forms!*formname* to Me. Such syntax is common in applications converted from Access versions 1 and 2. Me is a local reference within the form, meaning that Access Basic can resolve it within the context of the form. A reference to the Forms collection (as in Forms!*formname*), however, means that Access must look outside the form's namespace (into the collection) to resolve the call, making for slower code. One example of code you want to change is found in subforms, which in previous versions of Access referred to their parent form with the syntax Forms!*parentformname* and now should be rewritten to use the syntax Me.Parent instead.

▶ Use Me instead of Screen.ActiveForm when the intent of your code is to refer to the form running the code, not the form with the focus.

Caution
The use of Screen.ActiveForm instead of Me is a frequent source of application errors among coders who are new to the event model in Access.

▶ In general, form and standard module code that performs an operation on a form should act on a `Form` object (passed in as an argument) rather than refer to a form by name. Consider the two `Sub` procedures in Listing 12.2, which are structured the same as code that I see written by many new Access developers. The first `Sub` is in a form module for form `frmMe`, and the second is in a standard module. The first procedure calls the second to change the form's caption.

Listing 12.2   AES_Frm0.Mdb— Hard-Coded Routine to Effect a Form Property Change

```
Private Sub cmdChange_Wrong_Click()
' Purpose: Set this form's caption the wrong way

  Call FrmCaptionSet_Wrong(1, "New Caption Set - Hard-coded")

End Sub


Public Sub FrmCaptionSet_Wrong(rintForm As Integer, rvarCap As Variant)
' Purpose: Change the caption of a form by its index

  ' Decide which form to change
  Select Case rintForm
    Case 1
      Forms!frmMe.Caption = rvarCap
    Case 2
      Forms!frmAddNew.Caption = rvarCap
  End Select

End Sub
```

The performance of this code example, as well as the cleanliness of the code, is degraded by the absolute reference to form names in the `FrmCaptionSet` procedure, as well as by the `Select Case` structure, which must be modified each time a form is added to the application. The same objective would be served—and with faster, cleaner code—by passing `Me` to the caption routine as a form pointer, as in Listing 12.3.

Listing 12.3   AES_Frm0.Mdb—A Generic Routine to Effect a Form Property Change

```
Private Sub cmdChange_Click()
' Purpose: Show how to call a truly generic routine

  Call FrmCaptionSet(Me, "New Caption Set - Generic Routine")

End Sub
```

12

continues

Listing 12.3   Continued

```
Public Sub FrmCaptionSet(rfrm As Form, rvarCap As Variant)
' Purpose: Change the caption of the specified form
' Arguments: rfrm:=Form to change
'            rvarCap:=New caption

  rfrm.Caption = rvarCap

End Sub
```

Note that passing Me into the preceding procedure actually passed a variable of type Form. This feature enables your older code, which used to refer to Forms!*formname* explicitly, to be changed in many cases to refer to a Form type variable instead. In larger blocks of code, this new structure has the added benefit of increased performance because multiple references to the same Form object variable execute significantly faster than multiple references to the Forms collection.

 Tip

The discussion of form references in this section is directly relevant to working with reports as well. Substitute the words Form, Forms, SubForm, *formname*, and ActiveForm with Report, Reports, SubReport, *reportname*, and ActiveReport in the section and the information provided is equally accurate. The use of Me in report module code is identical to its use in forms as described here.

Working with Form Design Information

You do not have direct access to the saved layout information used by Access to draw a form. Form (and report) definitions are stored in a system table in your database as binary data, and the storage structure is not documented.

Therefore, in order to make Form Wizards, Property Wizards, and builders function, Access must support the ability to open Form and Report objects in design view and manipulate their properties programmatically. Microsoft's implementation of this activity in Access is not as philosophically "clean" as modifying database object properties in the DAO because modifying a form from code involves opening the form to make the design changes. Nevertheless, it works just fine.

Getting to a Form's Design

You can review or modify a saved form definition by opening the form in design view, changing properties, and then closing and saving the form. This is simply an automated variation of the steps you would take manually to do the same process via the Access interface.

To open a form in design view, use the syntax below in a VBA procedure, replacing the *formname* placeholder with the name of a form in your database.

```
DoCmd.OpenForm formname, acDesign, , , , acHidden
```

 Tip

The constant, acHidden, in the window mode argument will open the form without displaying it. If you do not include this constant, the user will see the form opening in design view, which may or may not be desirable.

Once the form is open, you can perform the following actions on it:

▶ You can read form properties as part of a search for specific settings or a documentation routine. See the example in the following section.

▶ You can modify properties of the form or its controls programmatically and save the changes made. See the example in the following section.

▶ You can create new controls on the form using the Access CreateControl function or delete existing controls using DeleteControl.

▶ You can insert Basic code into the form module using the InsertLines or InsertText method. See Chapter 20, "Applying Development Shortcuts," for an example.

A form opened for design becomes part of the Forms collection of open forms, despite the facts that it is open in design view and that it is hidden. Therefore, you can refer to it with the same syntax variations you use for referring to any open form:

```
Forms!formname
Forms![formname]
Forms("formname")
Forms(expression)
Forms(indexnumber)
```

12

Your code will be easier to read and modify and will run faster if you create a form variable whenever you work with the design of an open form. Once the form is open in design view, create a Form object variable and set it equal to the open form:

```
Dim frm As Form
DoCmd.OpenForm formname, acDesign, , , , acHidden
Set frm = Forms!formname
```

You can now refer to all properties and controls of the open form through this object variable. To refer to the properties of an open form, whether open in form view or design view, use the `Properties` collection of the form, which contains all the properties by name. For example, you can use a string variable along with the form variable `frm` to retrieve the `RecordSource` property from an open form, using any of these syntaxes:

```
' The direct approach
strSrce = frm.Properties("RecordSource")
' Property name "RecordSource" is in a variable
strSrce = frm.Properties(strRecSrce)
' Shorter, direct syntax
strSrce = frm.RecordSource
```

Although the third syntax is more common, shorter to type, and faster to run, the second syntax is useful when you need to supply the property name in a variable or as an argument to a procedure. The first syntax is infrequently used simply because it wastes space and typing effort. An example in the following section shows these techniques.

To refer to a control on an open form, whether open in form view or design view, use the `Controls` collection of the form, which contains all the controls by name, or use a bang to refer to the control directly. See the examples in the "Object References with a Bang (!)" section earlier in this chapter.

 Tip

The discussion of form references in this section is directly relevant to working with reports as well. Substitute the words `Form`, `Forms`, *formname*, `OpenForm`, `CreateControl`, and `DeleteControl` with `Report`, `Reports`, *reportname*, `OpenReport`, `CreateReportControl`, and `DeleteReportControl` in the section, and the information provided is equally accurate.

Performing Bulk Form Operations

There are times when you want to get a list of all forms in a database or open more than one form at a time, perhaps to perform bulk operations on multiple forms in an application. To work with multiple forms, your code must "walk" the list of saved forms and open each one by name. Because the `Forms` collection refers only to forms that are open, you will need to find another way to get a list of forms in a database.

The list of all saved forms in an Access database is held in the `Forms` container in the `Containers` collection, maintained by Jet in the Data Access Objects hierarchy.

The `Containers` collection is a Jet object that has multiple containers, some defined by Jet (such as `Tables`) and some defined by Access (such as `Forms` and `Reports`). One of the purposes of a `Container` object is to store references (called `Documents`) to objects created by Access that are not native to Jet (see Figure 12.1). Jet must maintain references to non-Jet objects so that it can implement its security model on those objects for the benefit of Access, for example, to enable you to set security permissions on forms.

Fig. 12.1

Form names are stored as Document *objects.*

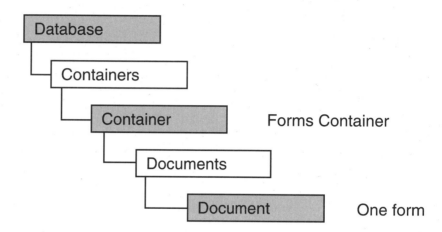

The `Forms` container has one `Document` object for each saved form; each `Document` has maintenance and ownership information for the form. The form's actual design layout is not known by Jet and is not in the `Document` object but instead is stored in a system table maintained by Access and hidden from users.

> α **Note**
>
> Forms are stored in a format known only to Access. Therefore, other products that can call Jet—Visual Basic, for example—cannot load and use the forms you create in Access. This is also why you cannot create, append, open, close, and otherwise manipulate `Form` objects through Jet in the same manner you work with `TableDefs` and `QueryDefs`; instead, you must use Access commands like `OpenForm` to do the work.
>
> Because Access' Forms engine is proprietary and difficult to separate from Access, it was not used as the basis for the new Forms 2 engine implemented in Excel, PowerPoint, and Word 97. Similarly, Access' Forms model was too proprietary to Access to replace with Forms 2. Thus, Access has a different set of form services than the other Office applications.

12

Knowing where the list of saved form names is stored, you can now walk through the list sequentially, using these steps:

1. Open the container of forms documents.

2. Get the name of each document (form).

3. Open the named document (form).

Listing 12.4 shows an example of this technique. The example goes through the list of saved forms, opens each form, and searches for occurrences of a specific value within a specific property. Figure 12.2 shows the result of running the listed code in the Debug window.

Listing 12.4   AES_Frm0.Mdb—Opening Each Form in a Database and Reading a Specific Property

```
Function FrmPrpFind(rstrPrpName As String, rvarPrpVal As Variant) _
    As Boolean
' Purpose:    Open all forms in design view hidden and look
'             for a specific property value in the named property
' Arguments: rstrPrpName:=property to search
'             rvarPrpVal:=value to find
' Returns:    True/False, True=found at least one
' Example:    FrmPrpFind("AutoCenter", False)

  Dim con     As Container
  Dim dbs     As Database
  Dim edoc    As Document
  Dim frm     As Form
  Dim iintCon As Integer

  ' Open the Forms container
  Set dbs = CurrentDb
  Set con = dbs.Containers!Forms

  ' For each document (Form object) in the container
  For Each edoc In con.Documents
    ' Open the form in design view
    DoCmd.OpenForm edoc.Name, acDesign, , , , acHidden
    Set frm = Forms(edoc.Name)
    If frm.Properties(rstrPrpName) = rvarPrpVal Then
      Debug.Print "Property value " & rstrPrpName & " = " & rvarPrpVal _
        & " was found in form " & frm.Name
      FrmPrpFind = True
    End If
    DoCmd.Close acForm, frm.Name
  Next

End Function
```

Fig. 12.2

This is the result of searching all forms for a specific property.

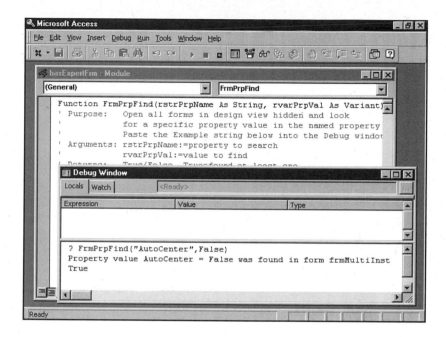

As a developer of expert forms, you will use this technique frequently to perform bulk form operations. The following are a few ideas:

▶ Audit forms for specific property settings before shipping an application.

▶ Set or retrieve the HelpFile and HelpContextID properties of forms after building user documentation.

▶ Build lists of forms for wizards, builders, and other tools.

▶ Find forms of a specific class and add code to each one. For example, if you use my naming conventions, you could write a routine to add a code snippet to all lookup forms based on the flkp tag in their names. Use the InsertText or other methods to manipulate VBA code as shown in Chapter 20, "Applying Development Shortcuts."

Using Custom Form Properties

Access has a rich built-in property model for forms. There are times, nevertheless, when it is necessary to add your own properties to forms. Access now provides two ways you can approach this situation, both built around variables.

12

Setting Custom Properties Using Variables

The simplest way to create a custom property is to create a module-level variable in the Declarations section of the form:

```
Public pstrCalledFrom As String  ' Name of the calling form
```

The variable becomes a repository where you can store information about the form; thus, it is similar to a property attached to the form. You address the variable as a property of the form from code outside the form by using the class name of the form, as in this syntax:

```
Form_formname.varname
```

The syntax for addressing form class objects with `Form_formname` was introduced in Access 95. If you are not familiar with this syntax, study the following Caution item and then read "Using Forms as Class Modules" later in this chapter.

Caution

The following syntax is also valid, but not in the context you would expect:

```
Forms!formname.varname
```

The latter syntax refers to a member of the Forms collection opened via the OpenForm method or the user interface, while the former syntax refers to a programmatic instance of the Form class. The code in Listing 12.5 clarifies what is happening and why a programmatic reference to a form must explicitly indicate the desired form instance.

Listing 12.5   AES_Frm0.Mdb—Using Multiple Syntax Variations to Open Forms Produces Multiple Instances

```
Form_frmOrigin.Visible = True  ' Open a programmatic instance
DoCmd.MoveSize 10, 10          ' Move to the upper left
DoCmd.OpenForm "frmOrigin"     ' Open the default instance
DoCmd.MoveSize 1200, 1200      ' Allow both to show

' At this point there are two forms open
Form_frmOrigin.lblOrigin.Caption = "Opened from code"
Forms!frmOrigin!lblOrigin.Caption = "Default instance"
```

When addressing the variable from elsewhere within the host form's module (as long as it has been declared `Public`), you can use the fully qualified syntax or simply use the name of the variable directly—as you would with any other variable:

```
Form_formname.varname = value
Me.varname = value
varname = value
```

 Note

Even though you are using the variable as a transitory property, you cannot address it using the following syntax, as you would with a built-in property:

```
Form.varname
```

 Caution

If you reuse variable names, your code may be hard to read with respect to scope. You can legitimately create variables in a form procedure, a form module, and a standard module that all have the same name. When your code calls any one of these variables, it may be hard for the reader and sometimes even Access to determine which variable you intended to actually address. Judicious use of naming conventions, as detailed in Chapter 6, "Leszynski Naming Conventions for Access," and demonstrated throughout this book, will help alleviate such problems.

As an example, assume that your application has a customer address form, frmCustAddr, that can be opened from several other forms. When this form is opened, it needs to know which of the other forms called it so that it can send information back to the calling form. The form frmCustAddr contains a module-level variable declaration for pstrCalledFrom, as shown at the beginning of this topic. A code snippet that opens the form and sets the custom property variable looks like this:

```
DoCmd.OpenForm "frmCustAddr"
Form_frmCustAddr.pstrCalledFrom = Me.Name
```

Once set, the variable's value is available until the form that contains it is closed. Code behind the form that contains the property can use the property setting at will:

```
Forms(Me.pstrCalledFrom).Requery   ' Re-query the calling form
```

Of course, creating custom form properties using this technique has limitations, including the following:

▶ Unlike the built-in properties of Access, runtime property values that you set using variables do not persist when the form is closed and reopened.

12

▶ Runtime properties are challenging to use when debugging a form. As you toggle between form view and design view, the values of form variables are cleared. Also, when code execution is reset, the variable values are reset as well.

Despite the limitations, setting custom properties via variables provides a clean, simple syntax for adding information to a form at execution time.

Setting Custom Properties Using *Property Let*

A more powerful way to create and invoke custom form properties is found in the new property procedures of Access. There are three varieties, as follows:

`Property Let` sets the value of a custom form property.

`Property Get` retrieves the value of a custom form property.

`Property Set` sets the value of a custom form property to an object.

As in the previous section's examples, the storage device for these custom form property procedures is a module-level variable. However, you now have the option to make the scope of the variable either `Public` or `Private`. In general, you will use `Private`.

Caution

If your property variable is declared as `Public` when using property procedures, then code outside the form can affect the variable's value without invoking the corresponding `Property Let` procedure. This circumvents the property code you have written and may lead to unexpected behavior in your application.

The purpose of property procedures is threefold, as follows:

▶ Property procedures intercept changes in custom properties so that other code operations can be run when the property is set or retrieved.

▶ They expose the custom property to viewers of the object. Custom property procedures are displayed in the Object Browser, even though the variables they use to do their work are not.

▶ These procedures can be written to validate a custom property setting against a limited range of values. This makes your form or class module more robust because it can be distributed to other developers and still carry its own value testing with it to discourage improper use.

Philosophically, custom property procedures provide developers with the tools in Access to create tighter class definitions. A saved form is a class module with properties and methods that provide a template for forms built on the class. Property procedures provide the mechanism for creating the custom property definitions that are saved with the class. See the section "Using Class Modules" later in this chapter for more details on form and standard class modules.

Let's explore a set of property procedures in use. The form for our example is `frmCust`, a simple form enabling entry and editing of multiple company name records. The form can be opened by several different code procedures in your application, and you need to be able to open the form in different data modes from the various procedures.

Although you can use various arguments of the `OpenForm` method to tailor the data-entry mode of a form, it is much cleaner programming style to be able to simply set a custom property value on the form (for example, `prpFormMode`). This enables code to run when the property is set and also allows any code to query the value of the form's custom property.

To create the custom property `prpFormMode`, you must first create a storage variable. Because two procedures, `Property Let` and `Property Get`, will both be making use of the variable, it must have module-level scope. For this example, we'll declare the following variable in the form module's Declarations section:

```
Private mstrFormMode As String
```

 Tip

I find property code more readable if the property variable and its property procedures share the same base name (in this case, `prpFormMode`).

Next, create the `Property Let` procedure. This function will accept the property value from the calling code and determine what actions to take. If the argument value is valid, the function should assign it to the storage variable, thus creating the form property. The syntax diagram for a `Property Let` procedure looks like this:

```
[Public ¦ Private][Static] Property Let procname ([arglist], value)
```

Listing 12.6 shows the `Property Let` function for the `prpFormMode` property.

Listing 12.6 AES_Frm0.Mdb—A *Property Let* Procedure to Assign the Value of a Custom Property

```
Public Property Let prpFormMode(rstrMode As String)
' Purpose:   Set the form mode when the form opens
' Arguments: rstrMode:=Form mode: Add/AddEdit/Browse/Edit
' Pseudocode:
'   1. Check the form mode argument for validity
'   2. Enable/disable buttons and features depending on argument
'   3. Set the custom property equal to the argument

  On Error GoTo prpFormMode_Err
  Const cstrProc As String = "prpFormMode"

  ' All form buttons are enabled on the saved form
  ' Disable specific buttons/properties based on the property
  Select Case rstrMode
    Case "Add"   ' All buttons are allowed
      Me.DataEntry = True   ' Data entry only
    Case "AddEdit"   ' All buttons are allowed
      ' Nothing to do
    Case "Browse"   ' No editing allowed
      Me!btnAdd.Enabled = False
      ' Make the form read-only
      Me.AllowAdditions = False
      Me.AllowEdits = False
      Me.AllowDeletions = False
    Case "Edit"   ' No add allowed
      Me!btnAdd.Enabled = False
      Me.AllowAdditions = False   ' No new records
    Case Else
      Err.Raise 65535   ' Raise a custom error
      GoTo prpFormMode_Exit
  End Select
  mstrFormMode = rstrMode   ' Set the property variable
  Me.Caption = Me.Caption & " [" & rstrMode & "]"   ' Show mode in caption

prpFormMode_Exit:
  Exit Property

prpFormMode_Err:
  If Err.Number = 65535 Then   ' Customize the error
    Call lci_ErrMsgStd(Me.Name & "." & cstrProc, Err.Number _
      , "Invalid value passed to property.", False)
  Else
    Call lci_ErrMsgStd(Me.Name & "." & cstrProc, Err.Number _
      , Err.Description, False)
  End If
  Resume prpFormMode_Exit

End Property
```

The property procedure is called by addressing the name of the property function attached to the class name of the form, as in the following code:

```
DoCmd.OpenForm "frmCust"
Forms!frmCust.prpFormMode = "Add"
```

 Tip

When calling a property procedure in the current form from code within the same form, you can use the Me keyword:

```
Me.prpFormMode = "Add"
```

Additionally, a form does not need to be open before setting a custom property from code. If you issue a command that creates a new class instance of the form (Access opens it hidden first), then set the property:

```
Form_frmCust.prpFormMode = "Add"
```

Note the following important features of the property function:

▶ The argument passed to the function declaration is the value to place into the property (the verb "Add" in this example). This argument is passed in on the right side of an assignment statement instead of in parentheses, as with other VBA procedures.

▶ The function has unique syntax elements: Property Let, Exit Property, and End Property.

▶ The error handling code in Listing 12.6 shows how a custom error message can be generated when an invalid value is passed into the function. This enables the property procedure to disallow invalid property settings.

▶ The property functions can have the same structure and logic as in any standard function, allowing for infinite logical possibilities as the custom property is set or retrieved.

To retrieve the custom property setting created by a Property Let procedure, create a Property Get procedure of the same name, as in Listing 12.7. This procedure must have its return value set to the same data type as the property storage variable and the argument in the corresponding Property Let procedure. Your code calls the Property Get procedure using syntax structured like the following example:

```
If Form_frmCust.prpFormMode = "Add" Then
```

12

Listing 12.7   AES_Frm0.Mdb—A *Property Get* Procedure to Retrieve the Value of a Custom Property

```
Public Property Get prpFormMode() As String
' Purpose: Return the saved form mode

  prpFormMode = mstrFormMode  ' Return the stored property value

End Property
```

The advantage of the property procedure technique over setting a module variable directly, as shown in the previous section, is the ability to run code routines as an event response to the setting of the custom property. Additionally, property functions are exposed to you and other developers who browse the form in the Object Browser. Figure 12.3 shows the custom `prpFormMode` property listed with the other properties for its form.

 Note

A form property is read-only when you create a `Property Get` function on a form but do not create a corresponding `Property Let` function. Code in the form module must set the value of the property variable directly before you can use the `Property Get` function to retrieve the value in the variable.

Fig. 12.3
Custom property procedures for a form are listed in the Object Browser.

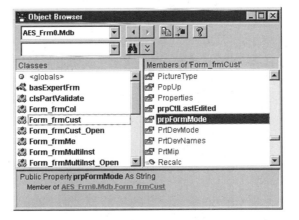

Tip

The data type and function structure for a custom property can be discerned from the syntax diagram for its `Property Get` function, as shown in the lower portion of the Object Browser in Figure 12.3.

Property procedures enable you to extend your forms by creating custom properties for specific application needs.

 Tip

Property procedures can be used with reports as well. The syntax is identical, except that you use the class descriptor for addressing `Report` objects—`Report`—where I have used the descriptor `Form` in this chapter, as in this example:

```
Report_rptCust.prpRptMode
```

Using Property Procedures with Objects

`Property Set` procedures are used when the procedure argument, or property value, must be an object data type. `Property Set` procedures are structured and used identically to `Property Let` procedures, with the following exceptions:

▶ A `Property Set` function's argument value must be of an object data type.

▶ `Property Set` functions can work with a corresponding, identically named `Property Get` function, which must return the same object data type.

▶ Assignments to a `Property Set` function must use the `Set` keyword.

Consider form `frmCust` again. You want this form to set a property that points to the last edited text box control so that other code in your application can check on the properties of the control. The code in Listing 12.8 provides a way to do this. This `Property Set` procedure accepts a form control as its argument and saves a handle to the control in the custom property.

12

Listing 12.8   AES_FrmO.Mdb—A *Property Set* Procedure to Set a Custom Property to an Object Pointer

```
Public Property Set prpCtlLastEdited(rctl As Control)
' Purpose:   Point to the last edited Text Box control
' Arguments: rctl:=Control on the form

  On Error GoTo prpCtlLastEdited_Err
  Const cstrProc As String = "prpCtlLastEdited"

  If rctl.ControlType <> acTextBox Then   ' Only allow text boxes
    Err.Raise 65535
  Else
    Set mctlCtlLastEdited = rctl   ' Set the property variable
  End If

prpCtlLastEdited_Exit:
  Exit Property

prpCtlLastEdited_Err:
  If Err.Number = 65535 Then   ' Customize the error
    Call lci_ErrMsgStd(Me.Name & "." & cstrProc, Err.Number _
      , "Invalid control type passed to the property.", False)
  Else
    Call lci_ErrMsgStd(Me.Name & "." & cstrProc, Err.Number _
      , Err.Description, False)
  End If
  Resume prpCtlLastEdited_Exit

End Property
```

To set the custom property, use the Set keyword and pass an object to the property procedure:

```
Set Me.prpCtlLastEdited = Me!txtCompnyName
```

The Property Get to match this Property Set procedure is shown in Listing 12.9. Notice that its return value is an object.

Listing 12.9   AES_FrmO.Mdb—A *Property Get* Procedure to Retrieve a Custom Property that Is an Object Pointer

```
Public Property Get prpCtlLastEdited() As Control
' Purpose:  Retrieve the last edited Text Box control

  Set prpCtlLastEdited = mctlCtlLastEdited   ' Get the property variable

End Property
```

Code elsewhere in your application can now access any property of the control pointed to by the custom property. For example, this syntax calls the Property Get procedure from

Listing 12.9 and returns the `ForeColor` property of the most recently edited text box on `frmCust`:

```
lngColor = Form_frmCust.prpCtlLastEdited.ForeColor
```

Advanced Uses of Property Procedures

As with any other function, property procedures allow multiple arguments. When you define more than one argument in `Property Let` and `Property Set` procedures, use the last (rightmost) argument to assign the property value. Because the last argument is passed in from the right side of the equal sign in a property assignment, only the other arguments need to be passed into the function by placing them inside parentheses. Figure 12.4 is a diagram showing how Access passes property arguments to a pair of sample property procedures that have three arguments.

Fig. 12.4

This diagram shows how Access passes custom property procedure arguments to property procedures.

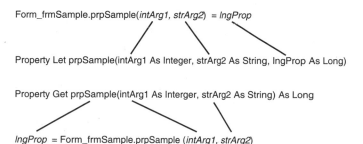

The capability to pass multiple arguments to property procedures enables you to provide as much context and information to the procedures as is required to set the custom property value. It also enables you to create property arrays using property procedures.

For example, a property procedure with two arguments can be coded to use the first argument as an array index and the second (last) argument as the property value to place in the array at the specified index. Assume you have an array dimensioned in your form module as follows:

```
Private mavarDayComment(vbSunday To vbSaturday) As Variant
```

The array has seven elements (rows), one for each day of the week. Through property procedures you can use this array to store seven values under one custom property name (`prpDayComment`). The `Property Let` and `Property Get` function definitions for such a technique are shown in Listing 12.10.

12

Listing 12.10   AES_Frm0.Mdb—*Property Let* and *Property Get* Procedures to Work with a Custom Property Array

```
Public Property Let prpDayComment(rintIndex As Integer _
, rvarComment As Variant)
' Purpose:   Set a comment property setting for a specified weekday
' Arguments: rintIndex:=Day of week, vbSunday through vbSaturday
'            rvarComment:=Comment

  If rintIndex < vbSunday Or rintIndex > vbSaturday Then
    Exit Property   ' Don't accept invalid property setting
    ' Alternately, you could trigger a custom error here
  End If
  mavarDayComment(rintIndex) = rvarComment   ' Set the property

End Property


Public Property Get prpDayComment(rintIndex As Integer) As Variant
' Purpose:   Return a comment property setting for a specified weekday
' Arguments: rintIndex:=Day of week, vbSunday through vbSaturday

  If rintIndex < vbSunday Or rintIndex > vbSaturday Then
    Exit Property   ' Don't accept invalid request
    ' Alternately, you could trigger a custom error here
  End If
  prpDayComment = mavarDayComment(rintIndex)   ' Get the property

End Property
```

These property procedures create a custom form property with seven elements, `prpDayComment(1)` through `prpDayComment(7)`. Lines of code to set the custom property look like this:

```
Me.prpDayComment(vbMonday) = "Company meeting"
Forms!frmCalendar.prpDayComment(vbMonday) = "Company meeting"
Form_frmCalendar.prpDayComment(vbMonday) = "Company meeting"
```

 Tip

Property procedures can also be created for standard modules. Such custom properties essentially become properties of the database file (application) itself. Custom properties attached to standard modules can be addressed with the property name only, as in `prpUserName`, or with the module name as a class designator, such as `basLogin.prpUserName`. I recommend the latter syntax for clarity of code.

If you intend to create custom properties in a standard module, define it as a class module when you first create it.

Using Class Modules

Access now fully supports the concept of class modules. A class is a saved object definition that includes properties and methods. In Access 95, class modules were implemented only through the `Form` and `Report` objects. Access 97 expands this concept to include the ability to have standard class modules of type `Module`, stored in the Modules tab of the Database window. The following are important points about class modules:

▶ An Access form or report as a class definition can also contain controls, but it does not have to. By contrast, standard class modules do not allow controls. Use a form class module when you need to present a visible interface to the user. For example, you can create your own advanced message box class object.

▶ An Access 95 class definition saved as a form or report but without controls can be converted to a standard class module in Access 97 by copying the code into a standard class module object.

 Tip

Alternately, you can set the `Hidden` attribute of a form using the Properties dialog box for the form, available from the <u>V</u>iew, <u>P</u>roperties menu option. Once hidden, they are not displayed to users in the Database window. Consider hiding the forms that you use as class modules from code only if you decide not to convert them to standard classes.

▶ Form and report class modules can only be opened in a single instance from the Database window but can be opened in multiple instances from VBA. Standard class modules cannot be opened from the user interface.

For the purposes of this chapter's discussion, I'll mix references to form and standard class modules because they are coded the same even though they may be used slightly differently.

Creating and Using Class Modules

The `New` keyword is used to create a new instance of an object. When the `New` keyword is used while declaring a form or class object variable, a new instance of the form, form class module, or class module is created. The instance is loaded into memory but is not displayed to the user until the object's `Visible` property is set to `True`. The following code creates a form variable and opens an instance of the form `frmMultiInst` but does not display the form:

12

```
Dim frmMultiInst As New Form_frmMultiInst
```

A variable declaration that defines an object *without* using the New keyword creates a placeholder for the object but is set to the value Nothing until an actual object (a form, for example) is assigned to the variable with the Set statement. Therefore, the next two lines of code achieve the same result as the previous single line of code:

```
Dim frmMultiInst As Form_frmMultiInst
Set frmMultiInst = New Form_frmMultiInst
```

In most cases, using the New keyword in the variable declaration is the appropriate approach because it creates both a variable and an instance of an object in the variable with a single command.

As an example of a class module, assume that your application requires reusable code routines to validate part numbers. One approach would be to place the same validation logic in every form procedure in the application that must validate a part. An alternative approach would be to place the validation code in a common library module. The newest approach is for you to create a class module to do the work. Because a class module is self-contained, it can be called from any place in the application, making it highly reusable and centralized. More importantly, the self-contained class module can be imported into multiple applications as a reusable validation object throughout your company.

We've already seen in this chapter how custom property procedures can be added to a class module. For the validation engine, create a class module called clsPartValidate (we'll use a standard class module because no interface is needed; alternately, using a form as a class module would work just as well but incur the performance burden of calling the forms engine to load it). Add a custom property, prpPartNum, to hold the part number passed in by any code that wants to use the validation class, as shown in Listing 12.11.

Listing 12.11   AES_Frm0.Mdb—*Property Let* to Define the Custom Part Number Property

```
' In the Declarations section of the class module
' Store the PartNum custom property
  Private mvarPartNum As Variant


' In the code inside the class
Public Property Let prpPartNum(rvarPart As Variant)
' Purpose:   Set the part number property
' Arguments: rvarPart:=Part number

  mvarPartNum = rvarPart   ' Set the property variable

End Property
```

Notice that Listing 12.11 does not include a `Property Get` sibling for the `Property Let` procedure. The validation engine accepts and checks part numbers but has no need to return the part number to the calling program because the program sent it to the class in the first place.

Next, create a custom method, `mtdPartValidate`, for the class. Custom methods are simply procedures within a class that are declared `Public` so that they can be invoked from anywhere in the application. Listing 12.12 shows a sample method to validate the part number set by the custom property in Listing 12.11.

Listing 12.12   AES_Frm0.Mdb—A Custom Part Number Validation Method in a Class

```
Public Sub mtdPartValidate()
' Purpose: Validate the part number property set in mvarPartNum

  Const cintFail As Integer = vbOKOnly + vbCritical
  Const cintPass As Integer = vbOKOnly + vbInformation
  Const cstrProc As String = "mtdPartValidate"

  ' Part number must be like A9999
  Beep
  If lci_IsBlank(mvarPartNum) Then
    MsgBox "Part number cannot be blank.", cintFail, cstrProc
  ElseIf Len(Trim(mvarPartNum)) <> 5 Then
    MsgBox "Part number must be five characters.", cintFail, cstrProc
  ElseIf Left(UCase(mvarPartNum), 1) < "A" _
    Or Left(UCase(mvarPartNum), 1) > "Z" _
    Or Not IsNumeric(Mid(mvarPartNum, 2)) Then
    MsgBox "Invalid part number format, must be like A9999." _
      , cintFail, cstrProc
  Else
    MsgBox "Part number is valid.", cintPass, cstrProc
  End If

End Sub
```

Once the class module has a property and a method, it can be used for part number validation from code. Because the class was created to serve as a background engine, it has no user interface and is never displayed to the user while open. The code in Listing 12.13 shows how to create an instance of the class, pass a part number to it, and initiate the validation routine.

12

> **Listing 12.13   AES_Frm0.Mdb—Invoking the Property and Method in a Custom Class**

```
Dim clsPartValidate As New clsPartValidate
clsPartValidate.prpPartNum = Me!txtPart  ' Set the part number property
clsPartValidate.mtdPartValidate  ' Invoke the validate method
Set clsPartValidate = Nothing
```

Using Forms as Class Modules

A form opened by a user from the Database window or OpenForm in code is called the *default form* because the object instance is unique to the application environment, meaning that only one instance of a specific form can be open at a given time if any of these invocation methods are used:

▶ Opening the form from the Database window

▶ Opening the form with DoCmd.OpenForm

▶ Using CreateForm to build a new form

▶ Using a Form type variable to refer to the instance

Unlike the default instance of a form, a form class module can be opened more than once from code and does not need to be explicitly closed because it is created via a code reference or explicit variable. When the variable or procedure goes out of scope, then the class form is closed by Access.

> **Tip**
> Despite the fact that Access closes the form class object for you, it is considered good programming practice to explicitly release the memory used by any object by setting the object variable to Nothing, as shown for the class module in Listing 12.13. I have seen rare instances when some objects will generate errors if they go out of scope without an explicit cleanup.

Your code can also create an instance of a form class without creating a variable by simply addressing it, as in this code:

```
Form_frmMultiInst.Visible = True
```

However, this creates an instance of the class with no attached object variable, which has the following potential pitfalls:

▶ This class is like an open default form—it does not go out of scope when the calling procedure is closed. You must do the cleanup yourself and close the form.

▶ This class does not have a referencing variable, making it harder to directly address. Your calls to the class object are not guaranteed to go to the correct object if more than one instance of the class is open, making for sloppy code and a sloppy application environment.

Form class objects in Access have some limitations. The most glaring is that the classes in a referenced database are not available to a referencing database, which would provide the ultimate in object reusability. You can create a Public function in a standard module of a referenced database, which *can* be called from referencing databases, and have that function invoke a class object in the referenced database, providing a workaround.

Another limitation is that class objects cannot be used in expressions that are handled by Access's expression service, which does not understand class objects. Thus a form or standard class module's custom property, for example, cannot be used in the Where clause criteria of a query. Consider a form frmCust, open as a class object, with a custom property prpCustNum. Assume that the following line of code properly retrieves the Customer Number property in the Debug window:

```
Debug.Print Form_frmCust.prpCustNum
```

In spite of this visibility of the form class's property to the Debug object and other code running in the application, a query would not work correctly if it attempted this syntax:

```
WHERE tblCust.CompnyName = [Form_frmCust].[prpCustNum]
```

A third limitation is that custom property information for a form class is erased by print preview mode. If your form class is displayed to the user and the user selects File, Print Preview from the menu, this action clears the module-level variables in the form class that hold your custom property settings. Upon returning to form view from preview mode, the form may no longer work as expected.

Despite these few limitations, class definitions in Access are still a powerful tool for creating reusable objects within an application.

Creating Multiple Form Class Instances

Because each instance of a class is a unique object, you can open multiple object variables against a single class definition. Therefore, if you had two forms open in an application to accept part numbers, each form could start and work with its own instance of the part validation class described earlier. Two procedures can contain exactly the same code to create exactly the same object variable, yet each procedure creates a unique instance of the object.

A class instance is destroyed when the code that creates it goes out of scope, so a form displayed to the user from code may not persist long enough for the user to manipulate it. The following code displays the target form for only an instant but does not do so by displaying the default form as previously described. Thus, the form is destroyed when the procedure ends:

```
Private Sub cmdOpen_Click()
' Open a form through code

  Dim frmMultiInst As New Form_frmMultiInst
  frmMultiInst.Visible = True

End Sub
```

The form is destroyed immediately because the procedure cmdOpen_Click stops running and the variable frmMultiInst goes out of scope. Here are three ways you can create a form through code and circumvent this problem:

▶ Create the form instance using a module-level variable. The scope of such a variable is equal to the life of the form that contains it. Therefore, the called form does not close until the calling form closes. The code in Listing 12.14 demonstrates this approach.

Listing 12.14   AES_Frm0.Mdb—Opening a Form Instance that Persists Using a Module-Level Variable

```
' In the calling form's Declarations section
Dim mfrmMulti As Form_frmMultiInst


' In the calling form
Private Sub cmdOpen_Click()
' Purpose: Open a form instance

  Set mfrmMulti = New Form_frmMultiInst
  mfrmMulti.Visible = True

End Sub
```

▶ Create the form instance from within a standard module with the form variable declared at the module level. Because a standard module variable never goes out of scope, the variable is not closed until the user decides to close the form. The code for this looks much the same as the code in Listing 12.14.

▶ Create the form using a variable declared as static within a procedure. Such a form variable is prescrved even when the containing procedure goes out of scope—due to its static nature. The code for this technique is shown in Listing 12.15.

Listing 12.15   Opening a Form Instance that Persists Using a *Static* Variable

```
Private Sub cmdOpen_Click()
' Purpose: Open a form instance

    Static sfrmMultiInst As New Form_frmMultiInst
    sfrmMultiInst.Visible = True

End Sub
```

Caution

Even though I show this static instance technique for demonstration purposes, I do not recommend it. If the user closes the form manually, the form instance is destroyed, but the static variable that refers to it is not alerted and does not release its memory. Application errors can be generated when this happens.

One of the great benefits of opening a form instance through code is the ability to set properties on a modal Form object from subsequent code. If the following lines of code employing OpenForm are used to open a form as a modal dialog box, the second line of code does not execute until the form is closed—the modality of the form causes the code to pause at the OpenForm method:

```
DoCmd.OpenForm "frmMultiInst", , , , , acDialog  ' Open a dialog box
' The next line is not reached while the form is open
Forms!frmMultiInst!lblMsg.Caption = "File not found."
```

In contrast, if code is used to open a form instance via an object variable, the code continues execution. Therefore, the following four lines replace the previous two lines, and all of the lines execute in immediate sequence:

```
Set mfrmMultiInst = New Form_frmMultiInst
mfrmMultiInst.Modal = True
mfrmMultiInst.Visible = True
mfrmMultiInst.lblMsg.Caption = "File not found."
```

With VBA, you can also create an array of classes, using syntax similar to Listing 12.16. A class array is dimensioned with multiple elements (rows), as with any other kind of array, but the data type of the array is set to a form class.

12

Listing 12.16   AES_Frm0.Mdb—Creating an Array of Class Objects

```
' In the form's Declarations section
Private mfrmMultiInst(3) As Form_frmMultiInst

' A procedure in the form
Private Sub cmdOpen_Click()
' Purpose: Open multiple form instances

  Dim iintLoop As Integer
  For iintLoop = 0 To 3
    Set mfrmMultiInst(iintLoop) = New Form_frmMultiInst
    mfrmMultiInst(iintLoop).Caption = "Instance " & CStr(iintLoop)
    mfrmMultiInst(iintLoop).Visible = True
  Next iintLoop

End Sub
```

Figure 12.5 shows the result of running this code. Be aware that an array of objects is resource intensive and should be used wisely.

Fig. 12.5

Four form class instances were created using a single form class array variable.

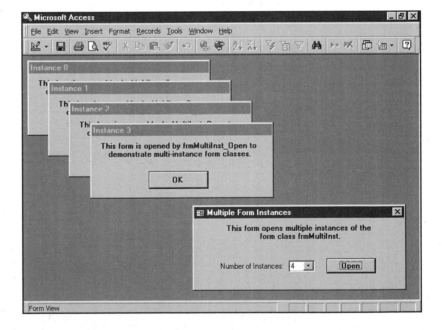

Using Collections to Work with Forms and Controls

VBA's new Collection object enables you to group several related objects together into a container where they can be subjected to bulk operations. Think of a Collection object as a one-dimensional array of pointers to objects. Unlike an array, which holds data, the only information the Collection object holds is references (pointers); thus, the elements referenced by a collection do not need to be of the same type. You can mix form, report, control, and data access object references together in a single collection. You can even make a Collection object a member of another Collection object.

Working with Collections

Before you add items to a Collection object, you must create it using the New keyword, as in the following example:

```
Private mcolData As New Collection
```

> **Tip**
>
> Most collections you create in a form module will be addressed by more than a single procedure in the form. Consequently, you will usually declare Collection objects in the form module's Declarations section as either Public or Private.

Adding items to a Collection object and working with them is easy and involves the following three methods:

Add *method* inserts an object reference (called a *member*) into the collection.

Item *method* returns an object reference from a specified location in the collection. The location is referenced by either a positional index number or an identifier called a key, defined later in this chapter.

Remove *method* removes a reference from the collection, either by positional index or key.

When adding an item to a Collection object, use this syntax:

```
collection.Add Item[, Key][, Before][, After]
```

> **Tip**
>
> Arguments in the Add method are *named arguments;* thus, you can specify them in any order as long as they are qualified by name, as in this example:
>
> ```
> colWidget.Add After:=3, Item:=rstWidget, Key:="Widget"
> ```

12

Unless otherwise specified, an item added to a collection is appended to the end and given the next available index value. Each Collection object has a Count property indicating the highest index number assigned to an object in the collection.

> **Caution**
>
> Unlike other Access and VBA collections and arrays, the lower bound of a `Collection` object is an index value of 1, not 0.

There are four `Add` method arguments, as follows:

Item. This argument provides the object reference to add to the collection. Any valid object reference is allowed, as in the following examples:

```
mcolData.Add Forms!frmWidget
mcolData.Add Item:=Forms!frmWidget!txtWidgetName
mcolData.Add Form_frmWidget!subComponent.Form.txtSupplier
mcolData.Add Me.RecordSetClone
```

Key. The key value provides an alternate string index to use when referring to the item in the collection. It enables you to reference an item without knowing its position in the collection and provides the ability to designate a unique identifier (think of it as a *primary key*) to directly address each object.

This argument is optional—if you do not provide one, none is assigned by Access. Without a `Key` value, an element must be retrieved by its position in the collection. The following syntax shows references to collection members by index versus by key:

```
mcolData.Add Forms!frmWidget!txtWidgetName, "WidgetName"  ' Add an item with a key
ctlWidget = mcolData(7)  ' Retrieve the seventh item by index
ctlWidget = mcolData(mcolData.Count)  ' Retrieve the last item by index
ctlWidget = mcolData("WidgetName")  ' Retrieve the Widget item by key
```

Before, *After*. With these arguments, you can note an optional, specific destination location for an object added to a `Collection` object. Only one of these arguments can be used at a time. Either note the index or the string key of an item you want the new item to precede or follow. You cannot insert an item into a collection before the index location of 1 or after the index location equivalent to the `Count` property of the collection.

The `Item` method of a `Collection` object retrieves an object reference to the designated member by index number or key string. Because the `Item` method is the default method for the collection, the `Item` keyword is optional; thus, these two syntaxes are equivalent:

```
ctlWidget = mcolData.Item("WidgetName")
ctlWidget = mcolData("WidgetName")
```

The `Remove` method removes an item reference from the `Collection` object. The original object is not affected in any way; only its relationship with the collection is destroyed.

To remove an object, refer to it by index number or by key string:

```
mcolData.Remove(7)
mcolData.Remove("WidgetName")
```

To loop through a `Collection` object, you can use either of the following variations of a `For` statement. The second syntax executes faster due to the presence of an object variable:

```
Dim iintLoop As Integer
For iintLoop = 1 To mcolData.Count
    Debug.Print mcolData(iintLoop).Name
Next iintLoop

Dim eobj As Object
For Each eobj In mcolData
    Debug.Print eobj.Name
Next eobj
```

Addressing Attributes of Collection Members

`Collection` objects are both strange and wonderful. The strange aspect derives from the mixed nature of objects in a collection. You cannot depend on the items in a collection to be homogeneous unless your code controls the object class of each item added to a collection. However, this feature also supplies collections with their "wonderfulness" because you can accumulate related but dissimilar object types together. In this section, I will provide some examples of how to take advantage of the wonderfulness without bumping into the strangeness.

Because a collection member is an object, you can append property and method designators to a collection reference as if applying them to the member object. The keyword must be appropriate for the collection member, as in the following examples:

```
mcolData.Add Forms!frmWidget!txtWidgetName, "WidgetName"  ' Add a text box item
MsgBox mcolData.Item("WidgetName").Name  ' Retrieve the text box name
MsgBox mcolData("WidgetName").Value      ' Retrieve the text box value
```

In a collection that contains a variety of objects, there is a risk of applying a method or property to a collection member that does not support the specified method or property. This situation results in an error. You can prevent the problem by using the `TypeOf` keyword to determine if the collection member is of the expected type, as in the following code:

```
If TypeOf mcolData(iintIndex) Is TextBox Then  ' If a text box
    ablnLocked(iintIndex) = mcolData(iintIndex).Locked  ' Get the property
End If
```

Another feature of collection members is the capability to use their object references in `With` statements. This capability is especially useful on forms where you may want to

12

work with several control property settings at a time. In the following example, the `With` statement is used to clarify and speed up code that changes the editable nature of controls in the collection based on a flag variable:

```
For iint = 1 To mcolCtlCust.Count
  With mcolCtlCust(iint)
    .Enabled = Not blnLock
    .Locked = blnLock
    .BackColor = IIf(blnLock, gclngColorGray, gclngColorWhite)
  End With
Next iint
```

Using Collections of Controls

Creating `Collection` objects whose members are form controls enables your expert forms to loop through the collection and manipulate each control. You can set control properties, retrieve control properties, invoke control methods, and perform any other legitimate control-related action.

In previous versions of Access, you performed such tasks by looping through the built-in `Controls` collection for a form, using code like the following:

```
Dim iint As Integer
For iint = 0 To Me.Controls.Count - 1
  Debug.Print Me.Controls(iint).Name
Next iint
```

This code also works in Access 97 and, indeed, is still useful for reviewing every control on the form. To perform an operation on subsets of controls with such code, however, you must loop through the form's entire control collection and test each control for specific attributes. By contrast, creating a custom `Collection` object pointing directly to only controls with the desired attributes is more efficient and executes faster.

 Tip

Because a form builds its own *object containing all of its controls, you can use the `Me` reference as the object of a `With` statement to loop through a form's control collection, as in this example:

```
With Me
  !txtCustName = "Jones"
    !txtCustPhone = "206-555-1212"
End With
```

You can load a control collection using *hard code* or *soft code*. Hard code points explicitly to controls by name, as in these lines:

```
Private Sub Form_Open(Cancel As Integer)

  ' Create a collection of customer order controls
  mcolCtlCust.Add Me!txtCustName
  mcolCtlCust.Add Me!txtCustNum
  mcolCtlCust.Add Me!txtOrderDate
  mcolCtlCust.Add Me!txtOrderNum

End Sub
```

Soft code identifies the controls to add to the collection by an attribute rather than by name. The examples in Listing 12.17 load the same collection in three different ways: by using each control's class (type), by using each control's LNC naming convention tag, and by using values placed in the Tag property of each control by the developer.

Listing 12.17   Three Different Ways to Load Controls into a *Collection* Object by Attribute

```
' All three examples use this module-level collection
Public mcol As New Collection


' All three examples use these local variables
Dim ctl  As Control
Dim iint As Integer

' 1. Use TypeOf to load all Text Box controls into a collection
For iint = 0 To Me.Controls.Count - 1
  Set ctl = Me.Controls(iint)
  If TypeOf ctl Is TextBox Then
    mcol.Add ctl
  End If
Next iint

' 2. Use LNC tag to load all Text Box controls into a collection
For iint = 0 To Me.Controls.Count - 1
  Set ctl = Me.Controls(iint)
  If Left(ctl.Name, 3) = "txt" Then
    mcol.Add ctl
  End If
Next iint

' 3. Use the Tag property to load all Text Box controls into a collection
'    This also uses the new For Each version of a form control loop
For Each ctl in Me.Controls
  If ctl.Tag = "Cust" Then
    mcol.Add ctl
  End If
Next
```

12

Code for working with control collections executes quickly and is quite efficient with system resources. The following are some examples of the use of control collections:

Bulk Validation. You can keep a collection of controls that must be checked together for some data condition, such as non-blank, a value range, or mutual dependencies.

Bulk Resets. The quickest way to clear a related set of controls on a form is to loop through a collection of the controls and set each control's value to Null or to its default value.

Bulk Property Changes. Groups of controls can be quickly enabled, disabled, resized, and so forth by virtue of their membership in a collection.

Chapter 14, "Navigating in Forms and Applications," provides examples of the use of control collections in form data validation.

A useful example of control collections derives from the need to group controls on your form. Assume that your form has related controls that should be set, cleared, or validated together. For example, your customer form has a set of address fields for the home address and another set for the business address. You would like your form to have some mechanism for identifying each control in each group.

First, declare a collection array, mcolCustAddr(), whose number of elements matches the number of groups, in this case two. Next, fill each element of the collection array with the address information. Finally, loop through the collection array and perform the bulk operation required. Listing 12.18 shows sample code to clarify this strategy.

Listing 12.18   AES_Frm0.Mdb—Creating a Collection Array for Controls in Two Different Control Groups

```
' In the Declarations section, create a collection array
  Private mcolCustAddr(0 To 1) As New Collection   ' One for each address group

Private Sub Form_Load()
' When loading the form, assign controls to their collection element

  mcolCustAddr(0).Add Me!txtHomeAddr   ' Becomes collection element (0)(1)
  mcolCustAddr(0).Add Me!txtHomeCity   ' Becomes collection element (0)(2)
  ...
  mcolCustAddr(1).Add Me!txtBusnAddr   ' Becomes collection element (1)(1)
  mcolCustAddr(1).Add Me!txtBusnCity   ' Becomes collection element (1)(2)
  ...

End Sub

Private Sub cmdCopy_Click()
' Copy home address to business
```

```
      Dim ectl As Control
      Dim iint As Integer

      For iint = 1 To mcolCustAddr(0).Count  ' Copy each collection element
        mcolCustAddr(0)(iint).Value = mcolCustAddr(1)(iint).Value
      Next iint

   End Sub
```

Using Collections of Forms

A `Collection` object can include references to open forms. In the same fashion that you use control collections to group controls with related attributes, you can also group forms with related attributes.

First, create a public collection declared in a standard module as `gcolFrm`. Next, in each form in the application, place code in the `Form_Open` event that loads a reference to the form into the custom form collection:

```
   gcolFrm.Add Me, Me.Name  ' Use the name as the key
```

For as long as the form is open, there will be a reference to it in the custom collection. You now have an additional reference method with which to manipulate the properties and objects on a form: `gcolFrm.Item("formname")` or simply `gcolFrm("formname")`.

A collection of all open forms has limited usefulness because Access has a built-in `Forms` collection that provides the same functionality. However, if you selectively add the `Form_Open` code line shown to only specific forms or, through some other mechanism, only add forms to the custom collection based upon some criteria, you will create custom form collections that hold an identified subset of the open forms. This is widely useful. For example, you can create a collection of forms that need to be requeried together based on a trigger provided by some application event and then quickly loop through the collection at any time and apply the `Requery` method to each member form.

As another example, you could create a collection of forms that nest within a parent form. Assume that your application allows for multiple forms to be opened simultaneously from a parent form and either minimized or hidden by the user. At any given time, several forms may be open that are dependent upon the presence of their parent form. In the parent form, create a collection to which you add members that point to child forms as they are being opened. When the user closes the parent form, you can loop through the collection and close each child form before closing the parent.

12

Caution

Once you have added a form reference to the custom collection, your code should explicitly remove the form from the collection when it closes. Otherwise, the collection maintains an erroneous pointer to the closed form. Referencing the collection element for the closed form will generate an error, as will attempting to add the form to the collection a second time (the next time the form opens). Use code like this in a form's Close event:

```
gcolFrm.Remove Me.Name
```

Recall that each key value in a single collection must be unique. In the current example, I am using Me.Name to pass the form name to the custom collection as the key. This strategy works fine when your code enforces the condition that each form will only be open once. However, if your code needs to open multiple instances of a single form, and each form instance must load itself into a collection, your code must also enforce a unique name for each form instance. You have the following two choices in such a scenario:

Do not use a key value. The key is a convenience index; if your code does not require such an index, you can simply add the form reference to the collection without specifying a key argument. This approach is only useful when you treat all members of the collection in aggregate; in other words, you always loop through the collection and do the same thing to each member, which does not require that you be able to index one specific member directly.

Create a unique key value when loading the collection. When you assign a form reference to the custom collection, modify the form name key to reflect its unique instance. For example, your code can add an instance number to the form name to create a unique key or even add a unique random number like the current value of the Timer function. This ensures that any form class can be opened with an unlimited number of instances, each of which generates a unique key value to identify its membership in the custom collection.

When using the second technique listed, it is convenient to store the key value of the form within the form itself. One way to do this is to create a module-level variable in each form to act as a custom property that stores the form's current key value from the global collection. This approach causes each form to travel with its own index into the collection. The code for this approach is shown in Listing 12.19.

> **Listing 12.19   AES_Frm0.Mdb—Setting and Clearing a Form's Membership in a Custom Form Collection**
>
> ```
> ' In the form's Declarations section
> Public mstrColKey As String   ' Index in global collection
>
>
> ' In the form's Open event
> mstrColKey = Me.Name & CStr(Timer)
> gcolFrm.Add Me, mstrColKey
>
>
> ' In the form's Close event
> gcolFrm.Remove Me.mstrColKey
> ```

With this structure in place, any code in the application can retrieve a form's membership location in the custom collection by using the form's `mstrColKey` custom property value.

Using Nested Collections

It is possible to add a `Collection` object to another collection as a member. With this technique, you can build collection hierarchies, similar to the way object collections are nested in the DAO.

For example, you can combine the two techniques previously described for creating form collections and control collections, as shown in Figure 12.6. The figure diagrams how each form has a `Collection` object, `mcolCtl`, with all the form's controls as members. Additionally, `gcolFrm`, a public collection, is loaded with all of the form control `Collection` objects.

Fig. 12.6

Two control collections are nested inside a third collection.

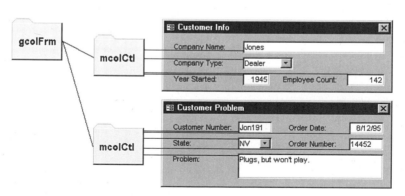

12

To address items in a nested collection set, follow these syntax examples:

```
gcolFrm.Item(1).Item(1)
gcolFrm(1)(1)
gcolFrm.Item("frmCust").Item("txtCompName")
gcolFrm("frmCust")("txtCompName")
```

Some Collection Considerations

Here are a few concepts to keep in mind when using collections on your expert forms or elsewhere in your application:

Do not store the index. An item's index into a collection is not a reliable address designation because the following events can alter the index numbers of some or all of the elements in a collection:

▶ Removal of a collection member via the Remove method.

▶ Insertion of a collection member at a specific index location using the Before or After arguments of the Add method.

If you need to reliably address a specific collection member, store and use the key value instead of the index.

You cannot retrieve or alter the key. The key value that uniquely indexes a collection member cannot be read or changed, unlike some ActiveX controls that have a Key property that can be read and written. (The Collection object is built internally as a doubly-linked list and provides a rather sloppy extension to VBA because it lacks access to the internal Key value.)

Collections need not be homogeneous. While the examples in this chapter keep apples with apples, you will sometimes need to mix different types of objects within a single collection.

You can set a collection to Nothing. To clear a collection, set the Collection object equal to the Nothing keyword. Because the collection contains a reference to, not a copy of, each member object, clearing the collection does not affect the underlying objects. Also, after all members have been removed from a Collection object, if the collection is not currently useful to the application, setting the collection equal to Nothing in your code may recoup some additional system memory and resources.

You can create a collection member by using an object variable. When you add an object variable to a collection, the collection reference receives from the variable a pointer to the underlying object, not a pointer to the variable itself. Consider the following code:

```
Dim frm As Form
Set frm = Forms!frmCust
gcolFrm.Add frm
```

In this example, the collection gcolFrm maintains a reference to the form frmCust even when the variable frm goes out of scope.

You can assign a collection member to an object variable. When you assign a collection member to an object variable, the variable reference is actually to the underlying object of the collection member, not to the collection element. Therefore, in the following code, the variable frm will still refer to frmCust after the form is removed from the collection gcolFrm or after the collection is set to Nothing:

```
gcolFrm.Add Forms!frmCust, "Cust"
Dim frm As Form
Set frm = gcolFrm("Cust")
gcolFrm.Remove "Cust"
```

 Tip
Even though the examples in this chapter are form-centric, collection members can include reports, their controls, and related data objects.

Creating Faster Forms

From the beginning, form loading has been one of the most difficult jobs for Access and one of the most serious complaints from users. As Microsoft adds 20 or 30 percent more features to forms with each release, forms load more slowly with each version as a result, even as other areas of the product get faster. Such is the price of progress. Fortunately, this trend was reversed with Access 97, which loads forms faster than its immediate predecessor.

When developing expert forms, you must balance the goal of enhanced usability with the fact that slow form loads and events offset much of your usability gains. The first and foremost mission I give to my staff when working on a new project is to communicate to the users the important role that a good infrastructure plays in successful deployment of Access applications. Access works your machine very hard and must be given adequate horsepower to do its considerably complex job.

Consider the racecar driver. Put an expert driver into a Ferrari, and you will see a fantastic combination of power and performance. Put the same driver into an old Volkswagen Beetle, and all of his skill and potential are wasted.

12

In the same vein, the single most important performance improvement for an Access application is not to tune the application but rather to tune its host machine. If you recall my performance benchmarks shown in Chapter 1, "Access as a Development Tool," simply doubling the RAM in a 486 machine from 8M to 16M more than halved the load time of Access and its forms.

Of course, simply beefing up the user's hardware does not remove the application tuning burden from the developer. Let's explore our development and architectural options for improving performance.

Access 97 introduced *lightweight* forms, or forms that have no code attached to them. Such forms load faster than identical forms with a code module. In order to qualify as lightweight, a form must have no code module (its HasModule property is False). Such a form does not need to utilize any services from VBA in order to load or run the form and does not need to post its type library information into the application's object model. Thus, a lightweight form does not appear in the Object Browser and cannot be referenced from an object variable. Use such forms for simple tasks and for subforms that do not have events.

Microsoft has published several help topics and articles over the years listing additional performance optimization suggestions for Access forms. I have pulled their best suggestions together into one list and combined them with some hints of my own in an attempt to produce a single comprehensive checklist of performance enhancement techniques for loading and using forms.

Data Techniques:

Index the data. In general, forms will be faster if the following fields are indexed:

▶ Fields in the form or subform's RecordSource that are used with criteria (in a Where clause) or for sorting (with Order By).

▶ Fields in a subform that link the data to the parent form.

▶ Fields used for criteria or sorting in large lookup tables that feed combo or list boxes.

Don't create an editable recordset. Set a form's RecordsetType property to Snapshot where possible in order to create a read-only version of the form. Note, however, that when Access creates a snapshot, it loads the recordset with all of the underlying records. In contrast, forms buffer their records in chunks when they are based on a dynaset. This means that if the form's recordset is more than a few hundred records, a snapshot may actually be slower; you may have to experiment.

Minimize the size of the form's recordset. You should minimize the number of fields (Select them by name) as well as rows (use a Where clause) that are provided to the form via the `RecordSource`, returning only the data items actually required by the form. Also, if the form's primary purpose is to create new records, use a `DataEntry` property value of `False` to ensure that the form loads with no records at all.

Use saved queries for `RecordSource` and `RowSource` properties. Queries are parsed and optimized by Jet when saved (essentially "compiled"), so a form or control based on a named query will usually populate faster than one based on an analogous SQL statement, which must be re-parsed and re-optimized each time the form or control calls it.

 Note

The Access group did some work to optimize the performance of `RecordSource` and `RowSource` properties in Access 97. When you save an SQL statement in one of these properties, Access creates a system-level saved query for the SQL statement and uses the saved (thus compiled) query when loading the form.

These system objects are visible in the `MSysObjects` system table but not in the Database window and are named using the syntax `~sq_fformname` for a form `RecordSource` and `~sq_fformname~sq_ccontrolname` for a control `RowSource`.

Use list callback functions to add speed to combo boxes and list boxes. Chapter 13, "Mastering Combo and List Boxes," described these techniques. Bear in mind that callback functions, even though driven by memory arrays, are not *automatically* faster than the internal recordsets in Access. This is because of the numerous re-dundant calls that combo and list boxes sometimes make to the callback function; this issue is documented in Chapter 13. If your combo or list box is loading more than a hundred records, you may need to experiment to determine if callback functions add any performance benefit.

Minimize `Memo` and `OLE Object` type fields. Jet stores the data for these field types sepa-rate from the rest of the related record, so fetching these items can introduce de-lays. If a specific form does not need to display these items in the underlying table(s), do not include fields of these types in the `RecordSource`.

Coding Techniques:

Compile the code. In Access 2, form code was loaded and compiled when the form was opened. Now, VBA code can be stored in a compiled state with the form. If Access does not need to compile a form's code, the form will load faster. See Chap-ter 11, "Expert Approaches to VBA," for more information on this subject.

12

Replace your IsLoaded *function with* SysCmd. Most Access developers write some version of the function I call IsLoaded for their libraries. This function's purpose is to loop through the Forms collection, checking to see if a specific form is loaded. The SysCmd() function can now be used for the same purpose and may be faster than checking the collection of open forms:

```
If SysCmd(acSysCmdGetObjectState, acForm, formname) _
   = acObjStateOpen Then
   IsLoaded = True
End If
```

Close forms not in use. If a hidden or minimized form will not be displayed for the user again for a reasonable period, close the form to free up system resources. However, balance this suggestion with the next one.

Don't close forms too soon. Forms that are used regularly will be much faster to display if kept open and hidden rather than constantly closing and reopening them. Chapter 14, "Navigating in Forms and Applications," provides suggested techniques for optimized form navigation of this nature.

Use explicit object class references. When creating object variables for forms or form controls, dimension the variables as Form, CheckBox, and so forth. Using the explicit class type produces faster code than using generic types, such as Object and Control. As a bonus, your code is actually more readable and more self-documenting.

Layout Techniques:

Minimize the use of graphics. If bitmaps or other pictures must be used, place them in the new Image control, and consider using black-and-white pictures instead of color.

Skip the background picture. While use of the form's Picture property to add a *wallpaper* (also called *watermark*) graphic to your form is a nice touch, it adds significant graphics overhead to form loads and repaints.

Don't stack controls. Placing controls on top of other controls—for example, locating a transparent Label control on top of a picture or rectangle—requires intensive repaint work from Access.

Consider the impact of domain functions and calculated controls. Basing ControlSource properties on expressions that include DLookup(), DSum(), IIf(), and similar functions can slow form performance, especially if these computed values are recalculated often. Consider alternative techniques for replacing these functions.

Minimize the use of ActiveX controls. Where they serve a valuable purpose, ActiveX controls can dramatically enhance the usability of your forms. ActiveX controls load more slowly than built-in controls, however, so rely on built-in controls first to supply specific interface needs. For example, replace any ActiveX tab controls you may have used in your Access 95 applications with the new intrinsic Tab control during conversion.

Separate primary from ancillary data. Include on the primary (first) page of a multi-page form only the fields that the user needs access to most frequently. Place lesser-needed fields on secondary pages. Some data for the non-displayed fields on additional pages will not be fetched by Jet until the user actually moves to the page (this is called *on-demand loading*)—this is especially true of Memo and OLE Object fields and Combo Box controls.

Move ancillary data to a second form. Sometimes it is prudent to move lesser-used data to a separate form, which is loaded by the user from a button or other device when the additional information is needed for viewing. This technique is discussed more in Chapter 15, "Protecting and Validating Data."

From Here...

In this chapter, I felt it was more important to focus on the areas of Access that appeal most to a developer of expert forms, rather than provide a complete tour of all the new features of Access forms. To review a complete list of new form features, search Access Help for "What's New." For more information about some of the topics discussed in this chapter, refer to the following:

▶ To understand the visual layout issues of expert forms, review Chapter 8, "Designing Effective Interfaces."

▶ To explore VBA's role in application and form development, see Chapter 11, "Expert Approaches to VBA."

▶ To continue the discussion of expert form techniques started here, read Chapter 13, "Mastering Combo and List Boxes," Chapter 14, "Navigating in Forms and Applications," and Chapter 15, "Protecting and Validating Data."

12

Creating Expert Forms

chapter 13

Mastering Combo and List Boxes

In this chapter

◆ **Responding to user changes—combo box values**

◆ **Adding values to these controls that are not in the primary underlying row source**

◆ **Getting maximum performance from combo and list boxes**

◆ **Tips for load combo and list boxes from nonstandard data sources**

◆ **Using list boxes for multiple selection**

C ombo and List Box controls are perhaps the most useful in the Windows application development environment. They allow the presentation of a large quantity of information using a minimum amount of screen space. You will come to rely heavily on these controls in your Access solution development efforts. In this chapter, I show you how to squeeze the maximum benefit out of these two controls.

Coping with a Changing World

Having been in the business of capturing and protecting clients' data for many years, I have learned to expect almost anything, so I try to design flexible applications that permit change. Since the early days of Access, we have used a combo box on our forms to reflect the values for Sex, with Male and Female in a lookup table.

Clients often ask why we do not use an option group instead because that type of control is much friendlier when dealing with a simple, two-option selection. My response has always been that if your applications are ready for anything, then changes cost you nothing.

Recently, certain political groups started an international lobbying effort to define five legal sexes, instead of the standard two, in an effort to include sexual minorities. If these efforts succeed, tens of thousands of computer applications worldwide will be thrown into chaos as the range of data options expands.

Our applications, however, would require only an addition of values to a lookup table—a one-minute process. Whether or not you agree with the way things are changing, combo and list boxes enable your applications to be ready for the changes.

Try to imagine a world without lists—the shopping list, the Christmas list, the voting ballot, and the multiple-choice exam question are all a part of daily life. Without lists, we don't have a way to easily represent choices or to organize information.

Access forms are also full of lists. Sales prospects can live in a defined list of states and provinces, inventory items can have subcomponents, and each employee works in a specific department. Even in their simplest form, the lists in Access Combo Box and List Box controls are powerful tools for easing the users' data entry burden and for providing data validation with no development overhead.

Yet many developers take for granted that—with a little extra effort and clever coding—these form controls can be made even more powerful. When building expert forms, you will rely heavily on Combo and List Box controls to restrict and validate data. In this chapter, we explore several ways to squeeze extra capabilities and performance out of these invaluable objects.

Expert Combo Box Techniques

Combo boxes are one of the most useful features in Access. Because they provide users with a limited range of options, they minimize data entry errors and confusion. Fortunately, two of the most common user complaints about combo boxes were addressed by the Access team with the Access 95 release, as follows:

Performance. Microsoft put considerable effort during both Access 95 and 97 development into speeding up the loading of combo boxes on forms. However, because there is never such a state as *too fast,* see the "Creating Faster Forms" section in Chapter 12, "Understanding Form Structures and Coding," for tips about squeezing still more speed out of combo boxes on forms.

Clearing Limited Lists. In earlier versions of Access, when your form had a combo box whose LimitToList property was set, you could not clear the combo box value from the keyboard. Starting with Access 95, your users can now clear the combo box value (in other words, set it to Null by deleting the characters in the combo box) and exit the field without producing the earlier error that the selected value is not on the list.

 Tip

Given this change in the Access response to Null values in a LimitToList combo box, you should review your converted applications for such controls. If one of the purposes of the LimitToList property in your application was to prevent Null values from being saved in a bound field, you will have to add new validation to the form.

These two enhancements reduce some of the major frustrations that developers experienced when they used combo boxes; thus, you will now be adding even more of these controls to your forms to increase their usability.

Trapping Additions to Combo Boxes

When loading a combo box with values to present to users, you usually provide list items for the control from a table or query using Table/Query as the RowSourceType value. The RowSource property usually contains a table name, query name, or SQL statement that refers to a *lookup table,* which is a table of values specifically defined to map short codes in the data to their longer values displayed on forms and reports.

13

In a data entry application, it is not always possible to anticipate the range of values that will be required by the users. Simply setting the LimitToList property of a combo box to False (No) so that users can enter data into the control that is not on the list is seldom an adequate solution because it removes the validation benefits of using the combo box.

Caution

Removing validation from combo boxes enables new lookup values to enter the form's data records without being added to the related lookup table; this destroys data integrity.

A solution to this problem is to help users select items that are not in the combo box's list and to trap such an event, recording and validating the entry. My favorite technique for this is to use a union query to place a new item marker in the control without having to add it to the underlying lookup data. Starting with Access 2, you can create SQL statements and saved queries that use the UNION operator to combine (append) values from two or more data sources. (For more information on union queries, see Chapter 10, "Creating Expert Tables and Queries.")

You begin the process of adding a new record marker to a combo box by creating a union query like the one in Listing 13.1, which produces a list of items with a new record marker at the top.

Listing 13.1   AES_Frm1.Mdb—Adding a Marker Item to a Combo Box List by Using an Expression

```
SELECT FirstName As SalesAgent
  FROM tblPeople
UNION SELECT "(add new)"
  FROM tblPeople
  ORDER BY SalesAgent;
```

By default, Access removes duplicate records from union query results, so only one record is returned by the expression "(add new)" as shown in the SELECT statement, and in Figure 13.1.

Fig. 13.1

The (add new) *on this list is not in the source table; it was added by the* UNION *operator.*

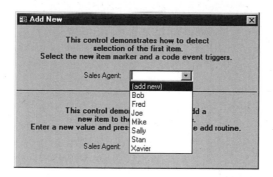

 Tip

You can create very powerful queries using the UNION operator to combine values from multiple tables and queries into a single combo box list. For example, even if American states, Canadian provinces, and Swiss cantons were stored in separate tables, you could combine them with UNION into one list for a RowSource property. However, union queries are among the slowest operations in Jet, so for the best results review the performance rules in the "Creating Faster Queries" section in Chapter 10.

Although the technique shown works quite nicely for adding an additional virtual (non-table) item to your list, I prefer to vary this *new record* marker technique to eliminate the need to hard-code the marker in the query definition. Because the (add new) expression shown in Listing 13.1 is stored with the QueryDef object (in the SQL), changing the string as the needs of the users change—or as the language base of the application is modified—becomes a significant development burden. Instead, you can create a table that you configure the new item marker in for the entire application without saving it into any queries or SQL strings used as RowSource properties. Then, use UNION to add the marker table value to lists as needed.

For example, to achieve the same result as in Listing 13.1, you can create a field called AddNewMarker in the defaults table zstblDefault and place the new item string in the table field. Any combo box RowSource properties that require a new item marker can refer to the table to get it, as in Listing 13.2. From the user's perspective, the combo box looks the same as in Figure 13.1.

Listing 13.2   AES_Frm1.Mdb—Adding a Marker Item from a Table to a Combo Box List

```
SELECT FirstName As SalesAgent
  FROM tblPeople
UNION SELECT AddNewMarker As SalesAgent
  FROM zstblDefault
  ORDER BY SalesAgent;
```

 Tip

The string that you use for the new item marker should be one that is guaranteed to sort to the top of the list for any data items your list might include. You can review character sort orders in the help topic "Character Set (0–127)" in Access (search for "character sets" in the index). The sort order of characters that sort before letters of the alphabet is shown in Table 13.1.

The (add new) example used here is enclosed in parentheses so it will sort above alphabetic and numeric characters. However, it will not sort above a space or seven other special characters (see Table 13.1), so if any data items on the combo list begin with the special characters that sort above the parentheses, you must change your method.

Although our clients sometimes choose to vary the new item marker to suit their tastes (for example <Add>, *New*, or -New-), Access itself uses parentheses for non-standard list markers in built-in lists, such as those on the Startup dialog box. My favorite method is to use (string) as well.

Table 13.1   Character Sort Orders in Access

Character	Character
space	,
!	-
"	.
#	/
$	0–9
%	:
&	;
'	<

Character	Character
(	=
)	>
*	?
+	@
A–Z	

When a user selects the new item marker from your combo box, your form can detect this event and run a code procedure. To trap when the user selects the new item marker, place a code snippet in the BeforeUpdate or AfterUpdate event of the Combo Box control to detect if the value selected by the user is the new value marker. Because your new value marker is designed to always sort to the first position on the list, your code knows the first item was selected when the ListIndex property of the control is zero, as in Listing 13.3.

Listing 13.3   AES_Frm1.Mdb—The First Item on a List Has a *ListIndex* Property of 0

```
Private Sub cboPeople_BeforeUpdate(Cancel As Integer)
' Purpose: Detect if the first item was selected

  If Me!cboPeople.ListIndex = 0 Then
    Beep
    MsgBox "New option detected. Add your code here to create " _
      & "a new list value.", vbInformation, "Add New - ListIndex"
  End If

End Sub
```

Although your objective may be for the new item marker to always appear at the top of the list, it is better coding style not to assume that it's there. Because the database administrator (or perhaps even users) can change the marker default in the table, it is not *guaranteed* to sort to the top of every list (and thus return a ListIndex of zero). A better strategy is to get the new item marker using a Dlookup() function on the zstblDefault table and then to compare the value of the combo box to the variable in your code. Listing 13.4 shows this method.

13

Listing 13.4   AES_Frm1.Mdb—Detecting When the First Item on a List Is Selected by Value

```
Private Sub cboPeople_BeforeUpdate(Cancel As Integer)
' Purpose: Detect if the first item was selected

  If Me!cboPeople.Value = DLookup("AddNewMarker", "zstblDefault") Then
    Beep
    MsgBox "New option detected. Add your code here to create " _
      & "a new list value.", vbInformation, "Add New - Default"
  End If

End Sub
```

 Tip

Listing 13.4 uses a `DLookup()` function to retrieve the new item marker on demand. If the user cannot change the new item marker in the defaults table while an application is running, you can load the new item marker into a global variable instead and access the variable repeatedly in your code. This technique can save scores of `DLookup()` calls during a single application session and thus improves performance.

When the user selects the new item marker from a combo list, your code can respond by prompting for an item to add, and then validating the item and adding or rejecting it. Your application can collect a new item value by displaying a pop-up form for data entry, or by displaying an `InputBox` dialog box for the new value using Basic code. Your code adds the newly entered value to the underlying lookup table and requeries the Combo Box control to show the new value. The techniques in the following section explain how to add the new value.

 Tip

This technique for adding a new item marker to a combo box works with list boxes as well.

Adding Values to a Combo Box List

In addition to—or instead of—a new item marker, your application can enable users to type an entry into a combo box that is not found in the combo's list. If this happens in a combo box whose LimitToList property is set to True (Yes), Access fires the NotInList event for the control. You can place code in the event to test the entered item for validity, and add it to the source of the list or reject it as required.

When the user types the new value and triggers the NotInList event, you can use code similar to that in Listing 13.5 to insert the value into the appropriate lookup table. Your code should also requery the combo box to display the new value in its sorted position.

Listing 13.5   AES_Frm1.Mdb—NotInList Event Code to Add a New Item

```
Private Sub cboAgent_NotInList(NewData As String, Response As Integer)
' Purpose: Add a new name to the underlying table for the list
' Pseudocode:
' 1. Create a Recordset against the list source
' 2. Add the user's item to the Recordset
' 3. Tell Access to requery the list and not alert the user

  Dim dbs As Database
  Dim rst As Recordset

  Set dbs = CurrentDb
  Set rst = dbs.OpenRecordset("tblPeople", dbOpenDynaset)
  ' A recordset gives better control than a RunSQL action
  rst.AddNew
  rst!FirstName = NewData
  rst.Update
  ' Tell the user what happened
  Beep
  MsgBox "Item '" & NewData & "' was added to the list and lookup table." _
    , vbInformation, "New Item"
  ' Tell Access to ignore its built-in error message
  ' and to requery the list
  Response = acDataErrAdded

  rst.Close
  dbs.Close

End Sub
```

13

In this listing, note that Access passes the value entered from the combo box to the NotInList event procedure as the NewData argument. This enables your code to test, display, or record the value. Also note that you can set the Response argument of the event in your code to select the disposition you want to trigger in Access. In this example, I set Response to an intrinsic constant (acDataErrAdded) that tells the event handler to requery the list, and not to display a warning message if the value is successfully found in the underlying table after the requery. The other constants for Response are the following:

> *acDataErrDisplay.* Tells Access to display the default warning alert ("The text you entered isn't an item in the list."), and does not add the entry to the combo box's list. This is also the default behavior if no event code exists when the OnNotInList event is triggered.

> *acDataErrContinue.* Tells Access not to display a message for the user, and does not add the entry to the combo box's list. This enables you to prohibit the entry and to provide a custom message that explains it to the user.

These three Response values enable you to handle any data entry situation activated in a Combo Box control.

Listing Combo Box Values as Properties

You can provide values for a combo box directly in the control's properties by setting the RowSourceType property to Value List and by listing the values in the RowSource property. The values must be separated with semicolons, as in Figure 13.2.

In general, setting combo box values as saved properties of a form is not a good design strategy. Over time, the values listed in a form's design will need to be changed as the user's needs change, requiring rework and redeployment of the form or its application by the developer. Basing list values on a table is usually a more flexible strategy.

However, there are some special circumstances when using the RowSource property to list combo box values might be a good strategy. What follows is a description of two such situations.

Fig. 13.2

You can set combo box values directly in a control's Property dialog box.

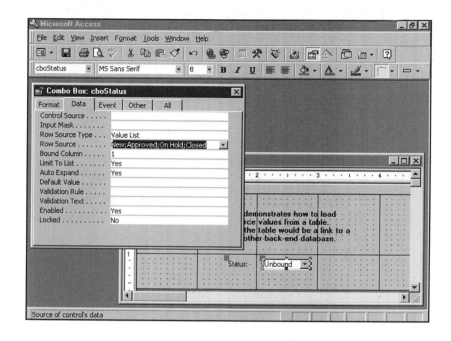

α Note

Any strategy for loading the RowSource property with a list of values is useful only when the total length of the concatenated values is not large because the maximum length of the string in the property setting can be only 2,048 characters.

Loading a Combo Box from a File

Assume for a moment that your company has a large mainframe system for its inventory data. The inventory system maintains purchase and shipment information about the goods that the company buys from suppliers. On any given day, there are 50 to 100 open orders in transit.

Your job is to write a receiving system for the loading dock. The entry form for the system needs a combo box that shows vendor number and purchase order number for the open orders only, so that the workers on the dock can match each incoming order against a valid purchase order. The list of active open orders, however, is kept on the mainframe.

You have convinced your Information Technology group to download the order data into a file for you each night. They will even post the file to your application's directory

13

after each download. Now, you need only to get the downloaded data to show up in your combo box.

Your first inclination might be to write a code routine to load the file into a table in the database each morning. The problem with this method is that someone must remember to run the load routine each morning. You'll need to write a scheduling routine, enforce a logout/login, add a button to a menu, and train all the users about when to press it. Or you'll need to find some other method to ensure that the new data is loaded each morning.

Your next inclination might be to have IT download the file as a *comma-separated value* (CSV) format file and to use the Access ISAM engine to link to the file directly. The format of the CSV file is simple, as Figure 13.3 shows.

Fig. 13.3

A file in comma-separated value (CSV) format has commas between the values and quotation marks around the strings.

To link to the file, create a link to the downloaded file in the Database window; Access then treats it like any other table. Figure 13.4 shows the Link Text Wizard in action against the file from Figure 13.3.

Fig. 13.4

The Link Text Wizard helps you establish links to non-Access data. The linked data can be used as a combo box RowSource.

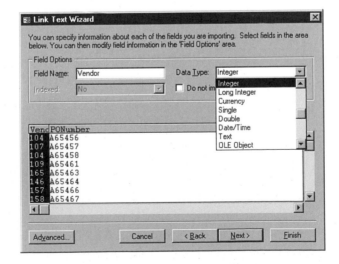

Tip

You can link text files using program code with the `TransferText` method of the `DoCmd` object.

With the file linked to Access, you can base your form's combo box upon the table link. The flaw in this strategy is that the loading-dock workers keep the entry form open all of the time. In such a scenario, the following problem occurs:

Your form locks the table, which...

...locks the linked flat file on disk, which...

...keeps IT personnel from being able to copy the new file over the previous file each night.

To solve this dilemma, you must find a way to set the combo box's row source from the data while not locking the underlying table and file. You can use the following strategy:

1. Add a combo box to your form, but do not bind the combo to the linked text file. Also, do not link the text file to your database at all, and do not enter any `RowSource` property for the combo box.

2. Ask the IT personnel to change the format of the downloaded file to use semicolons as the item separator, instead of the commas shown in Figure 13.3. (Semicolons are the required delimiter for value lists that are used as the source for a combo box, which makes this file easier to use directly from your application.)

3. Add code to the `Enter` event of the combo box to create the `RowSource` from the file on disk. The `Enter` event is used so that the list of values can be rebuilt each time the user moves to it, which guarantees that the latest data is always displayed. This ensures that the list is rebuilt from the daily download, even if the users never close the form and reopen it. In fact, even if the file on disk was changing minute-by-minute, using the `Enter` event would ensure that the list was rebuilt from the latest disk file every time the combo received focus.

4. Add code to the `Load` event of the form to initially populate the list and to set a monitor variable to detect whether or not the file has been updated. Have your code check the file status against the monitor variable and reload the combo box values only if the file has changed.

In effect, you have set up a background process that teaches the combo box to watch its own data source and to rebuild its list from the data source only when IT copies a new file over the old file. Such a strategy would be much more difficult to implement using

13

import routines to refresh a table because the form would have to be closed to run the routines, the database structure would be impacted as a table is deleted and rebuilt, and so on.

 Note

When implementing any variation of this particular solution, be alert to data integrity and data sharing issues. My example in this section does not discuss issues such as accidental deletions of the file, bad data inside the file, sharing the file on a network, and so forth. Also, there are interesting philosophical issues about strategies that allow data to live outside of its database, mostly related to data ownership and centralization.

Listing 13.6 shows the code that drives this strategy.

Listing 13.6   AES_Frm1.Mdb—Loading and Refreshing a Combo Box from a Disk File

```
' In the Declarations section of the form module
Private mvarFileDate As Variant ' Preserve date of data file
Private mstrOrderFile As String ' Path and file name

' When the form loads, load the combo and set the monitor variable
Private Sub Form_Load()

  ' File must be in the same path as this database
  mstrOrderFile = lci_DbsPathGet(CurrentDb) & "Order.Txt"
  ' Perform the initial load
  Call cboOrder_Enter
  ' Preserve the starting stamp of the file
  mvarFileDate = FileDateTime(mstrOrderFile)

End Sub

' Check the file status with each Enter event and refresh if needed
Private Sub cboOrder_Enter()
' Purpose: Reload the combo from the flat file
' Pseudocode:
' 1. If the file date/time has not changed, abort
' 2. Open the disk file
' 3. Fetch each line in the file and concatenate into one string
' 4. Set the combo source to the string
' 5. Set the monitor variable to the new file date/time

  ' See if the file date/time has changed
  If mvarFileDate = FileDateTime(mstrOrderFile) Then
    GoTo cboOrder_Enter_Exit ' Nothing to do
  End If
```

```
Dim intFile As Integer ' File number
Dim strInp As String ' Line from the file
Dim strWork As String ' Build the RowSource

DoCmd.Hourglass True
' Load the file items into one string
intFile = FreeFile()
Open mstrOrderFile For Input As #intFile
Do Until EOF(intFile) ' Cycle thru all rows
  Line Input #intFile, strInp
  strWork = strWork & ";" & strInp ' Add the delimiter
Loop
Me!cboOrder.RowSource = Trim(Mid(strWork, 2)) ' Ignore the first ;
Me!cboOrder.Requery
mvarFileDate = FileDateTime(mstrOrderFile)

End Sub
```

 Tip
This technique for loading a combo box from a file works with list boxes also.

Loading a Combo Box from Code

There are various data values that can be useful in an application that are difficult to maintain in a data table. One example is a list of database objects. Assume that you want to include on a form a list of all the forms in the current database. It will be challenging to keep all the current object names in a data table, and you can't expect a user or developer to maintain the list of forms accurately over time.

A more useful approach is to enable your code to query the Data Access Objects for the list of forms and to load this list into the RowSource property of the combo box. (See Chapter 12, "Understanding Form Structures and Coding," to learn how to get the names of all the forms in your database.)

Consider a second example, which was inspired by one of our clients. Assume your company has 400 users running Access applications at various times every day. Each application has a need for the same five combo boxes on most forms, providing static information, such as state names and customer type codes. The company wants to provide the source data for these five combo boxes in one centralized database. For our purposes, I'll call this database the "lookup database."

13

Jet does its best to manage and minimize locking situations that can arise in an environment like this. For example, Bob opens a form in data entry mode. The form has five combo boxes, each of which is bound to a table in his database. However, each of the five tables is actually a link to a table in the lookup database. How many locks does Bob have on the lookup database?

In fact, he hasn't locked any tables yet because he hasn't opened any of the combo boxes on the form, and Access does not request the data to fill the combo boxes until it's demanded by a user event. However, after Bob opens each of the combo boxes, Access has placed a read lock on each of the tables in the lookup database, totaling five locks.

Now, imagine that each user in the company tries to open a form with combo boxes that read from the lookup database. You have two immediate problems, as follows:

▶ Jet runs out of user locks at 255 users, so some users won't be able to access the lookup database.

▶ Two hundred fifty-five users multiplied by 5 read locks each is 1,275 locks, which will consume a share of server resources that could be used for other processes.

Because I've already noted that the lookup information is mostly static, you have the following options to resolve this problem:

▶ Make several copies of the lookup database and distribute users evenly across the copies.

▶ Copy or replicate the lookup table data to each user's local database or data (back-end) database at regular intervals.

▶ Devise a strategy to minimize the impact on the lookup database.

For the purposes of this example, proceed with the third option because it fulfills the goal of keeping a centralized lookup database. Because the lookup data is fairly static and the lists themselves are short, you can solve the problem by unbinding each form's combo boxes from the linked tables; then, create code in each form's Load event to populate the combo boxes from the linked tables. The code is simple, as Listing 13.7 shows.

Because the combo boxes now load from program code, any locks placed on their source tables exist only as long as the code is running rather than for the life of the form. This reduces the hypothetical server and Jet loads, described earlier, from hundreds of simultaneous locks to a handful—a significant improvement in server load and general performance.

Tip

As an added bonus, this strategy releases locks on the lookup database immediately after loading the combo box. This means that, overnight, no user workstations that still have the interface application open will hold any locks on the database, which enables any overnight processes (such as backup, updates, or repair and compact) to grab the exclusive database lock that they need.

Listing 13.7   AES_Frm1.Mdb—Code to Load a Combo Box from a Linked Table

```
Private Sub Form_Load()
' Purpose: Load combo box from a lookup database

  Dim dbs As Database
  Dim rsnp As Recordset
  Dim strWork As String

  Set dbs = CurrentDb
  Set rsnp = dbs.OpenRecordset("tlkpStatus", dbOpenSnapshot, dbForwardOnly)
  Do While Not rsnp.EOF
    strWork = strWork & ";" & rsnp!Status
    rsnp.MoveNext
  Loop

  Me!cboStatus.RowSource = Mid(strWork, 2) ' Ignore the first ;

  rsnp.Close
  dbs.Close

End Sub
```

To complete the example, remember the following few points:

▶ As you build the RowSource for each combo box, check it to be sure that it doesn't reach the 2,048 character-length limit. Combo box lists that exceed this limit will require a different technique for loading (a table, query, or callback function as the row source).

▶ To add performance, you can do away with table links altogether and open your Recordset objects in code against the lookup database directly (using the OpenDatabase method). You can also use forward-scrolling snapshot-type Recordsets instead of dynaset-type Recordsets, which will improve data access times (as in Listing 13.7).

13

▶ Because your value lists are built in the same order as the underlying recordset (the code simply walks through with MoveNext), consider storing the lookup tables in sorted order at all times. In this way, the application code for loading combo boxes does not have to force any sorting. If this is not possible, have your combo box routine call a saved query to sort the data instead of using an SQL statement to sort it ad hoc.

Careful planning and coding of combo boxes can sometimes squeeze significant extra performance out of applications with a high user count.

> **Tip**
> The technique in this section for loading a combo box from code works with list boxes as well.

Retrieving Lookup Values with the *Column* Property

Sometimes when the user selects a value from a combo box, your application may require more information based on that value. For example, the user selects a person from a combo box and your form has to display the person's phone number. You might currently solve this problem by using a domain function, such as DLookup() or DFirst(), to retrieve the related value from a table. In such a scenario, assume you have a combo box, cboPeople, in which the RowSource property is equal to the following:

```
SELECT FirstName FROM tblPeople
```

When using the domain lookup approach, you retrieve the phone number by placing a function into a text box labeled Phone. The function, located in the ControlSource property, will look something like this:

```
=DLookUp("Phone","tblPeople","FirstName = '" & [Form]![cboPeople] & "'")
```

Because the domain function must go to the table to retrieve the lookup value, however, the performance of this method will not be instantaneous. Worse, if you need to grab more than one value from the target table—such as the phone number into one text box and the phone extension into another—you must run multiple domain lookups in succession, which has a negative impact on performance.

An alternative approach to domain functions—with increased performance and usability—is to bring the desired lookup data into the combo box as an additional column value when the list first loads. Then, using the Column property of the control, you can retrieve the additional value(s) as needed, even if they aren't displayed on the form.

To use the `Column` property, include the phone number column from `tblPeople` in the `RowSource` of the combo box. This ensures that the phone number for each person is fetched from the table when the combo box loads:

```
SELECT FirstName, Phone FROM tblPeople
```

You can suppress the display of the phone column in the combo by setting the `ColumnWidths` property to zero for the second column. Even though the column is not displayed, the value is still available in the `Column` property of the control. In this example, because `Phone` is the second column in the list and Access column indexing is zero-based, you can refer to the `Phone` value for a displayed `FirstName` by using an expression in the `ControlSource` of your Phone text box, as Figure 13.5 shows.

Fig. 13.5

Information in a combo box column is available to a text box via the `.Column(n)` *syntax.*

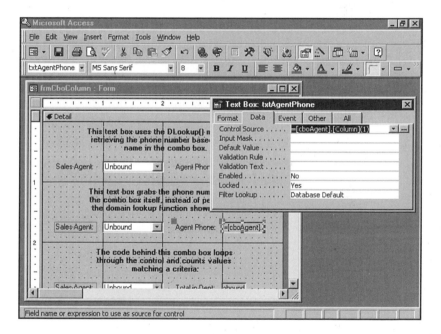

Compare the performance difference of the two methods. Using a domain lookup function to retrieve a value causes a query to run against a data table each time the function is executed, which occurs whenever the combo box value is changed or the form expressions are recalculated. By contrast, if the lookup data is pulled into the combo box list, all phone numbers are fetched in one pass from the table as the combo box loads. The latter approach runs much faster.

13

Note

This example placed the `Column` reference in the `ControlSource` property of a text box. Access will recalculate the expression in the text box as the combo box value changes. Instead, if you want more control over when the value assignment occurs, you can use the `Column` property in an expression in the form's code, usually in the `AfterUpdate` event of the Combo Box control. When the value for the text box is fed from your code, you can design your form with the text box as an editable or non-editable control. By contrast, when the text box value is fed by an expression in its `ControlSource`, the control is always made read-only by Access.

The real power of this technique is due to the fact that you can pull multiple columns of data into your combo box when it loads, and reference any or all of the values in code or in expressions on the form. This technique saves multiple domain lookups when a new combo box value is selected, and it greatly enhances form performance.

 Tip

The `Column` property is also available on List Box controls where it can be used in the same manner as described in this section.

Direct Addressing to Combo Box Values

Access now has the capability to address a specific combo list row. This makes the combo box into an array of addressable values. However, the syntax is convoluted compared to an array because the row index comes after the column index:

```
controlname.Column(column,row)
```

 Note

The indexing for the `Column` property is by column and row, rather than the commonly accepted row and column, because the row index was added to Access only recently (Access 95) and it was necessary to maintain backward compatibility.

This addressing scheme enables you to extract any value from a combo box once you know its location. Listing 13.8 shows a procedure that loops through the values in any combo box and dumps the value matrix to the debug window. The results of running this procedure against a simple name and phone number combo are shown in Figure 13.6.

Listing 13.8   AES_Frm1.Mdb—Looping Through a Combo Box as If It Were an Array

```
Public Sub CtlDump(ctl As Control)
' Purpose: Dump the contents of a combo box or list box 'array'

  Dim iintCol As Integer
  Dim iintRow As Integer

  For iintRow = 0 To ctl.ListCount - 1
    For iintCol = 0 To ctl.ColumnCount - 1
      Debug.Print ctl.Column(iintCol, iintRow),
    Next iintCol
    Debug.Print
  Next iintRow

End Sub
```

Fig. 13.6

The result of running the code in Listing 13.8 to loop through all the values of a Combo Box control.

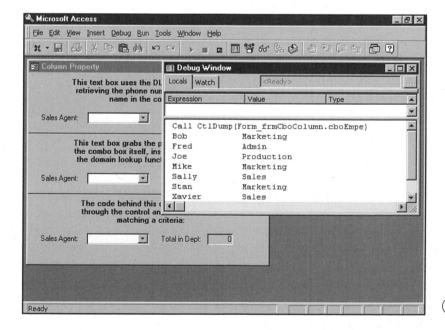

Now, let's find a practical application for this feature. Assume you have a combo box that lists the name and department of all employees. When the user of your form selects a particular employee, you want a Text Box control to display the total number of employees in the same department as the selected employee. The code in Listing 13.9 will achieve the desired result by employing the looping logic previously described. (The department name is in the second column (`ctl.Column(1)` in the combo box.)

Listing 13.9   AES_Frm1.Mdb—Looping Through Values in a Combo Box

```
Private Sub cboEmpe_AfterUpdate()
' Purpose: Count the employees in the selected department

  Dim cbo      As ComboBox
  Dim intCount As Integer
  Dim iintRow  As Integer

  Set cbo = Me!cboEmpe
  For iintRow = 0 To cbo.ListCount - 1
    ' Compare each row to the selected row
    If cbo.Column(1, iintRow) = cbo.Column(1) Then
      intCount = intCount + 1
    End If
  Next iintRow
  Me!txtDeptCount = intCount

End Sub
```

As with other uses of the `Column` property, the big win in this listing is performance. Previously, you would have had your code run a grouping query or `DCount()` function to count all of the members of a specific department. The technique shown here produces the same result without running the query engine, and without accessing any index or data pages in the database.

 Tip

The row offset argument described in this section is also available in the `Column` property of List Box controls.

Using One Combo Box to Replace Several

The following technique demonstrates how to replace several combo boxes with Text Box controls, with the text boxes sharing only a single combo box instead. As with other techniques in this chapter, the primary objective of this strategy is to add performance to forms that are not loading or running as quickly as desired.

The example uses the sample data in Figure 13.7, and is described as follows:

▶ Your company utilizes a standard accounting structure of GL (general ledger) codes and sub-codes.

▶ The GL also has three departments that receive separate treatment when budgeting and tracking expenses.

▶ Not all combinations of GL codes and sub-codes are valid for each department. For example, only the Administrative Department can charge expenses to GL code 240.02, Building/Grounds Mechanical.

Fig. 13.7

These sample GL codes, GL sub-codes, and GL department codes belong to the hypothetical company in this section's examples.

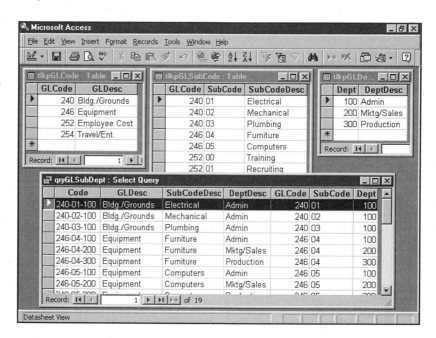

A standard approach to building a form to collect accounting information around this data structure would include three combo boxes, one each for GL Code, GL Sub-Code, and GL Department Code. The performance problem arises because there is a dependency between the GL Code combo and the GL Sub-Code combo (for each GL Code there is a valid set of sub-codes), and a dependency between the GL Code/Sub-Code combination and the GL Department codes (for each GL Code/Sub-Code pair there is a valid set of GL Department codes).

With a dependency between combo boxes, you must requery a dependent control whenever the value of its parent changes. For example, the following code is required in the GL Code combo box's event model to requery the lists in its two dependents:

13

```
Private Sub cboGL_AfterUpdate()
' Purpose: Requery dependent controls

    Me!cboSub.Requery
    Me!cboDept.Requery

End Sub
```

To express the dependency from the child's side, each control that relies on cboGL must include that control in its criteria selection. For example, the RowSource property for the cboSub control looks like this:

```
SELECT SubCode, SubCodeDesc
   FROM tlkpGLSubCode
   WHERE GLCode=[Forms]![frmCboConsolidate]![cboGL]
   ORDER BY SubCode;
```

Each requery takes time, and with multiple dependencies in place, the form makes several requeries per record.

 Note

To offset the negative performance of dependent combos, each such combo box provides the user with a carefully filtered list of codes and values, which clearly identifies the permitted data items. Thus, increased usability derives from decreased performance, and this tradeoff might be acceptable in some applications.

An alternative approach to dependent combo boxes is to allow the entry of the GL data into text boxes instead. This method presumes that most users, most of the time, will know the values they want to enter, thereby reducing the need for a limited combo list. However, the user should not be asked to live without a combo box completely because sacrificing usability for performance is not usually a good strategy.

The form in Figure 13.8 contains a Text Box control for each of the required values for GL Code, Sub-Code, and Department. Next to the text boxes, the form also contains a button with a Click event that displays a combo box of compounded values on top of the text boxes (see Figure 13.9). The combo box must contain all of the valid combinations for the three types of codes because it will be used in the following two ways:

▶ As a list of permitted combinations, the combo box can be used to validate the data entered into the text boxes.

▶ If the user is not aware of a valid combination that is permitted in the text boxes, the combo box can be opened and searched for the desired compound value.

Fig. 13.8

This form contrasts the two approaches described for entering compound values—using combo boxes and using text boxes.

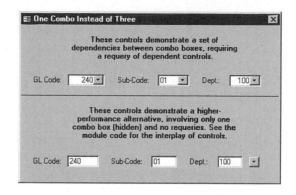

Fig. 13.9

This combo box feeds values to, and helps to validate, the text boxes hidden below it.

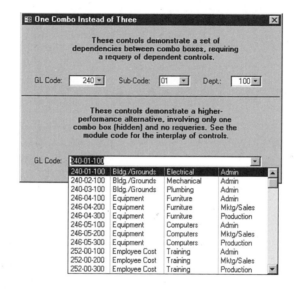

The flow of this form (specifically, the current example as shown in the lower half) is as follows:

1. The user enters values into the text boxes for GL Code, Sub-Code, and Department. You place VBA code behind the text boxes to validate the entered data against the hidden combo box, as shown in Listing 13.10. By validating against the combo box, validation is performed in memory and no disk access to a table or query is undertaken. (The columns with index values 4, 5, and 6 in the combo box hold the GL codes, sub-codes, and department codes, respectively.)

13

Listing 13.10   AES_Frm1.Mdb—Validating Text Box Values Using a Compound Combo Box

```
Private Sub txtDept_AfterUpdate()
' Purpose: To validate the combination of GL, Sub, Dept
' This validation example is not comprehensive,
' because it only validates on the update of one of the
' three related text boxes, to demonstrate the technique.
' In production you would place it in Form_BeforeUpdate.

  Dim blnFound As Boolean
  Dim cbo      As ComboBox
  Dim iintLoop As Integer
  Set cbo = Me!cboCombined

  For iintLoop = 0 To cbo.ListCount - 1
    If cbo.Column(4, iintLoop) = Me!txtGL Then
      If Me!txtSub = cbo.Column(5, iintLoop) _
        And Me!txtDept = cbo.Column(6, iintLoop) Then
        blnFound = True
      Exit For
    End If
  End If
Next iintLoop

  If Not blnFound Then
    Beep
    MsgBox "Combination of codes is not valid.", vbExclamation, "GL"
  End If

End Sub
```

2. When the user clicks the drop-down command button, code runs to hide the text boxes and to display the combo box in their place. Alternatively, you can display the combo box above or below the text boxes.

3. When the user makes a selection from the combo box, the individual values are parsed and used to feed the dependent Text Box controls, as Listing 13.11 shows.

Listing 13.11   AES_Frm1.Mdb—Sending Compound Combo Box Values to Dependent Controls

```
Private Sub cboCombined_AfterUpdate()
' Purpose: Send compound value into dependent controls

  If Not IsNull(Me!cboCombined) Then
    Me!txtGL = Me!cboCombined.Column(4)
    Me!txtSub = Me!cboCombined.Column(5)
    Me!txtDept = Me!cboCombined.Column(6)
  End If

End Sub
```

> **Note**
>
> The code to hide and show controls is not listed in this section. See the examples in the database AES_FRM1.MDB on the CD-ROM.

This technique tries to walk a very narrow line between two objectives that are often mutually exclusive: to provide power users and rapid data entry personnel with validation that doesn't slow their use of the form, and to maintain a way for unsophisticated users to get extra assistance when they need it.

Tricks like this provide increased performance to your forms. However, because they change the usability model of the form, you should be sure that users can understand and be comfortable with such nonstandard approaches to data entry.

Loading a Combo Box from a List Callback Function

If your applications require a combo box's value list to be filled with data that isn't available in a table or query, Access provides another mechanism beyond using value lists in the RowSource property. The technique involves creating a user-defined function to feed values to the combo box. The function is created as code in the form's module or in a standard module. To use the function, enter its name into the RowSourceType property of a Combo Box control.

A function used in this fashion must be coded to an exact structure, which enables Access to call it repeatedly, in order to fetch the values for the combo box. Programmers commonly use the term *callback function* to describe a procedure that is called repeatedly, so I will use the term *list callback function* to describe the technique here. (Microsoft called this type of function a *list function* in Access 1 and 2 documentation; other common terms for this technique used in the Access community include *fill-list function* and a *list-fill function*.)

To apply a list callback function, enter the name of the function in the RowSourceType (not the RowSource) property of a combo box, minus an equal sign and any arguments. Figure 13.10 shows a combo box with the RowSourceType property set to a callback function name.

Fig. 13.10

A user-defined list callback function is attached to a combo box by entering its name in the RowSourceType *property in the property sheet.*

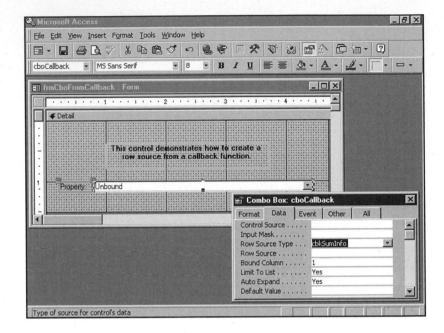

Structuring a List Callback Function

A callback function used with a combo box must follow a very specific model, or Access can't use it. The restrictive model means that Access can call the function expecting an action to happen, and the function will trigger the action on cue. The following are the various actions that occur in the callback function:

1. Access *initializes the function,* which creates the structure of the list data (in rows and columns).

2. The function tells the combo box *how wide* to display each column and what the *row count* is.

3. The combo box calls the function repeatedly to *fetch values* to load into its list. Then, the combo box may still continue to call the function to get more values as the user moves the cursor or browses the control's list.

4. The combo box calls the function one last time to *perform cleanup* when the form is closed.

The function declaration for a list callback function must have these arguments:

```
Function functionname(ctl As Control, varID As Variant, varRow As Variant _
    , varCol As Variant, varCode As Variant) As Variant
```

Note

I used my own argument names in the syntax example, but you can use any valid variable names. The variable data types and their positional location, however, must not be changed.

The values for the arguments to the callback function are explained in Table 13.2.

Table 13.2   Elements of a List Callback Function

Argument	Description
functionname	The name of the function. You can use any valid name. Note that the return value must be Variant.
ctl	A variable of type Control, which points to the target combo box.
varID	Access creates a unique ID for each control calling the function, so that multiple controls can share the same function.
varRow	The row number that the combo box tries to fill.
varCol	The column number that the combo box tries to fill or format.
varCode	Access sends a code to the function with each call, specifying the type of action for the function to perform.

 Note

Access doesn't seem to notice if you declare an actual control object class as the first argument, as in the string cbo As ComboBox instead of ctl As Control, so you can safely use this more explicit syntax if you choose.

An interesting feature of this type of function is that you call it from the RowSourceType property by its name only and you aren't permitted to pass in the arguments shown. Although the arguments are not listed in the property sheet, the control actually passes them back and forth to the function itself.

Note

The row and column numbers (`varRow` and `varCol` in the example) are zero-based numbers, like addressing values in a Combo Box control.

Because Access must initialize, fill, and then maintain the combo box list via your function, the combo box calls the function one or more times for each possible value of the `varCode` argument. Depending on the `varCode` passed in, your function executes a specified action and sets the return value of the function to describe the result of the action to the combo box.

Listing 13.12 shows a rough outline of a list callback function to illustrate how the function's structure depends on the `varCode` values coming from the control.

Listing 13.12   AES_Frm1.Mdb—An Outline of a List Callback Function's Structure

```
Private Function cbkCallbackShell(cbo As ComboBox, varID As Variant _
  , varRow As Variant, varCol As Variant, varcode As Variant) _
  As Variant
' Purpose: A code shell for a list callback function

  Select Case varcode

    Case acLBInitialize ' Initialization
      ' Initialize here

    Case acLBOpen ' When the control is opened
      ' Create a control ID here

    Case acLBGetRowCount ' How many rows?
      ' Set the number of rows here

    ' ...More varCode Case tests go here

    Case acLBEnd ' Close down the function
      ' Cleanup here

  End Select

End Function
```

The following `varCode` values are passed in to a list callback function. Each code value is represented by an intrinsic constant in Access, as shown parenthetically. Codes 2 and 8 are not used by the function or documented by Microsoft, and they are not listed here.

varCode=0 (acLBInitialize). This code causes the function to initialize, and is only passed in once as the combo box is awakened when the form loads. Your code should create the working list of combo box values in this block. The function should return True or any non-zero number if it can service the forthcoming load requests, or False (or Null) if it can't proceed.

varCode=1 (acLBOpen). This code is passed in when the combo box is fully created. Your function should return a unique, non-zero ID value for the current instance of the current control. The ID is passed back to the function when the function is called later to identify the calling control. Return False or Null here if the function can't proceed.

 Tip

Most programmers simply use the Timer function to create a unique ID for the control because this function does not create any duplicate numbers during one day (the 24-hour period from midnight to midnight).

---

varCode=3 (acLBGetRowCount). Your function is called only once with this code—when the combo box wants to know the total number of items that will be in the list. When it sees this code value, your function should return the number of rows that will be in the list, zero if no rows, or –1 if the row count is currently unknown. When you use –1, Access will continue to call your function with incremental row numbers looking for more data until you pass back a Null return value to signify the end of data (which will obviously run slower than passing back an absolute row count, and thus should be avoided if possible).

varCode=4 (acLBGetColumnCount). The combo box calls your function once with this code value to request the number of columns that will be in the list. The number your function returns for this action must be equal to the number saved as the ColumnCount property of the control.

 Tip

Your code can simply return the column count of the control back to it by using the syntax ctl.ColumnCount.

---

varCode=5 (acLBGetColumnWidth). Access calls your function with this code value (with the varCol argument set to a column number) to tell you which column's

(13)

information is being requested. Pass back to the combo box the column width (in *twips*) of the column specified, or return –1 to have the control use the setting from its `ColumnWidths` property.

 Tip

A twip is a unit of screen measurement. There are 1,440 twips in an inch and 567 in a centimeter. If your list's width measurements are in inches, multiply the value in inches by 1,440 to get a value in twips.

varCode=6 (`acLBGetValue`). Access will call your function repeatedly with this code value (with the `varRow` and `varCol` arguments set) to request the data item to place in the list at the specified position. Set your function's return value to send back the appropriate data item.

varCode=7 (`acLBGetFormat`). Access will call your function (with the `varCol` argument set) as rows are displayed for the user. Return a valid format string to format the data item in the specified column, or return `Null` to have the control use its existing `Format` property setting. Any string that can be used in the `Format` property, such as `>;` to format all characters as uppercase, can be utilized.

varCode=9 (`acLBEnd`). The control uses this code value to make one final call to your function before the form closes. Use this notification to close variables and to do other standard cleanup in your function. You do not need to set a return value for this code.

 Note

If the function sets the return value to `Null` or any invalid value for any `varCode` value passed in to your function, the combo box will not call your function again with the same code value. This gives you the ability to discontinue certain action calls to the function by switching them off. However, it also affords an opportunity for confusion when the return value is set improperly through a coding error—your function may no longer work as expected.

List callback functions are too complicated and their capabilities too powerful to explain them outside the context of a real-life example. The next two sections provide such examples.

Tip

The technique for creating functions to provide data for Combo Box controls works equally well with list boxes. As with combo boxes, the name of your custom function goes in the RowSourceType property of your list boxes.

Using a List Callback Function with One Control

Your list callback function must feed data back to the calling control, as requested, using row and column coordinates. Thus, your function must have data available in an addressable row and column format. Most commonly, such a structure is provided by an array within the function. When a varCode of zero is passed to your function to trigger initialization, your code must fill the array so that the values are available for all subsequent passes through the function.

Although filling an array from a table is straightforward, your application should probably not be using a callback function in the first place if the data source for the combo box is a table. Simply use the table directly (or a query that filters it) as the RowSource of the combo box.

 Note

The exception to the preceding paragraph occurs when you want to load a combo box from a table, but for performance reasons you do not want Access to maintain a link to the table. Thus the technique you learned for tuning lookup database access, in "Loading a Combo Box from Code" earlier in this chapter, is a good candidate for a callback function. The callback would load its array from a lookup table during initialization and then disconnect from the lookup database.

The real worth of a callback function is determined by the fact that it can provide values to a combo box that can be gathered only via program code. What follows are a few situations where a callback function is quite valuable:

▶ Callbacks can be used to list objects or properties in the *Data Access Objects* collections of a database. For example, your callback function can fill a combo box with the names of all of the forms in a database, or can use coding logic to return only specific form names. (Refer to the "Performing Bulk Form Operations" section of Chapter 12, "Understanding Form Structures and Coding," for an example that explains how to list all forms in a database.)

13

▶ A list of *disk files* matching a specific criteria can be built using a callback function. For example, your callback function can list all mainframe download files in a specified holding directory.

▶ *Automation* can be used from the callback to list information held in other Office applications or similar servers. For example, you can fill a combo box with items from your Schedule+ or Outlook task list.

▶ Callbacks can include *API calls* to the Windows system to list system information.

Before delving into a functional example, study Listing 13.13, which shows a code shell outlining the basic structure of a callback function. As you review the shell, note the following points:

▶ Because the function can be called multiple times, you need to use `Static` variables to preserve variable values that must persist between calls.

▶ The structure of the primary `Select Case` block provides a chunk of code for each of the possible `varCode` values passed to the function.

▶ Subordinate `Select Case` blocks are required where the function is passed a row or column index.

▶ This code shell will not run as listed; it is a framework for educational purposes only.

Read the listing carefully and be sure that you understand the components of a callback function before you proceed. It is apparent from the listing that a callback function is very rigidly structured.

Listing 13.13   AES_Frm1.Mdb—A Code Shell for a Simple List Callback Function

```
Private Function cbkCallbackShell(cbo As ComboBox, varID As Variant _
  , varRow As Variant, varCol As Variant, varCode As Variant) As Variant
' Purpose: A code shell for a list callback function
' Placeholders are in <brackets>, this code does not run

  Static sastrCallback() As String ' Array for data values

  Select Case varCode

    Case acLBInitialize ' Initialization
      '<Fill array sastrCallback() here>
      cbkCallbackShell = True ' Okay to proceed

    Case acLBOpen ' When the control is opened
      cbkCallbackShell = Timer ' Create a unique control ID

    Case acLBGetRowCount ' How many rows?
      'cbkCallbackShell = <n> ' Number of rows
```

```
      Case acLBGetColumnCount ' How many columns?
        cbkCallbackShell = cbo.ColumnCount ' Echo back the property value

      Case acLBGetColumnWidth ' How wide are the columns?
        Select Case varCol
          Case 0 ' First column
            'cbkCallbackShell = <twips> ' Set the width
            '<Add more cases here>
          'Case <n>
        End Select
      ' Alternately, use the defaults
      'cbkCallbackShell = -1 ' Use the default widths

      Case acLBGetValue ' Fetch one data item
        cbkCallbackShell = sastrCallback(varRow, varCol)

      Case acLBGetFormat ' Format one data item
        ' cbkCallbackShell = "<formatstring>"

      Case acLBEnd ' Close down the function
    End Select

  End Function
```

 Tip

This code shell is included in AES_FRM1.MDB on the CD-ROM as VBA code and can be used as a starting point for creating your own callback functions. A working list callback function is also included in the database.

Now, with the groundwork established, you can review an actual callback function that runs. The example in Listing 13.14 shows a function that fills a combo box with the property names and values for the SummaryInfo properties stored by Access in the database.

Listing 13.14   AES_Frm1.Mdb—A List Callback Function that Fills a Combo Box with Database Properties

```
Private Function cbkSumInfo(cbo As ComboBox, varID As Variant _
  , varRow As Variant, varCol As Variant, varCode As Variant) As Variant
' Purpose: Callback to fill a combo box with database summary info
' Arguments: cbo:=Control handle
'            varID:=Unique control ID
'            varRow:=Row number
'            varCol:=Column number
'            varCode:=Index to action item
```

13

continues

Listing 13.14 Continued

```
Dim dbs As Database
Dim doc As Document
Static sintRow As Integer
Static sastrPrp() As String  ' Array for data values

Select Case varCode

  Case acLBInitialize       ' Initialization
    ' Fill the array
    Set dbs = CurrentDb
    Set doc = dbs.Containers!Databases.Documents!SummaryInfo
    ReDim sastrPrp(doc.Properties.Count, 2)  ' Set the array size
    For sintRow = 0 To doc.Properties.Count - 1 ' Get each property
      sastrPrp(sintRow, 0) = doc.Properties(sintRow).Name
      sastrPrp(sintRow, 1) = doc.Properties(sintRow).Value
    Next sintRow
    cbkSumInfo = True         ' Okay to proceed

  Case acLBOpen             ' When the control is opened
    cbkSumInfo = Timer       ' Create a unique control ID

  Case acLBGetRowCount      ' How many rows?
    cbkSumInfo = sintRow     ' Number of rows

  Case acLBGetColumnCount   ' How many columns?
    cbkSumInfo = cbo.ColumnCount  ' Echo back the property value

  Case acLBGetColumnWidth   ' How wide are the columns?
    Select Case varCol
      Case 0                 ' First column
        cbkSumInfo = 1500    ' Set the width
      Case 1                 ' Second column
        cbkSumInfo = 3500    ' Set the width
    End Select

  Case acLBGetValue         ' Fetch one data item
    cbkSumInfo = sastrPrp(varRow, varCol)

  Case acLBGetFormat        ' Format one data item
    cbkSumInfo = cbo.Format  ' Echo back the property value

  Case acLBEnd              ' Close down the function
End Select

  dbs.Close

End Function
```

As you can see, Figure 13.11 shows the results of running the listed code, which fills the combo box with database properties.

Fig. 13.11

A user-defined list callback function loads database summary information into this combo box.

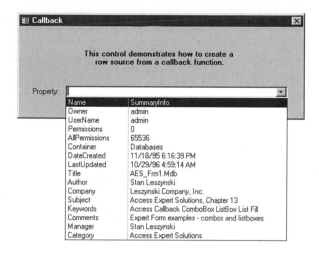

It is instructive to trace exactly how a callback function is called by Access. To illustrate the flow of a callback function in use, I placed Debug.Print statements throughout the function in Listing 13.14. It shows the sequence of varCode values passed to the function as its form opens and the combo box loads. Table 13.3 shows the results of the trace.

 Note

I limited the trace function to retrieve only the first two database properties in order to keep the example simple. Thus, the resulting array was two rows by two columns (indexed as 0,0 to 1,1). The trace function code is not shown here, but is in AES_FRM1.MDB on the CD-ROM.

Table 13.3   Tracing a Callback Function

User Action	varCode	varRow	varCol
Form open	acLBInitialize		
Form open	acLBOpen		
Form open	acLBGetColumnCount		
Form open	acLBGetColumnWidth		0
Form open	acLBGetColumnWidth		0
Form open	acLBGetColumnWidth		0
Form open	acLBGetColumnWidth		0

continues

13

Table 13.3   Continued

User Action	varCode	varRow	varCol
Form open	acLBGetColumnWidth		0
Open combo	acLBGetColumnWidth		0
Open combo	acLBGetColumnWidth		1
Open combo	acLBGetColumnWidth		0
Open combo	acLBGetRowCount		
Open combo	acLBGetValue	1	0
Open combo	acLBGetValue	0	0
Open combo	acLBGetFormat		0
Open combo	acLBGetValue	0	1
Open combo	acLBGetFormat		1
Open combo	acLBGetValue	1	0
Open combo	acLBGetFormat		0
Open combo	acLBGetValue	1	1
Open combo	acLBGetFormat		1
Form close	acLBEnd		

The values from the trace in the table should clarify exactly how Access uses your function code. Note the "better safe than sorry" approach Access takes in calling your function more than is really required to fetch and format each row.

Once you grasp the essential structure and flow of callback functions, you will find myriad ways to use them in your Combo and List Box controls.

Using a List Callback Function with Multiple Controls

If a list callback function can be used to replace the execution of a record fetch from a table or via a query, the performance of your form is almost always improved. On a larger scale, imagine the benefits of replacing several combo box queries with a single function. The performance benefits can be exemplary.

Caution

The following example is what we call "double-latté code" in Seattle. (A *latté* is a double-strength coffee espresso drink.) In other words, don't try to follow this code unless you're wide awake! Also, if you have not already done so, you should read the preceding two sections on callback functions and review the callback examples on the CD-ROM before you proceed.

You may recall that the second block in a callback function (where varID = acLBOpen) asks your function to provide an ID value for the calling control. This enables the function to uniquely identify a caller by its ID and to pass back the appropriate values. Such a structure enables your function to service more than one Combo Box control, as long as your code is set up to recognize the different callers (by ID values).

Note

The following example is from an application we created for a client. When we took a form with a dozen Combo Box controls, each fed by a query, and implemented the callback strategy described here on all of the combo boxes, the average load time of the form decreased by 70 percent.

For this example, assume that you are creating an application for a medical clinic, and that the application contains a form to log test results. The form has one combo box for each of the following six values:

Area

Diagnosis

Location

Machine

Procedure

Status

Normally, the values for combo boxes such as these would come from six lookup tables, such as tlkpArea, tlkpDiagnosis, and so on. In addition, you would use the lookup table names in the RowSource properties of the six Combo Box controls. However, such a

13

structure requires the form to create multiple recordsets against the back-end database, one for each lookup table/combo box combination. A better strategy is for the form to access the lookup data once, saving five "hits" on the back end.

To employ such a solution, structure the application as follows:

1. Combine the lookup values into one table so that they can be retrieved with one fetch to the back end.

2. Create an array behind the form to contain all of the lookup values.

3. Load the six combo boxes from the array using a callback function.

Figure 13.12 shows the single table structure that supports this method. Each lookup value (the Code field) must have a Type designation in the combined table so your function can tell the six value types apart.

Fig. 13.12

This lookup table combines and codifies multiple types of values, as opposed to creating a separate lookup table for each type.

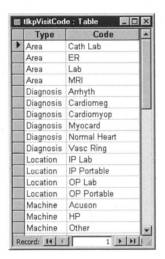

Next, you must declare the necessary array structures in the form's module, as shown in Listing 13.15.

Listing 13.15   AES_Frm1.Mdb—Declaring a Single Array for Multiple Boxes

```
Option Base 1   ' This code must be 1-based
Option Compare Database
Option Explicit

' mastrCode holds the lookup values Type and Code
' The array looks like this:
```

```
'   TYPE        CODE
'   Area        Lab
'   Diagnosis   Myocard
Dim mastrCode() As String

'  mastrControl holds indexes for the lookup array
'     The columns are: Type, count of type, starting array index
'     for type, ending array index for type
'  The array looks like this:
'     TYPE        ELEMENTS   START   END
'     Area        4          1       4
'     Diagnosis   6          5       10
Dim mastrControl() As String

Dim mblnArrayLoaded As Boolean
```

Note the following items of interest in the listing:

Option Base 1. VBA arrays can be zero-based or one-based, but I chose to make this code one-based for two reasons. First, the X-dimension (row) index of the control array (mastrControl) in the example is used as the varID for a control using the callback, and an ID value of zero is not permitted by callback functions. Second, one-based examples are easier to read and follow in print than zero-based code.

mastrCode array. This array holds the actual lookup table data used by the callback function. It has two Y-dimension items (columns), one for each field in the data (Type and Code). Sample records in the array look like the following:

(x,1)	(x,2)
Area	Lab
Area	MRI
Diagnosis	Myocard
Diagnosis	Normal Heart

mastrControl array. This array holds summary information used to index the data array (mastrCode) because that array contains information for more than one Type. The first column in mastrControl holds a Type value from the data array. The second column holds a count of the number of lookup values that match the given type. This number will be used to provide a row count to the combo box when it requests such information from the callback function. The third and fourth array columns hold the starting index and ending index for the first and last items of the given type in the data array.

13

I call this the *control array* because it provides a control structure for indexing the data array. (It has nothing to do with form controls, as the name might imply in a different context.) The structure of the array is shown in Figure 13.13. Items in the array are in the format `Type`, `Count`, `Start`, and `End`.

Fig. 13.13

This control array includes one item to index each unique `Type` code in the related lookup table.

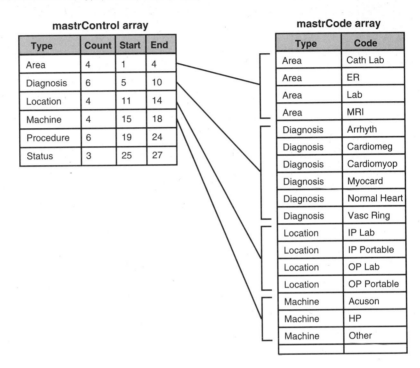

mastrControl array

Type	Count	Start	End
Area	4	1	4
Diagnosis	6	5	10
Location	4	11	14
Machine	4	15	18
Procedure	6	19	24
Status	3	25	27

mastrCode array

Type	Code
Area	Cath Lab
Area	ER
Area	Lab
Area	MRI
Diagnosis	Arrhyth
Diagnosis	Cardiomeg
Diagnosis	Cardiomyop
Diagnosis	Myocard
Diagnosis	Normal Heart
Diagnosis	Vasc Ring
Location	IP Lab
Location	IP Portable
Location	OP Lab
Location	OP Portable
Machine	Acuson
Machine	HP
Machine	Other

The next task is to load the data array. This will make the lookup values available to the callback function because the array has module-level scope. The code for the `cbfArrayLoad()` function that loads the array is shown in Listings 13.16 through 13.18; the three pieces in the listings combine into the single function.

Listing 13.16 shows the startup portion of the array load function. Notice that the size of the data (`mastrCode`) array is set to equal the number of records returned from the lookup table.

Listing 13.16   AES_Frm1.Mdb—Sizing a Data Array Based on Its Source Recordset

```
Private Function cbfArrayLoad() As Boolean
' Purpose: Load the lookup code and control arrays

  Dim dbs As Database
  Dim intCRow As Integer ' Current control array row
```

```
Dim intDRow As Integer ' Current data array row
Dim rst As Recordset
Dim strType As String ' Current Type value

' Load the array of lookups
Set dbs = CurrentDb
' The query sorts the data by Type, then Code
Set rst = dbs.OpenRecordset("qlkpVisitCode", dbOpenDynaset)
rst.MoveLast
ReDim mastrCode(rst.RecordCount, 2) ' Size the array
rst.MoveFirst
intCRow = 0
intDRow = 1
strType = ""
```

In Listing 13.17, each record in the lookup table is inserted into the data array. Each time a new value for the Type field is detected in the lookup table data, a counter (intCRow) is incremented. The counter is used to determine the size for the control array later in the code (see Listing 13.18).

 Note

Although the count of unique Type values in the lookup table can also be retrieved with another Recordset object running against a grouping query, operations on small arrays usually run faster than accessing a data table in the back-end database does.

Listing 13.17   AES_Frm1.Mdb—Loading a Data Array from a Recordset

```
Do While Not rst.EOF
  ' Load the array items from the table
  mastrCode(intDRow, 1) = rst!Type
  mastrCode(intDRow, 2) = rst!Code
  ' Count the number of unique Type items
  If rst!Type <> strType Then
    strType = rst!Type ' Reset the marker
    intCRow = intCRow + 1 ' Increment the count
  End If
  intDRow = intDRow + 1
  rst.MoveNext
Loop
```

13

The size of the control array is set in Listing 13.18, and the four array columns are loaded. While making a pass through the entire data array, the code captures unique instances of the Type value, stores the beginning and ending array index for each Type, and computes the count of items for the Type. These values are stored in the control array (refer back to Figure 13.13).

Listing 13.18   AES_Frm1.Mdb—Populating a Control Array that Indexes a Different Array

```
' Size the array based on the count of unique Types
ReDim mastrControl(intCRow, 4)

' Review the code array and place the first occurrence of each
' Type value in the index array, along with starting and
' ending indexes
intCRow = 0
strType = ""
For intDRow = 1 To UBound(mastrCode)
  If mastrCode(intDRow, 1) <> strType Then
    If intCRow > 0 Then ' Skip on the first pass
      ' Plug the values in the control array
      mastrControl(intCRow, 4) = (intDRow - 1) ' Ending index
      ' Set the number of elements
      mastrControl(intCRow, 2) = (intDRow - CInt(mastrControl(intCRow, 3)))
    End If
    intCRow = intCRow + 1
    strType = mastrCode(intDRow, 1) ' Reset the marker
    mastrControl(intCRow, 1) = strType ' New Type code
    mastrControl(intCRow, 3) = intDRow ' Starting index
  End If
Next intDRow
' Complete the last index
mastrControl(intCRow, 4) = (intDRow - 1) ' Ending index
' Set the number of elements
mastrControl(intCRow, 2) = (intDRow - CInt(mastrControl(intCRow, 3)))
cbfArrayLoad = True

rst.Close
dbs.Close

End Function
```

After the procedure in these listings has run, the form module has loaded all of the lookup values into a single data array in memory, and it has created a control array with all of the index information that's needed to retrieve specific lookup values from the data array.

The next task is to create the common callback function that will feed the six combo boxes on the form. The name of the function (cbkCode) is placed in the RowSourceType property of each of the six combo boxes because they share the routine. In addition, I place a marker value in the Tag property of each of the combo boxes that describes the Type code value that will feed the combo's list. For example, in the combo box that will load the area values, place Area in the Tag. This value will be used by the callback function.

The shared callback function cbkCode is structured using the standard callback layout described previously. The following descriptions illustrate the blocks of code from the function for the most important varCode values:

> *acLBInitialize*. The initialization code is called by Access once for each Combo Box control that shares the function. However, only the first of the six controls to call this function must load the arrays. After the first load of the arrays, the initialization block sets a flag (mblnArrayLoaded) so that the array loading routine is not called on subsequent iterations. The code looks like this:

```
Case acLBInitialize  ' Initialization
' Load the array (module-level) if not loaded
  If Not mblnArrayLoaded Then
    cbkCode = cbfArrayLoad()
    mblnArrayLoaded = True
  Else
    cbkCode = True
  End If
```

> *acLBOpen*. This code block is also called only once by each combo box. Based on the Tag property value we set in the Combo Box control, the function can identify which Type value will feed the control. The VBA code looks in the control array for the Type value matching the Tag of the combo. Upon finding a match, the routine uses the index of the matching array element as the unique ID for the control, like this:

```
Case acLBOpen  ' When the control is opened
  ' The control's ID will be set to the index into the control array
  ' For example, if the code Diagnosis is element 2 in the control
  '   array, the ID of cboDiagnosis is set to 2
  For iintLoop = 1 To UBound(mastrControl)
    If mastrControl(iintLoop, 1) = Trim(cbo.Tag) Then
      cbkCode = iintLoop
      Exit For
    End If
  Next iintLoop
```

On subsequent calls to the function, Access will pass this ID in as an argument that identifies not only the calling control, but the location in the control array of the combo box's information.

For example, if the `Type` value of Diagnosis was loaded into the control array as the second row, the callback would set the ID value of the combo box with Diagnosis in its `Tag` to an ID value of 2.

acLBGetRowCount. When the array load routine built the control array, it included a row count for each `Type` value. This count is now sent back from the callback function as the row count for the combo box:

```
Case acLBGetRowCount   ' How many rows?
  ' Number of rows for a Type are in the control index
  cbkCode = CInt(mastrControl(varID, 2))
```

acLBGetValue. When the callback function fetches data, the control array knows the starting point for that data in the data array. This offset value must be added to the row number requested by Access in order to find the exact target value in the data array:

```
Case acLBGetValue   ' Fetch one data item
  ' Compute the offset for the location of the data item
  '   in the code array, note that varRow is 0-based
  intRow = mastrControl(varID, 3) + varRow
  cbkCode = mastrCode(intRow, 2)
```

For example, the control array (in item `mastrControl(2,3)`) knows that `Diagnosis` type values start at row 5 in the data array. The callback adds the 5 to the requested row (such as `varRow = 3`) to arrive at the correct index (8) for the data in the `mastrCode` array.

A complete, working version of the callback function `cbkCode` is on the CD-ROM.

Figure 13.14 shows the destination combo boxes on a form, and the single lookup table that provides the values for all of the combo boxes via the code described in this section.

On forms with many Combo Box controls, this technique can save a lot of time when loading the form. In addition, passing table data through a function as it loads into a combo box enables you to perform auditing, formatting, or other code processes on the lookup values before the user sees them.

 Note

When using my example code to feed List Box controls instead of Combo Box controls, change the callback function argument `cbo As ComboBox` to `lst As ListBox`, and change other code that uses `cbo` accordingly.

Fig. 13.14

*A single lookup table
provides values for the
six combo boxes on this
form via a shared list
callback function.*

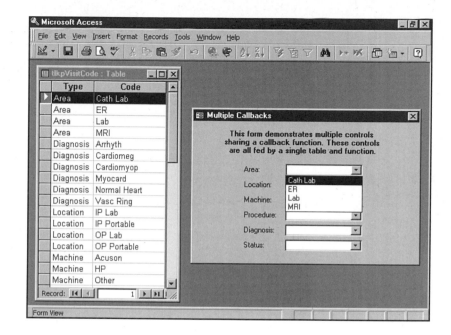

Creating Expert List Boxes

List boxes are as useful as combo boxes, and in many cases the decision to use one over
the other is a philosophical issue. Because the difference in the use of these controls is
less pronounced than the difference in form space consumed by them, combo boxes are
often used simply because insufficient space exists for a list box.

Combo Box and List Box controls share an almost identical property set. You probably
noticed in earlier sections of this chapter that most of the expert forms techniques that
were described for combo boxes will also work with list boxes.

The following sections provide two techniques for using list boxes more effectively. The
techniques are unique to list boxes and do not apply to combos.

Using Multi-Select List Boxes

Starting with Access 95, you had the ability to select more than one item in a list box on
a form, which is very useful in your applications. Using familiar keyboard and mouse
techniques, your users select any combination of items on a list; then, your program
code can determine the values in their selection.

13

Note

You can't multi-select within a Combo Box control.

The following listing briefly summarizes the new properties and methods added to List Box controls to support multiple selection.

▶ *MultiSelect Property*. Set this new property to None (0) to disable multiple selection, Simple (1) to enable each mouse click to select/deselect an item, or Extended (2) to emulate File Manager-type selection, which includes the use of Ctrl and Shift keys in conjunction with mouse clicks.

▶ *Selected Property*. This property is actually an array of Boolean values with the index of each array item matching the ListIndex of items in the list box. Thus, *listbox*.Selected(1) is True or False depending on the selection status of the list box item with a ListIndex of one.

▶ *ItemsSelected Collection*. This collection is different than most collections in Access because it does not hold objects. Instead, it is a Variant array of ListIndex numbers containing only the indexes of the items currently selected in the list box. Thus, if the first and third items in the list box are selected, the *listbox*.ItemsSelected collection will contain only the values 1 and 2.

▶ *ItemData Method*. This method returns the bound column value for a specified list box item, addressed by ListIndex number. Although any list box item is available using the syntax *listbox*.Column(*column*, *row*), this method provides a shortcut for such syntax. Thus, the following two lines of code are equivalent:

```
lst.Column(lst.BoundColumn - 1, 2)
lst.ItemData(2)
```

The remainder of this section provides two code listings that you will find useful in the following ways:

The listings contain *syntax examples* of actual usage of the primary properties and methods that affect the new list box features.

The listings represent *actual working code* that will make a good addition to your Access library because they are written as generic functions that can be called from any form. These functions are included in the sample database AES_FRM1.MDB on the CD-ROM.

The two listings show the *two aspects of an important need:* saving multiple selections into a table field and retrieving those selections from the table into a list box, as shown in Figure 13.15.

Fig. 13.15

The multi-select list box on this form provides delimited strings that are saved to a related data table.

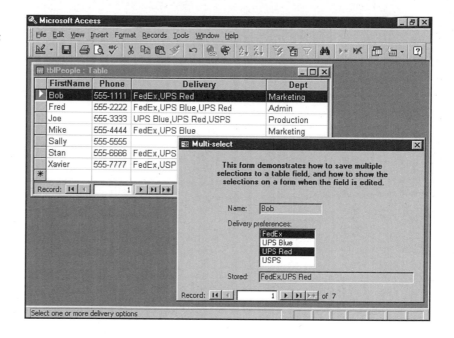

Saving Multi-Selected Values to a Table

For the following routines, assume that customer profiles are created when you enter a customer record into your application. The customer profile includes a field holding one or more values that reflect the customer's delivery preferences. You select these values from a list box, and the code stores them in the database field Delivery with commas between them—for example: "UPS Blue,USPS."

Listing 13.19 shows how to grab multiple selections from a list box and create a delimited string of those values. Note the following important elements in the listed routines:

Cycling through the ItemsSelected collection of the list box provides access only to the indexes of the selected items.

The new For Each...Next syntax is used to cycle through the elements of the ItemsSelected collection.

The Column property is used to retrieve a specified column value from a specified row in the list box.

13

Listing 13.19 AES_Frm1.Mdb—Creating a Delimited String of Selected List Box Values

```
' A procedure in the data entry form
Private Sub lstDelivery_AfterUpdate()
' Purpose: Create list for table field from selected list box items

   Me!txtDelivery = lci_LstItemSelDelim(Me!lstDelivery, ",", 0)

End Sub


' A library function in a standard module
Public Function lci_LstItemSelDelim(rctl As Control _
   , rvarDelim As Variant, rintCol As Integer) As Variant
' Purpose:   Return a delimited string with all selected items
'            from a list column
' Arguments: rctl:=List box control
'            rvarDelim:=Delimiter to place between items
'            rintCol:=Column number
' Returns:   Delimited list or Null
' Example:   lci_LstItemSelDelim(Me!lstPlace, ";", 1)

   Dim varRet  As Variant ' Build return value
   Dim evarRow As Variant ' Element in ItemsSelected

   varRet = Null
   For Each evarRow In rctl.ItemsSelected ' Cycle thru all selected items
     If IsNull(varRet) Then ' Trap first pass
       ' Start return string
       varRet = rctl.Column(rintCol, evarRow)
     Flse
       ' Build return string
       varRet = varRet & rvarDelim & rctl.Column(rintCol, evarRow)
     End If
   Next evarRow
   lci_LstItemSelDelim = varRet

End Function
```

 Note

The routine `lci_LstItemSelDelim()` returns a delimited list of values, such as "UPS Blue,UPS Red,USPS." Storing the list in a table field is one way to turn multi-select data into table data. Another way is to take each item in the selected list and write a record for the item in a table that is a child of the form's primary data table.

Selecting Multiple List Values from Table Data

For this section, assume that the delimited list of user shipping preferences created in the previous section is saved in the Delivery table field. The next routine reverses the process of saving the data by fetching the delimited data into a list box.

Assume that you want your form to display in a list box the multi-selected values that are saved in the Delivery field. Your code must dissect the table field when moving to a different record (as reflected in the Form_Current event) and select the appropriate list box items. The routines in Listing 13.20 show how to select multiple items on a form list box based on passed arguments. In this example, the arguments are items from the comma delimited list stored in the table field using the format described in the previous section: "UPS Blue,UPS Red,USPS."

Listing 13.20 also demonstrates the following list box and VBA techniques:

Passing multiple, unspecified values to a function using a ParamArray argument.

Cycling through the ParamArray array in the same way that collections are cycled, using a For Each...Next loop.

Listing 13.20   AES_Frm1.Mdb—Selecting Specific Values in a List Box

```
' An event in the form
Private Sub Form_Current()
' Purpose: Select items in the list box based on table data

    Dim blnRet As Boolean
    ' Clear the list by setting all selections to False
    blnRet = lci_LstItemSetAll(Me!lstDelivery, False)
    ' Select specific items in the list by their bound value
    ' The table data item has up to four delimited values
    blnRet = lci_LstItemSetByValue(Me!lstDelivery, True, _
    lci_DelimItemGet(Me!txtDelivery, ",", 1), _
    lci_DelimItemGet(Me!txtDelivery, ",", 2), _
    lci_DelimItemGet(Me!txtDelivery, ",", 3), _
    lci_DelimItemGet(Me!txtDelivery, ",", 4))

End Sub

' A library function in a standard module
Public Function lci_LstItemSetAll(rctl As Control _
    , rblnSet As Boolean) As Boolean
' Purpose: (Un)select all items in a list
' Arguments: rctl:=List box control
'            rblnSet:=Setting: True/False
' Returns:   True/False, True=success
' Example:   lci_LstItemSetAll(Me!lstPlace, True)

    Dim iintLoop As Integer ' Index into list box
```

continues

Listing 13.20 Continued

```
   For iintLoop = 0 To rctl.ListCount - 1 ' Cycle thru the list
      rctl.Selected(iintLoop) = rblnSet ' Set item selection
   Next iintLoop

End Function

' A library function in a standard module
Public Function lci_LstItemSetByValue(rctl As Control _
   , rblnSet As Boolean, ParamArray ravarItems()) As Boolean
' Purpose:   (Un)select specific list items by ItemData value
' Arguments: rctl:=List box control
'            rblnSet:=Setting: True/False
'            ravarItems:=Array of values to select
' Returns:   True/False, True=success
' Example:   lci_LstItemSetByValue(Me!lstPlace, True, "ID", "KS")

   Dim iintRow  As Integer ' Index into list box
   Dim evarItem As Variant ' Element in ParamArray

   For iintRow = 0 To rctl.ListCount - 1 ' Cycle thru the list
      For Each evarItem In ravarItems ' Cycle thru the ParamArray
         If evarItem = rctl.ItemData(iintRow) Then ' Found a match
            rctl.Selected(iintRow) = rblnSet ' Set item selection
            Exit For
         End If
      Next evarItem
   Next iintRow
   lci_LstItemSetByValue = True

End Function
```

α **Note**

The library routine `lci_DelimItemGet()` is called by code in the listing to parse a passed list and return the *n*th item. The code is not listed here, but is available in AES_FRM1.MDB on the CD-ROM.

Note that the list box routines in this and the preceding section are very generic: They can be called with a variable number of arguments, they can be passed to any List Box control object, and they can be used to work with either selected items or unselected items. Such routines follow the strategies for good reusable components as described in Chapter 11, "Expert Approaches to VBA," and Chapter 20, "Applying Development Shortcuts."

Reordering Values in a List Box

When your form must give users the ability to view items in a list and to rearrange the order of the items, the most common method in the past was to show users a subform of listed items and to require the users to place a unique sequence number into each record to sequence the values. However, List Box controls now provide a good mechanism for enabling the user to reorder a displayed list of values. Compared to the subform method, a list box provides both better performance and better usability.

Enabling a user to reorder items in a list box involves the use of the list callback function technique described earlier in this chapter. Review the section, "Loading a Combo Box from a List Callback Function," if you have not already done so.

As an example, we'll start with the list of shipping methods shown in the previous section, and we'll permit our user to view the various delivery options for a customer. Unlike the previous example, that selects a specific set of options for each customer; in this example, all options are considered valid for each customer. The user's only job is to order the options on a per-customer basis, to reflect the customer's stated preferences for shipping priorities.

The form for this example is shown in Figure 13.16. The basic structure of this form is as follows:

- The list box of shipping preferences is loaded from a callback function based on an array.

- When the user chooses to reorder items in the list, the array items are reordered and the list is requeried to show the change.

- The final order of the shipping list items is saved in the customer record using the delimited string technique, which was described earlier in this chapter, starting with the "Saving Multi-Selected Values to a Table" section.

There are several code routines that are essential to this technique. The first is shown in Listing 13.21, which presents the following steps:

A module-level array, `mavarDelivery()`, is created to contain the list items.

In the `Form_Load` event, the array is loaded. The load routine for the array is written as a callable `Sub`.

13

Fig. 13.16

This list box provides values that can be reordered by using the related command buttons. The ordered items are stored in delimited strings in a data table.

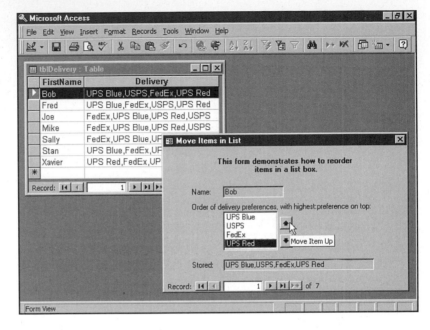

Listing 13.21   AES_Frm1.Mdb—Supporting Routines for the Delivery List Array

```
' A declaration in the Declarations section of the form module
Private mavarDelivery() As Variant  ' Delivery options

' The Load event for the form
Private Sub Form_Load()
' Purpose: Initialize the array

  Call cbfListLoad(Me!lstDelivery, "FedEx", "UPS Blue", "UPS Red" _
    , "USPS")

End Sub

' Routine in the form module to populate the array
Private Sub cbfListLoad(ParamArray ravarList() As Variant)
' Purpose: Load the items into the delivery list
' Arguments: ravarList:=One or more items to load

  Dim iintLoop As Integer
  ReDim mavarDelivery(UBound(ravarList) - 1)
  For iintLoop = 1 To UBound(ravarList)
    mavarDelivery(iintLoop - 1) = ravarList(iintLoop)
  Next iintLoop

End Sub
```

When the array is initially populated, it is used as the basis of the list callback function shown in Listing 13.22. This function feeds the array values to the list box.

Listing 13.22   AES_Frm1.Mdb—List Callback Function to Manage the Delivery List

```
Private Function cbkDelivery(lst As ListBox, varID As Variant, _
  varRow As Variant, varCol As Variant, varcode As Variant) As Variant
' Purpose: Load the delivery list

  Select Case varcode

    Case acLBInitialize ' Initialization
      ' Array is initialized at form load
      cbkDelivery = True ' Okay to proceed

    Case acLBOpen ' When the control is opened
      cbkDelivery = Timer ' Create a unique control ID

    Case acLBGetRowCount ' How many rows?
      cbkDelivery = 4 ' Number of rows

    Case acLBGetColumnCount ' How many columns?
      cbkDelivery = lst.ColumnCount ' Echo back the property value

    Case acLBGetColumnWidth ' How wide are the columns?
      cbkDelivery = -1 ' Use the default widths

    Case acLBGetValue ' Fetch one data item
      cbkDelivery = mavarDelivery(varRow)

    Case acLBGetFormat ' Format one data item
      ' Unused

    Case acLBEnd ' Close down the function
  End Select

End Function
```

Finally, when the user clicks the appropriate button to move an item up or down in the list, the code in Listing 13.23 handles the rearrangement of the array. When an array item is moved, sending the Requery method to the list box causes the control to rebuild its list from the new array order by using the callback function once again.

Listing 13.23   AES_Frm1.Mdb—Routines to Move Items Within a List Array

```
' A routine behind the form to move an item up the list by one
Private Sub cmdUp_Click()
' Purpose: Move an item up one position
```

13

continues

Listing 13.23   Continued

```
     Call cbfListMove(-1)

End Sub

' A routine behind the form to move an item down the list by one
Private Sub cmdDown_Click()
' Purpose: Move an item down one position

  Call cbfListMove(1)

End Sub

' A routine behind the form to perform the reorder and requery
Private Sub cbfListMove(rintMove As Integer)
' Purpose:    Move an item in the list box
' Arguments: rintMove:=Positive/negative offset for move
' Example:    cbfListMove(-1)

  Dim avarHold  As Variant
  Dim iint      As Integer
  Dim intNewPos As Integer
  Dim intOldPos As Integer

  If Me!lstDelivery.ListIndex = -1 Then
    Exit Sub
  End If
  avarHold = mavarDelivery() ' Preserve the original values
  intOldPos = Me!lstDelivery.ListIndex
  intNewPos = intOldPos + rintMove
  ' Make sure the move is to a valid location
  If intNewPos < 0 Or intNewPos > UBound(mavarDelivery) Then
    Exit Sub
  End If
  ' Swap the relocated items
  mavarDelivery(intOldPos) = avarHold(intNewPos)
  mavarDelivery(intNewPos) = avarHold(intOldPos)
  Me!lstDelivery.Requery
  Call lstDelivery_AfterUpdate ' Reset the text box

End Sub
```

The supporting routines for this technique that are not shown here are available in AES_FRM1.MDB on the CD-ROM. They include a Form_Current and a lstDelivery_AfterUpdate event on the form that synchronize the list box values to the string version of those values stored in the table. This code is very similar to the earlier example in the "Using Multi-Select List Boxes" section in this chapter. The work of creating, saving, and interpreting the delimited string versions of the list box items is handled by library functions, also included in the sample database.

This technique has myriad uses and, once again, highlights the utility of callback functions.

From Here...

In this chapter, you saw a variety of techniques for maximizing the value and performance of Combo Box and List Box controls used on forms.

  ▶ The library routines used in this chapter fit the model of reusable code described in Chapter 11, "Expert Approaches to VBA," and in Chapter 20, "Applying Development Shortcuts."

  ▶ Review Chapter 12, "Understanding Form Structures and Coding," for a discussion of the basic approaches to form development and performance tuning.

  ▶ To see how combo and list boxes fit my form design model for solid applications, read Chapter 17, "Bulletproofing Your Application Interface."

13

chapter 14

Navigating in Forms and Applications

In this Chapter

◆ **Controlling user movement between the forms in your application**

◆ **Providing switchboard forms for navigation**

◆ **Using menus and toolbars to navigate and to initiate application events**

◆ **Storing application information where forms can utilize it**

An expert solution does not point users to the Database window and let them guess what to do next. On the contrary, the hallmark of an expert solution is how well it guides the users to data and helps them understand it, manipulate it, and perfect it. This chapter describes techniques you can apply to your forms and program code to help your users navigate smoothly through your applications.

Paradigm Déjà Vu

Since our first Access application, we have always enforced a high degree of modality (one form at a time). To us, a linear model is the only choice for database applications because the developer is highly motivated by the needs of data integrity to force the user to finish one task before starting another.

Thus, in 1992 and 1993, when Microsoft was highly touting the *Multiple Document Interface* (MDI), we were building applications that were very linear, using a *Single Document Interface* (SDI) paradigm instead. We believed our users were not power hungry or sophisticated enough to be juggling multiple forms, records, or data management processes at the same time. Instead, we presented them with one form at a time and a clear path forward and backward between related records and forms.

So, it was with a sense of satisfaction that I observed a Microsoft presentation in 1994 and listened to an Excel program manager extolling the benefits of their new tabbed workbook layout. Their research had shown that users were most likely to work on one task at a time instead of tiling multiple windows. He also said that Microsoft had decided to downplay the use of MDI in their Office product line.

Although the Database window is a wonderful place for you as a developer to hang out, it's a dangerous place for users. They can delete your objects, modify your code, enter records into tables out of sequence, bypass batch processes, and generally make trouble (usually unintentionally). When you create a solid application centered around expert forms, you must consider whether your users should ever see the Database window at all. Or perhaps they should be directed through the application from start to finish.

Most of our applications do not provide the everyday user with access to the Database window. Instead, users navigate from form to form, occupying a very restrictive and well-defined application universe. Chapter 17, "Bulletproofing Your Application Interface," discusses strategies for locking the user out of the Database window.

Our preferred user interface model directs users through forms one by one, or at least limits them to some small, manageable groups of related forms at the same time (see Chapter 8, "Designing Effective Interfaces," for more information on user interface design). Data-bound forms really should be structured into cohesive, restrictive applications. Consider the following problems that can occur when you enable your users to open multiple Access forms at random:

▶ Users can enter dependent data out of sequence. For example, they might try to enter child records before parent records.

▶ Users can open multiple forms that point to the same record, introducing possible record locking challenges.

▶ Users can open too many forms at the same time, impacting application performance or losing track of their workflow.

▶ Users can keep multiple unsaved records open, usually by minimizing forms on the desktop without saving their edits. This situation prevents other users from seeing current data.

▶ Users can lock records, usually by minimizing forms that have edited records in an unsaved state (depending on the form's locking model). This potentially locks other users out of specific records for an unreasonable amount of time.

To prevent these situations, you can restrict how users interact with your applications by establishing limits that dictate the application flow. By enforcing only permitted behavior and events, users are guided through the application in a friendly and logical manner.

Providing your users with a directed path through the application entails some extra effort. It requires money or time or both. Consequently, when you are building expert forms, the best strategy is to develop repeatable systems and then use them in multiple applications, instead of reinventing the user interface paradigm with each new application that you create.

Your standard user interface model will include some or all of the following components:

▶ *A main switchboard menu form* enables users to navigate to the various features of the application.

▶ *Toolbars and menu options* aid navigation, but do not include any built-in Access options that are dangerous to the specific application.

▶ *Forms that open in a single-instance modal state* create a simplified environment in which the user performs one task at a time.

▶ *A controlled data mode* provides a filtered recordset with the ability to selectively add, edit, browse, and delete within the recordset, as appropriate to the context.

▶ *Keystroke trapping* provides form and record navigation. Don't assume that users always navigate with a mouse.

▶ *A limited feature set*, with features disabled when they are not needed in a specific context, gives users access only to options that they can use effectively to execute the task at hand.

▶ *A clear path to navigate* enables users to move forward and backward between application elements. The application must establish and enforce order in the workflow.

Using Switchboard Menus

At the top of almost every application's navigation pyramid is a switchboard menu. These are usually constructed as a single-page form with a button for each main functional area in the application. Each menu button contains attached code that opens a form, prints a report, runs a data process, or opens another switchboard.

There are as many varieties of switchboard menus as there are developers. The next four topics describe my favorite options for switchboard navigation in expert solutions.

Using and Extending Switchboard Manager Menus

In addition to switchboard variances between developers, Microsoft's examples for switchboard menus were not consistent in previous years. However, the new Switchboard Manager add-in defines a standardized approach for switchboard menus. You may opt to use this new look for your switchboards, and you may even choose to use the code generated by the add-in as a starting point for your switchboard functionality (see Figure 14.1).

Fig. 14.1

This simple menu was generated by the new Switchboard Manager add-in.

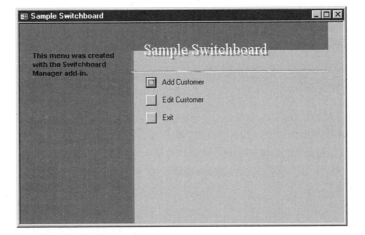

 Note

The type of switchboard created by the Access 97 Switchboard Manager is generally the same as the layout used in Access 95.

The Switchboard Manager's interface model uses a column of small buttons, each with a text descriptor next to it, as shown in Figure 14.1. The strength of this design style is the capability of conveying varying lengths of explanatory text to the user for each application option without creating wide command buttons.

The Switchboard Manager places eight buttons on the form and loads the text for each button from a table called Switchboard Items. The table has the structure shown in Figure 14.2. The Switchboard Manager also creates code behind the form, which loads the switchboard options and executes user selections based upon entries in the supporting table.

 Note

If you use the Switchboard Manager to create a switchboard and then later add, delete, or rename form objects in your application, the switchboard does not detect the changes and may no longer work. You may need to update the driving table or re-run the add-in.

Fig. 14.2

This menu item table supports the Switchboard Manager menu in Figure 14.1.

Switchboard Items : Table

SwitchboardID	ItemNumber	ItemText	Command	Argument
1	0	Sample Switchboard	0	Default
1	1	Add Customer	2	frmCust_Embedded
1	2	Edit Customer	3	frmCust_Embedded
1	3	Exit	6	
0	0		0	

Record: I◀ ◀ 1 ▶ ▶I ▶∗ of 4

Although the Switchboard Items table is created by the add-in, once you understand the structure you can modify the switchboard menu yourself by changing the table records. You can use the generated switchboard as a template, making changes to it to customize the look and functionality for your specific application. What follows is the table structure:

SwitchboardID *field.* This field is a Long Integer describing the "page" of the switchboard, starting with 1 for the first page. Each page is a grouped list of up to eight button items. To move between pages, you must designate one button on each page to move to the next page, and one button to move to the previous page (where appropriate). Note that the concept of *paging* here does not use actual form or tab pages; instead, it is implemented by simply rebuilding the text on the eight form buttons.

14

ItemNumber field. Each switchboard page can have up to eight items with `ItemNumber` values of 1 through 8 to prescribe the item sort order on the menu. An `ItemNumber` of 0 designates the switchboard name record whose `ItemText` value is placed in the form's caption. This type of record is evident in the data of Figure 14.2.

ItemText field. This field denotes the text that actually appears next to the button for the menu item, or the menu page caption, when used in the switchboard name record.

Command field. The code in the switchboard form executes the command designated in this field when the respective menu item is selected by the user. Available commands are tokenized with the following values:

1. Display the switchboard page whose `SwitchboardID` field contains the number designated in the `Argument` field for the record.

2. Open the form in add mode whose name is specified in the `Argument` field for this record.

3. Open the form in edit mode whose name is specified in the `Argument` field for this record.

4. Open the report in preview mode whose name is specified in the `Argument` field for this record.

5. Run the Switchboard Manager to customize the menu.

6. Close the current database (ending the application).

7. Run the macro named in the `Argument` field.

8. Run the function or `Sub` procedure named in the `Argument` field.

Argument field. This item provides the argument for the action numbers designated by the `Command` field, as follows:

1. The page designator for the switchboard page. This designation is only used when running the Switchboard Manager and it must be the string "Default" for the application's default menu page.

2. The name of the form to open for entry.

3. The name of the form to open for editing.

4. The name of the report to preview.

5. No value (blank).

6. No value (blank).

7. The name of the macro to run.

8. The name of the procedure to run. The procedure must be a `Public` function and must be stored in a standard module.

To create switchboards for expert forms, you can run the Switchboard Manager to build a switchboard form and its code, then you can add or modify table entries according to your application's needs. What follows are some suggestions and pitfalls related to Switchboard Manager menus:

Improve the display. You may want to add your own graphic to the menu using an Image control in the available area on the left side of the form.

Modify the navigation model. You may want to modify the switchboard form to follow the navigation model described in "Navigating Between Forms" later in this chapter, including the following:

▶ Hiding the switchboard when it opens another form.

▶ Changing the `BorderStyle` from the default of `Sizable` to `Dialog`.

▶ Removing the Control menu, Minimize and Maximize buttons, and Close button.

▶ Adding a `MenuBar` property entry to restrict the menubar options for the form.

Add your own events. You can create new custom events for a switchboard form by modifying its embedded code. The function `HandleButtonClick()` built by the add-in defines eight constants—one for each of the permitted `Command` field event tokens. To add your own events, create a new constant starting with the number 9, and add a test for the constant's value to the `Select Case` structure engine in the function. Listing 14.1 shows an example of custom code added to the `HandleButtonClick()` function.

Listing 14.1   AES_Frm2.Mdb—Custom Modifications to the
***HandleButtonClick()* Function**

```
[el]
' Run code.
 Case conCmdRunCode   ' Command = 8
   Application.Run rst![Argument]

 ' Print directly, added by developer.
 Case conCmdPrint   ' Command = 9
   DoCmd.OpenReport rst![Argument], acNormal

 ' Any other command is unrecognized.
 Case Else
   MsgBox "Unknown option."
```

14

Understand the event structure. Be aware that there are no button events for the switchboard buttons in the form's module. Instead, the click procedure is placed directly in the property page, such as =HandleButtonClick(1). Thus, if you copy code from a switchboard form to another form or use File, Save As Text to save the code, the event model exported will not be complete.

Watch for performance issues. The switchboard items are displayed by pulling options from a table on demand rather than by buffering items in a list box or some other optimized structure. On slower machines, menus using this model may not display pages or options as quickly as desired.

Note the naming conventions. The Access team misused LNC in this wizard. Do not confuse the code constants, such as conCmdGotoSwitchboard, in the code of these forms with Container variables, as the name might imply.

 Note

Once you have changed a switchboard's options, structure, or code, you may be unable to use the Switchboard Manager to maintain the form—depending on the scope of your modifications.

To execute a function whose name is stored in the Argument field of the table, the Switchboard Manager includes the following line of code in its forms:

```
Application.Run rst![Argument]
```

Note the use of the new Run method to execute a function whose name is supplied by an expression. This method provides a simple mechanism for executing a function without storing the function's name in the calling code. Previously, you used the Eval() function to run a procedure whose name was supplied as an expression or variable at runtime. Now, you might prefer to use Run as it is superior to Eval() in the following two ways:

▶ Run enables the referenced procedure to be a Sub procedure, and Eval() only executes a function procedure.

▶ You can supply arguments to the Run method that are passed to the called function by placing them after the function name expression, as in the following example:

```
' Pass one argument to the called function
Application.Run strProcName, Me.Name
```

Using the Switchboard Manager to shell out form menus can be an effective use of an Access add-in.

Using List Boxes in Menus

Unlike a button-based metaphor, a list box enables the list of menu options to be essentially infinite. For example, the list of options in a list box menu could conceivably exceed fifty or a hundred items.

As an additional bonus, a list box menu can be driven by a table containing its options, much like the Switchboard Manager metaphor shown previously. Modifying the application's capabilities becomes simply a matter of adding or editing the table's records. Figure 14.3 shows a menu layout built around a list box.

Fig. 14.3

A switchboard menu is built around a List Box control.

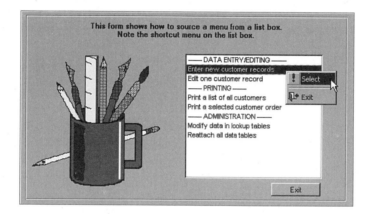

By altering the width of the List control, you can provide room to display the menu option information with the degree of clarity you want. For example, a list box several inches wide can display as many as a hundred characters of descriptive text for each menu option.

The table that supports the menu shown in Figure 14.3 is captured in Figure 14.4. The table specifies the sort order in which the menu items are displayed using a field called SortKey. Options in menu lists are usually grouped by functional area, then sorted based on any model that supports users. The following are the most common:

By process flow. In a process-oriented system, the order of menu options should follow the order that the tasks are executed. For example, many accounting processes have a logical flow; steps must be performed in sequence.

By frequency of use. Menu options can be listed in the order of frequency, with the most commonly used items at the top of each group.

Alphabetically. When all else fails…

14

Tip

Note in Figure 14.4 how I create numbering blocks for each group of menu options (for example, 20 through 29 are reserved for printing features). Such gaps enable you to add menu items later without renumbering the majority of table records.

Fig. 14.4

This menu item table supports the ListBox-*based menu in Figure 14.3.*

	SortKey	MenuItem	MenuProc	UserLevel
▶	10	—— DATA ENTRY/EDITING ——		2
	11	Enter new customer records	CustAdd	2
	12	Edit one customer record	MenuDummy	2
	20	—— PRINTING ——		2
	21	Print a list of all customers	MenuDummy	2
	22	Print a selected customer order	MenuDummy	2
	30	—— ADMINISTRATION ——		1
	31	Modify data in lookup tables	MenuDummy	1
	32	Reattach all data tables	MenuDummy	1

tmnuList : Table

Record: 1 of 9

The function MenuDummy listed repeatedly in the figure is a placeholder indicating that a menu function has not yet been created for the option. In your menus, the MenuProc column for each menu item would name the related function for the option.

The following are other techniques I've employed on the list box menu in Figure 14.3:

Security. The menu implements a layer of programmatic security by only listing options in the ListBox that are permitted for the current user. The UserLevel field in the table specifies the lowest number of user security level that can access a specific option. My program code places the security level in a hidden text box zhtxtUserLevel on the menu form as the form loads. (In this example, the security levels are 1 through 3, with 1 as the highest access level.) The list box's RowSource only displays items whose security level is within the range permitted for the current user:

```
SELECT MenuItem, MenuProc FROM tmnuList _
    WHERE UserLevel >= [Forms]![fmnuList]![zhtxtUserLevel] _
    ORDER BY SortKey
```

Shortcut menu. I've placed a shortcut menu on the list box to enable the user to execute an option via the right-mouse button. Because the shortcut menu must use a custom OnAction property to execute the user's selection, the code for running the option has been placed in a standard module rather than the menu form's module.

See the section "Navigating via Menus and Toolbars," later in this chapter, for a description of the new types of menus and toolbars.

Group headers. Using graphic characters from the Arial character set, I've created table records that provide the group delimiters displayed in the list that bracket related features. The header text is uppercase and delimited by the graphic characters to catch the user's eye. There is no function name associated with these table items; thus, nothing happens when the user selects a delimiter item.

Borderless form. If your form provides users with a button for closing the application, the form does not need a Control menu or a Close button. Once you remove these buttons—and the Minimize and Maximize buttons as well—you have the opportunity to create a "floating" form with no border, as Figure 14.3 shows. You remove a form's border by setting the BorderStyle property to None and leaving the form's Caption property blank.

Note

Without a title bar, a borderless form can't be moved by the user. Therefore, this style is most useful for modal menu forms, which are usually displayed by themselves on the screen and never on top of another form.

List box menus can be useful for applications that the feature set changes frequently, the process flow might frequently be redesigned, the order of options must change on a per-user basis, or development resources for friendlier menu forms are limited.

Creating Tabbed Menus

When you create a switchboard menu for a complex application, you might need to display dozens of options to users. Grouping the options together based upon their functionality or attributes enables you to present the menu options to users in manageable subsets.

One of the great interface devices for helping users navigate through subsets of information is the tabbed dialog box. Applying this model to switchboard menus is easy with the help of Access 97's new TabControl object.

Figure 14.5 shows a simple switchboard menu that uses the tab control to group menu items by functional area.

Fig. 14.5

This switchboard menu is built around the new tab control.

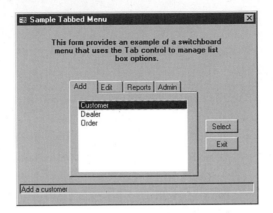

Tip

The sample menu in Figure 14.5 uses List Box controls embedded on tab pages to display items for users. Like other menus centered on list boxes, a table is used to feed user options to the list. The table for the tabbed menu in Figure 14.5 is shown in Figure 14.6.

Fig. 14.6

This menu item table supports the tabbed menu in Figure 14.5.

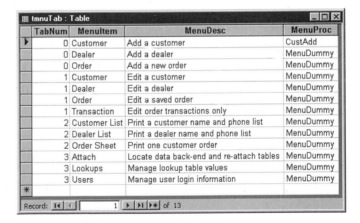

The table structure to support the tabbed menu includes a TabNum field containing the target tab (page) number for each item. When a tab is selected, the source for the list box is rebuilt to pull option information from the table for the selected tab, as Listing 14.2 shows.

Listing 14.2   AES_Frm2.Mdb—Rebuilding the List Box Items When a Tab Is Selected by the User

```
Private Sub tabMenu_Change()
' Purpose: Set the listbox focus

  Dim strLst As String

  ' The tab page number is in the control name
  strLst = "lstOption" & CStr(Me!tabMenu)
  Me(strLst).SetFocus  ' Move to the list box
  If Me(strLst).ListIndex = -1 Then  ' Nothing selected
    Me(strLst).ListIndex = 0  ' Select the first item
  End If
  Call cbfStatusSet  ' Set the status bar text

End Sub


Private Sub cbfStatusSet()

  ' The status label text is in the second column of the list
  Me!lblStatus.Caption = Me("lstOption" & CStr(Me!tabMenu)).Column(1)

End Sub
```

 Note

Form controls can bind with specific tabs of the `TabControl` object, hiding and showing with the parent tab. Nevertheless, the form itself is still aware of the controls and they can be addressed directly with `Me!controlname` or `Me(expression)`, as shown in Listing 14.2.

In a list box menu, the user selects an option by double-clicking a list item or by clicking the Select button. Note the following user interface devices that are employed in the tabbed menu in Figure 14.5:

Database window layout. This menu was designed specifically to mimic the layout to the Access Database window. The placement of the tabs, the list, and the buttons will be familiar to Access users.

Status Text. In order to provide the user with additional information about the menu items, my sample form contains a label to display status text. The `Click` event for the list box refreshes the text from the `MenuDesc` field of the associated menu

14

options table. Because this field has been pulled into the list box as its second column, the form displays the text instantly without a lookup, like this:

```
Me!lblStatus.Caption = Me("lstOption" & CStr(Me!tabMenu)).Column(1)
```

Executing an option. Also, I've pulled the `MenuProc` field into the list box from the options table as the third column, enabling the form to instantly execute the named code procedure without a domain lookup, like this:

```
Application.Run Me("lstOption" & CStr(Me!tabMenu)).Column(2)
```

Tabbed menus are less flexible than the simple list box menus shown in the previous section because the form layout is not completely table-driven. (In other words, a developer must add another tab to the control's layout each time a new group of options is needed, or write the code to do so dynamically.) Nevertheless, such menus are very attractive, well organized, and highly functional.

Creating Fast, Simple Switchboards

Although it is appealing to employ one of the three previously discussed menu techniques in your application, there are times when the old-fashioned, brute-force approach has more value than newer, advanced approaches. In the old-fashioned paradigm, your switchboard has buttons and the buttons have `Click` events that run code directly. Figure 14.7 shows a simple form that applies the older model.

Fig. 14.7

The simplest variety of switchboard form has only a few buttons and no underlying menu options table.

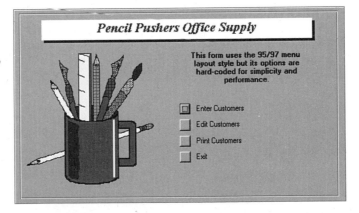

Compared to table-based menu forms, this option is very inflexible. To add a feature to the menu, a developer must add a button and its related code to the form. On the positive side, simple switchboards load and execute faster than forms tied to a menu options table, and might be better for very simple applications and for applications targeted to slower workstations.

Another positive aspect of button-based menus is the capability to selectively enable and disable features "on-the-fly" by toggling the `Enabled` property of each button. Achieving this result is much more difficult in a menu based on a list box, in which you must change a flag value in the underlying table and requery the menu. (Consequently, you must also keep the menu list in the local database so that table changes do not affect other users, which may adversely affect your application maintenance strategy.)

As an example, assume that the workflow required in a company using an invoice entry system is as follows:

1. Scott enters invoice records for payments.
2. Diana, the boss, approves each invoice in the batch.
3. Scott posts the batch to the ledger table when all the invoices are approved.

Each of the invoice entry tasks is controlled by a separate button on the main switchboard form. The following list describes how the buttons follow the workflow:

1. When Scott logs in, he presses the Invoices button on the main menu, which always is enabled, so that he can enter new invoice records. However, the Posting button on his menu is only enabled when all of the invoices he entered have been approved by Diana for payment.
2. When Diana logs in, the Invoices button on her main menu is enabled only if Scott has entered at least one invoice for approval since the last batch posting.
3. Each time Scott's application returns to the main menu form, code runs to detect whether or not every invoice in the batch has been approved for payment by Diana. If so, the application sets his Posting button to an `Enabled` state so that he can press the button to post the batch.
4. After Scott posts a batch, there are no invoices for Diana to review and approve until he enters another batch. Each time her main menu is displayed, logic runs to enable or disable the Invoice button depending on the availability of invoices to review.

Thus, Diana can see if she has any invoices to review by simply looking at the button status on her main switchboard, and Scott can also see from the menu if it is time to post a batch.

These very simple programming techniques convey immediate status information to the users via the menu form and also prevent the premature posting of a batch of invoices. In addition, the techniques produce large and highly visible results for the small amount of development time it takes to create a "smart" menu.

Navigating Between Forms

When you first create your application, you build table structures. Next, you produce the forms and reports that give your users access to their data.

Once your forms are created, you must add the navigation elements that differentiate a simple *database file* from a true *application:*

Switchboard Forms. An application may have one or more of these interface elements, as discussed in the preceding section.

Navigation Methodology. You must determine how users will get to each form, how forms will be opened and closed, and what toolbar and menu options will be utilized.

Navigation Code. You must implement code to move to and from the switchboards to the entry/edit forms. Further, your application will need code to move between related forms because some application navigation occurs outside the realm of switchboards.

The navigation code you implement must open, close, hide, and show forms in a desired sequence. Also, the code must never permit either too many forms or too few forms to be displayed to the user. The next three topics discuss the mechanics of this navigation.

Hiding versus Closing Forms

Opening Access forms can be one of the slowest areas of your application. As you move from frm1 to frm2, if you intend to return to frm1 when you are finished, there may be no need to close the form and reopen it later. Hiding frm1 instead, and re-displaying it when you need it, has great performance advantages.

For example, assume your application opens frmCust to edit a customer record. To change a customer's phone number, frmCustPhone must be opened from frmCust. When this occurs, you have three choices regarding how to handle the required navigation, as follows:

Close frmCust and open frmCustPhone. Later, when frmCustPhone closes, reopen frmCust. This technique produces the poorest performance because Access must close frmCust and then open it again a few moments later.

Leave frmCust open in normal or minimized view and open frmCustPhone on top; this produces a stacking effect. As a result, with two forms open on the desktop, users may get confused and their workspaces may get cluttered. If you are using modal forms (as you should when parent and child records are displayed separately), some confusion may result when users can't understand why frmCust is displayed on-screen, yet they can't move the focus to it.

Hide `frmCust` and open `frmCustPhone`. This is usually my preferred method for expert form navigation. The approach keeps `frmCust` in memory while removing it from current view in order to prevent user frustration and confusion. By simply redisplaying the hidden form when `frmCustPhone` is closed, it will appear almost instantly.

To hide a form, simply set its `Visible` property to `False` in your program code. To redisplay the form, set the property to `True` again. You can also use `DoCmd.OpenForm` `formname` to redisplay a hidden form. There is no performance advantage for either technique because `OpenForm` merely makes the form visible if it finds that the form is already loaded. The effect on the form's recordset is the same whether you change the `Visible` property or use an `OpenForm`. In either case, the data for the form is refreshed, but not requeried.

Tip

Applying the `OpenForm` method to a form that is already open but hidden enables you to alter the view, filter, `Where` clause, or `OpenArgs` as the form is redisplayed. However, be alert to the potential for confusion when users go back to a form they were viewing earlier and they find that its characteristics have changed.

Under what circumstances should you select one approach over the other? You should use `OpenForm` in an application that is not using expert forms techniques, but which is attempting to be user-friendly. Consider what happens in an application that the user can press a button on `frm1` to open `frm2`, yet neither form is made modal nor hidden in the process. Imagine the user moving the focus from `frm2` back to `frm1` and closing it, then returning to `frm2` and closing it. If `frm2` has any code to make `frm1` visible again by setting its `Visible` property, no instance of `frm1` currently exists, and an error results. In contrast, if the user gets in this situation and `frm2` uses `OpenForm` to return to `frm1`, the code will either redisplay `frm1`, if it is open and hidden, or open it again if it is closed. In either case, the code will not fail. Thus, if your interface is not highly restrictive, `OpenForm` provides an insurance policy that prevents navigation collisions.

It may seem at this point that `OpenForm` is a good way to navigate backward through forms, but there is a downside. Continuing our example, assume that `frm1` was originally opened with a `Where` clause supplied by its calling form. When the user closed `frm1` manually, then closed `frm2` and invoked an `OpenForm` on `frm1`, the `OpenForm` could not possibly know the filter information originally passed to `frm1`. Thus, when `frm1` is displayed on the way back from `frm2`, it has a different (that is, unfiltered) recordset than was originally presented to the user. Usually, this situation is quite inappropriate.

Not only should this example dissuade you from relying on OpenForm to navigate backward through forms, it should alert you to the dangers of enabling users to work with more than one form at a time. It should clarify why my preferred techniques for navigation depend upon hiding the first form as the second is opened, and redisplaying the first form with Visible = True when the second is closed.

When using the technique to hide and show forms during navigation, be wary that hiding a data entry or edit form may introduce several dangerous concurrency situations into your application, as follows:

▶ The hidden form may lock one or more records if it contains unsaved edits and it uses pessimistic locking (the RecordLocks property is set to Edited Record). To avoid this situation, always *validate and save* data on a form before hiding it.

▶ If the hidden form contains unsaved edits and uses optimistic locking (the RecordLocks property is set to No Locks), then other users can edit the same records that are dirty on the hidden form. When redisplaying the hidden form and attempting to save the edits, the user will receive a Write Conflict alert. Saving record edits before hiding a form will prevent this situation.

▶ Some data changes to items on a hidden form will not be reflected when the form is later redisplayed because the underlying recordset is not requeried when the Visible property is changed. For example, if a user in a high-volume database hides a form for an hour, during which fifty new records are added to the table that provides records to the hidden form, the form's recordset will be very antiquated when it is redisplayed. In contrast, if the application had closed the form during the hour and reopened it, instead of simply showing it, an accurate dataset would have been built as the form reopened.

Obviously, you must be consciously aware of data currency situations as you craft your application navigation. If a current operation (including data additions, edits, and deletions) might affect the accuracy of data on a hidden form, set a flag during the operation to requery the hidden form as it is displayed. Similarly, if the user edits lookup table values, or otherwise affects records in the combo or list boxes of a hidden form, the affected controls must be requeried by your code.

 Tip

Only requery the hidden object that is specifically affected by data changes. In other words, requery a combo box directly if only that control's data was affected, and only requery an entire form when absolutely necessary.

If your code must requery a form, remember that such an event changes the current record displayed to the first one in the form's recordset. If you want to display the same record to the user after the requery that was showing previously, store the primary key of the current record in a variable before sending the Requery method. After the requery, synchronize the form to the record that was originally displayed. This form synchronization technique is described in Chapter 16, "Presenting Data to Users."

Opening Forms in Sequence

When hiding and showing forms for navigation purposes, you must keep track, in your program code, of the forward flow of the application so that you can go backward to the appropriate object. The simplest method is to place commands in your form module code to display the calling form when a form is closed. This strategy, however, is too inflexible to be very useful. For example, if your code opens frm2 from frm1 then hides frm1, the Close button event code for frm2 might look something like this:

```
Forms!frm1.Visible = True
DoCmd.Close acForm, Me.Name
```

Because this code references frm1 by name, it does not enable you to call frm2 from any other form except frm1. In keeping with the expert forms objective of creating reusable objects, you should be able to call a properly coded form from practically any other form in the application. Thus, each form needs a custom property (let's call it CalledFrom) that can be used to store the name of the form that called it when it was loaded. Looking in the property, the form knows which form to redisplay as it closes itself.

What follows are several possibilities for providing a CalledFrom property setting to assist with form navigation:

OpenArgs. The OpenArgs property of a form can be set by passing a value to the appropriate argument of the OpenForm method. The following lines of code demonstrate this technique:

```
' In the calling form, pass its name to the called form via OpenArgs
DoCmd.OpenForm "frm2", , , , , , Me.Name
```

```
' In the called form, redisplay the calling form during close
Forms(Me.OpenArgs).Visible = True
```

Tag. If you are not generally using the Tag property of an application's forms, the name of the calling form can be set into this property after the called form is displayed. Use the following lines of code to facilitate this process:

```
' In the calling form, pass its name to the called form via the Tag
DoCmd.OpenForm "frm2"
Forms!frm2.Tag = Me.Name
```

```
' In the called form, redisplay the calling form during close
Forms(Me.Tag).Visible = True
```

Simple custom property. The simplest way to add a custom property to a form is to create a `Public` module-level variable for the form. This line of code will create a bin in which to place the name of the calling form:

```
Public mvarCalledFrom As Variant
```

The following two lines of code in the calling form will open the called form and set the property value:

```
DoCmd.OpenForm "frm2"
' Set the caller's name into a form property
Form_frm2.mvarCalledFrom = Me.Name
```

Custom property with `Property Let`*.* Using a `Property Let` statement, you can define a custom property for a form and set its value to the name of the calling form after opening it. Conceptually, this approach is similar in flow to using the `OpenArgs` or `Tag` properties of forms (as shown earlier), but it invokes your own special-purpose property that's created specifically for navigation.

The code in Listing 14.3 shows how to define and use `prpCalledFrom`, a custom navigation property procedure placed in each form.

Listing 14.3   AES_Frm2.Mdb—Passing the Calling Form Name into a Custom Property

```
' This routine is in the calling form frmPrpCalledFrom1
Private Sub cmdForm2_Click()
' Purpose: Open the dependent form

  DoCmd.OpenForm "frmPrpCalledFrom2"
  ' Set the caller's name into a form property
  Form_frmPrpCalledFrom2.prpCalledFrom = Me.Name
  Me.Visible = False

End Sub


' The remaining routines are in the called form frmPrpCalledFrom2
' In the Declarations section, create the property variable
Private mvarCalledFrom As Variant


Property Get prpCalledFrom() As Variant
' Purpose: Retrieve the calling form name from the custom property

  prpCalledFrom = mvarCalledFrom

End Property
```

```
Property Let prpCalledFrom(rvarForm As Variant)
' Purpose: Custom property for the calling form

  mvarCalledFrom = rvarForm

End Property


Private Sub cmdClose_Click()
' Purpose: Close the form

  DoCmd.Close acForm, Me.Name

End Sub


Private Sub Form_Close()
' Purpose: Open the calling form

 Forms(Me.prpCalledFrom).Visible = True

End Sub
```

Custom property procedures for forms (with `Property Get` and `Property Let`) are described in Chapter 12, "Understanding Form Structures and Coding." Property procedures provide the ability to detect the events generated by setting or reading the custom property. The code in the listing is for demonstration purposes; in reality, there would be little value in using the property procedures in a form navigation model as simple as the one shown. A custom form variable would work equally well.

System Control. The final option is what I call a system control (hidden from the user) to hold the name of the calling form—implemented with an invisible text box on the called form. Compared to the other three techniques, this approach is the least glamorous but it's quite practical. The code to use this property text box from the calling form looks like the following:

```
' This code resides in the calling form
DoCmd.OpenForm "frm2"
' Set caller's name into a form control
Forms!frm2!zhtxtCalledFrom = Me.Name
Me.Visible = False
```

Figure 14.8 shows a conceptual diagram of the various techniques for assigning a custom property value to a form. The options are equally effective, and any of them is an appropriate choice to use as a form navigation strategy.

14

Fig. 14.8

You can use a variety of methods to assign custom values (user-defined properties) to a form.

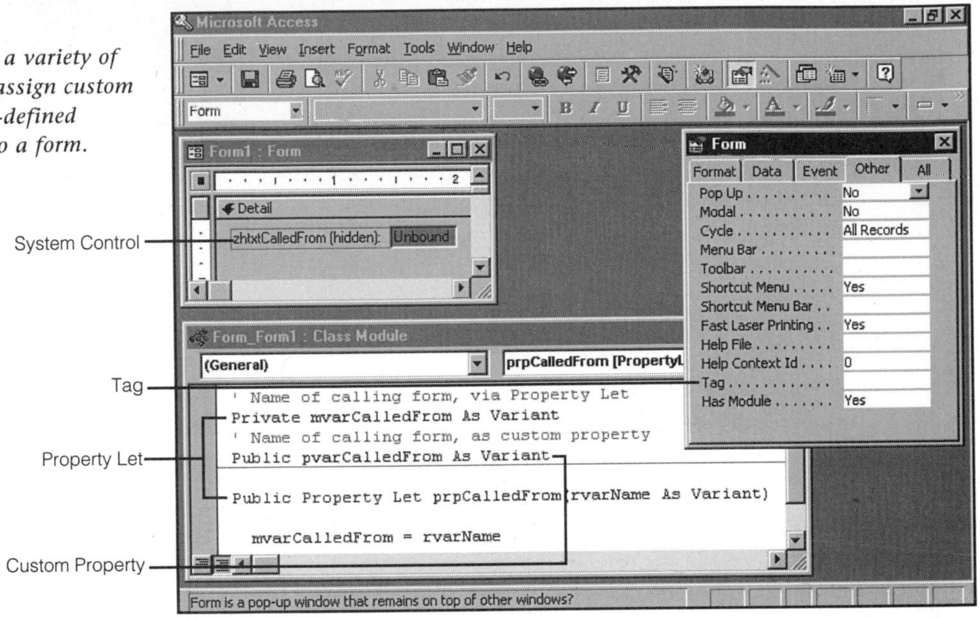

System Control

Tag

Property Let

Custom Property

Tip

You may want to try each of these techniques in a different application before you select a standardized approach for your development team. Each has strong and weak points, so one of the techniques will probably be a "best fit" for your unique development needs.

My development team and I favor two of these techniques. For new applications, we use the third option on the list: creating a simple property in each form as a module-level variable. It's very easy to implement—we simply modified our company Form Wizards to create the single-line property variable declaration in each new form. The only drawback is that, as a variable, the CalledFrom value is cleared during debugging if you select the Reset menu option or toolbar button. Thus, after a code reset, you may have to navigate backwards manually from the current form by using Window, Unhide to display the previous form.

For applications developed in Access 2, we have always used the last option on the list: a hidden system control placed on each form. We continue to use this in new Access 2 applications, and we keep the methodology in place when converting Access 2 applications to Access 97—there's no economic value for our clients to switch from the TextBox approach to the custom property approach.

The navigation techniques described in this section are highly flexible because you are no longer hard-coding the path back through your application's form stack. Because any given form no longer permanently points to a specific calling form, but instead points to the form that called it this instance, you can easily reorder the sequence of events in your application with no backwards navigation changes. You can also call one form from many different forms, thus achieving the objective of reusable objects.

Once you have standardized a form navigation strategy, you can formalize it by creating a library routine to make your coding tasks easier. Listing 14.4 shows our standardized routine for opening forms.

Listing 14.4 AES_Frm2.Mdb—A Standardized Library Routine for Opening Forms

```
Public Function lci_FrmOpenStd(rstrFormTo As String, _
  rstrFormFrom As String, Optional ByVal nvvarFlt As Variant, _
  Optional ByVal nvvarWhere As Variant, _
  Optional ByVal nvvarMode As Variant, _
  Optional ByVal nvvarWndMode As Variant, _
  Optional ByVal nvvarOpenArg As Variant) As Boolean
' Purpose:    Standardized form open
'             This routine plugs view argument to Normal only
'             Sets pvarCalledFrom and pintEditMode in the called form
' Arguments: Requires only the first two arguments
'             rstrFormTo:=Name of form to open
'             rstrFormFrom:=Name of calling form
'             nvvarFlt:=Filter name or Null
'             nvvarWhere:=SQL WHERE clause or Null
'             nvvarMode:=acAdd, acEdit, acReadOnly
'             nvvarWndMode:=acNormal, acHidden, acIcon, acDialog
'             nvvarOpenArg:=OpenArgs to follow the calling form name
' Returns:    True/False, True=form was opened
' Examples:   lci_FrmOpenStd("frmCust", Me.Name)
'             lci_FrmOpenStd("frmCust", "", "qfltCust", nvvarMode:=acAdd)
' Pseudocode:
'   1. Plug any missing Optional arguments to Null
'   2. Open the called form
'   3. Set the navigation properties
'   4. Hide the calling form

  On Error GoTo lci_FrmOpenStd_Err
  Const cstrProc As String = "lci_FrmOpenStd"
  Dim intLoc     As Integer

  ' Cleanup optional args
  If IsMissing(nvvarFlt) Then
    nvvarFlt = Null
  End If
  If IsMissing(nvvarWhere) Then
    nvvarWhere = Null
  End If
```

continues

14

Listing 14.4   Continued

```
  If IsMissing(nvvarMode) Then  ' Default data mode to Edit
    nvvarMode = acEdit
  End If
  If IsMissing(nvvarWndMode) Then  ' Default window mode to Normal
    nvvarWndMode = acNormal
  End If
  ' Set first argument of OpenArgs to calling form
  If IsMissing(nvvarOpenArg) Then
    nvvarOpenArg = Null
  End If

  ' Open the form
  DoCmd.OpenForm rstrFormTo, acNormal, nvvarFlt, nvvarWhere, nvvarMode _
    , nvvarWndMode, nvvarOpenArg
  ' Set the properties of the form, ignore if they don't exist
  On Error Resume Next
    Forms(rstrFormTo).pvarCalledFrom = rstrFormFrom
    Forms(rstrFormTo).pintEditMode = nvvarMode
  On Error GoTo lci_FrmOpenStd_Err
  ' Hide the calling form
  If Len(rstrFormFrom) > 0 Then
    Forms(rstrFormFrom).Visible = False
  End If
  lci_FrmOpenStd = True

lci_FrmOpenStd_Exit:
  Exit Function

lci_FrmOpenStd_Err:
  Call lci_ErrMsgStd(mcstrMod & "." & cstrProc, Err.Number _
    , Err.Description, Truc)
  Resume lci_FrmOpenStd_Exit

End Function
```

Why use a complex library routine to perform something as simple as opening a form? I can offer three justifications:

Standardization of approach. With all form open events centralized, the following benefits accrue: errors can be handled the same way each time; each form is required to have the same property variables, mandating a consistent design; using named arguments makes the complex code lines for opening forms easier to read than an `OpenForm`.

Organized team development. If you occasionally have six or more developers on a project, as we do, a variety of approaches among individuals can produce overly complex code. Requiring all team members to call the same library routine ensures consistency of code and approach throughout an entire application.

Extensibility. When all the forms in an application call the same library routine, a change in approach or adding new features can be performed simply—by changing the library routine rather than each affected form. For example, in a few minutes we can add event logging to our library routine to write an audit record to an ordered log each time a form is opened. Adding the same code to the individual forms in a large application would be much more costly.

If you keep too many hidden forms open at one time, the performance of your application may suffer. We have successfully nested forms twelve levels deep using the navigation techniques described here, but with an expected performance hit on the application. However, most applications are not—and should not be—designed to lead the user to so many layers in a particular logic path.

 Tip

If you find your application stacking more than four or five hidden forms at one time, consider reviewing the application logic and the users' needs in order to determine if the data entry/edit objective that produces this much stacking can be achieved by designing the task in another way. Users often find applications confusing when they must drill through many layers of forms to find a specific record or task.

Exploring Advanced Form Navigation Techniques

In the preceding section, we explored some standard approaches to navigating through forms and tracking the form call tree. The techniques described were adequate for handling the majority of your navigation needs, or for ideas that you can explore when devising your own approach.

In order to be comprehensive, in this section I'll mention some more advanced form navigation concepts. Although these concepts will not be applicable to all of your applications, they should give you food for thought nevertheless.

Opening Forms via Code Reference

Chapter 12 discusses how Access forms are now *class modules*, or templates from which multiple form instances can be created. It is possible to open a form by referring to a property of the form class directly in code, which invokes the *default instance* (a single instance) of the form. The following code line opens and displays the default instance of the frmCust form:

```
Form_frmCust.Caption = "Hi Mom"
```

The following are the features and limitations of such a direct-referencing scheme:

▶ A form opened by this type of code is instantiated without the creation of a variable because simply referring to any property of the form creates this default instance. The form is opened hidden and only displayed when the Visible property is set to True. Consequently, the following code line could legitimately serve as a replacement for a simple OpenForm method in your code:

```
Form_frmCust.Visible = True
```

However, there may be compelling reasons for *not* navigating this way—read on.

▶ Because this code invokes the default instance of the form, it can only be used to create one form instance. Repeated references to the named form will continue to refer to the single instance. In this respect, the default instance created by direct reference has the same characteristics as an instance created by OpenForm, which means that the new code technique has no tangible benefit over the older syntax.

▶ Because no variable is created in program code to refer to the form, the form is not closed when the calling procedure goes out of scope. However, because there is no variable created, all programmatic references to the form when it is opened must be hard-coded to the form's name, which produces the same inflexible code provided by OpenForm.

▶ The OpenForm method provides a simple mechanism for filtering records, setting the form window mode, and so forth, which makes it more powerful than the code reference technique.

Also, I noted in Chapter 13, "Mastering Combo and List Boxes," that forms can be instantiated via the use of form variables. The following code opens an instance of the frmCust form:

```
Dim frm As New Form_frmCust
frm.Visible = True
```

Unlike the previous syntax that opened the *default* instance of the form *without* a variable, the creation of a form variable in this manner enables multiple instances (via multiple variables) to be created from the same form class. This capability can be very useful when using forms as hidden classes that contain code engines. But I do not recommend creating programmatic form instances this way as a navigation strategy. The lifetime of the called form is limited to the lifetime of the calling procedure or the referencing variable, whichever expires first.

Advanced Form Stacking Concepts

"Opening Forms in Sequence" in this chapter explained strategies for keeping a "stack" of open forms by teaching each form how to return to its calling form. There are two other mechanisms for keeping a stack that should be mentioned here: a collection of forms and an array of form names.

Collections of forms are described in detail in the "Using Form and Control Collections" section of Chapter 12. Here, for our purposes, it is sufficient to note that the technique involves adding a reference for each form object to a collection of forms when they are opened. However, collections in Access have the following serious syntactic limitations (as described in Chapter 12):

▶ You can't retrieve the index number of a specific collection member.

▶ The location of an object in a collection can change as items are inserted into the collection.

These limitations make it very challenging to use a collection to determine which form to display when another form is closed. As forms are added to and removed from a collection, the "stack" becomes rearranged and this collection behavior makes it difficult to manage the restructure.

Thus, a collection of forms can serve a variety of purposes, but navigation is not one of them.

In contrast, maintaining an array with a form call tree is an easier proposition. Simply create a `Public` string array to contain form names:

```
Public gstrFrmStack() As String
```

As each form is opened, add its name to the array:

```
ReDim gstrFrmStack(UBound(gstrFrmStack) + 1)
gstrFrmStack(UBound(gstrFrmStack)) = Me.Name
```

When a form is closed, your code can determine where that form is located in the array, remove its entry, and walk backward through the array to the preceding item, which holds the name of the calling form. See the sample in Listing 14.5.

Listing 14.5   Finding the Calling Form's Name in a Navigation Array

```
Function FrmCallerGet(rstrName As String) As String
' Purpose:   To return the name of the next form down the stack
' Arguments: rstrName:=Name of called form

  Dim iint As Integer
  For iint = 0 To UBound(gstrFrmStack)
    If gstrFrmStack(iint) = rstrName Then
      Exit For
    End If
  Next iint
  FrmCallerGet = gstrFrmStack(iint [ms] 1)

End Function
```

Closing Forms in Sequence

In the previous section, "Opening Forms in Sequence," the code samples clearly reflected my preferred approach to closing forms. The code is summarized in Listing 14.6.

Listing 14.6   AES_Frm2.Mdb—Closing a Form and Opening the Calling Form

```
Private Sub cmdClose_Click()
' Purpose: Close the form

  DoCmd.Close acForm, Me.Name

End Sub


Private Sub Form_Close()
' Purpose: Open the calling form

 Forms(Me.prpCalledFrom).Visible = True

End Sub
```

The following are a few interesting points about closing forms:

Visible versus *OpenForm.* The simplest way to redisplay a calling form from a closing form is by setting the *Visible* property. Refer to the previous section "Hiding versus Closing Forms" for an explanation of the differences between these two syntax elements.

Locating the code. If your form has no Control menu or built-in Close button, and you rely on the user to close it through a code event (button click), you will probably locate the redisplay of the calling form in that code event (for example, cmdClose_Click()).

However, to be safe you should consider placing the code in the Form_Close() event, as shown in Listing 14.6. This ensures that the code will be called if the user finds a way to close the form that bypasses your custom event (the Ctrl+W keystroke, for example).

Explicit DoCmd.Close Reference. Notice in Listing 14.6 that the DoCmd.Close statement explicitly states that form to close (using Me.Name), even though the form name argument is not required by Access. It is good coding practice to explicitly declare the object that you intend as the target for such code instead of leaving it to Access to guess. DoCmd.Close by itself closes the current window, but as you move into a multithreading world you should not write code that assumes what the current window is. Explicit code is always safer than vague code, and usually runs faster.

Lagging behind validation. In many forms, the last major task is to validate and save the current record before closing. Should the validation fail, you do not want the burden of discerning whether or not the calling form has already been shown. This situation provides another reason to locate your display code very late in the form's event sequence (in the Unload or Close event). That way, it never fires too soon.

A slightly different variation on this philosophy occurs when you decide to write a library routine to handle the closing of forms. Listing 14.7 shows a standardized form close routine that works in conjunction with the standardized open routine shown in Listing 14.4.

Listing 14.7   AES_Frm2.Mdb—A Standardized Library Routine for Closing Forms

```
Public Function lci_FrmCloseStd(rfrm As Form) As Boolean
' Purpose:    Close the form and move back up the stack
'             Assumes the form to display next is in rfrm.pvarCalledFrom
' Arguments: rfrm:=Form object to close
' Returns:    True/False, True=form was successfully closed
' Example:    lci_FrmCloseStd(Me)
' Calls:      lci_IsBlank

  On Error GoTo lci_FrmCloseStd_Err
  Const cstrProc As String = "lci_FrmCloseStd"
  Dim varWork    As Variant

  On Error Resume Next
    varWork = rfrm.pvarCalledFrom
  On Error GoTo lci_FrmCloseStd_Err
  ' Show the calling form, ignore if doesn't exist
  If Not lci_IsBlank(varWork) Then
    Forms(varWork).Visible = True
  End If
  DoCmd.Close acForm, rfrm.Name
  lci_FrmCloseStd = True

lci_FrmCloseStd_Exit:
  Exit Function

lci_FrmCloseStd_Err:
  Call lci_ErrMsgStd(mcstrMod & "." & cstrProc, Err.Number _
    , Err.Description, True)
  If lci_FrmIsLoaded(rfrm.Name) Then   ' If the close failed
    Forms(varWork).Visible = False     ' Put stacked form away
  End If
  Resume lci_FrmCloseStd_Exit

End Function
```

Note that this library routine closes the named form; thus, it can't be located in a form's Unload or Close event. Such a routine usually goes in the event for your custom Close button on the form.

Caution

Locating the library routine in your button event brings to light the primary navigation challenge that will confront you: *your application can't enforce navigation unless you control how the user closes the form*. If a user can close a form with the Control menu or File, Close from the menubar, your navigation library routine will be skirted. Therefore, unless you are committed to absolutely controlling how the user closes a form, abandon the library routine and employ the simpler approach described at the beginning of this section.

Enforcing the Modal Interface

When you create your application according to the Single Document Interface principle, there will be only one form displayed at a given time. To facilitate this metaphor, you must tightly control the display properties of your application's forms.

Displaying Dialog Box Forms

Although one of our expert forms objectives is to reduce the number of objects displayed to the user at a given time, there are places in your applications where a form should "pop up" on top of a related form in order to gather additional information from the user. Such a form is called a *dialog form* or *dialog box*, as exemplified by the About dialog box that Figure 14.9 shows.

Fig. 14.9

An About dialog box is a common example of a modal pop-up form.

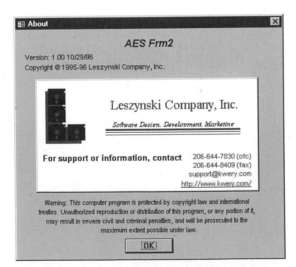

If a dialog box is displayed in a non-modal state, a user can click behind its window to the underlying form and "break free" of your intended navigation. To more strongly enforce the flow in this scenario, set the Modal property to True (Yes) for each of your dialog box forms. A modal form, once opened, will not release control (focus) to any other form until it is closed or hidden.

For dialog boxes that have command buttons like OK and Cancel, you should also set the PopUp property to True, which disables access to the menubar and toolbar. Finally, setting the BorderStyle property to Dialog creates the proper fixed border as in the dialog boxes in Office applications. The dialog box form in Figure 14.9 has the following settings:

```
Modal = True
Popup = True
BorderStyle = Dialog
```

A second technique for creating dialog forms is to open the form as a dialog box using the WindowMode argument of the OpenForm command, as in the following code sample:

```
DoCmd.OpenForm "frm1",,,,,acDialog
```

This command overrides the form's current settings for the Modal, PopUp, and BorderStyle properties to create a form that mimics the three property settings listed earlier for dialog forms.

As a general rule, the property settings (Modal, Popup, and BorderStyle) you set and save with a form are useful for determining how the user views the form from the Database window. Because it is important for a developer to control the form view that the user sees when the application is running, setting the window mode argument of a form from code during its OpenForm method is a critically useful habit you should develop.

 Note

Testing and debugging dialog forms is easier if you are able to open the forms non-modally from the Database window during development. To do this, you can keep the Modal and PopUp properties of your dialog box forms set to False, and instead have your code open these forms with the WindowMode argument of OpenForm set to acDialog.

The downside of this strategy is that the dialog box nature of your form will not be reflected in its saved properties. Thus, other developers reusing your form object will need to know the special OpenForm requirements of the form when they use it.

Dialog forms have some additional interesting characteristics, as follows:

▶ When you set a form's PopUp property to True or create a dialog form with OpenForm, you no longer have to disable the Ctrl+W keystroke combination for that form (you would want to disable this keystroke if it was necessary for users to only close the form via a button). Access automatically disables this method of closing dialog forms.

▶ When using OpenForm to create a dialog form, the actual values of the form's Modal, PopUp, and BorderStyle properties are not changed from their saved values. Thus, you can't detect from code that the form has been opened as a modal, pop-up dialog box by checking its property settings. This is an odd quirk in Access.

▶ When you set the BorderStyle property of a form to Dialog or create a dialog form with OpenForm, Access automatically removes the Minimize and Maximize buttons regardless of the MinMaxButtons property setting for the form.

Displaying Entry/Edit Forms

Because entry/edit forms usually make use of the menubar and toolbar, you should not set their PopUp properties to True nor open them as a dialog form via OpenForm.

However, when a form is set to be modal but *not* pop-up, the user can access the menubar and toolbar without having access to any other displayed forms. This is exactly the situation I want in the majority of my expert forms.

 Tip

You can open one modal form on top of another, so you can actually stack entry forms while still preserving the enforced navigation of your application. However, users might be confused by having forms shown to which they can't send the focus.

In addition to being a display concept, modality is also a navigation concept in the expert forms model, which states that the user should be doing only one thing at a time. To strictly enforce modal navigation, consider setting the ControlBox property to False (No) for each application form. Once removed, the user can't close the form without triggering an event that your code can trap.

In summary, I use the following settings to serve my entry/edit form navigation objectives:

```
Modal = True     ' Or alternately use OpenForm with acDialog
Popup = False
BorderStyle = Dialog  ' Or alternately use OpenForm with acDialog
ControlBox = False
```

Note

Regardless of the actual settings for the `MinMaxButtons` and `CloseButton` properties, when `ControlBox` is set to `False` on a form, the Close, Minimize, and Maximize buttons are not displayed.

The form in Figure 14.10 has no Control menu, Close button, Minimize button, or Maximize button. To completely control the application's flow, I eliminated the user's ability to go in any direction other than the one I intend.

Fig. 14.10

This expert form controls all aspects of user navigation.

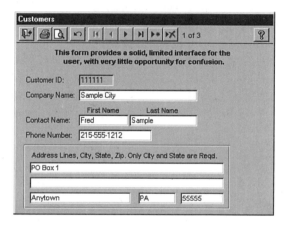

Of course, without built-in tools on the form that the user can click to close it, you must add your own Close button to each form, as Figure 14.10 shows. From the `Click` event of your Close button, you can trap the user's intention to close a form at a very early stage (before the form has actually started to close), and react accordingly in your code by validating the record or performing a related operation.

If you enable the user to close a data form with the Control menu or built-in Close button instead, you are forced to place your final code for validation and other operations in the form's `Unload` event. This event occurs *after* the current record is saved, which makes the flow of events in your form overly complex and makes validation and other processes difficult to connect to the form.

When you require users to close a form with your button, you intercept save and close events at a manageable point in the application flow. Thus, in achieving a navigation objective, you have also taken a step toward making your validation objectives easier to achieve. See Chapter 15, "Protecting and Validating Data," for a discussion of record validation on forms.

Handling Form Keyboard and Resize Events

Simply removing the Control menu and Close button from a form goes a long way toward putting your application in control of its form navigation events. However, Access enables the user to bypass your efforts by providing keyboard shortcuts that replace the buttons you've removed.

For an entry/edit form opened modally, the user can press Ctrl+W or Ctrl+F4 to close the form. However, you can disable these keystrokes throughout the application by simply redefining them to do nothing via the AutoKeys macro. Chapter 17, "Bulletproofing Your Application Interface," discusses this technique in detail.

For a dialog form, Access disables both of these keystrokes automatically. However, this doesn't mean you are out of the woods because Access provides the Alt+F4 keystroke combination as a shortcut for closing dialog forms only. Because this combination *cannot* be remapped in AutoKeys, you will not be able to prevent the user from applying it. Therefore, if your dialog form must be aware of the instant it begins closing, you must place code in the Unload or Close event to trap the user's intention. Alternately, you can attempt to detect and discard the Alt+F4 combination with a *keyboard handling procedure*, as described in Chapter 17.

Caution
When no dialog form is displayed, the Alt+F4 keystroke combination closes the current application and Access itself. Because this harsh exit may bypass some of your application code or potentially cause premature termination of a data process, you should discourage users from applying these keystrokes in *any* Access application or form.

In addition to undesirable keystrokes, your application should also be alert to one undesirable mouse event. If you choose to set a form's border to Sizable instead of my suggested Dialog value, users will be able to drag the form's border to a new size with the mouse. When they do this, they will expect your code to rearrange form control locations or sizes to fit the new form dimensions.

However, most forms are designed to be a specific size, and I've not built or seen more than a few applications over the years that trap the Resize event on a form and rearrange the size or shape of controls (this is very complex and expensive coding). Unless you intend to trap the resize and act accordingly, I can think of no good reason not to use the Dialog setting for your forms' borders.

Navigating via Menus and Toolbars

The form in Figure 14.10 used embedded (on the form) toolbar buttons to enable the user to move between records and close the form. Embedded buttons give the user of the form the ability to launch a form navigation or processing action.

 Note

In addition to buttons, you might enable the user to double-click a List Box, Text Box, Hyperlink, or Label control to open a form related to the current form. See "Synchronizing Record Displays" in Chapter 16, "Presenting Data to Users."

Instances arise in an application when navigation between forms with an embedded button is not efficient. The simplest example is provided by the ubiquitous About dialog box. You should not place an About button on each form simply to show this dialog box. Thus, you can add a menu option to the Help menubar, a custom menu, or a custom toolbar to display the dialog box. Because the About form *is* a dialog box, there are no associated navigation issues—simply open the form as a dialog box over the top of the current form and close the form when the user is finished, to return control to the current form. This procedure emulates that of Access and other retail applications.

A more complex situation arises when you choose to move beyond embedded buttons for navigation and you attempt to create complex menus or toolbars to help users move between forms and records.

Creating Your Own Record Navigation Routines

To enable users to navigate between records, you can very easily provide the internal Access record movement capabilities to a form. Simply enable any combination of the following features:

- The Edit, Go To menu option
- The toolbar buttons for record navigation
- The record navigation buttons control enabled via the NavigationButtons property on the form

If the capabilities of the Access navigation buttons are satisfactory to your users, the built-in features listed are highly useful and cost effective. On the other hand, some situations may arise that you choose to replace the built-in navigation options with your own navigation features. The following application needs provide examples of such situations:

> *Users are confused by the record number indicator.* I've never been a big fan of the record number box on the Access navigation buttons. In a relational database, records are not considered positional because data can be filtered and sorted many different ways, and because a record's identity is provided by its key—not its location in a recordset.

> *You prefer to embed your navigation features on the form.* Objects that are more completely self-contained and the ability to customize the look of navigation buttons are two benefits that accrue to your development effort when you create your own navigators.

> *Your program requires more control over navigation.* With a custom navigation strategy, your program will not have any reliance on menu or toolbar macros, and navigation events can more easily be trapped in the form's module. When using the standard Access navigation buttons, form events are already in motion (BeforeUpdate has fired) by the time your code gets the notification that a user is trying to move through the data. With custom buttons, you can detect the *intent* to move in the buttons' Click events, which is available before any actual movement has occurred.

I generally prefer to add my own First Record, Previous Record, Next Record, Last Record, and New Record navigation buttons to forms, and to attach the corresponding Click event code.

The following two sections discuss replacing the Access navigation buttons with your own if you choose to follow my lead.

Replacing the Record Number Box

Access displays a record position indicator in the record number box on a form's navigation button control. User's often assume that this is an identifier for the record. Thus, if the number 4 shows in the navigation buttons, a user may send e-mail to cohorts directing them to "review customer record 4," or reports to Technical Support asking why this week's record 4 is different than last week's. I have long wanted Access to enable us to remove this number from the navigation buttons (see the sidebar). In the absence of such a capability, you must remove the navigation buttons entirely and create your own record position indicator and navigators as required.

Everybody's Number One

In one of our first Access applications years ago, we created a form to track customer information for a client. When viewing the customer information form, the user could click a button that opened a second, pop-up form to display only the phone numbers for the current customer. We used the Access navigation control on the pop-up form, and because our client had only entered one phone number for each of his customers, each record that appeared on this pop-up had the number 1 in the record number box.

After using it for a few days, our client called and said, "Your program has a really big bug. Every customer in my application has exactly the same phone number." It took us just a few minutes to sort out the *real* problem.

Even though the phone number and the primary key of the phone number record were displayed differently on each pop-up, the client had focused on the positional number in the record number box, mistaking it for the phone number record key. Thus, to him, each time the pop-up loaded, the number 1 in the record number box indicated that this was the same record (with an *ID* of 1) that was displayed for all of his customers. (Never mind that the actual phone number on the screen was different, he based his opinion on the assumption that the record number was the primary key.)

The very next day, we threw up our hands, abandoned the built-in navigation button control, and started to code our own navigation button routines.

If your forms need to show a positional record number, Listing 14.8 shows how to get the same record number Access displays in its navigation buttons, by using the `AbsolutePosition` property of the form's recordset.

Tip

With Access 95, the record navigation control added the "of n" string to show a record's position in the recordset. You can include such information in your custom record number display by showing a record position label in the format "1 of *n*" instead of merely a record number. This listing includes this technique. Our clients agree that this format is less confusing than a record number by itself.

Listing 14.8   AES_Frm2.Mdb—Creating a Record Number Indicator from Code

```
Private Sub Form_Current()
' Purpose: Show current record position

  If Me.NewRecord Then
    Me!lblPos.Caption = "New"
  Else
    Me.RecordsetClone.Bookmark = Me.Bookmark
    Me!lblPos.Caption = CStr(Me.RecordsetClone.AbsolutePosition + 1) _
      & " of " & CStr(Me.RecordsetClone.RecordCount)
  End If

End Sub
```

Caution

A form does not have a Bookmark property when it's on a new record. If your navigation routines empower the user to move to a blank record, include a provision in the code for detecting the NewRecord property, as Listing 14.8 shows.

Tip

In addition to the AbsolutePosition property shown in Listing 14.8, experiment with the PercentPosition property, which shows the record location within the recordset as a percentage. Your users may find a percentage useful, yet less confusing than a record number. Note, however, that the PercentPosition property is not perfect either: it assumes that the first record in the recordset is at zero percent and that the last record in the recordset is something less than 100 percent. Thus, you may prefer to calculate the percentage position yourself in code, using the position and record count numbers provided in Listing 14.8.

Replacing the Navigation Buttons

To remove the Access *VCR* control from your forms, set the `NavigationButtons` property to `No`. Then, via code add any removed functionality that your users still require.

One approach is to place buttons directly on the form's header, creating our own navigation toolbar as shown in Figure 14.10. These navigation buttons can be made much more flexible and powerful than the Access buttons in the following ways:

You can selectively enable and disable buttons. You can't do this with the built-in navigation buttons, either on the Access menu system or dropped onto your own custom command bar. For example, when the user moves to the first record in a form's recordset, I disable both the First Record and Previous Record buttons to provide a clear signal that the user is at the beginning of the recordset.

You can immediately detect a button selection. When the user clicks a custom navigation button, your code can evaluate the state of the record, the permissions of the user, or any other status items before deciding whether to enable the navigation. Unlike the Access navigation buttons, your own buttons can choose not to initiate a navigation event, which is easier than trying to cancel a pending `BeforeUpdate` event already in progress.

You can add keyboard shortcuts. If your users have a familiar set of Alt key shortcuts for navigating between records, it is easy to add their favorite shortcuts to the navigation buttons. For navigation buttons containing text, select a character from the text caption and use the ampersand (&) prefix to denote the character is a hotkey. If the buttons contain graphics, you can assign a hotkey character using the `Caption` property of the button, and the button's graphic will conveniently override the display of the shortcut character. For example, we use &. as a caption for our Next Record button, which assigns it to the Alt+. keystroke for keyboard-centric users. (Users think this is actually the Alt+> shortcut but in fact they would have to include the Shift key to create that keystroke; surprisingly, few users ever notice this).

Coding homemade navigation buttons is not difficult. It requires a few global library routines and a smattering of `Click` event code attached to each button in the host form's module.

 Note

Even if you don't intend to adopt my techniques for record navigation, a close study of the code in this section should give you valuable insights about how to move within an Access form's recordset, how to trap various form conditions, and how to build upon a foundation of reusable library routines.

14

Listing 14.9 shows the `Click` event code behind our five standard custom navigation buttons: First Record, Previous Record, Next Record, Last Record, and New Record. The `Current` event for the form is also shown. The library routines called by code in the listing are explained after the listing.

Listing 14.9   AES_Frm2.Mdb—*Click* Routines for Form Navigation Buttons That Move Though a Form's Recordset

```
Private Sub btnAdd_Click()

  Call lci_FrmFocusSave(Screen.PreviousControl)
  Call lci_FrmNavGotoNew(Me)
  Call lci_FrmFocusRestore

End Sub


Private Sub btnFirst_Click()

  Call lci_FrmFocusSave(Screen.PreviousControl)
  Call lci_FrmNavGotoFirst(Me)
  Call lci_FrmFocusRestore

End Sub


Private Sub btnLast_Click()

  Call lci_FrmFocusSave(Screen.PreviousControl)
  Call lci_FrmNavGotoLast(Me)
  Call lci_FrmFocusRestore

End Sub


Private Sub btnNext_Click()

  Call lci_FrmFocusSave(Screen.PreviousControl)
  Call lci_FrmNavGotoNext(Me)
  Call lci_FrmFocusRestore

End Sub


Private Sub btnPrev_Click()

  Call lci_FrmFocusSave(Screen.PreviousControl)
  Call lci_FrmNavGotoPrev(Me)
  Call lci_FrmFocusRestore


Private Sub Form_Current()
' Purpose: Reset nav. buttons and show current record position
```

```
    Call lci_FrmNavCurrent(Me)

End Sub
```

Note that the routines in Listing 14.9 are quite similar and have the following characteristics in common:

> *Attention to Focus.* When the user clicks one of the navigation button controls on the form, focus moves from a data-entry field to the button. Our navigation routines track the previous control by storing a pointer to the control that had focus before the tool was clicked, and restoring focus back to that control after the navigation.

 Tip

The coding model shown in Listing 14.9 places the focus management in the event code behind the button. The focus code can just as easily be located in the library routines for navigation. However, I have located the focus routines with the form in order to keep the library routines more generic. In other words, the library routines *sans* focus management can be called from routines other than button events, but can only be called from controls if the focus information was moved into them.

> *Centralization.* Our navigation buttons always call central library routines. This enables navigation for all forms in an application to be modified by changing the central library routines only.

The library routines that support the navigation strategy in Listing 14.9 are shown in Listing 14.10.

Listing 14.10   AES_Frm2.Mdb—Library Routines that Support Form Navigation Buttons

```
Public Sub lci_FrmNavGotoFirst(rfrm As Form)
' Purpose: Goto first record in form recordset

  If rfrm.mtdValidate Then
    rfrm.SetFocus  ' Just to be sure
    Application.RunCommand (acCmdRecordsGoToFirst)
  End If

End Sub


Public Sub lci_FrmNavGotoLast(rfrm As Form)
```

continues

Listing 14.10   Continued

```
' Purpose: Goto last record in form recordset

  If rfrm.mtdValidate Then
    rfrm.SetFocus   ' Just to be sure
    Application.RunCommand (acCmdRecordsGoToLast)
  End If

End Sub


Public Sub lci_FrmNavGotoNext(rfrm As Form)
' Purpose: Goto next record in form recordset

  If rfrm.mtdValidate Then
    If Not lci_FrmNavIsLast(rfrm) Then
      rfrm.SetFocus   ' Just to be sure
      Application.RunCommand (acCmdRecordsGoToNext)
    End If
  End If

End Sub


Public Sub lci_FrmNavGotoNew(rfrm As Form)
' Purpose: Goto new record in form recordset

  If rfrm.mtdValidate Then
    If rfrm.AllowAdditions = True Then
      rfrm.SetFocus   ' Just to be sure
      Application.RunCommand (acCmdRecordsGoToNew)
    End If
  End If

End Sub


Public Sub lci_FrmNavGotoPrev(rfrm As Form)
' Purpose: Goto previous record in form recordset

  If rfrm.mtdValidate Then
    If Not lci_FrmNavIsFirst(rfrm) = True Then
      rfrm.SetFocus   ' Just to be sure
      Application.RunCommand (acCmdRecordsGoToPrevious)
    End If
  End If

End Sub
```

Note that I used the new RunCommand method in an attempt to speed up the record navigation code. In prior versions of Access, I utilized recordset operations to navigate, such as
the following alternative to the code in lci_FrmNavGotoFirst shown in Listing 14.10:

```
frm.RecordsetClone.MoveFirst   ' Move to the first record
frm.Bookmark = frm.RecordsetClone.Bookmark   ' Sync form
```

This type of navigation uses the form's RecordsetClone property, which is the only way to use DAO recordset operations like Move and Find operations on a form. The previous code shows how to synchronize the form's displayed record to the record that is current in the clone by synchronizing their respective bookmarks.

Navigation code based on recordsets still works fine in the current version of Access, so you can use either the recordset approach or the RunCommand approach in your navigation routines. My only rationale for using RunCommand is a secret hope that it executes a bit faster than the corresponding VBA code.

The next piece of our navigation puzzle involves creating the supporting library routines that are called by the navigation routines in Listing 14.10. These supporting routines test for the beginning and end of the form's recordset and are shown in Listing 14.11. The two location checking routines in the listing help the navigation routines determine what record a form is pointing to. Based on this information, the navigation buttons are enabled or disabled accordingly, as shown in Listing 14.12.

Listing 14.11   AES_Frm2.Mdb—Library Routines that Support Programmatic Record Navigation by Testing for the First or Last Record

```
Public Function lci_FrmNavIsFirst(rfrm As Form) As Boolean
' Purpose: Is form on first record in form recordset?

  Dim rst As Recordset   ' Form Recordset

  Set rst = rfrm.RecordsetClone  ' Get form recordset

  If Not rfrm.NewRecord Then
    rst.Bookmark = rfrm.Bookmark   ' Sync Recordset to the form
    If rst.AbsolutePosition = 0 Then
      lci_FrmNavIsFirst = True
    End If
  Else  ' On new record, just check for one more
    If rfrm.RecordsetClone.RecordCount = 0 Then
      lci_FrmNavIsFirst = True   ' No records yet
    End If
  End If

End Function


Public Function lci_FrmNavIsLast(rfrm As Form) As Boolean
' Purpose: Is form on last record in form recordset?

  Dim rst As Recordset   ' Form Recordset

  Set rst = rfrm.RecordsetClone  ' Get form recordset

  If Not rfrm.NewRecord Then
    rst.MoveLast   ' Get the record count
```

Listing 14.11   Continued

```
      rst.Bookmark = rfrm.Bookmark  ' Sync Recordset to the form
      If rst.AbsolutePosition + 1 = rst.RecordCount Then
        lci_FrmNavIsLast = True
      End If
    Else  ' New record is automatic last
      lci_FrmNavIsLast = True
    End If

End Function
```

The next component of the navigation puzzle to explore is the most interesting. In the preceding two listings, I showed you how to navigate within the form's recordset using command buttons. From the developer's perspective, this record navigation system is powerful, because each navigation event can be detected, enhanced, and controlled. From the user's viewpoint, however, simply moving between records is straightforward and almost boring. The best part of our custom navigation style, from the user's perspective, is that the forms self-configure the navigation buttons to indicate the user's position in the recordset.

Using the library routines we're exploring here, when the user is on the first record in the form, the First Record and Previous Record buttons are disabled. When the user is on the last record, these two buttons are enabled but Next Record and Last Record are disabled, and so on. The buttons provide visual clues about the form's recordset. In this respect, our custom navigation buttons are smarter than those in Access, which still do not self-configure properly, even in the 97 release. Access' built-in First Record button does not disable when the user is on the first record, nor does the Last Record button disable on the last record. Thus, if you use these controls on your custom menus, you inherit this odd behavior.

In order to self-configure the navigation buttons, a form's Current event must check and reset the buttons with each record move. Referring back to Listing 14.9 you'll see the Current event procedure for a form with custom navigation; the event calls the lci_FrmNavCurrent library function as shown in Listing 14.12. This routine configures the navigation buttons.

**Listing 14.12   AES_Frm2.Mdb—Library Routine that Supports
Programmatic Record Navigation by Setting Navigation Buttons**

```
Public Sub lci_FrmNavCurrent(rfrm As Form)
' Purpose: OnCurrent processing for forms with lci nav buttons

  rfrm!btnFirst.Enabled = Not lci_FrmNavIsFirst(rfrm)
  rfrm!btnPrev.Enabled = Not lci_FrmNavIsFirst(rfrm)
```

```
        rfrm!btnNext.Enabled = Not lci_FrmNavIsLast(rfrm)
        rfrm!btnLast.Enabled = Not lci_FrmNavIsLast(rfrm)

    End Sub
```

The final component of manual navigation is a record validation methodology. Note that the navigation routines in Listing 14.10 are careful to call the form's validation method before moving. This approach ensures that a form record is painstakingly validated by code before any navigation occurs. The validation method `mtdValidate` for the form is simply a `Public` function in the form that tests the record and returns a True/False value to the navigation routines. See Chapter 15, "Protecting and Validating Data," for an expanded discussion of this validation method.

With custom record navigation, your code always knows where it is in the recordset, your users see what you want them to see on the navigation buttons, and data-oriented events are detected as soon as they are triggered.

Exploring Toolbar and Menu Strategies

You may have noticed that my expert form examples in this book do not use the built-in toolbars of Access, but rather create custom interface devices: toolbar-like buttons directly on the forms (see Figure 14.11), customized toolbars using the new command bars technology, or customized menubars.

Fig. 14.11

This application form has embedded toolbar buttons only and a minimal bar menu.

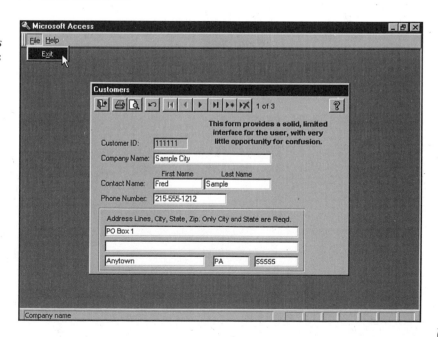

The use of embedded toolbars creates a form "component object" that is self-contained and provides your application with the highest degree of control over events triggered by user interaction. Other reasons for considering the use of embedded toolbars are explained in Chapter 15, in the "Deciding Between the Access Commands and Your Own" section.

You can also create a hybrid style, which uses a generic Access toolbar for operations that are truly generic (do not require custom code) and embeds custom tools on forms for the rest of the work, as in Figure 14.12.

Fig. 14.12

This application mixes custom embedded buttons on the form with the Access built-in toolbar buttons.

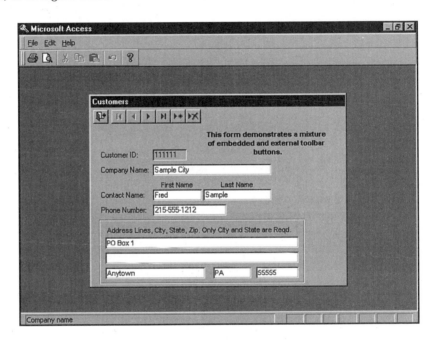

The following list offers some built-in toolbar buttons that you might consider as candidates for a generic entry/edit form toolbar.

    Close

    Print

    Undo

    Cut

    Copy

    Paste

    Help

Note that the listed tools do not change focus from the current record to another record; thus, they do not affect your navigation or validation strategies. Tools that cause a record save and all of its related events may be placed on an Access toolbar as well, but you will have to work harder to enable this approach. You will find that you have more control of the application environment if your code is aware of navigation and validation events.

For example, you must locate your record validation code in the BeforeUpdate event of any form that enables navigation from standard navigation buttons placed on an Access toolbar. You must also devise a strategy to cancel any record saves in progress that are initiated by a toolbar selection but that do not survive the validation process or meet your other criteria for allowing a record move. Although this may present no problem in some interface metaphors, forms with complex validation generally benefit from very tight application control over the saving and testing of records.

A detailed discussion of the benefits and liabilities of Access built-in features placed on form toolbars and menubars is in the "Selecting the Appropriate Menu Options" section of Chapter 15. However, in this chapter we are concerned with the mechanical aspects of implementing toolbar and menu strategies.

Although Access's menu macros from previous versions are still supported in Access 97, you will learn to appreciate the powerful but complex command bar technology for menu and toolbars. The next two sections provide an introduction to this technology.

Introducing Command Bars

As an active member of the review and testing process for each new release of Access, I see a lot of the feedback that the Access team gets from developers. Year after year, one of the top wishes from developers has been "Give us programmable menus, like in Visual Basic." With Access 97, these wishes became a reality.

Access actually didn't add programmable menus, it inherited them. The new CommandBar object, and its object model, is a feature of Office that Access leverages. The command bar model in Access is the same as the one in Excel, Outlook, PowerPoint, and Word. This situation is both a positive and a negative.

On the positive side, if you develop Office-centric solutions you need only learn one object model and create one code library to provide custom menus in multiple host applications. The negative aspect is that the Access team was not able to fine-tune command bars for Access; as a generic Office object they work as you would expect: generically. This means that command bars are not very aware of the special needs of Access.

As an example, the ability to call a custom form method from a custom toolbar function is not properly enabled in Access 97. You must instead create a "helper function" in a standard module, call that function from your command bar object, and have the helper in turn initiate the form's method code. (The function is called a "helper" because its

14

only purpose is to call the form code that the command bar cannot execute directly.) Another example of the lack of full command bar integration with Access is that you cannot nest command bars on an Access form or within a form control.

Despite the limitations, command bars are a viable and useful technology for creating navigation elements in expert solutions. The next three sections will show you how.

Using Command Bars for Form Menus

The best use of command bars in your applications is for form menus. Most applications have some kind of menu system. Based on the navigation models described in this chapter, you will decide to enable user navigation and other form operations via some combination of form Command Button controls, command bar toolbars external to the form (see the next section), and command bar menus.

To create a command bar menu, select View, Toolbars from the menu system or select Customize from the shortcut menu on the Access menu workspace. The Customize dialog box appears, as shown in Figure 14.13. From this dialog, you create, modify, and remove all of your application's command bars.

Fig. 14.13

Command bars are created and modified using the Customize dialog box.

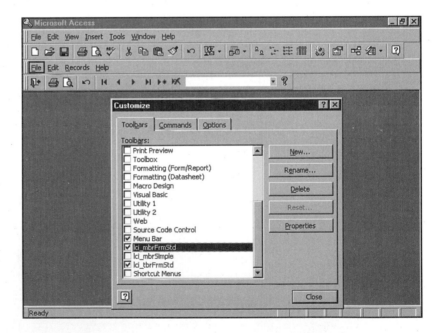

Notice in the figure that I have already created three custom command bars that are supplied in the custom database for this chapter: lci_mbrFrmStd, lci_mbrFrmSimple, and lci_tbrFrmStd. From my naming conventions you can probably divine that the first menu is a standard (default) menu bar object for use with forms, the second is a sparse menu with few options, and the latter is the default form toolbar. `lci_mbrFrmStd` and `lci_tbrFrmStd` are displayed in the figure.

To create a custom menu bar like the one shown in the figure, follow these steps:

1. *Create a new command bar.* Select New from the Customize dialog and name your new command bar.

2. *Set the properties for your new command bar.* Highlight it in the list of toolbars in the Customize dialog's Toolbars tab and click Properties. The Toolbar Properties dialog box appears, as shown in Figure 14.14. By default, new command bars are created as toolbars, but you can select the style for your custom toolbar using the Type drop-down as shown in the figure. Also note in the figure that I have opted not to show the standard form toolbar on the shortcut menu for toolbar selection (Show on Toolbars Menu is off) and have decided that users cannot modify the toolbar (Allow Customizing is off).

Note

When you are first building a new command bar, leave the Allow Customizing option in the Properties dialog on or you will not be able to add and modify menu options for the object. When you are finished designing the command bar, return to the Properties dialog and turn this option off.

Fig. 14.14

Customizing the at-
tributes of a command
bar with the Toolbar
Properties dialog.

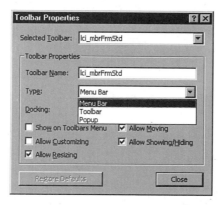

3. *Drag existing command items to the toolbar or create new commands.* To add an Access menu option to your toolbar, drag it from the Commands tab of the Customize dialog and drop it onto your command bar. To create a custom command bar item that does not tie to any built-in Access functionality, drag the item named Custom from the tab to your command bar, as shown in Figure 14.15. In the figure, the Custom option is being dropped between the Preview and Print... menu options, as indicated by the locator bar and mouse cursor.

14

The type of menu item created is a function of the destination that you drop it to. Dropping a built-in or custom menu option on the menu bar area creates another top-level option on the bar menu. Dropping a menu item onto a toolbar creates a new button. Dropping a menu option onto a drop-down for a menu bar item adds it to the drop-down. To place a new menu item onto a drop-down, you must first drag it to the bar menu item. As you hover over the item, it will open and reveal its drop-down. You can then drag the item downward onto the drop-down.

Fig. 14.15

Add a custom menu item to a command bar by dragging the Custom item from the Customize dialog to the destination location.

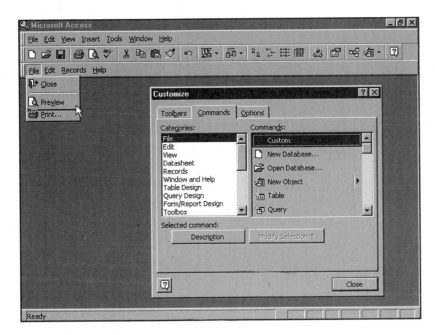

4. *Set the properties for the custom menu option.* Right-click on the menu option you want to customize and select Properties from the shortcut. The Control Properties dialog is displayed, as shown in Figure 14.16. For custom command bar menu items, you will want to set the menu caption, tool tip text, help file, help context ID link, and display style.

5. *Assign an action to the control.* When you create a new menu item by dragging an Access built-in menu item to a toolbar, the menu item inherits from Access the same event that would result from the item's selection from a built-in menu. In other words, if you add the built-in Undo menu option to your custom command bar by dragging it to the menu from the Commands list in the Customize dialog, it

will function the same way in every respect as the Undo option on Access' Edit menu. In contrast, if you create a custom menu item with the Custom option as described in step 3, you will have to designate the action to perform when the user selects the option.

Fig. 14.16

Property settings for an individual menu item on a command bar are made in the Control Properties dialog.

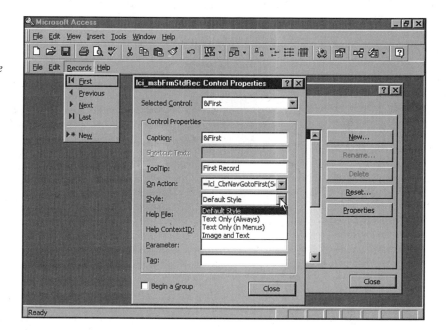

With the Control Properties dialog from step 4 still open, enter a custom action in the On Action property item. The entry here can be either a macro or a `Public Function` procedure in a standard module. The function procedure's name must be preceded by the = character and must be followed by parentheses even if no arguments are required. Here is the full text of the action entered into the On Action property setting in Figure 14.16:

```
=lci_CbrNavGotoFirst(Screen.ActiveForm, 1)
```

Once you've created a command bar menu and its custom menu options and an action, you can attach the menu to a form by entering the menu name in the form's `MenuBar` property. When the form opens, the menu is displayed, as shown in Figure 14.17.

When the user selects a custom menu option from your command bar menu, the function specified in the On Action property setting is run. In the case of our current example, selecting the custom Records, First menu option would run the function `lci_CbrNavGotoFirst` that was attached to the menu item in step 5. Listing 14.13 shows the code for this function.

14

Fig. 14.17

A custom menu built with command bars is attached to this form.

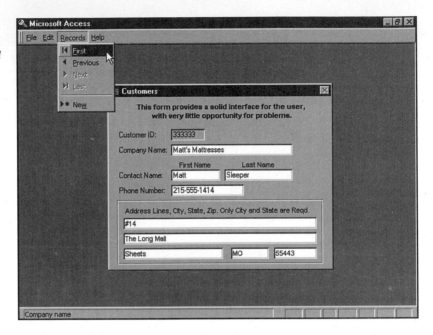

Listing 14.13   AES_Frm2.Mdb—A Function that Provides a Custom Menu Action for a Command Bar

```
Public Function lci_CbrNavGotoFirst(rfrm As Form, rbytCbr As Byte)
' Purpose:    Goto first record in form recordset
' Arguments:  rfrm:=Calling form
'             rbytCbr:=Which command bar is used:
'                 msoBarTypeNormal=0=toolbar, msoBarTypeMenuBar=1=bar menu,
'                 msoBarTypePopup=2=shortcut

  If rfrm.mtdValidate Then
    rfrm.SetFocus  ' Just to be sure
    Application.RunCommand (acCmdRecordsGoToFirst)
  End If

End Function
```

This code routine provides the ability for the user to navigate to the first record on a form by selecting a custom menu option. Because we code our expert forms using a component object model, the menu is generic and has no awareness of the specific form that it is attached to at the current moment. Thus, the function call from the menu to the library navigation routine must pass in a handle to the active form without knowing its name, so it uses Screen.ActiveForm. The library function receives this pointer to the current form object and moves the record pointer for the form.

You may have noticed that this library routine is almost identical to the library routine for navigation via embedded form toolbar buttons, `lci_FrmNavGotoFirst`, shown in Listing 14.10 previously. The only difference is that the menu bar action passes in an argument value of 1 to the function in the `rbytCbr` argument position. The function does not currently use the argument but provides a placeholder for it. This allows the function to be enhanced in the future to recognize the type of command bar that called it.

In Listing 14.12 previously, you explored the library routine `lci_FrmNavCurrent` that cleverly enables and disables a form's embedded navigation buttons. It is possible to follow a similar path, and to make your custom command bar menu selections come and go, based on context. This creates menus that are smarter than those provided by Access and are user-friendly to the highest degree possible.

In the `Current` event of a form using the custom menu bar shown in this section, I call the function provided in Listing 14.14 and pass in a handle to the form and the type of command bar to configure:

```
Call lci_CbrNavCurrent(Me, msoBarTypeMenuBar)
```

The listing not only shows how to smartly configure command bar menu items from code, it provides an opportunity for you to begin to explore the object model of the `CommandBar` objects that define the menus.

Listing 14.14   AES_Frm2.Mdb—*Current* Event Processing Allowing a Form to Configure its Menu Bar Options

```
Public Sub lci_CbrNavCurrent(rfrm As Form, rbytCbr As Byte)
' Purpose:   OnCurrent processing for forms with lci nav command bars
' Arguments: rfrm:=Calling form
'            rbytCbr:=Which command bar is used:
'                msoBarTypeNormal=0=toolbar, msoBarTypeMenuBar=1=bar menu,
'                msoBarTypePopup=2=shortcut

' The constants for the command bar name are set at the module level:
'   mcstrMbr = "lci_mbrFrmStd"
'   mcstrTbr = "lci_tbrFrmStd"

  Select Case rbytCbr
    Case msoBarTypeNormal   ' Toolbar
      CommandBars(mcstrTbr).Controls("btnFirst").Enabled _
        = Not lci_FrmNavIsFirst(rfrm)
      CommandBars(mcstrTbr).Controls("btnPrev").Enabled _
        = Not lci_FrmNavIsFirst(rfrm)
      CommandBars(mcstrTbr).Controls("btnNext").Enabled _
        = Not lci_FrmNavIsLast(rfrm)
      CommandBars(mcstrTbr).Controls("btnLast").Enabled _
        = Not lci_FrmNavIsLast(rfrm)
    Case msoBarTypeMenuBar  ' Bar menu
```

continues

14

Listing 14.14   Continued

```
        CommandBars(mcstrMbr).Controls("&Records").Controls("&First").Enabled _
          = Not lci_FrmNavIsFirst(rfrm)
        CommandBars(mcstrMbr).Controls("&Records").Controls("&Previous").Enabled _
          = Not lci_FrmNavIsFirst(rfrm)
        CommandBars(mcstrMbr).Controls("&Records").Controls("&Next").Enabled _
          = Not lci_FrmNavIsLast(rfrm)
        CommandBars(mcstrMbr).Controls("&Records").Controls("&Last").Enabled _
          = Not lci_FrmNavIsLast(rfrm)
    Case msoBarTypePopup      ' Shortcut
        ' Not implemented
    End Select

End Sub
```

The key difference between the way Command Button controls were enabled and disabled by the routine in Listing 14.12, and the way that command bar controls are managed in Listing 14.14, is in the addressing of the target object. A command bar object, whether menu or toolbar, has a `Controls` collection. Each control in the collection can be addressed by name or index. Thus, for a toolbar object, your code can address the navigation button `btnFirst` on the toolbar with this:

```
CommandBars("lci_tbrFrmStd").Controls("btnFirst")
```

For a menu bar object, each drop-down menu is a control on the menu bar. Within each drop-down menu object, however, is another `Controls` collection with the buttons on the drop-down. Thus the syntax elements must be nested to show this relationship. This line of code addresses the Records, First menu option:

```
CommandBars("lci_mbrFrmStd").Controls("&Records").Controls("&First")
```

 Note

Notice the different naming convention issues between toolbar buttons and menu options. Command bar items do not have an actual `Name` property; instead, the `Caption` serves as the item's name. For menu items, the caption displayed to users also provides the name of the menu item in the object model. Thus the reference in the previous code line to the command bar control `&First`. For toolbar buttons that display text, you will also provide a caption that has meaning to the user and inherit this caption as the menu item's object name. For toolbar buttons that display only a graphic and not the caption, I use an object name for the caption that follows LNC style, such as `btnFirst`.

Using Command Bars for Form Toolbars and Shortcut Menus

When you determine that a command bar toolbar is an appropriate addition to a specific form, you must first define the composition of the toolbar. Usually, a custom toolbar contains a mix of built-in buttons borrowed from Access and your custom buttons. For example, there is usually no need to write your own undo code when you can now place the Access Undo toolbar button on your custom toolbars and inherit that code. On the other hand, record deletions are often tightly managed by program code and will usually be custom-coded, as described in Chapter 15, "Protecting and Validating Data." Your custom code for record deletions on your expert forms can be invoked as an action of a custom toolbar button.

Creating a new custom toolbar is similar to creating a command bar menu as described in the steps and figures in the preceding section. The primary difference is that the Type value you select in the Toolbar Properties dialog box will be Toolbar as opposed to Menu Bar.

Toolbars are very flexible. In addition to button controls, you can place edit (text) boxes, drop-down list boxes, and combo box controls on a toolbar. You can also place a drop-down menu on a toolbar.

 Note

There is a control type in the command bar model for each toolbar control used in the Office applications, but most cannot be created from Access code. For example, the Style drop-down in Word, which mixes text and graphics, is a command bar object, as is the grid control in Word that allows you to identify the size of a new table. Hopefully these control types will be exposed to Access developers at some time in the future.

Unlike with the Windows 95 Toolbar control in the Office Developer Edition, you cannot attach ActiveX controls to a command bar toolbar or menu.

Figure 14.18 provides an example of the new toolbar capabilities introduced in Access 97. The figure shows a custom form toolbar that includes a combo box control allowing the user to navigate to a record in the form's recordset.

Fig. 14.18

A custom toolbar with a combo box control.

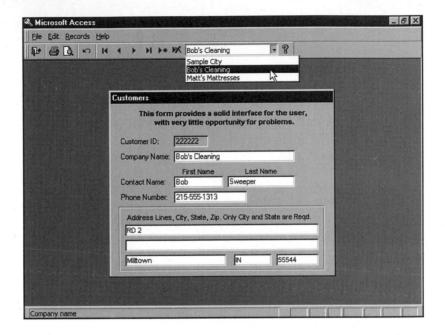

⚛ Tip

Minus the combo box control, which is useful but not mandatory for form navigation, the toolbar in the figure provides a good example of an optimal set of controls to provide to an expert form. The mixture shown allows a user to navigate, add, delete, undo, and print, but does not provide options, like bulk replace, that are dangerous to the data, nor provide controls that are only marginally useful.

For each custom toolbar control you create, you will assign the name of a `Public` function procedure to the On Action property; this attaches event code to the button click. For example, the action assigned to the combo box control shown in Figure 14.18 is:

```
=lci_CbrNavFrmSync(Screen.ActiveForm _
  , Commandbars!lci_tbrFrmStd.Controls!cboCust.Text)
```

This action calls the public helper function `lci_CbrNavFrmSync` and passes in two arguments: a handle to the active form, and the current value of the combo box control. The helper function is called only to activate the form code that the command bar cannot call directly; it contains this line:

```
Call rfrm.mtdSync(rvar)
```

The helper initiates a customized synchronization method (mtdSync) on the form whose purpose is to move the form to the record that is specified in the combo box control, as shown in Listing 14.15.

Listing 14.15   AES_Frm2.Mdb—A Custom Form Method to Move to a Specific Record, Initiated by a Command Bar Combo Box

```
Public Function mtdSync(rvarFind As Variant) As Boolean
' Purpose:    Synchronize the form to a specific record
' Arguments: Company name to find

  Dim rst As Recordset
  Set rst = Me.RecordsetClone

  rst.FindFirst "CompanyName = """ & rvarFind & """"
  If Not rst.NoMatch Then
    Me.Bookmark = rst.Bookmark
  End If
  rst.Close

End Function
```

The code in the custom method synchronizes the form's recordset to the value from the toolbar combo box, as passed in as an argument from the helper function. Notice the generic nature of this process: neither the toolbar button nor the helper function are aware of the name of the form, nor the contents of the form's custom method. This allows different forms to provide different features in their mtdSync method, and yet all of the forms can benefit from one standard toolbar coded to this method name.

 Tip

The action for the custom combo box control on the toolbar passes back the value displayed to the user (cboCust.Text). If the *position* of the user's selection in the combo's list is more important than the text, you can pass around the Index property of the combo box instead of the Text property.

Context (shortcut) menus can also be created using command bar objects. First, create a new command bar as a menu or toolbar and set the properties of the command bar and its controls. Then, change the Type property of the command bar to Popup in the Toolbar Properties dialog. This converts the command bar to a shortcut menu.

To view a shortcut menu for customization, you must display the container for all shortcut menus by selecting Shortcut Menus from the Toolbars list in the Customize dialog box, as shown in Figure 14.19.

14

Fig. 14.19

To customize a shortcut menu you must display the Shortcut Menus bar.

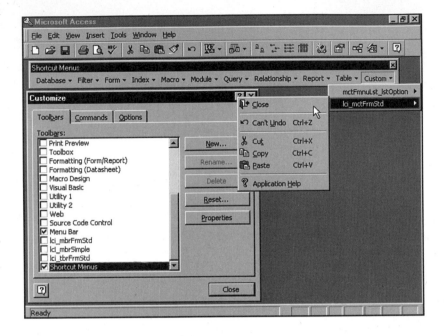

To attach a shortcut menu to a form, simply set the form's Shortcut Menu Bar property to the name of menu. Figure 14.20 shows my standard form shortcut menu, as designed in Figure 14.19, at work on a form.

Fig. 14.20

A custom shortcut menu used on a form.

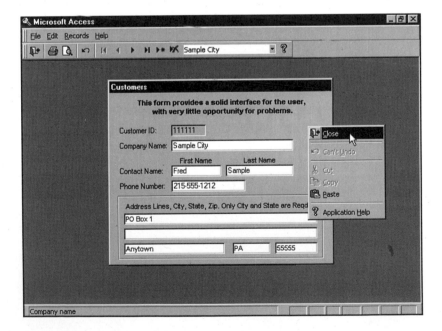

Programming Command Bars

Menu bars, toolbars, and shortcut menus are each simply command bars with specific property settings, as opposed to different object types. Thus, the command bar object model is actually simpler than it seems. Command bars in your applications will be primarily created in the user interface, but can also be created and modified from program code as required.

By creating a reference to their object model, command bars become programmable from Access. The object model is stored in the Office object library MSO97.DLL. You must create a reference to this file in the References dialog box in order to use program code to address the components of command bars.

There are three primary varieties of command bar objects. Each menu option and toolbar button is a CommandBarButton object in the object model. A CommandBarPopup object represents a context menu or a (cascading) submenu. A CommandBarComboBox control represents a text box, drop-down list box, or combo box control on a command bar. Each of these is programmable.

The three command bar object types are subordinate to a parent CommandBar object, which is a member of the CommandBars collection for the application. Within this collection, you can do most of the things you expect from a collection, such as inspect its Count property to see how many command bars are in the application or use the Add method to create a new command bar. The example code in Listing 14.16 creates a new menu bar and adds a drop-down with one item to the menu.

Listing 14.16   AES_Frm2.Mdb—Creating a New Menu Bar from Program Code

```
Dim cbr As CommandBar
Dim ctl As CommandBarControl
Dim pop As CommandBarPopup

' Create a new menu bar command bar object
Set cbr = CommandBars.Add(Name:="mbrTest" _
  , Position:=msoBarTop, MenuBar:=True)
With cbr
  .Protection = msoBarNoCustomize   ' Don't allow user changes
  .Visible = False  ' Do not display
End With
' Create a drop-down menu
Set pop = cbr.Controls.Add(msoControlPopup)
pop.Caption = "&Batch"
' Add an option to the drop-down
Set ctl = pop.Controls.Add(msoControlButton)
ctl.Caption = "&Post"
```

14

The Add method in the listing is used to create a new command bar or a command bar control, depending on the context. Setting attributes of a command bar or control is similar to setting properties for a built-in Access object.

You cannot create a CommandBarComboBox control (text box, drop-down list box, or combo box) from the user interface, you *must* use code. Thus, the combo box control shown on the form toolbar in the previous section was created using the code in Listing 14.17.

Listing 14.17   AES_Frm2.Mdb—Adding a Combo Box Control to a Toolbar from Program Code

```
Public Sub lci_CbrCboCreate()
' Purpose: Example of programmatically creating a combo box on a toolbar

' This code will not run if you do not own Office and set a reference
'    to its type library MSO97.DLL
    Dim cbr As CommandBar
    Dim cbo As CommandBarComboBox

    Set cbr = CommandBars("lci_tbrFrmStd")
    ' Create a combo box
    ' Control is located one position in from the right
    Set cbo = cbr.Controls.Add(Type:=msoControlDropdown _
      , Before:=cbr.Controls.Count, Temporary:=False)

    With cbo
      .Caption = "cboCust"
      .DropDownLines = 10
      .DropDownWidth = 180
      .ListHeaderCount = -1
      .OnAction = "=lci_CbrNavFrmSync(Screen.ActiveForm," _
          & "Commandbars!lci_tbrFrmStd.Controls!cboCust.Text)"
      .Width = 150
    End With

End Sub
```

The code in the listing simply appends another control (cboCust) to the existing named command bar. The Add method allows you to specify the location of the control on the toolbar; in this case, I chose to place the control just to the left of the rightmost control, the Help button, which is located in the Controls.Count (maximum) location on the toolbar.

Once the control is created, the code in the listing simply establishes its properties such as height, width, and action. If the values in the combo box's list were to be permanent, the listing could include AddItem method statements to insert items into the list. However, the purpose of the combo box, as demonstrated in the previous section, is to dynamically display records from a form's recordset in its list. Thus, the combo list values must be loaded from code as the form loads. This code is shown in Listing 14.18.

Listing 14.18   AES_Frm2.Mdb—Loading Values into a Combo Box Control on a Toolbar

```
Private Sub Form_Load()
' Purpose: Place record ID values in toolbar combo box

  Dim ctl As CommandBarControl
  Dim rst As Recordset

  Set ctl = CommandBars!lci_tbrFrmStd.Controls!cboCust
  Set rst = Me.RecordsetClone

  If rst.RecordCount > 100 Then
    ctl.Visible = False   ' Don't use if too many records
  Else
    With ctl
      While Not rst.EOF
        .AddItem rst!CompanyName
        rst.MoveNext
      Wend
      .Visible = True
    End With
  End If
  rst.Close

End Sub
```

The code in the listing simply moves through the form's recordset and adds the company name value for each record to the combo box list. For performance and usability reasons, the listing does not attempt to load the combo box if the form contains more than 100 records. The form code to move to an item as dictated by the combo box was shown previously in Listing 14.15.

The structure of the object model for command bars can be discovered by browsing the Object Browser and experimenting with the code I've provided on the CD. Command bars offer a wealth of possibilities for custom programming and dynamic configuration of the user's environment.

Passing Information to a Form

A form often needs information that originates outside of itself. One simple example of such information is the name or security level of the current user. Forms may find value in such information.

14

What follows are the various ways your program can supply information to a form:

The Tag *Property.* Your code can pass information to a form's Tag property immediately after opening the form, using code like the following:

```
DoCmd.OpenForm "frmCust"
Form_frmCust.Tag = "Sally"
```

Once set, the Tag property can be referenced from code in the form's module, using the syntax Me.Tag, or by form expressions, such as the DefaultValue property setting shown in Figure 14.21.

Fig. 14.21

The DefaultValue *property for this Text Box control refers to the form's* Tag.

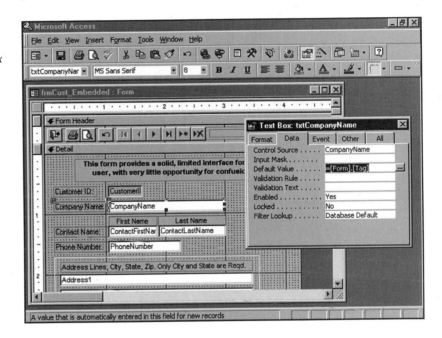

The OpenArgs *property.* Passing a value to a form's OpenArgs property is even easier than setting the Tag because only a single line of code is needed:

```
DoCmd.OpenForm "frmCust", , , , , , "Sally"
```

The OpenArgs property can be referenced in the same fashion—from code and from expressions—as the Tag property. The negative attribute of OpenArgs is that it's read-only once the form is opened. You can easily reset a form's Tag value repeatedly while the form is open, but resetting the OpenArgs value requires an additional OpenForm method, which is quirky.

Note

If your code opens a form as a dialog by using `OpenForm` with its `WindowMode` argument set to `acDialog`, the calling code pauses at the `OpenForm` line and does not continue until the form is closed. The only viable strategy for passing information to a form called this way is via the `OpenArgs` argument. Because the calling code pauses, any code after the `OpenForm` line that sets a form's `Tag`, custom variable, or custom property will not run until after the form closes, producing an error.

Public variables. Storing information in a variable declared `Public` makes it available from any code in the application, which is convenient. However, `Public` variables are out of scope in some expressions. For example, the `DefaultValue` property setting shown in Figure 14.21 could *not* be altered to reference a `Public` (or global) variable, as in this syntax:

```
=lci_gstrCurrentUser
```

The workaround is to create a function that returns the global variable, and to use the function in places where the variable can't be addressed. Thus, a `Public` function `lci_CurrentUserGet()` can be created whose return value is set to the value of the `lci_gstrCurrentUser`. The function could then be placed in the `DefaultValue` of a Text Box control.

Custom properties. Chapter 12, "Understanding Form Structures and Coding," explores various techniques for creating custom properties in forms, both as exposed variables and using property procedures. Properties created in this manner can be addressed by form code. For example, assume your form has the public navigation variable, `mvarCalledFrom`, described in "Opening Forms in Sequence" earlier in this chapter. The following reference in a control's `DefaultValue` will return the value of the custom property:

```
=[Form].[mvarCalledFrom]
```

Likewise, if the form contained a custom property created with `Property Let`, the matching `Property Get` procedure, called `prpCalledFrom`, can be used in a form expression as well:

```
=[Form].[prpCalledFrom]
```

A system control. You can create an almost unlimited number of value containers on a form as hidden Text Box controls (we call hidden controls used by program code *system controls*). For many new developers, these are easier to conceptualize and use than some of the more esoteric techniques, like custom properties. For example,

14

you can locate a hidden Text Box control called `zhtxtCalledFrom` on your form and set or get the form property in that text box at any time. Any code in the application can directly address the text box, like this:

```
Forms!frmCust!zhtxtCalledFrom = "Sally"
```

A system form. Most of the preceding options I listed involved placing information within the form's workspace to make is easily accessible to the form. The final technique provides a uniquely different approach, but only works for values that are application-wide (such as the user name), rather than form-specific (such as the calling form's name). The technique involves creating what we call a *system form*, or simply a collection of text boxes on a form designed only for holding global values.

The system form usually contains Text Box controls for the various values that might be needed by every form (and possibly report) in the system, such as the user name, access rights, login session ID, elapsed time in the session (imagine a text box fed by a form's `Timer` event), and so forth. System forms are hidden from the user and never displayed.

System forms have the following three distinct positive merits:

▶ *Ease of reference.* Once set, a value on a system form can be referenced with simple `Forms!zhfrmWorkspace!`*fieldname* syntax from program code as well as in form/report expressions.

▶ *Ease of testing/debugging.* Once the system form is loaded and in use, system values on the form can be reviewed by simply choosing <u>W</u>indow, <u>U</u>nhide... and reviewing the form's text boxes. This is faster and less cryptic than trying to dump variable values.

Better yet, imagine you are testing how a form responds to the system value for user security level. With a system form, you can set a value on the form, load and test a dependent form, then change the value on the system form and repeat the process. This is all very quick and simple compared to achieving the same result with variables.

▶ *Persistence.* When debugging, code execution problems sometimes necessitate a reset of program code, which clears variables in both standard and form modules. A reset does not, however, clear values on your system form—they remain ready for use.

▶ We've even bound our system form to a table and saved the values at regular intervals. This actually enables you to restore the most recent system values when restarting an application, which has great value in some application models.

To be fair, system forms also have a disadvantage: they do not appeal to programming *purists* who believe that everything important must happen in VBA code. If you are a purist, you will use global variables, a global array, or a global collection to store system-wide values that are transitory. I've reviewed six options for passing application information around between code and forms. You may want to evaluate each method and to select a single approach as a standard. Alternately, you may find that each application has unique needs and each expert form may even require its own special approach.

Navigation Issues for Reports

Why is a report issue cropping up in a forms chapter? Because, I prefer that my expert forms call reports in many cases when the user chooses to print, rather than simply printing the current form.

Why? What's so bad about printing the current form? It's true that Access forms can be made to print very attractively, complete with headers and footers whose DisplayWhen property ensures that they only show up on the hard copy, as Figure 14.22 shows. However, my style choice is based not so much on presentation quality, but rather on usability.

Fig. 14.22

This form has custom property settings that show the page header but not the form header when printing.

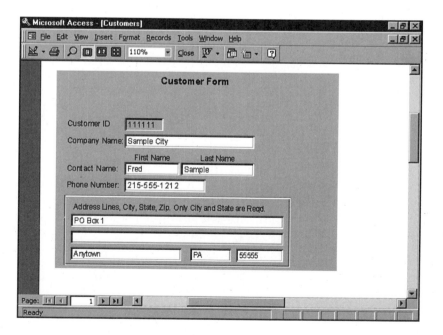

Consider the following issues that derive from print previewing a form:

Form settings are bypassed. In "Enforcing the Modal Interface" section earlier in this chapter, we explored some of the benefits of opening forms in a fixed-size, modal state, and without the Control menu or Close, Minimize, and Maximize buttons. When the user changes a form like this to print preview mode, Access adds these missing buttons to the form window. The user can now close the form (bypassing code on your custom Close button), resize the form (which affects the size of the form when preview mode is terminated), or maximize the window.

The latter selection even causes the form's window to stay maximized when preview mode is terminated, meaning that a modal form that you've disabled form maximization on is now stuck in a maximized state with no Restore button. When trying to create expert forms, these usability issues are indeed annoying.

The print preview toolbar is displayed. In print preview mode, forms display the Print Preview toolbar, which contains some buttons you may not want to expose to the user, including the Office Links button, the Database Window button, and the New Object button. (Fortunately, these buttons can be removed by creating a custom print preview toolbar and attaching the toolbar to each form.)

All records are printed. Unless you provide a mechanism for the user to select the current record before printing, Access prints all the records in the recordset. This is often more data than the user intended to see.

Graphics slow printing and consume toner. Printing a form, with its gray background and 3-D effects, is a much slower proposition and consumes more print toner or ink than printing a less visually complex report.

Printing forms is not paper-friendly. Most screen forms are designed to be four- to six-inches wide and display data from the top down, although most reports are eight inches wide and use the more space-efficient columnar layout. Thus, a report may use less than half the paper of a similarly detailed form.

The first two problems can be bypassed if you disable print preview and only provide users with direct printing from the form. But most users immediately notice and complain about the removal of print preview from an application. Chapter 18, "Creating Expert Reports," expands on this discussion of printing forms as reports.

Our expert forms approach is to create reports for those forms for which the user expects a printing option. The custom logic on a form's matching report can be made much smarter than the printing of a form by Access via a toolbar button. With custom printing logic, users can select only the current record, a range of records, or all records as determined by the reporting code that you write.

In addition, closing the print preview of a report does not close or otherwise affect the underlying form. You are also able to intercept the display problems noted previously with respect to a maximized window state by simply placing the following code in each report's Close event:

```
DoCmd.Restore
```

This code undoes a maximization state induced by the user during preview and returns your form to its original size.

From Here...

Creating the visual elements of a form does not take very long, but defining and building a robust user interface mechanism to make the form more usable and powerful can be very time consuming. This chapter defined some of the strategies for creating forms that guide users gently through your applications.

The following chapters in this book provide information about expert forms and related concepts:

▶ Chapter 8, "Designing Effective Interfaces," provides a detailed discussion of form design concepts.

▶ See Chapter 12, "Understanding Form Structures and Coding," for an overview of creating and coding forms.

▶ Chapter 15, "Protecting and Validating Data," discusses navigation issues that affect moving within a form's recordset and debates the merits of exposing users to various built-in Access commands.

▶ See Chapter 17, "Bulletproofing Your Application Interface," for concepts and techniques related to providing a solid and structured application interface.

14

Protecting and Validating Data

15

C reating forms that expose data to users is much easier than creating forms that *protect* the data from users. One of the reasons an application needs forms (as opposed to simply exposing users to datasheets) is because forms contain properties and code. Form and control properties and event code can be used to minimize the ways that a user can enter erroneous or incomplete data into a database. In this chapter, I provide practical advice for creating forms.

Nightmare Finding Elm Street

The suburb I grew up in is laid out in a near-perfect grid. Streets run north to south and east to west, with even house numbers always on the east and north sides of the street. There are ten blocks to a mile. Give me any address in my hometown and I can tell you how far it is from where I am standing and how to get there by walking, driving, or flying.

When I was in college, I sold real estate on the weekends to pay for tuition. I had to navigate all over Seattle, often late at night and far from the comfort of my hometown's orderly grid. In Seattle, streets like Elm and Maple are nowhere near Oak and Pine, and each street, lane, park, or court can run in any given direction for two blocks, turn 90 degrees for two more, and then double back on itself completely. Suffice to say, finding a building in Seattle requires good navigational aids.

When users work in your application, would you rather they savor the pleasure of its easy, orderly layout—like cruising the streets of my hometown—or struggle with a map and compass, lost in a big-city labyrinth of features and forms?

If you can keep complex applications from looking complex to their users, you can ensure that they easily will find the data and features they need. A little extra coding and layout effort, coupled with a few clever interface techniques, can make the difference between a navigable application and scores of lost, wandering users.

An expert form must find a delicate balance: it must lead the user to the data and then protect the data from the user. Regardless of their aptitude or training, users are human and will make mistakes in your application at some point, and those mistakes will cost somebody time and money. Expert forms are designed to minimize mistakes and should do the following:

▶ Remove any Access features that might cause problems or confusion for the user.

▶ Add routines and features to protect and check the data as the user works.

In Chapter 14, "Navigating in Forms and Applications," I describe the following concepts:

▶ Displaying forms in sequence

▶ Controlling form window modes

▶ Displaying as few forms as possible at one time

▶ Navigating via switchboards, menus, and toolbars

Each of these concepts is important to application usability. In this chapter, I drill-down from broad navigation concepts to specific form design techniques to regulate the interaction between users and data. The techniques in this chapter are optional and follow a very restrictive application interface paradigm. You may choose to use a subset of these techniques or create your own derivative techniques from my examples, but in either case the problems and concepts addressed in this chapter deserve thoughtful consideration as you construct applications. The code samples will also provide you with food for thought.

Protecting Data and Assisting Users

We've all heard the common question asked of parents, "It's 9 P.M.; do you know where your children are and what they are doing?" Parents like to know that their children are happy and safe. As a developer, this question translates to "It's 9 A.M.; do you know where your users are in the application and what they're doing?" Developers like to know that their users are happy and their data is safe. Creating this kind of environment means controlling how the users interact with forms and other objects and with data.

As you monitor user interaction, you must observe and respond to various actions, including the following:

- ▶ Keystrokes
- ▶ Mouse actions
- ▶ Moving between records
- ▶ Record saves
- ▶ Adding and deleting records
- ▶ Initiating built-in features

The following sections provide thoughts and tips for building applications in which such actions do not escape the notice of your underlying program code.

Trapping Dangerous Keystrokes

Access 97 provides you with more tools than ever to monitor the keyboard and to limit how users interact with your forms. As a bonus, several form coding techniques we heavily relied on in Access versions 1 and 2 have now become built-in product features, as discussed in the sections that follow:

- ▶ The *Cycle* property allows your forms to restrict navigation using the Tab key to the current page of a form.
- ▶ Startup property values can be set to control what level of interaction the user has with menus, toolbars, the Database window, and the keyboard.
- ▶ Keyboard monitoring routines can be written to trap keystrokes coming to the application.

Cycling: The Old Way and the New Way

When building Access expert forms, sometimes you will want to trap keyboard actions and provide the user with navigation assistance, directing the cursor to a specific location.

One simple navigation assistant is called a "tab sentry." A tab sentry is a control placed at a strategic location on a form to intercept Tab and Shift+Tab keystrokes and reroute the focus to a specific location or launch some other process. In Access 2, you most commonly placed a tab sentry at the bottom of each form as the last control in the tab order. When a user tabbed to the control, the Enter event of the sentry fired, executing code to intercept the intention of Access to move to the next record and "cycling" the focus back to the first control on the current form instead. In this manner, you could prevent the user from pressing Tab to move off the current record.

 Note

Using tab sentries differs from using a control's LostFocus event to detect movement out of a control because the tab sentry is designed to trap the use of the Tab and Enter keys when leaving a control; LostFocus is activated by mouse movements as well.

Sentries at the Gate

Many of my Access articles and speeches over the past several years have focused on helping developers create systems to control form navigation. Tab sentries have always been a featured topic in such presentations. Generally, despite the several dozen tips that I might include in a navigation presentation, tab sentries generate an overwhelming majority of the positive feedback. I've concluded the following from this fact:

▶ Although Microsoft wants us to live and die by our mouse, the reality is that there are plenty of keyboard-centric users and developers left, migrating slowly from mainframe and minicomputer terminals to PCs. These users want keyboard-friendly applications.

▶ Access does not provide enough built-in options to empower developers to develop keyboard-centric systems.

Thus, tab sentries remain a fact of life for expert forms developers.

15

The new Current Record setting for the Cycle property of a form now removes the need for tab sentries for "inter-record" navigation. Cycle is a form-level property with the following values and uses:

AlI Records. This setting turns off cycle control. Use it on forms when you intend for the user to tab freely between form pages and between records.

Current Record. With this setting, the user can press Tab to move between any fields on the current record (even spanning pages) but cannot tab to the next or previous record. Use this setting when you build forms where the user must consciously choose to move between records by selecting a button, a combo box value, or a similar navigation option.

Current Page. This setting prevents the user from tabbing off of the current page in a multi-page form. Use the setting when you prefer to have your users click a page number button or otherwise consciously choose to move between form pages on the current record.

Although the addition of the Cycle property solved the problem of users wandering from the current form record or page via Tab, the property still does not address other navigation situations. Therefore, even with the Cycle property, there are situations in which tab sentries can provide value to your forms. I'll give two examples.

The first useful placement of tab sentries is to control navigation into and out of single-record subforms. Subform controls present the following two navigation problems:

▶ When the user leaves the subform via a mouse, the focus inside the subform remains on the last control with the focus. The next visit to the subform via a Tab key returns the focus to the previous location in the subform, not the first control in the subform.

▶ Once inside a subform, the user cannot use the Tab key to exit the subform. In a continuous subform, the Tab key moves to the next record, as it should. In a single-record subform, however, you may desire the user to be able to tab off of the last control in the subform and return to the parent form.

To provide a more friendly subform navigation model, place Command Button controls at the locations desired for the sentries—one just before the Subform control, and one inside the subform as the last control in the tab order. For these sentries, set the Transparent property of the buttons to True. This setting enables each control to receive focus via a Tab keystroke yet does not display the control to the user. Finally, add code to the Enter event for each control to initiate the desired movement when the control receives the focus via a Tab key. To move focus into the subform, the `Enter` event uses this code:

```
Me!subSentry.SetFocus
Me!subSentry.Form!txtFirstName.SetFocus
```

 Note

You cannot move focus from a parent form directly to a control in its subform. The focus change requires the two steps shown in the previous code listing: one step moving to the `Subform` control and another moving to the subform's `Text Box` control.

The subform `Sentry` control's `Enter` event uses this code to move focus from the subform back to the parent form:

```
Me.Parent.txtFirst.SetFocus
```

 Note

You can also use a text box as a `Sentry` control, but doing so involves more work on your part. A text box whose `Visible` property is `False` is removed from the tab sequence, so you must keep the control visible and instead set the `BackColor` and `BorderColor` to match the form's background. This makes the text box seem invisible when the form is run. These settings make the control invisible in design view also which can be frustrating during your development work.

Figure 15.1 shows the design view of an example form with a subform and two tab sentries. Note the location of the transparent buttons that serve as sentries.

 Tip

Make your tab sentry buttons very small. Even though the tab sentries are transparent, the user can unintentionally click them, which may cause some confusion. You can type a small value such as 0.001 into the `Width` property of the `Sentry` control and Access will set the control to its smallest allowed size.

Alternatively, you can place a tab sentry control behind another control so that users cannot unknowingly click it.

Fig. 15.1

This form has a tab sentry on the parent form and another on the subform.

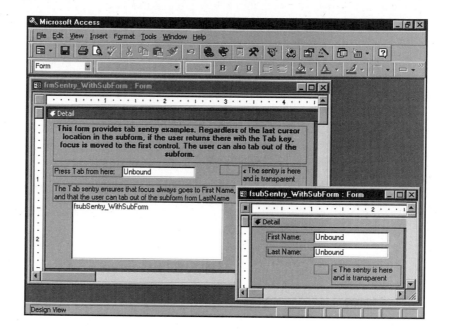

A second useful implementation of tab sentries is on multi-page forms. Simply setting the Cycle property to Current Page and teaching users to press PgDn and PgUp to navigate between pages may not provide the friendliest approach for some users. As an example, create a two-page form with text boxes on each page and the Cycle property set to Current Record. When you tab off the last field on page 1, Access only displays enough of page 2 to show the next control in the tab sequence, as shown in Figure 15.2.

Fig. 15.2

Pressing Tab in the last control on a page scrolls to the first control on the next page instead of synchronizing the page display.

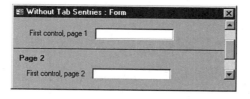

If users want to navigate between controls on consecutive form pages with the Tab and Enter keys and have the pages align properly, you need to employ tab sentries. To create a tab sentry for pagination, use a Command Button control with the Transparent property set to True. The user can tab to the button, triggering the Enter event, but the button does not display on the form. Attach to your tab sentry button an Enter event in code that performs the desired movement:

```
Private Sub zscmdSentry1_Enter()
  Me.GoToPage 2
End Sub
```

When the user tabs to the sentry button, the Enter event fires and synchronizes the form to page 2, making for a much more pleasurable form navigation. After you are on page 2, however, you have the problem of how to return to page 1 because using Shift+Tab to do so introduces the same out-of-sync display problem that occurs when moving forward through pages. To compensate, place a tab sentry at the top of page 2 to trap a Shift+Tab moving backward off the page. Each page now has a top sentry (to handle a Shift+Tab at the first control on the page) and a bottom sentry (to handle a Tab at the last control on a page).

Unfortunately, the top sentry on page 2 can receive focus in two different ways, as follows:

▶ As the user pressing Shift+Tab goes backward from the first control on page 2 heading toward page 1

▶ As the user presses Tab to move forward from page 1 to page 2

The challenge is that your code must trap and ignore the second situation while facilitating the first; otherwise, the sentry at the top of page 2 will receive focus as page 2 is displayed, execute its code, and bounce the focus right back to page 1. You will have created a nonsensical loop.

The sentry at the top of each multi-page form must cleverly know when the user is tabbing backward through the controls and wants to see the previous page, and when the user is coming from the previous page. The code in Listing 15.1 addresses this need.

Listing 15.1   AES_Frm3.Mdb—A Smart Page 2 Tab Sentry

```
Private Sub zscmdSentry2_Enter()

  ' If not moving to page 1, stay on this page
  If Screen.PreviousControl.Name <> "txtSecond" Then
    Me!txtSecond.SetFocus
  Else  ' Must be moving to page 1 from txtSecond
    Me.GoToPage 1
  End If

End Sub
```

α **Note**

When using tab sentries, you can safely use `Screen.PreviousControl` in the code to determine which control the user is tabbing from. Because tab sentry code is tied to the `Enter` event, which fires before the control's `GotFocus` event, `Sentry` controls technically never receive the focus and thus never register as a `PreviousControl`.

Now consider the ultimate navigation hybrid: buttons that serve as tab sentries for keyboard users that also can be clicked to navigate with the mouse. Such buttons must be located at form locations and in the tab sequence in a manner that enables them to fulfill both of these objectives, and they must not be set as transparent because users need to see the caption or graphic on the button to click it.

Figure 15.3 shows a form with tab sentries that also serve as visible navigation buttons. Because the Access Enter event is fired by both the keyboard movement to the button and a mouse click to the button, this single event provides the mechanism for both types of navigation from the same button.

Fig. 15.3

This form has three pages and tab sentries to allow users to use Tab *and* Shift+Tab *to move between the pages.*

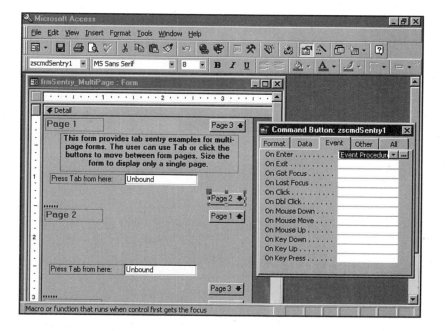

Tip

Tab sentries are very useful if you need to create a form that has pages aligned not only downward but across. You can create forms in Access that are wider than the screen display and use the `Right` and `Down` arguments of the `GoToPage` method to move the screen window from left to right to view the pages. Usually this technique is employed to create forms with more pages than can be created in the Access maximum form-section height of 22 inches. Because the user cannot use `PgDn` and `PgUp` to move to pages located to the right or left, tab sentries are your salvation in this situation.

Disabling Keystrokes with Startup Properties

Beginning with version 95, Access provided a new property for limiting some specific user keystrokes. The property is set in the Startup dialog box available from the Tools menu, as shown in Figure 15.4.

Fig. 15.4

The Startup options dialog box has an option to disable four powerful Access keystrokes.

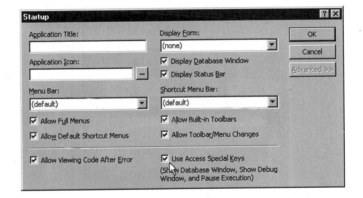

Clearing the check box labeled Use Access Special Keys disables the high-level keyboard shortcuts shown in Table 15.1. These keystrokes and the new Startup dialog box are explained in greater detail in Chapter 17, "Bulletproofing Your Application Interface."

Table 15.1   Keystrokes Disabled by the Startup Option Use Access Special Keys

Keystroke	Action
F11, Alt+F1	Shows the Database window
Ctrl+G	Shows the Debug window
Ctrl+F11	Alternates between menu bars
Ctrl+Break	Pauses code and displays the module window

Startup property settings travel with the database—not the workstation, so you need only clear the special keys check box once when building the application. You must close and reopen the database to see the effect of the setting.

In spite of this useful new feature, many other keystrokes still cause concern in an application, and they are not so easily disabled. The next two sections address further protective techniques you can use to watch the keyboard.

Disabling Keystrokes with *Autokeys*

Several Access keyboard shortcuts provide powerful functionality to careful users and developers. The same keystrokes can just as easily prove dangerous to an application's data, however.

Two convincing examples of dangerous keystrokes are the Ctrl+H shortcut to display the Replace dialog box and the Ctrl+A combination to select all records in a form's recordset. In both cases, an unsophisticated user can easily affect disastrous bulk changes on multiple records, perhaps even thinking that he or she is only altering a single record.

Many keystroke combinations like these can be disabled using an AutoKeys macro entry that maps the keystroke to do nothing by leaving the Action value blank, as shown in the AutoKeys macro in Figure 15.5. Restricting these keystrokes is described in more detail in Chapter 17, "Bulletproofing Your Application Interface."

Fig. 15.5

This AutoKeys *macro disables most built-in keyboard shortcuts for unsophisticated users.*

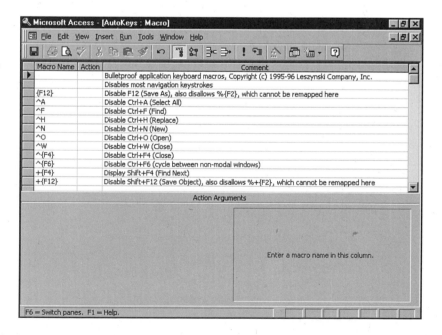

> **Tip**
>
> If your application's users are quite familiar with these Access keyboard shortcuts, some of them may be confused when familiar keystroke combinations stop functioning. To assist such users, you can place a MsgBox statement in the Action column of the macro instead of leaving the column blank, and your message box text can tell the user what menu or toolbar options they should use to replace the removed functionality. Alternatively, you can use a keyboard macro or a form keyboard handler to detect the standard keystroke and redirect it to run your own version of the feature.

A few keyboard shortcuts cannot be intercepted with keyboard macros. These keystrokes, such as Ctrl+Shift+Spacebar to select all records, are listed in Chapter 17, "Bulletproofing Your Application Interface." You must use code to trap these keys, as shown in that chapter and in the next section.

Trapping Keystrokes Coming to a Form or Control

You may want to add code to a form to watch the keyboard for specific events. Such code (often called a keyboard handler) is one of the ways to trap and discard keyboard shortcuts that you choose to disable on a specific form.

You can also use keyboard handlers to watch for keystrokes that have special meaning to the form or application. To trap keystrokes, use one of the following Access events:

KeyDown. This event fires when the user presses down a key or keyboard combination. KeyDown traps both the primary key and any key shift information (the state of Ctrl, Alt, and Shift). KeyDown (and its sibling, KeyUp) traps keystrokes that do not display a character to the user, including the following:

- ▶ Function keys
- ▶ Navigation keys (arrows, End, Home, and so on)
- ▶ Combinations of keys with Alt, Ctrl, and Shift

> **Note**
>
> KeyDown can fire multiple times if a key is held down, making it a poor choice for trapping keystroke combinations that should execute a process rather than a single action. Use KeyUp instead, subject to the caveat described for it.

KeyPress. KeyPress fires between KeyDown and KeyUp and will fire once for each related KeyDown event. KeyPress does not provide shift state information about a keystroke; it only returns the ANSI value of the primary keystroke. Put another way, this event detects the numeric value returned by using the Asc() function on the character displayed to the user by the keystroke.

KeyUp. This event fires when the user releases a key that was pressed down. It only fires once even if multiple KeyDown and KeyPress events were generated. KeyUp traps both the primary key and any key shift information (the state of Ctrl, Alt, and Shift).

You can trap keystrokes at the form level, the control level, or both. Each control, as well as the form itself, lists the three keyboard events. Setting the KeyPreview property of a form to True ensures that the form's keyboard events will fire before a control's events. The events are not mutually exclusive, meaning that a key pressed on txtCust fires the KeyDown event for the form first and then the same event for the text box.

Based on these event descriptions, you can discern that KeyDown is the most reliable overall choice for trapping keystrokes coming to a form or control. KeyPress is also useful but to a lesser degree—use it when the keyboard test does not need to provide shift key information and does not involve cursor movement keys.

As an example, assume that your new Access application replaced an older application where you could use the Ctrl+F2 key combination to highlight the remaining text in an entry field, much the same as Shift+End works in Access. Your users expect and want the Ctrl+F2 keystroke to function the same way in your Access application as in their previous applications.

Listing 15.2 shows a sample KeyDown event at the form level to trap Ctrl+F2 and provide the text highlighting functionality your users request.

Listing 15.2 AES_Frm3.Md—A Keydown Event Providing a Form-Level Keyboard Handler

```
Private Sub Form_KeyDown(KeyCode As Integer, Shift As Integer)
' Purpose: Trap the key combination Ctrl+F2 coming to a text box
'          control and highlight the remainder of the text.
'          The form's KeyPreview property must be True.

  Dim ctl    As Control  ' Active control
  Dim blnCtrl As Boolean  ' To test for Ctrl key

  Set ctl = Me.ActiveControl
  If ctl.ControlType <> acTextBox Then
    Exit Sub
  End If
```

continues

Listing 15.2   Continued

```
If blnCtrl And KeyCode = vbKeyF2 Then   ' Ctrl+F2 pressed
  If ctl.SelStart < Len(ctl.Text) Then ' Nothing to do if at end
    ctl.SelLength = Len(ctl.Text) - ctl.SelStart   ' Highlight text
  End If
End If

End Sub
```

 Tip

Use generic keyboard handlers whenever you want your form to be "smart" about keystrokes. In the previous example, notice that I created the keyboard handler at the form level rather than at the control level, then simply made the handler abort when the current control was not of the desired type. This type of centralized, generic keyboard handler is much easier to create and maintain than one placed in the keyboard events of each individual control.

Note in Listing 15.2 that the state of the Shift argument is detected by storing in a variable the comparison between the key state in the Shift argument and a keyboard constant (acAltMask, acCtrlMask, and acShiftMask are the intrinsic constants to use). The Shift argument is a bit field with bits 0, 1, and 2 flipped to represent Shift, Ctrl, and Alt respectively; thus, you must test their state with bitwise math (as in Shift And acCtrlMask).

If you intend to trap keystrokes to disable certain key combinations rather than to trigger an action, you can render keys inert by altering the KeyCode argument in the KeyDown and KeyUp events. Set the argument to 0 at the end of the event procedure to disable the keystroke, as in this code:

```
KeyCode = 0
```

To disable the key sent to KeyPress procedure, set the KeyAscii argument to 0 in place of the KeyCode.

 Caution

When detecting keystrokes coming to a control, be aware that the control that currently has the focus generates KeyUp and KeyPress, making these events somewhat dangerous for detecting navigation keystrokes. For example, if the user presses the Tab key, the current control receives the KeyDown event, then the focus moves to the next control in tab order. This second control actually executes its `KeyPress` and `KeyUp` events; these same events for the first control do not fire.

Using keyboard handlers, you can detect and discard or reroute keystroke combinations, such as Ctrl+Shift+Spacebar (<u>E</u>dit, Select <u>A</u>ll Records), that you do not want to be active in your application.

Determining Allowed Menu and Toolbar Options

You might have noticed that some of my expert form examples in this book do not use the Access built-in toolbars but rather place toolbar buttons directly on the forms, as shown in Figure 15.6.

Fig. 15.6

This form has embedded toolbar buttons only.

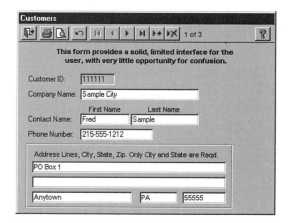

This embedded toolbar button model provides me with complete control of the user's environment with no activities assigned to macros or command bars and little else left to chance. Whether you agree with my metaphor, you should consider the relative merits and dangers of using Access menus, Access toolbars, and embedded toolbar buttons in various combinations.

 Note

If you have not done so already, read the section "Navigating via Menus and Toolbars" in Chapter 14, "Navigating in Forms and Applications," to gain a better understanding of the strengths and limitations of the new Access command bar technology.

Deciding Between the Access Commands and Your Own Commands

The navigation code shown in the section "Replacing the Navigation Buttons" in Chapter 14, "Navigating in Forms and Applications," can enable or disable embedded buttons at will or even hide, show, and rearrange buttons. This provides my application with control over its environment, a situation that does not arise when I rely on the Access toolbars, over which I have little control. Additionally, the following are a few other reasons why embedded form toolbars can prove useful:

Forms are self-contained. To reuse a form that employs a toolbar or menu bar in another application, you must import the form, its toolbars, and its standard module "wrapper" functions for the toolbars. You cannot import specific toolbars in Access 97; thus, you get all custom toolbars from the host database when you really only wanted a specific set. This effort is a bit of a hassle. By contrast, embedded buttons and their code travel with the form—the form is a completely self-contained object.

Embedding provides the least painful conversion path. You can create forms that use embedded buttons and thus wean yourself from the abandoned menu macro technology of previous Access versions without jumping into command bars. In the future, if you choose to change the embedded buttons to toolbar buttons, the toolbars mostly will be able to reuse the code in your form.

Buttons provide complete control of events. When the user clicks a tool on the Access toolbar, such as Delete Record or New Record, an event is immediately initiated. Your code must work very hard to detect the event, determine whether it is legitimate for the specific user and the specific record status, and try to cancel the event if it is not. This situation is much easier to handle with embedded buttons, so that all such status checking can be done *before* an event is initiated.

Embedding provides control of the button state. Access' attempts to make its toolbars "friendly" for the user may not match the model your users prefer. For example, Access cleverly disables the Next Record and Previous Record buttons when there is no next or previous record to move to, but it does not disable the First Record or Last Record buttons in the appropriate context. Your embedded buttons can handle this situation better with only a small amount of coding.

Despite this rationale, most developers are quite comfortable using custom or built-in toolbars and menus in their applications for specific forms or form groups. You will have to experiment and decide which style suits you best and when your needs warrant a more restrictive model.

It is also possible to create a hybrid style that uses a generic Access toolbar for truly generic tools and that embeds tools on forms for the rest of the work, as shown in Figure 15.7.

Fig. 15.7

This form mixes custom embedded buttons on the form with the Access built-in toolbar buttons.

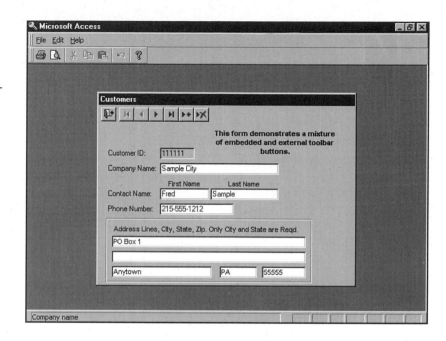

While it is tempting to assume that many Access toolbar buttons and menu options are good candidates for use with your forms, even some seemingly innocuous features can be dangerous. Consider the complexity of the following "simple" toolbar buttons:

Tools, Spelling. This button checks the spelling of the currently selected object, which is useful and painless when the object is a single form control or a single record. However, if the user is able to select all records in a form's recordset, the spelling action will check the entire recordset. Moving through each record in the recordset and making spelling changes will trigger Current, BeforeUpdate, and other events for the affected records, which may or may not fit cleanly with your form's validation model. Bulk spelling changes enable wholesale, and often erroneous, changes of data.

Edit, Cut/Copy/Paste. Using these options at the control (field) level does not have negative consequences. If the user can select a record or all records in a form, however, the Cut action will trigger a Delete event for each affected record, which may or may not fit cleanly with your form's deletion tracking model. Worse, the user can cut an entire form's recordset to the clipboard, effectively clearing an entire table.

My point here is that tools save or delete a record and all of its related events, and may cause problems when placed on a form toolbar or menu, so you should use them with caution or at least be alert to their power.

> **Caution**
> For any form with which you can navigate between records using the Access
> toolbar or menus, you must locate the form's record validation code in the
> BeforeUpdate event so that it will be called as the form navigates. Placing validation
> code on an embedded navigation button that can be circumvented by a toolbar or
> menu selection is dangerous.

In deciding how to balance the placement of Access' features against your coded routines (as embedded buttons on a form or custom options on a menu or toolbar), consider three more key points:

1. *Match toolbar options to menu options.* An old Windows rule of thumb states that every toolbar button must have a corresponding menu option. When you mix Access toolbars and menu bars with your customized interface elements, you should keep this maxim in mind. It is becoming more common, however, for toolbars to be present when menu options are not.

2. A primary concern is that keyboard-centric users must be able to initiate your custom features. When you place embedded buttons on a form and the buttons have no corresponding menu option, users may bemoan the loss of a keyboard activation method. To compensate, add keyboard shortcuts to your form buttons.

3. *Notice which object has the focus.* Remember that two different coding models are at work when you mix embedded form buttons with toolbar buttons and menu options. A custom command bar routine must look at the ActiveForm and ActiveControl objects to discern which form and control operates. An embedded form button must instead locate the PreviousControl object to achieve the same result.

4. *Decide how much control you need.* Placing buttons on forms versus using toolbars and menus is all about control. How much control you need will determine the model you adopt.

Crafting a balance between custom form buttons and built-in Access features is both an art (the art of user interface design) and a science (the science of coding). Consequently, you may find strong discussion among your fellow developers about the points I have made in this section.

Selecting the Appropriate Menu Options

Crafting retail-quality expert forms requires that you pay close attention to usability and interface design. While generally accepted interface guidelines require that you provide your users with a menu bar, you are sometimes faced with the conflicting desire to control the user's interaction with the form, and menu bars in Access have historically not facilitated this well.

The advent of programmable command bars has improved the developer's lot somewhat in this area. When building your user interface elements, you can now easily choose between using a built-in Access feature or creating a custom one. In either case, you can provide users with access to your feature set through menus or toolbars that look and work professionally.

Keyboard-centric users historically prefer a rich set of menu options, so if you lean toward embedded form buttons (as discussed in the previous section), they may feel slighted. On the positive side, you can balance your custom form options with standard menu options. In doing so, you can create generic, reusable menus for your application that perform standard tasks while still disabling the Access features that you want to replace and handle through form code.

For a menu bar or toolbar to be generic, it must apply to any kind of form your application might display: data-bound forms, fill-in dialog boxes, switchboard menus, and so on. Therefore, a truly generic menu is quite sparse, as shown in Table 15.2.

Table 15.2   The Truly Generic Access Menu Options

Menu	Option	Action or Code
File	Exit	`Application.RunCommand acCmdExit`
Help	Contents and Index	Launch the application's help
Help	About	`OpenForm` on a custom About dialog box

If you want to add more commands than these to your standard form menus, you must understand the advantages and dangers of each Access menu item exposed through the `RunCommand` method (the core command for your menu actions). Table 15.3 lists examples of the internal menu options that I would not normally use on an expert form.

Table 15.3   Some Built-in Menu Options Dangerous to Custom Forms

Menu	Option
File	New Database...
File	Open Database...
File	Get External Data
File	Save
File	Save As/Export...
File	Database Properties

continues

Table 15.3   Continued

Menu	Option
View	Design View
View	Toolbars
Tools	Relationships...
Tools	Analyze
Tools	Security
Tools	Replication
Tools	Startup...
Tools	Run Macro...
Tools	ActiveX Controls...
Tools	Options...
Window	all options
Help	Microsoft Access Help
Help	What's This

In your particular application, a feature in the preceding table may, in fact, provide useful capabilities to a specific form. Providing one of these native Access capabilities on your standard menu may expose too much opportunity to the user to modify the application objects or disrupt application flow. In such a case, replace the functionality that the Access menu option provides with a custom menu option that calls your own code routines that safely achieve the same objectives. The fact that the Access runtime mode provides none of the built-in menu options listed in Table 15.3 (except for the window and help options) reinforces their limited usefulness in applications.

The following list describes the commands that may be useful for your form menus and toolbars, subject to the concerns stated with each command. Note that a built-in command may perform its job in a way that is not fully appropriate to an expert solution, so I usually prefer making custom toolbars for many applications. (See examples of my highly customized menus and toolbars in Chapter 14, "Navigating in Forms and Applications.") In this list, commands that the runtime mode in Access provides are noted with an (r):

 File, Close. If you choose to include File, Close on your custom menu, you should call the custom close procedure code you have written for the form, not the Close method, which does a "brute force" form close. Enabling your form to validate in its Close event as triggered by File, Close can be difficult, so it is easier to close the form with a function that initiates your validation routines and does other cleanup work (see "Closing Forms in Sequence" in Chapter 14, "Navigating in Forms and Applications," for more information).

File, Page Setup. Users may need this option on a form if they are able to print the form itself. It is only useful in conjunction with the File, Print... option.

File, Print/Print Preview. These buttons print the current form, which is acceptable in some contexts, but I prefer that forms print a report for the displayed record rather than printing the form. Printed forms usually look cluttered, and reports provide more readable hard copy layouts. Further, allowing Access to manage printing may generate an error if the validation triggered by the save fails. Even if your code properly cancels the BeforeUpdate event, the print routine generates a confusing error: "You can't save this object at this time."

File, Send. This option enables your user to send a representation of the form and its data as an electronic mail message containing an Excel file, a Rich Text Format document, or a simple text file. Although you may find this option to be convenient, you can provide better content layout and more control of e-mail messages from program code.

File, Exit. Most applications will display this menu option to close and terminate the application. Depending on your validation model, however, this action may interrupt a pending database or code process, so be wary.

Edit, Undo/Cut/Copy/Paste. Most Windows users are familiar with the keyboard shortcuts to initiate these features, yet placing the commands on application menus makes the application friendly to the broadest range of users. Be aware, however, that the Cut operation at the record level will trigger Delete event code in your form and must be validated and audited in the same manner as any other deletion. Rarely will users need the ability to copy or cut a record to the Clipboard.

Edit, Paste Special. This option may be appropriate for forms that contain Bound Object Frame controls or have some other need for nonstandard paste functionality.

Edit, Paste Append. Because this option appends one or more new records to the form, I usually do not add it to menus unless it solves a particular need of the specific application. The user may be able to circumvent or confuse form navigation and validation routines by inserting records this way, and he or she must be a sophisticated user to apply the command correctly. If multiple records regularly come into the application from another source, consider creating an import routine to fetch and check the data instead of relying on the Clipboard.

Edit, Delete. Virtually every Windows user knows that the Del key removes the highlighted information, so one can debate the need for displaying this command. There is no harm in showing it, however.

Edit, Delete Record. Using Access instead of your code to delete a record could bypass any programmatic deletion logic and processes you've crafted, so be careful. However, a deletion that Access initiates does trigger the form's Delete event, so using this menu option may be safe if you code appropriately. For this and other reasons detailed in the "Deleting Form Records" section of this chapter, you may want to consider programming your own deletion routines.

Caution

Be careful when allowing users to apply the built-in Delete Record button or the Del key from the keyboard for two reasons. First, it's hard to intercept this type of deletion and write a log record of the deletion or create backup copies of the records to be removed. Second, did you know that a user can press Crtl+Shift+Spacebar to select all records in a form's recordset, then select Delete Record and wipe out all the records in the form's recordset? By controlling deletions from your own button and code, you can better control such situations.

Edit, Select Record. This option removes the focus from a field and selects the entire data record. If your application enables the user to initiate the Cut, Delete, or Spelling actions at the record level, then your form will require either this menu option or the form's record selector. In most applications, I prefer to include the record selection capability in the code that performs the deletion or spell check. This reduces the process for the user from two steps to one and enables me to control the record selection operation and its related save from code.

Edit, Select All Records. Because this feature is primarily useful for a mass copy or deletion, either of which are best controlled through program code, I do not frequently suggest exposing the built-in version of this command in an application.

Edit, Find. The find operation may move to other records and thus trigger an automatic record save of the current record or may move to a record without alerting other processes or objects bound to the current record. (For example, your code opens a recordset in the background with child records for the displayed record and needs to know when the displayed record is changed so that the recordset can be queried again.) On the other hand, a form in datasheet view or a lengthy subform may benefit nicely from this feature. Expert forms frequently provide a programmatic mechanism to assist users with finding records and don't require this menu option.

 Edit, Replace. We rarely permit users to do bulk replacements across a recordset; the consequences can be disastrous in a form with multiple records. If you provide this feature, place the Replace button on the form rather than the toolbar and disable it for nonadministrative users.

 *Edit, Go To, First/Previous/Next/Last.* Move operations trigger an automatic record save of the current record and generate the same concerns as with *Edit, Find...*, mentioned previously. If you provide these options, your form must have its validation code in the BeforeUpdate event to provide validation before the record move occurs. See Chapter 14, "Navigating in Forms and Applications," for more details on enabling user navigation between records.

Edit, OLE/DDE Links. If a form contains enabled (they can receive focus) OLE object fields (bound or unbound Object Frame controls), it is appropriate to place this command on the menu so that users can view and maintain OLE links to external documents.

Edit, Object. On a form with enabled (they can receive focus) OLE object fields (bound or unbound Object Frame controls), the user can use this menu option to launch the source (Automation server) application. If the form contains an ActiveX control, this command provides access to the control's property page. This option should be provided on menus in both of these cases.

 View, Form/Datasheet. These options should travel together on menus and should only be provided where a form can be displayed legitimately in both of these views with no negative repercussions for the users or the data.

View, Subform Datasheet. You should provide this option where a subform can be displayed legitimately in both form and datasheet views with no negative consequences for the users or the data.

 View, Zoom/Pages. If you provide users with access to File, Print Preview, you may want to provide these options as well so they can refine the preview layout.

 Insert, New Record. Be aware that this option triggers an automatic record save of the current record. Also, note that detecting a new record event from a toolbar button requires special coding in your form (checking the Me.NewRecord property in the Form_Current() event code).

Insert, Object. If a form contains a bound or unbound object Frame control that can receive the focus, the form's menu will need this option; otherwise, do not use it.

Format, Font, and so on. The Format menu is appropriate only for the datasheet view of a form's records. You should only provide the menu and its options via a custom menu attached to forms where datasheet view is accessible and user changes to datasheet layouts are encouraged.

All Records, Filter options. The filtration event triggers an automatic record save of the current record. Also, some users are sophisticated enough to work with filters while others are not, so you must dispense these features in proportion to your users' abilities. Finally, unless your code detects the filtration events, the application's expectations for the content of a form's recordset may be different from the current filtered recordset, causing problems in your code.

 Tip

If you provide users with the ability to filter a form's recordset, give them a button on the toolbar or form that shows them the current filter criteria. Otherwise, they often forget they have filtered the data and become confused when they cannot find a specific expected record. Simply have your button display a message box that shows the value of the `Me.Filter` property.

Records, Sort, Sort Ascending/Sort Descending. We usually open a particular form with a predefined sort order that solves a specific user objective. Sometimes users request the ability to resort a form's recordset on-the-fly, but in other cases users find the feature confusing.

 Caution

When you add the Advanced Filter/Sort toolbar or menu option to a custom menu, Access presents the user with several built-in menu options when in the query grid for filtration, even if you disabled these options on your custom menu. For example, the File and Tools menus are available even if the form's custom menu does not include them. If your application is not running in runtime mode, consider clearing the Allow Full Menus Startup property to remove the display of the most dangerous of these menu options.

Records, Save Record. Depending on how your form is structured, this option may be acceptable to enable users to do interim saves of a record without moving off the record or closing the form. If you enable this option, your validation code must reside in the form's `BeforeUpdate` event to provide validation before the save.

Records, Refre<u>sh</u>. Enabling users to get current data by refreshing the form's recordset is a fine idea, but note that this option initiates a record save and triggers related validation, which should be in `BeforeUpdate`.

Records, <u>D</u>ata Entry. The concept behind this option is valid—to filter out existing form records by setting the form's `DataEntry` property to `True`—but the implementation is flawed. Unlike other filters, the `ApplyFilter` event for the form does not fire when you enable this mode, even though the event does fire when you remove the data-entry filter. This behavior is too awkward for my taste. I prefer to create a custom menu option and/or button to enable data-entry mode through program code so that I can detect the event.

<u>T</u>ools, <u>S</u>pelling. In some applications, this option may be quite useful. Data entered into a database, however, is not frequently standard English syntax that is found in the dictionary, so users may find little practical value in this option. Also be aware that when this option is applied to the form's entire recordset, the user can make wholesale, and potentially inaccurate, changes to data items.

If you limit the spell check to the current record, then record saves and all related events are not initiated and the spell check operation does not move between records. To check only the current record, use code similar to that in Listing 15.3 from a form button or event. Note that you should save and validate the record before you call this code; otherwise, the `SelectRecord` action in the code will save it for you.

Listing 15.3   A Code Routine to Check Spelling Only on the Current Record

```
Private Sub RecordSpell()
' Spell check the current record

  Application.RunCommand acCmdSelectRecord
  Application.RunCommand acCmdSpelling

End Sub
```

<u>T</u>ools, <u>A</u>utoCorrect.... In some applications, it may be acceptable to enable the user to customize the AutoCorrect behavior of the application.

 Caution

AutoCorrect is a helpful but dangerous feature. You cannot detect and disable this option on the workstation through program code, so your application will inherit the AutoCorrect behavior installed on its user's workstation. You should teach your users about its existence and the vigilance required as data items are entered then changed by auto correction. If this feature is deemed too dangerous, disable it by setting the `AllowAutoCorrect` property to `No` on each Text Box and Combo Box control on a form.

You should also teach users that changes to the AutoCorrect behavior in one Office application trickles into the others. Access, Excel, PowerPoint, and Word all share the same ACL (auto correct list) file in the Windows directory, so any change to the behavior made in any other Office tool will trickle into the Access data-entry sessions!

For example, AutoCorrect as shipped changes the letters "CNA" to "CAN." If you have a customer named "CNA Shipping," AutoCorrect makes entering the customer's information in the database frustrating because it constantly changes it. In this example, you may have to customize the AutoCorrect behavior on each user workstation to remove the suggestion for "CNA" to protect data during entry and editing.

Tools, OfficeLinks. For most forms, there is no downside to enabling users to export the presented data using one of the OfficeLinks options as long as the export does not bypass any programmatic security routines. If your needs require more control over the export/merge process, you may decide to forego these tools in favor of programmatic export routines.

Tools, Add-Ins. You generally do not want users to have access to the entire list of add-ins. (For example, do you really want someone running the Database Splitter on your application database?) Instead, add a custom menu option to run a specific add-in if your application requires the tool. To run an add-in, you will need to call its entry function, which can be found by reviewing the add-in settings in the Windows Registry. See Chapter 20, "Applying Development Shortcuts," for more information.

Window, Tile/Cascade. If you enable the user to view multiple forms, especially in datasheet view, you may find value in these menu options. In most applications, though, these options will resize and relocate forms in a manner that is not appropriate for a friendly application interface.

0............... Unless users are able to minimize and restore multiple forms in an application, this option is not needed.

Window, Hide/Unhide. If your application relies on hiding and showing forms as a navigation strategy, you most likely do not want to expose these options to the user who could then disrupt your application flow by changing the display mode of open forms.

Window, Size to Fit Form. In an application that provides forms with a resizable border, this option is helpful to enable users to restore a form's size to the size that you intended for it when you designed it. If your form borders use a fixed size, this option is not needed.

 Help, Microsoft Access Help. It is unlikely that you will want your application to call the Access help system. You will probably want to replace the position of this item with an option that calls your application's own help topics.

 Help, What's This. You can add this feature to each form individually if the form supports What's This Help. A generic version of the command on the menu system is generally not useful in a custom application.

Help, About Microsoft Access. There is no need for your application to call the Access About dialog box, but in the same position on the menu you most likely will place an About option that shows the copyright information and credits for your application instead.

Carefully reading this lengthy listing of access menu and toolbar commands should leave you with the impression that almost every built-in Access menu option has a specific value in a specific application, but most options also have the ability to place power in the hands of the user that your application cannot easily detect or control. As you build an application, you must review this list and consider which built-in Access features are appropriate to place on your application's menu system, which features should be provided by program code instead, and which features are not appropriate at all.

Restricting Access from the Database Window

By definition, an application usually does not include the ability for users to wander in the Database window. Some applications built for sophisticated users may provide navigation from a switchboard menu as well as allowing some work to be done within the Database window. This provides the developer with a conundrum, as follows:

▶ Users need access to objects.

▶ Objects need to be protected from users.

Access security provides the only fail-safe mechanism for limiting users' ability to interact with your objects directly. In its absence, you can use the following techniques to limit the risk when users wander into the Database window:

Hide objects. Each Access object has a property available from its Properties dialog box that you can designate whether the object is hidden or displayed in the Database window, as shown in Figure 15.8. One strategy for selectively manipulating user access to objects is to hide all objects in the Database window except for those you want your users to see.

Tip

You may want to check and set a user's workstation options when he or she opens the database to disable the display of hidden objects. The following code resets the user's Show Hidden Objects option setting:

```
Application.SetOption "Show Hidden Objects", False
```

Note

When an object is hidden via the Properties dialog box, the attribute is stored as part of the object's `Properties` collection within its `Document` object in the DAO. The hidden attribute of the object is read-only within the document, and therefore can be determined but not set from code.

Fig. 15.8

Set the property to hide an object from its Properties dialog box.

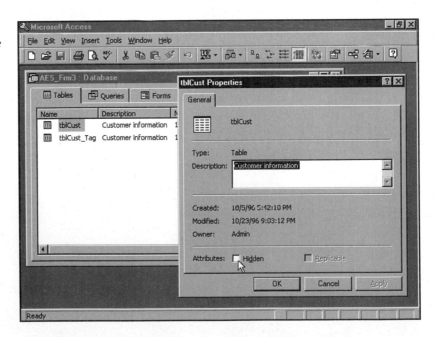

Move code to libraries. Placing code that is global to the application in a referenced code library removes standard modules from the current application database and moves them one step further away from the user.

Link Tables. Users browsing the Database window have full access to displayed tables, providing them with the ability to do serious damage to data. They cannot do damage to the underlying table structure, however, if your database contains only the links to tables that are located elsewhere. In this situation, a user will be able to delete the table link but not the table itself, which creates a condition that you or the user can remedy fairly easily.

Create self-policing forms. You can create forms that will not load from the Database window if specified conditions are not met. Simply place code in the Open event of a form that checks a condition and cancels the event if the condition is not satisfactory. A condition can be the presence of another form, the state of a variable, or any other detectable status.

Listing 15.4 shows code in a subform that will not allow the user to open the form unless the parent form is open, preventing the user from opening the form directly from the Database window.

Listing 15.4   AES_Frm3.Mdb—Preventing a Subform from Opening Except via Its Parent Form

```
Private Sub Form_Open(Cancel As Integer)
' Purpose: Don't allow opening from the Database window

  If Not lci_FrmIsLoaded("frmSentry_WithSubForm") Then
  Beep
  MsgBox "Open frmSentry_WithSubForm to see this subform.", _
    vbOKOnly + vbCritical, Me.Name
  Cancel = True
  End If

End Sub
```

Educate your users. Of course, teaching your users wise and unwise behavior in the Database window reduces the number of problems they can cause.

Lock the objects. You can "compile" an application database into the new MDE file format that places some limitations on the users' ability to interact with objects, especially the design of objects. See Chapter 17, "Bulletproofing Your Application Interface," for more information.

Additionally, Access provides a fairly clever capability that you can use to create self-policing objects, but unfortunately provides the capability only for reports and not for forms. The technique derives from a report's ability to execute its `Open` event before it actually looks for its `RecordSource` data. Using this capability, you can have a report link its own data tables into the database as it opens and delete the links as it closes. Thus, the tables are only available in the Database window while the report is printing, then they are gone from the user's view.

Listing 15.5 provides a sample of the `Report_Open()` and `Report_Close()` procedures that use this technique.

Listing 15.5 *Open* and *Close* Event Routines that Link a Report's Record Source

```
Private Sub Report_Open(Cancel As Integer)
' Purpose: Temporarily attach the report's source data

  Dim dbs As Database
  Dim tdf As TableDef

  Set dbs = CurrentDb
  Set tdf = dbs.CreateTableDef("tblCust")
  tdf.Connect = ";Database=C:\DATA\CUSTOMER.MDB"
  tdf.SourceTableName = "tblCust"
  dbs.TableDefs.Append tdf
  dbs.TableDefs.Refresh
  dbs.Close

End Sub


Private Sub Report_Close()
' Purpose: Detach the report's source data

  Dim dbs As Database

  Set dbs = CurrentDb
  dbs.TableDefs.Delete "tblCust"
  dbs.TableDefs.Refresh
  dbs.Close

End Sub
```

Note the following points about the techniques shown in Listing 15.5:

▶ The target database name and path are hard-coded in the example. A generic routine with arguments for these values may be more useful because you can call it from multiple objects in the same application.

▶ Linking tables on-the-fly increases the time it takes to load the report.

▶ You can use this technique with forms but not in a form's `Open` event. (A bound form looks for its data source before this event fires and will generate an error if the link is missing.) The workaround is to open forms from an application switchboard form and perform the table link operation in the switchboard's module just before opening the data form. The data form itself can still contain the code to remove the link in its Close event.

If users must see the Database window, the techniques in this section can at least reduce the number of unpleasant data situations that result from their interaction with application objects.

Deleting Form Records

Deleting the current record when using the expert forms model is not always as simple as allowing the user to press the Del key. Depending on the amount of control your application requires, you are faced with several techniques from which to choose.

There are many good reasons to control and monitor record deletions, not the least of which follow:

> *Data Integrity.* In many databases, dependencies between records cannot be represented by creating a table relationship. Accounting transactions provide a good example—transactions belong to batches, batch records post to journal entries, journal entries post to ledgers, and so on. You must write smart program code to assist your user with the removal of an entire record tree from such a system.

> *Quality of Alerts.* You may want your forms to provide high-quality information to the user before and after a deletion. When Access deletes records, however, the corresponding alerts tell nothing about the affected records except for the number of records targeted for deletion. You may want your deletion alerts to provide more information to users, such as the identities and counts of the affected dependent records.

There are essentially three different record deletion scenarios to consider when you create an application form, as follows:

▶ *Any user* can delete any record.

▶ *No users* can delete any records.

▶ *Some users* can delete some records.

To support the first scenario, simply ensure that the AllowDeletions property of your form is set to True, as in Figure 15.9, and provide the user with menu or toolbar options for the Delete Record action. Access will perform the deletion and provide the alerts for confirmation and if a problem occurs.

Fig. 15.9

The AllowDeletions *property of a form is located with its other data properties.*

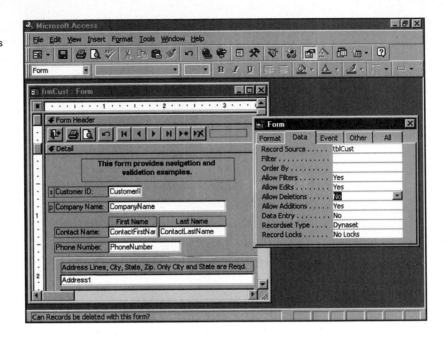

The second scenario is also easy to enable in its basic model. To disallow all deletions, merely set the AllowDeletions property of your form to False. If you have several forms in an application that allow deletions and other forms that do not, however, your users may not readily understand the selective limitations. If your forms have been set to disallow deletions, you cannot intercept the form's deletion events and show a message to the user explaining the situation (the form's Delete event no longer fires). In such a case, you must employ a combination of the techniques described in the following two sections to selectively trap deletion attempts and provide an alert instead of a deletion.

When you allow some users to delete some records while retaining strong program control of the event, you must use the deletion event model as described in the next section.

Detecting, Enabling, and Disabling Deletions

For users to use a form to delete records selectively, the form's code must determine who can delete which record and when. There are a variety of scenarios where you will want your forms to be this smart.

One example involves record ownership. Assume that each record in your form has an ownership field indicating that a designated department or user is responsible for the record. The form may need to determine whether the current user is in this ownership group for the record and disallow deletions if he or she is not.

> α **Note**
>
> Allowing and disallowing record deletions using program code is not a substitute for applying an Access security layer where appropriate. Some record ownership logic cannot be expressed by the security model alone, however, because Access security applies to tables and forms but not specific records. Many of your applications will need to balance both programmatic security and built-in security, and to disallow direct user interaction with table data.

You cannot disallow a record deletion at the form level unless your application watches each backdoor deletion provided to the user. In the following ways, a user can delete records:

▶ Select Edit, Delete Record from the menu.

▶ Click the Delete Record button on the toolbar.

▶ Press the Del key when a form record is selected.

▶ Press the Ctrl+Minus Sign (–) keyboard shortcut.

In addition, Access provides several very powerful and terribly dangerous bulk-deletion options. The existence of these options and their danger to unsophisticated users provides another good reason to regulate record deletions. A user can delete all the records in a form's recordset with the following techniques:

▶ Choose Edit, Select All Records from the menu and employ one of the deletion methods from the previous list.

▶ Press the Ctrl+Shift+Spacebar keyboard shortcut and employ one of the deletion methods from the previous list.

▶ Press the Ctrl+A keyboard shortcut and employ one of the deletion methods from the previous list.

To watch for deletion events, you most often place code in the Delete event for the form. This event is triggered at the point where the user initiates the deletion but before any built-in alert is shown or any actual action is taken. You have the following two choices when the Delete event fires:

▶ Cancel the Delete event and then execute your own code to handle the deletion. Note that your own code to manage the deletion cannot use the RunCommand acCmdDeleteRecord method to reinitiate the deletion because the Delete event will fire again and code recursion will result. Deletions must be done with program code in this scenario.

▶ Let Access manage the deletion, but add code to log or audit the deletion activity. When the `Delete` event fires, the target record has not yet been removed from the form's recordset and placed in the undo buffer. (This activity happens between the `Delete` event and the `BeforeDelConfirm` event.) Thus, your code is able to retrieve the unique key or other information about the record and act accordingly.

> **Ⅹ Caution**
>
> In addition to the `Delete` event, Access also provides the `BeforeDelConfirm` and `AfterDelConfirm` events. You can place code in these events to manage the display of the delete confirmation message and to test the post-deletion status of the action. These events do not fire if the user has cleared the Confirm Record Changes check box in the Options dialog box, however, so use these events at your discretion or fix the user's option setting during application initialization.
>
> Also be aware that when the `BeforeDelConfirm` event fires, the record has been removed from the form's recordset and the next record has become the current record. Consequently, any references in your event code to the current record in the form will not point to the deleted record.

It is possible to selectively allow and disallow deletions while letting Access manage the work:

1. In the `Current` event of a form, run code to detect whether the current user is allowed to delete the current record.

2. Set the `AllowDeletions` property of the form equal to the user's deletion rights. Changing this property setting does not cause Access to query again the form's recordset, so there is no negative visual or performance impact of this property change.

3. Access detects the property change and enables or disables the Delete Record menu option and toolbar button accordingly.

Let's examine the two approaches I just described for selectively allowing a deletion. Assume that your company's customer database has customer records with unique ID numbers starting at 2. The number 1 is reserved for your parent company to whom you sell (transfer) products as well. Under no circumstances should users be able to delete the record for the parent company.

You may approach this problem by disallowing a deletion of the parent company record via code in the form's `Delete` event. The code would look like the first event in Listing 15.6.

Alternatively, you can make the form smarter and the interface friendlier by disabling the built-in deletion capabilities of the form when the parent company record is the current record, as shown in the second event routine in Listing 15.6.

> **Listing 15.6   AES_Frm3.Mdb—Two Different Code Approaches to Disallowing Deletion of a Specific Record**

```
Private Sub Form_Delete(Cancel As Integer)
' Purpose: Do not allow deletion from UI of parent company record

  If Me!txtCustomerID = 1 Then
    Beep
    MsgBox "Cannot delete parent company record.", _
      vbOKOnly + vbCritical, "Disallowed"
    Cancel = True
  End If

End Sub


Private Sub Form_Current()
' Purpose: Turn off the form AllowDeletions property when ID = 1

  Me.AllowDeletions = (Me!txtCustomerID <> 1)

End Sub
```

Either method is equally effective; they simply have a different manifestation to the users.

 Note

Once you have set the AllowDeletions property of a form to False, your code cannot use the RunCommand method to initiate a deletion. Access will generate the error message: The command or action Delete Record isn't available now. You must use code in this circumstance.

Deleting Records via Program Code

With Access' innate abilities to manage record deletions and to alert users when they occur, under what circumstances would you simply not let an Access form provide record deletions? Actually, there are quite a few scenarios in which you may desire tighter control of record deletions. The following are a few examples:

You want to provide a custom message. When Access manages the deletion, your user sees the Access alert. You may want more control over the delete warning message and the timing of its display.

You want to audit the deletion. Perhaps your application places a record in an audit table for each deletion, noting the record key, the user, and the date/time of deletion. Alternatively, some users want their applications to make a copy of each important record (in its entirety) into an archive table before deleting it from a production table. This provides a permanent "undo" buffer for deletions.

You have implemented a custom lock strategy. If your application uses advanced locking strategies to manage user contention, take the locking model into account when doing deletions.

You want to disable all deletions except for programmatic deletions. If you want to set the `AllowDeletions` property of a form to `False` for a specific reason, deletions using the Access built-in capability will not work. You must write program code.

The deletion involves child records. When Access manages a deletion, if child (dependent) records are involved that will be deleted as a result of referential integrity enforcement, Access only provides a generic warning to that effect. The names of the affected dependent tables and the number of affected records are not shown.

The deletion cascades into nonrelated records. For example, in an accounting application that posts records to ledgers, deleting a posted transaction may require corrective logic to run, such as the programmatic creation of an adjusting entry record.

Bulk deletion is problematic. The Access `Delete` event fires once for each record deleted from the form's recordset. In a form that is regularly used for bulk deletions, the number of messages displayed may be onerous, and the user's confusion that results may be unpleasant.

In scenarios such as this, you may choose to delete records with program code. At the simplest level, you can use program code to delete a record by calling on the deletion capabilities of Access:

```
Application.RunCommand acCmdDeleteRecord
```

You can trigger such code from a menu or toolbar option or from a custom button on the form or other event. When you depend on Access to notify you of a deletion, place code in the `Delete` event for the form. This event has a `Cancel` argument that your code can set to `True` to override the built-in delete routine that would be provided by Access. The remaining code in the event can then proceed with your programmatic deletion, as in Listing 15.7.

Listing 15.7   A *Delete* Event Shell for a Programmatic Deletion Process

```
Private Sub Form_Delete(Cancel As Integer)
' Purpose: Code shell to enable programmatic deletions

  Cancel = True    ' Cancel the internal event
  ' Check the user's rights to delete the record
  ' Validate and save the record
  ' MsgBox to ask if the user is sure
  ' Create a backup copy of the record or audit log entry
  ' Delete the record

End Sub
```

You cannot rely on Access to notify you of a deletion when the AllowDeletions property of the form is set to False. This property setting causes Access to remove Edit, Delete Record from the menu and to disallow related keyboard shortcuts, such as Ctrl+Minus Sign (–). In such a case, you must add a custom delete function to your form and attach it to a custom event. The user can call the event by a button, a custom menu option, or a related event.

The code in Listing 15.8 shows a programmatic record deletion triggered by a custom button on the form.

Listing 15.8   AES_Frm3.Mdb—A Custom Single-record Deletion Routine Called by a Form Button

```
Private Sub btnDelete_Click()
' Purpose: Delete a record using program code

  On Error GoTo btnDelete_Click_Err
  Const cstrProc As String = "btnDelete_Click"
  Dim blnInTrans As Boolean
  Dim dbs        As Database
  Dim rst        As Recordset
  Dim wsp        As Workspace

  Beep
  If MsgBox("Permanently delete customer " & Me!txtCompanyName _
    & "?", vbYesNo + vbExclamation, "Delete") = vbNo Then
    GoTo btnDelete_Click_Exit
  End If

  ' If writing an archive record, save and test the record first
  '   so the archive copy can be un-archived and remains valid
  ' Alternately, send Me.Undo before deleting to clear edits

  If Me.mtdValidate Then    ' Save and test the record first
    Set wsp = DBEngine.Workspaces(0)    ' Current workspace
```

continues

Listing 15.8   Continued

```
    Set dbs = wsp(0)  ' Current database
    Set rst = dbs.OpenRecordset("SELECT * FROM tblCust WHERE CustomerID = " _
      & Me!txtCustomerID, dbOpenDynaset)
    wsp.BeginTrans
    blnInTrans = True
    ' Your deletion code could write audit records here
    '   or save a copy of the record before deleting
    rst.Delete  ' Delete the record on the form
    ' Your code can delete child or related records here
    wsp.CommitTrans
    blnInTrans = False
    Me.Requery
  End If

btnDelete_Click_Exit:
  On Error Resume Next
  rst.Close
  dbs.Close
  Exit Sub

btnDelete_Click_Err:
  Call lci_ErrMsgStd(Me.Name & "." & cstrProc, Err.Number _
    , Err.Description, True)
  If blnInTrans = True Then
    wsp.Rollback
  End If
  Resume btnDelete_Click_Exit

End Sub
```

Note the following points that Listing 15.8 reveals:

> *Transaction Wrapper.* The deletion and all its related events are wrapped in a transaction so that the deletion can be discontinued at any time before it completes. Therefore, if your routine's attempt to delete a record fails after an audit log and backup copy of the record have already been written or even after dependent records have been deleted, rolling back the complete transaction will cleanly undo any deletion work.

> *Error Trapping.* The custom delete routine provides error trapping. As dictated by your application's needs, the error handler can be expanded to test for specific error situations and take action as desired.

> *Validation.* Why would my code validate a record about to be deleted? In many applications, deletions are not really deletions, but rather are a movement of records from active tables to archive tables. In such a scenario, system administrators often have the ability to "undelete" records (return records from the archive to

the active tables). You would not want to return a record to a table that does not survive the validation requirements for that table; therefore, the deletion routine in the example does not allow invalid records to be archived.

Customized Alerts. Using programmatic deletions, you can place messages to the user anywhere in your code. Your code can also provide more information to the user than the Access built-in deletions can. The following are a few examples:

▶ Your code can ask users to confirm important or multi-record deletions more than once to make doubly sure they understand the ramifications.

▶ From code, you can place the actual record key or identifying string (such as customer name) in the alert to provide clarity on exactly what will be deleted.

▶ Access does not show how many records will be affected in related tables when the form's recordset referential integrity is active. Programmatic deletions can detect and display this information.

Caution

One simple way to delete a form record is to use the `RecordSetClone` object. You cannot wrap code lines using this object in a transaction, however; therefore, you cannot protect the following delete routine as well as you can protect the code shown in Listing 15.8:

```
Me.RecordsetClone.Bookmark = Me.Bookmark
Me.RecordsetClone.Delete
Me.Requery
```

Deleting records through code sounds like a winning strategy, and it is. It provides you, the developer, with complete control of one of the most important events in a database application.

Selectively Disabling Features

When your application needs to restrict access to specific controls or processes, it can "switch" form controls and features on and off as needed. Developers can easily give users selective access to specific features and controls in Access by using any combination of the following techniques:

Restricting Buttons. Just like retail Windows applications and Access itself, your application should note when a process is disallowed and disable the button for that process, setting its `Enabled` property to `false`. This technique applies to buttons embedded on forms as well as command bar buttons and menu options.

Disabling Control Groups. If you are going to disable form controls based on a particular user security or process status, locate the controls in a meaningful way, usually by grouping. If possible, try not to disable various controls throughout the form that can confuse the user. A better alternative is to place all the affected controls in a rectangle with a label stating why the options are disabled, such as "These data items are for managers only."

Tip

You can use the new `Tab` control in Access to create a group of controls bound to one rectangle, and enable or disable all of the controls together by simply setting the `Enabled` property of the tab.

Hiding Items. I generally prefer not to hide controls that become irrelevant in a particular context, opting instead to make them disabled as required. We have found that users can get confused when the screen layouts are not consistent between sessions. For example, imagine a user who learns how to perform data entry by watching a manager—who has access rights to all fields on the screen—and then returns to his or her workstation and finds that the application screens look differently because some controls are hidden for nonmanagers.

Limiting Forms. When possible, disable the button on a switchboard menu that calls a form that is currently restricted for some reason. This interface restriction is immediately obvious to the user. If this is not feasible, use the `Form_Open()` event procedure of the called form to check all circumstances required for the form to load, then set the `Cancel` argument of the event to `True` if the form should not be loaded. These events and activities occur before the form is displayed, so the form will not load and will not even flash on the screen.

Tip

If a significant number of controls or features apply to one group of users and not another, consider grouping the controls or features onto different form pages. Then you can simply disable the ability to go to a particular page for the restricted users. Limiting access to a form page involves trapping the keystrokes, including `PgDn` and `Tab`, that take users between pages, as described earlier in this chapter.

Validating Important Data

The most important and complex element of expert forms is data validation. Without good data, your application is worth nothing.

 Note

An application with an unfriendly interface is an annoyance, an application with imperfect features is a work in progress, but an application that does not collect accurate data and protect it is truly a disaster.

Depending on the needs of the application, the skills of your users, and your personal development style, potentially complex program code may be required to fully validate a record before saving it. Some brief guidelines to follow:

You may have to go beyond the ValidationRule property. This convenient feature—which Access provides for form controls, table fields, and records—is limited when it is applied to complex data needs and does not provide the developer with much control nor the user with much feedback. On forms, validation must kick in at a point where data problems can be caught before a record is saved; therefore, validation code should usually be placed in the BeforeUpdate event.

Programmatic validation routines are important for the following reasons:

▶ Built-in validation is not triggered unless the user actually dirties the record, and there may be cases when you want to validate the data regardless of whether the user makes an edit. For example, a form to scan all the records newly downloaded from the company mainframe is only useful if it helps trap errors in the records that were downloaded. Assume that at the end of the download, a user reviews the imported data in a form but the Access field-level validation—triggered only by edits on the field—will not kick in as the user reviews these records. In fact, even if a record is edited, individual fields that are not edited do not test the validation rule.

In this scenario, you would have to provide program code to more aggressively validate records as the users browse them to tie validation to the form's Current event or some other record navigation routine.

▶ Field and control validation are not triggered unless the user actually dirties the control. This means that if the user does not set focus to the control and perform an edit there, the Access validation for that field is skipped. This is unacceptable in most types of application forms. For example, Null values in required fields are not detected in this model.

▶ If a built-in validation rule fails, you can only show a message. On a validation failure, the user receives either a canned message from Access or one that you have added to the control's ValidationText property. In neither event can you run code on the validation failure, display a specific message for the given context, or fix up the erroneous data? (A ValidationFailure event on each control would be nice, wouldn't it?)

Batch your validation. Using the InputMask property of controls and the Access built-in type testing for bound control data, you can implement some simple validation at the control level. Because some controls may never receive focus as the user moves through the form, it is usually appropriate to sweep through a record looking for problems when data entry is complete for the entire record but before the record is saved. This is called bulk validation.

Validate before saving the record. It is much easier to validate a record before it is saved than to try to unsave a record if it fails muster. By hanging bulk validation on the BeforeUpdate event of the form or on your own record navigation buttons, a well-coded form notices a validation problem before a record is committed.

Make sure the user knows what data is required. I like to flag required controls on forms so that the user has a visual clue denoting how validation will work and is thus less likely to bump into it. Required controls can be denoted with a variety of visual clues, as described in the next section.

Use combo and list boxes to excess. Wherever possible, create look-up tables that list allowed values and use these lists to populate Combo and List Box controls on entry forms that feed values into fields. Additions to these lists should be considered high-priority and high-security data because the old maxim, garbage in, garbage out, will result from poorly maintained lists.

Remember to validate records during editing with the same fervor used for data entry. Both events are important, and both can introduce data errors. You may want to create various audit logs as records are changed, as described in Chapter 17, "Bulletproofing Your Application Interface."

The remaining sections in this chapter discuss these validation concepts and related techniques in greater detail.

Denoting Required Elements

Select your favorite phrase from the following two:

▶ Wrong answer, you dummy.

▶ Correct response—good job!

An application that does not tell the user what is expected of him or her regarding data validation and then pops up a host of validation failure alerts when it tries to save the record is essentially shouting the first phrase at the user. On the other hand, a friendly form that clearly denotes value ranges, required fields, and data types will enable the user to fill in data elements correctly most of the time. As each record slides smoothly past validation and out to some disk sector, the user receives the second phrase as implied feedback, and smiles wryly.

Application users have limited bandwidth that can be exceeded easily by the data-entry needs of a complex application if the following questions remain unanswered:

▶ What kind of data goes in this field?

▶ How do I spell this particular item?

▶ Where in the mainframe does this value post?

▶ What is the required format for telephone numbers?

Users crave information that will help them understand the application better and receive the least amount of negative feedback from it. Chapter 17, "Bulletproofing Your Application Interface," describes user feedback in more detail, so for the purposes of this section, we talk only about required fields.

Designating When a Value Is Required

The most common interface challenge in database development is denoting required fields to the user. No Office applications or Office Compatible documents give insight to Microsoft's recommended method for noting data-entry requirements, so you must contrive your own. We decided to use asterisks next to required fields. For the rationale behind this design strategy, review our user research on the issue described in Chapter 8, "Designing Effective Interfaces."

Using an asterisk to denote required fields is simple, and you can let Access do the work for you. We place a small, disabled (but visible) text box next to each required field. Each text box has a formula similar to the following:

```
=IIf(IsNull([txtCompanyName]),"*","")
```

This expression places a red * character next to the label of a required field as long as the control is Null. When the user enters data into the field and moves to another control, however, the expression recalculates and the asterisk disappears. Figure 15.10 shows a form with some required fields noted via this technique.

Fig. 15.10
Required fields on this form that are not filled in are denoted with an asterisk.

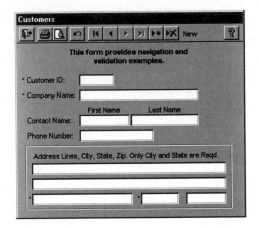

In addition to this simple technique, you can contrive more elaborate schemes to denote required fields. For example, using the KeyPress event, your code can watch each keystroke coming to a control and update the asterisk or some other marker as characters are typed into a control. This has the benefit of removing the required field marker as soon as the first keystroke is pressed, rather than delaying until the user moves focus from the control, as in our model.

Recently, we have taken to denoting required fields in the table design as well. We place the string (r) at the end of a field's Description property, regardless of whether the required nature of the field is enforced at the engine level (via the field's Required property or a validation rule) or by the application interface. The Description of the field is pulled into the StatusBarText property of related form controls, thus providing a message to users on the status bar that reinforces the data-entry requirements.

Conveying a Control's Data-Entry Requirements

Denoting required fields is only part of the equation. It is also desirable to tell users what type of data goes into each field tied to a control and what the size and "shape" of the data is. For this, you have five primary interface assistants, as follows:

InputMask Property. This powerful property gives you great flexibility to create entry masks that restrict characters coming to a control. A few points to consider about this property follow:

▶ The mask is not displayed until the user begins to type in the field. Therefore, the mask may not be useful to you as a required field indicator. The mask also doesn't convey its data requirements when the control does not have focus. In some cases, a label or other prompt that conveys further formatting information may be a useful addition to a control with a mask.

15

▸ Table and form input masks are not synchronized. The `InputMask` property of the field in a table definition is used for table datasheets. This mask is imported into the `InputMask` property of a form control bound to the field at the time the control is created, but any changes in the future to the property at either the field level or control level are not automatically synchronized between the two.

▸ You can change the `InputMask` property on-the-fly to convey data requirements that are specific to a record's characteristics. For example, a customer form has a combo box where the user indicates whether the customer is an individual or company. Based on the user's selection in the combo box, your code can change the `InputMask` of the `Tax Identification` field (a Text Box control) to mask for either a Social Security number or a Federal Tax ID number.

▸ You can set the `InputMask` property of a form control to `Password`, causing the control to display only asterisk (*) characters in place of the actual data values. This is useful when a form should not display sensitive information in a particular context.

StatusBarText Property. The status bar has been an attribute of Office programs for quite some time, and most users are familiar with its location and purpose. You can denote in the `StatusBarText` property of a control the data type, required nature, range of values, or any other information that will help the user survive data entry and validation.

ControlTipText Property. In this property, you can add pop-up tips to controls on your forms. Although you could conceivably provide a control tip for each control, complete with detailed data-entry instructions for the control, this proliferation of yellow tips when navigating between controls with the mouse would be annoying to many users. We sometimes place control tips on control labels instead of the controls themselves, as shown in Figure 15.11. The user is less likely to make these tips pop-up accidentally when moving through the form, yet can quickly get extra help for a field by passing the mouse over its label.

Fig. 15.11

Placing a control tip on a form control assists users with data-entry requirements for the related field.

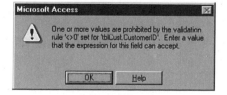

WhatsThisHelp Property. Setting the form's `WhatsThisButton` property to `Yes`, the `HelpFile` property to a file name, and the relevant controls' `HelpContextId` properties to help topic ID numbers will enable the user to get specific pop-up help information for individual controls. While this is the slowest method for showing data-entry information to a user, it nevertheless provides the most space for detail and clarity.

Form Labels. If space on a form allows, you can add additional Label controls to a form to provide clarification text that details data-entry requirements for specific fields or for the form in general.

Once you have conveyed the data-entry requirements to the user, you must communicate the breach of these requirements as well. Validating data and notifying the user of a validation failure is discussed in the next several sections.

Validating at the Field Level

The term validation is not represented only by complex rules applied to fields and records. When you use the Access features in its purest form to set a field's DataType and FieldSize properties, you are using the product's more subtle validation capabilities. The majority of validation that Jet provides to Access is in the form of rules, however.

Jet validation rules (often called *engine-level validation*) are entered into tables via the following properties:

ValidationRule *(Table)*. This property setting holds the 2,048-character string equivalent of a SQL Where clause without the keyword Where. (The string can be 64K when set using the DAO rather than the Access interface.) The ValidationRule string for a table can refer to other fields in the table but not to other objects, expressions, or functions.

ValidationText *(Table)*. This message is displayed when the ValidationRule for the table fails as a record is saved. If no message is provided, Access generates a default message similar to the one shown in Figure 15.12, whether in a table/query datasheet, or in a form.

ValidationRule *(Field)*. In Access, this property setting is the 2,048-character string equivalent of a SQL Where clause. (The string can be 64K when set using the DAO rather than the Access interface.) The validation expression for a field cannot refer to other fields, objects, expressions, or functions.

ValidationText *(Field)*. This 255-character message is displayed when the ValidationRule for the field fails as the focus leaves the field (in a datasheet) or a form control bound to it.

Required *(Field)*. Setting this property to Yes tests the field for a value (non-Null) when the record is saved.

Fig. 15.12
*Access displays a
default message when
a ValidationRule is
broken.*

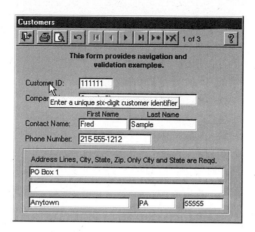

AllowZeroLength (Field). Setting the AllowZeroLength property to No will not allow the user to store a zero-length string in the field. A zero-length string (or "empty string") is different than a Null value, and it is entered into a field by some import processes and by the user consciously entering in the field (typing ""). This property setting provides a different type of validation than the Required property but in general has limited usefulness.

The simplest method of validating form data is to create engine-level rules and then enable the form to use them. The relationship between a form and the validation rules in its underlying tables follows:

▶ A control's ValidationRule runs as the user tries to exit the control. The rule is tested against the control bound to the field when the user saves a new record and also is tested against the control before the control's BeforeUpdate event fires as the user modifies a saved record.

▶ A control's BeforeUpdate event fires just after the control's validation rule is tested.

▶ A field-level ValidationRule is tested against the control bound to the field after the control's validation and BeforeUpdate is finished.

▶ A field-level Required property is also tested at save time on a new record and after the control's rule and BeforeUpdate are run when a saved value is modified.

▶ Table-level rules are tested when a form record is being saved, coming after all control and field rules have run.

▶ When a new bound control is created on a form, it inherits the ValidationRule property from the table definition for the bound field. If the validation rules for the form and the control are the same, they are only enforced once. If the rule is deleted from the control, the field-level rule is still enforced by the form. If you enter a rule in the control's property that is different from the field's rule, both rules are enforced by the form.

Field and table validation rules provide a straightforward way to validate data on a form. They do have a few negative characteristics, but many developers choose to live with the following annoyances:

▶ Table and form rules do not always manifest themselves in the same fashion to the user. For example, field-level validation alerts have a Help button but control-level alerts do not.

▶ Your code cannot control the caption of validation alerts produced by field, table, or control validation failure.

▶ Field rules are triggered as the focus moves from a bound control, interrupting the user's navigation between form controls and removing the user's ability to move the focus to another control that may assist with data entry (a Suggest, Defaults, or Undo button, for example).

▶ Rules on form controls are not automatically synchronized to revised table or field rules when a schema change is made to the table, nor are changes to validation properties on bound form controls trickled into their related table field definitions.

To determine your application's validation strategy, you will need to experiment with table-level rules and compare their strengths and weaknesses to other validation options.

Validating at the Control Level

As noted in the previous section, most Access form controls provide a `ValidationRule` property that can be used to mirror, replace, or augment a table-level rule for the bound field. A control-level rule is superior to a field-level rule in that it can call expressions, your functions, intrinsic functions, and object references.

In addition, the nature of form and control events provides several candidate events for you to consider when you place validation code on individual controls, as follows:

BeforeUpdate Event. This event is an excellent location to place validation code attached to a control because you can cancel this event by setting its `Cancel` argument to `True`. This event fires after the validation rule at the control level but before field and record-level tests are activated, giving you an early "sneak peek" at the data before Jet's rules see it.

AfterUpdate Event. You cannot cancel this event and therefore it makes a poor location for most validation code.

Exit Event. This event comes after the control and field validation have run and after the `BeforeUpdate` event code. You can also cancel this event and, therefore, it is a potential location for validation code. But it occurs a little late in the process for my taste.

LostFocus Event. You cannot cancel this event and therefore it provides no way to stop the movement out of the invalid control.

KeyDown Event. This event fires one or more times for each key pressed and can be used to write complex character-based validation. The `InputMask` property can often more easily provide much the same benefits as a keystroke-based validation routine, however.

KeyPress Event. This event provides a subset of the functionality available in the `KeyDown` event and can be used to test and/or discard most nonshifted keyboard characters.

Change Event. This event fires on Text Box and Combo Box controls only but can be used to test the total value of the control as opposed to checking each keystroke as pressed.

KeyUp Event. As with `KeyDown`, you can place code in this event to "screen" for allowed and disallowed keystrokes.

Error Event. In some validation models, you may want to add code to a form's `Error` event, which is triggered by data access and other user interaction errors on the form. Listing 15.13 shows an example of code in this event that traps for three specific table and field validation failures. Unfortunately, when this event fires, the `Err.Description` value does not match the `DataErr` argument, so you must build alert strings manually in the event procedure, as shown in Listing 15.13.

Listing 15.13   Making *Error* Event Messages More Explicit

```
Private Sub Form_Error(DataErr As Integer, Response As Integer)
' Purpose: Provide intelligent validation alert

  Const cintFldNull As Integer = 3314   ' Field can't be null
  Const cintFldZLS  As Integer = 3315   ' Field can't be ZLS
  Const cintTblRule As Integer = 3316   ' Table rule failed

  Select Case DataErr
    Case cintFldNull, cintFldZLS, cintTblRule
      Beep
      MsgBox "Validation failure in " & Me.ActiveControl.Name _
        & ": " & Choose(DataErr — 3313, "Null not allowed.", _
        "Zero-length string not allowed.", "Table rule failed."), _
        vbOKOnly + vbCritical, "Customer Form"
      Response = acDataErrContinue
    Case Else
      ' Let Access show its message
      Response = acDataErrDisplay
  End Select

End Sub
```

In summary, bear in mind that placing too many different types of validation on a single form can lead to awkward event models and potentially confusing alerts for users. Nevertheless, because control-level validation is more powerful than field-level validation, it is a superior choice when the runtime or Access security can guarantee that users will not be interacting with table datasheets directly and bypassing validation on the form.

For more regulation of the validation process than rules provide, use code in a control's BeforeUpdate event for unlimited flexibility in the approach to validation and the message to users. Finally, to test each individual keystroke, consider the keyboard and Change events.

Validating at the Record Level

Your users will help you to determine the best validation model to use either based on an existing preference or via their feedback on your applications. For us, many of our users have migrated to PCs from other computer systems and are not only accomplished typists but are accustomed to high data-entry throughput. Consequently, they have provided much feedback to us over the years stating a preference for bulk validation in applications as opposed to validation that tests each field as it is exited.

 Caution
Record-level validation works best when unencumbered by Jet validation rules popping up unpredictably. This means that stronger form validation comes at the cost of removing table-level and field-level validation. In applications that use the runtime or Access security, users do not have direct access to the underlying data without the form, and the lack of the regulation should not be a problem. In other situations, however, you must weigh the dangers of not using engine-level validation in favor of programmatic validation.

Bulk validation simply refers to the aggregate testing of an entire record at the end of the data-entry session, just before the record is saved. Users who are rapid typists or who are keying data into a system from hard copy often prefer to type all the information into a form record and only then to validate the data.

To facilitate bulk validation, place your testing code in the form's BeforeUpdate event procedure or at least call your validation routine from that event. BeforeUpdate is triggered when your code attempts to save the current record as part of navigation or closing the form as well as when the user saves the record via a menu selection or keyboard shortcut before heading for lunch. Listing 15.14 shows a sample event procedure calling a validation routine.

Listing 15.14   AES_Frm3.Mdb—A BeforeUpdate Event in a Form that Calls Record Validation

```
Private Sub Form_BeforeUpdate(Cancel As Integer)
' Purpose: Test and save the record

  If Not Me.mtdValidate Then  ' Didn't survive validation
    Cancel = True
  Else
    ' Stamp the log fields in the record before saving
    Call lci_FrmRecStamp(Me)
  End If

End Sub
```

Note

The record stamping function, `lci_FrmRecStamp()`, in Listing 15.14 is discussed in Chapter 17, "Bulletproofing Your Application Interface."

The validation routine, `mtdValidate`, referred to in Listing 15.14 is a public procedure in the form serving as a validation method that can be called from inside or outside the form to check the current record. It can be as simple or complex as needed to facilitate the objectives for the data. The following are three approaches to bulk validation:

> *Brute Force Validation*. The simplest way to validate controls on a form is to test each control in sequence, as shown in Listing 15.15. This approach enables each control's tests to be unique, creating flexible but verbose validation code.

Listing 15.15   AES_Frm3.Mdb—A Brute-Force Form Record Validation Routine

```
Private Function mtdValidate() As Boolean
' Purpose: Validate the current record
' Returns: True/false, True=Record is valid

  Dim blnValid As Boolean
  Dim ctl      As Control
  Dim strValid As String

  blnValid = True   ' Assume record is valid

  ' Let the user leave an empty record
  If Not Me.Dirty And Me.NewRecord Then
    mtdValidate = True
    GoTo mtdValidate_Exit
```

continues

Listing 15.15   AES_Frm3.Mdb—A Brute-Force Form Record Validation

```
End If

' Validate rules
If lci_IsBlank(Me!txtCustomerID) And blnValid Then
  Set ctl = Me!txtCustomerID
  strValid = "Customer ID is required."
  blnValid = False
End If

' Add additional rules here

If blnValid Then  ' Passed all validations
  mtdValidate = True
Else
  Beep
  MsgBox strValid, vbOKOnly, "Validation Failed"
  ctl.SetFocus
End If

mtdValidate_Exit:
  Exit Function

End Function
```

With the linear nature of the validation routine shown, you can structure the routine's response in one of two ways. Your code can abort at the first field that fails validation, show an alert, set focus to the form control that failed validation, and end. The code in Listing 15.15 follows this model. Alternatively, you could allow the code to run through the entire validation cycle and build a compound message string listing each control that failed, then show this string to the user.

 Tip

To make forms more friendly for our users, you'll notice in Listing 15.15 that I return focus to the first control that failed validation to make it easy for the user to begin the data correction process without requiring any focus changes.

Tagged Validation. Smart validation routines can use flags in the form controls themselves to perform validation. For example, if you place the marker NotNull (or other specific string you choose) in the Tag property of each control on a form that must be filled in, your validation routine can cycle through the form's Controls collection and test for required values.

Listing 15.16 shows an example of a validation routine that checks each form control for my NotNull string as the first part of the tag and validates all tagged controls for non-Null values. The routine also shows the user an alert string listing that prompts all of the controls that failed validation. (The prompt is also stored in each control's Tag.) This validation scheme is quite flexible because adding or removing a control from the validation loop is as simple as altering its Tag property.

Listing 15.16   AES_Frm3.Mdb—Form Record Validation Using the Tag Property

```
Private Function mtdValidate() As Boolean
' Purpose: Validate the current record
'          Build and display a string of failures
'          Required field tags format: "NotNull;prompt"

' Returns: True/false, True=Record is valid

  Dim ctl        As Control   ' First control to fail
  Dim ectl       As Control   ' Collection element
  Dim intFailed  As Integer   ' Number of failures
  Dim strValid   As String    ' Failure string

  ' Let the user leave an empty record
  If Not Me.Dirty And Me.NewRecord Then
    mtdValidate = True
    GoTo mtdValidate_Exit
  End If

  ' Validate all rules with a validation loop
  For Each ectl In Me.Controls
    If Left(ectl.Tag, 7) = "NotNull" Then
      If lci_IsBlank(ectl) Then  ' Failure
        If intFailed = 0 Then
          strValid = Mid(ectl.Tag, Trim(InStr(ectl.Tag, ";") + 1))
          Set ctl = ectl   ' First control to fail
        Else
          strValid = strValid & ", " _
            & Mid(ectl.Tag, Trim(InStr(ectl.Tag, ";") + 1))
        End If
        intFailed = intFailed + 1
      End If
    End If
  Next

  If intFailed = 0 Then   ' Passed all validations
    mtdValidate = True
  Else
    strValid = "The following required " & _
      IIf(intFailed > 1, "fields are", "field is") & " blank: " _
      & strValid
    Beep
    MsgBox strValid, vbOKOnly, "Validation Failed"
    ctl.SetFocus  ' Go to first failure
  End If

End Function
```

Note

Of course, there are more advanced types of validation than simply required fields. You can still handle a variety of validation needs with a tag loop by creating your own flags for different types of validation and including multiple flags in the control's `Tag`.

 Tip

For each control that fails validation in Listing 15.16, the string to display to the user indicating the control's name is pulled from the `Tag` value. Starting with Access 97, you can take an alternative approach to this model by retrieving the `Caption` property from the Label control bound to the control being tested.

Each form control now has a `Controls` collection pointing to its subordinate controls. For all controls except for the Tab and Option Group controls, this subordinate collection has only one member—the bound label. Thus, to address the label caption for the label attached to a text box, use this syntax:

```
Me!txtCustName.Controls(0).Caption
```

Grouped Validation. As an alternative to placing validation tags on controls, you can group controls that require the same type of validation into a collection or group their names into an array and review all collection/array members for a particular status.

For example, in the `Form_Open()` event, create a collection called `mcolNotNull` and add to it all the controls on the form that should not be `Null`. Next, create a collection called `mcolNonZero` and add in any controls that need to be validated for a positive integer value. Remember that a single control can be in multiple collections, allowing for compound validation on any control.

Your validation routines would loop through each collection in `Form_BeforeUpdate()` and apply the appropriate test to each member. Chapter 12, "Understanding Form Structures and Coding," describes how to create and iterate through control collections.

 Note

Your navigation and validation events must not collide. If necessary, place `Debug.Print` statements in your various form events to track and analyze the event flow of your validation scheme during testing. Alternatively, print out your code and review the event flow of your validation logic.

> Also, review Listing 15.10 for examples of code that carefully validate and save data before moving focus away from the current record.

All manner of simple and complex validation processes are available to you from VBA code. Some records require complex validation across multiple fields/controls while other forms demand that you create a recordset and perform domain operations to ensure the uniqueness of a value or the integrity of a relationship. Validation processes are limited only by the needs of your users and by your imagination.

From Here...

This chapter brought together a combination of concepts involving interface design, VBA coding, form event management, and data validation. Review the following chapters for more information on these subjects:

◆ Chapter 8, "Designing Effective Interfaces," discusses form layouts and other interface considerations that relate to navigation, menus, and toolbars.

◆ In Chapter 10, "Creating Expert Tables and Queries," you can review more information about Jet tables and their structure.

◆ To pull the concepts in this and the previous form chapters into sharp focus, read Chapter 17, "Bulletproofing Your Application Interface."

◆ Chapter 20, "Applying Development Shortcuts," elaborates on the use of code libraries as discussed in this chapter.

chapter 16

Presenting Data to Users

16

In this chapter

◆ **Determining how to layout forms and subforms to present information clearly**

◆ **Using form controls like tabs and list boxes to enhance the presentation of data**

◆ **Synchronizing the display of related records on related forms**

◆ **Creating forms that help users filter sets of records**

◆ **Creating a list wizard for the selection of multiple data values**

F orms are the windows through which users view their data. Forms are not useful if they present too little information, do not allow users to locate desired information, or allow users to become confused about the use of the application. In this chapter, I show you techniques for providing users with maximum value from your forms.

> ## A New Form of Angst
>
> Invariably, I have found that users think of a new application's forms as *outstanding* for roughly a week. After that time, they begin to discover the "design shortcomings." For example, users on design teams often feel that they do not want phone number text controls to take advantage of the Format property, finding it too restrictive. Once the application is deployed, however, they notice that users enter phone number data in various formats, and then they wish they had implemented tighter restrictions.
>
> Worse, users begin to understand the application better over time and then start comparing it to other applications (Access-centric or otherwise). As soon as they see a screen with a tab control in another application, for example, they wonder why they didn't get tabs in their application, disregarding the fact that it may not have even been an appropriate design option.
>
> I call this ending of the new application honeymoon "designer's remorse."

The difference between a "database" that contains forms and an "application" that also does is that an *application* has a mission. Forms in a *database* are often disjointed, created with the Access wizard, and not bulletproofed. Forms in an *application*, on the other hand, are meant to be friendly to use, to provide navigation to and from other forms, to present information in the way most useful to their users, and to protect the data.

This book concerns itself with the latter type of forms. Because forms are the gateway to data, they must find a balance between usability and data security. More importantly, the ultimate role of application forms is not simply to enter data; forms must make entered data accessible so that people can learn, draw conclusions, or make decisions from them.

Many developers fail to research, plan, or develop with this latter consideration in mind. The result of understanding the ultimate role of forms is that applications must place the same emphasis on presenting data as they do on protecting it during entry. Thus, research and design efforts must include asking users questions such as:

> *How will you need to locate existing records?* You must determine what are the data items that will be used to find existing data for review or editing. Developers think in terms of primary keys, but users may need to locate a record based on several different fields, singly or in combination.
>
> *What decisions will be made from the data?* Not all decisions are made from hard copy reports. As users become more mobile, your development efforts will need to address situations bred by laptops and telecommuters. Management people, for

example, may take a replica of the live database home and review a customer's data records in preparation for a pending meeting with the customer the next day.

How should the data be presented to match the problems you intend to solve with it? If users are coming in to a system with a specific objective, its forms should help them achieve the objective. When an invoice record is entered, for example, users need to create invoice details in a subform on the invoice form. When users later return to the invoice to input the DatePaid value, they may not need to see the invoice lines on the invoice form. Instead, it may be more useful to them to see the payment history for that invoice or customer.

Having asked these questions during your design work, you will have a better idea of how many different personalities of forms will be required to express the data in each table. A given table (or query result set of related records) may be represented on multiple forms in a single application, with each form providing different functionality.

In this chapter, I discuss various techniques for helping users explore and understand their data using forms. The techniques exemplify the two facets of working with existing data through forms: *presentation* and *selection*. Forms must fulfill both of these roles well in order to qualify as expert forms.

Presenting Records to Users

Access 97 introduced no significant new tools for presenting and displaying records within Access itself, with the exception of a tab control. The new Web publishing capabilities, while interesting, are not related to data presentation via forms. Forms, subforms, and list boxes are still the primary presentation instruments in applications. As these elements are combined to help users work with data, keep these considerations in mind:

Forms get crowded quickly. I see people regularly making use of small fonts and minimal blank space in order to cram dozens of data fields onto a single screen. Such forms indicate to me that the developer was either illiterate in creating multi-page forms, or was doing a "rush job" to avoid writing navigation code.

Form real estate, especially in a VGA-resolution environment, fills up fast. You must be willing to apply some creativity to find ways to display the required information within a limited space, as investigated in the section "Exploring Form Layout Options" later in this chapter.

Subforms provide development challenges. Subforms are remarkably powerful tools, but they have display limitations and provide unique event management and other coding challenges for developers. See the following section "Implementing Subforms" for a discussion of some of these issues.

Balance the performance load. As your forms get more complex, they may not perform as desired. When your application reaches this point, you are forced to depart from the standard form/subform layout and explore other options. See the topic "Exploring Form Layout Options" later in this chapter for a discussion of the alternatives.

Data entry, data editing, and data analysis are distinctly different processes. You may not be able to create one form that is all things to all users—a specific set of data may require an entry form, an edit form, a search/filter form, an approval/review form, and perhaps an analysis/summary form.

The following several sections discuss these issues in greater detail and provide suggestions and techniques for optimizing the use of forms.

Exploring Form Layout Options

Within the reasonable limits imposed by the Access forms engine, you can create some imaginative and powerful forms. The ability to nest forms within each other, to create multi-page forms, to display, hide, and resize controls at will, and to make use of event procedures provides you with a high degree of flexibility.

When you design forms in conjunction with your users, make certain that they are advised of their different options with respect to form layouts. Your job as a developer is to balance the users' objectives, usability, and access to data, with the capabilities of Access and the available budget.

The following four topics discuss some of the technical and structural options you can employ in your Access forms.

Selecting the Appropriate View of Data

I prefer to create one form for each specific view of the data, and optimize it for that view. In other words, select a `ViewsAllowed` property of either `Form` or `Datasheet` and create a form that works best only in that view. Changing views, especially from form to datasheet, may allow the user to circumvent some usability feature or validation that works better in one view than the other.

For example, datasheet view does not show command buttons, which may provide functionality critical to the user's mission. It is not possible to create a single form that has the same capabilities in datasheet and form views, thus the need to determine which view your users will be seeing.

You can trick Access to some degree by embedding a subform in datasheet view *inside* a parent host form in normal view. The host form provides the command buttons and display container; and the embedded subform provides the clean, gridded layout of a datasheet, as shown in Figure 16.1.

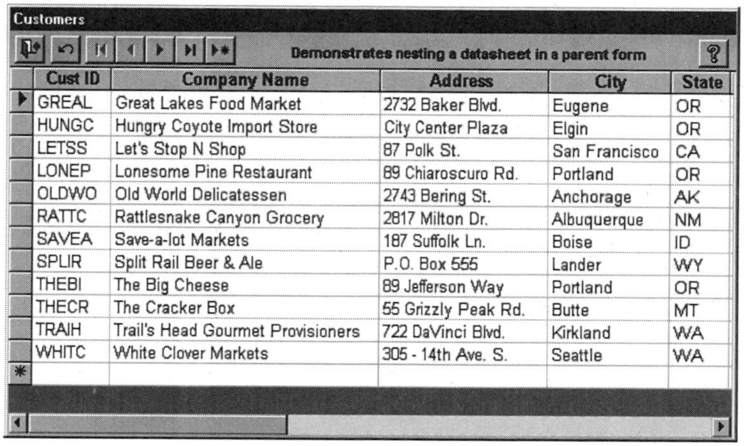

Fig. 16.1

A datasheet form can be made more usable by embedding it inside a host form.

Cust ID	Company Name	Address	City	State
GREAL	Great Lakes Food Market	2732 Baker Blvd.	Eugene	OR
HUNGC	Hungry Coyote Import Store	City Center Plaza	Elgin	OR
LETSS	Let's Stop N Shop	87 Polk St.	San Francisco	CA
LONEP	Lonesome Pine Restaurant	89 Chiaroscuro Rd.	Portland	OR
OLDWO	Old World Delicatessen	2743 Bering St.	Anchorage	AK
RATTC	Rattlesnake Canyon Grocery	2817 Milton Dr.	Albuquerque	NM
SAVEA	Save-a-lot Markets	187 Suffolk Ln.	Boise	ID
SPLIR	Split Rail Beer & Ale	P.O. Box 555	Lander	WY
THEBI	The Big Cheese	89 Jefferson Way	Portland	OR
THECR	The Cracker Box	55 Grizzly Peak Rd.	Butte	MT
TRAIH	Trail's Head Gourmet Provisioners	722 DaVinci Blvd.	Kirkland	WA
WHITC	White Clover Markets	305 - 14th Ave. S.	Seattle	WA

While datasheets are useful when comparing records or reviewing batches of data, developers place too much emphasis on the display of multiple records together on a single form. You should consider when you really need to present multiple records to users and when one record will suffice. Too much information can add unwanted complexity for users as well as developers.

Ponder the following display options as you design your forms, making sure you match the display of records with the tasks to be performed on them and the aptitude of the users:

▶ *A form displaying records in datasheet view* is the least structured way to present data to users and may be inherently dangerous because this layout exposes the data to multi-record operations (specifically deletions and bulk text replacement). Also, when the user wants to see only one specific record, he or she may not enjoy paging up or down through hundreds of other records to find the desired one.

▶ *A form displaying records in a continuous view* also has several shortcomings. The first is limited screen area, forcing you to display all of the information about a record in very little space. The second is propagation, where any *unbound* object on one record is displayed on all records, removing the ability to use some custom text and graphic techniques on the form. Thus, a message label, a status graphic, an unbound list box, and other useful interface objects may be unusable on forms using this display mode.

A third shortcoming—confusion—can arise in the usability of multi-record forms. Users can find it more difficult to locate the cursor or to clearly perceive which record among several shown will receive actions like deletion and printing.

▶ *A form with an embedded subform* is very useful to display related data together. However, you may opt for a single-record subform display over the crowded continuous subform. See the discussion in the "Implementing Subforms" topic that follows.

▶ *A form with an embedded list box* summary of child records is sometimes an adequate subform substitute, as long as the user can easily navigate from the list to an editable version of its data on another form. This style is discussed in the section "Replacing Forms With Lists" later in this chapter.

▶ *A form whose child records display on another form* may need no subform at all. In some situations, the performance of an application is greatly enhanced by moving child records from a subform to a separate, dependent form. Complexity for the user is also reduced. Consider a customer record and related transactions. If the transactions are in a subform on the customer form, for each customer record displayed a query must run to bring the related transactions into the subform. This takes time. If, on the other hand, your user research tells you that users need to view the transaction detail for a customer on only 20 percent of all visits to the customer form, it is wise to move the transaction records to a separate form and load the form from a button on the customer form. Because the dependent form is needed only 20 percent of the time, it is only loaded on demand, thus making the customer form without the subform data speedier the other 80 percent of the time.

You can see from these examples that the common thread when choosing a form layout is balancing these needs: protecting the data, solving the users' needs, and maximizing performance.

When you are building a form to display a large number of fields, you must consider using multiple pages on the form. You can provide the user with buttons to use to move between the pages, with each button issuing the appropriate `GoToPage` method.

 Tip

The `GoToPage` method has a `Right` argument that prescribes a horizontal offset for the page within the form window. You can use this to create a form with more pages than are allowed in the 22-inch maximum form height by creating two columns of pages within a single form.

Implementing Subforms

What subforms giveth they also taketh away, by which I mean that subforms provide the ability to cram related data onto a parent form, but in the process of "cramming" they also may become difficult to use. With limited space (most subforms consume the lower half of a form, sometimes even less), it can be challenging to display enough data in a subform to make it useful.

Additionally, subforms create development challenges on two fronts:

Managing Events. When a user can move freely between a parent form and its subform, detecting focus changes, record saves, and similar events becomes more challenging for the developer. For example, when moving from a parent form into a subform, the parent's record is saved. This action may trigger validation and other events that intercept or abort the focus move to the subform, providing a challenge for developers and confusion for the users.

Data Synchronization. Frequently, a subform and its parent have more in common than key field values. Subforms sometimes must fetch information *from* the parent, or display information *on* the parent, as in the example of subform detail records that are totaled and show the total on the parent form.

In a standard form/subform approach, developers often crowd multiple detail records into a subform on the parent form. In this layout, there is often not adequate space to display each value. In a crowded subform, for example, users may be required to press Shift+F2 regularly to zoom on a Comment field's data.

In general, users will not need to see multiple detail records in order to receive value from the subform. Thus, a crowded subform can be made uncrowded by exposing only a single record on it at one time.

 Note

It is interesting to watch the facial expressions of users (and sometimes even developers) when they are shown subforms with a layout other than continuous records. Subform examples in print and in demo applications are usually laid out with continuous records, thus many Access owners do not even realize that they have other layout options available to them.

If single-record subforms are usually more friendly and descriptive, why not use such a layout in all cases? Primarily because users will voice two common complaints when you use this layout:

An inability to quickly move to a designated record. If a subform shows three or four records at one time, a user can quickly locate a desired record in it, sometimes without even scrolling down through the records. In contrast, a subform with a single record requires the user to move through records one by one in order to find the targeted record.

Extra confusion for non-sophisticated users. Users who are not familiar with your form's design may not understand that the subform contains multiple records if only one is shown at a time.

Both of these situations can be resolved, fortunately, through creative form design. For example, the form navigation techniques suggested in Chapter 14, "Navigating in Forms and Applications," can also be used to build friendlier subforms as easily as with parent forms.

Review the form shown in Figure 16.2. The subform contains navigation buttons and positional information such as that found on its parent form. The navigation buttons provide a strong visual clue to the user that there are multiple records inside the subform area. Users are unlikely to be confused by this layout. In addition, the developer achieves two important objectives with it:

Consistency of Code. The developer can take advantage of the navigation and validation code developed for parent forms and use the code on subforms as well. Both the parent and child forms can call a common library of navigation code.

Fig. 16.2
This form and its subform use similar navigation strategies.

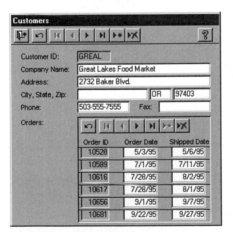

Consistency of Design. Using a similar metaphor for navigation on parent forms and their children reduces user confusion and, correspondingly, the training and documentation burden for the form. For example, users click a Delete button on the

16

parent form to delete the current parent record, or click a similar-looking Delete button on the subform to delete its record. This layout contrasts with the normal subform metaphor where record navigation, selection, and deletion are all handled from the record selector at the left of each record.

For data entry/edit forms, it can be quite useful to display subform records in the un-cluttered fashion shown in the previous figure. Users will be able to take advantage of standard form features such as combo boxes for selection, option group and check box controls, and text boxes that match the size of their average content.

However, if other types of forms are constructed against the same data, their use may dictate the display of the data in a different fashion. You have several creative options for altering the data display; a few examples follow.

Your first alternative is to create "exploding subforms." Because a subform control on an Access form can be resized programmatically, you can provide the user with the ability to "zoom" the subform on demand.

Assume that your subform control consumes the lower half of its parent form. You can place a Zoom button on the toolbar in the subform's header and toggle the zoom state of the subform between its normal size and a larger size, perhaps even filling the entire parent form. As you resize the subform, you can use the extra space to display additional controls that were hidden or increase the size of existing controls, such as showing ten lines of the Comment field where only one is shown in the default size.

Caution

Due to its unique window class, there are often display problems when you place other controls over the top of an Access List Box control—the list portion of the control may bleed through. You should not resize a subform to cover a list box located on the parent form.

Tip

If your application and user base comfortably support multi-page forms, you can place a subform on the second page of the parent form in order to provide it with the full height of the parent, but with a lower coding and usability burden than is attached to the zooming technique.

Alternatively, you can create a tabbed form layout with the parent form's controls on the first page of a tab control and the subform on the second page.

Another way to alter the display of subform data is to display only fields relevant to the form's specific purpose. A subform for data entry must usually provide access to all editable fields in the underlying recordset. In comparison, subforms on specialty edit or browse forms can be tailored to the task at hand.

For example, assume a customer form whose specific purpose is to flag orders for the customer as they are shipped. The parent form would display the customer information, and the subform would show the orders. There may be no need to display on the subform all of the order information in order to accomplish the task at hand. Instead, you could create a subform that displayed only the fields OrderID, OrderDate, and ShippedDate, which provide enough information for the user to indicate each invoice's payment status.

A subform with many records and few fields (thus a narrow display footprint) is a candidate for a taller display than is normally used with subforms. Figure 16.3 shows an order subform consuming the entire height of its parent form rather than located at the bottom. The subform shows only order date information and would be used by data entry personnel to enter or verify the Date Shipped values.

Fig. 16.3
This subform displays only a selected subset of fields and uses a non-standard layout.

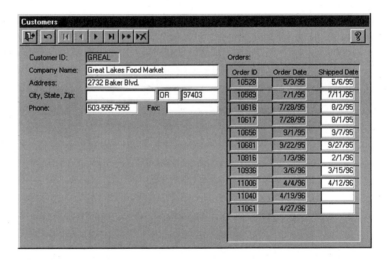

In some cases, a subform itself must be multi-page or must contain other subforms. Technologically, Access supports these needs. However, such complexity may be hard to use and will bump into serious space limitations on lower resolution monitors. At that point, you will need to consider making the subform into a form of its own, and creating methods for moving between the new form and its parent form. Techniques for synchronizing a form with its dependent form are discussed in the section "Synchronizing One Form with Another" later in this chapter.

A final option for creative subform displays is to use the datasheet view of information in a subform. Review Figure 16.1 in the prior section "Exploring Form Layout Options" for an example of this technique.

The primary challenge with a datasheet as a subform is that the program code must be keenly aware of whether the parent form or the subform has the focus. For example, in Chapter 14, "Navigating in Forms and Applications," I showed routines to support custom navigation buttons embedded on a form. The Last Record button on the example form in that chapter calls a library routine for navigation by passing it a handle to the form itself:

```
Call lci_FrmNavGotoLast(Me)
```

Consider instead the form shown in Figure 16.1, where the Last Record button is on the parent form but the actual records are on the subform datasheet. To navigate through the subform, the library routine must now receive a pointer to the subform's Form property, not the parent's; thus the button on the parent must issue this code instead:

```
Call lci_FrmNavGotoLast(Me!subCust_DS.Form)
```

As another example of the challenges of multi-record layouts, subform datasheets expose their data to bulk deletions. A subform datasheet with the record selectors showing allows for the selection of more than one record before an operation like Cut and Delete. Your code must determine how to best protect the data in such cases. For example, the SelHeight property of a datasheet indicates how many records are currently selected, so your subform's Delete event could contain this code:

```
If Me.SelHeight > 1 Then
  ' Show an alert and disallow the deletion
```

Replacing Forms With Lists

Whenever the updatability of a subform is not required, consider replacing a subform with a List Box control. Often, the nature of subform data prescribes that it need not be editable, so why incur the overhead of subform loading for no good reason?

Assume that you want to display on a parent form its related historical records, audit trail information, transactions, or similar non-editable dependent records. Displaying this information in a list box control instead of a subform would provide you with tangible performance benefits on two fronts:

▶ A ListBox is a native form control on the parent form and will load faster than a subform, which is an additional form object that must be loaded and embedded on the parent.

▶ Access creates a non-editable snapshot by default for a List Box control, so the data will load faster than with a subform due to the removal of multi-user management overhead.

In a similar vein, you can use list box controls on a form with no subform, replacing the form's continuous display mode with a continuous list. Obviously, if editability is an issue, a list box is not a sufficient replacement for a continuous form. However, you can create a hybrid form that includes both a list box *and* editable fields. See Figure 16.4.

Fig. 16.4

A list box control provides a handy device to navigate through form records.

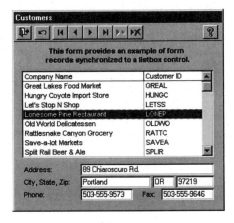

To keep the form data synchronized with the list box, use the Find methods against the form's recordset when the list box value changes. See the example in the upcoming section "Synchronizing a Form to a Value."

 Note

This model works best when the fields in the list box are *not* among those that are edited by the user. Because the list box is unbound from data, if the user changes a value in the editable portion of the form that is also reflected on the list, your code will need to requery the list to display the change.

Using a Tab Control

Before the advent of an intrinsic tab control in Access, we were forced to concoct workarounds for what is an excellent data management metaphor. Imagine a customer record that has multiple invoices, addresses, and contact people as child records. There is no better display model for information like this than a tabbed metaphor with one tab control and several attached subforms, one on each tab page for each of the three child tables.

Prior to a built-in tab control, developers used tab-style ActiveX controls in Access instead. However, you could not bind Access controls to the embedded tabs, because Access did not—and does not—support binding its controls to ActiveX controls. Thus, all movement between tabs and the display of information related to each tab was managed by program code. You can now discard your ActiveX tab controls and their workaround code in favor of the Access tab.

16

Let's explore a technique for managing parent/child information using the new tab control. Figure 16.5 displays the control on a form. This control has a "body" that hosts a Pages collection of Page objects. Each page can contain different controls that will be displayed only when that page is active (its tab is selected).

Fig. 16.5

This form uses the new tab control, shown here with two tabs.

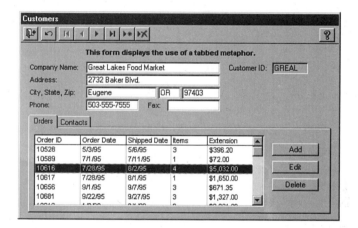

Working with the tab control is very simple. The current tab number provides the Value property of the control (zero-based), as well as the index into the Pages collection. Thus, for the form in Figure 16.5, the Debug window would return these values:

```
? Forms!frmCust_Tab!tabDetail.Value
0
? Forms!frmCust_Tab!tabDetail.Pages(0).Name
pgeOrders
```

A control on a tab page is still a member of the parent form (in its Controls collection), but is also a member of the Controls collection for its host page on the tab. Thus, a control on a tab page can be addressed in several ways, as shown in the examples in Listing 16.1. The statements in the listing were run in the Debug window while the form in Figure 16.5 was open.

Listing 16.1   Examples of Syntax for Addressing a Tab Control and its Child Controls

```
' A control on a tab is also in the forms Controls list
? Forms!frmCust_Tab.Controls(26).Name
lstOrder

' A control on a tab is also a child of the form
? Forms!frmCust_Tab!lstOrder.Value
10528

' Each tab page has a Controls collection
? Forms!frmCust_Tab!pgeOrders.Controls(0).Name
lstOrder

' Controls on a tab are children of the tab page
? Forms!frmCust_Tab!pgeOrders.Controls!lstOrder.Value
10528

' A tab has a Pages collection with child controls
? Forms!frmCust_Tab!tabDetail.Pages(0).Controls!lstOrder.Value
    10528
```

Figure 16.6 shows the second tab from the form in Figure 16.5. Note how a tab page makes a perfect host for a subform control.

Fig. 16.6

A tab control provides a mechanism for showing different information on each tab.

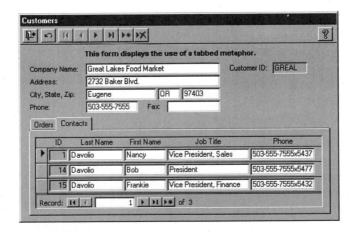

Synchronizing Record Displays

One of Access's strongest features is the seamless manner in which forms and subforms are linked. Not only are subform records automatically kept synchronized with the parent records, but information that cascades from the parent form to the subform or the reverse is refreshed automatically for the user.

As you build forms that are more complex than standard form/subform pairs, you will find new challenges related to keeping records synchronized. Forms can have relationships with each other; therefore, data on a particular form can have a relationship with data displayed simultaneously elsewhere.

The next several topics discuss some of the challenges and techniques related to synchronizing information between forms.

Synchronizing a Form to a Value

By using the FilterName or WhereCondition arguments of the OpenForm method, you can open a form to a single record or to the first record in a designated record source. However, there may be instances where you want to display a record to the user other than the first one. You can use program code to synchronize a form to a specific record.

The simplest technique for making a form's recordset display a specific record is using the FindRecord method. This method invokes the search engine from the Find dialog to locate a control value in the form's recordset.

To move a form to the first record whose CustID value is 100, for example, your form code would issue the following commands (presuming that the table field CustID is bound to text box txtCustID):

```
Me!txtCustID.SetFocus
DoCmd.FindRecord FindWhat:=100
```

The shortcomings of this technique are two-fold:

> *Error Handling.* If the find operation fails, an Access error is not generated. Your application must programmatically determine if there was no match or perhaps multiple matches.

> *Focus.* The FindRecord method operates on the control with focus. Either the user or your code must move the cursor to the target field before initiating the find operation. This may be an annoying change of focus for the user or require additional programming by the developer.

Note

If the value you are synchronizing the form to is not unique in the form's recordset, the first `FindRecord` operation may not locate the expected target. In such a scenario, you must provide users with the ability to initiate an additional `FindRecord` that starts searching at the current location, so that they can move among the several candidates and decide which match to stop at.

The `FindFirst` argument of the `FindRecord` method determines whether the search starts at the beginning of the form's recordset (`FindFirst` is `True`) or at the current record (`FindFirst` is `False`). Thus the following line would begin searching at (actually after) the current record.

```
DoCmd.FindRecord FindWhat:=100, FindFirst:=False
```

A second alternative for locating a specific record in a form's recordset using VBA code is to use the `FindFirst` method. Because `FindFirst` is a recordset operation, you must apply it to the form's recordset directly (via its clone). The code to synchronize a form's recordset with a List Box control, as described in the earlier section "Replacing Forms With Lists," would look like this:

```
Dim rst As Recordset
Set rst = Me.RecordsetClone
rst.FindFirst "CustomerID = '" & Me!lstCust.Value & "'"
Me.Bookmark = rst.Bookmark
```

 Note

To access a form's recordset, use the `RecordSetClone` property as shown. Move and Find operations applied to the recordset returned by this property do not cause the form to change its current record; thus, you can perform any valid DAO recordset operation against any record in the clone and only show results to the user when you deem it appropriate. The previous code shows how to synchronize the form's displayed record to the record that is current in the clone by synchronizing their bookmarks.

The advantages of the `FindFirst` approach shown over `FindRecord` are two-fold:

Easier error trapping. When a `FindFirst` does not discover a match, it sets the recordset's `NoMatch` property to `True`. Testing for this situation in code is easier than trapping for a failed `FindRecord`, which generates no error.

No change of focus. By operating against the form's recordset directly, this method does not rely on the cursor's location within a form and, consequently, does not need to relocate the focus to execute.

 Note

If your needs warrant, your code can call the other Find methods (`FindLast`, `FindNext`, and `FindPrevious`) against the form's recordset in the same fashion as previously shown.

Code to find a specific record can be used to improve a form's recovery from a forced requery. While the previous `FindFirst` example showed the use of a form recordset's `Bookmark` property to synchronize to a specified record, be aware that all bookmarks are invalidated when a recordset is requeried. Thus, you can save and reuse bookmarks when working with a form's recordset, but you cannot use a saved bookmark following a requery because all bookmarks are destroyed and rebuilt differently when the recordset is rebuilt. You can use the `FindFirst` method instead of a bookmark to move to a specified record in this scenario.

For example, when you run code to delete a record programmatically from a form's recordset, you must requery the form to display the change. The requery will cause the form to display its first record again rather than synchronizing back to the pre-requery location. A friendlier approach is to recreate the functionality provided by Access itself when the deletion occurs through the user interface—the record following the deleted record becomes the current record. To do this in code, your routine can preserve the ID (*not* the bookmark) of the record following the deletion target, then delete the record, requery the form, and finally resynchronize to the preserved location, as in Listing 16.2.

 Note

The code in the listing presumes that the `CustomerID` values are unique in the underlying table. When you use a strategy like the one shown to locate a specific record in code, make certain that you use a unique (usually primary key) value with the `FindFirst`.

Listing 16.2   AES_Frm4.Mdb—Resynchronizing a Form After a Deletion

```
Private Sub btnDelete_Click()
' Purpose: Delete a record and resynch the form to previous location

  Dim rst     As Recordset
  Dim varSave As Variant

  Beep
  If MsgBox("Are you sure you want to delete " _
    & Me!txtCustomerID & "?", vbOKCancel, "Delete") = vbCancel Then
    GoTo btnDelete_Click_Exit
  End If
  Set rst = Me.RecordsetClone
  rst.FindFirst "CustomerID = '" & Me!txtCustomerID & "'"
  If Not rst.NoMatch Then
    rst.MoveNext
    If Not rst.EOF Then
      varSave = rst!CustomerID   ' Save the return location
    End If
    rst.MovePrevious
    rst.Delete
  End If
  Me.Requery  ' Jumps to beginning of recordset
  ' Resynchronize the form
  If Not IsNull(varSave) Then
    Set rst = Me.RecordsetClone
    rst.FindFirst "CustomerID = '" & varSave & "'"
  End If
  Me.Bookmark = rst.Bookmark

btnDelete_Click_Exit:
  On Error Resume Next
  rst.Close
  Exit Sub

End Sub
```

An additional, and friendlier, approach to assisting users with form record navigation is to use a combo box on the form, populated with the same records as in the form's recordset. The combo box contains an AfterUpdate event procedure to synchronize the form to the user's selection, as in the following listing:

```
Set rst = Me.RecordsetClone
rst.FindFirst "CustomerID = '" & Me!cboCust.Value & "'"
Me.Bookmark = rst.Bookmark
```

If a form's recordset is large, the selection combo box will be lengthy; and you may decide to filter it to reflect a subset of the form's records rather than the entire recordset. A second combo box, a check box, or an option group are good candidate controls for enabling this feature.

Note

When you filter a selection combo, there is usually no need to filter the form's recordset itself to match that in the combo. The form can continue to include all records even when its selection control displays a subset. Requerying the form when its selector is rebuilt is an unnecessary performance hit given your objective, which is to give the user a list of all or some of the form's ID values from which to choose.

As an example, a combo box containing the states (the *filter combo*) can be placed next to the record *selector combo* that lists customers. When the user selects a state, only the records for that state will be displayed in the selection combo box, because the state list will rebuild the selection combo by issuing a `Requery` method on it.

In turn, the dependent selector combo box must utilize the information from the filter combo in its SQL statement:

```
SELECT CustomerID, CompanyName
  FROM tblCust
  WHERE State LIKE Forms!frmCust!cboState
```

 Tip

If one of the options in the filter combo box is an asterisk, the selection combo box's SQL statement must use the LIKE keyword as shown so that it will display all possible records when the user selects the "all" (*) filter. (You can learn how to add an "all" marker to a combo box in Chapter 13, "Mastering Combo and List Boxes.")

Because of the need to frequently requery a record selection combo, especially in an entry form where the recordset is changing regularly, you can implement a simplified method for locating form records through buttons. You can place multiple buttons on the form or its header, with the code for each button jumping to a specific location in the recordset.

As an example, you could place 26 buttons on a form whose record source is sorted alphabetically, with the alphabet characters *A* through *Z* as the button captions. Clicking a button would use the `FindFirst` method to synchronize the form to the first record beginning with the selected character:

```
Me!txtCustID.SetFocus
DoCmd.FindRecord FindWhat:= "w", Match:=acStart
```

> **Note**
>
> This method is useful for jumping to a relative location in a form's recordset, but not for finding a specific record, unless you can place a button on the form for each record in the recordset.
>
> Techniques for jumping to a specific location in a form's recordset often assume that the recordset is sorted in a manner that supplements the jump. Using the current example, jumping to the first state value that begins with the letter "w" does not provide the user with much worth unless the form's recordset is sorted by state, so that the user can see the other "w" records by moving forward through the recordset after the find operation.

The previous techniques enable you to make locating designated form records easier for your users. Note that the record location and synchronization techniques described in this section differ from the ability to *filter* a form, as provided programmatically through the `Filter` property or by using the <u>R</u>ecords, <u>F</u>ilter menu options in the user interface. Form filtration restricts the actual contents of the form's recordset, while navigating to a specific record preserves the recordset unaltered. Each feature is useful, but in different contexts.

Synchronizing One Form with Another

When two forms are related to each other, the need will arise to synchronize the information they display. In the simplest scenario, the user is on `frmCust` (the "calling form") and selects a related record to view on `frmOrder` (the "dependent form"). When `frmCust` opens `frmOrder`, code can pass a `WhereCondition` argument in the `OpenForm` method to display the desired record.

In this example, the recordset on `frmOrder` is restricted to a single record related to the calling form, so there is no need to resynchronize the forms in the reverse direction, from `frmOrder` to `frmCust`, when the dependent form closes.

A more complex situation arises when the calling form displays a dependent form with more than one record, and when both forms must be synchronized to each other. The synchronization must occur at one of two locations in the flow:

> *At every record movement.* If your forms are both displayed simultaneously, the calling form must be synchronized with the dependent form at each relevant `Current` event. For example, if `frmCust` and `frmOrder` are displayed side-by-side, and the user can browse all invoices, each time a different invoice is selected the form's code must determine if the customer showing on the customer form is the correct parent record of the current invoice and synchronize the calling form if not.

When the second form closes. If the calling form is not displayed while the dependent form is open, your code needs to synchronize the calling form only once. In the dependent form's Close event, you can place code to synchronize the calling form to the last value on the dependent.

Let's inspect a code sample that synchronizes the display between a calling form and a dependent form. We can utilize the same technique described in the previous section by exposing the calling form's synchronization routine as a Public procedure and calling it from the dependent form.

In this example, the calling form frmCust_Tab has a list box control from which to select a target order. The user can click an order in the list and then click Edit to launch frmOrder and see more detail for that order. Figure 16.7 represents this scenario.

Fig. 16.7

The list box on the customer form and the current record on the order form here are kept synchronized with each other.

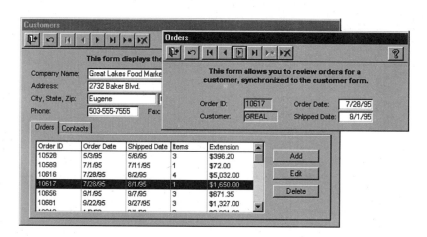

The objective is for the Edit button's event code to open frmOrder with a record source that includes all of the orders for the displayed customer, and then synchronize to the item selected in the list box.

The first step is to have the calling form open the dependent form and display on it only the related records:

```
Private Sub cmdEdit_Click()
' Show all orders for this customer

DoCmd.OpenForm "frmOrder", , _
    , "CustomerID = '" & Me!txtCustomerID & "'", , , Me!lstOrder
```

Note that the called form frmOrder is modal (its saved Modal property is True), thus the code in the calling form will halt when the called form is opened and wait for the form to close. Thus, any synchronization code cannot come after the OpenForm method in the calling form. Instead, the value used for synchronization must be passed to the modal form via its OpenArgs argument (the Me!lstOrder item in the code block shown above).

When the popup form opens, it synchronizes itself to the caller by applying the passed OpenArgs value to its recordset, as shown in Listing 16.3.

Listing 16.3 AES_Frm4.Mdb—Synchronizing a Form to a Value Passed to its Recordset

```
Private Sub Form_Load()

  Call cbfSynch(Me.OpenArgs)

End Sub

Private Sub cbfSynch(rvarID As Variant)
' Purpose: Synchronize the form to a passed value

  Dim rst As Recordset

  If Not IsNull(rvarID) Then
    Set rst = Me.RecordsetClone
    rst.FindFirst "OrderID = " & rvarID
    Me.Bookmark = rst.Bookmark
  End If

  rst.Close
End Sub
```

As the user browses through orders, the dependent form's code moves the selection in the calling form's list box to match the selection on the dependent form. Thus the order form's Current event has code like this:

```
Forms!frmCust_Tab!lstOrder = Me!txtOrderID
```

Notice how this example is in sharp contrast to the standard approach of simply opening the order form with a restriction to display only the single targeted order. In that model, the user must open and close the popup form each time a specific record's detail is desired. The example shown here is much more friendly and flexible.

In addition to the challenge of synchronizing the displayed records, dependent forms bring with them the additional burden of synchronizing data changes. For example, frmOrder and frmCust_Tab in Figure 16.7 both display the values for Order Date and Shipped Date. Changing one of these values on the order form will require a requery of the list box on the calling form:

```
Private Sub Form_AfterUpdate()
  Forms!frmCust_Tab!lstOrder.Requery
End Sub
```

You can probably envision even more complex derivatives of this example scenario, with dependent forms calling their own dependent forms, nesting the dependencies several levels deep. Regardless of the complexity of your scenario, you will still utilize the same techniques for synchronizing forms listed in this section.

Helping Users Locate Records

When users interact with form data, they must first be able to select a specific record or sets of records on which to operate. Access provides three *built-in* mechanisms for finding specific records: the new Filter By Form and Filter By Selection capabilities, and the standard Find dialog. However, your applications will sometimes require functionality more powerful than, or different from, these new features.

The section "Presenting Records to Users" earlier in this chapter demonstrated the use of Combo Box and List Box controls on a form to navigate within the form's recordset. When utilizing the record navigation techniques described in that section (as well as the new Access filter features), bear in mind that such approaches are generic in nature—users must know either the record they are looking for in advance, or the criteria for finding the record.

On the other hand, if the path the users will take most commonly to find or define a data subset is known at application design time, you can provide advanced record selection capabilities as you build the application. I have found that user satisfaction with our applications has increased as we have refined our ability to provide robust interfaces for record location/selection.

In a perfect world, the Access query grid would be an object that we as developers could program. It would be great to display a query grid to users, pre-populated with specific tables and fields, and have the user determine the criteria. Your applications could then use this information as a filter string or WHERE clause in an SQL statement.

In the absence of such niceties, you must determine what ad hoc query requirements your users will have, and how to provide them with these capabilities. The remainder of this chapter concentrates on several such data location techniques.

Implementing Query-By-Form

Every major application should have a system administrator. One of the tasks usually assigned to this person is to facilitate the users' ability to interrogate the application's data.

The simplest model employed is for people to e-mail their data extraction requests to the system administrator, who runs impromptu queries and forwards the results in a spreadsheet, document, or database table back to the requester. More complex models create read-only replicas of the application's data and let users do their own ad hoc queries off of the non-production copy of the data.

In between these two poles is a technique called "query-by-form." Precisely as the name implies, you must create a form to allow users to build queries. There is no standard model for a query-by-form interface; you simply create the layout that works best for the specific combination of users and application.

Figure 16.8 shows an example of a form that implements query-by-form. The form has these attributes:

Select a table or query. The form provides a combo box list of tables and queries from which the user can select fields. This list should be limited to those tables and queries that are the most frequently accessed for ad hoc query purposes.

 Tip

Most query-by-form screens do not allow the user to join tables, because creating an interface to support this task is programmatically challenging. Instead, create a set of saved queries designed specifically to join tables into datasets that will be useful when interrogating the database. Display these queries in the list of tables and queries on the query-by-form screen. See Chapter 10, "Creating Expert Tables and Queries," for information on the various types of saved joins you can create to help users explore data.

Select a field. When the user selects a source table or query, the form must display a list of fields in the source object. The user can select one or more fields to query.

Enter a value. After selecting a field, the user applies a comparison operator and a criterion against the field.

Add the operators. If your query-by-form screen allows multiple fields and criteria to be entered, you must provide a mechanism for the user to join the criteria with AND or OR operators, as demonstrated in the figure by the Connector option.

 Note

Unless users understand how SQL operators are applied, allowing the user to create multiple criteria values and apply AND/OR operators *between* each criteria comparison can create a confusing situation (as in "A OR B AND C OR D"). In many environments, it is safer to build a query-by-form screen that either allows the entry of only one set of criteria, or alternatively that applies the AND or OR operator to every criterion uniformly, as in the figure.

Fig. 16.8

A "query-by-form" layout is designed to assist users as they build an ad hoc search string.

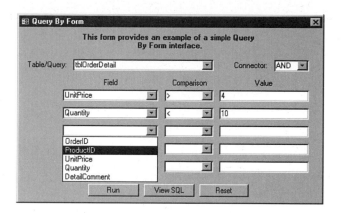

Here are some of the mechanical aspects of the form shown in the previous figure:

▶ The list of tables/queries for the combo box control must be derived from either a DAO routine or by querying against the Access system table MSysObjects, which lists all database objects. For example, this code in the RowSource of the combo box in the form pulls in a list of user-oriented tables and queries:

```
SELECT Name FROM MSysObjects
  WHERE Name Not Like "MSys*" And Name Not Like "~*" And Name Not Like "zt*" _
    And Type In (1,5)
  ORDER BY Name;
```

The Name field of the MSysObjects system table holds the names of objects known to Access, and the Type values 1 and 5 restrict the list to table and query names. The WHERE clause shown excludes system objects that the user should not be querying—Access system tables/queries ("MSys*" and "~*"), and temporary objects as identified by LNC ("zt*").

For your own query-by-form screens, you can build a selective list of tables and queries for the combo box by listing objects that fit a specific naming convention, creating your own "lookup table" of table names, or creating custom object properties to flag objects that can be queried by the users.

▶ My code makes use of the new Collection object in Access by creating a collection array with one dimension for each of the triads Field/Comparison/Value from the form. I define the collection, and the constants to use for indexing it, in the Declarations section of the form, like this:

```
Private mcolQBF(1 To 5) As New Collection  ' Collection of field sets

Private Const mcbytField As Byte = 1  ' Field item
Private Const mcbytComp  As Byte = 2  ' Comparison item
Private Const mcbytValue As Byte = 3  ' Value item
```

Then, whenever I need to visit all of the criteria controls on the form, I simply loop through the collection. For example, here is code from the Reset button to clear the criteria fields:

```
Dim ibyt As Byte

For ibyt = 1 To 5
  mcolQBF(ibyt)(mcbytField) = Null
  mcolQBF(ibyt)(mcbytComp) = Null
  mcolQBF(ibyt)(mcbytValue) = Null
Next ibyt
```

▶ The combo boxes that provide lists of fields have their RowSourceType properties set to Field List and their RowSource properties set dynamically to the name of the table or query in the Table/Query combo:

```
Private Sub cboTbl_AfterUpdate()
' Purpose: Reload the field lists on table/query selection

  Dim ibyt As Byte

  Call cbfReset(False)  ' Don't reset top line
  For ibyt = 1 To 5
    mcolQBF(ibyt)(mcbytField).RowSource = Me!cboTbl
    mcolQBF(ibyt)(mcbytField).Requery
  Next ibyt

End Sub
```

▶ The Run button builds and executes an SQL statement based on the criteria the user has entered. By looping through the control triads, as in the previous code sample, the code concatenates the user's criteria into a WHERE statement, and then prefixes it with SELECT * FROM *tablename* to create a result set (refer back to the figure). The code builds a temporary query to display the result set and displays it to the user:

```
Dim dbs    As Database
Dim qdf    As QueryDef
Dim strSQL As String

Set dbs = CurrentDb

strSQL = cbfSQLBuild()
If Len(strSQL) > 0 Then
  On Error Resume Next
  dbs.QueryDefs.Delete "ztqryQBF"
  On Error GoTo cmdRun_Click_Err
  Set qdf = dbs.CreateQueryDef("ztqryQBF", strSQL)
  DoCmd.OpenQuery "ztqryQBF", acNormal, acReadOnly
End If
```

Tip

I used the `acReadOnly` argument on the `OpenQuery` statement so that users cannot edit data presented to them by this ad hoc interrogation tool. If you need to allow system administrators to edit the results of ad hoc browsing, set this flag based on the current user ID and do not include it for administrators. This simple but effective security strategy gives the users some of the power of the query design grid without the complexity or direct access to data.

Alternately, in a secured environment you can set the `QueryDef` to run with user's permissions only, which will ensure that only people with editing rights can modify the raw data presented.

16

Figure 16.9 shows the temporary query that was built from the selections in the previous figure.

Fig. 16.9

This query result set was built from a temporary query written by code in the "query-by-form" object.

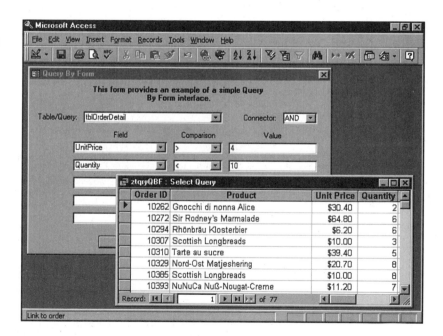

More complex versions of query-by-form screens can include these additional features:

▶ The ability for the user to name the query created by the process and save it for later reuse.

▶ Export capabilities to send the selected dataset to a table, to Excel, or to Word.

▶ The ability to edit the SQL statement before running it to enhance the WHERE clause syntax or criteria groupings.

▶ Controls that help the user build an ORDER BY clause to sort the resulting dataset.

A query-by-form interface such as the one shown presents users with an easy-to-use device for asking simple questions of their data. In many applications, the combination of comprehensive reporting and a simple query interface such as the one shown is adequate for all user requirements.

Creating a "Get" Form

An alternative record selection approach to the query-by-form tool is to create a form for filtering a specific dataset. Its record source would be specified in the design, and the form's purpose would be to help the user locate one record within a larger record set.

For example, users enter customer orders into an application. When customers call in later to ask questions about an order, the caller may not have the order number. Users of this system would require a tool for finding an order quickly while knowing only one or two of its attributes.

Figure 16.10 shows a form that assists users with this process. We call such a form a "Get" form because with it the user can easily get to one record.

Fig. 16.10

We build many of our applications around this proprietary Get form layout designed to help users filter and locate records.

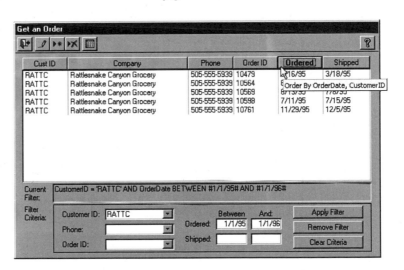

The Get form is arranged to help the user find records by applying the most convenient criteria information. The user can enter one or more criteria values and receive a filtered list of matches.

Note

Eighty percent of the time, your users will be trying to find records by searching only 20 percent of the application's table fields. If you correctly identify these fields and provide an interface to query them, you will have provided your users with a great benefit.

16

Here are a few features of our standard Get form:

Sorting. The form in the figure employs sort buttons above the list box columns to allow the user to easily sort the list items by any column, much like lists in the Windows 95 interface.

Simple Filtration. The user enters filter criteria into controls by typing or selecting values, then applies the filter. Removing the filter is also simple, and the currently applied filter criteria are displayed in a text box.

Fast Loading. If you have a small, predefined record set, you can load a Get form with all of the records in the set displayed in the list. In general, however, our model is to load the form with the list empty. This provides faster form loading and lessens user confusion by enabling users to select a range of criteria and narrow the scope of the list *before* they see any records.

Selection. Once the user has filtered the list to one or several records, the target record should be easy to locate. The user can then double-click the record in the list, or click the Edit tool on the top of the form to initiate a code event to display an edit form bound to the selected record.

Here are high-level steps to create a Get form like the one shown:

1. Add a List Box control to the form and create a row source for it if you want it to load populated, or leave the row source blank for faster loading. Size the list box columns to display the data cleanly.

2. Create a variable in the form's module to hold the raw SQL statement that provides the rows for the list box. The simple SELECT statement should have no WHERE or ORDER BY clauses:

```
Private Const mcstrSQL As String = _
    "SELECT CustomerID, CompanyName, Phone, OrderID, OrderDate, ShippedDate " _
    & " FROM qryCustOrder"
```

3. Place command buttons above the list box columns that will be used to sort the data. In the ControlTipText property of each button, place a control tip that will also serve as the ORDER BY clause when sorting the list. Such tip text would look like this:

```
Order By CompanyName, OrderDate
```

Note

I placed the ORDER BY clause in the ControlTipText property so that it is conveyed to users when they hover over a sort button with the mouse, and is also available to my code. Alternatively, you could store the ORDER BY information in the Tag property instead and create a different control tip string to show the user.

4. Add the filter display text box, and add as many criteria controls as are required to help the user work with the listed data. In general, you will select the most important records from the underlying data set to display in the limited width of the list box, then give the user a control for each column in the list in order to apply criteria to each important field.

 Tip

You do not have to squeeze all the relevant information into the width of the list box. Because list box controls can have a horizontal scroll bar, you can place more columns in the list than are displayed in its width. However, doing this removes your ability to have the sort buttons at the top of the columns because there is no way to match the button text and events to the columns as the user scrolls horizontally in the list.

5. Add the buttons that will provide the filtration capabilities. We use text on the buttons—Apply Filter and Remove Filter—that will be familiar to most Access users.

6. Now begin creating your code. I have not provided all of the code here, just a few listings to give you a sense of the mechanics; the remainder of the code is on the CD-ROM in AES_FRM4.MDB.

7. The form's Load event initializes a module-level variable that points to the currently selected button; this is used to retrieve the ORDER BY statement from the control tip (see step 9.) Initializing the variable in this event presets the sort order to use the first time the list is loaded. This event also places a help string in the filter text box to help new users understand how to proceed:

```
Private Sub Form_Load()
' Purpose: Set sort to first column

   Set mcmdSort = Me!cmdCustID  ' Set pointer to sort button
   mcmdSort.FontWeight = mcintBold  ' Bold current sort button
   Me!txtFilter = "<Click Remove Filter to display all records>"

End Sub
```

8. Next, create the code behind each sort button's `Click` event. This event must reset the pointer variable to reference the current sort order, and also sets the font effect of the button representing the sort order to bold. For example, the following code is in the `Click` event for `cmdCompany`, the button to sort by company name:

```
mcmdSort.FontWeight = mcintNormal   ' Unbold previous sort button
Set mcmdSort = Me!cmdCompany  ' Set pointer to sort button
mcmdSort.FontWeight = mcintBold   ' Bold current sort button
Call cbfRequery  ' Rebuild the list
```

16

9. Finally, build the query logic. This routine must traverse the criteria controls and build an SQL statement from those that are filled in. The SQL is used as the `RowSource` property for the list. The code (abbreviated) to build the search statement is shown in Listing 16.4.

Listing 16.4   AES_Frm4.Mdb—Building a RowSource for a Get Form List

```
Private Sub cbfRequery()
' Purpose: Build SQL and requery the list box

Dim strFilter As String

DoCmd.Hourglass True
If Not IsNull(Me!cboCustID) Then
  strFilter = strFilter & " CustomerID = '" & Me!cboCustID & "' AND"
End If
If Not IsNull(Me!cboPhone) Then
  strFilter = strFilter & " Phone = '" & Me!cboPhone & "' AND"
End If
...
' Code here continues adding other criteria to the string
...
  ' Cleanup the string
  If Right(strFilter, 3) = "AND" Then ' Strip trailing AND
    strFilter = Trim(Left(strFilter, Len(strFilter) - 3))
  End If
  If Len(strFilter) > 0 Then
    Me!txtFilter = strFilter   ' Show the filter to the user
    strFilter = " WHERE " & strFilter
  Else
    Me!txtFilter = "<none>"
  End If
  strFilter = strFilter & " " & mcmdSort.ControlTipText  ' Add ORDER BY clause
  Me!lstOrder.RowSource = mcstrSQL & strFilter  ' Put SQL in the list box
  Me!lstOrder.Requery
  DoCmd.Hourglass False

End Sub
```

Notice that your code must carefully construct the SQL statement depending on the values available. The SELECT portion of the SQL never changes and thus comes from the constant `mcstrSQL`. The order for the list comes from the `ControlTipText` property of the button object (mcmdSort) that designates the current sort order. Finally, the WHERE clause is built from the criteria or is left blank if the user has entered no criteria, which causes the return of all records into the list.

While Get forms of this type are simplistic, they have proven enormously popular with our clients and are not expensive to code. These forms are most useful for unskilled data entry and edit personnel; power users will prefer direct access to the data, Access's Filter by Form screen, or a query-by-form model as shown in the previous section.

As you become adept at Get forms, you can extend their capabilities. Here are some advanced options we build into this type of form:

Printing. Get forms provide a useful interface for printing a specific record without having to load it into a form. Add a Print button to the toolbar and print the default detail report for the displayed records or only the single selected record when the user clicks the button.

For example, you can create a Get form that lists open invoices, enables the user to click a specific invoice, select the Print button, and send a statement for that open invoice to the printer.

Multiple Selection. Access's new multi-select list box capabilities provide you with the ability to have users select more than one record from a list on the Get form, then execute a process against the list.

For example, the code behind the Edit button on the toolbar could check to see if multiple records were selected, create an SQL IN clause from the ID values of the selected records, and open an edit form with a recordset containing only the selected items.

Direct jump to a record. If the Get form is the only gateway to a particular edit form, the model I have shown here penalizes users who know the unique ID of the record they are searching for at the time the form opens. You can solve this by adding a text box to your Get forms and allowing the user to type a primary key value directly into the text box and click the Edit button. This circumvents the filtration features and proceeds straight to a designated record.

Browsing. The Get form shown in the figure includes a Browse button on the toolbar. Such a button can be enabled to display a datasheet that lets users browse all of the records listed in the list box. The datasheet is provided by creating a query that uses the same SQL statement that drives the list box, as in the following:

```
Set qdf = dbs.CreateQueryDef("ztqryGetOrder", Me!lstOrder.RowSource)
DoCmd.OpenQuery "ztqryGetOrder", acNormal, acReadOnly
```

Descending Sorts. To match the true Windows 95 interface model, multiple clicks of a button at the top of a list column should toggle the sort order for that column between ascending and descending. You can easily add code to your Get forms to enable this capability.

Whether you use this form model for your users or contrive a different approach, the principle demonstrated here will prove useful to you. As databases get larger, users need to be able to work with small subsets of data or they feel overwhelmed; and the application performance suffers as well.

Writing a List Constructor

Having spent any time in Access at all, you will have seen the selection list box pairs that are common in the wizards. A listbox-based selection metaphor places two list boxes beside each other with buttons in the middle to move items back and forth, as shown in the Table Wizard form in Figure 16.11.

Fig. 16.11

The Access Table Wizard provides a list box-based layout for selecting multiple values.

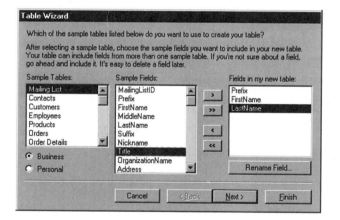

We call this combination of two list boxes and the selection buttons a "list constructor," because it is used to construct a selection list. To some extent, the usefulness of this interface tool has been lessened by the appearance of multi-select list boxes in Access. Nevertheless, a list constructor can do several things that a multi-select list cannot:

Display only the selected values. In a list box with multiple selections, the user must scroll up and down through the list to review selections and frequently will not see all of the selected values displayed in the list at one time. In contrast, the right-hand list in a list constructor pair shows only the selected values, providing less "clutter."

Allow for reordering of the selected values. In a multi-selected list, it is not possible to change the order of the selected items. To change item order, you need to be able to specify an item to move; but you cannot do so in a multi-select list without destroying the multiple selection. In other words, you can either select one record or multiple records, but you need both options in order to reorder.

A list constructor, on the other hand, allows you to select and operate on a specific individual record within the group of selected items.

Provide quick mass selection and de-selection of values. The Add All and Remove All buttons on a list constructor provide a quicker mechanism for selecting items in bulk than is provided by a single multi-select list.

Allow filtration. Using a list constructor, the available items list can be filtered, sorted, expanded, or contracted to show different blocks of information without losing track of the user's selection.

 Note

I will use the terms "available items list" and "selected items list" respectively to describe the left and right lists in a list constructor.

Figure 16.12 shows a list constructor based on the sample data used throughout this chapter. The tool in the figure allows a user to select one or more products and move them to the selected items list. The available items list can be filtered to remove clutter.

Fig. 16.12

This advanced selection wizard uses a pair of list box controls, list callback code, and a filtration combo box.

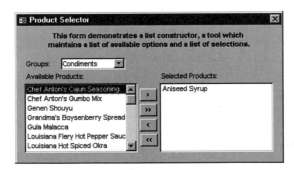

It would take an entire (lengthy) chapter to explain the workings of a list constructor in detail, so in this section I will only outline the concepts involved. Once you are familiar with list callback functions and working with arrays, you can tackle a list constructor.

> **Note**
>
> I have provided a library module of list constructor code and a working example in AES_FRM4.MDB on the CD-ROM for you to use as is or to reverse-engineer and improve.

The first concept that is important when building list constructors is an understanding of *callback functions*. (See Chapter 13, "Mastering Combo and List Boxes," to learn how these are built.) Both the available and the selected item lists make use of these handy devices.

The reason that callback functions provide value here is that both the available and selected item lists are fluid, rather than fixed. It is easy to drive a fixed list from a table or query; but in a list where the values change constantly, the performance hit of continuously writing and deleting available and selected items in work tables is not tolerable.

In contrast, a callback function can be constructed to derive its values from an array. Displaying items in the available and selected lists is actually enabled by setting flags on items in a master array and rebuilding both list boxes based on the flags.

Thus, the second important concept in a list constructor is the structure of the driving arrays. Listing 16.5 shows the Dim statements for the arrays I will use in this tutorial.

Listing 16.5   AES_Frm4.Mdb—Structures Used by the List Constructor

```
' Type structure for the display flags
Type typFlags
   blnSel   As Boolean
   blnAvail As Boolean
End Type

' Type structure containing selected & available pointers
Type typPtr
   intSel   As Integer
   intAvail As Integer
End Type

' List management arrays
Dim mastrLstWiz() As String   ' Contains the actual rows in the list
Dim matypFlags()  As typFlags ' Contains display flags
Dim matypPtr()    As typPtr    ' Contains the pointers to the master array items
```

The three arrays dimensioned in the code listing are used to do the majority of the work of the list constructor:

> `mastrLstWiz`. This *master values* array, shown in Table 16.2, stores the actual values used to fill the list (it is, essentially, the virtual table that provides each list's `RowSource`). The information in this array is delimited and stored in a single element, as in "17;Alice Mutton," so that our list constructor library routines can service a list with any number of columns. If you prefer not to use a single array element with a delimited compound string, your array can have one column element for each column in the list data.

> `matypFlags`. This array is displayed in Table 16.3. It has a row for each item in the master values array (`mastrLstWiz`) and two flags. The first flag (`blnAvail`) indicates if the item is currently part of the available list. The purpose of this flag is to enable filtration, not selection. An item is flagged as part of the available items list if it matches the filter criteria (as in the product group filter in the previous figure).

> The second flag in this array (`blnSel`) determines if the user has selected the item for inclusion in the selected items list. This flag is used to build the selected items list display.

> Whether or not an item that is flagged as available (`blnAvail`) is actually displayed in the available list is determined by the combination of this flag and its `blnSel` partner, in conjunction with the style of the list (copy versus move). List constructor code displays items in the available list based on the value pairs from this array, as shown in Table 16.1.

Table 16.1   How the Available List Is Displayed Based on the Two Flags in the *matypFlags* Array

List Type	blnAvail	blnSel	Show in Available List
Copy	True	False	Yes
Copy	True	True	Yes
Move	True	False	Yes
Move	True	True	No

> `matypPtr`. This array contains the array pointers to the items in the available and selected items lists, as shown in Table 16.4. Each value in this array is an *index* into the `mastrLstWiz` master array that extracts a specific value from the array when the list is filled by the callback function. This array is essentially a mirror of the two list boxes, with the available items listed in the `intAvail` array column and the selected items listed in the `intSel` column.

16

Tables 16.2 through 16.4 show the first three values in the three listed arrays after a constructor loads, and its arrays and list boxes have been initialized.

Table 16.2   The *mastrLstWiz* Array Stores all Available List Box Values, in this Case the Primary Key and Name for Each Product

Item	Value
(1)	17;Alice Mutton
(2)	3;Aniseed Syrup
(3)	40;Boston Crab Meat

Table 16.3   The *matypFlags* Array Determines How the Available and Selected Lists Display Their Values; Currently No Items Are Selected

Item	blnAvail	blnSel
(1)	True	False
(2)	True	False
(3)	True	False

Table 16.4   The *matypPtr* Array Mirrors the Structure of the List Boxes. Each Value Indicates an Index in the Master Array

Item	intAvail	intSel
(1)	1	0
(2)	2	0
(3)	3	0

The list callback derives its values from these structures by using the matypPtr array to locate a string in the mastrLstWiz array. Each time the callback fires to fetch a row to display in either the available or selected lists, it runs a line of code similar to this:

```
strValue = mastrLstWiz(matypPtr(vintRow).intAvail)
```

Using this line of code and referring back to the three previous tables, you note that if vintRow is 1, the value matypPtr(vintRow).intAvail translates into this string: matypPtr(1).intAvail, which (only by coincidence) happens to return a value of 1 (see the array contents in Table 16.4). This number provides the index for mastrLstWiz, so the command mastrLstWiz(matypPtr(vintRow).intAvail) translates into mastrLstWiz(1), which is

"17;Alice Mutton." Therefore, the previous code line fills the available list with "Alice Mutton" when fired in the callback function.

As you have divined by this point, if the callback makes its decisions by asking the matypPtr array for pointers to the available and selected list items, the majority of the work in moving items back and forth between lists becomes simply managing the values in this array.

Here is an outline of the processes to make a selection from the available list to the selected list:

1. Review the available list and see which item or items the user has selected. Flag the selected items in the flag array (matypFlags). Listing 16.6 provides a code snippet from this process.

Listing 16.6   AES_Frm4.Mdb—Determining the User's Selections

```
For Each varItm In rlstAvail.ItemsSelected
  ' Get the primary key value from the list
  varValue = rlstAvail.Column(0, varItm)
  ' Search in the master array for the selected item
  For iintLoop = 1 To mintMaxRow
    ' Find the primary key value in the master array
    If lci_DelimItemGet(mastrLstWiz(iintLoop), ";", 1) = varValue Then
      matypFlags(iintLoop).blnSel = True   ' Flag as selected
      Exit For
    End If
  Next iintLoop
Next varItm
```

2. Traverse the flag array (matypFlags) updated in the previous step and rebuild from it the pointer array (matypPtr), which mirrors the two lists shown to the user. Each item in the flag array is checked to see if it is available for display in the available list and, if so, is added to the pointer array dimension for that list. The process is then repeated for the selected list. Listing 16.7 provides a code snippet that helps demonstrate the process.

Listing 16.7   AES_Frm4.Mdb—Building the Selection Pointer Array

```
intCount = 0
' matypLst is an info array not described in the tutorial
' matypLst.intRows simply contains the number of rows in the matypFlags array
For iintLoop = 1 To matypLst.intRows
  If matypFlags(iintLoop).blnAvail And Not matypFlags(iintLoop).blnSel Then
    intCount = intCount + 1
    matypPtr(intCount).intAvail = iintLoop
  End If
Next
```

3. Requery the list boxes, which runs the callback function for each row in each list. As described earlier, the callback function walks down the pointer array and fetches the corresponding strings from the master array, adding them to the list boxes.

Tables 16.5 through 16.7 show the first three values in the three arrays after a user filters the available list to display only "Condiments," and then moves the value "Aniseed Syrup" (the second value in the master array) from the available to the selected items list.

16

Table 16.5   The *mastrLstWiz* Array Stores all Available ListBox Values; This List Is Unchanged after a Move Operation

Item	Value
(1)	17;Alice Mutton
(2)	3;Aniseed Syrup
(3)	40;Boston Crab Meat

Table 16.6   The *matypFlags* Array Indicates that Only Items Matching the Filter Are Available, and that Item 2 in the Array Has Been Moved to the Selected List

Item	blnAvail	blnSel	Comment
(1)	False	False	"Alice Mutton" is not in the "Condiment" filter
(2)	True	True	"Aniseed Syrup" *is* a "Condiment" and *is* selected
(3)	False	False	"Boston Crab Meat" is not in the "Condiment" filter

Table 16.7   The *matypPtr* Array Mirrors the Structure of the List Boxes. Compared to Table 16.4, the Available List Has Been Filtered and the Selected List Now Has One Item

Item	intAvail	intSel
(1)	9	2
(2)	10	0
(3)	17	0

The code to facilitate a list constructor can be fairly non-intimidating once you understand the flow described here. The routines shown in this tutorial, and on the CD-ROM in AES_FRM4.MDB, are more complex than in a simple list constructor because they take two factors into account:

1. *Multiple lists serviced by one set of routines.* When building list constructor library routines, a single set of routines can help manage more than one pair of lists on the same form if you allow each list pair to be uniquely identified wherever used. (The code routines for this chapter on the CD demonstrate this in detail.)

2. *Multiple-selection and filtration.* The complexity of your constructor routines goes up dramatically if you must provide these two advanced capabilities.

While building your first set of list constructors can take some effort, once you have created a reusable methodology and code library for this interface device, you will find yourself using it in most of your applications. The usability advantages of this interface metaphor—users are familiar with it, and it is visually uncomplicated yet powerful— make it an appealing choice to solve many data management problems.

From Here...

An application's interface is enhanced by the accurate and simple presentation of information to its users and by assisting the users when they need to find specific information. The foundation for the ideas in this chapter was laid in these related chapters:

▶ The philosophical issues involved in designing and building effective user interfaces are found in Chapter 8, "Designing Effective Interfaces."

▶ Chapter 13, "Mastering Combo and List Boxes," discusses key interface concepts used in this chapter, including list callback routines.

▶ In Chapter 14, "Navigating in Forms and Applications," techniques are described that make navigation within forms and subforms more friendly for their users.

▶ To understand how record selection and navigation routines must dovetail with your application's data protection layers, read Chapter 15, "Protecting and Validating Data."

Advanced Development Techniques

P A R T

IV

chapter 17

Bulletproofing Your Application Interface

17

In the previous seven chapters, I've given you a wealth of techniques for creating well-structured databases, code routines, and forms. Taken individually, these techniques are useful, but taken together they are an "application." In this chapter, I show you how to combine your Access components into a solid, reliable application by using a design concept that I call "bulletproofing." Bulletproofing is a set of guidelines and techniques that ultimately protects the data, guides the user, and collects status information.

> ### Start Access Up
>
> "From time to time, I like to visit Access events to see what folks are saying about our products. Stan's been giving a speech called 'Bulletproofing Access Applications' for quite some time, so in mid-1994 I stopped by his session at a developer's conference to see what was up. In his speech, Stan revealed the nuts and bolts of taking a '90 percent finished' Access application and bringing it up to a deployable state.
>
> "As Stan was talking, I noticed all the steps we made folks go through to get an application ready to ship. The steps weren't complicated—designate a form as the main menu, create an AutoExec macro, write some code that hides the Database window, and the like—but they were tedious. That's when I came up with the idea of the Startup properties dialog box for Access 95, which is nothing more than a simple way of declaring how you want to 'bulletproof' your application. Best of all, the properties can be applied with no coding effort.
>
> "Perhaps I should have called it the Bulletproofing properties dialog box instead, but then I might have had to pay Stan a royalty!"
>
> David Risher, Access Product Team Manager

If you are responsible for data and need to have control over its quality, Access is a dangerous product. Because your users can enter, update, and query important business data quickly and inexpensively, they get comfortable with the product. When they get comfortable, they lose their sense of fear and respect, and without the proper sense of seriousness, users can get sloppy. Because an Access application brings your users into very close contact with your crucial data, sloppy people can easily introduce "bad" data into a system or delete data or even delete objects! So, when you give users the power to enter, edit, and query data, you also must give them one of the following powers as well:

> ▶ *Design a robust application interface* that prevents accidents and errors and protects the data.

> ▶ *Provide intense ongoing training and supervision* so that the users understand the data and the application objects and grasp how to get the most from them while not doing any damage.

Many companies mistakenly calculate that the first option is more expensive because custom development may cost tens of thousands of dollars. The reality is that the second option is usually more expensive for the following two reasons:

> ▶ *It involves an ongoing commitment of time that never ends.* All new users must be fully trained, not only on Access, but on the data structures, ad hoc usage, and so on.

Then, any procedural or structural changes will trigger a need to retrain all users again. Also, if users regularly interact with data without an application layer, they will raise questions and cause data problems that will require at least a part-time database administrator.

▶ *It is not foolproof.* Even with good training, people make mistakes. For example, virtually nobody can enter data into an Access table datasheet day after day without generating data errors. Also, some users will eventually forget their training and revert to old habits.

Consequently, an application can often protect important data more cost effectively than good training in the use of Access. This is true, but not automatically true because a poor application is no better than none at all. Only a solid application is a better investment than training.

χ Caution

I am in no way downplaying the importance of training. Instead, I am saying that a particular dataset, deployed in an environment with a fixed and limited budget, will benefit more in terms of data quality and protection from a good application than from the same amount of money spent on training. Consider this question: "Is it more important that our users know how to use Access, or how to manage our inventory data?" With a well-written inventory application in place, most users will neither know nor care that Access is the engine.

As David Risher noted in the introductory quote to this chapter, creating a solid application (bulletproofing) takes a 90 percent complete application and brings it from a code-complete state to a user-ready state. What David failed to note is that setting a few of the new Access properties is not enough to make an application totally bulletproof by my definition. Instead, a developer must apply a rigorous methodology to hunt down and eliminate areas in an application where users can experience confusion or problems. This methodology is the essence of bulletproofing.

Many bulletproofing concepts are quite simple, but in my experience, they are often overlooked in the rush to ship an application—or because of budget constraints. Once developed and formalized, the bulletproofing strategy described in this chapter can be easily applied to all new applications.

Note

You can find most of the examples in this chapter on the CD-ROM in the file AES_BPRF.MDB. You will also find BULLETPF.DOC, a set of guidelines for application bulletproofing that you can print and use during development.

The Basics of Bulletproofing

Philosophically, bulletproofing assumes that database application users are most productive—and application development projects are most successful—when the application provides an organized and controlled environment layered over the data. Although the objective in application development is to put the power in the hands of the user, that power should be tempered by an interface that organizes the workflow, guides a user through the application in a directed manner, and validates important procedures. This approach minimizes the impact of a user's curiosity, inexperience, or improper keystrokes, and consequently protects the underlying data.

Bulletproofing safeguards data by controlling a user's access to it. It also presents an ordered and professional application interface to the user.

At the simplest level, an Access application consists of a set of base tables, some queries to group and sort the table data, entry/edit forms, reports, and perhaps some macro routines. I call such a collection of objects an "unstructured application" and do not consider it an expert solution. Instead, true applications are more than a collection of objects in an MDB file. Interface objects must be added to enhance usability, and Basic code routines must be provided to organize the application flow and perform repeated tasks reliably.

In an unstructured application, where users can roam the Database window, a user can easily edit or delete vital records directly or possibly open and redesign database objects. For most installations, this model shifts too much power and risk from the developer to the end user. A bulletproof application, on the other hand, does not expose the user to data directly or to design tools. Figure 17.1 shows the conceptual difference between these two application types.

Bulletproofing is the process of pulling together all the pieces of the application to which you've applied your expert solution techniques individually and "shrink-wrapped" the pieces inside a protective coating that makes the application more robust and the data better shielded. The protective layer you apply is simply the implementation of some basic features that enable the application to escort the user safely through the maze of its own data and objects.

Fig. 17.1

This conceptual diagram compares an unstructured application to a bulletproof application.

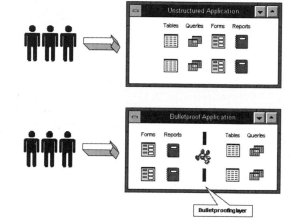

Before you finalize your application by bulletproofing it, make sure that it is complete in other respects and that you test the individual components. After you add the protective bulletproofing features, you must perform final testing on the application.

At its most basic level, a bulletproof application survives the following tests:

▶ *Do users understand the flow of the application the first time it is used?* Data entry, navigation, reporting, and process flow should be controlled by the interface, but their operation should be obvious to users.

▶ *Does the application flow prevent events from occurring out of sequence?* The user should not be able to initiate a process that depends on another, unfinished process.

▶ *Does the application trap data manipulation and other interaction that would have negative consequences?* It should be very difficult for the user to introduce invalid data into the system or to affect application objects.

▶ *Does the application provide feedback?* The user should receive constructive messages and suggestions, especially when an error occurs.

For applications to satisfy such tests and qualify as bulletproof, I use the following ten guidelines during the application development process:

1. Create a shortcut, icon, or other device to launch the application. Provide the feeling that the application has a life and personality of its own and is to be respected.

2. Use Startup options or an AutoExec macro to start the application when the database is opened. Put the application, not the user, in control from the start.

3. Remove the Database window and the toolbar from view. Those who use bulletproof applications should only see what you want them to see. Even if the application is not deployed with the runtime, it should be as solid as if the runtime were used.

4. Provide a login form to track users of the application. Even if you are not using Access security, this provides the impression of security and control to your users. Also, once you have captured the user's login ID, your application can make use of it, as shown in the sections "Logging In to an Application" and "Collecting Information from the Application" later in this chapter.

5. Display a main menu form and subordinate menu forms with simple and organized lists of options. Switchboard (form) menus provide organization and flow to the application.

6. Display only one form on the screen at a time and (where appropriate) one record at a time. I don't advocate using multiple forms simultaneously because doing so can introduce certain data integrity, record-locking, and usability pitfalls.

7. Organize the forms for maximum data protection. Every important feature should have a button and menu bar item, every dangerous feature (such as the Del key) should be trapped, and every unwanted feature (such as the View menu) should be removed.

8. Validate the data. Use combo boxes, list boxes, and option groups to limit entry of data where appropriate and test each important field before writing a record to the database.

9. Explain to the user what is happening. Use status bar texts, pop-up message boxes, control tips, hourglasses, and text on forms to give the user both positive and negative feedback and to educate.

10. Keep activity logs and audit trails. Leave a "bread crumb trail" for you and other developers to follow when reviewing how well the application works, which people use it, and how they use it.

α **Note**

This chapter makes the assumption that a bulletproof application guides the user, protects the data, and collects status information. It does not assume that even the best application can teach a worker how to do a job he or she does not know or understand. Sometimes, users are thrown at your application with not only a lack of knowledge of the application but a lack of knowledge of the workflow it automates as well.

In such a scenario, the bulletproof application particularly shines because an untrained or unskilled worker is the most dangerous of all, and your automated solution needs to help these people get their work done with a minimum of mistakes and frustration while protecting critical business data.

A bulletproof application can never fully compensate for a skills deficit, so make certain that your users understand their job "sans application" before they sit down in front of your application.

I discuss techniques for each of these guidelines in the sections that form the remainder of this chapter. Although some of the techniques are simple to understand and implement, building a truly bulletproof application requires some extra development effort and an intermediate-level of Access development skills. Those financing a development project sometimes see this final layer of "polish" on an application as unnecessary, so be wary that you may have to sell the concept on its merits, which I've detailed throughout this book.

 Tip

To justify the cost of the bulletproofing effort to project financiers, compare the cost of adding the features in this chapter with the cost of recovering and reentering lost data in this scenario: Near the end of the day, a user working in a table datasheet on a production version of the database accidentally selects all the records in a table and presses the Del key.

Deciding When to Use the Runtime or Strip Source Code

You've noticed that when I talk about bulletproofing, I don't automatically assume that the runtime is being used. Thus, the following two questions probably arise in your mind at this point:

Question 1: *Isn't an application installed with the runtime automatically bulletproof?* The answer is emphatically no because most of the ten features listed previously are usability features—application enhancements that exceed the simple protection provided by the runtime. Only the first three items on the list are automatically provided in any variation by installing an application with the runtime.

For example, the runtime hides features, but in some cases, the features are still there. In Figure 17.2, I opened a database with the /RunTime command-line option (to simulate the runtime). I then pressed the Del key. Note the message—I am in the process of deleting a table I can't even see! How? In runtime mode, the Database window is actually still on the screen but is colorized so that all colors match the Access desktop—in effect, it is transparent. My database file, opened in runtime mode, is actually less bulletproof than one running in a session of full Access where I've permanently removed the Database window via Startup properties, as I explain in "Setting Startup Options" later in this chapter.

Fig. 17.2

In a poorly constructed application, the runtime mode will not prevent the random deletion of an object that you can't even see on the screen.

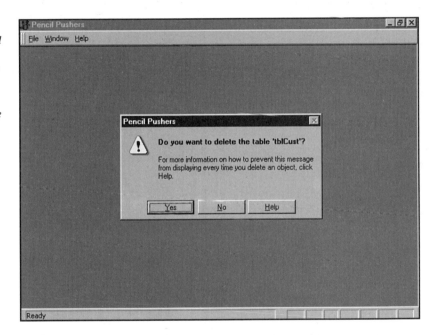

Question 2: *Shouldn't all applications be installed with the runtime?* When we create applications, we assume that the runtime will not be used (even if it will be) and we develop and code the application accordingly for the following three reasons:

▶ Many of those who use our applications will have full Access on their machines whether the application is installed with the runtime or not. We want the application to be smart and protected should users open the front-end MDB file from full Access.

▶ The application is better protected regardless of its distribution. For example, managers and power users may be more effective running the application with full Access so that they can administer the database or do ad hoc inquiries. These users should see the same application that other users see, whether using the runtime or full Access.

▶ Sometimes we prefer to use full Access. Testing and debugging applications with the runtime is very difficult because the context of coding errors is not shown. For testing, we prefer to have our users run an application under full Access so we can debug problems right there on the user's machine. Even so, we want the users to see the same application they will see if the runtime is later used for deployment.

You can see that good bulletproofing boils down to being able to say, "Users can use my application with full Access or with the runtime option, and in either case the application is solid and the data is protected."

Table 17.1 summarizes some of the features that the runtime adds to an application and shows how bulletproofing provides the same protection even when it runs in full Access.

Table 17.1   Runtime Features Matched to Features Provided by Bulletproofing Techniques

Runtime Feature	Bulletproofing Technique
Some menu options are not available.	Implement a custom menu bar and shortcut menu for the application or each form.
Built-in toolbars are not available.	Implement a custom toolbar for the application or each form.
Some keyboard shortcuts are available.	Use Startup properties, not AutoKeys macros, and event code to trap keystrokes.

If your application needs to know whether it is running in the Access runtime, your code can test the result of the SysCmd() function as follows:

```
blnRet = SysCmd(acSysCmdRuntime)
```

This function returns True or False depending on whether the application is running in runtime mode. Runtime mode is provided by the actual runtime executable as well as by full Access opened with the /RunTime command-line argument.

Starting with Access 97, you are now able to "lock up" the source code and structure of application objects before distribution without employing database security. When you use the menu option Tools, Database Utilities, Make MDE File..., Access creates a copy of your database with an .MDE file extension and does the following to the file:

▶ Compiles and saves the code

▶ Removes the VBA source

▶ Permanently locks forms, reports, and modules

▶ Compacts the database

The MDE file is now a fully functional application file, but without the capability to:

▶ View, add, change, or delete any VBA code

▶ View, add, change, delete, import, or export objects that contain code (forms, reports, and modules)

▶ View, add, change, or delete any references to object libraries or library databases

▶ Change any setting that affects VBA code (such as Conditional Compilation Arguments and Project Name settings in the Options dialog box)

▶ View code that contains a stop statement (the statement is ignored) or drop into code with the Break on All Errors setting (the setting is ignored)

 Note

The restrictions that apply to MDE files as previously listed apply from both the Access user interface and from VBA code. An MDE file's code cannot execute these tasks, either.

You can add, change, delete, import, and export tables, queries, and macros from within an MDE file.

How does an MDE file compare with an application shipped with the runtime? The runtime environment is a limitation placed on the Access executable, not the database file, while Make MDE... places limitations on a specific file. An application created for the runtime will still work in full Access, but it will work differently there (design views and full menus are available). In contrast, an MDE file's objects are locked in either environment.

Use Access's MDE capabilities to create a smaller (no source code), faster (can't decompile), protected (objects and code cannot be changed) version of your bulletproof application when development is complete.

Caution

Access has no capability to rebuild an MDB file from an MDE file. Do not lose the source file from which an MDE is created or your application can never be debugged or changed. Each time you need to enhance the application, do so in the source MDB file and then make a new MDE from it when deployment time arrives.

Launching an Application

In Windows 95 and NT 4, you can launch your Access application using any of the methods you use to start other programs, including from the Start menu, from a desktop shortcut, or from the Office Shortcut Bar. In Windows NT 3.x, you can create a program item in Program Manager for your application. In either case, the last thing you want your users to do is to double-click directly on the application's MDB file. This approach has several problems associated with it, as follows:

The user must know where the application file is. If users have to keep notes by their computers reminding them of the path and file name for your application and navigate to that path and file each time they want to use the application, they will not enjoy using it.

Access must be registered correctly. If users have multiple copies or versions of Access available on their machines, your application may not launch correctly if it relies on the fact that Access 97 is associated with the MDB file extension in the Windows Registry. If you encourage users to double-click an MDB file and the application does not load properly, you may take the blame for this even if you are not responsible for the configuration of a user's machine.

Note

For this same reason (reliance on registration), it is sometimes not a good idea to have the command line in a shortcut point only to an MDB file without specifying the location of the Access executable.

Users get too close to the file. Any excuse you give your users to look directly at your application file from the Windows Explorer or other tool increases the chance that they will delete, rename, or move the application file by accident.

The command-line arguments are not executed. Some of the options for correctly running an application may be contained in the application's icon or shortcut as command-line arguments. Opening an MDB file directly bypasses these command-line arguments and may alter the way the application runs.

Instead of requiring the user to hunt for the application, always create a shortcut or icon that specifically points to the copy of the Access executable that you want your application to launch (see Figure 17.3).

Fig. 17.3

An Access application shortcut is displayed on the desktop with the properties showing.

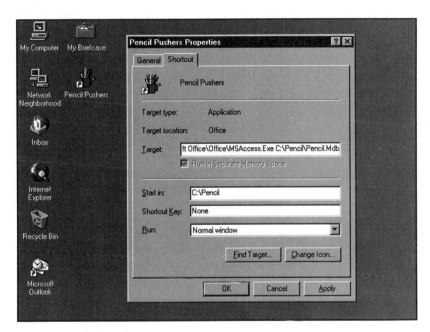

Using Application Graphics

Pay attention to the graphic image used as your program icon. Although it is tempting to use the Access icon or some icon readily available from Windows, the following are my two rules of thumb:

▶ *Your application icon should be unique.* Users should identify the icon with the program when looking at the shortcut and not be able to confuse it with other programs on their systems.

▶ *Your application icon should tie to other graphics in the application.* Specifically, the application icon, splash screen graphic, About dialog box graphic, and main switchboard graphic should all have a common design or theme.

At the least, your bulletproof application requires the following two graphic images:

A Shortcut Icon. The image used with your application shortcut should be a standard icon file of 32-by-32 pixels.

 Tip

If you do not have the tools to create icon files (ICO), assign a Windows bitmap file (BMP) to your shortcut instead of an icon. You can do this in Windows 95 even though its Change Icon dialog box does not show bitmaps as an option in the Files of type filter combo box. Note the following two special considerations:

▶ Windows 95 may add an odd shadow to your bitmap if you saved it as a 16-color bitmap from Paint; instead, use the 24-bit bitmap format when creating your own desktop bitmaps.

▶ Windows 95 clips off the outside pixel when displaying a shortcut bitmap (it does not do this with icon files). To compensate, make your bitmap no larger than 31-by-31 pixels.

An Application Icon. You can replace the Access icon in the control box position in the upper left corner of your application window using program code or Startup properties (see the section "Controlling an Application from Startup" to follow). Windows also uses this icon to represent the application on the taskbar. This icon is displayed in a 16-by-16-pixel area.

 Note

Even if you have the tools to create a Windows 95 format icon file (one that contains both 16-by-16- and 32-by-32-pixel icons), Access does not use the 16-pixel icon for the application icon. Instead, it takes the larger icon and shrinks it to 16 by 16 pixels. (Unfortunately, this flaw has carried forward from Access 95 to 97.) This means that you may decide to create a different icon for the application than the icon you used for the shortcut because the application icon will be designed to look best when reduced rather than when full size.

If you think you can cheat Access by creating a 16-by-16-pixel bitmap instead, you are unfortunately mistaken. It is possible to assign a 16-by-16-pixel bitmap file to the application icon property even though the Icon Browser dialog box does not show bitmaps as an option in the Files of type filter combo box. Access makes some color changes to the bitmap, however, that it does not apply to an icon file. This usually makes the bitmap appear less attractive than its icon alternative.

In addition to these small graphics, you can create a larger graphic to use for the application's dialog boxes and switchboard menus if you so desire. Figure 17.4 shows the Pencil Pushers sample application in this book, highlighting the application graphics assigned to it.

Fig. 17.4
The Pencil Pushers main graphic is shown with its matching icon.

Application Icon

Application Graphic

> **Tip**
> Numerous shareware applications for creating icon files are posted on CompuServe, the Microsoft Network, and elsewhere. If you choose to use bitmap files instead, you can create them with Paint, which ships with Windows 95.

Using Command-line Options

When your application is launched, Access enables certain optional command-line arguments that your shortcut can pass to Access and the application. You can add command-line options to your shortcut (or Program Manager item) following the path and file name string that loads Access. Listing 17.1 shows the syntax for starting Access with command-line options.

Listing 17.1   The Syntax for Access Command-line Options

```
\\path\MSACCESS.EXE databasename /Compact targetdatabase
/Convert targetdatabase /Excl /NoStartup /Profile userprofile
/Pwd password /Repair /RO /RunTime /User username /X macroname
/Wrkgrp workgroupfile /Cmd commandstring
```

Tip

The /NoStartup, /Profile, /RunTime, and /X option switches were introduced with Access 95.

The following list describes the command-line options that I think are important when you bulletproof an application:

databasename. Placing the name of a directory path and database file on the command line causes Access to open the database automatically. All bulletproof applications should be started this way.

When the user opens the file, your application will begin execution if it contains an AutoExec macro, a Startup macro specified on the command line (see the /X option later in this list), or a startup form (see "Controlling an Application from Startup" later in this chapter).

/Cmd commandstring. Use this option to pass information about the current shortcut, user, or workstation to your Basic routines in the application. The string following /Cmd up to the end of the command line (this option must be the last one in your argument list) is passed to Access and returned whenever you specify Command or Command() in your code, as in:

```
If Command() = "Browser" Then
  ' Do something
End If
```

Note

You can abbreviate the /Cmd string in your command line using a semicolon, as in the following example. However, I prefer to use the longer syntax, so that the command line is more readable and self-documenting.

```
\\path\MSACCESS.EXE databasename ;commandstring
```

In some applications, you can have your code test for various settings of the /Cmd argument and act accordingly. For example, you can assign different values to this argument for different types of users, then have your code branch to different logic depending on the user type returned by the Command() function.

Tip

When testing an application that expects a variety of values passed in from the command line, you can test your code without repeatedly changing the shortcut command line and restarting Access. The trick is to set the Command-Line Arguments option in the Advanced tab of the Options dialog box to mimic a string passed in to the application via the /Cmd option.

/Excl. When Access starts the application with this option, the database opens for exclusive use; only the current user can work with the database. Although this removes from the developer the burden of resolving multiuser issues in the application, few solutions are meant for only a single user.

Tip

If your application is created for a single user, opening an Access file for exclusive use adds up to a ten percent performance improvement for the user.

/Profile userprofile. Specifying a profile bypasses the standard Windows Registry settings for Access and passes the named user profile to Access instead. This option provides functionality that replaces the /Ini option in previous versions of Access, enabling you to set custom ISAM, Jet optimization, and application options via the Registry. See the Office 97 Developer Edition documentation for more information on custom profiles.

If your application was launched with this option, your code can detect the name of the specified *userprofile* by using the SysCmd function as follows:

```
varRet = SysCmd(acSysCmdProfile)
```

/Pwd password. This option relays the specified user password to Access security when Access starts. Although this is a convenient option, it is preferable to have the user login manually when using application security—I do not recommend listing the user's password in a visible place like a shortcut property.

/RO. When Access starts the application, the database is opened in read-only mode so that no data changes are allowed. This option can be useful when an application is installed for users or managers with the ability to browse data without initiating changes. This option is a convenience that should not be used to replace Access security or programmatic security where such features would provide a more solid protection layer.

/RunTime. This option starts Access as if it were the runtime executable. As a new option, it limits menus, removes design features, and enhances your ability to deploy applications to full Access users without having to deploy additional runtime files on their machines. It also enables developers to emulate the user's configuration when testing an application.

/User username. This option passes the specified user name to Access security when Access starts. Unless the password is also included on the command line with /Pwd, the Access security dialog box will still display. When using application security, you may prefer the user to login manually—I do not recommend listing the user's login name or password in a visible place such as a shortcut property.

/X macroname. Use this option if you need to override the AutoExec macro and start your application with the named macro. With this option, you can create different macro "entry points" to your application for different user shortcuts.

Tip

If your user opens the application file with File, Open... in full Access, the AutoExec macro will still run (if available) instead of the custom macro you designated in the shortcut with the /X argument. To trap this situation, you can include a /Cmd string in your shortcut and include code in your startup form to check the Command() function for this string. If the string is not found, the user has not started the application from a shortcut and your code can force an exit.

/WrkGrp workgroupfile. This option passes to Access the directory path and file name of a workgroup information file that specifies user preferences and user-level security information for the application to use. This option can be useful when different user shortcuts point to different applications created under different security models.

Note

The name of the workgroup information file was changed from SYSTEM.MDA to SYSTEM.MDW beginning with Access 95. Your code can detect the path and file name of the specified *workgroupfile* by using the SysCmd function as follows:

```
varRet = SysCmd(acSysCmdGetWorkgroupFile)
```

These following three command-line options are not used directly to launch a bullet-proof application, but may still have certain useful implementations:

/Compact *targetdatabase*. This option compacts the database in the `databasename` argument into a new database file described by the `targetdatabase` argument or into the same `databasename` if no `targetdatabase` argument is specified. Access is closed after the compact operation, regardless of any other command-line options.

/NoStartup. This option suppresses the display of the Access database dialog box—the dialog box in full Access that prompts a database file to open. Bulletproof applications will always specify a `databasename` argument, which implies `/NoStartup` and thus automatically suppresses this dialog box (regardless of the inclusion or exclusion of this command-line option).

/Repair. This option repairs the database named in the `databasename` argument. Access is closed after the repair operation, regardless of any other command-line options.

The following list summarizes my tips for using command-line options:

▶ A bulletproof application started with full Access from an icon will specify the `databasename` and `/RunTime` options in most cases. This restricts users from the design tools and the Database window.

▶ The `/Cmd` option enables your application code to inherit information passed from the shortcut.

▶ Advanced developers and their applications can use the `/Profile` argument to tailor application settings.

▶ Applications installed in a secured environment will use the `/WrkGrp` option.

▶ `/Excl`, `/Pwd`, `/RO`, `/User`, and `/X` are the least frequently used options.

Displaying an Early Splash Screen

Access 97 now includes the capability to create a bitmap graphic used as the application "splash" graphic—a form or graphic that displays before any application menu or dialog box. When you use the `databasename` argument in your shortcut, Access looks in the same directory as the specified database for a Windows bitmap file with the same root file name as the database and a BMP file extension (for example, `PENCIL.BMP` in the same directory as `PENCIL.MDB`). If Access finds a bitmap with the appropriate name, Access displays the graphic at startup instead of showing its internal splash graphic.

The positive aspect of this feature is that a graphic is displayed very soon in the application load cycle—quite a bit sooner than a splash screen supplied by a form in your application. (Your bitmap is actually drawn before Access has completely loaded into memory.) Thus, your users' perception of the load time of the application is favorably influenced because they see feedback almost immediately after launching the application. A second positive aspect of this feature is that the Access splash screen is replaced with your own, which enables the application to appear more "customized" to the user by hiding the programming platform.

Note

Your graphic is only shown while Access finishes loading itself into memory, which happens at different speeds on different machines. You cannot predict or control how long this graphic will be displayed.

On the negative side, the bitmap graphic does not show dynamic version or registration text or other information your application supplies—the bitmap's content is fixed and not programmable. Thus, using a bitmap does not reduce the need for a standard application splash screen coded as an Access form in your application.

Caution

Because the bitmap is stored as a file on disk and not inside the application file, it is not protected by any security in your application. Users can alter or remove the bitmap if they choose to.

How, then, do you best use this feature? I prefer to have Access display a startup graphic and still show my application splash screen because the two options are not mutually exclusive. I use the application graphic (which I call an "early splash" screen) to note that the application is starting up, and I use a fun graphic such as a stopwatch or hourglass for this effect. When Access finishes loading, I show the actual application splash form as the first form the application displays. Because I can control the length of time the application splash form is displayed, I place any text information there (such as a copyright notice or version information).

Figure 17.5 shows an early splash graphic that tells the user to wait while the application is loading.

Note

I have included on the CD-ROM several bitmap files that we use as early splash graphics. You can use these files—ESPLASH1.BMP through ESPLASH6.BMP—in your own applications.

Fig. 17.5

An early splash screen is a bitmap file with the same name and location as the application database file.

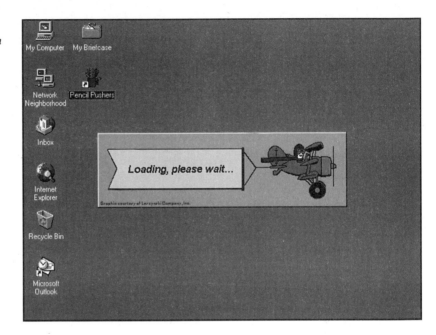

Controlling an Application from Startup

When users open your application, you want the application code to be in charge, not the user. In previous versions of Access, you created AutoExec macros to begin executing application code when each database file was opened. This technique is still useful and available in Access, but much of the work previously performed by AutoExec macro actions and the code they call can now be done by Access's new Startup options. Startup options not only control how the application appears when it is opened but what kind of interaction is allowed between the application's users and underlying Access features.

17

Wishes Can Come True

Frustrated by some of the shortcomings in the configuration options of earlier versions of Access, I had been writing and speaking on the subject of application bulletproofing since 1993. Over the years, various members of the Access team at Microsoft attended my presentations. Thus, when I first saw the Startup dialog box in Access 95, which solved many of the shortcomings in Access that I had highlighted in my speeches, I felt somewhat responsible. Later in the beta cycle, Microsoft acknowledged that my tricks in the bulletproofing sessions and articles had influenced them to design Startup options (see the introductory section of this chapter).

The point of this story is that the Access team at Microsoft, despite all their great ideas and momentum, doesn't home-grow every innovation—they do take notice of what people outside the company are saying about their product. If you have a suggestion on how to improve Access, don't be silent—you can phone your idea in to Microsoft at 206-936-WISH or fax it to them at 206-936-7329. If you submit a product "wish," there's a good chance that it will be reviewed by someone on the Access team. (I know because I wrote the database that manages the product wish list for Microsoft!)

Setting Startup Options

In a database, choose Tools, StartUp... to display the Startup dialog box, as shown in Figure 17.6. Options set in this dialog box are applied each time the database is opened with full Access or the runtime option.

 Note

Startup options are saved with the database file and travel with it wherever it goes—unlike the user preferences set in the Options dialog box, which are saved to the workstation and not the database.

In a bulletproof application, you will want to set each Startup property to tightly control the initialization and use of your application.

Fig. 17.6

The Startup options dialog box with the advanced options is displayed.

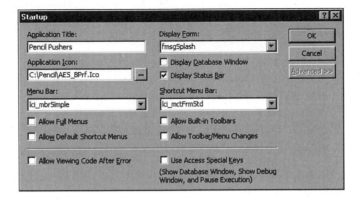

Caution

Startup options are applied before the `AutoExec` macro or a macro run with the `/X` command-line option is executed. If you use a combination of Startup options and an initial macro, be careful about any event collisions that might occur if they both open forms or initiate processes that could overlap.

Specifically, you can set the Display Form startup option to show a form when the application is launched. This form may contain code. After the form is opened and the code begins running, Access will begin execution of any `AutoExec` macro actions it finds in the database. Running your macro actions and form code in parallel may generate an error.

The following list details the options in the Startup dialog box and my suggestions for using each option:

> *Allow Built-in Toolbars.* Clearing this check box causes Access not to display its standard toolbars in your application. I prefer to clear this option and create custom toolbars for each application.

 Tip

You can display your own toolbars instead of those built in Access by using the `ShowToolbar` method from form and report code:

```
DoCmd.ShowToolbar "tbrPencilMain", acToolbarYes
```

Allow Default Shortcut Menus. Clearing this check box causes Access not to display the standard shortcut menus in your application. If you leave this option selected, your forms will show the standard shortcut menu with its filter options. Although giving the user access to filters does not seem overly dangerous, some developers prefer to have total control over a user's access to any options. Further, the filter shortcut menu for forms has a Save <u>A</u>s Query option and the standard report short-cut enables Save <u>A</u>s/Export..., either of which could enable your users to destroy existing objects in your application by saving filters or reports in place of objects with the same name. I prefer to clear this option and to create my own custom shortcut menus to attach to application forms and reports.

Allow full menus. This option limits the actions on the built-in menu bar, if your application displays it. With this option's check box cleared, the user can open database objects and work with the data in them, but the commands for designing objects or creating new ones are removed from the built-in menus.

α Note

Clearing this option is only useful if you also clear the Allow Built-in Toolbars check box; otherwise, a user can still access design options via the toolbar buttons even if the menu options are restricted.

If you create custom menu bars for all the forms and reports in your application and set a value for the Menu Bar Startup property (see the following), the setting in Allow Full Menus will not matter because any menu bar you designate for the application overrides the built-in menu system. In less-restrictive applications for well-trained users, however, you might choose to clear this setting in lieu of creating custom menus. Such an approach provides a limited subset of the Access standard menu options to your user with minimum effort by the developer.

Allow toolbar changes. This check box determines whether users have the ability to change your custom toolbars (or the built-in toolbars if they are used by your application). I prefer to clear this option, which disables the shortcut menu on all toolbars. (The Access toolbar shortcut menu, available with a click of the right mouse button on a toolbar, has a <u>C</u>ustomize... option that enables your users to add back to a toolbar the features that you painstakingly removed.)

α Note

Clearing this option also disables the <u>V</u>iew, <u>T</u>oolbars command from the built-in menus.

Allow Viewing Code After Error. Clearing this check box disables the <u>D</u>ebug button shown in the Runtime error alert. Access shows this alert (see Figure 17.7) whenever a code error occurs and no error handler is in effect. If your application is running with full (nonruntime) Access, is not an MDE file, and users can click the <u>D</u>ebug button in this dialog box, they will be able to view and modify your code.

Fig. 17.7

The Startup option Allow Viewing Code After Error controls the display of the <u>D</u>ebug button in this dialog box.

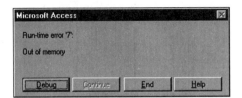

In theory, your users should never see this standard Access error dialog box because your code should have its own error trapping in every procedure. Clear this option before you ship your application, however, just in case the standard error alert pops up somewhere—you don't want users changing your underlying code without your knowledge.

Application Icon. With this option, you can specify an icon file to display in the control box position of the application window and on the taskbar. See the section "Using Application Graphics" earlier in this chapter for a complete discussion of icons.

 Tip

You should use the same icon or bitmap for the Application Icon property that you used when you created a shortcut to start the application.

 Note

The specified icon is not saved inside the Access database file—only the file path is saved. The users who receive the application file from you must have the icon file in the folder on their machines that matches the file path saved in this property. Alternatively, your application can include code to search for the icon, as shown in the example procedure `lci_AppIconCheck` in the database AES_BPRF.MDB on the CD-ROM.

Application Title. Set this to the application name you want to display in the Access window title bar and in the Windows taskbar and task list. Figure 17.8 shows an application title and icon set as database properties.

Fig. 17.8

This application's icon and title are defined by Startup *properties.*

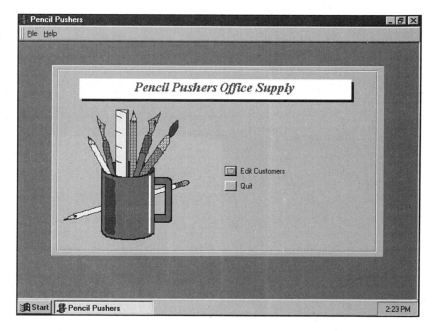

17

Display Database Window. You can clear the check box for this option to hide the Database window from the application's users. The Database window, however, once hidden, is displayed if the user presses the F11 key or selects the Window, Unhide... menu option. To prevent a user from showing the Database window once it has been hidden, you should also clear the Startup option named Use Access Special Keys, which disables F11, and make sure that the Window menu is not available in the application.

Display Form. This property enables you to name the first form you want to display when your application starts. The first form is usually a splash screen, a login dialog box, or the main switchboard menu. In the past, you opened this initial form via an action in the AutoExec macro.

 Tip

I mentioned in the section "Displaying an Early Splash Screen" earlier in this chapter that you might want to create a splash form that loads when your application starts. If you set the Display Form option to the name of your splash form, it will be the first form the user sees when the application has finished loading. You can place an `OnTimer` event in the form that triggers after three or four seconds, closes the splash form, and opens the main switchboard. Figure 17.9 shows the splash form displaying for the Pencil Pushers application.

Fig. 17.9

This splash form for the Pencil Pushers application is displayed by the Display Form setting.

Display Status Bar. This option enables you to remove the status bar shown at the bottom of the Access window. In most cases, you will keep this option's check box selected so that your users (and code) can benefit from the built-in status bar. You can clear this option, however, if you choose instead to use the ActiveX control `COMCTL32.OCX` from the Office Developer Edition to add a custom status bar or to handle status notifications through labels on your forms or another technique.

Menu Bar. With this property, you can designate a default menu bar that will be displayed anywhere in the application where no other menu bar is explicitly displayed. This assigned menu bar does not override the custom menu bars you connect to the `MenuBar` property of forms and reports but does override the built-in menu bar Access provides everywhere else. This option achieves the same result as setting the `MenuBar` property of the `Application` object from Basic code.

Caution

If you do not clear the Use Access Special Keys option when using the Menu Bar option, your user will be able to switch between your designated menu bar and the menu of Access by using the Ctrl+F11 key combination.

Shortcut Menu Bar. Setting the value of this property assigns a default shortcut menu that will be displayed throughout the application where no other shortcut menu is explicitly designated. The listed menu does not override custom shortcut menus you connect to the ShortcutMenuBar property of forms and reports but does override the built-in shortcut menus Access provides.

Note

When the ShortcutMenuBar property is set for a form, the designated shortcut menu will still be displayed even if you clear the Allow Default Shortcut Menus check box in the Startup dialog box.

Use Access Special Keys. Clearing this check box disables some of the keyboard shortcuts that let your users get past your application's bulletproofing layer. Specifically, the keystrokes in Table 17.2 are disabled.

Table 17.2   Access Keystrokes Disabled by the Use Access Special Keys Startup Option

Keystroke	Action
F11, Alt+F1	Shows the Database window when hidden or brings it to the front of the window stack when displayed.
Ctrl+G	Shows the Debug window when the user has dropped into application code by pressing Ctrl+Break or by clicking the Debug button in the Access runtime error alert.
Ctrl+F11	Alternates the menu bar between your custom menu bar for an object and the Access built-in menu bar for the object.
Ctrl+Break	Halts code that is executing and displays the Module window with the current line of code highlighted.

Note

If the application database is secured, revoke the Administer permission from the Database object for any users who should not be able to change Startup properties. (Without this permission, a user also cannot replicate the database and cannot create a database password for the file.)

Putting Startup Properties to Use

All the Startup options previously listed are actually stored in your database file as properties of the Database object. You can read these property values from your application code when you need to detect the setting of an option, and you can set them from Basic using code like this:

```
Dim dbs As Database
Set dbs = CurrentDb
dbs.Properties("AllowFullMenus") = False
```

A likely scenario where you would set Startup properties of a database from code occurs when you create a new database using program code and you want to create certain default options for it. You might also want to be able to detect a current application setting by reading a Startup property. Table 17.3 lists all of the Startup dialog box options and the Database object property name that is used to store each option.

 Note

Changes to Startup properties, whether through the interface or by code, do not take effect until the database is closed and reopened, with the exceptions noted in the following table.

Table 17.3 Startup Properties as Database Properties

Startup Dialog Box Option	Database Property
N/A	AllowBypassKey
Allow Built-in Toolbars*	AllowBuiltInToolbars
Allow Default Shortcut Menus*	AllowShortcutMenus
Allow Full Menus*	AllowFullMenus
Allow Toolbar Changes*	AllowToolbarChanges
Allow Viewing Code After Error*	AllowBreakIntoCode

Startup Dialog Box Option	Database Property
Application Icon	`AppIcon`
Application Title	`AppTitle`
Display Database Window*	`StartupShowDBWindow`
Display Form	`StartupForm`
Display Status Bar*	`StartupShowStatusBar`
Menu Bar	`StartupMenuBar`
Shortcut Menu Bar	`StartupShortcutMenuBar`
Use Access Special Keys*	`AllowSpecialKeys`

* None of the properties in the table exist as database properties for a new database. Starred items indicate properties created by Access the first time the Startup dialog box is used. I will divulge the importance of this information later in this current section.

Table 17.3 includes a `Startup` property, the `AllowBypassKey` property, that is not displayed in the Startup dialog box. This property determines whether the user can override Startup options and the `AutoExec` macro by holding down the Shift key when opening the database. This property only can be set from code, and you should only set it after you have completed development and testing and you're prepared to deploy the application.

 Tip

In a bulletproof application, once you have set the `AllowBypassKey` property to `False`, you can no longer override the Startup properties and design application objects. You may want to leave yourself a "backdoor" that helps you to re-allow this property so that you can further develop the database in the future.

One backdoor I use is to create a shortcut to unlock an application and install it on developers' workstations only. The shortcut has a special string in the /Cmd option of the command line, for example:

```
\\path\MSACCESS.EXE databasename /Cmd AllowShift
```

This command line passes the phrase `AllowShift` to the Access `Command()` function. I then add code to my application's startup form to check for the special string (`AllowShift`) in the `Command()` function and to set the `AllowBypassKey` property to `True` if the string is found. Because property changes don't take effect until the database is closed, my application code then closes the database after setting the property. A developer can then reopen the unlocked application while holding down Shift, which again provides access to the built-in menu system.

Startup properties are Access interface constructs as opposed to DAO constructs and do not actually exist in the Database object in Jet until Access determines that they should be stored there. The point at which this happens is not uniform. When you create a new database, none of the properties in Table 17.3 exist in the Database object's Properties collection. After you open the Startup dialog box and set at least one property (any one), the starred (*) items in the table are all created as database properties and persist for the life of the database.

The non-starred items (corresponding to the combo box options in the Startup dialog box) are created as properties on a case-by-case basis, however. In other words, each property is created when the property is set via the interface or code, and each only persists as long as the property has a value, after which it is deleted from the Database object.

The upshot of this confusing situation is that you can set and retrieve Startup properties from code, but you need to make certain that the property has been added to the Database object's Properties collection first or an error will occur. The code in Listing 17.2 shows how to test for the existence of a Database property and to create it if necessary. The function shown uses the example of setting the application title bar caption dynamically.

Although most Startup property changes do not take effect until the database is closed and reopened, you can repaint changes to the application title or application icon immediately with the RefreshTitleBar method on the Application object.

Listing 17.2   AES_BPrf.Mdb—How to Set a Startup Property from Code

```
Public Sub lci_AppTitleCheck()
' Purpose: Try to locate and set the application title
' Calls:    lci_IsBlank

  On Error GoTo lci_AppTitleCheck_Err
  Const cintErrPrpNotFound As Integer = 3270
  Const cstrProc As String = "lci_AppTitleCheck"
  Dim dbsCurr    As Database
  Dim prpTitle   As Property
  Dim strTitle   As String

  Set dbsCurr = CurrentDb
  ' If the property does not exist, the next line jumps to _Err
  strTitle = dbsCurr.Properties("AppTitle")  ' Get the title
  dbsCurr.Properties("AppTitle") = strTitle  ' Set the title
  Application.RefreshTitleBar  ' Repaint the screen to show the change

lci_AppTitleCheck_Exit:
  Exit Sub

lci_AppTitleCheck_Err:
  ' Trap the nonexistence of the property
```

```
If Err.Number = cintErrPrpNotFound Then
  ' Create the property in the database
  If lci_IsBlank(strTitle) Then   ' If none specified, use the constant
    strTitle = lci_gcstrAppTitle
  End If
  Set prpTitle = dbsCurr.CreateProperty("AppTitle", dbText, strTitle)
  dbsCurr.Properties.Append prpTitle
  Resume Next
Else
  Call lci_ErrMsgStd(cstrProc, Err.Number, Err.Description, True)
  GoTo lci_AppTitleCheck_Exit
End If

End Sub
```

Access has greatly improved your ability to control how much interaction the user has with your database objects outside of your application's interface. Additionally, testing an application is easier now that you can use the /RunTime option to tell full Access to emulate the runtime product.

𝒳 Caution

If you start an application without the /RunTime argument in full Access and the user has enabled the option Break on All Errors in the Options dialog box, this option setting will override any error trapping in your code. This situation is dangerous for you because your carefully crafted error traps are ignored. To protect your application from this situation, consider issuing the following line of code as the application starts:

```
Application.SetOption "Break on All Errors", False
```

Because you are changing an interface option that may be important to the user, you might want to store the initial setting in a variable before changing it and set the option back to its original state as your application closes. Also, note that if you are a developer testing an application, you may be using Break on All Errors as part of your debugging effort and choose not to disable the option.

Table 17.4 summarizes my recommended settings for Startup options in a bulletproof application. Note that I recommend that you disable almost every user feature listed in the Startup dialog box.

Table 17.4 Recommended Startup Options for a Bulletproof Application

Option	Setting	Comment
AllowBypassKey	False	Not available in the Startup dialog box; must be set from code.
Allow Viewing Code	False	Disables the Debug button After Error from the Runtime error alert.
Allow Built-in Toolbars	False	Removes access to the standard toolbars.
Allow Toolbar Changes	False	Removes the capability to change built-in and custom toolbars.
Allow Full Menus	False	Removes design actions from the built-in menu bar.
Allow Default Shortcut Menus	False	Removes built-in shortcut menus.
Application Icon	iconname	Specifies an icon file to represent the application.
Application Title	titlestring	Displays the application name in the Access window title bar.
Display Database Window	False	Hides the Database window from the users.
Display Form	formname	Displays the named form first.
Display Status Bar	True	Displays the Access status bar.
Menu Bar	menuname	Names the default menu bar to display when no other menu bar is designated.
Shortcut Menu Bar	shortcutmenuname	Names the default shortcut menu bar to display when no other shortcut menu bar is designated.
Use Access Special Keys	False	Disables keystrokes that bypass the application interface layer (see Table 17.2).

Startup options are an excellent new device for configuring the usability of your custom application, especially an application that may run in full Access instead of the runtime, where all control of the interface must be provided by the application.

Logging In to an Application

In most data-centric applications, users are expected to login (or logon) to the application by providing a name and password to validate their right to enter the system. If your application uses Access security, Access provides the login dialog box when the application starts. If the application is not secured, however, consider providing a login dialog box through your application for the following reasons:

▶ A login dialog box enables you to capture information about the current user and save it to a global form or variable. This information can be used throughout the application to create record stamps, activity logs, error logs, usage logs, e-mail signatures, and more.

▶ The application exudes the image that it is secured and important. Users will take the application more seriously, and would-be hackers in a hurry may be discouraged by the impression of a security layer.

If your application uses Access security, Access provides a standard login dialog box. After login, the user name is available to your application via the CurrentUser() function, as in this example:

```
lci_gstrUser = CurrentUser()
```

If you trap user logins with your own form in an unsecured system, you must design a strategy to supply login validation, if any. Bear in mind that any programmatic password validation your application does is not hacker-proof and provides validation as a convenience, not as true security. In some installations, however, the burden of setting up Access security and managing the workgroup information file(s) that define the group/user security model is greater than the expected return, so login validation through code may be an adequate model.

To validate user names with code, provide a name and password dialog box like the one shown in Figure 17.10.

Users often complain about having to reenter their name at each login to an application, so you might want to default the user name to the previous name used. You can default the user name at login in one of the following ways:

▶ Pass the default user name from the command line used to start the application if the application starts from a shortcut or program icon. To do this, use the /Cmd argument followed by the user name in the shortcut command line, as in this example:

```
C:\MSOffice\Access\MSAccess.Exe F:\PencilPusher.Mdb /Cmd Bob
```

As your login dialog box loads, get the user name ("Bob") using the built-in
Command() function, like this:

```
Private Sub Form_Load()
' Preload the user name

    Me!txtUserName = Command()  ' Retrieve the /Cmd parameter

End Sub
```

I personally do not use this technique because it always defaults the user name to
the owner of the workstation, as opposed to the person who last used the machine.
(Imagine when Bob is on vacation, and someone else is using his machine daily.
Your application will be more impressive if it remembers the new person's name
between sessions rather than using Bob's at every login.)

Fig. 17.10

*You can create an
application login
dialog box from an
Access form.*

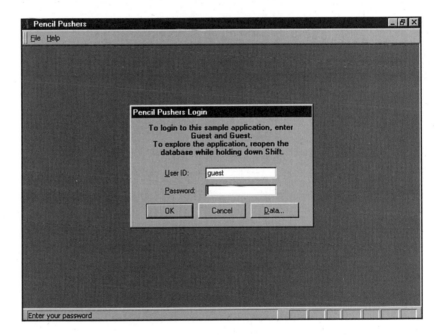

α **Note**

You cannot use the /User option to pass the user name into an application that
does not use Access security. In contrast to my previous example using /Cmd, the
/User option will cause the display of the Access security login dialog box, and any
user name typed in will be rejected because it is not a defined user in the
workgroup information file.

- ▶ Get the default user name from an initialization (INI) file or Windows Registry setting that you have created for the application. Information on using these options to store application values is provided in Chapter 11, "Expert Approaches to VBA."

- ▶ Store the user name in a table during login and retrieve the value for the next login. For example, you can use a default table zstblDefault, which is local to the front end of the application, and place a field LastUser in the table. At each login, write the user name to the LastUser field in the table (see Listing 17.4). At the next login, use a DFirst() function to retrieve the value of the LastUser field (the defaults table has only one record), and use the value as the default for the login dialog box's user name text box.

    I prefer this method of the three described here because the previous user name is stored in the database—an appropriate place for a data item. The code to retrieve the last user is shown in Listing 17.3.

Listing 17.3 AES_BPrf.Mdb—Seeding the User Name Text Box with the Prior Login Value

```
Private Sub Form_Load()
' Purpose: Preload the previous user name

  Me!txtUserName = DFirst("LastUserName", "zstblDefault")

End Sub
```

To validate the login name and user password through program code, I keep a table of users and passwords (tblUser) in the shared (back-end) database. The table is not linked to any interface (front-end) database, so a user somehow browsing through the linked tables in their local (application) database will not see it. After the OK button is pressed on the login dialog box, I use program code to validate the user name. See the example in Listing 17.4.

 Note

This technique requires that your code knows where on the network the data back-end file is located. Ideally, the back-end path and database name are stored in a table in your database, perhaps in the zstblDefault local table previously described if your application involves only one back-end database.

Listing 17.4   AES_BPrf.Mdb—A User and Password Validation Routine

```
' The Click event on your login form OK button
Private Sub cmdOK_Click()
' Purpose: Validate the user name and password

    Dim dbs        As Database
    Dim rst        As Recordset
    Dim intRet     As Integer
    Dim varBackEnd As Variant

    ' For this app, the user table is in the current database
    ' In a real app, use this next line instead:
    ' varBackEnd = DFirst("BackEndData", "zstblDefault")
    varBackEnd = CurrentDb.Name
    ' Look for user name in zhtblUser in back-end
    intRet = lci_UserValidate(Me!txtUserName, Me!txtPW, varBackEnd)
    Beep
    Select Case intRet
      Case -1
        lci_gstrCurrentUser = Me!txtUserName  ' Set global user name
        Set dbs = CurrentDb
        Set rst = dbs.OpenRecordset("zstlogLogin", dbOpenDynaset)
        ' Add record of login to log table
        rst.AddNew
        rst!UserName = lci_gstrCurrentUser
        rst!LoginAt = Now
        rst.Update
        rst.Close
        Set rst = dbs.OpenRecordset("zstblDefault", dbOpenDynaset)
        ' Update most recent user name for next login
        rst.MoveFirst
        rst.Edit
        rst!LastUserName = lci_gstrCurrentUser
        rst.Update
        rst.Close
        MsgBox "You are logged-in and validated." _
            , vbInformation, lci_gcstrAppTitle & " Login"
        If lci_FrmOpenStd("fmnuMain", "") Then
          intRet = lci_FrmCloseStd(Me)
        End If
      Case 1
        MsgBox "The user name you entered is not valid for this application." _
            , vbCritical, lci_gcstrAppTitle & " Login"
        Me!txtUserName.SetFocus
      Case 2
        MsgBox "The password you entered is not valid for this user name." _
            , vbCritical, lci_gcstrAppTitle & " Login"
        Me!txtPW.SetFocus
    End Select

End Sub

' The Declarations section of a standard module in the application
    ' Current application user, fed during login
    Public lci_gstrCurrentUser As String
```

```
' A function in the standard module
Public Function lci_UserValidate(rvarUser As Variant, rvarPW As Variant _
  , rvarDbs As Variant) As Integer
' Purpose:   Validate a user name and password against the table
'            zhtblUser in a remote database
' Arguments: rvarUser:=user name
'            rvarPW:=user password
'            rvarDbs:=database path and name
' Returns:   -1=both OK, 1=invalid user, 2=invalid password
' Example:   lci_UserValidate(Me!txtUserName, Me!txtPW, varBackEnd)

  Dim dbs  As Database
  Dim rtbl As Recordset
  Dim wsp  As Workspace

  Set wsp = Workspaces(0)
  Set dbs = wsp.OpenDatabase(rvarDbs)
  Set rtbl = dbs.OpenRecordset("zhtblUser", dbOpenTable)
  rtbl.Index = "PrimaryKey"
  rtbl.Seek "=", rvarUser  ' Find the user
  If rtbl.NoMatch Then  ' User not found
    lci_UserValidate = 1  ' Flag as invalid user
    GoTo lci_UserValidate_Exit
  End If
  If rtbl!UserPassword = rvarPW Then  ' Password is valid
    lci_UserValidate = -1  ' Flag success
  Else
    lci_UserValidate = 2  ' Flag as invalid password
  End If

End Function
```

Notice that the event procedure behind the command button stores the user name into a global variable (lci_gstrCurrentUser in the preceding example) for the application to use. (I show how to make use of this variable in the "Collecting Information from the Application" section later in this chapter.) If you use Access security, set the global variable to the value of the CurrentUser() function after the user has logged in to the workgroup so that your code can always refer to one variable (lci_gstrCurrentUser) whether the application is running on a secured or unsecured system. This enables you to write generic, reusable code.

Note that the login dialog box in Figure 17.10 has a <u>D</u>ata... button to refresh table links. The option to locate the back-end database in a new installation or when the network is reconfigured must be early in the application flow (before the first bound form is shown), and I find that the login dialog box is the best place for this option. See Chapter 7, "Understanding Application Architecture," for a discussion of linked tables.

Restricting User Interaction

For unsophisticated users of full Access, the Database window is an intimidating and dangerous place, full of dozens of strangely named objects in different bins. As a developer of bulletproof applications, you will remove the Database window and the object design features and instead provide a menu system that introduces more structure into the application.

Old Name, New Name

Nothing is more terrifying to me as a developer than to have a user of my database wandering around the Database window. Such a user can execute action queries at random, redesign my forms, and so on. This concept should terrify you as well.

Beginning with Access 95, a new reason to be terrified exists. Access now employs the Windows 95 metaphor for renaming objects by clicking once on the object name in the Database window to enter Rename mode. This is a terribly dangerous option to provide a user who may not understand that renaming a table object will immediately invalidate all dependent objects, such as queries and forms.

This feature is even dangerous for a developer who can click an object in an attempt to set focus, accidentally enter Rename mode, and inadvertently pass the next keystrokes to Access as the object's new name—and this entire sequence can occur unnoticed if the developer is working too quickly.

There is no way to disable this new feature, so be aware of the danger. The feature provides yet another reason to remove the Database window and reproduce its navigation benefits using application objects instead.

Another of the prime tenets of the bulletproofing regimen is to think through the various ways your user can get confused or into trouble in your application and to remove or restrict such opportunities.

Providing a Restrictive Interface

When you have removed the Database window and design features, the user requires a way to navigate through your application. One or more switchboard menus usually provide such navigation. In addition, the following considerations apply when you provide a restrictive yet navigable interface.

Startup Options. As you've discovered in the section "Setting Startup Options" earlier in this chapter, options in the Startup dialog box give you a great deal of control over database properties that affect the interface.

Menu Bars. Your application should provide a custom default menu bar and a custom default shortcut menu for the application (set via Startup dialog box properties). Additionally, you can provide custom menu bars and shortcut menus on individual forms and reports via the MenuBar and ShortcutMenuBar properties. You must first design the minimum subset of functionality that your users require for a given application or object, then provide those features through menus and toolbar buttons. See Chapter 8, "Designing Effective Interfaces," for a detailed discussion of menu and toolbar design, and Chapter 14, "Form Navigation Issues," for a discussion of how to implement the new menu and toolbar features in Access 97.

Datasheets. If your application enables users to browse table or query datasheets, you have limited control over restricting their user interface. If you do not provide a custom menu but clear the Startup option Allow Full Menus, the user will receive the appropriate menu options from Access when in table and query datasheet view but will not see options to switch to these objects' design view. Although this situation is useful for power users, it does not enable you to prescribe a specific menu for a table or query datasheet or to attach any code events to the datasheet. In bulletproof applications, I prefer to embed table or query datasheets in forms where I have more control of my users' interaction with the displayed data. An example of this technique is shown in Chapter 16, "Presenting Data to Users."

Trapping Dangerous Keystrokes

As you restrict the interface options to bulletproof an application, consider disabling the keyboard keystrokes in Table 17.5 to implement better control of the interface. With these keystrokes, the user can bypass a Close button and navigation buttons that you place on your forms or add and delete records via the keyboard—possibly skirting data validation and other important code routines. To disable each option, define a macro for the keystrokes in the Autokeys macro group, and leave the Action column blank.

Table 17.5   Dangerous Keystrokes that Can Be Masked with *Null AutoKeys* Macros

Feature	Keystrokes
Select all records	Ctrl+A
Display the Find dialog box	Ctrl+F

continues

Table 17.5   Continued

Feature	Keystrokes
Display the Replace dialog box	Ctrl+H
Open a new database	Ctrl+N
Open an existing database	Ctrl+O
Close the active window	Ctrl+F4 and Ctrl+W
Cycle between open windows	Ctrl+F6
Display next Find or Replace match	Shift+F4
Display the Save As dialog box	F12 and Alt+F2
Save the current object	Shift+F12 and Alt+Shift+F2

 Note

The key combinations Alt+F2 and Alt+Shift+F2 shown in the table cannot actually be remapped in AutoKeys. Their corresponding (sibling) keystroke combinations shown can be remapped, however, which causes the related key combinations to become disabled as well.

Table 17.6 lists keystroke options that cannot be disabled via AutoKeys settings or Startup dialog box options. Unfortunately, if users issue these keystrokes in your application, they could incur negative consequences. You will have to write code to trap these keystrokes as they are sent to each form.

Table 17.6   Dangerous Keystrokes that Cannot Be Masked with *AutoKeys* Macros

Feature	Keystrokes
Add a new record	Ctrl+Plus (+)
Delete the current record	Ctrl+Minus (−)
Move to the next page/record	PgDn
Move to the previous page/record	PgUp
Move to the next record	Ctrl+PgDn
Move to the previous record	Ctrl+PgUp
Select record	Shift+Spacebar

Feature	Keystrokes
Select all records	`Ctrl+Shift+Spacebar`
Save changes to the current record	`Shift+Enter`
Quit Access or close a dialog box	`Alt+F4`

To trap these keystrokes coming to a form, create a routine called a "keyboard handler" and discard the keystrokes that you consider dangerous. Listing 17.5 shows how to create a simple keyboard handler that uses the `KeyDown` event on a form to trap and discard the keystrokes for the Replace dialog box.

Listing 17.5   How to Disable Keystrokes Sent to a Form

```
Private Sub Form_KeyDown(KeyCode As Integer, Shift As Integer)
' Trap the Ctrl+H key combination to disable Replace
' The form's KeyPreview property must be True

  Dim intCtrl As Integer

  intCtrl = (Shift And acCtrlMask) > 0   ' Test for Ctrl key
  If intCtrl And KeyCode = vbKeyH Then   ' Ctrl+H pressed
    KeyCode = 0   ' Throw out the keystrokes
  End If

End Sub
```

A more comprehensive example of a keyboard handling procedure is shown in Chapter 15, "Protecting and Validating Data."

> **Tip**
>
> If you intend to use your keyboard handler from many forms, create a shared (library) routine to hold the keyboard testing code and call the routine from each form's `KeyDown` event. See the sample procedure `lci_FrmKeyIsAllowed` in `AES_BPRF.MDB` on the CD-ROM for an example.

Giving Some Features Back

Even though disabling features is a step forward in the protection of your data, it can be a step backward in overall usability if you do not offer alternatives to specific users for the features you remove from view as you bulletproof. Thus, for some useful features you disable, you must provide a replacement that is equally useful and more appropriate to the specific application.

For example, the database administrator might need the ability to reproduce a problem that a user is having and to pass meaningful information about the root of the problem to a developer. As such, the administrator would find value in being able to enter debug mode in the application. As a developer, your debugging strategy might include setting a conditional compilation constant in the Options dialog box to enable the application's debug routines. In a bulletproof application, users (including the administrator) will not have access to the Options dialog box, so your applications should provide a button on the administrator's menu (or some other device) to set the conditional compilation constant from code and thus toggle debug mode on.

As another example, if you clear the Use Access Special Keys property check box and the Display Database Window check box in the Startup dialog box, there is no way for the user to get to the Database window. Thus, even the system administrator and other power users (perhaps you yourself) are locked out of expected or needed features. To alleviate this situation, you can provide a backdoor or other mechanism for selected users to see the Database window. One approach is to provide a menu option on a maintenance menu that initiates the following command:

```
DoCmd.SelectObject objecttype, objectname , True
```

For this command, use any object type and name that will always be available in the application, such as the first table in the Database window. Because the third argument (InDatabaseWindow) of the command is set to True, Access forces the display of the Database window.

 Note

This trick further highlights the difference between a bulletproof application and a runtime application. The trick works for users of full Access, but it does not work when the /RunTime command-line argument is used—runtime mode never enables the Database window. Thus, an application that has an audience of sophisticated and unsophisticated users may be most usable when installed with full bulletproofing applied, yet without the /RunTime argument.

Further, in an application for sophisticated (and well-trained) users, you may choose to allow the database to be opened in some instances with the Shift key held down, which enables the user to bypass the Startup options. The /RunTime argument in a shortcut disables this override of Startup properties.

Providing Feedback to Users

A basic tenet of human nature is that people prefer positive over negative feedback. Then, why is most computer software so negative or vague when giving feedback to a user? As a simple example, if you assign a value greater than 32767 to an integer variable in Basic, you get an error message back from Access that simply states "Overflow." This might make sense to you as a developer, but it is going to cause confusion, frustration, even anger for any of your users viewing this message in an alert that your application shows. How many users will enjoy using your system if it evokes any of these emotions?

To minimize the impact of negative feedback, bulletproof application developers should give careful consideration to the messages that are displayed to users. The next four sections provide my suggestions on how you can make your applications provide the best possible feedback.

Crafting Friendly Alerts

To their credit, Microsoft developers have tried to "humanize" some of the error alerts generated by the Access 97 interface. Some messages include not only a problem description, but a suggested resolution, as shown in Figure 17.11.

Fig. 17.11

Access 97's built-in error alerts are friendlier than they used to be.

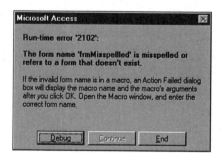

> **Microsoft Access**
>
> **Run-time error '2102':**
>
> **The form name 'frmMisspelled' is misspelled or refers to a form that doesn't exist.**
>
> If the invalid form name is in a macro, an Action Failed dialog box will display the macro name and the macro's arguments after you click OK. Open the Macro window, and enter the correct form name.
>
> [Debug] [Continue] [End]

 Note

Not all Access error messages are intelligible, however. Try to imagine the confusion of your users when they see an alert like the one for error number 97: "Cannot call friend function on object which is not an instance of defining class."

In a perfect world, all developers would create a table of frequently used error numbers in their applications and craft specific and informative messages for each error number. Most budgets don't allow for such niceties, however.

Because your applications will rely on error traps placed in the code, they will not be displaying Microsoft's built-in, friendlier alerts, which are not exposed to the developer. Thus, you're stuck with Access' `Err.Description` string as your primary alert text, which unfortunately leads back to messages like "Overflow" wrapped inside your application's message box.

Compare Figure 17.12 and Figure 17.13, both generated by a `MsgBox()` function placed in application code. The first figure shows an alert that uses the Access error number and message only. The style shown reflects the standard approach taken by most developers. The second figure shows a more polite and detailed wrapper around the standard error message. Even though the Access error message shown on the alert is the same, the alert contains additional helpful context information for the user to convey to the developer, and provides a suggested course of action. The alert in Figure 17.13 is far less intimidating and more useful than the one in Figure 17.12.

Fig. 17.12

A common alert placed in applications simply shows the internal error number and message.

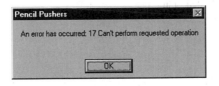

Fig. 17.13

A friendly error alert provides more information than the common, terse style.

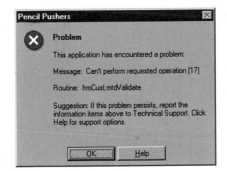

Well-written code can detect the most common negative situations and handle them with the least impact on the user. For some situations, your error trap should filter out specific errors by number with a `Select Case` statement and act on them accordingly, providing a customized message that improves upon the Access error description text. In other cases, it may not be necessary to show the user an alert every time an error occurs—specific nonfatal errors can sometimes be trapped by your code and discarded without giving any feedback to the user at all.

To create standardized, friendly alerts such as the one in Figure 17.13, write a centralized alert routine that each of your error handlers can call. The procedure should accept error information and display a formatted message box. Chapter 11, "Expert Approaches to VBA," discusses such standard error handlers in detail, including the one used in Figure 17.13.

The alert in the Figure 17.13 includes bold text in the message body. Access looks for an internal flag (the @ character) in your message string to facilitate this formatting for you. The message string you supply to the MsgBox() function can include one or two @ characters to delimit the message into three parts, like this:

```
MsgBox "headingtext@bodytext@solutiontext", vbOKOnly, caption
```

The three sections are displayed as follows in the message box:

> *headingtext*. This text is displayed in bold, and Access adds a line feed to the end for spacing. Use it for message headings such as "Problem," "Error," "Warning," and so on.

> *bodytext*. The body text is displayed in the normal font. Access adds a line feed to the end of the text for spacing.

> *solutiontext*. Access displays this second text block below the body text block, using the normal message box font separated by a blank line. You can use this *solutiontext* string to provide users with suggested courses of action or more information about the situation or application.

 Note

The total length of the combined string passed to the MsgBox function cannot exceed 1,024 characters.

Only a small amount of development effort is required to make your application produce alerts that are less intimidating and more useful than the error messages built into Access.

Funny but Not Friendly

In an attempt to lighten up the spirit of his application, a friend of mine once put a random number generator in his code to vary the information in the alerts the system produces. When an error occurred, his standard error dialog box randomly displayed messages such as the following:

You're History!

Ouch!

Incoming!

Bad Move!

You Broke It!

Although his idea was well-intentioned, this approach was not received with enthusiasm by the users. When new and unskilled users saw these alerts, they took the message seriously and assumed they had caused serious trouble. When skilled users saw these alerts, they craved a more useful and deeper level of information on the problem than was provided.

The humorous message text lasted only one week.

Telling Users What's Expected of Them

One primary approach to helping your application interact better with users is to prevent them from getting into trouble in the first place. In addition to good training, documentation, and supporting materials (help files, for example), you can employ various form design techniques to give users a better sense of what the program expects of them.

Place reminders on your forms wherever possible to help the user understand the right and wrong way to use the form and its controls. A reminder can be as simple as a label in an application stating "Press the Tab key to move to the next field" for many of the users who are new to Windows computing. Alternatively, reminders can be more complex, such as having the Enter event for each text box trigger the display of a long message on the form stating the data entry and validation requirements for the current control.

Access provides many ways of giving the user constructive information, including the following techniques:

StatusBarText Property. Each control on your form should have information in the StatusBarText property for the control. The status bar has been in Access and other Office applications for a long time, so most users will habitually look to that area of the screen for guidance on an option. Do not use this information only for Text Box controls—buttons, combo boxes, and any other control that can receive the focus through a Tab key or mouse click should be included.

ControlTipText Property. Also commonly called "tool tips," these small rectangles display when the mouse hovers over a control for about a second. You can add these tips to many of the controls on your forms, as shown in Table 17.7. Control tips are more than copies of the StatusBarText property for a control pasted into the ControlTipText property. This property gives you 255 characters of instant help text you can provide to your user—more than can be shown on the status bar— enabling you to give very explicit instructions to the user (see Figure 17.14). On the other hand, you may opt to have the tips more abbreviated than the status bar text because the yellow tip boxes are quite intrusive when they are displayed. You will have to decide the best model for your users.

Table 17.7   Suggestions for Using Form Control Tips

Control	Type of Tip
Bound Object Frame	Tell the user what kind of objects are allowed in the control.
Chart	Tell the user exactly what data the chart is based on.
Check Box	Tell the user the ramifications of selecting the box and any related events that are triggered.
Combo Box	Tell the user the source of the list and whether items not on the list are valid selections.
Command Button	Tell the user exactly what happens when the button is pressed.
Custom Control	Describe unique information about the control and its use.
Image	Tell the user whether clicking or double-clicking the object performs any action.
Label	Provide expanded information beyond that shown on the label.
List Box	Tell the user whether one or multiple list items can be selected and how to do it.
Option Button	Tell the user the ramifications of selecting the option and any related events that are triggered.
Option Group	Describe the purpose of selecting an option from the group.
Text Box	Provide information about data entry requirements or validation rules.
Toggle Button	Tell the user what happens when the button is selected.
Unbound Object Frame	Note whether the user can double-click to activate the object and the source of the object.

Note

The only controls that do not have `ControlTipText` properties are `Line`, `PageBreak`, `Rectangle`, `Subform`, and `Tab` controls.

Fig. 17.14

A control tip, shown here on a button, can provide useful, customized information.

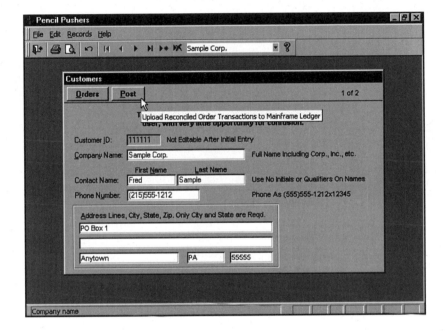

Field Formats. Setting an input mask for a form control validates the data as it is entered. It also provides the added benefit of allowing the user to see the structure of the data to be entered. For example, an `InputMask` property for a date field that shows four placeholders for the year removes any confusion about how the data should be entered. Similarly, an input mask that shows six placeholder characters (#) in a Customer ID field is very explicit about the number of characters and data type required from the user (see Figure 17.15).

Control Groupings. In some cases, you can economize on form text by grouping several controls together with a Rectangle or Line control and creating one label to describe the data entry requirements for the entire control group. See the example in Figure 17.15.

Check Box, Option Group, Combo Box, and List Box Controls. Of course, these control types limit the data entry options for the user and therefore are very explicit about the data entry requirements.

Fig. 17.15

`InputMask` *and control group techniques convey data entry restrictions to users.*

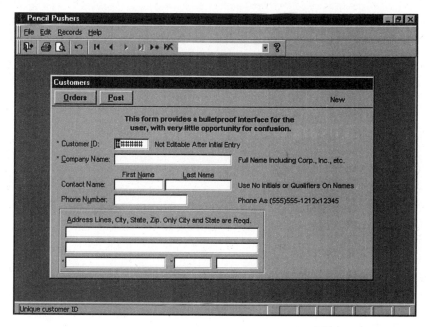

17

Form Messages. Depending on the amount of empty space on your form, you can often provide detailed messages by using labels on the form. Because a label's caption can be changed by program code, you can use one label on the form and change the text as needed, creating your own expanded version of status bar text on the form as the user moves the focus. For example, you can change the caption of a label attached to a Comment field by program code to describe the type of comment required for the specific Customer Type code chosen for the current record.

Visual Clues. Some companies or workgroups have preexisting user interface models that prescribe standards for informing users. For example, one client had us place "(mm/dd/yy)" at the end of all form labels for date fields because the mainframe screens had looked this way for years and the users expected it. Figure 17.15 shows a similarly explicit reminder attached to the Phone Number field.

Message Boxes. If the user steps out of bounds or needs a gentle reminder, the `MsgBox()` function is a ready tool for communicating information.

Help. With Access 97, you have an additional option for displaying help text for your user. As before, you can attach a custom help file to your application by setting the form's `HelpFile` and `HelpContextID` properties. This will take users to specific help topics when they press F1 in a form or control. If you prefer, you can now add the What's This button to a form and have Access display a customized pop-up help topic instead, which is launched when you click the button then click a Form control. See Chapter 8, "Designing Effective Interfaces," for information on implementing this feature.

The best way to measure your success or failure in this area is to watch how users interact with your application during the working model release or alpha testing phase of the development. Watch first-time users enter data records into your forms and encourage them to verbalize any confusion or mistakes; then you can make corrections to the application.

Telling Users What's Going On

Too many Windows applications rely almost exclusively on an hourglass mouse pointer to tell the user, "Please hold, the program will be back with you shortly...." Certainly, any feedback is better than no feedback, but the reality is that the hourglass pointer has become for most of us the ubiquitous reminder that we don't have enough horsepower in our machines to perform operations instantly, and we need to spend more money on hardware! Also, an hourglass does not by itself really answer any questions the user might have about the status of the application, such as:

What is the program doing right now?
In other words, is everything okay or is there a problem?

How long will I be waiting?
Should I go for coffee or is the application coming right back?

What can I do to help?
Is there something that I can do to make this process go faster?

With all the effort you put into making your application work well, it does not take much extra time to make it friendly for the user. When you have completed primary development, run the application on a slow machine (a 486/33 with 8M of RAM is a good candidate) and note where the application delays more than a few seconds. Each of these areas is a candidate for adding feedback for the user. The following are some good ways to give feedback:

Mouse Hourglass Pointer. Although I've already noted that this is not always the preferred option for asking users to wait, this is your fallback plan if you do nothing else. Whenever a form is loading or a long process begins running, set the `Hourglass` method to `True` until the process is complete.

 Tip
VBA now includes the same `MousePointer` property that you are used to if you program in Visual Basic. If you are writing code that you will move from Access to VB, consider using `Screen.MousePointer = 11` and `Screen.MousePointer = 0` in place of `DoCmd.HourGlass True` and `False`.

Status Bar Text. Using the `SysCmd()` function, you can alter the status bar text at any time. During a long process, you may want to tell the user what is happening (for example, "Posting invoices, please wait. Completed: 10"), and refresh the status at timely intervals (for example, update the message at every 10 invoices). Sample `SysCmd()` code lines follow to set and clear the status bar. Note that the function returns an empty variant value, which you can simply ignore in your code:

```
varRet = SysCmd(acSysCmdSetStatus, "Posting, please wait...")
varRet = SysCmd(acSysCmdClearStatus)
```

 Caution

When you use `SysCmd()` to set the status bar, text in the `StatusBarText` property of form controls will not override the status bar text you have set. Until you clear the status bar text with the code line shown, your form controls will not display status bar text.

Speedometers. With program code, you can create the same speedometer inside the status bar that Access uses to note query progress and similar processes. If your code runs a long operation and you are able to accurately estimate the number of looping increments or time units that the process will consume, you can display the partial progress on the status bar, as shown in the following code:

```
' Initialize the meter text and maximum value
varRet = SysCmd(acSysCmdInitMeter, message, maxvalue)
' Set the meter current value
varRet = SysCmd(acSysCmdUpdateMeter, value)
' Remove the meter
varRet = SysCmd(acSysCmdRemoveMeter)
```

First, initialize the status bar by setting the message prompt and the total number of units that will constitute 100 percent. Next, send repeated `SysCmd()` calls to update the value, and Access will compute the percentage to display as the *value* sent with the `acSysCmdUpdateMeter` argument divided by *maxvalue* sent with `acSysCmdInitMeter`. When the process is complete, make sure to remove the meter as shown.

Form Messages. You can provide detailed messages on a form by setting the caption of a label to describe a process that is running and to note its status. Use this technique if the Access status bar does not provide enough space for the desired message.

ActiveX Controls. ActiveX controls are available for you to create a variety of status speedometers embedded directly on a form, including the Status Bar control shipped with the ODE and the Kwery Gauge control. (A demo version of this Gauge control is on the CD-ROM.)

The upshot of using these techniques is that users should not have any questions about what is going on while the application takes control of their mice and keyboards.

Telling Users How to Get Help

At some point, the user may have exhausted the training materials, the system documentation, the screen prompts, and the help file and still not understand some feature of the application. When that happens, frustration mounts quickly, and your application can placate users with information describing how to get support or help. I suggest each of your bulletproof applications employ one or more of the following devices:

Helpful information within alerts. Rather than just having your alerts display an error message, they should also suggest possible resolutions to the problem at hand, for example, a "solution" block of text as shown in "Crafting Friendly Alerts" earlier in this chapter. For certain fatal error codes, consider having the alert message tell the user whom to call for help or how to get immediate assistance.

From the About Dialog Box. Applications, both custom and retail, normally provide an About dialog box option on the Help menu. For custom applications, consider listing support options on this dialog box, such as telephone numbers, pager numbers, or e-mail addresses for support or development personnel (see Figure 17.16).

E-mail Support Requests. On some applications at corporate sites that have their own PC support staff, we've added a Support option to the Help menu that creates the shell of an e-mail message and addresses it to the support personnel. It then displays the e-mail compose dialog box so the user can finish and send the message immediately.

The latter two options previously mentioned—an About dialog box and a Help support menu option—are especially useful if you make them available on the menu bar throughout the application.

Fig. 17.16
This About dialog box provides a variety of suggestions for getting assistance.

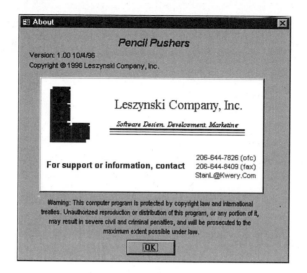

17

Collecting Information from the Application

Although bulletproofing is intended to minimize the potential for problems in the data and with the use of the application, issues often arise in a complex system that will benefit from an audit trail. My bulletproofing strategy includes creating the following four audit trails in all of our applications.

As I discussed in the "Logging In to an Application" section above, your application can collect and validate login information and set a global variable such as lci_gstrCurrentUser with the user identifier. Each of the audit routines that follow make use of this variable.

Collecting Login Information

The first level of auditing involves finding out who uses the system and when. This information can be useful for answering such questions as the following:

▶ Which people use the system and which do not?

▶ How often does each person use the system?

▶ How long does each user and the average user stay logged in to the system?

▶ Which users do not log out at night (may interfere with the backup process)?

▶ Which users are currently logged in?

To answer these questions, you can create an activity log table in the back-end database with a name like `zstlogLogin` and include the fields shown in Table 17.8.

Table 17.8   Fields for a Login Activity Table

Field	Data Type
SessionID	AutoNumber
UserName	Text 10
LoginAt	Date/Time
LogoutAt	Date/Time

When a user logs in to the application, write a new record to the login activity table, as shown in the first function in Listing 17.6. The login record stays open until the user logs out, at which point you close the record by stamping the logout time with the second function in the listing. This combination of a very simple table and two simple routines provides your application with a wealth of information.

Listing 17.6   Routines that Manage User Login and Logout

```
Public Function LoginStart() As Boolean
' Create a login record for the login activity table

  Dim dbs As Database
  Dim rst As Recordset

  Set dbs = CurrentDb
  Set rst = dbs.OpenRecordset("zstlogLogin", dbOpenDynaset)
  rst.AddNew
  rst!UserName = lci_gstrCurrentUser
  rst!LoginAt = Now
  rst.Update
  rst.Close

End Function

Public Function LoginEnd() As Boolean
' Close a login record on logout

  Dim dbs    As Database
  Dim rst    As Recordset
  Dim strSQL As String

  strSQL = "SELECT * FROM zstlogLogin WHERE UserName = '" _
    & lci_gstrCurrentUser & "' And LogoutAt Is Null; "
  Set dbs = CurrentDb
  Set rst = dbs.OpenRecordset(strSQL, dbOpenDynaset)
```

```
' In actual implementation, your code at this point should check
'   for more than one record in the dynaset, which would indicate
'   either a reboot or system crash on a previous session, thus
'   the activity record is still open, or a user logged in from
'   more than one workstation.  In either case, you would want to
'   notify the user or run some resolution code to decide which
'   user to logout.

    rst.MoveFirst
    rst.Edit
    rst!LogoutAt = Now
    rst.Update
    rst.Close

End Function
```

You'll note that the login activity table also has a sequential field, SessionID, which creates a unique number for each user login session. Because a named user can actually log in to the application more than once on the same or different machines, a login record must note the unique user login instance. This number can then be used to manage multiple logins for the same user, lock records or flag status values, track distinct user sessions, and so on. The following section gives more insights into using this value.

Collecting Activity Information

As your needs require, you can use a method similar to the login audit in Listing 17.6 to track other important application events, such as when a specific form is loaded, procedure is run, or record is added to a table. Simply copy and modify the code in Listing 17.6 to write an explicit message string to an activity table, zstlogActivity, that looks something like that in Table 17.9.

Table 17.9   Table Fields for an Activity Log Table

Field	Data Type	Description
ActivityID	AutoNumber	Primary key
UserName	Text 10	User name
Object	Text 65	Name of form or process
Table	Text 65	Name of affected table
RecordKey	Long Integer	Primary key of affected record
Records	Long Integer	Record count of affected records
Activity	Text 30	Activity description
ActivityAt	Date/Time	Time stamp

Whenever an event occurs that has value for tracking purposes, you can have your code write a record to this activity table. Table 17.10 shows a few examples of such events in the log table (minus the user name and time stamp fields). The code to create such activity records will be very similar to that in procedure `LoginStart` in Listing 17.6.

Table 17.10   Sample Records from an Activity Table

Object	Table	RecordKey	Records	Activity
frmCust	tblCust	15733	1	Added
frmCust	tblCust	15688	1	Deleted
frmInvcPost			42	Posted

Recalling the `SessionID` that was created for each unique user login in the previous section, you can optionally use the `SessionID` as an activity's owner instead of `UserName`. The session number indicates not only the user name but which unique user session triggered the event. To enable this feature, you will have to carry the `SessionID` in a global variable when the application is running and replace the user name variable in your logging code with the session variable. For most developers, however, this extra information is not highly useful; its greatest benefit comes when the same user (for example, Guest) can be logged in from multiple terminals/locations and thus can generate multiple simultaneous `SessionID` numbers for the same user name.

Note that the sample data in Table 17.10 has a mix of data in the `Records` field: For record modifications I write the actual record primary key affected, but for a process I write the quantity of records processed. If you prefer your activity records to be less free-form, you can separate this information into two fields.

With the affected table name and a record primary key in the activity table, you can now query the audit data by target table name and record key to get a picture of how records are affected and by which users. For example, a query where the `Table` field equals "tblCust" and sorted by the `RecordKey` and `ActivityAt` fields would show you the entire sequential history of each individual customer record.

You can have your application write to the log table at event triggers that you deem important, whether code events or user-generated events. For example, for some clients we add three more columns to the activity table—`Field`, `OldValue`, `NewValue`—and our audit routine tracks individual edits to critical fields. In some extreme cases, we even create a separate audit table for each major data table and place archive copies there of records that are edited before changes are saved.

Tip

If you have no need of special activity flags, such as "Posted" shown in Table 17.10, you can use built-in Access constants, such as `acAdd`, `acDelete`, `acEdit`, and `acSave`, to set values in your activity log table.

17

Collecting Record Edit Information

As a further audit technique, I always add to every major data table the fields shown in Table 17.11.

Table 17.11   Table Fields for Edit Logging in Each Data Table

Field	Data Type	Description
CreatedAt	Date/Time	When was record created
CreatedBy	Text 10	User ID of creator
ChangedAt	Date/Time	When was record last edited
ChangedBy	Text 10	User ID of last editor

Our applications update these fields when each record is created and edited, so we can easily track who has created a specific record and who changed it last. Attach to the `BeforeUpdate` property on each form a code routine that plugs the four fields with user and date information before the record is first saved and plugs only the changed fields when each edited record is saved. See the examples in Listing 17.7.

Listing 17.7   AES_BPrf.Mdb—The Routines Required to Track Record Edits

```
Private Sub Form_BeforeUpdate(Cancel As Integer)

  Call lci_FrmRecStamp(Me)

End Sub

Public Sub lci_FrmRecStamp(rfrm As Form)
' Purpose:   Timestamp current form record, called from Form_BeforeUpdate
' Arguments: rfrm:=Form object with recordset to stamp
' Example:   lci_FrmRecStamp(Me)

  rfrm!ChangedAt = Now
  If lci_IsBlank(lci_gstrCurrentUser) Then
```

continues

Listing 17.7 Continued

```
    rfrm!ChangedBy = CurrentUser()
  Else
    rfrm!ChangedBy = lci_gstrCurrentUser
  End If
  ' Only stamp Created fields if Null
  If IsNull(rfrm!CreatedAt) Then
    rfrm!CreatedAt = Now
    If lci_IsBlank(lci_gstrCurrentUser) Then
      rfrm!CreatedBy = CurrentUser()
    Else
      rfrm!CreatedBy = lci_gstrCurrentUser
    End If
  End If

End Sub
```

Note that the information in these audit fields might duplicate information that you place in the activity log described in the previous section. Even so, having this record creation and edit information in the table itself is very useful because it can be printed on reports, displayed on forms, or viewed when browsing the table directly. You can also add these fields to ancillary tables, such as lookup tables, that may not be audited by the activity log process.

 Note

You will need to capture the SessionID in numeric versions of the CreatedBy and ChangedBy fields instead of using the user name if you decide to track all activities by session instead of by user name, as I described in the section "Collecting Activity Information" immediately preceding this section.

Collecting Error Information

The final audit technique enables you to keep track of error messages that your application generates. I use a table, zstlogError, in the back-end database with the structure shown in Table 17.12.

Table 17.12 Table Fields for an Error Log Table

Field	Data Type	Description
ErrWhen	Date/Time	Time of error
ErrProcName	Text 130	Module.Procedure name

Field	Data Type	Description
ErrUserName	Text 10	User ID
ErrNumber	Integer	Err.Number value
ErrDescription	Memo	Err.Description string

Each time a code error is generated and your code jumps to its error handling routine, you can write a log record to this table. The table's information provides great value in the following two ways:

You can use it as part of the design process for future releases of the application. Running queries on the error log table will tell you the most frequently generated error numbers overall and the code routines and users who generate the most frequent errors. We review this table before going to meet with a client to discuss the next system upgrade so that we can be proactive and propose areas to strengthen within the application.

It protects you from exaggerated criticism. Every application seems to have at least one user who is totally intolerant of the fact that applications generate alerts by design. This person, who thinks that every message box signifies a bug, can poison a developer's reputation by overstating the number of error messages a system generates. With statistical data to show exactly how your system is performing, you can defend your reputation in such a situation.

The VBA code structures and procedures to support this table are detailed in Chapter 11, "Expert Approaches to VBA."

Additional Feedback Collection Techniques

Although the four primary audit routines described in the preceding section give you detailed information about the application and how users interact with it, they operate "behind the scenes." I find it handy to give users a chance to actively participate in the feedback process as well.

One mechanism for gathering feedback is to create a table and form to gather users' comments. Periodically print reports from the table to review user issues and suggestions. Another technique is to provide users with an e-mail dialog box or an e-mail-enabled form with which they can send their comments directly to a support or development person. Whichever of these options we employ, we usually place a Support or Feedback option on the Help menu to launch it from any form.

From Here...

Once you have developed a ritual for bulletproofing applications, your efforts accrue the following benefits:

Application training and documentation requirements are lessened because the application is friendlier to use.

Support calls are reduced because there are fewer ways for the user to be confused or to get into trouble.

Your application looks—and you look—professional.

Your data is protected. If your application is bulletproof, that dreaded telephone call, "Oops, I just deleted every row in the customer table; what do I do?" will never come!

The time investment to implement these bulletproofing techniques is small in contrast to the benefits described. For more information about related issues, consult the following chapters:

▶ To review the relationship between application structure and bulletproofing concepts, return to Chapter 7, "Understanding Application Architecture."

▶ Chapter 8, "Designing Effective Interfaces," provides information about menu and toolbar design and discusses various user interface elements used in this chapter.

▶ For coding techniques to support error handling, error logging, and other VBA concepts discussed in this chapter, see Chapter 11, "Expert Approaches to VBA."

▶ To understand more about form design and coding techniques that improve usability and data presentation, read Chapters 13 through 16 on the subject "Creating Expert Forms."

chapter 18

Creating Expert Reports

18

In this chapter

◆ The new reporting features added in Access 95 and 97 and how to capitalize on them

◆ How to create standardized report layouts that present a consistent interface to their readers

◆ How and when to print a form as a report

◆ How to create useful interfaces for users to filter a report's data

◆ How to beat common problems with embedded subreports

◆ How to use Access data and program code to publish data in Web-based reports

Putting data into an application that has no reports is like taking your daily newspaper from the front porch each day and locking it, unread, into a closet. Similarly, putting data into an application with poorly designed or inaccurate reports is like reading selective paragraphs from newspaper stories without reading the headlines or understanding the context. Because you work hard to collect and protect data with your expert solution, you should work equally hard to provide its users with high-quality reporting output so that the data stored in the solution can feed business processes and decisions.

There are many facets to creating good reports and to using the Access reporting engine. Consequently, there is no shortage of techniques to put in reporting chapters. The problem is that most reporting techniques are already in print in other Que books, and I wanted to provide unique value here. For this chapter, I try to identify strategies that I know will provide developers of expert solutions with value but are not covered widely in print.

Reporting the Facts

Sometimes creating solutions can be a thankless job. One example that comes to mind occurred when we were creating reports for a client recently.

For many years, our client had been using simple, columnar reports produced off of the mainframe. The manager reviewed these reports at the end of each month. We convinced the manager that these reports would be more detailed and visually appealing if they were produced from Access instead, so he authorized us to create a system to download and report the mainframe data.

When our database and reports were completed, the system was installed and the first month's worth of data was imported into it from the mainframe and printed out. The manager immediately called us and quite gruffly pointed out that there was a significant math error in our main inventory report. I apologized and sent someone over to have a look.

What the manager had noticed was that our reports did not arrive at the same average value as the mainframe reports that were run in parallel. As it turns out, we discovered on closer examination (and proved to the manager) that our report was accurate and the calculations on the mainframe report were wrong.

Because the manager placed great faith in mainframes and his legions of Cobol programmers, he had never checked the math on the original reports, and they had been in error for years. Due to his distrust for personal computers and inexpensive tools like Access, his review of our Access reports constituted the first time he had ever checked the validity of the inventory report calculations!

The Access reporting engine is extremely powerful. With its ability to nest multiple reports in a parent report (or to nest a subreport inside a subreport inside a report), Access allows you to express relational data easily and to group and sort information for very effective data presentations.

Over the years, you will devise common approaches to your complex reporting problems. To help you master your reporting challenges, I wanted to spark your interest here in some of the newer or more interesting facets of reporting. This chapter contains information about assisting users with report selection and filtration, about dynamically configuring reports, and about utilizing HTML-based Web pages to report Access data.

Exploring New Reporting Features

Access 95 introduced several new reporting properties and features of interest. In case you didn't discover them or are moving to Access 97 directly from version 2, I'll describe those that make reports more powerful and programmable:

Filter Property. This property contains an SQL WHERE clause (without the WHERE keyword) that places an additional filter over the recordset for the report. Generally, your reports will have a predetermined recordset or have the recordset established by code in the Open event of the report. However, there may be times when you want a report to have a base data set and a filtered data set, with the user able to switch between the recordsets at will. In such a case, you can set the Filter property string for the report and toggle from code the FilterOn property setting. The property value determines if the filter is or is not currently applied. When you set FilterOn to True, the report rebuilds and requeries its record source with the filter string applied. Here is code that filters a report:

```
Reports!rptCust.Filter = "LastName = 'smith'"
Reports!rptCust.FilterOn = True
```

HasData Property. This property returns -1 if the report has a recordset that contains records, 0 if the recordset has no records, and 1 if the report is unbound and has no recordset. You can use this property in place of the NoData event (its description follows) when you don't want to cancel an empty report, but instead want to reconfigure it on-the-fly, print it empty, or otherwise utilize it.

You can also use this property in the Format event of a section to determine whether or not to display a subform located on that section, as in this example:

```
Me!subKids.Visible = Me!subKids.Report.HasData
```

NoData Event. The NoData event fires as the report opens if it is bound to data but contains no records to display. You can use this event to cancel the report if there are no records that match the current record source or filter criteria. Place the following code in the NoData event procedure to cancel the report when it has no records:

```
Private Sub Report_NoData(Cancel As Integer)

  Beep
  MsgBox "No records match the report criteria." _
    , vbOKOnly + vbCritical, Me.Name
  Cancel = True

End Sub
```

18

Note

The `NoData` event does not fire for unbound reports. You can check the `HasData` property for a value of 1 instead to tell if a report is unbound (has no recordset).

Picture Property. You can set this property to the name of a graphic image file that will serve as the background for the entire printed area of the report. Because a background picture will slow printing and make the report more visually complex, this feature may not be useful in every application. However, your users may appreciate a very subtle "watermark" background picture that identifies all of an application's reports, or want you to use pictures selectively for reports that are distributed to a specific audience.

RepeatSection Property. This property applies only to group header sections, and determines if the header is repeated for each new page or column that displays the group's controls. This property will replace your workaround coding from prior versions to print repeating headers programmatically.

Access 97 dabbles very little with reporting—it introduces only one new report property. The `IsVisible` property determines whether a report control is going to be displayed for the current record on the current section or not. `IsVisible` is used when there is a dependency between controls and the driving control for the dependency has its `HideDuplicates` property set to `True`. You use `IsVisible` to determine if the control will be displayed for the current record or if it will be hidden, because it contains the value that duplicates the value in the prior record.

The `IsVisible` property is *not* the same as the `Visible` property. Assume that you have a Text Box control placed on a report's Detail section. The control's `Visible` property is set to `True` so that the control will attempt to print whenever its section prints. In addition, the control's `HideDuplicates` property has been set to `True` so that duplicate values repeated in the text box will not print as duplicate values on the report.

As each individual detail record is prepared for printing, the report evaluates whether or not to display the text box by checking to see if its value will be equal to its value from the previous record. If so, the report toggles the control to invisible to honor the `HideDuplicates` property for the control, and then temporarily sets the control's `IsVisible` property to `False`. The control's `Visible` property setting is left unchanged at `True`, and the control's `IsVisible` property setting is reset again when the report moves on to the next record.

To use `IsVisible`, your code can read the property as a record prints, and can set properties of related controls to dynamically display or hide them based on the specific

circumstances. For example, a Label control related to a Text Box control whose
IsVisible property is currently False can be hidden by your code at the same time:

```
Me!lblDivision.Visible = Me!txtTitle.IsVisible
```

 Note

You can only read and set the IsVisible property for a report control from the Print
event procedure attached to the parent section that contains the control, as in this
example:

```
Private Sub Detail_Print(Cancel As Integer, PrintCount As Integer)

    If Me!txtTitle.IsVisible Then
      ' Do something
    End If

End Sub
```

18

Creating Standardized Report Layouts

Report layout standards are very subjective and will vary by company, user team, and
sometimes even application. The Access report wizards actually do a fine job of satisfying
many reporting needs and producing reports that have a consistent look.

When defining report layouts, the key concept to keep in mind is this: A form displayed
or a report previewed within an application is "in context," meaning that the user can
discern the purpose and content of the form or report from its place in the application.
The hardcopy (printed) version of a form or report, on the other hand, is "out of context," because it may be circulated to people who do not know which application it was
generated from or the context in which it was printed.

That fact that hardcopies are out-of-context means that special care must be taken when
creating them to provide enough contextual information on the printout to clarify the
document for its readers. The next section will help you improve context information on
your reports.

Displaying Context on Reports

An expert report should carry with it all of the information required to identify its origin
and data set. As a general rule, good reports circulate much more widely than the developers or users initially expected. Thus, it is almost certain that an application's reports
will end up being read by people who are not users of the application itself. When these
people have a question about the report, they need to know its source and other information about how it was produced.

I like to create a standard reporting template for each project, and use the template for each report in the application. The template should be designed to provide the same look and layout to each report in the application. This allows users to quickly identify the source of the report by its layout.

 Note

I use the term *template* here in an expanded context when contrasted to how Access uses the word. A report template in Access is an actual report whose format settings for the report and its controls are automatically applied to each new report. By default, the report template for your new reports is a report you create and save named Normal (although any report can be used as a template by identifying the report's name in the Report Template item in the Options dialog box).

When applying a saved report template, Access reads only the property settings from the named template; it does not copy its controls. Thus, my concept of a template goes past Access' to include adding specific controls to a report and using the report *and its controls* as a template. This is achieved by making a copy of the template itself as the starting point for each new report. Read on for clarification of this approach.

A report template for an application should provide a layout format that meets the needs of the specific users. Some of the items that we place on a standard report template include:

Application Name. It is useful to give each application in an organization a unique name so that it can be identified apart from all others. Reports generated by the system should have the application's name prominently displayed in a label at the top or bottom of each report, for example "Friendly Foods Order Management System."

Report Title. Each report should be given a unique descriptive title, also displayed at the top or bottom of each report, such as the "Products on Backorder Listing." A report title should indicate a unique layout or content; although, the same base title may be used for reports that are similar but incorporate different levels of detail, such as the "Unshipped Orders Report—Summary" and its sibling, the "Unshipped Orders Report—Details."

Report Name. I like to put the actual object name, such as rptProdList, of each report in the Page Footer section so it repeats on each page. Users will describe a report to each other using the report title, but if they can describe it to developers using the actual name of the Access report object, I find that bug reports and enhancement requests are communicated much more accurately.

 Tip

Locate either the report title, the report name, or both on each page of a report, as well as the date and time of printing. Together, these identifiers describe one unique printed instance of a report, and if the pages become separated each one is clearly identified by these key values so that they can easily be reunited.

18

Record Source Description. I have found that users are appreciative when we place a brief description on each report page that describes the sort order and filtration applied to the report. For example, users may be able to print a report using two different sorting/grouping strategies in addition to applying a range of dates to the data. In the Page Footer of such a report, I would place a string like this: "Grouped by Category where Order Date between 1/1/95 and 10/15/95."

 Tip

You do not need to hard-code the sorting information shown on the bottom of a report. Your report can look at its own group-level information to learn how it's sorted and grouped.

For example, if a report has two sorting/grouping levels set by code and they are not static, placing the following expression in a text box on the report will show the current sorting information at the time of printing:

```
="Ordered by " & [Report].[GroupLevel](0).[ControlSource] _
    & ", " & [Report].[GroupLevel](1).[ControlSource]
```

For more information on group level properties, see the section "Changing Report Properties Dynamically" later in this chapter.

Page Numbers. Page numbers are an obvious necessity for multipage reports. You can specify the Page property in an expression to show the current page, or the Pages property to show the total number of pages for the report, as in the following:

```
="Page " & [Page] & " of " & [Pages]
```

Access now has a menu option called Insert, Page Numbers that inserts a text box with this string into your report.

Date and Time. The major reports in most business systems are printed at regular intervals, such as every Friday or the end of the month. However, unless the system prohibits printing outside of such a cycle, users are likely to print a report arbitrarily. For example, Sally might print a report, look for erroneous data on it, correct the data in the system, and then reprint and re-audit the report, all outside of the normal processing cycle. Without the date and time on each page of a report, how would she differentiate the audit printout from the weekly version if they both sat on her desktop?

Access now has a menu option—Insert, Date and Time—that places a text box with a date and/or time string onto your report.

Figure 18.1 shows a report that follows a standardized layout and contains the elements from the previous list.

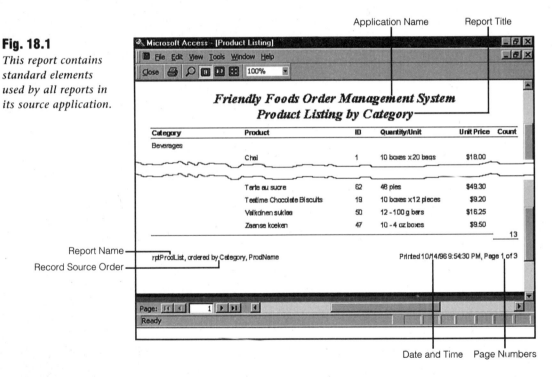

Fig. 18.1

This report contains standard elements used by all reports in its source application.

In addition to the descriptive elements shown in Figure 18.1, a more comprehensive reporting layout standard may include one or more of these elements:

Copyright/Confidentiality Notice. If a report contains sensitive or proprietary information, placing a notice "Copyright © 1997 *company name*" on a report may provide some legal protection for the document. Similarly, you can place a string akin to "***Private and Confidential***" on each page of a report that is deemed sensitive. Consult a legal advisor for more information on the use of these and similar proactive phrases.

User Name. Chapter 17, "Bulletproofing Your Application Interface," describes how to capture the user's name and store it for later use. Recall in that chapter that I suggested creating a global function (`lci_gstrCurrentUser`) that will return your application's current user, whether in a secured environment or not. In some applications, one use for such a function can be to print the name on reports to indicate their origin. You can use the function in an expression in a Text Box control:

```
=lci_gstrCurrentUser()
```

Subsystem Name. In some applications, different modules can produce very similar reports, leading to a need for indicating the module's name on the report itself. For example, the Sales subsystem and the Accounting subsystem of an application may both print a Sales Report, but with slightly different information (the Sales group's report will be interested in volume by salesperson while the Accounting version may be concerned about tax-related categories, like the purchaser's state). Giving them different names is preferable, but showing the subsystem name on the report is an alternative.

Audit Information. For some reports, printing the record source and other contextual information consumes too much space to use a page footer. You can create a separate audit information page on the report that shows exactly what parameters were used to print the report. This is very useful in highly complex reports that are used as master documents for audits and other financial recordkeeping. See the section "Creating Report Appendixes" later in this chapter for an example of an audit page.

A saved report used as a template can have any or all of these listed attributes. In addition, you can save standard printer and margin information and a default code module with your report template.

As an alternative to creating a report template that you copy and paste to create new reports, you can utilize the new AutoFormat feature, which saves report format information for reuse. Access ships with six default formats, and you can also create your own.

A report AutoFormat is a saved definition of properties for the objects listed in Table 18.1. The listed settings are saved for each section and control displayed on the report used as the basis for the template. Control settings can be saved for each type of control—even the new TabControl object and the ActiveX container control.

Table 18.1   Property Values Saved with a Report AutoFormat

Object	Property	Comment
Report	Picture	Background picture
Report	PictureAlignment	Layout of picture
Report	PictureSizeMode	How picture is sized
Report	PictureTiling	Whether picture is tiled
Report	PictureType	Embedded or linked
Picture	ObjectPalette	Palette for background picture
Section	BackColor	Background color
Section	SpecialEffect	Outline effect
Control	BackColor	Background color
Control	BackStyle	Transparency
Control	BorderColor	Outline color
Control	BorderStyle	Outline style
Control	BorderWidth	Outline width
Control	ForeColor	Foreground color
Control	FontItalic	Italicization
Control	FontName	Font name
Control	FontSize	Font point size
Control	FontUnderline	Underlining
Control	FontWeight	Font emphasis
Control	LabelX	Placement of attached label
Control	LabelY	Placement of attached label
Control	SpecialEffect	Outline effect
Control	TextAlign	Positioning of text

A report AutoFormat is applied at the control, section, or report level. The saved format contains information for each of these elements; and when you select Format, AutoFormat from the menu and pick a format, the format is applied to only the selected object in your report design window. For example, if only a text box is selected as opposed to the entire report, only the standard text box properties from the format are applied to the selected control.

To create a new AutoFormat, create a report with one control of each type and one section of each type and apply your desired property attributes to the objects listed previously in Table 18.1. Next, choose Format, AutoFormat from the menu, click Customize, and choose the option choose the Create a new AutoFormat option.

Note the difference between AutoFormat and the saved report template I discussed earlier in this section. AutoFormat applies the property formats listed in the previous table to existing sections and controls, but does not create new controls (such as your application's standard Report Footer labels). AutoFormat also does not set all of the properties on a report that may be part of your standard template, such as the width and margin settings for printing.

Using both a standard report template and an AutoFormat template together can provide an effective means for creating standardized reports. Here is an example of how you would do so:

1. Create a standard report template that has the default controls you want placed on all application reports, such as standard headers and footers. Save the template as a report.

2. Create another report, one that has one of each type of control, and set the control defaults specified in Table 18.1 for each control to the attributes you want on your standard reports. Choose Format, AutoFormat to save these property values together as your standard AutoFormat template.

3. Set any additional border, color, effect, and font settings for each control on the report and choose Format, Set Control Defaults for each control to save the control's properties as the default values for the report. Save the report as Normal or whatever name you've chosen for the default report template in the Options dialog box.

4. To create a new report, copy your company report template from step 1 to the Clipboard and paste it back into the application, giving it the name of the new report you want to create. Change the informational text strings in the default controls inherited from the template to the appropriate values for the current report.

5. Set the record source of the new report and populate it with the data-bound controls it needs. Each control, when created, will derive its properties from those you set on the control of the same type on the Normal report from step 3.

6. Apply the AutoFormat saved in step 2 using the Format, AutoFormat menu option. This sets the properties for sections and controls on the new report to values saved in the format template. Your report's attributes and layout should now match your defined standard for the application.

The AutoFormat information is saved in tables in the supporting database WZDAT80.MDT. If you want to preserve your auto formats in case of a crash, back up

18

this file. You can also copy the file to the workstations of other users in order to distribute your formats to them, but be aware that your file will overwrite theirs; and if they have any saved formats of their own, they will lose them. In a multideveloper environment, you can have one person be the owner of the master AutoFormat templates by changing them on his or her workstation, then distributing the master WZDAT80.MDT to all the other developers.

Tip
Saved AutoFormat templates can be created for forms in the same way as for reports.

Printing Forms as Reports

Access allows you to print forms. However, in keeping with the WYSIWYG (What You See Is What You Get) tradition of Windows, when Access prints a form it *looks* like a printed form, which is often quite unappealing. For example, Figure 18.2 shows the printed view of our standard Get form for filtering record lists, as described in Chapter 16, "Presenting Data to Users."

Fig. 18.2

The printout of an Access form usually looks too much like a form to make a useful hard copy report.

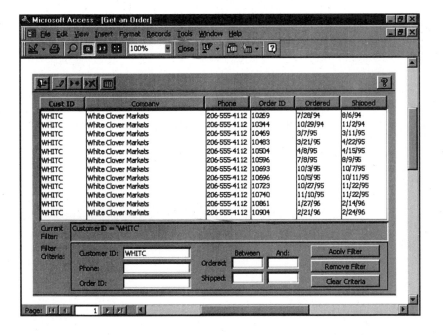

Note from Figure 18.2 that forms printed as reports do not provide the sorting, grouping, and dynamic control and section sizing features found in reports. Thus, only infrequently will you be motivated to print forms to paper.

In order to be print-worthy, your form should meet these criteria:

▶ *It can be displayed with only printable attributes.* When a form is printed, Access creates a *metafile* (a detailed type of Windows graphic file) in memory of the form's layout, then prints the metafile. The algorithm for converting the form's look on the screen to the metafile for printing sometimes produces less-than-perfect results.

For example, you have probably noticed that text on a Command Button control that displays satisfactorily on the screen may bleed off of the button when printed, depending on the font and point size. As a result, what you see on the screen may not be what you get on the printout. Command Button and ActiveX controls are the most common offenders in this respect. Test the hard copy look of your form on each of the printer models that will be utilized by its users before certifying the form as printable.

Also, many colors that display well on the screen may not print well on a black-and-white printer. In general, forms look best in hard copy when they use only black and white.

▶ *It does not need to be resized for printing.* Form controls and sections do not dynamically resize in the same fashion as with reports. A form that contains a list box filled with records, or a continuous form or subform, will only print the same number of records as are shown on the screen. This may result in incomplete information on the hardcopy version of the form. A printout showing a subset of the form's data is usually not useful.

▶ *The application does not need to detect printing events.* When a report prints, events such as Format and Print fire and allow the developer's code to control the printing operation to a fine degree. Forms, on the other hand, do not notify the developer at all when they are printed, and thus are inadequate substitutes for reports when customization of the printing process is required.

The form shown in Figure 18.3 provides an example of a form that qualifies as a better-behaved candidate for printing, because it has these attributes:

▶ The BackColor of the form is white. While the standard gray background color used for most application forms will print adequately, the shading on the hard copy is usually undesirable and a white background is preferred by most users.

▶ The List Box control shown is fed by a "top ten" query and thus will never show more than ten items; there will never be more items in the list than are displayed on the form. No data will be missing from the printout despite the fact that a printed list box does not resize to show all of its contents.

18

> ▸ The form layout is simple and needs no complicated visual attributes in order to be
> printed. If dynamic layout, color, or other property changes are desired during
> printing, a report provides better capabilities in this area than a form.

Fig. 18.3

*This simple form
makes a good candi-
date for a hard copy
printout.*

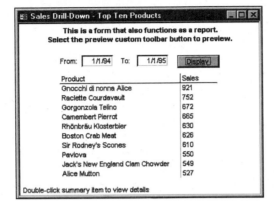

See Figure 18.7 in the next section to see this form in print preview mode.

Setting Properties for Printable Forms

In addition to providing a layout that prints well, your printable form must make proper
use of available property settings that help create a report-like appearance from the form
as it prints. The following property settings are important to help your form print well:

Dividing Lines. This form property should be set to No to remove horizontal dividing lines between the printed sections.

Border Style. Access clears the value in unbound controls on a form when the form
is printed and the Border Style property has a setting other than Sizable. In other
words, if I use the setting Dialog for the Border Style property of the form in Figure
18.3, when the form is printed the two unbound Text Box controls and the unbound List Box control will be blank, and they will also be blank upon returning to
form view from print preview. (Access 2 worked more appropriately by printing the
unbound values; this errant behavior was introduced in Access 95.)

 Note
Access is not able to print preview a form that has the Border Style property set to
Sizable and has been opened in dialog mode with the OpenForm method, like this:

```
DoCmd.OpenForm "frptProdOrderDet",,,,,acDialog
```

Attempting to preview a form opened this way produces runtime error number 2465. If your application needs to print preview a form that will be opened as a dialog with OpenForm, set the form's Border Style property to Dialog when originally designing the form.

Pop Up, Modal. The same errant behavior (unbound controls print without their values) that is initiated by a Border Style property other than Sizable is also initiated when a form's Pop Up or Modal properties are set to Yes. You must set both of these values to No for a printable form.

 Note

Controls that are bound to data fields (that have a Control Source value) are always printed just as they are displayed on the screen, regardless of the form's Border Style, PopUp, and Modal properties.

Page Header/Footer. For forms that you want to print, consider turning on the Page Header and Page Footer sections (from the View menu), because these are printing—not viewing—sections. Text placed in these areas appears on every page of a printout, but not on the screen, making them ideal for report titles and page numbers.

Display When. This property is available for the Form Header and Form Footer sections, as well as individual form controls. The setting determines whether the object will show on the screen, on hard copy, or on both. This setting allows you to define specific objects that will not show in one view or the other, giving the form distinctly different on-screen and printed appearances.

 Note

The Display When property setting for a section overrides that of any controls on the section. Thus, for example, a control whose Display When setting is Always will not show on a printout if it's located on a Page Footer section with Display When set to Screen Only.

Force New Page. Just as it does for a report, this property determines if a form section prints on a new page or the current page. It has no effect on the display of the form on the screen.

Layout For Print. For forms that you want to print, you may want to set the Layout For Print property value to Yes. This setting determines which *font set* will be used for the form. The font set is the list of fonts that appears in the Font list on the toolbar and in the Font Name property list in the property dialog. The font set is also used by Access when the form is printed.

Printers often install a font set that includes fonts with the same names as screen fonts, as well as fonts unique to the printer. Figure 18.4 shows a Font list from the Access form design toolbar displayed when Layout For Print is set to Yes. Note that the list includes True Type and printer fonts, denoted with separate symbols.

If Layout For Print is selected, when you make font assignments you are selecting printer fonts instead of screen fonts for the form's objects. Using printer fonts ensures that the way a form is displayed on the screen most closely matches the way it appears when printed. In contrast, using screen fonts to print can produce unpredictable results. For example, some printer drivers don't ship with a printable version of MS Sans Serif, Access' default font. Sending a form that uses this font to a printer will cause the printer to substitute a similar font from its font set in place of the screen font, and the printout may not appear as anticipated.

Tip

True Type fonts have both a display and a printer version of the font. Using these fonts for printable forms makes them independent of a specific printer driver and more useful across a large number of users with various printers. If you use only True Type fonts on a form that is printed, the value of the Layout for Print setting becomes unimportant.

Fig. 18.4

This toolbar combo box for font selection lists the fonts supported by the current printer.

When creating forms that may also be printed, Access allows you to tailor the form controls' properties to allow for two distinct views of the form: the on-screen view, and the printed view. The separate views are defined by the use of the Display When property on form sections and controls. The value for this property determines in which of the two form views the section or control will be displayed: Print Only, Screen Only, or Always.

When building forms that will also be printed, you can create two distinct form views (on-screen and hardcopy) by placing sections or controls on the form whose specific purpose is to add context when the form is printed. You may find it useful to provide additional information (the application name, for example) on the printed form versus the displayed form, because the printed version may be distributed to users unfamiliar with its source application.

 Note

The Page Header and Page Footer sections do not have a Display When property setting. By design, these sections display during print only.

18

Figure 18.5 shows a diagram of some of the display property settings for the form controls in the current example form. The form includes controls and sections that are specifically designed for display or printing, but not both.

Fig. 18.5

Setting the display properties of form objects determines in which view the objects are printed.

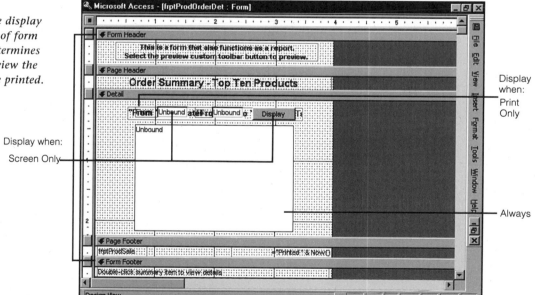

Figure 18.6 shows the form as printed. Controls and sections that are set to display in the Screen Only view are not displayed during printing (see Table 18.2). Contrast the printed version with the displayed version in Figure 18.3 shown previously.

Fig. 18.6

The form from Figures 18.3 and 18.5 is shown as it will print on the printer. Controls set to display on Screen Only *are not shown.*

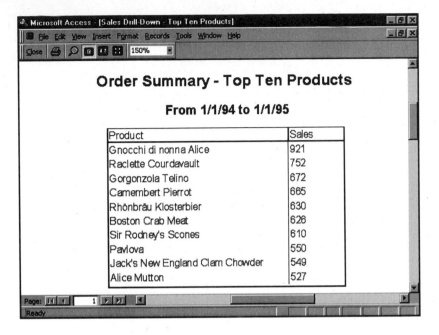

In the example form from the previous figures, I've set the display properties of the form and its controls as shown in Table 18.2, in order to create a form that displays well and prints well.

Table 18.2   Properties for Elements of a Printable Form in Figure 18.5

Object	Property	Value	Comment
Form	Border Style	Sizable	Allows printing of unbound values
Form	Layout For Print	Yes	Use printer fonts
Form	Modal	No	Allows printing of unbound values
Form	Pop Up	No	Allows printing of unbound values
Form Header	Display When	Screen Only	Text for screen view only
Detail	Can Grow	Yes	Show all information
Detail	Can Shrink	Yes	Resize to best size

Object	Property	Value	Comment
Detail	Display When	Always	Show on screen and report
Form Footer	Display When	Screen Only	Text for screen view only

Tuning the Display of Printable Forms

When you intend to allow users to print preview a form, it is likely that they will maximize the previewed form in order to see more of its data. Returning from preview to form view will leave the form in a maximized state. Add the following line of code to the Activate event of the form to restore the form's default size when preview mode ends:

```
DoCmd.Restore
```

Forms have no specific event that tells your code when a mode change between form view and preview takes place. Using Activate is a workaround that will usually prove adequate, because this event fires when a previewed form switches back to form view. However, be aware that this event also fires when the form is first opened and when focus moves to the form from another form, so any code you place in the event to solve reporting problems will fire in these instances.

When in print preview mode, you may not want the application's users to see Access' default preview menu, or toolbar, or custom menu, or the toolbar you've assigned for the form (see this chapter's sample database AES_RPTS.MDB on the CD-ROM for a sample custom print preview toolbar). You may instead want to provide your users with a custom menu bar or toolbar for the form while it's in preview mode. Your code can change the Toolbar property of the form as it enters preview mode, and then change it back to its previous setting on returning to form view. In the event procedure that previews the form, use code like this:

```
Me.Tag = Me.Toolbar
Me.Toolbar = "lci_tbrPrvw"
```

Notice that the code preserves the value of the current Toolbar property setting (hides it in the Tag) before the change, so that the original setting is not lost. Reverse this process when the form changes back to form view. This approach is shown in the Form_Activate procedure in Listing 18.1. (Chapter 14, "Navigating in Forms and Applications," describes custom command bars in more detail.)

In addition to showing how to toggle custom command bars, the following navigation techniques for a printable form are demonstrated in Listing 18.1:

- ▶ I've created a custom toolbar for the form, and on the toolbar is a Preview button to indicate to the user that it is a printable form. The form uses the *method procedure* `mtdPrntPrvw` to initiate preview mode from the toolbar button. This procedure is publicly exposed so that it can be called from the standard module procedure that is initiated by the custom toolbar button. This tangential invocation methodology is required, because a custom toolbar button cannot be used to call the form's method directly (refer to Chapter 14 for more information).

▶ The first line of the method procedure `mtdPrntPrvw` invoked to preview the form *deselects the current selection* in the List Box control on the form. This makes the control print more attractively and accurately (without a highlighted record in the list box). A list box selection is only valid in the context of the screen display—on the hard copy all items in the list are important, so the selection would be nonsensical. Consider doing this kind of cleanup as a form prints to make it more presentable.

▶ The method procedure `mtdPrntPrvw` *swaps the visible custom toolbar* displayed via the form's default setting to a custom toolbar that is specifically designed for print preview mode.

▶ The procedure `Form_Activate` *restores the form's default custom toolbar* and removes the custom toolbar used during print preview mode.

▶ The procedure `lstSale_DblClick` is used to launch a specific drill-down report from the form (more information on drill-downs is found in the section "Creating Drill-Down Reports" later in this chapter). In this procedure, the *form hides itself* so that the report owns the entire interface.

Listing 18.1   AES_Rpts.Mdb—Changing from the Default Toolbar to a Custom Toolbar and Back

```
Private Sub Form_Activate()
' Purpose: Reset toolbars and form size

   If Me.Tag <> "" Then
     ' When the toolbar is swapped during preview, its default
     '   value is stored in the Tag
     Me.Toolbar = Me.Tag
   End If
   DoCmd.Restore

End Sub


Private Sub lstSale_DblClick(Cancel As Integer)
' Purpose: Drill-down to more detail

   On Error Resume Next  ' Allow printing to be canceled
```

```
    If cbfValidate() Then   ' Don't drill-down when criteria invalid
      Me.Visible = False  ' Hide the form
      DoCmd.OpenReport "rptProdOrderDet", acPreview
    End If

  End Sub


Public Sub mtdPrntPrvw()
  ' Purpose: Change to preview mode, called by toolbar button

    Me!lstSale = -1   ' Deselect list item for printing
    Me.Tag = Me.Toolbar   ' Preserve the default value
    Me.Toolbar = "lci_tbrPrvw"
    DoCmd.OpenForm Me.Name, acPreview
  End Sub
```

The final element required for smooth navigation in this scenario is for the drill-down report (rptProdOrderDet) called by the form to redisplay the form as it closes. Recall that the form in the listing hides itself so that its drill-down report can be displayed, thus the drill-down report's Close event procedure must contain this line:

```
Forms!frptProdOrderDet.Visible = True
```

Filtering and Sorting Report Data

I see many users and developers create several—even dozens—of variations of a single report in order to present the same data to users in different layouts. For example, a telephone number report produced from a customer or contact database often must be printed in two different sort orders: sorted by last name, and sorted by company name. A nonsophisticated approach to reporting these items would result in two different reports. A more sophisticated approach to the same problem would allow your application to use a single core telephone number report in a variety of different ways, and thus reduce the size of the database file and the number of objects in it.

In order to produce "reusable" reports, you must enable them with some sense of self-awareness and provide the code to detect and react to different states.

Selecting Reports and Report Data

As you noticed in Chapter 13, "Mastering Combo and List Boxes," and Chapter 16, "Presenting Data to Users," my applications rely heavily on List Box controls to present users with multiple options. A list box is a natural choice when allowing users to select reports or reporting options in an application. Figure 18.7 shows a simple menu form fmnuReport for selecting a report to print. The list of available reports is driven by a database table containing report names and configuration settings. When a report is added to the application, I simply add the report name and its attributes to the table, which in turn causes the report and its description to appear in the form's list.

Fig. 18.7

A simple menu form can be used to allow users to select a report to print.

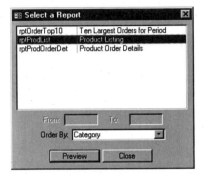

The reporting menu in the figure is self-configuring, making it a truly smart object. The configuration information is passed to the form from its settings table zstblReport. The table has the structure shown in Table 18.3. All of the table fields are of type Text.

Table 18.3   Table Fields that Feed a Reporting Menu

Field	Contents
ReportName	Name of the report
ReportDesc	Short description of the report
ToOpen	A flag (F/R) that notes whether to open a criteria form or the report itself
OrderBy	Values for the RowSource of a combo box filled with sort order options
DatesReqd	Whether the form must collect From and To dates

Figure 18.8 shows the table zstblReport with some values.

Fig. 18.8

A configuration table can be used to provide values to a report selection menu form.

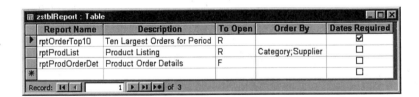

The menu form (refer to Figure 18.7) that drives report selection has a List Box control (to list the available reports), a Combo Box control (to select the chosen report's sort order), and two Text Box controls (to select the starting and ending date range for the report). For each report, the field values in OrderBy and DatesReqd determine which of these controls will be displayed for the user.

When the menu form loads, it pulls values from the configuration table into the List Box control (the control's RowSource property is set to zstblReport). This list control serves two roles. First, it gives the user a list of reports to print. Secondly, it contains in its columns (hidden) the configuration information that the form needs for each report. Thus, each of the five fields shown in Table 18.3 is loaded into the list box, but only the first two (ReportName and ReportDesc) are shown to the user. To hide the last three columns, the list box's Column Widths property is set as follows:

```
1";1.5";0";0";0"
```

When the user clicks a report name in the list box, code runs to reconfigure the form for that report. Reconfiguration is simply a matter of displaying the combo box (and filling it), enabling the text boxes so that the user can enter report criteria, or disabling all of these criteria controls, as determined by the OrderBy and DatesReqd (Column(3) and Column(4)) values in the list. The reconfiguration code is shown in Listing 18.2.

Listing 18.2   AES_Rpts.Mdb—Dynamically Enabling Criteria Selection Controls

```
Private Sub lstReport_Click()
' Purpose: Show the appropriate controls when a list selection is made

  Call cbfCtlReset
  With Me
    If Not !lstReport.Column(3) = "" Then   ' Show combo box
      !cboOrder.Enabled = True
      !cboOrder.RowSource = !lstReport.Column(3)   ' Set the RowSource
      ' Select the first order as default
      !cboOrder = !cboOrder.Column(0, 0)
    End If
    If !lstReport.Column(4) = True Then    ' Show text boxes
      !txtDateFrom.Enabled = True
      !txtDateTo.Enabled = True
    End If
  End With

End Sub


Sub cbfCtlReset()
' Purpose: Re-hide the selection fields

  With Me
    !cboOrder = Null
    !cboOrder.RowSource = ""
    !cboOrder.Enabled = False
    !txtDateFrom.Enabled = False
    !txtDateTo.Enabled = False
  End With

End Sub
```

When the user has clicked a report, entered the required selection criteria, and clicked the Print button on the form, the selected report or form is displayed, as enabled by the code in Listing 18.3.

Listing 18.3   AES_Rpts.Mdb—Checking the Criteria and Printing the Selected Report

```
Private Sub cmdPrint_Click()
' Print the report or show a criteria form

  If Me!lstReport.ListIndex = -1 Then  ' No report selected
    Beep
    Exit Sub
  End If

  If cbfValidate() Then
    If Me!lstReport.Column(2) = "F" Then  ' Open a reporting form
      DoCmd.OpenForm "f" & Me!lstReport
    Else  ' Open a report
      On Error Resume Next  ' Allow report to be canceled
      DoCmd.OpenReport Me!lstReport, acPreview
    End If
  End If

End Sub


Private Function cbfValidate() As Boolean
' Purpose: Check for valid report criteria

  Dim ctl As Control
  Dim strMsg As String

  With Me
    ' Validate combo box if showing
    If !cboOrder.Enabled = True And IsNull(!cboOrder) Then
      Set ctl = !cboOrder
      strMsg = "Must select an order."
    End If
    ' Validate text boxes if showing
    If !txtDateFrom.Enabled = True Then
      If IsNull(!txtDateFrom) Then
        Set ctl = !txtDateFrom
        strMsg = "Must select a start date."
      ElseIf IsNull(!txtDateTo) Then
        Set ctl = !txtDateTo
        strMsg = "Must select an end date."
      ElseIf !txtDateFrom > !txtDateTo Then
        Set ctl = !txtDateFrom
        strMsg = "Start date cannot come after end date."
      End If
    End If
    If Len(strMsg) > 0 Then
      Beep
      MsgBox strMsg, vbOKOnly + vbCritical, "Validation Failed"
```

```
    ctl.SetFocus
Else
    cbfValidate = True
End If
End With

End Function
```

You can make your report selection forms as complex as your application requires. For example, the form shown in this topic does not allow the user to choose between preview mode and print mode. If you do not need to have the user automatically preview each report before printing, your reporting selection form could provide an option group to allow the user to specify Preview or Print.

The key concept here is that reports, unlike all other application objects, usually continue to be added to a system after deployment. Creating a table-driven, self-configuring approach to report selection that allows for the easy addition of reports to a system is the correct methodology for an expert solution.

 Tip

Placing criteria selection fields on a reporting menu is only one of several ways to provide users with the ability to print subsets of data. Another example: if you allow users to create ad hoc filters for a displayed form, it's now easy to print the same data on a report that is displayed on the form. When the user clicks the form button that prints the report related to the current form, the button can run code to copy the form's `Filter` property into the report's `Filter` property as the report opens. This causes the report to apply the preselected filtration from the form to its recordset.

Additionally, you can use the form's `Filter` property setting in `WhereCondition` argument of the `OpenReport` method in the form code that opens the related report, like this:

```
DoCmd.OpenReport "rptCust", , , Me.Filter
```

Reports can also be based on parameterized queries. A query with a criteria parameter displays a dialog box prompt for each criteria when the report is run. The downside to this technique is that the parameter information is captive to the query engine and cannot be easily validated by code in the calling form or called report.

Finally, most of the techniques for passing information into a form during its load process that are described in the section "Passing Information to a Form" in Chapter 14, "Navigating in Forms and Applications," are also applicable to reports. These techniques include setting the `Tag` property or passing information to a report via global variables.

18

Creating Drill-down Reports

When analyzing data, it can be very useful to view summary information and then to "drill-down" from that summary information to the related details. In Access, you must facilitate this behavior with a form, because reports and their controls do not provide events like Click and DblClick that a developer can use to make them interactive.

To create a drill-down environment, create a form that summarizes the desired information in a datasheet view or a List Box control. Provide the form with code that detects a user event and responds to the event by showing another form or a report with details for the selected record. A click or double-click action on a record, or a button click on a Details button, are two mechanisms for enabling this behavior.

For example, the form in Figure 18.9 shows a list box with aggregated sales order data by product. The query driving the list box control is a Top Values query that only shows the top ten products by sales volume. The product information in the query is limited by a criteria using the date ranges entered on the form. The SQL for the list box's Row Source property value looks like the statement in Listing 18.4.

> **Listing 18.4   AES_Rpts.Mdb—An SQL Statement that Selects the Top Ten Products by Order Volume**

```
SELECT DISTINCTROW TOP 10
  tblOrderDet.ProdID,
  First(tblProd.ProdName) AS Product,
  Sum(tblOrderDet.Quantity) AS Sales
FROM tblProd
  INNER JOIN (tblOrder
    INNER JOIN tblOrderDet ON tblOrder.OrderID = tblOrderDet.OrderID)
  ON tblProd.ProdID = tblOrderDet.ProdID
WHERE tblOrder.OrderDate Between [Forms]![frptProdOrderDet]![txtDateFrom]
  And [Forms]![frptProdOrderDet]![txtDateTo]
GROUP BY tblOrderDet.ProdID
  ORDER BY Sum(tblOrderDet.Quantity) DESC
```

The first column of the list box (ProdID) is not displayed on the form, because it's required by code but not essential for the user.

The list box on the form shown contains a DblClick event procedure to open the related detail report for the ProdID value specified by the List Box control, as shown in Listing 18.5.

Fig. 18.9

From this summary form, a user can double-click a product name to drill-down to its details.

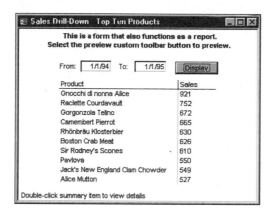

Listing 18.5   AES_Rpts.Mdb—Drilling-Down from a List Box to a Report

```
Private Sub lstSale_DblClick(Cancel As Integer)

  On Error Resume Next  ' Allow report to be canceled
  DoCmd.OpenReport " rptProdOrderDet", acPreview _
    , , "ProdID = Forms!frptProdOrderDet!lstSale" _
    & " And (OrderDate Between Forms!frptProdOrderDet!txtDateFrom" _
    & " And Forms!frptProdOrderDet!txtDateTo)"

End Sub
```

This code opens the detail report bound to the product information for the product and date range selected on the form.

In place of a list box, a continuous form or subform can be used to enable drill-down in a similar fashion. Place a button or event on the continuous form that allows the user to print more detail for a selected record.

 Tip

In a drill-down environment like the one described here, your application moves from forms to reports and back. Your users may appreciate the application more if each report displays itself maximized, and then cleans up after itself (restores the calling form's size) as it closes:

```
Private Sub Report_Close()

  DoCmd.Restore

End Sub


Private Sub Report_Open(Cancel As Integer)
```

```
        DoCmd.Maximize

    End Sub
```

The technique described here for drilling-down into reports from a controlling form is the easiest to enable, but is by no means the only way to implement drill-down. An alternative approach involves the use of command bars to allow the user to navigate from one record to another.

To drill-down using command bars, your application must provide users with a custom menu option on a menu bar, context menu, or toolbar button that allows them to indicate the desire to drill-down from the displayed report record. Your Drill-Down menu option will open a subordinate report with more information for the currently displayed record. The challenge in this technique is determining which record the user wants to see detailed. Reports do not provide an event model that allows the user to click or otherwise select a specific record. Thus, when the user selects your custom Drill-Down menu option, your code needs to be able to infer the context (in other words, deduce what the "current record" is). To detect the current report record, use this logic:

1. Create a report that displays only a single record per page.
2. When the user selects your drill-down option, determine which record is showing on the current report page (see code following).
3. Display a drill-down report for the target record.

When your report displays a single record per page and the user makes the menu selection to drill-down, your code can grab the ID of the item on the currently displayed report page and proceed to drill-down. The code in Listing 18.6 shows how to determine which report record is currently showing.

Listing 18.6   How to Determine Which Record Is Showing on a Report

```
' In the Declarations, establish a module-level recordset
Dim mdbs As Database
Dim mrst As Recordset

Private Sub Report_Open(Cancel As Integer)
' Purpose: On Open, establish a recordset matching the report's

  Set mdbs = CurrentDb
  Set mrst = mdbs.OpenRecordset(Me.RecordSource, dbOpenSnapshot)
  mrst.MoveLast   ' Cache all of the data

End Sub

Public Function mtdDrillDown()
```

```
' Purpose: Grab the displayed ID and drill-down

    mrst.AbsolutePosition = Me.CurrentRecord - 1
    DoCmd OpenReport "rptDrillDown", , , "CustID = " & mrst!CustID

End Function
```

Your custom command bar option for drilling-down would initiate the custom method mtdDrillDown shown in the listing.

The code in Listing 18.6 highlights these Access characteristics:

> *Lack of* RecordSetClone. When the report opens, the code shown creates a clone of the report's recordset. Reports do not provide the RecordsetClone property available in forms, so the code must create a recordset based on the RecordSource string that drives the report.
>
> *Recordset Positioning.* The code synchronizes the work recordset to the same record displayed on the report by setting the recordset's AbsolutePosition property, which moves to specific location in the recordset.
>
> *Use of* CurrentRecord. Reports expose a CurrentRecord property that describes the currently-displayed item's position within the report's data. Thus, the CurrentRecord value can be used to synchronize the work recordset to the report by placing the value in AbsolutePosition (subtracting 1 is necessary as shown because CurrentRecord is 1-based and AbsolutePosition is 0-based).

If this seems like a convoluted approach, it is. The technique shown is required, however, because of the nature of the report layout engine. The engine is preparing the next record for presentation while you are viewing the current one, so you cannot simply ask the report for the value on the displayed page as you might presume. Assume that your customer report is ordered by customer number and that you are viewing the report page for customer 1. Surprisingly, entering the following string in the Debug window will show 2, not 1, because the report is busy laying-up the display of customer 2 while you are viewing customer 1:

```
Debug.Print Reports!rptCust.txtCustID
```

Thus, the code in Listing 18.6 is needed to accurately grab the value of the displayed record by checking its CurrentRecord setting.

> ⚛ **Tip**
> Information that will help you understand how to implement command bars on reports is contained in Chapter 14, "Navigating in Forms and Applications."

Also, in that chapter I provide a technique for loading a combo box on a toolbar with the values in a form, and navigating within the form based on the user's selection from the combo. This technique could also be used to list records on a currently displayed report and to facilitate drill-down to a specific record from the toolbar.

Changing Report Properties Dynamically

Report properties, like form properties, can be changed "on-the-fly" from code in order to create flexible and self-configuring reports. From the developer's standpoint, adequate properties and events exist in Access to detect the majority of status changes as a report is printing, and to modify the look of the report on demand.

The highest level report property is its `RecordSource`. Access reports provide an interesting opportunity with respect to this property. Reports do not look for the table or query defined in their `RecordSource` until the end of the `Open` event procedure (unlike a form, which looks for the record source before the `Open` event). This allows you to change a report's `RecordSource`, or set a filter or sort order, in the `Open` event procedure without incurring a performance penalty, because the report doesn't create an initial recordset from its saved record source prior to the property change. This behavior is a great asset for developers.

Frustratingly, Access reports do not have the `OpenArgs` property that's available on forms. If `OpenArgs` were enabled in reports, it would be simple to change the record source for a report by passing in the new value as an `OpenReport` method argument and running code in the `Open` event like this:

```
Me.RecordSource = Me.OpenArgs
```

Unfortunately, reports are missing this capability. The mystery I mentioned earlier is now apparent: Your reports open awaiting record source information from your code, but provide no easy way to get it to them. To solve this situation, your code must pull any new `RecordSource` value from some external setting within the application.

Consider the drill-down form described in the prior section and shown in Figure 18.9. This form is used to open a detail report, and the example in the previous topic showed how to pass filter criteria to the report as the `WhereCondition` argument on the `OpenReport` method. While useful, the technique demonstrated in Listing 18.5 earlier is limited because it can only change the report's `WHERE` clause, and not the entire record source or any other attributes of the source data.

A more advanced approach to the same problem would allow the report to look back to the drill-down form from its `Open` event and determine how to build its own record source. The following code shows an example of such an event procedure:

```
Me.RecordSource = "SELECT * FROM qrptProdOrderDet" _
   & " WHERE ProdID = Forms!frptProdOrderDet!lstSale" _
   & " And (OrderDate Between Forms!frptProdOrderDet!txtDateFrom" _
   & " And Forms!frptProdOrderDet!txtDateTo)"
```

 Note

If the report in the current example used only one record source, it might run faster if the criteria shown were entered directly into the saved query `qrptProdOrderDet` and the query listed as the report's record source. The current example, however, assumes that the report's `Open` event has `If...End If` or `Select Case...End Select` logic to allow the creation of various different `RecordSource` properties during the report's launch.

18

In addition to the `RecordSource`, other report properties are equally good candidates for dynamic changes based on circumstances present at open or print time. Here are some other examples of property changes at print time that may prove useful:

Changing the sorting and grouping. A report has one `GroupLevel` property array element for each level of sorting or grouping assigned to it, and this property setting can be used to build your record source description string. In turn, the `GroupLevel` property has its own descriptive properties (one for each attribute in the Sorting and Grouping dialog box), such as a `ControlSource` that represents the value in the Field/Expression column of the dialog, and a `SortOrder`.

For example, the following line changes the primary grouping and sorting for a report on-the-fly in the `Open` event:

```
Me.GroupLevel(0).ControlSource = "Category"
```

Changing the location of controls. As a general rule, I usually prefer to have report layouts reflect the sort order of the data on the report, reading from left to right. Thus, if I create a report that can be sorted in different ways, I will often write code to change the order of Text Box controls on the report at the same time that the sort order changes. Simply modify the `Left` property of a control to move it horizontally on the page.

Hiding and showing information. Report data sometimes loses its context if a related piece of information is not present. In such a case, your report code can hide specific controls on a section to prevent confusion. Likewise, graphic elements of a report such as lines and boxes sometimes must be shown from program code, depending on context. In both of these cases, you can place code in the report's `Format` event to move, resize, hide, and show controls to dynamically alter a report's layout as it prints.

Creating Report Appendixes

Some reports are more valuable when followed with supplemental information. Programmatically, it's simple to print two reports back-to-back. However, a few special challenges arise that may trip you up and are worthy of discussion. I'll approach the situations by explaining both what works and what doesn't work, with the hope of teaching you how to think creatively when debugging reporting challenges.

Consider the case where you have two reports that have a relationship to each other (rptChain_1 and rptChain_2 for this example). Your code needs to print both reports back-to-back. Because the reports are related, it would be nice to have the page numbering sequence continue from rptChain_1 onto rptChain_2. To facilitate this, you would be inclined to add your standard text box to the first report's footer to show the page number, using the Page property:

```
="Page " & [Page]
```

Next, you might locate a page number text box on the second report and add the total number of pages from the first report to the page counter to show the compound number, like this:

```
="Page " & ([Page]+[Reports]![rptChain_1].[Pages])
```

While your approach would be valid conceptually, it would stumble on two roadblocks:

Timing. Staging reports with dependencies may present your application with a timing problem. Assume that your code prints rptChain_1 and then rptChain_2, like this:

```
DoCmd.OpenReport "rptChain_1", acViewNormal
DoCmd.OpenReport "rptChain_2", acViewNormal
```

There is no guarantee that Access will finish all of the pagination efforts for the first report before the second one begins opening. Thus, the page counter on the second report that refers to the first report may not be accurate.

 Note

Timing problems become more likely over time as applications like Access utilize the techniques for creating separate memory "threads" for different processes. In a multithreading environment, you would not be able to reliably predict that the first report would open or complete before the second report, because their processing would run parallel.

Pages Property Unavailable. Oddly, the Pages property is not initialized on a report unless it's needed. In the current example, you would not want rptChain_1 to print its total number of pages, because this number would not reflect the page count of the second report that follows it. Thus, you are unlikely to locate a text box on the first report that references its Pages property. However, if you do not, the property is not available in code and any lines of code or external references (like the incremental counter idea just shown) would return 0 for the uninitialized Pages property.

To beat the second limitation, you must create a text box on rptChain_1 and set the ControlSource equal to =[Pages], then make the control invisible. Now, the Pages property *will* be initialized as the report formats and it will be available to code and external references, while still not printing on the report.

However, you still have not resolved the timing problem that may arise from chaining the reports in code. Solving the problem entails creating a more rigidly enforced flow of events. Knowing that the Pages property of rptChain_1 will certainly be available by the time the report is done printing gives you alternative approaches to chaining the reports. You can move the code that opens rptChain_2 from the original driving procedure into the module for rptChain_1, putting it in charge of the order of events, like this:

```
Private Sub Report_Close()

  DoCmd.OpenReport "rptChain_2", acViewNormal

End Sub
```

This code structure means that the first report completes its print or preview processing before invoking the second report. The order of events appropriately meets your chaining objective. However, the fact that rptChain_1 is in the process of closing when it opens rptChain_2 means that the second report should not continue to make explicit reference to the first in its expressions (recall that you placed the following code in a control on the second report):

```
="Page " & ([Page]+[Reports]![rptChain_1].[Pages])
```

A wise strategy would be to gather the page counter information from the first report before it closes. (Ideally, if the OpenReport method had an OpenArgs argument, you could use that, but Access provides no such luxury.) To grab the page number from the first report, place code in the Open event of the second report, as shown in Listing 18.7.

> **Listing 18.7   AES_Rpts.Mdb—Grabbing the Page Count from the Previous Report**
>
> ```
> Public pintPage As Integer   ' Inherited starting number
>
>
> Private Sub Report_Open(Cancel As Integer)
>
>   pintPage = Reports!rptChain_1.Pages   ' Get starting number
>   DoCmd.Maximize
>
> End Sub
> ```

The code in Listing 18.7 ensures that whether the first report completes its closing process or not while the second report is running, the variable pintPage preserves the first report's page counter for reuse. The variable is created with Public scope so that it becomes a custom property of the second report and can be used in a text box to bump the printed page number by the first report's total page count:

```
="Page " & ([Page]+[Report].[pintPage])
```

You can also take a completely different approach to printing reports consecutively. By embedding one report inside another as a subreport, and locating the subreport on the footer of the parent report, the reports will print in sequence. The pagination problem is solved by this approach because the parent report's page footer provides the consecutive page numbering.

Consider the specter raised in the "Displaying Context on Reports" section earlier in this chapter, where I noted that it may be useful for some reports to include audit information. To print audit information, you can build a generic audit subreport and place the report on more than one parent report as required.

Figure 18.10 shows a subreport rsubAudit that is populated with unbound text fields. Each field derives its information from a property of the parent report.

To use the generic auditing subreport shown, place it in the report footer of a parent report.

Getting the subreport to print on its own page at the end of the parent report is a little tricky; you must establish the following environment in order for the subreport to print correctly:

> *Subreport Settings.* In order for a subreport to begin a new page within a parent report, it must contain at least one group header section. Setting the Force New Page property of the subreport to Before Section *does not* achieve this result—the New Page setting is ignored and the subreport begins printing within the parent's footer anyway.

Fig. 18.10

A subreport that does not refer to its parent report by name can be used as a component in multiple parents.

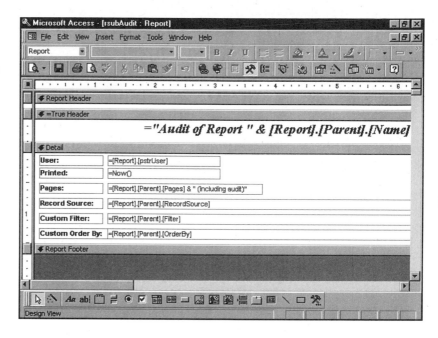

 18

Instead, add a bogus section break to the subreport, using any valid break expression. Set the Force New Page property of the section to Before Section, and Access will properly begin the subreport on a new page within the parent.

> ### 🔬 Tip
>
> In the example report in Figure 18.10, I created a group break on the expression =True, which serves as a bogus break expression. The value never changes; therefore, it does not introduce multiple group breaks into the report, yet it does solve the current problem.

There are two other requirements for successfully tricking Access into printing the subreport on its own page. The first technique is to ensure that the subreport has a visible but empty Report Header section. Do not place any controls in the header, or they will print before the group break forces its new page (in other words, in the parent report's footer).

The second technique is to use the dummy group break section as the subreport's page title instead of adding a control to the page or report header. Note in Figure 18.10 that I've placed the title of the audit report in the group break rather than the report header.

Tip

Set the `Repeat Section` property of the group header to `Yes` if the subform will span multiple pages. This setting instructs the group header to repeat on each new page, serving effectively as a page header for the subform.

Parent Report Settings. Having told the audit subreport to force itself to a new page, the final task is to make sure that the parent report allows this to happen. First, you must set the `Keep Together` property of the report footer on the parent report to `No` in order to ensure that the footer allows its subform to begin on a new page.

Second, you may not want the page header printed by the parent report to appear on the page containing the subreport. In such a case, the following code will disable the parent's page header on the last page of the report:

```
Private Sub phd_Print(Cancel As Integer, PrintCount As Integer)
' Purpose: Cancel the page header on the last page

  If Page = Pages Then  ' Last page contains audit subform
    Cancel = True
  End If

End Sub
```

The audit report's specific job is to display summary information about a report's properties at the end of a printout. The printed information in the example in Figure 18.10 includes the record source of the report, sorting information, and so on. The audit information could be expanded to include other properties of the parent, such as group-level information. Such audit pages on reports are useful when complex reports are printed and used for financial or legal purposes. The audit information clearly describes the exact content of the report as defined when it was printing.

You will be able to utilize the techniques in this topic to solve other situations that arise in your applications that are similar to the current audit report illustration. For example, you may need to print a detail report that is attached to a summary report, or an appendix to a report that lists references for the report.

 Tip

In addition to their usefulness for subreports used as report appendages, the techniques described here will work when you need to create embedded subreports in any section of a report. The same tricks used here to cause the subreport to begin on a new page must be used when the subreport is located on the Detail or other section of a report.

Reporting Access Data to the Web

With the explosion of interest in the Internet and corporate intranets, it was only natural that Access 97 include support for publishing Access data in World Wide Web format.

HTML, or HyperText Markup Language, is the layout language of the Web. From Access 97, you can create static or dynamic Web-based versions of your Access data by using the menu option File, Save As HTML. This option launches the Publish to the Web Wizard and walks you through the export process.

> **Tip**
>
> You can start the Publish to the Web Wizard from your application code. First, add a reference to the file WZMAIN80.MDE that ships with Access. Then, call the function `pub_modMain.pub_StartWiz` from your VBA code.

(18)

The Publish to the Web Wizard is a useful tool for creating one of the following three different types of data exports:

Static HTML. A static Web page is text that is "frozen"—a saved document with no data linkage. The data in these pages is only refreshed when the pages are overwritten with newer versions. (The value of static documents follows later in this section.)

> **Note**
>
> You can export tables, queries, forms, and reports to static HTML page format, and tables, queries, and forms to dynamic format. You cannot create dynamic Web-based reports from the Wizard.

Dynamic HTML via IDC/HTX. HTML pages that communicate with Access via IDC/HTX (Internet Database Connector/HTML Extension) format files perform an actual query against your database and retrieve the most current information into your Web pages. The connection between the Web pages and Access is facilitated by Jet drivers installed on a machine running Internet Information Server (IIS).

IDC files contain ODBC connection information and an SQL statement to send to the database server (Jet, in this case). HTX files are format files that tell IIS what HTML format to apply to the data set returned by the IDC. The end result of this Wizard process is a Web page that resembles the original Access data layout and includes the latest data from the original Access database. (Reports cannot be exported as dynamic HTML of either the IDC/HTX or ASP variety.)

Dynamic HTML via ASP. ASP (ActiveX Server Page) format files are the newest language for communicating with IIS version 3 and higher. An ASP file is a hybrid of the IDC/HTX pair, and includes HTML formatting information, one or more SQL requests, program code in the VBScript dialect, and commands to invoke ActiveX Controls within the browser. As with the IDC/HTX formatted output, a Web page using ASP format retrieves the latest data from your Access database and formats it to resemble a datasheet or form.

 Note

At the time of this writing, fully functional ASP technology was not available for my review in conjunction with Access 97. However, at first glance it appears that the ASP technology provides a significant improvement over the limited and frustrating IDC/HTX approach, so I encourage you to bypass IDC/HTX altogether if you have access to an ASP-compatible server by the time you read this.

One of the most notable benefits is the ability to include multiple SQL statements in a single ASP file, a capability not found in the IDC approach. Running more than one data request allows you to more easily create Web pages that truly resemble reports, with a report/subreport layout or aggregate computations such as totals.

When you run the publishing wizard (or, alternatively, use File, Save As/Export to save an object as HTML), the Web pages created by Access for viewing in a browser provide many of the same capabilities as their parent objects within Access. Internet Explorer provides background colors, various fonts, and colors approximating those from the original presentation, a tabular data layout format, and so on. On the other hand, Web-published data does not incorporate the more advanced reporting features built in to Access such as pagination, snaking columns, and expressions, so exporting data with the File menu options does not provide a comprehensive solution.

The remainder of this chapter goes beyond the File menu options for exporting Web pages from Access and focuses on programmatic approaches to Web publishing. We'll explore how to enable your applications to create static Web reports using VBA code.

When you can create dynamic Web pages from tables or queries (as described previously), and these pages can retrieve real-time Access data, why would you use static Web pages?

To reduce server load. While Jet can support 255 concurrent users querying a database, its response time increases significantly at a fairly light load (20 or so users, depending on the machine hosting it). If the data to be presented to users does not change frequently or does not need to be up-to-the-minute, providing static Web reports to users instead of reports that query the production database will free the database for more important tasks.

To expand the application's audience. The promise of Internet technology is to expand the audience for information. Historically, users interested in sales data needed access to the Sales Department's server, a copy of Access on their machine, and a login and password into the sales application. Now, the same users only need a copy of Internet Explorer and the location on the corporate intranet of the HTML-based sales reports exported weekly from the Access system. With static pages, the users will not need Access, ODBC, or rights to the Access database. In fact, the users will not even need a network connection. Static reports based on Web pages are small enough that they can be e-mailed to salespeople, telecommuters, and other workers that dial in periodically for messages but have no active network connection.

To create data snapshots. In some application environments, Web reports can be created from a database at regular intervals and will provide a library of historical data. For example, the company sales report can be run each week and saved as a new HTML file. The files for each week can be kept online for access by all employees, providing a friendly surrogate for the traditional file cabinet drawer filled with hard copies of the same reports.

To create portable reports. As the workforce becomes more mobile, more and more employees are unplugging from the corporate network and traveling to customer sites or working at home. Such a worker can download the latest static Web reports to his or her laptop while on the corporate network, and then review them later in their browser without the need for a network connection.

If your application must export Web-based reports to achieve one of the listed objectives (or a different one), you can write some fairly simple code to create attractive and accurate reports based on the original Access data. In general, you will write application code, as opposed to exposing the Publish to the Web Wizard to your users, if you are concerned about these two factors:

The Wizard exposes the database structure. Within the Wizard is a tab-based form that re-creates the Access Database window. According to the bulletproofing principles in this book, most of your users have no business being in the Database window and have insufficient knowledge of its objects to make proper use of it (picture a user wandering through your application's list of 200 queries). Your application will need to provide the users with more focused assistance in selecting the data to export than the Wizard does.

18

The Wizard exports data in bulk. The Wizard exports the data behind an object in total as opposed to allowing the user to select data sets (unless the object being exported is, or is based on, a parameterized query). Your application code can preselect specific records to export or provide a custom form to assist the user with doing so.

The following three topics introduce techniques for outputting Access data to HTML format from your applications.

Getting Started with HTML

Here it is—the dreaded HTML primer you were hoping you wouldn't find in this book. While everybody seems to have caught Internet Mania within the past year, I'm not writing this section because I'm Web-crazed. Actually, I believe that the Web will not replace the capabilities of Access to create user interfaces and to query and report data for a long time to come. This doesn't mean, however, that the Web cannot provide effective ways to disseminate information stored in Access databases—in fact, it can.

Given the limitations of Access 97, you can't export expert reports to expert Web pages without some knowledge of HTML syntax. In fact, you can't be a well-rounded solution developer in 1997 if you are unable to write program code to create Web documents from your applications. To do this, you must learn to output HTML pages from VBA. If you already speak HTML, skip onward to the next topic.

 Note

This section was devised to introduce you to HTML concepts that are specifically relevant to exporting Access data. It is not intended to cover this dynamic and complex language comprehensively.

Structuring an HTML Document

An HTML-based Web page is a file that is read into a browser application like Internet Explorer (IE) and displayed to the user. Formatting information in the file tells the browser how to lay out the text and other elements for display. Your HTML files can contain text, references to graphic files, and references (called *hyperlinks*) to other HTML files.

Within an HTML file, you create multiple *elements*. An element is a related pair of tags surrounding text, with the first tag (the *start tag*) toggling on a specific display attribute, and the trailing tag (the *end tag*) toggling the attribute off. Tags are always enclosed in the <> character pair, and an end tag is simply the same text as its start tag but preceded with /.

Here is an example of a tagged element from an HTML file. The start and end tag pair shown are predefined HTML syntax that turns on and off italics mode:

```
<I>This text is italicized!</I>
```

An attribute that is toggled on stays on until toggled off; thus, your file can nest tags within other tags for compounded effects:

```
Normal, <B>bold, <I>bold italics</I>, bold</B> and normal.
```

You've deduced the tags <B> for bold and <I> for italics from the previous example; the tag pair for underlining is <U> and </U>. Other font attributes are set with the <FONT> and </FONT> tags, which have three attributes that can be combined within the tag to define the font structure:

```
<FONT SIZE=n FACE="font-name" COLOR=color>
```

The SIZE= attribute allows you to specify a number from 1 to 7 to select one of the browser's built-in font sizes, with 1 as the smallest. The values for font color are found in Table 18.6 later in this section.

In addition to tag pairs, the HTML language has some directive statements that begin and end simply with a matched set of <> characters. Inline document comments are one example of such directives—a comment begins with <! and ends at the next >, such as the following:

```
<!Purpose: This is a sample document.>
```

HTML documents should begin with a standard information block. The first line in the document should be the <!DOCTYPE> tag, which describes the document version to the browser. See your Web administrator to learn what the syntax and standards for this heading are in your company. The simplest variation of this tag is shown as follows; more complex variations include HTML version information:

```
<!DOCTYPE HTML>
```

The second element of a standard header block is denoted with the <HEAD> and </HEAD> tag pair, which delimit the heading information for the document. In simple documents, the document heading is comprised of the document title, which displays in the browser's title bar and is delimited with <TITLE> and </TITLE>:

```
<HEAD>
<TITLE>Access Expert Solutions Sample Document</TITLE>
</HEAD>
```

More complex documents may contain reference information and browser directives in the heading. Consult a full HTML reference for more information.

18

The document body comes after the document heading, beginning with the <BODY> tag. The body element includes the main text and images for the page. Within the body element, carriage return/line feed information in the source document is ignored. Instead, you must physically tell the browser to insert a line break by using the <P> tag. When you place the following in an HTML file, you see two lines of text:

```
<BODY>
<P>
This is the
first paragraph.
<P>
This is the
second paragraph.
</BODY>
```

 Note

<P> is the only tag noted here that does not *require* the use of its mate </P>, because it functions much like the vbCrLf constant does in VBA and inserts a line break immediately. The concept of pairing in this situation is irrelevant.

After the body section, a document should close with the end tag </HTML>.

Beyond the basic structural mechanics described so far, another important element of an HTML document is a *hyperlink*. When clicked, a hyperlink causes the browser to load the referenced page into the current window and move the current document down one level in its stack (browsers usually cache more than one page in a stack that can be navigated forward and backward).

Hyperlink tags begin with A (for *anchor*), then HREF=, followed by a destination address, as in the following example. The text between the tag pair in the example would be underlined by the browser and would provide a clickable jump to my Internet site:

```
Visit the <A HREF="http://www.ldfinfo.com/">Access
Expert Solutions home site</A>.
```

Figure 18.11 shows a browser page demonstrating the tag examples shown so far in this section.

For showing outline-type structures within a document, HTML supports six levels of section heading tags—H1 through H6. These tags do not cause an outline view of the information, but they do allow you to define six different styles, one per heading, to give your information a nested look. The six styles are predefined by your browser but can be redefined in your style sheets as in the following example (see the section "Creating HTML Reports Based on Styles" at the end of this chapter):

```
<H1>Regions</H1>
<H2>West</H2>
<P>Total sales: $140,125
<H2>East</H2>
<P>Total sales: $152,180
```

Fig. 18.11

IE is showing a Web page with a title, paragraph breaks, text with attributes, and a hyperlink.

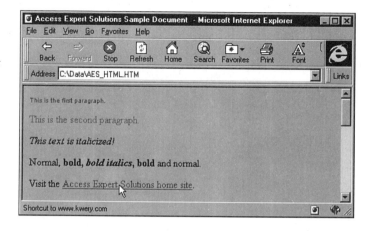

Table 18.4 lists a few more useful formatting tag pairs.

Table 18.4   Tag Pairs for Formatting Web Page Text

Tags	Meaning
<BLOCKQUOTE> </BLOCKQUOTE>	Indented text
<CENTER> </CENTER>	Centered
<LISTING> </LISTING>	Fixed (non-proportional) type
<PRE> </PRE>	Fixed (non-proportional) type

Figure 18.12 shows a browser page with examples generated by heading styles and the tags shown in Table 18.4.

Placing Tables in HTML Documents

With the basics of Web page layout in hand, we must move on to Web page tables. You cannot export tabular data from Access very attractively without some basic knowledge about how to lay out a table in HTML. The <TABLE> tag begins a table, but there are several important attributes that you can combine with this tag to determine the table's characteristics, in this fashion:

```
<TABLE attribute1=value ... attributen=value>
```

Fig. 18.12

IE is showing a Web page with styles H1 through H3, plus block quote and fixed text.

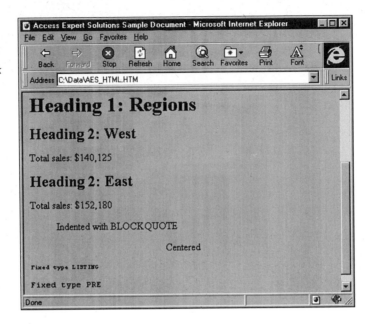

Table 18.5 lists some important table definition attributes.

Table 18.5   Attributes for Defining an HTML Table Layout

Attribute Name	Values	Comment
ALIGN=	LEFT,RIGHT	Horizontal alignment of table
BACKGROUND=	url	Path to bitmap file
BGCOLOR=	color	Background color (see Table 18.6)
BORDER=	n	Pixel width of border
BORDERCOLOR=	color	See Table 18.6
CELLPADDING=	n	Pixels between cell border and contents
CELLSPACING=	n	Pixels between table frame and interior cells
COLS=	n	Number of table columns
FRAME=	frame-type	See Table 18.7
RULES=	rule-type	See Table 18.8
WIDTH=	n	n%	Table width in pixels or percent of window

Table 18.6 lists the colors supported by Internet Explorer (other browsers may support different color values than those shown). These color values replace the placeholder *color* in the table syntax in Tables 18.5 and 18.9.

Table 18.6   Standard Color Values for IE

AQUA
BLACK
BLUE
FUCHSIA
GRAY
GREEN
LIME
MAROON
NAVY
OLIVE
PURPLE
RED
SILVER
TEAL
WHITE
YELLOW

Table 18.7 lists the values for the *frame-type* argument of the FRAME= tag shown in Table 18.5. This tag draws a border around all or part of the outside of the table:

Table 18.7   Types of Frames in the HTML *<FRAME=>* Tag

Value	Meaning
ABOVE	Border on top of table only
BELOW	Border on bottom of table only
BORDER	Border on all sides of table
BOX	Border on all sides of table
HSIDES	Border on top and bottom of table only
LHS	Border on left side of table only

continues

Table 18.7 Continued

Value	Meaning
RHS	Border on right side of table only
VOID	No borders
VSIDES	Border on left and right of table only

Table 18.8 lists the values for the *rule-type* argument of the RULES= tag shown in Table 18.5. This tag draws lines (inside borders) between cells within the table.

Table 18.8 Types of Cell Dividers in the *<RULES=>* Tag

Value	Meaning
ALL	All cells have lines
COLS	Vertical lines between columns
NONE	No cells have lines
ROWS	Horizontal lines between rows

To begin a table definition, establish a table format with the <TABLE> tag and specify its attributes. The prescribed formatting pervades the table(s) that follow until the next </TABLE> tag is reached, unless overridden by individual cell tags. The following HTML statement defines a table format that includes a thin blue frame and dividing lines between the columns:

```
<TABLE ALIGN=LEFT BORDER=1 BORDERCOLOR=BLUE CELLPADDING=2
    CELLSPACING=0 FRAME=BORDER RULES=COLS
```

After establishing the table format, your Web page must add table cells with these tags:

<TR> </TR>. This pair begins and ends the definition of a table row. Multiple format attributes can be included within the tag's brackets (such as <TR ALIGN=LEFT>); the attributes in the tag apply to all of the cells in the row(s) between the tag pair. These are some of the attribute values that can be specified within the table row tag (see Table 18.9 for information on their syntax): ALIGN=, BACKGROUND=, BGCOLOR=, BORDERCOLOR=, HEIGHT=, VALIGN=.

<TD> </TD>. This tag pair defines the beginning and ending of a cell within the table row. Multiple format attributes can be includes within the tag's brackets (such as <TD ALIGN=LEFT>); the attributes apply to the information in the cell. If no attribute is specified, the row's value for that attribute defines the formatting. These are some of the attribute values that can be specified within the table cell tag (see Table

18.9 for information on their syntax): `ALIGN=`, `BACKGROUND=`, `BGCOLOR=`, `BORDERCOLOR=`, `COLSPAN=`, `ROWSPAN=`, `VALIGN=`, `WIDTH=`.

`<TH>` `</TH>`. This tag pair defines a column heading. The attributes are identical to those for the `<TD>` tag pair. The difference between TH and TD tags is that cells in TH style are bold by default, and setting a `WIDTH=` value for the heading establishes the width of the table column it represents.

 Note

You must prescribe attributes such as font information for each individual cell in a table. Each new cell definition (TD) resets to the default attributes.

18

Table row and cell attributes and values are listed in Table 18.9.

Table 18.9   Attributes for Table Tags TB, TD, and TH

Attribute Name	Values	Comment
`ALIGN=`	`LEFT,CENTER,RIGHT`	Horizontal alignment
`BACKGROUND=`	*url*	Path to bitmap file
`BGCOLOR=`	*color*	Background color (see Table 18.6)
`BORDERCOLOR=`	*color*	See Table 18.6
`COLSPAN=`	*n*	Number of columns the cell spans
`HEIGHT=`	*n*	Height in pixels
`ROWSPAN=`	*n*	Number of rows the cell spans
`VALIGN=`	`TOP,MIDDLE,BOTTOM`	Vertical alignment within cell
`WIDTH=`	*n*	Width in pixels

Let's pull these table tags together into an example. Listing 18.8 shows HTML syntax to build a table; here's the process followed in the listing:

1. Build a header for the table by creating a single-cell table the same width as the data table below it and centering a heading string in the cell.
2. Using the `<TABLE>` tag, establish the general table attributes for the data table.
3. Apply a `<TR>` tag to define the overall row attributes for each row.
4. Finally, specify a `<TD>` tag element and corresponding string value for each table cell.

Listing 18.8   AES_HTML.Htm—Building a Simple Table with HTML

```
<!Begin a table>
<TABLE>
<!Top row is single heading cell>
<TR ALIGN=CENTER>
<TH ALIGN=CENTER WIDTH=120>
<FONT SIZE=3>
Table Heading
</FONT></TH></TR></TABLE>
<!Next come the column headers>
<TABLE ALIGN=LEFT BORDER=1 BORDERCOLOR=BLUE CELLPADDING=2
  CELLSPACING=0 FRAME=BORDER RULES=COLS>
<TR>
<TH WIDTH=40><FONT SIZE=2>
JAN
</FONT></TH>
<TH WIDTH=40><FONT SIZE=2>
FEB
</FONT></TH>
<TH WIDTH=40><FONT SIZE=2>
MAR
</FONT></TH></TR>
<!Next come the data rows, 3 cells wide>
<TR>
<TD ALIGN=RIGHT><FONT SIZE=2>
100
</FONT></TD>
<TD ALIGN=RIGHT><FONT SIZE=2>
200
</FONT></TD>
<TD ALIGN=RIGHT><FONT SIZE=2>
300
</FONT></TD></TR>
<TR>
<TD ALIGN=RIGHT><FONT SIZE=2>
400
</FONT></TD>
<TD ALIGN=RIGHT><FONT SIZE=2>
500
</FONT></TD>
<TD ALIGN=RIGHT><FONT SIZE=2>
600
</FONT></TD></TR></TABLE>
```

Figure 18.13 shows the table generated by the script in the previous listing.

The value of table formatting tags becomes apparent when you attempt to write code to publish higher quality Web pages from Access VBA than are available via the built-in export features. With a knowledge of table formatting and some simple code, your application can create Web-based reports that look outstanding.

Fig. 18.13

Dozens of commands are required to create this rudimentary table using HTML.

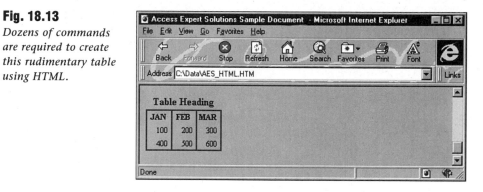

Creating Simple Web Reports Using *OutputTo*

The OutputTo method has been expanded in Access 97 to include HTML export in dynamic and static formats. Within your code, you can create export routines that call this command and pass it a subset of data to publish.

The syntax for this command is as follows:

```
DoCmd.OutputTo ObjectType
    [, ObjectName]
    [, OutputFormat]
    [, OutputFile]
    [, AutoStart]
    [, TemplateFile]
```

When exporting to HTML, you can specify an ObjectType argument of acOutputForm, acOutputQuery, acOutputReport, or acOutputTable. The values for the OutputFormat argument when creating Web pages are acFormatActiveXServer, acFormatHTML, and acFormatIIS. Because you cannot directly create dynamic Web pages from reports, these argument combinations are not allowed:

```
ObjectType:=acOutputReport, OutputFormat:=acFormatActiveXServer

ObjectType:=acOutputReport, OutputFormat:=acFormatIIS
```

For HTML-based output, use the AutoStart:=True argument with the OutputFormat:=acFormatHTML argument setting to launch IE immediately after export, loaded with the file specified by the OutputFile argument. The argument is ignored when the output format is IDC/HTX or ASP.

In the OutputTo command line, you can specify a template file that will be used to format the resulting Web page. If you specify a template file name but no path, Access looks in the HTML Template directory you've specified in the Options dialog box. If no path is specified, Access looks for the file in the default location \Program Files\Microsoft Office\Templates\Access.

HTML template files provide formatting information that is applied by the export routines to the exported data as it's moved to a Web page. Template files specific to Access contain custom commands (called *tokens*) defined for its export process. When you place a custom token in a template file, the export process replaces the token with data specific to the object being exported.

For example, place the following token in a template file:

```
<!--AccessTemplate_Title-->
```

During an export, Access replaces the token above with the name of the exported object, and wraps the object name in the standard HTML <TITLE> tag so that the string becomes the title for the Web page.

Table 18.10 shows the tokens that Access 97 understands in a template file. The tokens are shown in the order that they are usually located within a template file (the same order that a report flows in).

Table 18.10   Template File Tokens Applied to an Export

Token	Replaced With
<!--AccessTemplate_Title-->	Name of the object
<!--view onlyAcessTemplate_Body-->	Object's controls and data
<!--AccessTemplate_FirstPage-->	Hyperlink jump to first page of data
<!--AccessTemplate_PreviousPage-->	Hyperlink jump to previous page of data
<!--AccessTemplate_NextPage-->	Hyperlink jump to next page of data
<!--AccessTemplate_LastPage-->	Hyperlink jump to last page of data
<!--AccessTemplate_PageNumber-->	Page number

 Note

When Access exports a report, it creates one Web page (file) for each report page. The navigation tokens shown in Table 18.10 for moving between pages are used in your template file to tell Access to provide page navigation hyperlinks between the pages. If you are exporting a table, query, or form, only one Web page is created and you do not need the navigation tokens.

Also, if you export a single-page report, the navigation tokens still cause the creation of page jump hyperlinks in the Web page, but they are inert. If you are exporting from code and can determine the number of pages on a report, you can create a template file that does not have navigation tokens and specify it when you export single-page reports.

In addition to the listed tokens, your template file can include any valid HTML tags. The tags will be copied into the output file as the Web page is built. If dynamic ASP or HTX file output formats are chosen, the commands in your template file are merged with the commands in the ASP or HTX output file.

To create reports for Web publication from your VBA code, you have two options. The first approach involves exporting a report directly to HTML using OutputTo and a template file, as discussed in this topic. The second approach, discussed in the next section, is to write Web pages completely from code.

When using OutputTo to handle your application's formatting and export work, your report may look adequate if you stay within the following guidelines:

Simple Layout. Web reports expose data to a broader audience than simply the designated users of the Access application. It may not be useful to attempt to publish complex reports outside of the context provided by the application.

Sized for a Browser. A report that is designed for an 8"-wide printer does not view well in a 6"-wide (VGA) browser. Reports that are slated for online publication should be limited to 5" or 6" in width.

Don't use non-exportable controls. Access' export capabilities ignore Custom Control, Line, Rectangle, and Object Frame controls on the report. Reports you build for export should not make use of these.

Non-parameterized. When you export a report, Access executes the SQL in the report's RecordSource property. If the SQL statement has parameter values, the user is prompted for the parameters. This may not provide the desired friendly interface.

As an example, assume you want to export the report rptOrderTop10_Web from code. The report is shown in Figure 18.14 and has been created using the guidelines from the preceding list. For example, the report summarizes all of the data in a table as opposed to needing criteria parameters.

Fig. 18.14
This report is optimized for export as a Web page.

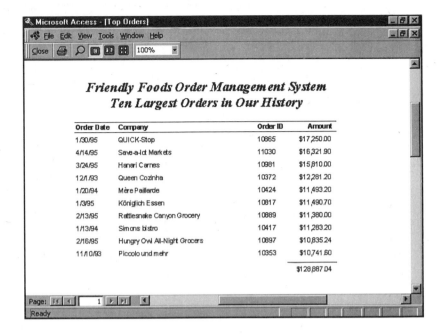

Use the following command line to export the report in the figure to an HTML page:

```
DoCmd.OutputTo acOutputReport, "rptOrderTop10_Web" _
    , acFormatHTML, "C:\Data\Top10Web.Htm"
```

The result of executing this command against the sample "Top Ten" orders report is shown in Figure 18.15.

Fig. 18.15
This Web page was created by exporting an Access report with `OutputTo`*.*

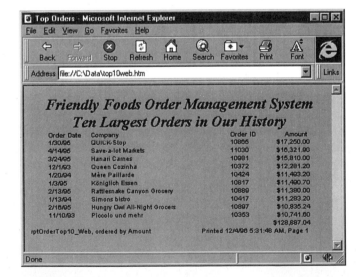

Notice that the Access export process did a decent job of creating a Web page providing the information from the source report. However, the formatting of the report was not fully carried into the exported Web page. For example, the graphic lines have been lost and the column headers are no longer bold. You are able to create Web pages from code that are more visually appealing than are produced by OutputTo.

Outputting Formatted HTML Reports

A alternative to using OutputTo involves exporting database data as well as the Web page layout information from your code. While OutputTo makes its "best guess" about the desired layout of the Web page, programmatic export gives you total control over the final look of the Web page and the information on it.

Consider the techniques you learned for creating Web pages and tables in a previous section "Getting Started with HTML." Armed only with the information in that section, you should be able to produce a Web report superior in appearance to one created by the OutputTo method (as shown in Figure 18.15 in the previous section).

In addition to improving on the look of the exported report, your code can improve on OutputTo in these ways:

Field Formats. You can format exported data using the Format function or other code technique to present it in the most user-friendly fashion. (By contrast, when OutputTo exports a Boolean value, it shows 1 and 0 in the Web page. This is not usually considered "user-friendly.")

Pagination. OutputTo creates a Web page for each page in your report. You are not required to use this approach when writing your own export routines. For example, HTML allows you to create hyperlinks that are inline jumps within the current document. Your code could create one Web page as a single report and use inline jumps with the <A NAME=> and <A HREF=> tag pairs to navigate between the pseudo-pages:

```
<!Jump to page 2>
<A HREF="#Page2">
...
<!Begin page 2>
<A NAME="Page2">
```

Using inline jumps into the current document as opposed to creating one Web page per report page improves performance, reduces disk clutter, and streamlines document management (cleanup, backup, forwarding, and so on).

You can output selected fields. OutputTo exports all of the fields and rows in the selected object's recordset. This may not always produce friendly output, as in the case of OLE Object fields; controls bound to this data type are exported as blank columns in the Web page table. Using code, your export can select only specific fields and records to output.

Let's create a set of routines to build a Web-based report similar to that produced by the bulk export of `rptOrderTop10_Web` in the previous section. Our objective for this code is to provide a more attractive report than the one shown in Figure 18.15.

Here are the steps we'll take to create a Web export engine:

1. Create a class object `clsWebReport` to contain all of the logic for Web reporting.
2. Add custom properties to the class object that are set with values that will control the export.
3. Add a custom method to the class to generate an HTML file based upon the property settings.

A modest amount of code is required to create the reporting engine. In describing the process, I assume that you are familiar with class objects and custom properties (from Chapter 12, "Understanding Form Structures and Coding") and with the basics of VBA such as file input/output, arrays, and user-defined types. The first step is to create the data structures used in the class object. Listing 18.9 shows the Declarations section of the module *clsWebReport*.

Listing 18.9   AES_Rpts.Mdb—Declarations for a Web Reporting Class Object

```
Option Base 1   ' 1-based arrays
Private Const mcstrQuote As String = """"
Private mdblSums() As Double   ' Column sums

' Structures for custom properties
Private Type mtypCols          ' Report columns
  strHeading As String         ' Column header display string
  strField   As String         ' Bound field name
  strFormat  As String         ' Column format
  intWidth   As Integer        ' Display width
  blnSum     As Boolean        ' Total the field
End Type
Private Type mtypWebReport      ' Structure for one web file
  intCols     As Integer        ' Number of columns: prpColumns
  strFilename As String         ' Output filename: prpFilename
  strName     As String         ' Report name: prpName
  strSQL      As String         ' Record source: prpSQL
  strTitle    As String         ' Report title: prpTitle
  tCols()     As mtypCols       ' Column information: prpCol
End Type
Private mtWebReport As mtypWebReport
```

The primary information storage device for the class is the variable mtWebReport based on the type structure mtypWebReport. It contains all of the settings required for a single Web export session: the number of columns for the report, the output filename to create, the SQL statement for the source data, and so forth. Each of the values for the structure is fed by a custom property procedure such as this:

```
Public Property Let prpFilename(rstrFilename As String)
' Purpose: Set the destination filename
  mtWebReport.strFilename = rstrFilename
End Property
```

When you use the class object, you set the custom properties in the same way you set an intrinsic property:

18

```
clsWebReport.prpFilename = "C:\Data\Top10VBA.Htm"
```

Notice that the custom property tCols() is an array variable based on another custom type definition mtypCols. This allows for the storage of multiple columns for the report and multiple attributes for each column: the column heading, the bound field name, and so forth. The custom property setting for this structure is a little more complicated than prpFilename, and is shown in Listing 18.10.

Listing 18.10   AES_Rpts.Mdb—Complex Custom Property Procedure to Set Values into a Custom Type Array

```
Public Property Let prpCol(rstrAttrib As String, rintCol As Integer _
, rvarValue As Variant)
' Purpose:   Set attribute of a report column
' Arguments: rstrAttrib:=Attribute name
'            rintCol:=   Report column number, 1-based
'            rvarValue:= Attribute value

  Select Case rstrAttrib
    Case "Heading"
      mtWebReport.tCols(rintCol).strHeading = rvarValue
    Case "Field"
      mtWebReport.tCols(rintCol).strField = rvarValue
    Case "Format"
      mtWebReport.tCols(rintCol).strFormat = rvarValue
    Case "Width"
      mtWebReport.tCols(rintCol).intWidth = rvarValue
    Case "Sum"
      mtWebReport.tCols(rintCol).blnSum = rvarValue
    Case Else
      Beep
      MsgBox "Invalid property name: " & rstrAttrib, vbCritical, "prpCol"
  End Select

End Property
```

For each report column, the calling code that populates the custom property in the listing must specify which element of the structure to populate. The calling convention to set the custom heading value for column 2 of the report using the custom property looks like this:

```
clsWebReport.prpCol("Heading", 2) = "Company"
```

The engine of the Web reporting class is, of course, the code that produces the HTML file. In the current example, the class object is generic enough that it could be used for a variety of purposes. However, the class is specifically tailored for reports with a few columns and no free-form leading or trailing text. Also, font and layout information is standardized in the code. However, any attributes that are in the code could just as easily be passed in as more custom properties on the class. Thus, the value of creating a class object is to make it self-contained enough that it can be reused in multiple applications, and also to make it generic enough that it can be used in a variety of ways.

Listing 18.11 shows the driving routine that generates the Web report. It is built as a custom method on the class. Notice how simple the process is:

1. Create an output file.
2. Write the standard HTML header information to the file.
3. Create the HTML table from the record source and add it to the file.
4. Write a report footer to the file.
5. Write the standard HTML file footer to the file.

Listing 18.11   AES_Rpts.Mdb—Driving Routine to Create a Web Report File

```
Public Sub mtdGenerate()
' Purpose: Generate a Web report

    Dim dbs     As Database
    Dim intFile As Integer
    Dim intLoc  As Integer
    Dim intPage As Integer
    Dim rtbl    As Recordset
    Dim strOut  As String      ' Output string

    intPage = 1  ' This routine does not deal with pagination yet

    ' Get standard strings
    Set dbs = CurrentDb
    Set rtbl = dbs.OpenRecordset("zstblWebReport", dbOpenTable)
    rtbl.Index = "PrimaryKey"

    ' Create output file
    intFile = FreeFile
    Open mtWebReport.strFilename For Output As #intFile
```

```
' Create HTML Header
rtbl.Seek "=", "HTMLHead"
strOut = rtbl!StringValue
intLoc = InStr(strOut, "{webreporttitle}")
strOut = Left(strOut, intLoc - 1) & mtWebReport.strTitle _
  & Mid(strOut, intLoc + 16)
Print #intFile, strOut

' Create report table
rtbl.Seek "=", "SystemName"
Print #intFile, cbfTableCreate(rtbl!StringValue _
  , mtWebReport.strTitle)

' Create report footer
rtbl.Seek "=", "ReportFooter"
Print #intFile, cbfFooterCreate(rtbl!StringValue, intPage)

' Create HTML footer
rtbl.Seek "=", "HTMLFoot"
Print #intFile, rtbl!StringValue

MsgBox "File " & mtWebReport.strFilename & " created."_
  , vbInformation, cstrProc

End Sub
```

In order to make the process of Web reporting truly generic, I've based the class on a table of standard strings, as demonstrated by the listing. Using a table means that each different application can customize the strings displayed by the Web browser or written into the HTML file's structure without modifying the code. Within the table strings are replaceable placeholders used by the code, such as {webreportdatetime} to tell the class to insert the date and time at the specified location.

Placing a string like the HTML file header tags in a database table provides three primary benefits. The first is that the class code is uncluttered by such mundane text. The second is that the programmer using the class does not need to pass the same information to the class over and over as a property. And the third benefit is that, when the HTML standard changes (as it does with regularity), reconfiguring the behavior of the class does not require opening the code—only the table. The configuration table is shown in Figure 18.16.

Building the table of report data values in the HMTL file is a very straightforward process, controlled by the procedure cbfTableCreate; here is the flow of the code for the function:

1. Establish the procedure's variables and structures, as shown in Listing 18.12. The calling code passes in one or more lines to use as the table caption, which are managed by Access' new ParamArray argument feature.

Fig. 18.16
The Web reporting class engine is customized by changing values in this configuration table.

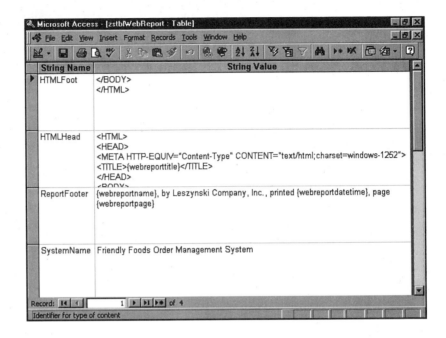

Listing 18.12   AES_Rpts.Mdb—Setup Portion of a Routine to Create a Web Report Table

```
Private Function cbfTableCreate(ParamArray avarHeadings() As Variant) _
  As String
' Purpose:   Create table of report data with headings
' Arguments: avarHeadings():=Heading lines

  ' Table cell constants
  Const cintHeight As Integer = 15   ' Cell height
  Const cintLeft As Integer = 30     ' Left-side offset for table
  Const cstrCellFont As String _
    = "<FONT SIZE=2 FACE=""Arial"" COLOR=BLACK>"
  Const cstrCellFontSum As String _
    = "<FONT SIZE=2 FACE=""Arial"" COLOR=BLUE>"

  Dim blnSumRow As Boolean   ' Make a row with column sums
  Dim dbs      As Database
  Dim iint     As Integer
  Dim intWidth As Integer    ' Total width
  Dim rst      As Recordset
  Dim strAlign As String     ' Cell alignment
  Dim strValue As String     ' Cell value
  Dim strWork  As String

  Set dbs = CurrentDb
  Set rst = dbs.OpenRecordset(mtWebReport.strSQL)

  ' Compute table width
  For iint = 1 To mtWebReport.intCols
```

```
      intWidth = intWidth + mtWebReport.tCols(iint).intWidth
   Next iint
   intWidth = intWidth ' + cintLeft
```

2. Create one or more table caption lines, using the code in Listing 18.13.

Listing 18.13   AES_Rpts.Mdb—Create the Caption Lines for a Web Report Table

```
' Create table caption headings
For iint = 0 To UBound(avarHeadings)
  strWork = strWork _
  & "<TABLE BORDER=0 CELLSPACING=0 CELLPADDING=0>" & vbCrLf _
  & "<TR HEIGHT=26>" & vbCrLf _
  & "<TD WIDTH=" & cintLeft & "></TD>" & vbCrLf _
  & "<TH WIDTH=" & intWidth & " ALIGN=CENTER><B><I>" & vbCrLf _
  & "<FONT SIZE=5 FACE=" & mcstrQuote & "Times New Roman" _
  & mcstrQuote & " COLOR=BLUE>" & vbCrLf _
  & avarHeadings(iint) & "</FONT></B></I></TH></TR>" & vbCrLf _
  & "</TABLE>" & vbCrLf
Next iint
```

3. Create a row of column headings. These are passed in to the class as the `strHeading` attribute of each column definition. This allows the developer to configure the report text. Alternately, the code shown could grab the `Caption` property of each field in the recordset and use that value as the column header. The code to create the column headings is in Listing 18.14.

Listing 18.14   AES_Rpts.Mdb—Create the Column Headings for a Web Report Table

```
' Create column heading row
strWork = strWork & "<P>" & vbCrLf _
  & "<TABLE BORDER=0 CELLSPACING=0 CELLPADDING=0>" & vbCrLf _
  & "<TR HEIGHT=" & (cintHeight * 1.2) & ">" & vbCrLf _
  & "<TH WIDTH=" & cintLeft & "></TH>" & vbCrLf

For iint = 1 To mtWebReport.intCols
  ' Columns that are summed are aligned right
  strAlign = IIf(mtWebReport.tCols(iint).blnSum, " ALIGN=RIGHT" _
  , " ALIGN=LEFT")
  strWork = strWork _
    & "<TH WIDTH=" & mtWebReport.tCols(iint).intWidth & strAlign _
    & "><B><U>" & cstrCellFont & mtWebReport.tCols(iint).strHeading _
    & "</FONT></B></U></TH>" & vbCrLf
Next iint

strWork = strWork & "</TR></TABLE>" & vbCrLf
```

18

4. Create each individual table cell. The code walks through the source recordset, formats each cell based on a Format property string also passed to the class, and creates the HTML for the table cell. The table cells are created in Listing 18.15.

Listing 18.15   AES_Rpts.Mdb—Create the Table Cells for a Web Report Table

```
' Create column data rows
rst.MoveLast    ' Pull all rows to cache
rst.MoveFirst
Do While Not rst.EOF
   strWork = strWork _
      & "<TABLE BORDER=0 CELLSPACING=0 CELLPADDING=0>" & vbCrLf _
      & "<TR HEIGHT=" & cintHeight & ">" & vbCrLf _
      & "<TD WIDTH=" & cintLeft & "></TD>" & vbCrLf
   For iint = 1 To mtWebReport.intCols
      ' Columns that are summed are aligned right
      If mtWebReport.tCols(iint).blnSum Then   ' Running sum
         blnSumRow = True
         strAlign = " ALIGN=RIGHT"
         mdblSums(iint) = mdblSums(iint) _
            + rst(mtWebReport.tCols(iint).strField)
         strValue = Format(rst(mtWebReport.tCols(iint).strField) _
            , mtWebReport.tCols(iint).strFormat)
      Else
         strAlign = " ALIGN=LEFT"  ' Default alignment
         strValue = rst(mtWebReport.tCols(iint).strField)
      End If
      ' Apply underline to last row for summed columns
      If rst.AbsolutePosition + 1 = rst.RecordCount _
         And mtWebReport.tCols(iint).blnSum Then
         strWork = strWork _
            & "<TD WIDTH=" & mtWebReport.tCols(iint).intWidth _
            & strAlign & ">" & cstrCellFont & "<U>" & strValue _
            & "</FONT></U></TD>" & vbCrLf
      Else  ' No format
         strWork = strWork _
            & "<TD WIDTH=" & mtWebReport.tCols(iint).intWidth _
            & strAlign & ">" & cstrCellFont & strValue _
            & "</FONT></TD>" & vbCrLf
      End If
   Next iint
   strWork = strWork & "</TR></TABLE>" & vbCrLf
   rst.MoveNext
Loop
```

5. The calling code for the class is allowed to specify if a column is to be summed (the blnSum flag on each column definition). Columns that are summed are added up into mdblSums as the recordset is processed, as shown in the previous listing. An array is used for summing so that more than one column can be totaled. Additionally, the code underlines the last value in each column in order to improve the display of totaled columns.

6. If any columns have been summed, a final row must be added to the table with the totals. This code is shown in Listing 18.16.

Listing 18.16   AES_Rpts.Mdb—Create a Row of Totals for a Web Report Table

```
' Create summary row
If blnSumRow Then
  strWork = strWork _
    & "<TABLE BORDER=0 CELLSPACING=0 CELLPADDING=0>" & vbCrLf _
    & "<TR HEIGHT=" & cintHeight & ">" & vbCrLf _
    & "<TD WIDTH=" & cintLeft & "></TD>" & vbCrLf
  For iint = 1 To mtWebReport.intCols
    ' Columns that are summed are aligned right
    If mtWebReport.tCols(iint).blnSum Then  ' Running sum
      strAlign = " ALIGN=RIGHT"
      strValue = Format(mdblSums(iint) _
        , mtWebReport.tCols(iint).strFormat)
    Else
      strValue = ""
    End If
    strWork = strWork _
      & "<TD WIDTH=" & mtWebReport.tCols(iint).intWidth _
      & strAlign & ">" & cstrCellFontSum & strValue _
      & "</FONT></TD>" & vbCrLf
  Next iint
  strWork = strWork & "</TR></TABLE>" & vbCrLf
End If

cbfTableCreate = strWork

End Function
```

The final piece of the puzzle is the code that sets the attributes and controls the process. While the class contains several powerful chunks of code, the ideal is that the investment in coding effort can be reused over and over, and can be reused very easily. Using custom properties that can be viewed in the Object Browser, and good naming conventions that help the user understand the class' structure make reusing even a complex object a very uncomplicated task.

Listing 18.17 shows the code that creates an instance of the class and tells it how to create a Web report file.

Listing 18.17   AES_Rpts.Mdb—Routine that Drives the Web Reporting Class

```
Sub WebReport()
' Purpose: Print report to Web page

  Dim clsWebReport As New clsWebReport

  clsWebReport.prpColumns = 4
```

continues

Listing 18.17   Continued

```
    clsWebReport.prpFilename = "C:\Data\Top10VBA.Htm"
    clsWebReport.prpName = "Top10VBA"
    clsWebReport.prpSQL = "qrptOrderTop10_WebExport"
    clsWebReport.prpTitle = "Ten Largest Orders in Our History"

    clsWebReport.prpCol("Heading", 1) = "Order Date"
    clsWebReport.prpCol("Heading", 2) = "Company"
    clsWebReport.prpCol("Heading", 3) = "Order ID"
    clsWebReport.prpCol("Heading", 4) = "Amount"

    clsWebReport.prpCol("Field", 1) = "OrderDate"
    clsWebReport.prpCol("Field", 2) = "CompName"
    clsWebReport.prpCol("Field", 3) = "OrderID"
    clsWebReport.prpCol("Field", 4) = "Extn"

    clsWebReport.prpCol("Format", 4) = "Currency"

    clsWebReport.prpCol("Width", 1) = 90
    clsWebReport.prpCol("Width", 2) = 210
    clsWebReport.prpCol("Width", 3) = 70
    clsWebReport.prpCol("Width", 4) = 80

    clsWebReport.prpCol("Sum", 4) = True

    clsWebReport.mtdGenerate

End Sub
```

Figure 18.17 shows the end result of the machinations in this section. Notice that the Web report produced by our class object is more attractive than the one produced by Access and shown in Figure 18.15. Using our code, we were able to improve the spacing and layout, use bold font for column headings, underline summed columns, add color, and otherwise fully control the appearance of the output.

The objective for the code in the previous listings was to produce an attractive report (more attractive than was available using built-in Access export features). With a few more additions, other objectives could have been achieved by the code instead. For example, once you have mastered writing static HTML reports from code, you can experiment with writing dynamic ones (HTML pages that extract their data from the source database using ASP files). Additionally, you can build drill-down reporting systems that place hyperlinks on Web reports to jump from a line of summary information to a related online detail report.

Fig. 18.17

This Web report was produced entirely by code in the Web Report class object.

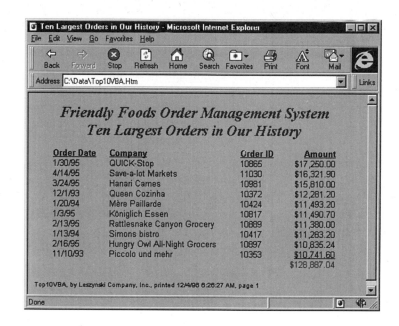

18

From Here...

Mastering Access' reporting capabilities takes a teaspoon full of examples, two tablespoons of information, and a cup of time. In this chapter, I've given you the information and the examples for some practical techniques to make your report authoring efforts more productive. Its up to you to supply the time to incorporate them into your expert solutions skill set.

▶ You can explore Microsoft's online HTML documentation by navigating on the Internet to **http://www.microsoft.com/workshop/author/ default.htm**. If this information has moved by the time you read this, simply search the Microsoft Web site for the keyword "HTML."

▶ See Chapter 13, "Mastering Combo and List Boxes," for more information on the creative use of Combo and List Box controls.

▶ Chapter 14, "Navigating in Forms and Applications," describes various switchboard menu and command bar menu systems for application navigation that can also be employed for report selection.

▶ This chapter covered issues related to hard copy and online reporting of data. For an exploration of the issues when selecting data, see Chapter 16, "Presenting Data to Users.

Exploring Client/Server Issues

19

N o doubt you've seen a client/server demo or read an article that provided information to this effect: "Run the Access Upsizing Wizard to move your tables from Jet to SQL Server, link your application to the server tables, and wham—you've got a client/server-based solution." This kind of presentation is like a plate piled high with whipped potatoes—lots of air, a little starch, and no meat.

Creating an expert solution that uses the teamwork between Access and the server-based data effectively involves more work than simply running a wizard. This chapter describes the required effort; it is crammed with as much client/server connectivity "meat" as I could provide in the allotted space.

> ## Making Connections
>
> If you are an old Visual Basic veteran like myself, you probably spent hundreds of hours over the years writing complex library routines that called the ODBC API directly to provide server data to your applications. Then, suddenly, along came the Jet database engine.
>
> What a godsend! Jet suddenly provided a connectivity tool that made gatewaying out from VB applications to server data much easier to code. Installing the Jet Compatibility Layer into Visual Basic 3 provided what seemed like "instant" access to server data.
>
> As an Access developer, close your eyes and contrast the difference in metaphors between life *with* Jet's connectivity capabilities and the alternative—a life *without* them. Because Jet invisibly manages connections, ODBC compatibility, and cursors, an Access developer can literally link to server tables, run the Report Wizard, and print a report from legacy data all in about five minutes. Without Jet's connectivity options, however, we'd all be using the API routines from our Visual Basic applications to login to a server, establish connections, create SQL statements, step through cursors, and fetch data into temporary tables simply to print the same report—a difference of 20 to 50 times more effort. Whew!
>
> Makes you feel like sending a thank-you card to the Jet Team, doesn't it?

Those of you who have worked with other database products prior to Access probably were quite impressed when you saw the Jet Database Engine—it's a remarkable tool. However, the true genius of Jet doesn't really become apparent until you incorporate a database server into your Access application. Doing so reveals in stark detail two important facets of Jet:

1. *Jet's Extensive Capabilities*. Human nature causes us to think that bigger is better. However, architects of server database engines must make substantial tradeoffs in order to accommodate high volumes of records, transactions, and users. Thus, when you contrast Jet to a server database engine, you immediately notice the "conveniences" in Jet that are not provided by its big brothers—features like:

   ▶ The breadth of updatable join combinations found in Jet are not available on higher-end servers.

   ▶ Jet adeptly handles nesting queries within queries (called "subqueries") going many levels deep, while many server products cannot handle a single nesting level. (Happily, the latest version of Jet now sends some types of subqueries to the server, where it previously did not send any.)

   ▶ The simplicity of creating and maneuvering through Jet recordsets contrasts sharply with the limitations of SQL cursors.

2. *Jet's Smart Connectivity.* If Jet provided only one way to connect to server data, we developers would probably still be grateful. Instead, we have several options to apply to our applications:

   ▶ Server tables can be linked to an MDB database file.

   ▶ Saved queries can point to linked tables.

   ▶ Saved pass-through queries can point directly to server data.

   ▶ Virtual (temporary) pass-through queries can be executed without creating any saved Jet objects.

   ▶ DAO recordsets can be built off of any of the objects in the four preceding bullet points.

   ▶ SQL pass-through statements can be executed directly against a Jet Database object, bypassing even the query engine.

In spite of Jet's powerful capabilities, if you could simply link a server table to your Access application and point a form to the link, there would be no need for this chapter. Unfortunately, there are many nuances in making Access rely on an external server for its data. Ponder just a few of the questions that arise:

   ▶ How are records validated when they are saved to the server?

   ▶ Will the performance gains of a server be lost by the necessity to pass all messages between Access and the server through an intermediary (an Open Database Connectivity driver)?

   ▶ Will the server's data management dialect understand the types of queries that Access forms and reports use?

In this chapter, I help you close in on the answers to questions like these. If you recall from Chapter 7, "Understanding Application Architecture," that there is no single way to combine application components, you will understand the fact that adding a server into your application's object mix introduces rewards and risks, advantages and obstacles. Thus, I use "close in on the answers" because often absolutes are hard to come by in a client/server model. Here I provide you with many techniques and options, but you'll need to employ and test the techniques in your specific environment and applications before their value can be measured with certitude.

The first part of this chapter discusses the basic workings of the Jet Database Engine and the new ODBCDirect component of the Data Access Objects in a client/server application, with Access on the front-end and a server (SQL Server 6.5 in these examples) on the back-end. Then it discusses some practical techniques for crafting Access forms and reports in client/server applications. This chapter is *not* a tutorial on upsizing. Instead, I assume that you have run the Access Upsizing Wizard already or manually created a server data structure for your application.

 Note

In spite of its lack of robust data and good naming conventions, the database Pubs that ships with SQL Server is used for the examples in this chapter and on the CD-ROM. Because it was not feasible for me to ship you a server database to run with my code samples, I opted to use a sample database that every SQL Server owner already has.

In my examples, the tables in the Pubs database are linked to an Access database using the tag tsql in front of each table name.

Manipulating Server Data

The relational data model that permeates the current database climate is based on—what else?—"relations," which are datasets of records and fields. SQL, the language of the relational model, thinks in terms of such datasets. That is why SQL places a higher emphasis on statements like SELECT, which return multiple records, than on a robust model designed to go to a particular record or to navigate between records.

Jet, however, provides the best of both worlds. Its use of an SQL dialect based on ANSI SQL (plus custom extensions) implements the positive aspects of the relational model. In addition, Jet provides recordset operations that exceed the capabilities of SQL cursors and enables very granular access to individual records and fields.

Likewise, when working with server datasets, Jet again breaks free of the SQL paradigm's restrictions and provides added value. The concept of returning sets of multiple records means that the obvious way for Jet to work with server data would be to fetch the entire results of an SQL statement from the server into its local buffer. Because this would not be time- or resource-efficient, Jet "cuts corners" for speed by pulling keys (indexes) down from the server and requesting specific records or blocks of records by their keys, as shown in Figure 19.1. Thus, Jet can get (and give) data in keyset-driven chunks rather than in entire dataset-driven superchunks. This optimizes the retrieval of server data when using dynaset-type recordsets (snapshots are retrieved in aggregate rather than chunks).

Fig. 19.1

Jet retrieves server data in chunks by keys rather than by entire result set.

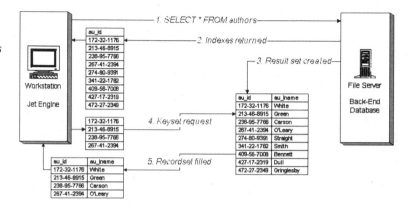

Mechanically, much of Jet's interaction with a server is handled through two components:

> *Query Engine.* This Jet service processes queries that you create, translates them into SQL statements, optimizes them, and compiles them.

> *Remote Manager.* When your query must communicate with the ODBC API to share requests and data with a server, this component translates Jet's communications into ODBC function calls.

In contrast to Jet's local workings, the new ODBCDirect engine attempts to offload as much work to the server as possible. It does this by employing ODBC's capability to use *cursors* (server-based recordsets). When the DAO passes a direct record request through to the server, it tells the server to create a cursor using server resources. DAO then fetches records from the cursor as required. In essence, ODBCDirect moves steps 2 and 4 in Figure 19.1 from the client side to the ODBC driver if the driver is connected to a server that supports the required cursor capabilities. This increases performance.

Linking to ODBC Data Sources

When running setup for Access or Office, choose the advanced (custom) installation option, which enables you to install the ODBC driver for SQL Server (select the Data Access option). The SQL Server driver SQLSRV32.DLL ships with Office and Access; other ODBC drivers are available from third-party vendors.

To configure your ODBC driver, you must first create a *data source*, which is a named configuration that includes a driver and a pointer to a data server. For example, to create a data source for the sample database included with this chapter, perform the following steps:

1. Select the ODBC icon from Control Panel. The ODBC Data Source Administrator dialog box appears.

2. Click Add in the dialog box.

3. Select "SQL Server" from the Create New Source dialog box. Click Finish.

4. In the ODBC SQL Server Setup dialog box, enter a Data Source Name, for example Pubs. Next, enter the name of your Server containing the Pubs database. Finally, enter Pubs as the Database Name option, as shown in Figure 19.2.

Fig. 19.2

Creating a new SQL Server data source.

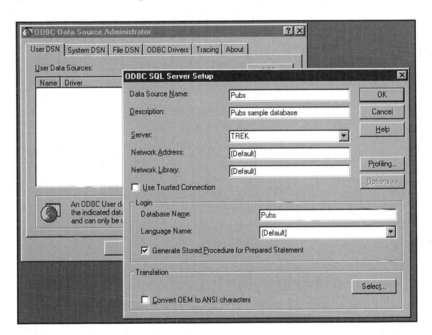

> ### ⚛ Tip
> You can create a disk file (DSN file) that saves data source information and that can be passed from one user to another (for example, it can be distributed with your Access application). Notice the tabbed layout for the ODBC dialog box in Figure 19.2. To create a data source that is visible only to the user currently logged in to the current machine, create it from the User DSN tab. To create a data source that is available to any user logged in to the current workstation, use the System DSN tab. To create a DSN file saved on disk, use the File DSN tab.

You also can create a data source entry in the Windows Registry using program code. This enables an Access client/server application to create or update the data source for its back-end tables as the application initializes. See the Help topic on the `RegisterDatabase` method for more information.

Having created a data source, you can now use the data source to link server tables to your client database. From the Database window, choose File, Get External Data, Link Tables... from the menu. In the Link dialog box, open the "Files of type" combo box and select "ODBC Databases ()" (hidden at the bottom of the list). The SQL Data Sources dialog box displays, as shown in Figure 19.3. Set the data source you require (notice that Pubs from our previous example is available in this dialog box).

Fig. 19.3

Selecting the data source that will supply the table to be linked.

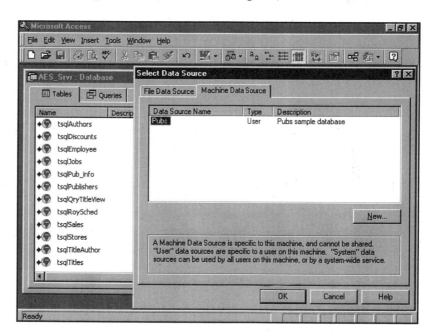

19

Next, an SQL Server Login dialog box is displayed. Enter the appropriate Login ID (for Pubs, this is sa). Normally, an entry in the Password text box will also be required, but Pubs has none.

 Note

Pubs is unprotected because it is a sample database. In general, you will *always* be using security and passwords with server databases.

Finally, a Link Tables dialog box displays the tables (and *views*, which are saved queries) in your server database, as shown in Figure 19.4.

Fig. 19.4

The Link Tables dialog box enables you to select the server tables to link.

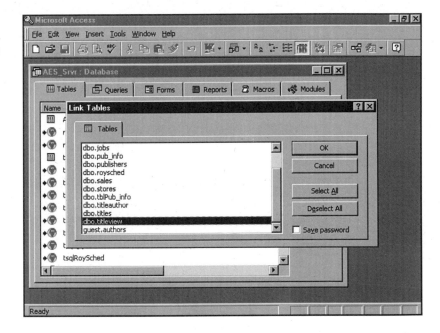

Note the following issues in the figure:

Tables and views are mixed. Server views are mixed in with tables, as indicated by the presence of the view dbo.titleview in the table listing in the figure. In fact, by default Jet requests that ODBC display all tables, views, system tables, synonyms, and aliases in this dialog box.

 Tip

A good naming convention like the one in this book makes it easier to distinguish server tables (which are usually updatable) from views (which usually are not). Appendix C, "Leszynski Naming Conventions for Microsoft Solution Developers," on the CD-ROM provides naming conventions for use with SQL Server databases and Jet databases that work with them.

The password can be saved with the connect string. The ODBC connect string is saved with the table link (in its Connect property). By default, Access does not save the password you entered when it saves the connect string. However, the Link Tables dialog box has a "Save password" option that enables you to save the password with the table link.

> **Caution**
> As you can imagine, saving the database password with the table link exposes it to anyone who can view or progammatically access the `TableDef's Connect` property. See the section "Setting Jet Options on the Server" later in this chapter for information on disabling local password storage.

Each linked table must have an index to be updatable. Jet cannot enable you to edit data in a remote table that does not have a unique index. When linking to server tables, if Access determines that the remote table does not have a unique index, it prompts you to select the combination of fields that will make the remote record editable. For example, Figure 19.5 shows the Select Unique Record Identifier dialog box displayed when you try to link to the `roysched` table in `Pubs`, which does not have a unique index. You need to select a combination of fields that uniquely identifies a record in order for Jet to create a unique local index map that will enable you to edit records in the table.

Fig. 19.5

When linking a table or view without a unique index, you are prompted to select the fields for Jet to use as an index; otherwise, editing will be unavailable or unreliable.

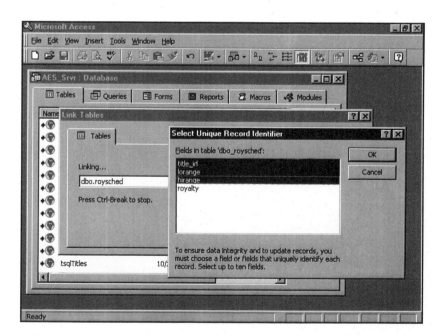

This last point cannot be overstressed. Consider the surprising situation in Figure 19.6, which shows the same table (roysched) linked twice from Pubs to an Access database. In the first link (roysched_unique), I properly specified all three columns required to create a unique index for the table (title_id, lorange, and hirange, refer to Figure 19.5). However, for the second link (roysched_nonunique), I specified only title_id as the key field, which is not a unique value. As a result, Jet displays the data in the datasheet incorrectly (see Figure 19.6), which shows how the records for the title_id field value BU1032 are displayed accurately when a unique key is used but inaccurately when displayed via the non-unique index.

Fig. 19.6

Datasheets that reflect two table links pointing to the same server table, with different Jet indexes for the links.

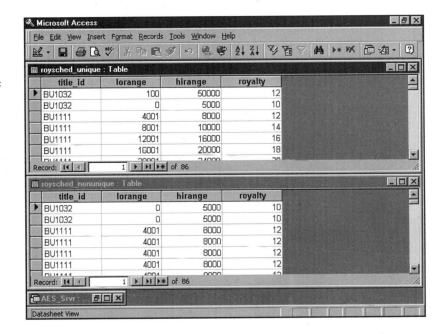

> ⚛ **Tip**
> Server databases, like Jet databases, should have a unique (primary) key on each table whenever possible. You should also make use of server time stamp columns in every table, if the server supports them (see the section "Updating External Recordsets" for more information on time stamps). Read/update problems such as those shown in the previous figure can be avoided with a good database structure.

When Jet links a table, it uses the name of the table as *supplied by the server*, and does any required name fixup. For example, table objects on SQL Server are always prefixed with the name of the object's owner (the default owner is dbo for "database owner") and a period.

When Jet receives this name from the server, it is unable to create a table link named dbo.authors due to its naming conventions (Jet does not allow the period), so it fixes the link name to dbo_authors.

Once a table is linked from a server to an Access database, it can be viewed in a datasheet, edited (index issues permitting), and used as the basis for recordsets, queries, forms, and reports. For your application and its users, a linked server table has many of the same attributes and capabilities of a local (Jet) table. In addition, like other linked tables, Access displays the connect string for a server table in the Description property in the Table Properties window available in design view.

If a linked server table (or view) is not updatable from Jet by default, you might be able to force it to be updatable by telling Jet to build a unique (local) *pseudo-index* for the table or view. First, link the table or view to the local database. Then, execute a CREATE INDEX statement through a Data Definition query to tell Jet which fields will be used for the index. Remember that the combination of fields you specify must uniquely identify a record (in other words, qualify as a "pseudo primary key"), as in this example:

```
CREATE UNIQUE INDEX idxRoySched
ON tsqlRoySched (title_id, lorange, hirange);
```

 Note
Jet does not actually build an index for the data, because it would not be able to keep the index synchronized with changes made by other users to the server data. Instead, Jet saves the index information with the definition of the linked table and uses it when creating the recordset of bookmarks (index values) that it builds at the time you open an editable recordset against the server.

When you create a unique pseudo-index with a Data Definition statement, the index is reflected in the table design view for the link as a primary key. (A primary key for the link is also indicated if you select the key fields when creating the link from the File menu.) However, you cannot create or alter the displayed primary key information for a linked table when in design view. You must use the CREATE INDEX and DROP INDEX statements to do so.

Note
Because pseudo-indexes are local, CREATE INDEX and DROP INDEX statements applied against them do not have any effect on the *real* indexes on the server.

Establishing Your ODBC Connection

When your application first communicates with an ODBC data source, it establishes a *connection*, which is a handle to a communication pipeline through which requests and results flow back and forth. Because it would be inefficient to establish a new connection each time your user sends a statement to the server, DAO saves the first connection you establish between the client and the server and reuses this channel for the remainder of the application's needs or until the connection times out.

DAO creates a connection the first time it actually needs to talk to the server. This is *not* when the Access application opens; instead, it occurs when the first table datasheet opens or query process runs that actually transfers a request to the server. Your applications can usually rely on the server's ODBC driver to provide a login dialog box for this purpose, but coding an application this way sometimes feels just a little "sloppy."

Instead, recall my admonition in Chapter 17, "Bulletproofing Your Application Interface," that every application has an Access form that serves as a login dialog box. The dialog box collects login information that is useful to the application's code routines. In a client/server application, you can extend the capabilities of your login form to create your application's initial server connection.

Figure 19.7 shows the login dialog box and the system defaults table we used in Chapter 17, modified to collect and supply the information required to establish an SQL Server connection.

Fig. 19.7

A login dialog box and supporting table for making an SQL Server connection.

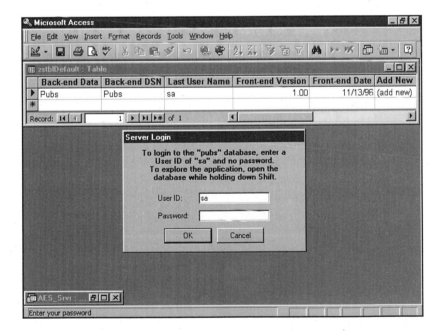

Listing 19.1 shows code that establishes an initial connection to the server from the OK button on the login form. The code actually establishes two preliminary connections: one for the default Jet workspace and one for the ODBCDirect workspace to use (see "Introducing ODBCDirect" later in this chapter to learn the difference). This strategy creates two buffers, one for each type of server access. Regardless of which type of connection (Jet or ODBCDirect) is utilized later by application code, a cached server connection should already exist after this login code has run.

Listing 19.1   AES_Srvr.Mdb—Logging in to an SQL Server and Creating an Initial Connection for Jet to Use

```
' A routine attached to the login form's OK button
Private Sub cmdOK_Click()
' Purpose: Create a connection to the server database

  Dim blnRet      As Boolean
  Dim dbs         As Database
  Dim rst         As Recordset
  Dim varBackEnd  As Variant
  Dim varDSN      As Variant

  Set dbs = CurrentDb
  varBackEnd = DFirst("BackEndData", "zstblDefault")
  varDSN = DFirst("BackEndDSN", "zstblDefault")
  blnRet = lci_ODBCValidate(varBackEnd, Me!txtUserName, Me!txtPW, varDSN)
  If blnRet Then
    Beep
    lci_gstrCurrentUser = Me!txtUserName  ' Set global user name
    Set rst = dbs.OpenRecordset("zstblDefault", dbOpenDynaset)
    rst.MoveFirst
    rst.Edit
    rst!LastUserName = lci_gstrCurrentUser
    rst.Update
    rst.Close
    MsgBox "You are logged-in and validated.", _
      vbInformation, lci_gcstrAppTitle & " Login"
    DoCmd.Close acForm, Me.Name
  Else
    Me!txtUserName.SetFocus
  End If

End Sub


' A library routine
Public Function lci_ODBCValidate(rvarDbs As Variant, rvarUser As Variant _
  , rvarPW As Variant, rvarDSN As Variant) As Boolean
' Purpose:   Create and validate an ODBC connect string
'            Also creates initial (cached) Jet connection as byproduct
' Arguments: rvarDbs:=database name
'            rvarUser:=user name
'            rvarPW:=user password
'            rvarDSN:=data source name
```

continues

Listing 19.1   Continued

```
' Returns:   True/False, True=logged in
' Example:    lci_ODBCValidate(varBackEnd, Me!txtUserName, Me!txtPW, varDSN)

    Const cstrProc As String = "lci_ODBCValidate"
    On Error GoTo lci_ODBCValidate_Err

    Dim cnn     As Connection
    Dim dbs     As Database
    Dim strCnn  As String
    Dim wsp     As Workspace

    ' Build a connect string
    "ODBC;DATABASE=Pubs;UID=" & rvarUser & ";PWD='';DSN=Pubs"

    ' Create a Database connection (Jet)
    Set dbs = OpenDatabase( _
        Name:="" _
      , Options:=False _
      , ReadOnly:=False _
      , Connect:=strCnn)

    ' Create a Connection connection (non-Jet)
    Set wsp = DBEngine.CreateWorkspace( _
        Name:="ODBC" _
      , UserName:="sa" _
      , Password:="" _
      , UseType:=dbUseODBC)
    Set cnn = wsp.OpenConnection( _
        Name:="" _
      , Options:=dbDriverCompleteRequired _
      , ReadOnly:=False _
      , Connect:=strCnn)

    ' Save the connection string for our own use later
    lci_gstrCurrentCnn = strCnn
    lci_ODBCValidate = True

lci_ODBCValidate_Exit:
    On Error Resume Next
    dbs.Close
    cnn.Close
    wsp.Close
    Exit Function

lci_ODBCValidate_Err:
    Call lci_ErrMsgStd(mcstrMod & "." & cstrProc, Err.Number, Err.Description _
      , True)
    Resume lci_ODBCValidate_Exit

End Function
```

Here are several important considerations about the routines in the listing:

▶ I store the database name and data source name in a table in the database (zstblDefault, the structure of which is shown in Figure 19.7). Although these values do not change frequently, having them in a table makes it unnecessary to change any code when the back-end database moves or is renamed. Also, there is no benefit in making the user enter these values into the login dialog box at each session, so they are seeded into the form from the table.

Note

The connect string in the example uses the DATABASE, DSN, PWD, and UID arguments. While all ODBC drivers must support the keywords DSN, PWD, and UID, DATABASE is an SQL Server driver-specific keyword. To make my routine into a generic routine for multiple servers, you would have to add special handling for such server-specific keywords.

▶ The login validation routine calls our standard library error handler lci_ErrMsgStd as documented in Chapter 11, "Expert Approaches to VBA." This handler builds a message string that includes all errors returned to Jet by ODBC by checking the new Errors collection in the DAO. This collection is particularly useful when working with ODBC data sources, which can return multiple error messages back to your application (all of which are trapped in the Errors collection). For example, the following code (similar to that found in our generic error message routine) demonstrates how to loop through the collection:

```
For Each eerrJet In DBEngine.Errors
  With eerrJet
    Debug.Print .Number
    Debug.Print .Description
    Debug.Print .Source
  End With
Next
```

To give you an example of the information logged in the Errors collection for ODBC events, Figure 19.8 shows an example of the results generated by this code loop after a simple pass-through query failure.

Note

If some parameters are missing or invalid, ODBC may display its own login dialog box to collect the required information. Canceling this dialog box produces error number 3059, "Operation canceled by user." If you desire, you can trap this specific error number in your code and close the application session during login.

Fig. 19.8

Two messages are in the Jet `Errors` *collection after a pass-through query failure.*

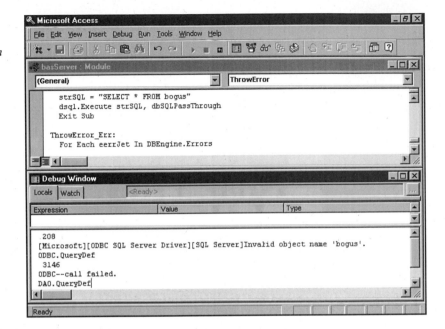

▶ If a connection is successfully established, my code saves the connect string to the public variable `lci_gstrCurrentCnn`, which can be reused elsewhere in the application for creating pass-through query connections. (If Jet can save and reuse connection information, why can't we take a hint and do the same?)

▶ The first connection in the example is built on a `Database` object that is attached to the default workspace. By definition, the default workspace is based on Jet. Thus, the second connection logic explicitly creates a non-Jet workspace and then a `Connection` object based upon it. If your application had no need for either the Jet connection or the ODBCDirect connection, it would remove the unneeded one from the login routine.

▶ Some developers yield to the temptation to simplify their work by skipping the creation of a login dialog box and simply letting ODBC supply the dialog box when the initial connection is made. Changing the `OpenDatabase` method shown in the previous code listing to the following line facilitates this:

```
Set dbs = OpenDatabase("", False, False, "ODBC;")
```

Caution

This syntax enables users to login to any database for which they know the location and password, even one that does not match the application they are running. Unless your application is a "universal client" of some sort that works with more than one back-end, I do not recommend this approach.

Similarly, the `OpenConnection` method could also be instructed to provide a login dialog box for the user by changing the option flag to `Options:=dbDriverPrompt`.

When DAO has successfully established and cached initial server connections, it can reuse the connections for each request your application makes to the server. For some servers, such as Oracle, one connection may be sufficient for your application because a single connection can handle multiple statements passed back and forth between client and server.

For other servers, with SQL Server as an example, a single connection can only process a single statement. However, a single DAO task may require more than one statement. Also, DAO may decide to perform multiple tasks asynchronously. In these cases, DAO clones the initial connection into additional connections as needed, without burdening the user with an additional login dialog box for each new connection. In fact, all programmatic and pass-through requests from your application that go to the same server and database as accessed by the initial connection are handled invisibly by DAO's creation of extra connections on-the-fly.

 Note

Despite SQL Server's limitation of one statement per connection, DAO is able to use a connection to the server for more than one purpose if the data source name and the database name are the same for the different requests. This clever connection management provides you with another good reason to store connection information in a variable as I've just shown, and reuse the connection information over and over in your code. When presented with a consistent connection string coming from different requests, DAO can do some optimization of ODBC traffic.

Linking to ODBC Tables

Frequently, you will code into your Access applications the capability to link tables dynamically from a back-end Jet database when the database's location changes. In contrast, it is rare for the name of a server or a server database to change. Nevertheless, there are occasions when it is useful to programmatically link server tables to Jet.

To link a table from an ODBC server to a local database programmatically, use code like that shown in Listing 19.2.

Listing 19.2   AES_Srvr.Mdb—Dynamically Linking an ODBC Table

```
Public Function lci_ODBCTblLink(rstrTblSrc As String, rstrTblDest As String) _
  As Boolean
' Purpose:   Link a table from an ODBC server
' Arguments: rstrTblSrc:=table name on server
'            rstrTblDesc:=table name in database
' Returns:   True/False, True=linked
' Example:   lci_ODBCTblLink("tblCust", "tsqlCust")

  Dim dbs As Database
  Dim tdf As TableDef

  Set dbs = CurrentDb
  Set tdf = dbs.CreateTableDef(rstrTblDest)
  tdf.Connect = lci_gstrCurrentCnn
  tdf.SourceTableName = rstrTblSrc
  dbs.TableDefs.Append tdf
  lci_ODBCTblLink = True

End Function
```

Data in a linked table can only be updated by the user or a process if it has a unique (primary) key on the server. If not, the data is read-only in all views. To determine if a recordset created from a linked table can be updated, use the Updatable property on the recordset, as in this example:

```
If rst.Updatable Then
```

Caution

Be careful not to test the Updatable property of the linked table itself instead of testing a Recordset object built from the table. The Updatable property of a TableDef object describes whether the *design* can be changed, not the data, and is always False for a linked table.

Introducing ODBCDirect

In the past, if you were a power-hungry developer or had power-hungry users, you had to find some way to invoke ODBC without the overhead of Jet when working with server data from code. You solved this problem either by writing code directly against the ODBC API, or by using the Remote Data custom control provided with Visual Basic 4.

The Access 97/Jet 3.5/DAO 3.5 toolset gives you a new weapon in the battle for improved performance. And unlike the two weapons previously mentioned, this one is actually easy to use. The tool is called ODBCDirect. ODBCDirect is simply the capability of the

Data Access Objects engine to communicate with ODBC without loading any of Jet. This new technology will provide a significant performance boost to some of your code routines.

All Access database activity has always taken place within a Workspace object. Prior to Access 97, DAO and Jet were unified, and as a result the only type of workspace available from DAO was a Jet-centric one. At its simplest level, ODBCDirect is nothing more than the addition of another type of workspace (an "ODBC workspace" or "ODBCDirect workspace") to the DAO.

To create an ODBCDirect workspace, explicitly create a Workspace object in your code with the appropriate Type flag:

```
Set wsp = DBEngine.CreateWorkspace( _
    Name:="ODBC" _
  , UserName:="sa" _
  , Password:="" _
  , UseType:=dbUseODBC)
```

The Name property of a workspace must be unique within the containing application and cannot exceed 20 characters.

The UseType argument flag has two values: dbUseODBC and dbUseJet. To create a Jet workspace using the previous code lines, simply change the UseType flag. Alternatively, leave the optional UseType argument off altogether because the default workspace created within Access uses Jet.

Note

If your application will use ODBCDirect more than Jet, you can change the default workspace type by changing the DefaultType property of the DBEngine object when your application starts up.

If your code needs a default Workspace object of the default type, you can still issue the syntax you are familiar with from previous Access versions:

```
Set wsp = DBEngine.Workspaces(0)
```

The key component of an ODBCDirect workspace is a Connection object. Think of this object as a surrogate for the Database object in an environment where the database is irrelevant (technically speaking). Whereas a Jet Database object provides a container for QueryDef and Recordset objects, in an ODBCDirect environment the Connection provides this parentage. The object's role is to establish a link with a server database and then manage the traffic for QueryDef and Recordset objects that ride along that link.

19

The next two sections continue the ODBCDirect tutorial, first by clarifying the differences between ODBCDirect and Jet, and then by providing examples of using ODBCDirect in your code.

Comparing Jet and ODBCDirect

The DAO object model has 17 objects (16 collections plus the DBEngine). Table 19.1 summarizes the version 3.5 object model and shows which objects are available in a Jet workspace, which can be used with ODBCDirect, and which apply to both.

The methods and properties listed in the table include only those that apply to the Database object. Methods and properties subordinate to other objects inherit their capabilities from their parent object and thus are not shown. For example, the ConflictTable property applies to a TableDef object; because a TableDef is not available in ODBCDirect, neither is the ConflictTable property.

 Tip
On the Access Help topic "Data Access Objects Overview," click the See Also link. The resulting topic list includes several useful comparisons of the properties and methods in Jet and ODBCDirect.

Table 19.1   DAO Object Model Comparison Between Jet and ODBCDirect

Object	Jet	ODBCDirect
Connections collection		X
Containers collection	X	
Databases collection	X	X
Documents collection	X	
Errors collection	X	X
Fields collection	X	X
Groups collection	X	
Indexes collection	X	
Parameters collection	X	X
Properties collection	X	X
QueryDefs collection	X	X
Recordsets collection	X	X

Object	Jet	ODBCDirect
Relations collection	X	
TableDefs collection	X	
Users collection	X	
Workspaces collection	X	X
Close method	X	X
CreateProperty method	X	
CreateQueryDef method	X	X
CreateRelation method	X	
CreateTableDef method	X	
Execute method	X	X
MakeReplica method	X	
NewPassword method	X	
OpenRecordset method	X	X
PopulatePartial method	X	
Synchronize method	X	
DBEngine object	X	X
CollatingOrder property	X	
Connect property	X	X
Connection property		X
DesignMasterID property	X	
Name property	X	X
QueryTimeout property	X	X
RecordsAffected property	X	X
Replicable property	X	
ReplicaID property	X	
Updatable property	X	X
V1xNullBehavior property	X	
Version property	X	X

19

When do you use ODBCDirect instead of Jet? When you need to write code to perform SELECT, INSERT, UPDATE, or DELETE operations from VBA against an ODBC back-end, try using ODBCDirect first. ODBCDirect is best suited to simple record-based operations against server data.

ODBCDirect does not fully replace Jet. Here are circumstances where you will still use a Jet workspace in your client/server coding:

> *Your code must talk to a Jet database.* ODBCDirect cannot be used to communicate with a Jet database. It requires a Level 2 ODBC driver, and the Jet driver only meets the Level 1 specification.
>
> *You must do heterogeneous joins.* If your SQL statements join tables between a server database and Jet or between two dissimilar server databases, ODBCDirect cannot help you.
>
> *You are designing database objects.* It may be simpler to code database structure definition statements in Jet. Your code can use TableDef and QueryDef objects within a Jet-based Database object, while ODBCDirect does not understand a TableDef and can only create a temporary version of a QueryDef.

 Note

While ODBCDirect cannot create a table by using the CreateTableDef method, it can be used to pass SQL CREATE TABLE, ALTER TABLE, and other data definition statements to a server database instead. This provides similar functionality.

The strongest similarities between Jet and ODBCDirect are their common use of QueryDef and Recordset objects. For both types of workspaces, these objects provide the engines for data manipulation work, and your code against these objects will be very similar.

The primary difference between a QueryDef in Jet and one in ODBCDirect is that the ODBCDirect object can execute asynchronously when requested, while the Jet object can never do so. The second difference is that ODBCDirect QueryDef objects are not saved to the database; they are always transitory.

A third difference between the two types of QueryDef objects involves ODBCDirect's capability to accept parameter values back from the server. These are placed in the Parameters collection you are already familiar with for the QueryDef object. Thus you can set the value of qdf.Parameters(0), have the value passed to the server, and accept a returned value back from the server into the parameter. See the example in the section "Checking Messages Returned by the Server" later in this chapter.

For Recordset objects, the most important difference in the two technologies are the defaults applied to the creation of a new recordset, and the variety of options available to override those defaults. In a nutshell, a Jet recordset tries to become a read/write dynaset by default, while the default ODBCDirect recordset is a read-only snapshot. The section "Comparing Dynasets and Snapshots" provides complete details of the OpenRecordset syntax for both types of workspaces.

Another important distinction evidenced in recordsets is that ODBCDirect manages caching more tightly than a Jet Recordset object, where you can set cache properties through code. An ODBCDirect recordset does not support the CacheStart property and FillCache method, and its CacheSize property cannot be set directly (these properties and methods are described in "Taking Advantage of Caching" later in this chapter). Instead, the cache attributes of an ODBCDirect Recordset object are inherited from its QueryDef. You can now apply the CacheSize method to a QueryDef, and the caching model defined will be propagated into any recordsets created from the query:

```
Set qsql = cnn.CreateQueryDef("")
qsql.SQL = "SELECT * FROM roysched"
qsql.CacheSize = 20  ' Arbitrary number for example
Set rsql = qsql.OpenRecordset()  ' Recordset's cache size is also 20
```

Other, more subtle differences between Jet and ODBCDirect objects will become evident as you read the next section.

Putting ODBCDirect to Work

With ODBCDirect, you can now write generic DAO code that runs against two different types of workspaces, often with no changes at all to the code. Generic code like this can sometimes benefit from knowing what kind of workspace it lives in. Your code can check the Type property of its parent workspace for the values dbUseJet or dbUseODBC to discern the workspace's character:

```
Public Function BatchUpdate(rwsp As Workspace) As Boolean

    ...
    If rwsp.Type = dbUseJet Then
    ...
```

Once you've established a workspace, your code must determine whether to use the Database or Connection object for its transactions. With a Jet workspace, you'll continue to use the traditional Database object. With ODBCDirect, you'll usually elect to use the new Connection object. The Connection object was designed specifically as a pipeline to server data. For example, it can manage multiple queries running simultaneously (asynchronously).

The object structure of the DAO makes it easy to prototype applications in Jet and then migrate them to a server. The switch is facilitated by the presence of a Connection object

19

as a member of the `Database` object, and the reverse. Assume you have written DAO code that uses a `Database` object, and the database is attached to a Jet workspace. Now, you change the workspace to use ODBCDirect. By checking the `Connection` property value, your code can discover that it is now running in an ODBCDirect workspace.

You test for the presence of ODBCDirect this way:

```
Dim dbs As Database
Dim cnn As Connection

' The next line will generate a trappable error if the workspace is Jet
' If Err.Number is still 0 after the line, ODBCDirect is present
Set cnn = dbs.Connection
```

On the other hand, if your code knows that it will be running under ODBCDirect, testing for it is unnecessary and a `Connection` object can be used from the start:

```
Dim cnn As Connection

Set cnn = wsp.OpenConnection( _
    Name:="wspWork" _
  , Options:=dbDriverCompleteRequired _
  , ReadOnly:=False _
  , Connect:="ODBC;DATABASE=Pubs;UID=sa;PWD=;DSN=Pubs")
```

Here are the arguments to this method:

> `Name`. This argument provides the object's name within its parent Connections collection and is required. However, you will usually refer to a variable pointing to a connection rather than the connection itself by name.

> You can specify a data source name as the `Name` argument, but you must leave the `Connect` argument blank. The DSN will be applied to the `Connect` property automatically. Alternatively, if you leave `Name` blank and include a `Connect` string, the `Connect` property is copied into the `Name` property. Finally, you can specify a `Name` property *and* a `Connect` property that are the same or different. The `Connect` property is used to establish the ODBC link in that case.

> `Options`. This argument is not required, but you can pass to it one of four flags:

>> ▶ `dbDriverNoPrompt` indicates that you will provide full connection information in the `Connect` argument and no dialog box should be displayed under any circumstances.

>> ▶ The `dbDriverPrompt` causes the display of the ODBC Data Sources dialog box in all cases, seeded with the `Connect` string information if any was supplied.

>> ▶ `dbDriverComplete` indicates that an attempt should be made to establish a connection using the `Connect` string provided. Only if the attempt fails will the ODBC Data Sources dialog box display. This flag is the default if none is supplied.

▶ The `dbDriverCompleteRequired` flag also attempts to use the information in the `Connect` property first. If the information is inadequate, the ODBC Data Sources dialog box is displayed but only the prompts for the missing or incomplete information are shown.

The value `dbRunAsync` can be added to any of the four previous flag values (as in `Options:=dbDriverComplete + dbRunAsync`) to tell the connection to establish itself asynchronously. The connection will be established immediately, without waiting for other connection-based processes to complete.

ReadOnly. This argument is optional and contains a `Boolean` flag that tells the connection to be read-only (`True`) or read/write (`False`, this is the default).

Connect. An optional ODBC connect string. You are probably already familiar with this property from working with Jet pass-through queries.

Once a `Connection` object is created, your code can create one or more `QueryDef` and `Recordset` objects against the connection. To create an ODBCDirect `QueryDef` object, you will use the same syntax you are familiar with from working with Jet:

```
Set qdf = cnn.CreateQueryDef("qsqlJobs", "SELECT * FROM jobs")
```

Notice that the `QueryDef` object is created against an ODBCDirect `Connection` object; this gives the query a direct pipeline to ODBC's routines for executing *prepared statements* (SQL strings). Also, the name of the `QueryDef` object is only used to identify it within the `QueryDefs` collection; with ODBCDirect, the object is never actually saved to the host database and a name string is optional.

With an ODBCDirect `QueryDef` object, you will generally either apply an `Execute` method to run an action query or an `OpenRecordset` method to create a `Recordset` object from the `QueryDef`. In either case, the syntax matches the structures you are familiar with from previous Access releases; the most noteworthy addition is the capability to use the new `dbRunAsync` flag on either method to prescribe that the query run in parallel with other processes:

```
qsql.Execute dbRunAsync
Set rsql = qsql.OpenRecordset(, dbRunAsync)
```

 Note

You cannot use `dbRunAsync` with `Execute` on a query hosted by a `Database` object; the query must be attached to a connection. However, you can use `dbRunAsync` on an `OpenRecordset` method attached to a `Database` object in the same manner that you can when a `Connection` object is involved.

When a query is running asynchronously, you can generate errors by attempting to access its result set before it completes its work. Your code must always check the query's processing via the StillExecuting property and wait for completion before addressing the resultant recordset:

```
Set rsql = qsql.OpenRecordset(, dbRunAsync)
Do While rsql.StillExecuting
Loop
rsql.MoveLast
```

You cannot have multiple processes running on the same connection. Check StillExecuting on a running process before issuing another process on the same connection. To run asynchronously, use multiple Connection objects.

If a process is still executing and your code needs to abort it, send the Cancel method to the object, as in:

```
rsql.Cancel
```

Note, however, that Cancel does not perform a rollback of the transaction in progress, it simply cancels it at the current point. You will generally want to wrap processes in a transaction if they can be canceled, and issue a Rollback statement in conjunction with the Cancel.

See "Comparing Dynasets and Snapshots" later in this chapter for a complete discussion of ODBCDirect-based recordsets.

Sending Queries to the Server

There are several ways to send queries to a back-end server:

▶ Saved queries can be based on tables linked from the server.

▶ Saved pass-through queries can send commands directly to the server, bypassing table links.

▶ Virtual (temporary) pass-through queries can be executed to send commands to the server without creating any saved Jet objects.

▶ Pass-through statements can be executed directly against a Database or Connection object using the Execute method, bypassing the query engine and any saved Jet objects. Pass-through statements can either utilize Jet or bypass it and go through ODBCDirect.

Whenever possible, a Jet workspace will try to transform your query into a request that the server can execute by itself, because any query processing that takes place on the client workstation slows your application. For example, if a user or process is allowed to join a local table with a remote transaction table, much of the value of the server is discarded—Jet will need to fetch indexes or records from the server and then perform the join work on the user's machine. (Jet *has* optimized this behavior in its latest incarnation, and will fetch only the server records that are needed to join to the local records, presuming you've joined the tables based on indexed fields.)

In contrast, an ODBC workspace does not have the same logic capabilities as Jet. ODBCDirect passes statements through to the server with little to no preparation or added value. Your syntax and your server must be tuned during construction.

You can optimize Jet query processing by ensuring that little or no work is done by Jet other than submitting a data request to the server and managing the result set. Techniques for achieving this result include:

Use standard SQL. Sending standard ANSI SQL syntax that is known by the server will not trigger any local processing. Most servers understand the DELETE, INSERT, SELECT, and UPDATE action keywords. In contrast, no servers understand the Access SQL extensions like TOP and TRANSFORM.

Use simple SQL. Even an SQL statement that looks simple and runs fine in Jet may not be digestible by the remote server. For example, Jet can process a query with multiple outer joins while SQL Server can process only a single one. Similarly, you can nest one query within another in Jet, several levels deep. Many such constructs, however, cannot be translated into a single SQL request to send to the server.

Locate all records on one server. Joining data across more than one data source (between servers or between a server and Jet) will cause Jet to send queries to the disparate servers to return the necessary data, and then process the join locally.

Don't use functions. Remote servers cannot process VBA functions and expressions applied to data columns, nor user-defined functions that you've written. Try to re-engineer a query that depends on these to do its math or display processing on the server, or against the resulting recordset *after* it's retrieved.

> ## α Note
> Jet will do *some* cleanup for you in an attempt to convert a function to a statement that can be sent to the server. Specifically, if your function or expression evaluates to a constant that can be placed in the WHERE clause as a criteria value, Jet does the evaluation in advance and passes the enhanced statement through to the server. Functions applied to table columns, however, require evaluation on a per-record basis and must be evaluated locally.

Skip Jet altogether. Bypass Jet and use ODBC directly when appropriate. Jet is useful or even required in certain situations (see the section "Comparing Jet and

ODBCDirect" earlier in this chapter). Outside of these situations, do not invoke the Jet engine's overhead if it is not needed.

Getting the best performance out of the DAO's connectivity to server data through ODBC involves carefully structuring your application to take advantage of the way the connectivity works.

Avoiding Common Query Pitfalls

In order to illustrate ODBC connectivity and the roles each of the three players in a Jet-based remote data request (Jet, the ODBC layer, and the data server) play, let's dissect the processing of two example queries. Each is based on a Jet table tsqlSales linked to the table sales in the Pubs sample database on SQL Server.

The first query, qsqlSelNet30Sales_SQL, selects all of the sales records where the terms include the string "30" using the standard SQL LIKE operator. The second query, qsqlSelNet30Sales_VBA, also selects sales records where the terms include the string "30" but uses the VBA InStr() function in its criteria.

Figure 19.9 shows these two queries in design view.

Fig. 19.9

Two sample queries against a linked table, one of which uses standard SQL and one that uses a VBA function.

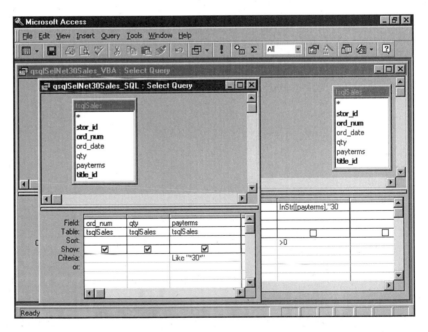

To understand Jet's interaction with the server, let's run these two queries and trace the interaction between Jet and the server as reflected in the ODBC trace files.

Note

Tracing server statements involves telling Jet to write log records to a disk file, as described in the "Determining What the Server Received" section later in this chapter.

Running the query `qsqlSelNet30Sales_SQL` produces the following interaction with the server (as summarized from the trace logs):

1. Jet executes an SQL statement (using ODBC's `SQLExecDirect()` function) to select the primary index values for the table that match the criteria. These values are copied into an ODBC result set, which essentially is an ODBC-managed recordset.

Because the string sent to the server has the appropriate standard SQL WHERE criteria, the result set contains only the eight requested *bookmarks* (index values). With this first request, Jet has not actually requested full data records yet, but instead has only asked for the three columns that make up the linked table's primary key:

```
SELECT stor_id, ord_num, title_id
FROM sales
WHERE ("payterms" LIKE '%30%' )
```

In Jet parlance, this bookmark-fetching query is called a *keyset population query*.

2. Jet then fetches (using ODBC's `SQLFetch()` and `SQLGetData()` functions) the indexes from the ODBC result set into its own temporary table. Jet selects only key values in the first pass in order to build a list of index values that will be useful in future data requests. For example, in order to scroll forwards *and backwards* through a datasheet or `Recordset` variable, Jet must be able to retrieve specific records on demand.

3. Next, Jet executes an additional SQL statement to select the actual table data you've requested in the `QueryDef`. In addition to the displayed fields, Jet again requests the key fields as part of this result set so that it can match its index recordset from the first two steps with its data recordset:

```
SELECT stor_id, ord_num, qty, payterms, title_id
FROM sales
WHERE ("payterms" LIKE '%30%' )
```

4. Finally, Jet fetches the data from the ODBC result set one record at a time into its own temporary table. This recordset is the data actually presented to your users or application through a datasheet, form, or DAO `Recordset` object.

In summary, Jet was able to grab exactly eight indexes and eight records from the server in two quick and simple operations, thanks to the query's use of standard SQL.

19

In contrast, the query `qsqlSelNet30Sales_VBA`'s use of the VBA function `Instr()` produces a more wasteful interaction with the server, as follows:

1. Jet executes an SQL statement (using ODBC's `SQLExecDirect()` function) to select the index values for the table. However, unlike the SQL-specific variation of this operation, Jet cannot pass an SQL WHERE criteria to the server, due to the presence of the VBA function. Consequently, Jet must ask the server for *all* indexes for the table.

   Further, Jet must request the value for the `payterms` field in addition to the three fields in the index, so that it will have the information necessary to do the `Instr()` evalution:

   ```
   SELECT payterms, stor_id, ord_num, title_id
   FROM sales
   ```

2. Jet then issues 21 fetches to get the fields from the ODBC result set into its own (internal) recordset (using ODBC's `SQLFetch()` and `SQLGetData()` functions). Jet then performs the VBA `Instr()` function against each retrieved value of the `payterms` field in the recordset, and builds a list of indexes that matches the records satisfying the function's criteria.

3. Next, Jet creates another SQL SELECT statement, this one with a WHERE clause to request specific records from the server—those that meet the VBA function's criteria. This operation uses the ODBC `SQLPrepare()` and `SQLBindParameter()` functions repeatedly to build a statement resembling the following:

   ```
   SELECT stor_id, ord_num, qty, payterms, title_id
   FROM sales
   WHERE stor_id = '7066' AND ord_num = 'A2976' AND title_id = 'PC8888'
       OR stor_id = '7067' AND ord_num = 'P2121' AND title_id = 'TC3218'
       OR <etc...>
   ```

   Jet then sends an ODBC `SQLExecute()` function call to execute the SQL string and build a result set containing only the desired records.

4. Finally, Jet fetches the data from the ODBC result set one record at a time into its own recordset. This recordset is then displayed to the user or exposed to program code.

These two contrasting examples serve to illustrate the inner workings of Jet against an SQL Server host. More importantly, the examples clarify that Jet must request much more data and do much more local processing when asked to perform a query operation that it cannot simply submit to the server for remote resolution.

Creating Pass-Through Queries

Using an SQL pass-through query, you can forward any command or set of commands to the receiving server that are valid on the server. Valid commands are not necessarily limited to SQL queries against data tables. For example, with an ODBC connection to SQL Server, the DAO can pass through any of these strings:

- An SQL data request or batch of requests using these commands: DELETE, INSERT, SELECT, UPDATE.
- The name of a stored procedure or multiple procedures.
- A Data Definition command such as ALTER TABLE or CREATE INDEX.
- Commands to create or alter system objects, including defaults, rules, stored procedures, security settings, or triggers.
- A command to check the consistency of a server object using SQL Server's database consistency checker.

In addition to providing your application with access to any features of the server exposed to ODBC (as in the previous list), the benefit of pass-through queries is that the Jet or ODBCDirect query parser ignores the query and simply sends it on to the server for evaluation. This moves the translation effort to the ODBC driver and the data host, which are the most capable devices for evaluating and complying with the request.

Stored procedures have a variety of uses on a database server. Because they are compiled, they provide a fast-executing method for performing repeated operations (in this respect, they have something in common with queries compiled and stored as Jet QueryDef objects).

Depending on the server's syntax capabilities, stored procedures can provide capabilities to accept arguments, create variables, return printed output, iterate through records, run SQL statements, and so on. Thus, any temptation you have to write VBA code against a recordset built from a server table should be moderated by first attempting to solve the same problem through a stored procedure on the server and using your application to invoke the stored procedure via pass-through.

 Note

By nature, a pass-through SELECT query saved in a Jet database can only return a non-editable snapshot-type recordset. This makes it an effective object for read-only DAO operations, for row sources in ComboBox and ListBox controls, and for report sources but not an effective query to supply forms with records that must be editable.

Editable recordsets can be created from QueryDef objects, but not from QueryDefs saved in Jet. Creating a Recordset based on a QueryDef based on a Database or Connection object linked directly to a server can produce an editable recordset.

19

You cannot create pass-through statements using the query design grid; you must use the SQL view of query design, as shown in Figure 19.10. Jet does not evaluate the information you type into the SQL text box, so you are responsible for the validity of the statement.

Fig. 19.10

*The SQL view of Access'
query design view for a
pass-through query, with
the Properties window
displayed.*

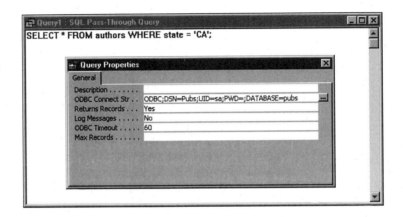

> ### ⚛ Tip
>
> Wherever possible when creating pass through queries that are SQL statements, link the server tables to an Access database first and use the query design grid to author the core of the request. When the request exceeds standard Jet join capabilities or syntax, change the query type from Select to SQL Pass-Through and finalize the query development in the SQL view text box. Delete the table links after you save the query.
>
> Alternatively, develop and test the pass-through statements in the Query Analyzer dialog box in the SQL Enterprise Manager, then copy and paste the string into Access' query design view.

Executing a pass-through query from code without the use of a QueryDef object involves the use of the Execute method against a Database or Connection object. When performed against a Jet Database object, include the pass-through constant dbSQLPassThrough as shown in the example in Listing 19.3.

Listing 19.3   AES_Srvr.Mdb—Using the *Execute* Method Against a *Database* and a *Connection* Object to Send a Pass-through Query

```
Dim cnn    As Connection
Dim dsql   As Database
```

```
Dim strSQL As String
Dim wsp    As Workspace

strSQL = "UPDATE publishers SET country = 'United States'" _
  & " WHERE country = 'USA'"

' Jet example
Set dsql = CurrentDb
dsql.Connect = lci_gstrCurrentCnn
dsql.Execute strSQL, dbSQLPassThrough
' RecordsAffected does not work against a Database object

' ODBCDirect example
Set wsp = DBEngine.CreateWorkspace("", "", "", dbUseODBC)
Set cnn = wsp.OpenConnection("cnn", , , lci_gstrCurrentCnn)
cnn.Execute strSQL
' RecordsAffected works against a Connection object
Beep
MsgBox CStr(cnn.RecordsAffected) & " records updated.", vbInformation, cstrProc
```

19

 Note

The `Execute` method flag `dbSeeChanges` has no effect on the `Execute` method with pass-through queries against a `Database` object. `dbSeeChanges` is useful for updatable recordsets, but not for pass-through queries that create snapshots or perform action queries. However, you must use `dbSeeChanges` when performing an SQL action against a linked table if the server table has an `Identity`-type column.

The `dbFailOnError` flag tells Jet to fail an entire bulk operation, as opposed to a partial failure that may arise under the default Jet behavior. Use this flag if your SQL statement is wrapped in a Jet transaction or you want Jet to create an implicit transaction that enables the operation to be fully rolled-back in the event of failure.

You can also use pass-through with a `QueryDef` object. This option is valuable to you if you want to save the pass-through query before or after it is executed, or to use the query to create a recordset. Here are the steps:

1. Create a `QueryDef` using the `CreateQueryDef` method on a `Database` object. Do not specify an SQL statement for the query during its creation:

   ```
   Set qspt = dbs.CreateQueryDef("qsptSelPublisher")
   ```

   Because a named `QueryDef` object is appended to the database immediately upon creation, an SQL string included at the time of creation as the second argument to `CreateQueryDef()` is evaluated by Jet and therefore must be a valid Jet SQL statement. By contrast, an SQL string added through the `SQL` property after the query has been assigned a connect string is *not* evaluated, and thus can be in a foreign server's syntax. For example, the name of a stored procedure is a valid command to pass to SQL Server, but would not survive Jet's scrutiny if parsed and compiled as a non-pass-through query.

Alternatively, to create a temporary pass-through query that is not saved in the database, leave the query name argument blank:

```
Set qspt = dbs.CreateQueryDef("")
```

> **Tip**
>
> A temporary (unnamed) `QueryDef` object like this produces the least possible impact on local (Jet) resources, because no `QueryDef` object is appended to the local database. Temporary query objects are ideal when your primary objective is to create a recordset from a pass-through SQL statement, like this:
>
> ```
> Set qspt = dbs.CreateQueryDef("")
> ' Set query properties here
> ...
> Set rsql = qspt.OpenRecordset()
> ```

With ODBCDirect, all `QueryDef` objects are temporary. When you create a `QueryDef` against a `Connection` object, the name is transitory and not required, and no object is saved to the database:

```
Set qspt = cnn.CreateQueryDef("")
```

2. For a Jet `QueryDef`, set the `Connect` property for the query to address the ODBC server:

```
qspt.Connect = lci_gstrCurrentCnn   ' Connect string saved from login
```

You do not need to set this property for an ODBCDirect `QueryDef`, which is attached to a `Connection` object and inherits that object's connection information.

3. Set the query's `SQL` property:

```
strSQL = "UPDATE publishers SET country = 'United States'" _
  & " WHERE country = 'USA'"
qspt.SQL = strSQL
```

4. Decide whether or not the query will return records, then set the `ReturnsRecords` property accordingly. A `SELECT` query *will* return records while `DELETE`, `INSERT`, and `UPDATE` queries will not:

```
qspt.ReturnsRecords = False
```

> **Caution**
>
> The default for the `ReturnsRecords` property is `False`, and Jet will *not* change the setting for you by checking the string assigned to the SQL property of the query. You *must* set the property to `True` yourself if the pass-through statement will return records.

5. If the query returns records (the UPDATE query in this example does not), it can be assigned to a snapshot-type Recordset object, as in this syntax:

```
Set rsnp = qspt.OpenRecordset(dbOpenSnapshot)
```

The example in Listing 19.4 pulls these steps together. The first block of code creates an action pass-through query, the second block assigns a row-returning query to a recordset.

Listing 19.4   AES_Srvr.Mdb—Three Pass-through *QueryDef* Objects Created from Code—One Action Query and Two Return Records

```
Dim cnn    As Connection
Dim dbs    As Database
Dim qspt   As QueryDef
Dim qsql   As QueryDef
Dim rsql   As Recordset
Dim strSQL As String
Dim wsp    As Workspace

' Jet example
Set dbs = CurrentDb
dbs.QueryDefs.Delete "qsptUpdPublishers_USA"
' Create and execute a pass-through action query
Set qspt = dbs.CreateQueryDef("qsptUpdPublishers_USA")
qspt.Connect = lci_gstrCurrentCnn
strSQL = "UPDATE publishers SET country = 'United States'" _
   & " WHERE country = 'USA'"
qspt.SQL = strSQL
qspt.ReturnsRecords = False
qspt.Execute dbFailOnError

dbs.QueryDefs.Delete "qsptSelPublisher"
' Create and execute a pass-through SELECT query
Set qspt = dbs.CreateQueryDef("qsptSelPublisher")
qspt.Connect = lci_gstrCurrentCnn
strSQL = "SELECT * FROM publishers WHERE country = 'United States'"
qspt.SQL = strSQL
qspt.ReturnsRecords = True
Set rsql = qspt.OpenRecordset(dbOpenSnapshot)
rsql.MoveLast
Beep
MsgBox CStr(rsql.RecordCount) & " records in Jet record set." _
   , vbInformation, cstrProc

' ODBCDirect example
Set wsp = DBEngine.CreateWorkspace("", "", "", dbUseODBC)
Set cnn = wsp.OpenConnection("cnn", , , lci_gstrCurrentCnn)
Set qsql = cnn.CreateQueryDef("", strSQL)
Set rsql = qsql.OpenRecordset(dbOpenSnapshot)
rsql.MoveLast
Beep
MsgBox CStr(rsql.RecordCount) & " records in ODBC record set." _
   , vbInformation, cstrProc
```

19

Access Help infers that, after a pass-through operation against a `Database` or `QueryDef` object, you can check the `RecordsAffected` property of the object to see how many records were altered by the most recent process, like this:

```
qspt.Execute
MsgBox CStr(qspt.RecordsAffected) & " records updated."
```

In fact, this property is only partially implemented, so use it wisely. If your `Execute` action runs SQL against a Jet table that is linked to a server table, this property is correctly set by `Execute` to reflect the number of records inserted, updated, or deleted. In contrast, if your `Execute` action operates as a pure pass-through statement directly against a named server table, not only is `RecordsAffected` not set, it is not reset. Thus, whatever value existed in this property from the last action against a Jet table or table link is still there. Do not query this property after a pure pass-through operation using Jet. The property *is* accurate when used with ODBCDirect `Execute` operations using a connection.

Caution

Once you assign a `Connect` property to the `QueryDef`, Jet determines that it is an SQL pass-through query. Oddly enough, Jet will then generate an error if you try to use the pass-through flag on the `Execute` or `OpenRecordset` statements, like this:

```
qspt.Execute dbSQLPassThrough    ' This generates an error
Set rsql = qspt.OpenRecordset(dbSQLPassThrough)   ' This generates an error
```

Using a `SELECT` pass-through `QueryDef` object, you can copy records into a table in your local database for more extensive processing using a Jet `SELECT INTO` query. As an example, replacing the `OpenRecordset` logic in the prior listing with the following statement would copy the selected records from the remote `publishers` table into a newly created local table `zttblPub`:

```
dbs.Execute "SELECT * INTO zttblPub FROM qsptSelPublisher"
```

To check the success of an insert operation like this, you will need to check for the existence of records in the target table. If the table is used for temporary processing, remember to delete the table when its usefulness expires.

Tip

Consider including a table name prefix on each field reference in SQL statements that you write in code. For example, the following code is very clear in its intent:

```
SELECT stores.stor_name, stores.city, sales.qty
FROM stores, sales
WHERE stores.stor_id=sales.stor_id;
```

Code like this is reliable even if the database structure expands. In contrast, if a `qty` field were added to the `stores` table in the future, and your query was saved with a non-qualified derivative of the syntax shown, the query would fail with an ambiguous reference because both tables would have a `qty` field.

Using Complex Pass-Through Queries

If your pass-through query returns multiple recordsets, the situation is slightly more complex than with a simple SELECT or UPDATE statement. Multiple result sets can be returned by calling a server's stored procedure or by sending the server a batch of commands in one pass-through statement.

DAO can handle multiple return sets, but not within Jet recordsets. Instead, you must tell Jet how to direct the returned records to tables, and the data returned will then be placed in your database in the designated tables. When using ODBCDirect, DAO supports multiple recordsets within one returned data set.

19

For the purpose of the following example, we'll use the stored procedure `byroyalty` in the `Pubs` SQL Server database. We'll modify the stored procedure to take two parameters (`percentage` and `percentage2`) instead of one, and to consequently return two result sets, as shown in Listing 19.5.

> **Listing 19.5   AES_Srvr.Mdb—Modifying the *byroyalty* Stored Procedure in the *Pubs* Database to Return Two Result Sets**

```
CREATE PROCEDURE byroyalty @percentage int, @percentage2 int
AS
SELECT au_id FROM titleauthor
WHERE titleauthor.royaltyper = @percentage
SELECT au_id FROM titleauthor
WHERE titleauthor.royaltyper = @percentage2
```

Assume you want to return two result sets from the server using this stored procedure, one with author ID values for authors where the royalty percentage is 50, and one for 75. The mechanism for using Jet is as follows:

1. Create and save a pass-through query that executes the statement which will return multiple results. In the current example, we want to run a single pass-through query that will return two recordsets.

   The following code creates a query that runs the stored procedure:

   ```
   Set qspt = dbs.CreateQueryDef("qsptMakByRoyalty_2Result")
   qspt.Connect = lci_gstrCurrentCnn
   strSQL = "byroyalty @percentage=50, @percentage2=75"
   qspt.SQL = strSQL
   qspt.ReturnsRecords = True
   ```

2. Execute the pass-through query by using a make-table Jet statement to direct the returned results to a table:

```
dbs.Execute "SELECT * INTO zttblRoyalty FROM qsptMakByRoyalty_2Result"
```

Obviously, Jet cannot return the two result sets from the single stored procedure into the single local table named in the statement, because there is no guarantee that the two result sets will have the same field structure (even though they do in my simple example). To solve the problem, Jet appends table version numbers to the name you prescribe for each table returned. Thus, in the previous example, the first dataset returned from the server is placed in a table named zttblRoyalty, but the second result set is directed to zttblRoyalty1.

3. Use the returned data as required, then delete the returned tables when they are no longer needed. Note that the tables created by this process are native Jet tables, and are divorced from any relationship with the server (thus my use of the zt prefix to specify that these are temporary, work tables).

 Tip

Because Jet is actually assigning table names for you in a process like this, you need to take care to allow Jet to use the names you expect, or you need to write a routine that checks the DAO for the most recently added tables so you can discern what Jet has done.

The cleanest scenario is to simply reserve specific table names for a specific process. Using the previous code as an example, only your routine to retrieve customer data from the server should make use of the table name zttblRoyalty; this table name should not be used by any other process. Consequently, your routine can safely delete zttblRoyalty and zttblRoyalty1 before executing the procedure that creates new versions of them, and thus the result sets created by your pass-through operation will be predictable in advance.

The process of handling multiple result sets in ODBCDirect is different than with Jet. ODBCDirect is able to retrieve multiple Recordset objects from a single statement (however, none of the result sets will be able to be updated). The technique involves telling the server not to use cursors to handle the data; this creates a fetch engine returning one record at a time. Under this model, SQL Server can return multiple result sets.

Here are the steps to get ODBCDirect working against a multiple `Recordset` result set:

1. Create a `QueryDef` and set its `CacheSize` property to 1. This causes DAO to request one record at a time from the server.

2. Open a `Recordset` against the `QueryDef`. Use the flag `dbOpenForwardOnly` and `dbReadOnly` to force the server to use no cursors.

3. Alternatively, set the `Workspace` object to use no cursors by setting `dbUseNoCursor` on the `Workspace`'s `DefaultCursorDriver` property. This achieves the same result as steps 1 and 2.

4. Walk through each recordset. First, traverse the initial recordset until the end is reached. Then, issue the `NextRecordset` method to determine if another result set is queued up. If it is, traverse that recordset, and so on.

Listing 19.6 shows the code for this process. It uses the `byroyalty` stored procedure that was created in Listing 19.5.

19

Listing 19.6   AES_Srvr.Mdb—ODBCDirect Code that Returns and Reviews *Two Recordsets* within a Single Result Set

```
Set wsp = DBEngine.CreateWorkspace("", "", "", dbUseODBC)
wsp.DefaultCursorDriver = dbUseNoCursor  ' Disable cursors
Set cnn = wsp.OpenConnection("cnn", , , lci_gstrCurrentCnn)
' Run the stored procedure; it returns 2 result sets
' OpenRecordset("sqlstatement1; sqlstatement2") would work too
Set rsql = cnn.OpenRecordset("byroyalty @percentage=50, @percentage2=75")

Do  ' Loop through the recordsets
  Debug.Print "Recordset:"
  While Not rsql.EOF
    Debug.Print rsql.Fields(0)  ' Dump the first field
    rsql.MoveNext
  Wend
  ' Get the next Recordset in the result set
Loop Until (rsql.NextRecordset = False)
```

In addition to calling a stored procedure with multiple result sets, your advanced pass-through queries can send any legitimate server syntax. One example is multiple SELECT statements, as in the following lines:

```
' Jet example
strSQL = "SELECT * FROM authors; SELECT * FROM discounts"
qspt.SQL = strSQL

' ODBCDirect example
Set rsql = cnn.OpenRecordset( _
  "SELECT * FROM authors; SELECT * FROM discounts")
```

These compound statements sent as a pass-through query will return two result sets back to your application.

Another example of compound statements involves multiple stored procedures. When sending more than one stored procedure name in a pass-through statement, use the EXEC keyword:

```
EXEC byroyalty 50
EXEC byroyalty 75
```

Inserting Records on the Server

When creating pass-through queries to insert records into a server table, you have more than one option for approaching the task. Which approach you select will be based upon the client/server coding model you adopt for Access applications, as well as performance and security considerations.

Here are the three options:

1. *Direct Insert.* Your code can insert records directly into a server table using the Execute method of a pass-through Database, QueryDef, or Connection object, as described in the previous section:

   ```
   dbs.Execute "INSERT INTO jobs VALUES ('Boss',50,100)", dbFailOnError
   ```

   Directly inserting records is the most straightforward solution, but not necessarily the fastest or wisest. Here are a few considerations:

   ▶ Always include the dbFailOnError argument so that DAO wraps direct inserts in a transaction. This provides integrity protection to ensure that all of the records were received by the server in good order; if not, none of them are committed.

> **Tip**
> Rather than rely on implicit transactions, it is a cleaner coding model to create an explicit transaction with BeginTrans in your code whenever you are performing an operation against a server. DAO will use your transaction for its SQL operations, and the transaction provides your code with a way to roll back the process for any reason it deems important.

   ▶ A direct insert may not be as fast as a compiled query or a linked table, because the INSERT statement is uncompiled and thus DAO must request the table structure from the server, review the query syntax, and perform other maintenance work as part of the insertion.

> ▶ You may want direct inserts to be filtered through a stored procedure on the server (see the next item) in order to benefit from integrity checking, logging, or other server-side mechanics.

2. *Insert via stored procedure.* Sometimes we build our SQL Server databases with a security layer that prevents users from directly altering table data via an ODBC connection. To implement this layer, direct inserts are disenabled and record insertions must instead be sent to a stored procedure, which performs the insert work. This technique and its benefits are described in the section "Applying Security with Stored Procedures" later in this chapter.

Insert via linked tables. Once you have linked a server table to your Access application, you can programmatically append records to the table in two ways:

> ▶ You can create a Jet or ODBCDirect recordset against the table and use the AddNew method to insert records into the remote table.
>
> ▶ You can execute an SQL INSERT statement that inserts records into the linked table.

3. Insert via query wrapper. From a performance standpoint, I've saved the most interesting option for last. Imagine a saved SELECT query in your application database that points to a linked server table but returns no records. If you ran such a query from the Database window, you would have an empty datasheet into which you could enter records—basically an append-only recordset.

Here are two examples of the SQL statements that can be used for such a query, which is saved as qsqlSelJobs and based on a table link tsqlJobs pointing to the server table jobs:

```
SELECT * FROM tsqlJobs WHERE False
SELECT * FROM tsqlJobs WHERE job_id = -1   ' Non-existent job
```

Having created and saved such a query, your code can issue INSERT statements directed at the query, such as this:

```
INSERT INTO qsqlSelJobs (job_desc, min_lvl, max_lvl)
VALUES ('Boss',50,100)
```

The benefit of this approach over simply inserting records directly into the server table with pass-through is that Jet has compiled the saved QueryDef object into which you are placing the new records. Thus, the initial "handshaking" burden, where DAO establishes a connection to the server and packages up the query for submission, is reduced by using information in the compiled QueryDef. While ODBCDirect operations are generally faster than analogous Jet operations, the ODBC connection will have to query the server for table structure information just as a Jet connection would have to, and thus a saved Jet

`QueryDef` may outperform ODBCDirect in this scenario. Test your specific application to see which option is best.

 Note

Did you observe that the previous INSERT statement specifically identified the target fields in the destination table by name? This syntax is not always required, but I selected the jobs table for my example specifically to make this point: The jobs table has a field defined as Identity type on the server (akin to Jet's AutoNumber type). This field is the first field (job_id) in the table. As such, a generic INSERT statement like the following

```
INSERT INTO jobs VALUES ('Boss', 50, 100)   ' This works
```

will run against the server directly, because no attempt is made to insert data into the Identity field. However, this similar syntax *will not* run against the server table linked to Jet, or any query wrapped around such a table link:

```
INSERT INTO qsqlSelJobs VALUES ('Boss', 50, 100)   ' This doesn't work
```

While this Jet behavior is odd, specifying the target fields for the insertion by name (and *not* including the Identity field in the list) will allow you to work around it. In general, you should specify column names in an INSERT statement if you are not inserting into all columns.

Unlike the security of working with Jet data, where you can create a recordset with LockEdits set to True to enable pessimistic locking and guarantee your updates, bulk operations on a server that don't support pessimistic locking are more risky. Therefore, always use a transaction wrapper around bulk server operations and roll back the transaction at the first sign of trouble.

In some applications, clever record inserts can be done *from* the server *to* the server, bypassing Jet altogether. Audit routines are a good example: When server data is manipulated, it causes a server process to be triggered that spawns another process (such as writing an audit log to a log table).

SQL server provides such capabilities for purely remote processing through stored procedures and *triggers*. A trigger is an event that fires when table data is modified. Triggers can contain some simple programming commands. You can create them on the server or using DAO pass-through statements.

For example, assume you need a trigger on the Pubs sample database that creates a new record in the discounts table whenever a new store record is inserted into the stores table.

Under no circumstances will your VBA code do this job faster than the server can, so it's a natural choice for embedding in a trigger. You would use a pass-through query to create an insert trigger to handle this task; the query would look like this:

```
CREATE TRIGGER trgCreateDiscount ON dbo.stores
FOR INSERT
AS
INSERT INTO dbo.discounts (discounttype, stor_id, discount)
SELECT ('<new>'), inserted.stor_id, (0) FROM inserted
```

 Note

In the previous example, the new record's ID is fetched from the table named `inserted`, which is a buffer in SQL Server triggers. It contains a copy of an inserted record until the insertion is committed.

Using Parameter Queries

Parameter queries are handy devices. Without them, the only option available for setting parameters in a saved query would be to open the `QueryDef` and somehow rewrite the WHERE clause.

Because server databases do not understand the Jet PARAMETERS keyword, your first intuition regarding parameter queries may be that Jet or DAO must send a broad request and then process the results locally. In fact, while DAO indeed must take such a query and prepare a statement for the server from it, DAO does so quickly and efficiently, and makes the server do the work.

 Note

It is a good idea to include the PARAMETERS keyword in your saved parameter queries destined for a server. If you do not explicitly assign a data type to each parameter in a query, Jet will make its best guess based on the context of the query's fields. (In earlier versions of Jet, queries without typed parameters were resolved locally. This behavior has been replaced by the "best guess.")

For example, review the code in Listing 19.7, which creates a parameter query programmatically. (The query also could be created through the Access interface; query parameters are assigned from the Query, Parameters... menu option). The query is based on a table tsqlJobs linked to the Pubs database on the server, and it is a parameter query expecting a single parameter value.

Listing 19.7   AES_Srvr.Mdb—Creating and Executing a Parameter Query Against a Linked ODBC Table

```
Dim dbs    As Database
Dim qsql   As QueryDef
Dim rsql   As Recordset
Dim strSQL As String

Set dbs = CurrentDb

' Create a parameter query pointing to the linked table
strSQL = "PARAMETERS MinLevel Byte;" _
   & " SELECT * FROM tsqlJobs WHERE min_lvl > [MinLevel];"
Set qsql = dbs.CreateQueryDef("qsqlSelJobLevel", strSQL)
qsql.Close

' Reuse the query over and over with this code
Set qsql = dbs.QueryDefs("qsqlSelJobLevel")
qsql.Parameters("MinLevel") = 150
' The following syntax is also valid in place of the previous line
' qsql!MinLevel = 150
Set rsql = qsql.OpenRecordset(dbOpenDynaset)
```

Tracing the interaction between Jet and the server when executing this parameterized query shows that Jet does *not* fetch all the records from the target table and evaluate them locally against the parameter value, which would be the slowest possible resolution method. Instead, Jet rebuilds the query's SQL statement with the parameter before sending it to the server, returning only the three desired records.

You might think that a parameter query using a linked table might not run as fast as creating the corresponding SQL statement in your program code and executing the statement as a pass-through query. Some of the time, you would be correct. However, in many cases the saved parameter query provides better performance than either Jet or ODBCDirect pass-through. Why?

The query is compiled. All saved Jet queries are compiled when saved. Even though a parameter query is missing a criteria value, enough of the query's resolution plan can be determined by Jet to enable the saved query to be optimized. Opening and submitting such a saved query to ODBC may be faster than the ad hoc handshaking that takes place when sending a raw SQL string.

The table link is cached. Even though Jet does not waste time compiling a pass-through query on its way to the ODBC driver, Jet must still establish a buffer for receiving the result set back from the server. When dealing with a linked table, Jet can discern the remote table's structure from the local link information, rather than having to query the server for table layout information in order to build a result buffer.

VBA string manipulation is slow. Creating long SQL statements in VBA involves concatenating multiple strings together, and often processing text values through functions like `Instr()` in order to create the string. Such VBA string operations may take more time than Jet takes to open and submit a compiled version of the same query.

Take great care to make certain that parameter values passed to the server are of the expected type, avoiding the temptation to grab a value from a form control or `InputBox()` function and pass it to a `QueryDef` object's parameter untested. In order to properly test values, your code should know the data type of the server field to which the parameter will be sent, and how to test the parameter value supplied by a user to see if it's valid for the target field.

In the previous code listing (19.7), the query passed a parameter value to the SQL Server field `min_lvl`, which is defined as the `TinyInt` type on the server. As such, the allowable range of values for the field is from 0 to 255. Jet's analogous data type to `TinyInt` is `Byte`, so I used this as the query parameter type.

In other cases, Jet may not have an analogous value to map to a server data type. Consequently, it is possible to pass a value to a parameter query that survives Jet's inspection but generates an error on the server.

χ Caution

Do not rely on Access to provide you with valid data type information that maps to the server's data type for linked tables, because the table design view does not have a way to represent non-Access data types. For example, if you were to look at the table link to the `roysched` table in design view, you would see the field type for `hirange` represented as a `Long Integer` in the Access property list, not a SQL Server `Integer` (its true data type). This disparity is shown in Figure 19.11.

Thus, if you had the SQL Server data structure in front of you and were building a parameter query in the Access design grid for the `roysched` table, you might be inclined to set the type of the parameter for the `hirange` field to `Integer` (the SQL data type). Unfortunately, this would restrict users, developers, and Jet from passing larger values to the server field—values that are quite acceptable. The corollary can also be true—sometimes Access will represent the closest field data type match in the table design grid and the match actually overstates the values accepted by the field. In this scenario, users or developers may attempt to pass a value to the server that is valid. Jet overflows the field type linked from the server, which will generate ODBC errors like these:

```
3146  ODBC—call failed.
 220  Arithmetic overflow error for type tinyint.
```

Fig. 19.11

Access does not represent the true data type of a server field in a linked table; it represents the nearest matching Jet data type.

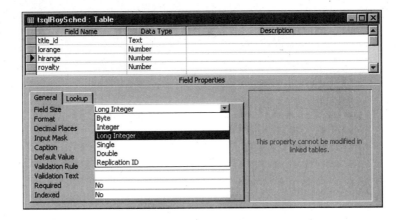

For a table that compares Jet data types to SQL Server data types, see the Help topic "Equivalent ANSI SQL Data Types."

Working with parameters in an ODBCDirect environment is somewhat different than with Jet. ODBCDirect supports SQL parameters but does not support them as named parameters. The syntax for a parameter in a statement that it sends to ODBC is the question mark (?) character in the location where Jet would use a parameter name. If you want to create a statement to send repeatedly to the server and change only the parameters, use one or more of the placeholder ? characters in the statement:

```
SELECT * FROM jobs WHERE min_lvl > ?
```

In the Parameters collection for the SQL statement, the placeholders become parameters with names Parameter1, Parameter2, and so on. Using parameters, you can create reusable ODBCDirect statements like the one shown in Listing 19.8.

Listing 19.8   AES_Srvr.Mdb—Creating and Executing a Parameter Query Using ODBCDirect

```
Dim cnn    As Connection
Dim qsql   As QueryDef
Dim rsql   As Recordset
Dim strSQL As String
Dim wsp    As Workspace

Set wsp = DBEngine.CreateWorkspace("", "", "", dbUseODBC)
Set cnn = wsp.OpenConnection("cnn", , , lci_gstrCurrentCnn)

strSQL = "SELECT * FROM jobs WHERE min_lvl > ?;"
Set qsql = cnn.CreateQueryDef("", strSQL)
```

```
' Set the parameter
qsql.Parameters(0) = 150
' The following syntax is also valid
' qsql!Parameter1 = 150
Set rsql = qsql.OpenRecordset(dbOpenSnapshot)
```

The value of parameterized SQL statements can be inferred from the listing. ODBC keeps a copy of the SQL string in its buffer as long as the QueryDef qsql exists; neither ODBC nor DAO need to re-evaluate the statement's structure when a parameter value is changed. Thus, the code above could create many recordsets in quick succession by simply setting the parameter value, creating a recordset from qsql, changing the parameter, creating a different recordset, and so on.

Checking Messages Returned by the Server

Some ODBC database servers are capable of passing status messages back to the client application after the execution of a pass-through query. To trap or ignore such status messages returned by a server, set the LogMessages property of a saved Jet query.

This property does not exist in Jet unless you create it from code when you build or modify a pass-through QueryDef object, or if you set the property in the Properties dialog box in query design view. The following lines show an example of creating the property on a new QueryDef object:

```
Set prp = qspt.CreateProperty("LogMessages", dbBoolean, True)
qspt.Properties.Append prp
```

Jet queries with the LogMessages property set to True will create a table to hold message strings returned from the server's execution of a pass-through query. In this context, a "message" is *not* an error string—errors are returned to the Jet Errors collection. Instead, *messages* are non-recordset information passed back from a server process. Different servers implement this functionality differently, but the simplest SQL Server example is afforded by the PRINT statement. This command can be placed in stored procedures to return a string back to the client application.

A message logging table will contain one or more server messages resulting from an action. The name of the message table is the name of the currently logged user, plus a space, a dash, a space, and a sequential number from 00 through 99. For example, if the current user is Admin, the message table names will be Admin—00, Admin—01, and so on.

To clarify this situation, let's once again modify the stored procedure byroyalty in the Pubs sample database, as shown in Listing 19.9. This time, we'll add a PRINT statement to the end of the procedure to echo back to the client application the parameter value that was passed in *to* the procedure, as follows:

Listing 19.9   AES_Srvr.Mdb—Modifying the *byroyalty* Stored Procedure in the *Pubs* Database to Return a Message with *PRINT*

```
CREATE PROCEDURE byroyalty @percentage int
AS
DECLARE @pct CHAR(5)
SELECT au_id FROM titleauthor
WHERE titleauthor.royaltyper = @percentage
SELECT @pct = '>>' + CONVERT(CHAR(3), @percentage)
PRINT @pct
```

From Access' perspective, the stored procedure returns a *result set* (table records) for the SQL SELECT statement, but a *message string* for the PRINT statement. Listing 19.10 shows an example of code that creates a query to run the revised stored procedure byroyalty, which generates a results table *and* a message table.

Listing 19.10   AES_Srvr.Mdb—Creating a Pass-through Query that Logs Server Messages in a Local Table

```
Const cintPct As Integer - 50
Dim dbs       As Database
Dim prp       As Property
Dim qspt      As QueryDef
Dim strSQL    As String

Set dbs = CurrentDb

' Create a pass-through query on the stored procedure
Set qspt = dbs.CreateQueryDef("qsptSelPrcByRoyalty_Msg")
qspt.Connect = lci_gstrCurrentCnn
' cintPct is the stored procedure argument
strSQL = "byroyalty @percentage = " & CStr(cintPct)
qspt.SQL = strSQL
qspt.ReturnsRecords = True

' Create the LogMessages property
Set prp = qspt.CreateProperty("LogMessages", dbBoolean, True)
qspt.Properties.Append prp

' Create the results table and messages table
dbs.Execute "SELECT * INTO zttblRoyalty FROM qsptSelPrcByRoyalty_Msg"
```

Figure 19.12 shows the contents of the message table generated when the code in the listing is run with a *percentage* argument value (cintPct) of 50.

Fig. 19.12

A table and record generated by the LogMessages *property on an ODBC pass-through query to a stored procedure.*

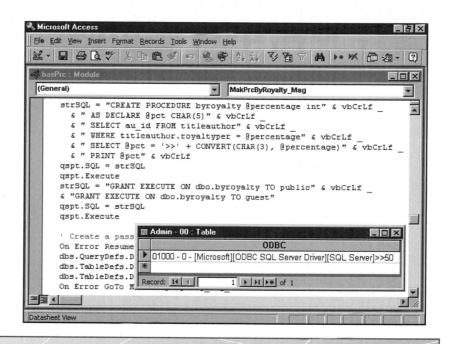

 Tip

When dissecting server messages like the one shown in the figure, your code will need to parse off the driver information prefix characters in order to retrieve the actual value returned. Consider adding special characters to the message string created by the server to facilitate this parsing, as demonstrated by the ">>" characters in my example.

The method for returning server information to an ODBCDirect operation is different from the table-based metaphor just described. The basis for passing values to and from a server operation in ODBCDirect is QueryDef parameters. There, I described how parameters in ODBC statements are represented with placeholder characters (?). This is ODBC syntax, not DAO or server syntax. The following syntax creates a statement with a replaceable parameter and sets the parameter to 150:

```
strSQL = "SELECT * FROM jobs WHERE min_lvl > ?;"
Set qsql = cnn.CreateQueryDef("", strSQL)
qsql.Parameters(0) = 150
```

This syntax construction can also be carried over to stored procedures, which have two different types of parameters: arguments and a return value. Consider the stored procedure created in Listing 19.11, which accepts a passed-in value and returns a different value (similar to the way a VBA Function procedure returns a value).

> ### Listing 19.11   AES_Srvr.Mdb—Creating a Stored Procedure that Accepts an Argument and Also Returns One
>
> ```
> CREATE PROCEDURE byroyalty @percentage int
>   AS UPDATE titleauthor
>   SET titleauthor.royaltyper = (@percentage + 1)
>   WHERE titleauthor.royaltyper = @percentage
>   RETURN @@rowcount
> ```

Return values from stored procedures provide the flexibility of Jet's message-logging table as described earlier in this section, but they provide a more graceful approach. The procedure in the previous listing does the following:

▶ Accepts a percentage value passed in as an argument.

▶ Updates all records matching the passed percentage argument to increase the percentage by one point.

▶ Returns back to the calling statement the number of affected records (the SQL variable @@rowcount is similar to DAO's RecordsAffected property).

To call this stored procedure from an ODBCDirect statement, you must use proper ODBC grammar:

```
Set qsql = cnn.CreateQueryDef("", "{? = CALL byroyalty(?)}")
```

The grammar rules evidenced by this statement are quite strict:

▶ The CALL statement is ODBC-specific syntax to execute a remote procedure.

▶ The brackets ({}) are required when executing a CALL statement.

▶ The argument placeholder (?) appears in the parentheses to provide a location for the query parameter to fill. If the procedure had multiple arguments, they would also appear in the parentheses, as in byroyalty(?,?,?).

▶ If the procedure returns a value, the value must be noted by the placeholder in front of the CALL statement. If the procedure has no return value, do not use the ? = prefix string.

In summary, the syntax to call a stored procedure with and without a return value looks like this:

```
Set qsql = cnn.CreateQueryDef("", "{? = CALL byroyalty(?)}")
Set qsql = cnn.CreateQueryDef("", "{CALL byroyalty(?,?,'Bob')}")
```

The placeholder arguments must be set somehow so that they become constants sent to the server, and the value returned by the server procedure also must have a destination. Both of these circumstances are facilitated by Parameter object values. The following code uses parameters to pass values to the stored procedure:

```
Set qsql = cnn.CreateQueryDef("", "{CALL byroyalty(?,?,'Bob')}")
qsql.Parameters(0).Value = 50  ' Replaces the first ?
qsql.Parameters(1).Value = 60  ' Replaces the second ?
qsql.Execute
```

The next code passes one value to a stored procedure and gets one back:

```
Set qsql = cnn.CreateQueryDef("", "{? = CALL byroyalty(?)}")
qsql.Parameters(1).Value = 60  ' Replaces the second ?
qsql.Execute
varRet = qsql.Parameters(0).Value  ' Gets value from first ?
```

 Note

The following syntax for a CALL statement with a return value is also valid according to the ODBC standard but generates an error when used from ODBCDirect:

```
{CALL ?=byroyalty(?)}
```

When using Parameter objects to set and get stored procedure values, you must provide a type constant to the parameter's Direction property so that it can establish the proper communication with its ODBC channel. Here are the values:

dbParamInput. Denotes a parameter that passes a value to the procedure argument.

dbParamInputOutput. Denotes a parameter that passes a value to the procedure argument and receives one back (using SQL OUTPUT syntax).

dbParamOutput. Denotes a parameter that receives a value back from the procedure argument (using SQL OUTPUT syntax).

dbParamReturnValue. Denotes a parameter that traps the return value from a procedure (using SQL RETURN syntax, as shown in the current example).

Listing 19.12 demonstrates code that calls the procedure created in Listing 19.11, setting and retrieving the procedure's argument values.

Listing 19.12   AES_Srvr.Mdb—Calling a Stored Procedure that Accepts and Returns a Value with ODBCDirect

```
Dim cnn    As Connection
Dim qsql   As QueryDef
Dim strSQL As String
Dim wsp    As Workspace

Set wsp = DBEngine.CreateWorkspace("", "", "", dbUseODBC)
Set cnn = wsp.OpenConnection("cnn", , , lci_gstrCurrentCnn)
```

continues

Listing 19.12   Continued

```
Set qsql = cnn.CreateQueryDef("", "{? = call byroyalty(?)}")

' Set the parameters
qsql.Parameters(0).Direction = dbParamReturnValue   ' Value from procedure
qsql.Parameters(1).Direction = dbParamInput   ' Value to procedure
qsql.Parameters(1).Value = 50
qsql.Execute

' At this point qsql.Parameters(0).Value contains the return value
```

Working With Recordsets

By default, when Access creates a recordset object to fetch server data, it asks Jet to make the recordset an updatable dynaset. When creating the dynaset, Jet does not actually fetch records until Access needs to display them. Instead, Jet fetches all the index values of the requested records and uses these keys to retrieve selected records as Access needs them.

Jet is actually quite efficient in optimizing this type of fetch operation. For example, when it retrieves a record from SQL Server that contains Text (memo) or Image (OLE object) fields, Jet does not request these fields from the server unless Access actually needs them, because fetching these field types is fairly inefficient.

Beginning with Access 97, your code can also bypass Jet completely and use the ODBCDirect capabilities of the Data Access Objects to communicate with server data directly. Using this new feature will provide a performance boost to your client/server code, and also give you almost unlimited control of the communication processes between client and server and the manipulation of data by the server, as the next three sections will make apparent.

Comparing Dynasets and Snapshots

Jet's dynaset processing is based on *keysets*, which fetch data from the server in chunks. With ODBCDirect, you can also use keysets, but you can utilize any other type of cursor processing available on the server as well. You can configure the behavior of ODBCDirect recordsets at a more detailed level than with Jet recordsets.

You can also tell DAO to retrieve records into a snapshot-type recordset, and all of the requested data for the records is returned back to the DAO for processing. This would seem to be less efficient than building a dynaset-type recordset, which initially fetches only keys and not data, and in fact it usually is. In general, creating a dynaset from a server will be faster than creating a snapshot (the larger the recordset, the more likely this is true).

> **Tip**
>
> Regardless of the type of recordset that you are using to fetch data from the server, always request only the fields your application actually needs.

The exception to the "dynaset is faster" rule-of-thumb occurs when the snapshot is small, in which case DAO can build the read-only snapshot faster than the dynaset because a snapshot executes a single query on the server and then returns the results. Dynaset creation executes multiple queries—one to populate the keyset and another to fetch the data corresponding to the records in that keyset. A *small* snapshot in this context is usually around 500 to 1,000 records, depending on the number of fields and other factors. You will need to experiment to determine where the performance threshold is in your specific application.

> **Caution**
>
> If your snapshot contains memo fields or OLE object fields, it will always be slower than a dynaset, due to the overhead of these specific field types. Use a dynaset when either of these field types must be retrieved.

Snapshots are primarily a Jet concept. ODBCDirect thinks primarily in terms of different types of dynasets. If you are using Jet and you have determined that a snapshot is more appropriate than a dynaset in a specific context in your application, consider whether or not the snapshot needs to scroll backwards through the data with MovePrevious. If not, you can pass the dbForwardOnly flag when calling the OpenRecordset method and create a forward-only snapshot. Creating and navigating the snapshot will be faster if Jet does not need to account for moving backwards.

This is also true of ODBCDirect recordsets, which can be set to move in a forward direction only, and can be configured for a variety of data access behavior. The following list describes the different types of ODBCDirect recordsets that you can create with OpenRecordset, including the related Type arguments. Because record navigation in ODBCDirect is performed by the server, a recordset's behavior is a function of the type of cursor built by the server to feed it:

> *Dynamic Cursor (dbOpenDynamic).* As the most robust cursor, this updates data in the recordset immediately after it is changed by any user. These cursors can be tricky because the underlying data can change underneath your process, and they use a lot of server resources.

Keyset Cursor (dbOpenDynaset). This cursor is quite dynamic and mimics what you are used to with Jet—changes to records are displayed and data is fetched in efficient chunks, but the order of the recordset data does not change once the keyset is built.

Static Cursor (dbOpenSnapshot). A static cursor is locked; it does not enable or display any changes to the underlying data.

Forward-Only Scrolling Cursor (dbOpenForwardOnly). A forward-scrolling cursor is dynamic in that it also operates on keysets, and whenever a new batch of data is fetched based on a keyset, the latest information is pulled into the recordset.

While Jet attempts to build an updatable dynaset when it can, ODBCDirect attempts by default to build the fastest Recordset, which is based on the dbOpenForwardOnly and dbReadOnly arguments and is non-editable. If you want an editable recordset you have to supply values that override this behavior.

When determining what type of recordset to use and whether to use ODBCDirect or Jet, your decision will be based on each type of data operation and its unique needs. ODBCDirect is superior to Jet in these areas: asynchronous queries, returning multiple Recordset objects, batch cursor processing, and record throughput.

However, ODBCDirect is also more restrictive than Jet. It does not enable you to select the index to use on your Recordset object, does not support Seek, does not allow for modification of server table objects via the DAO object model, and cannot perform FindFirst, FindNext, FindPrevious, or FindLast. Clearly, then, there will be times where you still want to employ Jet recordsets to solve specific problems.

ODBCDirect has five values that can be compounded in the LockEdits argument to tailor locking behavior:

dbOptimistic. Uses optimistic locking and only locks a page of records when an Update method is sent. This locking model is based on comparing the unique record values to determine if a record has changed (usually a timestamp).

dbOptimisticBatch. This locking model is quite unique—it keeps the recordset's data in a local cache, and clears the cache to the server only when you say to. To use this model, you must set the DefaultCursorDriver property on the workspace to dbUseClientBatchCursor before opening the recordset. Your code navigates through the recordset normally and makes updates as required, then when it is finished it must call recordset's Update method with the flag dbUpdateBatch. All affected records are then copied over their master copies on the server.

dbOptimisticValue. Another type of optimistic locking, this model forces the comparison of field values in two rows to determine if a record has changed.

dbPessimistic. The most punitive type of locking, this setting locks the page a record is on as soon as the Edit method is issued and keeps the lock until the Update method.

dbReadOnly. The recordset is not editable.

Finding the best mix of a recordset's type, options, and locking behavior will be a trial-and-error proposition given the newness of ODBCDirect. Nevertheless, its flexibility and power are a major step forward in client/server computing.

Updating External Recordsets

A recordset built on a linked table pointing to an ODBC data server will be updatable if the remote table has a unique key. When using such a recordset, the Edit method may be applied to the recordset to update the record via code, and the user can also edit data via a datasheet or form based on the table link.

Note, however, that Jet cannot utilize *pessimistic* locking on server datasets, so all ODBC-related locking will be optimistic and the LockEdits property of the recordset cannot be changed from False. Because optimistic locking is the default behavior for Access datasheets and forms, the locking behavior of these objects against linked server tables is similar to the default behavior you are familiar with against native Jet tables. Opening a Recordset object against a linked server table or a query pointing to it is no different than opening one against a Jet-based table or query:

```
Set rsql = dbs.OpenRecordset("qsqlSelJobLevel")
Set rsql = dbs.OpenRecordset("tsqlAuthors", dbOpenDynaset)
```

Jet will do its best to create an editable dynaset-type recordset where possible. To force the creation of a non-editable snapshot, use the dbOpenSnapshot flag instead of dbOpenDynaset.

 Note

Because Jet creates a dynaset by default when it can, the dbOpenDynaset flag is optional when working with linked tables.

Here are other OpenRecordset flags of interest when working with linked recordsets:

dbAppendOnly. Creates an empty dynaset for appending new records to the table. When the only requirement for the dynaset is to add records, using this flag will improve performance over the use of a populated recordset.

dbDenyWrite. You *cannot* issue this flag on an ODBC-linked table; Jet is not able to place exclusive locks on a recordset.

dbReadOnly. The recordset is established as read-only. You can step through records and retrieve their values, but you cannot issue the Edit method on the recordset. If you are creating a dynaset instead of a snapshot for the performance reasons described in the preceding section "Comparing Dynasets and Snapshots" but do not require an editable recordset, use this flag to maximize performance.

dbSeeChanges. This flag is required if you:

▶ Open a dynaset-type recordset in code against a linked table, and;

▶ The table has a counter-type field (such as SQL Server's Identity type), and;

▶ You need to insert records into the table.

dbSeeChanges tells Jet to refetch a row after it's inserted so that the newly created counter field value is available in the recordset.

 Note

This flag does *not* create pessimistic multi-user locking, although you might assume so from its name. Regardless of whether you include this flag, Jet still traps concurrency conflicts between different users *editing* the same linked table record, and produces the same "Data has changed; operation stopped" message that you are familiar with from working with native Jet tables.

If you open a recordset against a linked table that is already in use by another process on your machine (recordset, datasheet, or form) and do not use this flag, an error will be generated.

Jet's concurrency model for recordsets is based on key fields. Jet can be the most successful when updating records if comparing the key fields in its recordset with the key fields in the source record on the server produces an accurate comparison. You can do two things to help ensure this accuracy:

Use time stamps in all tables. If your server supports time stamping of records (like SQL Server's TimeStamp field type), Jet can use the time stamp information as a tie-breaker when resolving multi-user conflicts. A time stamp column is a server-maintained version stamp that is automatically updated whenever a record is changed. For Jet to check if a record you are sending to the server has been changed by another user, it must compare the values of some or all of the fields in your record with the fields in the server's record. This wastes precious time, and can be bypassed if Jet can simply compare record time stamps.

Caution

The presence of floating-point data columns in a server table can cause concurrency check failures if a time stamp is not present. If you have floating-point data anywhere in the recordset, you should include a time stamp column in the source table.

Do not use floating-point fields in indexes. Fields with decimal precision are subject to rounding variances and therefore do not make good index bookmarks.

The section "Linking to ODBC Data Sources" earlier in this chapter discusses the importance of unique keys in creating updatable recordsets, and the creation of local key information for linked tables.

Taking Advantage of Caching

When working with recordsets that are built from attached server tables, Jet enables you to configure its use of cache resources to optimize the effort of "loading the boat." Specifically, you can establish a cache (a memory buffer area on the workstation) and then fill it with a block of server records. Any time the recordset addresses a record that is in the cache, no server activity takes place. To a smaller degree, you can also tune the caching behavior of ODBCDirect recordsets.

I've Got a Boat to Cache

When I was wandering through Europe years ago, I came to an Italian port city to catch a boat to Greece. There was a line of hundreds of passengers waiting to be crammed into the small boat, and only a small gangplank going down to the dock.

The Italian officials wisely let 20 or 30 people down the gangplank to the dock, then wandered through the group checking passports and tickets. When they had inspected the entire group, it was hustled onto the boat and another 30 people were moved to the dock. In this manner, officials were processing people as fast as they could move through the small group, instead of waiting on each individual person to navigate the small gangplank down to the dock.

This batch processing is what "caching" is all about.

19

Jet provides the following properties and methods for use from code that addresses a DAO `Recordset` object built from server data and a `Database` object:

`CacheSize` *Property.* This property specifies the number of records to place in the cache. Valid values for the property are within the range of 5 to 1,200 (although the property's data type is actually `Long Integer`). To release the cache memory for use by other processes, set the `CacheSize` to 0.

`CacheStart` *Property.* This property specifies a *bookmark* from the recordset that indicates the first row to use when filling the cache.

`FillCache` *Method.* Executing this method fills the cache with server data starting at the row specified by the `CacheStart` bookmark and fetching the number of records specified by the `CacheSize` property. Figure 19.13 shows a diagram of this process.

Fig. 19.13

Jet can be told to retrieve a specific number of records into a cache.

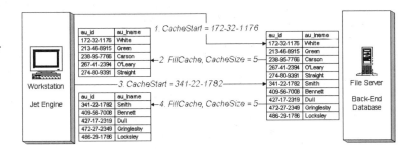

Listing 19.13 shows a routine that fills the cache and fetches records from it. The listing has these attributes:

Configurable `CacheSize` *Property.* The size of the cache can be configured by your code. In my example, the cache size is passed to the routine as an argument. This style allows you to test a routine at various cache sizes to gauge the setting that supplies the best performance to your application.

Positioning Within the Cache. The code keeps track of its position in the cache buffer so that it knows when it has reached the end of the cache and can refill the buffer with another block of records.

 Note

Issuing a `MoveNext` that positions the record pointer to a record outside of the cache will *not* generate an error. Jet merely fetches a record that is not in the cache from the server individually, circumventing your caching scheme and its benefits.

Linked Recordset. The listing demonstrates the use of a linked table to provide the server records to the recordset. The code would also work with a database object that points directly to the ODBC data source using a connect string, but in general, working with a linked table provides better performance.

Caution

You probably use the `Option Compare Database` or `Option Compare Text` statement in the Declarations section of your code modules. When using the `CacheStart` property in a procedure, the Declarations section of the containing module must have an `Option Compare Binary` statement instead. The bookmark of an ODBC recordset using the `CacheStart` property is unlike a standard Jet recordset bookmark, which is a string, and must be treated as binary data. (A remote recordset's bookmarks are actually created by compounding a record's primary key field values together.)

19

Listing 19.13   AES_Srvr.Mdb—Directing Jet to Fetch Data into a *Recordsetcache* by Blocks

```
' In the Declarations section
Option Compare Binary

' A procedure to demonstrate caching
Sub CacheExample(rlngCacheSize As Long)
' Purpose:   Use the FillCache method to cache records from server
' Arguments: rlngCacheSize:=Cache size from 5 to 1200

  Dim dbs    As Database
  Dim intRec As Integer
  Dim rsql   As Recordset

  Set dbs = CurrentDb
  Set rsql = dbs.OpenRecordset("tsqlRoySched", dbOpenDynaset)

  rsql.CacheSize = rlngCacheSize
  Do Until rsql.EOF
    If intRec = rlngCacheSize Then
      Debug.Print "Fill cache"
      rsql.CacheStart = rsql.Bookmark
      rsql.FillCache
      intRec = 0
    End If
    Debug.Print rsql!title_id
    rsql.MoveNext
    intRec = intRec + 1
  Loop

End Sub
```

Note

Data in the cache will no longer be current when another user has edited a record stored in a cache buffer. The `Requery` method of the recordset is not the appropriate way to refresh the data in the cache, because it will clear the cache and reset bookmarks. Instead, issue these commands (using the example in the previous listing) to see the latest data:

```
rsql.CacheSize = 0
rsql.CacheSize = rlngCacheSize
rsql.FillCache
```

ODBCDirect does not enable you to control caching to the same degree as Jet. An ODBCDirect recordset does not support the `CacheStart` property and `FillCache` method, and its `CacheSize` property is inherited from the `QueryDef` on which it was based. For example, you will apply the `CacheSize` method to a `QueryDef` object, and the cache configuration propagates into recordsets created from the query:

```
Set qsql = cnn.CreateQueryDef("")
qsql.SQL = "SELECT * FROM roysched"
qsql.CacheSize = 20   ' Arbitrary number for example
Set rsql = qsql.OpenRecordset()   ' Recordset's cache size is also 20
```

By default, Jet caches one record at a time, while ODBCDirect's default cache size is 100 records.

Squeezing Out the Last Drop of Performance

There are a variety of ways to increase performance when working with server data. For example, Jet will establish separate connections for retrieving keys and data when creating recordsets against SQL Server. However, if a recordset has 100 records or fewer, Jet can fetch both its keys and its data on a single connection. As a result, if you can tune your application to fetch data in small "bites" of under 100 records, it will run faster.

The next few sections provide additional tidbits on boosting the performance of your applications against a server. The collection of techniques is by no means comprehensive, because different servers have different personalities, and different applications have different performance logjams. However, I'll touch on the most important areas for optimization.

Retrieving the Smallest Possible Dataset

When retrieving records from a server, the conventional wisdom that you apply to native Jet SQL requests also applies here: "Request the smallest possible number of rows and fields that will answer the stated question." Obviously, a request for a large dataset takes longer to process than one for a smaller set of data, due to these three factors:

Network Traffic. The volume of network traffic is increased by each field or row added to the result set.

Server Index Processing. The amount of work required by the server is proportional to the amount of data requested. For example, a server that uses clustered indexes to group data will return related ranges of data very fast (as in "WHERE `value` BETWEEN `nnn` AND `nnn`"), while broader requests like "WHERE `value` IN (`nnn`, `nnn`, `nnn`)" may require that the server visits several different, noncontiguous index pages.

Server Data Processing. Larger result sets require more spins of the disk on the server and more disk head movement to return the data. In the case of certain types of data, the data items might actually be located quite physically distant from their siblings, adding a significant amount of work for the server. For example, Text fields and Image fields in an SQL Server database are not stored with the remainder of the parent table's data and can significantly slow a data request when included in the result set.

19

The concept of requesting a small dataset may mean doing some experimentation. For example, a recordset operation may require data from a Text or Image field (let's call them "large fields") on an SQL Server. We've already discussed in this chapter that pulling the data from large fields into a recordset may be a poor performance choice. Instead, you could create a separate recordset pointing only to the large fields and fill the recordset on demand with only a few records as required, using the caching technique described previously in this chapter. You would want to try timing tests on this approach and then contrast its performance against the alternative approach of sending a new SQL request to the server for each large field and creating single-record result sets as required.

Selecting Specific Records

If you are creating a recordset from a server for the purpose of sequentially reviewing the returned data, DAO can move forward and backwards through the recordset (cursor) with ease. However, DAO cannot use the Seek method on a recordset created from ODBC data, and only a Jet-based recordset can use the Find methods. Thus if your intent is to jump around the recordset to specific records, you will be relying on either the Find methods and a Jet recordset, or creating a very small recordset and moving sequentially through it in search of specific records.

You have two options when trying to give Jet a fighting chance to perform well in such a scenario. The example I'll use to describe both of these options assumes that you want to locate the records for Carson, Greene, and Hunter within the authors SQL Server table.

Note

While this table provides the most convenient example within Pubs, it does not contain enough records to be a good example against which to run timing tests. You will have to create a much larger table in order to fully evaluate the worth of these techniques.

The options to create the fastest Find methods are:

Select a smaller dataset. Consider the situation where you open a recordset on the server's authors table using pass-through, then execute a FindFirst to find each author, as in this example:

```
Set rsql = dbs.OpenRecordset("qsptSelAuthors")
rsql.FindFirst "au_lname = 'Carson'"
rsql.FindFirst "au_lname = 'Greene'"
rsql.FindFirst "au_lname = 'Hunter'"
```

If the authors table was actually quite large and the au_lname field was not indexed, these operations could take a significant amount of time. It would be wiser to apply the FindFirst method against one or more indexed fields instead.

An alternative, and usually faster, approach would be to create a recordset for just the selected records, and to base the selection criteria upon their unique indexes. Assuming that you know the primary key values for the three authors, this code provides a better approach than using FindFirst:

```
Set qspt = dbs.CreateQueryDef("")
qspt.Connect = lci_gstrCurrentCnn
qspt.SQL = "SELECT * FROM authors WHERE" _
  & " au_id IN ('238-95-7766', '527-72-3246', '846-92-7186')"
qspt.ReturnsRecords = True
Set rsql = qspt.OpenRecordset(dbOpenSnapshot, dbSQLPassThrough)
```

It is plausible to assume that your code could even create *three different* recordsets from SQL statements or parameter queries, each with a WHERE clause that returned only one of the desired authors in less time than it would take to do three FindFirst operations against a non-indexed field in a server table. This advice is even more relevant to ODBCDirect data sets, which must be made as small as possible due to the lack of Find altogether.

Optimize the Find methods. If you specifically need to find records within a server-based recordset using FindFirst, Jet will optimize the find operation if your criteria is based on a single, indexed field, and it uses the = or LIKE operators to do the comparison. Thus, the first line below will be fast if au_id is an indexed field, and the second line shown will also be fast if the au_lname field is indexed, as seen here:

```
rsql.FindFirst "au_id = '238-95-7766'"
rsql.FindFirst "au_lname Like 'Car*'"
```

 Note

In the previous line of code, notice that the Jet asterisk wildcard (*) was used rather than the ANSI SQL wildcard (%), even though the recordset was created from a pass-through query. This is because the FindFirst operation is applied to the recordset at Jet's level, not at the server's, and thus must use Jet syntax. Jet will translate the * to a % before sending the query to the server so that the server can still evaluate the LIKE predicate.

The previous examples of FindFirst operations assumed that the recordset created from the server was a dynaset. If you are working with snapshots instead, very different logic applies. Because a snapshot is copied to your local drive, a FindFirst on a small snapshot will be quite speedy, even though it does not use indexes. Conversely, a find operation on a larger snapshot will not have the benefit of the server's indexes and will be slower than the dynaset examples I've just given.

 Note

The discussion in this section has used FindFirst in all examples, but is equally relevant to its siblings FindLast, FindNext, and FindPrevious.

Relocating Lookup Table Values

Lookup table values are used frequently within an application, so they are an immediate candidate for tuning when optimizing a client/server application. Master copies of lookup tables must be located on the server with the remainder of the data, for three reasons:

Database Integrity. The lookup data must be allowed to benefit from the same server assets as the other data tables, specifically referential integrity, validation, centralized backup and recovery, centralized administration, and so on.

Security. The security layer applied to entry/edit work on lookup tables should be no less robust than that applied to the remainder of the data.

Performance. Joins between a transaction table and a lookup table will always perform at the best possible level when both of the tables are located in the same database.

19

Despite these considerations, you will usually find that local lookup tables load combo and list boxes in forms faster than tables on the server. (For our purposes, a *local* table is one that is located in the application database or in another Jet database that is on the same machine as the application database and linked to it. A lookup table that is linked to its application database from a Jet back-end database on a file server is not considered local.)

Taking advantage of local lookup tables requires that you "clone" lookup tables from the server database to the client database, effectively creating your own (one-way) replication mechanism. See the section "Loading Lists from Local Tables" later in this chapter for a discussion of the issues involved in this strategy.

Wrapping Processes in Transactions

DAO is quite an intelligent tool when sending batch processes to a server. However, the way it defines a "batch" of work may not be as efficient or useful to your application as if you were to define the batch yourself. Thus, you will want to train DAO to manage server transaction commits and rollbacks for the maximum benefit of your application.

By default, each bulk query statement (DELETE, INSERT, and UPDATE) that you send to a server is wrapped by DAO in an ODBC transaction. Thus, DAO defines a single one of these statements as its default batch size for action queries. DAO will roll back the transaction if it detects from the server that the operation failed.

 Note

As opposed to action queries, Data Definition queries and other types of special statements sent to the server are not automatically wrapped in a transaction, and in many cases will not be wrapped in a transaction even if your code specifies one. This behavior varies by server. For example, SQL Server does not support a Data Definition statement inside a transaction.

When you use the DAO to perform recordset operations on a linked server table, Jet creates a larger batch than simply a single action—it places a transaction around all the operations for a given recordset. This is quite efficient and requires no work on your part. However, this implicit transaction cannot be rolled back.

Thus, the greatest degree of control of a data process is achieved when you manually build your own transaction, and place the events in it that you want to manage as a batch. When you create an explicit transaction on a Jet workspace, Jet uses your transaction model rather than its defaults (inasmuch as they don't openly conflict).

DAO translates your BeginTrans and CommitTrans method statements into the appropriate ODBC syntax and passes it to the server, so there is no need to include server-specific transaction statements in a pass-through query that is already nested in a DAO transaction. (In fact, this situation might actually prove dangerous by attempting to get the server to nest transactions when it cannot.)

 Note

In VBA, you can nest transactions inside each other when coding against the DAO. However, ODBC does not support nested transactions, so any levels of transactions other than the first one are ignored when DAO packages up the batch for ODBC. Thus, coding nested transactions in an ODBC client/server application is a waste of your time, as well as a small amount of VBA/Jet processing time.

19

As an example, assume that your system "checks out" or borrows records from the server into a local work table. The user edits these records, then runs a code process to replace the records on the server with the newly edited ones. Your code could create a transaction around the code containing all DELETE and INSERT statements that execute this plan.

The lines of code in Listing 19.14 show that a transaction targeted for the server is structured much like a standard transaction based on Jet tables. The code uses a simple Pubs example that mirrors the scenario of deleting and inserting a record. The example contains both Jet and ODBCDirect syntax.

Listing 19.14   AES_Srvr.Mdb—Wrapping Workspace Transactions Around a Server Process

```
' Jet example
Set wsp = DBEngine(0)
Set dbs = wsp(0)
 wsp.BeginTrans
   Set qspt = dbs.CreateQueryDef("")
   qspt.Connect = lci_gstrCurrentCnn
   qspt.ReturnsRecords = False
   qspt.SQL = "DELETE FROM discounts" _
     & " WHERE discounttype = 'Customer Discount'"
   qspt.Execute
   qspt.SQL = "INSERT INTO discounts" _
     & " VALUES ('customer discount', '8042', NULL, NULL, 5)"
   qspt.Execute dbFailOnError
 wsp.CommitTrans
```

continues

Listing 19.14   Continued

```
' ODBCDirect example
Set wsp = DBEngine.CreateWorkspace("", "", "", dbUseODBC)
Set cnn = wsp.OpenConnection("cnn", , , lci_gstrCurrentCnn)
wsp.BeginTrans
  Set qspt = cnn.CreateQueryDef("")
  qspt.SQL = "DELETE FROM discounts" _
    & " WHERE discounttype = 'Customer Discount'"
  qspt.Execute  ' Can't use dbFailOnError with ODBCDirect
  qspt.SQL = "INSERT INTO discounts" _
    & " VALUES ('customer discount', '8042', NULL, NULL, 5)"
  qspt.Execute
wsp.CommitTrans
```

Caution

Set the IsolateODBCTrans property on each individual Jet Workspace object if you are going to attempt to run parallel transactions against ODBC. By default, all workspaces share a single transaction space, so a CommitTrans method on one workspace may actually end a transaction on a different workspace. Setting the IsolateODBCTrans property to True tells Jet to keep a transaction buffer for each Workspace object.

Tip

You will want to be familiar with the record locking model of your server. Many servers lock records affected by a transaction and do not release the lock until the transaction ends. Thus one large transaction can effectively prevent other users from working with the affected data.

Jet does not commit an open transaction unless you explicitly tell it to do so. If there is no matching CommitTrans in your code to pair with an open BeginTrans, Jet initiates a roll back when the procedure ends. ODBCDirect transaction behavior is less predictable, because a transaction is initiated on and controlled by the server.

Determining What the Server Received

What happens at your birthday or the holidays after you make your gift list?

▶ You launch a process (shopping) in motion, but you don't see how the process is resolved.

▶ You may or may not get something (a gift) back from the process.

▶ What you get back (a gift) may or may not look like what you really wanted.

This series of events is similar to what happens when your application sends a data request to a server—what you get back, and when you will get it, may not be predictable. But worse, if you don't get what you asked for, you have no idea why.

On your birthday or the holidays, you can solve this problem by going shopping with your loved ones, knowing that an involvement in the process brings a higher probability that you'll get what you requested. The same is true of working with servers. You can ask Jet to take you on its "data shopping" errands by asking it to expose to you the actual requests it makes to the server. This is called *tracing*.

Trace mode is enabled by setting values in the system Registry. These values are stored in the tree \HKEY_LOCAL_MACHINE\SOFTWARE\Microsoft\Jet\3.5\Engines\ODBC. Two trace mode values can be placed in this key:

TraceSQLMode. This Registry value is of type DWORD and has a value of either 0 (tracing is off) or 1 (tracing is on). When tracing is on, Jet will write a copy of the requests it sends to the ODBC driver into a file called SQLOUT.TXT. This file is located in the default directory (your "personal folder") for new databases.

TraceODBCAPI. This Registry value is of type DWORD and also has a value of 0 (tracing is off) or 1 (tracing is on). When tracing is on, the workings of the ODBC API are logged to a disk file ODBCAPI.TXT, also in the default new database directory.

Figure 19.14 shows the Windows Registry structure where you will find or create these keys.

Tip

When tracing ODBC calls, you may find the process easier if your requests go to the server synchronously. To enable this, create or find the key called DisableAsync (of type DWORD) in the same ODBC folder of the Registry as shown previously. Set this key's value to 1 to disable asynchronous queries. Remember to set this key back to 0 when you are done tracing to get the best performance from future ODBC calls.

Fig. 19.14

If the ODBC section of the Jet tree in the Windows Registry does not already contain the two keys for ODBC tracing, you can add them yourself.

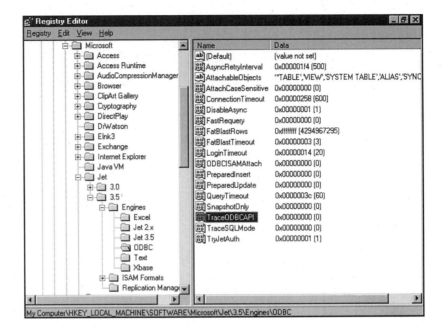

Let's send a simple request to the server and review the information in the log files. The SQL statement we'll send as a pass-through query from Jet is:

```
SELECT emp_id, fname, lname
FROM employee
WHERE job_lvl >200;
```

This SQL statement generates the following information in the SQLOUT.TXT log file:

```
SQLExecDirect:
  SELECT emp_id, fname, lname
  FROM employee
  WHERE job_lvl > 200;
```

Notice that the pass-through operation from Jet did exactly what was expected—it passed the SQL string unmodified directly to the ODBC driver. Jet sent the SQL request to the SQLExecDirect() ODBC function. This function passes the received string directly to the server with no parsing or preprocessing.

The abridged contents of the ODBCAPI.TXT trace file for the example SQL statement are shown in Listing 19.15, with my annotations.

Note

I have removed trace details (memory handles and so on) and duplicate statements that are not relevant to this discussion from the listing. I also have not dissected the individual attributes of each ODBC function in the listing, but instead have commented the file at a broader level. I've used apostrophe-marked comments and VBA-style line continuation markers to make the listing more readable; these characters are not in the actual log file.

Listing 19.15   Contents of the ODBCAPI.TXT Trace File After Running a Simple Pass-through *SELECT* Statement

```
' Establish a connection
SQLAllocEnv
  RETURN:   0 (SQL_SUCCESS)
SQLAllocConnect
  RETURN:   0 (SQL_SUCCESS)
SQLSetConnectOption
  RETURN:   0 (SQL_SUCCESS)
SQLDriverConnectW
  ARGUMENT: "DSN=Pubs;UID=sa;PWD=;DATABASE=pubs"
  ARGUMENT: <SQL_DRIVER_NOPROMPT>
  RETURN:   1 (SQL_SUCCESS_WITH_INFO)

' Check the attributes of the connection
SQLGetInfo
  ARGUMENT: <SQL_ODBC_API_CONFORMANCE>
  RETURN:   0 (SQL_SUCCESS)
SQLGetInfo
  ARGUMENT: 6 <SQL_DRIVER_NAME>
  RETURN:   [12] "SQLSRV32.DLL"
  ' The number in brackets above is the byte length of the return string
SQLGetInfo
  ARGUMENT: <SQL_TXN_CAPABLE>
  RETURN:   0 (SQL_SUCCESS)
SQLGetInfo
  ARGUMENT: <SQL_CURSOR_COMMIT_BEHAVIOR>
  RETURN:   0 (SQL_SUCCESS)
SQLGetInfo
  ARGUMENT: <SQL_CURSOR_ROLLBACK_BEHAVIOR>
  RETURN:   0 (SQL_SUCCESS)
SQLGetInfo
  ARGUMENT: <SQL_ACTIVE_STATEMENTS>
  RETURN:   0 (SQL_SUCCESS)

' Create a statement handle for passing statements
SQLSetConnectOption
  RETURN:   0 (SQL_SUCCESS)
```

continues

19

Listing 19.15   Continued

```
SQLAllocStmt
  RETURN:    0 (SQL_SUCCESS)
  RETURN:    HSTMT = 0x030c2920

' Once a statement handle is returned (a pointer to a connection),
'   the pointer is passed by Jet to each ODBC request from here onward
'   as in the following argument
SQLGetStmtOption
  ARGUMENT: 0x030c2920
  RETURN:    0 (SQL_SUCCESS)
SQLSetStmtOption
  RETURN:    0 (SQL_SUCCESS)

' Check for the configuration table
' See the section "Setting Jet Options on the Server" later in this chapter
SQLExecDirect
  ARGUMENT: "SELECT Config, nValue FROM MSysConf"
  RETURN:   -1 (SQL_ERROR)
SQLError
  RETURN:    0 (SQL_SUCCESS)  ' Informational—not fatal—error
  RETURN:    [78] "[Microsoft][ODBC SQL Server Driver][SQL Server] _
                  Invalid object name 'MSysConf'."
SQLError
  RETURN:  100 (SQL_NO_DATA_FOUND)

' Drop the statement handle to the invalid table
SQLFreeStmt
  ARGUMENT: 0x030c2920
  ARGUMENT: <SQL_DROP>
  RETURN:    0 (SQL_SUCCESS)

' Create a new statement handle
SQLAllocStmt
  RETURN:    0 (SQL_SUCCESS)
  RETURN:    0x030c2920
  ' Note that ODBC reuses the previous handle for efficiency
SQLGetStmtOption
  RETURN:    0 (SQL_SUCCESS)
SQLSetStmtOption
  RETURN:    0 (SQL_SUCCESS)
SQLGetStmtOption
  RETURN:    0 (SQL_SUCCESS)
SQLSetStmtOption
  RETURN:    0 (SQL_SUCCESS)

' Create a cursor to the desired table data
SQLExecDirect
  ARGUMENT: "SELECT emp_id, fname, lname FROM EmployeeWHERE job_lvl > 200;"
  RETURN:    0 (SQL_SUCCESS)

' Get information about the query result set
SQLNumResultCols
  RETURN:    0 (SQL_SUCCESS)
  RETURN:    3  ' Number of fields in result set
SQLGetInfo
```

```
  ARGUMENT: <SQL_DBMS_NAME>
  RETURN:    0 (SQL_SUCCESS)
  RETURN:    [20] "Microsoft SQL Server"
SQLDescribeCol
  ARGUMENT: 1   ' Column number
  RETURN:    0 (SQL_SUCCESS)
  RETURN:    [6] "emp_id"  ' Name of column 1
  ' The number in brackets above is the byte length of the return string
SQLDescribeCol
  ARGUMENT: 2
  RETURN:    0 (SQL_SUCCESS)
  RETURN:    [5] "fname"
SQLDescribeCol
  ARGUMENT: 3
  RETURN:    0 (SQL_SUCCESS)
  RETURN:    [5] "lname"

' Retrieve one record and its fields
SQLFetch
  RETURN:    0 (SQL_SUCCESS)
SQLGetData
  ARGUMENT: 1   ' Column number
  RETURN:    0 (SQL_SUCCESS)
  RETURN:    [9] "F-C16315M"  ' Row 1, column 1 data value
SQLGetData
  ARGUMENT: 2
  RETURN:    0 (SQL_SUCCESS)
  RETURN:    [9] "Francisco"
SQLGetData
  ARGUMENT: 3
  RETURN:    0 (SQL_SUCCESS)
  RETURN:    [5] "Chang"

' Retrieve the next record
SQLFetch
  RETURN:    0 (SQL_SUCCESS)
SQLGetData
  ARGUMENT: 1
  RETURN:    0 (SQL_SUCCESS)
  RETURN:    [9] "PTC11962M"  ' Row 2, column 1 data value

...
' The fetch/read process continues for all records

' The final fetch goes to the end of the cursor
SQLFetch
  RETURN:    100 (SQL_NO_DATA_FOUND)

' Release the statement handle and connection
SQLFreeStmt
  ARGUMENT: 0x030c2920
  ARGUMENT: 1 <SQL_DROP>
  RETURN:    0 (SQL_SUCCESS)
SQLDisconnect
  RETURN:    0 (SQL_SUCCESS)
SQLFreeConnect
  RETURN:    0 (SQL_SUCCESS)
```

19

The first few lines of the trace file contain the initial "handshaking" between Jet and the remote database. Jet first creates a connection, then a *statement handle* within the connection, which is a buffer for sending the SQL string to the server and for retrieving the records back from the server. Jet asks the buffer for information about what the server has sent (columns and rows), then the records are fetched individually as Jet needs them to populate its own record set.

Notice how much work Jet is doing for you "behind the curtain." Jet handles all the communication of your Access request to the ODBC driver, and all the retrieval of data through the driver from the server.

Let's look at a more complex example now, where Jet is sending a request to the server but is basing the request on a linked table `tsqlJobs` and not using pass-through. Here is the SQL statement:

```
SELECT job_id, job_desc, min_lvl, max_lvl
FROM tsqlJobs
WHERE tsqlJobs.min_lvl > 100;
```

For the purposes of this example, I executed the following steps:

▶ Ran this SQL statement as a saved query.

▶ Edited one record in the query datasheet.

▶ Closed the datasheet.

The information in the SQLOUT.TXT proves insightful. Listing 19.16 shows a summary of the relevant SQL submissions logged in the trace file.

Listing 19.16   Contents of the SQLOUT.TXT Trace File After Running a Query on a Linked Table and Editing the Data

```
SQLExecDirect:
  SELECT "dbo"."jobs"."job_id"
  FROM "dbo"."jobs"
  WHERE ("min_lvl" > 100 )

SQLPrepare:
  SELECT "job_id","job_desc","min_lvl","max_lvl"
  FROM "dbo"."jobs"
  WHERE "job_id" = ? OR "job_id" = ? OR "job_id" = ? OR "job_id" = ?
    OR "job_id" = ? OR "job_id" = ? OR "job_id" = ? OR "job_id" = ?
    OR "job_id" = ? OR "job_id" = ?

SQLExecute:
  (MULTI-ROW FETCH)

SQLPrepare:
  SELECT "job_id","job_desc","min_lvl","max_lvl"
  FROM "dbo"."jobs"
  WHERE "job_id" = ?
```

```
SQLExecute:
  (GOTO BOOKMARK)

SQLExecDirect:
  UPDATE "dbo"."jobs"
  SET "max_lvl"=?
  WHERE "job_id" = ? AND "job_desc" = ? AND "min_lvl" = ?
    AND "max_lvl" = ?
```

Compare this listing to the one from the prior example and you will notice these significant differences:

▸ *Jet does cleanup.* While Jet sent the pass-through query to the driver untouched, it sends a *compiled* query with extra information added. Jet has rewritten the query according to the attributes described to it by the ODBC driver. This includes items such as the table owner name (FROM "dbo"."jobs").

▸ *Jet fetches indexes.* When Jet needed to build a snapshot (from the pass-through statement), it only fetched the data. When working with a linked table, however, Jet is able to build a dynaset-type recordset. As a result, Jet must make an initial request to the server for the indexes of all of the selected records (the first SQLExecDirect call requesting the job_id field). This is because Jet builds a separate recordset for index values apart from the data recordset. This enables Jet to perform two significant operations for your benefit:

  1. *Buffering the data requests for best performance.* Jet initially retrieves only a small amount of data to display or populate your DAO Recordset object (in this case the first SQLPrepare statement asks for ten records). As you need more data (moving through a datasheet manually or a recordset programmatically), Jet uses the indexes to efficiently fetch another block of records.

  2. *Writing data to the server.* In order for you to be able to edit a record and send the edits to the server, Jet uses the record's indexes to check if the requested record can be edited, fetch the latest copy when you need it, and to send the changed record as an update back to the server.

▸ *Jet creates a prepared statement.* When Jet needs to simply execute a statement one time, it calls the SQLExecDirect function, which passes the request through to the server. However, when Jet learned that I intended to *edit* data in the datasheet, it decided to create a *prepared statement* and pass it to ODBC (using SQLPrepare). A *prepared statement* is pre-processed (grammar-checked and so on) by ODBC so that future uses of the statement will run faster by requiring no further checking. This is Jet's way of helping ODBC cache a frequently used statement.

  Next, Jet fetches the latest version of the record I want to edit by calling SQLExecute, which replaces the key value parameter with the ID of my record and runs the prepared statement.

> ▶ *Jet sends the updated record.* Finally, Jet takes my updates to the record and posts
> them to the server using another SQLExecDirect call, but this time with an UPDATE
> statement containing the changed value. Note that only the changed field is sent,
> not the entire record; this is a true reflection of the minimalist approach of an
> efficient client/server environment. Jet wraps the update in an explicit transaction,
> as can be seen in the following listing.

Listing 19.17 summarizes the contents of the ODBC trace file for the current data
request. I've included only the core statements from the trace file. All server processes
include events to establish a connection, retrieve the connection attributes, create statement handles, and release resources. Each of these tasks was shown in Listing 19.16 so I
have removed them from the following listing to keep it uncomplicated. I have also
removed many of the duplicate statements from the trace file for brevity and included
comments in their places.

**Listing 19.17   Contents of the ODBCAPI.TXT Trace File After Running a
Query on a Linked Table and Editing the Data**

```
' Fetch the initial key values into a keyset
SQLExecDirect
  ARGUMENT: "SELECT "dbo"."jobs"."job_id"
            FROM "dbo"."jobs"
            WHERE ("min_lvl" > 100 )"

' Get a record from the cursor
SQLFetch
' Get the index field from the record
SQLGetData

...
' Fetch/GetData repeat six times, once per index record,
'    until all index values are in the cache

' Create a prepared statement for filling the buffer
SQLPrepare
ARGUMENT: "SELECT "job_id", "job_desc", "min_lvl", "max_lvl"
            FROM "dbo"."jobs"
            WHERE "job_id" = ? OR "job_id" = ? OR "job_id" = ? _
              OR "job_id" = ? OR "job_id" = ? OR "job_id" = ? _
              OR "job_id" = ? OR "job_id" = ? OR "job_id" = ? _
              OR "job_id" = ?"

' Replace the ? parameters in the prepared statement above
'    with the actual values for the SELECT
SQLBindParameter
  ARGUMENT: 1  ' Bind a job_id from the keyset to the first argument
SQLBindParameter
  ARGUMENT: 2  ' Bind a job_id from the keyset to the second argument

...
```

```
' BindParameter repeats ten times, once for each job_id key value in
'    the keyset plus four dummies to fill out all ten

' Execute the prepared statement
SQLExecute

' Get a record from the cursor
SQLFetch
' Get the data values
SQLGetData
  ARGUMENT: 1  ' Retrieve first column
SQLGetData
  ARGUMENT: 2  ' Retrieve secon column
SQLGetData
  ARGUMENT: 3
SQLGetData
  ARGUMENT: 4

...
' Fetch/GetData repeats six times, once for each record; this
'    populates the datasheet

' At this point, I edit the first record in the datasheet

' Check the record for currency
' Before doing an UPDATE, Jet checks the record to see if has
'    has been edited by someone else or still matches the record
'    in the buffer
SQLPrepare
  ARGUMENT: "SELECT "job_id","job_desc","min_lvl","max_lvl"
             FROM "dbo"."jobs"
             WHERE "job_id" = ?"

' Replace the ? parameter in the previous statement with the
'    key value of the edited record
SQLBindParameter
  ARGUMENT: 1 ' Bind job_id for edited record to the argument

' Retrieve the record
SQLExecute
' Get a record from the cursor
SQLFetch
' Get the data values
SQLGetData
  ARGUMENT: 1

...
' GetData repeats four times, once for each field

' Comparison complete, okay to UPDATE

' Replace the ? parameters in the upcoming statement with the
'    appropriate values
SQLBindParameter
  ARGUMENT: 1  ' Bind first parameter to new max_lvl
```

19

continues

Listing 19.17   Continued

```
SQLBindParameter
  ARGUMENT: 2  ' Bind second parameter to job_id
SQLBindParameter
  ARGUMENT: 3
SQLBindParameter
  ARGUMENT: 4
SQLBindParameter
  ARGUMENT: 5

' Send the edited record to the server
SQLExecDirect
  ARGUMENT: "UPDATE "dbo"."jobs"
            SET "max_lvl"=?
            WHERE "job_id" = ? AND "job_desc" = ?
              AND "min_lvl" = ? AND "max_lvl" = ?"

' See if one row was affected
SQLRowCount

' Commit the transaction
SQLTransact
```

Why is it important to understand this communication process from client to server and back? Because once you comprehend it, you can review how Jet communicates your more complex statements to the server and gain insight into how to optimize the process. Even if you don't understand the ODBC function statements themselves, you can see the fetches of data and the SQL statements in these trace files and gain a greater understanding of how your application requests records.

For example, if you send a complex join for a report to the server and the processing is slow, reading the trace files will help you gain insight as to whether or not Jet sent the complete query to the server, or instead fetched data in "bite-sized chunks" and processed the query locally.

 Tip

After a long day of debugging, remember to delete your trace log files ODBCAPI.TXT and SQLOUT.TXT and to reset the tracing Registry keys before you go home. You'll forget about them by the next day and the log files will get large very quickly if tracing is left on unintentionally.

Using Access Forms Against a Server

In the past two years, we've created for one of our larger clients about a half-dozen Access applications that were each intended to be migrated to SQL Server within a year of creation. Consequently, we designed the applications with a client/server model in mind. In the end, the client's IT group decided that they were not ready to support our SQL Server databases yet, and these projects all stayed in Access. Because they were designed to move to a server, they are performing more slowly in Jet than we would like.

Mind you, we always try to do our best job on every project, but an application written to one model is not always optimized for another model. In the case of client/server applications, we usually "over-engineer" the system in several ways, expecting that the speed and capabilities of the server will compensate for the extra baggage. Here are four examples:

Manual Locking. We often create manual record locking systems in order to have finer control of user locks, error messages, and transactions.

Super-normalized. Database servers generally provide more CPU horsepower, larger drives, and bigger caches than file servers. Consequently, we can completely normalize a data structure and create scores of relation tables to track all conceivable many-to-many relationships. By contrast, in a Jet-based system we will often cheat for performance by convincing the users to let us simplify the data structure.

Bulk Operations. We make judicious use of transactions, and often do manual locking and advance lock-checking in order to ensure the success of record-altering operations before they are sent.

Minimal Dependence on Jet. We will not use coding techniques specific to Jet but disallowed when working with servers, such as the Seek method.

These engineering decisions often add code or complexity that de-optimizes the application when run under Jet, but enhances performance when working against a server.

Additionally, an application is usually selected as a candidate for a client/server model by virtue of a large amount of users or records. Leaving the data in Jet long after the record or user volume exceeds a comfortable level is one sure way to run slowly.

The moral of this story is that it's always nice to have an application ready to migrate to a client/server model, but constructing an application for a database server and then running it indefinitely on a file server is not a positive scenario.

When creating Access applications for use against a server, there are several general rules-of-thumb that can be applied to make the technology partnership run smoothly. The simple techniques include:

19

Use good naming conventions. Server databases are quite particular about object names, and you may have to work quite hard to move a non-server database to a server if the naming conventions you originally used are not supported by the server.

 Tip

Follow the naming conventions in Chapter 6, "Leszynski Naming Conventions for Access," and Appendix C on the CD-ROM to ensure that your database structure is "server-compatible" when migrated.

Index your data. A small database stored in Jet and running on fast machines may be able to perform adequately without indexes. When moved to the server, however, the indexing model will determine how efficiently Jet retrieves the data, and whether or not the data can be edited.

Bypass Jet when you can. Review your existing Access applications that interact with server data to determine if recordset operations performed in code can be moved from a Jet workspace to an ODBCDirect workspace. This should buy you a measurable performance gain and defer the time at which the application slows to an unusable state.

Do not rely on technology unsupported by the server. In a phrase, "Think SQL." There is more than one way to perform recordset operations in an Access application, but when you create applications with growth potential, you should rely on SQL statements over their VBA or DAO alternatives.

Design backwards. If your application is starting small but going to get bigger, plan for the "bigness" in advance and let the five year vision for the application be a factor in all architectural decisions. (I stress the importance of good planning and an understanding of a product's lifecycle in Chapter 3, "Preparing for Development.")

In addition to these general guidelines, there are plenty of nuances when working with server data, many of which are detailed earlier in this chapter. The next few sections discuss additional concepts specific to the architecture of forms in Access client/server applications.

Providing Records to Forms

Access forms are the cornerstone of your application, and also the biggest performance bottleneck. In order to work with server data, some minor paradigm shifts must take place. You must weigh each of these considerations as you design your forms:

Where are the performance concerns? For example, ComboBox and ListBox controls are a significant performance anchor weighing down your forms. While you can get away with large combo lists or complex callback functions when working against local data, moving the data to a server may mean a restructuring of your approach.

What is the composition of the data? A simple form dataset based on a table or inner join will probably open as swiftly off of a server link as from Jet data. In contrast, forms with multiple subforms may run more slowly with server data than Jet data depending on the index configuration, the type of data, and your form logic. Similarly, a form with a complex join may provide an editable recordset from Jet, but will be read-only when directed against a server.

How will relationships be managed? Without the luxury of Jet's relationships, your forms will have more difficulty performing cascading updates or deletes, or displaying the most current data.

How will users select records? Allowing users to open a form on a large recordset and "browse" may not be the most efficient interface model once data moves to the server. Similarly, you may need to stop relying on the Find methods or row-fixup to help users navigate to a different record in the form's recordset, and instead provide interfaces which enable the user to identify the target records in advance of opening the form.

How will security be managed? Jet's security model does not propagate onto the server—servers have their own security engine. A number of overlapping processes may be at work when the server, Jet, ODBCDirect, and the Access' forms engine are all trying to communicate security concerns back and forth.

When tying your forms to server data, your options are different than those when working with Jet data. The most significant difference is the decision as to whether or not server tables will be linked to your database and forms built on the links. If you select this strategy, your architectural decisions are basically behind you and pulling your application together becomes quite straightforward.

If, on the other hand, you intend to take into account the various techniques discussed in this chapter, your decision-making and development processes become more complex. For example, you must consider all of the following options for providing data to forms. Each option has strong and weak points.

▶ *Browse with snapshots.* You can create forms that are read-only and therefore create a snapshot of records. Small server snapshots are built quickly and such a form should load with reasonable swiftness. Set the value of the RecordsetType property to Snapshot for a form pointing to a table link to force this behavior, or base the form on a pass-through query, which is never editable.

▶ *Retrieve a single record at a time.* You must find a balance when applying this technique. On one hand, if your users need to browse multiple records with the form, it is more efficient to create a record source for the form that grabs all of the records at once than to repeatedly requery the form to fetch additional records. On the other hand, if users most often need to find a specific record, provide them a means to enter or select a specific record key and fetch only that record into the form. Loading a form with either more or fewer records than the user really needs is wasteful. Review Chapter 16, "Presenting Data to Users," for insights on how to optimize your application interface for performance and friendliness.

▶ *Open your forms unbound.* Do not open a form against a record source that is not appropriate for the user. In other words, do not open a form with a data record displayed simply for the sake of showing data. It is better to open a form with no record source, so that it loads quickly, and then alter the RecordSource property through code and requery when the user or code has decided which record is needed. For example, the data selection model I define in Chapter 16 (built around "Get" forms) is highly efficient in a client/server model.

▶ *Work with local data.* In some cases, it is easier to create your forms against local work tables and to batch the work of pulling records into the tables ("checking-out" from the server) and sending records back (with bulk updates). Working with local tables is especially useful in situations where a form is used only for data entry.

 Note

As mentioned earlier in this chapter, Jet relies on the server's locking methodology, not its own. Because most servers utilize optimistic locking, the setting for the RecordLocks property on your server-based forms should always be No Locks (the All Records setting is not allowed for remote data and Edited Record is ignored).

The various coding techniques required to create form record sources are covered earlier in this chapter.

Shifting the Data Entry Work Locally

Forms designed specifically for data entry do not necessarily need to point to server tables. Because an entry form does not fetch records, it can be tied to a local table that provides the appropriate validation, then an entire data entry batch can be moved from the local database to the server when complete.

> **χ** **Caution**
>
> Note the key word in the previous sentence: *validation*. Do *not* proceed with the following technique unless you have a good strategy in place for keeping your Access form and table validation in sync with the server's validation.

To enable such a local data entry strategy, follow these steps:

1. In the interface (client) database, create tables that match the exact structure of the target tables on the server.
2. Create validation rules in the tables that mirror the rules in the server.
3. Design data entry forms that tie to the local work tables.
4. Create any nonlinear validation that exceeds Jet's capabilities for business rules as form code (in other words, reproduce rules in VBA code that are enforced as stored procedures or triggers on the server).

When the user makes a menu selection to create a new batch of records, your application can either:

▶ Clear the work tables in preparation for a new batch (if they were not already cleared after the previous batch was posted).

▶ Create a unique batch identifier and assign it to each record entered in the batch. Using the batch identifier, only records in the specified batch should be copied to the server.

At the end of the batch entry process, the user closes the primary entry form or clicks a button that signifies that it is time to "post" the batch to the server. Your application must save any unsaved batch records, complete any pending validation, and then bundle up the batch records into a package and send it to the server. The entire batch of records should be sent to the server inside a transaction that either succeeds or fails as a unit.

> **α** **Note**
>
> The discussion in the "Inserting Records on the Server" section earlier in this chapter will clarify the options you have for posting the local records to the server.

The gaping hole in this strategy as described is exposed by the jobs table in Pubs, the source of many examples in this chapter. The table has an auto-increment field (of SQL

Server type Identity) that provides each job with a new number automatically. If your forms or application routines send records to the table with INSERT statements, this presents your application with two problems:

What numbers were assigned? If your code were to insert a batch of records into the remote table, the job_id values would be assigned by the server but would not be sent back to your application. Your application would have to work quite hard to get the assigned numbers back from the server, because simply looking at the last records in the jobs table does not guarantee that you are looking at *your* records. (Consider a high-volume database, where perhaps ten more jobs were inserted by other people an instant after yours.)

How do I maintain relations? The job_id field in Pubs is found not only in the jobs table but in the employees table. Assuming that your application wanted to insert both a job and its related employee records in a single batch, how would it know which job numbers to place in the employees table records, because the numbers are not assigned until the records are sent to the server?

The solution to these problems is actually quite complex. Essentially, you need to pre-assign server record numbers to records that you are creating locally, or you need to teach the server to handle your incoming batch and to process it for you. These approaches are described in the next two sections.

Pre-Assigning Record Numbers for Data Entry

Pre-assigning a record number from the server to the client is not always an appropriate approach, because to pre-assign a record ID number you must create a placeholder record on the server. Once the dummy record is created, it will show up in queries, reports, datasheets, and so on. Thus your bogus record essentially "pollutes" the database until plugged with the final values.

However, because pre-assigning is easier to manage then post-assigning, it *is* a worthwhile technique in the case of transaction records that feed to a transaction table. In other words, creating placeholder records is an acceptable strategy for server tables whose only purpose is to queue transactions for processing, and not to display records to users. During processing batches, any bogus records (unused placeholders) on the server are simply not carried into master data tables.

When creating placeholder records, you will need to create dummy field values that satisfy the validation requirements of the table on the server. In doing so, your data may look "live" when it really is not. To prevent the misinterpretation of a placeholder record, always include a "flag" field in your server record that says whether it is a placeholder or live data. Any server processes that run against the table must be taught to ignore the records currently flagged as placeholders.

As an example, assume that you have 100 order entry clerks taking orders in an Access application that is connected to server data. In order to minimize connections, lock contentions, and network traffic, you've designed the application to send a record or batch of records to the server via bulk inserts. This application would benefit from the ability to reserve one or more record numbers on the server, do local data entry, and then post the entry batch into the placeholders when complete. Overnight, the server should run routines that check the transaction tables for unused placeholder records (these indicate records that the user did not successfully post). It should also take records that *were* successfully posted and move them into production tables.

 Note

Reserving ID values is especially important in data entry situations where a "paper trail" is kept for auditing purposes. In the current example, if the clerks were keying in orders from hard copy, having the record number in advance would allow them to write the table record number on the hard copy when keying a record into the form.

Although the technique of pre-assigning record numbers *before or during* data entry can be used in a variety of ways, it works best under this combination of circumstances:

1. *A Single-record Batch.* In this scenario, the user will be adding one record at a time, then the record will be sent to the server. Thus, the placeholder record does not exist on the server for very long, and you do not often confront the problems of creating or deleting *multiple* placeholders.

2. *No Dependencies.* If the entered record is not going to be the parent to multiple child records, it is easy to make use of a single pre-assigned ID number. However, if the form will enable the entry of child records, and the child table has an Identity field on the server as well, you will not know how many record numbers to pre-assign for the children before data entry begins. You will have to pre-assign child record IDs as well, as each child is created. This unfortunately creates complex groups of placeholder records sitting on the server.

To pre-assign a record number, run a stored procedure on the server that creates a dummy record in the target table and returns to you the ID of the added record as a message. You can pre-assign the record number in one of two locations in the application flow:

▶ *Before the form is opened.* Once the user has indicated an intent to add a record, you can retrieve the next record number from the server before opening the form, and pass it to the form, perhaps as an OpenArgs property argument.

Alternatively, you can insert a placeholder record with the designated number into the local work table and open the form for *editing* against the table instead of entry.

Caution

If you pre-seed a work table with only a single record, you must make certain that the user cannot add additional records through the form. Set the form's `AllowAdditions` property to `False`.

▸ *Before a new record is added.* You can make use of the form's `BeforeInsert` event to detect the user's intention to create a new record, and fetch an ID number from the server within that event procedure.

Of course, once the user has completed entry of a record using the assigned ID value, your code must post the data to the server. Because you've already created a dummy record on the server, you will be using an UPDATE statement to send the user's values to the dummy record rather than appending a record with INSERT.

Note

Remember that your form must enable the user to undo the record entry process by selecting a "Delete" or "Discard" option of some sort on the form. In this situation, you must delete the record in progress in the local work table, *and* you must also delete the placeholder record that was created on the server, or cleverly reuse the placeholder for the next record entered.

This example illustrates these concepts using the Pubs database. First, a stored procedure is created on the server to insert the placeholder record:

```
CREATE PROCEDURE prcNextJobID
AS
DECLARE @ID char(6)
INSERT INTO jobs (job_desc, min_lvl, max_lvl)
  VALUES ('Dummy', 10, 10)
SELECT @ID =  '>>' + CONVERT(char(6), @@identity)
PRINT @ID
```

There are three important features to note about this server procedure:

▸ The dummy record is *flagged* as a dummy with a string Dummy in the `job_desc` field. (This is my best option given the Pubs structure. In your database, you would probably want to create a `Boolean` flag field instead.)

▶ The procedure returns the ID of the inserted record as a message back to Access (using the SQL Server global variable @@identity in this example).

 Note

See the section "Checking Messages Returned by the Server" earlier in this chapter for information on how the DAO can be taught to handle returned server messages.

▶ The dummy record must survive the target table's validation. In this example, the values for min_lvl and max_lvl in the table cannot be less than 10—thus my choice for plugging that value into those fields.

Next, create a simple pass-through query qsptAppNextJobID to call the stored procedure, with the single line:

```
prcNextJobID
```

Saving this call in a query allows you to use the stored procedure from code more easily than with the alternative method of creating a temporary QueryDef each time the procedure is to be run. However, a temporary QueryDef built on an ODBCDirect workspace may provide enough performance improvement over Jet to warrant bypassing the saved query.

Next, create a work table that mirrors the structure of jobs on the server. This table (tblJobs) has the same field names and validation rules as the server data, and will be used as the record source for an entry form. Finally, create a form based on the work table tblJobs and place code like that shown in Listing 19.18 in the form's module.

Listing 19.18   AES_Srvr.Mdb—Routines that Create a Placeholder Record on the Server and Assign the Record ID to the Form Record

```
' This routine is initiated when the user begins typing a new record
Private Sub Form_BeforeInsert(Cancel As Integer)
' Purpose: Assign a job number to the record

Dim lngID As Long
DoCmd.Hourglass True
lngID = cbfNextJobID()   ' Assign the ID
If lngID <> 0 Then
  Me!txtjob_id = lngID
Else
  Cancel = True
End If
DoCmd.Hourglass False

End Sub
```

continues

Listing 19.18   Continued

```
' This routine fetches the next ID number
Function cbfNextJobID() As Long
' Purpose: Add placeholder record to server table and return ID value
' Returns: Next ID number or 0 on failure

    Const cstrProc As String = "cbfNextJobID"
    On Error GoTo cbfNextJobID_Err

    Dim dbs  As Database
    Dim qspt As QueryDef
    Dim rsql As Recordset
    Dim str  As String

    Set dbs = CurrentDb

    ' Delete the messages table if it exists
    On Error Resume Next
    dbs.TableDefs.Delete CurrentUser & " - 00"
    On Error GoTo cbfNextJobID_Err

    ' Run the stored procedure to create the dummy record
    Set qspt = dbs.QueryDefs("qsptAppNextJobID")
    qspt.Execute dbFailOnError

    ' Get the ID number from the message table
    ' In your application, add code here to trap if the table doesn't exist
    '  or is empty
    Set rsql = dbs.OpenRecordset(CurrentUser & " - 00")
    rsql.MoveFirst
    str = Trim(Mid(rsql!ODBC, InStr(rsql!ODBC, ">>") + 2))
    ' In your application, add code here to make sure a Long was returned
    cbfNextJobID = CLng(str)
    Exit Function

cbfNextJobID_Err:
    Call lci_ErrMsgStd(Me.Name & "." & cstrProc, Err.Number, Err.Description, _
      , True)
    Exit Function

End Function
```

When the user begins keying a new record, the Form_BeforeInsert() event fires, a place-holder record is created on the server, and its ID number is displayed on the form. Figure 19.15 shows the results of this process.

When the user has completed data entry for the form, he or she clicks the Post button on the form and the form's data is sent to the dummy record on the server. Fields in the placeholder record shown in the figure are modified with their new values by an UPDATE statement. The code for this process is shown in Listing 19.19. Notice that the code first saves the edits in the form to the local work table. This validates the record before any attempt is made to send it to the server. Validation could also be provided by form code and the work table would not be necessary. Alternatively, each record could be saved to the work table after entry and all new records could be queued up and updated on the server by a bulk process.

Fig. 19.15

A form that is bound to a local entry table but whose record ID is assigned by creating a server placeholder record.

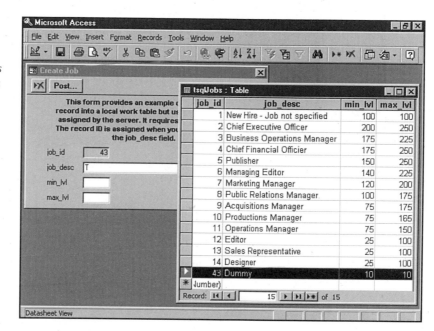

Listing 19.19   AES_Srvr.Mdb—Updating a Placeholder Record on the Server with Form Values

```
Private Sub cmdPost_Click()
' Purpose: Send the edits to the server
'          This routine could alternately be coded against ODBCDirect
'
  Dim dbs  As Database
  Dim qspt As QueryDef
  Dim wsp  As Workspace

  RunCommand acCmdSaveRecord  ' Save the record to validate it

  Set wsp = DBEngine(0)
  Set dbs = wsp(0)

  wsp.IsolateODBCTrans = True  ' Prevent overlapping transactions
  wsp.BeginTrans
    Set qspt = dbs.CreateQueryDef("")
    qspt.Connect = lci_gstrCurrentCnn
    qspt.ReturnsRecords = False
    ' The example here sends one record to the server
    ' It can pull the record's values from either the form or its table
```

continues

Listing 19.19   Continued

```
    ' In this example, the data is pulled from the form
    ' In the case of a form that allows multiple batch transactions,
    '   the batch records would be appended from the work table to
    '   the server as the form closes
    qspt.SQL = "UPDATE jobs SET job_desc = '" & Me!txtjob_desc _
      & "', min_lvl = " & Me!txtmin_lvl _
      & ", max_lvl = " & Me!txtmax_lvl & " WHERE job_id = " _
      & Me!txtjob_id
    qspt.Execute dbFailOnError
  wsp.CommitTrans

  RunCommand acCmdRecordsGoToNew  ' Ready for another one

End Sub
```

Assigning Record Numbers After Data Entry

Assigning record numbers *after* data entry is the best solution when the data entry process is complicated, involving multiple tables and record dependencies. The downside to this strategy is that the user does not see the final record ID value on the form while data entry is occurring, because the number is not yet assigned. On the positive side of the coin, the application can discard an abandoned entry process by simply clearing the local work tables. This does not encumber the server with the addition or deletion of placeholder records.

When you implement this scenario, you can send all of the records to the server in a batch, or send records individually. The former option is easier to code, because you need to assign fewer ID numbers in advance, and because it is easier to "plug" the ID values into your work tables when there is only a single record.

Here is a suggested approach toward implementing this process:

1. *Decide how many record numbers you need.* You must determine how many ID numbers are required for each of the primary/foreign key combination fields in the entry tables. You will need to create dummy records for each table in your batch that is on the *parent* side of a join.

 Tip

You do *not* need to assign record numbers for primary key values of tables that have no children in the entry batch. These records' ID numbers can be assigned by the server during record insertion, and do not need to be returned to your program because they do not propagate into other records.

2. *Create server placeholders.* When you know how many records to create on the server and in what table(s), insert the dummy records to the server using a process that returns the list of ID numbers that were allotted during the insertion.

3. *Change the temporary record numbers to the assigned values.* With cascading referential integrity enabled on your local work tables, you can change the temporary key values to their server-assigned values on the parent side, and the change will cascade into related child records. Using the list of ID values returned by the server, update the temporary ID field values in your work tables with the actual record numbers. Because your data entry tables should mimic their targets on the server, each table will have a temporary ID field that links it to its child table(s).

α Note

You cannot assign temporary record ID values in the work tables using Access' AutoNumber field type, because you will not be able to change this read-only ID number to reflect the actual number when assigned by the server.

The "easy" way to beat this dilemma is to assign temporary record keys by having the user or program code enter them into the form. For example, the user or a procedure can enter the first job record with an ID of 1, the second with 2, and so forth. This enables your work table to accrue temporary ID numbers and to link parent/child record pairs with no programmatic effort.

Your form code can mimic the functionality of the AutoNumber data type using VBA, so that each form's BeforeInsert procedure creates a new, "next available" number to assign to the record. One common approach to this is to grab the maximum record number from the work table (the DMax operator can do this) and increment it.

19

---

4. *Send the records onward.* Once the records have been "fixed-up" with the proper ID values to match their server placeholders, you can forward the records to their placeholders on the server using UPDATE statements within a transaction.

If this technique sounds complicated, that's because it is. One of the benefits of using a server is to shift as much work as possible from the client side to the server side. The process described does *not* do so. I've detailed the process anyway in order to provide you with food for thought. However, the actual approach I prefer to use is to post records to the server through stored procedures. We accomplish two objectives with this arrangement:

Using the server effectively. Stored procedures shift the insertion burden to the server, where it belongs. Transaction management, validation, and logging can all be accomplished from within the stored procedure.

Enabling security. Using stored procedures to perform record operations allows us to keep the server tables protected by a security layer that discourages table browsing. See the "Applying Security with Stored Procedures" section further on in this chapter for more information.

I'll summarize here one flow that your application could employ to use stored procedures to perform batch insertions. This flow requires no placeholder records and thus can feed data directly to "live" tables, as follows:

1. *Send the local records to the server.* Use INSERT statements to send the local work table records to holding tables on the server with the same structure. You will need to include a user or process ID in each record sent to server holding tables in order to identify the owner of the batch.

 Tip

If you are a fan of my auditing strategies described in this book (see Chapter 17, "Bulletproofing Your Application Interface," for examples), you can create a unique batch number and use that number in the posted records instead of a user ID. The batch number can be assigned by calling a stored procedure that creates a new batch log table record and returns the number assigned to the record (this is similar to the technique described in the preceding section for creating placeholder ID values).

Once the related batch process is complete or has failed, you can update the batch table record to log information about the success or failure.

2. *Call the stored procedure.* Invoke the stored procedure from your application, and pass to the procedure the unique user ID or batch ID that identifies the holding table records to be processed.

3. *Move records into production.* As the stored procedure executes, it must work through the records you submitted to the holding tables one record at a time, by processing a parent record first and then all of its children. This enables the stored procedure to create an Identity field value for the parent record and then propagate that value into the child records in the holding table before posting them onward, thus maintaining referential integrity. Listing 19.20 provides a pseudo code outline for such an operation.

Listing 19.20   AES_Srvr.Mdb—Logic for Stored Procedure-based Batch Addition Records to Data Tables

```
Start the transaction
Declare a cursor for the records in the parent holding table
Open the cursor
Fetch the first record in the cursor
Loop until the cursor is depleted
  Insert the parent record into the production table
  Capture the ID of the new parent record
  Update child records, placing the ID of the parent in their foreign keys
  Insert the child records into the production tables
  Fetch the next record in the cursor
End loop
Close the cursor
Delete all holding table records
Commit the transaction
Report the status to the calling program
```

19

4. *Check the status.* You must have your server process return a success or failure message to your application so that you can inform the user of its outcome, and clear the local tables or retry the process based on that outcome.

While writing DAO code is quicker and less frustrating than writing server routines like this one, shifting the batch insert load to the server is the appropriate use of the client/server paradigm.

Filling Combo and List Boxes

Form combo boxes and list boxes may sometimes load more slowly from the server than from a Jet database, increasing the load time for their forms. There are several different techniques at your disposal for providing records to these controls. For each application, you should review and potentially benchmark each of the following options in order to determine the best approach for the specific application.

 Note

For purposes of the following sections, I'll refer to combo and list box controls in aggregate as "list controls."

Regardless of the techniques you employ to load list controls, these two rules apply whether your list data is on the client machine or the server:

Index the data. Index any fields used in the WHERE clause of the selection criteria, as well as any fields used in sorting the list.

Restrict the data. Only return the fields you need in order to populate the list control. Never use a SELECT * statement or a table name as a list source if these will return fields that are not needed for display or used by form code.

Loading Lists From the Server

The key to successfully loading form list controls is to allow Jet or ODBC every opportunity to optimize the process. When you want to pull list items from server data, you can use any of these mechanisms as your list's row source:

Server tables linked to the local database. You can base a list control on a local table which is a link to a server table. This strategy is only useful if the table data is pre-sorted in the order needed by your list.

Queries or SQL statements based on linked tables. This scenario is the one most commonly used and the easiest to create.

 Tip

Raw SQL statements as row sources used to skirt the positive benefits of Jet's pre-compilation applied to saved queries. As a result, you previously favored saved queries over SQL statements in the RowSource of list controls. Access now saves a compiled query for list control row sources, so the performance benefit of a saved query as a RowSource has diminished.

Saved pass-through queries. Pass-through queries may or may not provide better performance than queries based on linked tables. You should evaluate both types of queries against the server database before deciding which to use in a particular application.

SQL statements using IN. The IN clause is a syntax structure not yet discussed in this chapter. Jet enables a syntax where you specify the connect string in your SQL statement, as in this example:

```
SELECT * FROM jobs IN "" [ODBC;DATABASE=Pubs;UID=sa;PWD=;DSN=Pubs];
```

In general, data will load more slowly using this construction than with the other alternatives stated here. In addition, embedding the connect string in the SQL statement makes code and queries harder to maintain than using the Connect property of a saved QueryDef object instead.

Program Code. You can use *list callback* functions to fetch server data and provide rows to list controls (callback functions are described in Chapter 13, "Mastering Combo and List Boxes"). In general, this approach will perform the slowest of those listed here, but it may be necessary to satisfy a specific user interface requirement. Of course, the source of your Recordset object used in the callback function can be any of the sources described in the previous bullet points.

 Note

When using program code to provide list values, you have two additional opportunities for fetching data: you can call the ODBC API directly from code, or you can use the new ODBCDirect techniques to fetch data using ODBC but skirting Jet.

Loading Lists From Local Tables

List controls are usually populated from lookup tables, which normally contain data that is fairly static. From a performance standpoint, your list controls will invariably load faster from a local table than a server table.

In order to populate lists from local data, you will need to "clone" the server tables onto the client workstation at regular intervals. Notice that I said "client workstation" and not necessarily "client database," because server lookup tables may be difficult to clone into the application database. The reason is that data must be "pulled" from the source databases by a client application's process, rather than being "pushed" to the client workstations by a central administrative process (I will clarify this concept in a moment).

The challenge provided by local lookup tables is to decide how often to update the values on the client workstation. You have these options:

Coordinate updates with releases. If the client application is updated frequently, and the lookup data is *very* static, the lookup values can be refreshed with each new build of the user interface. When the users run setup to install the new interface, the lookup tables come with it.

Update when the data changes. When the lookup data changes on the server, client copies of the data must be updated as soon as possible. You can program your application to check a flag in a server table when a user logs in to the system, begins a process, or even opens a form. Based on the flag setting, the user's lookup tables may be immediately rebuilt.

Push the values to the users. In centrally managed network environments in larger companies, automated processes usually exist to distribute software to user workstations from a central location (for example, using Microsoft Systems Management Server). Consequently, an overnight or periodic process can run on the central server to distribute lookup tables to each user's workstation.

19

> **Tip**
> Keeping lookup table values in a separate Jet database on the workstation, with the lookup tables *linked* to the client application, will allow the download process to overwrite lookup table values without destroying any saved personal objects (usually queries or reports) saved in the client application database.

Pushing data out to workstations can be problematic if the users do not log out from the application each evening. Any process that attempts to copy a new database file on top of a file in use will fail. To beat this situation, you can employ one of these three approaches:

▶ *Store the list items centrally.* You can place all lookup table values in one central Jet database and have users link to the database. When lookup tables need to be rebuilt, a process can run which synchronizes lookup table values with the server data using deletes, inserts, and updates. Client users simply need to requery in order to see the updated data. Note that this concept removes the performance gains incurred from storing the lookup values on the local workstation, and may not prove faster than simply relying directly on server data for list rows.

▶ *Push list values out as text.* In Chapter 13, "Mastering Combo and List Boxes," I show a technique for loading list controls from ASCII disk files. The discussion there is appropriate to this chapter because a central process can update lookup list text files on a user workstation without risking the file locks that may prevent copying an MDB file.

▶ *Replicate.* You may be able to replicate centrally stored lookup values from a Jet database (updated from the server) into lookup databases on the client workstations.

As network cards and server machines continue to get faster, the need to clone lookup values to user workstations will diminish and large numbers of concurrent users should be able to pull lookup values directly from the server tables.

Protecting Server Data

The ease with which users can create table links in their local databases and then edit server data directly should cause you much concern. To prevent problems introduced by this feature, you will need to implement a security layer on your server data tables that disables direct edits from Access.

How then can an application update tables that can no longer be updated? The simplest solution is to create different security levels for users and processes. The password that users login to the server with does not allow them to edit data. However, the password that *does* allow tables to be updated is passed to the server from code before running any process that alters server data. Access' security or Make MDE features can then be used to lock the modules that contain such code in order to prevent users from discovering the write password.

This scenario has two shortcomings:

▶ Storing security information in scores of program modules makes updating the program more difficult if the security model changes.

▶ Part of the security model is assigned to the client application when it would be more appropriate to centralize all security on the server.

I'll propose two other solutions to this security dilemma in the next two sections, in order to provide you with other options to explore.

Applying Security Via the Three-Tiered Model

One solution to the data security problem brings into sharp focus the value of the three-tiered architecture model as described in Chapter 7, "Understanding Application Architecture." Imagine creating a business object as an Access MDE file or Visual Basic Automation server whose job it is to post order records to the server. Your client application could perform data entry directly into tables managed by the business objects (if they are in a Jet database), or could set class properties in an Automation server application via VBA code.

In either case, the business objects would then take care of posting records to the server. The objects can have embedded password information that enables server updates but is compiled or otherwise secured from users.

Using common business objects allows for sharing of record operations between Access and non-Access users. In other words, a set of common business objects could also be used by Visual Basic and Excel client applications.

Applying Security with Stored Procedures

A second security model to use in client/server applications is to employ stored procedures to enforce a security layer. With stored procedures, all data operations are concen-trated onto the server, where they can benefit from the server machine's higher performance. In addition, developers benefit from the centralization of all data functions in one place, where they can be updated together, backed-up together, replicated to another site together, and so on.

For each data process (DELETE, INSERT, and UPDATE), you would create a stored procedure on the server to accept information from the client application and process it against the server. Set the stored procedure's rights to a level that enables it to update tables on the server. Only the procedure has these rights to base tables; users linked to the database from Access or wandering in it without the Administrator password would not have rights to alter data, and would need to know the syntax of a stored procedure to do any actual damage to data.

Data can be passed in to the stored procedure as arguments when calling it, or can be written to a non-secured table on the server from which the stored procedure retrieves the records and moves them into production. Refer to the previous section "Assigning Record Numbers After Data Entry," which provides a simple example of how stored procedures can be used to process data passed in from a client application.

Preserving Data Integrity

Another important issue in the protection of server data is preserving referential integrity (*RI*). Access provides such easy visual mechanisms for creating Jet table relationships and enforcing referential integrity that Access developers get just a little "spoiled." Most servers, however, do not provide such luxuries as graphical relationship builders. Some, in fact, do not even provide for stored relationships at all.

When you move your Access database to a server, you will need to establish referential integrity constraints there to ensure data integrity. In general, offloading this work to the server is the best approach from both a performance standpoint and a philosophical one.

Tip
SQL Server added some referential integrity capabilities starting with version 6.0. If you are using an older version you are still enforcing RI with triggers, in which case you might want to upgrade.

Your Access application should not have to enforce the RI of a remote database. In fact, it cannot do so because Jet cannot build referential integrity for linked ODBC tables. Nevertheless, any *local* batch data entry tables used for creating records that are posted to the server *should* enforce the same RI model as the server, in order to ensure a lower probability of posting failures.

When working against servers that do not have a robust RI model, client application code or stored procedures may be needed to "fake" referential integrity. For example, where cascading updates and deletes are not provided by the server, programmatic routines must be created to fill the void.

Setting Jet Options on the Server

When Jet establishes its first connection to a server database, it looks for a proprietary settings table called MSysConf that gives Jet/Access some connectivity behavior parameters. No Jet error occurs if the table is not found. You can create the table in your server databases using the following fields:

Config. Defined as a SmallInt type, this holds the ID number of the configuration setting record.

chValue. This field of type VarChar(255) holds the text portion of the configuration option.

nValue. This field of type Integer holds the numeric component of the configuration option.

Comment. This is a VarChar(255) column with the description of the option record.

You set the flags that Jet uses to determine how to interact with the server by adding records to this table. Currently, Jet only recognizes three Config field values:

101. Creating a record with this Config field value and a 0 value in the nValue field tells Jet never to store the user ID and password in a table link's property. With this option set to 0, the "Save password" check box on the Link Tables dialog box will always appear disabled. Any *secured* server database should have an MSysConf table with this value, because without it Jet defaults to enabling the user to store the password locally. (The nValue field in this record can be set to 1 if you need to emulate the default behavior and enable local password storage.)

102. A record with this Config field value and a number in the nValue column tells Jet how many seconds to pause between background fetches of data when the user is viewing a datasheet. By default, the Access UI tells Jet to pull another chunk of records into a memory (or disk) buffer every 10 seconds in order to slowly fill the buffer.

103. A record with this Config field value and a number in the nValue column tells Jet how many rows to grab on each background fetch. By default, Jet grabs 100 records each time.

> ### α Note
> Jet does not perform background population by default. All background record fetching is done by Jet at the request of the client (the Access user interface).

From Here...

Creating client/server applications is a very complex task. In this chapter, I've provided discussions of the most important issues and techniques involved when using Access against remote data. I've done much more than scratch the surface here, yet there are many application-specific issues that will crop up in your development work that I have not dealt with. To solve them, use the code in this chapter and the associated sample database on the CD-ROM to create test cases in your application. Run and refine the test cases to achieve the best combination of data protection, usability, performance, and load-balancing between Access and its server partner.

- ▶ Chapter 6, "Leszynski Naming Conventions for Access," and Appendix C on the CD-ROM, "Leszynski Naming Conventions for Microsoft Solution Developers," provide naming conventions to use when creating Access, Jet, and SQL Server objects.

- ▶ Refer to Chapter 7, "Understanding Application Architecture," for a discussion of Access' role in the client server model and in the three-tiered architecture paradigm.

- ▶ Handling Jet and remote (ODBC) errors with a central library routine is detailed in Chapter 11, "Expert Approaches to VBA."

- ▶ Some of the combo box and list box routines detailed in Chapter 13, "Mastering Combo and List Boxes," can be modified for use in your ODBC-centric applications.

chapter 20

Applying Development Shortcuts

20

In this chapter

◆ **How to create keyboard shortcuts to repeat common keystrokes**

◆ **Making the most of the component object model**

◆ **How to improve the communication within a development team**

◆ **Creating and installing code libraries, wizards, and builders**

t is unlikely that you will choose to do the same task over and over again when you have the option to challenge yourself with new tasks. In most expert solution development, new challenges are commonplace and provide much of the enjoyment of the development work. Thus, as a solution developer you are inclined to eliminate or at least streamline the drudgery of repetitive tasks from your workflow. To minimize repetitive tasks, you create tools and systems that aid your work.

> **Building Blocks**
>
> "Being a member the Microsoft Office product family has distinct marketing benefits for Access, but you may not realize that development benefits accrue as well. By replacing some of our home-grown components with common Office components—for example, File Open and Save dialogs, the setup engine, and command bars—the Access group saved one person-year of development time on Access 95, and more time than that on Access 97."
>
> Tod Nielsen, General Manager, Microsoft Access Business Unit

I've been a tool builder since my early consulting days, constantly tinkering with ways to make the development process more automated. (The tools that I built for developing in the R:BASE database product were so engaging to its publisher that the company bought the tools from me and sold them as retail products.)

So, naturally, the first day that I saw Access I was already thinking about how to extend it, build tools for it, and create development shortcuts. I was pleased with the extensibility I discovered in the product.

You may not realize the wealth of tools that you have at your disposal when doing development in Access. Some of the helpful devices are Access features or extensions that are exposed for your immediate use, and others are building blocks from which you assemble your own tools and shortcuts.

Here are some of the Access features that you can employ to make your development work easier and quicker:

AutoKeys *Macros*. You can redefine the keyboard with keyboard shortcuts that execute actions specific to your development style.

Custom Object Properties. You can tag database objects or the database itself with custom properties to store information that aids with object cataloging, object currency, and other aspects of your development efforts.

Built-in Builders and Wizards. Many developers find that these built-in tools do not provide features in the way *they* would have coded them, and consequently abandon the tools. Instead, you can modify some of the existing add-ins or learn enough from them to quickly create your own.

Custom Builders, Wizards, and Other Add-ins. Access provides an excellent extensibility model that allows you to create your own tools and "hook" them into the Access environment.

Central Code Libraries. You can remove some of the more mundane aspects of writing the same code repeatedly by creating core routines that perform everyday operations and calling these routines from multiple applications.

Generic, Reusable Application Objects. With a little extra development effort, many of the objects you create for applications can be built to work "generically." Such objects can be reused over and over in different applications.

In this chapter, we'll explore the various options for building a more enjoyable and productive application development environment for yourself.

 Note

I've included the macros, toolbars, wizards, and other utilities described in this chapter on the CD-ROM in the file AES_SCUT.MDB, AES_LIB.MDA, and AES_WIZ.MDA. Before you waste time typing one of this chapter's examples into Access, check the CD-ROM first to see if I've already provided it for you.

20

Employing Techniques that Streamline Development

No craftsman or mechanic can build or fix things without good tools. Software mechanics are no different—they rely heavily on their tools as well. Two of the first tools that developers usually build are keyboard shortcuts and code libraries.

Defining Keyboard Shortcuts

While much of your Access development work is mouse-centric, keyboard shortcuts are still a part of the core user interaction when working with any Office product (imagine life without the Cut, Copy, and Paste shortcuts Ctrl+X, Ctrl+C, and Ctrl+V).

Access provides the ability to define a single macro group called AutoKeys that contains your own special *keyboard shortcut* assignments. When the database containing the AutoKeys macros is opened, the keyboard is remapped by the commands in the macro group, and *hotkeys* are created that execute specific actions for you.

In Chapter 17, "Bulletproofing Your Application Interface," I discuss remapping the keyboard to provide a more restrictive and data-friendly interface for application users. My focus in this section, however, is on the needs of the developer, which are different from the user's needs.

Depending on both the requirements of the application, and the style of the developer, you issue certain commands more frequently than all others. In order to determine which keyboard shortcuts are useful for your specific style, you must observe your behavior and note which commands you heavily rely on.

Having listed the commands that are most important in your environment or development team, you must determine how to assign these commands to keystrokes. AutoKeys macros have significant limitations in the specific keystrokes that are allowed. Table 20.1 lists the keystroke combinations that you can map in AutoKeys. (You can also redefine the Insert and Delete keys, but this capability is marginally useful.)

Table 20.1 Keystroke Combinations that Can Be Remapped with AutoKeys

Combination	Syntax
A function key	{*functionkey*}
Ctrl plus a letter key	^*letter*
Ctrl plus a number key	^*number*
Ctrl plus a function key	^{*functionkey*}
Shift plus a function key	+{*functionkey*}

 Note

Each key combination in the preceding table that involves either the Ctrl or the Shift key can also be paired with both. For example, Ctrl+Shift+*functionkey* (^+{*functionkey*}) is a valid AutoKeys combination, as is the alternative syntax Shift+Ctrl+*functionkey* (+^{*functionkey*}). Both of these key combinations execute the same macro when pressed on the keyboard.

Table 20.2 shows the shortcut keys that are already in use by Access but meet the criteria for remapping as defined in the previous table. Use this table to determine if a keystroke combination that you want to remap is already in use, and what Access shortcut you will be replacing if you usurp the keystroke from the built-in functionality.

 Note

Access default shortcut keys that cannot be remapped are not shown here, such as Ctrl+; to insert the current date into a datasheet.

Table 20.2 Valid *AutoKeys* Combinations that Are Already Used by Access Itself

Keys	Action
Ctrl+A	Execute Edit, Select All
Ctrl+C	Execute Edit, Copy
Ctrl+F	Execute Edit, Find...
Ctrl+F2	Execute a builder
Ctrl+F2 (M)	Move focus to object combo box
Ctrl+F3 (M)	Find the next match for highlighted text
Ctrl+F4	Execute File, Close
Ctrl+F6	Cycle between open windows
Ctrl+F8 (D)	Toggle column move mode
Ctrl+F8 (M)	Execute Debug, Run To Cursor
Ctrl+F9 (M)	Execute Debug, Set Next Statement
Ctrl+G	Execute View, Debug Window
Ctrl+H	Execute Edit, Replace...
Ctrl+I (M)	Execute Edit, Quick Info
Ctrl+J (M)	Execute Edit, List Properties/Methods
Ctrl+L (M)	Execute View, Call Stack...
Ctrl+M (M)	Execute Edit, Indent
Ctrl+N	Execute File, New Database...
Ctrl+O	Execute File, Open Database...
Ctrl+P	Execute File, Print...
Ctrl+R (F)	Execute Edit, Select Form/Report
Ctrl+S	Execute File, Save
Ctrl+Shift+F2 (F)	Move focus to builder button
Ctrl+Shift+F2 (M)	Execute View, Last Position
Ctrl+Shift+F8 (M)	Execute Debug, Step Out
Ctrl+Shift+F9 (M)	Execute Debug, Clear All Breakpoints
Ctrl+Shift+F10	Display toolbar shortcut menu
Ctrl+Shift+I (M)	Execute Edit, Parameter Info
Ctrl+Shift+J (M)	Execute Edit, List Constants
Ctrl+Shift+M (M)	Execute Edit, Outdent

20

continues

Table 20.2 Continued

Keys	Action
Ctrl+V	Execute Edit, Paste
Ctrl+W	Execute File, Close
Ctrl+X	Execute Edit, Cut
Ctrl+Y (M)	Cut the current code line to the Clipboard
Ctrl+Z	Execute Edit, Undo
F1	Execute Help, Microsoft Access Help
F2 (D)	Toggle insertion cursor or expand hyperlink
F2 (M)	Execute View, Object Browser
F3 (M)	Locate the next find or replace match
F4	Open a combo box
F5 (D)	Go to the record number box
F5 (F)	Switch to form view from design view
F5 (M)	Execute Run, Go/Continue
F6 (D)	Cycle forward through sections
F6 (F, M)	Switch window panes
F7	Execute Tools, Spelling...
F8 (D)	Cycle forward through extend modes
F8 (M)	Execute Debug, Step Into
F9 (D)	Refresh/recalculate controls or fields
F9 (M)	Execute Debug, Toggle Breakpoint
F10	Activate the menu bar
F11	Display the Database window
F12	Execute File, Save As/Export...
Shift+F1	Display the What's This help pointer
Shift+F2 (D)	Display the Zoom box
Shift+F2 (M)	Execute View, Definition
Shift+F3 (M)	Locate the previous find or replace match
Shift+F4 (D)	Locate the next find or replace match
Shift+F6 (D)	Cycle backward through sections
Shift+F8 (D)	Cycle backward through extend modes
Shift+F8 (M)	Execute Debug, Step Over

Keys	Action
Shift+F9 (D)	Requery the underlying data
Shift+F9 (M)	Execute Debug, Quick Watch...
Shift+F10	Display current shortcut menu
Shift+F12	Execute File, Save

(D) Indicates shortcut keys that are used in datasheet view and form view

(F) Indicates shortcut keys that are used in form or report design view

(M) Indicates shortcut keys that are used in the Module window

 Tip

Scanning the previous table gives you a comprehensive understanding of almost all of the built-in keyboard shortcuts in Access.

20

Figure 20.1 shows an AutoKeys macro with sample keyboard mapping entries.

Fig. 20.1

Developers can use an AutoKeys *macro group to apply keyboard redefinition macros.*

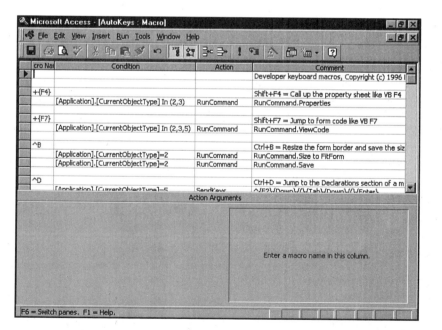

The following itemization provides some of my personal favorite AutoKeys combinations, in order to give you examples of using this feature and to supply you with a starting point for your planning. For each keystroke, I've listed the arguments to enter into the macro grid (table). The listing includes helpful key maps for each of the Ctrl key combinations that are not used by Access except for Ctrl+U. I've included a reminder to help you remember each keystroke if you choose to use it in your application development.

Shift+F4. I use these keystrokes to call up the property dialog in form and report design.

I selected this keystroke combination because it is similar to the F4 keystroke used in Visual Basic.

Macro Name	+{F4}
Action	RunCommand
Command	Properties

Shift+F7. These keystrokes display the code for the current form or report.

These keys mimic the work of the <u>F7</u> keystroke in Visual Basic.

Macro Name	+{F7}
Action	RunCommand
Command	ViewCode

Ctrl+B. This shortcut cleans up the display size of a form by resetting the border to the form's actual dimensions, then it saves the settings. This action is useful when changing from form design view to form view because Access does not correct the form's display size when you do so.

Think of "B" for "Border" to remember this shortcut.

Macro Name	^B
Action	RunCommand
Command	SizeToFitForm
Action	RunCommand
Command	Save

Ctrl+D. I've always wanted a built-in keyboard shortcut to jump back to the Declarations section of a module when I'm deep inside its code. In the absence of an Access-provided shortcut for this, I've built my own and assigned it to Ctrl+D.

 Think of "D" for "Declarations" to remember this shortcut.

Macro Name	^D
Action	SendKeys
Keystrokes	^{F2}{Down}{(}{Tab} {Down}{(}{Enter}
Wait	No

Ctrl+E. This combination resizes the current window using the MoveSize action. I use it to locate whichever window has the focus to the upper left corner of the Access desktop, then increase the height to fill the desktop. (Note that the value for Height can be increased to 4.5" when working in 800×600 resolution, and 5.5" on a 1024×768 display.)

 Think of "E" for "Enlarge" to remember this shortcut.

Macro Name	^E
Action	MoveSize
Right	0"
Down	0"
Height	4"

Ctrl+I. I use this shortcut to open the Tab Order dialog box from form design view.

 The "I" key stands for "Index," as in the affected TabIndex property.

Macro Name	^I
Action	RunCommand
Command	TabOrder

Ctrl+J. This combination executes the Size to Grid command against the selected form or report control(s). This allows you to easily clean up the size of a control or a selected group of controls.

Think of the phrase "Jump to grid" to remember this shortcut.

Macro Name	^J
Action	RunCommand
Command	SizeToGrid

Ctrl+K. This key combination duplicates the selected form or report control(s). I find it handy to be able to create one control with specific properties and then copy the control multiple times very quickly by pounding on these shortcut keys (this technique is especially useful when working with headings for columnar reports).

Think of the mnemonic "Kopy" to remember this shortcut.

Macro Name	^K
Action	RunCommand
Command	Duplicate

Ctrl+O. This shortcut opens the Options dialog box. (This sequence reuses the shortcut assigned by Access to File, Open, but I don't miss it.)

Remember "O" for "Options" as a reminder for this shortcut.

Macro Name	^O
Action	RunCommand
Command	Options

Ctrl+Q. I use this keyboard shortcut from query design view to execute the current query.

Remember "Q" for "Query" to use this shortcut.

Macro Name	^Q
Action	RunCommand
Command	Run

Ctrl+T. In the following section, I show you how to create custom toolbars for use during development and testing. I use this shortcut to display my personal toolbar with my favorite development utilities.

The "T" in this shortcut stands for "Toolbar."

Macro Name	^T
Action	ShowToolbar
Toolbar Name	tbrDevelopment
Show	Yes

With dozens of keys available for your redefinition, you can create a wealth of shortcuts to speed up your development work and build an environment optimized for your work habits.

 Tip

In an AutoKeys keyboard shortcut macro, you can enter an expression into the Condition column of the macro to cause it to execute the actions only in a specific context. For example, a keystroke sequence that you only want to execute when a form or report has the focus would be restricted by use of the following condition:

    [Application].[CurrentObjectType] In (2,3)

This restriction limits the keyboard shortcut so that it only executes if the current object with focus is a form (CurrentObjectType = 2) or a report (CurrentObjectType = 3). The values for the CurrentObjectType property are shown in Table 20.3. Refer back to Figure 20.1 to see an example of these restrictions in the macro design grid.

Table 20.3 Values for the *CurrentObjectType* Property When Used in *AutoKeys*

Value	Object
0	Table
1	Query
2	Form
3	Report
4	Macro
5	Module

Creating Development Utilities

The new command bar objects for user interface construction provides developers with a handy device for building tools. You can create small utility routines and attach them to the Access menu system or a custom toolbar for use during development.

 Tip

The keyboard shortcuts in the previous section can be coded as standard macros rather than keyboard macros if you prefer to use them with the mouse rather than the keyboard. By giving each keyboard macro a name rather than a keyboard assignment in the Macro Name column of the design grid, the named macro can then be called as the action for a custom menu item or toolbar button.

Let's examine two common development tasks that are easily automated and assigned to a toolbar.

Whether you are testing a form or debugging an application, there are times when you want the code to provide you with instant feedback when a problem is encountered. Unlike your users, for whom you create elaborate error handlers and polite messages, as a developer you want to jump to an offending line of code in order to debug and fix its problem. Access facilitates this nicely with the Break on All Errors option setting.

I create two custom toolbar buttons to help me toggle this setting on and off. These toolbar buttons are shown on my custom development toolbar in Figure 20.2. Each of the two debugging buttons calls the routine shown in Listing 20.1, which is a `Public` function in a standard module. One button calls the function with the argument value `True` to enable the Break on All Errors setting, and one calls the same function and passes `False`. Figure 20.2 shows the Control Properties dialog for the button that sets the Break on All Errors setting to `True`; notice how the name and argument for the custom function go in the `OnAction` property setting.

This utility is quite useful when unit testing a piece of code, or when integration testing an application. When you see an anomalous event or receive an error alert, click the custom toolbar that sets Break on All Errors. Repeat the event of interest and you will drop to the offending line of code, where you can debug the issue. When you are done fixing and testing the feature, click the button that returns Break on All Errors to its off setting, and continue your testing.

Fig. 20.2

*Command bars can
contain custom
toolbar buttons that
call utility functions.*

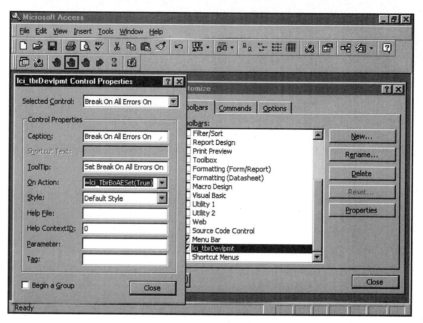

**Listing 20.1   AES_SCut.Mdb—A Utility Routine to Toggle the Break on
All Errors Setting**

```
Public Function lci_TbrBoAESet(blnState As Boolean)
' Purpose:   Turn Break on All Errors on or off
' Arguments: blnState:=True/False

  On Error Resume Next
  Application.SetOption "Break on All Errors", blnState
  Beep
  MsgBox "Break on All Errors has been set to " _
    & IIf(blnState, "True", "False"), vbInformation, "lci_TbrBoAESet"

End Function
```

α **Note**

The custom toolbar in Figure 20.2 shows several other handy tools that are useful
during development. Some of the tools are not explained in the chapter text. You
will want to explore the custom toolbar in the sample database file for this chapter
to learn how the other tools work.

Refer to Chapter 14, "Navigating in Forms and Applications," to learn how to create
toolbars using the new command bar technology.

Another example of a handy development utility that I often use is a routine to quickly view the code for the currently active form or report. When developing or testing an application, I'm often in a mode that re-creates the user's view of the system and thus does not provide access to the built-in toolbars. When using such a system, there is no menu option or toolbar button available to jump to the code behind the currently executing form or report. Thus, a routine that performs such a task makes a perfect candidate for a toolbar button on my development toolbar, which is even available when I'm testing applications. My custom toolbar button calls the Public function lci_TbrViewCode() in its OnAction property argument. The function, shown in Listing 20.2, determines the state of the currently selected form or report (either open or simply highlighted in the database window) and issues the appropriate RunCommand method to toggle to design view and show the object's module.

Listing 20.2   AES_SCut.Mdb—A Utility Routine to View the Code for the Current Object

```
Public Function lci_TbrViewCode()
' Purpose: Change form or report object into design view and show code
'          Issue from the Database window or on an open object

  Dim bytState As Byte
  Dim bytType  As Byte
  Dim strName  As String

  bytType = Application.CurrentObjectType
  strName = Application.CurrentObjectName

  If bytType = acForm Or bytType = acReport Then
    bytState = SysCmd(acSysCmdGetObjectState, bytType, strName)  ' Get state
    If bytState = acObjStateOpen Then  ' If open
      RunCommand acCmdDesignView  ' Toggle to design view
    End If
    RunCommand acCmdViewCode  ' Execute View Code
  End If

End Function
```

The code in this listing is assigned to the View Code button on my custom development toolbar (the second button from the left in Figure 20.2).

 Note

The Access toolbar also provides a tool to view code. The difference between the built-in toolbar button and my custom button is that the Access version is disabled when a form or report is running. My custom tool does not have this limitation, and is therefore more useful during debugging.

An additional opportunity to create development tools arises from the new `Module` object exposed in Access 97. A Module object is one module in an application's `Modules` collection. Access provides several methods and properties for a module that can be manipulated from code.

In Chapter 11, "Expert Approaches to VBA," I suggested placing an index at the top of each module during development that lists the procedures in the module. My indexes look similar to this:

```
' Index:
'  lci_TbrBasIndex      - Recreate module index
'  lci_TbrBoAESet       - Turn Break on All Errors on or off
'  lci_TbrHourglassOff - Turn off the hourglass cursor
```

By writing code against the new Module object, you can create a utility that generates this index automatically. The code in Listing 20.3 shows you how. Running this code from a toolbar button with a module open creates an index string comment block at the top of the module that matches my style.

20

Listing 20.3   AES_SCut.Mdb—A Utility Routine to Create a Module Index Comment

```
Public Function lci_TbrBasIndex()
' Purpose: Recreate module index
'          A module must have focus when this is called

    Dim blnRet       As Boolean  ' Result of Find
    Dim bytType      As Byte     ' Current object type
    Dim lngEndCol    As Long     ' Find method argument
    Dim lngEndLine   As Long     ' Find method argument
    Dim lngProcKind  As Long     ' ProcOfLine method argument
    Dim lngStartCol  As Long     ' Find method argument
    Dim lngStartLine As Long     ' Find method argument
    Dim bas          As Module   ' The module to search
    Dim strIndex     As String   ' The index

    bytType = Application.CurrentObjectType  ' Object with focus

    If bytType <> acModule Then  ' Object with focus is not a module
      GoTo lci_TbrBasIndex_Exit
    End If

    ' Get a pointer to the current module
    Set bas = Modules(Application.CurrentObjectName)
    strIndex = "' Index:" & vbCrLf

    ' Loop through the module and find each target string
    ' The find target is assembled in pieces so it is not found
    Do
      lngEndLine = bas.CountOfLines   ' Search to the end
```

continues

Listing 20.3   Continued

```
    blnRet = bas.Find("' " & "Purpose:", lngStartLine, lngStartCol _
      , lngEndLine, lngEndCol, True, True)
    If blnRet Then  ' The string was found
      ' Add the found line's procedure name and purpose to index string
      strIndex = strIndex & "  '  " _
          & bas.ProcOfLine(lngStartLine, lngProcKind) & " - " _
          & Trim(Mid(bas.Lines(lngStartLine, 1), 11)) & vbCrLf
      Else
        Exit Do
    End If
    ' Increment the start of next find
    lngStartLine = lngStartLine + 1
  Loop
  ' Insert the index at the top of the module
  bas.InsertLines 1, strIndex

End Function
```

The listing introduces you to some of the new methods and properties of the Module object; refer back to the listing to see each of these properties and methods in action:

CountOfLines. This property contains a Long Integer specifying the number of lines of code in the module.

Find. The Find method locates a specified string in the module. The arguments to the find are the target string and four Long Integer variables. The variables specify, respectively, the starting line and column and the ending line and column for the search. If a Find operation is successful, Access resets these variables to values indicating the location of the found text.

InsertLines. This method inserts one or more code lines into the module starting at the specified line number.

Lines. This property contains the contents of one or more lines, as specified by arguments for the starting line and the number of lines to return.

ProcOfLine. This property holds a string indicating the name of the procedure containing a specified line in the module.

Add-ins you create that manipulate modules can be run as toolbar buttons, as in this example, or as wizards or expression builders, as explained later in this chapter.

Using Component Objects

The greater the percentage of each day that you spend in Access application development, the more highly motivated you are to reuse your code and objects wherever possible. Coding the same routine twice or building the same form over and over does not increase job satisfaction for a majority of developers. Instead, you will attempt to create "component objects" (easily-reusable items).

As you create application objects, constantly ask yourself this question: Under what circumstances would I or another developer use this object again? Many objects and procedures that have a very narrowly defined purpose in an application can be easily expanded to provide broader functionality. I have found that a very specific object or routine can usually be made generic with an extra effort of only 10 to 30 percent.

For example, assume that you must create a routine to check specific fields on a form to ensure that they are not Null. The routine inspects specific form controls by name, as in this code:

```
If IsNull(Me!txtCustName) Then...
```

When designing this routine, it occurs to you that almost every form you will create for this and other applications will need a similar routine. You determine that a standard, generic routine that can be used on any form would solve not only the current problem, but future similar problems. You create a module-level collection of controls mcolNonNull at form load, and the improved validation routine simply checks all of the controls in the collection, without need of their names:

```
For Each ectl In mcolNonNull
  If IsNull(ectl.Value) Then...
```

 Note
Refer to Chapter 12, "Understanding Form Structures and Coding," if you are not familiar with the use of control collections.

Let's assume that the original (hard-coded) approach would have taken you 20 minutes to write. It is unlikely that the new routine, employing a different metaphor but not more lines of code, would take you more than 30 minutes to create instead. This provides the benefit of a 20 minute time savings the very next time the routine is used, for only a 10 minute extra investment up front.

As you create routines like this (and component objects), you must store the master copy of each object in a central location from which all developers can extract the reusable objects. The "object store" is such a central repository. An *object store* of Access objects can be built as an Access database.

One of the keys to success with reusable objects is to enable them with the flexibility to support various arguments or application statuses. The next few sections provide a few examples of this.

Reusing Tables and Queries

Data tables are one of the most difficult objects to reuse, because each application has unique data collection needs. Nevertheless, lookup tables, system tables, and other non-transaction tables can frequently be moved from one application to the next with little or no change.

The simplest example of this point is provided by the ubiquitous *state* table. Lookup tables of states, provinces, cantons, districts, or similar geographic fixtures are quite static, and can be used in different databases. Because these lists are non-variable, a single table object with this type of data can often be used throughout an entire company by placing it in the object store and letting developers pull it out from there into new databases as needed. Alternatively, one central copy of such a table can be kept in an object store and all applications in the company can link to the shared table.

Component tables of data that are less static provide a slightly larger problem. It is not possible to simply place the master of such a table in an object store, make its availability known to potential users, and then forget about it. Instead, an *object owner* must be designated to manage the table's data to keep it current.

Such an object owner has two primary responsibilities:

▶ To audit the underlying data in the table periodically for currency, and update the data if it's not timely.

▶ To notify affected parties when the data in the table changes, so they can refresh their versions of the table already in use.

Consider the example of telephone area codes, which change several times a year. Without an object owner, an area code table template in an object store would quickly grow "stale" and inaccurate. To be useful to the development team, this kind of component object must be kept current and the team must be notified when the master version of the object changes. Notification that the master has changed allows a developer to update any copies of the master object already in existing applications.

Because queries reflect table data and not their own, component queries do not suffer from a lack of timeliness. Instead, the key challenge with reusable queries is understanding what they do and why they are valuable.

For reusable queries, you should label them in such a fashion that their dependencies are easily identified and that they always travel with the table or tables on which they're based. A good naming convention, system documentation, and strategy for using the query's `Description` property will help with this process.

Reusing Forms and Reports

Obviously, if a component table for states is placed in the object store, then the table's primary query, its entry/edit form, and its reports should be placed there along with it. At the point where you have five or ten component objects that depend on each other like this, your object store becomes complex enough that it cries out for a documentation or tool-based solution to help users dissect its dependencies.

Thus, the biggest challenge when reusing forms and reports is to help developers understand which tables, queries, and code objects are also required in order for the form or report to function when copied into an application. In other words, developers require an easy way to determine which object they want from the store, and to extract that object and its related components from the store. Here are a few suggestions for managing this challenge:

Create Documentation. The owner of the object store should keep documentation on the objects in the store and their relationships. From the documentation, a developer would be able to determine that when the state lookup maintenance form flkpState is extracted from the store into an application, the related table tlkpState and query qlkpState and report rlkpState must also be extracted.

Create an Extraction Tool. If an object store is an important part of your development methodology, you can create a tool to help other developers use it. The simplest form of object extractor is a macro that controls the extraction process. Create a macro group named somthing like zsmcrObjIndex in the object store. In the group, create one macro for each primary object in the store; the name of each macro is the same as the object that it extracts, such as flkpState for the macro that extracts the form of the same name. Within each macro are a series of TransferDatabase actions that simply pull one or more objects from the store into the current database.

As a developer, you use the macro index by importing the latest version of it from the object store into your current application database. Select Tools, Run Macro... to see the Run Macro dialog box. From the list of macros in the dialog, select the macro stored in the zsmcrObjIndex group that has the name of the object you want to import. When the macro is selected, it runs and imports the chosen object and all of its dependents.

The macro management tool is quite simple. Of course, at the other end of the spectrum from macros, you can create an object store indexing and extraction tool as an Access application itself, using forms, tables, and code to help developers select and extract components.

Use a Naming Convention. We've dabbled with various strategies for showing relationships between objects in an object store by using intelligent naming conventions, but creating a foolproof system has proven elusive. The example shown previously in this list of a form, table, query, and report with the same base name (State) provides a usable approach that works in limited cases.

The problem with this approach is that one component may actually be the child of several parents, so showing complex dependencies in object names simply becomes unworkable. As a simple example, the table of states is a child component of the state form, but also of the form and report that maintain area codes, which are organized by state, and the form and report for postal rates.

Create Intelligent Objects. You can create objects in the store that list all of their own dependencies. Techniques for listing dependencies are limited only by your imagination; the simplest one is to place a comment in the Declarations section of the object stating the related items. For example, if a developer needs a state lookup form flkpState in his database, he imports it from the store, opens up the form's module, and imports every child object for the form that is listed in the module comments.

Carrying this technique a step further, instead of using comments you can create a dummy Sub procedure in each form or report object that includes all of the code required to import the related objects from the store. Each line in the procedure is simply a TransferDatabase method that imports one component from the store. When a form or report object is imported from the store into an application, the developer opens up the object's module, copies the import procedure to the Clipboard, pastes it into a blank new module, and presses F5 to run the code. The second challenge when reusing form and report object types involves consistency. Pulling two or three component forms or reports from an object store into an application, only to discover that they were built using different interface metaphors and must be reworked, does not maximize the value of reusable objects.

Before you create an object store for forms or reports, your team should define interface standards that will be used for all objects placed in the store. This ensures a consistency of "look and feel," as well as coding style.

Reusing Code

Code dependencies can be quite complex. Assume that you pull ProcedureA() and its module from the object store, only to find that it calls and requires ProcedureB(), which is in a different module. After pulling the module for ProcedureB() into your application, you discover that it calls yet another function ProcedureC() in a different module, and so on. Code dependency trees like this can become quite convoluted and thus are difficult to diagram and manage.

You can select one of three methodologies to help your team manage the situation I've just described:

Note the dependencies. During your coding efforts, or after their completion, create a dependency map that shows how procedures are related and reliant. Use this document to identify affiliated objects when importing code routines from the object store.

 Tip

You may have noticed in my code samples that I create a comment at the top of some routines labeled "Calls:" where I list the other procedures that the current procedure invokes. This gives us a quick idea of specific dependencies as we work with a code routine.

This technique is only valuable if the comment is kept accurate, and is not a good surrogate for comprehensive dependency documentation.

20

Group the dependencies. In some circumstances, it is possible to collect all related procedures into a single module or class object. A common example is provided by string manipulation routines that change the case of strings, parse strings for specific values or delimiters, and so on. Routines like these often depend entirely on other string routines. All related routines can be collected into a single module in the object store and brought into an application from there together by importing the module.

Skirt the dependencies. Sorting out code dependencies is only an issue if you reuse procedures or modules individually. If you are comfortable keeping all central modules together instead, you can reuse code according to one of these two models:

▸ Import *all* reusable code into an application whenever a single routine is needed from the object store. This ensures that all dependency requirements will be met and also makes all of the shared routines available to the application during development.

▸ Create a library database and reference the database from your applications. This approach provides all reusable code in one central repository that is "cloned" from the object store.

Note

Tips for creating generic, reusable code procedures are found in the section "Building Library Routines" later in this chapter.

Improving Team Development

Access developers who also work in environments like Visual C++ or Visual Basic have expressed frustration year after year with the lack of internal mechanisms to do version control on Access objects. Developers have had to select between a few add-on products that attempt to assist in this area, or create their own tools or policies. However, the wait is over—Visual SourceSafe and Access now communicate with each other to allow version control of Access application objects.

There are two primary issues of importance in team development of Access applications. I'll briefly describe each one.

Communicating Application Changes

Developers need to advise each other when a new object is added to an application or is completed. There is no formal notification process for this within Access.

As a result, object concurrency problems may arise by virtue of the fact that the Database window does not refresh dynamically in a multi-user development environment. Without background refreshes, a developer viewing the list of objects in the window is not guaranteed to see the most current list of objects, or the current values for the objects' properties. This can produce dangerous situations.

For example, suppose Wade has been viewing the list of tables in the Database window for several minutes and has not forced the list to refresh. He observes that nobody has created the table tblCust required by the application yet, and spends several minutes creating the table.

In actual fact, Curt created the table ten minutes ago, but without a refresh of the Database window, and Wade did not see it in his table object list. When Wade tries to save the new table, Access will detect that the name conflicts with an existing object and either Wade's or Curt's time will have been wasted.

Fortunately, developers can be made aware of this situation and can learn to avoid it. Access refreshes the Database window with changes to the database made by another user (additions, deletions, and object renaming) when you do the following:

▶ Save a new object.

▶ Save changes to the design of an existing object.

▶ Rename an object.

▶ Delete an object.

▶ Move to another tab in the Database window and then move back to the current tab.

The one object activity that does not refresh the Database window is opening an object in its default view. Thus, developers must be made aware that actions such as working in table or query datasheets, viewing forms or reports, or reviewing code do not cause a refresh of the Database window when completed.

 Tip

If you work in a multi-developer environment, viewing the latest application object changes is important. You can create a utility routine that helps keep the Database window current by building a form that has an `OnTimer` event procedure with this line of code:

```
Application.RefreshDatabaseWindow
```

Set the form's `TimerInterval` property value to 5000 (for five seconds, or whatever interval your group deems important). Teach each developer to keep the utility form open at all times (you can hide the form so it doesn't clutter the workspace). At each regular interval when the timer fires, the form event will run and refresh the current object list in the Database window, ensuring that each developer sees additions and deletions instigated by the other.

While creating or enhancing an application, developers should utilize good habits like regularly forcing a refresh to see the most current objects. However, simply seeing the latest objects does not provide an indication of what they do or how they have been changed by another developer. Team development procedures must include regular project status meetings or an e-mail policy that forces developers to advise each other of critical object additions and enhancements.

Tip

You can create a table in the application database to act as a running development log. We use the following table structure for `zstblLog`:

```
LoggedAt        Date/Time

LoggedBy        Text 10

LoggedObjects   Text 255

LoggedActions   Memo
```

We create a keyboard shortcut Ctrl+L in `AutoKeys` to open this table from anywhere in the database and jump to the bottom, where we log each development activity in a new record there. This provides an ongoing audit of work done, for the benefit of both the client and the remainder of the development team. In a multi-developer environment, you should be able to review the entire history of an object by simply reading the development notes for the object added by other developers to this log table.

Controlling Object Versions

Development teams require a mechanism for ensuring that only one member of the team "owns" a specific object at a given time. This situation is known as "check in/check out," and is facilitated by products commonly called "version control software."

Version control software, such as Visual SourceSafe, relies on the ability to compare (or "diff") files, and on the ability to place the files in a central repository. Because Access objects are somewhat captive to their host database file, and because of the unique binary format in which they are stored, commercial version control software has not worked with Access applications in the past. That left developers with several choices, all less than perfect. Even with the addition of code control to Access, these other techniques are still available to you and may prove useful.

The first control technique is to assign objects directly to developers as a matter of policy. Thus if Sid is working on reporting, he would need to "own" all of an application's reports, and potentially the code that drives the reports and the objects on which they are based as well. Other developers needing to modify any objects related to Sid's work on reports would need to coordinate their efforts with him.

While this situation requires a significant amount of planning and ongoing communication, for many development teams this is the only affordable approach to multi-person application development.

A second approach to team development is to check out the entire application to a single developer at one time. Extending the earlier example, at the point in the development cycle where Sid needs to work on reports, he would "own" the database and work in the application in Exclusive mode to ensure that no other developers have access to it while he adds his pieces.

This model is actually quite effective for smaller projects (several hundred hours or less), subject to scheduling considerations:

▶ Other developers must be given another project to work on while Sid has exclusive access to the application.

▶ Development in this model occurs in a linear fashion and much of the expediency value of "multi-threading" with multiple developers is lost.

A third approach is to create a "poor-man's" version control system, which allows developers to flag objects with ownership without providing true version control.

The easiest way to implement a simple ownership strategy in Access is to use the custom Description property available on each object. This property can be set from the user interface in the Database window by selecting <u>P</u>roperties from the <u>V</u>iew menu, or from the <u>P</u>roperties option on the shortcut menu for a database object. Each developer on the team must set the Description property to his or her name or initials before beginning development work on an object, then remove the property value when work on that object is finished.

All developers on the team must select <u>D</u>etails from the <u>V</u>iew menu in order to show the Description property setting in the Database window. With this scheme in place, a developer follows these steps to "check out" an object:

1. Refresh the contents of the Database window.

2. Note the Description property of the desired object or objects.

3. If the objects are not currently checked out (the description is empty), set the Description property for each desired object and then begin development.

Figure 20.3 shows a Database window with this strategy in place.

This tactic requires discipline on the part of each developer or it will fail. Remembering to check objects out and check in is a primary responsibility of each developer, and one forgetful team member can create a mess for all members.

You can modify this technique by building a simple add-in that all developers can use to provide a list of database objects, select and check out a specific object, check objects back in, and test to see if any items remain checked out to the current user before closing the database for the day.

20

Fig. 20.3

The Description *property shown in this Database window is used to hold checkout information for multi-developer work.*

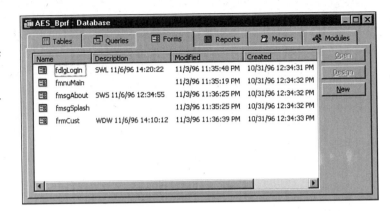

Another option for version control is to create your own home-grown automated control application. Such a tool must be written in Access, preferably as an add-in, in order to effectively manage Access objects. This methodology works as follows:

1. An Access application database under development has a "master" database, which serves as the repository for current copies of all its objects.

2. The application also has a "working" database (a copy) for each developer working on it.

3. When a developer begins work for the day, he or she runs the custom add-in to *check out* the needed objects into the working database. This process makes a copy of the object from the master database into the working database, and also flags the object in the master database as owned by the developer. This process prevents any other developers from checking out a copy until the modified object is returned to the master.

4. During the process of copying the desired object into the working database, the add-in also fully synchronizes the working database with the master by updating it with any objects that are newer in the master than in the copy. This update is done without checking out the updates to the current developer. This process allows developers the benefit of receiving updates of work done by other members of the team.

5. When development is complete on an object, the developer checks it back in to the master.

As with the other version control schemes discussed in this topic, this one requires discipline on the part of each participating developer, and introduces an extra time drain on the development process.

Note

Access' new replication capabilities can be used to distribute new objects to replica databases, but shotgunning objects out to developers' working copies of a project does not resolve the version control issues discussed here.

The newest version control technique for Access is the integration of Access 97 with Visual SourceSafe (VSS) to manage the versions of Access objects.

 Note

Version control integration between Access and VSS is enabled by purchasing the Office Developer Edition (ODE) product. However, the ODE only includes the Access-specific tool for VSS integration, not VSS itself. You must purchase VSS version 4.0 or higher separately, or purchase Visual Basic Enterprise Edition, which includes it.

In a nutshell, source code control in Access 97 using VSS allows you to:

▶ Check an object out of a central repository and prevent other developers from changing the object while you are working.

▶ Check an object back in to the repository when changes are complete.

▶ Review a historical change log for a database object maintained by the repository.

▶ Revert to a previous version of an object stored in the repository.

The previous version control techniques I've discussed in this section are developer-centric, and rely on the initiative of the development team to enforce the controls. The VSS model is more restrictive. A database must be added to source code control, then developers for that database must be added. Past that point, Access integrates with VSS for object version control while you work in the Database window. For example, when you open an object in design view in a version-controlled database, Access either asks if you would like to check out the object or it opens the object's design read-only if another developer currently has the object checked out.

When a non-module object is checked out of the repository for the benefit of a developer, no other person can check it out. However, multiple developers can check out the same module. The different changes made by different developers at the same time are merged as each developer checks a module back in. This can make VBA development on a team somewhat more complex than under your current model.

In order to facilitate integration with VSS, Access must save a Database window object as a text definition file. The file is what actually gets checked in to VSS. Upon checkout, Access retrieves the text definition and re-creates the object in your database file. For non-Database window objects like command bars, database properties, and relationships, Access sends these items to VSS as binary information. All of these operations take time and will noticeably impact your workflow as you create your solutions.

Creating Wizards, Builders, and Libraries

Zooming In

"When we were building Access 1.0, we were very concerned that users and developers would not be able to figure out how to extend Access using Access itself. So, we set ourselves the task of trying to find a simple example of how to enhance the product without C code, in order to prove to ourselves and our users that it could be done.

"We finally conceived of the *Zoom box*, and wired it into the Shift+F2 key combination. The Zoom dialog was built as an Access form, and while it was a simple example, we were undeniably pleased that we had shown that Access was extensible."

Tod Nielsen, General Manager, Microsoft Access Business Unit

For developers, one of the hallmarks of a "good" development tool is whether or not it can be extended to include non-native functionality. Fortunately, Access passes the test of a "good" tool by allowing you to build your own extensions using Access and VBA, and to hook the extensions into the retail product quite easily.

Extensions to Access are generically call "add-ins." There are four subsets of the classification *add-in*, and the lines between them are a bit fuzzy:

▶ *Menu Add-In*. These extensions are installed on the Tools, Add-Ins submenu. They can perform any task that you deem important, such as printing database documentation or creating new objects. If your add-in displays a wizard-style (step-by-step) dialog, it may qualify as both a menu add-in and a wizard.

▶ *Library*. In general, a library database in Access terminology is defined as a database filled with code routines that can be called from other databases. By adding a reference from an application database to a library database, utility procedures in the library can be called from the application. A library database allows you to reuse code across multiple applications and/or users.

With the ability to protect your intellectual property by creating library files free of source code (see the description of MDE files in Chapter 17, "Bulletproofing Your Application Interface"), you will be using code libraries more in Access 97 than in previous versions.

▶ *Builder*. A builder is generally a single-task dialog that is displayed to help create an object or its properties (the Expression Builder is a familiar example). Builders are usually launched from a build button (one with three dots).

▶ *Wizard*. A wizard is essentially a complex builder. It presents multiple screens inside a dialog form, and guides the user through a specific task from start to finish. Wizards can be launched as an add-in, from an application process, or by a user selection when creating a new database object.

 Note
I will use the terms "add-in" and "extension" to refer generically to the four types of tools in the previous list.

20

Access 97 does not present significant opportunities for creating new types of custom add-ins that you could not construct in prior versions, because Access has supported add-ins well for several releases. The most notable changes from Access 95 are the empowerment of module code builders through a fix to an InsertText method defect, and the exposure of the Module object and the code lines within it.

Access 95 and 97 each defined a slightly different model for connecting extensions to Access than their predecessor. The detailed steps for creating, installing, and using the specific types of add-ins are itemized in the topics that follow. Note, however, that there are several concepts that apply to all add-ins:

Registry Entries. Access uses entries in the Windows Registry to determine how to find and initiate add-ins. For each type of add-in, there is a specific Registry value model to follow.

Installation. In order to place the required entries into the Registry, you must provide users with installation instructions or create a setup program. Access provides a technique to use for creating Registry entries.

Coding Methodology. There are specific considerations to apply when creating code for Access extensions. Procedures and tools that are intended to simplify database development or record maintenance work for a defined audience must be written to the quality standard that provides the most value to that audience. As a general rule, add-ins should be "bulletproofed" as if they were retail products.

Each of these points will be clarified as we work through the actual steps to create add-ins.

Creating Code Libraries

It is easy to get into the mindset that the list of intrinsic functions and constants in Access and VBA is fixed. Developers get familiar with the limitations of Access early on in their interaction with it, and often develop a habit of writing similar routines over and over to perform tasks that are not built-in to the product. Visit any development team using Access and review the code of each developer, and you will find the same task's code written again and again in different applications by different coders.

You can minimize this wasteful overlap of effort by creating a standard library of code routines for your entire development team. The library should contain procedures that solve problems commonly experienced in almost every application.

Some of the issues addressed by library routines are generic to all Access users (such as checking to see if a form is loaded is one example of a routine that every developer needs). Other library routines evolve to satisfy needs specific to a user community (for example, a company heavily involved in telemarketing may get great benefit from a central routine that returns the name of the state that contains a passed-in area code value).

Locating and Versioning a Library

A code library can be applied to your applications in two ways:

▶ Standardized routines are grouped into modules by functionality. For each new application, developers import into the application the code library routines that will be most useful to the project.

▶ Standardized routines are kept in a separate library database file and referenced from any other application database that requires them.

The first of these two options is generally easier to implement, because the embedded library code modules travel with their application. Installation and debugging are simpler in this model, because application code and library code are in the same database file.

The ongoing enhancement of library routines during application development is also facilitated by this setup, because a library is "frozen" (or "versioned") in each specific application that it ships with. The master library can then be modified for the benefit of future applications without impacting its existing users, because the changes are not retroactively applied to library code in applications already in use.

 Note

I've seen environments where developers use library code as a template only. The library code is copied into a project and then can be freely modified for that application; no attempt is made to update the master library with the modifications.

By contrast, locating library routines in a separate library database file from the application code creates and solves a different set of problems than the embedding of library code into applications. The issues that must be dealt with are best illustrated by an example.

Consider a library routine `lib_FrmIsLoaded()`, stored in a central library database AES_Lib.Mda on a shared server, and referenced by every application in the company. This arrangement provides you with the following opportunities and challenges:

▶ Disk space consumption in the company is favorably impacted, because only a single copy of the routine exists companywide. If the routine were embedded in each application, hundreds or perhaps thousands of copies of it would exist.

▶ Minor changes to the routine can be redeployed to the entire company by simply altering the central master procedure. This allows for performance tuning, improved error handling, and similar enhancements to be "trickled" into the routine. The corollary to this point is that it can be difficult to modify the central routine if other users have active references to it or its database. Centralized maintenance of a library database sometimes requires that all of its users close all open instances of Access, in order to guarantee no contentions (locks).

▶ The performance of a library routine is lessened by placing it in a separate database apart from the application database. While the performance decrease can be minimized by placing a copy of the library database on each user's workstation rather than a shared server, this deployment model removes some of the benefits of centralization gained by using a library database.

▶ Creating and maintaining Access' references to its library databases places an additional configuration burden on users and technical support personnel.

20

It should be apparent to you that there is no single "correct" way to deploy a set of library routines. You will have to weigh the factors discussed here and adopt the best model for your organization.

Referencing a Library

Code in an add-in library database is not available to an open database unless the library database has been *referenced* by creating a link through the References dialog. Once a library database is properly referenced, routines that are `Public` in it can be run by referencing applications. Figure 20.4 shows the References dialog with a reference for the sample library file provided with this chapter.

 Note

You can only address routines in a referenced database that are stored in standard modules and are declared as `Public`. You cannot initiate routines that are stored in a library database's class modules or forms from code outside the library.

Fig. 20.4

References to library databases are created via the Access References dialog.

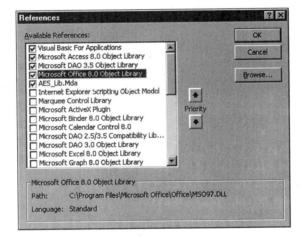

Here are the steps to manually create a reference:

1. Open any module.

2. Choose Tools, References....

3. Select the reference from the Available References list in the References dialog, or click Browse... to locate a file to be referenced.

4. Order the new reference with respect to the other references, if the order is important. How Access uses the order of references in this dialog is discussed later in this section.

Note

References to a library database become invalid when a user moves the library file. References are stored in the *referencing* database, but Access does not detect the move of a referenced file and update the links accordingly. The user must manually re-create a reference to a relocated library file, or your code must do so.

There are several ways to call a routine in a referenced library database. Because `Public` variables and routines in a library database are available to the current application database as if they were local, you can call a library routine in the same fashion as with a routine in the current database:

```
blnRet = lib_FrmIsLoaded("frmCust")
```

You can also use the `Run` method to call a referenced routine. With this method, you can optionally specify the project name of the database in which the routine resides. Thus the three syntax examples in Listing 20.4 are equivalent.

20

Listing 20.4   Using *Run* to Invoke a Library Routine

```
' The standard version
Application.Run "lib_FrmIsLoaded", "frmCust"
' You can include the project name
Application.Run "AES_Lib.lib_FrmIsLoaded", "frmCust"
' The Application object is optional
Run "lib_FrmIsLoaded", "frmCust"
```

 Note

An Access 97 database file's project name is set on the Advanced tab of the Options dialog. By default, it is the same as the name of the database file (without the .MDB extension), but you can set it to a different string if you prefer. A file's project name is displayed in the Object Browser and the References dialog.

In the previous example, AES_Lib is the project name assigned to library database. If I was using the full database name as the project name, the prior line of code would need to look like this:

```
Application.Run "AES_Lib.Mdb.lib_FrmIsLoaded", "frmCust"
```

Note these issues that differentiate a standard call to a library function from the use of the `Run` method:

▶ A standard call to a library routine loads into memory the "potential call tree" of the module containing the routine in the referenced database. This means that Access retrieves all of the code that *could be* called by all of the routines in the affected module. This is wasteful of memory resources. In contrast, the use of the Run method causes Access to load only the module containing the library procedure. This makes Run the faster-executing option in many cases.

 Tip

You should structure your library code carefully to ensure that it executes efficiently regardless of which of these methods is used to initiate routines in it. Where practical, group your library routines together so that procedures that refer to each other are in the same module.

▶ Attaching the library database's project name to a Run method call allows you to have routines with the same name in multiple databases without generating a name space collision. The project name in the Run statement makes it abundantly clear to Access which routine to execute. On the other hand, including a project name with a Run statement creates code that is "hard-wired" to a specific database file. Any reorganization of library routines in the future into multiple database or a change in the project name of the library database would create the necessity for code changes to the calling code.

 Note

You cannot qualify a procedure name with a project name when *not* using Run, as in this example:

```
blnRet = AES_Lib.lib_FrmIsLoaded("frmCust")   ' This fails
```

▶ Using Run can make your code easier to read and debug. By attaching the library database name to each procedure name invoked with Run, the structure of your application and its library dependencies are very clear.

▶ A standard call must be used to library functions that return values. Access discards the return value of a procedure called using the Run method. Thus, the examples here using Run to call the library routine lib_FrmIsLoaded() would not be useful if the calling code was dependent on receiving a return value from the library function.

If a procedure name is duplicated in multiple places, you can directly reference a non-local procedure without using Run if the procedure is in a referenced library and the name of its containing module is unique. Simply prefix the procedure name with the module name, as in this example:

```
blnRet = lib_basSample.lib_FrmIsLoaded("frmCust")
```

▶ A standard function call allows you to pass procedure arguments using named parameters. The Run method, on the other hand, does not support named parameters, thus only the first syntax of this pair is valid:

```
blnRet = lib_FrmIsLoaded(rblnBeep:=True, rstrForm:="frmCust")
Application.Run "lib_FrmIsLoaded", rblnBeep:=True, rstrForm:="frmCust"
```

Library routines do not load into a global name space, as in previous versions of Access, but instead are loaded "on demand." This allows you to have routines with the same names in different application and library databases. If a routine exists in several places, Access uses this hierarchy to determine which one to use:

1. A routine in the local database with the given name will be run if found.

2. If the routine is not local, Access will check the referenced databases for the named routine *in the order of the references in the References dialog*, and then run the first routine it finds with the target name.

3. Alternatively, Access will run a named non-local routine in the location specified if the Run method is used with the project name qualifier, or if the function call includes a module name prefix as described earlier in this topic.

α **Note**

Users of an application that is distributed with the run-time executable are not able to create references in the application database because they do not have access to the Tools menu. Consequently, before you distribute an application database that requires a library database, you must create the reference to the library in the application database. Because the reference includes a drive and path designation, the library must be located in the referenced directory or the reference search path for each user of the application (the search model is explained following the next code listing).

Alternatively, your application must include a routine that loads the File Open dialog for the user or calls the new FileSearch object to locate the referenced file (see Chapter 11, "Expert Approaches to VBA," for an example of code that uses the FileSearch object). Once located, the original reference can be updated by updating the new References collection information, as shown in Listing 20.5.

Listing 20.5   AES_SCut.Mdb—Using the *Remove* and *AddFromFile* Methods to Update a Reference

```
Private Sub cmdUpdate_Click()
' Purpose: Refresh a reference

  Dim eref As Reference

  ' Find and remove the existing reference
  For Each eref In References
    If eref.Name = "AES_Lib" Then
      References.Remove eref
      Exit For
    End If
  Next
  ' Update the reference
  References.AddFromFile (Me!txtRef)
  Beep
  MsgBox "Reference to " & Me!txtRef & " has been set." _
    , vbOKOnly, "cmdUpdate_Click"

End Sub
```

There are a few special noteworthy characteristics of the Access reference model that affect library code. For the purpose of explaining these nuances, assume that your working database is AES_SCut.Mdb, which contains a reference to a library database C:\Program Files\Microsoft Office\Office\AES_Lib.Mda:

▶ Access will try to update a reference if it cannot find the referenced database in its original location. Access looks in the current directory, the Access directory, the Windows directory, and the Windows\System directory when attempting to correct a reference.

For example, you move C:\Program Files\Microsoft Office\Office\AES_Lib.Mda to the C:\Windows\ directory. The next time you open AES_SCut.Mdb and view the References dialog, you'll see that the previous reference to C:\Program Files\Microsoft Office\Office\AES_Lib.Mda has been changed to C:\Windows\AES_Lib.Mda. Alternatively, if you moved C:\Program Files\Microsoft Office\Office\AES_Lib.Mda to the S:\Libs\ directory, Access would not be able to update the reference for you in this fashion because the library is not in the reference fixup path.

 Tip

The upshot of this reference-updating behavior is that you will be most successful distributing library databases to users if you mandate that they place the library in the same directory as their MSACCESS.EXE file, which is searched by the reference fixup logic.

▶ You can add additional directory paths to the hierarchy that Access searches by creating a Registry key called RefLibPaths. If Access sees this entry, it searches in the specified location before searching elsewhere. The key looks like this:

```
\HKEY_LOCAL_MACHINE\SOFTWARE\Microsoft\Office\8.0\Access\RefLibPaths
```

Create a string value within this key for each library you want to establish a search path form. The value name for the entry is the name of the library database, and the value data is the path to search.

▶ You can cheat the reference model and "hard-wire" the location of a specific library without creating a reference to it by using a Registry key. Create a key called \HKEY_LOCAL_MACHINE\SOFTWARE\Microsoft\Office\8.0\Access\LoadOnStartup. Enter a value name under this key that is the path and file name for a library database, with the value data set as "RO" if the library is read-only, or "RW" for read/write. See Figure 20.5 for a diagram of this key.

Once you've created this direct Registry reference to a library, you can call procedures in the library using the Run method and the qualified name of the procedure, as in this example:

```
Run "AES_Lib.Mda.FocusExample
```

You cannot directly call a library function in a database with a Registry reference and no reference in the References collection—you must use Run. Because Run cannot return a value and because a library referenced like this through the Registry does not appear in the Object Browser, the value of the trick is somewhat diminished.

Fig. 20.5

The LoadOnStartup *Registry key allows your application to find a library without a reference.*

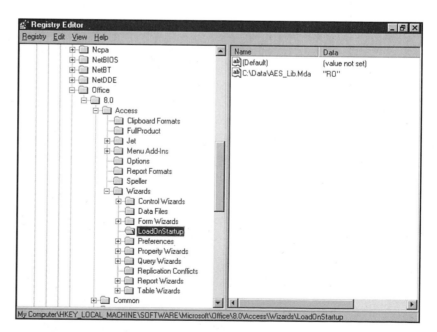

See the section "Installing Add-ins Via Self-Registration" later in this chapter for more information on creating Registry keys.

Building Library Routines

When creating code that will be located in a library database and shared repeatedly, or copied into an application database from a library template, consider these points while you are coding:

▸ Passing object arguments to functions makes them more generic than calling objects directly from within the function. For example, passing a form name into a function as an argument makes the code more generic than calling a form directly (with `Forms!formname`) from that function.

▸ Use optional arguments whenever possible, to allow a specific procedure to be called in various ways and with varying degrees of information depending on the context required by the developer. The `OpenForm` method in Access provides an excellent example of this point—it can be called with as few as one argument or as many as seven, providing the user with enormous flexibility when using it.

▸ Use *flags* in a library routine to allow its users to further customize the procedure's behavior. A "flag" is usually a `Boolean` argument with a `True` or `False` value or a `Byte` argument with a narrow range of values, each with a specified meaning.

For example, we frequently structure library routines with a `True/False` argument that serves as a flag telling the routine whether to display error messages itself if it fails, or to simply pass the `Err.Number` value back to the calling routine.

▸ A function is more useful than a `Sub` procedure for most library tasks. Because functions return values to the calling routine, the caller is always able to know if a library process succeeded or failed, or returned a particular value. By contrast, a `Sub` does not communicate such information to its caller, so you are forced to handle a failure or other status in the `Sub` itself. This removes some flexibility in how the routine can be used.

▸ Be certain that your library code understands where the tables and queries it needs to use are located. You can create `Recordset` objects in the library database and use them from code by creating their database object variable from the `CodeDb` function rather than the `CurrentDb` function.

As an example, assume that the code in Listing 20.6 is in a library database but invoked from another database.

```
Dim dbsCode As Database
Dim dbsCurr As Database
Dim rstCode As Recordset
Dim rstCurr As Recordset

Set dbsCode = CodeDb
Set dbsCurr = CurrentDb

Set rstCode = dbsCode.OpenRecordset("MSysObjects")
rstCode.MoveLast
Debug.Print "Objects in code database: " & rstCode.RecordCount

Set rstCurr = dbsCurr.OpenRecordset("MSysObjects")
rstCurr.MoveLast
Debug.Print "Objects in current database: " & rstCurr.RecordCount
```

The first recordset in the code in the listing points to a table in the library database (the CodeDb), while the second recordset points to the current database (the CurrentDb).

▶ You cannot bind form, report, and control properties in a library database directly to data in the current database. RecordSource and other object properties in library database objects reference other objects in the *library*.

▶ When a routine in the library references a database object by using the OpenForm, OpenQuery, OpenReport, or OpenTable methods, Access looks for the named object in the *library* database first, then in the current database.

▶ When a domain aggregate function (DAvg(), DCount(), DLookup(), DMin(), DMax(), DStDev(), DStDevP(), DSum(), DVar(), or DVarP()) is used in code or from an expression in the library, the domain specified in the function is assumed to be in the *current* database. Thus, this code in a *library* database counts the number of objects in the *current* database:

```
intStat = DCount("*", "MSysObjects")
MsgBox "Objects in current database: " & CStr(intStat)
```

▶ Library code routines cannot call code routines in the current database. The ability to call a library routine from the current database *and* call a routine in the current database from the library is called "circular referencing," and is not allowed.

▶ When using macros and toolbars from a library routine, good coding policy dictates that you will generally store these objects in the library database if they are needed by library routines. (In past versions of Access, if a menu or toolbar was invoked from a library database routine but not found there, Access also looked in

20

the current database for the object. In Access 97, this functionality is broken and a library database cannot do a ShowToolbar method on a command bar outside of a library database.)

▶ When you create library routines that may be imported into application databases, consider the names used for your Public library procedures and variables carefully. A library function or variable name should be unique across all of the possible applications into which it might be introduced, so you may want to prefix your library functions and variable names with a unique identifier (for example, your company initials).

▶ Consider language implications if you will distribute your libraries internationally as part of a retail product or internal company tool. As with any other application intended for wide distribution, you should make it easy to change the strings displayed to users by your library routines. Strings that are publicly exposed can be stored in a table in the library database, or can be defined as constants at the beginning of each library procedure. Both of these methodologies facilitate quick localization of the messages into a different language.

 Tip

Because versions of Access in different languages may not have the same keystrokes and strings that are in the language used for your library routines, you should avoid the use of the SendKeys statement in any application that may be used in other countries.

Defining the composition of a library begins with determining the types of tasks that are performed most frequently by a development team, and creating a list of candidate procedures to write. Additionally, you can analyze current code that exists in your organization to see what kinds of tasks are coded repeatedly.

If you do not have an existing code base, or have not been developing Access applications for very long, you can select between these two directions:

▶ Review code written by others outside of your organization (such as the sample databases shipped with Access and the many databases posted in the public domain on CompuServe, The Microsoft Network, Microsoft.Com, and other sites on the Internet). Make a list of the types of routines used commonly by others.

▶ Design a hypothetical, complex application that will be used as the basis for your library planning. Specifying and reviewing the needs of a complex application, whether real or imagined, will give you a good picture of the most useful components that belong in your library.

Having listed the types of routines that will appear in the library, the next step is to determine what the scope of your library will be. If you work exclusively in Access, you can write functions with no thought to portability to other platforms. If you work in other VBA-aware applications, as is quite common, you may consider writing library routines that can be used in multiple environments as much as is practical. Some VBA routines written in Access will work in other platforms with no changes; other routines will require minor platform-specific variations.

Next, standardize how your library routines will be coded, and by whom. It is helpful to decide how libraries will be organized and managed before getting started—changing them after they have been implemented in one or more user application is troublesome. Also, it may be difficult to have multiple developers working in the same library simultaneously—changes can be lost and objectives can clash, so you may wish to designate a *librarian*, someone who either codes all the library processes or monitors who is coding each piece, to ensure better code control.

Here are some development areas that you may want to consider for standardization as you create library code:

20

Naming Conventions for Objects and Variables. It can be very helpful to use a consistent object naming strategy across an entire library. See Chapter 6, "Leszynski Naming Conventions for Access," for suggestions on creating object names and their descriptors.

Naming Conventions for Procedures. Decide how to name your routines consistently. You can place a unique prefix on all library functions (for example, `lib_`), or on all the functions in a specific library module (for example, `lib_Frm`). I use both of these naming conventions in the example databases for this book.

Naming Conventions for Code Modules. Visual Basic modules are stored as files on disk, while Access modules are embedded in a database. If you are writing library routines for both of these hosts, you must decide if your Access and VB module names will mirror each other, or follow some other defined scheme. For example, we take a module name in Access like `lci_basFrm` and turn it into the similar Visual Basic file name LCI_FRM.BAS.

Code Commenting Techniques. Many development teams standardize how code comments are located, structured, and maintained across all of their library functions. See Chapter 11, "Expert Approaches to VBA," for more discussion of this subject.

Version Control Methodology. It is very important to define who will maintain each library routine, how new releases are to be distributed to users, and if backward compatibility is or is not an objective when updating libraries.

Security Model. Generally, a library routine has only a few people that are designated to maintain it. Allowing a non-designated user to browse or edit the code, either from the Object Browser or by opening the library database directly, can be disastrous. You will probably want to define a security model that protects library code from unauthorized access.

Creating team development standards for library code is certainly optional (because Access doesn't care), but doing so feeds an important standardization goal that should drive all of your Access development work, including the creation of libraries—you should be able to sit down with code created by anyone on your team and navigate comfortably through the code as if you had written it yourself.

Creating Builders and Wizards

The primary difference between wizards and other types of add-ins and tools you will buy or create is that wizards enforce a linear, step-by-step approach to a single task. Commonly, your wizards will follow a prescribed interface metaphor similar to that found in the Access wizards.

A *builder* is a simplified wizard. While the distinction between the two tools is somewhat arbitrary, a builder is usually distinguished from a wizard by virtue of its single-screen, more utilitarian layout.

 Note

Wizards provide an interesting terminology problem in that they can also be launched from a build button (and thus are also a type of *builder*) and from the Tools menu (acting as an *add-in*). Within your organization, you will have to decide which of these terms you will apply to a specific wizard functioning in one of these additional capacities.

The invocation process for wizards in Access that you are most familiar with is from the New Object dialog box displayed when you choose to create a new Access database object. As an example, the process of creating a new form displays the dialog box shown in Figure 20.6. The list in this dialog box includes six wizards.

This list is displayed by Access based on settings in the Windows Registry. Therefore, you can add your own custom wizards to the list by creating additional Registry entries. Figure 20.7 shows the Registry entries for the form wizards shown in Figure 20.6.

Fig. 20.6

The New Form dialog displays six form wizards that are included with Access.

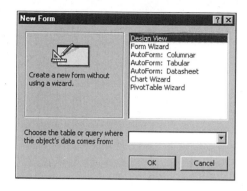

Fig. 20.7

The default form wizards are listed and launched via these Registry entries.

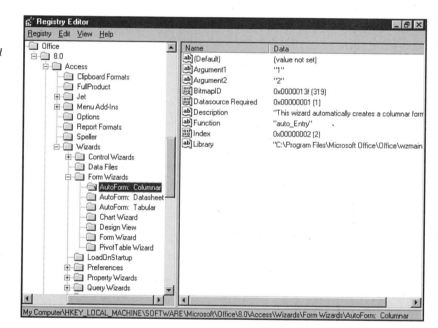

Designing Builders and Wizards

Creating builder and wizard-style add-ins for Access is not quite as simple as just producing a quick form with some code behind it. Two important concepts come into play when creating these types of tools:

> *Solidity.* Add-ins are often widely distributed, sometimes to a user community including all Access users in a company, and sometimes even more broadly as retail products or shareware/freeware. Thus, it is generally accepted that your builders and wizards be solidly coded and tested in order to generate a minimum support burden. Good error handling and smart detection of operating conditions are a de facto requirement for high-quality tools.

Usability. By definition, builders and wizards assist users in performing a process, with the objective of saving them time or demystifying a process. To achieve either of these objectives, your add-ins must be intuitive, simple to use, and self-explanatory. The quality of form layouts, screen prompts, status messages, and on-line help will all impact the successful reception of a tool by its users.

In general, wizards usually operate on objects, while builders operate on settings. This rule of thumb is only a guideline, and you can mingle wizards and builders as the needs of your users dictate. By using these general guidelines, and modeling your builders and wizards after the tools shipped with Access, you will derive guidelines for add-in development that resemble these:

▶ Builders and wizards employ a simple interface that solves only one problem or accomplishes only a single task. Their forms are opened modally and have no Min or Max buttons.

▶ Wizards use a multi-screen flow enforced by the use of Cancel, Back, Next, and Finish buttons. By contrast, a builder usually displays only a single-page form with OK and Cancel buttons.

▶ Wizards employ helpful prompts and graphics on each screen that explain the task at hand.

▶ The usual outcome from interacting with a wizard is the creation, modification, or deletion of a database object or data records, while the creation or modification of a property setting is usually the result of running a builder.

Figure 20.8 shows a standard wizard form and notes the components of the form.

Fig. 20.8
*Wizard forms
follow this commonly
accepted layout.*

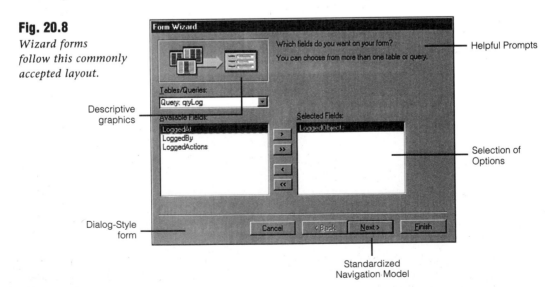

There are two common technical metaphors for structuring a wizard form. The first design (the one often employed in Microsoft's wizards) places a Subform control on a parent form. As the user navigates through the wizard, and the parent changes the SourceObject property of the Subform control in order to display another wizard "page." In this model, there is a saved form loaded as a subform for each *page* of the wizard, and the parent form provides only the wizard's "shell," or container with the navigation code and buttons.

The second wizard design model utilizes multiple form pages to simulate the different wizard screens. Thus, clicking the Next button on the wizard form simply displays the next page moving downward through one form. Table 20.4 summarizes the strengths and weaknesses of the two different wizard layouts.

Table 20.4   A Comparison of a Wizard Using Subforms with a Wizard Using Pagination

Area	Multiple Subforms	Multiple Pages
Loading	Faster than the multi-page model for complex wizards	Faster than the subform model for simple wizards
Navigation	Offers unlimited number of "pages"	Pages limited to the size of an Access form
Persistence	Requires that the parent form's code has a structure to save the user's selections before a new subform is loaded	User selections are retained on the pages where they are entered
Componentization	A single page (subform) can be used in more than one wizard form	Pages are captive to the parent form
Data	Each subform contains its own code, properties, and record source	Does not provide for multiple record sources, or continuous or datasheet layouts

20

A third approach to wizard pagination is to use the new Tab control as a container for controls, and to bring a specific tab to the top as a means of going to a "page." This method is a variation on the multi-page model described above and works well, with the drawback that it increases form load time because all of the wizard's controls and code are in a single form.

Navigation in a wizard form can be slightly challenging, primarily because you must keep track of which "pages" are allowed and disallowed in the current context. In other words, for a particular task or based on a particular user selection, it may or may not be appropriate to display a particular page of the wizard in the current context. The routines driving the Back and Next button navigation must account for this situation.

After you've created a layout and chosen a navigation model for your wizard or builder, you must engineer the code. As I implied earlier, your wizard code should always utilize advanced error handling and provide the user with high-quality feedback and a recovery mechanism in the event of a builder or wizard error situation or failure.

Another key concept driving add-in coding is to empower your add-ins with enough flexibility to operate on a variety of objects or to respond to various inputs. You can economize on your add-in code and use one tool for more than one task with a little extra planning and coding effort.

For example, a wizard to create a new Text Box control can be hard-coded to work against a form object only, or it can be written to be applicable to both forms and reports with only about 20 percent more effort.

The steps for creating a builder or wizard are very similar to the steps for creating any Access application:

1. *Describe the objective.* Because a builder or wizard is oriented toward accomplishing a specific task, you must narrowly define the task before starting. Unlike an application, which has a flexible and extensible layout, a builder or wizard gives you only a few screens in which to affect your result, and may be difficult to change once widely deployed.

   Work with your users to define the audience that will use the tool, their primary needs, the unique terminology they use in their job roles, and the level of aptitude and experience they have. Weigh each of these factors as you create the prompts, graphics, and layouts for the add-in.

2. *Describe the inputs, outputs, and objects.* You must determine what information will be passed to the add-in, and what information will be entered by the user. In the case of a property builder, for example, the inputs are defined by the fixed structure of the entry function (see the section "Invoking Builders and Wizards" later in this chapter). For a more powerful tool, like a New Account Wizard, your tool may pull information from application variables (such as the ID of the current user) and information from the currently open form (a customer number, for example).

   Next, define the value or object returned by the tool back to the current Access session. A control or property builder or wizard returns a pre-defined value by virtue of its calling structure, but an object wizard can create one or multiple objects, add records to tables, create a new database, or perform any other task within the realm of VBA's and the DAO's capabilities.

3. *List what to collect and how to collect it.* In order to economize on-screen space, you must determine the builder or wizard's prompts with an eye toward simplicity and size. You must also determine how to supply data to controls and prompts. Because a wizard can draw information from both its own library database and the current application database, you have two sources for providing records to combo box controls, filling lists, and so on.

4. *Create a prototype target object.* For a new object wizard, it is convenient to work backwards from the desired result. Define the minimum set of properties and attributes of a new object to be created by the wizard, and engineer the wizard to collect enough information to achieve that objective.

5. *Create the database structure.* All of your company's builders and wizards can reside together in a single library database (MDA file). Alternatively, you can create multiple libraries, grouping tools by functionality or target audience. Before you begin development, you must define where each tool will reside and what components it will share with other tools.

6. *Build the required objects.* An add-in will be built from some or all of the components on the following list:

> *Supporting Tables.* If your tool has combo box or list box controls, or provides validation of entered data, it may require multiple *lookup tables* in the library database. Also, builders and wizards that are intended for translation into multiple languages often use *message tables* to provide strings to the interface.
>
> `Public` *Constants and Variables.* As with any programming effort, you may need to create constants in the library database for use by one or more add-in. Additionally, `Public` variables are useful in builders and wizards because they provide a mechanism to pass return values from the tool's modal form back to the entry function. (This technique is exemplified in the wizard code samples later in this chapter.)
>
> *An Entry Function.* An add-in is invoked based upon a defined user process, at which point Access calls your entry function that starts the add-in. The structure of such a function is narrowly defined (see the following section "Invoking Builders and Wizards"), and the procedure must be declared `Public` so it can be invoked from outside of the wizard's database.
>
> *One or More Forms.* Almost all add-ins contain a single form which collects and processes inputs from the user. A builder can actually be run without any forms, collecting information from the Access environment or using the `InputBox()` function to collect user feedback. At the other end of the spectrum, a wizard can display multiple screens via a single form and embedded

20

subforms, or can even *chain* from one form to another to gather information in very complex situations.

 Tip

Forms used with add-ins are generally dialog-style, with a dialog border, no scroll bars or record selectors, standard Windows color schemes, and the OK/Cancel button combination (for builders) or the Cancel/Back/Next/Finish button combination (common to wizards).

Library Code Routines. Builder and wizard code can primarily reside in the form(s) that are displayed to the user, but if you include multiple builders and wizards in a single library database you will be able to create shared routines (error handlers, for example) that can be used by more than one add-in.

7. *Refine the user interface.* Some application processes (administrative tasks provide the best example) can make an assumption about the skill level of the people that will execute them. In contrast, most builders and wizards are "for the masses," and must be written to your *lowest common denominator* user (the one with the lowest skill level). When you have prototyped the user interface for your add-in, have your lesser-skilled users review the interface and see if they find the tool self-explanatory, simple to use, and difficult to get lost in.

8. *Write the code.* When creating add-ins, don't use macros—you must write VBA code in order to create appropriate error-handling mechanisms. The principles defined in the "Building Library Routines" section of this chapter for creating library code are applicable when authoring builder and wizard code as well.

9. *Create an installation procedure.* In order to easily deploy your add-in, you must create a setup procedure for the user to execute. See the section "Installing Add-ins Via Self-Registration" later in this chapter for information on installing add-ins.

10. *Create documentation and define a support mechanism.* As with any software application, the users of add-ins will benefit from some combination of What's This help, a standard help file, and printed documentation. Additionally, tool users in a large organization should be able to quickly determine how to receive technical support on the tool.

11. *Test, test, test.* Before wide deployment of your add-in, test it under a variety of inputs, user aptitudes, and hardware environments.

Tip

You can modify the existing wizards shipped with Access to customize them for your specific user base. However, the wizard code shipped with Access is secured, so you must download the unsecured version of the code from CompuServe or other public forums where Microsoft has placed it. (In past versions of Access, the unlocked wizard code has been posted publicly, but at the time of this writing it was not clear whether the Access 97 wizard code would be posted unsecured.)

Be aware that the unsecured wizard libraries do not contain the performance optimizations made to the secured version. If you replace a secured version with its unsecured copy, your Access performance will suffer. Also, you cannot redistribute modified versions of Microsoft's wizard or library code with retail add-ins or applications.

Code in a builder or wizard must be aware of the fact that two databases (the add-in's library and the user's database) are active at once. Refer to the information in "Building Library Routines" earlier in this chapter for further explanation of this issue.

20

Once the process of creating and installing add-ins is demystified for them, companies with large numbers of Access licenses find that the creation of a small, core set of tools and utilities dramatically improves the productivity of its users and developers.

Installing Builders and Wizards

Adding your own wizards to the Access interface is easy when you understand how the object wizard Registry trees are structured:

▶ New *table wizards* are listed in the Registry in
   \HKEY_LOCAL_MACHINE\SOFTWARE\Microsoft\Office\8.0\Access\Wizards\Table Wizards. The three default wizards in this tree are the Table Wizard, the Import Table Wizard, and the Link Table Wizard.

▶ The Registry entry
   \HKEY_LOCAL_MACHINE\SOFTWARE\Microsoft\Office\8.0\Access\Wizards\Query Wizards lists the four *query wizards*.

▶ New *form wizards* are listed in the Registry in
   HKEY_LOCAL_MACHINE\SOFTWARE\Microsoft\Access\7.0\Wizards\Form Wizards. This tree includes six form wizards, as shown in Figure 20.6 earlier.

▶ There are five *report wizards* for creating new reports. Their Registry keys are under
   \HKEY_LOCAL_MACHINE\SOFTWARE\Microsoft\Office\8.0\Access\Wizards\Report Wizards.

Note

The order of wizards presented by Access in the four lists noted previously is controlled by the `Index` key of each wizard's Registry entry. For example, to reverse the order of the *AutoForm: Columnar* and the *AutoForm: Tabular* wizards on the list of new form wizards, swap their `Index` key values.

In addition to providing you with the ability to launch these object wizards, Access allows you to define two types of specialty builders and wizards in its Registry structure:

> ▶ *Property wizards* (and builders) can be invoked to create property settings from within the property dialogs in table, query, form, and report design views. These wizards are defined by Registry settings under the key `\HKEY_LOCAL_MACHINE\SOFTWARE\Microsoft\Office\8.0\Access\Wizards\Property Wizards`. Placing a key in this tree with the name of the designated property causes Access to add a build (...) button to the property box in the Properties dialog in design view. Selecting the build button launches the wizard (or builder) defined in the Registry entry.

> ▶ *Control wizards* (and builders) are launched when the user creates a new form or report control, as defined by the Registry settings under the key `\HKEY_LOCAL_MACHINE\SOFTWARE\Microsoft\Office\8.0\Access\Wizards\Control Wizards`. Access ships with control wizards for `ComboBox`, `CommandButton`, `ListBox`, `OptionGroup`, `Subform`, and `Subreport` controls, but you can add your own wizards for these controls as well as for the other control types.

The following list summarizes the various invocation methods for the builders and wizards you can add to Access:

> ▶ Object wizards are invoked by selecting Table, Query, Form, or Report from the Insert menu, clicking the New button on any of these four Database window tabs, or clicking the New Object button on the toolbar.

> ▶ Control builders and wizards are invoked when a new control is created on a form or report and the Control Wizards toggle button in the toolbox is depressed.

> ▶ Property builders and wizards are invoked by clicking the build button next to a property setting's text box in the Properties dialog.

You can add your own builders and wizards to the locations in the preceding list by creating additional Registry keys and values below the keys noted earlier in this section. A combination of the following Registry values are needed in a Registry key that launches a builder or wizard:

▶ *Bitmap*. This string value is used only for object wizards, and specifies the name of the bitmap file that is displayed in the New Object dialog when the specified wizard is highlighted on the list.

▶ *Can Edit*. This value, of type DWORD, determines if your builder or wizard can be used to edit existing settings (the value's data is 1), or only to create new settings (the value's data is 0). The setting is used with control and property builders and wizards.

For control builders and wizards, a data setting of 1 for this value causes the add-in to be invoked when creating a new control and also from the shortcut menu; a setting of 0 causes the add-in to be disabled on the shortcut menu.

For property builders and wizards, a data setting of 1 displays the build button next to the property value, while a setting of 0 removes the build button.

This value is not required for object wizards.

▶ *Datasource Required*. This DWORD value is used only by the object wizards for new forms and reports. It determines whether the user is required (the value's data is 1) or not required (the value's data is 0) to select a source table or query from the combo box in the New Object dialog.

▶ *Description*. This string value is used in various ways to provide information about the builder or wizard to the user. For object wizards, this data value is shown below the bitmap in the New Object dialog.

For control and property builders and wizards, this value is not displayed except in the case where more than one builder or wizard has been defined for a specific property or control type. In such a case, Access displays a Choose Builder dialog and shows the *Description* values for the related builders in the dialog.

▶ *Function*. For all builders and wizards, this string value defines the function that will invoke the add-in. Such a function is called the "entry point" into the add-in.

α Note

I use the terms *entry point* and *invocation function* interchangeably in this chapter to refer to the procedure that Access calls to start your builder or wizard.

▶ *Index*. For object wizards, this DWORD value determines the wizard's relative location in the list box control that shows wizards in the New Object dialog.

For control and property builders and wizards, this value is not required and is ignored if entered.

▶ *Library*. For all builders and wizards, this string value defines the location of the entry point procedure defined by the Function value.

Figure 20.9 provides examples of these values in the Windows Registry structure for a custom property builder.

Fig. 20.9

These Windows Registry entries define how to launch a property builder.

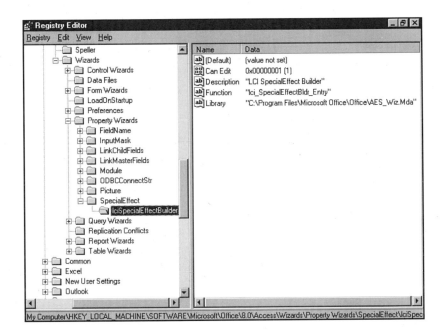

While manually creating these Registry entries to support a builder or wizard is not a difficult challenge for a developer, distributing add-ins to non-sophisticated users requires a simpler, automated setup process. Access provides such a process, as detailed in "Installing Add-ins Via Self-Registration" later in this chapter.

> **α Note**
>
> A library database with installed builders and/or wizards does not automatically receive a reference, nor does it need one to run these add-ins. Without a reference, Access can invoke the add-in but your code cannot call procedures in a builder or wizard library. If the wizard database will also serve as a code library, it must also be installed as a referenced library, as described in the section "Referencing a Library" earlier in this chapter.

> The entry points for builders and wizards are available (exposed) to Access by virtue of their supporting Registry settings. This is how Access can invoke an add-in *without* having referenced its database. The entry points are not shown in the Object Browser.

Invoking Builders and Wizards

There are two requirements for invoking a builder or wizard. The first is that Windows Registry entries must be created that point to the invocation function. These entries are described in the previous section.

The second requirement is the creation of properly structured *invocation functions* (also called *entry points*). The entry point for a builder or wizard is a function located in the builder or wizard's library database. This function must be structured with specific arguments, because Access calls the defined entry point and passes certain arguments to it, depending on the type of builder or wizard.

The invocation function is merely a "launching point" for your add-in. You do not need to do any work in the function itself; you can open a form or forms to collect information, or call a subsidiary procedure to do the bulk of the work. The invocation function has only two purposes:

1. To allow Access to pass information to your add-in via the entry point's arguments.
2. To allow your add-in to return information back to the calling object by setting the return value of the entry function.

The builder and wizard examples that follow exemplify both of these points.

Invoking Control Wizards

Control builders and wizards are launched when a new control is created on a form or report, but only if the Control Wizards toggle button in the toolbox is depressed.

When Access calls a control builder or wizard, the entry point must define two arguments:

1. Access first passes to the invocation function the name of the target control.
2. The second argument is the name of the target control's label.

Here is the invocation function syntax for control builders and wizards:

```
Public Function name(controlname As String, labelname As String) _
    As Variant
```

Note

You can replace the placeholders *controlname* and *labelname* in the function template shown with any valid variable names. Although Access prescribes a specific *structure* for entry point functions, it does not care what actual procedure or variable names are used in the structure.

 Tip

Because their structure (arguments list) is fixed and defined by Access, I use a naming convention suffix _Entry for entry point functions in order to clearly identify them, as in this example:

```
Public Function lci_TxtBldr_Entry(rstrCtlName As String, _
    rstrLblName As String) As Variant
```

Obviously the target control's name is not valuable without a pointer to its form or report object parent. When your control builder or wizard first starts, it should create an object variable that points to the target control's parent object. Listing 20.7 provides an example of code that does this.

Listing 20.7 The Entry Point Function for a Control Builder Should Begin by Setting a Pointer to the Object that Called It

```
Dim obj As Object
Select Case Application.CurrentObjectType
  Case acForm
    Set obj = Screen.ActiveForm
  Case acReport
    Set obj = Screen.ActiveReport
End Select
```

The variable must be set before your entry point opens another form for use by the builder or wizard, because once a builder or wizard form opens, the ActiveForm property will return *it* rather than the original calling object.

With a pointer to the calling form or report, and the name of the target control, your builder or wizard can manipulate the target control and/or its label, changing properties as required by the add-in.

Note

Your control builder or wizard must directly manipulate the target control. Expecting this, Access ignores the return value of its entry point function for these add-ins. You do not need to set the invocation function's return value at the completion of a control builder or wizard.

Let's examine a sample control builder which asks the user to define the base name for a text box control, then creates an LNC name for both the control and its label. Figure 20.10 shows the Registry entries for the builder.

Fig. 20.10
Windows Registry entries that launch an example Text Box control builder.

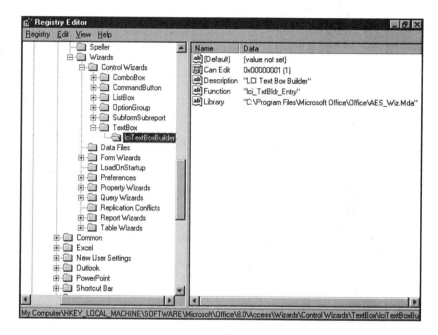

After creating the Registry entries shown, the presence of a control builder in the Registry causes the Build... option to appear enabled on the shortcut menu for TextBox controls, as shown in Figure 20.11.

The code in Listing 20.8 provides an example of a builder that names text boxes and their labels. Notice that the function name in the listing matches the name of the entry point function installed for the builder in the Registry, as shown previously in Figure 20.10. Also, when Access starts the builder invocation function, it automatically passes in two argument values. The pseudocode in the listing explains the flow of the builder code.

Fig. 20.11

Control builders and wizards appear on the shortcut menu as a Build... button in form design.

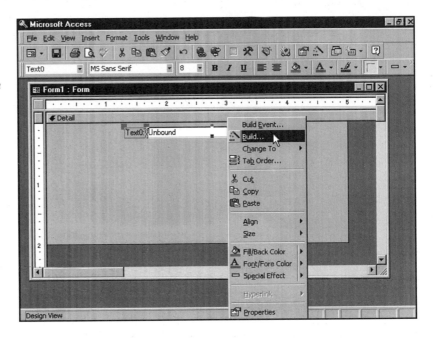

Listing 20.8   LCI_Wiz.Mda—A Builder that Requests a Name and Label for a Text Box from the User and Applies the Entered Properties to the Control

```
Public Function lci_TxtBldr_Entry(rstrCtlName As String, _
   rstrLblName As String) As Variant
' Purpose:   Entry point for text box builder
' Arguments: All control builders have these arguments:
'            rstrCtlName:=Current control name
'            rstrLblName:=Current label name
' Pseudo Code:
'   1. Create an object variable on the active object
'   2. Suggest and collect the control's base name
'   3. Create LNC text box and label names from the base name
'   4. Suggest and collect the label's caption

   Dim obj     As Object
   Dim lbl     As Label
   Dim strBase As String
   Dim txt     As TextBox

   ' Set a pointer to the calling object
   Select Case Application.CurrentObjectType
     Case acForm
       Set obj = Screen.ActiveForm
     Case acReport
       Set obj = Screen.ActiveReport
   End Select
```

```
Set lbl = obj(rstrLblName)
Set txt = obj(rstrCtlName)

' Suggest the ControlSource as the base name
strBase = Nz(txt.ControlSource, "")
' If the ControlSource is an expression, make no suggestion
If Left(strBase, 1) = "=" Then
  strBase = ""
End If
' Collect the control base name
strBase = InputBox("Enter the control's base name:", "Base Name", strBase)
If Len(strBase) = 0 Then  ' User aborted
  GoTo lci_TxtBldr_Entry_Exit
End If
' Create object names
txt.Name = "txt" & strBase
lbl.Name = "lbl" & strBase
' Suggest the base name as the prompt
If Left(lbl.Caption, 4) = "Text" Then  ' Not a good prompt
  strBase = strBase & ":"  ' Build prompt from base name
Else  ' Prompt is good, add only a colon if needed
  strBase = lbl.Caption
  If Right(strBase, 1) <> ":" Then
    strBase = strBase & ":"
  End If
End If
' Collect the prompt
strBase = InputBox("Enter the label caption:", "Caption", strBase)
If Len(strBase) <> 0 Then  ' Didn't abort
  lbl.Caption = strBase
End If

End Function
```

The code in the example demonstrates a builder that does not rely on a form to collect information. Instead, the builder makes some judgment calls of its own, and then requests user feedback by employing the InputBox() function.

Invoking Property Wizards

Property builders and wizards are invoked by clicking the build (...) button next to a property setting's text box in the Properties dialog.

When Access calls a property builder or wizard, the entry point must define three arguments:

1. Access first passes the name of the target object to the invocation function.

2. The second argument passed to the add-in is the name of the current control, if any.

Caution

Some properties to which you can attach a builder or wizard apply to objects that are not controls. In such a case, the controlname argument of your invocation function will receive the name of an object that is not a control. Your invocation function must detect such instances and react appropriately.

For an example of code that deals with this issue, see Listing 20.9.

3. The third argument passed to your invocation function is the current value of the desired property for the target object.

Here is the invocation function syntax for property builders and wizards:

```
Public Function name(objectname As String, controlname As String, _
    currentvalue As String) As String
```

Listing 20.9 shows a sample invocation function for a property builder to help the user set the SpecialEffect property. See Figure 20.12, which shows the builder form, when reading the listing. Note in the figure that the presence of the builder is indicated by the Build button (the ellipses ...) on the SpecialEffect property in the Label control's Properties dialog box.

Fig. 20.12

A single-screen builder form to collect SpecialEffect property information from the user.

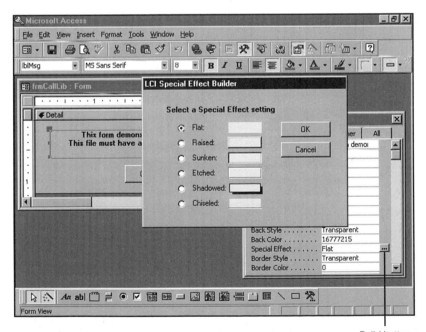

Build button

Listing 20.9   LCI_Wiz.Mda—Core Routine for a *SpecialEffect* Property Builder

```
' The entry point in a standard module
Public Function lci_SpecialEffectBldr_Entry(rstrObjName As String, _
  rstrCtlName As String, rstrCurVal As String) As String
' Purpose:    Entry point for SpecialEffect property builder
' Arguments: All property builders have these arguments:
'               rstrObjName:=Current object name
'               rstrCtlName:=Current control name
'               rstrCurVal:=Current property value

  On Error GoTo lci_SpecialEffectBldr_Entry_Err
  Const cstrProc As String = "lci_SpecialEffectBldr_Entry"
  Dim ctl      As Control
  Dim obj      As Object
  Dim varArgs  As Variant

  ' Set a pointer to the calling object
  Select Case Application.CurrentObjectType
    Case acForm
      Set obj = Forms(rstrObjName)
    Case acReport
      Set obj = Reports(rstrObjName)
  End Select

  ' Must check for a current control name that is actually a section
  '   by setting the passed argument to a control variable and trapping failure
  On Error Resume Next
  Set ctl = obj(rstrCtlName)
  If Err.Number <> 0 Then  ' Not a control, must be a section
    varArgs = "1" & rstrCurVal  ' Set the flag for a section
  Else
    varArgs = "0" & rstrCurVal  ' Set the flag for a control
  End If
  On Error GoTo lci_SpecialEffectBldr_Entry_Err

  ' The form places the code shell in global gstrEffect
  DoCmd.OpenForm "lci_fwzmSpecialEffectBldr", , , , , acDialog, varArgs
  If Len(gstrEffect) > 0 Then
    lci_SpecialEffectBldr_Entry = gstrEffect  ' Return the form's input
  Else
    lci_SpecialEffectBldr_Entry = rstrCurVal  ' Return the original value
  End If

lci_SpecialEffectBldr_Entry_Exit:
  Exit Function

lci_SpecialEffectBldr_Entry_Err:
  Call lci_ErrMsgStd(mcstrMod & "." & cstrProc, Err.Number, Err.Description, 0, True)
  Resume lci_SpecialEffectBldr_Entry_Exit

End Function
```

continues

Listing 20.9   Continued

```
' Form: lci_fwzmSpecialEffectBldr
' Code in the builder form's Load event to manage the object type
Private Sub Form_Load()
' Purpose:   Pre-select the form values
' Arguments: OpenArgs has two values, concatenated:
'                Is control (0) or is Detail section (1)
'                Current value setting

    Dim varArg As Variant

    With Me
      varArg = Mid(.OpenArgs, 2)   ' Current value
      ' Three settings are not valid for a Detail section
      If Left(.OpenArgs, 1) = "1" Then   ' Disable some if a Detail section
        !optEtched.Enabled = False
        !txtEtched.Locked = False
        !optShadowed.Enabled = False
        !txtShadowed.Locked = False
        !optChiseled.Enabled = False
        !txtChiseled.Locked = False
      End If
      !grpSpecialEffect = _
        Switch(varArg = "Flat", 0 _
            , varArg = "Raised", 1 _
            , varArg = "Sunken", 2 _
            , varArg = "Etched", 3 _
            , varArg = "Shadowed", 4 _
            , varArg = "Chiseled", 5)
    End With

End Sub
```

Note three important points about the builder code in the listing:

1. The entry point code (the first procedure in the listing) uses an error trap to detect if the `controlname` argument passed to it actually reflects a control or not. This is important because the `SpecialEffect` property applies to form and report *sections* as well as *controls*. However, the property only has three settings for sections, but has six for controls. Consequently, the builder must detect which type of object is being affected, and limit the selections on its screen to only those that apply.

   The example entry point function deals with this by passing a flag to the builder form via the `OpenArgs` property. The second procedure in the listing (the form's `Load` event) checks the flag value in `OpenArgs` and disallows the user from selecting a property setting that does not apply in the current context.

2. The entry point code also uses `OpenArgs` to pass to the builder form the current value of the property before the builder was invoked. The builder form's `Load` event executes a `Switch()` function against the passed value and pre-selects the current property setting on the form. This makes the builder more "friendly" for its users.

3. The return value of the entry point function is passed back to Access and written into the Properties dialog in place of the current value found there. The code that facilitates this is in the cmdOK_Click() procedure for the builder form. The routine sets the global variable gstrEffect to return the user's selection from the modal form back to the invocation function:

```
gstrEffect = Choose(Me!grpSpecialEffect + 1, "Flat", "Raised", "Sunken" _
    , "Etched", "Shadowed", "Chiseled")
```

Your entry point function should return either the user's new property value, or the original value if the builder is canceled. Do not return an empty string to indicate cancellation of the builder.

Access also provides a special derivative of property builders and wizards that can be used to build or edit module code. These *expression builders* are installed on the <u>B</u>uild option on the shortcut menu in module design view, as shown in Figure 20.13.

Fig. 20.13

An expression builder is invoked from <u>B</u>uild on the module design shortcut menu.

The entry point function for such add-ins is a derivative of the standard property builder invocation function syntax:

```
Public Function name(modulename As String, _
    procedurename As String, currentvalue As String) As Variant
```

When invoking an expression builder or wizard, Access passes these arguments to your entry point:

•1. The first argument is the current module's name, as in the following examples. The first example is the name of a standard module, and the second is a form module:

```
lib_basFrm
Form_Form1
```

2. The second argument passed to your expression builder is the name of the current procedure, based on the location of the cursor when the add-in was invoked. If the user was viewing the Declarations section of a module, this argument is empty.

3. If the user has selected any text in the module editor before invoking the builder or wizard, the currently selected text is passed in to your entry point as the third argument.

The return value of an expression builder or wizard's invocation function should be a string of valid VBA code. If the user has selected text in the module editor before starting your invocation function, Access replaces the selected text with the function's return value. If there is no selection, the text is inserted at the cursor's current location when the builder or wizard ends.

Figure 20.14 shows a very simple form interface for an expression builder that creates an LNC-compatible procedure code shell in the current module.

Fig. 20.14

*This example proce-
dure builder screen
collects information
used to create a VBA
code shell.*

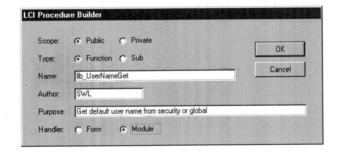

The Registry entries to support the procedure builder shown in the previous figure are in Figure 20.15. Note that these entries are similar to the entries from other property builders.

Listing 20.10 shows the invocation function that drives the sample expression builder. The function's only purposes are to display the form to collect user input, and to send the code shell back to Access as the function's return value. The builder code for creating the procedure text from the user's selections in the form is located in the form's module.

Fig. 20.15

These Windows Registry entries define how to launch an expression builder.

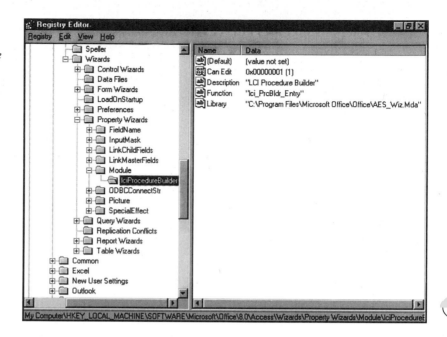

Listing 20.10   LCI_Wiz.Mda—The Entry Point or "Invocation Function" for a Simple Procedure Builder

```
' The entry point for the procedure builder
Public Function lci_PrcBldr_Entry(rstrModName As String, _
   rstrPrcName As String, rstrCurVal As String) As Variant
' Purpose:   Entry point for procedure builder
' Arguments: All expression builders have these arguments:
'              rstrModName:=Current module name
'              rstrProcName:=Current procedure name
'              rstrCurVal:=Currently selected text

  ' The form places the code shell in gstrPrcText
  DoCmd.OpenForm "lci_fwzmPrcBldr", , , , , acDialog
  lci_PrcBldr_Entry = gstrPrcText

End Function


' Form: lci_fwzmPrcBldr
' The code in the builder form's module that creates gstrPrcText
Private Sub cmdOK_Click()
' Purpose: Shell out the code

  Const cstrErrForm As String = _
    "Call lci_ErrMsgStd(Me.Name & ""."" & cstrProc, Err.Number," _
    & " Err.Description, True)"
```

continues

Listing 20.10   Continued

```
Const cstrErrMod  As String = _
  "Call lci_ErrMsgStd(mcstrMod & "".""" & cstrProc, Err.Number," _
  & " Err.Description, True)"
Dim strErr As String
Dim strTop As String

strTop = Choose(Me!grpScope, "Public", "Private") & " " _
  & Choose(Me!grpType, "Function", "Sub") & " " _
  & Me!txtName & "() " _
  & Choose(Me!grpType, "As Variant", "") & vbCrLf _
  & "' Purpose: " & Me!txtPurpose & vbCrLf _
  & "' Arguments:" & vbCrLf _
  & Choose(Me!grpType, "' Returns:" & vbCrLf, "") _
  & "' Authors: " & Me!txtAuthor & " " & Format(Now, "MM/DD/YY HH:MM") & vbCrLf _
  & "' Calls:" & vbCrLf _
  & "' Example: " & Me!txtName & "()" & vbCrLf & vbCrLf

strErr = "  On Error GoTo " & Me!txtName & "_Err" & vbCrLf _
  & "  Const cstrProc As String = """ & Me!txtName & """" & vbCrLf & vbCrLf _
  & Me!txtName & "_Exit:" & vbCrLf _
  & "  Exit " & Choose(Me!grpType, "Function", "Sub") & vbCrLf & vbCrLf _
  & Me!txtName & "_Err:" & vbCrLf _
  & "  " & Choose(Me!grpHandler, cstrErrForm, cstrErrMod) & vbCrLf _
  & "  Resume " & Me!txtName & "_Exit" & vbCrLf & vbCrLf _
  & "End " & Choose(Me!grpType, "Function", "Sub") & vbCrLf

gstrPrcText = strTop & strErr
DoCmd.Close acForm, Me.Name

End Sub
```

When the user clicks OK in the builder, the code in the previous listing runs and creates a text string that is the shell of a VBA procedure. The code shell is passed back to the invocation function in a global variable, which in turn passes the shell back to Access. Access pastes the code shell in at the current cursor position. Figure 20.16 shows the result of executing the builder shown in the listing.

Using the programmable Module object introduced in Access 97, you can perform a wide variety of operations from an expression builder. See the previous section "Creating Development Utilities" for more information on the Module object.

Invoking Form and Report Wizards

Form and report wizards can be very complex to write. The big challenges in such an effort include the following:

▶ Managing the variety of fonts and screen resolutions available on different users' machines.

▶ Determining the location of controls and automatically creating an aesthetic layout.

▶ Collecting and setting property values for the controls.

Fig. 20.16

The output from a simple procedure builder is pasted to the Module window.

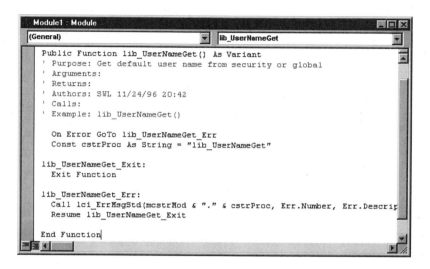

```
Module1 : Module

(General)                                              lib_UserNameGet

Public Function lib_UserNameGet() As Variant
' Purpose: Get default user name from security or global
' Arguments:
' Returns:
' Authors: SWL 11/24/96 20:42
' Calls:
' Example: lib_UserNameGet()

    On Error GoTo lib_UserNameGet_Err
    Const cstrProc As String = "lib_UserNameGet"

lib_UserNameGet_Exit:
    Exit Function

lib_UserNameGet_Err:
    Call lci_ErrMsgStd(mcstrMod & "." & cstrProc, Err.Number, Err.Descrip
    Resume lib_UserNameGet_Exit

End Function
```

20

Invoking your own object wizards, however, is a simple task. They are invoked by selecting Form or Report from the Insert menu, clicking the New button on the Form or Report tabs in the Database window, or clicking the New Object button on the toolbar.

Access manages the job of invoking these object wizards for you, by providing these services:

1. Access places your wizard on the list shown in the New Form or New Report dialog box. Access does this automatically if you install your wizard in the property Registry tree, as described in the earlier section "Installing Builders and Wizards."

2. Access enforces the user's selection of a record source for the new object, if you opt to use such enforcement. (The enforcement is triggered by the Datasource Required Registry key, also described in the "Installing Builders and Wizards" section.)

The entry point for a form or report wizard has one required argument—the record source for the object. Access passes to this argument the table or query name selected by the user in the combo box labeled "Choose the table or query..." in the New Object dialog. If the Datasource Required Registry key for your wizard is set to 0, the user is not required to select a record source and Access passes an empty string to this argument. Here is the syntax for a form or report wizard entry point:

```
Public Function name(recordsource As String) As Integer
```

Note

If you browse the Registry entries for the form and report wizards shipped with Access, you will notice that some entries have values named `Argument1` and `Argument2`. These Registry settings cause Access to pass additional values from the Registry to the wizard's invocation function as arguments. This allows a form or report wizard to pass information about the type of the wizard to the entry point. The information passed in the additional argument slots does *not* come from the current Access instance, as is the case with other invocation arguments, but instead comes from the Registry arguments.

For example, the Access wizard called "AutoForm: Columnar" is installed with Registry data of 1 for the `Argument1` value in its key, and Registry data of 2 for the `Argument2` value. When this wizard calls its invocation function, these Registry values are passed in as the second and third arguments, as shown in the invocation function for this wizard:

```
Function auto_Entry(stRecSrc As String, iPaneContent As Integer, _
    iDocType As Integer) As Integer
```

The invocation function in this example uses the first argument value to determine the type of process to run (an `iPaneContent` argument of 1 causes the wizard code to create a columnar form). The second argument specifies the type of object to create, with the value 2 designating a new form.

Knowing about this hack in the Registry allows you to pass one or two arguments from the Registry to your form wizards as well. The arguments do not need to be of the same name or data type as shown in the example here.

You cannot create special Registry values `Argument1` or `Argument2` for any other types of builders and wizards—Access only supports the additional arguments for form and report wizards.

Form and report wizards are launched without regard to the current object in the Access interface. In other words, they are intended to create a new object and thus do not care if the current object is a form, report, table, the Database window, and so on. Your wizard code must build the shell of the new object before placing controls on it or setting any properties. Use the `CreateForm` and `CreateReport` methods at the beginning of your wizard to achieve this result.

Creating Menu Add-ins

Menu add-ins are utilities that locate themselves on the <u>T</u>ools, Add-<u>I</u>ns menu. They usually provide tools and extensions that are not application-specific, but instead are appropriate to general database development or usage.

 Note

> You cannot prescribe that a specific add-in expose itself on the <u>T</u>ools menu only within a particular context, because Access does not trigger user-interaction events that you can trap. For example, there is no way to detect when the user is working within a form in design view and to enable a specific add-in only in this context. However, your add-in entry point code can test the environment using the `CurrentObjectType` property of the application to determine what kind of object currently has the focus.

When Access starts up, a menu add-in item is placed on the <u>T</u>ools menu for each key in the tree `\HKEY_LOCAL_MACHINE\SOFTWARE\Microsoft\Office\8.0\Access\Menu Add-Ins`. The key name in the Registry becomes the add-in's listing on the Add-<u>I</u>ns submenu. You can include an access key designation in the Registry key name to underline the access key on the menu. (An *access key designation* is an ampersand preceding the character to use as the Alt key shortcut for the menu item.)

Figure 20.17 shows the Registry entries for the add-ins shipped with Access, as well as the custom Last Update add-in that we will write in this section.

As with builders and wizards, a menu add-in is launched by Access' call to an invocation function. When your add-in is selected from the menu, Access executes the invocation expression defined in the Registry for that add-in. These are the menu add-in Registry entries:

> `Expression`. This string value describes the entry point of the add-in, in the following format:
>
> `=functionname()`
>
> `Library`. This string value defines the location of the entry point procedure defined by the `Expression` value.

20

Fig. 20.17

These Windows registries define how to launch menu add-ins.

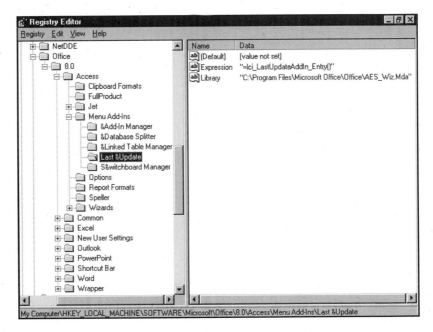

Menu add-ins are most useful for creating new database objects or performing bulk operations on a database. As an example, consider the code in Listing 20.11. This routine loops through the object containers in a database and finds the object with the most recent update date. Because this is a database-wide operation, it makes a perfect candidate for an add-in routine.

Listing 20.11   LCI_Wiz.Mda—A Simple Menu Add-in to Identify the Most Recently Updated Object

```
Public Function lci_LastUpdateAddIn_Entry() As Variant
' Purpose: Entry point for last update add-in
' Returns: Nothing

    Dim con    As Container
    Dim dbs    As Database
    Dim dtmMax As Date
    Dim edoc   As Document
    Dim iintCon As Integer
    Dim strCon As String
    Dim strObj As String

    Set dbs = CurrentDb

    ' Open each container and find the most recent date
    For iintCon = 1 To 5
```

```
        strCon = Choose(iintCon, "form", "module", "report" _
          , "script", "table")
        Set con = dbs.Containers(strCon & "s")

        ' Check each document in the container
        For Each edoc In con.Documents
          ' Identify the item with the most recent date/time
          If edoc.LastUpdated > dtmMax Then
            dtmMax = edoc.LastUpdated
            If strCon = "table" Then
              strCon = "table/query"
            End If
            strObj = strCon & " " & edoc.Name
          End If
        Next
      Next iintCon

      Beep
      MsgBox "The last updated object in the database " _
        & dbs.Name & " is the " & strObj _
        & ", updated " & Format(dtmMax, "mm/dd/yy hh:mm:ss") & "." _
        , vbOK, "Last Update"

    End Function
```

The add-in shown in the listing displays only a message box with the result of its search. It could, however, easily be made to display one or more forms, create a new database object, or perform any other legitimate Access operation.

Figure 20.18 shows the Registry entries that cause the function in this listing to be invoked by an option on the Tools menu.

Installing Add-ins via Self-registration

Access 97 makes it easy to create the Registry keys required by your add-ins. Each add-in database should travel with a system table USysRegInfo that contains the information required for the Add-In Manager to create Registry keys for the add-in.

The Add-In Manager uses two information items to help users install add-ins. The first is the database properties of the add-in, and the second is the Registry key information in the USysRegInfo table.

There are three database properties that you should set in any add-in database. The Add-In Manager retrieves these properties from an add-in database and displays them in its dialog box, as diagrammed in Figure 20.18.

Each of the specified database properties is found on the Summary tab of the Database Properties dialog box:

Title. This property value displays in the Add-In Manager dialog's "Available Add-ins" list box, from which the user selects to install or uninstall the add-in. Because this list box has a fixed width, limit your entries in the property to about 40 characters—the dialog's list box will truncate *Title* values that are too long.

Company. The name of your company, or the add-in's author, or any other descriptive single-line string can be placed in this property. The value in this property is displayed below the list box in the add-in dialog. The dialog will display around 50 characters from this property in its single line.

Comments. This property is displayed at the bottom of the add-in dialog on four lines (or roughly 220 characters). Use it to describe your add-in in greater detail.

Fig. 20.18

Custom database properties are retrieved from an add-in database and displayed in this dialog box.

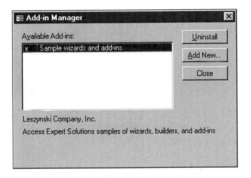

When the Add-In Manager is invoked, it scans all of the MDA files in the Access directory, and displays each in the list box of its dialog. (You can select the Add New button in the dialog to add additional libraries to the list that are not located in the Access directory).

When you highlight an add-in's description in the dialog's list box and click the Install button, Access scans the USysRegInfo table in the add-in's file and builds Registry entries from it. Each add-in that will be installed from the Add-In Manager must have entries in this table.

> **α Note**
>
> Tables that begin with USys (or MSys) are not displayed in the Database window by default. Once you have created this table in your add-in database, you will need to select Show System Objects in the Options dialog box in order to display and work with the table, or create a query that provides a datasheet with records from the hidden table.

Access provides a template that you can use to help you build the USysRegInfo table. Here are the steps to use it:

1. Import the table named Sample USysRegInfo from the WZTOOL80.MDE database in your Access directory into your current library database. Open the table.

2. Modify the sample records to install your add-in, or delete the samples and create new records with the required Registry entries. Required Registry entries for different add-in types are described in earlier sections of this chapter.

3. Rename the Sample USysRegInfo table to USysRegInfo before deploying your add-in.

For each add-in that you want to install, there will be multiple records in the USysRegInfo table—a header record, then one record for each Registry key to create. If there are multiple add-ins in a single library database, there will be several records in this table with matching Subkey field values for each add-in to install. (For our purposes here, I will call a set of records with identical Subkeys a *block*. One block defines the keys for one add-in.)

Records in this table must match a pre-defined structure. The first field is called Subkey; it names the key to create in the Windows Registry for the add-in. It is the same for each record in the table that relates to a single add-in.

Regardless of the type of add-in being installed, the first record in each block will have only Subkey and Type field values. The Type value will be 0 to indicate that a new key must be created, and the ValName and Value fields are blank.

The Subkey field specifies the full name of the key to create, and starts with one of these two placeholder strings:

> HKEY_CURRENT_ACCESS_PROFILE. This placeholder is replaced with the Registry tree structure for the current Access instance if Access was started with a user profile (using the /Profile switch at the command line). If Access is running without a profile, this placeholder is replaced with the standard Access key tree:
>
> ```
> \HKEY_LOCAL_MACHINE\SOFTWARE\Microsoft\Office\8.0\Access\
> ```
>
> HKEY_LOCAL_MACHINE. Regardless of whether or not Access is running with a user profile, this placeholder is always replaced with the standard Access key tree and the add-in will be available to all users of the workstation:
>
> ```
> \HKEY_LOCAL_MACHINE\SOFTWARE\Microsoft\Office\8.0\Access\
> ```

To complete the Subkey field entries for a block, append to one of the two placeholder strings the remainder of the key name to be created, using these syntax templates:

```
HKEY_CURRENT_ACCESS_PROFILE\Wizards\wizardtype\itemtype\addinname
HKEY_LOCAL_MACHINE\Menu Add-Ins\addinname
```

20

The values for *wizardtype* and *itemtype* can be any of the combinations shown in Table 20.5.

Table 20.5 Values for Wizard Registry Keys

wizardtype value	*itemtype* value
Control Wizards	BoundObjectFrame
Control Wizards	CheckBox
Control Wizards	ComboBox*
Control Wizards	CommandButton*
Control Wizards	Image
Control Wizards	Label
Control Wizards	Line
Control Wizards	ListBox*
Control Wizards	OptionButton
Control Wizards	OptionGroup*
Control Wizards	PageBreak
Control Wizards	Rectangle
Control Wizards	SubformSubreport*
Control Wizards	TabControl
Control Wizards	TextBox
Control Wizards	ToggleButton
Control Wizards	UnboundObjectFrame
Control Wizards	*OLEcontrolclassname*
Form Wizards	*wizardname*
Query Wizards	*wizardname*
Property Wizards	BackColor*
Property Wizards	BorderColor*
Property Wizards	FieldName*
Property Wizards	ForeColor*
Property Wizards	InputMask*
Property Wizards	LinkChildFields*
Property Wizards	LinkMasterFields*
Property Wizards	Module

wizardtype value	*itemtype* value
Property Wizards	ODBCConnectStr*
Property Wizards	Picture*
Property Wizards	ShortcutMenuBar*
Property Wizards	*propertyname*
Report Wizards	*wizardname*
Table Wizards	*wizardname*

 Note

The *itemtype* values in the table with a star reflect Registry trees that will already exist to support the builders and wizards shipped with Access.

Figure 20.19 shows two USysRegInfo blocks from the sample database AES_WIZ.MDA on the CD-ROM. The first block shows entries for a menu add-in, and the second shows a control wizard (builder). The CD-ROM file contains all four sample add-ins built in this chapter.

Fig. 20.19

Data from this USysRegInfo table drives the creation of Registry entries for add-ins.

```
Microsoft Access - [USysRegInfo : Table]
File  Edit  View  Insert  Format  Records  Tools  Window  Help

Subkey                                                      Type   ValName      Value
HKEY_CURRENT_ACCESS_PROFILE\Menu Add-      0
Ins\Last &Update
HKEY_CURRENT_ACCESS_PROFILE\Menu Add-      1    Expression   =lci_LastUpdateAddIn_
Ins\Last &Update                                                        Entry()
HKEY_CURRENT_ACCESS_PROFILE\Menu Add-      1    Library      |AccDir\AES_Wiz.Mda
Ins\Last &Update
HKEY_CURRENT_ACCESS_PROFILE\Wizards\Contr  0
ol Wizards\TextBox\lciTextBoxBuilder
HKEY_CURRENT_ACCESS_PROFILE\Wizards\Contr  4    Can Edit     1
ol Wizards\TextBox\lciTextBoxBuilder
HKEY_CURRENT_ACCESS_PROFILE\Wizards\Contr  1    Description   LCI Text Box Builder
ol Wizards\TextBox\lciTextBoxBuilder
HKEY_CURRENT_ACCESS_PROFILE\Wizards\Contr  1    Function     lci_TxtBldr_Entry
ol Wizards\TextBox\lciTextBoxBuilder
HKEY_CURRENT_ACCESS_PROFILE\Wizards\Contr  1    Library      |AccDir\AES_Wiz.Mda
ol Wizards\TextBox\lciTextBoxBuilder
HKEY_CURRENT_ACCESS_PROFILE\Wizards\Prope  0
rty Wizards\Module\lciProcedureBuilder
HKEY_CURRENT_ACCESS_PROFILE\Wizards\Prope  4    Can Edit     1

Record: |◄| ◄|          1  |►|►I|►*| of 18
Datasheet View
```

In addition to the `Subkey` field, `USysRegInfo` tables have the following three fields (refer to the previous figure for sample values):

Type. This field contains a flag describing what type of value to create in the Registry key named in the `Subkey` field. The flag is 0 to denote the first record in an add-in entry block. Subsequent records in the block are flagged in this field with 1 if the Registry entry to create is of type `String`, or 4 if the entry should be a `DWORD`.

ValName. This field provides the name of the value to create in the Registry key described in the `Subkey` field.

For example, most add-in Registry entries have a value named "Library," which appears once in this field for each add-in information block.

Value. Each of the key values named in the `ValName` field must have a corresponding data value in this field. The data value is a number or a string, depending on the type of value created in the Registry (as determined in the `Type` field setting).

For example, a value named "Library" may have a corresponding entry in the `Value` field.

Tip

You can use the placeholder "|AccDir\" in front of the name of a library database specified in the `Value` field. During creation of the Registry value, Access replaces this stub with the path providing the current location of Access (by default, C:\Program Files\Microsoft Office\Office\).

Note

The actual combinations of `ValName` and `Value` entries for builder and wizard add-ins are specified in the section "Installing Builders and Wizards," and the entries for menu add-ins are found in "Creating Menu Add-ins." Both of these sections are located earlier in this chapter.

This table-driven, automatic registration process for add-ins is easy for the developer to construct and for the users to employ. Adding to the simplicity and usability is the fact that tools installed this way are available in the current session of Access immediately after closing the Add-In Manager, without the need to close and reopen either the current database or Access itself.

From Here...

This chapter detailed the nitty-gritty of writing and installing add-ins. Your development efforts can be more enjoyable and more productive if you have quality libraries and tools that you can rely on.

- ▶ See Chapter 6, "Leszynski Naming Conventions for Access," for suggestions on how to name library and add-in objects.
- ▶ The code commenting techniques described in Chapter 11, "Expert Approaches to VBA," will help you standardize how you document your shared code.
- ▶ You can create add-ins to assist with many of the tasks carried out as you develop the types of expert forms described in Chapters 13 through 17.
- ▶ For the user's perspective on AutoKeys macros, read Chapter 17, "Bulletproofing Your Application Interface."

20

Appendixes

What's on the CD-ROM

This appendix lists and describes the files included on the CD-ROM.

> **Note**
>
> A document version of this appendix is in the root folder of the CD-ROM as CD_INDEX.DOC. The document may contain information that is more current than this appendix.

Installing the Sample Files

Before using a sample file, you will want to copy it to your local drive or a network disk from the CD-ROM. Files on the CD-ROM are read-only, which will inhibit your ability to explore and modify the samples as you learn.

There may be dependencies between multiple sample files for the same chapter. Thus, keep an entire chapter folder's contents together when copying.

Using the Sample Files

Here are some general considerations for using the database files included with this book:

Break on All Errors setting. Code in the sample databases may make use of a standard error trapping methodology that allows errors to occur and then traps and manages such errors. Consequently, if your Access environment settings include a Break on All Errors option setting of `True`, some routines on the CD-ROM drop into code when they are run. Make sure this option setting is cleared when running code included with this book.

> **Note**
>
> The file AES_VBA.MDB contains a routine `lci_AppBoAECheck` demonstrating how to check for this setting in the startup of an application.

Object Descriptions. Each object in the sample database files has a `Description` property string. The comment describes the use of the object or the example it conveys. Use <u>V</u>iew, <u>D</u>etails in the Database window to display these descriptive comments.

Library Routines. The sample databases share many common library routines; these procedures are stored in modules beginning with the tag `lci_bas`. The library routines have been synchronized between the various sample files—all modules with the same name in different databases are identical.

References. Some database sample files here were shipped containing a reference to the Microsoft Office 8.0 Object Library (MSO97.DLL) or other support files. A pointer to the Office library is required when Access code is used to program the Office Assistant, Office File Search, Office Command Bars, and other shared components. Files that are dependent on this object library or others are noted in this appendix.

When you open a file requiring the reference to an object library, view the References dialog box using Tools, References.... If the dialog box indicates that the referenced library is missing, you must locate it manually using the Browse button. When you have restored the reference, compile the application to verify that Access recognizes the library.

Files for Chapter 2

The file for this chapter provides information on the Leszynski Development Framework.

File LDF-SUMM.DOC

Title: Leszynski Development Framework (LDF) Summary

Description: Summarizes the core objectives and principles of LDF and outlines the precepts of the framework

Details: This document provides a summary of the development framework that guides the book and the files on the CD-ROM. The document includes the LDF model diagram and a listing of LDF precepts.

Usage: Print this file to discuss the merits of LDF in your environment or use the document as a starting point for creating your own framework.

Files for Chapter 3

The file for this chapter provides information useful in project planning.

File PRE-PLAN.DOC

Title: Database Software Project Pre-Planning Survey

Description: A brainstorming document that helps collect facts useful in the discussion of a new project

Details: This document helps design team members gather their initial thoughts on a proposed application and bring their structured input to design meetings to improve the communication process at such meetings. This survey may also be taken by prospective users of a new system.

Usage: Print this file and distribute the hard copies to the design team to help them prepare for the initial meeting on a new development project.

Files for Chapter 4

The files for this chapter provide tools to help you create design specification documents.

File SPECSHEL.XLS

Title: Schema design workbook

Description: Sample database design tool in Excel for use when developing a specification

Details: This workbook provides an example of the tool that Leszynski Company, Inc. uses to design database structures. Data entered into the spreadsheet is extracted and used by the Schema Builder tool in SCHEMA.MDB (see Chapter 10).

Usage: Copy and rename this file each time you start a new development project. Define the database tables, fields, properties, and indexes in the sheets of the workbook. Then use the Schema Builder to extract the information and create a new database from it.

File SPECSHEL.DOC

Title: Database Software Project Design Specification Outline

Description: Outline for a design specification document

Details: This document provides a suggested outline for a database application design specification that meets the LDF guidelines. The outline contains helpful notes to help you create a comprehensive design document, and uses {bracketed text} placeholders that prompt you to fill in required specification text.

Usage: Copy and rename this file each time you start a new development project. Use the file as a template to guide the authoring of each new project plan you create.

Files for Chapter 5

The file for this chapter provides examples of consistent object naming conventions.

File AES_NAMG.MDB

Description: Examples of consistent naming conventions for Chapters 5 and 6

Details: This database provides examples of objects employing consistent naming conventions. The examples apply the Leszynski Naming Conventions to database application objects.

Usage: Copy the file to your disk drive and review it in conjunction with Chapters 5 and 6. The purpose of the database is to demonstrate consistent naming conventions only; the database does not provide a working application and none of its objects actually are usable.

 Note

This database also demonstrates the use of carefully structured object descriptions, which can be used to group and sort objects in the Database window. You can sort the Database window by the `Description` column to see how the object descriptions provide an alternative sort order; the order is independent of the naming convention tags.

Files for Chapter 8

The file for this chapter provides examples of the various user interface components you need to build a friendly application.

File AES_UI.MDB

Description: Examples of user interface components that are visually uncomplicated and easy to use

Details: This database provides examples of forms and command bar objects that are designed for maximum user satisfaction. The examples show user interface elements that are easy to use and follow accepted standards for Windows components.

Usage: Copy the file to your disk drive and review it in conjunction with Chapter 8. The database contains references to the Office 8.0 Object Library (MSO97.DLL) and the Common Dialog ActiveX control (COMDLG32.OCX); you must check and update these references when first using the database.

 Note

This database provides an example of the use of the Common Dialog ActiveX control. The control is shipped with the Office Developer Edition and must be present on your system and properly registered in order to use the form frmComDlg. You may need to reinstall the control on the form in order to use it; follow these steps:

1. Install the Office Developer Edition tools on your system.

2. Open the form in design view.

3. Delete the Common Dialog control from the lower right of the form.

4. Insert the Common Dialog control onto the form, using the Insert, ActiveX Control... menu option. Name the control cdlg.

5. Update the reference to the control by locating the control file COMDLG32.OCX with the Browse button in the References dialog box.

6. Recompile the database.

Files for Chapter 9

The files for this chapter are useful when completing and distributing an Access-based solution.

File AES_ISSUE.MDB

Description: Examples of the structure of an issue management system

Details: This database provides sample tables that track issues discovered during the development process. The examples show how to capture feedback from users and testers in an organized structure.

Usage: Copy the file to your disk drive and review it in conjunction with Chapter 9.

File PRE-SHIP.DOC

Title: Database Software Application Pre-Release Checklist

Description: A list of application areas to review before certifying that the application is complete

Details: This document helps application developers and project managers compare an application against the standard requirements for shipping a "solid" application, as defined by LDF. An application should be reviewed against this document before being released to wide (beta) test.

Usage: Copy the file to your disk drive and print it when testing guidelines are required.

Files for Chapter 10

The files for this chapter provide examples of defining and building database table structures.

File AES_TBL.MDB

Description: Examples of table structures that solve common data management problems

Details: This database provides examples of table structures and query definitions that convey the relationships between real-world data items. The file also includes code examples that demonstrate specific features of the Jet database engine.

Usage: Copy the file to your disk drive and review its objects in conjunction Chapter 10.

File SCHEMA.MDB

Description: Sample tool to build a database structure from a definition table

Details: This database provides an example of the tool that Leszynski Company, Inc., uses to automate the building of database structures. Data entered into the spreadsheet SPECSHEL.XLS (see the section "Files for Chapter 4") is extracted and used by this tool to build tables and fields.

Usage: Copy the file to your disk drive and review its code. Also copy the file SPECSHEL.XLS from Chapter 4. Complete the definition information for a database's design in SPECSHEL.XLS, then use the form in this database to build tables from the design in the workbook.

Note

The database contains references to the Office 8.0 Object Library (MSO97.DLL), the Common Dialog ActiveX control (COMDLG32.OCX), and the Excel 8 object library; you must check and update these references when first using the database. See the section "Files for Chapter 8" for assistance.

Files for Chapter 11

The files for this chapter provide examples of using Visual Basic for Applications.

Files AES_VBA.MDB and AES_VBA.ICO

Description: Examples of working with VBA

Details: This database provides examples of structured code, error handling, and the use of Automation to drive Access. The icon file provides an example of a custom Access application icon.

Usage: Copy the files to your disk drive and review the database in conjunction with Chapter 11. Before using the Automation examples in this database, you must know the path to the Northwind sample application on your system, and you must disable the startup form in Northwind: open NORTHWIND.MDB using Access and set the Display Form option in the Startup options dialog box to *(none)*.

This database application contains initialization routines that demonstrate how an application can find its own components at startup. The routines are initiated by the Startup options for the database, which opens a hidden form zhfrmInit. To view the hidden form, select Hidden Objects on the View tab in the Options dialog box.

Note

The database contains a reference to the Office 8.0 Object Library (MSO97.DLL); you must check and update this reference when first using the database. See the section "Files for Chapter 8" for assistance.

Files for Chapter 12

The file for this chapter provides examples of some foundation techniques required before you can master Access form development.

File AES_FRM0.MDB

Description: Examples of various form development techniques

Details: This database provides examples of form techniques for bulk form operations and for new form coding techniques including collections, custom properties, class modules, and multiple object instances.

Usage: Copy the file to your disk drive and review its objects in conjunction with Chapter 12.

Files for Chapter 13

The files for this chapter provide examples of advanced techniques for using combo and list boxes on forms.

Files AES_FRM1.MDB and ORDER.TXT

Description: Advanced combo and list box examples

Details: Provides examples of form techniques for maximizing the use of List Box and Combo Box controls. The forms demonstrate solutions to common application development problems, including adding a marker value to a control's value list and loading a combo box via program code.

Usage: Copy the files to your disk drive and review the database in conjunction with Chapter 13. The text file is used by the form `frmCboFromFile` to show how combo box values can be loaded from static disk files.

Files for Chapter 14

The file for this chapter provides examples of advanced techniques for application navigation.

File AES_FRM2.MDB

Description: Examples of navigating within forms and between forms

Details: This database provides examples of form techniques for navigating between application elements. Various strategies are explored for creating switchboard menus, for creating and using the new command bar menu objects, and for passing information between two forms.

Usage: Copy the file to your disk drive and review it in conjunction with Chapter 14.

 Note

This file contains a reference to the Office 8.0 Object Library (MSO97.DLL). If code in the database does not run or compile correctly, check that this library is correctly referenced in the Tools, References... dialog box.

Files for Chapter 15

The file for this chapter provides examples of advanced data entry and validation techniques.

File AES_FRM3.MDB

Description: Examples of form routines that protect and validate data

Details: This database provides examples of form techniques for protecting data from erroneous entries, edits, and deletions. Routines that monitor the keyboard in various scenarios are also included.

Usage: Copy the file to your disk drive and review it in conjunction with Chapter 15.

Files for Chapter 16

The file for this chapter provides examples of techniques for the presentation of data on forms.

File AES_FRM4.MDB

Description: Examples of various data presentation scenarios

Details: This database provides examples of various user interface metaphors for selecting and displaying data using forms, including the propriety Leszynski Company, Inc. "Get" form model.

Usage: Copy the file to your disk drive, and review it in conjunction with Chapter 16.

Files for Chapter 17

The files for this chapter provide examples of techniques for "bulletproofing" an application to make it retail quality.

Files AES_BPRF.MDB, AES_BPRF.BMP, AES_BPRF.ICO

Description: Examples of a bulletproof application

Details: These files provide examples of a bulletproof interface that guides users through the application flow, protects the data, and provides feedback. The application model is very restrictive.

Usage: Copy the files to your disk drive and review the database in conjunction with Chapter 17. The bitmap file and the icon file must be placed in the same directory as the database file.

 Note

This database contains a reference to the Office 8.0 Object Library (MSO97.DLL). If code in the database does not run or compile correctly, check that this library is correctly referenced in the Tools, References... dialog box.

This database also contains startup property settings that restrict access to the Database window, menu design, and other aspects of the development environment. To browse the database, you must open it while holding down the Shift key to bypass the startup settings.

File BULLETPF.DOC

Title: Database Software Application Bulletproofing Guidelines

Description: Guidelines for creating a bulletproof application interface

Details: This document contains guidelines that help application developers and project managers create a "solid" application by applying specific usability and data-protection enhancements to the application interface. The document lists the LDF requirements and suggestions for creating a bulletproof application.

Usage: Copy the file to your disk drive and review it in conjunction with Chapter 17. Print the file and use it as a guide during application development and testing.

Files ESPLASH1.BMP Through ESPLASH6.BMP

Description: Early splash screen graphics

Details: Access will display a custom bitmap in place of the standard splash screen if the bitmap is located in the same directory as the database file and has the same filename prefix. These files can be used as an application early splash screen.

Usage: View these files in a graphics program and determine which one you would like to use for a specific application. Copy the selected file to the same directory as the application database you want it to work with, and change the leading portion of the file name to the same name as the related database file (for example, to use ESPLASH2.BMP with the database MYAPP.MDB, change the name to MYAPP.BMP).

Files for Chapter 18

The files for this chapter provide examples of techniques to create applications that use advanced Access reporting capabilities.

File AES_RPTS.MDB

Description: Examples for advanced reporting techniques

Details: This database provides examples of reporting techniques that assist users with data selection, summarize data and allow drilling-down from the summary, allow reports to be chained together, and export data to Web page reports.

Usage: Copy the file to your disk drive and review it in conjunction with Chapter 18. You must have Internet Explorer on your computer in order to view the Web-based output from this database.

Files AES_HTML.HTM, AES_VBA.HTM, and AES_WEB.HTM

Description: Sample files related to Web-based reporting

Details: These three files help demonstrate HTML syntax and the routines in AES_RPTS.MDB that export HTML files.

Usage: AES_HTML.HTM provides examples of the HTML tags described in the chapter text. AES_WEB.HTM demonstrates a report that has been exported to the Web using Access' native capabilities. AES_VBA.HTM shows a Web-based report created completely with code in the chapter. View each of these files in Internet Explorer.

Files for Chapter 19

The files for this chapter provide examples of using Access as a front-end for data stored in SQL Server.

File AES_SRVR.MDB

Description: Examples of using Access as a server client

Details: This database provides examples of using Access, DAO, and Jet as gateways to data stored in SQL Server databases, including SQL pass-through and ODBCDirect technology.

Usage: Copy the file to your disk drive and review it in conjunction with Chapter 19. You must have a connection to a running SQL Server and the Pubs sample database to use the examples.

 Note

You must create a saved data source on your workstation that tells Access how to locate the Pubs database. See the chapter text for instructions on creating a data source.

This database contains startup property settings that force you to login to Pubs each time the database is opened. The login event creates a cached connection to the server that is reused by Access to improve performance, and also creates a variable with a server connect string that is useful as you explore the examples. To bypass the login dialog box, open the database while holding down the Shift key.

Files for Chapter 20

The files for this chapter provide examples of creating tools to make your development work with Access more productive and enjoyable.

Files AES_SCUT.MDB, AES_LIB.MDA

Description: Examples of development shortcuts

Details: AES_SCUT.MDB provides examples of development shortcuts such as AutoKeys macros and custom toolbars. It also demonstrates calling a remote function in the library database AES_LIB.MDA.

Usage: Copy the files to your disk drive and review them in conjunction with Chapter 20. Before you use AES_SCUT.MDB, you must open it and update the reference to AES_LIB.MDA to point to the location of the file on your computer. Use the References dialog box to update the reference, then compile all modules to make sure the new reference is intact.

File AES_WIZ.MDA

Description: Wizard and builder examples

Details: This database provides working examples of a property wizard, a control wizard, and a menu add-in.

Usage: Copy the file to the Access directory (the location where the Access executable file resides) on your disk drive. Open the file and review its objects in conjunction with the chapter text. Then, install the sample wizards and add-ins contained in the file. First, use Tools, Add-Ins, Add-In Manager from any open database to start the Add-in Manager dialog box. Then, select the item "Sample wizards and add-ins" from the list, which is the identification string for this file, and click Install.

After the wizard database is installed, it cannot be opened with Access. Make a second copy of the file from the CD-ROM to your disk drive if you want to review the code again.

See the chapter text for information on using the custom add-ins.

Miscellaneous Files

In addition to the preceding materials directly related to the chapter text, the CD-ROM contains the following helpful files.

File CONVRT97.DOC

Title: Converting Existing Microsoft Access Applications to Access 97

Description: Tips for converting you applications

Details: This document provides a detailed and definitive reference for converting any application built with a prior version of Access to the current version.

Usage: Copy the file to your disk drive and print it to use as a reference when you begin a conversion procedure.

File KCCPAK1.EXE

Description: Kwery Control Pak 1 demonstration files

Details: This file contains a fully functional demonstration version of Kwery Corporation's Control Pak 1 ActiveX control suite. Control Pak 1 provides five ActiveX controls that you can drop into your Access or Visual Basic applications or on to your Web site pages.

Usage: Copy the self-extracting setup file to your disk drive and run the file. Multiple controls will be extracted and registered on your machine. Once setup is complete, you can open the demonstration file CTRLPAK1.MDB and explore the examples in it.

File LNC97DEV.HLP, LNC97DEV.CNT

Description: The Leszynski Naming Conventions for Solution Developers Help file and supporting contents file

Details: This Windows Help file provides a reference document to the Leszynski Naming Conventions as described in the chapter text. You can keep the Help file open on your desktop as you work. The file provides detailed information on naming convention issues and includes the LNC object tags for Access, Office, Visual Basic, SQL Server, and other Microsoft tools.

Usage: Copy the files to your disk drive and create a shortcut on the Windows desktop to LNC97DEV.HLP or add a shortcut to your Start menu.

Files UTILITY.MDA, WZLIB80.MDE, WZMAIN80.MDE, WZTOOL80.MDE, and WIZARD97.TXT

Description: Source code for the Access 97 wizards

Details: In the retail version of Access, you can't view the VBA code for wizards. This special version of the wizards contains viewable (unlocked) wizard code for you to use as a learning tool.

Usage: The four wizard library databases must be installed in place of the wizard databases that shipped with your copy of Access. To install these files, see the instructions in WIZARD97.TXT or follow these steps:

1. Close Access.
2. Create a backup directory to hold the wizard files that came with your retail version of Access.
3. From your Access directory, move the files UTILITY.MDA, WZLIB80.MDE, WZMAIN80.MDE, and WZTOOL80.MDE to the backup directory you created in step 2.
4. Copy the four wizard files from the CD-ROM to your Access directory.
5. Start Access.

Once installed, you can open the wizard files directly for exploration, or you can create a reference from within any Access database to any wizard file and explore the file with the Object Browser.

To stop using the unlocked wizard code, close Access and copy the backup files you made in step 2 previously back into your Access directory.

Index

Check out Que® Books on the World Wide Web
http://www.mcp.com/que

As the biggest software release in computer history, Windows 95 continues to redefine the computer industry. Click here for the latest info on our Windows 95 books

Make computing quick and easy with these products designed exclusively for new and casual users

Examine the latest releases in word processing, spreadsheets, operating systems, and suites

The Internet, The World Wide Web, CompuServe®, America Online®, Prodigy® —it's a world of ever-changing information. Don't get left behind!

Find out about new additions to our site, new bestsellers and hot topics

In-depth information on high-end topics: find the best reference books for databases, programming, networking, and client/server technologies

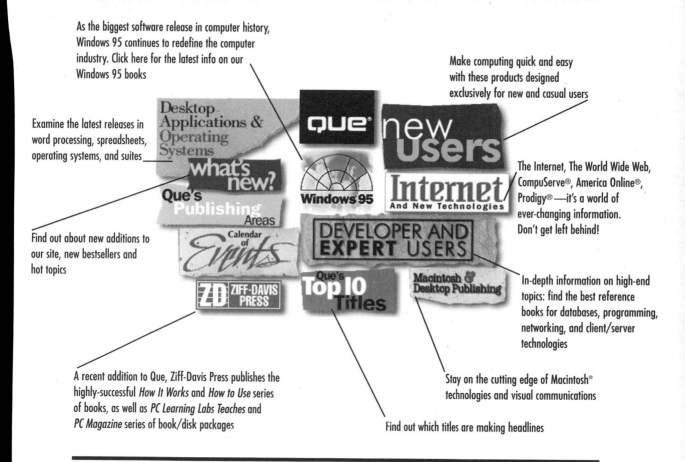

Desktop Applications & Operating Systems

Que's Publishing Areas

what's new?

Windows 95

que®

new users

Internet And New Technologies

DEVELOPER AND EXPERT USERS

Calendar of Events

ZD ZIFF-DAVIS PRESS

Que's Top 10 Titles

Macintosh & Desktop Publishing

A recent addition to Que, Ziff-Davis Press publishes the highly-successful *How It Works* and *How to Use* series of books, as well as *PC Learning Labs Teaches* and *PC Magazine* series of book/disk packages

Stay on the cutting edge of Macintosh® technologies and visual communications

Find out which titles are making headlines

With 6 separate publishing groups, Que develops products for many specific market segments and areas of computer technology. Explore our Web Site and you'll find information on best-selling titles, newly published titles, upcoming products, authors, and much more.

- Stay informed on the latest industry trends and products available
- Visit our online bookstore for the latest information and editions
- Download software from Que's library of the best shareware and freeware

que®

MACMILLAN COMPUTER PUBLISHING USA

A VIACOM COMPANY

Technical Support:

If you can not get the CD/Disk to install properly, or you need assistance with a particular situation in the book, please feel free to check out the Knowledge Base on our website at **http://www.superlibrary.com/general/support.** We have answers to our most Frequently Asked Questions listed there. If you do not find your specific question answered, please contact Macmillan Technical Support at **(317) 581-3833**. We can also be reached by email at **support@mcp.com**.

Complete and Return this Card
for a *FREE* Computer Book Catalog

Thank you for purchasing this book! You have purchased a superior computer book written expressly for your needs. To continue to provide the kind of up-to-date, pertinent coverage you've come to expect from us, we need to hear from you. Please take a minute to complete and return this self-addressed, postage-paid form. In return, we'll send you a free catalog of all our computer books on topics ranging from word processing to programming and the internet.

Mr. ☐   Mrs. ☐   Ms. ☐   Dr. ☐

Name (first) [＿＿＿＿＿＿＿＿＿] (M.I.) ☐   (last) [＿＿＿＿＿＿＿＿＿＿＿＿＿＿]

Address [＿＿＿＿＿＿＿＿＿＿＿＿＿＿＿＿＿＿＿＿＿＿＿]

[＿＿＿＿＿＿＿＿＿＿＿＿＿＿＿＿＿＿＿＿＿＿＿]

City [＿＿＿＿＿＿＿＿＿＿]   State [＿＿]   Zip [＿＿＿＿＿＿]

Phone [＿＿＿] [＿＿＿＿] [＿＿＿＿]   Fax [＿＿＿] [＿＿＿] [＿＿＿＿]

Company Name [＿＿＿＿＿＿＿＿＿＿＿＿＿＿＿＿＿＿]

E-mail address [＿＿＿＿＿＿＿＿＿＿＿＿＿＿＿＿＿＿＿＿]

1. Please check at least (3) influencing factors for purchasing this book.

Front or back cover information on book .... ☐
Special approach to the content .... ☐
Completeness of content .... ☐
Author's reputation .... ☐
Publisher's reputation .... ☐
Book cover design or layout .... ☐
Index or table of contents of book .... ☐
Price of book .... ☐
Special effects, graphics, illustrations .... ☐
Other (Please specify): _____ ☐

2. How did you first learn about this book?

Saw in Macmillan Computer Publishing catalog .... ☐
Recommended by store personnel .... ☐
Saw the book on bookshelf at store .... ☐
Recommended by a friend .... ☐
Received advertisement in the mail .... ☐
Saw an advertisement in: _____ ☐
Read book review in: _____ ☐
Other (Please specify): _____ ☐

3. How many computer books have you purchased in the last six months?

This book only .... ☐   3 to 5 books .... ☐
books .... ☐   More than 5 .... ☐

4. Where did you purchase this book?

Bookstore .... ☐
Computer Store .... ☐
Consumer Electronics Store .... ☐
Department Store .... ☐
Office Club .... ☐
Warehouse Club .... ☐
Mail Order .... ☐
Direct from Publisher .... ☐
Internet site .... ☐
Other (Please specify): _____ ☐

5. How long have you been using a computer?

☐ Less than 6 months   ☐ 6 months to a year
☐ 1 to 3 years   ☐ More than 3 years

6. What is your level of experience with personal computers and with the subject of this book?

	With PCs	With subject of book
New	☐	☐
Casual	☐	☐
Accomplished	☐	☐
Expert	☐	☐

Source Code ISBN: 0-7897-0367-x

7. Which of the following best describes your job title?

- Administrative Assistant ☐
- Coordinator ☐
- Manager/Supervisor ☐
- Director ☐
- Vice President ☐
- President/CEO/COO ☐
- Lawyer/Doctor/Medical Professional ☐
- Teacher/Educator/Trainer ☐
- Engineer/Technician ☐
- Consultant ☐
- Not employed/Student/Retired ☐
- Other (Please specify): _____ ☐

8. Which of the following best describes the area of the company your job title falls under?

- Accounting ☐
- Engineering ☐
- Manufacturing ☐
- Operations ☐
- Marketing ☐
- Sales ☐
- Other (Please specify): _____ ☐

9. What is your age?

- Under 20 ☐
- 21-29 ☐
- 30-39 ☐
- 40-49 ☐
- 50-59 ☐
- 60-over ☐

10. Are you:

- Male ☐
- Female ☐

11. Which computer publications do you read regularly? (Please list)

_____
_____
_____
_____
_____
_____
_____
_____
_____
_____

Comments: _____
_____
_____

Fold here and scotch-tape to mail

Licensing Agreement

By opening this package, you are agreeing to be bound by the following:

This software product is copyrighted, and all rights are reserved by the publisher and author. You are licensed to use this software on a single computer. You may copy and/or modify the software as needed to facilitate your use of it on a single computer. Making copies of the software for any other purpose is a violation of the United States copyright laws.

This software is sold *as is* without warranty of any kind, either expressed or impied, including but not limited to the implied warranties of merchantabliity and fitness for particular purpose. Neither the publisher nor its dealers or distributors assumes any liabilty for any alleged or actual damages arising from the use of this program. (Some states do not allow for the exclusion of implied warranties, so the exclusion may not apply to you.)